ZION-BENTON PUBLIC LIBRARY DISTRICT

D0151239

Zion-Benton
Public Library District
Zion, Illinois 60099
DEMCO

WARS
OF THE
AMERICAS

A Chronology of
Armed Conflict
in the New World,
1492 to the Present

DAVID F. MARLEY

Santa Barbara, California
Denver, Colorado
Oxford, England

Library of Congress Cataloging-in-Publication Data
Marley, David.
Wars of the Americas : a chronology of armed conflict in the New World, 1492 to the present / by David F. Marley.
p. cm.
Includes bibliographical references and index.
1. America—History, Military—Chronology. I. Title.
E18.75.M374 1998
355'.0097—dc21 98-21209
CIP

ISBN 0-87436-837-5

Typesetting by Letra Libre

04 03 02 01 00 99 10 9 8 7 6 5 4 3 2

ABC-CLIO, Inc.
130 Cremona Drive, P.O. Box 1911
Santa Barbara, California 93116-1911

This book is printed on acid-free paper ♾.

Manufactured in the United States of America

Dedicated to the memory of my beloved father,
Frank Lewis "Pancho" Marley
(12 July 1917–27 November 1996),
who at the age of 19 departed Canada aboard the S.S. Calgary
for a life of adventure in Africa, and the world beyond

Contents

Preface

Twist all our victories into one bright wreath,
On which let honor breathe. . . .
—William Cartwright (1611–1643)

INEVITABLY, ANY ATTEMPT to compress 500 years of warfare into a single volume must entail certain compromises. As a result, minor confrontations may have inadvertently been ignored or underreported in this book, and the very geographic limitations imposed by such a project—of describing only conflicts occurring within the territorial boundaries of the New World since the arrival of the Europeans—also means that descriptions of several colossal global efforts such as World War II appear strangely stunted, because most of their action happens to have been played out overseas.

Nevertheless, the narrow continental focus of this work also serves to reveal certain historical trends, common to virtually every modern nation-state in the Americas. The earliest explorers, for example, encountered lands already embroiled in warfare and used native divisions to facilitate their own campaigns of subjugation—by playing off Arawak against Carib, Tlaxcaltecan versus Aztec, northern Inca against southern Inca, and so on—as described in Part 1: Discovery and Conquest.

French, English, and Dutch sailors then arrived to scavenge from Spain's sprawling new empire (*see* Part 2: Seaborne Challengers), eventually setting up shore establishments of their own in defiance of Madrid's opposition (*see* Part 3: Rival Outposts). In time these footholds came to be contested as minor prizes during larger European conflicts (*see* Part 4: Intercolonial Friction) before finally flourishing to such an extent as to become the primary cause—and active participants—in a worldwide struggle for economic supremacy (*see* Part 5: High Tide of Empire).

The evolution of most American colonies then culminated with them seeking their own independence (Part 6), which in turn inaugurated a distinctly new—and oftentimes painful—transitionary phase into full nationhood (Part 7). Lastly, the gradual emergence of the United States as the world's dominant superpower brought an end to all foreign designs on the New World (Part 8) and ushered in our own contemporary era. It is to be hoped that this volume will provide both scholarly and amateur historians alike with rapid access to information about past conflicts and, in particular, considerable detail on some of the lesser-known hostilities of the New World.

In conclusion, the author would like to acknowledge the kind and patient assistance received from countless esteemed colleagues and friends during the compilation of this book, most especially Dr. Basil Kingstone, Head of the French Department, Dr. Berislav Primorac of the Classical and Modern Languages Department, and Dr. Ronald Welch of the Geography Department of the University of Windsor, Ontario, Canada; the entire staff of the Archivo General de la Nación, Mexico City; Dr. Pedro González García, Director of the Archive of Indies in Seville; Dr. José Ignacio González-Aller, Director of the Museo Naval in Madrid; Mr. André Gousse, Military Curator of Parks Canada; Dr. Leo M. Akveld, Curator, and Mr. Ron Brand, Deputy Librarian, of the Prins Hendrik Maritime Museum in Rotterdam; Mr. Robert Elliott, Ms. Maureen Souchuk, Mr. Graham Staffen, Mr. Donald Tupling, and Mr. Kenneth W. Badder of the Leddy Library of the University of Windsor; Ms. Hendrika Ruger, Ms. Joan Magee, Ms. Yvette Bulmer, and Mr. Mark Tupling; Ing. Adolfo Langenscheidt F. and Dr. Jodie S. Randall of Mexico City; Dr. Jean Starr of Edinbugh, Scotland; Mr. René Chartrand of Hull, Quebec; etc.

—David F. Marley
Windsor, Ontario

Adoption of the Gregorian Calendar

By the late 1500s, the Julian calendar—named in honor of its ancient Roman reviser, Julius Caesar—no longer coincided with the seasons, or new moons. Therefore, in March 1582, after lengthy studies by the Neapolitan astronomer Aloysius Lilius and many others, Pope Gregory XIII issued a bull declaring that a new calendar was to be introduced: the day following the feast of Saint Francis on 4 October 1582, rather than being reckoned the fifth day of the month, was instead to be designated 15 October, so as to restore all subsequent equinoxes to their proper cycle. This change was accepted in most of Italy, Spain, and Portugal on this day and in France two months later—passing from 9 to 20 December 1582—while the Netherlands and Germany introduced it in 1583.

Protestant England, however—being opposed to any hint of Catholic suzerainty—refused to comply. Consequently, from 1582 through 1700 their "Old Style" Julian calendars lagged ten days behind the "New Style" Gregorian calendars used by the Spanish, French, Dutch, and Portuguese, which difference increased to eleven days in March 1700. It was not until September 1752 that the English finally adopted the modern Gregorian calendar, still used today.

For purposes of this book, all dates are given in Gregorian style, unless specifically marked "(O.S.)" for "Old Style."

Part 1: Discovery and Conquest (1492–1572)

We only come to sleep,
we only come to dream;
it is not true, no, it is not true,
that we come to live upon this earth.

—ancient Aztec verse

Initial Contacts (1492–1498)

Friday morning, 12 October 1492: Genoese explorer Christopher Columbus steps onto an island, called Guanahaní by its Arawak-speaking Taíno inhabitants. He renames the island San Salvador (generally believed to be Long Bay, Watling Island, Bahamas). Having led a trio of Spanish vessels across the Atlantic in hopes of establishing a new trade route between Europe and Asia, Columbus erroneously assumes he is somewhere near Japan.

After briefly exploring San Salvador's adjoining islands, Columbus coasts along northeastern Cuba, where he becomes separated from his caravel *Pinta,* commanded by Martín Alonso Pinzón, then visits the northern side of an island he names Española (literally, the "Spanish" Island because of its strong resemblance to Spain's coastline; this name will later be Anglicized to Hispaniola). Here his flagship *Santa María* is accidentally wrecked on 24 December, but the Spaniards are generously granted asylum the next day by Guacanagarí, the local chieftain.

With only one ship remaining to him, Columbus decides to leave some crewmembers behind and return toward Spain. The Arawaks prove amenable, in turn hoping these visitors will protect them against their more ferocious Antillan neighbors, the Caribs, who have been raiding from seaward for several generations. *Santa María's* timbers are used to construct a small fortress on the beach, which Columbus dubs Navidad—"Christmas," in honor of the day he and his men were welcomed—then installs a 36-man garrison under officers Diego de Arana, Pedro Gutiérrez, and Rodrigo de Escobedo.

Setting sail with his remaining caravel on 4 January 1493, Columbus overtakes *Pinta* two days later, just east of present-day Monte Cristi. On 13 January, the two vessels encounter a Carib war party in Samaná Bay, their faces "blackened with charcoal." After an uneasy parley, fighting erupts when a seven-man Spanish boat party is set upon by 55 natives. The Spaniards' steel weapons frighten and scatter the Caribs, and three days later Columbus stands back out into the Atlantic for Spain.

Upon his return to Europe, the explorer proclaims his discovery of new islands, and his glowing account of exotic, fertile lands—rich with gold and inhabited only by primitive peoples—encourages a much larger expedition to gather around him for a second voyage intended to establish a permanent foothold.

May 1493. In order to avert a potential Hispano-Portuguese rift over Columbus's discovery, Pope Alexander VI issues his *Inter caetera* bull suggesting that a dividing line be drawn between both poles running 300 miles west of the Cape Verde Islands and Azores Islands, with Spain claiming all lands to the west of this boundary and Portugal all lands to the east.

3 November 1493. Columbus returns to the Antilles with the title "admiral of the ocean seas," heading a fleet comprising five Spanish ships and a dozen caravels, bearing 1,500 people (as well as several score of horses and other domesticated animals). The first island he sights is named Dominica in honor of this day—it being Sunday—while the next is named Marie Galante after the admiral's flagship *Santa María la Galante; Marigalante* to its Spanish seamen.

Other islands are spotted as the fleet picks its way through the Leeward Islands then passes northern Puerto Rico en route to Columbus's original outpost of Navidad (Haiti). A handful of Caribs are seized on the way, but no major clashes occur. Upon reaching Hispaniola, the Spaniards find their compatriots dead, apparently from a war against the rival chieftains Caonabó and Mayreni. Columbus orders a new settlement constructed nearby, calling it Isabela in honor of the Spanish queen. The colonists—many of them criminals banished from Spain—soon become disillusioned at the hardships, disease, and poverty they experience, and frictions develop among them and with local tribesmen.

20–21 January 1494. Having established a secure base, the Spaniards dispatch two expeditions in opposite directions on Santo Domingo, searching for the natives' goldfields.

2 February 1494. Twelve of Columbus's vessels return toward Spain under Capt. Antonio de Torres, bearing messages, a few exotic articles, and requests for reinforcement.

12 March 1494. Columbus, after recuperating from a brief illness, leads a small army inland to the supposed goldfields around Cibao. Nearly one week later he arrives there, building a second fort named Santo Tomás and installing Capt. Pedro Margarit as commander with a garrison of 56 men. Returning to Isabela, Columbus then sends another 70 men to reinforce

Engraving of a fifteenth-century round ship

Santo Tomás because of rumors of an impending native attack.

9 APRIL 1494. Concerned by the overcrowding of his original Isabela encampment, Columbus sends Capt. Alonso de Ojeda and more than 400 men overland toward Santo Tomás, hoping to expand his foothold there. During this march some minor incidents occur with the Arawaks because of heavy-handed Spanish punishments against theft.

24 APRIL 1494. In order to find the "Asian" mainland, Columbus sets sail with three vessels to explore farther west. Probing southern Cuba as far as Isla de Pinos, he turns back then slowly circles Jamaica and passes the southern side of Hispaniola.

JUNE 1494. During Columbus's absence, frictions on Hispaniola increase among the Spaniards and between colonists and local natives. When the admiral's brother Bartholomew arrives with an additional trio of ships from Spain, he finds discipline so badly deteriorated that Margarit and his followers immediately board one of these vessels to set sail toward Europe.

7 JUNE 1494. In Europe, the Treaty of Tordesillas is signed between Spain and Portugal, who agree to recognize a dividing line running approximately 1,110 miles west of the Cape Verde and Azores Islands as the boundary between their overseas claims.

29 SEPTEMBER 1494. Exhausted and sick, Columbus puts back into Isabela, bitterly disappointed at his inability to find any trace of either China or Japan.

26 MARCH 1495. ***Defeat of Caonabó.*** Columbus, after a lengthy convalescence, and his brother Bartholomew march inland on 24 March leading 200 Spaniards, 20 horsemen, and a score of fighting dogs to do battle with Caonabó, the principal leader of Arawak resistance. Two days later they defeat a mass of Indians in what the Spaniards later call the Battle of Vega Real (or Royal Plain), capturing the chieftain, condemning him to transportation to Spain, and executing many of

his followers. This massacre, coupled with disease and enslavement, effectively ends organized Arawak opposition on Hispaniola.

10 MARCH 1496. Still plagued by his failure to locate Asia as well as by negative reports circulating in Spain, Columbus decides to visit Europe. He sets sail aboard the caravels *Niña* and *Santa Cruz* (the latter known as *La India,* being the first European vessel to be constructed in the New World), which are crowded with 225 Spaniards and 30 Indian passengers including the captive chieftain Caonabó. Running short on provisions, the Spaniards fight their way ashore at the island of Guadeloupe, seizing food and a dozen Carib captives before departing again on 20 April toward Madeira. The admiral chose this unusual route to avoid a French fleet rumored to be blockading Spain's coast.

24 JUNE 1497. At 5:00 on this Saturday morning, 47-year-old John Cabot—an Italian navigator residing in Bristol and commissioned by Henry VII of England—sights the northern tip of Cape Breton (Canada) after traversing the North Atlantic via Iceland. Briefly exploring this region with his 50-ton, 18-man *Matthew,* he names Capes Ray and Saint George and the islands of Saint Pierre and Miquelon before sailing past Cape Race and out into the Atlantic again, returning to Bristol by 6 August convinced that he has reached Asia—"the country of the Great Khan."

SUMMER 1498. Reinforced with two ships and 300 men, Cabot returns to North America, determined to find "Cipangu," or Japan. After briefly exploring southern Greenland, he sights Baffin Island at approximately 66 degrees north latitude, then coasts south as far as the 38th parallel without encountering any sign of a major Asian kingdom. Disappointed, he returns to Bristol late in the autumn of 1498, dying shortly thereafter.

MAINLAND EXPLORATIONS (1498–1519)

THE INITIAL BELIEF THAT A NEW FAR EASTERN trade route has been found gradually gives way to disillusionment, especially since these newly discovered islands apparently have little commercial value. Thus, the urgency of the push to establish a fortified Spanish outpost and monopolize this western route against other European rivals, such as the Portuguese and Italians—who have earlier done much the same during their explorations of Africa and Asia—soon begins to evaporate. In case after case, the Antillan natives prove to be simple folk, eking out a subsistence living while possessing barely any clothes or tools, much less valuable barter items.

This alters the Spanish colonists' attitude as well, from one of mercantile adventurism to that of settlers bent upon occupying land. In the absence of better economic prospects, they lay claim to increasingly extensive plots and begin clearing these areas to plant crops, eventually importing slaves to help in this work. Those natives who befriend the Spaniards are decimated by disease, whereas those who resist are unable to match the Spanish weaponry and armor. The church encourages assimilation in order to gain converts. Thus, as the search to reach Japan, China, or India continues in vain, the Caribbean islanders go under.

31 JULY 1498. His prestige at court fully restored, Columbus returns to the New World, this time having followed a more southerly route across the Atlantic in hopes of spotting the chimerical Asian continent. Having quit Spain at the head of a squadron of four ships and two caravels with 500 men, the admiral sends three craft directly from the Canaries toward Hispaniola while leading the other trio farther south. Thus, he discovers the island of Trinidad, the Gulf of Paria, and Margarita Island (Venezuela) before continuing toward Hispaniola, where he arrives on 20 August.

During Columbus's absence, Isabela has been abandoned by his brothers Bartholomew and Diego in favor of a new town on the southeastern coast, which they christen Santo Domingo. A serious insurrection has also developed among the Spanish settlers, most of whom have sided with Francisco Roldán against the Columbus brothers. The admiral finds his own authority greatly diminished among the disgruntled inhabitants, forcing him to enter protracted negotiations with Roldán, who he eventually appoints lieutenant governor.

18 OCTOBER 1498. Five Spanish ships depart Hispaniola to recross the Atlantic, sighting the South American coast again during their voyage.

SUMMER 1499. In Spain, Bishop Juan Rodríguez de Fonseca has increasingly begun acting as minister for

West Indian affairs, authorizing rival captains to make independent explorations in spite of Columbus's supposed primacy over such matters.

One of the first challengers to sail is Columbus's erstwhile subordinate, Alonso de Ojeda, who departs Seville in mid-May 1499 with two ships piloted by the admiral's former sailing master, Juan de la Cosa, and accompanied by another pair under the 48-year-old Florentine navigator Amerigo Vespucci. After sighting land near Guyana, the first two explore the northeastern shores of South America from the Gulf of Paria as far west as Cape de la Vela, naming this stretch of coastline Venezuela, or "Little Venice." At Chichiriviche, a Spanish landing party clashes with Carib warriors ashore, suffering one dead and a score wounded. On 9 August they christen Cabo San Román, by 24 August they explore the Laguna de Maracaibo, and by 30 August they quit Cape de la Vela for Santo Domingo.

The second group under Vespucci meanwhile veers southeast, probing the Brazilian shoreline well past the mouth of the Amazon River before turning back at 6 degrees 30 minutes south latitude on 23 August. Vespucci then visits the island of Trinidad and the Gulf of Paria, continuing west in Ojeda's wake. After receiving a hostile reception from natives on the mainland, he rests on Curaçao and Aruba before venturing farther southwest and eventually swinging around to rejoin Ojeda at Santo Domingo.

JULY 1499. A third expedition enters the Gulf of Paria, consisting of a single 50-ton caravel with 33 crew members under Pedro Alonso Niño—another of Columbus's former pilots—and his partner, Cristóbal Guerra, who have quit Spain in late May. After they successfully barter for pearls in the gulf, their caravel is attacked upon exiting the Dragon's Mouths (near modern Port of Spain, Trinidad) by 18 Carib war canoes, which the Spaniards drive off with considerable difficulty by firing their artillery to frighten the occupants, capturing one craft.

Niño and Guerra then trade peaceably at Margarita and Cumaná for several weeks before venturing west and reaching Golfo Triste by November. When they attempt to land near Chichiriviche, however, several hundred warriors confront them on the beach, compelling the Spaniards to retrace their course toward Cumaná. After spending three weeks acquiring more pearls and visiting the nearby Araya salt pans, Niño and Guerra set sail for Spain on 13 February 1500. The profits from their voyage will encourage imitators.

5 SEPTEMBER 1499. Having completed his exploration of Venezuela, Ojeda calls at Yáquimo (southern Santo Domingo) to replenish his supplies. When Lieutenant Governor Roldán visits his ships on Sunday, 29 September, news of Bishop Fonseca's granting of licenses to explore the New World helps revive the Spanish settlers' resentment against the Columbus brothers, who have always sought to monopolize these affairs. Several months of turmoil ensue, culminating with numerous arrests, banishments, and even executions on the admiral's orders.

Ojeda, meanwhile, sails north with Vespucci on his return passage toward Spain, traversing the Lucayas (Bahamas) and enslaving 232 natives before recrossing the Atlantic via the Azores, Canaries, and Madeira, reaching Cadiz by mid-June 1500.

LATE JANUARY 1500. Vicente Yáñez Pinzón appears with four caravels off the eastern tip of Brazil, exploring its coast in a northwesterly direction. Near Maranhão one of his landing parties is set upon and 11 members are killed; many others are wounded by arrows as they rush to their companions' aid. Near the mouth of the Amazon 36 natives are taken captive, after which Yáñez Pinzón continues as far as the Orinoco River, the Dragon's Mouths, and the island of Tobago before reaching Santo Domingo on 23 June. After refreshing his supplies, he presses on toward the Bahamas, but two of his vessels are sunk by a hurricane in July; the remaining pair retire to Santo Domingo for repairs. The explorer subsequently strikes out across the Atlantic, returning to Spain by 30 September.

Another two-ship expedition under Diego Lepe follows a similar course up the South American coast and back toward Spain around this same time, although it does not make many contacts ashore.

22 APRIL 1500. A dozen large Portuguese trading ships under Adm. Pedro Álvares Cabral (also known as Pedro Álvares de Gouveia) and Vice Adm. Sancho de Toar sight the Brazilian coast near 19 degrees south latitude. Although this region nominally lies within the Portuguese sphere of influence as defined by the Treaty of Tordesillas (*see* 7 June 1494), Cabral has in fact not come in search of this territory; his actual destination is India via the Cape of Good Hope, but having departed Cape Verde (West Africa) Cabral has circled too far out into the Atlantic, thus inadvertently coming within sight of South America.

His vessels spend the next fortnight coasting south, occasionally going ashore to refresh provisions and to trade with local inhabitants. After holding Easter Mass on land, they name this shoreline Terra da Vera Cruz (Land of the True Cross); on 3 May they stand out into the South Atlantic again, bound toward the Cape of Good Hope. Cabral detaches Capt. Gaspar de Lemos's caravel to carry word of this discovery back to King Manoel I, but this report is greeted with scant enthusiasm, as the commercial prospects of the Far East command much greater attention.

23 AUGUST 1500. Francisco Bobadilla, knight of the Order of Calatrava, arrives at Santo Domingo with the caravels *Goda* and *Antigua,* with plenary powers to investigate reports of deteriorating conditions upon the island. He finds Columbus inland at Vega Real and his brother Bartholomew at Xaragua dealing with rebellious settlers, and so he immediately assumes office as governor. The admiral is then recalled to the capital, arrested in early October, and—along with his brother—taken aboard ship in chains to set sail early this December back toward Spain.

EARLY 1501. Rodrigo de Bastidas, commanding two ships piloted by Juan de la Cosa, expands upon the Spaniards' mainland reconnaissances by arriving to barter with natives from Cape de la Vela as far southwest as the Gulf of Darien, in the process discovering and naming the ports of Santa Marta and Cartagena. Their vessels weakened by teredo worms, Bastidas and de la Cosa then visit Jamaica and western Santo Domingo before being wrecked in a hurricane and arrested by governor Bobadilla on charges of tax evasion.

Meanwhile Vespucci also returns to the New World during the same summer, leading a Portuguese expedition that sights the Brazilian coast on 10 August then slowly reconnoiters down past modern Rio de Janeiro (January River, so named because it is discovered on 1 January 1502) and the River Plate, perhaps reaching as far south as Patagonia by late January 1502 before eventually reversing course. When he reaches Lisbon again on 22 July, reports of this and similar immense distances of new coastline convince Vespucci and a growing body of scholars that these territories cannot be part of Asia but rather are part of a completely new world.

3 FEBRUARY 1501. The Spanish crown repeats an earlier ban of 1499, prohibiting all foreigners from traveling to the West Indies. Such restrictions will be reiterated a number of times over the next two decades, to little avail.

SPRING 1501. Cristóbal Guerra and his brother Luis return to the Gulf of Paria aboard their 50-ton caravel to barter for more pearls. During their westward progress they endure some clashes with natives and enslave a number of them before returning to Spain this November.

12 MARCH 1502. ***Ojeda's Failure.*** A colonizing expedition arrives off pearl-rich Margarita Island (northeastern Venezuela) under Ojeda comprising the ships *Santa María de la Antigua* under Capt. García de Ocampo, *Santa María de la Granada* under Juan de Vergara (both partners to Ojeda), plus the caravels *Magdalena* of Pedro de Ojeda (the commander in chief's nephew) and *Santa Ana* under Hernando de Guevara. The expedition becomes separated, and a shortage of supplies leads some Spaniards to attack a peaceful native settlement at Cumaná on 2 April, killing 78 Indians at the cost of one Spanish fatality.

Continuing westward, Ojeda and his men eventually reach the port of Santa Cruz (Bahía Honda, Colombia), so called because it is discovered on 3 May (Feast Day of the Holy Cross). Here they are joined by Juan de Buenaventura, one of Rodrigo de Bastidas's men who has been earlier left behind at nearby Santa Marta (*see* early 1501) and learned the natives' language and customs. Shortly thereafter, when Ojeda attempts to erect an establishment ashore, his Spaniards are pelted with arrows by local tribesmen, obliging his expedition to come ashore in full armor to subdue these opponents. Ojeda then erects three small fortresses to protect his new town while skirmishing with the Indians farther inland and detaching Vergara's *Granada*—as well as his nephew's *Magdalena* later—to hunt for provisions.

On Vergara's return passage from Jamaica, where he has ventured to secure food, 25 of his men go ashore to forage at Valderrábano (24 miles southwest of Bahía Honda), suffering 19 slain before regaining the safety of the ship. By late May Ojeda's fledgling colony is in such dire straits that Ocampo and Vergara lure their partner aboard *Granada,* clapping him in irons to convey him toward Hispaniola, thus abandoning Bahía Honda.

MID-APRIL 1502. The first contingent of a massive new colonizing expedition reaches Santo Domingo from Spain under Nicolás de Ovando, the governor-designate and knight of the Order of Alcántara, which—when joined by its second group 15 days later—totals 32 ships bearing 2,500 men (among these the chronicler-priest Bartolomé de Las Casas). De Ovando immediately deposes Bobadilla as governor and sets about extirpating the last seeds of rebellion

Crude drawing of a Spanish disembarkation on a Caribbean island

from this island, preparing to send troublemakers home aboard the returning fleet under Capt. Antonio de Torres.

Just as this gets under way early in July, Columbus (pardoned but not restored to power after he was taken back to Spain in chains in 1501) passes by the island with four ships, heading farther west in another attempt to find Asia. He has been ordered not to touch at Santo Domingo until its situation is stabilized, so he merely sets some messages ashore along with a recommendation that Torres's fleet not weigh anchor because of signs of an impending hurricane. His advice is ignored, and all but two ships and a handful of lesser vessels are subsequently destroyed by a violent storm, costing Torres, Bobadilla, Roldán, the imprisoned chieftain Guarionex, and countless others their lives (among the few survivors is Rodrigo de Bastidas).

Columbus's quartet of ships rides out this hurricane at Puerto Hermoso, then is blown well past Jamaica toward southern Cuba. From here, the admiral spends many months working his way down the Central American shoreline, from Guanaja Island as far south as Veragua, without encountering any major kingdoms.

6 FEBRUARY 1503. Tired of being buffeted by contrary winds and storms, Columbus sends 70 men inland at Veragua, establishing a brief trade in gold pieces with its natives. This soon degenerates into hostility, with the local *quibián,* or chieftain, being captured by the Spaniards, then escaping.

SPRING 1503. On Santo Domingo, de Ovando as new governor declares war upon the natives of Saona Island for having killed eight Spaniards who were circling round to the north to settle. Capt. Juan de Esquivel leads a punitive expedition that defeats these tribesmen, along with their mainland overlord, Cutubano, at Higüey.

Around this same time, four Portuguese ships visit Brazil, returning home with several captives and tropical wood.

APRIL 1503. ***Columbus's Defeat at Veragua.*** His ships dangerously deteriorated after long exposure in the tropics, the admiral tows three out to sea in anticipation of departing Veragua (*Gallega* being left behind as unseaworthy). However, his shore parties are attacked by 400 infuriated natives before he can set sail; seven of his 20 men at the base camp under Capt. Diego Méndez are killed, and all but one of Capt. Diego Tristán's 12-man boat party are slaughtered when they venture upriver. The remainder finally fight their way off shore.

LATE JUNE 1503. Exhausted, Columbus reaches Jamaica with his two remaining ships (another having been scuttled) and sends to Santo Domingo for help, which takes more than a year to appear. This marks the end of the great explorer's efforts in the New World.

On Hispaniola, meanwhile, de Ovando has brought order to the settlers' lives and crushed the last shreds of Indian resistance by a brutal massacre at Xaragua. With 70 riders and 300 infantry he visits Anacaona—Caonabó's widow and native queen of the southwestern portion of this island—luring her with a false invitation to dine, only to seize the queen and burn her principal followers alive on suspicion of plotting a revolt. Spanish units under Diego Velázquez and Rodrigo Mejía subsequently subjugate this entire region, establishing new towns; three months afterward they hang Anacaona.

Shortly thereafter de Ovando receives news that the nine-man Spanish garrison installed this same spring at Higüey under Capt. Martín Villamán has been massacred by disgruntled natives, one man surviving to bring word of the disaster. The governor promptly orders Capt. Juan de Esquivel to prepare another punitive expedition for the east, comprising 300–400 Spaniards under Lts. Juan Ponce de León and Diego de Escobar plus numerous native auxiliaries. It takes about ten months to hunt down chief Cutubano and execute him, after which this territory is completely occupied.

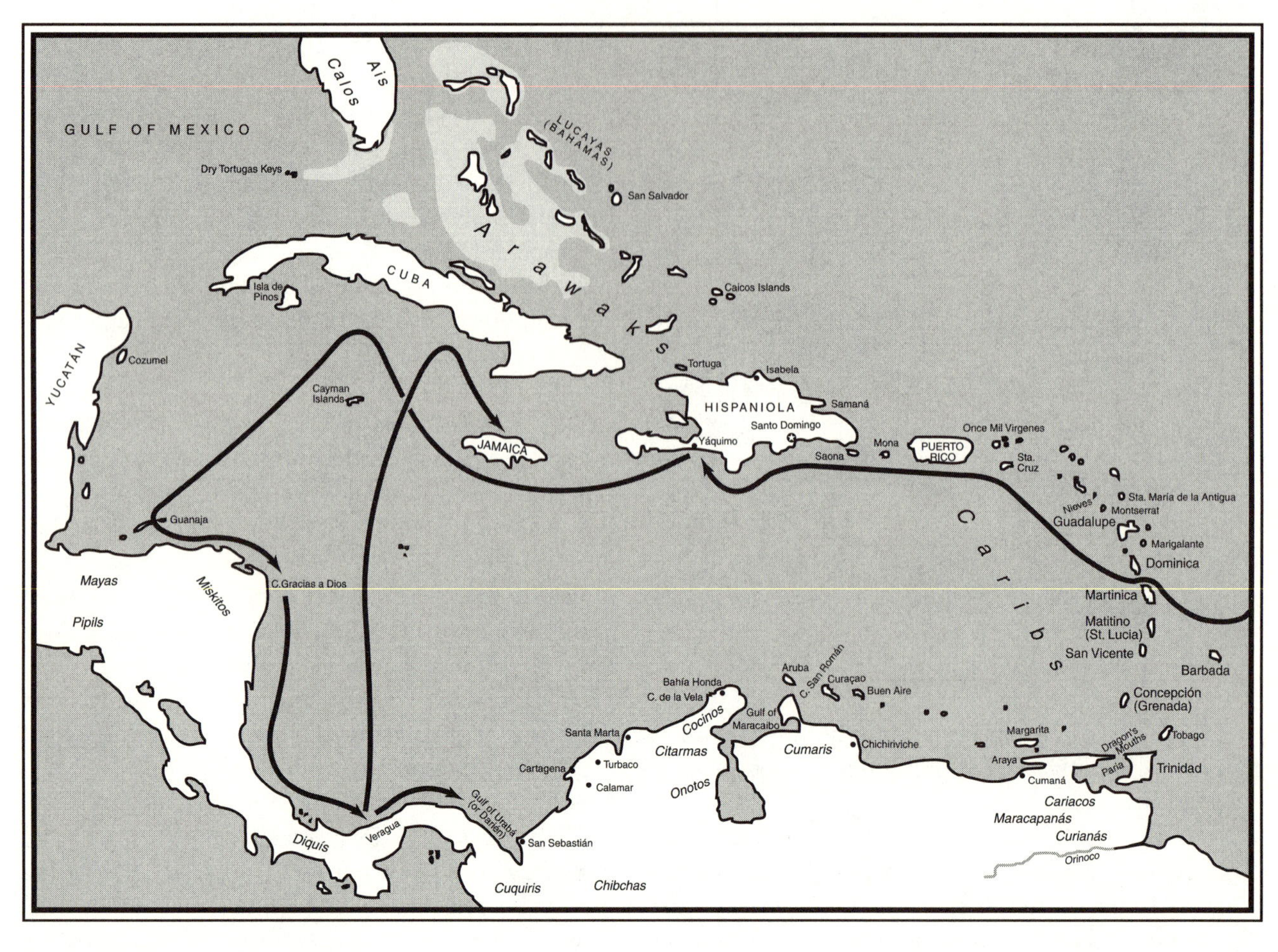

Columbus's voyage through the Caribbean

SPRING 1504. Cristóbal Guerra returns to the Caribbean with a small colonizing expedition, meeting the ships of Juan de la Cosa near Cartagena later this summer; the former chooses to remain and attempt settlement at this place while de la Cosa presses southwest to the Gulf of Darien, searching in vain for a passage farther west. Eventually Guerra sends his fellow explorer a message begging for help against Indian attacks, but none can reach him before he is slain. De la Cosa meanwhile beaches his ships because of extensive damage by teredo worms, camping uneasily ashore with 200 men while building two smaller brigantines from the remains of his larger vessels. Yellow fever and native attacks take a heavy toll, and only 50 Spaniards reach Jamaica, subsequently being rescued from Santo Domingo. Early in 1506, de la Cosa returns toward Spain with his survivors.

1505. Vicente Yáñez Pinzón is granted a license by the Spanish crown to settle unconquered Puerto Rico. He evidently fails to carry out this project, instead supposedly sailing around Cuba—thus proving it to be an island—before returning to Spain.

SUMMER 1506. Alonso de Ojeda, released from his legal entanglements (*see* 12 March 1502), returns to the Caribbean with a small expedition, supposedly to establish a stronghold in the Gulf of Urabá. He actually only coasts from Paria as far west as Panama before retiring to Santo Domingo.

EARLY 1508. Capt. Sebastián de Ocampo, a veteran from Columbus's first explorations, is ordered by Governor de Ovando to sail with two caravels from Santo Domingo to explore Cuba. He circles around, starting on its northern shore, returning eight months later to confirm it is an island.

SUMMER 1508. Vicente Yáñez Pinzón and Juan Díaz de Solís are authorized to attempt another exploration of the New World's mainland, the former aboard the hired merchantman *San Benito,* the latter aboard *Magdalena.* Failing to find any passage toward Asia's long-sought Spice Islands, they nonetheless expand upon Columbus's original Central American reconnaissance (*see* mid-April 1502) by sailing west from Hispaniola until sighting land, then traveling northwest from Cape Gracias a Dios as far as the northeastern tip of Yucatán—and perhaps even beyond, to the Gulf of Mexico—before returning to Spain in frustration in August 1509.

12 JUNE 1508. ***Occupation of Puerto Rico.*** The 48-year-old veteran Juan Ponce de León sets sail from his town of Salvaleón de Higüey (near the Yama River in eastern Santo Domingo), to reconnoiter and occupy the adjacent island of San Juan de Borinquen, or Puerto Rico, where Columbus and other sailors have often touched for water and wood. Ponce de León's first attempt flounders when his *caravelón* (large caravel) bearing 42 people—many of these natives from his Dominican plantation—runs aground on 3 August in Hispaniola's Ynaa Harbor during a storm, its provisions thus becoming spoiled. After a quick visit to Mona Island, the explorer continues his passage, reaching southwestern Puerto Rico a few days later and establishing friendly relations with its local chieftain, Agüeybana.

Another storm beaches Ponce de León's vessel on 10 August; while it is being refloated he explores Puerto Rico's interior with his host. Learning that several gold-bearing rivers empty onto its northern coast, he returns for his *caravelón,* then circles around the eastern tip of the island; after two abortive attempts he establishes a small fortified base named Caparra, two miles inland. Crops are duly planted and some gold gathered, after which Ponce de León returns toward Santo Domingo to report to de Ovando, leaving two Spaniards behind at Caparra. De Ovando acknowledges Ponce de León's accomplishment by appointing him governor and chief justice of Puerto Rico—subject to confirmation from Spain. The explorer returns to Caparra by May 1509.

10 JULY 1509. Diego Columbus, son and heir to the great admiral, leads a sizable convoy to Santo Domingo to succeed de Ovando as its governor. His ships are largely destroyed by a hurricane shortly thereafter, and he finds the island's native population—100,000 upon his father's first contact—shrunk to a mere 30,000.

Among his retinue is Cristóbal de Sotomayor, who bears a commission from King Ferdinand as governor of Puerto Rico. Ponce de León is therefore deposed, but once de Ovando reaches Spain he sees to it that Sotomayor's appointment is overturned, and Ponce de León is reinstated. The latter in turn delegates Sotomayor as deputy governor, who soon resigns and retires to his allotted native village, named Villa de Sotomayor. Eventually Ponce de León's commission is invalidated a second time, leading him to seek opportunities elsewhere.

Meanwhile other captains continue to probe the Panamanian coast, which is soon named Castilla de Oro (or Golden Castille); Juan de Esquivel prepares to establish a small Spanish colony on Jamaica; Ojeda receives title to the coastline stretching east from Colombia's Gulf of Darién (renaming this whole area New Andalucía) while 44-year-old Diego de Nicuesa arrives from Spain with five vessels and a similar grant farther west at Veragua, prompting arguments between both leaders as to the future boundary between their jurisdictions.

10 NOVEMBER 1509. ***Repulse at Cartagena.*** Seconded by Juan de la Cosa, Ojeda sets forth south from Hispaniola with two ships and two brigantines, bearing 225 men to establish his new colony at San Sebastián de Urabá (near the Colombia-Panama border). Four or five days later his expedition appears off Cartagena, pausing to storm ashore with 100 soldiers and kidnap natives to serve as slaves. Ojeda's column surprises a village called Calamar, slaughtering many of its inhabitants and securing some 60 captives; but when his raiders then press on against the larger town of Turbaco, things begin to go awry.

Its inhabitants flee into the underbrush, and the Spaniards disperse in hot pursuit. They quickly lose contact with one another and are destroyed piecemeal by Indian counterattacks in the jungle, suffering 70 deaths—among these de la Cosa, who is captured alive and tortured before succumbing. Ojeda is heavily beset yet manages to win free and be rescued. His vessels are joined some days later by the five-ship, 700-man expedition of his rival Nicuesa (who has quit Santo Domingo on 20 November), so that both Spanish contingents now unite to throw 400 fighting men ashore and raze Turbaco. The two expeditions then part company: Nicuesa presses on toward his destination of Veragua while Ojeda limps toward the Gulf of Urabá.

Ill fortune then descends upon Nicuesa, whose squadron is scattered by a heavy storm, his own flagship being lost upon the Panamanian coast. It takes three months for him and other survivors to straggle to the mouth of the Belén River (on the Mosquito Coast), where his remaining vessels are riding at anchor under Lope de Olano, unaware of their leader's fate.

MARCH 1510. Ojeda's reduced company establishes a new settlement at San Sebastián de Urabá but is soon beleaguered within the town by the region's ferocious natives. A renegade named Bernardino de Talavera arrives, having run away with a Genoese ship from Cape Tiburón (southwestern Santo Domingo) with 70 followers. Despite their reinforcement, the Spaniards continue to suffer thanks to Indian ambushes until Ojeda himself is wounded in the thigh by a poison arrow. Cauterizing the injury with hot irons, Ojeda waits in vain for further reinforcements and resupply to reach him from his financial backer on Santo Domingo, Martín Fernández de Enciso.

Eventually the wounded leader offers to sail toward Hispaniola in person aboard Talavera's ship for provisions, promising his colonists that if he does not return within 50 days they are free to abandon San Sebastián. His proposal is accepted, and Ojeda departs, leaving his colony under the temporary command of one of his soldiers, Francisco Pizarro. During their passage, Ojeda and Talavera are driven far northwest, being shipwrecked east of Jagua (Cuba). It takes many weeks before a caravel under Pánfilo de Narváez arrives from Jamaica to rescue them.

SUMMER 1510. Unaware of Ojeda's tribulations, Fernández de Enciso sets sail from Santo Domingo with a ship and smaller brigantine, bearing 150 men to carry provisions to San Sebastián. After clearing port, a stowaway named Vasco Núñez de Balboa is found hidden aboard in a barrel, fleeing from his creditors. Upon arriving opposite Cartagena, Fernández de Enciso finds the survivors of Ojeda's expedition limping away from their deserted outpost; having waited the stipulated 50 days, Pizarro and his subordinate Valenzuela have quit with the two brigantines left them. The latter sinks with all hands near Fuerte Island, leaving Pizarro to seek refuge ashore near Cartagena with his 30–40 remaining followers.

Fernández de Enciso incorporates these into his command and sails for San Sebastián, finding its stockade and 30 shacks already burned by local tribesmen. Uncertain how to proceed, Fernández de Enciso is convinced by Núñez de Balboa to sail farther west to the Gulf of Darien (which the latter knows from his earlier service under Rodrigo de Bastidas). Here they quickly establish a new town named Santa María la Antigua del Darién, but quarrels soon break out among its new inhabitants. Fernández de Enciso is deposed, thrown into prison, and deported back to Spain; the charismatic Núñez de Balboa assumes overall command. His bravery and just dealing soon win the allegiance of local tribesmen as well.

OCTOBER 1510. Having reunited his command at the mouth of the Belén River, Nicuesa leaves a small contingent behind under Alonso Núñez while venturing southeast himself to establish his governorship over Veragua (northern Panama). After being repelled by the natives of Portobelo, he comes ashore at Nombre de Dios in October, gaining a shaky foothold despite the hostility of local residents.

MID-NOVEMBER 1510. Nicuesa's lieutenant, Rodrigo de Colmenares, arrives at Santa María la Antigua from Santo Domingo with 60 reinforcements plus abundant supplies and arms. Noting how Núñez de Balboa's unofficial new Santa María settlement is flourishing—yet with a faction remaining opposed to his self-proclaimed rule—Colmenares proposes that Nicuesa take over as town governor.

LATE DECEMBER 1510. Desperate to hang on at Nombre de Dios, Nicuesa recalls Alonso Núñez's small contingent from the mouth of the Belén River to better resist the hostilities of the surrounding natives. This meager infusion of strength allows Capt. Gonzalo de Badajoz to lead a 20-man foray inland from Nombre de Dios, winning the Spaniards some breathing room; but the Indians then adopt a different tactic, retiring as far into the jungles as they can, leaving the 60–70 invaders isolated upon the coast.

At this juncture Nicuesa is joined by Colmenares, who holds out the promise of usurping command of Núñez de Balboa's settlement at Santa María la Antigua. The governor readily accedes, sending a caravel ahead under Juan de Quincedo to openly announce his intent while he gathers up the rest of his flotilla. This advance warning allows Núñez de Balboa to prepare by organizing a protest to greet Nicuesa upon his arrival, obliging the latter to retreat toward Santo Domingo aboard his brigantine.

EARLY 1511. A native uprising occurs on Puerto Rico, directed against the Spanish occupiers. Among the first victims are Ponce de León's former lieutenant governor, Cristóbal de Sotomayor, and his nephew Diego; Villa de Sotomayor is also torched. Some 80 Spaniards are killed before this rebellion can be crushed by Ponce de León, who divides his forces into three companies under Capts. Miguel del Toro, Diego de Salazar, and Luis de Almansa.

The deaths on Puerto Rico prompt Queen Juana, back in Spain, to issue a decree on 3 June authorizing Spaniards to make war upon the Caribs anywhere in the New World, treating any prisoners they seize as slaves. The chronic labor shortage in the Antilles means this law will be eagerly seized upon as an excuse for slaving raids against outlying islands.

NOVEMBER 1511. ***Conquest of Cuba.*** The jovial 46-year-old giant Diego Velázquez de Cuéllar, deputy governor for the western half of Santo Domingo, departs Salvatierra de la Sábana with 330 Spaniards and some native auxiliaries aboard four ships in pursuit of the Arawak chieftain Hatuey, who has fled west and reestablished himself on Cuba in the wake of de Ovando's Xaragua massacre (*see* late June 1503). Velázquez's small Spanish army disembarks at Puerto de Palmas near Cuba's Guantánamo Bay, where it is shortly joined by another contingent under Velázquez's lieutenant, Pánfilo de Narváez, who takes charge of the actual military operations against Hatuey.

The latter is soon defeated and burned at the stake, so that by early 1512 Velázquez can establish the first official Spanish settlement on Cuba—Nuestra Señora de la Asunción de Baracoa. From this northeastern corner he drives west to Camagüey, then regains the southern shore, where he establishes a new capital named Santiago de Cuba. Over the course of the next couple of years, Velázquez's cohorts gradually pacify this large island, moving ever farther west: the town of San Salvador del Bayamo is founded in 1513, Puerto Príncipe (modern Camagüey) in 1514, and, successively, Sancti Spíritus, Remedios, San Cristóbal de la Habana, and others.

EARLY JANUARY 1513. Capt. Cristóbal Serrano reaches Santa María la Antigua with 150 soldiers aboard two ships, bearing a royal commission appointing Núñez de Balboa governor of Darien. The latter has spent the previous two years exploring and pacifying this region, capturing the *cacique* (chieftain) Careta at Mosquitos Point, as well as subduing the tribes of Ponca and Comagre.

3 MARCH 1513. ***Exploration of Florida.*** Having again been deposed as governor of Puerto Rico two years earlier in favor of Diego Columbus's appointees, Ponce de León proposes to search north of Cuba for a land called Bimini, which according to Indian legend has waters of marvelous curative powers—the so-called Fountain of Youth. He sets sail from San Germán de Puerto Rico with three vessels on Thursday afternoon, 3 March, traversing the Caicos and Bahamas. On 27 March he sights land, subsequently deciding to name this territory Florida (because the date is Easter Sunday—in Spanish, *Pascua Florida*). He disembarks north of modern Saint Augustine on 2 April, taking possession of this area for Spain six days later. He then explores the coast south, and on 21 April he clashes with a party of Ais natives just below the Saint Lucie River despite his best attempts to establish friendly relations. Two Spaniards are wounded and an Indian is seized a few days later to be trained as interpreter.

Rounding the Florida Keys on 8 May, Ponce de León heads up Florida's western coast to at least 26 degrees 30 minutes north (and perhaps even higher). On Friday, 4 June, while careening his carrack *San Cristóbal* near Sanibel Island, his followers are attacked by 20 Calos warriors in canoes—some lashed two-by-two; he sinks five of these, killing numerous occupants and capturing four while suffering one dead. Another Calos flotilla appears on 11 June, ineffectually showering arrows upon the intruders until Ponce de León decides to reverse course three days later. The Dry Tortugas are visited on 21 June, where the Spaniards obtain a fresh supply of meat before retiring toward Cuba and the Bahamas, then finally regaining Puerto Rico by 15 October after weathering a hurricane.

Returning to Spain next year, Ponce de León receives a knighthood and appointment as governor of the "Island" of Florida, although he will not actually attempt to conquer this territory until 1521.

29 SEPTEMBER 1513. ***Discovery of the Pacific.*** Earlier this year, Núñez de Balboa received word that his previous deposal, arrest, and deportation of Fernández de Enciso has been deemed illegal in Spain (*see* summer 1510). Judgment having already been passed against him as a usurper, Núñez de Balboa is anxious to achieve some great success before the order for his recall can arrive. He therefore decides to act upon a rumor he has heard, from the friendly chieftain Comagre, of a great ocean on the far side of Panama's mountains linked to the gold-rich kingdom of Peru. On 1 September, the conquistador sets out from Santa María la Antigua with 190 Spaniards, 810 Indian auxiliaries, and numerous war dogs aboard a brigantine and ten large canoes. These travel west to the port of Acla, establishing a base camp in the village of chief Careta (Núñez de Balboa's father-in-law), from where his expedition then ventures inland.

Passing through the territory of their vassal Ponca, the Spaniards are confronted farther south by a native army of several hundred led by the Cuarecuan *cacique* Torecha, whose followers are easily scattered by the invaders' firearms, then cruelly slaughtered. Núñez de Balboa occupies the dead Torecha's village on 23 September; two days later from a nearby mountaintop he catches sight of a vast new body of water farther south. Descending into the valley between, his army subdues the tribesmen of chief Chiapes, in whose village the conquistador rests while three 12-man patrols are sent ahead under Francisco Pizarro, Juan de Ezcaray, and Alonso Martín to find the shoreline of this new ocean. Martín succeeds two days later, returning to report to Núñez de Balboa. The whole Spanish force then advances, wading fully armored into its waves on 29 September—Saint Michael's Day—for which reason this particular body of water is dubbed the Gulf of San Miguel; the entire Great South Sea, as it is named, is claimed for Spain.

Núñez de Balboa remains on the Pacific Coast, setting sail with 70 soldiers aboard eight native canoes on 17 October to conquer some offshore pearl islands. Instead, his expedition is washed onto the mainland beaches in the territory of chief Tumaco, who promptly submits to Spanish rule and pays tribute. On 28 October his town is renamed San Lucas, where the conquistadores remain until 3 November before marching northwest in search of fresh territories. Shortly thereafter the Spaniards capture the hated regional overlord, Pacra, condemning him and three subordinates to be torn to pieces by war dogs to ingratiate the Spaniards with the lesser tribes. Núñez de Balboa resumes his progress early in December, defeating chiefs Bocheriboca, Chiorisco, Tubanamá, and Pocorosa in quick succession before regaining his ally Comagre's village of Acla (now ruled by his son Panquiano, as the aged *cacique* has since died) by 14 December.

Recuperating for a month from this ordeal, Núñez de Balboa sets sail on 17 January 1514, returning triumphantly to Santa María la Antigua two days later. He at once sends messengers with presents of gold and pearls to Ferdinand, announcing his discovery. Fully as the conquistador expects, the king's displeasure is reconciled by his vassal's feat. Although Núñez de Balboa will not be confirmed as governor of Darien (this post having already been granted to the well-connected Pedro Arias de Avila, who sets sail from Seville on 12 April 1514 with Martín Fernández de Enciso and 2,000 men aboard 22 ships), he is nonetheless appointed by March 1515 *adelantado,* or military governor, for the newly discovered territories of Panama and the South Seas.

3 JUNE 1514. The 72-year-old Pedro Arias de Avila (whose name is commonly contracted into Pedrarias Dávila) reaches Dominica with his followers, pausing a few days later at Santa Marta to send three barks inshore to lay claim to this port. Its local natives react with hostility, obliging the Spaniards to open fire before retiring.

LATE JUNE 1514. Dávila's expedition reaches Santa María la Antigua, and he relieves Núñez de Balboa as governor. (Among the new arrivals are such famous future conquistadores as Bernal Díaz del Castillo, Diego de Almagro, Pascual de Andagoya, Sebastián de Velalcázar, Hernando de Soto, and Francisco Vázquez de Coronado.) Núñez de Balboa is briefly detained to answer charges of having deposed Fernández de Enciso but is soon released.

MID-JULY 1514. Capt. Juan de Ayora—one of Dávila's favorites—ventures west from Santa María la Antigua with a ship and three or four caravels, pillaging its friendly coastal tribes despite instructions to the contrary. He returns to port by early October, sailing for Spain shortly thereafter with his ill-gotten booty.

AUTUMN 1514. One of Dávila's nephews is sent northeast across the Gulf of Darien with 450 men aboard two ships to ascend the Cenú River (Colombia) and locate its Tarufi gold mines. The local natives, upon being informed that the pontiff has ceded these lands to Spain, reply that "the pope must have been drunk, for giving away what is not his." They then contest the Spaniards' advance, eventually compelling Dávila's nephew to turn back after three months with only 200 slaves and a little gold to show for his efforts, having suffered 150 casualties.

LATE 1514. Ponce de León returns to the West Indies from Spain at the head of a small expedition intended to conduct reprisals against the Caribs on Guadeloupe. Pausing off this island to refresh following their transatlantic crossing, the Spaniards suffer the ambush of one of their laundering parties, which is carried off into the jungle along with its escort of soldiers, before Ponce de León proceeds toward Puerto Rico.

20 MARCH 1515. Two caravels reach Santa María la Antigua, bearing Núñez de Balboa's appointment as *adelantado,* or military governor, for Panama and the South Seas, which Dávila grudgingly confirms on 23 April. An ambitious and covetous man, the governor is consumed by jealousy for his subordinate's better prospects. A distinguished veteran of warfare against the North African Moors, Dávila's ferocity and aggressiveness have earned him a reputation for cruelty among Santa María's natives (he is nicknamed *Furor de*

Dios, or Wrath of God) but scant profit. In contrast, the more humane Núñez de Balboa is popular; moreover, there is feverish excitement throughout the Spanish Caribbean about his latest push south, which Dávila realizes will reduce his own Darien governorship to secondary importance.

EARLY APRIL 1515. Before Núñez de Balboa is promoted, Dávila dispatches an expedition northwest along Panama's coast from Santa María la Antigua under Capts. Gonzalo de Badajoz and Alonso Pérez de la Rúa to sail toward Portobelo and attempt to cross the isthmus. They pillage their way inland until their greed leads them to treacherously assault the natives under chief Paris—even after being generously greeted with four chests of gold dust. This plan backfires: Pérez de la Rúa is killed along with almost half the Spanish force, the chests are lost, and the survivors must retreat to the coast.

When news of this disaster reaches Dávila, he sends out Capt. Gaspar de Espinosa with 200 men to recover this rich prize. De Espinosa first crosses the Tubanamá Range and cruelly subdues the province of Chepo, establishing his headquarters at Natá before advancing against Paris. The chief is eventually burned alive while defending his capital, which goes up in flames.

LATE SPRING 1515. Another of Dávila's favorites—Capt. Gaspar de Morales, seconded by Francisco Pizarro—departs Santa María la Antigua with 80 men to conquer the offshore Perla (also called Rica) Islands in the Gulf of Panama. These campaigners compel the *caciques* Chiapes and Tumaco to furnish them with canoes, which they then use to fight their way ashore, defeating and enslaving the inhabitants. The main island is renamed Flores, its chieftain made to promise an annual tribute of pearls before Morales and Pizarro retire to the mainland. Their return march toward Santa María la Antigua is complicated by a general Indian uprising, but they fight their way through by early August, Morales taking ship for Spain shortly thereafter.

LATE JULY 1515. Núñez de Balboa and fellow captain Luis Carrillo quit Santa María la Antigua with 150 men aboard five vessels to venture southward to the Gulf of Urabá and up the Darién River, in search of the legendary Dabaybe goldfields. After traveling as far as they can by ship, Núñez de Balboa and Carrillo continue with 50 men aboard four canoes until they are ambushed midstream by a native flotilla. About 30 Spaniards are wounded, including their leader; Carrillo is killed, and the survivors are forced to retreat to Santa María by the end of August.

1515. During this year, a series of Spanish *indiero,* or Indian-hunting expeditions, under Capt. Diego de Salazar nets 2,000 natives from Curaçao and Bonaire; they are shipped as slaves to Santo Domingo.

EARLY 1516. While Dávila is absent on an expedition to Acla (Panama), Núñez de Balboa secretly recruits 60 followers aboard a ship from Cuba to sail toward Nombre de Dios and lead another enterprise across the isthmus to the Pacific. The governor suddenly returns to Santa María la Antigua, however, arresting Balboa for attempting to disobey orders and detaining his vessel. Relations between Dávila and his subordinate are eventually patched up when Núñez de Balboa marries the governor's daughter María; Balboa is later sent with 80 men to reestablish the former Spanish base camp at Acla.

2 FEBRUARY 1516. The veteran explorer Juan Díaz de Solís arrives from Spain opposite present-day Montevideo (Uruguay), with 60 men aboard one 60-ton ship and two 30-ton vessels. His mission is to discover a new route around the South American continent to link up with Núñez de Balboa's southwesterly probes out of Panama. Díaz de Solís duly lays claim to the mouth of the River Plate in a formal ceremony then sails northwest up its course in the mistaken belief this will lead him to the Pacific. As this waterway gradually narrows, he continues with his smallest caravel alone until some Indians are sighted opposite Martín García Island and signal the Spaniards to land. Díaz de Solís ventures ashore with two officers and six seamen, all of whom are suddenly massacred by the natives. His expedition then returns to Seville on 4 September under his brother-in-law Francisco de Torres, minus one ship that has run aground at 27 degrees south latitude (opposite Santa Catarina Island, Brazil).

EARLY 1517. Still suspicious and envious of his son-in-law and subordinate Núñez de Balboa, who is at Panama's Pearl Islands preparing his seaborne expedition south toward Peru, Dávila lures him back to the town of Acla with a crafty message and throws him into prison on a trumped-up charge of treason. After spending nearly two years in incarceration, the Pacific discoverer is executed in January 1519, allowing Dávila to transfer his capital from the unhealthy Santa María la Antigua; he founds Panama City on 15 August 1519.

LATE 1519. Gaspar de Espinosa departs Panama City west with two brigantines—formerly commanded by Núñez de Balboa—piloted by Juan de Castañeda. He explores the Central American coastline as far as the Gulf of Nicoya before returning.

LATE NOVEMBER 1519. ***Magellan's Circumnavigation.*** The 39-year-old Portuguese explorer Ferdinand Magellan appears off Brazil with his flagship *Trinidad, San Antonio* of Juan de Cartagena, *Concepción* of Gaspar de Quesada, *Victoria* of Luis de Mendoza, and *Santiago* of Juan Rodríguez Serrano. After entering a bay they name Santa Lucía on 13 December (probably Rio de Janeiro), they rest for two weeks before departing, rounding Cape Frío on 10 January 1520 and sighting Montevideo. The River Plate is explored for the next three weeks by the small *Victoria* and *Santiago* while the three remaining ships chart its estuary. Convinced the waterway does not lead west to the Pacific, Magellan resumes his passage south on 3 February, finally coming to anchor at San Julián on 31 March.

Two nights later, Captains Cartagena and Quesada lead an armed mutiny of Spaniards against their commander, who next morning blocks the exit with *Trinidad, Victoria,* and *Santiago.* When *San Antonio* attempts to slip past during the night of 2–3 April it is boarded and recaptured; *Concepción* surrenders the next day. By 7 April more than 40 mutineers have been condemned to death, but only Quesada is actually executed; Cartagena and another accomplice are sentenced to be marooned. The expedition then winters, somewhat uneasily. Rodríguez Serrano's *Santiago* is sent out on a coastal reconnaissance and wrecks on 22 May near Santa Cruz River.

On 11 August Cartagena and his companion are set ashore, and Magellan's four remaining ships weigh on 24 August. By 21 October they come within sight of the Vírgenes Cape; as the expedition begins to probe its entrance a sudden storm blows *San Antonio* and *Concepción* directly into this passage—thus the Strait of Magellan is discovered. The expedition disperses and explores this waterway for another month, during which *San Antonio*'s crew rises against its new captain, Alvaro de Mezquita, and sails back toward Spain. After awaiting his consort's reappearance in vain, Magellan stands into the strait on 21 November, emerging on its far side one week later to stand out directly across the Pacific toward Asia.

CONQUEST OF MEXICO (1517–1521)

MORE THAN A GENERATION HAS PASSED since Columbus's initial contact with the New World. With no rich Asian trading countries found, Spanish efforts increasingly focus on colonization rather than commerce. Parties raid the Carib islands and South American mainland to capture natives for slave labor, while penniless adventurers and soldiers continue to emigrate from the Old World in much larger numbers than merchants—in hopes of winning large land holdings by dint of arms.

Cuba's acting governor, Diego Velázquez, having secured his hold over the terrified populace, decides to investigate rumors of other unknown "islands" due west of his newfound colony. Apparently these refer not to Florida or Honduras but to another, much richer land. He organizes a small reconnaissance force under Francisco Hernández de Córdoba, who sails for what we know today as Mexico.

8 FEBRUARY 1517. Hernández de Córdoba departs Santiago de Cuba aboard *San Sebastián,* accompanied by one other ship and a brigantine, with a total complement of 110 men (including the famous pilot Antón de Alaminos and future chronicler Bernal Díaz del Castillo). He circles through the Windward Passage before coasting along the north side of Cuba to replenish supplies, then strikes westward from Cape San Antonio.

20 FEBRUARY 1517. ***Discovery.*** Hernández sights Isla Mujeres off northeastern Yucatán and, shortly thereafter, its mainland. He is greeted off Cape Catoche by fully dressed Mayans in boats; the chieftain comes aboard next day and invites the Spaniards to land. Despite the friendly beginning, a contingent of Spanish soldiers is soon attacked by local warriors when they penetrate the jungle near the modern town of Porvenir. Fifteen Mayans are killed by crossbow and harquebus fire, and a like number of Spaniards are wounded (two of these will succumb).

Hernández obtains several finely wrought gold pieces and two native captives before venturing around the peninsula and landing near Champotón (in the vicinity of Campeche) to take on water. Camping ashore overnight, he and his men awaken next dawn to find themselves surrounded by warriors painted in black and white; the leader, Mochcouoh, launches an immediate attack. Twenty Spaniards are killed, two others are captured, and Hernández is compelled to make a fighting retreat to his boats, suffering numerous personal wounds. So many of his men are killed or wounded that he abandons his brigantine and sails directly to the southwestern tip of Florida for resupply, only to again be attacked by Indians in canoes. Limping back to Cuba two months after his departure with only 54 men, Hernández reports to the governor and dies shortly thereafter.

Notwithstanding Hernández's initial rebuff, Velázquez and other Spaniards are intrigued by his account of this new land's wealth and relative sophistication. Its natives are clothed (unlike the more primitive Arawaks or Caribs of the Caribbean), capable of erecting stone houses, and practice many other skilled crafts. Another expedition quickly begins to form, this time under the governor's 28-year-old nephew, Juan de Grijalva.

LATE JANUARY 1518. ***Reconnaissance.*** Grijalva sets sail from Santiago de Cuba with two ships (both called *San Sebastián*), the caravel *Trinidad,* and the brigantine *Santiago,* bearing a total of 200 men. His three principal captains are 32-year-old Pedro de Alvarado y Mesía, Francisco de Montejo, and Alonso de Avila; his expedition is further strengthened by several culverins (light cannons) and war dogs. A lengthy layover on the north shore of Cuba follows, during which *Santiago* turns back and is replaced by the brigantine *Santa María de los Remedios.* Grijalva's force finally quits Cape San Antonio toward the end of April.

3 MAY 1518. Grijalva sights the island of Cozumel (northeastern Mexico), which he explores for four days before heading south and discovering Ascensión Bay. Reversing course, he then rounds the Yucatán Peninsula, following Hernández de Córdoba's earlier route.

26 MAY 1518. Grijalva comes ashore near Champotón with three cannons, several harquebusiers, and a sizeable contingent of troops. The natives allow him to draw water and even present him with some gold gifts before ordering the Spaniards to leave. Grijalva refuses, and two days later his company is confronted at dawn by an army in war paint. This time the natives fail to press home their attack because of the Spaniards' frightening artillery discharges; this battle ends indecisively, with one Spanish fatality and about 40 wounded (of whom 13 later succumb), plus an unknown number of Mayan casualties. This night Grijalva stands out to sea, heading farther west.

8 JUNE 1518. After resting at the Laguna de Términos, Grijalva passes the mouth of a large river, which is christened with his name; some days later Pedro de Alvarado makes a reconnaissance up another large river, which in turn is given his name. (These are today's Grijalva and Alvarado Rivers, Mexico.)

17 JUNE 1518. Grijalva reaches an island near the site of present-day Veracruz, where there are signs of a recent human sacrifice, so he names it Sacrificios Island. The local Totonac Indians offer him an elaborate welcome, hoping to ingratiate themselves with these powerful new strangers and use them to throw off Aztec rule.

24 JUNE 1518. Grijalva receives a minor embassy from the distant Mexican emperor, then ceremoniously lays claim to the island of San Juan de Ulúa before detaching Alvarado a few days later to return to Cuba with a report and booty. In the meantime, Grijalva presses deeper into the Gulf of Mexico, eventually reaching as far north as Cape Rojo before turning back. Despite importuning by his men, he refuses to establish any permanent beachhead ashore, preferring instead to make a protracted reconnaissance before retiring toward Cuba.

During Grijalva's prolonged absence, Governor Velázquez grows increasingly restive, for this wealthy new find has not been fully claimed, and he fears usurpation by Spanish rivals. He therefore sends out a single ship under Cristóbal de Olid in a vain attempt to locate Grijalva while preparing a third expedition.

23 OCTOBER 1518. After offering command of the latest enterprise to various individuals, Velázquez selects a 34-year-old *alcalde,* or magistrate, at Santiago de Cuba named Hernán Cortés. Velázquez intends for Cortés merely to secure a foothold in this new territory and await the governor's arrival with a main body; Velázquez is soon disconcerted by the speed and scope of his subordinate's preparations, for within a matter of weeks Cortés musters seven vessels and more than 300 eager volunteers. Alarmed, the governor decides to replace him at the last minute with Luis de Medina, only to have Cortés get wind of this proposed change.

18 NOVEMBER 1518. Rather than allow himself to be superseded, Cortés weighs immediately from Santiago de Cuba with his flagship *Santa María de la Concepción* and five other vessels, sailing along southern Cuba and gathering more recruits and supplies while openly defying Velázquez's repeated recalls.

18 FEBRUARY 1519. After three months, Cortés has gathered 11 vessels off the western tip of Cuba bearing 530 troops (12 harquebusiers and 30 crossbowmen among them), 50 sailors, 16 horses, 14 large artillery pieces, numerous smaller pieces, war dogs, a doctor, two interpreters, a dozen women, and several hundred Cuban porters and black slaves. He strikes out toward Cozumel but is scattered by a nocturnal storm, so his fleet straggles into port over the course of several days, with one ship missing.

13 MARCH 1519. While preparing to resume his voyage from Cozumel, Cortés is joined by a Spanish castaway named Gerónimo de Aguilar, who has been living among the Indians of Yucatán for eight years and can provide valuable intelligence about local conditions. After watering at Isla Mujeres, Cortés rounds the Yucatán Peninsula and locates his missing ship, anchored off the Laguna de Términos. He probes up the Grijalva River, where he comes upon the large town of Potonchan.

24 MARCH 1519. ***Initial Clashes.*** After several days of tense negotiations with the Chontal Mayas, a fight erupts. Using artillery, the Spaniards overrun Potonchan, killing, wounding, or capturing 400 Indians; 20 Spaniards are injured.

Attempting to forage farther inland some days later, Cortés becomes embroiled in a much larger battle at Centla, which is decided by his cavalry, now fully deployed ashore. Never having seen horses before, the Mayas are panic-stricken by the swift-moving riders and suffer several hundred deaths. Sixty Spaniards are injured.

After accepting the natives' surrender, Cortés remains for three weeks and renames Potonchan as Santa María de la Victoria (literally, Saint Mary of the Victory), also receiving a young Indian slave woman named Malinali or Malinche as booty. Able to speak Náhuatl, the language of the inland Aztec empire, Doña Marina (her name becoming Hispanicized) will prove invaluable as interpreter, confidant, and lover to Cortés during his forthcoming campaign against Mexico.

17 APRIL 1519 (PALM SUNDAY). Cortés's expedition resumes its journey westward, anchoring off the island of San Juan de Ulúa on 20 April.

22 APRIL 1519 (GOOD FRIDAY). Cortéz comes ashore with about 200 soldiers as well as horses, artillery,

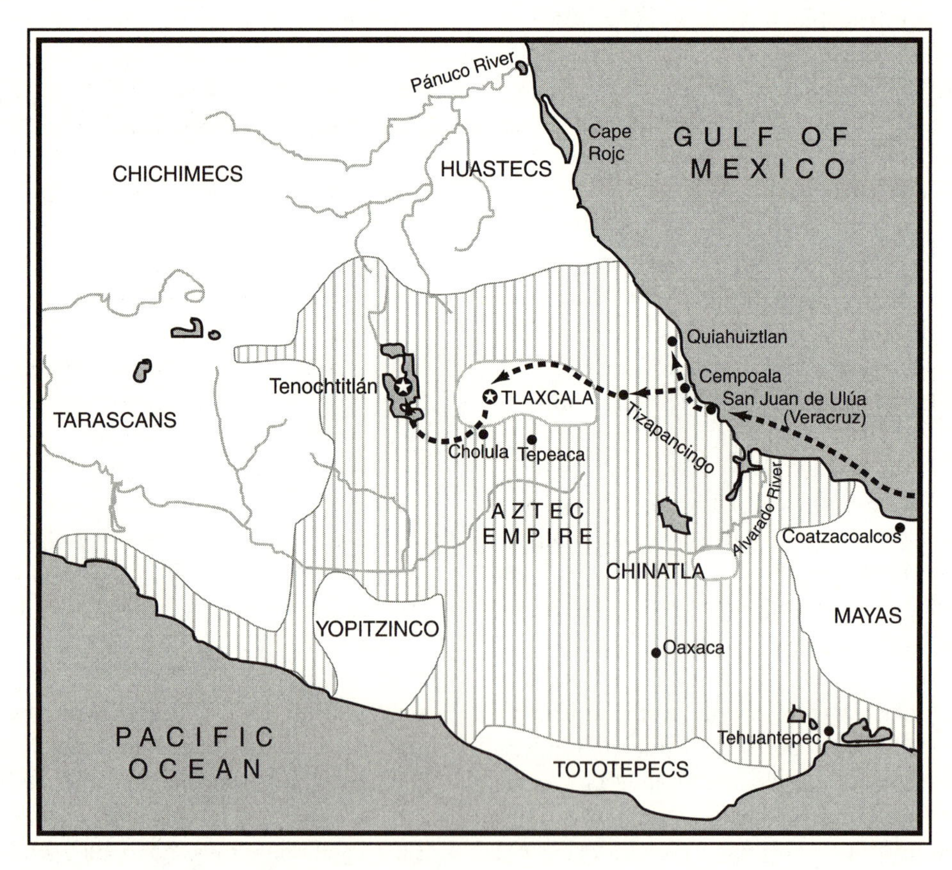

Cortés's advance on the Aztec capital

Cuban servants, and several dogs, getting a friendly reception from the local Totonac Indians. A like welcome is extended over the next few days by the Aztec representative Teudile, who assigns 2,000 natives to wait upon the Spaniards and exchanges rich presents with their leader.

1 MAY 1519. Aztec emissaries arrive from inland to shower wealthy gifts upon Cortés—thus unwittingly exciting the Spaniards' greed—while discouraging these new strangers from visiting their capital of Tenochtitlán (modern-day Mexico City) or meeting with their emperor, Montezuma II. Cortés insists on doing exactly that, and while awaiting a reply he receives a delegation of Totonac Indians from nearby Cempoala that reveals how a number of subject tribes are resentful of Aztec rule.

Shortly thereafter Teudile reappears, withdrawing the 2,000 native servants and cutting off the food supply. Cortés sends his lieutenant, Pedro de Alvarado, nine miles inland with 100 soldiers, 15 crossbowmen, and six harquebusiers; they return after pillaging several abandoned Indian towns. Two brigantines with 50 men apiece are sent northwest under Capts. Francisco de Montejo and Rodrigo Alvarez Chico to search for a better landing site.

During these absences, Cortés convenes a general meeting of his small army to agree to found a new Spanish settlement in Mexico, to be named Villa Rica de la Vera Cruz (literally, Rich Town of the True Cross); he is elected mayor. This legal fiction allows him to sever all ties with Velázquez and report directly to the king in Spain.

7 JUNE 1519. Once his two brigantines return, Cortés decides to transfer his base 40 miles northwest of San Juan de Ulúa to the more sheltered harbor of Quiahuiztlan, in Cempoalan territory. He marches overland with 400 men, all his horses, and two small artillery pieces while his ships circle round with the remaining force. The Spanish army is splendidly received by Tlacochcalcatl, the immensely fat chief of Cempoala, who proposes to Cortés than an alliance with the inland tribes of Tlaxcala and Huejotzingo will overthrow the Aztecs.

28 JUNE 1519. Completing his journey to Quiahuiztlan, Cortés establishes a fortified town then receives a large Aztec delegation. These inform him that while the Spaniards may now travel to Tenochtitlán, they may possibly not be received by Montezuma. Cortés returns a smooth reply while secretly encouraging the Cempoalans to refuse paying any more tribute to the Aztecs.

When news of this tax rebellion spreads, Aztec collectors flee to their local garrison, Tizapancingo, where the Cempoalans soon report an army is mustering. Cortés advances swiftly upon this outpost with most of his soldiers, scattering the Aztec host through sheer fright and overrunning the base. Upon returning triumphantly, Cortés further throws down Cempoala's native idols, building a church atop its principal temple.

1 JULY 1519. Once again harbored in Quiahuiztlan, Cortés's fleet is reinforced by a single caravel arriving from Cuba under Francisco de Saucedo bearing 60 men and several additional horses. More importantly, this officer brings word that Velázquez is authorized by Spain to take possession of any new lands discovered west of his Caribbean colony.

Such news prompts Cortés to quickly prepare three vessels to sail directly toward Europe, with messages and gifts to win crown approval of his independent campaign. Certain disgruntled elements within Cortés's army, who remain loyal to the Cuban governor, are put down by means of several arrests and a pair of executions.

Finally, in order to discourage any further talk of turning back, Cortés persuades the masters of the other nine ships riding in the harbor to beach and disassemble their craft, incorporating the sailors into his army ranks. Only the flagship *Santa María de la Concepción* and two caravels remain; Cortés dispatches these toward Spain on 16 July bearing treasure and letters.

8 AUGUST 1519. Cortés marches inland at the head of 300 soldiers, 40 crossbowmen, 20 harquebusiers, 15 horses, 150 Cuban servants, 800 Cempoalan auxiliaries, and many war dogs. Shortly after his departure, word arrives that four Spanish vessels have been sighted off the coast. These prove to be under the command of Alonso Alvarez de Pineda, who has been sent by Francisco de Garay, the governor of Jamaica, to reconnoiter and lay claim to the entire coastline of the Gulf of Mexico. Cortés returns hastily to Quiahuiztlan with 100 of his men, arresting Alvarez's men who dare step ashore and forcing the rival flotilla to stand off.

16 AUGUST 1519. Having rejoined his army from the coast, Cortés resumes his advance inland. Most Indian tribes prove hospitable—until the Spaniards enter the territory of the Tlaxcaltecans some ten days later.

At the border, an engagement erupts immediately between Cortés's mounted vanguard and several thousand Tlaxcaltecan warriors; two horses are killed and three others wounded before the natives scatter. The conquistadores carefully conceal the horse carcasses so they cannot be found and examined.

EARLY SEPTEMBER 1519. ***Tlaxcala Battles.*** Pushing deeper into Tlaxcaltecan territory the next day, Cortés's army confronts a huge throng of warriors and engages them in a hard fight until sundown. The Indians succeed in capturing a Spanish mare, which they sacrifice to their gods; they nonetheless suffer heavy casualties.

Cortés remains in possession of the battlefield, leading deliberately punitive raids against surrounding villages to brutalize the Indian populace in hopes of sowing terror among their ranks. Still, the Tlaxcaltecan armies return repeatedly to give battle over the next two weeks, even launching a night attack. Many Spaniards are wounded by obsidian-tipped swords, javelins, and arrows, but only 45 actually die from their wounds while many hundreds of Tlaxcaltecans—perhaps even thousands—are killed.

These losses eventually persuade the tribal leadership to offer terms; Tlaxcala's military commander, Xicotencatl the Younger, enters Cortés's camp and asks forgiveness for his attacks. The Spaniards are duly propitiated and welcomed to the capital of Tlaxcala by 18 September amid great festivities.

12 OCTOBER 1519. Having refreshed his troops (and sent two lieutenants, Pedro de Alvarado and Bernardino Vázquez de Tapia, to make an unobtrusive visit of the Aztec capital of Tenochtitlán), Cortés resumes his march inland, reinforced by several thousand Tlaxcaltecans. A couple of days later, his army enters the very large city of Cholula, a major Aztec satellite.

18 OCTOBER 1519. ***Cholula Massacre.*** Convinced the Cholultecans are in league with Montezuma to prevent his progress toward Tenochtitlán—and perhaps even to attack the Spaniards within the city streets—Cortés summons several hundred city noblemen to an assembly. His men then seal the doors and massacre all within; the city is cruelly pillaged over the next two days.

The Aztec emperor sends propitiatory messages to Cortés, denying all knowledge of this projected perfidy by his subjects and renewing his invitation for the Spaniards to visit his capital—while secretly arranging other obstacles to further delay the Spanish advance.

1 NOVEMBER 1519. Cortés's army departs Cholula, still determined to reach the Aztec capital. Although the Cempoalan auxiliaries retire toward the coast at this point, they are replaced by perhaps 1,000 Tlaxcaltecans.

Hearing rumors that an Aztec ambush may be planned along the main highway leading to Tenochtitlán, Cortés veers into the mountains, thus passing through the gap (elevation 13,000 feet) between the volcanoes of Ixtaccihuatl and Popocatepetl—still called the Paso de Cortés) today—before descending into the Valley of Mexico beyond.

8 NOVEMBER 1519. The Spanish army marches out across a vast lake along a long causeway, being personally welcomed to Tenochtitlán (population 200,000) by the reluctant Emperor Montezuma and nobly housed.

14 NOVEMBER 1519. After several days' entertainment in the Aztec capital, Cortés receives word of a clash between some of his forces left behind at Quiahuiztlan and an Aztec contingent farther to the north. Seven Spaniards and many Cempoalans having been killed, the conquistador now possesses a convenient excuse to confront Montezuma.

Visiting the emperor at his palace with about 30 armed men, Cortés surprises Montezuma by launching into a complaint then insists the chief return to the Spaniards' quarters under guard. After a lengthy discussion, the cowed emperor agrees, creating a sensation among his people. A few days later the offending Aztec commanders are brought in captive from the coast; on Cortés's orders they are burned alive in the main square of Tenochtitlán.

The Spaniards spend several months living peaceably in the wary Aztec capital, learning everything about its empire, receiving vast amounts of tribute, and reconnoitering outlying provinces.

APRIL 1520. Word reaches Cortés of another Spanish expedition off the coast of Veracruz, larger than his own. This force departed Cuba on 5 March comprising 11 ships and seven brigantines under Velázquez's lieutenant, 45-year-old Pánfilo de Narváez. The Cuban governor has already learned of Cortés's effort to circumvent his authority by dispatching treasure ships directly toward Spain; he is determined to arrest and hang this usurper, much as Dávila did to Núñez de Balboa (*see* early 1517).

Narváez has lost one ship and 40 men during a Gulf storm before reaching San Juan de Ulúa on 19 April. Here he finds a single ship awaiting him,

A romanticized nineteenth-century portrayal of Cortés and his conquistadores gazing across the Lake of Mexico toward the Aztec capital for the first time

bearing Judge Lucas Vázquez de Ayllón, who has been dispatched from the island of Santo Domingo to prevent any fighting between the two rival Spanish contingents. Narváez contemptuously sends this lawyer home and disembarks his army of 1,400 men (including 80 riders, 70 harquebusiers, and 90 crossbowmen) to begin building a base. Though numerous, the army is not entirely loyal to Narváez, many troops being more impressed instead by tales of Cortés's prowess in dealing with the powerful Aztec empire.

EARLY MAY 1520. Cortés departs Tenochtitlán with 80 Spanish soldiers, leaving another 120 behind as an occupation force under his lieutenant, Pedro de Alvarado. After marshaling another 260 Spaniards at Cholula, the conquistador strikes eastward to meet Narváez, Cortés unaccompanied by any native auxiliaries. Although outnumbered four to one, the clever and charismatic Cortés nonetheless sways many members of the rival expedition thanks to a steady stream of messages and gifts sent to Narváez's camp at Cempoala.

28–29 MAY 1520. ***Narváez's Defeat.*** Confident of victory, Narváez goes to sleep, high atop Cempoala's main pyramid, on the rainy night of 28 May. Cortés moves against him in the dark, hastening a company of troops up its familiar steps to fall upon Narváez and his closest companions before any alarm can be raised. In the confused fighting that ensues, Narváez's right eye is torn out, after which the thatched covering to his abode is set ablaze. He surrenders, and shortly thereafter his army follows suit. At the cost of only two dead (15 being killed among Narváez's men), Cortés incorporates this vast new army into his ranks.

A company of 120 Spaniards is then sent northward under his lieutenant, Juan Velázquez de León, to settle the Gulf Coast beyond Pánuco; a similar number is sent southward under Diego de Ordáz to establish a colony at Coatzacoalcos, thus ensuring Cortés's hold over the entire Mexican shoreline against any rival claimant.

However, the detachments are soon recalled by news that Alvarado, during Cortés's absence from Tenochtitlán, has massacred a large group of natives celebrating the festival of Toxcatl (16 May), having misconstrued their traditional festivities as a war dance in anticipation of a surprise attack against the garrison. Alvarado's brutality precipitates a vengeful descent upon the Spanish quarters in the Aztec capital, which abates after Alvarado forces Montezuma onto its rooftop to quell this angry crowd.

24 JUNE 1520. Cortés returns to a silent Tenochtitlán, having first circled warily around its lake to make a reconnaissance, at the head of more than 1,000 Spanish soldiers and fresh Tlaxcaltecan levies. Only five or six of Alvarado's men have actually been killed, but the garrison is isolated and shunned by the Aztecs; Cortés reproves his lieutenant for his poor judgment and is also angry with Montezuma, having learned the emperor secretly contacted his antagonist Narváez during the recent coastal campaign, promising friendship.

25 JUNE 1520. Wishing the Mexican markets to be reopened to obtain food for his troops, Cortés releases Montezuma's brother Cuitláhuac, lord of Ixtapalapa, to arrange these matters. Instead, this chieftain immediately begins rallying Aztec resistance.

Cortés then sends Diego de Ordáz into the narrow city streets with 300 troops, who are attacked by swarms of warriors, killing four or five Spaniards and wounding many others with stones and arrows. Retreating to their quarters, the Spaniards are besieged, enduring repeated attacks over the next several days. Cortés directs Montezuma to again address the mob from the rooftop, protected by Spanish soldiers. But the unhappy emperor is stoned by his own people and dies shortly afterward. Cuitláhuac is now the acknowledged leader of the Aztecs.

30 JUNE–1 JULY 1520. ***Noche Triste Retreat.*** Thirsty, hungry, and beleaguered, the Spaniards decide to cut their way out of Tenochtitlán after midnight, cloaked by mist and drizzle. They pass undetected across several bridges before finally being descried and attacked along the Tacuba causeway. Countless war canoes appear out of the night, filled with archers and enraged fighters. Cortés's men, being crowded together, make easy targets, and they cannot deploy their cannons or cavalry. Some 600 perish during this night, one of the last to emerge from this city being Alvarado. (According to legend he vaults across a gap in the causeway, still known as Puente de Alvarado—Alvarado's Bridge.)

Eventually reaching the mainland town of Popotla, Cortés pauses beneath a large tree to weep, giving rise to the story of the *Noche Triste* (Sad Night). He then leads his battered survivors back toward Tlaxcala, determined to recoup his fortunes. Cuitláhuac's forces hound this retreat, engaging the Spaniards heavily at Otumba on 7 July, only to be turned back by desperate counterattacks. As few as 340 Spanish soldiers and 27 horsemen stagger back into Tlaxcala; the Aztecs remain behind their frontier to attend to their own losses.

1 AUGUST 1520. After 20 days' recuperation, Cortés leads his army on a punitive expedition against the province of Tepeaca, an Aztec tributary near Tlaxcala. His aims are to discourage lesser assaults against isolated Spanish units and to propitiate his fierce Tlaxcaltecan allies, who clamor for this campaign.

Six days later the Spaniards and Tlaxcaltecans overrun Tepeaca, killing 400 warriors in a pitched battle before its gates. The town and its surrounding area are then cruelly ravaged, most citizens being enslaved and branded on the face by the Spanish or sacrificed and eaten by the Tlaxcaltecans. Such atrocities prompt many other Aztec satellites to refrain from attacking the invaders and instead offer terms to abandon the Aztec cause.

7 SEPTEMBER 1520. Cuitláhuac is officially elected emperor in Tenochtitlán, but aside from repairing fortifications and stockpiling weapons, he takes no offensive steps against his foreign enemies. Smallpox soon appears within the valley as well, causing many thousands to sicken and die; among these is the new emperor himself, who succumbs on 25 November. He is eventually succeeded by his cousin Cuauhtémoc, the late Montezuma's nephew.

OCTOBER 1520. At Tepeaca—now renamed Segura de la Frontera—Cortés instructs shipwright Martín López to travel to Tlaxcala with his assistants and begin cutting the necessary wood for 13 40-foot brigantines.

Nineteenth-century watercolor of Aztec warriors

A trickle of Spanish reinforcements continues to arrive at Quiahuiztlan: a half-dozen individual vessels bearing 200 adventurers for Cortés's ranks, more than 20 horses, and military stores. The conquistador dispatches four vessels to seek help from Hispaniola and a similar expedition to Jamaica to buy mares.

EARLY DECEMBER 1520. Gonzalo de Sandoval, one of Cortés's lieutenants, marches northward from Tepeaca with 200 Spanish soldiers, 12 crossbowmen, and 20 riders to secure the supply route from its coast by dispersing the Aztec garrisons at Zautla and Xalacingo. He succeeds with very few losses, thus further shrinking the Aztec empire.

27 DECEMBER 1520. Marshaling all his forces at Tlaxcala, Cortés sets forth with 550 Spanish troops and 10,000 native auxiliaries under the Tlaxcaltecan general, Chichimecatecutli. Four days later they reach the city of Texcoco, on the shores of the Lake Tenochtitlán, meeting little opposition. Although the frightened rulers of the city initially offer allegiance, Cortés discovers most of the populace fleeing into the Aztec capital and so sacks Texcoco. After three days' occupation he is approached by a few minor outlying chieftains, who agree to switch sides.

4 JANUARY 1521. Leaving Sandoval in command of his main force at Texcoco, Cortés sets out with 200 soldiers (including 18 riders, 10 harquebusiers, and 30 crossbowmen) plus 3,000–4,000 Indian auxiliaries to attack the city of Ixtapalapa 20 miles away. Despite the Aztecs' best efforts, he destroys this place and retires, losing only one Spaniard.

A similar expedition is sent under Sandoval against Chalco some time later to expel its Aztec garrison at the behest of the inhabitants. This proves successful, Chalco switching sides.

LATE JANUARY 1521. Concerned by such defections, Cuauhtémoc leads his army down the eastern shores of Lake Tenochtitlán, cowing these vassals into submission once more. Cortés replies with countersweeps of his own, even marching around the entire circumference of the lake, thus reversing many of these allegiances.

He also detaches Sandoval with a small company to fetch the brigantines that Martín López has been constructing at Tlaxcala. En route, Sandoval eradicates the town of Calpulalpan, where a party of Spaniards have been ambushed and sacrificed the previous year.

15 FEBRUARY 1521. ***Lake Warfare.*** Sandoval returns to Texcoco with Tlaxcaltecan bearers in a column six miles long and 10,000 strong, under the direction of Chichimecatecutli. Two thousand are carrying food, but the remainder bring countless planks and timbers, which when assembled will constitute López's vessels. With their tall sails, long oars, and swivel guns, these brigantines completely outclass the Aztecs' canoes and eventually permit Cortés to win control over the waters of the lake.

News also arrives shortly thereafter of another Spanish relief force that has reached the coast of Veracruz, sent by Rodrigo de Bastidas of Santo Domingo and comprising the ship *María* plus two small caravels. These add 200 men and 60 horses to Cortés's ranks.

5 MARCH 1521. The ship of Alonso de Mendoza quits the Gulf Coast, bearing messages and gifts from Cortés directly toward the king of Spain.

Valley of Mexico at the time of the Spanish conquest

Early this same month, Sandoval probes far beyond the Valley of Mexico with 200 soldiers, 20 riders, a dozen crossbowmen, and 1,000 native allies, defeating an Aztec army near Yecapixtla with the loss of only a single man.

15 MARCH 1521. The Indians of Chalco and Huejotzingo stave off a large Aztec army that descends upon them to reimpose Cuauhtémoc's rule, thus further diminishing the emperor's prestige.

APRIL 1521. At the head of 300 soldiers and 25 riders, Cortés strikes out on a widespread foray around the Aztec capital, overrunning the town of Cuernavaca on 13 April and Xochimilco two days later, amid very heavy fighting. Perhaps a dozen Spaniards are lost before Texcoco is regained on 22 April, some being dragged off to human sacrifice—a fate greatly feared by the invaders.

From 25 April through 29 April, Cuauhtémoc's official coronation ceremonies are celebrated within the Mexican capital.

28 APRIL 1521. López's brigantines are launched at Texcoco amid great rejoicing by the Spaniards and their allies. The largest is about 65 feet long, flat-bottomed, and armed with iron cannons; the remaining craft average 50 feet, have double or single masts and small bronze swivels, and are capable of carrying 25–30 men apiece. These are to reach Lake Tenochtitlán via a mile-and-a-half channel 12 feet deep and 12 feet wide, dug by 8,000 native levies.

The conquistador then calls upon all his newfound allies to provide him with men and supplies for one final effort against Tenochtitlán. The Aztecs' past tyrannies now come back to haunt them, as tens of thousands of natives rally around Cortés's flag. He commands nearly 90 Spanish riders, 120 crossbowmen and harquebusiers, and about 700 infantrymen, which he subdivides into four roughly equal battalions under himself, Alvarado, Sandoval, and Cristóbal de Olid.

His own unit is to man the brigantines and fight the Aztecs upon the lake while the remainder occupy the towns at the end of three of the four causeways: Tacuba, Ixtapalapa, and Coyoacán (the fourth, which reaches Tepeyac, is left open so as to furnish the Aztecs with a tempting avenue of escape). Cortés's aim is to weaken his densely concentrated foes by denying supplies to the city, then gradually fight his way inside.

22 MAY 1521. Alvarado's and Olid's contingents depart Texcoco to circle the lake and seize Tacuba and Coyoacán on its far bank. During this march—26 May—they destroy the aqueducts at Chapultepec, thus cutting off Tenochtitlán's water supply.

31 MAY 1521. As the first two Spanish battalions fight their way into position, Sandoval's unit departs Texcoco toward Ixtapalapa.

1 JUNE 1521. Cortés sorties with his brigantines and a large number of Texcocan war canoes under Ixtlilxóchitl to support Sandoval's advance. While traversing the lake Cortés destroys the Aztec base on Tepeapulco Island then defeats a large fleet of canoes sent against him from Tenochtitlán. Size and swiftness allow the brigantines to plow right through the native formations; the Spaniards use their guns and crossbows to finish off any survivors. Despite such advantages, Cortés's own flagship is boarded briefly by Aztec fighters during this particular fray, his person being saved only by the brilliant swordplay of shipwright—now chief pilot—Martín López.

Following this victory, Cortés disembarks and seizes the Acachinanco strongpoint on Tenochtitlán's Ixtapalapa causeway, intelligently seconded by Sandoval.

The Spaniards then beat off repeated counterattacks from the Aztec capital until well into the night.

2 JUNE 1521. Heavy fighting continues along both the Ixtapalapa and Tacuba causeways, where Alvarado is also slowly advancing. Brigantines protect the Spanish flanks, allowing them to advance almost to the outskirts of the city itself, although they are obliged to withdraw every night.

Seeing that operations are becoming drawn out, Cortés orders Sandoval to circle to the north side of Tenochtitlán with 23 riders, 18 crossbowmen, 100 Spanish soldiers, and several thousand natives to cut off the remaining Tepeyac causeway as well.

10 JUNE 1521. After failing to penetrate the Aztec defenses, Cortés leads a major effort from the south, fighting his way into Tenochtitlán's main square, hoping to be joined by Alvarado and Sandoval. Their attacks do not prosper, however, and Cortés is forced to retreat at nightfall, losing one of his cannons.

15 JUNE 1521. Cortés again fights his way to the city center, his native allies leveling many of its houses so that his cavalry might have room to maneuver. Desperate Aztec counterattacks throw the invaders back once more.

Tlaxcaltecan warrior, with plumed regalia on his back

16 JUNE 1521. Realizing that his tactic of razing buildings deprives the enemy of high positions from which to pelt down missiles and frees up space for his artillery and cavalry, Cortés returns to the capital over the next couple of weeks on a series of attrition raids, gradually tearing down more and more edifices until the Spaniards and their allies have pushed halfway into Tenochtitlán.

30 JUNE 1521. Hoping to hasten the end of Aztec resistance, all three Spanish columns launch a concerted drive toward the main remaining suburb of Tlaltelolco, but their assault fares badly. Cortés himself is lucky to emerge alive; Alvarado's standard is captured by the Aztec chieftain Tlapanecatl, 20 Spaniards are killed, another 53 captured. The latter are then sacrificed within plain view of their horrified comrades. As many as 2,000 Indian allies also perish this day; four horses, a cannon, and a brigantine are lost as well. Shaken by these setbacks, the Spaniards refrain from renewing their assaults for another four days as most of their local auxiliaries quit the Spanish side in fright.

This Aztec triumph prompts some outlying tribes to rise, and Cortés is obliged to detach Andrés de Tapia with ten riders and 80 soldiers to aid Cuernavaca's chieftain against the warrior-priests of Malinalco. Sandoval leads a similar expedition against Matalcingo a few days later, then defeats an Aztec relief column approaching from Tula. These three Spanish victories do much to restore the besiegers' prestige by mid-July, as does a foray into Tenochtitlán by the Tlaxcaltecans under Chichimecatecutli, which nets a large bag of Aztec prisoners during heavy fighting. Soon, Cortés's native auxiliaries begin returning, reassured by Tenochtitlán's palpable weakness.

The Spaniards are further heartened by the arrival of a ship at Quiahuiztlan bearing gunpowder, crossbows, and a few more soldiers (having formed part of Ponce de León's recent failed expedition to settle Florida; *see* spring 1521 under Expansion).

27 JULY 1521. Alvarado's contingent fights its way to the very center of Tlaltelolco, planting a new flag atop the main pyramid against increasingly enfeebled opposition.

12 AUGUST 1521. Pressed into a small northwestern section of Mexico City, the Aztecs continue to resist

heroically despite disease, starvation, thirst, relentless military defeats, and Cortés's repeated offers of terms. On this day a major assault by the Spanish on Tenochtitlán occurs in which many thousands of Aztec noncombatants are savagely massacred in their shelters.

13 AUGUST 1521. ***Fall of Tenochtitlán.*** The end at hand, Alvarado and Olid drive their battalions through the last remaining Aztec enclave; Cortés observes the action from afar. The defenders being largely powerless, a one-sided slaughter ensues. In a bid to reach the north shore of the lake, the defeated Emperor Cuauhtémoc flees during this afternoon aboard a canoe with a score of his courtiers, only to be overtaken and captured by García Holguín's brigantine. Brought before Cortés, the emperor's surrender marks an end to the conquest of Mexico and the Aztecs, during which at least 100,000 people have died.

EXPANSION (1521–1535)

CORTÉS'S CONQUEST OF THE AZTEC EMPIRE inspires a host of imitators. In addition to spreading out so as to secure outlying vassal states, many Spanish captains also penetrate beyond Mexico's borders in quest of additional native kingdoms to subjugate. Despite his own wealth and prestige, Cortés is constrained to head new exploratory efforts on behalf of less fortunate followers.

SPRING 1521. ***Ponce de León's Repulse.*** While the conquest of Mexico is proceeding, Ponce de León departs Puerto Rico in early March with a two-ship expedition bearing 200 men and 50 horses, hoping to establish a permanent colony in Florida by military means. He reaches Estero Island on Florida's western side and rests his people ashore before advancing inland and confronting the local king, Escampaba. Escampaba is dubbed *cacique Carlos* (chief Charles) by the Spaniards, and his tribal seat is on Mound Key. The invaders cannot speak the Calo dialect, and the ferocity of these nomads proves their undoing. In a sharp engagement the explorer is badly wounded in the thigh, his men driven back aboard ship.

Defeated, Ponce de León retires toward Cuba, one of his ships becoming separated and sailing to join Cortés in Mexico (*see* 30 June 1521). Ponce de León meanwhile limps into Havana, where he dies in June 1521.

LATE 1521. Because Spanish fighting men are draining toward Mexico, numerous Cuban natives begin rebelling and running away from their masters, some seeking refuge in the highlands of Baracoa under a chieftain named Guama. Eventually these uprisings are contained, with 28-year-old Vasco Porcallo de Figueroa leading 18–20 horsemen in a sweep inland from the port of Trinidad toward Sancti Spíritus, terrifying the Indians into submission.

21 JANUARY 1522. ***González Dávila's Exploration.*** From the Pearl Islands (Panama), a four-ship expedition sets sail under Gil González Dávila and his pilot Andrés Niño. Their water casks become damaged in a storm, and so González Dávila is compelled to disembark with 100 men in the territory of chief Burica (at modern-day Burica Point) to campaign inland until he can rejoin Niño at San Vicente Gulf. Leaving two ships here with gold treasure, González Dávila and Niño then press northwest separately, being greeted hospitably by two chiefs, Nicoya and Nicoraguamia (or Nicorao). González Dávila discovers the lake of Nicaragua in the latter's territory and is attacked on 17 April by 3,000–4,000 warriors under chief Diriangen, compelling him to retire; meanwhile Niño sails as far as the Gulf of Fonseca before rejoining his commander once more at San Vicente. Their expedition eventually regains Panama City on 25 June 1523. They report to Gov. Dávila, who prepares an expedition under Capt. Francisco Hernández to lay claim to the new territory.

LATE JUNE 1523. Gov. Francisco de Garay reaches Havana from Jamaica with 900 men aboard 11 ships, hoping to proceed farther west and conquer the Mexican province of Pánuco (*see* 8 August 1519). Learning that Cortés has already taken possession of this territory, Garay agrees to defer his campaign.

6 DECEMBER 1523. ***Alvarado in Guatemala.*** Cortés's lieutenant, Pedro de Alvarado, leads an expedition out of Mexico City comprising 130 mounted Spaniards, 300 Spanish infantry, and a host of native auxiliaries to conquer kingdoms to the south. He reaches the Pacific port of Soconusco and enters

what is today Guatemala in early 1524, finding the local Quiché and Cakchiquel Mayan tribes locked in civil war.

Temporarily allying himself with the second of the two tribes, Alvarado defeats 10,000–12,000 Quichés near Zapotitlán on 20 February 1524—personally running through their chieftain, Tecún Umán, with a lance—then burns the defenseless capital of Xelajú (modern Quetzaltenango) on 7 March amid fearful slaughter by the Spaniards as well as their 2,000 Cakchiquel cohorts.

On 12 April the conquistadores reach the Cakchiquel capital of Iximché, remaining five days before pressing on to destroy the Zutuhils—nearby native rivals—by 18 April. In short order Alvarado also reduces the Cakchiquel to subservience; he razes Atacat on 9 May then progresses farther southeast, entering the territory of the Pipil Indians (modern El Salvador) by June and slaying their leader, Atlacatl the Elder. His successor, Atlacatl the Younger, fights on; Alvarado's drive is halted by rumors of a possible Cakchiquel uprising, which obliges him to return to Guatemala by 21 July.

After extorting a huge ransom from the terrified Guatemalan inhabitants, Alvarado founds Santiago de los Caballeros de Guatemala on 25 July 1524 upon the site of Iximché, further petitioning Charles V to be appointed governor over this vast new territory. On 26 August many of his remaining Cakchiquel vassals flee into the jungle, prompting the conquistadores to chase them and fight a pitched battle on 5 September, after which the natives melt into the bush and launch a protracted guerrilla war.

Alvarado meanwhile resumes his Salvadoran campaign and defeats Atlacatl the Younger, and by 1 April 1525 his brother, Gonzalo, is able to found the city of San Salvador on the ruins of the Pipil capital of Cuzcatlán. (Soon after, however, the Salvadoran outpost falls under the jurisdiction of the ever-ambitious Pedrarias Dávila, governor of Panama, who is attempting to conquer Central America from the south.) On 7 February 1526 Alvarado destroys the hidden Cakchiquel capital of Xepau, compelling its survivors to seek sanctuary on the mountain retreat of Holom Balam (literally, "tiger head"—near Iximché).

One year later Alvarado is formally granted the title of governor of Guatemala, and his territory is declared to be an independent captaincy general. He and brother Jorge then transfer their capital of Santiago to Almolonga at the base of Agua Volcano—now known as Ciudad Vieja. The following year (1528) brother Jorge wrests El Salvador from the forces of Dávila, moving its capital of San Salvador to the Valley of La Bermuda.

3 MAY 1524. After visiting Cuba and renewing his loyalty to Governor Velázquez, Cortés's former subordinate, Cristóbal de Olid, lands on the north coast of "Hibueras" (Honduras) with a colonizing expedition and founds the town of Triunfo de la Cruz. When Cortés learns of this defection, he dispatches two small counterforces under his cousin, Francisco de las Casas, and González Dávila, who are encountered separately and captured.

(Although their men are released, de las Casas and González Dávila are held prisoner in Olid's household at Naco. Eventually they stab him one night in bed and, although he flees, de las Casas persuades the soldiery to overtake Olid next day and slit his throat.)

OCTOBER 1524. Cortés leaves Mexico City with a large following of conquistadores to personally put down Olid's rebellion in Honduras. He leaves the government in the hands of a triumvirate of officials—treasurer Alonso de Estrada, accountant Rodrigo de Albornoz, and lawyer Alonso de Zuazo. As an added precaution against Indian uprisings he takes the captive emperor Cuauhtémoc and other Aztec chieftains with him. This expedition easily travels down to the mouth of the Coatzacoalcos River but thereafter penetrates into trackless jungle, which greatly hampers progress.

Cortés spends many months forging into this wilderness until it becomes widely believed in Mexico that he and his followers are lost forever. When he reaches Izancanac (or Xicalanaco) in February 1526, he orders Cuauhtémoc, the captive lord of Texcoco Cohuanacoxtzin, and the Franciscan friar Juan de Tecto hanged on 20 February, suspects in a plot. By the time the conquistadores finally emerge at Naco, they discover that Olid is already dead at the hands of de las Casas. Cortés therefore lends aid to the new settlers of Trujillo (on the north coast of Honduras), and even wishes to explore Nicaragua; instead he opts to return to Mexico upon learning of a revolt by Gonzalo de Salazar and Peralmíndez Chirinos against the interim government.

LATE 1524. Francisco Cortés—cousin and deputy of the famous conquistador—leads an army north from Colima (Mexico) toward Ahuacatlan and Tepic, meeting some resistance at Tetitlan and elsewhere before returning via the coast.

4 MAY 1526. After a difficult, year-long voyage from Spain via Santo Domingo and Santiago de Cuba, Gov.-designate Nuño Beltrán de Guzmán reaches San Esteban del Puerto (modern-day Pánuco, Mexico) and assumes office. In order to improve the prospects of its 45 impoverished households, he authorizes slave-catching raids into the interior.

24 MAY 1526. After visiting Havana—where his former antagonist, Governor Velázquez, has died in early October 1524—Cortés returns to Veracruz. News of his miraculous reemergence from the Central American jungles, where many feared him dead, ignites a popular uprising against the usurpers Salazar and Chirinos, and Cortés reenters Mexico City in triumph this June. He learns that during his prolonged absence his secretary has secured him a knighthood in the Order of Santiago, as well as other privileges, from Spain.

JUNE 1526. Three Spanish ships under 50-year-old Sebastian Cabot (son of John Cabot; *see* 24 June 1497) appear off the eastern tip of Brazil, commissioned to round South America and gain Asia. Coasting south until opposite Santa Catarina Island, Cabot finds three survivors from Díaz de Solís's earlier expedition (*see* 2 February 1516), who give such glowing accounts of this country's wealth that the navigator decides to switch objectives.

Penetrating the River Plate by February 1527, he spends the next two years trying to advance up both the Paraná and Paraguay Rivers before finally admitting defeat and retracing his course in December 1529. Regaining Seville in August 1530, he is condemned to four years' banishment for having failed to fulfill his original commission.

MID-SEPTEMBER 1527. Pánfilo de Narváez enters Santiago de Cuba from Santo Domingo with 460 men he has brought from Spain aboard a half-dozen vessels to conquer Florida. Two of his caravels sail ahead to the port of Casilda under Vasco Porcallo and Alvaro Núñez Cabeza de Vaca for supplies while Narváez remains at anchor with the remainder off Cape Cruz (Manzanillo Bay). A hurricane sinks his first two vessels, with the loss of 60 out of 90 men plus 30 horses.

JANUARY 1528. More Indian uprisings are subdued on Cuba by Vasco Porcallo and Gonzalo de Guzmán.

23 FEBRUARY 1528. Narváez departs Jagua (Cuba) with five vessels, to proceed with the conquest of Florida. Bad weather and the inexperience of his pilot, Diego Miruelo, leads this ill-fated expedition deep into the Gulf of Mexico, coming ashore at Espíritu Santo Bay. Eventually only his lieutenant, Cabeza de Vaca, and three other men survive this ordeal, reaching Mexico City nine years later.

8 DECEMBER 1528. Nuño de Guzmán reaches Mexico City from Pánuco and assumes office as president of New Spain's first *audiencia,* or high court.

1528. A large Carib war party from the Leeward Islands assaults the Franciscan monastery at Aguada (Puerto Rico), slaying five of its missionaries.

21 DECEMBER 1529. ***Nuño de Guzmán's Campaign.*** Uneasy at the prospect of Cortés's return from a lengthy stay in Spain, during which the Mexican *audiencia* has often acted against his local interests, President Nuño de Guzmán decides to resign his office and depart the capital via Jilotepec with an army of 150 riders, 350 infantry, 12 cannons, and 7,000–8,000 Indian auxiliaries to conquer Mexico's northwestern highlands.

After crossing the Lerma River at Nuestra Señora de la Purificación Ford near Conguripo and entering the already subject realm of Michoacán, Guzmán tortures its Tarascan king, Tangaxoan II—whom he has brought along from Mexico City as a hostage—to relinquish his wealth, afterwards burning him alive on 14 February 1530. The Spanish commander then gathers a further 10,000 natives into his ranks as porters before venturing west into the territory of the hostile Chichimecs.

(Despite exaggerated accounts of Guzmán's cruelty later circulated by his enemy Cortés, this *conquistador* undoubtedly resorts to vicious acts throughout his expedition, apparently hoping to terrify his foes into submission.)

1529. A Carib raiding party captures a Spanish launch within the roadstead at San Juan de Puerto Rico, sending it to the bottom and making off with passengers and crew.

MARCH 1530. Nuño de Guzmán's army crosses the Río Grande below Puruándiro into Jalisco (Mexico), marching downstream for three days before turning northwest for another three, then capturing Coina. The Spaniards and their allies subsequently make a devastating sweep through this district's

Spanish conquistadores and their Indian allies, armed with swords

communities of Coca-speaking Tecuexe farmers, defeating the chieftain of Cuitzeo in a one-sided battle near Ocotlán before throwing him alive to their war dogs.

After erecting a fortress at Jamay, Guzmán proceeds through Pancitlán, reaching Tonalá by 25 March and subjugating its queen along with numerous subchieftains. The Spanish army then strikes north, repelling a native ambush at Tetlán before dividing at Teul in April. Guzmán's contingent marches southwest to recross the Río Grande and continue toward Ahuacatlán and Tepic; meanwhile, his subordinate, Pedro Almendes Chirinos (also known as "Peralmindes"), takes a more direct route north through Huichol territory into the Sierra Madre Range, pressing toward Comanja and Zacatecas.

13 MAY 1530. Nuño de Guzmán reaches Tepic (Nayarit), to find Chirinos already waiting outside. The Spaniards combine forces and attack this town, then detach Cristóbal de Oñate's company to explore inland toward Huejotitlán, Teocaltiche, Aguascalientes, and Nochistlán while Guzmán leads the main body down toward the coast for a respite.

5 JUNE 1530. Nuño de Guzmán's army, now refreshed, departs Tepic toward Huaristemba. Two days later (Sunday), it traverses the Santiago River near Ixcuintla and captures Sentispac.

Penetrating deeper into hostile territory, the Spaniards are set upon by 2,000 warriors near Cilan, defeating these after two hours' hard fighting. The invaders then cut a bloody swathe of destruction throughout this region, allegedly torching 800 villages before gaining Aztatlán and settling in to wait out the rainy season.

Many of Guzmán's men subsequently die of illness or hunger in this pestilential backwater, but their commander is able write to the king in Madrid about his successful conquest, claiming this territory as "New Castille." The crown responds by the end of this same year, appointing Guzmán governor over the new lands (which are instead to be called "New Galicia").

OCTOBER 1530. A Carib force 500 strong disembarks from 11 large war canoes on the eastern shores of Puerto Rico, marching inland to devastate the Luquillo mines before withdrawing.

The Spanish crown responds to this and similar seaborne aggressions by ordering the construction of a small keep on Puerto Rico's coast to prevent future landings, as well as by dispatching two brigantines from Seville under Capt. Juan de Júcar to conduct reprisal raids against the Caribs on Dominica and adjacent islands.

LATE OCTOBER 1533. Diego Becerra de Mendoza departs Tehuantepec (Mexico) to explore the Pacific Coast with Cortés's ship *Concepción*. A month later 22 crewmembers mutiny, led by pilot Fortún Jiménez, Becerra being killed and his adherents marooned on the Motines Coast. These mutineers head northwest on 9 December, reaching La Paz, where most are killed by Indians. Eventually, about ten survivors manage to sail back to Nueva Galicia with some pearls.

MID-NOVEMBER 1534. A slave uprising occurs at the Jobabo goldfields (near Bayamo, Cuba), which is promptly put down by a mounted company under Gov. Manuel de Rojas.

LATE APRIL 1535. ***Cortés in Baja California.*** The famed conquistador Cortés leads three ships from Nueva Galicia across the Gulf of California, landing in Santa Cruz Bay (modern Pichilingue) by 3 May. So many volunteers have flocked to his new expedition that the trio of ships must make several trips to fetch all of the men. Within a month, 300–400 Spaniards and many black slaves are encamped ashore, believing this to be an island. It soon proves harsh and inhospitable, so that by November 70 Spaniards and 50 horses have succumbed to starvation and native skirmishes.

Early in 1536 Cortés returns to the Mexican mainland, leaving Francisco de Ulloa in charge of the 30 or so Spaniards who choose to remain at Santa Cruz. Although intending to reinforce this outpost, Cortés is instead ordered to evacuate Baja California by the new Mexican viceroy, Antonio de Mendoza.

Hernán Cortés

CONQUEST OF PERU (1524–1539)

WHILE MOST SPANIARDS REMAIN ENGROSSED in the subjugation of Mexico and Central America, another explorer, Pascual de Andagoya, sails in the opposite direction—southeast out of Panama City—in search of another tribe of legendary wealth known as the Birú or Virú. Traveling some 200 miles down modern Colombia's Pacific shores, he ascends the San Juan River but fails to find signs of anything other than primitive coastal peoples. Eventually his ships and plan are taken over by a trio of investors: Francisco Pizarro, his lieutenant, Diego de Almagro, and a priest, Hernando de Luque (representing the recently created judge of Panama, Gaspar de Espinosa).

14 NOVEMBER 1524. ***Probes.*** The veteran Pizarro quits Panama City with a 47-ton ship and two large seagoing canoes, bearing 110 men and some horses, to explore southeast down the Pacific coastline. (He is to be followed shortly thereafter by his lieutenant, de Almagro, with a slightly smaller force.) After touching at Taboga and the Pearl Islands, Pizarro's expedition ascends the Birú River, then reverses course, frustrated at finding the village of Biruquete abandoned by its natives. The Spaniards next endure considerable deprivation while encamped on the ocean shore before eventually

being resupplied from the Pearl Islands by Captain Montenegro.

Venturing still farther south, they reach Candelaria by 14 April 1525, then continue to Puerto Quemado to careen and repair their vessel on land. While doing so, Montenegro ventures inland with 60 men; he is suddenly ambushed by a large body of warriors, suffering several losses. Before he can rejoin Pizarro's encampment, it too is assaulted by a native army, which is repelled. Nevertheless, the Spaniards suffer 17 killed and five wounded during these two actions, including Pizarro (who is wounded seven times, his injuries being cauterized with boiling oil). The expedition therefore limps back to Chochama in the Pearl Islands to recuperate.

Almagro, meanwhile, misses Pizarro while sailing south with his own 70 men and endures a hostile reception at Puerto Quemado as well, during which he loses an eye. Undaunted, he and his men eventually press as far as the mouth of the San Juan River (4 degrees 10 minutes north latitude), before finally turning back and overtaking the convalescent Pizarro at Chochama. Almagro then reports to Dávila at Panama City, who, although distracted by Hernández's recent revolt in Nicaragua, nonetheless sends Almagro back to the Pearl Islands with 110 men and a commission as cocaptain for future ventures against the "Pirú" (a corruption of the name Birú).

SPRING 1526. ***First Contact.*** Having assembled another 170-man expedition at the Pearl Islands, Pizarro and Almagro strike out on a second reconnaissance aboard two ships and three piraguas. They spend the next several months exploring the coast between the Cartagena and San Juan Rivers, often confronted by hostile natives, yet also noticing impressive signs of wealth and civilization. Almost exhausted, Pizarro's expedition decides to remain off this coast while sending pilot Bartolomé Ruiz farther south to reconnoiter and Almagro back toward Panama for reinforcements.

Ruiz's 70-day voyage provides the first actual contact with the northernmost fringes of the Inca empire, as he sights Gallo and Gorgona Islands, San Mateo Bay, Atacames, and San Lucas by 18 October, followed by Cape San Antonio on 3 December. Off Coaque, a native vessel is captured with two youths and three women passengers, after which Ruiz sails as far south as Capes Pasado and San Francisco before finally turning back. Upon rejoining Pizarro, he finds the Spaniards worried by continual losses—especially the 14 companions recently slaughtered while venturing upriver in a canoe—yet still willing to persevere upon receipt of his news. Almagro has meanwhile regained Panama by September 1526, only to discover that Dávila has been replaced as governor by Pedro de los Ríos. After meeting this new official on 14 December, Almagro sets sail again on 8 January 1527 with 40 additional soldiers to rejoin Pizarro.

Once reassembled, the expedition shifts farther south to establish itself ashore, visiting Gallo Island before disembarking at the town of Terapulla (renamed Santiago) in San Mateo Bay. Soon after, the Spaniards are beset by a large Indian army, being compelled to seek sanctuary on Gallo Island. Almagro departs in June 1527 for more Panamanian help, leaving Pizarro with only 85 followers. Upon regaining the isthmus in July, Almagro is detained by Governor de los Ríos; the same thing happens to pilot Ruiz when he returns on 28 August. The governor instead sends out his own subordinate, Pero Tafur, on 14 September to recall Pizarro, who refuses to leave Gallo Island. Only 13 of his followers remain with him, soon transferring to Gorgona Island, where they are eventually joined by Ruiz with a small ship in March 1528.

Still determined, Pizarro sails as far south as Tumbes with his few Inca captives, releasing them among their compatriots, thus being well received. He next sails to Paita, Coaque, and Manta without incident, leaving a few volunteers behind when he reverses course toward Gorgona, and returns to Panama by the end of 1528. From here, Pizarro crosses the isthmus and takes ship toward Spain to secure royal backing for his projected invasion of Peru.

SPRING 1530. Pizarro returns to Panama from Spain with a license from the crown to conquer Peru. He is accompanied by four of his brothers—Hernando, Juan, Gonzalo, and Francisco Martín de Alcántara—plus 300 men aboard a trio of ships (a third of these men soon die from disease). The rest of this year is spent preparing for the forthcoming campaign.

31 JANUARY 1531. ***Beachhead.*** Pizarro sets sail from Panama City with 180 men aboard three ships, touching at the Pearl Islands to gather another waiting contingent before proceeding south toward San Mateo Bay. Here the cavalry are disembarked to advance overland while the ships follow along the coast. When the Spaniards reach Coaque in April, its residents abandon it in fear. Pizarro establishes a base ashore while dispatching three ships under Bartolomé de Aguilar toward Panama and Nicaragua for more volunteers, bearing gold and precious stones as proof of the new land's wealth.

The first of these reinforcements—30 men from Nicaragua under Sebastián de Velalcázar—do not arrive until September, just as Pizarro is preparing to march still farther south. His progress among the coastal tribes is mostly peaceable, and by October his expedition reaches Portoviejo, where it is refreshed and reinforced by another ship. Upon reaching Puná Island the Spaniards suspect treachery and so arrest chief Tumbala and 17 of his lieutenants, handing them over to their mortal enemies—the Indians of Tumbes—for execution. A brief uprising occurs on the island but is quickly put down by Pizarro.

In March 1532 Hernando de Soto arrives from Nicaragua with more men, and the expedition begins rafting across to Tumbes. Now it is the Spaniards' turn to be betrayed, as the waiting natives quietly slaughter the first boat parties while beckoning others to come ashore. Hernando Pizarro, having disembarked farther south with the cavalry, is able to scatter the startled warriors from their rear then occupy their abandoned city. Chief Cacalami is promptly obliged to sue for peace, after which Pizarro installs a 50-man garrison; on 16 May he marches inland, eventually reaching Tangara (renamed San Miguel de Piura in mid-September). En route he learns that the Inca emperor, Huayna Capac, has died a few years earlier along with his heir-apparent, Ninan Cuyuchi, so that Peru is now torn by civil war between two rival successors, Huascar and Atahualpa.

24 SEPTEMBER 1532. ***Opening Campaign.*** Pizarro marches out of San Miguel at the head of 62 horsemen and 106 soldiers, having left another 60 Spaniards to maintain the outpost. By 6 November he reaches Saña; two days later he strikes up into the Andes after being greeted by an embassy from Atahualpa (who has recently defeated and imprisoned Huascar). After passing numerous Inca strongholds, on 15 November the Spaniards come within sight of Cajamarca, outside of which the emperor is encamped with a large army. Next evening, when Atahualpa visits Pizarro's lodgments within this town, he is treacherously seized, several thousand of his courtiers and servants being massacred in a two-hour bloodbath. The Inca army does nothing, and next day it disperses upon commands from Pizarro and Atahualpa.

Noting the avarice with which the Spaniards then fall upon his treasure, the captive emperor offers to fill a room with gold items as ransom for his release. Pizarro accepts, and while waiting for this booty to be gathered he uses Atahualpa's authority to keep Peru calm. The rival emperor Huascar is also brought prisoner from Cuzco but is murdered by his Inca guards at Andamarca—just short of Cajamarca—allegedly at Atahualpa's order.

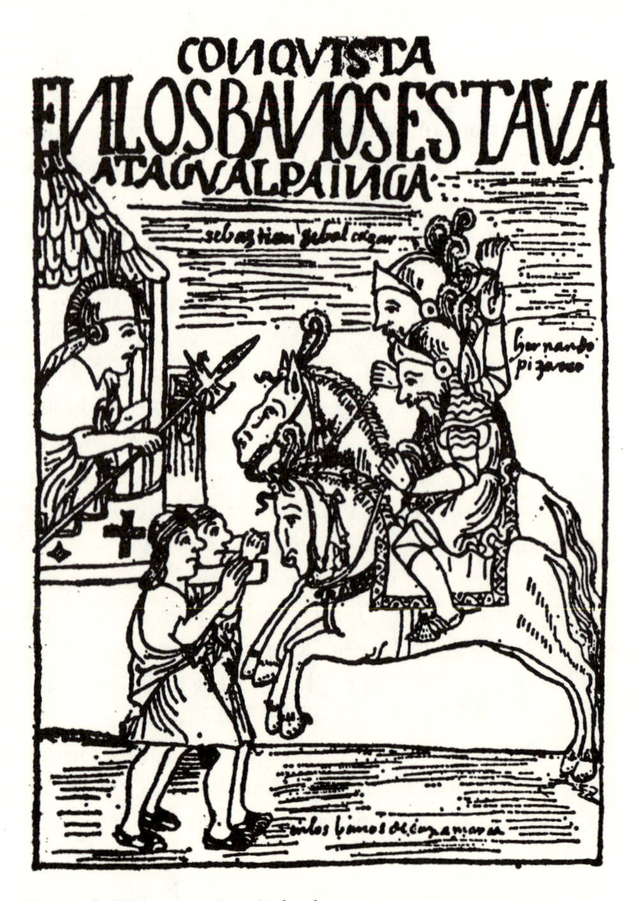

Hernando Pizarro meeting Atahualpa

5 JANUARY 1533. Growing restive at Cajamarca, Pizarro sends his brother Hernando with 20 riders and some foot soldiers to investigate rumors of an Inca army massing at Huamachuco. These rumors prove groundless, but the Spaniards avail themselves of this opportunity to travel on for another three weeks toward the great temple of Pachacamac on the coastal desert (south of modern-day Lima). Finding its gilt decorations removed, Hernando Pizarro remains there throughout most of February, searching in vain for the missing treasure.

15 FEBRUARY 1533. Another contingent of three Spaniards departs Cajamarca for Cuzco with Inca envoys to speed the gathering of Atahualpa's ransom.

EARLY MARCH 1533. Hernando Pizarro quits Pachacamac to rejoin the main body, meeting peacefully with the Inca general Chalcuchima amid his 35,000-strong army at Jauja on 17 March. The Spaniard convinces Chalcuchima to accompany him

Capture of Emperor Atahualpa

with a small retinue on this journey, thereby depriving the Incas of one of their mightiest leaders.

14 APRIL 1533. Diego de Almagro arrives at Cajamarca from the coast with 150 fresh Spanish troops and 50 horses. Atahualpa realizes this portends a full-scale Spanish invasion and so fears for his fate.

25 APRIL 1533. Hernando Pizarro returns to Cajamarca with Chalcuchima, who is henceforth treated as a captive and then tortured to reveal the whereabouts of treasure.

12 JUNE 1533. Hernando Pizarro departs Cajamarca for the coast, taking 100,000 *castellanos* and a report for the king of Spain.

16 JULY 1533. Pizarro makes a massive distribution of booty to his followers in Cajamarca.

26 JULY 1533. ***Atahualpa's Murder.*** Although having fulfilled his ransom pledge, the captive emperor is led into Cajamarca's square this Saturday evening, garroted, then burned at the stake on the unfounded fear that his general, Rumiñavi, is approaching with a vast army. Pizarro and Almagro next invest Huascar's younger brother Tupac Huallpa (whom they also hold prisoner) as new emperor in early August, marching south out of Cajamarca on 11 August toward the distant Incan capital of Cuzco. By mid-September they are in Recuay, where they rest for 12 days before resuming.

11 OCTOBER 1533. Having entered the part of Peru occupied by the Quito faction, Pizarro's expedition encounters increasing signs of hostility. He, Almagro, and de Soto therefore gallop ahead of their main body with 75 riders plus 20 foot soldiers to guard the chained general Chalcuchima.

At Jauja on 11 October they are greeted as liberators by the oppressed inhabitants; Chalcuchima's former Quitan army—now commanded by Yucra Hualpa—withdraws to the far bank of the Mantaro River in battle array. When a column of warriors is sent back to fire the large storehouses within Jauja, Pizarro's cavalry attacks, scattering the warriors with great slaughter. The Quitan army then retreats farther south to join Quisquis's forces near Cuzco, harried for almost 16 miles by Spanish riders who kill many and demoralize the rest. Pizarro's main body enters Jauja on 19 October under Capt. Alonso Riquelme; soon thereafter the puppet emperor Tupac Huallpa dies of natural causes.

24 OCTOBER 1533. In anticipation of resuming his march from Jauja toward Cuzco, Pizarro sends de Soto ahead with 70 riders to capture some vital bridges along its royal highway.

27 OCTOBER 1533. After installing an 80-man garrison in Jauja under Riquelme, Pizarro departs at the head of 30 riders, 30 foot soldiers, some native auxiliaries, and the captive general Chalcuchima to overtake de Soto.

29 OCTOBER 1533. At dawn, de Soto's flying column surprises Yucra Hualpa's retreating army at Vilcas while most of the men are absent hunting or gathering. This evening, the Quitans launch a furious counterattack to free their women and children, pressing the Spaniards so hard that a white horse mounted by Alonso Tabuyo is killed, another two injured. Next morning the Incans resume their assault, this time led by banners made from the mane and tail of the slain horse. Despite killing some 600 attackers, de Soto is eventually obliged to release his captives in order to

withdraw back into this town and wait for his enemy to retire with their loved ones.

8 NOVEMBER 1533. ***Ambush at Vilcaconga.*** Not wishing to wait for Pizarro before entering Cuzco, de Soto strikes on alone with only 40 riders. While ascending a steep hill toward Vilcaconga on this Saturday noon—dismounted, dispersed, and leading their mounts—the Spaniards are suddenly surprised by 3,000–4,000 of Quisquis's warriors attacking from above. They scatter to avoid an opening barrage of stones, then struggle to ride up toward the top through a hail of missiles. Five Spaniards are killed and 11 wounded during this affray, along with 14 horses, at a cost of 20 Inca fatalities. De Soto retreats and spends an uneasy night encamped nearby but is reinforced before dawn by another 40 riders under Almagro. On 9 November the invaders push forward again, and the Incas fall back.

13 NOVEMBER 1533. Pizarro overtakes Almagro and de Soto at Vilcaconga; while marching on toward Jaquijahuana he is met by a 19-year-old fugitive Inca prince named Manco, son of Huayna Capac and bitter foe to both Atahualpa and Chalcuchima. At Manco's instigation, the captive general is burned alive in Jaquijahuana's square this evening for having sent secret messages to Quisquis advising him where and how to attack the Spaniards.

14 NOVEMBER 1533. In an effort to reach Cuzco before Quisquis's Quitan occupiers can set it ablaze, a flying column of 40 Spanish riders surges ahead, only to be repelled in a clash at a pass outside this city; three horses are slain.

15 NOVEMBER 1533. Pizarro and Manco enter Cuzco together (without opposition, as Quisquis's army has retired); next day the Inca princeling is proclaimed emperor. Some 5,000 Cuzcan auxiliaries are quickly raised and set off with 50 riders under de Soto to pursue the retreating enemy into the Condesuyo Mountains. Thanks to the rugged terrain—though his rearguard is severely mauled—Quisquis is able to gain safety across Apurímac Gorge, burning the suspension bridge near Capi after crossing. De Soto and his allies are unable to fight their way over and so return to Cuzco by the end of December, where the Spaniards are busily gathering booty.

23 JANUARY 1534. In Guatemala, the conquistador Pedro de Alvarado—having learned of the rich new kingdom being subdued farther southeast by Pizarro—sets sail from the port of Poseción to take part with 100 crossbowmen, 400 soldiers, 119 horses, and 4,000 native auxiliaries aboard a dozen commandeered ships.

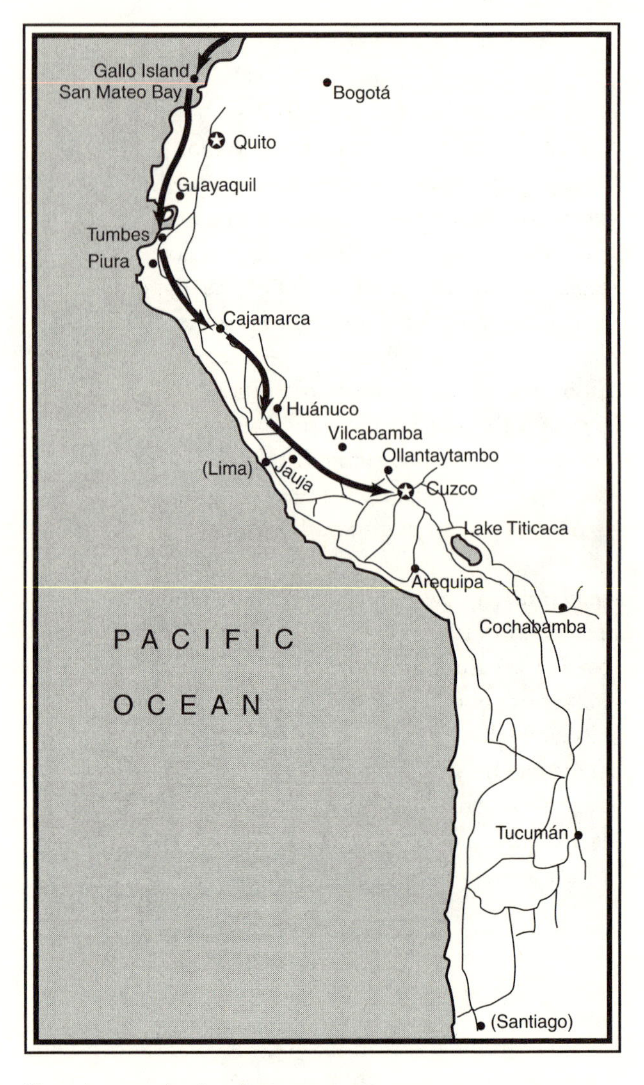

Pizarro's penetration into Peru

LATE JANUARY 1534. Being informed that Quisquis's army is retreating north toward Jauja, Pizarro sends Almagro and de Soto with 50 riders and 20,000 Cuzcan allies to reinforce the 80-man Spanish garrison under Riquelme.

MID-FEBRUARY 1534. ***Jauja.*** Before any Spanish reinforcements can arrive from Cuzco (though a small contingent does come up from the coast under Capt. Gabriel de Rojas), Jauja is attacked by Quisquis in a bungled pincer operation. Approximately 1,000 warriors are to circle through Jauja's hills, slip across the Mantaro River, and occupy the rocky heights behind, launching a coordinated surprise attack when Quisquis's 6,000-strong main body marches up the valley. Instead, the Quitans are discovered while traversing a bridge 50 miles downstream from Jauja; their 1,000-man contingent also arrives and attacks one day early. Riquelme easily repels this initial assault across the bridge with ten riders and some crossbowmen.

Next afternoon Quisquis appears, camping a mile outside Jauja. Riquelme boldly attacks his army with 18 horses, a dozen Spanish foot soldiers, and 2,000 local allies. The Quitans retreat across a swollen stream and pelt the Spaniards with rocks and arrows as they attempt to ford, killing one Spaniard, three horses, and numerous native auxiliaries before the Spaniards come to grips with the Quitans, defeating them and inflicting heavy losses. Pursued into the hills, Quisquis is unable to rally his men until Tarma is reached, after which he retires to a mountain stronghold near Bombón, on Lake Junín.

25 FEBRUARY 1534. ***Rival Spanish Expedition.*** Alvarado comes ashore at Portoviejo (Ecuador) with his large contingent, mistreating the coastal tribesmen before striking inland toward modern Guayaquil. News of this challenger's arrival prompts Pizarro's lieutenant, Sebastián de Velalcázar, to set out from San Miguel de Piura in early March with 200 Spanish soldiers and 62 horses to conquer Quito—the last active center of Inca resistance—before this intruder can intervene.

7 APRIL 1534. Almagro reaches Saña with a small contingent from Vilcas, alarmed at hearing of Alvarado's appearance. He attempts to overtake and assume command of Velalcázar's contingent but is driven back by native opposition along the Quito road.

MID-APRIL 1534. Pizarro and Manco reach Jauja and begin assembling an army to drive Quisquis out of his entrenched positions farther north.

LATE APRIL 1534. Velalcázar's column is approached while resting near Zoro Palta (possibly Paquishapa, in southern Ecuador) by the Inca general Chiaquitinta. As the Spanish commander is scouting in advance of his troops with 30 riders he is able to panic and scatter the Quitan warriors, who have never seen horses before.

3 MAY 1534. ***Teocajas.*** After being reinforced at Tumibamba by the Cañari and other subject tribes who hate the Incas, Velalcázar's army pushes north into the Andes, emerging into a highland valley. While approaching Teocajas, a vanguard of ten Spanish horsemen under Capt. Rui Díaz encounters the main Quitan army drawn up in battle array, under General Rumiñavi. One rider returns to advise Velalcázar's army, as the other nine skirmish with masses of enraged Quitan warriors, until they are reinforced by another 40 cavalrymen. But despite wreaking fearful destruction among the natives' ranks, this Spanish company is unable to make the Incas retreat, suffering four conquistadores and a like number of mounts killed before finally retiring for the night. It is not until next morning that the Spaniards at last break the Quitans' desperate resistance and compel the host to withdraw.

EARLY MAY 1534. Almagro quits San Miguel de Piura for a second time, determined to overtake Velalcázar to confirm his continuing loyalty to his cause and that of Pizarro.

MID-MAY 1534. De Soto and Gonzalo Pizarro march north out of Jauja with 50 Spanish horses and 30 foot soldiers, accompanied by 4,000 Cuzcan warriors under Manco plus numerous local levies. By the time they come into contact with Quisquis's army, it is once more retiring toward Quito. The Spaniards and their allies pursue this enemy as far north as Huánuco, fighting a series of sharp engagements before returning triumphantly to Jauja by early June.

22 JUNE 1534. After detouring down to the lowlands and reascending the Andes around Lake Colta and Riobamba, Almagro and Velalcázar's army succeeds in fighting its way to Quito, which is deserted, having been evacuated and burned by Rumiñavi five days earlier. Capt. Rui Díaz is quickly sent with 60 riders to pursue the Inca general into Yumbo province, but the latter eludes him.

Rumiñavi then adds the forces of the Latacunga chieftain Tucomango, Quingalumba of the Chillos, and Governor Zope Zopahua of northern Ambato to his own so as to launch a surprise counterattack against the Spanish occupation force at Quito. This descent is made stealthily by 15,000 warriors at night, but nonetheless the defenders are alerted and man their ramparts. The attack ignites numerous buildings, and vicious hand-to-hand fighting ensues by the light of these blazes. Dawn, however, permits the deployment of Velalcázar's cavalry, which smashes the Inca army and captures its camp. Significantly, seven local chieftains come in next day to submit to the conquistadores.

JULY 1534. Velalcázar marches north from Quito toward Cayambe and Otavalo, searching in vain for the Incas' vanished treasury, venting his fury by massacring the women and children of Quinche. Eventually, Almagro and Velalcázar abandon Quito, encountering further opposition in the Chillo Valley and on the right bank of the Pinta River. On either the Liribamba or Chambo River, the Spaniards find a small Inca army drawn up for battle on the far side; they attack despite losing 80 Cañari allies by drowning in the torrent. Twelve horses succeed in swimming across, though, dispersing these enemies.

From prisoners, Almagro and Velalcázar learn of the proximity of Alvarado's expedition, which has suffered terribly, losing 85 members and almost all its horses during a harsh passage over the Andes.

MID-AUGUST 1534. Alvarado's larger but emaciated army captures eight scouts sent ahead by Almagro and Velalcázar, and soon both expeditions warily confront each other, sleeping on their weapons for fear of a sudden attack. Eventually a deal is struck on 26 August between the leaders, whereby Almagro agrees to buy Alvarado's ships and equipment for 100,000 pesos, the latter to return toward Guatemala, leaving his men in Peru under Pizarro's orders. Two days later they all ride back toward Quito, where Velalcázar remains in command of 400–500 Spaniards while Almagro and Alvarado proceed farther south toward Peru.

En route, Almagro and Alvarado blunder into the vanguard of Quisquis's retreating army. This contingent, under an Inca leader named Sotaurco, is surprised holding a pass in Chaparra province and quickly dispersed. Realizing the main body is nearby, the two Spanish commanders lead a nocturnal dash with all their available cavalry, coming within sight of Quisquis's sprawling camp next evening. The Inca general immediately orders his warriors to hold a steep hill under one of Atahualpa's brothers, Huaypalcon, while noncombatants flee in the opposite direction. This stratagem works, as the Spaniards are unable to ride over Huaypalcon's position, and both native formations eventually disappear into the night. When overtaken next day by the pursuing Spaniards, the Inca rearguard again takes up a defensive posture on rocky high ground, killing 14 Spaniards and three horses and wounding 20 other mounts.

Yet even though Quisquis has succeeded in winning free, his army's morale collapses upon approaching Quito, finding it already occupied by many more Spaniards. When the general orders his officers to march on to a remote sector to continue resistance, he is murdered. The forces of both Rumiñavi and Zope Zopahua are hunted down and exterminated over the next few weeks by Velalcázar, marking the end of the Inca empire.

FEBRUARY 1535. Velalcázar sends his lieutenant, Diego de Tapia, from Quito to pacify the Quillacinga Indians on the Angasmayo River.

MARCH 1535. Fighting almost erupts at Cuzco between pro-Pizarro and pro-Almagro factions among the Spaniards.

LATE MAY 1535. Pizarro reaches Cuzco, mediating a deal with Almagro, whereby the latter is to lead a new expedition farther south and conquer Chile.

3 JULY 1535. Almagro quits Cuzco at the head of 570 Spanish riders and foot soldiers, 12,000 Inca allies under Paullu (the puppet emperor Manco's brother), plus great trains of native porters to conquer Chile. Pizarro returns to the coast to continue founding new cities; de Soto sails toward Spain.

EARLY NOVEMBER 1535. Because of increasing Spanish excesses and his own lack of power, the emperor Manco attempts to slip out of Cuzco, only to be ridden down and cruelly imprisoned by Juan and Gonzalo Pizarro. Isolated Spaniards also begin to be murdered, prompting the two brothers to lead a punitive expedition against Ancocagua, which is besieged and overwhelmed.

JANUARY 1536. Hernando Pizarro returns to Cuzco from Spain, releasing Manco from bondage and treating him well (the court at Madrid has disapproved of any disrespect toward monarchs). Nonetheless, the young Inca emperor is now secretly determined to drive the Spaniards out of Peru. Thus, weapons are secretly manufactured and troops slowly marshaled to fall upon Cuzco once the rainy season ends.

18 APRIL 1536. ***Manco's Revolt.*** The emperor Manco leaves Cuzco with Hernando Pizarro's permission, supposedly to attend some religious ceremonies in the Yucay Valley—but actually to mobilize his gathering army. On Easter Saturday, 21 April, news of this plot reaches Cuzco. Juan Pizarro is immediately sent with 70 riders to disperse the assembling Indians, fighting his way to Calca and capturing part of the Inca train. But after three to four days of occupation, his contingent is abruptly recalled by word of an im-

mense native army gathering outside Cuzco proper, under general Inquill. The cavalry fight their way back inside the capital and watch as perhaps 50,000 warriors slowly gather outside. Hernando Pizarro has only 110 soldiers and 80 riders at his disposal; he divides the riders into three companies under Gabriel de Rojas, Hernán Ponce de León, and Gonzalo Pizarro. But when the mounted Spaniards sally, they find the Indians much wilier, remaining on high ground to blunt the weight of cavalry charges, killing a rider and horse on 30 April.

Emboldened, Inquill's army then institutes a close siege of Cuzco, launching a massive dawn assault on Saturday, 6 May, preceded by a hail of heated stones that ignite many of the city's thatched roofs. By sheer weight of numbers, they fight their way into the streets, pushing the desperate defenders back into two buildings facing each other at the east end of its main square.

After several days of ferocious sallies and countersallies, Juan Pizarro leads 50 riders in a wild dash at sunrise on 16 May, which succeeds in circling out into the countryside and almost capturing the Sacsahuaman citadel above Cuzco from the rear. Juan Pizarro dies from a head wound this day, but his brothers Hernando and Gonzalo press home infantry assaults for the next few days, which eventually carry this fortress amid terrible slaughter. Virtually all of its 2,000 Inca defenders are either slain or commit suicide. Native reinforcements appear and attempt to recapture Sacsahuaman for three more days, finally giving up at the end of May. Nevertheless, hard fighting persists in and around Cuzco until at least August, when the natives' siege slackens.

MID-MAY 1536. Having learned of Manco's revolt on 4 May while at his new coastal capital of Lima, Francisco Pizarro quickly sends a relief column of 30 riders toward Jauja in the mountains under Capt. Francisco Morgovejo de Quiñones, followed by another 70 horses under a relative, Gonzalo de Tapia. The latter climbs inland near Huaitará but is ambushed in a defile on the upper Pampas River by Quizo Yupanqui's army, which annihilates the trapped Spaniards with rock slides. Its few survivors are sent as prisoners to Manco at Calca.

Quizo Yupanqui meanwhile continues north and, near Parcos, destroys a second Spanish contingent—60 men under Diego Pizarro marching down the Mantaro River toward Huamanga. Morgovejo is eventually obliged to turn back as well; he is killed before he can regain the coast.

MID-JULY 1536. Francisco Pizarro dispatches 30 foot soldiers from Lima under Francisco de Godoy to reinforce Jauja. While nearing this town, the relief column learns it has already been overrun by Quizo Yupanqui's army and the 30-man Spanish garrison slaughtered. De Godoy therefore retires to Lima by early August with this news.

AUGUST 1536. ***Defense of Lima.*** Flush with his victories in the Andes, Quizo Yupanqui descends to the coastal plateau with a huge army to extirpate Pizarro's stronghold. Capt. Pedro de Lerma is sent out of this city with 70 riders to check the enemy advance, fighting a sharp engagement in which one Spaniard is killed and many others wounded; he is unable to halt the Incas' progress. Thus, Lima is assaulted, but a surprise sally by Pizarro's hidden cavalry breaks the warrior ranks, persuading Quizo Yupanqui to retire to a defensive position atop San Cristóbal Hill.

After six days of close investiture of the city, the native general decides upon an all-out attack from three directions. He personally marches at the head of the eastern column with his senior staff, which receives the brunt of two squadrons of cavalry streaming out of Lima under Pizarro. Quizo Yupanqui is killed along with most of his officers and countless followers, shattering the resolve of his army, which begins to melt away that night.

LATE AUGUST 1536. In Cuzco, the Inca siege has slackened sufficiently for Hernando Pizarro to go over to the offensive against Manco, who has transferred his headquarters from Calca to the formidable fortress of Ollantaytambo, 30 miles downstream in the Yucay Valley. The Spaniards fight their way out of their city with 70 horses, 30 foot soldiers, and a large contingent of native auxiliaries, leaving Gabriel de Rojas behind with a small garrison. However, once coming within sight of this impregnable fortification—bristling with masses of archers and warriors—Pizarro realizes it cannot be taken; he retreats to Cuzco after heavy fighting.

Heartened by this success, the emperor sends his army once more to attempt to carry Cuzco, but these columns are defeated in open country by Spanish cavalry charges, so a stalemate develops, with both sides exhausted, remaining within their bases throughout the rainy season.

8 NOVEMBER 1536. Alonso de Alvarado leaves Lima at the head of 100 horsemen, 40 crossbowmen, and 210 foot soldiers to reconquer the interior of Peru. As he enters the Andes 25 miles east of Lima, he endures a

Undated engraving of a Spanish rider

fierce skirmish with an Indian contingent under Illa Tupac, killing 30 and capturing 100. The latter are maimed by having their hands and noses cut off, then released to spread news of their horrific fates among the region's natives. Another engagement occurs on 15 November in Olleros Pass, but Alvarado presses on toward Jauja, sowing destruction.

MID-JANUARY 1537. After being reinforced at Jauja by a further 200 men under Gómez de Tordoya, Alonso de Alvarado resumes his slow drive toward Cuzco. Major opposition is encountered at Rumichaca, a stone bridge over the Pampas River below Vilcas, but the Spaniards nonetheless continue east toward Abancay.

EARLY APRIL 1537. Almagro returns to central Peru from his failed Chilean expedition, sending a peace embassy ahead to call upon Manco at Ollantaytambo and listen to his grievances against Pizarro. The Inca emperor at first seems inclined to make peace with the rival conquistador but changes his mind once Almagro enters Calca (25 miles from Ollantaytambo) with his vanguard of 200 riders. Paucar, the young Inca commander for this region, launches a surprise attack with 5,000–6,000 warriors, obliging the Spaniards to fight their way across the river, reaching Cuzco after nightfall on 18 April. Almagro immediately deposes Hernando and Gonzalo Pizarro, imprisoning them along with a handful of supporters while he assumes overall command of the city.

12 JULY 1537. In order to ensure his hold over Cuzco, Almagro dispatches his lieutenant, Rodrigo Orgóñez, with a strong contingent and 10,000 native auxiliaries under Paullu to subdue Alonso de Alvarado's relief force approaching from the coast. Orgóñez meets this Spanish army at night near the Abancay River crossing, overwhelming it almost without bloodshed by sunup on 13 July.

LATE JULY 1537. ***Flight of the Emperor.*** Despairing of ever beating the Spaniards upon the battlefield, Manco abandons Ollantaytambo to seek safety in Peru's interior. Almagro instantly orders the victorious Orgóñez to pursue the fleeing emperor with 300 riders and foot soldiers. These overtake Manco at Amaibamba, defeating his rearguard; the emperor himself escapes afoot toward Vitcos. The next day, Orgóñez reaches this place as well, pausing to loot it, thus allowing Manco to escape into the mountains. The Spanish column then returns to Cuzco by the end of July with enormous booty and many thousands of prisoners, discovering that Paullu has in the interim been crowned the new puppet emperor.

MID-SEPTEMBER 1537. Almagro opens negotiations with Francisco Pizarro on the coast over ownership of Cuzco. The latter's position hardens when his brother Gonzalo escapes confinement and Hernando is exchanged. Eventually, fighting erupts between both factions, and Hernando Pizarro leads an invasion of the central highlands.

26 APRIL 1538. ***Almagro's End.*** After pressing the followers of the infirm, 63-year-old Almagro back to Cuzco, Hernando Pizarro and Alonso de Alvarado fight a pitched two-hour battle a few miles south of this city against Almagro's lieutenant, Rodrigo Orgóñez. He defends himself bravely until being wounded in the forehead by a harquebus round; he is then captured and beheaded. Some 200 of his troops are also slaughtered, another 150 wounded; only 25 or

26 are killed among Pizarro's ranks. Cuzco is then occupied, and Almagro is imprisoned. A vengeful Hernando Pizarro has him quickly tried and garroted on 8 July.

LATE JULY 1538. At Manco's instigation, the Lupaca tribe in Collasuyu province attacks their traditional foe, the Colla, now vassals to the Spaniards. Hernando Pizarro and Paullu march to their subjects' relief, defeating the Lupaca in a difficult battle on the banks of Desaguadero River. Hernando Pizarro then retraces his steps toward Cuzco, leaving his brother Gonzalo and the puppet emperor to mop up.

AUTUMN 1538. The Conchuco tribes in the hills bordering the upper Marañon rise against Spanish rule, sweeping south with Manco as far as Jauja, where the Huanca refuse to join them. The rebuffed Inca emperor therefore moves his army south to Ayacucho, threatening Spanish communications between Cuzco and the coast.

Francisco Pizarro reaches Cuzco in November and detaches Illán Suárez de Carvajal with 200 horses and a large force of auxiliaries to deal with this menace. After marching west to Vilcas, the Spaniards learn of Manco's headquarters in the hilltop village of Oncoy. Hoping to trap their elusive foe, Suárez remains on one bank of the Pampas River with his cavalry while a captain named Villadiego stealthily seizes the bridge crossing with a company of infantry. But rather than remaining, the eager young officer presses on with only 30 men (including five harquebusiers and seven crossbowmen) to personally attempt to capture the Inca chieftain and thereby gain great credit. Instead his contingent is discovered and massacred after a two-hour fight; only six Spaniards survive.

Inspired by this victory, Manco's generals, Paucar Huaman and Yuncallo, attack and defeat a large force of Spaniards and Indian allies at Yuramayo, killing many. Finally, Pizarro sorties from Cuzco on 22 December with 70 riders, compelling the Indians to retire.

DECEMBER 1538. ***Cochabamba.*** Gonzalo Pizarro's 70 Spanish soldiers and Paullu's 5,000 native auxiliaries spend five days fighting their way to wild and remote Cochabamba Valley (Bolivia). Huge numbers of warriors led by the Chicha general Torinaseo then trap them inside, under the overall strategic guidance of the emperor's uncle, Tiso Yupanqui. After a furious, day-long confrontation, however, the Chicha army finally breaks, leaving 800 dead upon the field. The Spaniards next work their way through the valley, reinforced early the following year by strong contingents under Hernando Pizarro and Martín de Guzmán, which have circled over the Andean Range and thus help subdue all valley tribes. Even Tiso surrenders in February 1539 after being granted amnesty, entering Cuzco on 19 March with Gonzalo Pizarro's triumphant army.

APRIL 1539. ***Chuquillusca.*** Gonzalo Pizarro marches out of Cuzco at the head of 300 Spanish fighting men and a host of native auxiliaries under Paullu to track down Manco at his remote new capital of Vilcabamba, deep within the Amazonian forest. The jungle beyond Vitcos proves so dense that the Spaniards are obliged to leave their horses behind. Nevertheless, they fight their way through until reaching a rocky hill called Chuquillusca, where 36 are suddenly killed in a native ambush, forcing the rest to retreat.

Ten days later, after being reinforced, Gonzalo Pizarro resumes his attack, delegating 100 Spaniards to storm Chuquillusca while leading his main body in a flanking maneuver. Manco flees, and his followers melt into the wilderness, leaving Vilcacamba, 14 miles away, to be destroyed by the Spaniards. This expedition returns to Cuzco in July with numerous captives, including the empress Cura Ocllo.

LATE SEPTEMBER 1539. Francisco Pizarro returns to Cuzco from Arequipa, hoping to negotiate Manco's surrender.

OCTOBER 1539. After a fierce eight-month campaign in Condesuyo province by Capt. Pedro de los Rios, the high Inca priest Villac Umu submits to the Spaniards.

NOVEMBER 1539. Manco rebuffs Pizarro's peace overture by slaughtering his envoys. In retaliation, the Spaniard has the empress Cura Ocllo stripped, beaten, and shot to death with arrows, her body being floated down the Yucay River in a basket to be found by the emperor's men. Villac Umu, Tiso, and many other prominent captives are burned alive.

1539. Despite Manco's continuing defiance in the eastern jungles, effective Inca resistance is at an end. Guerrilla warfare persists in certain regions for a number of years, but Peru is largely subdued. The Spaniards begin managing their vast new estates or dispersing for further adventures.

Conquest of Venezuela and Colombia (1529–1541)

In Europe during the spring of 1528, the Habsburg emperor Charles V—hoping to realize some immediate financial gains from his fast-expanding New World properties—leases mainland Venezuela to the German banking house of Welser (in Spanish, Velzare or Belzare), which is headquartered in the city of Augsburg. Along with this lease goes the right to establish towns, develop mineral deposits, and import African slaves into the new American territory.

A convoy of three ships and a caravel duly departs Seville on 7 October this same year, bearing 200 men under García de Lerma and Pedro Márquez, to begin the process of exploring and settling these new lands. These vessels rendezvous in January 1529 at the Antillan island of Santo Domingo with another contingent of 100 fighting men raised locally by a tough German mercenary—named in Spanish records as Ambrosio de Alfinger, though more likely Talfinger or Dalfinger—who assumes overall command of the enterprise. The first of several thousand Yoruba, Ibo, and Fon slaves are also brought across the Atlantic from West Africa.

The subsequent zeal displayed by these German conquistadores expanding out of Venezuela will prompt their Spanish neighbors at Santa Marta to competitive efforts so as to secure their own Colombian hinterland. Both groups will also be fired by native legends of El Dorado (literally "The Golden Man"—an allusion to the Chibcha coronation ritual whereby a new leader appears at dawn standing on a raft in sacred Lake Guatavita, coated with resin and gold dust, to dive into the water and emerge as new overlord).

24 February 1529. Alfinger reaches the town of La Vela de Coro (Venezuela) to establish a Welser beachhead and becomes its first governor.

Early August 1529. ***Alfinger's Opening Campaign.*** The new German governor appoints Luis Sarmiento as his deputy and departs La Vela de Coro with a small army of 180 men to venture southwest against the inland natives. By 8 September he discovers the shores of Lake Maracaibo, having sown terror in his path. Alfinger's brutality—which is calculated to cow the numerous dispersed Indian tribes and includes such atrocities as branding them on the face to establish Welser ownership—quickly earns him the sobriquet "cruelest of the cruel." He is also resented by his Spanish followers, discontented at what they regard as foreign leadership in their own American territories.

Alfinger conquers a native town on the site of present-day Maracaibo and renames it Ulma in honor of his German birthplace, Ulm. Disease and lack of provisions eventually oblige him to return toward La Vela de Coro with only 7,000 pesos' worth of booty.

12 January 1530. The 28-year-old mercenary Nicolaus Federmann der Jüngere (the Younger—also a native of Ulm) arrives at the Paraguaná Peninsula on the eastern side of what is today the Gulf of Venezuela from a stopover on the island of Santo Domingo. With 123 Spaniards, two dozen German miners, and ten horses aboard a bark owned by the Welsers, his mission is to support the efforts of Alfinger in exploring and securing this new region.

Federmann disembarks most of his men and horses to march overland toward the main town of La Vela de Coro under Georg Ehinger while he himself returns aboard his bark and stands away from the coast at 2 A.M. on 15 January, beating upwind toward Santo Domingo.

8 March 1530. Having taken on further horses, oxen, cattle, and provisions at Santo Domingo and nearby San Germán de Puerto Rico, plus being joined by another Welser vessel out of Spain, Federmann drops anchor off the Venezuelan port of La Vela de Coro to be greeted by Alfinger's Spanish deputy, Sarmiento. Federmann unloads his bark and sends it back toward Santo Domingo on 22 March to continue its homeward passage to Spain.

18 April 1530. Three more Welser vessels reach La Vela de Coro from Seville, bringing further reinforcements under a new acting governor, Hans Seissenhofer—whose difficult last name means he becomes known as Juan Alemán ("John German") or Juan el Bueno ("John the Good") to the Spaniards. Seissenhofer is sworn into office with Federmann as his deputy, as it is by now feared that the long-absent Alfinger must either be dead or lost.

3 May 1530. After a nine-month absence, a sickly Alfinger staggers back to La Vela de Coro with 110 survivors of his inland campaign, the remaining 70 having been lost due to disease, battle, or execution. He is immediately restored into office as governor, Seis-

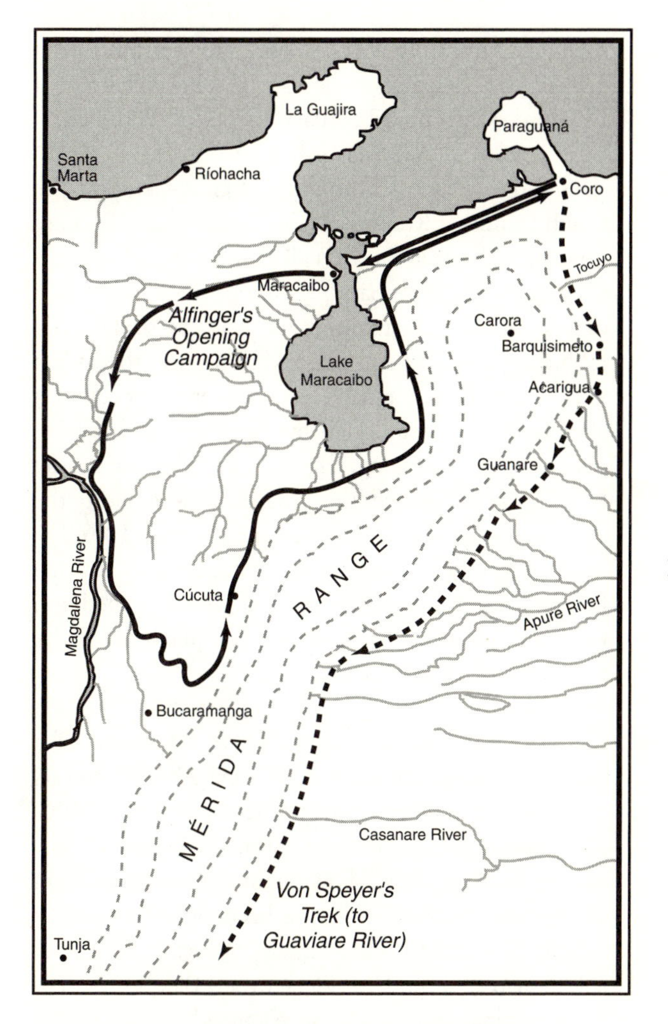

German-Spanish explorations of Venezuela and Colombia

senhofer choosing to pursue other interests (he dies about 18 months later).

26 JULY 1530. ***González de Leiva's Incursion.*** Alfinger designates Luis González de Leiva as his lieutenant governor for Maracaibo, sending him back along the coast with 60 soldiers and two large war canoes—wrested from the Indian chieftain Manaure—to reoccupy that advance base.

González de Leiva encounters steady resistance during his advance, especially from the Cumari tribesmen, who kill three of his men and injure several others. Nevertheless, the Spaniards succeed in capturing 222 prisoners, sending 50–60 to the frontier outpost of Santa Marta (Colombia) under Capt. Iñigo de Vascuña to be sold as slaves. The remainder are dispatched by ship toward Santo Domingo, but when the vessel sinks en route its survivors are instead sold at Jamaica.

1 AUGUST 1530. Still infirm from his prolonged military campaign, Alfinger departs La Vela de Coro aboard the ship *San Antón* to convalesce on the island of Santo Domingo, leaving Federmann as his acting governor.

12 SEPTEMBER 1530. ***Federmann's First Venture.*** During Alfinger's absence, Federmann in turn deputizes Bartolomé de Santillana as his acting governor and quits La Vela de Coro with a small army of 16 Spanish riders, 98 Spanish soldiers, and 100 native Caquetío porters to penetrate the jungles. He strikes southwest in the general direction of modern San Luis, hoping to expand the Welsers' Venezuelan holdings by driving toward the long-sought Pacific Ocean (called the Mar del Mediodía—Midday Sea—by these early explorers).

27 JANUARY 1531. Having recuperated from his previous illness, Alfinger returns to Venezuela from Santo Domingo, reassuming office as its governor from Santillana.

17 MARCH 1531. After six months' campaign through the interior of western Venezuela, Federmann's sickly army returns to La Vela de Coro, emerging from the jungle far to the southeast at the mouth of the Yacaruy River (near present-day Puerto Cabello). In contrast to Alfinger, his foray has managed to establish almost uniformly friendly relations with the mountain tribes, the Cayones being the only people to offer serious resistance to these intruders.

Angry at finding his deputy absent upon his own return, Alfinger orders Federmann exiled from Venezuela for four years.

9 JUNE 1531. ***Alfinger's Final Campaign.*** The German governor reappoints Santillana as his deputy and leads another major expedition out of La Vela de Coro to continue his expansion farther to the west and southwest. He explores the region in and around his advance base of Maracaibo until 1 September, when he is rejoined by González de Leiva's contingent and officially founds a town, appointing Francisco Venegas its first lieutenant governor.

Alfinger subsequently ventures farther north up to the Guajira Peninsula with 40 mounted Spaniards, under Capt. Hans von Casimir of Nuremberg, and 130 infantrymen divided into three companies under Capts. Luis de Monserrat, Gómez de Anaya, and Francisco de Quindos. The governor is seeking to establish a fixed inland boundary with the nearby Spanish colony of Santa Marta (Colombia), by circling southwestward in the general direction of the Magdalena River.

7 JANUARY 1532. After roaming out of Guajira Province (northeastern Colombia) and far southward into its mountains, Alfinger detaches his subordinate, Iñigo de Vascuña, with 24 foot soldiers to return to Maracaibo and La Vela de Coro, bearing 24,000 *castellanos*' worth of gold booty (weighing approximately 350 pounds) and to bring back further reinforcements.

Eighteen months later, it is learned that this detachment never reaches its destination, instead becoming lost in the trackless tropical jungle until its desperately hungry survivors are obliged to bury their gold under a large tree and abandon their companions one by one. Eventually all of them—except for one Francisco Martín—die of exposure.

24 JUNE 1532. Grown increasingly anxious to be reinforced and resupplied, Alfinger detaches his German lieutenant and interpreter, Stephan Martin (in Spanish, Estéban Martín), with 20 soldiers to carry dispatches out of the jungle northward to Lake Maracaibo. The latter reaches the Spanish settlement of Maracaibo 34 days later to find Lieutenant Governor Venegas absent on a retaliatory raid against Onoto tribesmen, who have massacred 14 local Spaniards.

Quite ill, Martin remains at Maracaibo while a subordinate conveys Alfinger's letters northeastward to La Vela de Coro. Soon a company of 50 soldiers returns overland from that port; Martin is thus able to rejoin Alfinger a few weeks later with 82 Spanish soldiers and a large body of native porters. With this renewed strength, the governor attempts to continue his campaign through the Andean sierras (foothills), only to be obliged to give up because of the daunting vegetation and towering heights.

For nearly another year, Alfinger will continue to probe southward and eastward through these ranges, inflicting untold brutalities upon the primitive mountain tribes; otherwise he finds no major cities or rich gold deposits to conquer and hold. Eventually he is struck in the throat by a poison arrow during a skirmish on 27 May 1533, dying four days later. His exhausted army is taken over by Pedro de San Martín, who finally strikes out toward the shores of Lake Maracaibo, sending a few survivors ahead to limp back to La Vela de Coro on Monday, 2 November 1533.

Around this same time Alfinger's deputy governor, Santillana, is deposed by the Spaniards, who, having grown increasingly restive at being ignored by their German rulers, dispatch Luis González de Leiva and Alonso de la Llana toward Spain as their spokesmen on 18 January 1534 to petition Charles V to retract the Welsers' privileges. Instead, a new German governor is sent out from Europe—Georg Hohermuth von Speyer (in Spanish, Jorge de Espira), who will arrive at La Vela de Coro on 6 February 1535 with 700 men.

13 JANUARY 1533. ***Founding of Cartagena.*** The tough Spanish adventurer Pedro de Heredia—his nose missing as a result of a Madrid street brawl—enters Cartagena Bay from Santo Domingo with a ship, two caravels, and a smaller consort, bearing 150 soldiers and 22 horses. The next day he goes ashore near the Indian village of Calamar, and three days later he occupies it after finding it abandoned by the frightened inhabitants. The city of Cartagena is duly founded on this site by 20 January while the two caravels explore the nearby port of Zamba and coasts of Cenú. Heredia's men clash with the natives of Canapote and Turbaco before inspecting Zamba. After a 22-day expedition toward the Magdalena River, the conquistadores retire to Zamba and then Calamar to rest.

15 MAY 1535. ***Von Speyer's Trek.*** Because of a food shortage precipitated by his expedition's arrival, the new German governor immediately sends a 100-man contingent inland, then appoints Federmann (returned to Venezuela following his four-year exile in Europe; *see* 17 March 1531) as his deputy governor at La Vela de Coro. On 15 May, von Speyer himself leads a 400-man army and 90 riders toward Barquisimeto to begin campaigning toward its plainlands.

On 20 May, this main body reaches Tocuyo, where it is joined by the smaller veteran unit of Lope Montalvo de Lugo and Stephan Martin, who are foraging for provisions. Eight days later this combined force passes south into hostile territory and attacks native villages to subdue these and secure slaves to act as porters.

On 26 June, von Speyer's army—which has divided into smaller contingents to facilitate its advance—comes together to assault the large town of Oyrabo (unknown today), overrunning this at the cost of three conquistadores; shortly thereafter he fights another pitched battle at Catimayagua. Indian resistance continues strong, although Indian weapons are no match for those of the invaders, who persistently push further south. On 16 July the invaders reach the shores of the Cojedes River, where they encounter the remnants of their 100-man vanguard, retiring with many wounded. Von Speyer reaches Acarigua on 20 July, where he remains for several days, terrorizing the district. Many men are sick, and the German governor leaves them at Acarigua to recuperate under Capts. Sancho de Murga and Andreas Gundelfinger, then plunges west into unexplored jungles with 30 riders and 100 infantrymen on 18 August.

AUGUST 1535. In La Vela de Coro, the restless Federmann dispatches a strong contingent west toward La Guajira—200 Spanish soldiers under Capt. Antonio de Cháves, supported by 70 horses and numerous Indian porters—which the German lieutenant governor intends to meet at Cape de la Vela by circling with more men aboard ship for a concerted sweep throughout the peninsula.

Cháves therefore marches to the bar of Maracaibo, traverses it by canoe, then proceeds north to La Guajira, where he encounters 50 Spanish soldiers out of Santa Marta (Colombia) under Capt. Juan de Ribera. The latter has been sent by the acting governor, Dr. Rodrigo Infante, to reassert Santa Marta's claim over the area following Alfinger's far-ranging western campaign of 1531–1533. Contrary to his instructions, Ribera agrees to incorporate his soldiers into Cháves's army for Federmann's forthcoming campaign.

LATE SEPTEMBER 1535. Deep in the interior, von Speyer's column—its ranks growing increasingly sick—reaches a prosperous native village on the banks of the Masparro River; he sends Stephan Martin to recall his main body from Acarigua for a joint attack. Awaiting their arrival, von Speyer's company is attacked at dawn by 600 native warriors, emboldened by the Spaniards' evident weakness, but the Indians succeed in slaying merely one horse and wounding several conquistadores before being defeated and dispersed. The Acarigua contingent is also ambushed during its march, suffering eight men and nine horses killed.

OCTOBER 1535. ***Guajira.*** The German lieutenant governor, Federmann, delegates his office at La Vela de Coro to Francisco Venegas, then sets sail with an additional force of 100 soldiers and 20 horses toward Cape de la Vela (Colombia). In February 1536, having united with the companies under Cháves and Ribera, Federmann is further strengthened by the arrival of two ships directly from the island of Santo Domingo bearing 80 more volunteers.

But the German lieutenant governor's hopes of effecting a lasting conquest in this region are dashed by the lack of any significant native concentrations. The local Guajiro and Cocino nomads resist fiercely, then simply melt back into their inhospitable terrain. Federmann attempts to establish a town named Nuestra Señora de las Nieves near present-day Ríohacha (Colombia), then sends Capt. Diego Núñez deep into Macuira province with 60 soldiers to found another town; both attempts fail. Finally, frustrated and hungry, his army heads south in search of easier prey.

CHRISTMAS 1535. Much further south, von Speyer's lost army is crippled by disease and want, spending an entire month encamped around Coharabichan. Limping into Ithibona by 9 January 1536, the commander leaves behind 130 sick soldiers and 19 riders under Capts. Sancho de Murga and Andreas Gundelfinger, with orders to rejoin the main column once their health is restored. (They never do; after a year in Ithibona, during which two-thirds of their number succumb, survivors retrace their route toward La Vela de Coro.)

Von Speyer continues his progress southward on 25 January 1536 with 49 riders and 150 infantrymen.

JANUARY 1536. The governor-designate for Santa Marta (Colombia), Pedro Fernández de Lugo, arrives from Spain with 1,200 men. One of his first tasks after assuming office is to use this considerable host to prevent Federmann's smaller army from pressing out of western Venezuela's Guajira province and infringe upon Santa Marta's territory. Fernández de Lugo therefore delegates 26-year-old licenciate Gonzalo Jiménez de Quesada to precede Federmann to the Magdalena River Valley and arrest the German lieutenant governor should he break the frontier.

Learning of this plan, Federmann instead orders the bulk of his army to retire to the Carora Plains under Diego Martínez while he returns toward La Vela de Coro for reinforcements and resupply.

1 APRIL 1536. Deep in the hinterland, von Speyer's lost army enters Guaypíe territory, fighting a ferocious battle at Guachimena. The stench of burned Indian bodies quickly obliges them to abandon the town.

5 APRIL 1536. Jiménez de Quesada quits Santa Marta at the head of a 600-man Spanish army, advancing south to rendezvous with another 200 troops, who will circle aboard some brigantines to travel up the length of the Magdalena River and meet him. After an arduous trek, the two contingents come together at La Tora, where Jiménez installs himself; he learns of another rich Indian nation, rumored to be flourishing still further upriver—the Chibchas or Muiscas. After refreshing his army over the winter, the young licentiate heads to a high central plateau early in 1537 with fewer than 170 Spanish soldiers.

MAY 1536. Federmann returns to La Vela de Coro and briefly resumes office, although a cloud of surly disapproval greets his failure at Cape de la Vela. He therefore remains only until 14 December, when he departs again with what men he can recruit to continue campaigning in a more southeasterly direction. (Meanwhile his previous expedition suffers cruelly in the Carora Plains, losing 120 men to disease, want, and native attacks.)

Federmann and his lieutenant, Pedro de Limpias, meanwhile inflict very harsh treatment upon Barquisimeto and Acarigua's Indians, but they otherwise accomplish little of lasting military value during their southeastern foray, soon turning back.

1 DECEMBER 1536. After several months of attempting to ford the Opía River, von Speyer's lost army finally crosses and fights deeper into Guaypíe territory. Passing into Punignigua lands shortly thereafter, the invaders find gold and silver artifacts within an abandoned village, prompting the German commander to detach his lieutenant, Stephan Martin, with a contingent of troops to again seek a pass westward through the mountains.

During his absence, von Speyer's men successfully weather a dawn attack by local natives. Martin returns with many prisoners—but without having found any route over the range. On 19 January 1537, the invaders turn south into fertile plainlands and are welcomed at a prosperous Indian town, which is renamed Nuestra Señora (Our Lady; today's San Juan de los Llanos). An inspection reveals that the army's strength is now reduced to a mere 102 men.

After a brief rest, von Speyer continues his weary march, again encountering hostile tribes.

LATE FEBRUARY 1537. Somewhere between the banks of the Yari and Caguan Rivers, von Speyer detaches his principal lieutenant, Stephan Martin, with 40 men to search for a ford. The rainy season is now fully raging, and these scouts are further beset by hostile bands. Many are injured before turning back, including Martin himself, who dies a few days after rejoining the main body.

Weary and dispirited by the loss of this valuable officer, von Speyer's men insist upon being led back toward La Vela de Coro. The German governor opposes this view, personally leading another foray at the head of 40 loyal followers; 60 stay behind under Capt. Santa Cruz. This attempt proves to be von Speyer's last gasp, as he is unsuccessful in finding any hope of emerging from the endless jungles further south. Returning to Santa Cruz's base camp, von Speyer eventually orders his surviving band of 100 men and 40 horses to turn back on 13 August.

EARLY MARCH 1537. ***Subjugation of Colombia.*** With 166 troops, the young Spanish explorer Jiménez de Quesada advances up the Opón River (tributary to the Magdalena River) and emerges into a high, lush plateau that is home to five major Chibcha tribes. The tribes share a fertile region delineated by the modern departments of Cundinamarca and Boyacá; the Spaniards name it the Valley of Los Alcázares. Its native peoples are several hundred thousand strong and maintain large standing armies—with a professional warrior caste and draftees—but their leadership is riven by intertribal disputes. Thus, Jiménez de Quesada will be able to use tribal differences to form valuable alliances, pit one group against another, and defeat each of the Chibcha nations in turn.

Fighting begins toward the end of 1537 and lasts into the following year, with the city-states of Tunja and Sogamoso providing especially valuable plunder to Jiménez's army. However, combat is hardly ferocious, the Spaniards suffering only minor casualties in a few skirmishes; most of the Indians are spared and become docile tributaries. The conquest ends with the largest Chibcha nation, located in the south under its *zipa,* or chieftain, Bogotá, being forced to surrender; a new capital named Santa Fé de Bogotá is founded on this site by 6 August 1538. Jiménez names this new territory Nuevo Reino de Granada (New Kingdom of Granada), which is soon shortened to Nueva Granada (New Granada).

LATE DECEMBER 1537. ***Federmann's Southern March.*** Desperate for a success to bolster his sagging prestige, the German lieutenant governor of La Vela de Coro (Venezuela) decides to make a more determined effort southward, setting out with a small army and marching through the nearby Valley of Tocuyo.

Here he is rejoined by the remnants of his unhappy army from the Carora Plains, then encounters a rogue Spanish unit under Capts. Juan Fernández de Alderete and Martín Nieto, who have rebelled against the rule of the new governor of Paria (eastern Venezuela), Jerónimo Dortal, and ventured westward on their own account. Federmann therefore arrests these two captains and sends them back to La Vela de Coro to stand trial, incorporating their men into his company. This gives him a total strength of some 300 Spanish troops, 130 mounts, and a host of native bearers.

Sixteenth-century drawing of Spanish riders on the march

With this force, Federmann strikes out south-southwest in the wake of von Speyer's lost army, skirting the northern Andean foothills. He crosses the Apure River in April 1538 but misses the survivors of von Speyer's expedition—some say deliberately, so as to avoid falling under his superior's orders again—who are now wearily retracing their steps northward. In order to make it easier for troops to forage, Federmann subdivides his small army into three companies, advancing by separate roads and only occasionally reuniting. After four months' march, his expedition gathers at the town of San Juan de los Llanos (called Nuestra Señora or La Fragua—The Forge—by these early explorers), where it is overtaken by another small company of Spanish troops from La Vela de Coro under Capt. Juan Gutiérrez de Aguilón.

27 MAY 1538. Von Speyer's 20 surviving riders and 80 infantrymen reemerge from the jungle at La Vela de Coro, very sickly and worn after three years' campaign against the Indians. Another nine cavalrymen and 40 foot soldiers will return separately under Capts. Sancho de Murga and Andreas Gundelfinger, having been left behind during the march on the banks of the Sarare River.

Von Speyer finds that during his prolonged absence he has been suspended from office for almost a year, being replaced on 27 July 1537 by Dr. Nicolás Navarro, who has been sent to investigate conditions in the colony. After protracted hearings, the German governor reassumes power toward the end of December, although hampered by Navarro.

JUNE 1538. Another Spanish army—nearly 500 strong—departs Popayán (southwestern Colombia) under Sebastián de Velalcázar, intending to penetrate the Andes independently from a westerly direction and capture the legendary El Dorado.

FEBRUARY 1539. After searching in vain for a pass westward through the Andes, Federmann learns that the local Ariare Indians trade gold objects with native tribes on the far side of the mountains, so he pushes up toward the headwaters of the Arrari River, losing many Indians and horses to the cold weather around Sumapaz.

Some 40 days later he descends to southeastern Colombia's Fosca Valley with 230 surviving men and 90 horses, only to discover that the entire region has already been subjugated by Jiménez de Quesada. Velalcázar also arrives in the neighboring Neiva province around this same time, leading 150 well-armed men (having detached another 300 to garrison the towns he has occupied along his route eastward through the Andes from Popayán). Both Federmann and Velalcázar contend that this newly conquered territory lies within their respective jurisdictions; they submit their dispute for arbitration by Madrid.

EARLY JUNE 1539. Jiménez de Quesada, Federmann, and Velalcázar quit Guataquí (Colombia), to travel down the Magdalena River together aboard some brigantines, arriving at Cartagena on 20 June after a few minor skirmishes with Indians along the way. They continue their journey via Jamaica across the Atlantic toward Spain to resolve their jurisdictional disputes.

11 JUNE 1540. Von Speyer dies at La Vela de Coro, just as he is about to depart after naming Juan de Villegas deputy governor; he had intended to join a 150-man advance unit already gathered at Barquisimeto under Capt. Lope Montalvo de Lugo to make another expedition southward.

7 NOVEMBER 1540. Bishop Rodrigo de Bastidas reaches La Vela de Coro from the island of Santo Domingo with 200 fresh troops and 150 mounts. Finding von Speyer dead, the bishop appoints Philipp von Hutten—a 29-year-old native of Birkenfeld, Germany, and veteran of von Speyer's previous three-year march southward—to temporarily succeed him in this post.

1 AUGUST 1541. ***Von Hutten's Campaign.*** The new acting-governor departs La Vela de Coro at the head of 100 riders and a few foot soldiers to campaign southward. Montalvo de Lugo has already refused to place himself under von Hutten's orders, leading his own, larger contingent away from Barquisimeto some months earlier toward the headwaters of the Casanare

River, from whence he gains the far side of its nearby mountain range and enters the service of New Granada (Colombia).

Von Hutten therefore remains at Barquisimeto until the end of January 1542, hoping further volunteers will join his standard. He too then ventures southward, following von Speyer's old trail. By August von Hutten's small army traverses the Opía River, there learning of a rival Spanish expedition that has crossed the Andes eastward from Colombia under Hernán Pérez de Quesada in search of El Dorado. Von Hutten follows this new contingent's path until about Christmas, when he enters the territory of hostile Choque tribesmen. After repeated skirmishes, his column veers southeastward, reaching Caguán by January 1543 and pausing to rest.

Capt. Pedro de Limpias descends Caguán's river with 28 horsemen, sweeping through numerous Choque towns and winning considerable booty over the next three months before rejoining von Hutten's encampment on 8 May 1543. Advancing further southeastward, the main body then suffers numerous losses battling the Choque until the end of the year. Making a fighting retreat northward to the land of the Guaypíes, von Hutten's exhausted survivors remain at the town of Nuestra Señora (San Juan de los Llanos) until the end of 1544, during which he further probes the adjacent Omegua territory, finding its inhabitants "strong and bellicose."

Convinced he needs greater numbers of soldiers to conquer all these regions, the young commander decides to retrace his steps northward at the beginning of 1545 and head for the Venezuelan coast. By May he reaches the Pauta River, where von Hutten's weary army rests for several months before detaching a vanguard of 20 soldiers under the youthful Bartholomäus Welser and the grizzled Pedro de Limpias to precede them to La Vela de Coro and send provisions to Barquisimeto to refresh the main body upon its homeward leg.

However, upon reaching Acarigua, Limpias and his followers refuse to obey the young German, instead striking out toward Cubagua to sail for the island of Santo Domingo and forsake the Welser service altogether. This mutinous column is then ambushed by a band of natives near Maracapaná—just short of Cubagua—who kill three horses and a Spaniard, wounding six others, and force the remainder to retreat to Barquisimeto Valley.

Here the Spaniards discover that an independent settlement has been established the previous year, called Nuestra Señora de la Concepción de Tocuyo, whose self-proclaimed "governor"—Juan de Carvajal—refuses to acknowledge the Welsers' authority. When von Hutten and young Welser reach this place with their 60 surviving soldiers on 24 April 1546, Carvajal wins over most of their Spanish followers, then attempts to arrest the two young Germans. The pair pushes past and continues toward La Vela de Coro with a reduced band, but a couple of weeks later they are overtaken in the Jirajaras Range and captured while resting in hammocks. Carvajal has iron collars placed around von Hutten's and Welser's necks, then orders his black slaves to behead them.

1546. Although the Welsers will continue to hold legal title to Venezuela for another 11 years—their lease does not officially lapse until 1557—for all practical purposes their influence extends little beyond the mid-1540s, when the Spaniards reassume de facto government of this region.

Consolidation (1538–1572)

Having secured the most densely populated, sedentary kingdoms of Mexico, Peru, Colombia, and Venezuela, the Spaniards now turn their efforts to creating a whole new colonial society by concentrating on the erection of cities, farms, and businesses. Military activity becomes reduced to exploratory probes against the more remote nomadic tribes, with occasional flare-ups of internal strife.

7 June 1538. Hernando de Soto, a veteran of Pizarro's campaign in Peru (*see* 31 January 1531 and subsequent entries) and now a knight of the Order of Santiago, arrives from Spain to assume office as new governor of Santiago de Cuba, further accompanied by a 950-man expedition intended to conquer a fiefdom in nearby Florida. He and his family are traveling aboard the 800-ton flagship *San Cristóbal* of Capt. Nuño de Tovar, leading the similar-size *Buena Fortuna* of Luis Moscoso de Alvarado and *Magdalena* of Andrés de Vasconcelos; the slightly smaller *Concepción* of Arias Tinoco and *San Antón* of Alonso Romo de Cardeñosa; the 500-ton *San Juan* of Diego García; the caravel *Santa Bárbara* of Pedro Calderón; plus two brigantines.

De Soto is installed in office next day, quickly appointing Bartolomé Ortíz as his deputy to administer

Santiago de Cuba while he concentrates on broader duties and the forthcoming Florida venture. Word reaches him of a French raid upon Havana (*see* May 1538 in Part 2), necessitating the immediate detachment of a relief force under military engineer Mateo Aceituno. Tovar is also deposed as second-in-command of de Soto's expedition, being replaced by Vasco Porcallo. His ships then set sail toward Havana at the end of August while de Soto himself departs Santiago de Cuba on 15 September to travel overland with 50 riders under Porcallo and inspect the length of the island before rejoining his fleet at Havana one month later.

EARLY SEPTEMBER 1538. De Soto's pilot Juan de Añasco quits Havana aboard a brigantine to reconnoiter the Florida coastline. He returns two months later, having failed to obtain reliable information because of bad weather, so he is sent out again in mid-November with a pair of brigantines. This second exploration lasts three months but is more successful, Añasco returning to Havana with four Florida Indians plus a detailed map of Espíritu Santo Bay.

19 MAY 1539. ***De Soto in Florida.*** The governor finally departs Havana with five ships, two caravels, and two brigantines, together bearing 513 soldiers and 337 horses, to launch his long-delayed Florida campaign. Six days later the fleet drops anchor in Tampa Bay and on 30 May they go ashore, enduring their first skirmish with local warriors on 1 June; two horses are killed and several others wounded. A few days later a band of friendly Indians is encountered, among them a Spanish survivor of Narváez's earlier expedition (*see* 23 February 1528) named Juan Ortiz, who has lived as a native for a decade.

Through Ortiz, De Soto is able to arrive at an accommodation with the local chieftain, Mucozo, then penetrates farther north in search of wealthier and more advanced tribes than the coastal nomads. He encounters no major civilizations, and his expedition is steadily eroded by hostile ambushes. Near the Suwannee River, a band of 400 warriors is defeated when they attempt to rescue their captive chief, after which the Spaniards winter near modern Tallahassee, being joined by their ships from Tampa. A brigantine explores the Gulf Coast westward, returning in February 1540 to report on the excellent harbor at Pensacola. It is agreed to send the ships back to Cuba for supplies and then rendezvous at Pensacola in the autumn.

De Soto's army resumes its northward progression on 3 March 1540, soon suffering greatly from hunger, thirst, and disease. By early October it has veered far enough inland to enter Choctaw territory (south-central Alabama) and de Soto treacherously seizes the local chieftain, Tuscaloosa—the Black Warrior. He guides them to a trap at Mobila (near the confluence of the Alabama and Tombigbee Rivers), which the overconfident de Soto enters with only 15 riders while his troops forage outside. Hidden Choctaw warriors stream out of huts, almost overpowering the Spanish leader and killing five of his companions. Captive Indians simultaneously rise within the invaders' baggage train, carrying powder and supplies inside the palisades. A savage fight erupts for Mobila, which ends with the Choctaw garrison massacred and buildings being consumed by flames. The Spaniards suffer 22 dead, 148 wounded, and the loss of most of their materiel.

Although his relief fleet is waiting at Pensacola, de Soto suppresses the news and marches further northwest in hopes of reversing his fortunes. After entering Chickasaw territory, the Spanish camp is infiltrated during the night of 3 March 1541 by several hundred warriors bearing firebrands concealed in earthenware. These are used to set the place ablaze, and the Spaniards suffer a dozen deaths and the loss of 50–60 precious horses through stampede before repelling the enemy. Now in desperate straits, the Spaniards reach the banks of the Mississippi River by Sunday, 8 May 1541, building barges near present-day Sunflower Landing for a month while hostile native flotillas patrol offshore. Slipping across, de Soto next forms an alliance with the Casqui tribe and attacks their enemy, the Quapaw, on 26 June.

After wintering near the confluence of the Canadian and Arkansas Rivers, he and his surviving 300 men and 40 horses head south toward the Gulf of Mexico, but de Soto dies of exhaustion and fever en route. Luis Moscoso de Alvarado becomes his successor, failing to march this army out; he instead winters on the banks of the Mississippi River to build boats. Finally, on 2 July 1543 they set sail: 322 Spaniards, 100 Indian slaves, and 22 horses aboard seven pinnaces and a host of dugouts. Natives harass their passage, compelling Moscoso to abandon all the horses by the time they reach the Gulf on 16 July. Eventually, 311 survivors reach safety at the Spanish settlements on the Pánuco River on 10 September.

JULY 1539. Francisco de Ulloa departs Acapulco and reaches the abandoned site of Santa Cruz (Baja California) with two ships by early September. He then crosses to Sonora and follows its coast to the Gulf of California's head before starting down its western side in late September. By 13 October he has reached Bahía de la Concepción, and five days later he reenters Santa Cruz, remaining 11 days and making several incursions inland. Cabo San Lucas is rounded with some difficulty in November, after which both ships run up the Pacific to Almejas, where a landing party clashes with Guaycura warriors. He explores Magdalena Bay 4–17 December, after which he follows the coast farther north. Early in January 1540 the expedition reaches Cedros Island—one ship remains there for three months while de Ulloa continues to Punta Baja; both return to Mexico later that spring.

FEBRUARY 1540. ***Coronado Expedition.*** The newly appointed governor for the northern Mexican province of Nueva Galicia—40-year-old Francisco Vázquez de Coronado—departs Compostela with 250 cavalry, 70 Spanish infantry, and several hundred Indian auxiliaries plus baggage animals and cattle. His objective is to find the legendary "seven cities of Cíbola," reputedly rich in gold, but these prove a chimera. After reaching the Zuñi pueblos of New Mexico by July, Coronado presses on through northeastern Arizona and the Grand Canyon before eventually wintering on the Rio Grande (Tuguez) and becoming reinspired by Indian tales of another rich city farther to the northeast called Quivira.

Coronado strikes out across the Texas plains in April 1541, venturing ahead of his army with about 30 riders as far as central Kansas before finally rejoining the main body on the Rio Grande in October. By spring 1542 he is compelled to admit defeat, leading the tattered remnants of his expedition back to Mexico.

10 APRIL 1541. ***Mixtón War.*** In northern New Galicia (modern Zacatecas, Mexico), the hitherto pacific Caxcán Indians have for several months refused to pay tribute to the Spaniards. A contingent under Miguel de Ibarra therefore enters the district, but on 10 April—during a solar eclipse—they are attacked and defeated by warriors from Nochistlán, only the captain and two of his men escaping the ambush alive.

Rebellion then grips the neighboring towns of Tlaltenango, Juchipila, and Teocaltiche as well, 10,000 natives soon being gathered atop Nochistlán Heights under their leader, Tenamaxtle (called "Diego el Zacateco" by the Spaniards). This example is also emulated by the more contentious Tecuexe and Coca peoples, as far southwest as the Nayarit Range—all being members of the much larger, seminomadic Chichimec nation. Through brutal land grabs and the imposition of their strange new culture, the conquistadors have alien-

Mexican Viceroy Antonio de Mendoza

ated most of these far-flung tribesmen, whose spiritual leaders promise their warriors divine rewards for any extraordinary feats performed during the forthcoming struggle.

After Spanish settlers are pushed south into central Jalisco, reinforcements begin rushing to their aid from other parts of Mexico. The first such company, under Lt. Gov. Cristóbal de Oñate, is defeated; a second led by the veteran Capt. Pedro de Alvarado fares little better. Twice repulsed while attempting to fight his way up Yahualica Ravine, Alvarado is accidentally crushed on 1 July by the falling horse of his scribe, Baltasar de Montoya, dying three days later, thereby bringing this second relief expedition to dissolution.

Emboldened by these successes, Tenamaxtle ventures farther south out of his mountain fasts, eventually attacking the city of Guadalajara on 28 September (at its original site, a native town formerly called Tlacotán, three miles west of modern Tlacotlán). Despite heavy losses, the garrison manages to resist—although once the throngs of attackers withdraw, leaving behind thousands of dead from disease and malnourishment, its 63 frightened Spanish householders decide to abandon this place and transfer their capital 15 miles farther southwest, beyond a large ravine into the safer Atemajac Valley (where the modern city of Guadalajara now stands).

On 22 October Viceroy Antonio de Mendoza at last quits Mexico City with 300 Spanish riders, 200 infantry, 50 harquebusiers, a like number of crossbowmen, plus perhaps as many as 50,000 loyal native auxiliaries—who in a special dispensation are permitted to wield Iberian weaponry, ride horses, and enslave local Indians during the ensuing campaign. This host is joined by additional contingents during its march northwest and, after scattering a rebel concentration at Payacuarán, arrives before Tenamaxtle's mountain stronghold of Nochistlán by 19 November. Although only commanding 12,000 Caxcán supporters, the latter refuses to surrender when called upon next day; de Mendoza therefore cuts off the defenders' water supply and by 24 November succeeds in fighting his way to the top, capturing 8,000 prisoners—among them Tenamaxtle.

The rebel survivors then make a final, desperate stand at nearby El Mixtón de Juchipila, atop Coina or Coinan Peak, and de Velasco again calls for their surrender. The defenders ask to speak to their captive leader first, but when Tenamaxtle is brought forward, they instead free him with a bold surprise attack. Furious, the viceroy orders El Mixtón besieged, its stone walls pounded with artillery. On 7 December, native turncoats guide a Spanish column to the summit via a hidden route, and next dawn its garrison are overwhelmed, some 1,500 Chichimecs being slain during the opening onslaught. Many others among the 3,000 prisoners are savagely executed afterward as a warning against further rebellion.

Although Tenamaxtle escapes from the massacre atop El Mixtón, this battle brings large-scale hostilities to a close. Thousands of Indians have died or have been enslaved, and a string of small keeps are subsequently established along the *camino real* (King's Highway) to maintain an uneasy peace. Nevertheless, minor raiding persists for another half-century.

26 JUNE 1541. ***Almagro's Revolt.*** In Lima on this Sunday morning, a group of about 20 embittered supporters of Diego de Almagro the Younger force their way into the undefended palace of Francisco Pizarro and hack the 63-year-old marqués to death along with his half-brother Francisco Martín de Alcántara. This uprising has been prompted by the fact that former supporters of Almagro's father (executed three years earlier; *see* 26 April 1538) have been systematically excluded from any division of Peru's spoils. In a desperate gamble, they proclaim Almagro's teenage son—the product of a liaison with a native woman from Panama—as new governor and captain general.

Young Almagro is soon opposed by the royal envoy, Cristóbal Vaca de Castro, who lands in northern Peru and is joined by an army under Alonso de Alvarado, loyal to the dead Pizarro. Together they press south, their ranks swelling with many adherents, until the two factions finally confront each other at Chupas, just outside Huamanga. A pitched battle is fought on 16 September 1542, resulting in Almagro's defeat and flight. He is overtaken with a few lieutenants in the Yucay Valley, 25 miles from Cuzco, and carried into the city to be executed. A few of his followers find sanctuary at the fugitive Manco's jungle camps, instructing the Incas in Spanish tactics.

JUNE 1542. Juan Rodríguez Cabrillo departs Puerto de la Navidad (Mexico) with two ships to continue de Ulloa's exploration of Baja California—also known as Cardona Island. He travels up its west coast during July–September, making disembarkations at Cabo San Lucas, Cedros Island, and San Quintín Bay before dying among the Channel Islands, leaving Rodríguez's survivors to return to Navidad by 14 April 1543.

SEPTEMBER 1544. The first Peruvian viceroy—Blasco Núñez Vela, in office only four months—is deposed by Lima's *audiencia* for his heavy-handed zeal in implementing Spain's new laws designed to protect the Indians. Gonzalo Pizarro enters Lima the following month, having rallied popular support because of fears of an alleged Indian uprising; shortly thereafter he compels the viceroy to quit the capital.

Núñez Vela lands in northern Peru and makes his way toward Quito, organizing a rival government. Pizarro eventually marches north against him during the summer of 1545, defeating the viceroy and his followers on 18 January 1546 at the Battle of Añaquito (just north of Quito). Núñez Vela is killed, leaving Pizarro undisputed master over all of Peru.

LATE 1544. The fugitive Inca emperor Manco is treacherously murdered at Vitcos while playing horseshoes with Diego Méndez and six other Spanish renegades, to whom he has given shelter. The latter attempt to ride to Cuzco to claim credit for their dastardly deed but are overtaken in the jungle by troops under Rimachi Yupanqui and put to death.

APRIL 1545. A silver deposit of immense wealth is discovered at Potosí (Bolivia).

AUTUMN 1546. A royal emissary from Spain, Licenciado Pedro de la Gasca, advances into northern Peru, gathering adherents against the usurper Gonzalo

Pizarro, whom he pronounces guilty of treason in December.

8 SEPTEMBER 1546. After probing north from Nochistlán into the central Mexican highlands, a band of Spanish explorers under Juan de Tolosa—alias Barbalonga or "Long Beard"—discovers a huge silver ore deposit at the foot of a rocky promontory he nicknames La Bufa (Basque for "pig's bladder"). Less than 18 months later, this site is settled and becomes the city of Zacatecas.

21 OCTOBER 1547. Gonzalo Pizarro defeats a royalist army under Alonso de Alvarado at Huarina, on the southeastern shores of Lake Titicaca.

9 APRIL 1548. ***Jaquijahuana.*** Despite the Huarina setback, Gasca's royalist army succeeds in driving on Cuzco, and on this day the two armies meet on the Jaquijahuana or Sacsahuana Plain, a few miles west of the city. Some 45 of Gonzalo Pizarro's closest followers are killed during the battle; most of the remainder run across the field to join the royalist ranks. Gasca loses only one man during this fighting and orders Pizarro executed the next day, thus restoring Madrid's hold over Peru.

13 NOVEMBER 1553. ***Hernández Girón's Revolt.*** The Spanish citizens of Cuzco rebel, this time under a respected *hacendado* (landowner) named Francisco Hernández Girón, against Madrid's continuing efforts to introduce pro-Indian legislation to Peru. The cities of Huamanga and Arequipa soon join this insurrection, and for the next year the Spaniards of the southern Andes are in a curious state—rebels who nonetheless loudly proclaim their loyalty to Charles I while demanding a freer hand in exploiting the region's native population. A royalist army raised by the *audiencia* (high court) at Lima eventually defeats Hernández Girón at the Battle of Pucará, north of Lake Titicaca, on 8 October 1554. He is captured at Huamanga in November and beheaded in December.

11–18 JANUARY 1567. A plot by certain Peruvian mestizos (offspring of Spaniard-Indian unions)—who call themselves *montañeses*—to assassinate peninsular Spaniards and seize their lands is foiled in both Cuzco and Lima.

MARCH 1572. A Spanish envoy, Atilano de Anaya, is murdered while en route to visit the new Inca emperor Tupac Amaru at Vilcabamba.

Indians with native prisoner

14 APRIL 1572. ***Vilcabamba.*** In retaliation for de Anaya's slaying, the Peruvian viceroy Francisco de Toledo ends the Spaniards' long-standing truce with the remnants of the Inca empire by declaring war upon Tupac Amaru; two weeks later he dispatches an advance unit from Cuzco to prepare the way for an invasion of the last surviving outpost in remote Vilcabamba. This is followed by a main army of 250 mounted Spaniards under Martín Hurtado de Arbieto, accompanied by thousands of native warriors and auxiliaries. A second force of 70 Spaniards under Gaspar Arias de Sotelo is to close in from Abancay while a third, 50 under Luis de Toledo Pimentel, is to occupy Cusambi Pass so as to prevent any escape.

Thirteen miles short of Vitcos, at a place called Coyao Chaca, the 50-man Spanish vanguard under Capt. Martín García de Loyola blunders into a native ambush on 1 June, obliging the attackers to retire after two and a half hours' heavy fighting. Three days later the Spaniards resume the advance, finding Vitcos abandoned; they then push higher up the valley. After resting at Pampaconas 3–16 June, Hurtado de Arbieto drives deeper into the jungle and learns from an Inca traitor that Tupac Amaru's army is fortified at Huayna Pucará, about ten miles away. The Spanish expedition comes within sight of it on 20 June, and next dawn a flanking party climbs unseen to some nearby heights, obliging the surprised defenders to retreat toward their keep. When Hurtado de Arbieto follows up with a vigorous frontal assault, the Inca general Colla Topa abandons his position. The same occurs the next day, when a Spanish scouting party comes upon another fortification called Machu Pucará, which is forsaken after token opposition.

At 10:00 A.M. on 24 June, Hurtado de Arbieto's army marches into empty, smouldering Vilcabamba. Flying columns are immediately dispatched to overtake the scattering Indians; after a lengthy pursuit, Capt. Martín García de Loyola succeeds in tracking down Tupac Amaru and his last surviving general, Huallpa Yupanqui, capturing both. The Spaniards return triumphantly to Cuzco on 21 September and, three days later, the last Inca emperor is beheaded on Viceroy de Toledo's orders.

Part 2: Seaborne Challengers (1526–1609)

I would like to see the clause in Adam's will which
excludes France from the division of the world.
—King François I (1494–1547)

Franco-Spanish Wars (1526–1559)

As Spain's settlers forsake their original Antillan outposts for the rich new kingdoms of the American mainland, traders from other West European nations begin drifting into the void. Madrid attempts to curtail the transatlantic traffic, embittering the envy already taking hold against the Spaniards' rising fortunes. Old World conflicts soon become transposed into the New World, beginning during the first half of the sixteenth century, when the rulers of Spain and France fight a series of intermittent conflicts known collectively as the Habsburg-Valois Wars (so named for dynastic surnames). They are largely territorial disputes originating in Italy and Flanders that flare into open warfare in 1494–1495, 1499–1505, 1508–1514, 1515–1516, 1521–1526, 1526–1529, 1536–1538, 1542–1544, and 1552–1559; in fact they constitute a nearly continuous period of strife from 1494–1559.

The accession of 19-year-old Charles V as Holy Roman Emperor in 1519 intensifies the rivalry. Already king of Spain and duke of the Netherlands, his dominions now completely encircle France. The ensuing round of hostilities (called the First Franco-Spanish War, 1521–1526) features as a minor sidelight numerous depredations by French privateers off the coasts of Spain, the Canaries, and the Azores Islands, waylaying Spanish vessels bound to and from the Americas. It is not until the next round of fighting, in 1526–1529, that the first French corsairs actually strike out across the ocean and into the West Indies proper.

Early 1526. The 130-ton Spanish galleon *San Gabriel* of Rodrigo de Acuña, separated from Garci Jofre de Loaysa's expedition into the South Pacific via the Magellan Strait, is attacked by three French vessels off Brazil.

1528. A French corsair vessel, accompanied by a Spanish caravel seized off Lanzarote in the Canary Islands, traverses the Atlantic and appears before Margarita Island (Venezuela). Shortly thereafter the same pair attacks and sinks a Spanish caravel near Cape Rojo (Puerto Rico) before sacking and torching the inland hamlet of San Germán and then standing away.

August 1529. In Europe, Franco-Spanish relations are temporarily patched up by the Treaty of Cambrai (known as the Ladies' Peace because it is negotiated between Margaret of Austria and Louise of Savoy).

30 April 1531. Fearful of French designs against South America, a small expedition under Martim Afonso de Sousa enters Rio de Janeiro to establish a Portuguese colony. Although a tiny fortification is erected and peaceable relations are established with the Tamoio natives, the isolated settlement does not prosper and is soon abandoned.

10 May 1534. The 42-year-old explorer Jacques Cartier arrives off Newfoundland with two ships and 61 men from Saint Malo (France), searching for a northwest passage to Asia. After charting part of the shorelines of New Brunswick and Quebec, he returns to Europe by 5 September.

1535. Relations between Paris and Madrid again begin to deteriorate, numerous French corsairs taking up station off the western approaches to Spain and threatening returning ships (especially those bearing treasure from recently conquered Peru). As a result, the Spanish crown orders the reestablishment of its *Armada de la Guardia de la Carrera de Indias* (Guard Fleet for the Indies Route).

9 August 1535. Cartier returns to Newfoundland with three vessels, penetrating the Saint Lawrence Seaway as far southwest as Hochelaga (modern-day

Montréal) by 2 October before retiring to winter at the mouth of the Saint Charles River (modern-day Quebec City). Although disappointed at not discovering a passage to the Far East, the Frenchman is nonetheless convinced this new territory is "rich and wealthy in precious stones." He thus kidnaps a dozen natives and carries them home to Saint Malo by 16 July 1536. Cartier's hope is to spark interest and thus be granted crown permission to found a colony in this land, which he mistakenly believes is called "Canada"—actually the Huron-Iroquois word for village.

SPRING 1536. War again erupts between France and Spain.

FEBRUARY 1537. A lone French corsair vessel is sighted capturing a Spanish merchantman near the port of Nombre de Dios as it arrives with a consignment of horses from Santo Domingo.

15 MARCH 1537. Apparently this same French vessel materializes before Havana, prompting Gov. Gonzalo de Guzmán to order three 200-ton Spanish merchantmen to sortie under Lt. Juan Velázquez. They overtake the intruder three days later off Mariel but run aground in shallow waters and are boarded. Two of the Spanish vessels are burned; the third becomes the prize of the triumphant Frenchmen, who return before Havana to extort ransom from its hapless villagers.

Other French trespassers are also sighted near Santo Domingo.

31 MAY 1537. A French corsair vessel enters Santiago de Cuba's harbor and carries off some merchantmen.

14 JUNE 1537. A dozen Spanish warships and two caravels sortie from Seville under Capt. Gen. Blasco Núñez Vela to escort the outward-bound American convoy, reinforce garrisons throughout the Caribbean, and lift Havana's blockade.

SPRING 1538. Numerous French privateers attack Spanish merchantmen off Santo Domingo and Santiago de Cuba, bringing Spanish maritime traffic in these waters almost to a complete standstill.

4 APRIL 1538. A large, 80-man French ship pillages a Spanish brigantine exiting from Santiago de Cuba and penetrates the harbor the next day; it engages the caravel *Magdalena* of Diego Pérez and a small, two-gun battery ashore. The shallow draught of Pérez's craft allows him to gain the Frenchmen's quarter; he thus peppers the intruders with his four culverins from 11:00 A.M. until they withdraw an hour past midnight, after sustaining about a dozen casualties. Three Spaniards die during the affray.

MAY 1538. A French corsair ship appears near Havana, robbing several houses and churches ashore. The island's new captain general, Hernando de Soto, dispatches military engineer Mateo Aceituno with 100 men from Santiago de Cuba; within a few weeks they throw up the six-gun Castillo de la Fuerza to guard the entrance (*see* 7 June 1538 in Part 1).

JUNE 1538. San Germán de Puerto Rico is sacked and burned by 80 French raiders from a Norman ship. Retiring back to their boats, they are overtaken by 30 mounted Spaniards in a rainstorm, who attack while the Frenchmens' powder is wet. Fifteen raiders are killed and another three taken prisoner; they are exchanged for San Germán's looted church bells and other booty.

15 JUNE 1538. In Europe, French and Spanish plenipotentiaries agree on a ten-year truce (negotiated at Nice by Pope Paul III). However, word of the cessation of hostilities does not reach the New World for some time.

EARLY JUNE 1540. French corsairs disembark from a ship near San Germán de Puerto Rico, sacking and burning the town and its outlying district.

AUGUST 1540. A leaking, 400-ton English ship under a French pilot commandeers a Spanish merchantman laden with sugar and hides off Cape Tiburón (southwestern Haiti), setting the crew ashore before transferring into the prize. They send their original vessel to the bottom and sail home.

1541. Franco-Spanish relations again begin to fray, and in May a 35-man French corsair vessel ransacks a Spanish caravel off Puerto Rico. The same craft sinks another victim off Mona Island before disembarking some men to loot ashore. It then proceeds to Cape de la Vela (Colombia) and robs a Spanish caravel of 7,000–8,000 ducats' worth of pearls at Portete.

SUMMER 1541. Cartier returns to Canada with five ships, having brought an advance contingent of a few hundred settlers from France to establish the foothold for a new colony. The titular head of this enterprise—

the impoverished, 41-year-old courtier Jean François de La Rocque, seigneur de Roberval—is to follow next year with many more colonists, hoping to rebuild his fortune by serving as "lieutenant general of Canada" and exploiting its rich mineral deposits.

While awaiting this arrival, Cartier erects a small fort called Charlesbourg Royal at Cap Rouge (nine miles above modern-day Quebec City) and explores the Saint Lawrence River until wintertime.

MID-DECEMBER 1541. Thirteen well-armed French vessels ransack a Portuguese caravel off Guyana; they are later joined by three additional vessels to press deeper into the Caribbean.

8 JUNE 1542. Roberval reaches Newfoundland with the ships *Valentine, Sainte Anne,* and *Lèchefraye,* bringing hundreds of French colonists to join Cartier at Charlesbourg Royal (Quebec). Instead he is surprised to meet his subordinate at Saint John's. Cartier earlier abandoned the advance foothold because of the harshness of the past winter and hostility from the Iroquois and is now retiring toward France with his survivors.

Undismayed by Cartier's withdrawal, Roberval proceeds to Charlesbourg Royal, reestablishes that outpost, then begins exploring Canada. Although Roberval's following is too numerous to be directly assaulted by Indians, many of the French settlers are ill-prepared to withstand the ensuing winter and suffer cruelly from cold, famine, and disease. Next summer they are retrieved by a rescue mission under Paul d'Austillon, seigneur de Sauveterre. France's North American colony thus is entirely forsaken.

1542. Hostilities between France and Spain erupt once more in Europe.

FEBRUARY 1543. Two French ships and a small auxiliary attack San Germán de Puerto Rico, burning it and making off with four caravels lying in the harbor. A pair of Spanish galleons and two lateen-rigged caravels on the neighboring island of Santo Domingo are manned with 250 volunteers and set out in pursuit under Ginés de Carrión, captain of the galleon *San Cristóbal.* Five days later he returns, having captured the enemy flagship and 40 of its crew and sunk the smaller French consort. Despite this victory, San Germán's inhabitants are too frightened to return to their dwellings, preferring instead to resettle at Guayanilla.

16 JUNE 1543. ***Antillan Sweep.*** Five French corsair ships and a smaller consort assault Venezuela's Margarita Island then burn the pearl-fishing town of Nuevo Cádiz on adjoining Cubagua. According to some Spanish sources, the raiders are commanded by Roberval ("Robertval" or "Roberto Baal"), but this seems highly unlikely; rather it is possible the French raiders have been intending to visit his Canadian colony on their homeward leg.

16 JULY 1543. Four of these same large French corsair vessels and a smaller consort arrive undetected before Santa Marta (Colombia), landing 400–500 men at noon the next day to occupy the port. They remain seven days, destroying everything of value before retiring with four bronze cannons and other booty.

24–25 JULY 1543. Under cover of darkness, the French squadron deposits 450 raiders near Cartagena, carrying the Colombian port with ease in a three-pronged attack. Bishop Benavides and an overawed populace surrender 35,000 pesos in specie—plus another 2,500 from the royal coffers—to help persuade the enemy to withdraw.

7 SEPTEMBER 1543. A single, 20-man vessel detached from this same French squadron pillages a rich Spanish merchantman off Santiago de Cuba then attempts a disembarkation, only to be repelled by the two-gun battery under Andrés Zamora.

31 OCTOBER 1543. The homeward-bound French squadron appears before Havana, disgorging more than 200 men at the San Lázaro Inlet. Advancing across open country, the invaders are checked by fire from La Fuerza Fortress. They leave behind 20 dead as they retreat to their ships, then depart the Caribbean altogether via the Straits of Florida.

18 SEPTEMBER 1544. The Treaty of Crépy is signed in Europe, marking an end to the latest round of Franco-Spanish hostilities, although some fighting still persists in the New World. Cuba and Puerto Rico, in particular, continue to be harassed by French interlopers.

LATE OCTOBER 1544. Three French ships prowl past San Juan de Puerto Rico, landing at San Germán to pillage and burn the town. Off Cape de la Vela (Colombia), another trio of French interlopers intercepts passing vessels and sells contraband items to the local Spanish citizenry.

1545. Five French corsair ships and a small auxiliary surprise Ríohacha (Colombia), seizing five Spanish vessels lying in the roadstead. Unable to disembark, the raiders arrange a truce with the residents, eventually selling them 70 slaves. A similar visit by these same Frenchmen—albeit entirely peaceful—follows at Santa Marta.

17 JANUARY 1546. More than 100 French raiders under one Hallebarde disembark from a caravel and a smaller vessel, ransacking Baracoa (northeastern Cuba) and scattering most of its inhabitants inland. The second of the two Huguenot craft—after becoming separated from the other in a storm—proceeds west to Havana, where its crew extorts 700 ducats from the terrified citizenry to spare the dwellings.

17 APRIL 1546. Hallebarde sneaks into Santiago de Cuba under cover of darkness, boarding a Spanish caravel recently arrived from Tierra Firme (Venezuela-Colombia) at dawn. In little more than an hour he carries it out with its crew locked below decks to loot at his leisure—an action described as one "of great daring" by Gov. Antonio de Chávez.

SPRING 1547. Two privately raised Spanish coast-guard caravels capture a French ship off Mona Island.

SEPTEMBER 1547. A French ship approaches Santa Marta (Colombia) but retires when its 16-man boat crew is lured inshore and captured.

LATE MAY 1548. A French corsair vessel is sighted prowling off Santo Domingo.

AUGUST 1548. A French two-master sneaks into the harbor at Santa Marta under cover of darkness. Although crewed by only 40 men, it sends a boarding party to seize Pedro Díaz's merchantman lying in the roads. Next dawn the rovers threaten to burn the prize if a ransom is not paid by the town, and when local garrison Cmdr. Luis Manjarrés calls out his militia the French bombard the town's buildings throughout most of the day, killing two black slaves.

Shortly thereafter the same attackers seize two Spanish caravels farther east off Cape de la Vela as they make from La Yaguana (modern-day Léogâne, Haiti) toward Nombre de Dios. Both Spanish craft are robbed and scuttled.

NOVEMBER 1548. A trio of French vessels is seen prowling off San Germán de Puerto Rico, Mona Island, and Santo Domingo, allegedly wishing to trade, but the region's Spanish inhabitants remain too mistrustful to oblige.

AUGUST 1549. A
18 oars per side, f
ish convoy off
laden with su
slaves, and tw

NOVEMBER
French
two stragg
repelled by the
scend upon La Yagua
pillaging a pair of Spanish ve
ing off with one as a prize.

LATE DECEMBER 1551. French Capt. Guilla
Testu, sailing past the island of Trinidade after explor-
ing Brazil, clashes with two Portuguese ships and sustains heavy damage before winning free and returning to Europe.

APRIL 1552. With hostilities flaring up in Europe between France and Spain, French corsairs execute various disembarkations on Puerto Rico and Santo Domingo and intercept four Spanish merchantmen.

18 JUNE 1552. A French ship becomes becalmed before Nombre de Dios, and its 14-man crew is captured by Nombre de Dios residents.

29 AUGUST 1552. Three Spanish warships and an auxiliary, manned by 130 men—the coast-guard force for Hispaniola under Cristóbal Colón (Columbus's grandson)—are lost in a hurricane; 16 galleons anchored in Santo Domingo's harbor are also destroyed.

SEPTEMBER 1552. A French corsair ship and a smaller consort pillage a Spanish vessel off Santo Domingo before retiring to Saona Island. The same Frenchmen return to Santo Domingo's southeastern shore to make off with a ship recently launched at the Zoco River.

EARLY FEBRUARY 1553. A Spanish caravel serving as a dispatch vessel, or *aviso,* is taken by French rovers off Mona Island.

MARCH 1553. Havana, San Germán de Puerto Rico, Mona Island, and Saona Island all report depredations by French blockaders, the latter three being visited by a trio of royal warships and other privateers led by peg-leg François Le Clerc (alias Jambe de Bois or Pie de Palo), Jacques de Sores, and Robert Blondel.

Engraving of a sixteenth-century warship, by Pieter Brueghel

29 APRIL 1553. Five French ships, a storeship, and three lesser craft led by Le Clerc, Sores, and Blondel deposit a landing force to sack Monte Cristi (northern Santo Domingo). La Yaguana (modern-day Léogâne, Haiti) is also overrun before the raiders stand away toward Puerto Rico. Local Spaniards feel powerless to resist; four of the craft are galliots "whose oars ensure none can escape [them]," and they carry a total of 800 men, half of whom are harquebusiers.

29 APRIL 1554. Off Cabo Frio (Brazil), the French ship *Marie Bellote* of Dieppe captures a Portuguese vessel.

LATE SPRING 1554. Three French ships appear before San Juan de Puerto Rico; on Palm Sunday they raid more than three miles inland near San Germán. Afterward they take up station off Saona Island, intercepting Spanish vessels. They later switch operations to Mona Island.

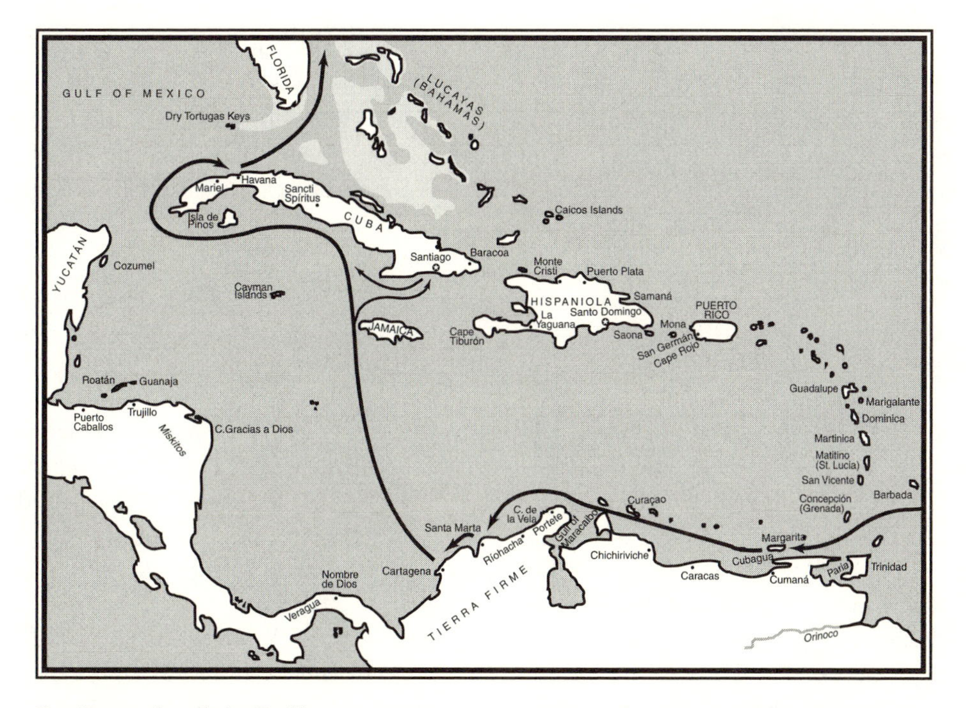

French sweep through the Caribbean

1 JULY 1554. ***Destruction of Santiago de Cuba.*** The Huguenot corsairs Le Clerc and Sores of La Rochelle lead four ships and four smaller auxiliaries into the harbor of Santiago de Cuba under cover of darkness, slipping 300 men ashore who fall upon the sleeping residents and occupy the city without resistance. Bishop Uranga and a half-dozen other prominent citizens are held hostage for almost a month and a half until a ransom of 80,000 pesos can be raised. The French then destroy Santiago's fortress and burn several buildings before retiring on 16 August, sparing the church in exchange for all its silver plate.

AUTUMN 1554. Five Spanish merchantmen and nine caravels depart Santo Domingo for Spain, encountering four French corsair vessels off San Germán de Puerto Rico, which pursue as far as the Azores. The caravel *Tres Reyes Magos* of Master Benito García becomes becalmed and is taken along with *Nuestra Señora de Guadalupe* of Alonso González; *Santa Catalina* of Francisco Morales Camacho is ransacked and later sinks.

OCTOBER 1554. French blockaders encircle Santiago de Cuba.

MARCH 1555. Three French ships disembark 150 men on southern Cuba; the force marches inland and burns Sancti Spíritus.

10 JULY 1555. ***Sack of Havana.*** At dawn, two sails are spotted disgorging several score corsairs under the Huguenot leader Sores a mile and a half away at San Lázaro Inlet. They advance inland and take Havana's 12-gun Fuerza battery from the rear, burning its wooden door to gain access and thereby compelling the two dozen defenders under *Alcalde* Juan de Lobera to surrender by sunup on 12 July. The French occupy the town and bring four vessels into its roads to careen.

While in possession of Havana Sores demands a ransom of 30,000 pesos, bread, and meat in order to spare the buildings; he also demands 500 pesos for every Spanish captive he holds and 100 pesos for each slave. Instead, Gov. Dr. Pérez de Angulo (who has managed to escape into the interior) launches a surprise assault at dawn on 18 July with 35 Spanish, 220 black, and 80 Indian volunteers, only to be repelled; the startled French corsairs slaughter their 30 Spanish prisoners (except for Lobera).

Next morning a wrathful Sores hangs numerous slaves by their heels at prominent places along Havana's outskirts, further using them for target practice in a brutal gesture intended to discourage further Spanish attacks. His men then level the town and the surrounding countryside up to five miles inland before retiring to sea on 5 August with the fort's 12 cannons.

AUGUST 1555. French Huguenots land at Santa Marta, sacking and burning its churches.

30 SEPTEMBER 1555. A boatload of 12 French raiders from Guy Mermi's trio of ships—anchored off Mariel (Cuba)—cut out a Spanish caravel laden with hides.

4 OCTOBER 1555. A trio of French ships penetrates Havana's harbor, landing 50 men to occupy the town. Discovering that Havana is still defenseless since Sores's July raid, they are followed within a few days by at least a dozen other intruders, who rest their crews and careen. Foraging parties also probe inland, securing some commercial booty (principally hides) before putting back out to sea some three weeks later.

During this month a French assault also occurs at Puerto Plata (northern Santo Domingo).

10 NOVEMBER 1555. ***Villegagnon in Brazil.*** Two well-armed vessels arrive in Rio de Janeiro's uninhabited bay (known to the French as Iteronne, or Genève) with a few hundred Calvinists under 45-year-old Nicolas Durand—Chevalier de Villegagnon, knight of Malta, vice admiral of Brittany, and veteran Brazilian explorer—who is bearing orders from Adm. Gaspar, Comte de Coligny, to found a new settlement in the region to be called *France australe,* or "southern France" (also *France Antarctique*—"Antarctic France"). His colonists disembark on Laje Island then transfer northwest to nearby Sergipe Island (in the process changing its name to Villegagnon—modern Villegaignon—Island), on which they erect a redoubt named Fort de Coligny, also emplacing a smaller two-gun battery to command its channel. A town named Henryville is founded, and a couple of relatively prosperous years ensue, with the settlers planting crops and enjoying peaceable relations with their Tamoio and Tupinambá neighbors.

Nicolas Durand, Chevalier de Villegagnon

In March 1557 the French are reinforced by a second expedition of three ships (under the flagship *Rosée*) bringing an additional 18 cannons and 300 people under Villegagnon's nephew Paris Legendre, sieur de Bois Le Compte Le Meaux. But this second contingent also brings with it religious dissension, which eventually fractures the colony's harmony and prompts Villegagnon to revert to Catholicism. He quits Rio de Janeiro in 1559, shortly before the first Portuguese attack in March 1560.

EARLY 1556. A lone French vessel raids Santa Marta, Cape de la Vela, Puerto Plata, Havana, and Margarita Island.

5 FEBRUARY 1556. In Europe, a truce—the Treaty of Vaucelles—is arranged between France and Spain; although meant to endure for five years, it quickly breaks down.

SUMMER 1556. A couple of skirmishes occur off Jamaica, as local Spanish authorities succeed in capturing a few French smugglers coming to trade.

1558. With tensions again escalating between Paris and Madrid, French corsairs renew their depredations. Full-scale warfare soon resumes in Europe, and off Saona Island the Spanish merchantman *Ascención* of Capt. Bernaldino Rizo is taken. Also, four French ships out of Bayonne and Saint-Jean-de-Luz sack Puerto Caballos (modern-day Puerto Cortés, Honduras).

JUNE 1558. French vessels appear within Santiago de Cuba's harbor, occupying the desolated town for about ten days before departing after receiving a meager ransom of 400 pesos.

EARLY 1559. Seven French corsair vessels under Jean Martin Cotes and Jean Bontemps appear off Santa Marta (Colombia), taking a small amount of booty after facing token opposition.

3 APRIL 1559. In Europe, the Treaty of Cateau-Cambrésis is signed between Philip II of Spain and Henry II of France, marking an end to the Habsburg-Valois Wars.

Private Warfare (1559–1587)

The recent agreement signed between two Catholic sovereigns at Cateau-Cambrésis does little to restrain the activities of Huguenot corsairs, who continue to visit the New World in pursuit of their own ends. Such independent behavior is further exacerbated by the death three months later of 40-year-old Henry II in a jousting accident, leaving France's central government greatly weakened.

But the corsairs' heyday proves short-lived, for in April 1562 a civil war erupts in France between a Catholic faction led by François, duc de Guise, and the Huguenots under Louis de Bourbon, prince de Condé. The resulting violence—36 years known collectively as the French Wars of Religion—drains the Huguenot rovers of much of their expansionist vigor, for they must concentrate upon fratricidal struggle rather than overseas campaigns.

The resultant decline in French sea power gradually makes way for a rise in English interventions. Throughout the first half of the sixteenth century England has remained Spain's ally in its struggles against France, although the relationship begins to sour as 1550 approaches. By the late 1550s English cooperation dwindles on account of Spain's growing might, its championing of the Catholic Counterreformation, and its steadfast refusal to open its American markets to foreign traders. Following Elizabeth I's ascension to the English throne in November 1558 the frictions evolve into open hostility.

11 April 1559. Off Cartagena five French privateering ships appear under Jean Martin Cotes and Jean Bontemps and set ashore 300 harquebusiers, who brush aside the three dozen Spanish defenders and overrun the city. The raiders then pillage residences, finally agreeing to spare Cartagena's empty buildings in exchange for 4,000 pesos.

11 June 1559. ***Spain's Florida Failure.*** In order to establish a permanent outpost to guard its homeward-bound plate fleets, Madrid delegates a 49-year-old Mexican *hacendado* named Tristán de Luna y Arellano—veteran of Coronado's 1540 Florida expedition—to found a settlement in the Gulf of Mexico. After a preliminary reconnaissance by Guido de Bezares in September 1558, Luna recruits 500 soldiers (mostly from Oaxaca, Zacatecas, and Puebla); then with 240 horses and 1,000 colonists he departs Veracruz on 11 June 1559. His 13 vessels endure a rough traverse, pausing at Miruelo (modern-day Tampa Bay) in July to refresh supplies before proceeding to Bahía Filipina (Mobile, Alabama) by 14 August. Two ships are detached to carry a report to Spain; the colonists divide into two contingents to probe inland.

While this exploration is conducted a hurricane destroys the Spaniards' coastal camp along with most of the provisions and ships. News of the disaster reaches Mexico City by 27 September, and although relief is quickly sent out, Luna's venture is doomed. Two sickly settlements are established—one on the coast, the other inland at Santa Cruz de Nanipacana; neither prospers. Disease and want take their toll. Luna himself falls ill and departs for Mexico in the summer of 1560; he is succeeded by Jorge Cerón. Angel Villafañe is later appointed governor, but his efforts also fail, and the survivors disperse to healthier, more prosperous lands.

August 1559. The rich Spanish caravel *Sanctus Spíritus* of Master Domingo González, arriving from Veracruz, is looted outside Havana by a French corsair.

1560. French corsairs sack Campeche, Puerto Caballos (modern-day Puerto Cortés), and Trujillo (Honduras). The Spanish in turn capture a 30-man French vessel off Guanaja Island, summarily executing three Huguenot crewmembers and conveying the remaining prisoners to Guatemala.

Elsewhere, three Spanish galleons are ransacked, one being the 200-ton merchantman *Santa María* of Master Bartolomé Rodríguez, homeward-bound from Honduras.

Early March 1560. ***Portuguese Counterstroke.*** In Brazil, the energetic new governor-general, Mem de Sá, departs the capital of Baía de Todos os Santos on 21 February with a large expedition aboard ten galleons under Adm. Bartolomeu de Vasconcellos da Cunha to assault the French Huguenot settlement at nearby Rio de Janeiro.

Coming upon the interlopers' trenches on Villegagnon Island, de Sá's men surprise the French defenders and easily overrun their positions. The attack is aided by the fact that Gov. Bois Le Compte is exploring inland with his best troops, a company of Scottish Calvinists. The 74-man garrison at Fort Coligny manages to resist for two days before being outflanked on the night of 15–16 March by de Sá with 120 Portuguese soldiers and 140 Indian auxiliaries under Martim Affonso. After the garrison is obliged to surrender the victors blow the fortifications and sail off toward Baía with 100 Huguenot captives, having scattered the rest into the jungle.

The French survivors reemerge and build new defenses outside Glória Bay and on Paranapuan (modern Governador) Island with the aid of native allies. Eventually, the Huguenots launch minor counterstrikes against São Paulo and other Portuguese outposts. Villegagnon attempts to organize another relief expedition from France the following year (1561), gathering the carrack *Aigle* and seven other vessels at Le Havre. But because of growing religious dissension within the home country that force never sails to rescue Rio de Janeiro.

7–8 JULY 1561. Near Campeche, three small Huguenot vessels disembark 30 men, who slip into the sleeping town under cover of darkness. The terrified citizenry and garrison flee into the night, but next morning they realize how few attackers there are and so pursue them as they exit aboard a captured bark laden with booty, carrying five women captives. The Spaniards use another bark and two shallops to overtake the Frenchmen, killing 15 and capturing five; the rest swim back out to their waiting ships.

JULY 1561. Off Havana, a French corsair vessel obliges an arriving Spanish ship to land its cargo nearby so as not to risk losing it in battle.

30 APRIL 1562. At daybreak an expedition from Le Havre sights Florida near present-day Saint Augustine. Two ships and a large sloop bearing 150 Huguenots under Jean Ribault of Dieppe explore as far north as modern-day South Carolina, building a fort near what is today Parris Island. Ribault departs on 11 June, leaving two dozen volunteers behind under Capt. Albert de la Pierria and vowing to return within six months with reinforcements.

Unfortunately, religious strife in France prevents him from keeping the promise. Despairing of relief, Ribault's settlers murder de la Pierria and put to sea aboard a crude boat, eventually being rescued by an English bark.

AUTUMN 1562. The 120-ton Spanish merchantman *San Miguel* of Master Vicente Martín is captured by some Englishmen while homeward-bound from La Yaguana (modern-day Léogâne, Haiti).

APRIL 1563. Plymouth merchant John Hawkins arrives off northern Santo Domingo with his 120-ton flagship *Solomon,* the 100-ton *Swallow* of Capt. Thomas Hampton, a shallop, and a Portuguese prize, hoping to sell 300 West African slaves. Despite the Spanish crown's ban against such trade, the Englishmen are allowed to dispose of their cargo at La Isabela with the connivance of Lic. Lorenzo Bernáldez, commander of a 120-man cavalry patrol sent to stop them. Hawkins then consigns some goods received in payment toward Seville aboard Spanish vessels, where the fraud is discovered and the merchandise is impounded.

Jean Ribault

22 JUNE 1564. Ribault's lieutenant, René Goulaine de Laudonnière, returns to Florida with 300 Huguenot settlers aboard the 200-ton *Élisabeth* of Capt. Jean Lucas, the 120-ton *Breton* under Michel Vasseur, and the 80-ton *Faucon* of Pierre Marchant. They build a triangular compound called Fort Caroline at the mouth of the Saint Johns River (near modern-day Jacksonville) then endure a harsh year of disease, mutiny, and starvation. Two shallops are apparently stolen by some men and used for unsuccessful piratical cruises, and the native chieftain, Holata Outina, attacks a French foraging party on 27 July 1565, killing two and wounding 22 others.

EARLY 1565. A Carib war party surprises Guadianilla (Puerto Rico), killing three residents and carrying off

30 captives, mostly women. The island's governor, Francisco Bahamón de Lugo, ambushes the retiring raiders, slaying 77 and setting the captives free; during the fight a horse is shot from beneath him and he receives two arrow wounds.

LATE FEBRUARY 1565. In Brazil, two Portuguese galleons bearing 300 soldiers depart Baía de Todos os Santos under Estácio de Sá (nephew of the governor-general) to attempt to eradicate the remaining French Huguenot settlers at Rio de Janeiro. Arriving outside by 1 March, de Sá establishes a defensive position below Pão de Açúcar; five days latter he is attacked by Tamoio Indians loyal to the French.

A second assault occurs after three ships arrive from France with reinforcements on 1 April, but this too is repelled, after which a stalemate ensues. It is not until another Portuguese contingent can be sent from Baía a year and a half later that the impasse is broken and the French are defeated.

MARCH 1565. Hawkins returns to the West Indies with the Queen's 30-gun, 700-ton flagship *Jesus of Lübeck,* lesser consorts *Solomon* and *Swallow,* the 50-ton *Tiger,* and three small prizes, bearing more than 400 slaves from Sierra Leone. After watering at Dominica he is refused trade by the Spaniards at Margarita Island but then enjoys better fortune upon arriving on 3 April at Borburata (east of Puerto Cabello, Venezuela). Contacting the residents ashore, Hawkins arranges a show of force on 18 April to overawe local authorities and thereby is allowed to transact business.

19 MAY 1565. Hawkins enters Ríohacha (Colombia) this Saturday morning, remaining 11 days after employing the same tactic as at Borburata—using a show of force to compel the crown treasurer, Miguel de Castellanos, to permit him to sell off his remaining cargo.

3 AUGUST 1565. While on his homeward leg to England, Hawkins visits Ribault's Huguenot settlement at Fort Caroline (Jacksonville, Florida), furnishing its sickly inhabitants with a 50-ton bark, victuals, shoes, and other stores.

28 AUGUST 1565. Ribault arrives at Fort Caroline from France, bringing out 600 more Huguenot settlers aboard his 32-gun flagship *Trinité;* the 29-gun vice-flagship *Émérillon* of Nicolas d'Ornano (a Corsican nicknamed Corsette); the ten-gun hired Dieppe transports *Perle* of Jacques Ribault (the commander in chief's son), *Levrière* of Vivien Maillard, and *Émérillon* of Vincent Collas; plus the auxiliary *Épaule de Mouton* (a type of sixteenth-century sail rig). This expedition has been joined during its passage by a privateer ship from La Rochelle under Capt. Jean Du Boys and two small Spanish prizes seized off La Yaguana (modern-day Léogâne, Haiti).

4 SEPTEMBER 1565. ***Ribault's Massacre.*** At dusk Adm. Pedro Menéndez de Aviles, knight of Santiago, and Vice Adm. Diego Flores de Valdés—sent from Spain to expel the intrusive French settlement in Florida—sight the enemy flotilla anchored before Fort Caroline. The startled French crews immediately cut their cables and flee out to sea, outrunning Menéndez's 1,000-ton flagship *San Pelayo* and four other consorts overnight.

The Spanish admiral puts into Saint Augustine (35 miles south) and entrenches ashore. Two of his shallops are detached to fetch cavalry mounts from Santo Domingo; farther north, Ribault takes the desperate gamble of hastening virtually his entire garrison aboard his four largest ships—which have rejoined after their nocturnal escapade—to attempt a surprise seaborne descent against Menéndez's position. The Huguenots come within sight of Saint Augustine by 10 September but are struck by a storm before disembarking.

The Spanish admiral meanwhile begins his overland march toward Fort Caroline on 16 September (once the storm abates) with 400 men, including 200 harquebusiers. On the rainy night of 20 September he bursts into Fort Caroline two hours before dawn in three columns, sending the 16 defenders fleeing through the marshes toward their remaining ships. Without suffering a single casualty the Spaniards kill 112 French inhabitants and capture 70 women and children by evening. Among the 27 survivors who manage to swim out to the anchored vessels *Perle* and *Levrière* (getting under way toward France by 25 September) is Laudonnière; 40 seamen are already aboard the ships, including Ribault's son.

Having thus secured the settlement, Menéndez renames it Fort San Mateo (Fort Saint Matthew, on whose feast day this victory is won), then installs Capt. Gonzalo de Villarroel as garrison commander with 300 troops. Returning to Saint Augustine with his other men, the Spanish admiral soon learns that Ribault has been shipwrecked to the south and is stranded ashore without food, water, or arms. During the next few days the 600 survivors are hunted down and pitilessly exterminated by the Spaniards, Ribault's own party of 200 eventually surrendering of exhaustion by 10 October. Save for five youngsters, the Huguenots' hands are tied behind their backs and their throats are cut at a place later named Matanzas ("killings" or "slaughter" in Spanish).

Menéndez concludes his ruthless campaign by departing for Havana on 30 October with three ships and the bulk of his men, leaving a small garrison behind in Florida. Two days later he finds another 150 French survivors entrenched on a beach near Cape Canaveral; they surrender on condition that their lives will be spared. (Shipped toward Havana aboard *San Pelayo,* the prisoners subsequently overwhelm their guards and seize control of Menéndez's flagship and carry it across the Atlantic to Denmark.)

LATE 1565. A galleon conveying Havana's former governor Diego de Mazariegos back to Spain is intercepted opposite Mariel by a pair of French corsair galleys under Captains Fornoux and Lacroix. A hefty ransom demand is sent into the Cuban capital, but the new governor—Adm. Francisco García Osorio de Sandoval—prolongs negotiations until Capt. Pedro Menéndez Márquez (nephew of Ribault's slayer) can sortie and take the corsairs by surprise. He kills 15 and frees the captives, bringing 50 prisoners back to Havana to work upon its fortifications.

3 JUNE 1566. Spanish Adm. Sancho de Archiniega arrives at Dominica aboard his 480-ton flagship *Tres Reyes,* accompanied by 13 ships, two caravels, and a shallop bearing 1,500 troops as reinforcements for the Puerto Rico, Santo Domingo, Cuba, and Florida garrisons.

26 JUNE 1566. Menéndez de Aviles returns to Havana aboard a small craft after destroying Ribault's Florida colony; he reports spotting 22 enemy sail in the Bahama Channel.

SUMMER 1566. The Spanish ship *Santa Catalina* of Juan de Parras spots a sail near the Colorados Islands (north of Cuba) and gives chase. It proves to be *Nazarena,* a raider with a Portuguese captain and a mixed French-English-Portuguese crew; they beach the vessel in Matanzas Bay and flee inland into the Yumurí Valley, only to be captured and carried into Havana along with their refloated ship.

OCTOBER 1566. Menéndez de Aviles sorties from Florida with six warships, a frigate, and a pinnace to cruise the Caribbean in search of foreign interlopers. He leaves 150 soldiers and some artillery to fortify Santo Domingo, 100 soldiers and some guns at San Juan de Puerto Rico, 50 soldiers at Puerto Plata (northern Dominican Republic), and a few more at Santiago de Cuba. He captures five rich prizes at nearby Manzanillo—the port of Bayamo—and enters Havana in January 1567 to deposit another 200 soldiers and six artillery pieces.

18 JANUARY 1567. ***Fall of French Rio.*** In Brazil, Portuguese Gov.-Gen. Mem de Sá decides to lead a final expedition from the capital of Baía de Todos os Santos to eliminate the French Huguenot settlement at Rio de Janeiro. Going aboard the recently arrived squadron of Cristóvão de Barros, he sails first to Espírito Santo to recruit a contingent of native auxiliaries under chief Ararigboia, then pauses at São Vicente (Santos) for further reinforcements.

Arriving before Rio by 18 January with 11 ships, the governor-general joins the beleaguered Portuguese contingent already occupying Villegagnon Island under his nephew, Estácio de Sá. The combined Portuguese force then falls upon the outnumbered French two days later, easily overrunning their defensive positions at Uruçu Mirim (Flamengo Beach)—held by only 11 Frenchmen and a handful of Tamoio warriors—and nearby Paranapuan or Paranapucuí (Governador Island).

De Sá consummates his victory by refortifying Rio's entrance and appointing his nephew—badly

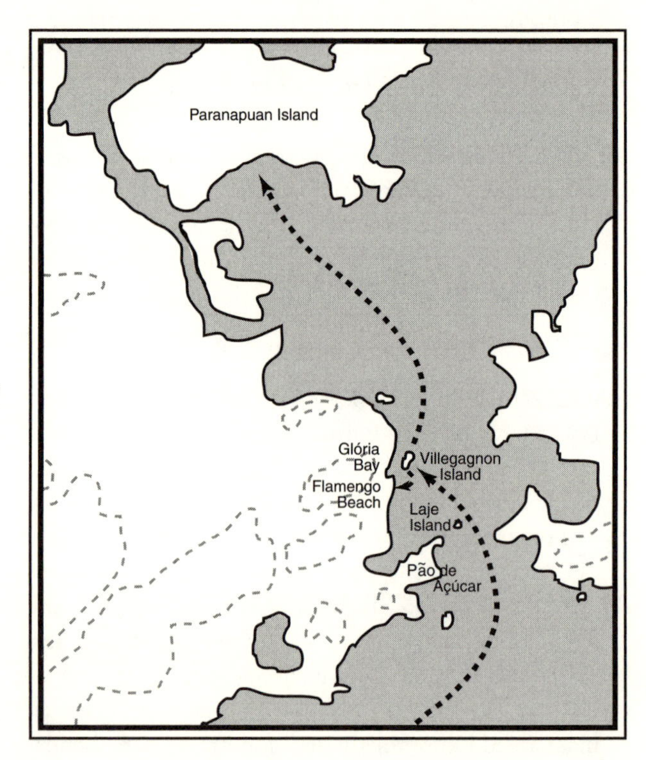

Portuguese counteroffensive against French settlements in Rio de Janeiro

wounded by an arrow in the face during the Uruçu Mirim assault—as the town's new governor. Estácio de Sá subsequently dies of his injury on 20 February and is succeeded as Rio's governor by another nephew of the governor-general, Salvador Correira de Sá e Benevides.

SPRING 1567. English slaving ships—the 200-ton *Powell* of James Hampton, the 100-ton *Solomon* of James Raunce, the 40-ton *Pascha* of Robert Bolton, and a smaller consort—arrive at Margarita Island (Venezuela). Although nominally under the orders of John Lovell, they secretly belong to Hawkins, whose youthful kinsman, Francis Drake, is serving aboard.

8 MAY 1567. At daybreak the French privateer Bontemps appears outside Ríohacha (Colombia) with four large ships, bearing West African slaves. The Spaniards send their noncombatants inland and mass upon the beach, and a boat arrives inshore requesting permission to trade. Treasurer de Castellanos agrees to discuss the proposal with other local leaders and reply the following day.

Next dawn the boat returns, but de Castellanos rejects the offer. Bontemps clears for action, begins a bombardment, and dispatches three armed boats inshore that are unable to disembark because of Spanish defiance. After four hours Bontemps recalls his boats and again suggests a trade. Once more rebuffed, he sails away that afternoon to surprise nearby Santa Marta on the morning of 10 May, holding a rich merchantman in its roads for ransom.

17 MAY 1567. ***(Whitsunday or Pentecost).*** Lovell's four English slavers appear outside Ríohacha, having traded peaceably with the Spaniards at Margarita Island and Curaçao Island (although also having united with Bontemps to skirmish with the authorities at Borburata). Entering Ríohacha's harbor, Lovell anchors on Monday, 18 May, and requests permission to trade; he is rejected by de Castellanos.

After spending a week smuggling a few pieces ashore the Englishmen depart on Saturday, 23 May, leaving behind 92 slaves (for which they receive no payment). Lovell subsequently touches Santo Domingo before returning to Plymouth by October.

SEPTEMBER 1567. Coro (Venezuela) is surprised by Nicolas Valier's French privateering squadron, his Huguenot followers desecrating the church among other excesses. Bishop Agreda barely escapes capture, although his deacon is taken. (It is believed the same raider has ransacked Margarita Island very recently.)

LATE MARCH 1568. Hawkins arrives at Dominica on his third slaving voyage with the hired Queen's ships *Jesus of Lübeck* and the 300-ton *Minion,* his own *William and John* of 150 tons, *Swallow* (100), *Judith* (50), *Angel* (40), and a Portuguese caravel captured off West Africa's Cape Blanco. The English are further accompanied by a pair of French privateering craft under Capitaine Planes and an eight-gun, 150-ton Portuguese prize that Planes has seized off Africa (incorporating it into Hawkins's squadron under the name *Grace of God,* commanded by Drake). They bear a total of 400 crewmembers and 500 slaves.

In early April they call on Margarita Island (Venezuela), peaceably selling trade items and slaves to the Spanish residents over the next eight days.

14 APRIL 1568. Hawkins proceeds to Borburata (near Puerto Cabellos, Venezuela) and trades with the Spanish inhabitants while careening his ships. He sends a detachment inland to the town of Valencia. He also sends *William and John, Grace of God,* and *Swallow* toward Curaçao for provisions, as well as *Judith* and *Angel*—under Drake—to Ríohacha as an advance party to contact the authorities there. His main body refreshed, Hawkins weighs for Ríohacha by 1 June.

24 APRIL 1568. ***De Gourges's Revenge.*** The Gascon rover Dominique de Gourges surprises the tiny Spanish garrison left guarding Fort San Mateo (Jacksonville, Florida) with two ships and a smaller consort bearing 180 Huguenot privateers. After enduring a brief siege the outnumbered defenders of Captain Villarroel attempt to flee south toward Saint Augustine under cover of darkness but suffer 30 killed and 38 captured during the flight. To avenge the massacre of Ribault's followers, de Gourges then puts all prisoners to death before sailing away for France on 3 May.

4 JUNE 1568. Drake arrives opposite Ríohacha (Colombia) and sends a boat inshore to request permission to water. Its local official, de Castellanos, orders his three-gun battery to open fire, and after a protracted exchange Drake retires out of range, instituting a close blockade.

9 JUNE 1568. This evening Hawkins's main squadron rejoins Drake off Ríohacha and slips 200 men ashore a mile away the next noon. They defeat a Spanish company drawn up to bar their path, and they occupy the

town. On 15 June Hawkins sends a detachment—led by a runaway Spanish slave—on a nocturnal march deep into the jungle, seizing Ríohacha's hidden treasures and noncombatants. The English then compel Castellanos to halt all resistance and permit trading.

LATE JUNE 1568. Four French ships arrive off Rio de Janeiro, only to find that the Huguenot colony has been eradicated by the Portuguese and Villegagnon Island occupied (*see* 18 January 1567). When the French attempt to disembark they are attacked by local contingents under Gov. Salvador Correira de Sá and his subordinate, Martim Affonso, who chase the trespassers back out to sea as far west as Cabo Frio, where one of the interloper ships is boarded and overwhelmed by the Portuguese pursuers.

10 JULY 1568. Hawkins's squadron departs Ríohacha (Colombia) and comes within sight of Santa Marta at dusk. Sending a message ashore, he meets the next morning with its governor, who agrees to allow trade—allegedly after a mock battle is arranged so that the Spaniard might maintain appearances with his superiors back in Madrid. The English remain in the harbor for a few days.

16 JULY 1568. Hawkins arrives outside Cartagena (Colombia) and, after a request for trade is rebuffed by Gov. Martín de las Alas, *Minion* bombards the defenses from long range while boats are sent into the bay to scrounge for provisions. Everything taken is scrupulously paid for with barter goods in hopes of encouraging further trade, but Hawkins is nonetheless compelled to quit Cartagena empty-handed by 24 July.

He scuttles his Portuguese prize and allows one of his French consorts to part company and prowl the West Indies, then lays in a northerly course across the Caribbean with his eight remaining vessels. After sighting Isla de Pinos his fleet is engulfed in a hurricane while attempting to round western Cuba. *William and John* becomes separated and eventually returns alone to Ireland.

The storm abates on 11 September to reveal that Hawkins is off the Triángulos Reef, deep within the Gulf of Mexico. Intercepting a passing Spanish coaster under Francisco Maldonado, the English learn that the only place to leeward where they might repair is the island of San Juan de Ulúa, opposite Veracruz. Hawkins's squadron limps toward that haven, capturing two outward-bound Mexican vessels (thereby precluding any alarm from being raised).

15 SEPTEMBER 1568. ***Hawkins at San Juan de Ulúa.*** At dusk Hawkins's ten English vessels anchor within sight of the Spanish island fortress of San Juan de Ulúa, its lookouts mistaking the squadron for advance elements of the annual plate fleet daily expected from Spain. Next morning, Hawkins gets under way with false colors, luring San Juan de Ulúa's pilot boat close enough to capture all of its welcoming dignitaries. He then passes the island's batteries—which are busily firing salutes—to moor directly under its walls before garrison Cmdr. Antonio Delgadillo can realize that these are foreign intruders. Having thus secured San Juan de Ulúa, the English send a message to the mainland authorities across the harbor at Veracruz, explaining their action and promising to depart once repairs are complete.

At sunrise on 17 September, however, Adm. Francisco Luján's flagship *San Pedro* appears outside San Juan de Ulúa escorting a half-dozen galleons. His second-in-command, Juan de Ubilla, soon brings another five up over the horizon with the vice-flag *Santa Clara*. They carry the new viceroy-designate for New Spain, Martín Enríquez de Almanza (sent to restore crown rule in Mexico City following an attempted usurpation by Martín Cortés, son of the famous conquistador).

Mexican Viceroy Martín Enríquez de Almanza

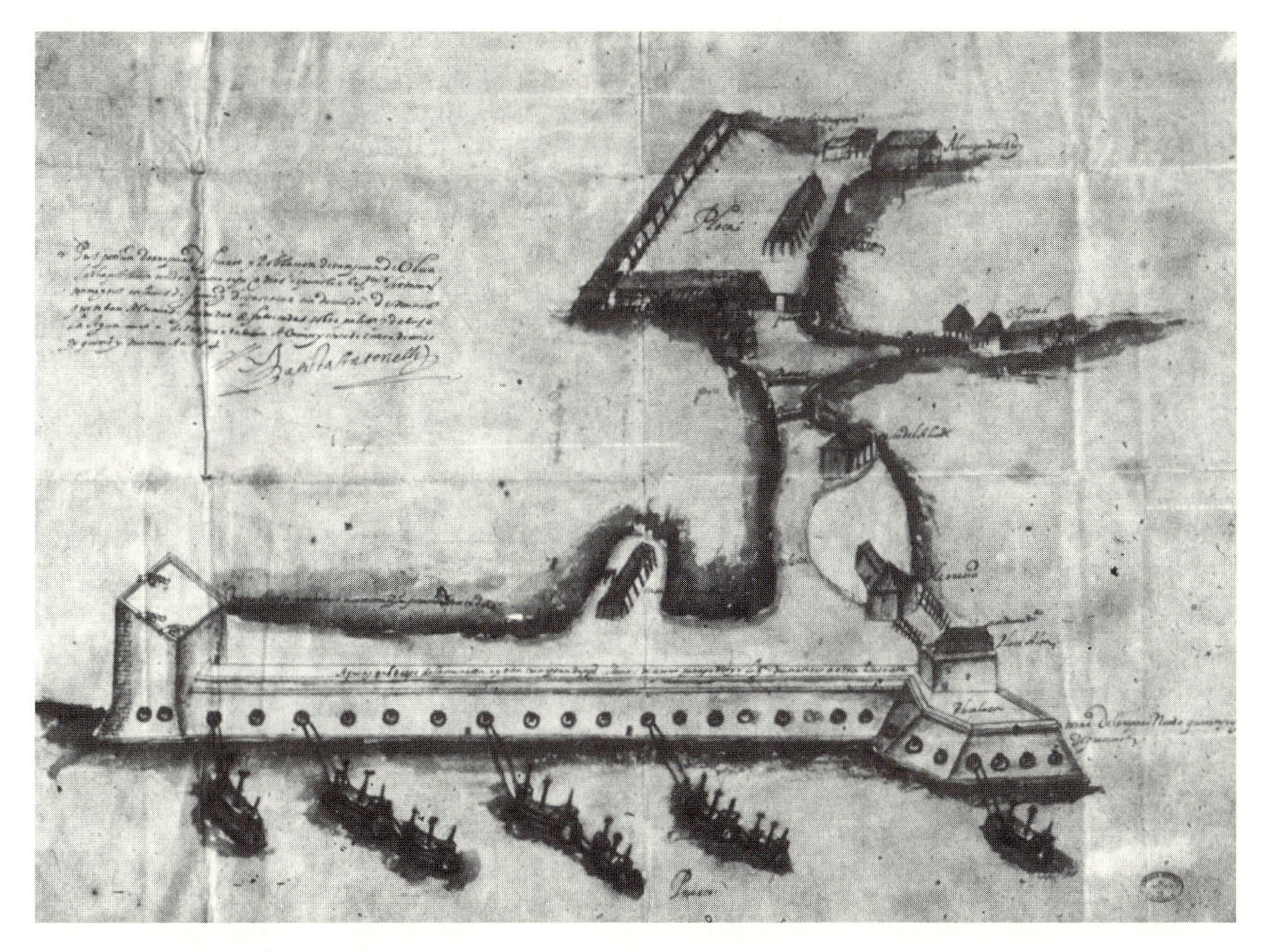

Sixteenth-century drawing of San Juan de Ulúa

A boat dispatched by Delgadillo warns these arrivals of Hawkins's occupation, and shortly thereafter the English commander delegates Delgadillo to relay his terms for permitting the plate fleet to enter: the Spaniards must agree to let Hawkins refit in peace or he will dispute their entrance. Short of food and water and on a dangerously lee shore, Luján and Enríquez have no choice but to comply—although they harbor little intention of honoring the extortionate demand. Contrary winds prevent their entrance until 21 September, but the two fleets are soon moored side-by-side within their crowded berths. Under cover of darkness Spanish troops are then slipped aboard Diego Felipe's dismasted hulk *San Salvador,* which is lying nearest to the English vessels.

At 10:00 A.M. on 23 September a suspicious Hawkins opens fire on the hulk, and most of his ships get under way. Taken thus by surprise—they had not planned on attacking for another hour—the Spaniards nonetheless react well, overrunning the Englishmen remaining on the island and regaining control of the batteries. In a day-long exchange all English vessels are either destroyed or captured except for *Minion* and Drake's tiny *Judith,* which escape out to sea via the perilous eastern channel to anchor overnight off Sacrificios Island. They leave behind several score dead and captured comrades as well as the sunken *Santa Clara.*

Drake sails directly for England that night, leaving Hawkins with more than 200 survivors crammed aboard *Minion,* which creeps as far north as Pánuco by 8 October. With little food or water, he allows 114 men to surrender to the Spaniards while resupplying *Minion* as best he can, setting sail eight days later for Europe with the 100 others. A nightmarish voyage ensues, with as few as 15 reaching England alive. This incident becomes a rallying cry for all Englishmen, who regard it as an example of Spanish perfidy.

1569. French corsairs sack and burn Guadianilla (Puerto Rico).

1570. Drake returns to the West Indies with the small ships *Dragon* and *Swan;* little is known about his activities on this cruise.

1571. Drake again ventures into the Caribbean, this time with *Swan* alone, pillaging several rich Spanish barks off Chagres (Panama) before returning to Plymouth.

This same year the French rover Bontemps lands on Curaçao with 70 men, being confronted in a driving rainstorm by its principal Spanish landowner, Antonio Barbudo, who exploits the invaders' temporary lack of firepower to inflict a stinging defeat. Bontemps dies after receiving an arrow wound in his throat; his head is then carried into Santo Domingo as a trophy.

28–29 JULY 1572. Having returned to the West Indies with 73 men aboard Hawkins's 70-ton *Pascha* and the 25-ton *Swan,* Drake is joined off the Spanish Main by James Raunce's 30-man ship. Assembling a combined boat party, Drake leaves Raunce in charge of the anchor watches while leading a stealthy entry into the roadstead at Nombre de Dios (Panama).

Discovered as they approach the beach at 3:00 A.M., the English have a sharp exchange with the hastily assembled town militia in the main square, during which Drake receives a wound. Before Nombre de Dios can be fully secured Drake faints from loss of blood, his men retreating back to the boats. Raunce subsequently quits the joint venture, leaving Drake to establish a small base in the Gulf of San Blas.

From September 1572 through January 1573 Drake harries the Spanish Main as far east as Curaçao.

JUNE 1574. Learning that the English privateer John Noble is making captures off Escudo de Veraguas Island (Panama) with a four-gun, 30-man ship, Gov. Pedro Godinez Osorio orders 30 Spanish harquebusiers out of Nombre de Dios aboard a "rowing frigate." With a brigantine and a launch out of Concepción de Veragua they trap the interloper and kill or execute all crewmembers, except for two young boys who are condemned to the galleys.

14 DECEMBER 1574. The 20-gun, 120-man French privateer ship of Captain Silvestre attacks Concepción de Veragua (Panama). Disappointed by the scant booty but informed of other potentially rich Spanish targets from runaway slaves (*cimarrones*), he detaches a pair of smaller auxiliaries two days later to assault Chagres farther east and the Desaguadero (or mouth) of Nicaragua's San Juan River to the northwest.

Three Spanish barks are seized at the Desaguadero, and the town is occupied for three months. The rovers—now reinforced by Gilbert Horsley's 32 recently arrived English adventurers aboard a seven-gun ship—even attempt to ascend the river and surprise Granada, intercepting some Spanish frigates traveling downstream.

15 MARCH 1575. At dawn the Silvestre-Horsley frigates set 40 harquebusiers ashore at Concepción de Veragua (Panama), attempting a surprise assault. But the raiders are discovered on the beach and are repelled; their vessels bombard the town for the rest of the day.

2 APRIL 1575. Horsley anchors behind Cape Honduras, and during the evening he sends a boat party nine miles south to raid Trujillo. Its defenders are alerted just past midnight, but the Englishmen nevertheless cut out an anchored Spanish frigate and make off with it by next dawn, steering west.

Lt. Gov. Diego López sends a shallop for Puerto Caballos (modern-day Puerto Cortés, Honduras) with a warning, but Horsley's rovers intercept it 60 miles away on the afternoon of 3 April along with the coaster of Juan Antonio. The Spanish merchantmen of Martín Monte and Vicencio Garullo enjoy better success, however, beating off an attack by the same rovers opposite Triunfo de la Cruz.

The Englishmen return past Trujillo on the evening of Tuesday, 5 April, before continuing east toward Cape Camarón, eventually regaining Plymouth by June.

MID-JUNE 1576. Spanish Adm. Cristóbal de Eraso enters the Caribbean with a plate-fleet escort, scattering seven Franco-English corsair vessels off Margarita Island (Venezuela), one of which scuttles itself rather than face capture.

LATE JUNE 1576. After departing England on 19 April and traversing the Lesser Antilles, 40-year-old Capt. John Oxenham—a native of Plymouth and former subordinate of Drake—reaches the Spanish Main west of Cartagena with his 11-gun, 57-man, 100-ton frigate. Concealing it along the shoreline, he then strikes west-southwest aboard a captured Spanish frigate and two pinnaces to intercept coastal traffic visiting the plate fleet at Nombre de Dios (Panama).

MID-AUGUST 1576. The Bristol merchant Andrew Barker reaches the Antillan island of Trinidad with 70 men aboard the barks *Ragged Staff* and *Bear* of William Cox to avenge the earlier detention of his factors and impoundment of properties by the Spanish Inquisitors at Tenerife. After refreshing provisions for six days, the Englishmen pillage a small Spanish ship off Margarita Island (Venezuela), then take on water at Curaçao—suffering 14 men injured at this latter place during an ambush.

26 AUGUST 1576. The English explorer Martin Frobisher claims modern-day Frobisher Bay (Canada) for Elizabeth I.

29 SEPTEMBER 1576. Oxenham transfers his English frigate and two Spanish prizes with 18 prisoners to Pinos Island (north of Acla, Panama), leaving a 40-man anchor watch aboard while exploring inland with 12 men guided by black *cimarrón* allies. During his two-week absence, Oxenham's vessels are surprised and captured by a Spanish frigate and brigantine bearing 20 soldiers out of Nombre de Dios, all his men except a young French page escaping ashore.

1576. French corsairs raid Guadianilla (Puerto Rico), capturing a large number of women. But the rovers are overtaken in a rainstorm before regaining their boats, suffering many casualties and losing the captives.

LATE JANUARY 1577. ***Oxenham in the Pacific.*** After building a 24-oar launch, Oxenham rafts down the Chucunaque and Tuira Rivers (eastern Panama) with 50 Englishmen and ten *cimarrón* allies to the Gulf of San Miguel. His expedition then falls upon the offshore Pearl Islands by 20 February (Ash Wednesday), pillaging them over the next three weeks and intercepting Spanish coastal traffic between Peru and Panama.

Learning of this threat from two escapees who reach Panama by canoe on 6 March, Gov. Dr. Gabriel de Loarte prepares his defenses, dissuading Oxenham from trying a surprise attack next evening. As the English withdraw toward the Pearl Islands, they seize a rich bark arriving from Guayaquil and so return into the Gulf of San Miguel with considerable booty. Meanwhile de Loarte on 13 March dispatches a 200-man counterexpedition under Pedro de Ortega Valencia aboard a half-dozen boats to hunt down the intruders.

This Spanish contingent meets the rich Peruvian galleon *Miguel Angel,* a 50-man detachment guiding it safely into Panama by 28 March. De Ortega meanwhile continues his search for the retiring Englishmen, while Vice Adm. Miguel de Eraso (Don Cristóbal's son) delegates two frigates from his plate fleet at Nombre de Dios—plus a Panamanian coast-guard frigate and brigantine—to cut off Oxenham's retreat on the Atlantic side of the isthmus, personally bringing 30 harquebusiers to reinforce Panama City.

After ascending the Tuira River for eight days until his vessels can go no farther because of shallow water, de Ortega proceeds afoot along the Chucunaque River's banks with 60 soldiers. After another four days' march, at 10:00 A.M. on 2 April he overtakes 30 Englishmen and 80 *cimarrones* eating near the "Piñas" confluence (either the modern-day Tupisca or Chico River), slaying nine of the former, capturing four—a wounded sailor and three boys—plus scattering the rest into the jungle. Oxenham's 12-man party is attacked two days later at the village of "Catalina" (possibly modern-day Yavisa), winning free after suffering three killed in an hour-long defense of their extemporized fort. The four English captives are then carried back to Panama by 18 April, along with the bulk of their supplies and booty.

In May 1577, 40 Spanish soldiers under Capt. Luis García de Melo travel from Panama City to Nombre de Dios with two English captives to destroy Oxenham's launches, hidden underwater on the north coast. Instead Adm. Cristóbal de Eraso appropriates the prisoners, delegating Gabriel de Vera's 80-man royal warship to carry out the mission. Eventually, both Spanish contingents unite and raise the launches together, after which García de Melo rampages south through *cimarrón* territory with 60 soldiers in a punitive sweep, emerging into the Gulf of San Miguel, while de Vera sails to Cartagena.

Without any means of escape, the English survivors remain in midisthmus until late August, when they are surprised by another 120 Peruvian troops in two columns under recently arrived Diego de Frías Trejo, who seizes Oxenham and eight of his followers. Other captures follow in mid-December 1577 and early February 1578, until 13 Englishmen are executed in Panama by April, and Oxenham with four others in Lima (Peru) some time later.

SPRING 1577. The Biscayan renegade Pedro de la Cruz raids Chagres and the Veragua Coast (northwestern Panama) with 80 Huguenot followers, establishing a base offshore.

APRIL 1577. After being pursued off Cartagena by Vice Adm. Miguel de Eraso's galleon and two frigates, Barker captures a Spanish frigate three days later off Tolú (Colombia), reputedly casting 28 soldiers overboard and holding an important passenger—Judge Juan Rodríguez de Mora—for ransom before being chased again by de Eraso and escaping toward Nombre de Dios (Panama).

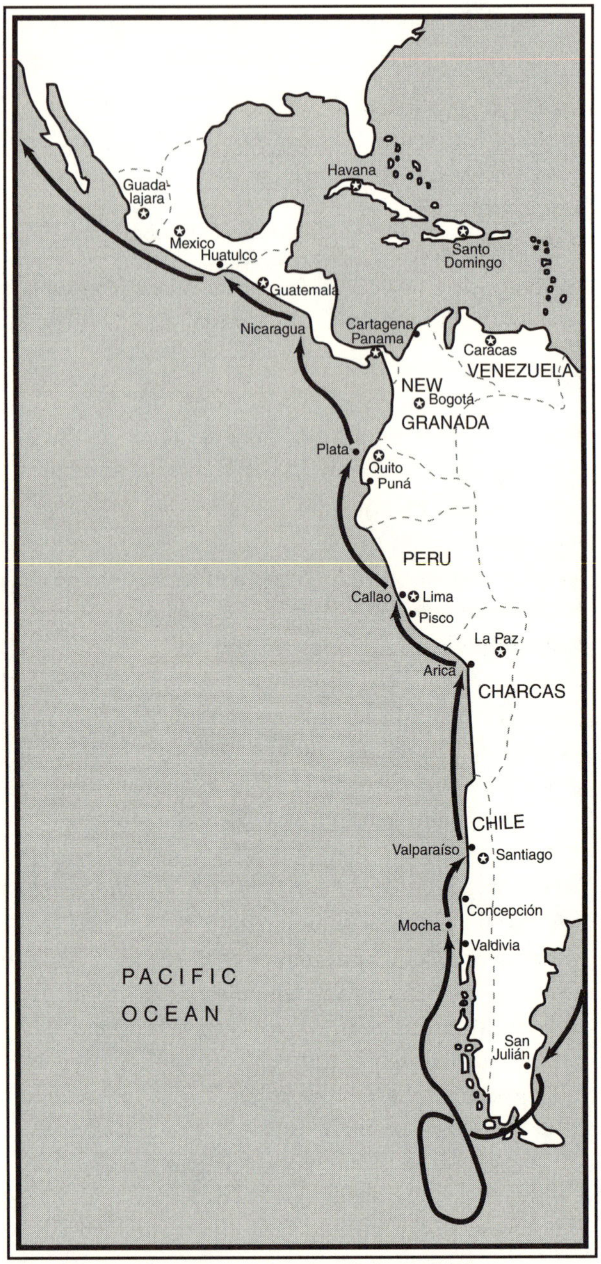

1 AUGUST 1577. Having pillaged the coast of Veragua (Panama), scuttled *Ragged Staff* in favor of a captured Spanish frigate, then coasted up eastern Honduras, Barker reaches Roatán Island. Two days later his second-in-command Cox mutinies, setting Barker ashore with a few loyal hands.

Less than two weeks afterward, López quits the mainland port of Trujillo with a demigalley and brigantine to rid the island of interlopers. Disembarking stealthily on its north coast, he leads 23 Spaniards in a dawn attack against the 30 Englishmen ashore on Saturday, 17 August, killing Barker and a dozen others. The 30 men aboard Cox's ships open fire, covering their survivors' retreat before retiring to another island three miles away. López then carries the heads and hands of the 13 dead Englishmen back into Trujillo.

JANUARY 1578. Two French corsair vessels occupy Manzanillo (Cuba), dispatching two boatloads of marauders up the Cauto River toward Bayamo. Its governor, Lic. Santistéban, ambushes these invaders with 30 harquebusiers as they come upriver, inflicting heavy losses and sinking both boats.

LATE FEBRUARY 1578. After one of his two small vessels has capsized off Cape San Antonio (western Cuba), drowning 14 crewmembers, Cox returns to Honduras with 35 men for one final raid. Despite carrying Trujillo in a nocturnal assault, the English boats are then chased away by superior Spanish forces, suffering one killed and seven captured—of whom a half-dozen are subsequently executed, only a young cabin boy being spared.

APRIL 1578. Drake appears off Brazil from West Africa on a secret but ostensibly peaceful mission to round the Strait of Magellan with six vessels and explore the Pacific Coast of South America. He brings along a captured Portuguese pilot, Nuño da Silva, who is knowledgeable about these waters.

After four months exploring Brazil and Argentina as far south as San Julián—and executing a mutinous subordinate named Thomas Doughty—Drake replenishes supplies and sets sail on 17 August with only his 150-ton flagship *Pelican,* the 80-ton *Elizabeth* under Capt. John Winter, and the 30-ton *Marigold* of John Thomas to attempt the famous passage.

SEPTEMBER 1578. ***Drake in the Pacific.*** Favored by good weather, Drake's squadron traverses the Strait of Magellan in 14 days, entering Spain's closed Pacific waters. He is greeted by storms on the western side that sink *Marigold* with all hands during a September night and oblige *Elizabeth* to turn back in early October. Although driven as far south as 57 degrees latitude by 20 October, Drake claws his way north to Mocha Island by 25 November. Upon attempting to go ashore, however, his 11-man boat crew is attacked by local tribesmen who kill two, capture two more, and wound Drake in the face.

Drake's cruise up the Pacific Coast of Spanish America

5 DECEMBER 1578. Drake sacks Valparaíso, capturing Licenciado Torres's ship, laden with wine and gold, in the harbor and securing its pilot, who possesses a chart of the Pacific Coast. After pausing at 30 degrees south

latitude in the vain hope of having his two lost consorts rejoin—then losing a man when a watering party is attacked ashore by the Spaniards—Drake resumes his northern heading on 19 January 1579.

5 FEBRUARY 1579. Drake raids Arica (Chile), burning a Spanish vessel at anchor and making off with another owned by one Felipe Corso.

13 FEBRUARY 1579. Drake's *Pelican* assaults Callao, boarding about a dozen vessels lying in the roads and cutting their cables; when they drift ashore they are destroyed. From captives he further learns that the Spanish merchantman *Nuestra Señora de la Concepción* (nicknamed *Cacafuego*) has recently departed northwest toward Panama City bearing a valuable cargo of silver. The English instantly set off in pursuit.

1 MARCH 1579. After taking a few minor prizes Drake overhauls *Cacafuego* near Cape San Francisco (south of Punta Galera, Ecuador). With *Pelican* and a large pinnace he draws along both sides of the lumbering, unarmed galleon at 9:00 P.M., challenging its master, San Juan de Antón, to strike. The Spaniard refuses, and the ship is quickly subdued. Reversing course to what is today Plata Island, Drake transfers 360,000 pesos in gold and silver aboard his ship, renaming it *Golden Hind,* then releases *Cacafuego.*

MID-MARCH 1579. Drake appears off Nicaragua, intercepting a Spanish bark bearing two veteran pilots of transpacific crossings aboard the Acapulco-Manila galleons, thus securing charts and sailing instructions for the route.

13 APRIL 1579. Drake ransacks Huatulco, Mexico (also spelled Guatulco), replenishing water supplies and releasing all his Spanish captives. *Golden Hind* then continues northwest, perhaps reaching as high as 42 degrees before reversing course. Careening outside San Francisco harbor—presumably in Drake's Bay—from 17 June to 23 July, the English dub this region Nova Albion and leave behind a commemorative plaque that has never been found. By late July *Golden Hind* quits the Americas for Mindanao (the Philippines).

11 OCTOBER 1579. Mistakenly assuming Drake will retrace his course into the Atlantic via the Strait of Magellan, Peru's viceroy, Francisco de Toledo, dispatches two ships south from Callao to intercept: *Nuestra Señora de Esperanza* (flag) under Capt. Pedro Sarmiento de Gamboa, and vice-flag *San Francisco* of Juan de Villalobos, armed with two guns each and carrying 112 men. They fail to sight the enemy, who has sailed west toward Asia; they therefore map the strait while traversing from west to east.

31 JANUARY 1580. In Europe, the death of the epileptic cardinal-king, Henry of Portugal, leaves Philip II of Spain as nearest claimant to the throne. His succession is disputed by the Portuguese people, so Philip recalls 72-year-old Gen. Fernando Alvarez de Toledo, duque de Alba, from enforced retirement; the latter crosses the border at the head of an army in late June. Aided by a Spanish fleet under 54-year-old Adm. Alvaro de Bazán, Marqués de Santa Cruz, Alba wins a smashing victory at Alcántara and compels Lisbon to surrender by 25 August.

Philip is officially proclaimed Portugal's king by the Cortes (Portuguese parliament) on 15 April 1581, thus adding 1 million subjects, a strong fleet, and more overseas possessions to his already vast empire. Despite minor resistance headed by a rival claimant—the prior Dom Antônio de Crato—Portugal will remain under Spanish domination until December 1640, when it revolts and regains independence.

1 FEBRUARY 1580. In the Strait of Magellan, Sarmiento de Gamboa loses contact with Villalobos's *San Francisco,* which returns to Peru. Emerging into the South Atlantic 23 days later, Sarmiento decides to sail to Spain and advise Philip II to fortify this vital waterway to prevent future incursions into the Pacific such as Drake's.

25 MARCH 1582. ***Sarmiento's Counterexpedition.*** Sarmiento de Gamboa—now governor-designate for the Strait of Magellan—reaches Rio de Janeiro from Spain with veteran Adm. Diego Flores de Valdés, knight of the Order of Santiago (*see* 4 September 1565) and Vice Adm. Diego de la Rivera aboard the 700-ton flagship gallease *San Cristóbal* of Juan de Garay; 500-ton vice-flagship *San Juan Bautista* of Alonso de las Alas, plus *San Estéban* of Juan Gutiérrez de Palomar; 1,100-ton, French-built *Jesús María* of Juan de Aguirre; 450-ton *María de Jesús* of Gutierre de Solís; 400-ton *Concepción* of Gregorio de las Alas, *María* of Francisco de Nevares, *Sancti Spíritus* of Villaviciosa Unzueta, *Santa Marta* of Gonzalo Meléndez, *Trinidad* of Martín de Zubieta, plus an unknown Galician ship under Martín de Quirós; 360-ton *San Nicolás* of Captain Vargas; 300-ton *Santa Catalina* (alias *Corza*) of Diego de Olavarri; 260-ton *San Estéban* of Estéban de las Alas, and *Santa María de San Vicente* of Hernando

Morejón; 230-ton *Santa María de Begonia* of Pedro de Aquino; 180-ton, Peruvian-built *Nuestra Señora de Esperanza* of Pedro Estéban de las Alas; plus 80-ton frigates *María Magdalena* of Diego de Ovalle, *Santa Catalina* of Francisco de Cuéllar, and *Santa Isabel* of Suero Queipo.

The original complements of 672 sailors and 1,330 soldiers are bolstered by 670 settlers destined for southern Chile under Gov. Alonso de Sotomayor. Another 206 are to fortify the strait under the supervision of military engineer Juan Bautista Antonelli. Storms, disease, and bad supplies have sapped their numbers, however, 153 men having succumbed during the transatlantic crossing; another 200 are carried ashore sick.

12 AUGUST 1582. The Spanish galley *Leona* and galliot *Santiago* reach the West Indian island of Dominica under Ruy Díaz de Mendoza, knight of the Order of Saint John, to take up station six days later as coastguard vessels operating out of Santo Domingo.

2 NOVEMBER 1582. After a miserable layover in Rio de Janeiro, during which Sarmiento and Admiral Flores have a falling out, the expedition resumes its voyage to colonize the Strait of Magellan. *Santa María de San Vicente* is left behind as useless, and on the night of 29–30 November—after several days of heavy weather—Gutiérrez de Palomar's *San Estéban* sinks with 300–350 hands. Flores lays in a course for nearby Santa Catarina Island (Brazil) to recuperate; upon arrival *Santa Marta* and a storeship run aground and are thus lost.

11 DECEMBER 1582. The English Cmdr. Edward Fenton appears off Brazil at approximately 28 degrees latitude with his 400-ton flagship *Leicester* (ex-galleon *Bear*) under second-in-command William Hawkins Jr.; the 300-ton vice-flagship *Edward Bonaventure* under Luke Ward; the 50-ton frigate or pinnace *Elizabeth* under Thomas Skevington; and the 40-ton bark *Francis* under John Drake (Sir Francis's nephew). Having crossed the Atlantic from West Africa, they intend to enter the Pacific and emulate Drake's exploits, eventually gaining China. However, after refreshing ashore the Englishmen intercept the 46-ton Spanish bark *Nuestra Señora de Piedad* on the morning of 17 December, bound from Brazil toward the River Plate with 21 settlers under Francisco de Vera. From him they learn of Sarmiento's recent departure from Rio de Janeiro to fortify the Strait of Magellan. Three days later the rovers release their prize, continuing south on 22 December.

31 DECEMBER 1582. Unsure of being able to win past Sarmiento's new settlement in the Strait of Magellan, Fenton reverses course this evening, heading north toward the Brazilian port of São Vicente. This same night John Drake's 18-man *Francis* parts company, eventually becoming wrecked; he is marooned for 15 months at the River Plate before surrendering to the Spaniards.

30 JANUARY 1583. Fenton reaches São Vicente Bay (Brazil) with *Leicester, Edward Bonaventure,* and *Elizabeth,* dealing peaceably with the Portuguese residents of nearby Santos.

3 FEBRUARY 1583. ***Fenton at São Vicente.*** At 4:00 P.M. the Spanish galleons *San Juan Bautista, Concepción,* and *Santa María de Begonia* appear outside the Brazilian bay of São Vicente. They have been detached from Flores's fleet at Santa Catarina Island to return to Rio de Janeiro under Commo. Andrés de Equino, bearing the many sick and injured (*see* 2 November 1582). Having stumbled upon the English intruders—the Spaniards are aware of the interlopers because of the released bark *Piedad* (*see* 11 December 1582)—Equino clears for battle and stands in at 11:00 P.M., bearing down upon the anchored English trio and initiating a moonlight exchange that lasts until 4:00 A.M., when a rainstorm interrupts.

Dawn on 4 February reveals *Begonia* sunk in shallow water, the attackers having suffered 32 killed and many wounded, compared to eight Englishmen slain and 20 injured. Equino's remaining two ships nonetheless defend themselves vigorously when action resumes at 10:00 A.M.; Fenton finally breaks off the fight and stands out to sea four hours later.

Ward's *Edward Bonaventure* eventually becomes separated from its consorts on 8 February and sails alone toward England after touching at Fernando de Noronha Island; Fenton visits Salvador before returning.

17 FEBRUARY 1583. Having detached another three galleons from his damaged fleet at Santa Catarina Island (Brazil) to transport Sotomayor's Chilean settlers toward the River Plate, so that they might continue their journey overland toward their destination, Admiral Flores appears at the mouth of the Strait of Magellan with only five vessels, bearing Sarmiento's shrunken following. Discouraged by the daunting shoreline, the Spanish naval commander—without venturing inshore—reverses course and returns north toward Brazil despite Sarmiento's heated protests.

9 MAY 1583. After rejoining Equino's battle-scarred *San Juan Bautista* and *Concepción* at São Vicente (Brazil) on 27 February, Admiral Flores reenters Rio de Janeiro. He learns that two of three galleons he has earlier detached toward Buenos Aires with Sotomayor have also been wrecked; even the presence of Adm. Diego de Alcega with four additional galleons at Rio—bearing supplies and reinforcements—cannot revive his spirits.

2 JUNE 1583. Delegating Vice Adm. Diego de la Rivera and Commo. Gregorio de las Alas to remain at Rio de Janeiro and make a second attempt at establishing Sarmiento's colony in the Strait of Magellan with five warships and 500 men, Admiral Flores meanwhile sails north toward Baía de Todos os Santos (Salvador) with his flagship *San Cristóbal, San Juan Bautista, Concepción,* the frigate *Santa Isabel,* and Alcega's galleons *Santa María* and *Santa Cruz.*

3 JUNE 1583. After reconnoitering and bartering up the Brazilian coast, an English expedition appears off Margarita Island (Venezuela) under William and Richard Hawkins, pausing for a few weeks to gather pearls from the 300-ton flagship *Primrose,* the 180-ton vice-flag *Minion,* the 100-ton bark *Hastings,* two 100-ton ships owned by Sir Francis Drake, an 80-ton pinnace, and a smaller consort. Despite its peaceful conduct the formation bears a privateering commission from Dom Antônio de Crato—pretender to the Portuguese throne (*see* 31 January 1580)—to attack Spanish interests.

5 JULY 1583. While working inshore nine miles west of La Isabela (northern Hispaniola) to anchor overnight, the Spanish galliot *Santiago* of Capt. Diego Osorio strikes a shoal an hour and a half after dark and breaks up; crew and slaves are rescued the next day by Ruy Díaz's consort *Leona.*

13 JULY 1583. Admiral Flores reaches Baía de Todos os Santos (Salvador, Brazil) from Rio de Janeiro, detaching his second-in-command, Alcega, toward Spain with the galleon *Santa Cruz* while laying up his other five warships in ordinary.

20 JULY 1583. Before dawn slave oarsmen mutiny aboard the coast-guard galley *Leona*—anchored for the night off Cape Engaño (eastern Santo Domingo)—killing Commo. Ruy Díaz and three loyal hands and wounding a dozen more Spaniards before reversing course northwest with the commandeered vessel. Led by the convict Pedro de Vargas and numerous French prisoners, the mutineers attempt to stand into Puerto Plata the next day, only to be discouraged by its alerted defenses under Capt. Pedro Rengifo de Angulo. Instead, 60 armed rebels go ashore at La Isabela, slaughtering beef cattle and releasing their captives before steering toward Bayahá. There they lure an unsuspecting crown official aboard, after which they destroy the harbor castle and pillage the town and its outlying district for four days before departing toward La Yaguana (modern-day Léogâne, Haiti) with a prize in tow.

22 JULY 1583. William and Richard Hawkins appear off Puerto Vargas (near Guadianilla, in western Puerto Rico), anchoring for repairs and taking on wood and water. They depart by the morning of 30 July toward the Mona Passage in company with three recently arrived English ships. While reembarking, one of their shore parties is ambushed by a half-dozen Spaniards under Diego Rodríguez de Castellanos; two interlopers are captured and put to death.

1 AUGUST 1583. After being repelled at La Yaguana (modern-day Léogâne, Haiti), the rebel galley *Leona*—its mutinous crew suffering one killed and another seriously injured—anchors 25 miles farther west at Guava (Petit Goâve) to begin gathering provisions so Vargas's followers can burn their prize and sail another captive consort (the ship brought from Bayahá) toward Europe. On 9 August they intercept a second merchantman arriving from the Spanish Main, incorporating it into the flotilla.

Next day, Captain Osorio reaches La Yaguana after a forced march overland to attempt to recapture the galley. Outnumbered, he fails to persuade the local militia to help; he therefore visits the mutineers' 50-man fortified camp at Guava on 13 August to offer pardons to anyone willing to surrender. The rebels become divided and shift the galley to La Yaguana on 20 August while retaining their camp and two other vessels at Guava.

Eventually, *Leona* departs north on 26 August, pausing at Atibonico (Artibonite) two days later to rustle cattle and then proceeding to Guanahibes (Gonaïves) on 6 September to rejoin the two companion ships. Some 90 mutineers go aboard that pair to sail for France, marooning 60 unwilling colleagues ashore. Osorio arrives during the evening of 7 September and recaptures the stripped galley just before it can be burned by its 50 remaining crewmembers; otherwise he is powerless to pursue the escaping pair out to Tortuga Island or into the Atlantic.

15 AUGUST 1583. Humphrey Gilbert lays claim to Newfoundland (Canada) for Elizabeth I of England.

1 DECEMBER 1583. Spanish Vice Admiral de la Rivera departs Rio de Janeiro with five vessels to attempt to deposit Sarmiento's colonists in the Strait of Magellan. For two months contrary winds prevent them from penetrating the waterway; therefore on 1 February 1584 330 Spaniards go ashore in the lee of Cape Vírgenes—wrecking their galleon *Trinidad* in the process—to proceed overland to their destination.

After tracing out a settlement named Nombre de Jesús, Sarmiento leads 94 of his healthiest men on a 200-mile trek (suffering one killed and ten badly wounded in skirmishes with Patagonian natives) to establish an eight-gun outpost called Rey don Felipe at the narrowest point of the strait. He is now supported by only the galleon *María;* de la Rivera's flagship and the frigates *Santa Catalina* and *Santa Magdalena* have retired to Brazil because of the ceaseless storms.

Repressing a mutiny by hanging its four ringleaders, Sarmiento departs the wretched colony of Rey don Felipe aboard *María* on 25 May 1584 to visit his original camp at Nombre de Jesús. Fierce weather precludes his landing, however, and after beating about in vain for 20 days, *María* stands away to Brazil.

3 JANUARY 1584. Antonio de Berrio leads a Spanish expedition eastward down the Casanare River and Meta River (central Venezuela) in search of Manoa, the legendary city of *El Dorado,* or Golden Man—a religious figure who would dive into a pool during rituals covered in gold dust, to emerge cleansed. Before reaching the Atures, the exhausted Spaniards turn back.

JANUARY 1584. In London, Elizabeth I expels the Spanish ambassador, Bernardino de Mendoza, for his role in the Throckmorton assassination plot against her, effectively severing diplomatic relations with Spain.

1 MARCH 1584. ***French Paraíba.*** Spain's Admiral Flores quits Baía de Todos os Santos (Salvador, Brazil), sailing north toward Pernambuco Province (Recife) to await the arrival of a Portuguese expedition of 100 cavalry, 300 infantry, and 3,000 native auxiliaries who are marching overland to expel French trespassers from Paraíba Bay.

After numerous delays, Flores circles around from Pernambuco with his five galleons, appearing before Paraíba. One French vessel escapes out to sea past his warships, but Spanish boat parties discover another four careening inside, the largest being of 200 tons. It is captured, although 150 Frenchmen torch the other three and their dwellings before disappearing upriver with their Pitiguara allies. In order to prevent their return, the victors establish a fortified camp upon this site—dubbed Filipeia in honor of Philip II—and garrison it with Portuguese Gov. Fructuoso Barbosa's contingent and a company of Spanish troops under a captain named Castrejón.

10 JUNE 1584. In France, the death of François, duc d'Anjou—the younger brother of the childless Henri III—leaves the Huguenot Prince Henri de Navarre next in line for the throne, prompting the revival of the Catholic League as an oppositionist force under Henri, duc de Guise. He secretly signs the Treaty of Joinville with Spain in December 1584, Philip promising to aid his coreligionists in supporting Charles, cardinal de Bourbon, as a rival claimant against the Protestant contender; in England, Queen Elizabeth I backs the Huguenot cause.

13 JANUARY 1585. Having dispatched a 40-ton relief bark from Brazil for his starving Spanish colonists in the Strait of Magellan, Sarmiento follows in a larger vessel, only to turn back because of foul weather. (Sarmiento later sails aboard a Portuguese caravel to beseech Philip's assistance from Spain in maintaining the remote outpost; he is intercepted by three of Sir Walter Raleigh's privateers off the Azores and held captive in England and France until 1590.)

MARCH 1585. In France, the eighth War of Religion erupts between the Huguenot faction of Henri de Navarre, the Catholic League of Duke Henri de Guise, and the royalist forces of King Henri III (thus becoming known as the War of the Three Henries). The nation is wracked by civil strife for the next four and a half years, with foreign mercenaries joining in on all sides.

17 MAY 1585. The 42-year-old adventurer Sir Richard Grenville reaches Dominica with his 140-ton flagship *Tiger* and a smaller consort plus several Spanish prizes, part of a seven-ship convoy bearing colonists toward Raleigh's projected new colony at Roanoke (North Carolina). Three days later Grenville approaches Las Boquillas—30 miles east of Guadianilla, in southern Puerto Rico and dubbed Mosquito Bay by the English—setting 400 men ashore on 25 May to build a temporary fort and a pinnace.

On 29 May he is rejoined by the 50-ton consort *Elizabeth* under Capt. Thomas Cavendish, departing on the morning of 3 June after burning the fort and surrounding countryside. Grenville's second-in-command, Ralph Lane, lands 20 men at Cape Rojo on 6 June to poach salt despite the presence of several Spanish cavalry patrols. The Englishmen then pause off Mona Island, intercepting a passing Spanish bark on the evening of 8 June and a frigate the next morning, holding both in order to extort fresh food, water, and mounts from the residents of nearby San Germán before steering northwest.

11 JUNE 1585. Grenville's five ships and prizes reach La Isabela (northern Hispaniola). They receive such a friendly reception from local Spanish officials and those of nearby Puerto Plata that they remain until 17 June, when they continue their voyage to North America.

MID-JULY 1585. Grenville reaches Roanoke (North Carolina), establishing a small colony in Raleigh's name. He leaves it under Lane and returns to England.

JULY 1585. In Europe, Henri III of France signs the Treaty of Nemours, aligning himself with the Catholic League and its Spanish backers.

20 AUGUST 1585. Elizabeth I signs the Treaty of Nonsuch, committing England to send 6,000 troops under her favorite, Robert Dudley, Earl of Leicester, to aid the Protestant Dutch in their revolt against Spain by December 1585.

10 SEPTEMBER 1585. While homeward-bound from North Carolina to England, Grenville's *Tiger* intercepts the 300-ton Spanish ship *Santa María de San Vicente* of Master Alonso de Cornieles near Bermuda. The rich prize is sailed into Plymouth by 28 October.

10 JANUARY 1586. ***Sack of Santo Domingo.*** At 8:00 A.M. Drake resumes his West Indian campaigns by materializing off Hispaniola with 2,300 men aboard 23 vessels—including two on loan from Elizabeth I (his 600-ton flagship *Elizabeth Bonaventure* and *Aid* of 250 tons)—plus Martin Frobisher's private merchantman *Primrose* (vice-flag), the 400-ton galleon *Leicester, Tiger, Minion,* and *Swallow.* Having captured a Spanish bark that carried a Greek pilot, Drake learns that the best disembarkation point lies at the mouth of the Jaina River (10 miles west of Santo Domingo's capital); he proceeds to that place this evening and begins landing 800 troops under Christopher Carleill.

Sir Francis Drake

Next day, Drake's fleet menaces Santo Domingo's seaward defenses, causing the Spaniards to scuttle two ships in a vain attempt to block up the entrance. When Carleill's small army unexpectedly approaches overland at noon Spanish will collapses, leading to a wholesale flight of the tiny garrison led by Gov. Lic. Cristóbal de Ovalle. The English hold Santo Domingo for a month, during which they pillage the city; they then begin burning buildings to extort ransoms from the inhabitants in the interior. Having raised 25,000 ducats, Drake departs on 11 February.

19 FEBRUARY 1586. ***Drake at Cartagena.*** Gov. Pedro Fernández de Bustos, having ample warning of the English approach, has amassed 54 riders, 450 harquebusiers, 100 spearmen, 20 armed black slaves, and 400 Indian archers. Furthermore, out in the harbor lie two well-accoutered galleys, recently arrived from Spain under veteran Cmdr. Pedro Vique Manrique. Yet rumors of the unprecedented size and armament of the enemy fleet sap the defenders' morale.

Drake leads his vessels directly into Cartagena's outer harbor, landing 600 men under Carleill that evening. While they circle north, Frobisher probes the Boquerón Fortress with pinnaces in the dark until

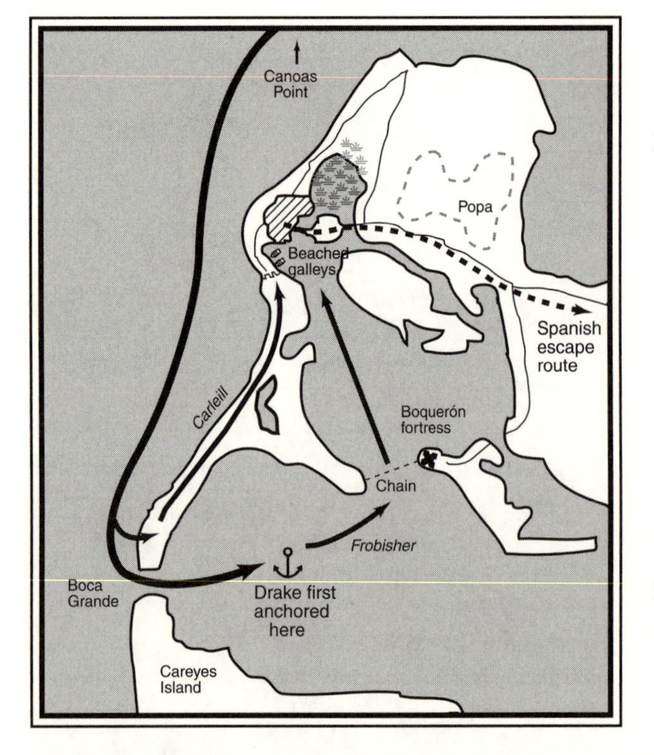

Drake's assault on Cartagena

obliged to withdraw. Next morning, Carleill's column brushes aside a line of trenches, spreading panic throughout Cartagena's garrison. Vique's galleys are run ashore, their crews abandoning ship as the slaves revolt. By 21 February all resistance ceases. Only seven or eight Spaniards lose their lives during the fighting compared to 30 Englishmen. The city is ransacked, its vacant buildings being ransomed for 107,000 ducats—against which Drake extends a receipt. With sickness weakening his men, he remains until 24 April (O.S.) before setting sail for Cuba.

10 APRIL 1586. The French corsair Captain Richard approaches the vicinity of Bayamo (southern Cuba) with two vessels, intending to ransom the merchant frigate of Hernando Casanova—which he holds captive—by selling it back to the Spaniards. Apparently unaware of the heightened state of alert caused by Drake's presence in West Indian waters, Richard is surprised by Cuban militia under Capt. Alvaro Pérez de Maya, who kills eight Frenchmen and captures numerous others (including Richard with his flagship) while liberating the Spanish frigate. Only the second French vessel, commanded by Richard's son, succeeds in escaping; his father is carried into Bayamo for execution.

30 APRIL 1586. In Roanoke (North Carolina), the death of local *werowance* (chieftain) Ensenore soon leads to hostilities between the natives and the surviving English colonists under Lane.

21 MAY 1586. Richard's ship returns to Santiago de Cuba with three other French corsair vessels to avenge his father's capture. Two deposit 80 rovers at Juragua Beach; they fight their way inland against local Cuban militia under Capt. Gómez Patiño. Meanwhile the other two French ships penetrate Santiago's roadstead and disembark more men, who torch the main church and several lesser buildings. Unable to carry the entire town, however, the French are driven off by Spanish reinforcements from Bayamo under Capt. Hernán Manrique de Rojas; they allegedly kill 50 invaders and wound another 30.

29 MAY 1586. Drake's fleet passes Havana, watched by more than 1,000 militia marshaled under Gov. Gabriel de Luján. The English are shadowed until they pass Matanzas and head north into the Straits of Florida. On 7 June Drake descends upon the Spanish outpost of Saint Augustine, whose handful of residents flee into the bush. After systematically throwing down its defenses and devastating the town, the English admiral continues north to visit Raleigh's fledgling colony at Roanoke (North Carolina).

19 JUNE 1586. Drake pauses at Roanoke, offering its distressed settlers the 70-ton bark *Francis* and two pinnaces, along with food and equipment. Unfortunately a storm disperses the English fleet shortly thereafter, with *Francis* and numerous boats being lost. Discouraged, the 109 remaining colonists opt to return to England with Drake, abandoning their settlement by 28 June. (Approximately one week later a 100-ton relief ship sent out by Raleigh arrives. Ten days later three more ships arrive under Grenville, who leaves 15 men behind as a second holding party and then departs.)

After touching at Newfoundland, Drake returns to Portsmouth by early August, having lost 750 men during the campaign—three-quarters due to disease. Despite having seized a considerable amount of booty, it does not cover the expedition's costs.

4 NOVEMBER 1586. Cavendish appears off Brazil from West Africa with his 140-ton flagship *Desire,* the 60-ton *Content,* and the 40-ton bark *Hugh Gallant,* manned by slightly more than 100 men. Like Drake and Fenton before him, he intends to round the Strait of Magellan into the Pacific and raid Spain's American empire before crossing to Asia. One week later his

squadron anchors off São Sebastião Island (east of Santos), refreshing provisions until 3 December.

27 DECEMBER 1586. Cavendish's formation pauses in a large uninhabited bay—dubbed Port Desire in honor of his flagship (modern-day Puerto Deseado, Argentina)—before resuming a southerly course toward the Strait of Magellan. A few days later the English rescue several "poore starved Spanyards" who are walking north from Sarmiento's failed colony (*see* 1 December 1583), learning that only 22 defenders remain alive.

11 JANUARY 1587. ***Cavendish in the Pacific.*** Entering the Strait of Magellan, Cavendish's three English vessels reach Sarmiento's ruined settlement of Rey don Felipe by 19 January, removing six cannons. The rovers emerge into the South Pacific by 5 March, steering north toward Mocha Island, which they sight on 24 March. Cavendish disembarks farther north at Santa María with 80 heavily armed men and is peaceably received by the local inhabitants.

20 JANUARY 1587. An English squadron arrives off the River Plate from Sierra Leone, dispatched by George Clifford, third Earl of Cumberland: the 260-ton, 130-man flagship *Red Dragon* under Robert Withrington; the 130-ton, 70-man vice-flagship *Clifford* under Christopher Lister; the "rear admiral" *Roe* under Captain Hawes; and pinnace *Dorothy,* on loan from Raleigh. They capture a pair of small Portuguese slavers that same day. Although intending to round the Strait of Magellan into the Pacific like Drake, Fenton, and Cavendish, they instead decide to reverse course northward on 6 March to attack Brazil.

9 APRIL 1587. Cavendish's three vessels put into Quintero Bay (north of Valparaíso, Chile). A shore party is ambushed two days later by local Spaniards, who kill seven Englishmen and capture another nine. Yet the interlopers remain until 15 April when they stand back out into the Pacific.

21 APRIL 1587. ***Salvador.*** The small English squadron under Withrington and Lister enters Baía de Todos os Santos (Salvador, Brazil) despite fire from its batteries and the eight ships and a caravel anchored inside. Four of the vessels are cut out by the raiders on the moonlit night of 23–24 April, a 24-gun, 250-ton Flushinger providing most of the opposition.

After riding out a storm, Withrington and Lister take their prizes nine days later to a bay northwest of Baía; shore parties are repeatedly attacked by several hundred local militia on both 12 and 16 May. Tiring of their subsequent blockade of Baía, the English finally sail away by 1 June and, after seizing several more inconsequential prizes off the coast, lay in a course for England by 3 August—reaching home on 29 September (O.S.) with scant profit.

APRIL 1587. In central Venezuela, de Berrio leads a second Spanish expedition eastward across the Casanare and Meta Plains, searching for Manoa—home of El Dorado. Despite reaching the eastern shores of the Orinoco River, the column is obliged to turn back one year later because of weakness and ill health.

3 MAY 1587. Cavendish captures a large Spanish ship and four barks at Arica (Chile), sacking and burning all except one, which is renamed *George*—its seizure having occurred on Saint George's Day (23 April [O.S.])—and incorporated into the squadron before resuming progress northwest two days later.

14 MAY 1587. Cavendish reaches Pisco (Peru), then intercepts two Spanish merchantmen three days later, which he pillages and burns. The English next descend upon Paita shortly after 20 May, capturing a bark in the harbor and setting 60 men ashore to occupy the town while its 300 inhabitants flee inland. The citizens refuse to raise any ransom, so the rovers set the dwellings ablaze before sailing north.

12 JUNE 1587. While resting on Puná Island (Ecuador), about 16 of Cavendish's men are surprised by several score Spaniards and Indians out of Quito under Capt. Juan de Galarza, who kills about a half-dozen Englishmen and captures several more. In retaliation, Cavendish orders all of Puná's buildings, ships, and crops burned before he departs on 21 June.

29 JUNE 1587. The 120-ton flagship *Lion* reaches Dominica from England, accompanied by a flyboat and pinnace, bearing 150–160 new settlers under John White, the governor-designate for Raleigh's colony at Roanoke (North Carolina). Three days later they go ashore at Saint Croix to refresh; by 8 July they sight Puerto Rico, which they skirt without incident before proceeding northwest toward the Caicos Islands and their final destination.

2 AUGUST 1587. White's expedition reaches Roanoke; he goes ashore with 40 armed men, finding no trace of the 15 men left behind the previous year

(*see* 19 June 1586). Nevertheless, all 120 remaining settlers disembark, being joined two days later by a flyboat under Edward Spicer (who had become separated). White returns to England shortly thereafter aboard the flyboat to hasten out fresh provisions and reinforcements the following spring but will be prevented by the general embargo to combat the Spanish armada in the English Channel.

7 AUGUST 1587. Cavendish surprises Huatulco (Mexico), looting it over the course of a week before setting its dwellings ablaze along with a merchantman in the harbor.

24 AUGUST 1587. Puerto de la Navidad (west of Manzanillo, Mexico) is visited by Cavendish, who imprisons the Spanish lookout and then torches a pair of 200-ton ships being built in the yards. Compostela is sighted by 18 September, Mazatlán on 27 September, after which the Englishmen cross to the southwestern tip of Baja California to await the annual Manila galleon.

14 NOVEMBER 1587. This morning, Cavendish's lookouts spot a large ship approaching out of the northwest; it proves to be the 700-ton Philippine galleon *Santa Ana* of Capt. Tomás de Alzola. *Desire* and *Content* chase it until noon, when they come within range and open fire. The galleon has no guns mounted—never expecting to encounter enemies along this route—yet repels two boarding attempts before being pounded into submission. Approximately a dozen Spaniards and two Englishmen are killed during the exchanges.

Cavendish works his prize back to Cabo San Lucas by 16 November, depositing 180 captives ashore and looting *Santa Ana* nearby. Eventually, 40 tons of rich Asian goods are transhipped before the raiders torch the galleon and strike out west into the Pacific on 30 November. Meanwhile the Spanish survivors build a raft from their ship's wreckage and use it to summon help from Santiago (Colima); they are rescued and carried into Acapulco by 7 December.

ELIZABETHAN WARS (1588–1603)

BY THE SPRING OF 1588 FRICTIONS BETWEEN King Philip II of Spain and Queen Elizabeth I of England become so intense that hostilities blaze forth openly. The so-called Invincible Armada—130 Spanish ships bearing 2,400 guns and 22,000 sailors and soldiers—appears off southwest England on 29 July bent on running up the channel to transfer the veteran army of Alejandro Farnesio, duque de Parma, out of the Low Countries in order to invade Kent. Persistent English counterattacks, lack of proper Spanish coordination, and heavy weather doom the enterprise; less than two-thirds of the vessels and half the men reach home again.

Although all of England's seamen are initially concentrated in home waters to resist the Spanish menace, victory soon permits them to switch to the offensive. During the ensuing 15 years of conflict, 100–200 privateering ventures set sail every year, bringing in £150,000–200,000 per annum in prizes. While most of the expeditions operate in the North Atlantic, a number also raid Spain's New World empire.

LATE JUNE 1588. The English privateers *Drake, Examiner, Hope,* and *Chance*—raised by the merchant John Watts and dispatched out of London early in March (prior to the Armada scare)—hover in the Old Bahama Channel for two weeks, hoping in vain to intercept Spanish ships arriving at Havana. After scanty results *Drake* steers toward the Azores; the other three vessels visit Newfoundland then set course toward England by mid-August with a single French prize.

LATE APRIL 1589. The 70-ton, 40-man privateer *Black Dog* of Capt. William Michelson appears off Hispaniola, driving a Spanish frigate ashore and pillaging it; later it visits like treatment upon another coaster. Michelson then roams southern Cuba as far west as Cape San Antonio, looting several more vessels before parting company on 14 May with ten men aboard a captured Spanish frigate to reconnoiter the approaches to Havana. There he joins three other English ships in mounting a blockade that intercepts two Spanish merchantmen arriving from the Canaries. One of them runs aground and is partially stripped before troops can push out from shore and drive the rovers away.

Meanwhile *Black Dog*—under pilot Roger Kingson and Master William Mace—weighs from Cape San Antonio on 18 May to chase a passing Spanish ship of 120 tons bearing a cargo of wrought iron and wine. Contrary winds and currents carry the privateersmen and their prize into the Gulf of Mexico, where they attack a large Spanish merchantman

Thomas Cavendish, painted upon his return from circumnavigating the globe. His body is wrapped with pearl ropes, and hundreds of others are sewn to his cloak and tunic, as part of the booty he captured off Spanish America.

loading in Campeche's harbor 20 days later. The assault is beaten off, but when Kingson and Mace attempt to extort a ransom of 5,000 ducats to depart, they are lured aboard by the Spaniards and stabbed; Mace manages to swim away with a handful of others. *Black Dog* then captures another wine-bearing Spanish ship while returning to Cuba. Although unable to find Michelson, *Black Dog* eventually returns to Plymouth by 20 September with three Spanish prizes.

2 AUGUST 1589. At Saint Cloud (France), King Henri III—now openly backing the Protestant cause—is assassinated by a fanatical young Dominican friar, Jacques Clément, thus clearing the way for Huguenot champion Henri de Navarre to claim the throne. Fighting escalates as Catholic forces redouble their efforts to impede his succession.

SEPTEMBER 1589. ***Chidley's Failure.*** The 120-ton, 90-man *Robin* (formerly *Delight*) of Capt. Andrew Merrick and Master Robert Burnet arrives off Brazil from Cape Blanco (West Africa), having become separated from an English expedition intended to round the Strait of Magellan into the Pacific. Its 24-year-old leader, John Chidley, sights South America shortly thereafter with his 300-ton, 180-man flagship *Wildman* (formerly *Susan*) under Master John Ellis; the 340-ton, 140-man *White Lion* (formerly *Elizabeth Bonaventure*) of Capt. Thomas Polwhele and Master Benjamin Wood; plus the tiny pinnace *Wildman's Club* of Richard Glover and another unknown auxiliary. Only *Robin* succeeds in gaining Puerto Deseado (Argentina), from where it attempts to enter the Strait of Magellan on 10 January 1590. A 15-man boat party is lost off a place called Penguin Island, and another five Englishmen are slaughtered by Patagonian natives near the derelict Spanish outpost of Rey don Felipe. The disheartened survivors on 22 February refuse to go any farther, so *Robin* reverses course out of the strait two days later and sails back up Brazil toward Europe; it eventually wrecks off Cherbourg, France.

19 MARCH 1590. De Berrio heads east down the Casanare River (central Venezuela) with a third Spanish expedition, determined to explore the Orinoco and discover the legendary city of El Dorado. One year later he reaches the Caroní confluence, leaving a garrison six miles downstream at Carapana (Morequito Province, opposite Tórtola Island) before reaching the Atlantic Coast and visiting the offshore island of Trinidad on 1 September 1591, then proceeding west to Margarita for reinforcements.

5 MAY 1590. The six-gun, 30-man bark *Young* of 60 tons, captained by William Irish (a 29-year-old gentleman of the retinue of Sir George Carey—later Lord Hunsdon), arrives off southern Puerto Rico. Ten days later he captures a 40-ton Spanish merchantman bound from Santo Domingo toward Havana with sugar and hides. Irish subsequently unites with *Falcon's Flight* off Cape Tiburón (southwestern Haiti) to capture another Spanish vessel before steering north toward Newfoundland accompanied by his first prize.

10 MAY 1590. A privateering expedition reaches Dominica, having been raised by the London merchant John Watts Sr.: the 22-gun, 160-ton flagship *Hopewell* (alias *Harry and John*) under Capt. Abraham Cocke; the 160-ton *Little John* of Christopher Newport; and the 35-ton pinnace *John Evangelist* of William Lane. Two days later the flagship and pinnace steer northwest toward Puerto Rico, leaving *Little John* temporarily off Dominica to intercept arriving Spanish vessels; all three later rendezvous at Saona Island.

29 MAY 1590. Cocke's reunited trio of vessels blockades the southern coast of Santo Domingo for two weeks, capturing the 60-ton Spanish merchantman *Trinidad* and two smaller island frigates on 17 and 24 June.

12 JULY 1590. ***Cape Tiburón.*** This morning off southwestern Haiti, Cocke's formation is joined by Edward Spicer's 80-ton *Moonlight*—also called *Mary Terlanye*—and the 30-ton pinnace *Conclude* of Joseph Harris (alias Master Harps). Around noon 14 Spanish sail approach out of the east, being five days out of Santo Domingo and bound toward the plate fleet assembly point at Havana escorted by Capt. Vicente González's galleon.

Most of the Spanish convoy scatters southwest, pursued until nightfall by the eight English privateers, who take a single small prize. Next dawn, *Hopewell, Moonlight,* and *Conclude* find the 350-ton, nine-gun Spanish vice-flagship *Buen Jesús* of Capt. Manuel Fernández Correa and Master Leonardo Doria anchored nearby, securing it despite a stout, four-hour resistance; four of the 68 Spanish crewmembers are killed and six are wounded by the long-range fire.

Little John and *John Evangelist* chase González's main body toward Jamaica, exchanging broadsides with the flagship and driving two merchantmen aground before the six or seven Spanish vessels that survive reach Santiago de la Vega (modern-day Kingston). English boat parties then refloat both beached vessels, one of which sinks; the other is sailed northwest toward Cape Corrientes (western Cuba) when Newport's triumphant pair of privateers quits Jamaica's coastline on the morning of 14 July.

18 JULY 1590. Toward sunset, Newport's *Little John* and *John Evangelist* sight three Spanish merchantmen off Los Organos Keys (west of Havana); they prove to be stragglers from Commo. Rodrigo de Rada's Mexican convoy, which has entered the Cuban capital five days ago. The English open fire in the darkness, compelling one ship to reverse course toward Veracruz.

Next morning the rovers close in on the remaining pair: Master Miguel de Acosta's *Nuestra Señora del Rosario* and Juan de Borda's 60-ton pinnace *Nuestra Señora de la Victoria.* The Spaniards lash both vessels together, and after a long-range artillery exchange the English fight their way aboard *Victoria.* In hand-to-hand combat, Newport's right arm is struck off; five of his men are killed and 16 are wounded before the Spanish can be driven from the vessel.

The victors then discover *Victoria* to be so badly holed that it sinks within 15 minutes. *Rosario* meanwhile retreats inshore, suffering two killed and eight injured before running aground on the western end of Los Organos, which allows its crew to escape ashore.

21 JULY 1590. Cocke arrives off Cape San Antonio (southwestern Cuba) with *Hopewell, Moonlight, Conclude,* and the prize *Buen Jesús,* becoming becalmed and thus watching impotently as the Cartagena treasure fleet of Adm. Juan de Uribe Apallua passes by farther out at sea. It enters Havana safely on 29 July.

16 AUGUST 1590. While at Notre Dame Bay (northern Newfoundland) with his captive Spanish consort, Irish's bark *Young* is attacked by seven French fishing ships and 15 pinnaces of the Catholic League under Jean Blondel; his prize is wrested away after a day-long struggle.

LATE MAY 1591. The 150-ton Spanish merchantman *Nuestra Señora del Rosario* of Master Francisco González is captured off La Yaguana (modern-day Léogâne, Haiti) by *Margaret* of 60 tons under Capt. Christopher Newport and Master Cuthbert Grippe; the 50-ton *Prudence* under Capt. John Brough and Master Thomas Harding; the 120-ton *Centaur* under Capt. William Lane and Master John Gall; the 80-ton *Pegasus* under Capt. Stephen Michell and Master Abicocke Perry; the 150-ton *Little John* of Capt. Michael Geare and Master William Bendes; and pinnace *Fifth Part.* The first pair and the latter foursome have only recently arrived in the West Indies, meeting and uniting forces to attack the Spaniards. *Rosario*'s crew is released and their vessel pillaged.

9 JUNE 1591. Having earlier become separated from Lane's quartet of English privateers, the 200-ton *Hopewell* (alias *Harry and John*) of Capt. William Craston and Master George Kennell meets with the following fleet between Saint Kitts and Puerto Rico: the 130-ton bark *Burr* of under Capt. William Irish; the 35-ton *Swallow* under Capt. Ralph Lee and Master Anthony Daniel; and the 30-ton *Content* under Capt. Nicholas Lisle and Master William King. They have been sent by Sir George Carey to raid Spanish targets in the Caribbean and proceed west together with *Hopewell* toward Cuba.

23 JUNE 1591. ***Corrientes.*** At 5:00 A.M. *Burr, Hopewell, Swallow,* and *Content* arrive between Capes Corrientes and San Antonio (southwestern Cuba),

sighting six sail. Believing they might be treasure ships from Cartagena, the English close, only to discover the force is Admiral de la Rivera's 700-ton flagship *Nuestra Señora del Rosario,* Vice Adm. Aparicio de Arteaga's 650-ton *Magdalena,* two other large galleons, and a pair of galleys bent upon giving battle.

A long-range exchange erupts at 7:00 A.M. and lasts for the next three hours, after which the English formation scatters. *Burr* explodes from a fire in the magazine; Captain Irish and 16 survivors are rescued by *Swallow.* The 100-ton galleys *San Agustín* and *Brava* chase the smaller English vessels into the shallows before they finally slip away at nightfall.

29 JUNE 1591. *Hopewell* and *Swallow* return to Cape Corrientes (Cuba), finding de la Rivera gone. They unite with *Centaur, Pegasus, Little John, Prudence, Fifth Part,* and Capt. John Oker's *Lion* out of Southampton. Three days later—while part of the formation is watering inshore—*Pegasus* and *Centaur* intercept the passing 150-ton Spanish merchantmen *Santa Catalina* of Master Martín Francisco de Armendáriz, and the 100-ton *Gift of God,* while *Lion* and *Swallow* take another prize; all are bound from Santo Domingo to Havana.

The English agree, on 5 July, to sail together with their prizes until they pass the Cuban capital. Upon reaching Matanzas *Prudence* and *Lion* continue up the Old Bahama Channel toward England with the prizes; *Centaur, Pegasus, Hopewell, Little John, Swallow,* and *Fifth Part* reverse course to take up station west of Havana and await incoming ships.

15 JULY 1591. Early this morning the English privateers *Pegasus* and *Little John* intercept the 300-ton Spanish merchantman *San Juan* of Master Agustín de Paz as it approaches Havana from Veracruz. It is pillaged and burned; four smaller coasters are also captured by other ships in the squadron as they arrive from Santo Domingo.

Early the next day, the first elements of the main Spanish convoy arrive from Mexico under Admiral Navarro; the 240-ton merchantman *Santa Trinidad* of Master Alonso Hidalgo is far ahead and is taken at 1:00 P.M. by *Centaur* and *Little John.* The prize proves so rich that the rovers decide to quit their watch outside Havana and sail home before the rest of the Spanish plate fleet sorties on its homeward leg.

14 APRIL 1592. ***Newport's Sweep.*** An English privateering expedition arrives at Dominica from the Canaries: the 150-ton flagship *Golden Dragon* under Capt. Christopher Newport and Master Robert Keble; 70-ton *Prudence* under Capt. Hugh Merrick and Master John Paul; 50-ton flyboat *Margaret* under Capt. Robert Thread and Master James Bragge; and the 30-ton pinnace *Virgin* under Capt. Henry Kedgell and Master Cuthbert Grippe. Despite commanding only 200 men, Newport intends to use his force for more than seaborne interceptions. He aims to make amphibious descents to conquer and hold such places as La Yaguana (modern-day Léogâne, Haiti) for an advance English base.

After refreshing provisions the rovers seize a 300-ton Portuguese slaver bound for Cartagena, diverting it to San Juan de Puerto Rico, where they land two wealthy prisoners on 18 April to raise ransom for the slaves. Tired of waiting, Newport coasts west toward Aguada, selling captives and scuttling the ship before standing away toward Mona Island.

18 APRIL 1592. After enduring calms during the transatlantic crossing to Brazil and suffering through a storm off the River Plate, Cavendish makes a late-season attempt to round the Strait of Magellan into the South Pacific with his 400-ton galleon *Dudley* (flag; formerly *Leicester*), the 240-ton *Roebuck* of John Cocke, the 140-ton *Desire* of John Davis, and *Black* pinnace of Captain Toby (a bark called either *Delight* or *Dainty* having turned back earlier). Fierce winter weather and contrary winds oblige the fleet to reverse course one month later; on the night of 21–22 May (O.S.) Davis leads *Desire* and *Black* pinnace into what the English call Port Desire (Puerto Deseado, Argentina), leaving Cavendish and Cocke to continue north alone to São Vicente Bay (Santos, Brazil).

Upon reaching that place the two are unable to cross the bar; with boat parties being attacked by local Portuguese forces they proceed farther east-northeast to Espirito Santo, where they suffer 55 men killed or captured in an attempt on two anchored ships. That night *Roebuck*'s master, Robert Tharlton, parts company with *Dudley* and lays in a course for England; Cavendish returns southwest in a desperate bid to refit. Again meeting with hostility off São Sebastião Island, he maroons his sick and steers for England, but he succumbs en route.

20 APRIL 1592. An English expedition reaches Dominica after raiding the Canary Islands during its transatlantic passage: *Salomon* of 26 guns, 200 tons, and 100 men under Capt. William King and Master John Wildes; and *Jane Bonaventure* (6/35/26) under Capt.

William Richards and Master James Perryman. Having refreshed provisions, the rovers seize a 100-ton slaver with 270 blacks from Guinea (West Africa), which they carry toward Puerto Rico. A captive 70-ton English merchantman is also cut out from San Juan's harbor during a nocturnal descent; afterwards most of the slaves are sold on the western half of the island, the 70-ton merchantman is scuttled, and the 100-ton slaver is detached to England under prize Master George Simson.

King subsequently visits Mona and Saona Islands, Cape Tiburón (southwestern Haiti), Jamaica, Grand Cayman, Cape Corrientes, and the Tortuga Keys (Florida), intercepting a handful of small coastal craft.

25 APRIL 1592. After touching at Mona and Saona Islands—and intercepting three small Spanish coasters—Newport makes a nocturnal descent upon Ocoa (Dominican Republic). Its inhabitants sight his ships at dusk and so disappear inland; little booty is found in the town and aboard two frigates in the harbor.

EARLY MAY 1592. De Berrio's lieutenant, Domingo de Vera Ibargüen (or Ibargoyen), reaches the Antillan island of Trinidad with a Spanish contingent from Margarita, founding a settlement called San José de Oruña by 19 May. De Berrio arrives some time later, delegating de Vera to continue exploring up the Orinoco River for El Dorado while himself rebuffing attempts by the rival Spanish governor at Cumaná—Francisco de Vides—to lay claim to Trinidad.

19 MAY 1592. Newport's squadron intercepts a Spanish coaster outside Trujillo (Honduras) then sends boat parties inside the harbor to attack a handful of anchored vessels despite fire from its batteries.

25 MAY 1592. Newport makes a descent upon Puerto Caballos (modern-day Puerto Cortés, Honduras), occupying the town without opposition—its inhabitants fled inland upon learning of the raiders' approach. The 200 empty buildings are pillaged until next evening, when the English reembark and reverse course east. Later they sight a 200-ton Spanish merchantman, anchored offshore, which is set ablaze and abandoned by its crew before the English can board.

4 JUNE 1592. After refreshing provisions on Trinidad Island following a transatlantic crossing, an English expedition reaches Margarita Island (Venezuela): *Challenger* of 120 tons under Capt. Benjamin Wood and Master John Tomlyn; *Mineral* (100 tons) under Capt. Richard Vavasour and Master Richard Cawson; *Pilgrim* (90 tons) under Capt. Thomas Coche and Master William Elsemore; and *Flight* (formerly the French *Florissant*) (50 tons) under Capt. Thomas Turner and Master Robert Abraham. They coast westward, touching at Cape de la Vela, Ríohacha (Colombia), and Santa Marta without taking any prizes. *Mineral* and *Flight* lose contact during a storm.

16 JUNE 1592. Newport's three privateering vessels make a second assault upon Trujillo (Honduras), only to be repelled by the fully alerted defenses. A storm scatters the English squadron and its prizes, so each commander makes his best way to England by circling Cuba and touching at Florida.

22 JUNE 1592. Wood's *Challenger* and *Pilgrim* meet the 50-ton privateer *Moonshine* of Capt. John Myddelton and Master John Hore off Hicacos Point (northeast of Cartagena, Colombia), accompanied by a 30-ton Spanish prize under Robert Barrett (alias Frost). Together the rovers attempt to capture a beached frigate but suffer numerous men drowned and killed by a Spanish counterattack; in addition, 13 are captured, including Barrett. The English then stand away toward Cuba.

EARLY JULY 1592. King's pair of privateers appears outside Havana and is fired upon for an hour by the defending batteries; it is chased west an hour later by the galleys *San Agustín* and *Brava* ("having 27 banks on a side," according to an English eyewitness). The rovers then coast to Cabañas, which they pillage before besting the pursuing galleys in a three-hour, long-range exchange on 11 July.

15 JULY 1592. King's *Salomon* and *Jane Bonaventure* are joined 20 miles north of Cabañas (Cuba) by Wood's *Challenger, Pilgrim, Mineral,* and perhaps *Flight;* Lane's *Centaur, Affection,* and *Little John* (having returned for another West Indian campaign; *see* 15 July 1591); Henry Roberts's 140-ton *Exchange* out of Bristol; and the 60-ton bark *Randall* (alias *Canter*) of Capt. George Kennell and Master Thomas Smith. Together they run down and pillage a 50-ton Spanish ship, whose crew flees ashore, then steer toward Havana to mount a close blockade.

28 JULY 1592. This morning the English privateers blockading Havana sight a vessel approaching out of the west, which they pursue. It proves to be a 60-ton merchantman arriving from Puerto Caballos (modern-day Puerto Cortés, Honduras), which puts into Chorrera Inlet—three miles short of the Cuban capital—in a desperate bid to gain sanctuary.

As nine privateer pinnaces close in on the prey, 50 Spanish harquebusiers and musketeers under Capt. Francisco de Rojas race along the beach from Havana to the rescue, seconded by the galleys *San Agustín* and *Brava* under Capt. Cristóbal Pantoja. The troops succeed in fending off the English encroachments with long-range volleys until 4:00 P.M., by which time all valuables have been removed from the ship. The raiders then carry off the empty vessel, sending it to England under prize Master Lawrence Cocke.

AUGUST 1592. After refitting *Desire* and *Black* pinnace at Port Desire (Argentina) and suppressing a mutiny, Davis makes a second attempt to round the Strait of Magellan. The pinnace is lost with all hands; *Desire* eventually returns to its original starting place.

MID-JUNE 1593. The 31-gun *Edward Bonaventure* of Capt. James Lancaster, homeward-bound after a trading venture to the Far East, reaches the Gulf of Paria (eastern Venezuela) in hopes of refreshing provisions before continuing its Atlantic voyage. After pausing for eight days the English sail northwest to Mona Island to refit.

AUGUST 1593. An English expedition raised by the Earl of Cumberland sights Saint Lucia: *Anthony* of 120 tons and 70 men under Capt. James Langton and Master John Paul; *Pilgrim* (100/55) under Capt. Francis Slingsby and Master John Dix; and *Discovery* (a pinnace). They refresh provisions for three days on Martinique and capture the Portuguese caravel of Domingo Díaz before steering to Margarita Island (Venezuela), where one night 38 men are set on the eastern coast to raid the pearl fisheries. They overrun the town of El Macanao and receive 2,000 ducats in order to spare buildings; they reembark five days later and coast westward.

EARLY SEPTEMBER 1593. After several months exploring Guiana and Trinidad for Raleigh, another English expedition arrives off Margarita Island (Venezuela), hoping to effect its conquest: *Roebuck* (flag) of 300 tons under Capt. Sir John Burgh and Master John Bedford; *Golden Dragon* (150) under Capt. Christopher Newport and Master Andrew Shillinge; *Prudence* (100) under Capt. Thomas Wally and Master Thomas Warne; *Virgin* (50) under Capt. Henry Kedgell and Master Cuthbert Grippe. Burgh, a 31-year-old veteran of military campaigns in the Low Countries, disembarks 100 men before dawn at Pueblo del Mar, striking inland to occupy the principal town of Asunción. He is ambushed en route by Gov. Juan Sarmiento de Villandrade, who, roused by Langton's raid in August, has marshaled a militia force at nearby Pampatar to repel such attacks. The grassland is ignited behind the invaders, who are obliged to retreat to their boats, suffering 16 casualties.

4 SEPTEMBER 1593. This Saturday afternoon, Langton's three English privateers appear off Punta de Araya (Venezuela) with their small Portuguese prize but do not disembark because of the Spanish militia gathered farther south at Cumaná under Lt. Gov. Francisco Gutiérrez Flores. Next morning Langton attempts leading a boat party inside Cariaco Gulf to raid Ostias. He is intercepted by a piragua bearing 20 Spanish soldiers and is obliged to retire after a long-range exchange with the rest of the town's defenders. After stripping and releasing the prize, the English subsequently stand away westward.

25 SEPTEMBER 1593. Having refreshed on Aruba and Curaçao, Langton appears outside Ríohacha (Colombia), only to find its defenders alerted and all valuables, along with noncombatants, sent inland. Rather than storm the beaches for little profit, the English loose off a few rounds, implement a desultory blockade, and depart north by the evening of 27 September.

28 OCTOBER 1593. Richard Hawkins—the 33-year-old illegitimate son of Sir John Hawkins—arrives off Brazil (6 degrees south latitude) with his 300-ton, 20-gun flagship *Dainty* (formerly *Repentance*), the 100-ton, eight-gun storeship *Hawk,* and the 60-ton pinnace *Fancy,* intending to round the Strait of Magellan into the Pacific.

10 NOVEMBER 1593. Richard Hawkins's flotilla approaches Santos (Brazil), pausing to refresh provisions before anchoring off Santa Ana Island five days later to set up camp ashore. Half his original 200 men having

died of disease, Hawkins scuttles his storeship and redistributes its crew among his two remaining vessels. Native Portuguese militia also attack his encampment, and a few passing coasters are intercepted.

30 NOVEMBER 1593. Battered by a storm in his unsuccessful bid to reach Newfoundland from northwestern Hispaniola (Haiti), Lancaster's *Edward Bonaventure* returns to Mona Island. Two or three days later a five-man anchor watch cuts the cable and maroons 19 companions ashore, only to be wrecked at Azua (the north side of Ocoa Bay, Dominican Republic) and captured by the Spaniards shortly thereafter.

NOVEMBER 1593. Governor Sarmiento of Margarita Island (Venezuela) is killed in an engagement between a Spanish galley and an English or Flemish interloper.

MID-DECEMBER 1593. After refreshing at Cape Tiburón (southwestern Haiti) and slowly coasting clockwise around Hispaniola, Langton appears at the mouth of the Zoco River and leads a boat party about 15 miles upstream to plunder Spanish ranches. The English return to their ships and shift operations to Caucedo Point on the eastern side of Santo Domingo Bay, mounting a two-and-a-half-month blockade that nets nine small prizes.

28 DECEMBER 1593. Richard Hawkins quits his anchorage off Brazil to attempt the Strait of Magellan. Four days later his pair of privateers intercepts a 100-ton Portuguese ship bearing the new governor-designate and 50 soldiers for Angola; the English strip it of all provisions before releasing it on 4 January 1594.

11 JANUARY 1594. Sailing south from Brazil toward the Strait of Magellan, Richard Hawkins's flagship *Dainty* loses contact with the pinnace *Fancy* of Master Robert Tharlton in the vicinity of the River Plate; the latter reverses course and makes for England.

4 FEBRUARY 1594. This Friday afternoon off Pedernales Point (near Ocoa, Dominican Republic), the Spanish frigates of Capts. Juan Montero and Juan Fernández de Santana—having sortied from Santo Domingo—surprise an English pinnace, which earlier had been detached from Langton's squadron to sweep west along this coastline. Next morning Langton's flagship *Anthony* and a second English pinnace intercept the victorious Spaniards as they return toward Ocoa, capturing Fernández de Santana's frigate after a bloody struggle and compelling Montero to strike.

MID-FEBRUARY 1594. Tiring of his Santo Domingo blockade, Langton proceeds to Jamaica, where he seizes two Spanish barks and combines their cargoes aboard one before detaching it to England with a nine-man crew. (Near Europe, the 40-ton prize is pillaged by an 80-ton French Catholic League privateer out of Le Havre.)

20 FEBRUARY 1594. Richard Hawkins's *Dainty* stands into the Strait of Magellan, emerging into the Pacific by 8 April and steering north. On 25 April the English interlopers pass Valdivia (Chile), anchoring off Mocha Island four days later.

16 MARCH 1594. ***Langton at Puerto Caballos.*** Having separated from his consort *Pilgrim* off southwestern Cuba, Langton appears before the Honduran port of Puerto Caballos (modern-day Puerto Cortés) with his flagship *Anthony* and a captured Spanish frigate. Flying false colors, the English seize the harbor pilot boat then demand the surrender of the seven merchantmen awaiting cargo inside under Diego Ramírez. Rebuffed, Langton stands in next morning and engages in a day-long gun duel with the Spanish anchor watches, finally launching a blazing, 20-ton prize against Ramírez's flagship on 18 March, which breaks the defenders' will and convinces them to abandon ship.

The rovers subsequently board Ramírez's 250-ton *San Diego* (whose master, Luis de Sevilla, lies slain), Andrés del Corro's 200-ton *Espíritu Santo,* Benito González Urrazo's 120-ton *San Antón de la Magdalena,* Baltasar de Riberol's 140-ton *Presentación,* and three lesser vessels, holding them for ransom. When the Spaniards ashore refuse to pay, Langton burns a couple of the merchantmen; concentrating all his booty aboard Ramírez's former flagship, he then departs with the prize. The English return to Plymouth "amid great rejoicings and excitement" by 25 May.

17 APRIL 1594. Having earlier joined forces off Cape Verde (West Africa), William Parker of Plymouth and Jérémie Raymond of Cherbourg capture the Spanish bark *Nuestra Señora de Loreto* off Saona Island, sending the prize to England.

25 APRIL 1594. The English privateers *Golden Dragon* of Christopher Newport and *Prudence* of John Brough shoot their way into Puerto Caballos (Honduras), seizing the four deserted Spanish vessels in its roadstead. They venture ashore briefly at 6:00 P.M. before retiring back aboard ship and submitting a ransom de-

mand. When it is rejected next day by Gov. Gerónimo Sánchez de Carranza, Newport fires two of the empty prizes and sails off with the other pair.

2 MAY 1594. ***Hawkins in the Pacific.*** Having refreshed provisions at Mocha Island (Chile), Richard Hawkins stands out to sea once more and weathers a ten-day storm. He then penetrates the roadstead at Valparaíso, pillaging four anchored merchantmen while Spanish militia watch impotently from ashore under Gov. Alonso de Sotomayor, knight of the Order of Santiago. The English also seize a fifth coaster as it arrives from Concepción. They then restore all of the prizes to the Spaniards in exchange for a ransom of 25,000 ducats before departing north a few days later for Coquimbo and Arica.

Word of the depredation reaches García Hurtado de Mendoza, Marqués de Cañete and viceroy of Peru, by 17 May. Having been forewarned of the English presence off South America, he instantly orders his brother-in-law, Beltrán de Castro y de la Cueva, knight of the Order of Alcántara, and veteran Adm. Alonso de Vargas to prepare to sortie from Callao with their 26-gun, 500-ton flagship *San Pedro y San Pablo,* the 28-gun, 600-ton vice–flagship *San Francisco y Nuestra Señora del Rosario,* the smaller galleon *San Justo,* and three lesser consorts, manned by 500 men.

Shortly after sailing the Spaniards sight their opponents at 9:00 A.M. on 31 May between Chincha Alta and San Vicente de Cañete but are unable to close before nightfall because of high winds, which damage their vessels aloft. *Dainty* thus slips through under cover of darkness, proceeding northwest to Puná Island (Ecuador); the dismasted Spanish flagship, the galleon *San Justo,* and the pinnace *San Juan* limp back into port for repairs. Realizing that his enemies only have one ship and a pinnace with 75 crewmembers between them, de Castro soon puts back to sea with *San Francisco y Nuestra Señora del Rosario* and a 14-gun galley-zabra under Miguel Angel Felipón to continue the pursuit.

3 MAY 1594. After a two-hour exchange of gunfire off Cape Saint Nicholas Môle (Haiti), the English privateer *Centaur* of Capt. William Lane captures the French Catholic League traders *Espérance* and *Princesse* out of Le Havre.

15 MAY 1594. This dawn four privateer ships, two frigates, and three pinnaces under Parker and Raymond materialize outside Trujillo (Honduras), intercepting the dispatch vessel of Francisco Rodríguez as it departs, who yields information about the weakness of nearby Puerto Caballos (modern-day Puerto Cortés). Moreover, a young black slave named Diego de los Reyes or Diego el Mulato is aboard, willing to turn against his Spanish masters. (He later becomes a famous rover in his own right; *see* 15 July 1633, 11 August 1633, 23 June 1634, and 28 July 1634 in Part 3).

17 MAY 1594. ***Parker and Raymond at Puerto Caballos.*** Shortly after midnight the Anglo–French formation under Parker and Raymond, guided by Diego de los Reyes, deposits 55 men from two pinnaces near the sleeping Honduran port of Puerto Caballos and silently secures its outposts. Parker and Raymond divide their landing party into two columns, surrounding the houses of Governor Sánchez de Carranza and naval Commander Ramírez before resistance can be mounted.

The Spaniards flee into the jungle, leaving the town in enemy hands for the next two weeks, during which buildings are ransacked and the plunder is loaded aboard four barks in the harbor. Parker and Raymond set sail with their prizes but become separated ten nights later. One of Parker's barks subsequently founders at sea; the other loses contact with the flagship *Richard* off Newfoundland on 11 July. Both regain Britain by the end of the month.

EARLY JUNE 1594. Newport's *Golden Dragon* unites with John Myddelton's *Affection* off western Cuba to waylay Spanish vessels making for Havana.

24 JUNE 1594. After refreshing provisions for four days in Atacames Bay (near Esmeraldas, Ecuador), Richard Hawkins spots a vessel out at sea and detaches his pinnace to investigate. At 9:00 A.M. next day he weighs with his flagship *Dainty* and takes up station farther west off Cape San Francisco for two days before returning and discovering his dismasted consort in nearby San Mateo Bay.

The English duo is preparing to stand back out into the Pacific by the morning of 29 June when another two sail come around Cape San Francisco. Believing them to be Peruvian treasure ships, Hawkins sends his repaired pinnace out to reconnoiter, only to see it chased back by Felipón's 14-gun galley-zabra. De Castro's *San Francisco y Nuestra Señora del Rosario* follows close astern and attempts to run aboard *Dainty* but is checked by a heavy broadside. The pinnace's crew meanwhile strives to regain their flagship and concentrate forces but are intercepted by the galley-zabra; a few survivors manage to clamber aboard over the bowsprit.

Both sides then exchange long-range salvos for the next couple of days, the English toppling Felipón's mainmast on 30 June before finally surrendering to the Spaniards by the afternoon of 1 July. Hawkins suffers a half-dozen personal wounds, 27 killed, 17 wounded, and 29 captured among his crew; Spanish losses total 28 dead and 22 injured out of 300. De Castro installs Felipón as prize master and tows the badly damaged *Dainty* to the Pearl Islands, reaching Perico (west-northwest of Panama City) to a tumultuous reception on 19 July. Despite being promised honorable terms, most of the English captives are tried by the Inquisition and condemned as galley slaves, Hawkins recuperating and eventually regaining England. *Dainty* is renamed *Nuestra Señora de la Visitación* and incorporated into the Peruvian squadron.

30 JUNE 1594. Myddelton's *Affection* intercepts a small Spanish caravel approaching Havana, seconded by the 130-ton English privateer *Jewel* of Capt. Richard Best and Master Edward Farrier.

1 JULY 1594. Lane's *Centaur* captures the Mexican merchantman *Nuestra Señora de la Soledad*—outward-bound from Trujillo (Honduras)—between Cuba's Organos Keys and Havana. Despite the sickness ravaging the Spanish crew, Lane sails his prize home to England, arriving by August.

6 JULY 1594. Myddelton's *Affection* sights a 100-ton Spanish merchantman 35 miles west of Havana; the crew beaches the vessel to escape ashore. The English refloat the prize and send it to England.

MID-JULY 1594. Myddelton makes another interception outside Havana—only to be captured himself when two Spanish pinnaces push out of the harbor and overwhelm his seven-man boat party. The English captain is eventually sent to Spain as a prisoner aboard the 1595 plate fleet.

28 JULY 1594. Best's *Jewel* finds a Spanish merchantman of 1,100 tons adrift in the Gulf of Mexico, without foremast and bowsprit and abandoned by its crew. The English board the vessel, strip it of remaining goods, and set it ablaze.

SUMMER 1594. A French vessel under Capt. François Riffault arrives off northern Brazil, separated from two other consorts intended to found a colony in the region. Discouraged, Riffault returns home, leaving a small group of settlers on Maranhão Island (near modern-day São Luis) under Charles Des Vaux. The latter befriends the local Tupinambá natives, residing among them for several years and helping them fight their Tobajare neighbors, who consequently become allies of the Portuguese.

Tupinambá warrior, by Albert Eckhout

(A decade later Des Vaux returns to France and persuades Henri IV that the foothold might be expanded into France Équinoxiale ["Equinoctial France"], prompting the king to assign that task to Huguenot sea Capt. Daniel de La Touche, sieur de La Ravardière. He makes two reconnaissances of the area in 1604 and 1609, followed by a major colonization effort in 1612.)

16 JANUARY 1595. In Europe, France officially declares war against Spain.

JANUARY 1595. Near Puerto Rico, Geare's flagship *Michael and John* (formerly *Little John*) and the pinnace *Handmaid* under Thomas Stokes intercept the 40-ton, 14-man Spanish supply ship *Nuestra Señora de la Concepción* of Master Juan Camacho, which is conveying building materials and supplies from Seville to the plate fleets wintering at Havana. Its Spanish captain, Nicolás Lafora, ransoms the vessel and cargo by raising £200 in pearls and silver at Santo Domingo, presenting it to his captors.

The English also pillage a small Spanish frigate off Santo Domingo, as it arrives from San Juan de Puerto Rico, before steering west to blockade Cuba.

9 FEBRUARY 1595. The 20-year-old English nobleman Robert Dudley sights the West Indian island of Trinidad with his 200-ton, 140-man flagship *Bear* (formerly *Peregrine*) and a pair of captured Spanish caravels from the Canaries renamed *Intent* and *Regard,* commanded by Benjamin Wood and one Wentworth. The illegitimate son and impoverished heir of Elizabeth I's former favorite, the Earl of Leicester—and inheritor of the deceased Cavendish's *Dudley* and *Roebuck* (*see* 18 April 1592)—Dudley originally intended to round the Strait of Magellan into the Pacific but has been dissuaded by the queen. He therefore aims to chart Trinidad and the mouth of the Orinoco River for the establishment of an English colony.

Anchoring off Cedros Bay, the young adventurer refreshes provisions and explores Trinidad's shoreline for two weeks before detaching his prizes toward England on 24 February. By 2 March he sends a 13-man boat party under cousin Thomas Jobson to explore the mainland around the Orinoco; the latter returns 16 days later with a partial report. Having been joined on 13 March by an English pinnace under George Popham, Dudley sets sail north with his new consort by 22 March.

23 MARCH 1595. Shortly after midnight Dudley captures a small Spanish merchantman 75 miles north of Grenada after a chase.

28 MARCH 1595. Dudley arrives off Puerto Rico, circling the island before anchoring off Cape Rojo three days later to set his Spanish prisoners ashore in hopes of raising ransom for their captive vessel. When payment is not forthcoming the English strip the prize on 3 April and burn it before standing away northeast toward Bermuda next day.

MARCH 1595. The large English privateer *Rose Lion* of Capt. Thomas West captures the hired Dutch ship *Fortuin* "with smale fight" near Santo Domingo (it is transporting Spanish cargo from Seville). West carries this prize into Plymouth by June, where a protracted—and eventually unsuccessful—legal battle brought by the Dutch owners ensues.

1 APRIL 1595. ***Raleigh's Adventure.*** In a bid to restore his influence with Elizabeth I, the disgraced courtier Sir Walter Raleigh arrives at Trinidad with a ship under Capt. James Whiddon and Master John Douglas and a small bark under Captain Cross. He has lost contact with two other consorts during the transatlantic crossing and failed to rendezvous with either Dudley or Popham, recently departed from this same coastline (*see* 9 February 1595). Raleigh disembarks 100 soldiers on 4 April and captures Trinidad's principal Spanish settlement of San José de Oruña, along with Gov. Antonio de Berrio.

After refreshing provisions and exploring for a fortnight, the English are rejoined by their two missing ships—*Lion's Whelp* of George Gifford and another under Lawrence Keymis—thus raising their total numbers to 300–350 men. Steering south to the mainland opposite, Raleigh probes the numerous streams of the Orinoco delta before leaving his ships anchored offshore late in May, leading 100 men upriver to make a detailed exploration aboard a small galley, barge, two wherries, and a boat. Roaming through myriad waterways and establishing peaceful relations with the natives, the English return to their vessels a few weeks later, then circle west to unsuccessfully assault Cumaná (Venezuela) on 22 June, depositing de Berrio and departing empty-handed two days later.

(Upon returning to England Raleigh exaggerates the wealth of this new land in hopes of being commissioned by the queen to lead a military expedition for its conquest or raising private capital toward this same end; neither prospect succeeds.)

3 APRIL 1595. Spanish Vice Adm. Sebastián de Arencibia sorties from Havana with a galleon, caravel, and two shallops to patrol the coastline in anticipation of the arrival of the Mexican plate fleet.

9 APRIL 1595. The 973-ton galleon *Nuestra Señora de Begonia,* flagship of the Tierra Firme plate fleet bound for Spain, is damaged by a hurricane and staggers into San Juan de Puerto Rico almost a month after departing Havana. Aboard are 2–3 million pesos in silver, which Adm. Sancho Pardo y Osorio transfers into the citadel of Gov. Pedro Suares. An *aviso* is then dispatched across the Atlantic to request that Philip II

Raleigh's destruction of San José de Oruña and capture of Gov. Antonio de Berrio of Trinidad; a stylized contemporary engraving

send a squadron to the rescue—but word of the treasure also reaches the English court via a privateer, prompting Elizabeth I to instruct Drake and Hawkins to attempt its capture.

14 APRIL 1595. Having prowled past Havana and commandeered an abandoned Spanish coaster, Geare is lying off Cabañas with his flagship *Michael and John,* Stokes's *Handmaid,* and their prize when they sight Vice Admiral de Rencibia's squadron at dawn. Due to faint breezes the Spaniards have difficulty closing the six miles separating the formations but eventually manage to row their caravel and two shallops into action.

Geare's flagship repels the attack of the caravel and shallop *Coloma,* killing 13 of the 30 soldiers aboard the shallop under Ensign Guerrero and wounding another seven or eight while fighting their way aboard. Nevertheless, the English are compelled to forsake the vessel and retreat out to sea once Rencibia's heavy galleon is finally towed into range by its two boats, leaving Stokes's *Handmaid* and Geare's first prize to fall into enemy hands. The English suffer eight killed and 17 captured (including Stokes) compared to 16–18 killed and numerous injured among the Spaniards.

After pursuing Geare's *Michael and John* along the coast, Rencibia's galleon returns to Havana by 21 April to refit; the rest of the formation follows two days later. The English flagship departs alone across the Atlantic.

APRIL 1595. John Ridlesden arrives in the West Indies with his 60-ton bark *Bond* and the pinnaces *Scorpion* and *Violet* (alias *Why Not I?*), intercepting a small Spanish coaster. Having plundered the prize, *Bond* sails for England, leaving both pinnaces to patrol the Caribbean until the end of July, when they depart for the Azores and home.

4 MAY 1595. Wood and Wentworth's caravels appear outside Ríohacha (Colombia), requesting permission from its governor, Lic. Francisco Manso de Contreras, to trade. He refuses, and the English depart.

16 MAY 1595. Parker again returns to raid Puerto Caballos (modern-day Puerto Cortés, Honduras) with a 200-ton flagship, three 40-ton consorts, and two pinnaces. Finding the town abandoned by its residents, the next day the English detach their two pinnaces farther west to probe into Golfo Dulce (Izabal Lake and El Golfete, Guatemala). They reverse course nine days later after securing little plunder.

Parker subsequently retires offshore to Guanaja Island, where he meets the vessels under Wood and Wentworth. The rovers sail north together to take up station off Cuba's Cape San Antonio.

18 MAY 1595. Captains Amyas Preston and George Somers reach Dominica with their privateer ships *Ascension* and *Gift,* Captain Jones's *Darling* (owned by Raleigh), William Prowse's *Angel,* and a pinnace to make amphibious descents throughout the Spanish West Indies. For this purpose they are bringing a disembarkation force of 300 men—many of them professional soldiers; they are further accompanied by Capt. Moses Willis's *Archangel* and two other vessels out of Southampton, which they have met at sea. After refreshing for six days the English steer south to Los Testigos Islands (Venezuela), celebrating a muster ashore on 28 May before continuing southwest against Margarita Island.

29 MAY 1595. The Preston-Somers expedition sights Margarita Island, exploring nearby Coche Island next day; they capture a Puerto Rican caravel and a few Spanish pearl fishermen.

1 JUNE 1595. Eight English privateer vessels and a small prize under Preston and Somers appear before Cumaná (Venezuela), seizing three caravels in the bay but otherwise finding the residents alerted to their presence. Having lost the element of surprise, the English accept a modest ransom of foodstuffs to depart in peace next evening.

6 JUNE 1595. ***Caracas.*** After anchoring off Guiacamacuto (a mile and a half east of La Guaira, Venezuela), Preston and Somers lead a 300-man force overland, surprising the small, mostly empty fortress of La Guaira and occupying it without opposition. Next afternoon a patrol of 40–50 Spanish riders descends out of the mountains from Caracas (the full name is Santiago de León de Caracas), but they withdraw when a like number of English musketeers emerge from the keep under Captain Roberts and offer battle.

Convinced the rovers must soon depart without attempting anything further, the Spanish concentrate their strength along the main road leading up to Caracas but fail to maintain close watch upon their enemies' movements. This allows Preston and Somers to march a column undetected through the rain during the night, up a little-known track high into the mountain range, and appear unexpectedly outside Caracas by afternoon on 8 June.

Again little resistance is encountered since most of the city's militia is gathered along the main road. The noncombatants flee inland while a lone elderly Spanish rider named Alonso Andrea de Ledesma bravely attempts to check their progress with his lance and shield; he is shot dead. The invaders enter the city by 3:00 P.M., remaining in possession for five days before finally setting it ablaze and returning to La Guaira by noon on 14 June with some booty (having failed to secure any ransom). Next day Preston and Somers also set the fortress afire and depart west.

16 JUNE 1595. This morning the Preston-Somers squadron appears outside Chichiriviche (Venezuela), Somers leading in a boat party that burns three anchored Spanish vessels.

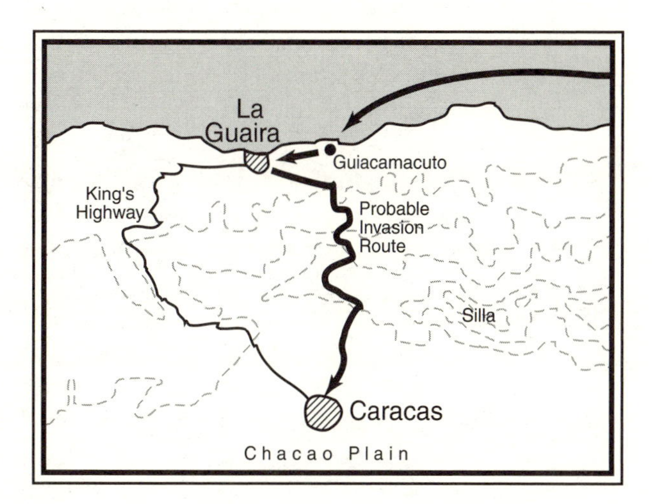

Preston and Somers's capture of Caracas

20 JUNE 1595. ***Coro.*** Having groped his way along the coast, Preston this morning leads his formation into Coro Bay (Venezuela) and ferries all his troops ashore by 11:00 P.M. The English attempt a nocturnal approach on the town but are checked at a roadside barricade, which the Spaniards defend "very strongly." Yet the invaders fight their way through, gaining Coro by the next morning with relatively few casualties.

Nevertheless, its buildings stand empty; the residents, having received ample warning of the advance, have fled inland with their valuables. Around this same time, Preston learns that a storm has struck the English anchorage, thus parting the cables of Somers's 50-man pinnace and driving it out to sea. Preston therefore orders Coro torched, hastening his column back to the coast by 22 June to set sail in search of his colleague. Somers is located next evening; after gingerly probing the Laguna de Maracaibo's entrance, the discouraged raiders steer away toward Hispaniola on 26 June.

30 JUNE 1595. The Preston-Somers squadron sights Hispaniola and next day anchors off Cape Tiburón (southwestern Haiti) to refresh provisions. Dysentery rages throughout the vessels, killing 80 men and destroying morale. When the formation resumes its cruise on 8 July Preston's *Ascension* and Somers's *Gift* are forsaken by all their consorts, except for a pinnace.

12 JULY 1595. The trio of privateer vessels under Preston and Somers anchors off Jamaica, remaining four days before proceeding toward the Caymans, reaching Cape Corrientes (southwestern Cuba) by 22 July.

16 JULY 1595. Raymond materializes before Puerto Caballos (modern-day Puerto Cortés, Honduras) with three French privateer ships, a pinnace, and a galliot. After attacking and burning the town he passes on toward Golfo Dulce (Izabal Lake and El Golfete, Guatemala) before retiring east to Utila Island. There he is surprised by a Spanish force out of Trujillo and is killed.

23 JULY 1595. Raleigh's trio of vessels sights the three privateers under Preston and Somers off Cape San Antonio (western Cuba), remaining in company for a week and chasing a couple of Spanish frigates before losing contact.

4 AUGUST 1595. Preston and Somers quit their blockade outside Havana and steer for England.

7 NOVEMBER 1595. Off Guadeloupe, five Spanish frigates under Commo. Pedro Tello de Guzmán—sent to retrieve the silver bullion from Puerto Rico—spot two small sail and give chase. One of these is overtaken while the other (a small English vessel called the *Delight*) is pursued to within sight of a much larger fleet, compelling the Spaniards to sheer off. Their lone prize proves to be the 35-ton *Francis* of one Captain Wignol with 24 crewmembers. Captured sailing instructions reveal that the nearby fleet is under Drake and Hawkins, bound to attack the silver galleon at San Juan de Puerto Rico. Tello de Guzmán therefore hastens to that destination, arriving six days later.

13 NOVEMBER 1595. Tello de Guzmán warns Admiral Pardo of the approach of Drake and Hawkins. At a general conference attended by all senior Spanish commanders and Bishop Antonio Calderón it is decided to resist the English within port rather than out at sea. San Juan's garrison of 400 troops is augmented by the galleon's 300 seamen, 500 from Tello de Guzmán's frigates, and 300 Puerto Rican militia. A log boom is also stretched between the harbor castle (*morro*) and Cañuelo Key; the galleon and frigates are anchored close to the entrance, ready to be sunk as blockships.

The English meanwhile pause at the Virgin Islands for three days, holding a muster before action. Hawkins has fallen ill on 8 November, his condition deteriorating so rapidly that Drake assumes overall command of the royal warships *Garland, Defiance* (flag), *Elizabeth Bonaventure* (vice-flag), *Hope, Adventure, Foresight,* and a score of lesser auxiliaries. His original 2,500 men are now much reduced by disease.

22 NOVEMBER 1595. ***Drake's Defeat.*** At dawn the English fleet comes within sight of Escambrón Point, standing in so close as to be fired upon by the four-gun Boquerón battery under Ens. Pedro Vásquez. It proceeds west toward the capital behind a flotilla of boats taking soundings, arriving opposite San Juan early this afternoon to anchor near Cabrón Inlet—just as Hawkins dies. At 5:00 P.M. the five-gun Cabrón battery under Capt. Alonso Vargas opens fire, sending one round directly into the cabin of Drake's *Defiant,* narrowly missing the commander in chief but killing Gen. Sir Nicholas Clifford and seriously wounding three other officers. Drake consequently moves his fleet out to sea, returning under cover of darkness to anchor farther away, off Cabras Island.

The raiders spend 23 November reconnoitering the shoreline for a nocturnal assault. At 10:00 P.M. 25 boats crammed with several hundred men row around Cabras and Cañuelo Islands into San Juan's harbor, attacking the anchored Spanish ships with incendiary devices. The shore batteries and anchor watches blaze away blindly, unable to prevent the English boats from reaching and igniting the frigates *Santa Isabel, Santa Magdalena,* and *Santa Clara.* However, when they burst into flames they also illuminate the attackers' craft, facilitating a counterfire that compels the English to draw off with 50 dead and missing and a similar number wounded. Spanish casualties total 40 dead; the frigate *Santa Magdalena* burns to its waterline.

Drake's fleet gets under way at 8:00 A.M. the next day, circling out to sea and returning toward San Juan's harbor mouth by 4:00 P.M., prompting the defenders to scuttle a large merchantman and two lesser vessels as blockships. The English instead heave-to, anchoring halfway between Cabras Island and the mainland. On the morning of 25 November seven or eight English boats probe as far east as Boquerón before withdrawing; that afternoon several blockaders pursue an arriving Spanish caravel until it runs aground at Cangrejos Beach, its crew escaping ashore.

Discouraged, Drake and Col. Gen. Thomas Baskerville (second-in-command since Hawkins's death) decide to sail away in search of easier prey at Panama. The Spanish are left exultant at their unexpected success. On 20 December they dispatch a pair of frigates and two smaller escorts with the silver, which reaches Spain safely.

14 DECEMBER 1595. Baskerville overruns Ríohacha (Colombia) by disembarking his troops from boats, then is joined by Drake's main fleet from the marshaling point off Cape de la Vela. The Spaniards have already withdrawn inland, so the English spend two weeks fruitlessly attempting to extort a ransom from Governor Manso de Contreras to spare its empty buildings. Eventually the city is set ablaze on 29 December, along with nearby La Ranchería and Tapia, after which the raiders sail southwestward.

30 DECEMBER 1595. Drake and Baskerville capture Lt. Gov. Francisco Ordóñez Flores of Santa Marta (Colombia) but find his city abandoned, so they burn it and depart. Too weak to assault Cartagena because of the diseases raging throughout their crews, the English press on toward the Panamanian coast.

6 JANUARY 1596. ***Defense of Panama.*** Drake and Baskerville drop anchor at Nombre de Dios without opposition, its few Spanish defenders retreating into the jungle. Baskerville quickly pursues with 600–700 men and occupies Venta de la Quebrada two days later, but at 8:00 A.M. on 9 January he encounters 70 Spanish troops under Capt. Juan Enríquez Conabut dug in atop Capirilla Hill to bar their advance across the isthmus.

This terrain is well chosen, the English suffering heavy casualties while vainly attempting for three hours to dislodge the defenders from this narrow pass. When the Spaniards are reinforced by an additional 50 harquebusiers under Capt. Hernando de Lierno Agüero, Baskerville orders a retirement. Sick and demoralized, his contingent rejoins Drake at Nombre de Dios by 22 January, and three days later the invaders depart westward.

20 JANUARY 1596. Drake and Baskerville's expedition anchors off Escudo de Veraguas Island (Panama), ravaged by disease. A 37-man party is massacred by the Spanish residents of Santiago del Príncipe when it attempts to draw water from the Fator River on the mainland opposite. Eventually Drake orders the fleet to sail east toward Portobelo on 2 February but dies of dysentery aboard his flagship *Defiance* off Buenaventura Island the night of 28–29 January 1596 (O.S.) and is buried at sea next morning. Baskerville assumes command of the fleet and, after contemplating a repeat attack against Santa Marta, steers his disheartened followers toward Jamaica.

28 FEBRUARY 1596. After relieving San Juan de Puerto Rico, 13 Spanish galleons sortie from Cartagena under Adm. Bernardino Delgadillo y Avellaneda. On 11 March they sight 14 of Drake's surviving ships anchored in Guaniguanicos Cove on Pinos Island (Cuba), taking on wood and water. The Spaniards immediately attack, scattering their opponents while Vice Adm. Juan Gutiérrez de Garibay's three-ship vanguard captures a 300-man English prize; the prisoners are put to work on Havana's fortifications. The Spaniards suffer 80 casualties and a sunken ship.

22 MARCH 1596. John Crosse's English pinnace *Little Exchange* is captured near Havana by elements from Delgadillo's Spanish fleet.

MAY 1596. Captain Anthony Hippon's pinnace *Scorpion* captures a Portuguese ship bound from La Yaguana (modern-day Léogâne, Haiti) to Cartagena.

SPRING 1596. Dutch traders build a fort called Ter Hooge on a small island at the confluence of the Cuyuni, Mazaruni, and Essequibo Rivers of the "Wild Coast" (near present-day Bartica, Guyana). A

A late-sixteenth-century Spanish galleon; modern drawing by Berenguer

Hispano-Portuguese counterexpedition destroys the stronghold later this year.

SUMMER 1596. ***Sherley's Cruise.*** After receiving at least 80 casualties in a brief occupation of Santiago in the Cape Verde Islands during his transatlantic passage, the 31-year-old adventurer Sir Anthony Sherley (or Shirley) arrives at Dominica with his 300-ton *Bevis,* the 150-ton *Black Wolf,* the 250-ton galleon *Constance,* the 200-ton *George,* the 140-ton *George Noble,* the 80-ton *Little John,* a galley, and a pinnace. Having refreshed, the English steer south toward Margarita Island (Venezuela), eventually prowling as far west as Santa Marta (Colombia), obtaining little booty. At Santa Marta Sherley is forsaken by one of his consorts, then leads his remaining seven ships northwest against Jamaica.

AUTUMN 1596. Newport arrives at Dominica with his privateer ship *Neptune,* accompanied by Michael Geare's pinnace. Despite cruising off Hispaniola and Honduras, they fail to take many prizes. When the vessels part company en route from Cape Corrientes toward "the Crown" (near Havana), Newport is left without his auxiliary and must return to England, largely empty-handed.

4 FEBRUARY 1597. After reconnoitering as far west as Point Negril, Sherley reverses course and anchors his squadron opposite Jamaica's principal town of Santiago de la Vega (Spanish Town—near modern-day Kingston), sending 230 armed men inshore. The Spanish governor, Lic. Francisco de Nabeda Alvarado, initially considers opposing the disembarkation with his few militia, but upon perceiving the invaders' overwhelming strength he instead retreats into the jungle with all residents.

The English consequently remain in undisputed possession of the harbor, being joined by the Dutch *Maen* of Middelburg and Geare's English pinnace. After 40 days they depart together west-southwest to attack Puerto Caballos (modern-day Puerto Cortés, Honduras). Although that assault proves successful, pickings continue to be sparse; by the time Sherley appears off Havana on 23 May he has been abandoned by all other consorts. (Geare, for example, steers toward Campeche, where he captures 12 tons of logwood and at least one prize.)

Reaching Newfoundland by 25 June Sherley returns to England the following month, "alive but poor."

EARLY JUNE 1597. ***Ransom of Ríohacha.*** After chancing to meet in the West Indies, the following ships unite for a combined assault against the Colombian port of Ríohacha: *Centaur* (flag) of 120 tons under John Watts Jr.; *Affection* (120) under Henry Middleton; *Pegasus* (80) under Richard Knottesford; *Golden Dragon* (150) under Anthony Hippon; *Mosquito* (pinnace); and *Little David* (auxiliary). Accompanied by three or four other vessels—possibly prizes—the flotilla takes and sacks the town, holding it for ransom. Part of the payment is intercepted while being delivered to Watts by Humphrey Reynolds's 90-ton *Lion's Whelp;* Reynolds is compelled to surrender the booty to his more powerful colleague shortly thereafter.

At this point *Mosquito* loses company with Watts's formation, taking a prize near Havana before returning home to England by August. Next month Reynolds's *Whelp* also reaches London with another Spanish prize.

SUMMER 1597. After exploring the coast of Guiana, 37-year-old John Ley captures a Spanish frigate off Cumaná (Venezuela) with his bark *John,* renaming this prize *Black Ley* and sailing it to England by late August.

21 SEPTEMBER 1597. ***Parker at Campeche.*** Having separated from Sherley, Parker appears before the Mexican port of Campeche with his 120-ton flagship *Prudence,* the 25-ton *Adventure* under Capt. Richard Henne, and a pinnace. After examining the shoreline from a distance, the English feint a retirement out to sea that evening but return under cover of darkness—guided by a Spanish turncoat named Juan Venturate—

and stealthily set a landing party ashore. The men penetrate the suburb of San Román and surprise Campeche's sleeping residents, stampeding the frightened survivors into San Francisco convent; general looting erupts.

Next dawn, Alderman Francisco Sánchez assembles numerous volunteers at his country estate farther inland, marching to the rescue. Upon approaching, he is joined by other Spaniards sallying from the beleaguered convent under Alderman Pedro de Iterián; together they oblige the raiders to retreat back aboard their ships after two hours of heavy fighting in the main square, during which Parker (among many others) is wounded. Among the prisoners left behind in Spanish hands is Venturate, who, after a swift trial, is put to death by red-hot tongs.

The defenders then sortie aboard a commandeered merchant frigate to pursue Parker farther out into the Gulf of Mexico. Soon the Spaniards are unexpectedly joined by a coast-guard frigate under Capt. Alonso de Vargas Machuca, sent from Caucel by the governor of nearby Yucatán. The pair of vessels corner *Adventure,* subduing it after a ferocious exchange in which 11 of 16 English crewmembers are killed. The Spanish frigates return to Campeche with their prize; Parker follows and remains outside for the next 17 days hoping in vain to ransom his colleagues.

SEPTEMBER 1597. Watts's *Centaur* takes a Spanish vessel off the north coast of Hispaniola, sending the prize home to Bristol.

1 JUNE 1598. Cumberland arrives off Dominica with his 600-ton flagship *Malice Scourge* captained by Watts, plus the 400-ton vice-flagships *Merchant Royal* of Sir John Berkeley and *Ascension* of Robert Flick; the 400-ton merchantman *Alcedo* of Thomas Coche (later John Ley), and *Prosperous* of John Langton; 300-ton *Centurion* of Henry Palmer, *Consent* of Francis Slingsby, and *Sampson* of Henry Clifford; 250-ton galleon *Constance* of Hercules Fulgham or Foljambe; 210-ton *Guyana* of Christopher Colthurst; 200-ton *Margaret and John* of Edward Dixon; 190-ton *Royal Defence* of Henry Bromley; 120-ton *Affection* of William Fleming, and *Anthony* of Robert Careless; 80-ton *Pegasus* of Edward Goodwin; the "old frigate" *Discovery* of William Harper; pinnace *Scout* of Henry Jolliffe; bark *Ley* of John Ley; plus two unnamed barks.

These bear 1,700 men, whom Cumberland intends to lead in the conquest of Puerto Rico, thereby securing a major English stronghold in the West Indies. After refreshing his fleet for a week, the Earl transfers to the Virgin Islands on 11 June, celebrating a final muster three days later before laying in a course for San Juan.

16 JUNE 1598. ***Seizure of Puerto Rico.*** This morning Cumberland disembarks 700 men at Cangrejos Bay (about a dozen miles east of San Juan), then marches until nightfall, when he is checked at a bridge one mile short of the city by ten Spanish regulars and 80 Puerto Rican militia under Capt. Bernabé de Sierra Alta. The first English assault is repelled with 20 deaths and a like number wounded; the Spaniards suffer four fatalities, including Sierra Alta.

Next morning the English use their boats to outflank the Spanish position, disembarking at Escambrón Point while bombarding Boquerón Redoubt (called Red Fort by the English). By evening all the defenders have been obliged to retreat, so on 18 June Cumberland sweeps unopposed into San Juan's streets, finding the citizenry has fled; 250 Spanish soldiers are ensconced within the Morro Citadel under Gov. Antonio de Mosquera.

A formal siege is instituted—artillery being ferried ashore from the English fleet—until the Spaniards request terms on 30 June. Next day surrender is consummated; Mosquera and his followers are repatriated to Cartagena several weeks later. Meanwhile disease sweeps through the English ranks, causing so many deaths that within a month and a half Cumberland relinquishes his conquest. Sailing for England with some ships on 14 August, he is followed by his main body under Berkeley on 23 September. The campaign costs 700 English lives: 60 due to battle, 40 from accidents, the remainder on account of illness.

JANUARY 1599. The English ship *Neptune* of Capt. John Paul, accompanied by the pinnace *Triton,* captures a Spanish vessel near Puerto Rico.

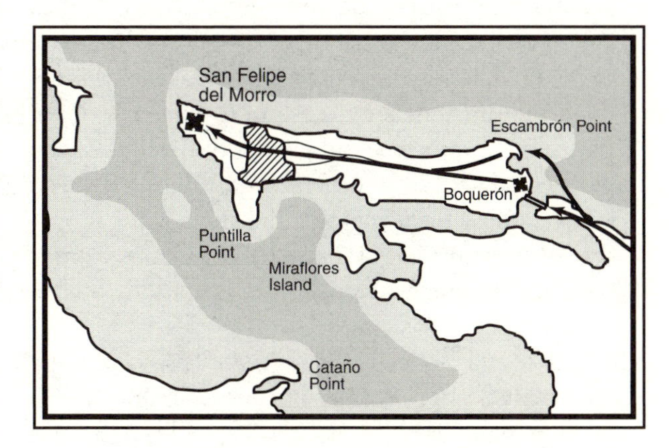

Cumberland's capture of San Juan de Puerto Rico

9 FEBRUARY 1599. A Dutch squadron arrives at Rio de Janeiro from Guinea, composed of *Mauritius* (flag) of 250 tons and 24 guns under Olivier van Noort; *Hendrik Frederick* of 300 tons and 25–28 guns under Jacob Claeszoon van Ilpendam; plus the 50-ton *Hoop* under Jacob Janszoon Huydecoper and *Eendracht* under Pieter Esaiszoon de Lint. The squadron wishes to buy fresh provisions, but the Brazilian residents—Portuguese vassals to the Spanish king—offer token assistance. Van Noort therefore slips a party ashore, which is ambushed; seven men are killed and several are captured.

The expedition's objective is to round the Strait of Magellan, trading or fighting with South America, then gain the Dutch commercial outposts of the Far East. Feeling the season too far advanced for such an attempt, van Noort scuttles *Eendracht* and sails off to winter at either Saint Helena or Ascension Island. Failing to discover either of his destinations, he instead puts into a bay near Puerto Deseado and Cape Vírgenes (southern Argentina), subsisting on penguins and fish.

6 APRIL 1599. Another Dutch squadron arrives from West Africa off the eastern approaches to the Strait of Magellan:

Ship	*Tons*	*Guns*	*Men*	*Commander*
Hoop (flag)	500–600	28	130	Simon de Cordes
Liefde (vice-flag)	300	26	110	Gerard van Beuningen
Geloof	320	18–20	109	Sebald de Weert
Trouw	220	18	96	Jurien van Bockholt
Blijde Boodschap	150	16	56	Dirck Gerritszoon Pomp (alias Dirck China)

Jacob Mahu, the expedition's original leader, died during the transatlantic crossing, being succeeded by Cordes.

Like van Noort's enterprise, this one is intended to penetrate the Pacific, trade with South America, then sail on to the Far East. But Cordes ignores the advice of his English pilots to immediately make an attempt upon the strait, preferring instead to winter in Great Bay (subsequently renamed Cordes Bay). This decision proves costly, as 120 crewmembers die during the next few months—including van Bockholt, who is succeeded in command of *Trouw* by Baltasar de Cordes, the admiral's younger brother.

JUNE 1599. The English ships *Golden Phoenix* of Capt. John Adey and *Flying Hope* of Capt. William Cabreth (plus the pinnace *Handmaid*) intercept a Spanish vessel near Havana and send it to London.

3 SEPTEMBER 1599. ***Pacific Penetrations by the Dutch.*** After quitting its Patagonian anchorage on 23 August, Cordes's squadron stands into the Strait of Magellan, becoming scattered by high seas and mist. The flagship *Hoop* and vice-flag *Liefde* stand on separately toward their agreed rendezvous of Santa María Island (opposite Concepción, Chile); *Geloof* and *Trouw* turn back to aid the damaged *Blijde Boodschap.* Five days later, they lose sight of *Blijde Boodschap,* being driven south by strong contrary winds. On 26 August, *Geloof* and *Trouw* seek refuge in a bay nine miles north of the western mouth of the strait, remaining anchored until 2 December.

4 NOVEMBER 1599. *Liefde* reaches the Santa María rendezvous to find that Captain van Beuningen and 27 men have been slaughtered while attempting to trade on Mocha Island.

7 NOVEMBER 1599. Having been accorded a friendly reception by the natives of the Chonos Archipelago, Cordes steps unwarily ashore at Lavapié Point with 23 men, only to be set upon and massacred by its Indians. The flagship's survivors sail on to Santa María next day, where they meet the vice-flag *Liefde.*

13 NOVEMBER 1599. Having departed the haven near Puerto Deseado, van Noort's trio of ships begins a separate attempt to penetrate the strait, taking three and a half months to accomplish the feat because of unfavorable weather.

17 NOVEMBER 1599. After being driven far south by fierce winds, Gerritszoon and 22 survivors aboard *Blijde Boodschap* surrender to the Spanish at Valparaíso, their vessel being sailed to Callao as a prize.

24 NOVEMBER 1599. The Spanish inhabitants of Valdivia (Chile) are massacred by an Indian uprising.

27 NOVEMBER 1599. Unable to achieve anything more off South America, *Hoop* and *Liefde* strike out west into the Central Pacific, the latter being lost with all hands. (The flagship eventually reaches Japan, where its English pilot, William Adams, lives and prospers for about 20 years, providing the inspiration for James Clavell's novel *Shogun*).

2 DECEMBER 1599. News of the Dutch penetrations into the Pacific reach the Peruvian viceroy, Luis de Velasco, at Lima. Six days later, the captive *Blijde Boodschap* (*see* 17 November 1599) is sailed into Callao, prompt-

ing de Velasco to prepare eight armed vessels and a launch, bearing 1,119 men, to protect the coast against the enemy.

11 DECEMBER 1599. After putting out into the South Pacific once more, de Weert's *Geloof* becomes separated from *Trouw,* compelling him to reverse course in despair, so as to regain the Atlantic via the strait.

16 DECEMBER 1599. While traversing the strait from west to east, de Weert's *Geloof* encounters van Noort's trio beating in the opposite direction. Neither group is able to offer the other succor, so de Weert reluctantly continues his passage and exits into the Atlantic on 21 January 1600. *Geloof* will be the only one of Cordes's five vessels to regain Holland, 36 crewmen still alive.

28 DECEMBER 1599. Morale on van Noort's struggling vessels reaches such a low point that Vice Admiral Claeszoon is tried for mutiny and marooned. This squadron does not gain the Pacific until 29 February 1600.

DECEMBER 1599. The 100-ton, 77-man English ship *Trial* of Capt. Thomas Cowper prowls off Margarita Island (Venezuela), making several captures before returning to Bristol by May 1600.

1 JANUARY 1600. Two Spanish galleons and a patache bearing 300 men are sent from Peru to locate the Dutch intruders off Chile; another half-dozen warships remain off Pisco under Juan de Velasco—the viceroy's nephew.

FEBRUARY 1600. The English ships *Golden Phoenix* of John Adey and *Flying Hope* of William Cabreth, plus the pinnace *Handmaid,* intercept a 25-ton Spanish bark near Barbados bound from Guiana to Cartagena with 120–130 black slaves. The captors sell the prisoners at Margarita Island (Venezuela) for 60 ounces of pearls, before venturing farther west and raiding Ríohacha (Colombia).

MARCH 1600. *Trouw* of Baltasar de Cordes, after becoming separated from de Weert and seeing his crew reduced to about 50 men, receives a friendly reception from the natives of Carelmapu (overlooking Chiloé Island).

Meanwhile Juan de Velasco escorts the annual Peruvian treasure convoy from Callao to Panama without encountering any Dutch; he is eventually shipwrecked and drowned off California.

21 MARCH 1600. Having become separated from *Hendrik Frederick,* van Noort's *Mauritius* and *Hoop* arrive off Mocha Island, where the admiral goes ashore and trades peaceably with its natives. Four days later, while sailing between Mocha Island and Santa María Island, the Dutch sight the Spanish ship *Buen Jesús* of Francisco de Ibarra, capturing it the next day. On 28 March, van Noort burns another two vessels and captures a third (*Picos*) off Valparaíso.

At Huasco on 1 April he scuttles his two Spanish prizes then releases most of the captives. Shortly thereafter van Noort strikes out into the Pacific, eventually becoming the fourth commander—and the first Dutchman—to circumnavigate the globe.

SPRING 1600. Two Dutch forts, named Nassau and Orange, are built by Zeeland settlers on the eastern banks of the Xingu River, deep within the Amazon Delta (near modern-day Porto de Moz, Brazil).

APRIL 1600. Baltasar de Cordes occupies the Spanish settlement of Castro by deceiving its commander, Baltasar Ruiz del Pliego, into believing that it is about to be attacked by a horde of hostile natives.

2 MAY 1600. *Hendrik Frederick* intercepts a Spanish vessel off Concepción (Chile).

4 JUNE 1600. After occupying Castro for a few weeks, Baltasar de Cordes's men are routed by a company of Spaniards led across from Osorno by Capt. Francisco del Campo. The Dutch suffer 26 killed; 23 survivors hasten back aboard *Trouw* to stand out into the Pacific, eventually reaching Tidore in the Far East. Meanwhile del Campo executes nearly 50 Indians at Castro for aiding the Dutch intruders.

18 JUNE 1600. *Hendrik Frederick* captures a Spanish vessel off Arica (Chile).

11 AUGUST 1600. *Hendrik Frederick* seizes a becalmed Spanish vessel in the Gulf of Panama before proceeding west-northwest past Costa Rica and Nicaragua; eventually it strikes out across the Pacific.

FEBRUARY 1601. ***Portobelo Strike.*** After raiding Cubagua Island (Venezuela) and capturing a Portuguese slaver off Cape de la Vela (Colombia), Parker appears off Portobelo (Panama) with his flagship *Pru-*

dence, accompanied by the 60-ton *Pearl* of Capt. Robert Rawlins and a 20-ton pinnace. They slip past the harbor castle and surprise the city proper, driving its 100 defenders inland under Gov. Pedro Meléndez. The raiders then set fire to the suburb of Triana and stand out to sea with 10,000 ducats of booty.

JULY 1601. The English ship *Archangel* of Capt. Michael Geare and the pinnace *James* of David Middleton roam off the Venezuelan coast.

OCTOBER 1601. A Spanish coast-guard galley from Cartagena (Colombia) sights an English pinnace with two prizes near Ríohacha, capturing Capt. Simon Bourman and 38 of his crewmembers. (Born of a Spanish mother, Bourman is eventually released upon the official cessation of hostilities three years later.)

JANUARY 1602. Geare's *Archangel* and Middleton's *James* operate off Cuba, taking three prizes before sailing for England.

MAY 1602. Newport returns to the Caribbean with his flagship *Neptune,* accompanied by *Diana* of Capt. Edward Glanvill; they take prizes off Guava and near Havana before recrossing the Atlantic to England.

NOVEMBER 1602. While lying at the smuggling outpost of Guananahibes (northern Hispaniola), three English vessels—Geare's *Archangel,* Newport's *Neptune,* and Hippon's *Phoenix*—form a partnership with five French slavers to attack a pair of Spanish galleons expected soon at Puerto Caballos (modern-day Puerto Cortés, Honduras).

24 JANUARY 1603. While making for Puerto Caballos (modern-day Puerto Cortés, Honduras), the combined Anglo-French flotilla of Geare and Newport raids Jamaica for supplies, only to be repelled with some losses.

17 FEBRUARY 1603. ***Raid on Puerto Caballos.*** Eight Anglo-French ships of 300–350 tons apiece stand into the Honduran port of Puerto Caballos (modern-day Puerto Cortés), detaching seven boats with 200 men and light artillery to board two partially laden Spanish galleons at anchor in the roads: Capt. Juan de Monasterios's 600-ton *Nuestra Señora del Rosario* and Francisco Ferrufino's 400-ton *San Juan Bautista.* The galleons put up a stout resistance, repelling their attackers for eight hours before finally surrendering, having suffered 11 killed and 16 wounded.

The triumphant rovers loot the vessels and buildings ashore for the next 18 days before falling out along national lines over their captives' fate. (Spanish eyewitnesses later declare that the French wished to kill them all, with the English refusing to do so.) Eventually, both groups depart with *San Juan Bautista* as their sole prize, *Rosario* being left behind a stripped hulk. The French tack upwind to Guanahibes (Hispaniola) while the English steer downwind toward Cuba.

LATE FEBRUARY 1603. Captain William Fisher's *John and Francis* captures nine Spanish pearling vessels off Ríohacha (Colombia), holding them for ransom.

LATE MARCH 1603. Fisher's *John and Francis* takes a Spanish prize off Cuba.

30 APRIL 1603. Fisher captures another Spanish vessel off Cuba.

MAY 1603. Geare, Newport, and Hippon take an additional pair of Spanish prizes near Havana before standing out through the Straits of Florida into the North Atlantic toward England.

This same month the ship *Elizabeth and Cleeve* and a smaller pinnace under Capt. Christopher Reeve—recently arrived in the West Indies from London—briefly occupy Santiago de Cuba, relieving its church of assorted booty. He subsequently makes an unprofitable descent upon Jamaica before seizing a prize off Cape San Antonio.

1 AUGUST 1603. Spanish Adm. Fulgencio de Meneses arrives from across the Atlantic at Guadeloupe with a 30-vessel plate fleet, most of it bound for Mexico. His wood and watering parties are unexpectedly attacked by Carib warriors ashore, suffering 20 killed and 30 wounded. In the resulting confusion, Meneses's 700-ton flagship *San Juan Bautista* and two other galleons run aground; set ablaze by their panic-stricken crews, they are consumed down to their waterlines.

28 AUGUST 1603. Cleeve's pair of English vessels, in company with Capt. Andrew Miller's ship *Neptune* and the pinnace *Dispatch,* take two Spanish prizes in the Old Bahama Channel north of Cuba. Earlier they were detached from Admiral Meneses's plate fleet at Guadeloupe to convey the new governor-designate of Florida and other passengers and cargo to Havana.

An English privateer ship firing salutes while standing into the French Huguenot port of La Rochelle

The rovers instead deposit their captives at Baracoa before standing away with their prizes—renamed *Christopher* and *Andrew*—for the smuggling port of Guanahibes on the northern coast of Hispaniola.

(Upon his eventual return to Plymouth in May 1604 Cleeve is forced to restore much of this booty after the Spanish ambassador brings a lawsuit through the courts of King James I.)

Lesser Hostilities (1604–1609)

The death of Elizabeth I on 24 March 1603 (O.S.) leads to the succession to the English throne of Scottish-born James I, who concludes peace with Spain by signing the Treaty of London in August 1604. Both nations are in effect drained and their treasuries bankrupt, so that for a period only minor frictions plague the New World.

29 April 1604. At dawn two dozen armed Frenchmen slip ashore near Manzanillo (Cuba) from the ship and smaller auxiliary of Gilbert Giron to seize hostages in reprisal for money and goods owed him by local Spanish traders. (The previous year Lt. Gov. Lic. Melchor Suárez de Poago has used a company of troops to arrest almost 100 Spaniards in and around Bayamo, thus discouraging the region's traffic with foreign seamen. Consequently, Giron finds himself unable to collect because of the new climate of fear and so resorts to more drastic methods.)

At Yara Hacienda he captures Bishop Fr. Juan de las Cabezas y Altamirano, Canon Francisco Puebla, Friar Diego Sánchez, and several other Spaniards, carrying them back aboard his ship. Eight days later the bishop is released, but when Giron comes ashore with ten musketeers and eight pikemen to claim his ransom he is set upon by 27 Spaniards under Gregorio Ramos and is killed along with most of his landing party. (Giron also leaves his name to Playa Girón, the beach where the Bay of Pigs invasion will be halted centuries later; *see* 17 April 1961 in Part 8.)

July 1605. In Madrid, the Spanish crown issues a *real cédula* (royal decree) ordering its American officials to execute any foreign corsairs or smugglers found in the New World, without allowing for any appeals.

2 August 1605. The governor of Santo Domingo and 150 Spanish soldiers appear at Bayahá (a town on the northwest coast of the island) to read aloud a proclamation from Philip III, complaining of its inveterate traffic with foreign smugglers and commanding that every resident be transferred to the south shore. The troops then begin putting buildings to the torch—along with structures at nearby Puerto Plata,

Monte Cristi, and La Yaguana (modern-day Léogâne, Haiti)—in order to hasten the evacuation.

Once complete, this "scorched-earth" policy will backfire for Madrid: rather than deny European traders contact ashore, it will instead present them with empty, beckoning establishments. The Spanish residents are obliged to leave behind planted crops plus the thousands of cattle and pigs roaming the fields; ships thus will find easy means of refreshing their provisions—and a tempting place for occupation.

6 NOVEMBER 1605. ***Araya Massacre.*** Fourteen Spanish galleons and four other ships bearing 2,500 men under Adm. Luis Fajardo materialize off Araya (Venezuela), carrying orders to exterminate the foreign poachers who have been gathering salt from its pans. Nine Dutch ships are sighted at anchor within Ancón de Refriegas, their crews salting ashore. Fajardo's men storm the beaches, and a one-sided bloodbath ensues, during which many of the Dutch are shot down or drowned while attempting to escape. Masters and pilots are then separated and hanged on hastily erected gallows; survivors are condemned to the galleys. Some 400 Dutchmen perish this day.

Fajardo's expedition remains another month, making seven more captures. One of them is a 100-ton Dutch ship with 26 men aboard, who kill 14 Spaniards in a desperate resistance before surrendering. All are put to the sword, except for one young man from Antwerp. The Spanish armada then stands away toward Santo Domingo, leaving behind evidence of their visit. When news of this action reaches the Netherlands a wave of outrage sweeps the Dutch nation, redoubling its resolve.

JANUARY 1606. Fajardo arrives off Manzanilla (northern Santo Domingo), setting a large contingent of troops ashore to help round up its remaining Spanish inhabitants and transfer them to the south side of this island in accordance with Madrid's depopulation plan. Word arrives of a large gathering of foreign smugglers farther west at Manzanillo (Guacanayabo Gulf, Cuba), so the Spanish admiral detaches his second-in-command, Juan Alvarez de Aviles, with six galleons and some support craft to deal with the interlopers.

7 FEBRUARY 1606. Alvarez comes upon 24 Dutch, six French, and one English vessel off Cape Cruz (Cuba) and engages. In the resulting affray the Spanish vice-flag is grappled by a Dutch ship commanded by Abraham Du Verne; the Spanish vessel's magazine

Sea battle between Dutch and Spanish warships

explodes, taking both to the bottom. The other smugglers escape in the confusion, after which Alvarez limps to Havana, accidentally losing his flagship and a flyboat in Jardines de la Reina Archipelago.

(The Fajardo-Alvarez fleets eventually reunite and return to Europe, where they are caught at anchor off Gibraltar in April 1607 by a powerful Dutch fleet, which destroys all vessels and slaughters most survivors in the water in retaliation for Araya.)

JUNE 1606. A small Dutch force attempts to capture a pair of Honduran galleons at anchor off Santo Tomás del Castillo (northern Guatemala). The Dutch lose a ship in their first attempt and are defeated again a few days later during a second try.

SUMMER 1609. ***Yanga's Revolt.*** In Mexico, raids by runaway slaves (*cimarrones*) become a serious nuisance in the region between Córdoba and Orizaba, where they burn farms, rob travelers, and kidnap wealthy citizens. Their leader is a fat, intelligent, aged African named Yanga, brought to New Spain as long ago as 1579. Having escaped his master, Yanga seeks refuge in the jungles around Orizaba's volcano, eventually establishing an independent fiefdom fed by a steady stream of runaways and delinquents.

By the summer of 1609 their activities are becoming so notorious they attract the attention of the reform-minded viceroy, Luis de Velasco ("the Younger"), in Mexico City; he orders Pedro González de Herrera to lead a military contingent from Puebla against their hideouts. Although no match for the Spaniards, who possess superior weaponry and armor, the *cimarrones* put up a spirited resistance. Yanga's principal lieutenant, an Angolan named Francisco de la Matosa, is finally captured and leads the Spanish army into the rebels' camp at night. Yanga escapes deeper into the jungle, only to be taken with his few remaining followers a short time later.

Impressed by the tenacity and fighting ability of the *cimarrones,* de Velasco decides to spare the rebels, resettling them in a new town named San Lorenzo de los Negros (literally, Saint Lawrence of the Blacks, 12 miles southeast of Córdoba) on condition that thereafter they serve His Catholic Majesty during wartime.

Part 3: Rival Outposts (1604–1659)

It is no good to fight the pirates and rebels in Indies by honest means; they must be intimidated by bloody war.
—Instructions from Philip IV to a Spanish admiral, the Marqués de Cadereyta (1633)

Early Footholds (1604–1619)

At the beginning of the 1600s, the West European powers lay spent from their exertions: the rebellious United Provinces have fought Spain to a standstill, as England did before them, while France remains racked by religious turmoil. For the New World there ensues a brief interlude of calm, as war-weary Europe begins rebuilding its economies, shaking off the horrors of war. However, this same truce inaugurates a somewhat more subtle form of aggression in the Americas, as the seaborne interlopers who previously visited Spanish America to smuggle and raid are now joined by law-abiding emigrants hoping to establish settlements ashore. In time, these colonies will prove infinitely more lethal to Spain's claims upon this continent than will any military or naval ventures.

8 April 1604. Daniel de La Touche, sieur de La Ravardière, appears off the mouth of the Amazon River with a ship and smaller auxiliary, anchoring the next evening opposite Yapoco. He explores the region in the direction of Cayenne until 18 May before visiting the pearl fisheries of Margarita Island (Venezuela) while returning home toward Europe.

20 August 1605. *Olive Branch* of Capt. Nicholas St. John sights Saint Lucia, having been blown off course during an attempt to reach Sir Olive and Charles Leigh's fledgling English colony in Guyana. Rather than continue beating south against contrary winds and currents, St. John and 67 settlers remain on Saint Lucia. Its natives initially prove friendly, but after a few weeks the English endure a massive attack by Carib raiders from nearby Saint Vincent, under chief Augramert. Only 19 settlers survive a ten-day onslaught, cowering behind a barricade of sea chests, after which they slip away at midnight on 26 September aboard a tiny craft.

26 April 1607 (O.S.). ***First Anglo-Powhatan War.*** The 100-ton ship *Susan Content* of veteran explorer Christopher Newport; the 40-ton *Godspeed* of Bartholomew Gosnold; and the 20-ton *Discovery* of John Ratcliffe arrive on the Atlantic Seaboard of North America from London, bearing 100 men and four boys to establish a new colony in Virginia. It takes them 17 days to work up a river they call the James (in honor of their monarch), founding a settlement called Jamestown with a triangular fort. Wilderness conditions are harsh, and the Indian chief Powhatan and his Algonquian vassals prove hostile; before too long only 38 Englishmen remain alive. One of these is 28-year-old Capt. John Smith, whose emergence as a leader will eventually ensure the colony's survival.

The First Anglo-Powhatan War of 1609–1614 sees these settlers—plus further reinforcements from England—gradually skirmish their way up the James, gaining control from Chesapeake Bay to the fall line thanks to superior weaponry and body armor. One of the few English defeats occurs in November 1609, when a force bent upon stealing corn is decimated by the Pamunkey subchief Opechancanough. But by the time Powhatan's favorite daughter, Pocahontas, is kidnapped by Samuel Argall in the summer of 1613, the native cause is essentially lost. As the line of tribal descendance runs matrilineally, Powhatan agrees to a truce with the English colonists next spring, after his daughter converts to Anglicanism and prepares to marry the planter John Rolfe. The aged Indian leader dies three years later, heartbroken by news of Pocahontas's death while she was visiting England.

Summer 1609. English brothers Robert and Michael Harcourt sail to the Guianas and leave a few colonists ashore before returning to England; the fledgling colony does not prosper.

28 July 1609. The Virginia Company flagship *Sea Venture,* bearing reinforcements under the veteran Adm. George Somers of Dorsetshire (*see* 18 May 1595 in Part 2) for the new English colony at Jamestown, is wrecked on the east end of Bermuda. Its survivors spend the next ten months building two

ships, *Patience* and *Deliverance,* to carry them to their destination. They finally reach Virginia in 1610, but they find conditions so harsh that they quickly return to Bermuda.

Somers dies shortly thereafter, and his body is carried home to England, along with glowing accounts of this new island. The survivors' adventures inspire William Shakespeare to write his play *The Tempest.* More settlers emigrate to Bermuda, and the island becomes known for a while as Somers Island.

30 JULY 1609. Samuel de Champlain leads a band of French settlers that, along with their Algonquian and Montagnais allies, defeat an Iroquois war party near Crown Point (modern-day Ticonderoga, on the banks of Lake Champlain between Vermont and New York State). Champlain slays two Iroquois chieftains with his harquebus, prompting the other warriors—who have never faced gunfire—to flee.

14–19 JUNE 1610. Champlain and his Huron and Algonquian allies defeat an Iroquois war band near the mouth of the Richelieu River.

MID-AUGUST 1610. The 55-ton *Discovery* of Capt. Henry Hudson arrives off Labrador, rounding Ungava Peninsula in hopes of discovering the Northwest Passage. After steering south, he becomes embayed and winters here, beginning his homeward voyage on 28 June 1611, only to have his crew mutiny and set him adrift in a small boat along with his 18-year-old son John ("Jack") and four loyal hands. None survives; only five of the 11 mutineers reach England.

26 JULY 1612. ***Equinoctial France.*** The ships *Régente, Charlotte,* and *Sainte Anne* arrive at Upaon-mirim Island (modern-day Guyavas, Brazil—temporarily renamed Sainte Anne by the French settlers, as they make landfall on this feast day). The expedition consists of 500 men under several captains: Daniel de La Touche, sieur de La Ravardière; Nicolas de Harley; François, sieur de Rasilly (also spelled Razilly or Rassily); Jacques de Riffault; and Charles Des Vaux. Eighteen years previously Des Vaux established a foothold in this region (*see* summer 1594 in Part 2), which the French crown now hopes to transform into a permanent colony.

Des Vaux reconnoiters upstream, reestablishing friendly relations with natives. A landing is made and a stronghold erected 50 miles from the sea on Maranhão Island (near modern São Luis), named Fort Saint Louis. This region is designated *France Équinoxiale* ("Equinoctial France"), after which Rasilly departs toward France for more colonists. When word of the settlement reaches Madrid, Philip III orders his Portuguese subordinates to drive the trespassers out. It will not be until two years later, however, that Brazilian Gov. Jerónimo de Albuquerque can assemble sufficient men and ships to challenge the French.

JULY 1612. Some 60 British settlers are sent aboard the Virginia Company ship *Plough* to help expand Bermuda; the island becomes a thriving English colony over the next few years.

JULY 1613. The French settlements at Saint Sauveur and Port Royal (modern-day Annapolis Royal, Nova Scotia) are attacked, sacked, and burned by 60 men under Capt. Samuel Argall on orders from Gov. Sir Thomas Dale of Virginia.

1 SEPTEMBER 1613. The French leader Champlain departs Huronia with a native war party for an expedition against the Iroquois. On 10 October they are ambushed by the Onondogas, Champlain being wounded; his Franco-Huron contingent is compelled to retire into its home base by 23 December.

SUMMER 1614. The English explorer John Smith arrives off Maine with two ships from London, surveying from Penobscot to Cape Cod during July and August, naming this shoreline New England.

LATE AUGUST 1614. ***Portuguese Retaliation.*** Jerónimo de Albuquerque, governor of Pernambuco and northern Brazil, disembarks 300 Portuguese militia and 230 native warriors from eight ships at the mouth of the Maranhão estuary (near modern-day São Luis), to begin operations against the intruder settlement of *France Équinoxiale* 50 miles upstream. A few months previously, Albuquerque has reconnoitered this region, installing a 40-man garrison at Rosário under Capt. Manuel de Sousa Dessa. The governor now rallies 1,000 Tobajara auxiliaries from around the base and advances as far as Guaxenduba by 26 October, entrenching his army at a place he dubs Fort Santa Maria del Maranhão—directly opposite the French fortification of Saint Joseph d'Itapary.

On the night of 11 November the first French counterattack occurs, when four barks glide downstream and board three Portuguese craft before the alarm can sound. Two hours before dawn on 19 November a much larger assault follows, when La Ravardière leads 200 French soldiers and 1,500 Tupinambá allies to attack Albuquerque's camp aboard four ships, three gunboats, and a host of canoes. La Ravardière succeeds in destroying many Portuguese vessels but loses 115 Frenchmen killed and nine captured during the assault. Thus, a truce is arranged two days later, whereby both sides agree to allow the territorial dispute to be decided by their respective governments back in Europe.

(But the 400 French Huguenot settlers are effectively doomed, being cut off from the sea by Albuquerque's forts; moreover, Paris is loath to antagonize Madrid early in the following year, when the Queen Regent Marie de Médici is arranging the marriage of her 13-year-old son, Louis XIII, to the Spanish princess, Anne of Austria. Very little diplomatic pressure is therefore exerted on La Ravardière's behalf.)

11–12 OCTOBER 1615. South of Lake Ontario in the Oswego region (modern-day New York State), Champlain unsuccessfully besieges a Seneca fort with a band of French, Huron, Algonquian, and Montagnais followers.

31 OCTOBER 1615. Nine more Portuguese ships bearing 600 troops arrive at Maranhão from Pernambuco under Capt. Gen. Alejandro de Moura, who quickly breaks the truce by advancing upriver, obliging the French to surrender Fort Saint Louis, their last remaining stronghold, by 15 November. Five days later La Ravardière signs a capitulation whereby he agrees to be transported to Lisbon as a prisoner while his followers are evacuated toward France. More than 400 sail away aboard three ships, leaving their properties to the Portuguese, thus marking an end to *France Équinoxiale.* (Their Tupinambá allies are also crushed by the Portuguese when they rise against the new masters in 1618.)

16 NOVEMBER 1616. ***Tepehuán Revolt.*** In Mexico's northern province of Nueva Vizcaya, 2,000 Tepehuán Indians rise in a concerted rebellion, slaughtering 270 Spanish settlers at the missions of Santa Catalina, Atotonilco, Guatimape, Santiago Papasquiaro, and Zape. This insurrection soon spreads to the neighboring Xixime, Acaxee, Tarahumara, and other lesser tribes of the Topia Range, who unite and march—allegedly 25,000 strong—against the capital of La Guadiana (modern-day Durango City). Gov. Gaspar de Alvear y Salazar scatters the host and executes 65 ringleaders, but Indian rebels continue to resist in its mountainous terrain for the next couple of years.

17 NOVEMBER 1617. ***Raleigh's Last Venture.*** Fifteen English vessels appear off the Orinoco River under 65-year-old Sir Walter Raleigh, who has been released from 13 years' incarceration in the Tower by James I on the understanding he will secure the El Dorado mines for England—without antagonizing Spain. Having contracted sickness during a stopover at the Canaries, Raleigh anchors his 36-gun, 400-ton flagship *Destiny* at Galeota Point (Trinidad) before detaching his second-in-command, Lawrence Keymis, with five vessels—the largest being the 160-ton, 18-gun *Encounter* of Captain Whitney—to advance up the Orinoco with several hundred men, including Raleigh's 25-year-old son, Walter, and nephew George.

Keymis reaches this river mouth by 31 December (O.S.), working his way upstream until Santo Tomé—

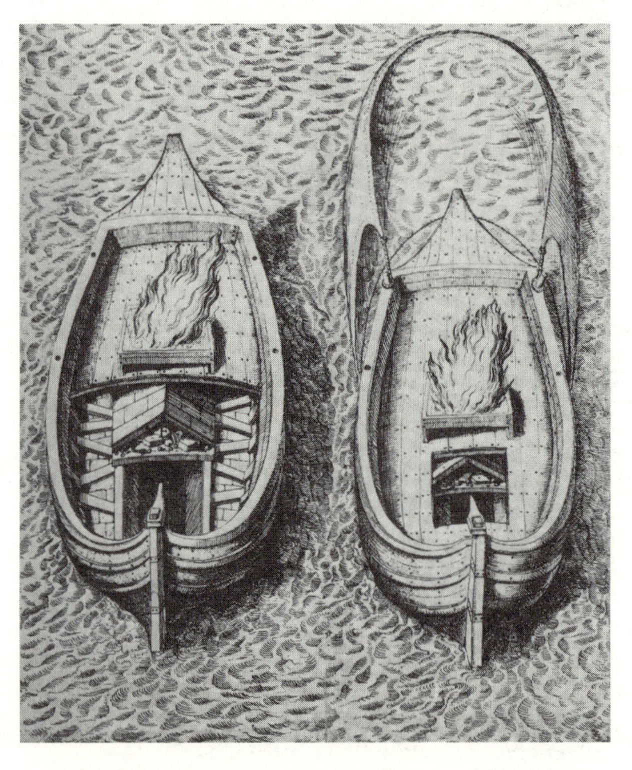

Methods for distributing and igniting combustibles in a seventeenth-century fireship; from a contemporary manual

near Jaya Island, between the Caroní confluence and Atayama Point (six miles west of Los Castillos)—is sighted three weeks later. Its recently installed Spanish governor, Diego Palomeque de Acuña, has been forewarned of the English approach by native scouts, so Santo Tomé's citizenry flees while 37 militia are mustered, supported by two small cannons and four swivel guns plus some Indian auxiliaries. This force is easily brushed aside by Keymis, with Palomeque and several others being killed—among these Raleigh's son, slain in hand-to-hand combat with a Spanish captain named Erineta. Finding the town empty, the English press farther upriver until ambushed near Ceiba by ten Spanish harquebusiers and as many native archers, hidden on the banks under Capt. Jerónimo Grado.

Retiring into Santo Tomé, the English suffer disease and a counterassault by 23 Spaniards and 60 Indians on the 27th day of occupation, obliging Keymis to retreat. He reports to Raleigh at Trinidad, who, in his anguish at facing ruin and the loss of his son, reproves his subordinate so harshly that the latter commits suicide. Raleigh's expedition quickly disintegrates, at least five captains parting company to prowl the Caribbean; Raleigh returns to England to meet his fate (being executed on 29 October 1618 [O.S.]).

23 MAY 1618. In Europe, most powers become embroiled for the next several decades in the Thirty Years War, which begins as a revolt against the newly elected king of Bohemia, Ferdinand II, who attempts to impose central Catholic rule over his Protestant noblemen. This regional conflict eventually spreads through Austria and Germany to engulf practically all of Europe. Its underlying impetus remains the struggle between Catholicism and Protestantism, exacerbated by diplomatic maneuverings in virtually every European capital. (Madrid, for example, supports Ferdinand in his religious and absolutist efforts, whereas Holland and Sweden favor their Protestant coreligionists; Paris weighs in against its traditional Spanish foe.) The resultant decades of warfare indirectly affect developments in the New World.

AUTUMN 1618. Three ships and 400 Huguenots out of Dieppe under Capt. Charles Fleury arrive to prowl the Caribbean for the next 11 months.

SPRING 1619. Five of Raleigh's former vessels—three large and two small—are lying near Santo Domingo when they are attacked by a like number of Spanish ships under Capt. Alonso de Contreras, knight of the Order of San Juan, who has arrived recently from Seville with two royal galleons and 200 troops to reinforce the garrison at San Juan de Puerto Rico. Having continued into Santo Domingo with two additional Spanish coasters and being joined by a Cape Verde (West Africa) slaver, de Contreras exits and engages the five English vessels, chasing them away.

Next, he calls at Santiago de Cuba with only a single ship (*Buen Jesús?*), subsequently proceeding along the island's southern shore toward Cape San Antonio, where he chances upon another of Raleigh's consorts, anchored off Isla de Pinos. Contreras captures that vessel, along with 21 crew members, carrying them into Havana. He ends his Caribbean foray by incorporating his galleon into the plate fleet of Adm. Carlos de Ibarra, knight of the Order of Alcántara, which sails for Spain on 28 July.

HOLLAND'S "GREAT DESIGN" (1613–1649)

ONE OF THE FEW NATIONS TO RISE ABOVE the destructive cycle of the Thirty Years War will be the Netherlands, which becomes the greatest maritime power in the world during the first half of the seventeenth century. The provinces of Holland, Zeeland, Utrecht, Gelderland, Overijssel, Groningen, and Friesland have already won independence by compelling Madrid to sign the Twelve Years Truce in the spring of 1609. Now their overseas ambitions also rise, Dutch vessels arriving in the New World in ever increasing numbers, proving themselves tenacious and resourceful traders who are anxious to acquire more outlets.

Eventually this commercial interest persuades the Dutch to allow their truce with Spain and Portugal to lapse on 31 March 1621, with hostilities resuming the next day. Both sides have grown increasingly restive under this arrangement, the Dutch wishing to develop their lucrative American market (which they realize Madrid will oppose), but also fearing the Spanish armies massed in the neighboring Palatinate under Marshals Ambrogio di Spinola and

Johann Tzerclaes, graf von Tilly. Therefore, for both strategic and philosophical reasons, the Dutch opt to intervene in the Thirty Years War on the Protestant side.

This decision will have profound effects in the New World, as Dutch expeditions begin crossing the Atlantic to attack Spanish shipping and to conquer new colonies. These efforts are greatly abetted by the Westindische Compagnie (West Indian Company, or WIC), created in May 1621 to inflict losses upon Spain while seeking commercial profit.

SUMMER 1613. Zeeland colonists found two new settlements: one up the Essequibo River (Guyana), the other up the Courantyne (in Dutch, Corantijn) River (the modern-day boundary between Guyana and Suriname). In August, 12 Spaniards and a priest from the island of Trinidad plus 20 more men from Santo Tomé (eastern Venezuela) rendezvous to expunge the Dutch establishments. It takes them 60 days to reach the Corantijn, creeping upon its sleeping Dutch lodgment at night and calling for the inhabitants to surrender. When the Dutch refuse, the Spanish attackers ignite the palm-thatched roof, and all the colonists perish in the flames. The Essequibo River colony is also eliminated before the Spaniards retire.

13 DECEMBER 1614. At dawn, *Groote Zon, Groote Maan, Æolus,* and *Morgenster,* plus the yachts *Jager* and *Meeuw,* appear off Brazil under a veteran commodore named Joris van Spilbergen. His orders are to penetrate the Strait of Magellan, reconnoiter Spain's American empire, then cross the Pacific in the wake of the Acapulco-Manila galleons to link up with the new Dutch trading outposts in the Moluccas.

One week later his formation drops anchor before Rio de Janeiro, spending nearly a month refreshing provisions from the uninhabited islands and tending to the sick. On 31 December a watering party that ventures upriver is captured by Portuguese irregulars, and on 6 January 1615 two of *Meeuw's* seamen are executed for mutiny. Van Spilbergen then sets sail on 15 January, arriving near Santos to trade three days later. Fighting erupts with the Portuguese inhabitants a fortnight later, and the Dutch retaliate by intercepting a bark arriving from Rio. On 4 February van Spilbergen gets under way again for the strait.

SPRING 1615. A group of 280 Dutch colonists settle at Cayenne (the modern-day capital of French Guiana) under Theodore Claessen of Amsterdam, transferring into Suriname shortly thereafter.

16 APRIL 1615. ***Van Spilbergen Enters the Pacific.*** After beating against contrary winds, the Dutch squadron (except *Meeuw,* which has parted company) emerges into the Pacific and begins working its way up South America. Because of the Twelve Years Truce, its progress is a blend of aggressiveness and goodwill: in some places, the Dutch fight pitched battles against the Spaniards, in others they trade peaceably with local residents. By 29 May, van Spilbergen's five vessels arrive between Punta Lavapié (Chile) and Santa María Island. After a guarded reception from the island's Spanish residents, hostilities erupt two days later, when van Spilbergen leads three companies of soldiers and sailors ashore at dawn to sack the town. Four Spaniards are killed, two Dutchmen wounded.

Getting under way again on 1 June, van Spilbergen enters Valparaíso 11 days later at sunup, prompting the Spaniards to scuttle their lone merchantman while firing on the advancing Dutch boats. Van Spilbergen forges ashore with 200 troops, but the Spanish militia cavalry melt away, obliging the Dutch to reembark during the evening and proceed farther north. After watering at Quintero on 13–17 June, the commodore continues slowly, arriving opposite San Vicente de Cañete (Peru) one month later to a hostile reception from fortified militia.

17 JULY 1615. ***Cañete.*** The Peruvian viceroy, Juan de Mendoza y Luna, Marqués de Montesclaros and knight grand cross of the Order of Santiago—alarmed by van Spilbergen's progression up South America—has earlier dispatched four men-of-war and a hired storeship under nephew Rodrigo de Mendoza, knight of the Order of Santiago (plus veteran Vice Adm. Pedro Fernández del Pulgar), to intercept these intruders; the formation probes as far south as Valdivia and reverses course, without sighting the Dutch. The viceroy therefore dispatches Peru's annual bullion shipment toward Panama aboard the 32-gun, 400-ton *San José* and the 20-gun, 250-ton *Nuestra Señora de la Visitación* (formerly Hawkins's *Dainty; see* 2 May 1594 in Part 2), leaving only two men-of-war at Callao.

When word subsequently arrives that van Spilbergen is at Cañete, the Spaniards must sortie with their 600-ton flagship *Jesús María*—pierced for 30 guns but only mounting 22—and manned by 400 men under Captain Delgado; plus the 350-ton vice-flagship *Santa*

Ana—pierced for 30 but bearing just 12 cannon—and manned by 200 men under Captain Bustinza. This understrength force is supplemented by the private merchantmen *Carmen* of Captain Coba, with eight guns and 150 men; *San Diego* of Capt. Juan de Nájera, with no guns and 80 men; *Santiago* of *Maestre de Campo* Pedraza, with four swivels and 80 men; and auxiliary *Rosario* of Capt. Juan de Alberdín, with 50 men. Overall command is held by the viceroy's nephew, de Mendoza, with Fernández del Pulgar as his vice admiral, and *Maestre de Campo* Diego de Sarabia as third-in-command.

The Spaniards exit Callao at dawn on 17 July, coming upon the enemy squadron at 4:00 P.M. 15 miles off Cañete in a light breeze (having scuttled a coastal trader and the shallop of Juan Bautista González, which they intercepted arriving from Arica). Although advised to engage next day, de Mendoza closes with van Spilbergen that evening, his *Jesús María* accompanied by the vice-flag *Santa Ana* and tender *Rosario.* Around 9:00–10:00 P.M., the five Dutch ships hoist lanterns and fire a blank signal gun to call for a parley; after a brief exchange of hails de Mendoza replies with two shotted guns, and the battle is joined. Several hours' gunplay ensues, during which *Rosario* is sunk (Captain de Alberdín and a few other survivors being rescued by *Jesús María*); all combatants receive some sort of damage because scanty winds prevent maneuvering out of harm's way.

Next morning—Saturday, 18 July—the action resumes, and after another prolonged exchange the Spanish flagship staggers out of the engagement with 60 dead and 80 wounded. Fighting now rages around Fernández del Pulgar's vice-flag *Santa Ana,* which resists until 8:00 P.M., when it surrenders and shortly thereafter plunges beneath the waves, a 12-man Dutch prize crew still aboard. Only a half-dozen survivors are plucked from the waters next dawn (another 60 being left to their fate by the Dutch, among these a woman named Catalina de Erauso, dressed as a man and known to the Spaniards as the Monja Alférez, or Nun Ensign). Van Spilbergen has suffered 40 killed and 48–60 wounded, principally aboard *Groote Maan* and *Morgenster.* On 20 July he appears off Callao to exchange a few shots with its batteries, then coasts north one week later with a small prize. Meanwhile *Jesús María*—de Mendoza fearful of encountering the Dutch squadron—limps toward Pisco to deposit its wounded, then continues into Panama for repairs.

8 AUGUST 1615. After refreshing at Huarmey (Peru), van Spilbergen appears this evening off Paita, disembarking four companies—300 musketeers—next morning to forage for provisions. Its defenders are commanded by Paula Piraldo, wife of the absent Piura *corregidor* Juan de Andrade y Colmenero; their sole defense is a trench parallel to the beach, which the Dutch probe at the cost of one ensign killed and three soldiers wounded before retiring to their waiting ships. On the morning of 10 August, van Spilbergen sends greater numbers ashore to resume the attack, supported by close bombardment from *Æolus, Morgenster,* and *Jager.* Outnumbered and outflanked, the Spanish flee to an adjacent hill, watching as the raiders, who will remain at anchor for another fortnight, ransack and burn Paita.

10 OCTOBER 1615. This evening, van Spilbergen's squadron arrives outside Acapulco, hoping to stand in the next day. Light winds slow entry until the afternoon, when the Spanish battery inside opens up a desultory fire. The Dutch commodore sends a boat inshore under a flag of truce, requesting permission to buy supplies. The surprised Spanish governor, Gregorio de Porres, agrees, and van Spilbergen's crews spend a week refreshing and visiting ashore.

The rovers depart on 18 October, prowling farther up the Mexican coast toward California hoping to intercept the Manila galleon. They capture a small Spanish pearling frigate on 26 October and skirmish with Mexican militia at Salagua Bay on the morning of 11 November while attempting to forage. Discouraged and tired, van Spilbergen then gives up his watch on 20 November, steering out into the Pacific.

6 DECEMBER 1615. At daybreak, the 220-ton Dutch *Eendracht* (19 guns and 12 swivels, manned by 65 men under Capt. Willem Corneliszoon Schouten of Hoorn), and the 110-ton yacht *Hoorn* (eight guns, four swivels, and 22 sailors under his brother, Jan Corneliszoon Schouten), reach the Atlantic Coast of South America. The expedition's leader is Jacob Le Maire of Amsterdam, who aims to discover a new passage into the Pacific (the Strait of Magellan and the Cape of Good Hope being claimed by competing Dutch monopolies, barring others from commercial access to Asia). Next midday, *Eendracht* and *Hoorn* anchor in Olivier van Noort's former haven of Puerto Deseado (Argentina), refreshing for more than a month before striking out on 13 January 1616 to sail around Tierra del Fuego. By 26 January they reach 57 degrees south latitude, successfully passing an island they name Cape Hoorn and entering the Pacific via this new route. Le Maire reaches the Juan Fernández Islands by 1 March, pausing briefly before

continuing out into the Central Pacific toward New Guinea.

SPRING 1616. The Zeeland ship *Goude Haan* of Pieter Adriaanszoon Ita arrives on South America's Wild Coast, where it deposits 150 Dutch settlers at the Ginipape River. They build a fort and remain for six years, bartering for tobacco with local natives.

Also in the spring of 1616, two more Zeeland ships and a smaller auxiliary under Aert Adriaanszoon Groenewegen—confusingly rendered Cromwegle by the English and Llanes or Yanes by the Spanish—sail up the Essequibo River to reoccupy Fort Ter Hooge (*see* spring 1596 in Part 2). Finding it abandoned by the Portuguese, Groenewegen builds a new fort named Kijkoveral on the site. An experienced South American hand, having previously served the Spaniards as factor on the Orinoco River, the Catholic Groenewegen establishes excellent relations with the natives by marrying a chieftain's daughter, thus helping his establishment flourish for the next half-century.

2 JANUARY 1621. After a lengthy pursuit, two Spanish caravels under Capts. Martín Vázquez de Montiel and Benito Arias Montano—patrolling on orders from the captain general of Cartagena—overtake a Dutch, an English, and two French ships off Tortuga Island (Haiti), capturing three of the ships and slaughtering 300 crewmembers at a cost of five Spanish dead and 25 wounded.

20 SEPTEMBER 1621. Word reaches Gov. Diego de Arroyo Daza at Cumaná that a half-dozen Dutch vessels are anchored at nearby Ancón de Refriegas to gather salt, establishing a six-gun camp ashore. He leads 30 men down the Bordones River aboard four small, armed craft to drive out the poachers, who are soon reinforced by ten Dutch ships and resist vigorously. The outnumbered Spaniards conduct guerrilla warfare until the Dutch withdraw of their own accord, leaving behind more than 20 dead (mostly from disease).

15 JANUARY 1622. Two large Dutch merchantmen are prevented from gathering salt near Araya (Venezuela) by Governor de Arroyo, who ambushes their landing parties with 40 Spanish militia and some native archers, killing 13 and capturing nine. But de Arroyo's 120-man company retires when another 27 Dutch vessels appear the next day and set ashore 500 men, who erect two small redoubts of five and three cannons each.

27 NOVEMBER 1622. More than 40 Dutch merchantmen arrive off Araya to poach salt, discovering that a small Spanish fortification has been erected by de Arroyo the previous summer (Fort Santiago de Araya, manned by militia under Lt. Juan de Vargas Machuca). Over the next three days the interlopers cannonade the Spanish entrenchments and disembark a large force, assaulting the ramparts. Suffering several fatalities, the Dutch eventually break off and reembark two weeks later.

12 JANUARY 1623. Some 41 Dutch merchantmen appear off Cumaná, bombarding its small fortress for two days before proceeding to the far side of the bay and disembarking several hundred men to gather salt under the protection of harquebusiers. The Spaniards, forewarned and reinforced from nearby Margarita Island by a company of soldiers and native archers under Capt. Jorge Gómez, eventually drive the poachers out by 24 January with a series of ambushes.

20 MAY 1623. Portuguese Capt. Luis Aranha de Vasconselhos reaches Belém (Brazil) with a dozen soldiers aboard his eight-gun, 60-ton caravel, as well as reinforcements from São Luís do Maranhão aboard a launch, to spearhead an expedition aimed at pushing foreign settlers out of the nearby Amazon Delta. With a total of 70 Portuguese and 400 native allies crammed aboard his launch, a brigantine, and 40 canoes, Aranha de Vasconselhos sets out again on 11 June, circling northwest around Joannes Island five days later to surprise the twin Dutch outposts at Maturu called Forts Oranje and Nassau—southeast of the mouth of the Xingu River. The victors subsequently retire with 36 Dutch captives, plus 100 local Indians and Angolan slaves, while Belém's garrison Cmdr. Bento Maciel Parente arrives off the delta with yet another force.

This second Portuguese contingent gradually sweeps the western shoreline toward the English settlement at the mouth of the Okiari River—established three years previously by Roger North's Amazon Company—where the surviving Dutch, English, and Irish residents rally under Captains Ita of Flushing and Charles Parker. On 22 August Aranha de Vasconselhos returns with his caravel from depositing the prisoners at Belém, joining Maciel Parente at Sapanapoco. Both Portuguese units then attack the interlopers but fail to overwhelm the Ita-Parker combined force (despite compelling the former to torch his two-gun, 32-man Dutch flagship when it runs aground).

Aranha de Vasconselhos concludes the campaign by standing away toward Europe—being intercepted before arriving by two Moroccan vessels out of Salé, in concert with a Dutch warship—while Maciel Parente retires to Mariocay, building 50-man Fort São António before eventually regaining Belém. This new fortress is destroyed shortly thereafter by a Dutch counteroffensive.

27 FEBRUARY 1624. ***The "Nassau Fleet."*** A Dutch squadron emerges around Cape Horn into the South Pacific, intent upon reconnoitering Spain's American empire and possibly gaining a foothold in this region:

Ship	*Guns*	*Men*	*Tons*	*Commander*
Amsterdam (flag)	42	237	800	Leendert Jacobszoon Stolck
Delft (vice-flag)	40	242	800	Witte Cornelis de Witte
Orangien (rear admiral)	32	216	700	Laurens Janszoon Quirijnen
Hollandia	34	182	600	Adriaen Tol
Eendracht	32	170	600	Jan Ijsbrantszoon
Mauritius	32	169	560	Jacob Adriaenszoon
Arend	28	144	400	Meyndert Egbertszoon
Koning David	16	79	360	Jan Thomaszoon
Griffioen	14	78	320	Pieter Corneliszoon Hardloop
Hoop	14	80	260	Pieter Harmanszoon Slobbe
Hazewind or *Windhond* (yacht)	4	20	60	Salomon Willemszoon

The expedition has been assembled by Prince Maurice of Nassau with financial backing from the Dutch East India Company and States General, so is commonly referred to as the "Nassau Fleet." Its commanders are the 42-year-old Huguenot Jacques l'Hermite (the Younger) of Antwerp and the 24-year-old Gheen Huygen Schapenham of Rotterdam. After weathering a storm in the Strait of Le Maire, during which a yacht and Portuguese prize sink, the formation proceeds up the South American coast out of sight of land in hopes of intercepting the annual convoy bearing Peru's silver toward Panama.

MID-MARCH 1624. Three Dutch ships under Pieter Schouten arrive at Barbados, having been dispatched by the WIC to conduct an extensive Caribbean reconnaissance. Over the next three months, Schouten—veteran of previous West Indian cruises—explores the Spanish mainland as far as the Gulf of Maracaibo, plus all of Santo Domingo and southern Jamaica, gathering valuable intelligence and establishing friendly relations with natives.

EARLY MAY 1624. The Dutch ship *Nieuw Nederland* arrives at Manhattan (New York) with 30 Protestant Walloon families to establish a colony under Gov. Cornelis Jacobszoon Mey. Only eight individuals remain on the island, more than half the families choosing to continue up the Hudson River to found Fort Orange (Albany).

7 MAY 1624. ***Callao Blockade.*** The Nassau Fleet is spotted bearing down on Lima's port, alarming residents. The Spanish silver convoy—comprising the private galleon *Santiago;* the 400-ton, 32-gun *San José,* vice-flagship of the South Sea Fleet; and the 16-gun *San Felipe y Santiago*—has departed Callao for Panama four days previously, bearing 8 million pesos in treasure. The only men-of-war left on station are the damaged, 900-ton armada flagship *Nuestra Señora de Loreto*—none of its 44 guns being mounted—plus the 150-ton, eight-gun auxiliary *San Bartolomé.* Hastily summoned from a bullfight, Viceroy Diego Fernández de Córdoba, Marqués de Guadalcázar and Conde de las Posadas, instantly orders the militia called out.

Not realizing they have already missed their chance at capturing the bullion, several hundred Dutchmen disembark next morning and march upon Callao, being repulsed by the maneuverings of a large mass of Peruvian riders in the distance. The Spaniards, meanwhile, strengthen their defenses; when the Dutch return three days later, the garrison is better prepared. L'Hermite attempts to penetrate the harbor in boats, only to be repelled with some losses. Fighting now focuses around the port, prompting the Spaniards to build a number of armed launches and floating batteries. L'Hermite dies of disease on 2 June and is succeeded by the more youthful and inexperienced Schapenham.

8 MAY 1624. ***Capture of São Salvador.*** A Dutch fleet materializes off Brazil under Adm. Jacob Willekens of Amsterdam and Vice Adm. Pieter Pieterszoon Heyn of Rotterdam: the 28-gun, 300-ton flagship *Hollandia* and 26-gun, 350-ton vice-flagship *Tijger;* 36-gun *Zeelandia;* 34-gun *Sampson;* 28-gun *Neptunis;* 24-gun *Groningen;* 20-gun *Eendracht, Oranjeboom, Provincie van Utrecht,* and *Ster;* 18-gun *Gulden Zeepaard, Haan, Hoop, Oude Roode Leeuw,* and *Sint Christowfel;* 17-gun *Vier Heems Kinderen;* 16-gun *Nassau, Overijssel,* and another unnamed ship; 14-gun *Oranjeboom;* 12-gun yacht *Vos;* ten-gun *Hazewind,* and *Zeejager;* eight-gun *Postpaard;* plus *Sint Martien.*

The 1,500-man landing force is to be directed by Col. Johan van Dorth, lord of der Horst and Pesch,

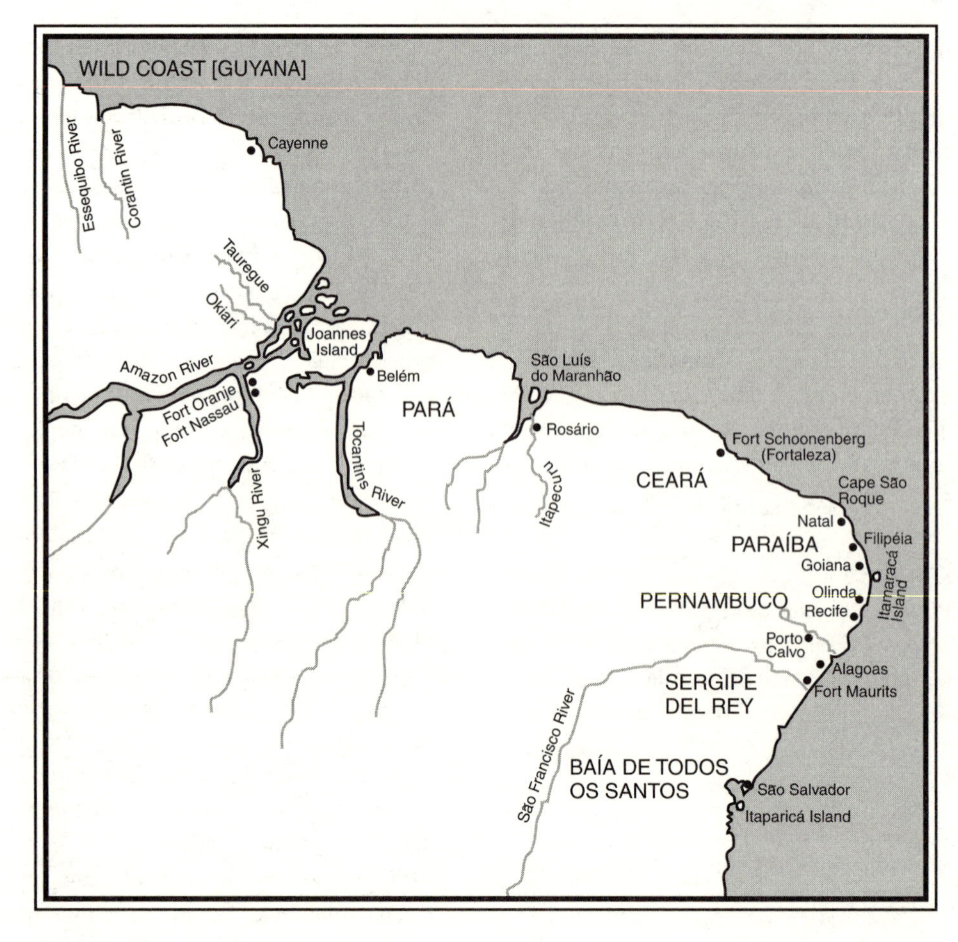

Dutch Brazil

who is further to assume office as governor of any newly conquered territories. This WIC expedition has been sent out to secure a permanent trading outpost in the New World, Brazil having been chosen because its Portuguese inhabitants are resentful of Spanish rule and friendly toward Dutch smugglers.

Spanish Gov. Diego de Mendoza Hurtado has had little advance warning of the enemy's approach; he can muster but a token defense. The landward face of São Salvador, capital of Baía de Todos os Santos, is protected by Fort San António to the east and Fort San Filipe to the west; a temporary six-gun battery is being erected on its beach, and streets are barricaded. Unimpressed, the Dutch sweep into the bay, dividing into two squadrons: One proceeds toward San António Beach some distance from São Salvador's walls to begin disembarking troops; the other—under Heyn—anchors opposite the city and opens fire. During the night the seaward defenses are neutralized by Heyn's efforts, and next morning more than 1,000 Dutchmen begin circling the city, dragging two field pieces. Seeing this, de Mendoza's 3,000 Portuguese militia—mostly reluctant peasant levees and black slaves—desert in droves. The governor is left with only 60 loyal troops; São Salvador is easily overrun at a cost of 50 Dutch casualties.

Willekens and Heyn immediately install a new garrison, planning to leave it under van Dorth's orders while they depart on further missions, in accordance with their instructions from Holland. Four ships are detached to carry booty and news back to the Netherlands while the city defenses are improved by deepening its moat and erecting additional ramparts, after which numerous Portuguese slaves are enticed to join the Dutch cause by promises of freedom and land. Nevertheless, the Brazilian interior remains hostile, guerrilla warfare springing up at the urging of Bishop Marcos Texeira, who has escaped inland. When Willekens and Heyn finally depart in separate directions by early August, São Salvador seems secure, its garrison enjoying improved defenses, three to four months' provisions, and the promise of timely relief from Holland. But shortly thereafter, van Dorth is killed leading a sally, and morale sags.

6 JUNE 1624. Schapenham decides to detach two contingents from his squadron to raid other points along the Pacific Coast while his main body maintains

its blockade of Callao. The first of these—*Mauritius* and *Hoop,* under Vice Adm. Jan Willemszoon—arrives undetected off Guayaquil, seizing three frigates, two brigantines, and four lesser craft from its estuary before pressing upriver to fall upon the city proper. Caught by surprise, *Corregidor* Diego de Portugal and his 200 ill-prepared militia can do little more than cover the civilians' evacuation. The Dutch sack Guayaquil, although their retirement toward their boats is harried by Spanish riders, resulting in some losses. After plundering nearby Puná Island and burning most of their prizes, the Dutch withdraw.

11 JUNE 1624. Schapenham's other detachment—*Eendracht, Koning David, Griffioen,* and *Hazewind,* under Cornelis Jacobszoon—falls upon Pisco but enjoys less success as its boat parties are sighted before they can disembark, the initial landing being repulsed from the beaches by Capt. Diego de Carvajal's men. Next dawn, seven boatloads of Dutchmen slip ashore and begin marching on Pisco. Cavalry shadows their advance, and the attackers are unable to fight their way through Pisco's trenches, retreating back to their ships a few days later after losing five men; they finally sail away by 15 June.

JUNE 1624. In the Gulf of Mexico, Schouten raids and destroys Zilam and Sisal (Yucatán) before striking out toward Cuba.

JULY 1624. One of Schouten's vessels, having become separated from his flagship, intercepts the annual Honduran convoy off Cape San Antonio (western Cuba), capturing the galleon *San Juan Bautista* of Francisco Hernández y Moreno. The exultant Dutch begin towing their prize home, only to wreck their own ship on Florida's Dry Tortugas Bank shortly thereafter. Transferring aboard the galleon, they continue their voyage and eventually reach the Netherlands safely by November.

5 AUGUST 1624. Having forsaken his blockade of Callao, Schapenham attempts a second assault against Guayaquil with four ships and 600 men. These penetrate as far as the Ataranzas and burn two brigantines upon their stocks before being repelled by Ecuatorian militia under the new *corregidor,* José de Castro. Schapenham tries more disembarkations on 25–28 August, again without success. Twenty-eight men are taken captive, and he sails for New Spain.

28 OCTOBER 1624. Schapenham's squadron forces its way into Acapulco without opposition. The Spanish garrison commander, Pedro de Legorreta, is without ammunition and leaves the Dutch undisturbed for a week before they depart northwest in hopes of intercepting the annual Manila galleon. Failing to find it, Schapenham quits the Mexican coast a few weeks later, striking out across the Pacific.

EARLY 1625. Capt. Hendrick Jacobszoon Lucifer's *Zwarte Arend* deposits a new Dutch colony—including 80–100 soldiers under Capt. Nicolas Oudaen—in the Amazon Delta, followed a few weeks later by Geleyn van Stapels's eight-gun, 90-ton *Vliegenden Draak.*

29 MARCH (EASTER SATURDAY) 1625. ***Reconquest of São Salvador.*** A Hispano-Portuguese fleet appears before Baía de Todos os Santos (Brazil), its Spanish contingent consisting of the 55-gun flagship *Nuestra Señora del Pilar y Santiago,* and 60-gun vice-flagship *Santiago de Oliste;* 60-gun *Concepción de la Siempre Virgen María;* 54-gun *Nuestra Señora de la Anunciación;* 40-gun *Nuestra Señora de Atocha,* and *San Juan Bautista;* 36-gun *San Nicolás Tolentino;* 32-gun *Nuestra Señora del Rosario;* 26-gun *San Juan Bautista,* and *Santa Ana la Real;* 24-gun *Nuestra Señora de la Victoria, San Francisco, Santa Teresa,* and *Santísima Trinidad;* 22-gun *Nuestra Señora de la Atalaya, San Pedro,* and *Santa Catalina;* 20-gun *San José, San Juan de la Veracruz, San Miguel,* and *San Pablo;* 30-gun storeship *San Salvador;* 20-gun storeships *Enrique,* and *San Miguel* (alias *Turquillo*); 18-gun storeships *Esperanza, Rey David,* and *San Pablo;* 16-gun storeship *Puerto Cristiano;* 16-gun tender *San Jorge;* plus 14-gun tender *Carmen.* Overall command is exercised by Adm. Fadrique de Toledo y Osorio, Marqués de Villanueva de Valdueza; his Spanish vice admiral is Juan Fajardo de Güevara, knight of the Order of Calatrava, and his rear admiral is Martín de Vallecilla, knight of the Order of Santiago.

The Portuguese formation is led by Adm. Manuel de Meneses, knight of the Order of Cristo, aboard his 60-gun flagship *São Martinho;* 30-gun *Santana;* 26-gun *São José;* 16-gun *Caridade, São Pedro,* and *São Roque;* 14-gun *Santa Isabel, São Alberto, São Antônio,* and *São João;* 12-gun *São Bartolomeu, São Estêvão, São Luis, São Martinho,* and *São Mateus;* ten-gun *São Sebastião,* and *Varejão;* 18-gun storeship *Sul Dourado;* 16-gun storeship *São João;* 14-gun storeship *Cão Caçador;* plus 12-gun storeship *Grifo.* Both fleets are further accompanied by five caravels, two Marseillean tartans, and four Biscayan pinnaces. The 9,400 troops are commanded by Pedro Rodríguez de Santiestéban, Marqués de Cropani and knight of the Order of Calatrava, seconded by the veteran *Sargento Mayor* Diego Ruiz.

This is Madrid's response to the fall of São Salvador (news of the event had reached Madrid before it had reached the Hague). Forming a huge crescent to prevent escape, de Toledo anchors his fleet and lands 4,000 troops at São António Beach, three miles outside this city, during the next afternoon to join up with local guerrillas and occupy the São Pedro high ground. The Dutch are forced back within their walls, warping their 18 ships beneath the protection of their batteries. Siege warfare ensues, with the Spaniards driving saplines toward the Dutch ramparts while the defenders launch sporadic counterattacks. During one of these sallies, *Maestre de Campo* Pedro Osorio and 71 Spanish officers and soldiers are killed; another 64 are seriously wounded—but progress continues. One night the Dutch also send two fire ships against the anchored Spanish fleet without success; Heyn's reduced squadron reappears from West Africa during the siege but is powerless to assist.

After a few weeks—when the siege lines finally reach São Salvador's moat—the Dutch request terms. A capitulation is signed on 30 April whereby 1,912 Dutch, English, German, and French defenders surrender to the Spaniards, being allowed to exit with their baggage to travel back to Holland. The triumphant de Toledo takes possession of 18 flags, 260 cannon, 500 *quintales* (hundredweight) of gunpowder, 600 black slaves, and considerable amounts of money and merchandise.

22 MAY 1625. Some 33 Dutch ships bear down upon Baía de Todos os Santos in two columns, being a belated relief force under Adm. Boudewijn Hendricksz and Vice Adm. Andries Veron. The Spanish commander, de Toledo, having advance warning of their approach, is prepared to receive them: the surrendered Dutch garrison is held aboard five German storeships in the harbor, and shore batteries are fully manned. Six Spanish men-of-war exit, hoping to lure the latest Dutch arrivals into a murderous crossfire. Hendricksz refuses to be drawn once he perceives the huge Spanish fleet anchored inside, instead veering back out to sea. Spanish warships attempt a halfhearted pursuit, ending abruptly when the galleon *Santa Teresa* runs aground. No further action is taken, the Dutch sailing away toward Pernambuco in search of supplies, leaving the Spaniards in uncontested possession of São Salvador.

(Dutch and Spanish leaders are later criticized for not having shown more—Hendricksz abandoning São Salvador without a fight, de Toledo suffering a major enemy fleet to roam unchallenged down Brazil's coast.)

23 MAY 1625. Having stealthily approached from Belém with 50 Portuguese soldiers and 300 native auxiliaries, veteran Capt. Pedro Teixeira attacks Oudaen's new Dutch outpost at Mandiutuba (Amazon Delta). Its defenders flee downriver next day after losing seven or eight men, eventually uniting with English and Irish settlers at the mouth of the Okiari River to resist their pursuers.

Teixeira defeats a combined force of 80 foreign interlopers in open country, killing 60—including Oudaen and the English leader Philip Purcell—and capturing the remainder. Another 20-man stronghold nearby also surrenders, after which the Portuguese withdraw in triumph.

JULY 1625. Hendricksz implements the second part of his instructions by subdividing his fleet and quitting Brazil. His vice admiral, Veron, heads toward Africa with a dozen sail; a convoy of prizes is detached for Holland while Hendricksz himself steers his 18 remaining vessels north on 4 August to assail the Puerto Rican capital of San Juan. He arrives at the island of Saint Vincent by late August, pausing two weeks to refresh and attend to his many sick; he then continues the voyage, weathering a hurricane with the loss of *Geele Sonne* before gaining Puerto Rico.

24 SEPTEMBER 1625. ***Hendricksz's Defeat.*** This afternoon, 17 Dutch ships bear down upon San Juan de Puerto Rico, whose Spanish governor—naval and military veteran Juan de Haro—has been in office less than a month. Nevertheless, he prepares to receive the enemy as best he can, sending his predecessor, Juan de Vargas, to nearby Boquerón with militia to hinder any landings in Escambrón Inlet.

Yet Hendricksz implements a much bolder plan. At 1:00 P.M. the next day the entire Dutch fleet sails directly into San Juan's harbor: *Roode Leeuw, Witte Leeuw,*

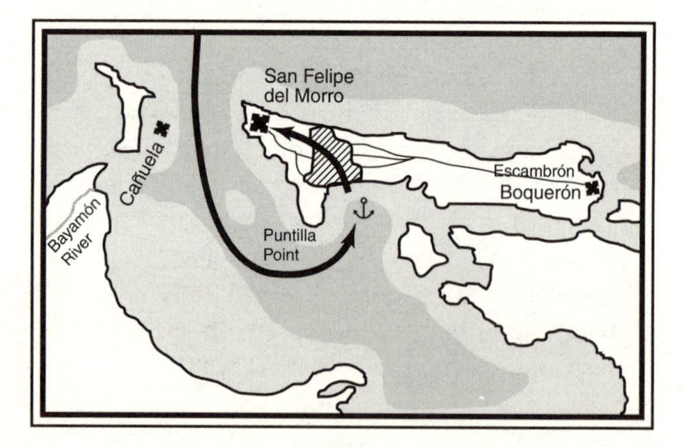

Hendricksz's failed attack on San Juan de Puerto Rico

Seventeenth-century Spanish painting commemorating Hendricksz's defeat at San Juan de Puerto Rico; by Eugenio Caxés

Leyden, Blauwe Leeuw, Goude Valck, Utrecht, Nieuw Nederlandt, Hoop van Dordrecht, Kleyne Tijger, Hoorn, Medemblik, Gouden Molen, Vlissingen, West Kappel, Goude Sonne, Koningin Hester, and *Jonas.* They exchange shots with the harbor castle, inflicting superficial damage and slaying four Spaniards while gaining a safe anchorage within the roadstead off Puntilla Point, beyond range of de Haro's artillery. However, shoals prevent an immediate disembarkation, allowing Spanish noncombatants to flee inland while the governor marshals his slender strength within San Felipe del Morro citadel. Six additional bronze 12-pounders are installed in its embrasures, 330 men gathering inside (220 effectives, but with abundant supplies).

On 26 September, Hendricksz leads 700–800 men ashore and occupies the empty city plus its smaller Cañuela Fortress two days later; the main citadel proves impossible to storm, so the Dutch begin digging saplines and installing a six-gun battery atop Calvario Heights by 29 September. At 9:00 A.M. the next day Hendricksz calls upon de Haro to surrender but is rejected, so action resumes. Capt. Jan Jasperz de Laet of *West Kappel* exits on 1 October to chase away a Spanish ship arriving with supplies, and on the night of Friday, 3–4 October, the Spaniards sally out of their citadel in two companies of 40 men apiece under Capts. Sebastián de Avila and Andrés Botello, accomplishing little. They enjoy better fortune at noon on 5 October, when 50 men under Capt. Juan de Amézquita y Quixano destroy the advance Dutch works, killing a captain, a sergeant, and eight sappers.

Guerrillas from the interior under Capt. Andrés Vázquez Botello de Carrera also begin plaguing the besiegers. On the night of 5 October they slay *Nieuw Nederlandt*'s captain and a 20-man boat party in the harbor; ten days later they destroy a similar force up Bayamón River. By 16 October the guerrillas have grown so bold as to reconquer Cañuela Fortress, using two launches and 30 men to kill two of its Dutch occupiers, capturing another 14. Faced with this increased pressure, Hendricksz finds himself trapped inside the harbor. Once more he calls upon de Haro to capitulate on 21 October, threatening to burn the city, but he is rebuffed. San Juan is therefore put to the torch, and the Dutch reembark at 10:00 A.M. the next day, hotly pursued by Puerto Rican units. The invaders must now run the gauntlet of Spanish artillery in order to escape, hesitating for a full fortnight before finally dashing past on 2 November. The 30-gun, 450-ton *Medemblik* runs aground and is left behind for the exultant Spanish, Juan de Amézquita boarding and extinguishing the slow fuse that is burning toward its magazine. De Haro is unable to savor the victory because a cannon explodes near him during these final exchanges, spraying him with two dozen fragments and eventually causing his death.

Hendricksz, meanwhile, retires into San Francisco Bay for a month to recover from the setback. In addition to *Medemblik,* numerous other Dutch vessels have sustained damage, and 200 men have perished (as opposed to 17 Spanish fatalities during the siege). Hendricksz nonetheless detaches his five best vessels on a privateering cruise toward Santo Domingo before attempting to lead his entire fleet west again in late November. Driven back by storms, he cruises south toward Margarita (Venezuela), despite advance warnings preceding him.

22 FEBRUARY 1626. Hendricksz bears down upon Margarita's port of Pampatar, dividing his fleet into two. One squadron approaches its keep and opens fire; the other deposits 500 men in nearby Lance de los Burros inlet. After an hour and a half, a chance Dutch shot explodes the fort's only bronze cannon, putting an end to Spanish opposition. Hendricksz's arrival overland with his landing party breaks the last of the defenders' will, forcing them to flee under Gov. Andrés Rodríguez de Villegas, after which the keep is stripped of its ordinance and razed along with the tiny town. But when the Dutch press on to the southern harbor of Puerto del Mar (modern Porlamar), two miles south of the capital of Asunción, they are again checked by Spanish soldiers and native archers. Discouraged by this resistance and the shallow approaches, Hendricksz withdraws.

Over the next few weeks, he raids such minor places as Coche and Cubagua Islands, Mochima, Santa Fé, and Araya, being repelled at the last place by its newly erected Santiago del Arroyo Fortress under Lt. Juan de Arroyo. Standing away from the Spanish Main on 5 April, Hendricksz intercepts a frigate bearing dispatches three days later before laying in a course for Bonaire.

10 APRIL (EASTER SUNDAY) 1626. Hendricksz arrives at Bonaire, rustling many sheep and gathering wood. The Dutch admiral now decides to attempt the third part of his instructions: attacking the Spanish plate fleet as it traverses the Gulf of Mexico between Veracruz and Havana. He begins working northwest, timing his movements so as to arrive off Cuba by midsummer, when the silver convoys traditionally depart. During this advance, his fleet splits into units of three or four vessels apiece so as to sweep the Caribbean.

Numerous captures are made, and in the Mona Passage the Dutch are reinforced by two men-of-war under Lucifer, who has come north after provisioning a small new Zeeland colony in the Amazon. After rendezvousing off San Felipe Key (near Isla de Pinos), the entire fleet rounds Cape San Antonio at the western tip of Cuba.

14 JUNE 1626. At 8:00 A.M. this Sunday, Hendricksz's 15 large and eight small vessels enter Cabañas (northwestern Cuba), encountering no resistance. Its few Spanish residents are supervising construction of a new galleon for Juan Pérez de Oporto and flee inland. The Dutch spend three days refurbishing supplies before burning the half-built galleon and standing out to sea.

19 JUNE 1626. Hendricksz arrives before Havana and institutes a close blockade. The plate fleet has not yet appeared from Veracruz, yet Dutch hopes are dashed two weeks later when their commander suddenly dies on 2 July from illness. His successor, Adriaen Claeszoon, is unable to maintain the weary fleet intact, most captains opting for a return to Europe. After pausing at Matanzas to deposit more than 50 prisoners, refresh provisions, and burn prizes they do not want, the Dutch disperse into the Straits of Florida.

6 JULY 1626. A fresh Dutch fleet arrives at Barbados, having been sent under the wily veteran Heyn to reinforce Hendricksz:

Ship	*Tons*	*Guns*	*Sailors*	*Soldiers*	*Commander*
Amsterdam (flag)	300	40	140	64	Piet Heyn
Hollandia	300	30	134	44	Jan Janszoon Zuyl
Geldria	300	34	130	50	Jan Karstenszoon (Christiaenszoon)
Zutphen	170	28	111	44	Pieter Gerritszoon Roodt
Pinas	100	18	66	—	Laurens Simonszoon van der Graft
Raaf (yacht)	15	5	14	—	Willem Joosten
Sperwer (yacht)	15	4	19	—	Jan Coenraedszoon
Walcheren (vice-flag)	280	30	150	25	Cornelis Corneliszoon Oele
Arend (yacht)	80	12	60	—	Claes Pieterszoon Wittebaerdt
Neptunus (rear admiral)	230	20	107	37	Pieter Stoffelszoon van Eyken (Cromeijk)
David (yacht)	60	14	58	—	Thomas Cornelis Condé
Oranjeboom	300	33	152	—	Gerrit Janszoon Eisens
Gouden Leeuw	250	28	119	71	Hendrik Best
Vos (yacht)	70	16	80	—	Jan de Braam

Heyn quickly resupplies then sails to join Hendricksz off Cuba. From a Spanish coaster taken near Cape San Antonio he learns of the latter's death in late August, then receives word that the Mexican plate fleet has already entered Havana. Heyn therefore takes up station off the bank of Florida's Dry Tortugas in hopes of snaring some Spanish stragglers.

He is lying there when the Tierra Firme treasure fleet appears, escorted by 13 powerful galleons under Adm. Tomás de Larraspuru. Despite being tempted, the Dutch must allow the rich Spanish convoy to pass. Frustrated, Heyn waters his ships at Cape Canaveral before striking out into the Atlantic to fulfill the next phase of his instructions: a descent upon Brazil. Contrary winds and currents force him to circle as far east as the Azores and Africa before finally steering back toward South America.

EARLY MARCH 1627. Heyn sights Brazil and shortly thereafter stands boldly into Baía de Todos os Santos, sinking or capturing 26 Iberian ships. This marks the beginning of a brilliant, summer-long privateering campaign, during which Heyn terrorizes the Brazilian coast and seizes countless prizes, some of which are used to augment his own fleet. In July, four of his ships are dispatched back to the Netherlands with booty, after which another attack is made against Baía de Todos os Santos, resulting in even more captures. Heyn finally quits these waters in October, sailing home to a hero's welcome.

8 JULY 1627. A Spanish merchant convoy escorted by two warships, bound from Tierra Firme and Honduras toward Cuba, is attacked opposite Cojímar by three Zeeland vessels under Lucifer. The Honduran *almiranta* (vice-flag; *San Antonio* of Capt. Miguel Ramírez) is seized after a heated fight in which Lucifer receives a mortal wound; the Spanish flagship gains Havana by Monday, 12 July. Nonetheless, the value of this single prize is so great that it nets the expedition's shareholders a profit of 1.2 million guilders.

LATE JULY–EARLY AUGUST 1627. Lt. Diego Vázquez de Hinestrosa (or Hinostrosa), commander of three Cuban coast-guard vessels and 150 men, guides some Honduran merchant ships into Havana through the Dutch blockade. Skirmishes are reportedly fought all the way from Cape San Antonio to the Cuban capital's entrance.

15 MARCH 1628. A dozen WIC men-of-war arrive in the Caribbean from the Netherlands, intent on conducting privateering operations under veteran Cmdr. Pieter Adriaanszoon Ita. Within a few weeks his forces

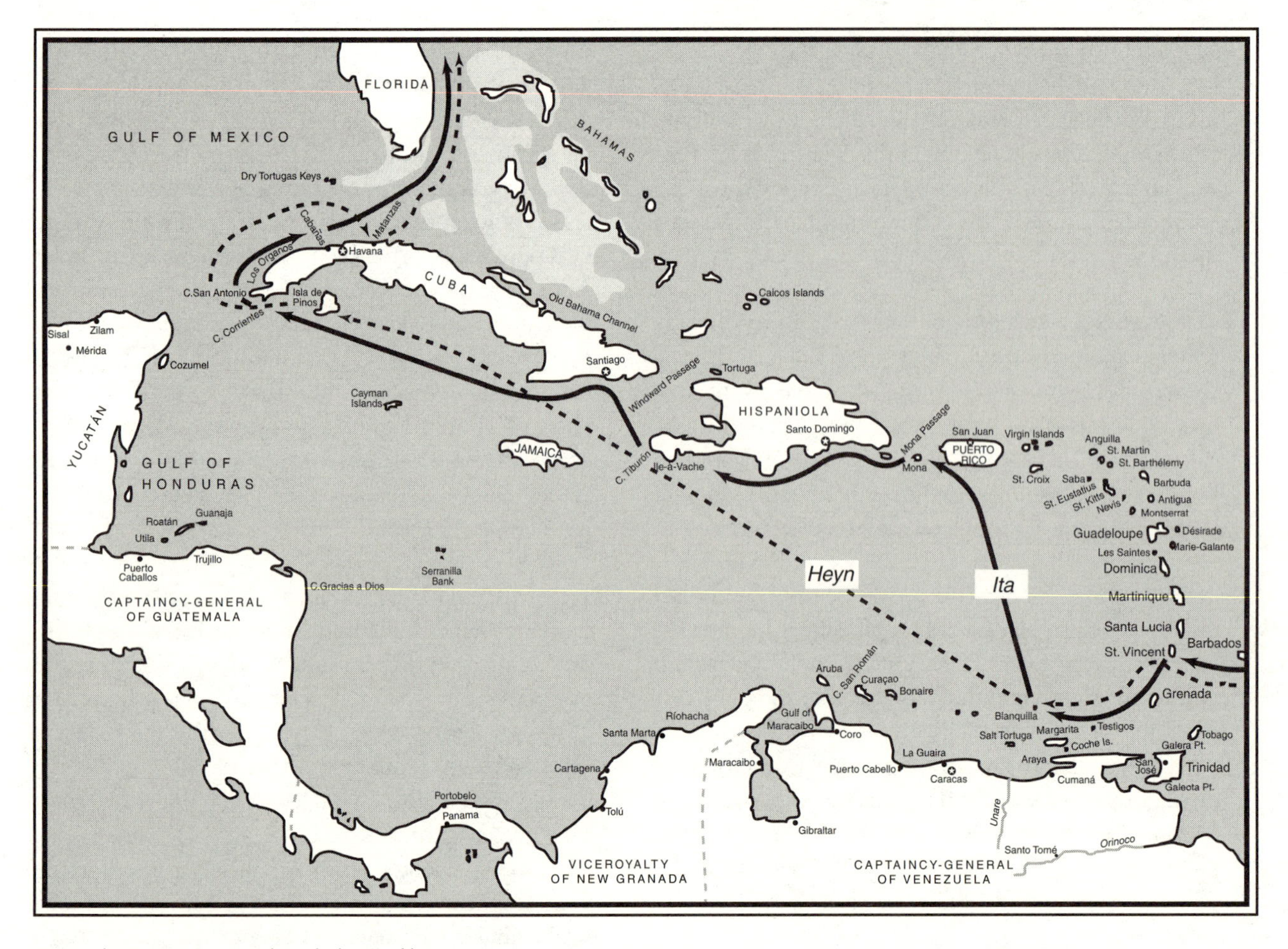

Ita's and Heyn's campaigns through the Caribbean

capture four substantial Spanish prizes and contemplate an assault upon Santiago de Cuba, although the plan is eventually postponed. After cruising independently, Ita's ships rendezvous at Cape Tiburón (southwestern Haiti) before rounding Cape San Antonio and taking up station off Florida's Dry Tortugas Bank. Their goal is to intercept the Spanish treasure galleons arriving from Honduras.

12 JULY 1628. Another powerful Dutch fleet arrives at Saint Vincent under 51-year-old Piet Heyn, now the WIC's senior admiral:

Ship	*Tons*	*Guns*	*Sailors*	*Soldiers*	*Commander*
Amsterdam (flag)	500	50	166	84	Witte Corneliszoon de With
Hollandsche Tuin (vice-flag)	400	36	130	67	Allert Janszoon
Hollandia	300	30	125	50	Thomas Sickenszoon
Gelderland	300	32	125	52	Pieter Gerritsz Root
Provincie van Utrecht	300	30	131	53	Hendrik Jacobszoon Kat
Witte Leeuw	250	26	?	?	Jan Janszoon van Hoorn
Zwarte Leeuw	180	24	75	32	Pieter Franszoon
Vergulde Valk	150	26	85	42	Marcus Martenszoon
Roode Leeuw	250	24	120	41	Albert Hendrikszoon
Haarlem	220	22	120	42	Frans Claeszoon

Ship	*Tons*	*Guns*	*Sailors*	*Soldiers*	*Commander*
Pinas	100	8	60	26	Claes Franszoon de Vries
Muiden (yacht)	60	16	(48 men total)		Cornelis Leendertszoon
Naarden (yacht)	60	14	(15 men total)		Hans Cools
Eenhoorn (yacht)	60	10	(47 men total)		Hendrik Janszoon Lang
Zwarte Ruiter (yacht)	60	14	(50 men total)		Michiel Gijsbrechtszoon
Langebark (yacht)	20	2	(20 men total)		Jacob Barents
Neptunus (vice-flag)	200	24	100	55	Joost van Trappen (Banckert)
Tijger	120	24	106	45	Lucas Pol
Goude Zon	160	18	(109 men total)		Willebrod Danen
Postpaard (yacht)	70	12	66	12	Willem Corneliszoon Domburgh
Oud Vlissingen (yacht)	50	12	(45 men total)		Willem Willemszoon
Utrecht (rear admiral)	300	35	159	50	Cornelis Claeszoon Melkmeid
Dordrecht	250	24	106	41	Willem Gerritszoon Ruijter
Neptunus	230	26	102	53	Bastiaan Jakobszoon
Tijger (yacht)	57	14	70	20	Cornelis Jakobszoon Gleijnbeet
Monnikendam	300	30	(168 men total)		Cornelis Symonszoon Groen
Griffoen	250	32	141	53	Jan Corneliszoon Keerlekoe
Ooievaar (yacht)	90	14	55	22	Samuel Willemszoon
Goude Leeuw	250	28	143	47	Pieter Walighszoon
Dolfijn (yacht)	150	20	98	34	Hendrik Corneliszoon Dreven
Vos (yacht)	70	12	(74 men total)		Jan de Braams

This huge force is to intercept the Spanish plate fleets before Havana. Heyn begins cautiously working his way west with stops at Blanquilla Island and Isla de Pinos but refraining from any overt act that might forewarn the Spaniards of his presence.

1 AUGUST 1628. Off Mariel, Ita's ships intercept a small Honduran *patache* (tender) at dawn, learning that two treasure galleons are following close astern, bound for Havana. They appear shortly thereafter, prompting the Dutch to give chase. The galleons' commander, Alvaro de la Cerda, having been advised of the blockade before departing, has reinforced his vessels with 100 musketeers under Ens. Juan de las Herrerías. Running toward Havana, the Spaniards are overtaken by Ita's faster ships around noon, and a fight ensues. Hard pressed, de la Cerda works close inshore late this afternoon, grounding his galleons two to three miles from La Punta Fortress in a desperate bid to save his cargo. De la Cerda is wounded three times, and both his galleons are set ablaze by their crews; a pair of Cuban coast-guard frigates and another smaller vessel—bearing a total of 180 men under *Sargento Mayor* Diego Vázquez de Hinestrosa—sally from Havana, only to be driven back.

The Honduran vice-flag goes up in flames, but Ita's boarders put out the fire aboard de la Cerda's *capitana* (flagship), towing it off with its indigo, ginger, silver, and hides still intact. The triumphant Dutch then depart into the Straits of Florida with their prize, bound toward the Netherlands. Such a dramatic retirement convinces many Spaniards that these waters are now safe—little realizing that this very day Heyn's much more powerful fleet is taking up station off the Dry Tortugas.

22 AUGUST 1628. After three weeks out of sight of land, Heyn's fleet closes upon Havana and institutes a blockade, anticipating the arrival of a plate fleet. *Mariscal de Campo* Lorenzo de Cabrera y Corvera, knight of the Order of Santiago and governor of Havana, attempts to send warnings across the Gulf of Mexico, but these are either intercepted or come too late. The Dutch, meanwhile, struggle to remain on station, being driven almost as far east as Matanzas by 7 September due to contrary winds and currents.

8 SEPTEMBER 1628. ***Capture of the Mexican Plate Fleet.*** Early this Friday morning, Heyn learns that one of his outlying ships has intercepted a Spanish vessel, an advance unit for the approaching bullion fleet. Veering northeast, the Dutch admiral sights 12 more sail, capturing nine of them over the course of the morning. Around noon he spots another nine or ten vessels to the southeast, a half-dozen being so large that they are doubtless the Spanish flagship and its consorts—the only vessels authorized to carry treasure.

These vessels are in fact *Santa Ana María* (flag) of Adm. Juan de Benavides y Bazán, knight of the Order of Santiago, plus the galleons *Santa Gertrudis* (vice-flag) of Baltasar de Amezquita, *San Juan Bautista* of Alonso de Ayspuru, and *Nuestra Señora de la Antigua* of Francisco Ortuño de Olano, plus a couple of lesser craft. They have departed Veracruz a month earlier, only to be scattered by a storm and then blundering past the proper longitude for Havana. Heyn immediately orders a pursuit, his vice admiral, Joost van Trappen (alias Banckert), hastening ahead of the Spaniards with nine sail to prevent any flight eastward; Heyn's main body steers southwest to cut off any similar retreat into Havana.

Toward evening, the encircled Benavides leads his galleons into Matanzas, hoping to make a stand until the king's bullion can be off-loaded. But the heavy galleons run aground on uncharted shoals inside, their broadsides not bearing upon the entrance. Panic spreads among the Spanish crews as numerous Dutch ships gather in the moonlight, firing upon the Spanish boats that are plying to and from shore. Discipline finally dissolves, and the four Spanish galleons and two smaller ships are boarded during the next morning without a fight. More than 300 Spaniards die this night and another 600 are wounded, against negligible Dutch losses. Heyn takes a full year's Mexican silver shipment plus countless private hordes. All captives are released ashore, and the Dutch occupy themselves for the next eight days transferring the riches aboard their vessels to return home. Eventually all except the four large Spanish galleons and another prize are burned, Heyn weighing from Matanzas by 17 September.

He and his vice admiral, Hendrick Corneliszoon Loncq, are given a joyous reception upon regaining Holland, the gross profits from their coup being 11.5 million guilders. Spain is plunged into a commensurate financial crisis by the loss of its entire Mexican fleet, Benavides and his second-in-command, Juan de Leoz, knight of the Order of Santiago, being court-martialed upon returning home. The admiral is eventually executed in Seville on Thursday, 18 May 1634; Leoz is banished to an African garrison for the remainder of his life.

1 APRIL 1629. A Dutch fleet under Adriaen Janszoon Pater arrives off Grenada, dividing into two smaller

squadrons to raid Spanish America. Having once served three years as a galley slave at Cartagena (arrested for poaching salt at Araya by Adm. Luis de Fajardo), Pater bears the Spaniards little love. For more than two months, his contingents—reinforced by numerous foreign mercenaries living in the Antilles—roam unchecked, until a rendezvous is effected off southwestern Cuba.

APRIL 1629. A mixed colonizing expedition of Dutch, Irish, English, and French settlers reaches the Amazon Delta from Holland, erecting a stockade on the Tauregue River. This outpost is besieged one month later by 40 Portuguese soldiers and 800 Indians out of Belém under Capt. Pedro da Costa. The defenders, under Capt. James Purcell, resist successfully, obliging the Portuguese to withdraw into Fort São António do Gurupá to recuperate.

MID-JUNE 1629. His command reunited and further augmented by two Zeeland ships, plus other reinforcements from Holland under Vice Adm. Jan Janszoon van Hoorn, Pater rounds Cape San Antonio and takes up station off Florida's Dry Tortugas Bank in hopes of intercepting another treasure fleet. The Spaniards—fully aware that 26 Dutch ships are hovering near Havana—refuse to budge from Portobelo, Cartagena, and Veracruz. Nevertheless, the blockade helps deepen Spain's financial crisis by preventing any silver bullion from crossing the Atlantic this year.

SEPTEMBER 1629. Tiring of blockading Havana, Pater sends nine ships and prizes home from the Bahamas and leads the remainder of his fleet southeast to Barbados, arriving by early November. He then detaches van Hoorn to investigate conditions on Saint Kitts and Nevis following de Toledo's campaign (*see* 16 September 1629) while proceeding with his 20 other ships under alternate Vice Adm. Maarten Thijssen to probe the nearby Orinoco.

28 SEPTEMBER 1629. Teixeira appears a half-mile from the new Dutch outpost on the Tauregue River in the Amazon Delta, with 120 Portuguese soldiers and 1,600 native auxiliaries aboard 100 boats. After disembarking, they advance next day and completely encircle the outnumbered garrison by 30 September.

Numerous sallies and countersallies ensue, until Purcell requests terms on 17 October. Teixeira proves generous, so an armistice is arranged by 19 October, with the actual surrender to take place on 22 October. At the last moment Purcell asks for a three-day extension, having secretly learned that a relief ship has arrived off the coast from Zeeland, accompanied by 100 new English colonists under William Clovell aboard the 90-ton *Amazon* of Capt. Francis Neville and 50-ton *Sea Nymph* of Master John Ellinger. When the Portuguese belatedly discover this fact, they compel the 80 defenders to capitulate on 25 October, razing the fort before withdrawing next day.

Amazon and *Sea Nymph* appear on 29 October with a captured pinnace, suffering four killed by native archers when they attempt a disembarkation; they stand away to found their own new colony elsewhere in the delta.

DECEMBER 1629. It takes Pater and Thijssen three weeks to work up the Orinoco River to Santo Tomé, which they attack with a landing force several hundred strong supported by 14 siege guns. With Gov. Luis de Monsalve absent on the island of Trinidad, Spanish resistance quickly collapses. The Dutch briefly occupy the town before returning to the Caribbean to visit like treatment upon Blanquilla Island, Bonaire, and Puerto Rico.

14 FEBRUARY 1630. ***Pernambuco Occupation.*** A Dutch colonizing expedition of 52 ships and 15 sloops under Hendrick Loncq (Heyn's former vice admiral; *see* 8 September 1628) appears before the Brazilian province of Pernambuco, bearing 1,170 guns, 3,780 sailors, and 3,500 soldiers. Two large landing parties disembark at Pau Amarelo and advance upon the capital of Olinda and the nearby port of Recife from opposite directions, along the Doce and Topado Rivers, forcing Gov. Matías de Albuquerque, Conde de Alegrete, to order the ships in its roadstead burned and all inhabitants to flee inland. The Dutch occupy the abandoned towns by 2 March, renaming the area Nieuw Holland ("New Holland"); de Albuquerque organizes a guerrilla campaign headquartered at Fort Arraial do Bom Jesus.

26 FEBRUARY 1630. Pater's 20 sail descend upon Santa Marta (Colombia) at 3:00 P.M. on this Tuesday, having learned from intercepted letters of its weakened condition. The initial bombardment silences the Spaniards' four bronze cannons and kills the ancient gunner, after which 1,000 Dutchmen disembark from 18 swivel-armed boats, overrunning both the fortress and the town within the next few hours. Spanish Gov. Gerónimo de Quero flees up Mamatocos River with 50 loyal militia, leaving Santa Marta to its fate. Pater remains a week, wreaking much destruction—although

A young Dutch adventurer; seventeenth-century oil by Pieter Codde

allegedly sparing a few dwellings in exchange for a ransom of 5,500 *reales* raised by the local clergy—before retiring out to sea on 5 March.

Shortly thereafter—in late April—Pater sails for home, despairing of further reinforcements reaching him from the Netherlands and of intercepting the Spanish treasure fleets. He arrives to a hero's welcome in June 1630.

5 MAY 1630. Six Dutch ships with 655 men quit Olinda in Pernambuco under Commo. Dierick Ruyters, a belated reinforcement for Pater in the Caribbean; this force is followed shortly thereafter by another eight ships with 545 men under Admiral Ita (leaving only 17 Dutch ships at Pernambuco).

Both units arrive in the Antilles to find Pater already departed and so cruise independently. On 17 August they unite with a small fleet under Jan Gijsbertszoon Booneter, which has also been prowling the Caribbean, to blockade Havana. Learning of this latest deployment, the Spanish admiral, de Larraspuru—commanding this year's Tierra Firme plate fleet—resorts to the extraordinary expedient of sailing his vessels directly out of the Caribbean via the Windward and Caicos Passages without touching at Cuba. This gamble pays off when he reaches Spain safely with 7 million pesos in silver.

14 APRIL 1631. Pater returns to the Americas, arriving at Recife with 17 ships to relieve its Pernambuco garrison. (Other vessels have preceded him out of Holland under his vice admiral, Thijssen.) The Dutch use this renewed strength to launch a counterattack against the Hispano-Portuguese guerrillas, who are bedeviling them, by sending an expedition including German-born Cols. Sigismund von Schoppe and Christovam Artichoksky (or Arciszewsky) north with 20 to 30 sail to conquer the southern tip of Itamaracá Island and erect a small offshore citadel called Geduld (later renamed Oranje). Pater then allows seven or eight of his largest ships to cruise south as far as Baía de Todos os Santos in search of prizes.

17 APRIL 1631. A Dutch squadron materializes off Havana under Booneter, who maintains a close blockade until 18 May, then stands away the next day to refresh provisions at Matanzas before steering out into the Straits of Florida on 4 June for Holland.

26 APRIL 1631. Commo. Jonathan de Neckere departs Pernambuco to reinforce Booneter in the Caribbean with *Domburg* (flag) of 22 guns, 260 tons, 60 sailors, and 45 soldiers under de Neckere; *Otter* (vice-flag) with 60 sailors under Cornelis Cornelis-zoon Jol; and *Phoenix* of 12 guns, 120 tons, and 50 sailors under Reynier Pieterszoon. Jol, already a veteran of three previous New World cruises, is better known to the Dutch as Houtebeen ("Peg-Leg")—the Spaniards calling him Pie de Palo—and will further burnish his reputation during the forthcoming campaign.

De Neckere reaches Barbados by 12 May, visits adjacent Saint Vincent, then arrives at Île-à-Vache by mid-June, missing Booneter by three days (he has gone on ahead to blockade Havana). De Neckere therefore prowls south toward Santa Marta, taking several prizes. He then sails for Europe, leaving Jol to continue hunting independently.

10 JULY 1631. Six piraguas arrive at Tortuga Island (Venezuela), disembarking 40 Spanish militia and 117 native auxiliaries under veteran Capt. Benito Arias Montano. These have been dispatched by Gov. Francisco Núñez Melián to chastise Dutch interlopers in these waters. After concealing themselves throughout the day, a small platoon under Pedro Lobera reconnoiters two Dutch merchantmen anchored offshore—one of 600 tons and 20 guns, the other of 300 tons and six guns—which have set landing parties ashore to load water and salt.

After nightfall, Arias divides his company into two contingents, sending one under subordinate Felipe Gómez de León to ambush the Dutch shore parties; he leads the remainder to attack the anchored vessels with boats. He approaches quite close before being discovered, yet he carries the larger ship by storm, killing its captain, sailing master, quartermaster, and several crewmembers. The smaller Dutch consort attempts to flee but is likewise subdued, and Gómez de León also wins his encounter on land. The interlopers' huts are burned and their craft are carried triumphantly into La Guaira six days later.

11 JULY 1631. This night, 27 Hispano-Portuguese men-of-war under Adm. Antonio de Oquendo, Vice Adm. Francisco de Vallecilla, and Rear Adm. Nicolás de Massibradi enter Baía de Todos os Santos with reinforcements from Lisbon. This fleet is to return toward Europe shortly, escorting the homeward-bound Brazilian sugar convoy.

19 AUGUST 1631. Word reaches Pater and the Dutch authorities at Recife of the arrival of de Oquendo's fleet farther south, so the admiral prepares to sortie.

Spanish Admiral Antonio de Oquendo, ca. 1626, with the red sash and baton of a captain-general

Because of a shortage of crews, he does not quit port until 31 August, then steers south with only 18 ships, reinforced by troops from the Pernambuco garrison.

3 SEPTEMBER 1631. De Oquendo exits Baía de Todos os Santos with his 44-gun, 900-ton flagship *Santiago de Oliste* and 28-gun, 700-ton vice-flagship *San Antonio;* 30-gun *Nuestra Señora de la Concepción;* 28-gun *Nuestra Señora del Buen Suceso;* 26-gun *Nuestra Señora de la Anunciada;* 24-gun *San Carlos;* 22-gun *San Buenaventura;* 20-gun *San Blas, San Francisco,* and *San Pedro;* 18-gun *San Bartolomé,* and *San Martín;* plus the requisitioned French pinnaces *Lion Doré* of 10 guns (renamed *San Antonio*), and *Saint Pierre* of 8 guns (renamed *San Pedro*).

These Spanish men-of-war are accompanied by the 28-gun Portuguese warship *São Jorge;* 20-gun *Santiago;* 19-gun *São João Baptista;* 18-gun *Nossa Senhora dos Prazeres (Maior),* and *Nossa Senhora dos Prazeres (Menor);* plus the unarmed *Nossa Senhora da Boa Nova, Nossa Senhora do Rozario, San António, Santa Cruz,* and *São Jeronimo.*

This force is protecting ten unarmed Brazilian caravels bearing 1,200 troops under the Neapolitan-born Cmdr. Giovanni Vincenzo de San Felice, Conde de Bagnuoli, intended to reinforce the town of Paraíba in addition to 20 Lisbon-bound sugar merchantmen. Standing away from the coast, the entire formation is driven southeast by contrary winds and currents into the vicinity of the Abrolhos (rocks 200 miles off Brazil at about 18 degrees south latitude, their name deriving from the Portuguese phrase *abre olhos*—"open eyes"—intended as a warning of the half-submerged dangers). On the evening of 11 September the Hispano-Portuguese fleet is sighted by Pater, who clears for action overnight.

12 SEPTEMBER 1631. ***Los Abrolhos.*** During Pater's voyage two of his ships have become separated, leaving the Dutch admiral with his 46-gun, 1,000-ton flagship *Prins Willem* and 50-gun, 800-ton vice-flagship *Geunieerde Provintien;* 38-gun *Provincie Utrecht;* 34-gun *Walcheren;* 32-gun *Griffoen,* and *Groeningen;* 30-gun *Hollandia,* and *Oliphant;* 28-gun *Amersfoort,* and *Goeree;* 26-gun *Mercurius;* 24-gun *Dordrecht;* 22-gun *Medemblik;* 20-gun *Fortuijn,* and *Wapen van Hoorn;* plus 14-gun *Nieuw Nederlandt.*

At first light the admiral summons his captains for final instructions, then drinks a toast of Brunswick beer to the day's success. The Dutch bear down in faint east-northeasterly breezes upon de Oquendo, who is six miles distant, having ordered his 17 Spanish and Portuguese galleons to interpose in a half-moon crescent between the enemy and the convoy. *Anunciada, Buenaventura, San Carlos,* and *San Bartolomé* lag astern.

Fighting begins around midmorning, when Vice Admiral de Vallecilla's *San Antonio* opens fire on Thijssen's advancing *Geunieerde Provintien,* which closes in to board along with *Provincie Utrecht.* About 15 minutes later de Oquendo and four other galleons open fire on Pater's flagship, which steers directly toward *Santiago de Oliste* with *Walcheren.* The Dutch hold their opening broadsides until point-blank range, then fire and grapple. A murderous engagement erupts around each flagship and vice-flag, both sides firing repeatedly into their opponents—yet unable to board. The smallest Portuguese galleon, *Nossa Senhora dos Prazeres (Menor)* of Capt. Cosme do Couto Barbosa, attempts to support *Santiago de Oliste,* only to drift helplessly beneath the combined guns of *Prins Willem* and *Walcheren* and be sunk. Its place is taken by the much larger *Concepción* of Capt. Juan de Prado.

Eventually, about 4:00 P.M., a chance shot from de Oquendo's flagship starts a blaze aboard *Prins Willem,* which the Spanish admiral cleverly directs his musketeers to fire at, so as to hamper Dutch fire-fighting efforts. The flames gain hold and finally drive Pater into the water, along with a few survivors, where he drowns. About this same time, de Vallecilla's vice-flag, *San Antonio,* breaks up and goes down by its stern, taking most of the complement; its Dutch foe *Provincie Utrecht* sheers off in flames and later sinks. Thijssen's *Geunieerde Provintien* is battered but in possession of a single prize—*Buenaventura* of Capt. Alonso de Alarcón y Molina, who has sailed to *San Antonio*'s side during the fighting, only to lose his life and ship. The remaining Dutch vessels are content to fire from long range—*Hollandia, Amersfoort,* and *Fortuijn* being the only others to become closely engaged—while the Spaniards respond in kind.

The day ends in a Spanish victory, although Spanish losses prove somewhat greater. A vice-flagship and galleon are sunk and another is taken, with 585 dead and missing (240 of these aboard the captured *Buenaventura*) plus 201 wounded. The Dutch flagship and another man-of-war disappear beneath the waves, leaving 350 dead and missing plus more than 80 seriously wounded. However, Thijssen shows no inclination to renew action the next day, preferring to limp back to Recife with his mauled fleet on 21–22 September. De Oquendo meanwhile deposits his reinforcements at Barra Grande of Porto Calvo—only 700 of them actually reach Fort Arraial do Bom Jesus—before continuing toward Europe with his sugar convoy. The Dutch garrison at Pernambuco subsequently evacuates Olinda in November in order to concentrate its strength around Recife.

5 DECEMBER 1631. Five boats from three large Dutch ships attempt a cutting-out operation at La Guaira, only to be repelled by Gov. Francisco Núñez Melián.

30 APRIL 1632. A trio of Dutch ships is spotted at sundown stealing upon La Guaira. The next morning the ships are engaged and driven off by Governor Núñez Melián while their boats attempt to tow them into harbor.

15 MAY 1632. Having stabilized the situation at Pernambuco and left a squadron under Commo. Jan Mast of *Walcheren,* Admiral Thijssen arrives at Barbados with 22 Dutch ships to cruise against Spanish possessions in the Antilles. His summer-long campaign proves uninspired, failing to surprise any significant target. After blockading Havana throughout August in hopes of intercepting a plate fleet, Thijssen departs for the Low Countries by early September.

NOVEMBER 1632. After residing on the uninhabited island of Sint Maarten for more than a year under WIC representative Jan Claeszoon van Campen, a group of Dutch settlers completes a 34-gun fortress that is capable of sustaining a 100-man garrison.

26 APRIL 1633. Veteran Commodore van Hoorn quits Pernambuco with four ships, three yachts, and three sloops, manned by 500 sailors and 400 soldiers (among these the gifted Capt. "Peg-Leg" Jol). Van Hoorn's instructions are to attack the Brazilian fortress of Ceará; visit the two-year-old Dutch base of Sint Maarten in the Windward Islands; then raid Trujillo, the staging point for the Honduras galleons. Instead, with the consent of the Dutch authorities at Pernambuco, he reconnoiters the Brazilian port of Maranhão before proceeding directly toward Barbados to commence his West Indian campaign.

22 JUNE 1633. Some 55 Spanish sail—24 of them men-of-war—appear off Saint Barthélemy under Adm. Lope Díez de Aux y Armendáriz, Marqués de Cadereyta, and his veteran vice admiral, Carlos de Ibarra, knight of the Order of Alcántara. The force comprises three distinct fleets: the annual Tierra Firme convoy under Adm. Luis Fernández de Córdoba; the Mexican convoy under Adm. Lope de Hoces y Córdoba, knight of the Order of Santiago; plus Cadereyta's own battle group. In addition to fetching Spain's American silver, this expedition is intended to eradicate Sint Maarten, the newest Dutch settlement in the Antilles.

Arriving by mistake off neighboring Saint Barthélemy, the Spaniards next day sight five interloper vessels anchored off its southern coast; four immediately get under way while abandoning the fifth (a ten-gun vessel) to its fate. Cadereyta learns from his *sargento mayor,* Juan de Irrazaga, that the fleet is at Saint Barthélemy; he therefore lays in a course for Sint Maarten that night.

24 JUNE 1633. ***Reconquest of Saint Martin.*** At noon, a Spanish reconnaissance reveals that Dutch settlers have a 22-gun fortress covering Sint Maarten's approaches, so Cadereyta sends an emissary ashore from his flagship, *Nuestra Señora de Aranzazu,* to demand the garrison's surrender. (This officer is Capt. Benito Arias Montano—*see* 10 July 1631—who has recently been appointed governor of Araya and Cumaná and is returning to Venezuela aboard the Tierra Firme fleet to take up his new post.) Approximately 150 Dutch defenders and 40 black auxiliaries under "Lambert

Franchrisperi" (perhaps a Spanish misspelling of Jan Claeszoon van Campen) reject Cadereyta's overture.

Several Spanish galleons then bear down, engaging the fortress in a heated exchange during which seven Spanish crewmembers perish while smaller boats seek a disembarkation point. At 2:00 A.M. the next day, 1,000 troops and 300 sailors are set ashore under Vice Admiral de Hoces and *Maestre de Campo* Luis de Rojas y Borgia with two small field pieces. They make an arduous march through the jungle, suffering at least six deaths from heat exhaustion before finally emerging behind the Dutch fortress and storming its walls on 26 June. Musket fire halts them, de Hoces receiving a crippling wound in his left elbow and side. The Spaniards inaugurate formal siege proceedings, bringing ashore four heavier guns to install in a battery, then launching another 100-man assault the night of 28 June during which veteran naval Capt. Tiburcio Redín is injured.

By 1 July, a badly wounded van Campen and his 62 Dutch and 15 black survivors request terms, which are granted. Cadereyta occupies the fortress the next day, deciding to keep it for Spain and strengthening its works; he adds four 24-pounders, four 18-pound demi-culverins, and five 12- to ten-pounders to its armament, plus a permanent garrison of 250 Spanish soldiers and 50 auxiliaries under Capt. Cebrián de Lizarazu, knight of the Order of Santiago. The Spanish fleet then clears for San Juan de Puerto Rico, arriving with its prisoners and three Dutch prizes by 13 July.

15 JULY 1633. Van Hoorn's ten vessels steal upon Trujillo (Honduras), surprising the port and battering it into submission within two hours at a cost of seven Dutch lives. However, most of its Spanish inhabitants succeed in fleeing inland, leaving van Hoorn with little booty (a few cannons plus some hides). Subsequent ransom demands also produce meager results (20 pounds of silver) so van Hoorn sails away six days later intending to attack Campeche. No Dutch raider has yet penetrated so deep into the Gulf of Mexico, but van Hoorn is encouraged by a mulatto rover named Diego de los Reyes (Diego Grillo, born a slave at Havana and better known to his Spanish-American victims as Diego the Mulatto or Diego Lucifer), who is in company. Having once resided at Campeche, Diego is familiar with its roadstead and defenses and so leads the way.

4 AUGUST 1633. Off Los Organos Keys (northwestern Cuba), the Spanish galleon *Triunfo de la Cruz* of Capt. Miguel de Redín—separated from Adm. de Hoces's convoy bound toward Veracruz—is engaged from dawn until 10:00 A.M. in a brutal exchange with a 46-gun Dutch ship. De Redín's leg is blown off by the second Dutch broadside, which kills him along with 15 of his crew and wounds many more. The two battered antagonists eventually drift apart, leaving de Redín's second-in-command, Juan de Llano, to pilot *Triunfo* into Havana ten days later.

11 AUGUST 1633. ***Van Hoorn's Sack of Campeche.*** Thirteen sail bear down this Friday noon, depositing more than 500 Dutch, English, French, and Portuguese raiders under Diego the Mulatto and peg-legged Cornelis Jol on the Campeche outskirts next morning. Although a cluster of armed boats covers their approach from offshore, the attackers' initial assault is repelled by 50 harquebusiers under Capt. Domingo Galván Romero, who is entrenched along the western circuit with three artillery pieces. But when the assault recedes, the defenders rise from their trenches and set off in pursuit, only to be trapped in open country. Galván and about a dozen others are shot down, the way into Campeche now lying open. The invaders pour into the city streets, unchecked until they encounter another 300 Spaniards drawn up in the main square. A ferocious firefight ensues, ending with more than three dozen Spanish being killed and many more taken captive; terrified survivors flee toward San Francisco Campechuelo.

Van Hoorn, Jol, and Diego remain in Campeche for the next two days, and although they strip it of everything of value and seize 22 vessels lying in its roads, they are unable to extort ransoms from the interior. They therefore spike its guns and sail a dozen miles up the coast before releasing their captives; they retain nine prizes, sell another four back to the Spaniards, and burn the rest. Van Hoorn departs toward Holland on 24 August, leaving Jol and Diego to continue operations.

25 AUGUST 1633. At Cumaná, the new governor, Bernardo Arias Montano, inaugurates his rule by organizing an expedition of 95 Spanish militia and 200 native archers to sail west aboard 14 piraguas and investigate reports of an intruder colony at the mouth of the Unare River (central Venezuela). During the voyage he is reinforced by 25 natives from Borracha Island plus another 30 from Cumanagoto.

On 28 August Arias's flotilla reaches Uchire Beach and disembarks, dispatching two scouts inland at noon. They return early that afternoon with news of a

Dutch fortress and ten ships at the nearby Unare salt pans, prompting Arias to leave two Spaniards and 50 natives behind to guard his piraguas while he marches overland with the main body. He comes within sight of his objective at 8:00 P.M., causing a stir within the Dutch stronghold.

Next dawn, the Spaniards storm the walls despite fire from eight cannons and the ships offshore; 80 Dutch defenders are slaughtered and another 36 are captured—among them Capt. Wybrand Cornelis-zoon—at a cost of only five to six badly wounded attackers. The vessels in the roads flee out to sea, leaving the Spaniards victorious. Later that same afternoon some Spanish soldiers are attacked by native allies of the Dutch, suffering a number of casualties. Next day (30 August), Arias orders the fortress razed, then retires with his captives and booty.

25 SEPTEMBER 1633. Shortly after returning to Cumaná, Arias leads 12 piraguas on a second foray 75 miles west-northwest against the Dutch salting operation on Tortuga. The island is easily overrun; a few Dutchmen are slain ashore and five anchored vessels are chased away before the intruders' huts are burned and their salt pans flooded.

DECEMBER 1633. A Dutch expedition out of Recife, led by Gov. Matias van Ceulen and Adm. Jan Corneliszoon Lichthardt, attacks Natal (Brazil). Two Portuguese caravels under Francisco de Vasconcelos da Cunha are seized in the Potenji River estuary, then a landing force disembarks to invest the Reis Magos harbor castle and secure Rio Grande do Norte Province. Upon the Portuguese surrender, the fortress is renamed Ceulen or Keulen.

JUNE 1634. The battle fleet of Admiral de Oquendo, escorting the Tierra Firme treasure convoy of Vice Adm. Nicolás de Judice y Fiesco from Spain, pauses at Sint Maarten during its outward-bound passage to resupply the Spanish garrison.

23 JUNE 1634. The Dutch ships *Groot Hoorn* of 40 guns, *Eenhoorn, Brack,* and *Engel Gabriel* and two Biscayan sloops arrive at Barbados, bearing 400 men—225 of them soldiers—to secure a new WIC base in the Antilles now that Sint Maarten has been lost. Their commanders are Jan van Walbeeck, a veteran in his 30s, plus Pierre Le Grand, a professional French Huguenot soldier who has distinguished himself in Brazil and is charged with the military contingent. Together they are to conquer Curaçao and Bonaire, guided by Jan Janszoon Otzen, a man who has visited these islands as a Spanish captive.

Next day the expedition reaches Saint Vincent, where the yacht *Brack* is detached to reconnoiter La Guaira. The main body meanwhile proceeds to uninhabited Bonaire, where van Walbeeck awaits his scout's return before finally standing toward Curaçao on 6 July. With Otzen's faulty intelligence the Dutch sight their objective, only to be carried too far west by winds and currents, continuing as far as Santo Domingo before eventually beating back to Bonaire by 26 July. During this digression they capture a Spanish bark and are joined by another Dutch ship plus the vessel of mulatto privateer Diego de los Reyes.

28 JULY 1634. ***Seizure of Curaçao.*** Van Walbeeck appears again, this time entering unopposed in single file through narrow Saint Ann Bay and emerging into the spacious Schottegat. The only Spanish inhabitants are Lope López de Morla and some 40 men, women, and children plus several hundred Indians. They are powerless to contest a Dutch disembarkation, although López stations about 50 Indians in a trench opposite the main beach. After two days' reconnaissance, van Walbeeck starts landing his troops with seven boats while Diego de los Reyes parleys with López from offshore. By the time the Spaniard realizes it is a full-scale invasion—rather than a foraging raid—the Dutch are already ashore. Next day (31 July), López abandons his principal settlement after setting it ablaze and poisoning its wells.

The Dutch press the defenders inland, suffering a brief setback at Santa Bárbara on 5 August, when they are attacked in a driving rainstorm by native archers, losing 25 men while their powder is damp. Yet by 17 August they have overrun the tiny hamlet of Ascensión in the western part of the island, nailing a surrender demand addressed to López upon a tree. The latter is at last cornered in the San Cristóbal Hills four days later and compelled to capitulate. He and 32 Spanish followers, plus 402 loyal Indians, are transported to Venezuela aboard two Dutch yachts and a Spanish fishing boat to be released about 15 miles outside Coro. Van Walbeeck remains in possession of Curaçao, from where the Dutch eventually occupy Aruba and Bonaire as well.

NOVEMBER 1634. Lichthardt's fleet sails north from Recife (Brazil), depositing a Dutch army under von Schoppe and Artichoksky near the mouth of the Paraíba River to expand into Portuguese territory. The attackers first subdue Fort Santa Catarina do Cabedelo on its southern bank, followed by Santo Antônio opposite, then São Bento Bastion in midstream, and finally São Filipe three miles upriver. This allows them to occupy the inland city of Filipéia de Nossa Senhora das Neves unopposed, renaming it Frederickstad.

15 MARCH 1635. Having returned to the West Indies with dispatches from Holland, "Peg-Leg" Jol's *Otter*—now mounting 18 guns—sorties from Curaçao on 3 March accompanied by the *Brack* of Capt. Cornelis Janszoon van Uytgeest. Twelve days later they penetrate the narrow confines of Santiago de Cuba's harbor, masquerading as Spanish men-of-war. In addition to flying false colors, the Dutch captains disguise themselves as members of the Spanish military orders of Cristo and Santiago; they hail its harbor castle in Spanish, thus being allowed to pass, after which they prepare to anchor in its roadstead and storm the beaches. At this point they are approached by Santiago's pilot boat, whose officer realizes their true identity, but he is already too close; he is fired upon and killed, his crew surrendering. This outburst warns the batteries ashore, who open up on the intruders. The Spaniards are so unprepared that at first only 14 gunners man their posts under Gov. Juan de Amezquita Quijano before militia can be summoned from the surrounding countryside.

Frustrated in their attempt to surprise the city, the Dutch search the half-dozen merchantmen in its roads, hoping to find rich cargos of copper ore. Most prove empty, so during a lull the privateer coolly offers to ransom the vessels and his prisoners, which the Spanish governor refuses; the battle rages until evening. Getting under way with the land breeze, Jol and van Uytgeest carry out a fully laden Spanish frigate (after attempting in vain to burn the remainder), unloading and firing the lone prize outside the harbor before releasing all captives two days later and making off.

SUMMER 1635. Having prowled past Havana, Jol stations himself off Cartagena with *Otter* and another yacht, one day pursuing a pair of Spanish coasters close inshore. Four coast-guard frigates suddenly emerge to give chase, forcing Jol out to sea. Here he meets another pair of Dutch vessels under Pieter Janszoon van Domburgh, who joins him to engage the coast-guard quartet. The Spanish vice-flagship is captured after a hard-fought battle; the other three escape. Jol releases his 150 prisoners with a note to Cartagena's governor asking him to reciprocate in kind. When only two Dutchmen, a few hens, and some fruit are returned, Jol burns his prize. After cruising through the Caribbean and making many more captures, Jol sails for Europe in the autumn.

26 NOVEMBER 1635. Some 30 Spanish and Portuguese ships appear off Jaraguay Point, near the Dutch base of Recife in Pernambuco. The Spanish contingent is led by Adm. Lope de Hoces and Vice Adm. José de Meneses; the Portuguese are directed by Adm. Rodrigo Lobo and Vice Adm. João de Sequeira. They examine the Dutch defenses and nine vessels anchored in its roads from a distance, demurring to attack. Instead they steer south to land supplies and 2,500 Spanish, Portuguese, and Neapolitan reinforcements at the Lagunas under veteran Gen. Luis de Rojas (*see* 24 June 1633), who is to assume command of the guerrilla campaign from Capt. Gen. Matías de Albuquerque.

The Brazilians have become increasingly hard-pressed, being driven out of Arraial do Bom Jesus and Fort Nazaré on Cabo de Santo Agostinho by recent Dutch offensives. This brings much sugar-growing land under the invaders' control and reduces the number of Pernambucans still loyal to Portugal to approximately 7,000. The disembarkation requires a fortnight to complete, during which the Hispano-Portuguese fleet is menaced by 11 small Dutch vessels, which retire on 5 December without pressing home any attack. Two days later, de Hoces's fleet stands out to sea, continuing toward Baía de Todos os Santos.

18 JANUARY 1636. A Dutch army under Colonel Artichoksky defeats de Rojas's Hispano-Portuguese forces at Mata Redonda, the Spanish general being killed and his survivors retreating toward Porto Calvo under Bagnuoli.

14 FEBRUARY 1636. De Hoces—having failed to overrun Pernambuco—departs Baía de Todos os Santos with his flagship, vice-flag, and an auxiliary to assault Curaçao. During the passage up the Brazilian coast he is attacked by eight smaller Dutch vessels, fighting a running battle on 19–20 February before finally driving them off. At this point the Spanish admiral decides to turn back to Baía for repairs. He exits again on Wednesday, 26 March, to escort the Brazilian sugar convoy part way out into the Atlantic before parting company and laying in a course for the Spanish Main.

SPRING 1636. Some 50 Dutch colonists under Pieter van Corselles disembark from Jan Snouck's vessels to found a settlement on uninhabited Sint Eustatius. They erect a fort on the ruins of an old French one, plant a

Oil painting by the Spanish court painter Juan de la Corte—a student of Velázquez—depicting the arrival of Admiral de Hoces's fleet off Dutch Brazil

crop of tobacco, and temporarily rechristen this island Nieuw Zeeland. Meanwhile Snouck returns to Vlissingen (Flushing) to lay his claim before the WIC. Its settlers flourish, and four years later they occupy adjoining Sabá as well, building another small fort.

9 MAY 1636. De Hoces arrives at Cumaná with his trio of warships to be joined on 25 May by Sancho de Urdanivia's four storeships and four tartans out of Spain, so as to mount a counterinvasion against Dutch Curaçao. However, de Urdanivia has lost the Spanish siege train during his passage (a fifth storeship having been wrecked on Matalino Island), and his remaining four ships are to immediately continue toward Cartagena, so the plan is abandoned. Criticism is eventually leveled against de Hoces upon his return to Spain for not having achieved more in either Brazil or Venezuela.

SUMMER 1636. A Catalan officer named Juan de Orpín leads 100 men out of Caracas to reestablish Spanish control over the Cumanagoto Coast, where rebellious Indians have been dealing with visiting Dutch ships. Generally through peaceable means he resurrects the abandoned town of Santa María de Manapir, in addition founding Nueva Barcelona and Nueva Tarragona—thereby preserving the region for Spain.

DECEMBER 1636. Reinforced by a company of 40 Spanish militia sent by Margarita's Gov. Juan de Eulate, Capt. Martín de Mendoza y Berrio raises a sizeable contingent—allegedly 400 soldiers and 3,000 native auxiliaries—from the towns of Santo Tomé (eastern Venezuela) and San José de Oruña to launch a counteroffensive against the foreign establishments on Tobago and northeastern Trinidad. He takes a fortification at Galera Point plus two more on Tobago—the main 65-man Dutch stronghold of Fort Vlissingen under Cornelis de Moor and Jacques Onsiel falling by 1 January 1637—gathering 160 captives of diverse nationalities and 42 cannons. Most of these prisoners are subsequently hanged on Margarita, their leaders transported to Spain.

23 JANUARY 1637. An able new governor-general for Netherlands Brazil—32-year-old Johan Maurits, graaf (count) van Nassau-Siegen—reaches Pernambuco and, one month later, leads an army to oust Bagnuoli's Portuguese guerrillas from their hilltop fortress

at Porto Calvo and the region north of the São Francisco River. After a siege of several days, Porto Calvo's 500-man garrison surrenders early in March, the Dutch subsequently laying waste Alagoas and compelling their enemies to retire into Sergipe del Rey.

22 JULY 1637. A small Dutch expedition from Essequibo (Guyana) bursts upon the newly reconstructed Santo Tomé, up the Orinoco River. This town has shifted to a new locale earlier this year under the direction of Cristóbal de Vera. Its inhabitants succeed in fleeing inland, along with Gov. Diego López de Escobar and a handful of troops. The Dutch put the empty buildings to the torch before withdrawing.

3 AUGUST 1637. Once more in the Caribbean, "Peg-Leg" Jol sights 26 sail of the Tierra Firme treasure fleet as it departs Cartagena under Vice Adm. Francisco de Mexía, escorted by the battle fleet of Adm. Carlos de Ibarra, knight of the Order of Alcántara. The Dutch are no match for this strength, Jol's new 260-ton, 28-gun flagship *Zwolle* being accompanied by a gaggle of smaller yachts—mostly independent privateers out of Curaçao with scant discipline. The rovers scatter when the Spanish men-of-war bear down on them, reforming once danger passes to follow in the plate fleet's wake, hoping to snap up a straggler. A Spanish merchantman indeed lags behind during the subsequent crossing to Havana, but the pursuers are so jealous of sharing any booty that they allow the potential victim to escape in the confusion. Disgusted, Jol takes up station off Cuba, hoping for a second chance.

6 SEPTEMBER 1637. Jol sights 16 Spanish merchantmen standing out of Havana, escorted by four men-of-war. *Zwolle* and its smaller accompanying privateers fall in astern, but at this moment another 33 Spaniards emerge from port, threatening to trap Jol's vessels between both Spanish formations. The Dutch sheer off, Jol taking one small prize from Puerto Rico. He then returns toward Holland, where his complaints about missed opportunities gain him command of a major WIC expedition intended to help reconquer Brazil's Baía de Todos os Santos and intercept a Spanish plate fleet in the Caribbean.

7 OCTOBER 1637. Two hours before sunrise, the Dutch rover Abraham Hendriksz's 17-gun ship overtakes a small Spanish frigate approaching Sint Maarten after a lengthy chase. It proves to be conveying the garrison's annual *situado* (payroll) from Veracruz, guarded by Ens. Francisco Fernández Núñez and three soldiers. They resist the Dutch boarding parties as best they can but are quickly overwhelmed and captured—along with their money chests. (Spanish reports indicate Hendriksz has intercepted Puerto Rico's *situado* the previous year.)

14 OCTOBER 1637. A small Dutch expedition from the Wild Coast destroys San José de Oruña (modern-day Saint Joseph, seven miles inland from Trinidad's capital, Port-of-Spain). The town's buildings are thrown down, and when the Dutch retire and San José's inhabitants attempt to return they find local natives hostile as well. Peace is not restored until Capt. Martín de Mendoza arrives with a small contingent.

NOVEMBER 1637. Von Schoppe advances out of Recife (Brazil) to attack the Portuguese in the captaincy of Sergipe del Rey, compelling Bagnuoli to retreat within 40 miles of São Salvador, the capital of Baía de Todos os Santos. The northern captaincy of Ceará is also overrun before year's end by two companies of soldiers under Maj. Joris Garstman, who destroys the small Portuguese fortress near the mouth of its river. Three years later a new citadel named Schoonenberg is erected on its ruins by Matias Beck.

MARCH 1638. ***Maurits's Defeat.*** Before Jol can recross the Atlantic to further reinforce Pernambuco, Governor-General Maurits decides to launch his own preemptive strike against the Hispano-Portuguese stronghold of Baía de Todos os Santos, believing its forces on the verge of collapse. Maurits departs Olinda with 3,600 Dutch troops and 1,000 Brazilian auxiliaries aboard 45 vessels, hoping to smash his demoralized enemy under Bagnuoli and Gov. Pedro da Silva. But he is unable to gain a quick victory and, after losing 500 men during a 40-day siege of São Salvador, he is compelled to withdraw by 18 May, abandoning considerable materiel. Returning into Olinda by mid-June, Maurits finds Jol's fleet at anchor.

8 MAY 1638. At Tortuga Island (Venezuela), 150 Spanish soldiers and a like number of native auxiliaries arrive before dawn aboard 13 piraguas, led by Cumaná's Gov. Bernardo Arias Montano and military engineer Juan Bautista Antonelli (the Younger) to expunge a newly constructed Dutch fortress. After being discovered by an anchored Dutch ship and three guard boats, Arias captures one of the latter and disembarks his forces on the western tip of Tortuga, marching on the interlopers' wooden stockade.

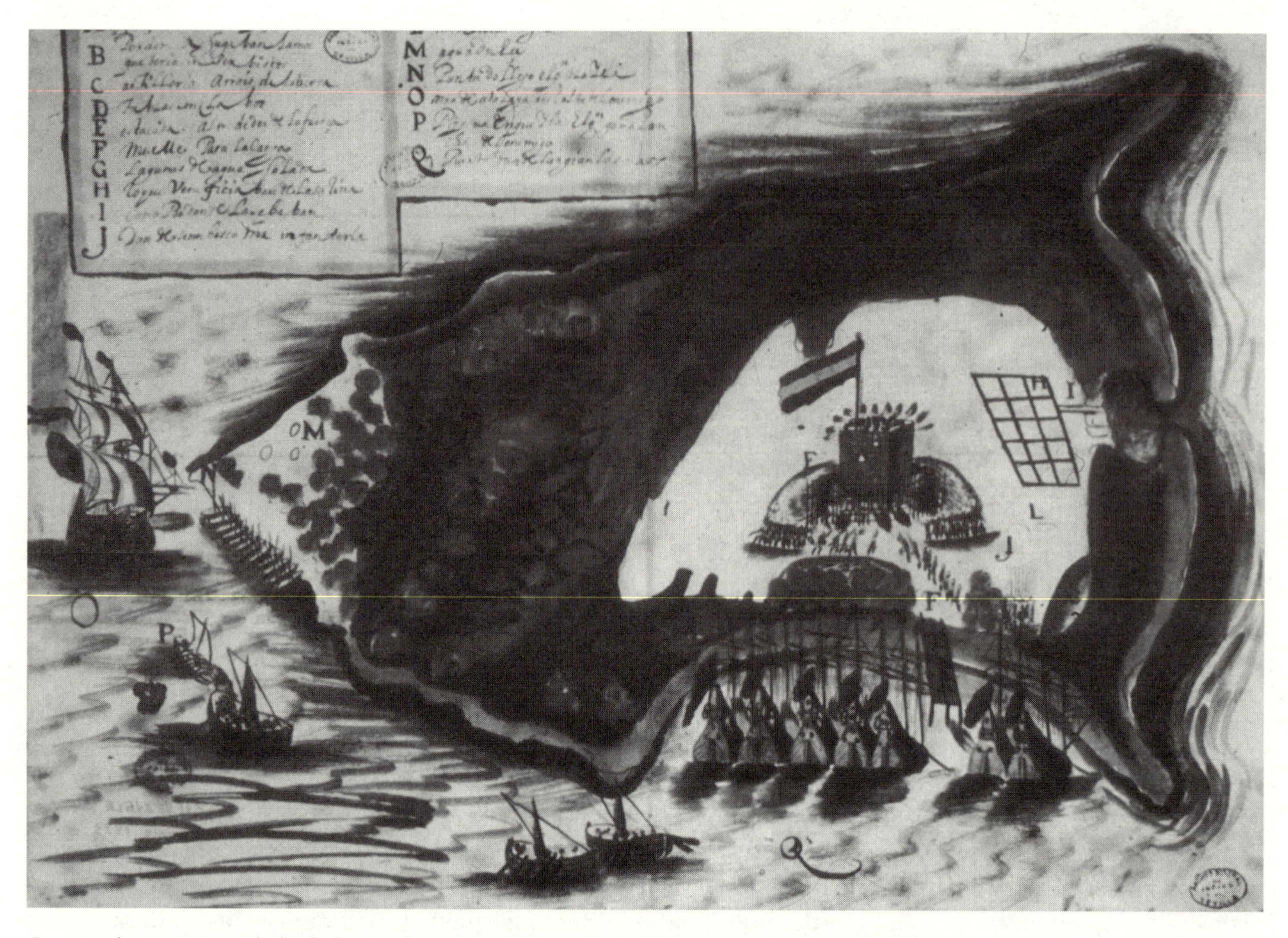

Seventeenth-century Spanish sketch showing the conquest of the Dutch fortress on Venezuela's Tortuga Island

The structure possesses eight small artillery pieces, sharpened stakes, and other defenses; Arias does not attack until sunrise on the following Sunday, fighting his way inside after a four-hour firefight to massacre the 40 defenders at a cost of seven Spaniards and four natives killed plus 20 wounded. The eight Dutch ships flee out to sea, after which Arias orders the fort destroyed and its harbor channel obstructed, so as to discourage future Dutch encroachments. By early June he is back at Cumaná, installing the eight Dutch cannons into Araya's fortress.

8 JUNE 1638. Jol arrives at Olinda to prepare for another cruise against Spanish plate fleets in the Caribbean with his 54-gun, 600-ton flagship *Salamander;* 44-gun *Hoop;* 34-gun *Oranje;* 32-gun *Graaf Ernst* (or *Ernestus*); 28-gun *Zwolle;* 26-gun *Mercurius;* 24-gun *Goeree,* and *Overijssel;* 18-gun *Wapen van Rotterdam;* 12-gun *Tholen;* 16-gun yacht *Brack;* 11-gun yacht *Postpaard;* eight-gun yacht *Kanarievogel;* and bark *Goyana.* He is reinforced by four additional ships, 600 men, and provisions at Pernambuco, getting under way again on 22 June with about 15 sail, 900 sailors, and 600 soldiers.

LATE JUNE 1638. The Spanish plate fleet bound for Tierra Firme under veteran Adm. Carlos de Ibarra—recently ennobled as Vizconde de Centenera—pauses at Tortuga Island (Venezuela) to ensure that it is clear of Dutch inhabitants before proceeding into Cartagena.

LATE JULY 1638. After stealthily traversing the Caribbean and being joined by the small squadron of Vice Adm. Abraham Roosendael, Jol stations himself off Florida's Dry Tortugas Bank to await either the Mexican or Tierra Firme treasure fleet. Numerous West Indian privateers augment his formation, so he divides his force to maintain watch upon Havana while masking his true strength. Retaining six ships off Florida's Cape Apalache, Jol detaches five more to hover off Matanzas; another 17 patrol between Cape San Antonio and the Dry Tortugas. This tactic proves effective. Although Francisco Riaño y Gamboa, governor of Havana and knight of the Order of Santiago, learns of the Dutch blockaders, he is confused by the repeated sightings, thus completely underestimating Dutch strength in his reports to the Spanish admirals.

30 AUGUST 1638. This afternoon, the Tierra Firme fleet of Admiral de Ibarra materializes off Cabañas, expecting to encounter a half-dozen Dutch cruisers. Instead he sights 17 or 18 enemy sail bearing down in a stiff breeze and prepares to give battle next day. The Spanish battle fleet comprises the 600-ton, 54-gun flagship, *San Mateo;* the 860-ton vice-flag, *San Marcos,* of Pedro de Ursúa; the 700-ton galleon *Nuestra Señora de Regla;* and the 600-ton galleons *Santiago, San Juan, Angel de la Guardia,* and *Carmen.* They are escorting seven merchantmen and a smaller *patache* (tender).

31 AUGUST 1638. ***Los Organos.*** At sunrise the Dutch fleet steers in two squadrons toward the Spaniards, who form up in single column to await them near Los Organos Keys, protecting the more distant convoy. De Ibarra's *San Mateo* is soon grappled by Jol's *Salamander*—seconded by *Wapen van Rotterdam* and then *Tholen*—while de Ursúa's *San Marcos* is attacked by Roosendael's vice-flag; Dutch Rear Adm. Jan Mast engages Sancho de Urdanivia's 20-gun *Carmen* (which is prominently displaying two pennants, giving the impression it is another flagship). A fierce eight-hour battle rages, in which the huge Spanish men-of-war acquit themselves well, repulsing every attempt at boarding. Both Roosendael and Mast are killed, after which de Ursúa's *San Marcos* moves to the aid of de Ibarra's flagship, obliging Jol to retire three miles out of range.

The Dutch admiral is furious to learn many of his ships did not join the battle but instead remained in the middle distance, viewing events. Jol reproves these recalcitrant captains and attempts to renew the engagement an hour later, only to notice the same reluctance; he consequently abandons this second attack before nightfall. The Dutch suffer approximately 50 dead and 150 wounded, as opposed to 82 dead and 134 injured among the Spanish. Both fleets also sustain considerable damage and spend the next two days repairing ships within sight of one another. Jol tries to resume the fight on 3 September with 13 ships, but the Spaniards now enjoy the wind, and some Dutch commanders remain as laggard as before. Only the crippled *Carmen* can be further damaged before the Dutch draw off at the approach of de Ibarra's menacing *San Mateo.* The rescued galleon, with 20 dead and 28 wounded, seeks refuge in nearby Bahía Honda, from where it will eventually be escorted into Havana by two Cuban coast-guard galleys.

De Ibarra persists in gaining Havana until the afternoon of 5 September, when he reverses course to sail across the Gulf of Mexico and seek sanctuary in Veracruz. Jol's ships remain off Cuba until 17 September, when they cruise as far west as the Organos Keys, searching in vain for the vanished prey. The Spanish treasure fleet enters Veracruz one week later amid great rejoicing. When word reaches Madrid, de Ibarra is elevated to Marqués de Taracena. Jol meanwhile sends one of his squadrons back to Brazil and allows another to prowl through the Caribbean while returning to Holland with his remaining ships. There he is awarded a gold chain and medal for his efforts; seven of his captains are court-martialed for cowardice.

FEBRUARY 1639. A group of Dutch rovers raids the island of Guanaja (north of Trujillo, Honduras).

EARLY 1639. Some 46 Hispano-Portuguese ships reach Baía de Todos os Santos under Portuguese Adm. Fernando de Mascarenhas, Conde de la Torre, bearing 5,000 reinforcements for Brazil. However, another 3,000 have succumbed during the lengthy transatlantic passage, prompting de la Torre to ignore his instructions for an immediate assault upon Dutch Recife in favor of recuperating at São Salvador.

JULY–AUGUST 1639. Dutch raiders prowl northern Honduras, landing at Puerto Caballos (modern-day Puerto Cortés) before coasting west to the Ulúa River and Omoa, clashing briefly with a Spanish landholder and his retainers. The rovers then proceed into Amatique Bay, and a 20-man sloop even penetrates Golfo Dulce—El Golfete—to forage until opposed by the merchant bark of Francisco Santillán.

SEPTEMBER 1639. Two Dutch privateers appear off Utila Island (Honduras), landing to set fire to the tiny Spanish settlement. They then visit a like treatment upon Roatán Island, frightening the few Spanish inhabitants into fleeing to the mainland. Over the next few years, these uninhabited islands become an increasingly popular haven for poachers, smugglers, and pirates.

12–17 JANUARY 1640. ***Itamaracá.*** Some 87 Hispano-Portuguese sail, under the overall direction of the Conde de la Torre, appear off the eastern tip of Brazil from Baía de Todos os Santos, steering for the northern part of Itamaracá Island and Goiana. The battle fleet comprises 23 Portuguese warships under Adm. Francisco Melo de Castro and Vice Adm. Cosme de Couto Barbosa, plus 18 Spanish men-of-war under Adm. Juan de Vega Bazán and Vice Adm. Francisco Díaz Pimienta. Their objective is to land 1,200 reinforcements under

Luis Barbalho Bezerra to bolster the guerrillas surrounding the Dutch enclave of Pernambuco, then proceed toward Europe with the annual Brazilian sugar convoy.

Before any disembarkation can be effected, however, 20 Dutch ships emerge from Recife under Adm. Willem Corneliszoon Loos and Vice Adm. Jacob Huygens to engage the formation as it straggles past. Although the action soon degenerates into a confused melee, with Loos being killed on the first day, his second-in-command continues the pursuit, and on 14 January he fights another pitched battle against the Hispano-Portuguese fleet off Paraíba. The latter is compelled to continue northwest without touching land, enduring another day-long pounding on 17 January before Río Grande, after which it deposits its troops at Cape São Roque—too far away to pose any danger—then stands out into the Atlantic toward Cumaná.

Only the Portuguese galleon of Capt. Antonio de Acuña Andrade is actually captured during these confrontations; another Spanish vessel runs aground and is boarded while fighting the Dutch *Zwaan*. Loos's flagship sinks, taking down the admiral, but these are the only losses incurred. The battle is regarded as a Dutch victory because the Spanish disembarkation is impeded. Portuguese Admiral de la Torre is arrested upon reaching Spain, charged with not doing his utmost—further embittering Hispano-Portuguese relations.

20 FEBRUARY 1640. Dutch raiders from the Wild Coast penetrate the Orinoco River, torching Santo Tomé (Venezuela). The Spaniards reconstruct their town once more and two and a half years later receive veteran Capt. Martín de Mendoza from Trinidad as the new governor.

26 MARCH 1640. Some 28 Dutch ships, manned by 2,500 soldiers and sailors, arrive at Recife from Holland under the shared leadership of Admirals Jol and Lichthardt. The former is to exercise seniority during Caribbean operations, the latter during Brazilian ones. (Lichthardt is an experienced officer who speaks fluent Portuguese—having lived many years in Lisbon—and was previously stationed at Pernambuco; *see* December 1633.) Shortly afterwards, Lichthardt departs with his squadron to cruise southwest and raid São Salvador, destroying 27 sugar mills before returning to Recife by June. Jol then prepares the entire fleet to hunt for a Spanish treasure convoy in the Caribbean.

4 JULY 1640. A small Dutch colonizing expedition returns to the Unare River (*see* 25 August 1633) to reestablish its claim over the salt pans. Although not numerous, the group is well organized, arriving with a prefabricated 22-gun fortress with 60 musket slits, which is assembled within a week.

14 JULY 1640. Jol departs Pernambuco with 2,000 sailors and 1,700 soldiers manning *Salamander* (flag); *Aemilia* (Lichthardt's flagship); *Middelburg* (Vice Adm. Bartel Wouters); *Witte Leeuw; Witte Eenhoorn; Alkmaar; Goeree; Utrecht; Zaaier; Tijger van Amsterdam; Keizerin; Graaf Ernst* (or *Ernestus*); *Sint Pieter; Nassau; Kampen; Bol van Hoorn; Haas; Maagd van Enkhuizen; Regenboog; Schop; Tijger van Rotterdam; Leiderdorp;* and *Cattenbau*. It is his aim to enter the Caribbean and steal upon Cuba, again intercepting a homeward-bound Spanish plate fleet. By 10 August he reaches Île-à-Vache (Haiti), pausing a week to refresh supplies before proceeding to his familiar hunting grounds off Havana.

26 AUGUST 1640. At the Unare River (Venezuela), a Spanish force under Capt. Juan de Orpín launches a dawn assault against the newly reestablished Dutch fortification. The attackers consist of 80 militia from the town of Nueva Barcelona, 40 from Nueva Tarragona, and numerous native allies. Daunted by the fort's imposing appearance, de Orpín deliberately makes his initial attack with a single weak column, keeping two others in ambush. When this force breaks and scatters, the Dutch sally from behind their walls, only to be surprised by the hidden companies and engulfed in a general melee. Francisco Tiquisper, son of a *cacique* (Indian chieftain), distinguishes himself during the action by personally slaying five Dutchmen.

Once out in the open, the Dutch cannot disengage, rushing forth reinforcements for an action in which they are heavily outnumbered and beyond the protection of their walls. The day ends with a crushing Spanish victory, 100 Dutchmen being slaughtered compared to 17 dead and 14 wounded among the attackers. As de Orpín's men pour into the fort, the surviving Dutch set it ablaze and flee aboard their ships, standing out to sea. The Spaniards extinguish the flames, leaving behind a garrison to occupy the place and prevent future Dutch reoccupations.

1 SEPTEMBER 1640. Jol arrives off northwestern Cuba with 36 sail, having been reinforced during his Caribbean crossing by two yachts from Curaçao plus ten privateers. Detaching three vessels to watch over Cape San Antonio and Florida's Dry Tortugas, Jol reorganizes his remaining fleet into squadrons of seven ships and four yachts apiece under his own flag and

those of Lichthardt and Wouters. The Dutch then send a single vessel two days later to look into Havana—confirming no plate fleet has arrived—before settling down to a blockade.

However, the new Spanish governor, Alvaro de Luna Sarmiento, knight of the Order of Alcántara, has already learned of Jol's approach and written to warn the treasure fleet commanders at Veracruz and Cartagena. Thus, Jol cruises unavailingly until the afternoon of 11 September, when his fleet is struck by a hurricane out of the north-northwest that blows itself out four days later. Seven ships are gone: three driven deep into the Old Bahama Channel while *Alkmaar, Bol van Hoorn, Keizerin,* and *Cattenbao* were wrecked on the coast between Havana and Mariel. *Sargento mayor* (garrison commander) Lucas Carvajal is delegated by de Luna to extract salvage from their remains, returning to the capital with 261 Dutch prisoners, 17 bronze cannons, 48 iron guns, and assorted equipment retrieved from Jarmanita, Bagne, Mosquitos, and Herradura.

Jol attempts to ransom his countrymen one week later (20 September), then quits the blockade altogether by 28 September. Pausing at Matanzas to refresh, the Dutch admiral sends foraging parties inland until 7 October, when his fleet exits the Straits of Florida toward Pernambuco.

1 DECEMBER 1640. Portugal revolts against Spanish rule, proclaiming the seventh Duke of Bragança as King João IV in place of Philip IV. The 60-year-old union with Spain has never proved popular with the masses; some Portuguese nobility and bourgeoisie have supported it at first for the security it afforded and for the possibilities of tapping into the markets of Mexico and Peru. By 1640, however, Spain's decline is so palpable that its military support is useless, and Portuguese merchants are systematically excluded from the Americas. Added to this are the centralizing tendencies of Minister Gaspar de Guzmán, conde-duque de Olivares, who seeks to subordinate Portugal's administration to that of Castile while steeply elevating taxes to meet Spanish needs.

The Dutch initially greet news of the Portuguese rebellion with enthusiasm, expecting the latter to become their natural allies against Spain. However, hope soon founders on the realization that Holland does not wish to restore Portuguese territories it seized during the war.

30 MAY 1641. Despite hospitably receiving Portuguese and Brazilian emissaries, Governor Maurits of Pernambuco continues prosecuting Holland's war effort by dispatching an expedition of 20 ships, manned by 850 sailors and more than 2,000 soldiers (including 240 Indians) under Jol and Vice Admiral Huygens, to seize Portugal's slaving depots in Angola before any treaty can be concluded back in Europe—thus greatly outraging Portuguese sentiment.

12 JUNE 1641. In Europe, a ten-year truce is signed between Portugal and the Netherlands.

15 OCTOBER 1641. ***Sack of Gibraltar.*** Four Dutch men-of-war of 20, 14, eight, and four guns, respectively—plus a Spanish prize sloop, intercepted as it arrives from Jamaica—appear off Maracaibo's bar under Commo. Hendrik Gerristz. This expedition of 250–275 men has been sent by the new governor of Curaçao, Jan Claeszoon van Campen (prisoner to the Spaniards eight years previously on Sint Maarten; *see* 24 June 1633), to raid the Spanish Main, its defenses having been seriously weakened by a massive earthquake on 11 June. After seizing a tiny vessel performing salvage work under Vicente Viana and Mateo Cornieles on a recently wrecked Spanish frigate just inside the bar, Gerristz works his 20-gun flagship *Neptune* and four consorts across to approach Maracaibo (then called Ciudad Rodrigo; later Nueva Zamora) by Friday, 18 October.

Instead of immediately storming the walls, Gerristz bypasses the place next morning, hurrying across the Laguna in hopes of falling upon the southeastern town of San Antonio de Gibraltar, where a rich tobacco crop has just been harvested. Two other Spanish boats are intercepted that same afternoon, and another next day (20 October), all of which the Dutch incorporate into their flotilla in place of Viana's prize, which is burned. After landing briefly at Barbacoas de Moporo to plunder, Gerristz presses on toward Gibraltar, encountering Diego Suárez's six-gun vessel, which has been sent out to reconnoiter. This is chased into the shallows, where it runs aground and is abandoned. The Dutch then arrive before Gibraltar, storming ashore the next morning with 200 men, encountering scant opposition as Gov. Félix Fernández de Guzmán and fellow citizens flee inland. Gerristz spends the next five days stripping Gibraltar's outlying districts of tobacco and cacao; he also refloats Suárez's vessel and incorporates it into his flotilla.

Reversing course after torching Gibraltar, Gerristz visits a like treatment upon the villages of Moporo and Tomocoro before reappearing off Maracaibo the morning of 31 October. Its garrison of 230 Spanish militia, 120 native auxiliaries, and three artillery pieces is now well prepared to resist under Dep. Gov. Francisco Cornieles Briceño, and a heated artillery exchange ensues between 11:00 A.M. and 3:00 P.M., until Gerristz sends a flag of truce inshore to propose a cease-fire. The Spaniards refuse, loosing off two more shots, but this battle is effectively over. The Dutch hover out of range until nightfall, when they set their prisoners ashore and sail back out of the Laguna three days later. Provincial Gov. Ruy Fernández de Fuenmayor (*see* 4 January 1634) organizes a belated relief force of 100 Spanish troops and 400 Indian auxiliaries at La Guaira and Coro to be shipped aboard three frigates, but the plan is soon canceled.

NOVEMBER 1641. São Luis Island and the Itapecuru lowlands at Maranhão, including Fort Monte Calvário, are captured by the Dutch out of Pernambuco, giving them control over more than 1,000 miles of Brazilian coastline.

5 OCTOBER 1642. ***Bonaire Counterraid.*** In retaliation for Gerristz's foray, Governor Fernández with considerable difficulty raises a force of 300 reluctant troops—half Spanish militia, half native auxiliaries—to venture out of Caracas and attack Bonaire and Curaçao. Arriving off the former island during the night of 5–6 October in rough seas, his expedition almost ends disastrously when many boats capsize during the disembarkation, which is followed by an arduous march toward the distant Dutch stronghold. However, the 40-man garrison is so frightened that it sets fire to the fort and retreats aboard a single ship, sailing away to advise the newly installed governor of Curaçao, Pieter Stuyvesant.

Fernández remains at Bonaire until 17 October, wreaking havoc and slaughtering many horses and cattle to hinder future Dutch reoccupation. He then returns to La Guaira without attacking Curaçao, his strength now being enfeebled by drownings and disease and also having lost the element of surprise.

LATE NOVEMBER 1642. Seeking to avenge the Spanish attack on Bonaire, Stuyvesant sends a pair of Dutch ships under Captain "Jacob" to assault Puerto Cabello, where it sinks four Spanish frigates. A second descent farther west against Coro and adjacent Cape San Román during the second week of December proves less successful, as the marauders are checked by 18 Spanish militia and 50 Indian allies under *Maestre de Campo* Joaquín de Belgarra. Despite this, the Dutch rustle 2,500 cattle, sheep, and goats to help restock Bonaire.

3 MAY 1643. ***Brouwer's Failed Colony.*** The WIC ships *Amsterdam, Eendracht, Vlissingen,* and *Dolfijn* appear off the Chiloé Archipelago, hoping to establish a base among the Araucan natives. The expedition arrives with several engineers, assorted construction materials, and 92 cannons to erect a stronghold capable of resisting Spanish counterattacks. Its commander, Hendrik Brouwer, quit the Texel on 6 November 1642 with *Amsterdam, Eendracht,* and *Vlissingen,* touching at Pernambuco to refresh supplies and gain another two ships—*Oranje* then being lost—before putting to sea again on 15 January 1643 to round Cape Horn.

The Dutch begin their South Pacific sojourn by seizing the tiny Spanish outpost at Carelmapu; on 6 June they disembark a force of musketeers and pikemen near Castro (southern Chile). Gov. Francisco de Herrera attempts to resist with a body of horse; after he is killed his followers scatter. Brouwer remains in possession of the town until 17 August, when he succumbs to disease. His successor, Elias Herckemans, continues the Dutch progression north toward Valdivia, backed by his Araucan allies. However, illness and discord drain his forces; the Dutch instead dig in, erecting a small fort and 60 houses near the seashore.

They remain almost a year, enduring want and occasional clashes with natives. Finally the survivors sail away, reaching Pernambuco by 28 October 1644. Shortly thereafter a Peruvian expedition arrives aboard 13 vessels to occupy the abandoned fortification, installing a 700-man garrison under *Maestre de Campo* Alfonso de Villanueva Soberal.

28 FEBRUARY 1644. São Luis, the principal Dutch town in the Brazilian region of Maranhão, falls to Portuguese guerrilla forces. Approximately 450 WIC personnel flee to Curaçao under David Adam Wiltschut, arriving during the first week of April. When provisions on the island begin to run scarce, many of the soldiers are then shipped farther north to New Netherland (New York) to assist its regional director, Willem Kieft, in his Indian campaigns.

20 MARCH 1644. ***Stuyvesant's Defeat.*** Gov. Pieter Stuyvesant of Curaçao leads five large Dutch vessels, a pink, and two tenders on a campaign to reconquer the former WIC base of Sint Maarten. After pausing at Saint Kitts to recruit English and French volunteers, he arrives off the eastern shores of Sint Maarten at dawn on 20 March, accompanied by a half-dozen merchantmen that continue north; Stuyvesant's squadron veers inshore to bombard the lone Spanish fortification, then anchors nearby and

disembarks several hundred troops. The Dutch spend the next two days installing a three-gun battery atop some heights; on 22 March they call on Spanish Gov. Diego Guajardo Fajardo to lay down his arms. Despite low morale, poor equipment, and insufficient rations, the 120-man Spanish garrison refuses to surrender, and Stuyvesant initiates a long-range bombardment next dawn.

A chance Spanish countershot carries off the Dutch commander's right leg while he is standing beside his battery, requiring Stuyvesant to be carried back aboard ship for amputation below the knee. The injury leaves the small army leaderless, undermining its resolve. On the night of 31 March–1 April an assault column steals under cover of darkness toward the Spanish positions, almost escaping the sentinels' detection because all are musketeers (and hence carry no lit cords). Once the Dutch intruders are discovered, however, a firefight erupts until dawn; at least five Dutch attackers are killed, as opposed to a single Spaniard. A second, even more halfhearted attempt is made at 9:00 P.M. on 3 April, which is easily repelled; no further assaults are made. On the night of 15–16 April, a Puerto Rican coaster under *Sargento Mayor* Baltasar de Alfaro lands refreshments for Guajardo's garrison, snapping the besiegers' will. The Dutch retire to their ships; a rearguard blows up the siege guns and fires the encampments by 17 April, and the flotilla departs toward Sint Eustatius and then Curaçao. Stuyvesant eventually returns toward Holland in August to convalesce from his wound.

On Sint Maarten, meanwhile, the Spaniards—notwithstanding their victory—are more reluctant than ever to remain in such an exposed outpost, being seldom resupplied or reinforced. Consequently, they request evacuation from Puerto Rican Gov. Francisco de la Riva Agüero, knight of the Order of Santiago, who complies three years later.

13 JUNE 1645. Despite the uneasy accommodation reached four years previously between Lisbon and the Hague—the former agreeing to recognize Dutch sovereignty over Pernambuco in exchange for support in the rebellion against Spain—a plot is hatched by 43-year-old João Fernandes Vieira, a Portuguese planter living in northeastern Brazil, to lead a local uprising against Dutch rule. When the conspiracy is betrayed, Fernandes Vieira is compelled to begin his revolt prematurely at Ipojuca.

The Portuguese governor of Baía pretends to help the Dutch by sending two regiments (800 men) into Pernambuco under Martim Soares Moreno and André Vidal de Negreiros, who disembark at Tamandaré. They are escorted by eight warships under 51-year-old Adm. Salvador Correia de Sá e Benevides, who remains off the coast before continuing toward Portugal with the Brazilian sugar convoy.

3 AUGUST 1645. ***Tabocas.*** The Dutch react to Fernandes Vieira's insurrection by dispatching a 500-man column under Lt. Col. Hendrik van Haus toward Ipojuca, another 300-man unit under Major Blaer toward Várzea, and a third company north under Paul de Linge. Van Haus drives Domingos Fagundes's rebels out of Ipojuca, but they retreat and join up with Amadeu de Araújo's company before uniting with Fernandes Vieira's main body and marching up Tabocas Hill—the highest point of the Comocim Range, 30 miles outside Recife.

Van Haus finally overtakes his opponents on 3 August, launching an attack that same afternoon against 1,000–1,200 Brazilians under Fernandes Vieira and António Dias Cardoso (possessing only 200 firearms between them). Nevertheless, the defenders repel every assault, defeating the 400–500 Dutchmen and their 300–500 Tapuia Indian allies after five hours' heavy fighting. By sundown, van Haus is in full retreat into Recife; ten days later Fernandes Vieira joins up with the guerrilla contingents of black leader Henrique Dias from Rio Grande do Norte and the Petiguar Indian chieftain (and knight of the Order of Cristo) António Filipe Camarão of Paraíba. Meanwhile Soares Moreno and Vidal de Negreiros have reoccupied the Serinhaém district and recaptured Fort Nazaré before rejoining the main Portuguese body by 16 August. Next day, another Dutch force is defeated at Casa Forte, but Admiral de Sá fails to attack Recife from the sea. Nevertheless, the revolt against Dutch rule quickly spreads to many other Portuguese settlements, encouraged by these early successes.

9 SEPTEMBER 1645. A Dutch fleet under Lichthardt attacks the remaining 14 Portuguese caravels and two lesser craft at Tamandaré under Vice Adm. Jerônimo Serrão de Paiva, which earlier deposited the Baía contingent. This formation is annihilated, ten caravels being burned and three others carried into Recife as prizes, only one escaping.

SEPTEMBER 1645. Portuguese insurgents recapture much of the provinces of Paraíba and Sergipe del Rey from the Dutch, including Porto Calvo and Fort Maurits on the São Francisco River. By the end of this year, the Dutch have lost most of their sugar-producing

Brazilian caboclo, *or mestizo militiaman, ca. 1641, by Albert Eckhout*

lands, being confined to Recife and its immediate vicinity.

FEBRUARY 1647. Some 26 Dutch ships and 2,400 men under Colonel von Schoppe occupy Itaparicá Island in Baía de Todos os Santos. This action prompts the Portuguese government to authorize a full-scale counterexpedition from Lisbon, 15 ships and almost 4,000 men setting sail by 18 October under Gov.-Gen.–designate António Teles de Meneses, Conde de Vila Pouca de Aguiar, followed next month by seven more ships under Salvador de Sá.

14 DECEMBER 1647. Von Schoppe's expedition forsakes its occupation of Itaparicá Island.

30 JANUARY 1648. With the signing of the Treaty of Westphalia at Münster, peace is officially concluded between the Netherlands and Spain. For Madrid, this represents the failure of its 80-year-old quest to subdue the Protestant Dutch rebels and is followed in October 1648 by the end of the Thirty Years War in Central Europe—another strategic and religious setback for the Spaniards. Bankrupt and weak, Spain is left to fight on alone against Cardinal Jules Mazarin's resurgent France while hampered by revolt in Catalonia and hostility with Portugal.

MID-MARCH 1648. Veteran Adm. Witte Corneliszoon de With begins reaching Pernambuco with 17 scattered warships and two dozen consorts, bearing 3,000 sailors and 3,000 soldiers. The reinforcement prompts 31-year-old Brazilian Gov. Francisco Barreto de Meneses—recently escaped from captivity in Recife—to mass troops for an all-out assault against the Dutch stronghold. He closes in on the Dutch enclave from the south with 3,200 troops, advancing in four columns under Vidal de Negreiros, Fernandes Vieira, the black leader Dias, and chief Camarão.

16 APRIL 1648. ***First Battle of Guararapes.*** Von Schoppe marches out of Recife with five field pieces and 5,000 men in five regiments commanded by Colonels Brinck, van den Brande, van Elst, Hautyn, and Heerweer. His aim is to overrun Fort Barreta in the Portuguese rear, thus compelling the enemy to abandon designs on Pernambuco. A sixth regiment under Col. Hendrik Hous is to destroy Várzea before rejoining the main Dutch army.

Barreto de Meneses responds by leaving detachments to hold Forts Olinda, Arraial, and Bateria while he concentrates his army in the narrow Guararapes Plain, nine miles south of Recife. Von Schoppe appears before that position on 19 April, launching a diversionary frontal assault while he sends troops in a flanking maneuver through hills on the Portuguese right. Barreto delegates Fernandes Vieira and Dias to ambush the Dutch column, which is surprised and defeated amid the jungle undergrowth. Von Schoppe's army remains hard-pressed until Colonel Hous's reinforcements arrive, which permits the Dutch to attempt another flanking maneuver. Barreto detaches 500 Portuguese soldiers to bolster Dias on the right, but they refuse to serve under the black leader and fight independently to little effect.

Nevertheless, this day ends with a Portuguese victory. Von Schoppe is wounded and obliged to retire into Recife with 1,000 men lost through death, injury, or capture—Colonel Hous and a field piece are among the Portuguese booty—as opposed to 80 killed and 400 wounded in Barreto's ranks.

AUGUST 1648. Barreto's forces, threatening Pernambuco, are reinforced by another Portuguese infantry regiment from Madeira and the Azores under Francisco de Figueiroa.

DECEMBER 1648. A Dutch fleet sails into Baía de Todos os Santos, destroying 23 sugar mills; it remains there unopposed for a month.

JANUARY 1649. In Europe, Spain offers to ally itself with the Netherlands against Portugal. Because of Amsterdam's and Friesland's reluctance, however, no joint declaration of war is made, only a few individual provinces issuing letters of reprisal.

17 FEBRUARY 1649. ***Second Battle of Guararapes.*** Some 3,500 Dutch troops march out of Recife under Colonel Brinck, two mornings later confronting 2,600 Portuguese defenders under Governor Barreto dug in on the Guararapes Plain. Brinck intends to seize Moribeca, but he cannot get past Barreto's position, even stronger than it was the previous year, when the Dutch were defeated at the same place. Toward midday Brinck orders a retirement without engaging, his army having sweltered under a blazing sun with little water.

At this point, the Portuguese storm across the plain, Fernandes Vieira attacking on the left, Vidal de Negreiros on the right. The Dutch respond well, but in the confusion a gap appears in their center through which Barreto sends his reserves. Brinck's army disintegrates, the commander himself falling mortally wounded. Dutch losses total 1,045 dead, wounded, or captured, as opposed to 45 Portuguese killed and 200 wounded.

APRIL 1649. The Dutch of Pernambuco recapture Ceará.

MAY 1649. Admiral de With begins an ineffectual blockade of Rio de Janeiro.

1649–1654. Luso-Dutch hostilities persist for another five years but with few major confrontations in the New World. Holland's strategic thinking gradually shifts away from conquest. The United Provinces only has about 1.5 million people at this time, and large overseas territories such as Brazil prove to be a burden that the small nation can ill afford to maintain. Holland therefore prefers to retain a string of trade outposts around the globe for its commercial traffic—now the world's largest—but otherwise sheds its extraterritorial ambitions.

The First Anglo-Dutch War erupts in May 1652, and the Portuguese avail themselves of its distraction to rid Brazil of the last Dutch occupiers. A fleet of 77 ships appears off Recife on 20 December 1653 under Pedro Jacques de Magalhães and Francisco de Brito Freire, besieging the defenders. They capitulate on 27 January 1654 and are given three months to depart. Many of the 1,200 Dutch colonists who subsequently evacuate Pernambuco resettle on Guadeloupe, Martinique, and other West Indian islands. The Hague and Lisbon eventually settle their differences by treaty on 6 August 1661, whereby Portugal pays 4 million cruzados as indemnity for the loss of Brazil.

OTHER COLONIAL STRUGGLES (1622–1640)

IN THE SHADOW OF DUTCH EXPANSION, other European nations also gain outposts in the New World. The first ones are shore bases for clandestine trade with Spanish America, later expanding into larger plantations for growing cash crops such as tobacco, indigo, logwood, and sugar. Virtually all are owned or operated by private monopolies that import indentured servants and slaves to work the estates with little direct involvement from their home governments. The early settlements remain vulnerable to Spanish and native counterattacks as well as to the vagaries of international politics.

22 MARCH 1622 (O.S.). ***Second Anglo-Powhatan War.*** At dawn this Good Friday, the new Algonquian chief *werowance* (leader) Opechancanough breaks the truce with Virginia's English settlers, executing concerted surprise attacks at many different locations. Opechancanough and his chief adviser—the mystical medicine man Nemattanew, called "Jack of the Feathers" by the English—have patiently crafted a plan to arm their followers while lulling their enemies into a false sense of security. They are helped by tribal resentment at the increasing English land grabs (spurred by a boom in London tobacco prices), in addition to the naive leadership of the new governor, Sir Francis Wyatt, and his religious cohort, George Thorpe.

Opechancanough himself feigns conversion to Anglicanism in late 1621, so when the onslaught begins colonists are caught completely unprepared. The ruthlessness of his attack appalls the English; within the first few days the Indians butcher 330 people—a third of all the Virginia colony's inhabitants—without taking prisoners. Jamestown barely escapes destruction when a friendly Indian gives last-minute warning on the very morning of the attack. Opechancanough's stroke inaugurates the Second Anglo-Powhatan War, and for several weeks the English reel from their losses, which are further exacerbated by famine and disease. Even when they mount some sort of counteroffensive, they find their enemies much more tenacious and skillful than before. In autumn 1624 a contingent of Virginia musketeers fights a fierce, two-day gun battle with about 800 natives deep within Pamunkey territory, forcing them to retire with great difficulty. Raids and counterraids ensue, in which Indians and colonists are systematically worn down.

A truce is eventually arranged in 1632, but mutual distrust remains. Although the natives admit defeat, the English remain resentful of their former neighbors, harboring lasting enmity.

JULY 1622. Scottish settlers begin reaching Nova Scotia, authorized by a grant from Britain's James I to William Alexander, despite prior French claims to the territory.

15 JANUARY 1624. A feud between the Mexican viceroy, Diego Carrillo de Mendoza y Pimentel, Marqués de los Gelves y Conde de Priego, and Archbishop Juan Pérez de la Cerna erupts into rioting when the latter is ordered deported to Spain, halting

all religious services. The unpopular Gelves attempts to summon Mexico City's 4,000 militia to his aid, but they ignore his repeated calls, leaving him besieged within his palace and protected by only a handful of ceremonial guards. Toward evening a mob fights its way indoors, and a disguised Gelves flees to a Franciscan monastery. Mexico is governed into late October by its *audiencia* (high court), until the new viceroy, Rodrigo Pacheco y Osorio, Marqués de Cerralvo, can arrive from Spain.

28 JANUARY 1624. ***Founding of Saint Kitts.*** Sixteen English colonists arrive at Saint Kitts aboard Thomas Warner's small ship. As a member of North's failed colonizing effort in Guyana four years previously, Warner has reconnoitered this West Indian island for several months before returning to England in 1622. Convinced it will make a safe and profitable tobacco colony, Warner forms a partnership with a London merchant named Ralph Merifield to finance the venture.

Warner's settlers erect a fort and some houses and begin planting crops. They are soon joined by a group of French colonists who have been deposited in Guiana earlier by Captain Chantail of Lyon and have now been driven out of the territory by local Indians. Because of their small numbers and mutual fear of Carib hostility, both groups agree to share Saint Kitts.

SPRING 1624. In England, the heir to the throne (who soon becomes Charles I) and the favored George Villiers, first Duke of Buckingham, persuade Parliament to authorize a naval war against Spain, which is refusing to allow relief to reach the Protestants of Central Europe. Although the cause itself proves popular with the English people, the House of Commons refuses to vote funds for operations on the continent, thus hampering prosecution. Thus, even though England remains officially at war with Spain for the next six and a half years (until the signing of the Treaty of Madrid in November 1630), its military efforts prove insignificant, with no major expeditions being dispatched to the New World.

SEPTEMBER 1625. A four-gun French brigantine with 40 men under Capt. Urbain Du Roissey, sieur de Chardonville—seconded by his good friend, 40-year-old Pierre Belin d'Esnambuc—engages a Spanish ship off southern Cuba, becoming badly mauled. Limping east in search of refuge, the Frenchmen chance upon Saint Kitts two weeks later, where they are given sanctuary by the Anglo-French settlers. Erecting a tiny fort at the northern extremity called Pointe de Sable, Du Roissey and d'Esnambuc remain for six months before sailing to France with a cargo of tobacco. In autumn 1626 they persuade the royal minister, Cardinal Armand Jean Du Plessis de Richelieu, to create the Compagnie de Saint Christophe for the colonization and commercial exploitation of Saint Kitts.

NOVEMBER 1625. Some 500 Carib raiders arrive on Saint Kitts but are repelled by its few score Anglo-French settlers.

DECEMBER 1625. Another Carib foray is defeated by the Anglo-French defenders of Saint Kitts.

MARCH 1627. In England, recently crowned Charles I—already fighting a listless war against Spain—becomes enmeshed in France's religious strife as well when he offers succor to the hard-pressed Huguenots within La Rochelle. His declaration of war proves worthless—the royal favorite, Buckingham, leads a motley force of 6,000 men across the English Channel, only to lose half—while drawing England into a two-year conflict with France.

8 MAY 1627. D'Esnambuc and Du Roissey return to Saint Kitts, hoping to convert it to a French colony. D'Esnambuc has shipped 322 men aboard his vessel *Catholique* from Le Havre; Du Roissey brings 210 Bretons aboard *Victoire* and *Cardinale.* Their transatlantic crossing is difficult, and fully half the men reach the Antilles dead or dying.

During the leaders' absence, the Anglo-French inhabitants at Saint Kitts have had a serious falling out with the local natives, killing many and driving most of the others off the island. Fearful of Carib reprisals, the English and French therefore agree to cooperate despite the official hostilities back in Europe, signing a partition treaty on 13 May whereby d'Esnambuc will govern the north of Saint Kitts around Pointe de Sable, Warner the center around Fort Charles, and Du Roissey the south around Basseterre.

MARCH 1628. The Anglo-French brothers David and Lewis Kirke quit Boston with three ships, armed with a letter of marque to assault French settlements in Canada. After seizing Miscou Island, they enter the Saint Lawrence seaway, ravaging Tadoussac and Cape Tourmente before calling upon Governor de Champlain to surrender Quebec City. He refuses, and the Kirkes withdraw.

Below Tadoussac on 17 July, however, they encounter a relief convoy near Barnabé Island arriving from France under Claude Rougement de Brison, whom they compel to strike colors next day after a prolonged exchange in which each side fires off 1,200 heavy shot. The Kirkes retire to New England with their prizes.

22 JULY 1628. An Irish planter named Anthony Hilton arrives at Nevis in the Leeward Islands with 100 men, founding a new English colony.

24 APRIL 1629. In Europe, the Treaty of Suze (or Susa) marks an end to the war between England and France.

SPRING 1629. ***Quebec Campaign.*** Unaware of the peace, New England resumes its offensive against French Canada, William Alexander Jr. landing two shiploads of colonists and soldiers at deserted Port Royal (Annapolis Royal, Nova Scotia) to erect Fort Charles; another 60 Scottish settlers reach Cape Breton under James Stewart, Lord Ochiltree, to build Fort Rosamar (later Louisbourg).

Meanwhile the Kirkes penetrate the Saint Lawrence seaway as far as Tadoussac, from where 32-year-old David sends his younger brothers Lewis and Thomas with three ships to once more call upon Governor de Champlain to surrender Quebec City. The main New England fleet intercepts a lone French relief ship under Emery de Caën, persuading Champlain to finally capitulate on 19 July. Next day, Thomas Kirke goes ashore with 150 men, beginning the evacuation of Quebec City and the installation of a British garrison. De Champlain and the first French prisoners reach Tadoussac by 1 August, Quebec's final evacuation occurring on 9 September.

Off Cape Breton, a French relief fleet arrives too late; instead it drives the Scots out of Fort Rosmar, building a new fort nearby with 40 soldiers before returning toward France. (Three years later, on 29 March 1632, Quebec is restored to French rule by the Treaty of Saint Germain en Laye.)

LATE JULY 1629. Six French men-of-war arrive at Saint Kitts under François de Rotondy, sieur de Cahuzac, led by *Trois Rois* (flag). They have been sent by Richelieu to aid the French settlers against their English neighbors, who have grown much more numerous and contentious. (Originally, the cardinal's intent has been to dispossess the English altogether, but this objective changes once the Treaty of Suze is signed in April.) English Gov. Sir Thomas Warner is absent in London, so his son, Edward, is told to withdraw certain colonists who have encroached upon French territory. When the Englishman hesitates, Cahuzac sails to Fort Charles and opens fire upon a half-dozen vessels lying in the roads. Three are driven ashore and the rest are cut out by French boarding parties, despite a brisk counterfire from the British batteries. The English sue for terms, so Cahuzac returns his three prizes; the island's partition treaty is reconfirmed in late August.

Cahuzac then detaches his second-in-command, Captain Giron, to make a reconnaissance through the West Indies while he proceeds to Sint Eustatius to install another French colony and fort. He eventually sends *Cardinale* back to France while allowing two of his other ships to cruise independently against Spanish America.

16 SEPTEMBER 1629. ***Spanish Countersweep.*** A Spanish expedition materializes unexpectedly off Nevis, consisting of two fleets. The first is under Adm. Fadrique de Toledo and his vice admiral, Antonio de Oquendo, and consists of the galleons *Nuestra Señora de Atocha, Nuestra Señora del Rosario, Nuestra Señora de la Victoria, San Sebastián, San Martín, Nuestra Señora de los Angeles,* and *San Pedro de Cuatro Villas* and ships named *San Bartolomé, San Carlos,* and *Natividad.* The second is a plate-fleet escort under Adm. Martín de Vallecilla, composed of Diego Alberto de Porras's *Santiago,* Sebastián de Anda's *Anunciada,* Juan Bautista de Garay's *Santísima Trinidad,* Felipe de Santa María's *Nuestra Señora de Begonia,* Miguel de Molina's *San Felipe,* Juan de Campo's *Tres Reyes,* Francisco Campi's *San Juan Bautista,* Agustín de Vivaldo's *Jesús María,* plus two other unnamed galleons. All are between 500–600 tons, thus representing a formidable fighting force, and are accompanied by seven merchantmen and other lesser vessels.

Next morning de Vallecilla probes Nevis's port with four galleons, scattering ten English tobacco ships inside, of which all but two are captured as they emerge through the shallows. (One vessel, commanded by the Earl of Carlisle's representative, Henry Hawley, cuts its cable and succeeds in carrying a warning to neighboring Saint Kitts.) Capt. Tiburcio Redín's *Jesús María* runs aground during the pursuit within range of a two-gun battery at Pelican Point, which strikes it repeatedly until de Oquendo leads a landing party ashore, killing 22 English defenders and driving the rest into the jungle. By the morning of 18 September the English deputy governor, John Hilton—his brother Anthony

Admiral de Oquendo's red battle flag

being absent in England—agrees to capitulate, and shortly thereafter the fort is dismantled; warehouses and other buildings are put to the torch.

De Toledo then presses on against Saint Kitts, first weathering a brief storm. Once regrouped, his fleet probes Du Roissey's defenses at Basseterre then disembarks a large force near the principal English defense of Fort Charles on the western side of the island. Its beaches are protected by an extensive trench system, but the Spaniards fight their way through; the outnumbered defenders finally break and flee inland. Du Roissey and d'Esnambuc hastily evacuate the island's northwestern quarter, 400 people being crammed aboard two ships. The Spanish meanwhile begin demolishing Fort Charles, at which time they are approached by English and French plenipotentiaries, under a flag of truce, who surrender their remaining populations.

De Toledo's booty amounts to 129 cannons, 42 mortars, 1,350 muskets and harquebuses, abundant ammunition, plus 3,100 prisoners. Of the latter, 2,300 are repatriated to Europe aboard a half-dozen prizes; the remaining 800—all Catholic—are carried to Cartagena when the Spanish fleets depart Saint Kitts on 4 October. However, de Toledo does not leave any garrison behind, and the islands are soon reoccupied by Sir Thomas Warner, d'Esnambuc, and Giron.

SPRING 1630. Following de Toledo's eradication of the Nevis colony, Anthony Hilton returns to gather up its few survivors, transferring them to join a handful of French and English hunters on Tortuga Island (Haiti). In order to ensure regular visits by passing merchantmen, Hilton and his lieutenant, Christopher Wormeley, sign an agreement with England's Providence Company, which is also attempting to colonize the nearby Bahamas. (For a time, Tortuga therefore becomes known as Association Island among the English, although its original Spanish name eventually prevails.) A six-gun battery is erected to cover the southern harbor; further emigration occurs.

NOVEMBER 1630. In Madrid, English and Spanish plenipotentiaries sign a peace treaty, marking the end to a conflict that has lasted more than six years.

LATE JANUARY 1631. Portuguese Cmdr. Jacome Raymundo de Noronha departs Pará (Brazil) with a contingent of soldiers aboard 13 craft, reinforced at Cametá by another 23 boatloads of native warriors, to press westward and attack the English Guiana Company's settlement in the Amazon Delta. This sickly establishment—named Fort North in honor of principal shareholder Sir John North and known by its local name, Pattacue—is quickly overrun in February, 86 defenders being slain and another 13 captured. Dep. Gov. Thomas Hixon attempts to escape downriver at night with a boatload of survivors, only to be overtaken by Indian canoes, who use their paddles to splash water into the English craft, soaking the gunpowder and slaughtering all aboard. Only seven Englishmen escape into the jungle.

9 JULY 1632. A Portuguese contingent under Feliciano Coelho de Carvalho captures a new outpost of 40 half-starved Englishmen at Cumahu near Point Macapá in the Amazon Delta. Their leader, Capt. Roger Fry, is taken five days later when he returns from a reconnaissance. (During his subsequent detention at São Luís do Maranhão, Fry studies the eclipse of April 1633, forwarding his observations to John Bainbridge, professor of astronomy at Oxford University.)

12 MAY 1633. Three militia companies and 50 native auxiliaries quit Margarita Island (Venezuela) aboard three large piraguas, under Julián de Eulate—eldest son of the island's Spanish governor. His mission is to investigate a foreign colony recently established on Trinidad. De Eulate arrives to find a small group of English settlers, capturing 11 of them along with 20 Indian allies. Back on Margarita Island, they confess to being an advance party for Sir Henry Colt's larger colonizing expedition, which has been diverted to Saint Kitts.

22 MAY 1633. Champlain returns to Quebec.

Spanish Adm. Lope Díez de Aux y Armendáriz, Marqués de Cadereyta

4 JANUARY 1634. Four Spanish warships slip out of the city of Santo Domingo with 100 soldiers under Capt. Francisco Turrillo de Yelva (or Yebra), circling the island to meet up with 150 lancers riding overland toward Bayahá under 30-year-old Capt. Ruy Fernández de Fuenmayor. Both contingents continue toward Tortuga Island together.

21 JANUARY 1634. ***Eradication of Tortuga.*** Under cover of darkness and guided by an Irish lad named John Murphy—who has recently fled Tortuga's buccaneer colony after killing a man during a dispute—the Spaniards disembark through the surf and take Tortuga's 300 inhabitants completely by surprise. Anthony Hilton, the self-proclaimed English governor, is butchered along with 194 followers; another 39 are captured, including three women. (One of the few who manages to escape is Lieutenant Governor Wormeley, aboard a ship crammed with his own goods and servants; later convicted of cowardice, he resettles in Virginia.) Tortuga's six-gun battery is thrown down, two prizes in its harbor are burned, and another is sailed back to Santo Domingo, laden with 123 captured muskets and ammunition. But the Spaniards neglect to leave behind any garrison, and the remaining buccaneers soon reoccupy their base,

eking out a meager existence under Nicholas Skinner during 1635–1636 and William Ludyard until 1640.

FEBRUARY 1635. In Europe, the Franco-Hapsburg War erupts, in which Paris—apprehensive of Spain's support of Austria's Ferdinand II in Central Europe—joins the Thirty Years War on the side of Holland and other Protestant states. Hostilities between France and Spain will last for more than 24 years, ending with the Treaty of the Pyrenees in November 1659.

LATE JUNE 1635. A French colonizing expedition arrives at Guadeloupe aboard a pair of Dieppe ships under Charles Liénard, sieur de l'Olive (former deputy governor of Saint Kitts) and naval Capt. Jean Duplessis, sieur d'Ossonville (veteran of Cahuzac's West Indian campaign; *see* late July 1629). The settlers soon endure famine and disease.

1 SEPTEMBER 1635. ***Occupation of Martinique.*** D'Esnambuc, governor of the French half of Saint Kitts, leads 150 subjects southwest to lay claim to Martinique, his motivation being the recent occupation of Guadeloupe by l'Olive and Duplessis, whom he views as rivals for Richelieu's favor. Dropping anchor off Rivière Du Fort, d'Esnambuc orders a three-gun fortress erected on its northern bank, naming it Fort Saint Pierre and installing Jean Du Pont as commander before departing by mid-November. During his return passage toward Saint Kitts, d'Esnambuc pauses opposite Dominica on 17 November to set another small force ashore under Lt. Philippe Levayer de La Vallée; he completes his sweep by populating Sabá before regaining Saint Kitts.

At Martinique, meanwhile, Du Pont's garrison is given a hostile reception by suspicious Caribs, who summon more than 1,000 allies from neighboring Dominica, Guadeloupe, and Saint Vincent to expel the interlopers. Du Pont remains watchful within the fort; when the Indian army finally bursts upon the outpost, he lures them directly beneath its artillery before unleashing a volley of grape. The sudden carnage shatters the Caribs' resolve, sending them reeling. Over the next several months, Du Pont succeeds in winning their confidence, establishing peaceable relations.

26 JANUARY 1636. ***Conquest of Guadeloupe.*** The plight of Guadeloupe's French colonists has grown so desperate because of want that Governor l'Olive decides to attack the friendly Indians. His more humane partner Duplessis having died on 4 December 1635, l'Olive is free to launch a surprise attack against a large Carib encampment in the vicinity of the modern-day capital of Basse-Terre. Although only a few casualties are inflicted, the unexpected brutality convinces most of Guadeloupe's natives to flee to neighboring Dominica and Saint Vincent, from where they will launch harassing raids against the French for the next three years.

SEPTEMBER 1636. Some 66 Spanish militia sortie under Juan de Vargas from Santiago de los Caballeros (north-central Santo Domingo), advancing upon this coast to ambush a French watering party in Cruz Bay. The Spaniards use the captured boat to row out and surprise the anchored ship, which proves to be a 12-gun slaver out of Saint Kitts under a captain known as Jambe-de-Bois ("Peg-Leg"). De Vargas subsequently employs this vessel to raid the foreign settlements on Tortuga Island, then sails to engage a group of runaway slaves entrenched at Bayahá. He compels the latter to surrender, promising liberty to their leader; he then sells the remaining 48 at Santo Domingo's slave market.

LATE JANUARY 1637. In Sancti Spíritus (Cuba), Ens. Agustín Pérez de Vera is murdered when he attempts to collect royal taxes. Although troops are dispatched by Havana's Gov. Francisco Riaño y Gamboa, knight of the Order of Santiago, they prove unable to detain the perpetrators.

SPRING 1637. Colonists out of New England, assisted by Narraganset and Mohegan warriors, attack and destroy the Pequot fort at West Mystic (Connecticut), thus crushing the influence of the Pequot chief Sassacus, who has been resisting expansion of the settlements. More than 700 Indians are killed; a like number of women and children are sold into slavery on Bermuda.

LATE 1639. A slave revolt erupts around Mount Misery, in the northwest quarter of Saint Kitts, requiring the newly installed French governor-general—Commo. Philippe de Longvilliers de Poincy, knight commander of the Order of Saint John of Jerusalem—to dispatch 500 troops.

LATE JANUARY 1640. ***Anti-Carib Campaigns.*** De Poincy dispatches 132 men from Saint Kitts under Maj. Gen. Jean Soulon, sieur de Sabouïlly, followed shortly thereafter by a similar contingent under Roi de Courpon, sieur de La Vernade, to assist the hard-pressed colonists of Guadeloupe in resisting

Carib attacks. Sabouïlly chases the seaborne raiders away after a clash off the coast that results in the death of 30 Indians and two Frenchmen.

MID-MAY 1640. Off southern Guadeloupe, the boats of Major General Sabouïlly encounter a Carib war fleet. Heavily outnumbered, his 24 harquebusiers retreat to a tiny atoll among the group of islands known as the Saintes, fending off repeated attacks for the next 30 hours thanks to their superior firepower. The Caribs eventually draw off at the approach of a French relief flotilla under La Vernade.

ENGLAND'S RESURGENCE (1640–1659)

ENGLAND IS THE ONLY EUROPEAN POWER TO AVOID direct involvement in the Thirty Years War. The foreign policy of its self-centered Stuart monarchs—James I (who rules from 1603 to 1625) and Charles I (from 1625 to 1649)—although superficially neutral, in fact precludes England from any substantive role in developments on the continent and overseas. Such unassertiveness eventually becomes one of the complaints leveled against Charles; serious disputes with Parliament erupt followed by civil war.

Despite such ineffectual crown leadership, private English expeditions nonetheless continue to press into the New World—hardly surprising for a vigorous island-nation of 7.5 million people who have already tasted the riches of the Americas. Numerous West Indian islands support sizable English colonies, leading to ongoing frictions with neighbors. Yet it is not until the home country undergoes the ordeals of civil war (1642–1646) and the First Anglo-Dutch War (1652–1654), that the English government can at last resume its imperial aspirations. The result is Oliver Cromwell's so-called Western Design; England thus conquers Jamaica in 1655.

SPRING 1640. Two Spanish galleons and six frigates, having sortied from Cartagena under *Sargento Mayor* (military adjutant) Antonio Maldonado, arrive to expel the English settlement on Providencia Island (150 miles east of Nicaragua's Mosquito Coast, called Santa Catalina by the original Spanish discoverers but renamed Providence by the English occupiers in the late 1620s; today it belongs to Colombia). Maldonado circles the reefs, looking in vain for a spot to disembark despite being shelled by the onshore batteries. He eventually draws off in defeat, having lost two captains and 100 soldiers during a disastrous landing attempt.

AUGUST 1640. The English settlement on Saint Lucia is devastated by a Carib assault from neighboring Martinique and Dominica, which forces the colonists to flee. The English suspect the attack has been instigated by Jacques Dyel Du Parquet, French governor of Martinique, but the natives are actually seeking vengeance for a treacherous English merchant captain who has tricked a number of their Dominican brethren on board and then carried them off into bondage.

17 MAY 1641. ***Spanish Reconquest of Providencia.*** Determined to expel the English, the Spanish crown orders veteran Adm. Francisco Díaz Pimienta to take his battle fleet—awaiting the annual treasure convoy at Cartagena—to expunge the intruder settlement. Díaz Pimienta appears off Providencia Island with his 400-ton flagship *San Juan;* the 800-ton, foreign-built vice-flag *Sansón* under Jerónimo de Ojeda; the 400-ton galleons *Jesús María del Castillo* and *San Marcos;* the 300-ton ships *Santa Ana, Teatina,* and *Comboy;* the 230-ton Portuguese man-of-war *Virgem de Ajuda;* the auxiliary *San Pedro;* and three lesser craft of 70–80 tons apiece. The expedition bears a total of 600 sailors and 1,400 soldiers; a high proportion are Portuguese and hence of suspect loyalty to Spain because of the recent rising against Madrid's rule (*see* 1 December 1640 in preceding section).

The attackers are again stymied by Providencia's reefs, spending several days searching for a safe landing place. On 19 May *San Marcos* strikes an outcropping and is severely damaged; it must retire toward Cartagena, taking 270 troops and one-third of the Spanish siege train. Díaz eventually decides to make a thrust directly into the main English harbor at dawn on 24 May with 1,200 men, hoping to catch his enemy off-guard. The gamble pays off: Spanish troops wade through the surf and storm the intricate system of English trenches and parapets with cold steel. The defenders are driven back within their keep, and the Spaniards manhandle English artillery pieces into new emplacements to open up a close-range bombardment. At this point, Providencia's residents send out two flags of truce, requesting terms.

The next day (25 May), Díaz accepts the surrender of the fort along with 40 guns, 380 slaves, and all English goods on the island. The 770 inhabitants surrender on the understanding they will be repatriated to Europe; the Spanish commander-in-chief installs a new garrison under Vice Admiral de Ojeda. Díaz's fleet then prepares to weigh, except for the Portuguese *Ajuda,* which attempts to desert its Spanish consorts but is wrecked on Providencia's reefs. Furious, Díaz orders two of its officers shot and their bodies displayed on the twisted wreckage as a warning to other would-be runaways.

(This is not the last such incident: after the fleet returns to Cartagena the Portuguese land commander, Juan Rodríguez de Vasconcellos Sousa, Conde de Castel Melhor—whose brother, Capt. Nicolás de Sousa, gave his life in the reconquest of Providencia—is arrested on 29 August 1641 and charged with plotting to seize the Spanish-American port for João IV. Although condemned to death, the *conde's* sentence is never carried out, and he eventually escapes to Portugal.)

The victorious Spanish admiral is accorded a hero's welcome at Cartagena, later being invested with a knighthood in the Order of Santiago. He leaves his English prisoners behind when the fleet subsequently escorts the silver convoy across to Portobelo, and Cartagena's captain general refuses to honor the terms of their capitulation, putting more than 500 to work as forced laborers clearing the Magdalena River.

JUNE 1641. In Canada, a skirmish near Trois Rivières (Quebec) marks the beginning of a new French-Iroquois war.

MID-JANUARY 1642. In England, the long-simmering political dispute between Charles I and Parliament comes to a head when the king withdraws from London to western England to assemble an army. The House of Commons responds in kind, and springtime witnesses the opening rounds of civil war, plunging the nation into conflict for the remainder of the decade (ending with the execution of Charles in 1649 and victory for Oliver Cromwell).

MAY 1642. The longtime West Indian resident and engineer François Le Vasseur quits Saint Kitts with a ship and 40 Huguenot followers, bearing a commission from Governor-General de Poincy to seize Tortuga Island (Haiti) and aid the French residents who have been complaining about their English leader, Capt. James Flood. Le Vasseur reaches Port à Margot, 20 miles east of Tortuga, installing himself on a tiny key named Refuge and rallying 40–50 buccaneers to his standard; he then sends a message to Flood and his English subjects ordering them to forsake Tortuga.

JUNE 1642. ***Jackson's Reprisal.*** Despite the eruption of England's civil war, three ships quit London under Commo. William Jackson, bearing a privateering commission from Robert, Earl of Warwick, Parliament's Admiral of the Fleet. It calls for a punitive strike against Spanish America in retaliation for the earlier extirpation of the Providence Island Company's colony (Warwick happens to be a member of its board).

Jackson reaches Barbados with his 30-gun flagship and two consorts, remaining a month and a half, during which he recruits additional volunteers, engages another private ship, and builds landing craft. His 30-gun vice-flagship then sails to Saint Kitts for more reinforcements, after which both contingents—totaling perhaps a half-dozen sail and more than 1,000 men—rendezvous off Los Testigos to attack Margarita Island (Venezuela). A fully laden Canary frigate is captured in its roadstead and incorporated into the English formation, after which 800 men disembark and are repelled with ten killed and 20 wounded. Two days later Jackson proceeds toward Tortuga Island (Venezuela), before laying in a course for La Guaira.

20 AUGUST 1642. In Canada, 40 French soldiers constructing Fort Richelieu (modern-day Sorel, Quebec) successfully repel an attack by 300 Iroquois warriors. Nevertheless, the outpost is abandoned four years later, then burned down in 1647.

31 AUGUST 1642. Le Vasseur sails to Tortuga and lands unopposed. Outnumbered and unable to count upon his *boucanier* allies, Flood leaves the island for New Providence (Bahamas) while Le Vasseur assumes office and temporarily renames the place New Normandy. He also uses his engineering skills to begin constructing a large fortress upon a promontory; when completed it will be called Fort de La Roche and offer the roadstead such good protection as to produce an upsurge in French buccaneering activities throughout the region.

14 DECEMBER 1642. Jackson's five large ships and three sloops are detected approaching La Guaira, creating alarm among the Spaniards. Governor Fernández de Fuenmayor, advised at Caracas around 8:00 P.M., makes a hurried nocturnal march to the coast with a sizable contingent of militia, arriving by midnight. On

the morning of 15 December, Jackson's five warships stand in to commence bombardment of La Guaira's Maiquetía battery, only to be repulsed. That night the three sloops attempt to creep into the harbor and cut out a hired English merchantman at anchor inside. However, the crew has been reinforced by 50 soldiers under Capt. Jacinto Sedeño (former governor of Spanish Jamaica) and is supported by a three-gun battery ashore; it proves impossible to board.

Next dawn (16 December), Jackson sails west, making minor disembarkations at Cata and Ocumare during daylight to search for water and provisions. On the morning of 17 December he slips into Puerto Cabello and lands 140 troops, who suffer two killed and seven wounded before dispersing a handful of Spanish defenders. Puerto Cabello is plundered of its six guns and other goods, then the raiders depart. Jackson calls at Dutch Curaçao, where he is well received and provided with a pilot named Abraham (a veteran of Gerristz's foray into the Laguna de Maracaibo the previous year; *see* 15 October 1641 in preceding section).

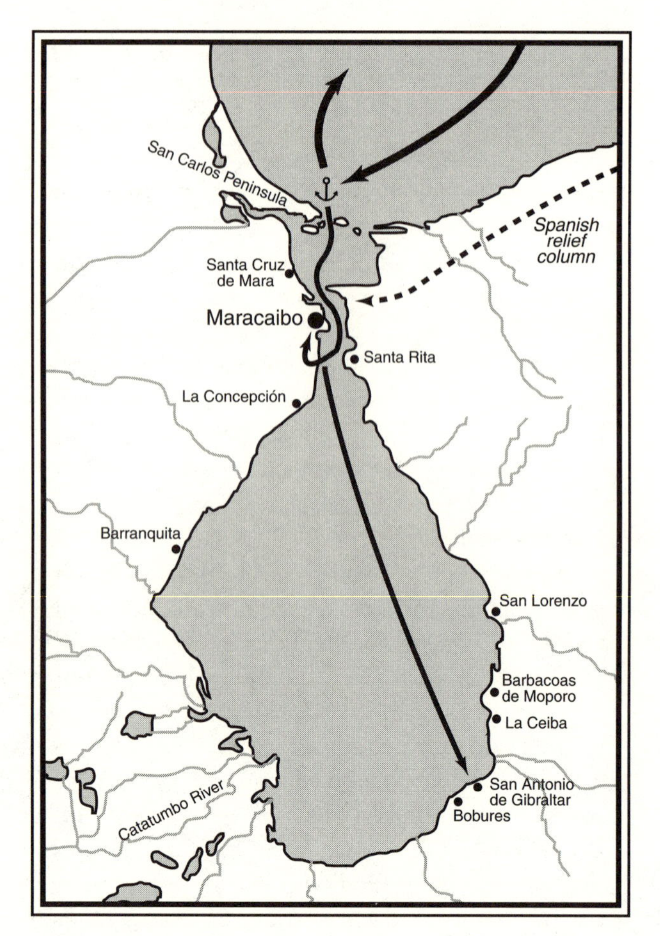

Jackson's Maracaibo raid

23 DECEMBER 1642. Arriving before Maracaibo's bar, Jackson leaves his heavy flagship with 120 men outside to mount a blockade while working his remaining seven vessels and almost 1,000 men over the shoals. Spanish lookouts convey word of the incursion to *Maestre de Campo* Manuel de Velasco in Maracaibo; he musters 250 militia in anticipation of an assault. The English do not resume their advance until 26 December, thereby giving the Spaniards ample time to prepare. But Jackson—aware that most of the Maracaibo defenses face seaward—surprises de Velasco by circling past at 11:00 P.M. that night, landing two contingents of 400 men apiece five hours later, two or three miles farther south at Los Bebederos. They march inland to take Maracaibo from the rear. The Spanish militia are obliged to abandon their prepared trenches and fight in the dark jungle, where they are quickly stampeded by fears of superior English numbers. Maracaibo falls next day, de Velasco and most of his followers being driven into the hinterland; four vessels are seized from the roadstead.

The English remain until 27 January 1643, when they receive a ransom payment and depart across the Laguna, hoping to attack the southeastern town of Gibraltar. Next morning, a Spanish relief column arrives overland from Coro under Fernández de Fuenmayor, who circles Maracaibo warily until learning that it is deserted; he then reoccupies the city on 29 January and begins to refurbish its defenses. The English commander in chief, meanwhile, finds scant booty at Gibraltar, its residents having long since fled upon word of his approach. A few days later he recrosses the Laguna, and by 8:00 A.M. on 9 February his vessels are again sighted southeast of Maracaibo. Fernández de Fuenmayor sorties that afternoon with 400 Spanish militia and 130 native archers to lay an ambush at El Palmar. Jackson ignores the Spaniards' bait—a cattle herd—and instead anchors out of range of Maracaibo's walls, offering to exchange his captives.

The transaction is completed by 21 February, after which the invaders retire toward the Laguna's bar, anchoring near Zapara Island for several days before working their way out to rejoin Jackson's flagship; they sail away on 4 March. (Shortly thereafter one of the prizes, a Maracaibo frigate formerly belonging to Capt. Francisco Barbero, becomes dismasted and is driven ashore near the Cocinas; its 89 English officers and crew fall into Spanish hands.) Fernández de Fuenmayor quickly dispatches a missive from Coro with Ens. Alonso de Cuevas, aboard the sloop *San Francisco y San Antonio,* to warn the Spanish authorities on Jamaica that their island is Jackson's next target. The governor remains at Maracaibo until September 1643, supervising construction of a small pentagonal fort on the Laguna's bar to impede future incursions.

28 MARCH 1643 (PALM SATURDAY). Spanish Ens. Alonso de Cuevas, aboard the sloop *San Francisco y San Antonio,* arrives at Jamaica from Coro (Venezuela) to warn its residents that their island is about to be attacked by Jackson's expedition. Its few inhabitants doubt the veracity of the report; they are in no position to resist in any event due to poverty and the small, scattered plantations.

3 APRIL 1643 (EASTER FRIDAY). The squadron of William Jackson—now 11 vessels strong following his campaign through the Laguna de Maracaibo—materializes before Jamaica, disembarking 500 men and taking possession of the Spanish island. He remains more than a month, eventually sparing the unprepossessing capital of Santiago de la Vega for a tiny ransom; he eventually disperses his auxiliaries and sails for England.

30 MARCH 1644. In Canada, a contingent of French settlers is defeated by an Iroquois war party that is intent upon attacking Montréal.

APRIL 1644. ***Last Anglo-Powhatan War.*** In Virginia, steady inland encroachments by English settlers provoke a second violent reaction from the Algonquian *werowance* (chieftain) Opechancanough. Although now almost 80 years old, he retains a hatred for whites and lays careful plans for a coordinated attack upon their forward elements. His warriors strike suddenly and, within the first two days, kill perhaps 500 trappers, traders, and farmers; but the English are now much more numerous—approximately 15,000 people—and more experienced in irregular warfare. Over the next two years they crush the Algonquian tribes, finally capturing Opechancanough, who is shot in the back in his Jamestown jail cell. His successor, Necotowance, is obliged to sue for terms by October 1646, agreeing to retire his people to a reservation north of the York River and acknowledge Charles I as his lord.

13 APRIL 1645. The 41-year-old Charles de Menou d'Aulnay, governor of Port Royal (modern-day Annapolis Royal, Nova Scotia), crosses the Bay of Fundy with some ships and 200 men to capture Fort La Tour (Saint John, New Brunswick), stronghold of his hated 53-year-old French rival, Charles de Saint Etienne de La Tour, who has switched allegiance to the English. After installing a two-piece battery ashore, the besiegers call upon Fort La Tour's 47-man garrison to surrender. They refuse, resisting heroically under the governor's wife, Françoise Marie Jacquelin de La Tour, whose husband is absent in Boston.

By evening of 16 April (Easter Sunday), eight defenders have been killed and several others wounded, and a gaping hole has been effected in the parapet. D'Aulnay's troops storm through the opening, and Madame de La Tour surrenders on the understanding her followers will be spared. All but two are hanged, and she dies in captivity a few days later; her infant son is sent to France.

APRIL 1645. Puerto Rican Gov. Francisco de la Riva Agüero dispatches an officer named Francisco Vicente Durán with 100 men aboard a frigate to exterminate a foreign settlement discovered on Santa Ana (among the Virgin Islands). Durán slays its leader and 13 other trespassers, captures 15, then scatters another 30 inland before burning the huts and returning to Puerto Rico.

14 JULY 1645. French settlers in Canada sign a peace treaty with the Iroquois.

LATE JANUARY 1646. ***Poincy's Revolt.*** On the French half of Saint Kitts, Governor-General de Poincy resists being replaced by the Compagnie des Îles d'Amérique's Noël de Patrocles, seigneur de Thoisy, as directed by Paris. A secret disembarkation is therefore made at the northwest tip of the island by Governor Du Parquet of Martinique—one of the new governor-general's supporters—who rallies 300–400 men and arrests de Poincy's nephews, Robert de Longvilliers and de Treval. De Poincy instantly marches with 2,000 militia (mostly Englishmen from adjoining districts) to confront the challenger, defeating Du Parquet in a clash at Pointe de Sable in which 60 Frenchmen die.

APRIL 1646. The Puerto Rican governor sends his son, Fernando de la Riva Agüero, with 50 soldiers aboard a frigate and two storeships (*urcas*) to again sweep Santa Ana and Saint Croix in the Virgin Islands. Santa Ana is easily overrun, but at Saint Croix the Spanish expedition unwittingly anchors beneath the lone battery. After a vigorous exchange of shot, the redoubt is captured and thrown down; the Spaniards then retire.

26 JUNE 1646. Rioting breaks out on Martinique—led by a former Parisian glovemaker who assumes the title "General" Beaufort—in protest

against the Compagnie des Îles d'Amérique's appointment of a new governor-general. A chaotic fortnight ensues; Martinique's deputy governor, Jérôme Du Sarrat, sieur de La Pierrière, lures Beaufort and 20 intimates to a meeting, where they are murdered. Trouble nonetheless spreads to Guadeloupe, where the new governor-general's residence is besieged by several hundred armed men, who are dispersed next day by Major General Sabouïlly.

De Thoisy transfers to Martinique on 3 January 1647 in anticipation of returning to France while full-blown rioting engulfs Guadeloupe. An expedition is sent after the governor-general ten days later, arresting de Thoisy and delivering him to archenemy de Poincy at Saint Kitts by 25 January in exchange for the captive Du Parquet.

EARLY APRIL 1647. Embarrassed by the continued incarceration of his rival de Thoisy, de Poincy orders him deported to France aboard a merchantman.

MAY 1647. A small Spanish expedition out of Puerto Rico removes an English colony from Saint Croix.

30 JUNE 1647. Five Spanish vessels under Capts. Francisco Vicente Durán and Celedonio de Escobedo return to Puerto Rico, having evacuated the infirm Saint Martin garrison from the Leeward Islands. Spain, its treasury impoverished, is no longer able to maintain the outpost. Within a year Saint Martin is reoccupied by Dutch and French settlers; sick Spanish soldiers further introduce the plague into Puerto Rico, causing the deaths of more than 500 people, including Bishop Damián de Haro.

LATE SEPTEMBER 1647. Some 60 French colonists under Jean Pinart, driven from Saint Kitts by Governor-General de Poincy, are deposited in the Virgin Islands (possibly on Saint John or Vieques) by Captain Le Verrier's bark. The establishment is soon discovered by Spaniards on nearby Puerto Rico; they send a contingent of soldiers aboard five vessels to eliminate the intruders. After a brief resistance the French are overwhelmed and carried into captivity at San Juan.

OCTOBER 1647. Capt. William Sayle returns to Bermuda from England with several volunteers, 400 muskets, and provisions for an attempted colonization of the Bahamas.

LATE FEBRUARY 1648. Dutch Capt. Martin Thomas arrives at Sint Maarten with a small band of settlers, having been sent to reoccupy the island by Abraham Adriaanszoon, governor of Sint Eustatius.

LATE MARCH 1648. Robert de Longvilliers Poincy—nephew of the French governor-general for the Windward Islands—and Lt. Col. Savinien de Courpon, sieur de La Tour, reach Saint Martin with 300 men to stake France's claim. The Dutch agree to share the island; a partition treaty is drawn up whereby the French receive its northern half, the Dutch its southern.

SPRING 1648. Sayle arrives off Eleuthera Island (Bahamas) from Bermuda with 70 settlers aboard his 50-ton *William* and a six-ton shallop. His flagship is wrecked on reefs near Governor's Bay, compelling Sayle to go for help with eight men aboard his consort. Eventually he returns from Virginia with 60 more colonists and, in March 1650, receives a shipload of provisions from Boston. (In gratitude, he sends back 10 tons of braziletto wood as a gift; its sale contributes substantially to Harvard University's initial endowment.)

JUNE 1648. English raiders under a leader known only as Abraham sack the Mexican town of Salamanca de Bacalar (southeastern Yucatán, near Belize). Women captives are carried offshore to Islote de los Cayos; they are rescued by Spanish militia and native auxiliaries.

LATE AUGUST 1648. An unidentified buccaneer ship appears off Havana with two small Cuban prizes. Gov. Diego de Villalba y Toledo, knight of the Order of Santiago, presses two private galleons into service, manning them with troops and guns. Upon exiting, however, the Spanish pursuers run aground and are wrecked, obliging the governor to send out a rescue expedition—and to indemnify the masters for their losses.

16 MARCH 1649. In Canada, 1,000 Iroquois warriors attack the French missions at Saint Ignace and Saint Louis, torturing the Jesuit priests to death.

17 MARCH 1649. ***Grenada Occupation.*** An expedition of 145 French settlers under Governor Du Parquet of Martinique, crammed aboard two barks commanded by Jean Lepelletier (known as "*Capitaine* Le Pas") and Captain Lorimer, enter Saint George's harbor to occupy a base previously explored by Captain La Rivière. Within eight days they erect a palisade named Fort Annunciation—25 March being Day of

the Annunciation in the church calendar—and Du Parquet appoints his 55-year-old cousin, Jean Le Comte, as Grenada's new governor, departing on 6 April.

The Carib residents under chief Kairouane remain suspicious yet nonhostile—until November, when 11 large canoes arrive bearing several hundred warriors from nearby Saint Vincent bent upon avenging an insult in the Grenadines. Le Comte's followers retreat within their stockade and spend eight anxious days while the Indians destroy their properties before withdrawing.

MAY 1650. Four Cuban warships with 350 troops under Capt. Francisco de Villalba y Toledo materialize under cover of darkness opposite Roatán to eradicate English buccaneering camps. Disembarking two hours before dawn, the Spaniards attempt to rush Roatán's defensive works, only to be discovered and fired upon. De Villalba attempts to outflank the system of trenches and ramparts with 30 men but is hampered by surrounding swamps. When ammunition runs low, the Spanish withdraw and sail to Santo Tomás del Castillo (Guatemala) for rearmament and reinforcements.

26 MAY 1650. Governor Du Parquet reaches Grenada from Martinique with 300 men, joining his subordinate (and cousin) Le Comte for a sneak attack upon the natives, who have been killing isolated settlers. Guided by a Carib traitor, 60 French musketeers steal up a hill overnight, surrounding a camp of perhaps two score sleeping Indians at the edge of a precipice overlooking the sea. When the French begin shooting, their crossfire proves so effective that the natives are either massacred or leap to their deaths (the spot becoming known as Morne des Sauteurs—Jumpers' Promontory). Du Parquet then orders the construction of a second small keep on Grenada, which he names Fort Saint Jean and garrisons with 70 men under Capt. Yves Le Cercueil, sieur Le Fort, before departing on 7 June.

JUNE 1650. While returning toward Martinique, Du Parquet detaches 35–40 men under Capt. Louis de Kerengoan, sieur de Rosselan, to occupy uninhabited Saint Lucia. They disembark on the western coast, near modern-day Castries, erecting a fort with double palisades, moat, and artillery on the banks of the Carenage River. De Rosselan, who is married to a Carib woman, proves a successful governor.

LATE JULY 1650. ***Roatán Counterattack.*** De Villalba's expedition of four Cuban warships returns to Roatán a second time, having been resupplied with powder and shot by the *audiencia* of Guatemala. The Spaniards' ranks have also been augmented by 50 soldiers from Chiquimula, under Capt. Juan Bautista Echavarría, and a like number from Guatemala City under Capt. Martín de Alvarado y Guzmán. On this occasion the attackers disembark some distance from the English defenses and advance with four small field pieces, which allow them to blast a breach and overrun the trench system. Although the attackers take no prisoners, the buccaneers melt into the jungle. De Villalba therefore retires empty-handed toward Cuba, leaving the English to reoccupy their base.

AUGUST 1650. ***Struggle for Saint Croix.*** Some 1,200 men out of Puerto Rico overwhelm the English colony on Saint Croix, forcing its settlers to evacuate to Saint Kitts. The Spaniards install a 60-man garrison, which captures two Dutch barks that arrive from nearby Sint Eustatius (the Dutch expecting to find Saint Croix uninhabited). A few weeks later the Spaniards are in turn besieged within their keep by 160 French buccaneers who slip ashore under the sieur de Vaugalan, sent from Saint Kitts by Governor-General de Poincy. The Spaniards surrender and are repatriated to Puerto Rico; 300 more Frenchmen arrive from Saint Kitts under sieur Auger to convert Saint Croix into a French colony.

26 MAY 1651. At 4:00 A.M., 25 Franco-Dutch raiders shoot their way into Alvarado (Mexico), killing ten residents and wounding nine others before withdrawing with their booty to a pair of waiting ships.

18 SEPTEMBER 1651. Parliamentary Commo. Sir George Ayscue arrives at Saint Vincent with his 50-gun, 280-man flagship *Rainbow;* 36-gun, 150-man vice-flagship *Amity* of Richard Pack; 30-gun, 90-man *Success* of Edmund Witheridge; 30-gun, 80-man *Ruth* of Edward Thompson; 24-gun, 70-man frigate *Brazil* of Thomas Heath; plus the 36-gun hired merchantmen *Malaga* of Henry Collins and *Increase* of Thomas Varwell. The expedition has been sent from England to establish Cromwell's rule over Barbados, which remains loyal to exiled Charles II. After refreshing supplies for ten days, Ayscue beats slowly upwind toward his objective, hampered by the "ill sailing" of *Success, Brazil,* and *Malaga.*

25 OCTOBER 1651. ***Ayscue at Barbados.*** The parliamentary squadron arrives off Barbados this evening, splitting early next morning to make simulta-

neous descents upon Carlisle Bay and Austin's Bay. Captain Pack enters the former with *Amity, Success, Malaga,* and an unnamed merchantman under Captain Totty, surprising 14 Dutch traders at anchor. Two of these deliberately run aground, but the other dozen are boarded and brought off by Pack; batteries at Carlisle Bay open fire without inflicting damage. Pack then dispatches a shallop to advise Ayscue, who sails from nearby Austin's Bay to rejoin his second-in-command. While passing Needham's Point, Ayscue's *Rainbow* is fired upon by a fort; at first he responds with a signal shot to leeward, still hoping to secure Barbados without bloodshed. But when bombardment continues his ships crash out full broadsides, suffering one man killed and two wounded before clawing out of range.

Next day (27 October), Ayscue sends an officer and trumpeter inshore to call for the surrender of Barbados "for the use of the Parliament of England." The royalist governor, Francis, Lord Willoughby of Parham, has arrived from his plantation 12 miles outside Bridgetown and assembled 400 riders and 6,000 militia. His answer: he knows "no supreme authority over Englishmen but the King"; to further outrage parliamentary sensibilities he addresses his reply to "His Majesty's ship *Rainbow.*" Faced with such intransigence, Ayscue institutes a close blockade, intercepting arriving merchantmen (mostly Dutch; this will unwittingly contribute to deteriorating relations in Europe, hastening the eruption of the First Anglo-Dutch War next year.)

Stalemate ensues until a packet arrives from England on 18 November with news of Cromwell's victory over the last royalist army at Worcester on 3 September (O.S.). Buoyed by these tidings, Ayscue sends 200 seamen under Captain Morris to destroy the four-gun battery at The Hole on the night of 2–3 December, spiking its cannons and coming away with 30 prisoners. The royalists' morale flags further on 11 December; the parliamentary ship *John* of Capt. Robert Dennis and frigate *Guinea* of Capt. Edmund Curtis (each mounting 32 guns) appear with 13 vessels bound to subdue Virginia. Temporarily reinforced by this second squadron, Ayscue sends 400 seamen and 150 Scottish soldiers—paroled after their defeat at Worcester—to attack the small fort at Speight's Bay early on the morning of 17 December. The Barbadian militia is forewarned, and Colonel Gibbs awaits the disembarkation with three troops of horses and 1,200 foot soldiers. Despite their superior numbers, the defenders break and run in the darkness, leaving behind four cannons, 500 small arms, and 80 prisoners (mostly wounded). Ayscue cunningly orders the prisoners treated and released in hopes of spreading sedition among the royalist ranks. A desperate Willoughby orders two returnees hanged and prohibits the reading of documents brought from the blockading fleet.

On 24 December the Virginia squadron departs and proceeds toward Saint Kitts, leaving Ayscue to begin a secret correspondence with Sir Thomas Modyford, colonel of the Windward Regiment stationed at Austin's Bay near his plantation. Although a longtime royalist, Modyford believes the stalemate is ruining the island's economy; he therefore agrees to change sides and, on 13 January 1652, turns his 800-man regiment inland, allowing Ayscue to come ashore at Austin's Bay. Once assembled, the parliamentary forces total 2,000 foot soldiers and 100 horse troopers; they are opposed by 2,000 foot and 400 horse under Willoughby a quarter-mile away. An immediate clash is averted by a week of rain, after which the royalists ask for terms. The response is generous: the Barbadians receive their own government, with no retaliations sought. Articles are signed at the Mermaid Inn near Austin's Bay on 21 January; the next day the fortifications are occupied by commonwealth officers. Ayscue installs his aide, Daniel Searle, as new governor. About mid-March Ayscue sails for Montserrat, Nevis, and Saint Kitts, which also submit to parliamentary government before the squadron returns for England in May.

SPRING 1652. ***Rupert's Counteroffensive.*** Shortly after Ayscue departs, the royalist commander, Prince Rupert (Count Palatinate of the Rhine, Duke of Bavaria and of Cumberland, Earl of Holderness, etc.), arrives in the West Indies from Europe, hoping to shore up monarchist resolve. Although only 33 years old, the German-born Rupert—nephew of the executed Charles I—is already acclaimed as a brilliant campaigner, having fought at his uncle's side throughout most of the civil war. But once driven out of Britain and pursued into the Mediterranean by Cromwellian Adm. Robert Blake, Rupert's royal squadron has become depleted; now it is reduced to the men-of-war *Swallow* and *Honest Seaman* plus a few unarmed prizes with mutinous unpaid crews. This force is wholly inadequate to reverse the recent assertion of parliamentary rule throughout the Windward Islands, so Rupert traverses them without attempting any attack.

While approaching the Virgin Islands his squadron is engulfed one evening by a storm, during which his own flagship is almost destroyed. Next morning only *Swallow* and two prizes remain afloat, his younger brother, Prince Maurice of Nassau, being lost on the south shores of Anegada Island with the prize-ship *Defiance.* Discouraged, Rupert returns to France in the spring of 1653.

SUMMER 1652. On Saint Kitts, Governor-General de Poincy becomes so alarmed by the growing independence of the Huguenot colony under Le Vasseur at Tortuga Island (Haiti), that he commissions naval officer Timoléon Hotman, Chevalier de Fontenay, and his own nephew, de Treval, to sail for it with two frigates. They rendezvous at Port à l'Éu (north shore of Hispaniola), but before they proceed word comes that Le Vasseur—who has alienated Catholics and Protestants alike by his increasingly autocratic behavior—has been assassinated by two confidants named Tibaut and Martin. De Fontenay and de Treval therefore hasten to Tortuga, the former assuming office as the new governor.

LATE AUGUST 1652. Buccaneer raiders from Tortuga Island (Haiti) ravage the defenseless Cuban town of San Juan de los Remedios, carrying away many citizens as hostages.

14 OCTOBER 1652. Near Montréal (Quebec), 34 Frenchmen under Maj. Lambert Closse repulse about 200 Iroquois warriors.

9 FEBRUARY 1654. ***Spanish Conquest of Tortuga.*** At midday, the French and English inhabitants of Tortuga spot four Spanish vessels bearing down. This counterattack has been prompted by the buccaneers' sack of Santiago de los Caballeros, in 1650, and that of the Cuban port of San Juan de los Remedios in August 1652. Consequently, a punitive expedition has slipped out of the capital of Santo Domingo on 4 December 1653, bearing 200 soldiers and 500 volunteers under Capt. Gabriel de Rojas y Figueroa, who is seconded by the former Irish renegade John Murphy (now promoted to *maestre de campo* and invested with a knighthood in the Order of Santiago; *see* 21 January 1634).

This Spanish squadron has captured a trio of buccaneer craft off Monte Cristi before sighting Tortuga. Gliding past its harbor, the Spaniards bombard the vessels in the roads, then continue two or three miles farther down the coast to disembark several hundred troops at the hamlet of Cayonne, marching back to besiege the island's principal fortress. On the night of 12 February, Rojas sends a company with grappling lines to scale the heights behind the keep and install siege artillery. By 18 February the French and English request terms; two days later de Fontenay surrenders. More than

Contemporary Spanish drawing of the Franco-English fortress on Tortuga Island, Haiti

500 captives are taken, among them 330 *boucaniers.* All are allowed to sail for France aboard a pair of ships—under de Fontenay and Tibaut and Martin, respectively—save two leaders who are kept as hostages; the Spanish seize 70 cannons in the fortress and shore batteries, three ships, a frigate, and eight lesser craft as booty.

These attackers also decide to hold their hard-won conquest by leaving behind a garrison of 100 troops under Murphy. (A few months later Santo Domingo's authorities send Capt. Baldomero Calderón Espinosa with 150 soldiers to relieve the Irishman, whom they do not trust.) On 13 September 1654, Madrid issues a *real cédula* ordering Tortuga evacuated after first throwing down its fortifications.

14 APRIL 1654. ***Franco-Carib War.*** On Grenada, warriors arrive from Saint Vincent and begin attacking the scattered French settlements, sending survivors flying south for protection from Governor Le Comte's stronghold at Beausejour. One month later it too is overrun, the French garrison escaping by the providential appearance of a Cayenne ship with 300 soldiers. They help restore the situation by occupying Fort d'Esnambuc on Morne des Sauteurs and then driving back the Caribs. A two-pronged counteroffensive eventually strikes north, killing 80 Caribs and temporarily clearing Grenada of invaders. But Governor Le Comte is drowned while retiring along the coast

from the campaign, so the Caribs return aboard 24 war canoes, landing at Grande Anse (south of present-day Saint George's) to resume their rampage until finally being defeated at Fort d'Esnambuc a month after.

Minor hostilities persist on Grenada and neighboring Saint Lucia for some time, prompting Martinique's Governor Du Parquet to send 150 men under his deputy, de La Pierrière, to attack the Carib bases on Saint Vincent aboard four ships (respectively mounting 12 guns; four guns and two swivels; two guns and four swivels; and two swivels). They find the Caribs waiting behind a breastwork, which they erected by placing canoes end to end on the beach and filling them with sand. After bombarding the emplacements from offshore without effect, de La Pierrière sends boats in close, luring the Caribs out into the open, where they are decimated by grape from his ships. Sweeping ashore, the French then inflict fearful punishment upon the western half of Saint Vincent before retiring to Martinique.

Trouble soon erupts on that island as well when 2,000 Caribs and blacks rise against the French. The outburst is put down thanks to the chance arrival of four large Dutch merchantmen, who disembark 300 men and assist the beleaguered Martinicans. Having broken the Carib-black army, Governor Du Parquet delegates his subordinate, Guillaume d'Orange, to complete the extirpation.

13 JULY 1654. Maj. Robert Sedgewick, the British commander on the New England coast, departs Boston to attack French Acadia farther north in reprisal for attacks upon British vessels. He captures Fort Sainte Marie, Port Royal (modern Annapolis Royal, Nova Scotia), and Fort Penobscot, which are restored to France in November 1655 by the Treaty of Westminster.

24 AUGUST 1654. Five buccaneer vessels return to Tortuga (Haiti), hoping to reoccupy the island. The force includes 100 of the original French settlers under de Fontenay. They sailed only as far as Saint Kitts to recruit greater strength—rather than return to France, as promised—and now disembark intending to reestablish ownership. After eight days' fruitless combat they are compelled to reembark and, while opposite Monte Cristi, are intercepted by three Spanish men-of-war hastening from Santo Domingo to rescue the garrison. One buccaneer ship is captured with 50 men, half being Dutch, the remainder French. The Dutch are spared and carried prisoner into Santo Domingo; the French are hanged from the yardarms for violating their paroles. De Fontenay escapes and sails back to France, never again visiting the West Indies.

28–31 JANUARY 1655 (O.S.). An English fleet straggles into Barbados, having been sent by Oliver Cromwell to conquer a major stronghold in the West Indies:

Name	*Guns*	*Men*	*Commander*
Swiftsure (flag)	60	380	Jonas Poole
Paragon (vice-flag)	54	330	William Goodson
Torrington (rear admiral)	54	310	George Dakins
Gloucester	54	310	Benjamin Blake
Marston Moor	54	310	Edward Blagg
Indian	44	210	Captain Terry
Lion	44	260	John Lumbert
Mathias	44	230	John White
Dover	40	190	Robert Saunders
Laurel	40	190	William Crispin
Portland	40	190	Richard Newberry
Bear	36	180	Francis Kirby
Great Charity	36	150	Leonard Harris
Selby	24	?	John Clark
Grantham	24	?	John Lightfoot
Martin (galley)	12	60	William Vessey

These are escorting the 30-gun transports *Convertine* of John Hayward, *Heart's Ease* of Thomas Wright, and *Katherine* of Willoughby Hannam; 28-gun *Halfmoon* of Bartholomew Ketcher, and *Rosebush* of Richard Hodges; 25-gun *Golden Cock* of William Garrat; 24-gun *Gillyflower* of Henry Fenn; 20-gun *Adam & Eve* of William Coppin, *Arms of Holland* of Robert Story, *Crow* of Thomas Thompson, *Marigold* of Humphrey Felsted, *Sampson* of John Hubbard, and *Westergate* of Samuel Hawkes; 18-gun *Cardiff* of John Grove, and *Tulip* of Jeffrey Dane; 24-gun flyboat *Falcon* of Thomas Fleet; 12-gun fireship *Falcon* of William Tickell; plus *Hound* of Richard Rooth, and *Falmouth* of Robert Mills. They are further accompanied by a pair of ketches, a hoy, and the dogger *Adventure.* (A convoy of victuallers also awaits them at Barbados.) Overall command is exercised by 33-year-old William Penn, Admiral of the Blue, with William Goodson serving as vice admiral.

The somewhat ill-prepared formation has departed Portsmouth on Christmas Day 1654 (O.S.), with Gen. Robert Venables, 2,500 soldiers, and 38 horses. Sloops are immediately detached to prevent news of the expedition from spreading throughout the Caribbean; also, 18 Dutch traders in Carlisle Bay are embargoed (among them three ships under Pieter Stuyvesant, who is returning from Holland to resume his posting at New Netherland—modern-day New York). Penn and Venables use the layover to recruit auxiliaries, eventually raising 5,000 volunteers on this and other Antillan isles to supplement their forces. After giving these a rudimentary training, the expedition—augmented by numerous prizes—departs Carlisle Bay on 31 March (O.S.) bound for Santo Domingo via Nevis and Saint Kitts.

23 APRIL 1655. ***Assault on Santo Domingo.*** The English expedition stems the Mona Passage and materializes unexpectedly before Santo Domingo's capital at 1:00 P.M., taking the garrison completely by surprise. The island's new governor—Bernardino de Meneses Bracamonte Zapata, Conde de Peñalba—has been in office only since 5 April, his regulars numbering scarcely 300 musketeers and pikemen. The English fleet divides into two segments an hour later, Penn bearing down on Santo Domingo's defenses with his men-of-war to create a diversion while Vice Admiral Goodson leads the transport fleet west to search out a suitable disembarkation point. Because of uncertainty regarding shoals, 9,000 soldiers and sailors and 120 horses do not begin landing until the next day; they come ashore 30 miles away, between Nizao Point and Haina, an absurdly long distance that allows the heavily outnumbered Spanish time to recover from their shock and fortify the capital.

The English troops, moreover—unaccustomed to campaigning in tropical climes—soon begin to succumb to heat, insalubrious drinking water, exotic fruits, and mosquito-borne disease. The vanguard cannot struggle through the jungle to the outskirts of Santo Domingo until 27 April; when Venables's main body arrives the next day, the general does not immediately storm its ramparts but instead withdraws several miles to the Jaina River to permit the enfeebled troops to resupply with fresh food and water from the fleet. The attackers resume their advance on 4 May and are bloodied the next afternoon by 300 militia lancers and 250 Spanish musketeers around Fort San Jerónimo, which effectively ends the English offensive.

Growing increasingly infirm within their camps, the invaders begin reembarking by 8 May, completing the withdrawal by 12 May. They leave behind more than 600 graves, 200 prisoners, two siege guns, eight flags, and all of their horses. The Spanish have lost 30 men killed and a like number wounded during skirmishes. Hoping to salvage something from this fiasco, the English decide to turn on smaller Jamaica two days later.

20 MAY 1655. ***Conquest of Jamaica.*** On 19 May, two Spanish turtle hunters spot the English expedition rounding Point Morant and warn Gov. Juan Ramírez de Arellano at Santiago de la Vega (modern-day Spanish Town). Like their compatriots on Santo Domingo, Jamaica's Spaniards—perhaps 1,500 men, women, children, and slaves—are caught utterly off-guard by the unannounced English aggression. During the night Penn's expedition heaves-to before Caguaya Point (later Port Royal; mispronounced "Cagaway" or "Cagway" by the invaders), and next dawn the admiral shifts his flag aboard the frigate *Martin* to lead a flotilla of lighter craft into the harbor around 10:00 A.M. *Martin* and a few other vessels run aground, but after a brief exchange the Spanish batteries are abandoned by the handful of inexperienced gunners under a hastily appointed *maestre de campo,* Francisco de Proenza, who is actually a local planter or *hacendado;* the frigate is refloated. Sick, General Venables refuses to step ashore, so Penn lands a force of volunteers at Esquivel, meeting no opposition.

On 21 May the English advance six miles and overrun Santiago de la Vega, where Ramírez beats for a parley. Venables comes ashore on 25 May to dictate terms: the inhabitants are to abandon their island within a fortnight, on pain of death. Ramírez temporizes for two days but eventually signs the arrangement on 27 May; shortly thereafter he sails for Campeche, dying en route. Not all Spanish residents recognize this arrangement, however, and *Maestre de Campo* de Proenza—after evacuating many noncombatants by boat toward Cuba from northern Jamaica—establishes his headquarters at the inland town of Guatibacoa, allying himself with the *cimarrones* (runaway black slaves) of the mountainous interior to inaugurate a guerrilla war against English occupation.

The English suffer severely from disease and want of provisions, dying by the hundreds. Within a year the 7,000 English officers and troops are reduced to 2,500. Soon sickness spreads to the Spanish, leaving de Proenza blind; he is succeeded by Cristóbal Arnaldo de Issasi, who continues a rather ineffectual resistance for three more years.

5 JULY 1655. Not wishing to tarry on disease-ridden Jamaica, Penn prepares for a quick return to England by careening his ships (during which *Discovery* is accidentally consumed by fire); off-loading all but six weeks' provisions to help feed the unhappy army; and appointing Vice Admiral Goodson as naval commander in chief of the station with *Torrington* (flag), *Martin, Gloucester, Marston Moor, Laurel, Dover, Portland, Grantham, Selby, Hound, Falmouth,* and *Arms of Holland.*

Penn departs at dawn on 5 July with *Swiftsure, Paragon, Lion, Mathias, Bear, Indian, Convertine, Heart's Ease, Halfmoon, Rosebush, Gillyflower, Sampson, Westergate, Little Charity, Marigold, Cock,* and *Tulip* (plus the flyboat *Falcon,* the fire ship *Falcon,* and *Adam & Eve,* bound for New England). His formation circles western Cuba by 19–20 July—possibly hoping to intercept a Spanish treasure convoy—but at noon three days later (Friday, 13 July [O.S.]), Penn's vice-flag *Paragon* accidentally catches fire and explodes with a loss of 110 men; the admiral presses on toward England. (He reaches Spithead by evening on 31 August [O.S.], only to be incarcerated within the tower three weeks later—along with Venables—on order from Cromwell, who is furious at the miscarriage of his Santo Domingo scheme.)

11 JULY 1655. Stuyvesant reaches New Netherland (New York City) from Curaçao, delayed due to being embargoed by Penn at Barbados. Nevertheless, he is still in time to lead seven Dutch vessels and several hundred men in a military sweep that recaptures Fort Casimir; he then occupies Fort Christina (Wilmington, Delaware), annexing the entire colony of New Sweden to Dutch rule.

8 AUGUST 1655. The Spanish garrison occupying Tortuga Island (Haiti) is withdrawn in compliance with Madrid's decree of 13 September 1654—as well as to bolster Santo Domingo's defenses against the recent English offensive. Captain Baldomero Calderón complains about the decision, which not only compels him to abandon Tortuga to the buccaneers but also obliges him to bury its 70 cannons rather than carry them off. As expected, Tortuga Island is soon reoccupied by English and French interlopers under a leader named Elias Watts (or Ward), who arrives from Jamaica with his family and about a dozen colonists some time during 1656, obtaining a commission shortly thereafter from Gov. William Brayne of Jamaica making him "governor" of Tortuga.

10 AUGUST 1655. ***Sack of Santa Marta.*** A month after Penn's departure, Goodson sails with his squadron to patrol the Spanish Main, leaving a few ships at Jamaica to defend it during his absence. He tacks 450 miles upwind to Santa Marta, which he takes, sacks, and burns, although for scant booty (except for 30 guns). Moving west-southwest toward Cartagena, he deems his force insufficient to attempt an assault and so returns to Jamaica by mid-November 1655 "to refit and consider of some other design."

MAY 1656. ***Ríohacha Raid.*** Goodson again visits the Spanish Main, having sailed from Jamaica on 25 April with ten ships (smaller than those of his previous foray). After devastating Ríohacha with 450 men—for little reward except four brass cannons—he departs on 18 May after torching the buildings. Proceeding down the coast, he waters at Santa Marta from 21–23 May before capturing a small Spanish ship bearing wines from Cadiz. Anchoring impotently before Cartagena on 24 May, Goodson returns toward Jamaica after leaving his second-in-command with three craft to maintain watch over the Spanish base. Meanwhile Goodson intercepts another small Spanish vessel bound from Santo Domingo toward Mexico, then arrives back at Jamaica on 2 June. He is followed into port 11 days later by his second-in-command.

JULY 1656. Goodson weighs from Jamaica, sailing to join the 14 sail he has earlier detached to hover off western Cuba in hopes of intercepting a Spanish treasure fleet. By 20 July he comes up with Commo. John Lambert's *Lion, Indian, Success, Dover, Selby,* and *Martin* off Cape San Antonio (*Arms of Holland* having previously exploded). A month later Goodson proceeds toward Havana with ten sail, arriving by 27 July to unite with his other squadron and institute a close blockade. On 29 August he decides to send his flagship *Torrington* home to England along with *Gloucester, Dover, Portland,* and *Laurel;* he shifts his flag into Capt. Christopher Myngs's *Marston Moor,* the others parting company four days later.

Abandoning his Havana blockade on 31 August (O.S.), Goodson beats slowly upwind toward Nevis, arriving by 19 October to begin embarking 1,400 settlers who are scheduled to emigrate toward Jamaica. Having completed the mission, Goodson remains in and around Jamaica until January 1657, when he shifts into *Mathias* and sails for England, arriving in late April complaining of ill health. Myngs follows a month later with a three-ship convoy, bringing *Marston Moor* into Dover by July.

LATE 1656. In the Capesterre region of Guadeloupe, Angolan slaves, under the leadership of two men named Pedre and Jean Le Blanc, rise against their masters. Their hopes of being joined by the Cape Verde slaves of the Basse-Terre region are not realized, leaving the rebels to melt away into the jungle after two weeks' violence. They are soon tracked down by a 20-man company of musketeers under a Walloon named Despinay, who brings in Pedre and Le Blanc to be drawn and quartered.

18 OCTOBER 1657. The Caribs of Martinique sue for peace, which is granted by Governor Du Parquet. Unable to travel because of illness, Du Parquet next day delegates his subordinate, d'Orange, to visit the native encampments at Capesterre, getting leaders to promise they will no longer harbor runaway black slaves (whom the French greatly fear).

20 FEBRUARY 1658 (O.S.). Commodore Myngs returns to Jamaica from England as new commander in chief of the station, having captured six Dutch merchantmen for illegal trading during his stopover at Barbados. Claiming all six as legitimate prizes, he is annoyed when only one is so deemed by Jamaica's admiralty court, the rest being released on technicalities.

APRIL 1658. The French ships *Gaspard* of Captain de Fontenay (former governor of Tortuga, Haiti) and *Renommée* of Captain Forant rush the entrance to Buenos Aires, engaging three hired Dutch vessels that are inside loading Spanish cargo. After a protracted engagement in which de Fontenay is killed and *Gaspard* captured, *Renommée* emerges with a single prize.

20 MAY 1658. ***Spanish Landing at Río Nuevo.*** Four Spanish troop transports anchor off northern Jamaica and deposit the Tercio Mexicano (Mexican Regiment): 31 captains, 31 ensigns, 28 sergeants, and 467 soldiers recruited in New Spain to wrest the island from English control. Two days later a trio of English coast-guard vessels chances upon the Spanish transports still at anchor but are chased away by gunfire. The English scouts nevertheless report to Gov. Edward d'Oyley, who appears at Río Nuevo on 25 June with 700 soldiers aboard ten ships, disembarking nearby.

The Mexicans, who in the meantime have been joined by perhaps 50 tattered Spanish guerrillas, choose to fight from behind a redoubt, despite the heavy firepower advantage enjoyed by the English. The invaders are pulverized in a two-day pitched battle, suffering at least 300 deaths before dispersing into the jungle, leaving behind 11 flags, six guns, numerous prisoners, and most of their arms and ammunition. The English suffer 60 fatalities and convey the Spanish artillery back to their island capital, installing it into the defenses.

SUMMER 1658. ***Myngs's First Foray.*** Alarmed by reports of the arrival of a large Spanish fleet at Cartagena, English Commodore Myngs sails from Jamaica with 300 soldiers (aboard *Marston Moor, Hector, Coventry, Blackamoor,* and *Cagway*) to examine the base from the sea, then veers south to assault Tolú. After burning that place, along with two ships in its roads, Myngs circles northeast to surprise Santa Marta, where his troops march 12 miles inland; he withdraws three days later. Returning to Jamaica after a ten-week cruise, Myngs also brings in three Spanish merchantmen—intercepted while bound from Cartagena toward Portobelo—which are sold to men who in coming years will prove to be formidable corsairs: Robert Searle, the Dutch-born Laurens Prins ("Lawrence Prince"), and John Morris.

SEPTEMBER 1658. Martinique's acting governor, Médéric Rolle, sieur de Gourselas, assembles 600 militia to exterminate the last Caribs in the northern Capesterre region. Five barks under François Rolle de Loubière are to carry 200 attackers around by sea while another 200 attackers are to advance overland around Mount Pelée; a similar force is to circle by way of Morne des Gommiers. The outnumbered and outgunned natives are quickly defeated, fleeing toward Dominica and Saint Vincent while their villages go up in flames. De Loubière completes the heartless campaign by erecting a small fortress on Martinique's northern coast that hinders the Caribs' return.

EARLY JANUARY 1659. ***Myngs's Second Cruise.*** Having enjoyed success on his first foray, Myngs's frigates *Marston Moor, Hector, Diamond,* and *Cagway* are joined by numerous freebooters for another raid against the Spanish Main. In order to surprise different targets Myngs patiently tacks hundreds of miles farther east than he or Goodson have previously operated. This pays handsome dividends when his formation bursts upon Cumaná, seizing and ransacking the unprepared port. Myngs hurries west with the prevailing winds and currents, falling upon Puerto Cabello before any alarm can be carried overland; he repeats the tactic by racing farther west to make a rich haul at Coro.

At Coro he seizes at least 22 chests—each containing 400 pounds of silver ingots—from two Dutch merchantmen flying Spanish colors in the roads. But when Myngs returns to Jamaica on 23 April (O.S.) the chests are found to have been opened; the commonwealth officials suspect a great deal of bullion has been extracted rather than surrendered to the state's coffers. Myngs does not deny some looting has occurred, dismissing it as customary among privateers after a battle. The officials take a dimmer view, believing Myngs to be taking justice into his own hands because the admiralty court earlier refused to condemn his Dutch prizes

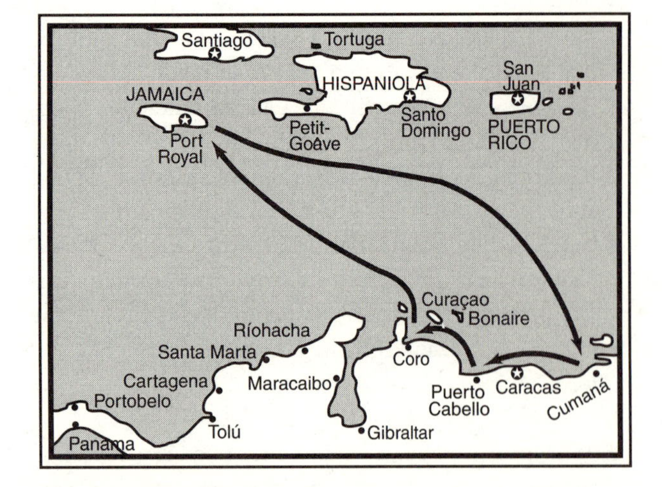

Myngs's campaign against the Spanish Main

(*see* 20 February 1658). Governor d'Oyley therefore suspends him and orders *Marston Moor* home, where Myngs is to stand trial for defrauding the exchequer.

(Myngs arrives in England during the spring of 1660, when the nation is distracted by the restoration of Charles II. An early supporter of the monarch, Myngs is cleared of all charges at a sympathetic hearing in June and restored to his Jamaica command shortly thereafter; *see* July 1662 in Part 4.)

5–9 APRIL 1659 (EASTER WEEK). ***Santiago de los Caballeros.*** Some 400 English and French buccaneers depart Tortuga Island (Haiti) aboard the frigate and three lesser vessels of Captain de l'Isle, under a letter of reprisal issued by Governor Watts. They land near Puerto Plata to march inland, attacking the border town of Santiago de los Caballeros on Good Friday night. Some 25–30 Spaniards are killed, the town is ransacked, and a number of hostages are seized. But the buccaneers must then make a fighting retreat toward their ships, beset by fearsome *cincuentenas* (Spanish militia cavalry organized in companies of 50—in Spanish, *cincuenta*—hence the nickname).

Shortly thereafter, a French adventurer named Jérémie Deschamps de Moussac et Du Rausset arrives at Jamaica from Europe, bearing letters from both the French and English governments appointing him governor of Tortuga. Rather than resist, Watts packs his family and goods aboard a ship and sails away to resettle in New England. Next day, Du Rausset assumes office, although he soon transfers from Tortuga to the more salubrious Petit Goâve, leaving his nephew, Frédéric Deschamps de La Place, to govern the offshore island.

LATE JULY 1659. A private French ship arrives at Marie Galante with 100 soldiers under the Chevalier Robert Houël, the disgruntled younger brother to Charles Houël, governor of Guadeloupe. Having previously been promised one-third of brother Charles's holdings, Robert was dismissed two years previously and returned to France. Determined to reassert his rights, Robert proclaims himself governor of this tiny offshore island then continues to Guadeloupe's *quartier* of Grande Anse to raise support. He circles to the capital of Capesterre, disembarking a small army to directly challenge his brother. Charles orders the local militia to march against Robert, but they refuse, forcing the governor to accept a compromise and share his lands.

Part 4: Intercolonial Friction (1660–1700)

If the king of Spain shall refuse to
admit our subjects to trade with them,
you shall in such case endeavor to procure and
settle a trade with his subjects in those parts by force.

—Instructions to the Jamaican governor, Lord Windsor (1662)

No Peace beyond the Line (1660–1665)

Two years after Oliver Cromwell's death, the English monarchy is reinstated, Charles II returning from exile in May 1660 to assume his ancestral throne amid popular rejoicing. Despite a general cessation of hostilities throughout Europe, however, little tranquillity is enjoyed in the New World. Treaties signed by Spain with both England and France avoid any mention of their American holdings, which Madrid eventually hopes to reconquer. This attitude helps feed the hostile undercurrent already prevalent in the American theater.

February 1660. On Saint Kitts, a conference is held between English Govs. James Russell of Nevis, Christopher Kaynall of Antigua, and Roger Osborne of Montserrat—plus French Governor-General de Poincy and Guadeloupe's cogovernors, Charles and Robert Houël. They draw up an agreement pledging mutual aid against Carib attacks, further recognizing that Dominica and Saint Vincent are to be left to the Carib natives. Funds for the new defensive alliance are to be deposited at Basseterre on Saint Kitts, to be disposed of by Charles Houël and Osborne; Houël is also to sign a peace treaty with the Caribs on behalf of all members.

31 March 1660. Fifteen Carib chieftains gather at Gov. Charles Houël's residence (Houëlmont, Guadeloupe), to sign a peace treaty with the French and English. By its terms, the natives agree to desist from seaborne raiding, in exchange for being allowed to live peacefully on Dominica and Saint Vincent.

2 May 1660. In Canada, 16 French voyageurs, 40 Huron allies, and four Algonquians under the Montréal garrison's youthful commander—Adam Dollard, Sieur des Ormeaux—are surprised by 200 Onondaga Iroquois warriors at an abandoned fortification at Long Sault on the Ottawa River (near modern-day Hawkesbury, Ontario). Although the defenders are able to repel the initial Iroquois assault, the latter summon several hundred Mohawk and Oneida reinforcements from the Sorel Islands at the mouth of the Richelieu River. Once they arrive, 30 Hurons also defect from Des Ormeaux's camp, which is easily overwhelmed by 15 May. All the Frenchmen are slain, Iroquois losses totaling 14 killed and 19 wounded.

Early 1662. At night, a 30-man Jamaican expedition under Col. James Arundell lands on Tortuga Island (Haiti), marching upon the home of the French acting governor, Frédéric Deschamps de La Place, to arrest him and restore English rule. Deschamps is asleep elsewhere but hears the commotion and surrounds his residence with followers, who disarm the English usurpers. Arundell and his Jamaicans are expelled, their ship shortly thereafter falling prey to a Spanish vessel that carries them into Santiago de Cuba (where Arundell subsequently dies).

July 1662. The 35-year-old governor-designate of Jamaica—Thomas, seventh Baron Windsor of Stanwell—arrives at Barbados from England with HMS *Centurion* of 46 guns and *Griffin* of 14 guns (both under Commo. Christopher Myngs, newly reappointed station chief for Port Royal; *see* early January 1659 in Part 3). While refreshing after the transatlantic crossing, Windsor sends *Griffin* to Puerto Rico and Santo Domingo, asking the Spanish governors if they will admit English ships to trade now that peace prevails.

Commodore Christopher Myngs; a modern portrait

This inquiry—which Windsor fully expects to be rejected—is actually meant to furnish a pretext for hostilities, for the governor brings with him secret instructions from Whitehall: if trade is refused, he might impose it by force. Windsor resumes his voyage a few weeks later, reaching Port Royal by August. Having brought out the back pay for its English garrison, he releases more than 1,000 soldiers from duty with full wages and a gratuity, replacing them with five volunteer militia regiments distributed throughout the island. Work is also accelerated upon the harbor castle (renamed Fort Charles in honor of the king); a local assembly is convened and an admiralty court established so cases need no longer be appealed to London.

SEPTEMBER 1662. Following the reappearance of *Griffin* carrying Spanish dispatches denying his requests for trade, Windsor inaugurates an aggressive new policy: privateering commissions are once more made available, and volunteers are summoned for a major expedition to be led by Myngs against the Spaniards. Many old hands are delighted, and within three days 1,300 men assemble—many of them former soldiers; *Centurion* and *Griffin* are joined by ten privateering vessels, including a tiny craft commanded by a 27-year-old militia captain named Henry Morgan. The commodore is to lead the force against Santiago de Cuba, which—having been the Spaniards' advance base in their recent efforts to reconquer Jamaica—is particularly detested by the English.

1 OCTOBER 1662. Myngs's flotilla quits Port Royal, slowly rounding Point Negril in light winds. Landfall is made a few score miles east of Santiago de Cuba, where the rogue privateer Sir Thomas Whetstone is spotted at anchor. Myngs obtains recent intelligence from him as to Spanish dispositions then decides to burst directly into the enemy port, taking it by surprise. Joined by Whetstone and seven more Jamaican privateers who belatedly overtake his expedition, Myngs steers west in scanty winds.

18 OCTOBER 1662. ***Destruction of Santiago de Cuba.*** At daybreak the English come within sight of the towering harbor castle guarding Santiago's entrance but cannot close because of faint breezes. Finally, late in the afternoon Myngs decides to veer toward Aguadores Village, two miles distant at the mouth of the San Juan River. By nightfall he puts 1,000 men ashore with no resistance; the English advance inland through darkened woods by torchlight.

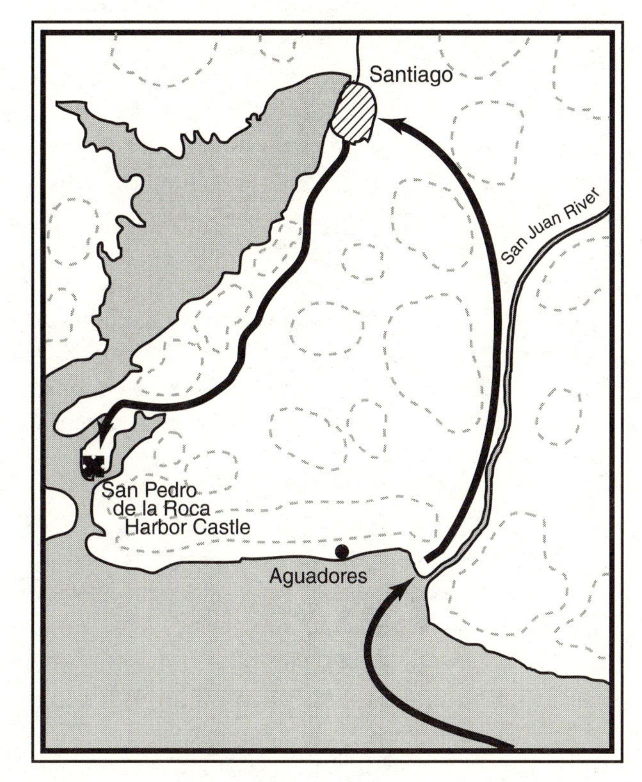

Myngs's assault on Santiago de Cuba

Next dawn they emerge six miles from the coast and three miles from Santiago, which they rush at midmorning. The assault is met at Las Lagunas outside the gates by 170 hastily mustered Spanish regulars and two field pieces under Gov. Pedro de Morales, backed by 200 militia under Cristóbal Arnaldo de Issasi (former guerrilla leader on Jamaica; *see* 20 May 1655 in Part 3). The overmatched defenders are quickly routed, the English gaining mastery of the city and seven vessels lying in its harbor by noon. Next day, 20 October, Myngs detaches a column to attack the San Pedro de la Roca harbor castle from behind in conjunction with a naval bombardment from his flotilla offshore. Such efforts prove unnecessary, however, for the isolated 30-man garrison has already deserted; the English ships enter unchallenged.

The invaders spend the next five days pursuing the Spaniards inland, hoping to seize their riches. Frustrated, the freebooters raze Santiago while Myngs uses 700 barrels of powder from its magazines to demolish the fortifications and principal buildings, leaving Santiago's harbor castle completely leveled. (It will take the Spaniards more than a decade to repair the redoubt.) Finally, Myngs departs on 25 October with his six prizes—the seventh being scuttled—having lost a half-dozen Englishmen killed in action and another 20 dead through accident or illness.

1 NOVEMBER 1662. Myngs returns to Port Royal and finds the political situation has changed: Governor Windsor has sailed for England three days earlier complaining of ill health, leaving power in the hands of Jamaica's newly created local assembly—to which Myngs has been elected during his absence. Encouraged by their easy success at Santiago, most privateers put to sea again to plunder other Spanish targets; the Jamaican Council votes on 22 December to authorize another raid, this time against Campeche. Myngs's flagship *Centurion* is refitted, and freebooters once more marshal under commanders such as Edward Mansfield and William James.

EARLY JANUARY 1663. The Jamaican privateer Robert Blunden (or Munden) quits Port Royal, accompanied by Col. Samuel Barry and a retired naval captain, Abraham Langford, to woo the French *boucaniers* of Tortuga Island (Haiti) over to English rule, in compliance with instructions from Whitehall. They sail to western Santo Domingo aboard Blunden's *Charles* but, upon arriving, learn that the Tortugans are hostile to any such notion in light of Arundell's abortive attempt (*see* early 1662). Blunden refuses to proceed farther; over Barry's objections the delegates instead visit the French at Petit Goâve, where a different band of *boucaniers* is persuaded to acclaim Blunden their chieftain and raise an English flag. Disapproving, Barry returns to Jamaica several months later; Blunden's partner, Langford, sails for England to petition Charles II for appointment as governor of "Tortuga and the coasts of Hispaniola" but is eventually denied.

21 JANUARY 1663. This Sunday, two Royal Navy warships and approximately ten privateers depart Port Royal under Myngs to attack Campeche. Working his way down Yucatán's treacherous coastline, Myngs loses contact with vice-flag *Griffin* and several privateers before finally coming within sight of the target.

8 FEBRUARY 1663. ***Myngs's Sack of Campeche.*** Under cover of darkness, the British commodore sneaks almost 1,000 men ashore at Jámula Beach, four miles west of Campeche, and begins his advance upon the sleeping city. At first light on 9 February Spanish lookouts spot Myngs's smaller vessels opposite the disembarkation point and two larger men-of-war farther out to sea. They sound the alarm but are too late, as the freebooter army bursts out of a nearby woods at 8:00 A.M. Despite being surprised and outnumbered, the 150 Spanish militia put up a spirited resistance, and Myngs receives serious wounds in the face and both thighs while leading the opening charge. As Myngs is carried back aboard *Centurion,* the privateer chief Mansfield assumes overall command. After two hours of heated fighting, the defenders are subdued, suffering more than 50 fatalities (as opposed to 30 invaders slain). Some 170 Spanish captives are rounded up, and many of the city's thatched huts go up in flames.

Next morning the only Spanish official still free—*Regidor* Antonio Maldonado de Aldana—agrees to a truce in exchange for good treatment of the prisoners, leaving the English undisturbed within the city. By 17 February Myngs is sufficiently recuperated to order the release of four prominent captives, with a message to Maldonado offering to spare Campeche's buildings and release the remainder of his prisoners unharmed upon withdrawing if the raiders can draw water from the nearby Lerma wells. The Spaniard accedes, and as a token of good faith Myngs releases all but six of his most important hostages before watering. On 23 February his fleet gets under way, carrying away booty and 14 vessels (described by a Spanish eyewitness as "three of 300 tons, the rest medium or small, and some with valuable cargo still on board"). The heavily laden formation then beats its way back around Yucatán against contrary winds and currents, taking so long that concern begins to mount at Jamaica. *Centurion* eventually reaches Port Royal on 23 April under its flag-captain, Thomas Morgan, followed by the rest of the expedition. Myngs's wounds require a lengthy convalescence, so he sails for England in early July.

11 MAY 1664. An expedition arrives at Dutch-held Cayenne (Guiana) under Alexandre de Prouville, Marquis de Tracy and "lieutenant general"–designate for France's New World colonies. His mission is to reimpose government rule over all French settlements, supplanting the private merchant-adventurers who have exercised control till now. Tracy commands the 50-gun *Brézé* (flag) of Captain Forant, *Aigle d'Or, Saint Sébastien,* and *Sainte Anne,* bearing 850 sailors and soldiers, plus three transports with 650 colonists.

Disembarking 750 men at Cayenne under Antoine Lefebvre, Seigneur de La Barre, the marquis cows Dutch Gov. Quirijn Spranger at Fort Nassau (formerly Fort Céperou) into surrendering four days later, replacing him with Lefebvre de La Barre's brother, Jean Hérault Lefebvre de Lézy. Tracy then continues into the Lesser Antilles, being well received at Guadeloupe and Martinique in June, although his subsequent efforts to eliminate free trade meet with only grudging success.

Alexandre de Prouville, Marquis de Tracy, ca. 1660

JUNE 1664. Francis, Lord Willoughby—reinstated as royal governor-general for the English Antilles (*see* 25 October 1651 in Part 3)—sends 1,500 men from Barbados aboard five vessels (two of these armed with 36 guns), plus 600 Caribs in 17 war canoes, to occupy Saint Lucia. This is home to a 14-man French garrison under Jean Bonnard, who is driven off toward Martinique, leaving Saint Lucia entirely to the English and several thousand Carib residents.

Willoughby justifies this seizure by the presence of Thomas Warner among his expedition, he being of mixed-race heritage, the natural son of a Carib woman and Sir Thomas Warner (*see* 28 January 1624 in Part 3); as nominal leader to the Indians, the younger Warner has therefore "sold" Saint Lucia to England. French Lieutenant General de Tracy lodges a formal protest, but before any accommodation can be reached between London and Paris the new English colony succumbs to a series of disasters; it is abandoned by January 1666.

14 JUNE 1664. The new Jamaican governor, 44-year-old Sir Thomas Modyford (*see* 25 October 1651 in Part 3), reaches Port Royal from Barbados aboard Captain Stokes's HMS *Marmaduke.* On 26 June he proclaims "that for the future all acts of hostility against the Spaniards should cease," adding that every English privateer must return into port to surrender his commission.

AUGUST 1664. ***Seizure of New Amsterdam.*** English Commo. Robert Holmes arrives from conducting peacetime reprisals against Dutch interests in West Africa. Upon reaching New England, he discovers that as of March Charles II has annexed all disputed territories bordering on the Dutch colony of New Netherland—from the west side of the Connecticut River to the east side of Delaware Bay plus all of Long Island—merging them into a new English province; he grants proprietorship to his brother, James, Duke of York.

James in turn delegates Col. Richard Nicolls as new governor, dispatching him with a small expedition to take control. Backed by Holmes's four warships and New England's Gov. Sir Robert Carr, Nicolls wins over New Amsterdam's burgomaster and several other prominent Dutch citizens, compelling Stuyvesant to surrender without bloodshed. The English flag is raised on 18 September, New Amsterdam becoming New York City; Fort Orange changes to Fort Albany, and so on.

SEPTEMBER 1664. The Jamaican privateer Robert Searle returns to Port Royal with two rich Spanish prizes. In order to underscore his new policy of peaceful coexistence with the Spaniards, Governor Modyford orders the prizes restored to Santiago de Cuba; Searle's rudder and sails are impounded.

15 NOVEMBER 1664. In Paris, Governor Du Rausset—imprisoned in the Bastille for offering to sell Tortuga Island (Haiti) to England the previous year for £6,000—agrees to make it over to the Compagnie des Indes Occidentales for 10,000 livres. The directors then appoint 52-year-old veteran planter Bertrand d'Ogeron, sieur de La Bouère, in June 1665 as governor of the 700–800 Frenchmen living on Saint Domingue and Tortuga.

MID-FEBRUARY 1665. A renegade expedition of a few vessels and 200 Jamaicans under John Morris and Dutch-born David Martien—seconded by Captains Freeman, Jackman, and Henry Morgan—cut an eight-gun Spanish frigate out of Campeche one night. Despite the peace recently promulgated by Governor Modyford, the commanders have chosen to slip away in January, feigning ignorance of his decree, so as to continue their depredations against Spanish America.

Sailing their prize down past the Laguna of Términos, they anchor on 19 February opposite Santa María de la Frontera, at the mouth of the Grijalva River. Some 110–120 buccaneers then disembark and travel 50 miles upriver, coming within sight of the provincial capital of Villahermosa de Tabasco.

24 FEBRUARY 1665. ***Tabasco Raid.*** At 4:00 A.M., English rovers fall upon the sleeping city of Villahermosa, capturing most of its inhabitants in their beds. A general sack ensues, after which the booty and captives are loaded aboard a coaster. The marauders pause at nearby Santa Teresa Ranch to release their women captives; they retain the men, for whom they demand a ransom of 300 cattle. Farther downriver they come upon a second coaster bearing flour, which they also seize.

Nearing the mouth of the Grijalva River, they discover their waiting ships have been captured during their absence by three Spanish frigates and 270 men, sent by Campeche's Lt. Gov. Antonio Maldonado de Aldana. This Spanish flotilla has sighted the interlopers' anchored trio on 22 February, boarding the ten-gun English flagship and eight-gun prize while the anchor watches flee aboard the third vessel. With their retreat now cut off, the main freebooter army releases the remaining hostages and begins moving west along Tabasco's shoreline with their two coasters, hoping to find another means of escaping out to sea.

17 MARCH 1665. This afternoon, Morris and Martien's raiders are overtaken opposite Santa Ana Cay (Tabasco) by Spanish *guardacostas* sailing the privateers' former ten-gun flagship and eight-gun prize, crewed by 300 volunteer militia from Campeche. Their commander, José Aldana, sends a boat inshore to call upon the buccaneers to surrender, but they pretend not to understand. When an interpreter approaches shore next morning, Morris and Martien reply that they will not give up without a fight; the Spaniards, somewhat reluctantly, disembark. But they discover that the rovers have used the delay to entrench behind a palisade, reinforced with sandbags and bristling with seven small cannons brought from Villahermosa. The Spanish force—mostly armed civilians—show little stomach for an assault and are easily repelled without a single loss among the freebooters.

Next day (19 March), the Spanish ships are found conveniently run aground, thus allowing the raiders to sail away unchallenged aboard their two coasters. Morris and Martien proceed north, hugging Yucatán's coast and making occasional forays ashore to obtain supplies. Off Sisal they loot a vessel laden with corn before finally rounding the peninsula and making off south.

SECOND ANGLO-DUTCH WAR (1665–1667) AND WAR OF DEVOLUTION (1667)

IN EUROPE, MERCANTILE JEALOUSIES BETWEEN English and Dutch interests lead to increased tensions, and both nations begin reinforcing their navies. The English unofficially open hostilities by sending an expedition to take over Dutch possessions in West Africa and North America in 1664; they also attack a homeward-bound Dutch convoy from Smyrna off Gibraltar on 29 December. The Dutch retaliate, and on 14 March 1665 Charles II declares war against the Netherlands.

FEBRUARY 1665. News of the imminent rupture between England and Holland reaches Port Royal, where Governor Modyford determines to send an expedition of Jamaican privateers against Dutch Sint Eustatius, Sabá, Curaçao, and Bonaire. He assigns the task to his lieutenant governor, Col. Edward Morgan (uncle of Henry Morgan), a professional soldier of fortune with extensive service in the Thirty Years War and England's civil war.

11 FEBRUARY 1665. The Dutch-born Jamaican subject Laurens Prins ("Lawrence Prince"), having sortied from Port Royal in command of Robert Searle's eight-gun frigate *Cagway* with 61 "mostly English" freebooters, falls upon unsuspecting Bonaire four hours before daybreak on 11 February. He remains six days, during which his followers wreak considerable damage.

5 APRIL 1665. Five English privateers depart Port Royal, the advance elements of Col. Edward Morgan's flotilla against Dutch possessions in the eastern Caribbean.

28 APRIL 1665. Colonel Morgan quits Jamaica aboard Capt. Maurice Williams's 18-gun privateer

Speaker, accompanied by three other sail, bound to assault the Dutch in the Lesser Antilles. Once united, the colonel's force will muster 650 buccaneers aboard his flagship; the 16-gun *Civilian* of Garret Garretson; the 12-gun *Saint John* of John Harman; the ten-gun *Pearl* of Robert Searle; the six-gun *Olive Branch* of John Outlaw and *Trueman* of Albert Bernardson; the two-gun *Susannah* of Nathaniel Cobham; the single-gun *Mayflower* of John Bamfield; and an unnamed galliot under Abraham Malarka (or Malarkey).

However, the rovers show scant enthusiasm for such a foray, being much more inclined to raid their traditional Spanish-American foe, an attitude further hardened when Morgan's flotilla puts into Santo Domingo to buy provisions, firewood, and water only to be refused. Nevertheless, their long upwind beat continues, until Montserrat is raised by 17 July.

29 APRIL 1665. ***De Ruyter at Barbados.*** At 10:00 A.M., a Dutch fleet appears out of the Atlantic under Adm. Michiel Adriaenszoon de Ruyter, bent upon punishing England's American possessions:

Ship	*Guns*	*Men*	*Commander*
Spiegel (flag)	68	315	Michiel Adriaenszoon de Ruyter
Noorderquartier (vice-flag)	50	258	Joan Corneliszoon Meppel
Provincie van Utrecht	58	265	Commo. Gidion de Wildt
Geloof	50	220	Willem van der Zaen
Princes Louise	40	175	Aert van Nes
Caleb	36	150	Govert 't Hoen
Middelburg	36	165	Isaak Sweers
Rode Leeuw	36	150	Dirk Gerritszoon Pomp
Edam	34	135	Jacob Corneliszoon Swart
Harderwyck	34	150	Jan van Nes
Rotterdam	34	124	Leendert Haexwant
Damiaten	32	135	Hendrick Adriaenszoon
Groene Kameel (cargo flute)	10	30	Enno Doedeszoon Star

De Ruyter has spent the past several months patrolling the Guinea Coast (West Africa) and, after repeatedly clashing with English vessels in and around Holland's slaving stations—plus receiving reports of deteriorating relations back in Europe—has boldly struck out across the ocean to launch a preemptive strike in the Caribbean.

At 11:00 A.M. the next day, he leads his fleet into Carlisle Bay, where 29 Barbadian merchantmen and a single man-of-war are about to weigh. De Ruyter does not bother returning the fire of the shore batteries or that of the anchored vessels until his ships are within point-blank range. Both sides then exchange furious volleys over the next several hours, de Ruyter's *Spiegel* and a number of other ships sustaining considerable damage. Despite destroying much of the English convoy, the Dutch admiral cannot dent the defenses and is obliged to withdraw to the neutral French port of Saint Pierre (Martinique) for repairs, arriving there on 1 May.

5 MAY 1665. While his fleet refurbishes, de Ruyter quits Martinique with seven ships and, during a sweep through the Lesser Antilles, learns the Second Anglo-Dutch war has officially begun back in Europe. After seizing the 20-gun English merchantman *Africa* and several other lesser prizes off Montserrat and Nevis, he sights Saint Kitts by 12 May, then pauses at Sint Eustatius on 14 May to deliver supplies, being rejoined by his Martinique consorts under van Nes.

The entire Dutch fleet (a dozen men-of-war, one provision ship, the fire ship *Martha,* the Rotterdam merchantman *Sint Petrus,* and five English prizes) quits the Caribbean three days later, exiting around Saint Martin toward Bermuda. De Ruyter passes Bermuda by 31 May and, having already decided that New York (former New Amsterdam) is too difficult for his depleted forces to attempt, reaches Newfoundland two weeks later. There he captures a few English fishing boats and anchors in Saint John's from 16 June to 20 June before proceeding out into the North Atlantic toward the Netherlands. (Upon returning home, he will be made "lieutenant admiral" of Holland and play a distinguished role in subsequent North Sea fighting.)

29 JUNE 1665. ***Sack of Granada.*** This spring, the rogue band of Jamaican privateers under John Morris and David Martien—including Henry Morgan—traverse the Bay of Honduras and gain Roatán, pausing to take on water. Continuing toward Trujillo, they overrun that port and seize a vessel in its roads before proceeding toward Cape Gracias a Dios and the Mosquito Coast, where nine native guides join them. Sailing south to Monkey Point (Punta Mono), the buccaneers hide their ships in an inlet and head up the San Juan River in lighter boats. More than 100 miles and three waterfalls later, they emerge into the Lago de Nicaragua, crossing it by nocturnal stages and sneaking up on Granada, so as to take it by surprise.

At dawn on 29 June they march undetected into the main square, loosing a sudden volley. The rovers then herd 300 captives into the principal church and plunder for 16 hours before leaving. Retracing their course across the lake, they ransack a 100-ton Spanish vessel and Solentiname Island, finally regaining their anchored vessels and returning to Port Royal by late August.

(Having learned the Second Anglo-Dutch War has since erupted, they know their illicit raids will be pardoned by Governor Modyford; only the Dutchman Martien does not return, preferring to instead continue toward the French *boucanier* stronghold of Tortuga Island. His withdrawal from Jamaican service is short-lived, however, for one year later he is being actively recruited by Modyford.)

30 JUNE 1665. Governor-General de Tracy arrives in Quebec City (population 500) from Martinique with four companies of French West Indian troops, 11 days after the first of 1,000 soldiers of the Carnigan-Salières Regiment have also begun disembarking from France. These reinforcements will allow for the construction of a chain of forts along the Richelieu River, expanding Canada's boundaries.

17 JULY 1665. ***Fall of Sint Eustatius.*** Having reached Montserrat, the nine-vessel privateering expedition of Col. Edward Morgan pauses to gather strength and procure landing craft. Shortly thereafter they run northwest before prevailing winds, coming within sight of Dutch Sint Eustatius. Morgan leads 350 buccaneers in a charge ashore, easily defeating the outnumbered and surprised garrison—although the colonel suddenly dies of a heart attack.

His Jamaican privateers remain at Sint Eustatius, renaming it New Dunkirk and deporting 250 residents to Barbados, as well as sending a single vessel with 70 men under Maj. Richard Stevens to occupy adjoining Sabá. Despite gaining 910 slaves and much booty, Morgan's death deprives the buccaneers of any incentive to attack other Dutch islands. Each captain splits off on an independent cruise, leaving Lt. Col. Thomas Morgan (apparently no relation to the colonel or to Henry) as governor of Sint Eustatius.

Captains Searle and Steadman make a subsequent descent upon the Dutch island of Tobago with 80 freebooters, who begin destroying everything they cannot carry away. While thus engaged, they are joined a few days later by Governor-General Willoughby, with a half-dozen vessels and 350 men from Barbados, who convinces the Jamaicans to refrain from such vandalism and replaces them with a 50-man occupying force.

18 JULY 1665. Although not yet officially commissioned to attack Dutch interests, English privateer John Wentworth of Bermuda disembarks 36 men from his small frigate *Charles* this morning and surprises the 130-man, seven-gun Dutch garrison on Tortola in the Virgin Islands, securing it unopposed. Next day he raises the English flag, and roughly half of the island's inhabitants swear fealty to Charles II. Later this same day the brigantine *Hazewind*—which belongs to the captive Dutch governor, Willem Houten—comes in and is seized.

On 24 July Houten and his retinue are sent away in a bark, Wentworth appointing Lt. Thomas Bicknell (or Bignoll) to act as temporary governor in his place. Four days later *Charles* sails for Bermuda, carrying 67 black slaves and *Hazewind* as prizes; he arrives eight days later to find his action deemed illegal.

NOVEMBER 1665. Because of continual victimization of neutral Spanish-Americans by English privateers, Governor Modyford convenes a rover meeting at Bluefields Bay (Jamaica) to recall them to their duty. Eventually 600 buccaneers answer his summons, reassuring the governor they are "very forward" to attack the Dutch; they even accept instruction for a descent against Curaçao. But once they depart the rogues lay in a course for southern Cuba, supposedly to buy provisions for their forthcoming campaign.

A Spanish bark is intercepted among the Cayos and its 22 crewmembers are murdered, after which the buccaneers seize the port of Júcaro around Christmas. Some 200–300 raiders then march 42 miles inland, taking and firing Sancti Spíritus on 26 December without suffering a single casualty; they carry their prisoners back to the ships to be ransomed for 300 cattle. (Some of the rogues later justify the depredations by alleging they hold Portuguese commissions issued by the French governor of Tortuga in addition to their English ones.) Having thus disposed of their supply problem, the privateers choose Mansfield to be their admiral and, by mid-January 1666, begin the long upwind beat toward Curaçao.

But their good intentions soon evaporate, the flotilla dispersing to again attack Spanish targets. From Bocas del Toro (Panama) eight privateer vessels roam east to descend upon Natá while Mansfield leads another seven west against Costa Rica.

9 JANUARY 1666. The recently arrived, 39-year-old governor of New France—Daniel de Rémy, Sieur de Courcelle—departs Quebec City with 300 troops of the Carnigan-Salières Regiment, plus 200 Canadian volunteers, to mount an expedition against the Mohawks farther south. The expedition is reinforced at Fort Sainte Thérèse by more men out of Montréal before it continues across the wintry landscape.

On 17 February, Courcelle reaches Schenectady (New York), his followers being too exhausted to attack the main Mohawk villages, still three days beyond. After being resupplied by its Anglo-Dutch residents, Courcelle's force returns to Canada by 17 March, having suffered 19 men killed and two captured during the campaign; Mohawk losses are three dead and five wounded.

26 JANUARY 1666. In Europe, Louis XIV declares war against England, entering the hostilities as a Dutch ally.

EARLY MARCH 1666. At Jamaica, Modyford decides to bow to popular demand and unilaterally authorizes the granting of "letters of marque against the Spaniard"—despite London's peaceful relations with Spain. The governor's reasons are manifold: to better control his unruly privateers, who are attacking Spanish-Americans anyway and carrying prizes into French Saint Domingue; the need for a steady flow of booty to maintain Jamaica's economy; plus the usual complaints against Spanish *guardacostas* and officialdom throughout the Caribbean.

19 MARCH 1666. News of the outbreak of Franco-English hostilities reaches Martinique, prompting Gov. Robert Le Frichot Des Friches, Seigneur de Clodoré to begin refurbishing its defenses and to recruit a company of tough black rebels, under leader François Fabulé, as extra militia.

8 APRIL 1666. ***Costa Rican Invasion.*** Seven English buccaneer vessels under Edward Mansfield arrive before Portete, capturing its lookout before any alarm can be sent inland. After anchoring off Punta del Toro, several hundred raiders burst upon Matina, snapping up its 35 Spanish citizens. But an Indian named Esteban Yaperi flees from the smaller hamlet of Teotique, carrying word of the incursion to the Costa Rican governor, *Maestre de Campo* Juan López de Flor. It is Mansfield's intent to take the capital of Cartago by a surprise overland march, but Yaperi's action spoils his plan. By 15 April hundreds of Spanish militia are mustering at the mountain stronghold of Turrialba, ready to dispute the invaders' passage. Mansfield meanwhile experiences considerable hardship penetrating the jungle, his men succumbing to hunger, thirst, and fatigue. When the buccaneers encounter some Costa Rican natives with bags of ground wheat, they begin fighting among themselves over the meager spoil.

López, heartened by this report, advances with his more lightly armed troops, and Mansfield retreats. By 23 April the exhausted survivors stagger back aboard their ships at Portete, retiring into Bocas del Toro shortly thereafter. Two ships desert Mansfield, leaving him in the awkward position of being regarded as a failure both by his mercurial followers and crown officials on Jamaica (for not attacking the Dutch as instructed). In an effort to vindicate himself, Mansfield decides to assault the Spanish garrison on Providencia Island, which once belonged to English settlers (*see* 17 May 1641 in Part 3).

MID-APRIL 1666. As news of France's entry into the Anglo-Dutch conflict spreads through the Windward Islands, the nonaggression pact between English and French residents on Saint Kitts is strained by mutual distrust, and both sides commence rearmament. The English soon begin concentrating all their regional strength upon this particular island, Lt. Col. Thomas Morgan bringing over his 260 Jamaican buccaneers, who have been occupying Dutch Sint Eustatius since Edward Morgan's conquest.

22 APRIL 1666. ***Pointe de Sable.*** At dawn, the outnumbered French settlers on Saint Kitts attack their English neighbors, firing outlying plantations. This prompts English Gov. William Watts and Lieutenant Colonel Morgan to march with 1,400 men against the smaller French concentration at Pointe de Sable. Cresting a hill shortly before noon, the English descend through canefields to engage 350 defenders under Robert Longvilliers de Poincy. Confident of victory, Morgan's buccaneers drive directly toward the French center, only to be ambushed by a company of musketeers, under Bernard Lafond de l'Esperance, that was hiding behind a hedge. The buccaneers fight their way through with horrific casualties, emerging against the main French body and fatally wounding Longvilliers. But the Jamaicans receive a heavy artillery blast that fells Morgan, destroying the last of their courage. Of the 260 who plunged into the firefight, only 17 emerge unhurt.

Seeing the tough buccaneers falter, Watts warily circles the French positions with his staff, hoping to find a better line of advance for his own force; but he too is ambushed, a single volley dropping him and most of his retinue. His militia, now leaderless, blaze away ineffectually from long range over the next two hours before finally running low on powder and withdrawing. The demoralized English then stampede back to their half of Saint Kitts, offering no resistance when Lafond's columns arrive to consummate the French conquest of the island.

LATE APRIL 1666. ***Nau's Maracaibo Campaign.*** A French buccaneer named Nau—alias "l'Olonnais," being originally from Les Sables d'Olonne—sets sail from Tortuga Island (Haiti) with colleague Michel Le Basque. He is leading eight small vessels and 660 men toward Bayahá for an additional party of *boucaniers* and provisions. Three months later (in late July) the formation stands into the Mona Passage, where Nau captures a neutral 16-gun Spanish vessel that has just departed Puerto Rico for Mexico, sending it back to Tortuga to be off-loaded. Nau remains off Saona, intercepting a second eight-gun Spanish ship carrying gunpowder and payrolls for the Santo Domingo and Cumaná garrisons. When the first prize rejoins him, the *boucanier* chieftain makes it his flagship, then proceeds with his entire flotilla to the Spanish Main, which he has combed the previous year.

Sailing into the Gulf of Venezuela, Nau and Le Basque disembark their *flibustiers* near the 16-gun battery guarding Maracaibo's bar, quickly overwhelming the feeble fortification and passing into the Laguna. Two days later they reach Maracaibo, abandoned by its 3,000 citizens. After occupying it for two weeks and unsuccessfully sending out patrols to bring in rich captives, Nau crosses the Laguna to Gibraltar (near modern-day Bobures), which the Spaniards have reinforced with several hundred troops. His *flibustiers* mount a ferocious assault, Gibraltar falling after a brutal battle in which 40 buccaneers are killed and 30 wounded; the Spaniards suffer disproportionately heavier casualties, their dead being loaded onto two old boats, which are then towed a mile out into the Laguna to be sunk.

The town is pillaged for a month, after which Nau demands 10,000 pesos' ransom to leave the buildings intact. Once paid, his *flibustiers* recross the Laguna and extort 20,000 pesos and 500 cattle to spare Maracaibo as well; they quit the Laguna altogether two months after entering. Eight days later they touch at Île-à-Vache (Haiti) to divide the spoils; they visit Jamaica before reentering Tortuga a month later.

MAY 1666. The sieur Des Roses, French governor of Saint Martin, leads 300 men aboard *Harmonie, Concorde,* and three barks, which have been sent to rescue his colonists. However, he instead uses them in an assault against nearby Anguilla, where they burn the houses, bringing away two English prisoners and three cannons.

25 MAY 1666. ***Seizure of Providencia.*** At noon, Mansfield's two frigates and three sloops raise Spanish-held Providencia Island, gliding down its northern coast this evening to anchor unobserved by 10:00 P.M. Around midnight the moon rises, and by its glow 200 buccaneers row in through the reefs. The force comprises more than 100 English, 80 French from Tortuga—unaware or indifferent to their country's recent declaration of war against England—plus a few Dutch and Portuguese. They march across the island, rounding up the more isolated Spanish residents before storming the lone citadel at first light on 26 May, suffering not a single fatality. Eight Spanish soldiers are asleep inside, the remaining 62 being scattered around their civilian billets. Mansfield grants all Providencia's inhabitants quarter; the French *flibustiers* prevent the English from ransacking the church.

Ten days later Mansfield sets sail with 170 Spanish captives, whom he has promised to repatriate. Captain Hatsell is left as "governor" of Providencia with 35 privateers and 50 black slaves, until Mansfield or some other English authority can return. On 11 June Mansfield pauses at Punta de Brujas (Panama) to deposit his prisoners before standing away toward Jamaica. He arrives at Port Royal with two ships by 22 June, learning of Modyford's fortuitous resolution of three and a half months earlier authorizing depredations against Spanish America (*see* early March 1666). Thus, Mansfield finds his unauthorized seizure of Providencia retroactively approved.

28 JULY 1666. Lord Willoughby, governor-general of the English Windward Islands, having just learned of the French victory on Saint Kitts, commandeers a merchant convoy about to depart Barbados that he uses to assemble a relief expedition: two Royal Navy frigates, 12 large vessels, three barks, a fire ship, and a ketch, bearing more than 1,000 men. He aims to sail northwest toward Nevis, Montserrat, and Antigua for further reinforcements and then reconquer Saint Kitts.

His fleet arrives off Martinique two days later, cruising ineffectually for a day before continuing toward Guadeloupe and hovering before its coast on 2–3 August. Watchful French militia cavalry patrols prevent the English from disembarking, so Willoughby detaches his vice-flag—the 26-gun frigate HMS *Coventry* of Capt. William Hill—with a bark and a ketch to seize two French West Indiamen anchored at the nearby Saintes.

4 AUGUST 1666. ***Willoughby's Shipwreck.*** Capt. William Hill bursts into the French anchorage at the Saintes, engaging its tiny battery, commanded by Captain Des Meuriers; he then closes on the merchantmen *Bergère* of Captain Reauville and *Marianne* of Captain Baron. Baron sets his own ship ablaze to prevent its capture; *Bergère* is boarded. The English then disembark troops, who overrun the Saintes's small redoubt, scattering the defenders inland.

However, this evening the weather changes, and a hurricane blows in by midnight. Willoughby's entire expedition is destroyed over the next 24 hours; only a dismasted flute gains Montserrat, and a fire ship staggers into Antigua. The other 18 English vessels are lost between the Saintes and Guadeloupe with horrific loss of life, including the governor-general. The French later salvage Hill's *Coventry* and rename it *Armes d'Angleterre,* giving command to Captain Bourdet, whose *Saint Sébastien* has foundered at Martinique during the same hurricane.

11 AUGUST 1666. François Rolle de Loubière arrives at Martinique with *Saint Christophe,* bringing 120 reinforcements from France plus news that further assistance is on the way.

14 AUGUST 1666. Under cover of darkness, Governor Claude François Du Lion of Guadeloupe leads seven boats with 450 militia and two guns across to the neighboring Saintes, where numerous English survivors from Willoughby's shipwreck are entrenching under Captain Hill. Du Lion attacks the extemporized fortifications overnight and again next day, eventually forcing the English to surrender by the morning of 16 August, suffering 33 killed and 80 wounded (as opposed to negligible French casualties). Prisoners are transferred to Guadeloupe.

17 AUGUST 1666. Four French ships and two barks reach Guadeloupe from Martinique, with 400 men under Captain de Loubière. This afternoon they sight eight smaller English vessels tacking upwind from Nevis toward the Saintes under Henry Willoughby (the nephew of the dead governor-general), who is hoping to rescue marooned compatriots. The largest English warship mounts only 12 guns, whereas de Loubière's smallest has 14; thus, the French commodore waits until his opponents arrive off Basse-Terre before attacking. The English are hopelessly outclassed, young Willoughby escaping in a bark along with his four smallest vessels while leaving his three largest to de Loubière. Some 200 English captives are carried into Guadeloupe and set to work.

EARLY SEPTEMBER 1666. A single French bark under Gilles Gaspart of Grenada deposits a tiny landing force on English-held Tobago (which was captured from the Dutch the previous year) and in the darkness tricks the garrison into surrendering. The French remain until March 1667, when they fire Tobago's buildings and withdraw shortly before Commo. Abraham Crijnssen's Dutch relief force appears (*see* 17 April 1667).

14 SEPTEMBER 1666. In Canada, Governor-General de Tracy and Governor Courcelle depart Quebec with 700 soldiers, 400 volunteers, plus 100 Huron and Algonquian allies to make a punitive sweep south against the Mohawks. Encountering scant opposition, they burn four major abandoned villages and destroy numerous crops before returning home by 5 November.

15 SEPTEMBER 1666. Eight French infantry companies from the Navarre and Normandie Regiments—400 soldiers under the *maréchal de bataille* Chevalier de Saint Leon and his military engineer, Jean Blondel—arrive at Martinique aboard the 28-gun *Saint Sebastien* of de Pas de Jet (de Paget?), the 26-gun *Aigle d'Or* of Du Maine, the 16-gun *Aurore* of Du Pré, the eight-gun *Cher Ami* of Jullien, and the 16-gun hired merchantman *Eglise* under Acard.

1 OCTOBER 1666. The new lieutenant general for the Antilles, Antoine Lefebvre, seigneur de La Barre, reaches Martinique from France aboard the 28-gun West India Company vessel *Florissant* with *Mercier, Irondelle, Lion d'Or, Dorothée, Pucelle,* and two lesser vessels, bearing reinforcements.

25 OCTOBER 1666. After strengthening Martinique's defenses, Lefebvre de La Barre departs with an expedition raised in conjunction with Governor Clodoré and a local West India company representative named Chambré to attack English Antigua. To secure greater numbers, the force pauses at Guadeloupe during its passage north, receiving further help from Governor Du Lion.

Lefebvre de La Barre puts to sea again on 2 November with the company ships *Florissant* (flag), 40-gun *Lis Couronée,* 32-gun *Justice,* 26-gun *Saint Christophe* and *Saint Sebastien,* 18-gun *Vierge,* 14-gun *Afriquaine,* and eight-gun *Bergère.* The frigate *Armes d'Angleterre* and a smaller craft follow later.

LATE OCTOBER 1666. While the French are marshaling on Martinique and Guadeloupe, the Dutch privateer Gerart Bogaert arrives at French-held Saint Kitts from Curaçao and recruits 100–120 compatriots—refugees driven out of Dutch Sint Maarten and Sint Eustatius by the English. Reinforced by 50 French soldiers, the expedition sets sail toward Sint Eustatius to besiege the remnants of Thomas Morgan's Jamaican garrison within their fort.

4 NOVEMBER 1666. ***Capture of Antigua.*** Lefebvre de La Barre's fleet, flying false English colors, appears off Antigua. This allows *Saint Christophe* and *Vierge* to enter Five Islands Harbor and silence its eight- and six-gun platforms while *Florissant* and *Justice* open fire on the main fort, stampeding the startled English garrison at the first salvo. Some 200 men under Captain Rémi Guillouet, seigneur d'Orvilliers (Lefebvre de La Barre's son-in-law) disembark, thus securing the port.

Lefebvre de La Barre comes ashore and next dawn permits d'Orvilliers and an adventurer named Baston to advance against English Gov. John Bunckley's stone residence, a mile and a half inland. This is rather ineffectually defended by Col. Robert Carden, who is captured along with 30 men. On the morning of 6 November, Governors Clodoré and Du Lion lead the main French army in from the beach but are checked by about 400 English defenders behind a palisade near Carden's house. This force is directed by Col. Charles Guest, who succeeds in halting Du Lion's initial rush, wounding the French governor and many followers. But the support columns under Clodoré and d'Orvilliers soon arrive and fight through, seriously wounding Guest before scattering his company. French casualties total 50–60 men, and this action marks an end to hostilities on Antigua. Next day Lefebvre de La Barre offers Bunckley terms, and by 10 November a capitulation is signed aboard *Armes d'Angleterre* in Saint John's harbor.

15 NOVEMBER 1666. Having overrun Antigua, Lefebvre de La Barre visits nearby Saint Kitts, where he learns a small Franco-Dutch force has besieged the 200-man English garrison at Sint Eustatius (*see* late October 1666). To aid that effort, the French lieutenant general detaches *Saint Sebastien* and *Saint Christophe* with 150 men under d'Orvilliers; their arrival persuades the English defenders to surrender.

Meanwhile the six-gun French *Pigeon* escorts 350 Englishmen and their families from Saint Kitts toward Jamaica. Lefebvre de La Barre—after failing to convince his French colleagues to assault Nevis—returns southeast to continue refortifying Martinique, delegating command of the forces on Saint Kitts to Clodoré.

30 NOVEMBER 1666. Eleven French vessels return to Saint John's harbor (Antigua) from Saint Kitts with almost 1,000 men under Clodoré, learning that 900 Englishmen have marshaled in the northern district (Pope's Head) from neighboring Barbuda and Nevis under Col. Daniel Fitch. Many English residents that were paroled when Antigua surrendered to the French appear in Fitch's ranks. The French commander therefore sails toward Pope's Head and disembarks his small army, seconded by Pierre Hencelin and Jean Blondel. They immediately charge the motley English force, scattering its members back aboard ship without suffering a single loss. Having thus reasserted French domination, Clodoré continues toward Martinique.

4 FEBRUARY 1667. ***Conquest of Montserrat.*** Having reappeared at Saint Kitts from Martinique and raised another large expedition, Lieutenant General Lefebvre de La Barre sails southeast against Montserrat. His flagships *Florissant* and *Justice* and ten other vessels sight the westernmost tip of this island by 4 February; while waiting for the remainder of his fleet to beat upwind Lefebvre de La Barre bombards the principal English fort until well past nightfall, without effect. Eventually, the French commander decides to disembark his 1,000 troops a few days later—despite having lost the element of surprise—because he learns Gov. Roger Osborne's 900-man English garrison includes many Irish Catholics who are serving unwillingly. The French landing force of *Maréchal* Saint Leon fights its way ashore under covering fire from a brigantine; the force comprises 300 men of the Navarre Regiment under Captain Sanson, 200 of the Normandie Regiment under Captain de l'Ecossais, and 500 Saint Kitts militia under Pierre Giraud Du Poyet.

This evening Lefebvre de La Barre's flotilla is further joined by a trio of French warships bringing two prizes from Barbados, who add 150 more soldiers of the Poitou Regiment to Saint Leon's army. Next day the French advance under Lefebvre de La Barre, Saint Leon, and the governor of Saint Kitts—Claude de

Roux, Chevalier de Saint Laurent—seeking 600–700 Englishmen who are believed concentrating in a nearby valley called the Gardens. No contact is established, but after a few days the lieutenant general detaches his son-in-law d'Orvilliers with a company of French troops and Carib auxiliaries to scour Montserrat's jungles. They capture Osborne's wife and another 80 English noncombatants, obliging the governor to sue for conditions a few days later.

By these terms, more than 300 English colonists become prisoners; also seized are 16 guns, 40 barrels of powder, 500 muskets, 3,000 shot, and a large number of slaves, horses, and cattle. Montserrat's 2,000 Irish residents agree to become subjects of Louis XIV, remaining under the interim governorship of the sieur de Praille (backed by 80 French soldiers and two frigates). Lefebvre de La Barre returns to Saint Kitts by 19 February.

26 FEBRUARY 1667. ***Reconquest of Suriname.*** Zeeland's commodore, Abraham Crijnssen—known to the English as Captain Crimson—appears out of the Atlantic with his 34-gun, 140-man flagship *Zeelandia;* the 28-gun vice-flag *West-Cappel* of Simon Lonck; the 34-gun, 167-man *Zeeridder* of Pieter de Mauregnault; the 14-gun, 75-man yacht *Prins te Paard* of Salomon Le Sage; the six-gun, 13-man hooker *Wester-Souburg* of Rochus Bastaert; plus the flute *Aardenburg* of Abraham Trouwers and an unnamed snow under Hayman Adriaensen. These are manned by almost 1,000 sailors and soldiers with orders to reconquer Dutch Guiana, ally with the French in the Windward Islands to ravage English outposts, then attack Virginia, New York, and Newfoundland on the homeward passage. (Crijnssen's force has been raised by Zeeland alone, hoping to improve upon de Ruyter's poor fortune two years ago; *see* 29 April 1665.)

William Byam, Suriname's English governor, refuses Crijnssen's initial call to surrender, so next morning the Dutch squadron opens fire upon Paramaribo's incomplete fortress and sets 700 men ashore. Byam flees inland without a fight, finally agreeing to capitulate five days later and evacuate Suriname with most of his English followers. Crijnssen meanwhile begins rebuilding Paramaribo's fortifications and on 27 March is reinforced by the 26-gun frigate *Visschersherder* of Boudewijn Keuvelaer.

4 MARCH 1667. The 32-year-old Royal Navy veteran John Berry arrives at Barbados with the hired men-of-war *Coronation* (flag, 56 guns), *Colchester, East India,* and *Quaker,* escorting a merchant convoy. This is the first contingent of a fleet being hastened out from London under 42-year-old Rear Adm. Sir John Harman to bolster English strength throughout the theater. Berry adds the local vessels *Pearl, Constant Katherine, William, Companion, Phoenix,* and *John and Thomas* to his forces, departing Carlisle Bay on 31 March to establish his base of operations at Nevis.

Shortly thereafter the new English governor-general for the West Indies—William Willoughby, younger brother of the deceased Francis—reaches Bridgetown (Barbados) with 800 soldiers under Sir Tobias Bridge plus abundant supplies of artillery, powder, and shot.

EARLY APRIL 1667. Learning of the arrival of Berry's English squadron, Lieutenant General Lefebvre de La Barre sets sail from Basseterre (Saint Kitts), hoping to beat back to Martinique with his frigate *Armes d'Angleterre* and a small brigantine. But he is intercepted off Charlestown (Nevis's capital) by the 48-gun *Colchester,* which Berry has detached on patrol. After a lengthy chase, the English warship overhauls Lefebvre de La Barre's frigate, engaging in the moonlight. A ferocious firefight ensues; the decrepit *Colchester* sinks, and the badly damaged *Armes d'Angleterre* staggers away west-northwest toward Saint Croix.

MID-APRIL 1667. After reaching Nevis, Berry blockades French-held Saint Kitts. Some Martinican and Guadeloupan vessels run the gauntlet, disembarking 250 reinforcements on the eastern shores. The speedy French frigate *Notre Dame de Bon Port* is also sent to retrieve Lieutenant General Lefebvre de La Barre from Saint Croix, returning him to Martinique.

17 APRIL 1667. Crijnssen sails from Suriname toward Berbice (modern-day New Amsterdam, Guyana), detaching *West-Cappel* and *Aardenburg* on separate services—the former to cruise for English prizes, the latter to carry captured sugar toward La Rochelle. After touching at Berbice and being joined by the yacht *Windhond,* Crijnssen reverses course west-northwest, reclaims abandoned Tobago by installing a 29-man garrison with four guns, then continues toward Martinique by 4 May, arriving three days later.

14 MAY 1667. Having agreed to a combined attack against Nevis, Crijnssen's Dutch squadron is joined at Martinique by French "Admiral" de La Barre, "Vice Admiral" de Clodoré (Martinique's governor), and "Rear Admiral" Du Lion (Guadeloupe's governor) with the 38-gun flagship *Lis Couronnée* of d'Elbée; 32-gun vice-flagship *Justice* of Jacques Gauvain

and "rear admiral" *Concorde* of Jamain; 34-gun *Saint Jean* and *Saint Sebastien* of Chevalier; 32-gun *Harmonie* of Pingault; 30-gun *Florissant* of La Jaunay; 26-gun *Hercule* of Garnier and *Saint Christophe* of Séguin; 24-gun *Armes d'Angleterre* of Bourdet and *Mercier* of Tadourneau; 14-gun *Irondelle* of Mallet; ten-gun *Nôtre Dame de Bon Voyage* (plus 12 swivels) under Du Vigneau; 18-gun transport *Marsouin* of Sanson; plus the fireships *Cher Ami* of Lescouble and *Souci* of Ferrand. They are further strengthened by 600 volunteers raised on Martinique plus another 500 picked up two days later at Guadeloupe; they steer toward Nevis on 18 May.

20 MAY 1667. ***Battle off Nevis.*** Rounding the southern points of Nevis during the early morning hours, the Franco-Dutch fleet is sighted by English reconnaissance boats, which carry a warning into Charlestown. By 8:00 A.M., 17 English sail exit under Berry, 13 of which immediately bear down on the attackers. The French line disintegrates into confusion while preparing to engage. Crijnssen's *Zeelandia* closes upon Berry's *Coronation,* but the Dutch flagship is driven off by two fire ships; after a desultory long-range exchange between both fleets, Lefebvre de La Barre sheers off toward Saint Kitts by 11:00 A.M., compelling his Dutch ally to follow. It is believed the English lose two or three small vessels and perhaps 80 men in this indecisive confrontation, as opposed to 20 casualties among the Franco-Dutch fleet.

Disheartened at the poor showing, Crijnseen decides to part company with the French, sailing north by 27 May with *Zeelandia, Zeeridder, Visschersherder, Prins te Paard,* and *Wester-Souburg.* Lefebvre de La Barre's fleet accompanies the Dutch as far as Saint Barthélemy before veering round and being chased south toward Martinique by some of Berry's cruisers.

24 MAY 1667. In Europe, peace negotiations are progressing between England, France, and Holland when Louis XIV declares war against Spain. His objective is to uphold wife Maria Teresa's claim to Brabant and other parts of the Spanish Netherlands following the death of her father, Philip IV. This separate, year-long conflict will become known to the French as the Guerre des Droits de la Reine (War of the Rights of the Queen); in England it is called the War of Devolution—France seeking the legal return, or "devolution," of the territories.

5 JUNE 1667. Henry Willoughby brings reinforcements into Nevis from Barbados aboard the 40-gun HMS *Jersey, East India,* and a supply ship. He is soon followed by the 60-gun *Saint George* and two other Royal Navy warships that have arrived in late May, part of a series of units being hustled out to recoup England's fortunes in the region before peace can be finalized. When added to local volunteers raised by Nevis's Governor Russell and members of Commodore Berry's squadron, English forces total 3,200 men, 14 ships, and a like number of smaller vessels—sufficient to contemplate an invasion of nearby Saint Kitts, which is held by 2,000 French under Governor Saint Laurent.

11 JUNE 1667. ***Crijnssen's Virginia Raid.*** Crijnssen's Dutch squadron appears undetected off Chesapeake Bay, snapping up a Carolina-bound shallop plus another English merchantman. Learning of a convoy assembling up the James River to convey the annual tobacco crop to London, Crijnssen orders English colors hoisted on his ships four days later and follows his captured shallop in past Point Comfort. English-speaking crewmembers call out the soundings, and passing vessels are hailed in English, so that everyone they meet is deceived. Nine miles upriver the raiders come upon the sole Royal Navy vessel for the station: the 20-year-old frigate HMS *Elizabeth* of 46 guns, which arrived from across the Atlantic the previous month. Undergoing repairs and with only a 30-man skeleton crew on board, *Elizabeth* is blasted with a broadside; Crijnssen boards the man-of-war but cannot haul it off, so he burns it at its mooring.

The Dutch reverse course downriver, seizing everything in their path. Of 17 merchantmen they take, seven are scuttled for lack of seamen, but the rest are kept as prizes. (*Wester-Souburg* is also destroyed around this time, being used as a fire ship.) The Virginians under Gov. Sir William Berkeley mount only a feeble resistance, few merchant masters being willing to match broadsides with Crijnssen's veterans; the Dutch commodore departs unmolested on 21 June.

16 JUNE 1667. ***Repulse on Saint Kitts.*** News of an imminent English assault reaches the French on Saint Kitts, and next dawn Henry Willoughby's 30 sail appear from Nevis, splitting into two contingents: one makes toward Old Road Town, the other toward the French capital of Basseterre. After anchoring out of range overnight, Willoughby signals before daybreak on 18 June to begin the disembarkation north of Palmetto Point, near Pelham River. By the time

Governor Saint Laurent gallops there with a handful of French militia, 300 Englishmen are ashore, and boats are bringing in more. Although the beach offers a good landing site, it is encircled by steep bluffs, with a single narrow path leading inland. Thus, Saint Laurent, with aides Giraud Du Poyet and Dominique Des Vergers de Sanois and less than a dozen others, are able to contain the English advance until more cavalry arrives.

The invaders then attempt to outflank Saint Laurent's position by circling north, only to be checked by the timely arrival of Captain d'Orvilliers with 120 men of the Poitou Regiment. A body of horses and four companies of the Navarre Regiment deal a similar setback to another English maneuver in the opposite direction, after which the invasion force becomes pinned down at the base of the cliffs. Offshore, Willoughby sends three boatloads of men in a desperate attempt to open yet another flanking movement; they are checked at the shore as well. After six hours of hopeless struggle, the English landing force surrenders, having suffered 506 killed, 284 wounded, and 140 captives. Defeated, Willoughby retires toward Nevis.

18 JUNE 1667. Rear Admiral Harman reaches Barbados from England with his 68-gun flagship *Lion;* the 50-gun *Crown* (formerly *Taunton*); the 44-gun *Newcastle;* the 40-gun *Dover, Bonadventure,* and *Assistance;* the 32-gun *Assurance;* two fire ships; and a pair of ketches. His squadron is quickly dispatched toward Nevis by Governor-General Willoughby to support the operation against French-held Saint Kitts.

21 JUNE 1667. Harman reaches Nevis and, after learning of Henry Willoughby's debacle, cruises impotently before Saint Kitts then opts to blockade Martinique. Setting sail southeast from Nevis on 25 June with his original squadron, plus *Jersey* and *Norwich* (for a total strength of nine ships of the line, a fire ship, and an auxiliary), Harman sights 19 French West India Company vessels and 14 Martinican traders huddled beneath Fort Saint Pierre by midday of 29 June. At 4:30 P.M., his formation stands into the bay, only to be driven off by the combined fire of the anchored ships and batteries. This tactic—drawing Martinique's fire—is to become part of Harman's strategy, for he knows the defenders are short on powder.

30 JUNE 1667. This afternoon Harman's flagship *Lion* and three frigates lead the English fleet into Saint Pierre's Bay (Martinique), precipitating a four-hour firefight that ends with the attackers' vessels becoming becalmed, obliging them to be towed out of range—their rowers suffering heavily.

2 JULY 1667. Harman again assaults Martinique's main harbor, engaging in a spirited three-hour exchange with its anchored warships and batteries under Lieutenant General Lefebvre de La Barre, Governor Clodoré, and Commodore de Loubière before the English are obliged to withdraw.

4 JULY 1667. At 10:00 A.M., Harman makes his third attack against Saint Pierre (Martinique), obliging its French defenders to expend a good deal of their remaining powder during a two-hour exchange.

6 JULY 1667. ***Harman's Martinican Bonfire.*** Once more, the English admiral leads his fleet into Saint Pierre, the French counterfire growing increasingly slack. During a lull, an English fire ship slips through the smoke to grapple *Lis Couronée,* setting it ablaze. This conflagration quickly spreads to *Saint Jean, Mercier,* and *Lion d'Or,* which are consumed down to their waterlines; panicky French crews abandon other ships. (Adding to the confusion, the fire ship *Pucelle* is set ablaze by its own French crewmembers, who then swim ashore.) After five hours the English retire, leaving the badly shaken French resolved to scuttle their remaining vessels should any other attack occur.

The very next day Harman leads his warships in to unleash a point-blank bombardment against Saint Pierre's battered redoubts. Fort Saint Robert already lies demolished, but Governor Clodoré and militia Capt. Guillaume d'Orange resist bravely from Saint Sebastien, supplementing their meager magazines from the fire ship *Souci.* But when Harman retires an hour and a half later 23 French vessels are left sinking, burning, or destroyed. The English have suffered 80 dead and numerous wounded plus considerable damage to their warships; Harman therefore quits Martinique before dawn on 11 July, returning to Nevis for repairs.

26 JULY 1667. Having refurbished his men-of-war, Harman discovers that his forces—when united with local contingents under Henry Willoughby—total 22 ships and 3,000 troops, sufficient to contemplate a second invasion of French-held Saint Kitts. The admiral therefore circles that island on 26 July with 12 vessels, coasting north from Basseterre to Pointe de Sable, bombarding strategic points. However, a 500-strong French cavalry unit under Governor Saint Laurent keeps pace, preventing any disembarkation. Disillusioned, Harman returns to Nevis and informs

Willoughby that he will lead an expedition against French Cayenne (Guiana) while leaving Commo. William Poole with a small squadron in the Leeward Islands.

31 JULY 1667. The Treaty of Breda is signed in Europe, signaling peace between England, France, and Holland. By its terms Antigua, Montserrat, and half of Saint Kitts are to be restored to English rule within six months. However, word of the pact does not reach the New World until a month and a half later—with official notification not arriving until Christmas—and it does not mark an end to Franco-Spanish hostilities.

AUGUST 1667. While at anchor near San Juan de los Remedios (Cuba) the French buccaneer Nau l'Olonnais learns that a ten-gun Spanish galliot is approaching to capture him. Instead, the *flibustier* sneaks up on it during the night with two boats, taking it by surprise while resting off the coast. He allegedly slaughters the entire crew save for one black slave, who is spared to carry word of the event back to Havana's governor.

22 SEPTEMBER 1667. On the Wild Coast, Admiral Harman—apparently still unaware of the peace in Europe—appears before Cayenne with nine of the line and 850 troops, overrunning and dispersing the tiny French garrison under Governor Lefebvre de Lézy within three days then giving the colony over to the sack. After loading their squadron with captured guns, ammunition, and 250 slaves, the English depart by 9 October.

13 OCTOBER 1667. ***Seizure of Suriname.*** Venturing west along the Guianas, Harman appears before Suriname's capital of Paramaribo, disembarking his troops a half-mile below Fort Zeelandia, then surrounding and calling upon its 250-man garrison under Maurits de Rame to surrender by nightfall. The Dutch refuse, so following a four-day lull occasioned by a lack of winds, on 17 October the English launch a combined land-sea assault. After heavy fighting in which Capt. Thomas Willoughby of the ketch *Portsmouth*—among others—loses his life and the defenders suffer 50 casualties, de Rame requests terms. While they are being finalized, some English soldiers stealthily swim around its defenses and occupy the fort.

When a fleet arrives two weeks later from the Netherlands to announce that this colony is to be restored to Holland according to the Treaty of Breda, Governor Willoughby refuses to comply, instead destroying its fortifications and many other properties. Harman meanwhile reenters Barbados by 20 November, in anticipation of returning to England.

BUCCANEER HEYDAY (1668–1672)

ALTHOUGH PEACE HAS BEEN RESTORED IN EUROPE, local frictions remain in the New World. Jamaica, in particular, experiences a period of renewed anti-Spanish fears in late 1667, prompting Governor Modyford to commission Henry Morgan—recently promoted colonel of the Port Royal militia—"to draw together the English privateers [throughout the region] and take prisoners of the Spanish nation, whereby he might inform of the intention of that enemy to invade Jamaica." Such open-ended license is meant to go well beyond mere intelligence-gathering; it is intended to bestow the unofficial mantle of buccaneer "admiral" upon Morgan following the death of Edward Mansfield several months previously.

Duly armed with his permit, Morgan attracts hundreds of rovers to his rendezvous off southern Cuba, including such notable commanders as John Morris and Edward Collier (as well as many French *flibustiers,* who can at least claim that their country is at war with Spain). After various consultations, Morgan leads his dozen ships and 700 men to Santiago de Cuba by 1 March, briefly blockading it before proceeding into the Gulf of Santa María.

27 MARCH 1668. ***Puerto Príncipe Raid.*** At dawn, Morgan sets a large party ashore at Santa María (modern-day Santa Cruz del Sur) to raid the inland town of Puerto Príncipe (modern-day Camagüey). The Spaniards attempt to dispute the invaders' passage next sunrise with 800 militia cavalry and native spearmen, but they are helpless before the superior firepower of the buccaneers, who inflict several hundred casualties—including more than 100 deaths—before carrying Puerto Príncipe by storm this same afternoon. Fifteen days of pillage ensue, yet the raiders withdraw by 1 April with only 50,000 pieces of eight, a disappointing sum when redistributed among so many. But the Spaniards in addition eventually provide 500 cattle to ransom their hostages, so Morgan leaves Cuba well supplied to head toward Cape Gracias a Dios.

There his two national contingents part company. Morgan has suggested a descent upon Portobelo, but

19-year-old Henry Morgan, painted shortly before he left Britain for Jamaica in the late 1650s

the French—already resentful at the meager profit obtained at Puerto Príncipe—refuse to join the enterprise, preferring to sail off on their own. With four frigates, eight sloops, and less than 500 men left to him, Morgan reaches Bocas del Toro (Panama), transferring his men into 23 piraguas and smaller boats to row 150 miles east against his chosen target.

SPRING 1668. On Saint Domingue (Haiti), the buccaneer chieftain Nau l'Olonnais sorties with 700 *flibustiers,* 300 of them aboard the large Spanish prize he has brought from Maracaibo (*see* late April 1666). Accompanied by five smaller craft, he proceeds into Bayahá to take on salt meat, then cruises southern Cuba as far as the Gulf of Batabanó, seizing boats for a proposed ascent of Nicaragua's San Juan River to sack Granada. But when Nau attempts to clear Cape Gracias a Dios on the Mosquito Coast he is thwarted by lack of wind, so he drifts along northern Honduras. Running low on provisions he sends foraging parties up the Aguán River and eventually prowls as far west as Puerto Caballos (modern-day Puerto Cortés).

There he captures a Spanish merchantman armed with 24 cannons and 16 swivels and occupies the town. Two terrified captives are persuaded to lead his 300 *flibustiers* inland toward San Pedro Sula; the remainder stay behind to garrison Puerto Cabellos under his Dutch-born lieutenant, Mozes van Klijn. Less than ten miles into the jungle the French are waylaid by a party of Spaniards, and more ambushes are sprung as they advance. The Spanish even repel Nau's initial assault upon San Pedro Sula before being allowed to evacuate under flag of truce. The city and its outlying district are then pillaged during the next few days and burned to the ground when Nau retires toward the coast.

Upon returning to Puerto Caballos, Nau learns a wealthy Spanish galleon is due to arrive at nearby Amatique Bay; he posts a pair of lookout boats on its southern shore while crossing to the west side of the Gulf of Honduras to careen. Three months elapse until word is finally received that the galleon has arrived. Nau attacks, but the Spaniard has 42 cannons and 130 men. His own 28-gun flagship and a smaller consort are beaten off, but four boatloads of *flibustiers* storm the galleon. Its booty proves disappointing, however, as most cargo has already been off-loaded. Discouraged, Nau's confederates van Klijn and Pierre Le Picard quit his company. Nau runs aground some time later among the Cayos de Perlas (near Bluefields, Nicaragua), eventually reaching the Gulf of Darien in a small boat; there he is massacred by natives.

25 APRIL 1668. The Dutchman Crijnssen returns to Suriname with the frigates *Suriname* and *Zeelandia* plus the flute *Land van Beloften,* bearing 270 sailors and 180 soldiers, to reclaim the former colony for the Netherlands. Crijnssen sails into Paramaribo's harbor and threatens to open fire if its recalcitrant English occupiers do not surrender. They submit and are eventually made to pay for all property damages; Crijnssen remains as new governor (he is succeeded on 16 February 1669 and dies shortly thereafter).

10 JULY 1668. ***Sack of Portobelo.*** Morgan's flotilla of boats arrives in the vicinity of Portobelo, four nights after quitting Bocas del Toro (*see* 27 March 1668). His men disembark, and Morgan leads them on a swift nocturnal march, taking the town by surprise at daybreak on 11 July. The citizenry is secured without a single buccaneer being lost; the 80-man citadel holds out for a couple of hours until Morgan rounds up a group of captives—including the *alcalde mayor,* two friars, several women, and nuns—to act as a human shield for an assault party that approaches the main gate with torches and axes. The Spanish defenders reluctantly

open fire, wounding two friars and killing an Englishman, but are unable to prevent the enemy sappers from reaching their gate. While the defenders are thus distracted another band of buccaneers uses scaling ladders to enter on the far side of this fortress; the attackers carry the citadel in a bloodbath that results in the deaths of 45 Spanish soldiers and the remainder being wounded.

Next morning Morgan leads 200 buccaneers across Portobelo Bay and forces 50 Spanish soldiers holding out in the harbor castle to surrender after token resistance. That allows his ships to enter once they arrive from Bocas del Toro; Portobelo is thus taken at a cost of 18 buccaneers dead. Wealthy Spanish residents are tortured to reveal their riches, and other excesses are committed. On 14 July Morgan writes a letter to the president of the *audiencia* (high court) of Panama, offering to spare Portobelo for 350,000 pesos. The acting president, Agustín de Bracamonte—already marching to Portobelo's relief with 800 militia—brusquely refuses. Morgan digs in to receive the relief column; it proves too weak to assault Morgan's positions when it arrives before Portobelo the next day, and the Spaniards are obliged to remain within the jungle for a week.

Finally, on 24 July, Bracamonte orders a retreat, leaving a subordinate to negotiate Portobelo's ransom. It is set at 100,000 pesos and paid during the first days of August; Morgan thus sails away, reentering Port Royal by 27 July.

EARLY OCTOBER 1668. Morgan sorties from Jamaica, calling on freebooters to join him at Île-à-Vache (Haiti) for another quasi-official venture against Spanish America. When the 34-gun royal frigate *Oxford* reaches Port Royal shortly thereafter—having been sent out from England for use against piracy—Governor Modyford sends a crew of 160 men under veteran privateer Edward Collier to reinforce Morgan.

Collier departs on 20 December and, upon arriving at Île-à-Vache, detains the 14-gun, 120-ton French corsair *Cerf Volant* out of La Rochelle (the vessel has recently plundered a Virginia merchantman). Captain Vivien and his 45-man crew are sailed into Port Royal for adjudication; *Cerf Volant* is quickly condemned, renamed *Satisfaction,* and then reincorporated into Morgan's fleet.

12 JANUARY 1669. At Île-à-Vache 900–1,000 freebooters have gathered with Morgan and his consorts, who decide their strength is sufficient to try for Cartagena; they feast to celebrate the forthcoming voyage and the English new year (2 January [O.S.]). Captains Aylett, Bigford, Collier, Morris, Thornbury, and Whiting join Morgan for dinner while seamen carouse upon *Oxford's* forecastle. Suddenly its magazine explodes, killing more than 200 crewmembers; only six men and four boys survive, Morgan and Collier being among the lucky few.

Such heavy loss of life ends any prospects for a major campaign. Collier departs with *Satisfaction* on a cruise against Campeche; for his part Morgan transfers into the 14-gun frigate *Lilly* and leads his remaining forces east, hoping to raid either Trinidad or Margarita. But by the time he reaches Saona, at the eastern end of Santo Domingo, three more of his ships desert, leaving only eight with 500 men under Capts. John Morris, Jeffery Pennant, Edward Dempster, Richard Norman, Richard Dobson, Adam Brewster, and one other. One of Morgan's French followers then suggests raiding Maracaibo in a repeat of Nau l'Olonnais's foray three years earlier. Morgan and his colleagues agree; after visiting Dutch Aruba a few weeks later to reprovision, the buccaneer fleet steers toward the Gulf of Venezuela.

4 FEBRUARY 1669. A French squadron under Commodore Jean, Comte d'Estrées, arrives at Martinique bearing the new governor-general, Jean Charles de Baas Castelmore, who takes up residence at Saint Pierre. D'Estrées is also supposed to curb foreign trade into France's colonies, but he performs that service rather indifferently before returning toward Europe.

9 MARCH 1669. ***Maracaibo Campaign.*** Reaching Maracaibo's bar, Morgan's raiders discover it has been fortified with a small, 11-gun castle; the freebooters disembark to besiege it. Only a single Spanish officer and eight soldiers are within the keep; they put up a brief show of resistance before slipping out in the night. After spiking the guns, Morgan's ships navigate through the shoals and proceed south to Maracaibo, which they find abandoned by the terrified citizenry. The buccaneers send parties into the surrounding countryside to round up scores of prisoners, who are tortured to reveal their riches.

Three weeks later, Morgan crosses to the southeastern side of the Laguna, visiting a like treatment upon Gibraltar (near Bobures). By 17 April he returns to Maracaibo with a captive Cuban merchant ship and five smaller piraguas, ready to head out into the Caribbean; but while the freebooters have been ransacking the Laguna's interior Spain's West Indian squadron (the *Armada de Barlovento*) has arrived outside the bar, thus bottling the interlopers inside.

Spanish Adm. Alonso de Campos y Espinosa has the 412-ton flagship *Magdalena* of 38 guns; the 218-ton frigate *San Luis* of 26 guns under his second-in-command, Mateo Alonso de Huidobro; plus the 50-ton sloop *Nuestra Señora de la Soledad* (alias *Marquesa*) of 14 guns—all manned by 500 officers, troops, and sailors. Having found the fortress devastated, Campos reoccupies it with 40 harquebusiers, repairs six of the guns, and then dispatches messengers inland calling for further assistance. After several days he also lightens his warships and crosses them over the bar before sending a letter to Morgan in Maracaibo calling for surrender.

20 APRIL 1669. In Madrid, news of Morgan's Portobelo raid prompts Queen Regent Mariana to authorize Spanish-American officials to issue privateering commissions against English vessels.

25 APRIL 1669. ***Battle of the Bar.*** After a week's preparation Morgan's 13 vessels approach Maracaibo's bar, arriving within sight of the anchored Spaniards. Two days later, at 9:00 A.M., Morgan—led by his large Cuban prize flying an admiral's insignia—rushes Campos's armada. The Cuban prize bears down on Campos's flagship and grapples; when the Spanish surge over the bulwarks they find the enemy decks lined with wooden dummies—and 12 buccaneers hastily decamping over the far side. The Cuban ship then bursts into flames, and *Magdalena* becomes engulfed, forcing Campos to leap into the water along with his panic-stricken crew. Seeing this terrifying spectacle, de Huidobro's smaller *San Luis* and *Marquesa* cut their cables and run for the shelter of the fort, pursued by buccaneer craft. Both Spanish vessels run aground and are deliberately set ablaze by their crews, although *Marquesa* is soon boarded and saved by the privateers.

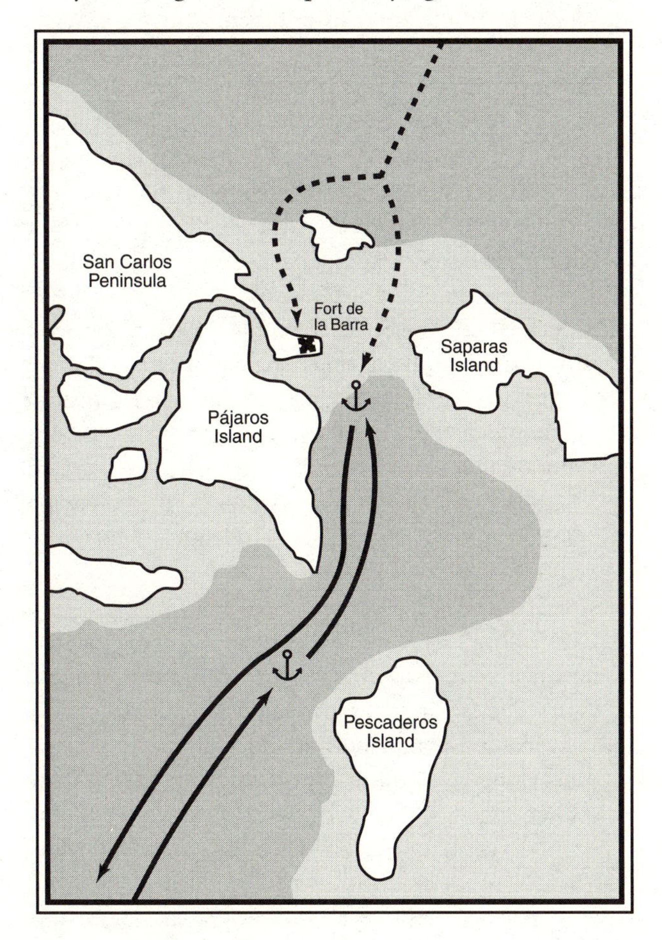

Morgan's victory at the bar of Maracaibo

Despite the victory, Morgan's flotilla is still unable to get past the fort, its garrison having been augmented by 70 militia from the interior plus most of the armada crews. The buccaneers attempt a land assault the next day but are easily beaten off, so Morgan retires into Maracaibo. After offering to exchange his Spanish captives for free passage out to sea—rebuffed by Campos—Morgan returns to the bar a few days later, setting his boats busily plying back and forth near the Spanish fort. Believing the English are depositing an assault force, Campos's garrison manhandles the few guns into the landward embrasures and brace for a nocturnal attack. But Morgan has again deceived the Spaniards, his boat movements being merely a feint; no buccaneers disembarked. Instead, his ships weigh and slip past the Spanish fortress under cover of darkness, depositing the prisoners outside before sailing triumphantly off. By 27 May Morgan is back in Port Royal.

SPRING 1669. The Jamaican privateer Joseph Bradley sails his 80-man frigate (*Mayflower*) into the Gulf of Mexico, accompanied by the brigantines of Dutch-born Rok Brasiliano and Jelles de Lecat, to campaign against the Spaniards. For two to three weeks the trio hovers off Campeche then attempts some disembarkations on the coast, before Bradley finally captures a Cuban vessel laden with flour and the raiders retire into the Laguna de Términos. They remain two months, Brasiliano's brigantine being careened while de Lecat lays in logwood. At the end of this interlude Bradley and de Lecat return to blockade Campeche while Brasiliano's brigantine hauls up close inshore off Las Bocas, four leagues southwest.

24 JUNE 1669. Jamaica's Governor Modyford proclaims the English crown's latest prohibition against anti-Spanish hostilities.

18 DECEMBER 1669. Three armed Spanish ships sortie from Campeche, chasing away the intruder vessels of Englishman Joseph Bradley and Dutch-born Rok Brasiliano. The latter wrecks shortly thereafter on Chicxulub Beach (east of modern-day Progreso), where a Spanish cavalry patrol finds him as he is burying a cannon and two swivels. Brasiliano's men flee aboard their boats, later being rescued by his Dutch colleague, de Lecat, and transferred aboard Bradley's frigate for conveyance to Jamaica.

3 JANUARY 1670. Gov. Pedro de Ulloa of Cartagena issues a privateering commission to Portuguese-born Manuel Rivero Pardal to attack English interests in the West Indies. Rivero sets sail three days later with 70 men aboard his *San Pedro* (alias *Fama*). It is his intent to raid Point Morant (Jamaica) for slaves, but unfavorable winds carry him past to the Cayman Islands, where he burns English fishing shacks; he then takes a ketch, a canoe, and four children captives into Cuba.

In Cuba Rivero learns of an English privateer lying at Manzanillo (the port for Bayamo). The vessel proves to be the 18-man *Mary and Jane,* commanded by an old Dutch rover named Bernard Claesen Speirdyke, who has been dispatched under flag of truce by Governor Modyford of Jamaica to carry letters and to restore some Spanish prisoners. When Speirdyke stands out of Manzanillo, he is intercepted by Rivero's *Fama,* which opens fire and fights him until dark. Next day the Spaniards close to board, but the men on *Mary and Jane* put up a staunch resistance, killing or wounding a third of Rivero's men before the vessel is carried. Five of *Mary and Jane*'s crew lay dead—including Speirdyke; the Portuguese corsair sends nine English prisoners back to Port Royal and boasts of his victory. This creates an ugly mood on Jamaica, and Modyford is hard pressed to prevent retaliatory strikes by his buccaneers.

Rivero meanwhile sails his prize back to Cartagena, arriving by 23 March. A fiesta is held to celebrate his cruise, and other corsairs come forward to emulate his example. One month later, two more vessels are fitting out in Cartagena's roads; Rivero flies a royal standard as "admiral" to the motley force.

APRIL 1670. Some 150 colonists from England and Barbados disembark at the mouth of the Ashley River and establish South Carolina. Spain regards the action as an infringement upon its Florida colony, which is headquartered farther south at Saint Augustine.

EARLY MAY 1670. On Tortuga Island (Haiti), Governor d'Ogeron learns that his French West India Company deputy, de Renou, has been overthrown at Léogâne by an unruly mob for attempting to prevent trade with two large Dutch merchantmen under Capts. Pieter Constant and Pieter Marck. D'Ogeron sails to the rescue aboard *Irondelle,* freeing de Renou. But when he attempts to reinstate his subordinate at Petit Goâve, *Irondelle* is fired upon by a large crowd of angry buccaneers, and he retreats into Tortuga.

11 JUNE 1670. The Spanish corsair Rivero reappears off northern Jamaica, having sortied from Cartagena at the end of May; he is accompanied by *Gallardina* (onetime French privateer seized two years previously). Flying false English colors, they pursue William Harris for an hour and a half when he arrives in a sloop to trade. The English master eventually beaches the sloop and escapes inland, firing at Rivero's men as they come ashore. The vessel is refloated by the rogues and then sailed to Cuba along with a canoe found on the beach. One week later *Fama* and *Gallardina* return, landing 30 men to burn settlements at Montego Bay before retiring to Cuba again.

LATE SPRING 1670. The Dutch-born Jamaican privateer and plantation owner Laurens Prins ("Lawrence Prince"), along with English colleagues Harris and Ludbury, take it upon themselves to retaliate for Rivero's nuisance raids by sailing up Colombia's Magdalena River to sack Mompós. Their raid is checked by fire from a fort recently installed upon the river; the trio therefore heads west in August, hoping for better fortune on the Mosquito Coast.

3 JULY 1670. The Spanish corsair Rivero appears off Jamaica a third time, having manned his captured sloop at Santiago de Cuba. Some 40 mounted Jamaican militia watch the trio of vessels for an hour before it stands off to leeward. Next day the Spanish raiders land 50 miles away and burn two houses; the following night they post a letter ashore, challenging Morgan to a ship-to-ship duel.

9 JULY 1670. Incensed by the Spanish corsair Rivero's nuisance raids, Governor Modyford and the Jamaican Council pass a resolution commissioning Morgan—"admiral and commander-in-chief of all the ships of war belonging to this harbor [Port Royal]"—to draw a force together to "attack, seize, and destroy all the enemy's vessels that shall come within his reach." Morgan sets sail on 11 August with 11 privateer vessels and 600 men, his flag flying aboard *Satisfaction,* now armed with 22 guns. He has also called for a freebooter gath-

ering at Île-à-Vache; first, however, he ventures to southern Cuba, where he leaves John Morris's ten-gun *Dolphin* on watch before tacking east with his main body.

MID-AUGUST 1670. Three Spanish ships under Juan Menéndez Marques, accompanied from Saint Augustine by 14 piraguas, arrive outside the new English settlement at Charleston (South Carolina) to expel its colonists. Having been forewarned by friendly tribesmen, the English are prepared for a siege, and Menéndez retires without attempting an attack after a storm drags his ships' anchors.

EARLY SEPTEMBER 1670. Three English privateer-captains—Prins, Harris, and Ludbury—ascend Nicaragua's San Juan River—despite the new fort installed following the raid by Morris and Martien five years earlier—stealing across the lake to surprise Granada. They wreak considerable destruction upon the city, driving home their demand for 70,000 pesos' ransom by "sending the head of a priest in a basket" to provincial authorities before finally withdrawing with their booty.

12 SEPTEMBER 1670. After touching at Tortuga Island (Haiti), Morgan and his privateer fleet continue south toward their rendezvous off Île-à-Vache. Four days later Morgan detaches six vessels under Edward Collier to gather provisions and intelligence from the Spanish Main.

25 SEPTEMBER 1670. Deputy Governor de Renou of Saint Domingue (Haiti) reaches French Governor-General de Baas at Saint Kitts, requesting assistance on behalf of d'Ogeron to suppress a buccaneer mutiny (*see* early May 1670). Eventually the royal frigate *Aurore* of Capt. Louis Gabaret is detached from Grenada to help.

Reaching Tortuga, Gabaret escorts d'Ogeron back to Léogâne, where several hundred buccaneers swear fealty to France but refuse to abide by its West India Company rule. A like reception awaits at Petit Goâve, where d'Ogeron storms angrily ashore and disperses the mutineers before returning to Tortuga. Gabaret then sails for Europe, leaving d'Ogeron to resolve the issue (he will moderate his conditions and grants a general amnesty by the end of April 1671).

24 OCTOBER 1670. At daybreak Collier's half-dozen English privateers appear off Ríohacha, disembarking a force to march against the tiny, four-gun fort. In the harbor lies the Spanish corsair *Gallardina,* whose crew is terrified at the prospect of falling into buccaneer hands. Ríohacha's fort holds out for a day and night before surrendering, after which Collier conducts a pair of executions and tortures several prominent captives for their wealth. He weighs almost four weeks later to rejoin Morgan with meat, maize, 38 prisoners, *Gallardina,* and one other prize.

MID-OCTOBER 1670. Off southeastern Cuba, Morris's ten-gun, 60-man privateer *Dolphin* is forced into a small bay by a threatening storm. Two hours later, just before dark, Rivero sails in for the same purpose with his 14-gun *Fama;* the Spanish corsair is delighted to find the smaller Jamaican ship embayed. Setting men ashore to cut off escape, the Spaniards prepare to attack at dawn—but Morris moves first the next morning, bearing down upon *Fama* with the land breeze and boarding on his first attempt.

Rivero is killed and his crew jumps into the sea. Some drown, but most are slaughtered by the English privateers; only five Spaniards reach shore alive. Later this month, Morris leads *Fama*—now renamed *Lamb*—to Morgan's rendezvous off Île-à-Vache. Despite the death of their Spanish tormentor, the English press on with their plans for a major blow against Spanish America.

29 OCTOBER 1670. The English privateer-captains, Prins, Harris, and Ludbury, return to Jamaica from their rampage through Central America; they are mildly reproved by Governor Modyford for attacking Spanish America without permission. They are then ordered to join Morgan's expedition, which is regrouping after being scattered by a storm off Île-à-Vache.

1 NOVEMBER 1670. A 29-year-old unemployed Royal Navy captain named John Narborough enters the Strait of Magellan from Patagonia aboard *Sweepstakes,* a private frigate of 36 guns, 300 tons, and 80 men, to trade with Spain's Pacific colonies. After passing Cape Pilar on the last day of November, *Sweepstakes* anchors in Valdivia Bay by Christmas (15 December 1670 [O.S.]), receiving a friendly reception. But the Spaniards arrest a four-man landing party three days later, and Narborough finds the port closed to him. Unable to recover his men and without authorization to take any offensive actions, he departs on 1 January 1671 to return through the strait, arriving in England by June.

18 DECEMBER 1670. Morgan's fleet quits Île-à-Vache, having swelled to 38 privateer vessels and more than 2,000 English, French, and Dutch freebooters. Although his intended target is Panama, Morgan first lays in a course for Providencia Island, which on two previous occasions has belonged to England.

24 DECEMBER 1670. Early this morning, Morgan's buccaneer fleet appears before Providencia Island, forcing the Spanish garrison to surrender the next day.

28 DECEMBER 1670. Morgan detaches 470 men under "Lieutenant Colonel" Joseph Bradley of the frigate *Mayflower,* "Major" Richard Norman of the ten-gun *Lilly,* and Dutch-born mercenary Jelles de Lecat of *Seviliaen* to sail ahead of the main body and seize Chagres, where Morgan intends to disembark his main army to advance across the isthmus.

6 JANUARY 1671. ***Capture of Chagres.*** At noon, Bradley's three ships disgorge 400 freebooters within sight of San Lorenzo Fort, making their initial assault that afternoon. The 360 defenders wait confidently under *Castellano* (Castle Commander) Pedro de Elizalde, halting Bradley's first and second charges with deadly volleys. As dusk falls, the English commander switches tactics, leading his men through some gullies to toss grenades and firepots inside, igniting the wooden stockades. Fires spread throughout the night, consuming the defenses and detonating San Lorenzo's magazines. In the darkness 150 Spanish soldiers desert, but enough remain to again break Bradley's first two assaults the next morning.

A French print from 1688, showing a soldier igniting a hand grenade

During the third assault a contingent of *flibustiers* from Tortuga fights its way inside; Elizalde and his 70 surviving defenders fight bravely to the last man. At least 30 buccaneers are killed and another 76 injured during the assaults—including Bradley, who is shot through both legs. Norman assumes overall command while Bradley convalesces; five days later, just as Morgan's ships heave into view, Bradley dies.

12 JANUARY 1671. Having departed Providencia a few days after Bradley, Morgan's fleet comes within sight of Chagres. As his flagship *Satisfaction* leads the way in it strikes a reef and sinks, along with another four vessels astern. Ten men drown, but losses are otherwise minimal. After a week refurbishing Fort San Lorenzo and ensconcing 300 defenders under Norman, Morgan ventures upriver with 1,500 men, seven small ships, and 36 boats. An epic, seven-day trek ensues through the jungle, the Spaniards shrinking away before the English host. Nonetheless, climate, terrain, hunger, and thirst prove to be formidable obstacles.

20 JANUARY 1671. In Panama City, 52-year-old Gov. Juan Pérez de Guzmán, knight of the Order of Santiago, rises from his sickbed and rides forth next day with 800 militia to camp at Guayabal, awaiting news of Morgan. But as the enemy continues to advance, Spanish morale plummets; by 24 January the governor wakes to find two-thirds of his army gone. Retreating into Panama, Pérez de Guzmán orders all able-bodied men to muster at Mata Asnillos (a mile outside the city) while noncombatants are evacuated by ship.

27 JANUARY 1671. At 9:00 A.M., Morgan's vanguard breasts a hill and sights the Pacific. Toward noon the buccaneers come upon a plain filled with cattle, which they eat. Thus refreshed, they press on; this afternoon they see the tiled roofs of Panama City, the Spanish army drawn up a mile outside to bar their path.

28 JANUARY 1671. ***Sack of Panama.*** Morgan begins his final advance at sunrise, 1,200 buccaneers marching steadily into battle. Gov. Pérez de Guzmán has 1,200 militia infantry drawn up in a line six deep at Mata Asnillos, with two companies of 200 militia rid-

ers apiece on either flank. But his inexperienced troops have few firearms and no artillery, and thus are no match for the better-armed, veteran freebooters.

Morgan's 300-man vanguard under "Lieutenant Colonel" Prins and "Major" Morris are still advancing up a hillock on the Spaniards' right when Pérez de Guzmán's unwieldy throng launches an undisciplined dash against the buccaneers, who break the wild Spanish charge with steady fusillades. More than 100 militiamen are killed with the first volley. The murderous fire, to which the defenders can scarcely reply, smashes their spirit and causes wholesale panic. The Spaniards break and flee, leaving 400–500 casualties on the battlefield, as opposed to 15 buccaneers.

Panama is occupied, but many of its buildings are set ablaze as the raiders enter; most riches have already been removed offshore. Thus, although Morgan remains for the next four weeks, he finds the wealth largely gone. Despite cruel tortures inflicted by the frustrated invaders, relatively little booty can be extracted from Panama or the outlying district. When the army marches back to Chagres and makes the final division of spoils, the rank-and-file buccaneers receive only £15–18 per head, prompting ugly talk about fraud.

16 MARCH 1671. Morgan hastily departs Chagres aboard the dead Bradley's *Mayflower,* accompanied by Prins's *Pearl,* Morris's *Dolphin,* and Thomas Harris's *Mary.* They reach Jamaica a couple of weeks later to find English policy reversed: A new treaty has been signed with Madrid, and attacks against Spanish America are now out of favor.

Three months later, HMSS *Assistance* and *Welcome* enter Port Royal with a new governor, Sir Thomas Lynch. Some time later he arrests his predecessor, Modyford, and deports him to London to answer Madrid's complaints about West Indian depredations.

SUMMER 1671. Two French warships and three frigates arrive in the West Indies under Commo. René de Gousabats de Villepars to restore government rule following the buccaneer revolt against d'Ogeron at Saint Domingue (Haiti—*see* early May 1670).

15 JULY 1671. French Governor-General de Baas officially restores half of Saint Kitts to Sir Charles Wheeler, newly appointed governor-general for the English Leeward Islands. This action fulfills the terms of the Treaty of Breda, signed almost four years earlier.

NOVEMBER 1671. An arrest order for Morgan arrives at Jamaica. Governor Lynch is loath to comply, fearing it will alienate privateers, upon whom he relies for the island's defense. He therefore defers the detention until mid-April 1672, when the freebooter admiral is conducted aboard the 36-gun royal frigate *Welcome* of Capt. John Keene to travel toward England in comfort as part of a three-ship merchant convoy.

1672. Morgan's legendary luck continues to hold. By the time he reaches London, in August 1672, the crown is distracted by the Third Anglo-Dutch War. When England's French allies declare war against Spain the next year, there is no longer any need to appease Madrid—so all charges are dropped. In July 1673 Morgan is consulted as to the best methods of ensuring Jamaica's security. By November 1674 he is knighted and appointed deputy governor of Jamaica, returning to Port Royal on 15 March 1675; he serves in office until his death 13 years later.

THIRD ANGLO-DUTCH WAR (1672–1674) AND FRANCO-SPANISH WAR (1673–1679)

IN ENGLAND, CHARLES II TREACHEROUSLY DECLARES WAR against the Netherlands in March 1672, being joined by his secret French allies one month later. Although Britain regards Holland as a commercial rival, this particular conflict proves unpopular with the public; it has been engineered by Louis XIV of France (whose armies quickly invade the Low Countries). The French forces are checked, however, and the new Dutch leader, William III, forms alliances with Brandenburg, the Holy Roman Empire, Spain, and Lorraine; the strengths even out. A discouraged Britain soon retires, leaving the continental powers to fight it out.

LATE JUNE 1672. Gov. Sir William Stapleton of the English Leeward Islands leads an invasion force against Sint Eustatius, being joined shortly thereafter by a French contingent from Saint Kitts. The outnumbered Dutch garrison surrenders to the English by the end of the month, as does neighboring Sabá by 4 July, plus Tortola and Virgin Gorda in the Virgin Islands somewhat later. The French meanwhile seize Saint Martin without loss.

18 DECEMBER 1672. Bridge arrives off Tobago from Barbados with his flagship *King David,* accompanied by 600 volunteers aboard a half-dozen lesser craft. After five or six hours' intense fighting, the 400 Dutch residents under Gov. Pieter Constant agree to surrender New Walcheren and be transported to Barbados. Two days later a French frigate also arrives from Martinique with a similar hostile intent, only to find Tobago already in English hands.

MID-FEBRUARY 1673. San Juan de los Remedios (Cuba) is surprised by buccaneer raiders; 14 women are carried off as hostages.

18 FEBRUARY 1673. The 50-gun French warship *Ecueil* and the smaller *Petite Infante* arrive at Tortuga Island (Haiti), having rounded Môle Saint Nicholas with 400 volunteers from Léogâne and Petit Goâve under Governor d'Ogeron.

The force is being raised to join Governor-General de Baas in the Windward Islands. Having learned during the latter half of 1672 of the outbreak of Franco-Dutch hostilities in Europe, de Baas is organizing a strike against Curaçao; he thus has detached the two warships to Saint Domingue with orders to rejoin him off Saint Croix by 4 March. Almost immediately after touching Tortuga, d'Ogeron gets under way again, having been further reinforced by many volunteers aboard a half-dozen privateer vessels.

25 FEBRUARY 1673. This night, d'Ogeron's *Ecueil* runs aground through navigational error near Arecibo (northwestern Puerto Rico); more than 500 men struggle ashore through the surf. D'Ogeron sends Lieutenant Brodart and nephew Jacques Nepveu, sieur de Pouançay, to the local Spanish authorities to request aid. But buccaneers have long victimized these shores, and both emissaries are thrown into jail; a host of Spanish militia descends upon the remainder, subduing it after a one-sided clash in which ten Puerto Ricans die and 12 are wounded, as opposed to 40–50 fatalities among d'Ogeron's group. Gov. Gaspar de Arteaga y Aunavidao then orders the 460 French survivors marched around the island to San Germán, where they are settled under a loose guard of 60 Spanish soldiers. Six months later, d'Ogeron escapes.

EARLY MARCH 1673. After awaiting in vain for the arrival of d'Ogeron's Saint Domingue contingent—only *Petite Infante* appears with 100 buccaneers—French Governor-General de Baas quits his Saint Croix rendezvous and steers toward Curaçao with his 70-gun royal flagship *Belliqueux* under Capt. Dumé d'Amplimont, the frigates *Sibylle* and *Fée,* and three transports bearing 600 volunteers from Martinique, Guadeloupe, and Saint Kitts.

After arriving off this coast on 13 March and disembarking next day on the north shore of Santa Barbara Bay (eastern side of Curaçao), Baas skirmishes with the defenders of tiny Fort Tolcksburg and attempts to advance overland with his small army, only to become disconcerted by the strength of Acting Gov. Jan Doncker's defenses and the number of Dutch ships lying inshore covering the approaches into its capital of Willemstad. After hurriedly consulting with his military engineer, Louis Ancelin de Gémosat, Baas retreats, reembarking his men by 16 March and sailing away two days later.

MARCH 1673. Zeeland's Commo. Cornelis Evertsen de Jongste ("the Youngest"; nicknamed Kees the Devil) arrives off Suriname with his 44-gun, 186-man flagship *Swaenenburgh* (formerly HMS *Saint Patrick*) under Evert Evertsen Corneliszoon; the 30-gun, 157-man *Schaeckerloo* of Passchier de Witte; the 25-gun, 158-man *Suriname* (formerly the English *Richard and James*) of Evert Evertsen Franszoon; the six-gun, 22-man snow *Zeehond* of Daniel Thijssen; the six-gun, 34-man ketch *Sint Joris* of Cornelis Eewoutsen; plus the four-gun, 30-man victualler *Eendracht* of Maerten Andriessen. His aim is to scour the West Indies, reinforcing Dutch colonies while simultaneously attacking Anglo-French interests. After disembarking troops and provisions at Fort Zeelandia on 25 March, Evertsen proceeds northwest into the Lesser Antilles six weeks.

LATE MARCH 1673. The English privateer Peter Wroth approaches the mouth of the Suriname River from Barbados with his 20-ton, six-gun sloop *Little Kitt,* manned by 30 men, intending to raid the turtling camp at Three Creeks. He finds the waterway blocked up by the Dutch but then learns of Evertsen's arrival; he immediately departs with this intelligence, which is eventually forwarded to London.

22 MAY 1673. At noon, Evertsen sights a half-dozen vessels off Cul de Sac Bay (Martinique) flying French colors. When he bears down, they prove to be Commo. Jacob Binckes's (or Benckes) two-year-old frigate *Noordhollandt* (flag) of 46 guns and 210 men; three other men-of-war; and a pair of prizes. Having

left Amsterdam the previous December on a similar mission, both commodores agree to join forces and attempt the French harbor entrance that night, but contrary winds prevent them from doing so.

Thus, they proceed toward Guadeloupe, seizing the French merchantmen *Saint Joseph* and *Françoise* off the coast; shortly thereafter they take the island trader *Nouveau France* and *Saint Michael* of Galway from beneath the English batteries at Monserrat. Nevis and Saint Kitts are also bombarded in passing before Sint Eustatius is reached by 29 May. When its acting English governor John Pognon refuses to surrender, the Dutch open fire on the fort and disembark 600 men, quickly overwhelming its defenders. Two prizes are also captured offshore, along with 200 slaves, and Sabá is liberated a few days later. The English garrisons are then deported to Saint Kitts, while those Dutch residents who have sided with the invaders are transported to Curaçao. With too few loyal inhabitants left to hold Sint Eustatius and Sabá, Binckes and Evertsen destroy their installations, then strike north by 8 June for Virginia.

JUNE 1673. The Cuban-born mulatto buccaneer Diego Grillo, with his 15-gun vessel, intercepts a Spanish merchant frigate bound from Havana to Campeche. A few days later 150 Spaniards exit Havana aboard a ship and two frigates to engage the raider. Instead, they are defeated off Nuevitas, Grillo executing the 20 peninsular-born Spanish captives before releasing the remaining ones.

MID-JULY 1673. Binckes and Evertsen raid the coast of Virginia, being resisted in Chesapeake Bay by the Royal Navy's hired vessels *Barnaby* and *Augustine*. The Dutch rovers then continue up the Atlantic seaboard toward New York.

28 JULY 1673. ***Reoccupation of New York.*** Binckes and Evertsen appear off New York City (formerly New Amsterdam) and oblige the English governor to surrender by 9 August. Having reinstated Dutch rule, the two commodores then detach Capt. Nikolaas Boes with four ships to raid Newfoundland while they sail the main body into the Atlantic.

(During their New World cruise Binckes and Evertsen have captured 34 English and French ships and destroyed at least 150 others. However, their reoccupation of New Amsterdam is disapproved by The Hague, which is already deep in negotiations to conclude a separate peace with England. New York is therefore restored to English domination, and nothing more is said about the damages wrought by Binckes and Evertsen's American campaign.)

AUGUST 1673. Following a particularly audacious raid several months previously by a small English vessel against Coatzacoalcos, in which three villages are ransacked and eight Indians carried off, the Mexican viceroy, Antonio Sebastián de Toledo Molina y Salazar, marqués de Mancera, orders Veracruz's new *sargento mayor* (garrison commander), Mateo Alonso de Huidobro, to pursue the interlopers with a frigate and three piraguas. He overtakes them near Santa Ana Bar (Tabasco), forcing them to beach their vessel and set it ablaze before disappearing into the jungle.

Upon de Huidobro's return to Veracruz, accounts of further nuisance raids arrive, and two enemy ships are reported inside the Laguna de Términos. Thus, a second, larger enterprise is mounted, de Huidobro quitting Veracruz again on 14 August with three frigates, a sloop, and 300 soldiers from San Juan de Ulúa's garrison. This expedition arrives undetected off Xicalango Point, where it is approached by three piraguas. Belatedly realizing the danger, the approaching craft suddenly veer round and flee into the Laguna while de Huidobro's men storm ashore. One interloper is killed, several others are wounded, and abandoned huts and boats are burned, but the Spanish men-of-war draw too much water to pass over the bar. A brigantine can be seen heading deeper into the Laguna; de Huidobro has no choice but to continue toward Campeche. En route he chases another piragua manned by a mixed crew of English, French, and Indians, who escape when a storm sets in.

After visiting Campeche, de Huidobro reverses course toward Veracruz. This time he intercepts—outside the Laguna—the brigantine that eluded him before, along with a Spanish prize. The Dutch captain, Jan Lucas, is carried with the crew into Veracruz by late October.

7 OCTOBER 1673. Governor d'Ogeron, having returned to Saint Domingue after a harrowing escape from Puerto Rico (*see* 25 February 1673), raises 500 *flibustiers* at Tortuga Island to rescue his imprisoned men. Pausing at Samaná Bay for reinforcements, the expedition appears before Aguada (Puerto Rico) by mid-October, learning—incorrectly—that Spanish Governor de Arteaga might consider an exchange. Therefore, despite the peace prevailing between France and Spain, d'Ogeron blunders ashore with 300 men and tries to seize hostages, marching as far as six miles inland on his third day before being ambushed

and forced to retreat after losing 17 men. The Spaniards allegedly lose double that number and, in their wrath, butcher the French wounded; de Arteaga also orders the execution of 40 prisoners at San Germán, the rest being placed in strict confinement.

D'Ogeron cruises helplessly off Puerto Rico for the next couple of months until word arrives that France and Spain are officially at war, dashing his final hopes of ransoming his followers. Discouraged, he returns to Tortuga by 29 December.

15 OCTOBER 1673. In Europe, after several months of strained relations, France declares war on Spain.

6 MARCH 1674. After winter-long negotiations, the second Treaty of Westminster is ratified and proclaimed in Europe, reestablishing peace between Britain and the Netherlands by promising to restore Sint Eustatius, Tobago, and Sabá to the Dutch and New York to the English.

EARLY JULY 1674. The Dutch corsair Jurriaen Aernouts arrives at New York with his frigate *Vliegende Postpaard,* commissioned by Gov. Jan Doncker of Curaçao to attack English and French interests. Learning that New York is soon to be restored to English rule by the Treaty of Westminster, Aernouts decides to attack the French farther north in Acadia (Maine and New Brunswick).

While preparing for the Acadia enterprise he meets Capt. John Rhoades of Boston, who is well acquainted with the settlements. Aernouts enlists Rhoades and several other Anglo-Americans, sailing into the Bay of Fundy to land 110 men. Advancing against the French stronghold of Penobscot (Pentagoët), the invaders overwhelm the 30-man garrison on 11 August after a one-hour fight. French Gov. Jacques de Chambly, wounded in the arm by a musket, is captured; the defenses are thrown down. Aernouts then ravages several smaller outposts before entering the Saint Jean River and seizing the secondary French fort at Jemsec. Its lieutenant governor, Pierre de Joybert de Soulanges et de Marson, is also taken, and Aernouts renames the entire territory New Holland before retiring into Boston.

Prior to departing for the Antilles, Aernouts appoints Rhoades acting governor of the new colony on 11 September, furnishing him with two small armed vessels. The Massachusetts authorities later refuse to acknowledge Dutch jurisdiction.

19 JULY 1674. ***De Ruyter's Defeat.*** With England's withdrawal from the alliance against the Netherlands, the Dutch are free to take the offensive against France's overseas empire. At 3:00 P.M., Admiral de Ruyter and Vice Adm. Cornelis Evertsen "de Jonge" (the Younger) materialize before Martinique with:

Ship	*Sailors*	*Soldiers*	*Guns*	*Commander*
Zeven Provinciën (flag)	486	80	80	Michiel de Ruyter
Zierikzee (vice-flag)	305	85	60	Cornelis Evertsen
Spiegel (rear admiral)	296	83	70	Engel de Ruyter
Provincie van Utrecht	198	111	60	Joan de Witte
Schieland	202	88	60	Adriaan Poort
Geloof	183	99	58	Thomas Tobiaszoon
Gelderland	237	41	56	?
Oisterwijk	206	98	56	Pieter van Middeland
Tijdverdijf	197	71	52	Graaf van Stierum
Bescherming	188	91	50	Pieter de Sitter
Vlissingen	220	70	50	Karel van der Putten
Caleb	198	33	46	Jan Muys
Burg van Leyden	?	?	44	Philis de Munnik
Zeelandia	183	61	42	Pieter de Liefde
Jupiter	166	31	40	Pieter Bakker
Utrecht	128	41	36	Barent Rees
Damiaten	96	72	34	Cornelis van der Zaan
Delft	120	89	32	Adriaan Bankert

They are supported by the 12-gun snow *Hoen* of Klaas Portugaal; eight-gun snows *Bonte Haan* of Zeger Corneliszoon Potter, *Bruinvis* of Matthys Laurenszoon, *Faam* of Jakob Hoek, *Griffioen* of Evert de Liefde, and *Tonijn* of Philips Melkenbeeke; four-gun fireships *Groene Draak* of Willem Willemszoon, *Leidster* of Jan van Kampen, *Louisa* of Jan Danielszoon van den Rijn, *Maria* of Dirk de Munnik, *Zaaijer* of Cornelis Boermans, and *Zalm* of Arent Ruighaver; four-gun storeship *Haas* of Klaas Huigen; four victuallers; three galliots; a water hoy; plus 15 troop transports bearing 3,400 soldiers under Col. Jan van Uyttenhove.

The French have been forewarned of de Ruyter's approach, but their strength is concentrated at their capital of Saint Pierre, up the coast. Being familiar with that island, which he visited nine years earlier (*see* 5 May 1665), and now carrying aboard the Huguenot turncoat Charles de Birac of Gascony, de Ruyter bears down on the principal harbor of Fort Royal (modern-day Fort de France), which the French consider to be impregnable and so have left unprotected. The Dutch admiral fails to take it the first day because his fleet becomes becalmed.

During the ensuing night 118 hastily assembled men under de Baas de l'Herpinière (nephew of the French governor-general, who is ill at Saint Pierre) work frantically to shore up Fort Royal's defenses, supplemented by crews from the vessels anchored in its roads: Capt. Thomas Claude Renart de Fuch Samberg, Marquis d'Amblimont's royal frigate *Jeux,* of 44 guns

A Dutch dispatch yacht bearing down on de Ruyter's flagship Zeven Provinciën *off the Texel, with orders for his fleet to weigh for Africa and the New World; contemporary painting by Willem van de Velde the Younger*

and 150 men; the 22-gun merchantman *Saint Eustache* of Saint-Malo; *Sagesse* of Bordeaux; *Notre Dame* of Ciotat; and *Saint Joseph* of Toulon. The latter two are scuttled as blockships while their 25 crewmembers go ashore under Masters Antoine Ganteaume and Joune—plus Ensign de Martignac, a sergeant, and 16 marines from *Jeux*—to bolster the garrison.

By dawn the French have assembled enough men under Guillaume d'Orange to stretch booms across the harbor mouth and work their batteries while 65-year-old Gov. Antoine André de Sainte Marthe de Lalande (a distinguished military veteran) arrives by boat to assume overall command. When de Ruyter enters the morning of 20 July, he is greeted by heavy gunfire; and when Uyttenhove's troops disembark at 9:00 A.M., they encounter positions of great natural strength. The French fortifications sit high atop rocky cliffs, and the Dutch columns soon become caught by a crossfire between the batteries on one side and d'Amblimont's *Jeux* and Captain Beaulieu's *Saint Eustache* out in the harbor. The 1,000 Dutch attackers have no siege pieces, scaling ladders, or support fire from de Ruyter's distant ships, their discipline further collapsing when a rum warehouse is breached.

The Dutch land commanders attempt to regroup in the lee of a nearby cliff, but d'Amblimont quickly lands a half-dozen guns from his frigate and opens fire upon the new position. Uyttenhove is seriously wounded and Dutch will snaps; by 11:00 A.M. the invaders are streaming off toward their boats, returning at 2:00 P.M. under Vice Admiral Evertsen and Rear Admiral de Ruyter for a second try. Again the assault troops suffer heavily from the combined French fire; two hours later they retire to their transports in defeat when Michiel de Ruyter hoists the white recall signal from *Zeven Provinciën.* Dutch casualties total 143 killed and 318 wounded compared to 15 French dead—among them d'Orange.

Not yet realizing they have won a great victory, the masters of *Saint Eustache* and *Sagesse* set their ships aflame and go ashore during the night while the nervous d'Amblimont sits aboard his royal frigate preparing to do the same. Dawn of 21 July breaks, revealing that de Ruyter is gone, having staggered north toward Dominica to recuperate. From here, a few Dutch ships return south on 25 July, although the main Dutch body continues north, passing Guadeloupe by 26 July and visiting the English on Nevis. Eventually de Ruyter steers toward Europe, sickness raging throughout his crowded transports.

13 APRIL 1675. John, Lord Vaughan (new governor of Jamaica), issues a proclamation at Port Royal ordering all English privateers to refrain from serving under foreign flags now that Britain is at peace. However, with France still at war against both Spain and Holland—and thus freely issuing commissions—many ignore the injunction and continue roving.

APRIL 1675. The English privateer John Bennett—his 20-man brigantine bearing a commission from Governor d'Ogeron of French Saint Domingue to campaign against the Spaniards—intercepts the 50-ton hired frigate *Buen Jesús de las Almas* of Bernardo Ferrer Espejo as it approaches the coast of Hispaniola with 46,471 pesos in payrolls for that island.

SUMMER 1675. The Dutch corsairs Jurriaen Aernouts and Jan Erasmus Reyning make a descent on Grenada with about 100 raiders. They quickly occupy the principal French fort (garrisoned by only eight men) but fail to notice the arrival of enemy reinforcements, who besiege the Dutchmen inside the keep and starve them into submission. Aernouts, Reyning, and the other captives are conveyed to Martinique aboard the warship *Émerillon* of Capt. Chadeau de La Clicheterre; they escape and eventually regain Curaçao by 1676.

17 JUNE 1675 (O.S.). ***King Philip's War.*** In New England, the Algonquian tribes have grown increasingly restive because of Puritan expansion inland out of Plymouth (Massachusetts) and are offended by religious proselytization and other mistreatment. As a result, the *sachem* or chieftain Metacomet—known to the English as Philip—begins organizing his Wampanoag tribes around Mount Hope for an uprising.

On 17 June (O.S.), Indian bands begin raiding Puritan farms, resulting in a warrior being shot next day at Swansea. Hostilities around this settlement quickly escalate and burst into open warfare by 24 June (O.S.). Isolated Puritan farms and hamlets are destroyed before 500 militia can be raised at Plymouth and Boston to advance into Wampanoag territory four days later. Philip's followers fall back into the Pocasset Swamp, from where they burn Swansea and Dartmouth, also attacking Taunton and Rehoboth before slipping across the Taunton River on 28 July (O.S.); they are scattered by 50 loyal Mohican Indians four days later.

The defeated Philip escapes into neighboring Nipmuk territory with only 40 warriors and 250 noncombatants, prompting the Puritans to disband their militia. However, on 2 August (O.S.) 20 Connecticut troopers under Capts. Edward Hutchinson and Thomas Wheeler are ambushed while peacefully approaching a Nipmuk gathering near Brookfield, suffering eight killed and five wounded. The town is leveled by a war band led by chief Sagamore John, its 83 terrified survivors being rescued two evenings later by 73-year-old Maj. Simon Williard with 46 troopers and five loyal scouts from Groton. Again, an additional 350 militia rush into the area, only to find the hostiles gone.

An Indian band is eventually attacked near Hatfield late in August by Capts. Richard Beers and Thomas Lathrop, who slay 26 Nipmuks at a cost of ten English dead. This provokes the natives under chiefs Manaco—alias One-Eyed John—and Sagamore Sam to attack Deerfield in retaliation on 1 September (O.S.), destroy Northfield next day, then devastate Beers's 36-man relief column just south of here on 3 September (O.S.), killing the captain and 20 of his men. Lathrop's demise occurs on 18 September (O.S.), when his 90-man wagon train is ambushed after evacuating Deerfield, being almost totally annihilated five miles south at Bloody Brook. Frightened English settlers abandon the Connecticut Valley to huddle around Hatfield and Hadley; Springfield is attacked but not entirely overrun on 5 October (O.S.).

On 2 November (O.S.), the New Englanders declare war against the Narragansett tribe of Rhode Island as well, convinced they have been abetting the hostiles. Five weeks later, seven companies of Massachusetts militia—527 men—under Maj. Samuel Appleton depart Dedham, uniting at Pawtuxet on 11 December (O.S.) with an additional 158 from Plymouth under Maj. William Bradford and Capt. John Gorham. Together they sweep through Narragansett territory for the next seven days, destroying minor villages and killing or capturing three-score natives, before meeting 300 Connecticut troops and 150 Mohican allies under Maj. Robert Treat at Petasquamscot. After a seven-hour trek across a frozen swamp through heavy snow, the army surprises 3,000 Narragansetts within a fortified camp at noon on 19 December (O.S.). The English fight their way inside after three hours' intense combat, during which they suffer 68 dead and 150 wounded; the natives are driven into the wilderness after enduring several hundred casualties. Still, the exhausted victors cannot hold their prize after the so-called Great Swamp Fight, instead retiring toward Wickford with considerable hardship.

Gov. Josiah Winslow of Plymouth subsequently attempts to maintain pressure on the scattered Narragansett bands with 1,500 militia, but the discouraged

New Englanders disband by 6 February 1676 (O.S.). Four days later, Philip with 300–400 Narragansett and Nipmuk warriors razes Lancaster in a dawn raid, departing before any rescuers can appear. On 21 February (O.S.) he burns 40–50 houses at Medfield, then evades a pursuing column under Major General Denison. Numerous hit-and-run raids by the Indians ensue during the unusually mild winter: Weymouth is attacked on 28 February (O.S.), Groton three days later, the outskirts of Plymouth on 12 March (O.S.), Warwick five days later, Marlboro on 26 March (O.S.), Seekonk and Longmeadow two days later, Bridgewater and Billerica on 9 April (O.S.), Chelmsford six days after, then the natives descend upon Sudbury—15 miles outside of Boston—in great numbers early on the morning of 21 April (O.S.), inflicting heavy casualties before withdrawing.

Despite these successes, spring sees a revival in English fortunes as the natives succumb to famine and disease. When a band of warriors approaches Hadley on 11 June (O.S.), they find it defended by 500 troops and so retire without attacking. Morale among the hostiles soon collapses, each small band looking to its own survival; some surrender to the English while others are hunted down and exterminated. On 12 August (O.S.), Capt. Benjamin Church surprises Philip's camp near Mount Hope and kills him, his head being carried into Plymouth on a pole. During the course of these yearlong hostilities, 600 colonists have died—one out of every 16 English males of military age in Massachusetts and Connecticut.

JULY 1675. Rogue Doeg and Susquehannock Indians (Siouan-speaking natives driven out of their traditional homelands by Iroquois pressure) slip across Virginia's border to rob and murder several English settlers before retiring into Maryland. They are pursued by Virginia militia, who attack and kill a number of raiders before withdrawing.

Such clashes are not uncommon occurrences, but this particular incident gains greater significance when the Maryland authorities contact Gov. Sir William Berkeley of Virginia, proposing a joint operation. As a result, Berkeley orders John Washington and Isaac Allerton to raise a company of militia in late August to campaign with the Marylanders. Both contingents meet and advance upon the principal Susquehannock stronghold, arriving in late September to accuse its inhabitants of participating in the summer raid. The natives vigorously deny the accusation; unconvinced, Washington and Allerton lead away five chieftains to be executed. The English then besiege the stronghold, but a few nights later the Susquehannocks escape.

JANUARY 1676. Enraged by the summary execution of five of their chieftains the previous autumn, the Susquehannocks take revenge by attacking the English settlements along the Rappahannock and Potomac Rivers, killing 36 people. News of the foray creates panic throughout Virginia, with Governor Berkeley attempting to control passions and protect friendly Indians.

APRIL 1676. ***Bacon's Rebellion.*** Convinced they are about to endure a massive Indian attack because of Berkeley's inaction, Virginia hotheads rally round a new councilor named Nathaniel Bacon to advance into the wilderness southwest of Henrico County and hunt natives. They join a band of friendly Indians and attack a group of Susquehannocks, but after this victory they fall out with their new allies, destroying their village before retiring.

In the meantime a furious Governor Berkeley has marched with 300 men to intercept Bacon; arriving too late to prevent his departure, Berkeley removes him from the council and declares him in rebellion. Finding much pro-Bacon sentiment, the governor then decides to dissolve the assembly and call for the first general elections in 14 years. Bacon is easily elected burgess for Henrico County, but when he arrives off Jamestown in his sloop to take his seat on 5 June the vessel is fired upon and he is arrested. Brought before Berkeley, he begs forgiveness, is pardoned, and is allowed to return upriver to his plantation (apparently having been promised command of a forthcoming Indian campaign).

The assembly meanwhile remains in session until the end of the month, when Bacon suddenly reappears in Jamestown with 500 armed men, terrorizing assembly members into giving him his Indian command—plus restitution of his sloop—before marching off into the wilderness. Scouting around the falls of the James during the summer and early autumn, Bacon learns the governor has again declared him a rebel. Retracing his steps toward Jamestown, Bacon forces Berkeley to flee to Accomack on the Eastern Shore (Chesapeake Bay) and attempts to assume control over the entire government.

In order to reconfirm his reputation as the people's champion, Bacon sets off once more against the Indians, destroying the main encampment of the Pamunkeys on the pretext they are secretly aiding the Susquehannocks. During Bacon's absence, Berkeley reoccupies Jamestown; upon Bacon's return the town is besieged, forcing the governor to retreat for a second time to his Accomack stronghold. On this occasion, however, Jamestown is burned to the ground, after which the rebellion begins to fall apart. Bacon dies of disease a month later, freeing Berkeley to stamp out the last vestiges of the rebellion during the coming winter. The governor is nonetheless recalled to London shortly thereafter, where he dies in disgrace; more than 1,000 troops are sent out from England under Commo. Sir John Berry to reassert royal rule.

4 MAY 1676. ***Binckes's Campaign.*** At Cayenne (French Guiana), recently promoted Vice Adm. Jacob Binckes of Amsterdam returns to the Americas with three ships of the line of 56–44 guns; six frigates of 36–24 guns; a fire ship; and numerous transports. He disembarks 900 troops and advances upon the principal stronghold of Fort Saint Louis, calling upon Gov. Jean Hérault Lefebvre de Lézy to surrender. The French official initially refuses but capitulates, along with his 300-man garrison, once the Dutch reach his walls. Within the next two days Binckes installs a new garrison under Quirijn Spranger then proceeds northwest to visit a like treatment upon Marie Galante.

MID-JUNE 1676. Binckes materializes off Marie Galante. The French residents—many unhappy over stringent new trade regulations imposed by the royal minister, Jean Baptiste Colbert—offer no resistance, even agreeing to emigrate to the new Dutch colony that Binckes intends to establish on Tobago. After throwing down Marie Galante's fortifications and embarking the inhabitants, Binckes sights Guadeloupe on 16 June. He considers its defenses too strong and so passes, pursuing a trio of French vessels offshore without success.

LATE JUNE 1676. Binckes arrives at Saint Martin to disembark 500 men and reconquer the island from the French. The French offer a spirited resistance under Governor de Magne from behind a recently constructed fortress and parapet near its salt pans. During the fight the defenders apparently fire upon Dutch emissaries sent to negotiate terms; Binckes orders no quarter is to be given. The Dutch eventually surmount a hill overlooking the parapet, shooting down into it and killing de Magne—after which the French settlers scatter. Angry, Binckes commandeers 100 slaves and a large number of cattle before departing but does not install a garrison; the French soon reoccupy the devastated stronghold.

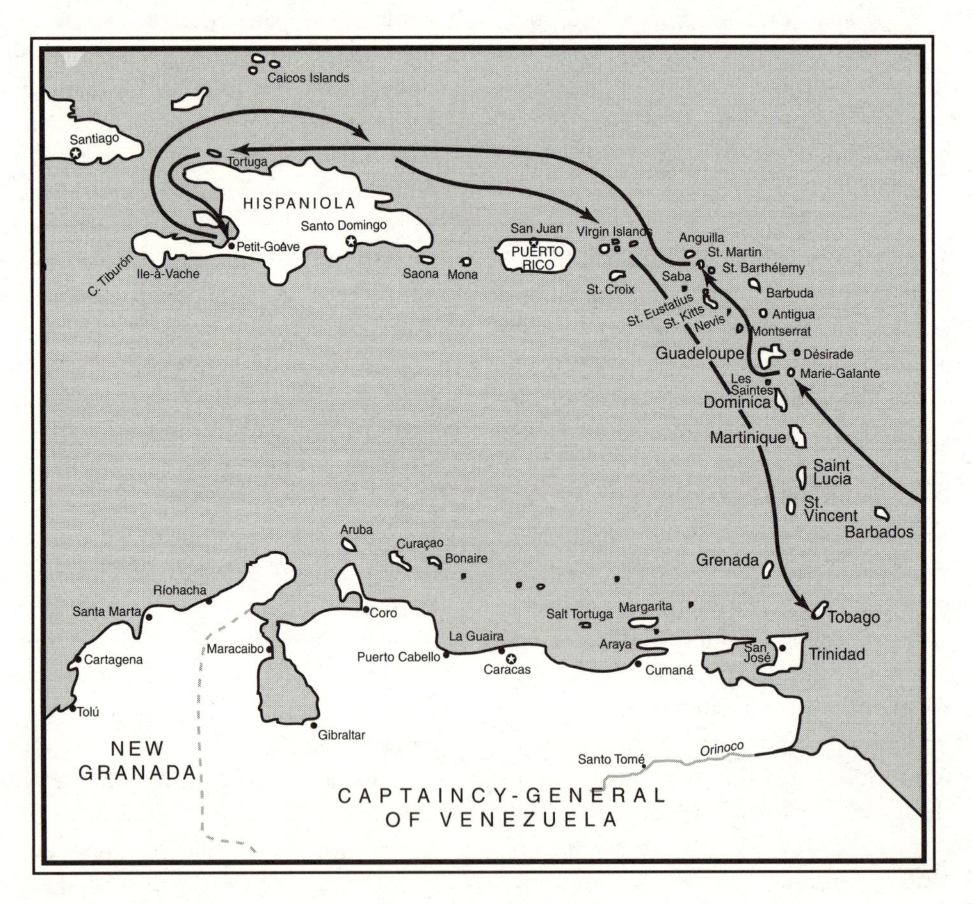

Binckes's sweep through the West Indies

From Saint Martin, Binckes divides his command, directing Commo. Jan Bont to sail toward Tobago with a squadron bearing colonists under the Swedish-born governor-designate, Hendrik Carloff, to begin reestablishing "New Walcheren" (*see* 18 December 1672); the admiral meanwhile probes farther west with a larger force hoping to incite a revolt among the *boucaniers* of Saint Domingue (Haiti), who are known to be resentful against the high tariffs of France's West India Company.

16 JULY 1676. Having failed to persuade any French residents along Saint Domingue's coast to reject Parisian rule, Binckes arrives before Petit Goâve with his 50-gun flagship *Bescherming;* the 44-gun *Zeelandia* under Pieter Constant (former governor of Dutch Tobago); the 24-gun *Popkesburg* of Pieter Stolwyck; and the privateer sloop *Fortuijn* of Jan Erasmus Reyning, sighting the following loading tobacco in its roads:

Ship	*Guns*	*Men*	*Commander*
Saint René of Nantes	14	28	Pierre Chevalier
Florissant of Nantes	14	40	?
Dauphin of Havre	18	50	Jean Dupont
Alcyon of Dieppe	18	50	Jean Pimont
Roi David of Honfleur	16	35	Martin
Marie of Dieppe	2	14	?
Lis Couronné	22	40	Jean Ducasse

Binckes launches a lopsided battle in which the French resist gamely, suffering many killed and wounded, before their merchantmen are boarded during the night. The Dutch seize three prizes, judging the surviving vessels to be too heavily damaged. However, they cannot go ashore because of the timely overland arrival of French reinforcements from Tortuga Island under acting Gov. Pierre Paul Tarin de Cussy. After dispatching his prizes toward the Netherlands, Binckes reverses course through the Antilles toward Tobago.

1 SEPTEMBER 1676. Binckes reaches Tobago to discover that all the colonizing vessels of Commodore Bont's detached squadron have arrived, save for three minor vessels intercepted off Nevis by a pair of French men-of-war under Commo. Rouxel de Médavy, Marquis de Grancey d'Argentan, plus Bont's own flagship (which the latter has inexplicably sailed back to Europe; eventually he is beheaded for desertion). The admiral begins organizing the island defenses, erecting a fort called Sterreschans (Star Bastion) at Klip Bay (modern-day Rockly Bay) as well as a smaller bulwark nearby, in anticipation of a French counteroffensive. Dutch morale is boosted in February 1677 by the appearance of a relief convoy bearing 150 soldiers, more settlers, and provisions.

17 DECEMBER 1676. ***D'Estrées's Counteroffensive.*** Ten French ships, two frigates, and three sloops appear off Dutch-held Cayenne (Guiana) under haughty 52-year-old Vice Adm. Jean, Comte d'Estrées. They have been sent by Louis XIV to reverse the gains made by Binckes. A veteran field marshal before joining France's royal navy, d'Estrées disembarks 800 troops and forms them into two columns, heading one himself and delegating the other to Captain Panetié of *Précieux*. Commo. Louis Gabaret of *Intrépide* blockades the Armire roadstead with five men-of-war while the remaining French warships close in on Cayenne's principal stronghold two days later to support d'Estrées's columns.

The attackers call upon the Dutch garrison commander, Quirijn Spranger, to surrender, but he refuses. Before dawn on 21 December the French soldiers storm the ramparts, achieving victory in half an hour at a cost of 40 French dead and 105 wounded (including Panetié, whose jaw is shattered). D'Estrées accepts the capitulation of 219 defenders and restores Lefebvre de Lézy as governor of Cayenne. After refreshing his ships and dispatching 260 Dutch prisoners toward Europe (where they are very badly mistreated), d'Estrées presses northwest.

19 JANUARY 1677. D'Estrées reaches Martinique, hoping to gain intelligence about Dutch defensive measures at his next intended target (Tobago) and to be reinforced by *flibustier* contingents. Governor-General de Baas dies on 24 January from protracted illness; d'Estrées sets sail on 12 February, slowly making for Tobago. His strength gradually expands to ten men-of-war; six lesser warships (*Fanfaron, Coche, Bayonnais, Entreprenant, Adroite,* and *Assurée*); a fire ship; some victuallers; and more than 4,000 men.

18 FEBRUARY 1677. On Tobago, Binckes receives word of two small French vessels reconnoitering the approaches to Klip (Rockly) Bay, correctly surmising them to be advance units from d'Estrées's approaching fleet. Overnight the Dutch admiral also receives intelligence from the English on Nevis (brought by a Dutch auxiliary, Jan Erasmus Reyning), advising of Cayenne's fall and d'Estrées's recruitment of West Indian privateers.

Next day, Binckes and his 1,700 followers count nine unidentified sail off the coast; the force increases to 14 by 20 February. The ominous buildup leads the admiral to redouble his defensive preparations, marshaling soldiers and sailors around the Sterreschans fort while ferrying noncombatants out to ships anchored in the harbor.

21 FEBRUARY 1677. This evening, d'Estrées disembarks seven infantry companies and 200 sailors (more than 1,000 men in all) at a quiet inlet, marching under Lt. Col. Hérouard de La Pirogerie and Maj. Chevalier d'Andigny de Grandfontaine toward the distant Dutch stronghold on Tobago. By 23 February a French emissary approaches the Sterreschans fortress, calling upon the defenders to surrender; he is rejected. The French army resumes the advance, skirmishing with Dutch units until coming within sight of Sterreschans a few days later, then emplacing a siege battery.

The French commanders are daunted by the imposing, well-armed fortification with its encircling river. But d'Estrées—worried over dwindling provisions—eventually orders a probe that is made between 9:00–10:00 P.M. and is supported by 14 light vessels feinting against the harbor entrance. The assault does not prosper, and the French are seriously considering lifting their siege when d'Estrées decides to make a last, desperate storm by both sea and land.

3 MARCH 1677 (ASH WEDNESDAY). ***First Battle of Tobago.*** At first light d'Estrées, piloted by a Dutch turncoat, heads into Klip Bay with his 72-gun, 445-man flagship *Glorieux;* 58-gun, 350-man *Précieux* of Mascarany; 46-gun, 280-man *Émerillon* of de Méricourt; and 38-gun, 250-man *Laurier* of de Machault. Closer inshore, his second-in-command Louis Gabaret leads the 56-gun, 320-man vice-flagship *Intrépide;* 62-gun, 380-man *Fendant* of Charles, Comte de Blénac; 48-gun, 300-man *Marquis* of the Chevalier de Lézines; 50-gun, 300-man *Galant* of de Montortié; 36-gun, 240-man *Soleil d'Afrique* of de La Borde; and 38-gun, 240-man *Jeux* of de La Cassinière. They are further accompanied by a pair of *avisos* or dispatch sloops, a fireship, and a galliot. D'Estrées's audacity has caught the Dutch fleet off guard, for they have stripped their warships of fighting men to reinforce the defenses ashore.

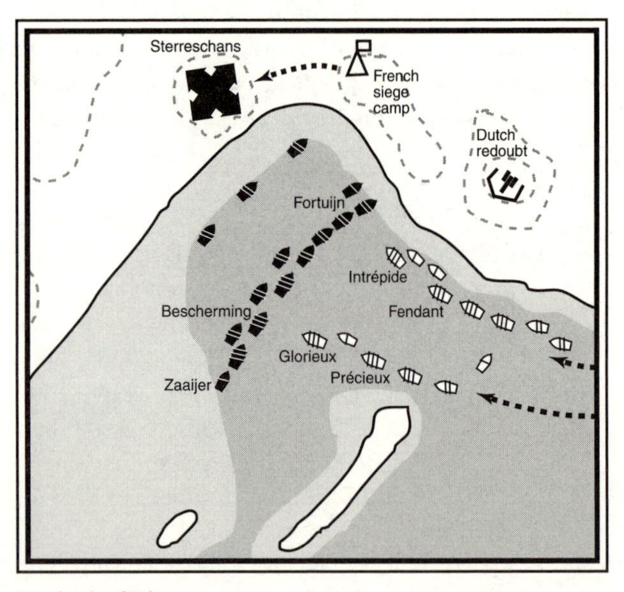

First battle of Tobago

Awaiting the French, in a curving anchored line, are:

Ship	*Guns*	*Men*	*Commander*
Zaaijer (fireship)	—	13	Heertje Carstenszoon
Zeelandia	44	118	Pieter Constant
Alcyon (French prize)	24	25	Cornelis Stolwyck
Bescherming (flag)	50	153	Jacob Binckes
Duc de Yorck (victualler)	26	35	Frederik Sweers
Huis te Kruiningen (vice-flag)	56	128	Roemer Vlacq
Gouden Monnik (victualler)	31	25	Dirk Schoen
Middelburg	36	83	Jan Swart
Gouden Ster	28	74	Pieter Coreman
Popkesburg	24	52	Pieter Stolwyck
Leyden	34	73	Galtje Galtjes
Fortuijn (sloop)	—	25	Jan Erasmus Reyning

Behind these lie the beached hulk *Starrenburg,* a neutral Portuguese vessel, and the 12-gun transport *Sphaera Mundi,* which is crammed with more than 200 women and children, several hundred slaves, and its regular 30-man complement.

D'Estrées's fleet enters with guns blazing, expending more than 1,000 shot against the Dutch batteries before reaching the moored warships. Inshore, *Marquis* closes upon *Leyden* despite ferocious countersalvos while, farther out, *Glorieux* sinks the fire ship *Zaaijer* then grapples with *Huis te Kruiningen.* The Dutch vice-flagship is promptly boarded and carried by the Chevalier d'Hervault while, nearby, *Précieux* begins a losing struggle against the Dutch flagship *Bescherming.* On land, Colonel de La Pirogerie sends storm columns against Sterreschans, only to be turned back by the efficient Dutch artillery. Twice more the French soldiers rush the walls, suffering almost 200 casualties before giving up.

The repulse of the French land force allows Binckes to shift his attention to the harbor, where flames soon begin spreading among the vessels, multiplied by heated shot from Sterreschans. Eventually, conflagrations take hold throughout both fleets, d'Estrées's own *Glorieux* nearly being destroyed when *Huis te Kruiningen* explodes (the French admiral himself is wounded in the head). His flagship subsequently catches fire and burns down to the waterline, along with *Marquis* and *Assurée.* Ten of the 13 Dutch vessels are also consumed, the badly damaged *Bescherming, Zeelandia,* and *Alcyon* surviving. Two French vessels—*Intrépide* and *Précieux*—also run aground and are captured, despite d'Estrées's cold-blooded command that they be burned, even though wounded still groan upon their decks. *Fendant* and *Galant* are dismasted; *Émerillon* sustains considerable damage as well.

All told, the French suffer more than 1,000 casualties (among them Colonel de La Pirogerie, Commodore Gabaret, Captains de Lézines and de La Borde). Dutch casualties are 344, with Captains Vlacq, Galtjes, Sweers, Constant, and Coreman among them. Three days after withdrawing into Palmyt Bay, six miles from Sterreschans, d'Estrées limps away toward Grenada and Martinique, proclaiming victory despite his retreat and heavy losses. (By early July he is back in Versailles reporting to the king, who orders the admiral to return to the West Indies and complete the mission.)

7 MARCH 1677. A buccaneering expedition sneaks upon the Mexican town of Jalpa before sunrise. It has departed the Laguna de Términos six days earlier, led by a French rover named André Ribaut with 35 men aboard his three-gun frigate. Another 117 freebooters sail aboard the frigate and brigantine of an English captain named George Rivers, who has also bolstered Ribaut's crew with an additional 70 men. The rovers' intent is to seize a rich cargo of silver and arms recently salvaged from Campeche's coast-guard frigate *Pescadora,* which sank near the entrance to the Grijalva River in mid-November 1676 while returning from Veracruz under Capt. Fermín de Huidobro.

The buccaneers anchor their vessels near Barra de Dos Bocas and advance up the Seco River, guided by a mulatto prisoner named Bartolomé Saraos. Fording streams on more than 20 occasions during the trek, 150 heavily armed freebooters eventually appear outside Jalpa before sunrise on Sunday, 7 March, attacking and overwhelming the sleeping Spanish citizenry. However, the treasure and arms have already been shipped back toward the coast with the mule train of José Tenorio; 40 buccaneers pursue to the coastal town of Amatitlán but they arrive too late. They kill three teamsters and capture the rest of Tenorio's men, but only the slow-matches and powder flasks remain behind, everything else having been placed aboard ship for transfer to Campeche.

The frustrated Ribaut and Rivers therefore evacuate Jalpa at 10:00 A.M. on 8 March, taking whatever booty and prisoners they can. Before any Spanish militia from outlying areas can react, the raiders are back aboard their ships; they suffered not a single loss during the entire incursion.

EARLY SUMMER 1677. A small English squadron under the veteran Capt. Sir John Berry reaches Virginia, bringing 1,000 reinforcements because of concerns about Indian uprisings and Bacon's Rebellion (*see* April 1676). Finding the situation largely stabilized, Berry returns shortly thereafter to England.

LATE JUNE 1677. The French privateer Pierre La Garde attacks Santa Marta (Colombia), seconded by English mercenaries under Capts. John Coxon and William Barnes. They surprise the port at dawn and take many captives, including the governor and the bishop, Dr. Lucas Fernández y Piedrahita, who they hold for ransom while ransacking the buildings.

10 JULY 1677. The 240-ton Spanish warship *San Juan* (formerly the French *Dauphine,* more commonly called *Princesa* or *Francesa*); the 200-ton *Nuestra Señora del Camino;* and the 200-ton *Santo Cristo del Buen Viaje* (alias *Mogoleño*) arrive at Cartagena; they are intended to reconstitute Spain's West Indian squadron (the Armada de Barlovento, or "Windward Fleet"). Capts. José de Arizmendi, Felipe de Diústegui, and Francisco López de Gómara report to their new *capitán general* (armada commander), Antonio de Quintana, a 20-year veteran of Cartagena's coast guard.

The trio is immediately dispatched, along with two hired merchantmen and 500 troops, to rescue Santa Marta, which is still being occupied by La Garde, Coxon, and Barnes. Quintana's flotilla supposedly bombards the invaders before being driven off by a storm (but Spanish observers later charge that the men-of-war engage only reluctantly, being heavy-laden with European imports). By the time they return to the attack a few days later, the buccaneers have withdrawn with their hostages, most of whom are released at Port Royal, Jamaica.

3 OCTOBER 1677. Admiral d'Estrées departs Brest with *Terrible* (flag); vice-flag *Tonnant* under the Marquis de Grancey; *Belliqueux* under Rear Adm. Charles de Courbon, seigneur de Romegeux and Comte de Blénac (and the new governor-general for the French West Indies, replacing the deceased de Baas); ships of the line *Duc, Prince, Étoile, Alcyon, Hercule, Brillant, Bourbon,* and *Émerillon;* transports *Dromadaire* and *Tardif;* a hospital ship; the fire ships

Périlleux, Maligne, and *Brutal;* plus a *barco luengo* and a caïque.

During the outward passage in early November, d'Estrées destroys the Dutch slaving station at Gorée (West Africa), entering the West Indies later that month and steering toward Tobago.

6 DECEMBER 1677. ***Second Battle of Tobago.*** The abrupt reappearance of d'Estrées finds Tobago's Dutch defenders completely unrecovered. Binckes has sent the repaired French prize *Intrépide* under a badly wounded Constant toward the Netherlands to beg for reinforcements, but none have arrived. Within Klip (Rockly) Bay lie the damaged flagship *Bescherming* and prize *Précieux,* plus three minor vessels. On land, the Dutch garrison is reduced to less than 500 effectives following the first defense and subsequent bouts of disease. Binckes's sole ally is the weather: torrential downpours hamper the French disembarkation and advance from Palmyt Bay.

Yet d'Estrées quickly throws almost 1,000 troops and a siege train ashore under Grancey and Blénac, who march upon the Sterreschans fortress while brushing aside 200 Dutch troops. By 10 December d'Estrées comes ashore and begins installing his siege battery under the direction of military engineer de Combes (brought specifically aboard Chadeau de La Clochetterie's *Brillant* for this work). Having launched a suicidal, all-out assault in the First Battle of Tobago, d'Estrées is determined to proceed more prudently the second time by instituting a formal siege.

On 12 December his chief gunner, Landouillette, begins firing ranging shots against Sterreschans, laying odds he will blow it up on the third attempt. Incredibly, Landouillette's third round lands squarely inside the fort's magazine and causes a mighty blast that kills Binckes and 250 other Dutch defenders and paralyzes the remainder. The French swarm exultantly over the ruins, and Dutch resolve collapses. *Étoile, Hercule,* and *Bourbon* enter Klip Bay to seize 16 vessels; rounded up are a total of 525 prisoners from land and sea as well as 45 artillery pieces and 30,000 shot. (One of the few Dutchmen to escape is the privateer Reyning, who carries word of the disaster to Curaçao aboard a tiny boat.) D'Estrées remains in Tobago until January 1678, when he retires toward Grenada after throwing down the fortifications and depopulating the island.

APRIL 1678. After resting at Saint Kitts throughout March, d'Estrées transfers his fleet to Martinique in April, calling for *flibustiers* from as far away as Saint Domingue (Haiti) to rally for a descent against Curaçao, the last remaining Dutch outpost in the West Indies. Supremely confident, the French expedition quits its rendezvous off Saint Kitts by 7 May, comprising 18 royal warships and more than a dozen *flibustier* craft. The admiral intends to lead them down the Lesser Antilles and then west past the Orchila, Roques, and Aves groups—despite warnings from local pilots that such a heading can be treacherous. *Étoile* and a buccaneer vessel are sent ahead to sweep for any dangers.

11 MAY 1678. ***Aves Islands Shipwreck.*** At 9:00 P.M. on this Wednesday, one of d'Estrées's *flibustier* consorts suddenly begins firing musket shots, followed by a heavy gun. It is signaling that the French fleet is too far south and about to sail onto the reefs surrounding Aves Islands. The warning comes too late, however, and many ships begin to strike bottom in the darkness. The dawn on 12 May reveals that the following vessels lie beneath the waves:

Ships	*Guns*	*Men*	*Commander*
Terrible (flag)	70	500	Admiral d'Estrées
Tonnant (vice-flag)	66	400	Marquis de Grancey
Belliqueux	70	450	de Nesmond
Bourbon	56	300	de Rosmadée
Prince	56	300	Saint-Aubin d'Infreville
Hercule	56	300	de Flacourt
Défenseur	50	200	Marquis d'Amblimont
Dromadaire (transport)	36	60	Périer
Unnamed caïque	24	250	?
Roi David (hired merchantman)	14	36	Julian

In addition, three corsair vessels of 18, 12, and six guns—bearing 400 men between them—have also been destroyed. A total of 500 sailors and soldiers are drowned, and the French siege train is mostly lost along with almost 500 naval guns.

The admiral has no choice but to retire toward Saint Domingue on 16 May with the remaining warships and the 800–900 survivors who are plucked from the water. Once reassembled at Petit Goâve early in June, his fleet is reduced to the 56-gun, 300-man flagship *Duc* under the Comte de Sourdis; men-of-war *Brillant, Alcyon,* and *Émerillon;* the transport *Tardif;* three fire ships; and a victualler pinnace. By the time d'Estrées staggers back to France, the war with the Netherlands is virtually ended.

10 JUNE 1678. ***Grammont's Maracaibo Campaign.*** Rather than retreat with d'Estrées following the Aves Islands disaster, many *flibustiers* prefer an alternate project under the veteran corsair sieur de Grammont. Having no interest in tackling the tough Dutch

garrison at Curaçao, they materialize in the Gulf of Venezuela by 10 June with 2,000 men aboard six large ships and 13 smaller ones under commanders such as La Garde, Archambaud, Stel, Le Gascon, Nicolas Le Fée, Desmoulins, Aymé, Gouin, Mathieu, Josee, and Grenezé.

Grammont disembarks half his force and marches along the San Carlos Peninsula toward the fort guarding its bar, knowing its artillery to be pointed mostly seaward. The garrison commander, Francisco Pérez de Guzmán, is able to stave off an immediate assault by stationing 100 harquebusiers outside the walls, but heavy guns are landed from the buccaneer flotilla, and after a brief bombardment the Spanish surrender. Grammont passes his ships over the bar, leaving his six largest to blockade the entrance while he presses on toward Maracaibo with the other 13. Maracaibo and its outlying district are thrown into panic, the ancient, sickly governor, Jorge Madureira Ferreira—in office for only one week—being unable to inspire confidence. Citizens begin fleeing in every direction and are soon followed by Madureira himself, who retires to Maicao with a handful of regulars. Thus, Grammont occupies Maracaibo largely unopposed on 14 June and gives it over to the sack. *Flibustier* columns strike out into the countryside, pursuing the Spanish governor and other notables, scattering them ever farther afield.

By 28 June Grammont abandons the gutted remains of Maracaibo to cross the Laguna and fall upon Gibraltar. But that town is already deserted, and after Grammont bombards its walls the 22-man garrison gives up. Emboldened, Grammont marches 425 buccaneers almost 50 miles inland to Trujillo, which is defended by a regular fort with 350 troops and four artillery pieces. Again the corsair chieftain prevails, storming the fortification from the rear on 1 September "by some hills where it seemed impossible to do so." Once more, terrified citizens crowd the roads, straggling 75 miles southwest into Mérida de la Grita. Having defeated or dispersed every Spanish concentration he has met, Grammont retraces his steps toward the Laguna and eventually reenters Gibraltar, which is stripped bare and put to the torch on 25 September. The invaders sail away with an 18-gun merchantman from the "Coulouba" (Catatumbo?) River, remaining in the region almost until the end of the year. On 3 December Grammont finally departs the Gulf of Venezuela after razing the fort guarding the bar of San Carlos Peninsula. His ships are laden with 77 captured cannons, booty, and numerous captives; he arrives at Petit Goâve by Christmas Eve.

6 JULY 1678. Two English buccaneer ships under Capts. George Spurre and Edward Neville—bearing French commissions—anchor near Jaina (Mexico) with eight piraguas in tow. Neville departs that night to reconnoiter the nearby port of Campeche with his sloop, rejoining the main body at daybreak on 7 July to report that all is calm. Both captains then slip ashore with 160 freebooters, leaving instructions for their vessels to bear down upon Campeche at dawn two days later.

The land party approaches the town by nocturnal stages, capturing every person it meets. Some are tortured to reveal the best access into Campeche, and one is persuaded to deceive its guard. An hour before daybreak on Sunday, 10 July, the disguised raider column materializes before a small city gate, where the terrified captive answers the sentinel's challenge and gains them entry. In the gloom the sentry assumes the shadowy figures are Indians coming early to market; the attackers march swiftly toward the central plaza and "with a great shout fire a heavy volley" before the governor's residence. Campeche's garrison is taken utterly by surprise; only nine soldiers are on duty instead of the usual 60. The garrison commander (*sargento mayor*), Gonzalo Borrallo, is taken in his nightshirt along with virtually every other prominent citizen.

Spurre's *Toro* and Neville's sloop appear on schedule, two huts being fired to signal them to enter. Captives are terrorized into raising ransoms, and every building is ransacked during the next few days. Although the buccaneers remain in Campeche only until the evening of Tuesday, 12 July, they withdraw with the ship *San Antonio,* a *barco luengo,* a boat, plus money and foodstuffs. They also carry off 250 black, mulatto, and Indian townspeople to sell as slaves at the Laguna de Términos; they proceed to Jamaica by the end of October to spend their ill-gotten gains.

10 AUGUST 1678. In Europe, Louis XIV signs the Treaty of Nijmegen, marking an end to French hostilities with the Netherlands. By the terms of the treaty France retains the wartime conquests of Tobago and Cayenne (Guiana).

27 AUGUST 1678. At nightfall, the French buccaneer Pierre de Frasquenay leads 800 *flibustiers* ashore at Justicia Inlet to fall upon nearby Santiago de Cuba while its citizenry sleeps. (He further believes its defenses to have been weakened by a devastating earthquake on 11 February.) However, the invaders are guided through winding jungle trails by a simpleminded Spanish captive named Juan Perdomo. They become

so confused that one column fires upon another in the darkness. The element of surprise thus being lost, Frasquenay has no choice but to retire to his waiting ships by 28 August.

17 SEPTEMBER 1678. France and Spain sign a separate treaty at Nijmegen, marking an end to their European conflict. But, unlike the recent peace treaty between France and Holland, this one does not contain any reference to the Americas—where fighting continues.

EARLY DECEMBER 1678. Two French ships and a pair of caïques arrive at Martinique under Commodore Forant, the young Marquis de Langeron, and Captain Paris. They have been sent to salvage the remains of Admiral d'Estrées's fleet from Aves Islands, which is accomplished after recruiting another two ships and four island traders and spending several months working the site. Eventually, 364 guns and 3,000 shot are recovered.

EARLY JULY 1679. D'Estrées returns to the West Indies ostensibly to demand prisoners from the Spanish-American authorities at Cartagena and Havana; he actually intends to reestablish France's naval prestige throughout the theater. His 74-gun flagship *Triomphant* is accompanied by the 56-gun *Bon* of Jean Gabaret; the 48-gun *Galant* of the Comte de Sourdis; the 44-gun *Faucon* of de Nesmond; the 38-gun *Tigre* of Saint-Aubin; the 34-gun *Tempête* of de Flacourt and *Mignon* of de Béthune; the frigates *Bouffone* and *Moqueuse;* the bark *Utile;* plus the transport *Chameau*. The arrival of this powerful squadron causes consternation throughout the Antilles, as it is believed to portend another outbreak in Europe.

When d'Estrées appears off Jamaica on 18 July, the English governor, Lord Carlisle, mans the defenses while Port Royal's citizenry flees inland; but one of d'Estrées's subordinates—the Comte d'Erveaux, knight of the Order of Malta—merely comes ashore to request permission to take on water and provisions at Bluefields Bay (it is granted). The French squadron subsequently works its way through the Greater Antilles, piloted by the Marquis de Maintenon, before finally visiting Havana on 18 October then continuing to France from Matanzas.

IRREGULAR WARFARE (1679–1688)

NOTWITHSTANDING THE CESSATION OF HOSTILITIES in Europe, frictions persist in the New World, especially as French authorities in the West Indies continue to issue privateering commissions against Spanish America because of Madrid's refusal to acknowledge the legitimacy of their existence.

21 FEBRUARY 1679. ***Repulse at Guanaja.*** An expedition under Grammont disembarks from three ships, two brigantines, and four lesser craft, advancing upon the town of Guanaja (Cuba) with 600 *flibustiers.* The inhabitants flee inland, allowing the invaders to enter unopposed to find buildings empty. Meanwhile some 600 Spanish militia gather under *Alcalde Mayor* Benito de Agüero, harrying the buccaneers' retreat so much that upon regaining the coast by 25 February Grammont must improvise a redoubt to cover his reembarkation. Eventually he suffers 70 killed before Dutch-born colleague Laurens Cornelis Boudewijn de Graaf can extricate the contingent (inflicting 67 Spanish fatalities).

20 JANUARY 1680. Manuel Lobo, newly appointed Portuguese governor of Rio de Janeiro and knight of the Order of Christo, arrives at San Gabriel Island (Uruguay) with three infantry and one cavalry companies—200 soldiers—plus 100 laborers and 18 cannons aboard the 30-gun, 300-ton flagship *Santa Veríssima* of Capt. Antônio Fernandes Poderoso; 14-gun, 250-ton vice-flagship of Manuel Carneiro da Costa; ten-gun, 200-ton vessel of Captain Mainardt; six-gun, 150-ton frigate *Jesus, Maria, Joseph* of naval Lt. Feliciano Inácio da Silva; and a small supply boat. This expedition disembarks on the mainland opposite and by 4 February begins erecting a stockaded fort called Colônia do Sacramento. The Spaniards across the River Plate in Buenos Aires consider this frontier outpost an infringement on their territory.

6 FEBRUARY 1680. Spanish piraguas steal into Mexico's Laguna de Términos under *Alcalde Ordinario* (town magistrate) Felipe de la Barrera y Villegas to strike against some English logwood cutters who have been selling trees to outward-bound Jamaican vessels. De la Barrera manages to surprise some interlopers, returning to Campeche with a few prizes. Encouraged by this success he leads a second expedition several weeks

later—consisting of a *barco luengo,* two piraguas, and 115 men—netting a 24-gun English merchantman.

12 APRIL 1680. Promoted *teniente de capitán general* (lieutenant governor) of Campeche, de la Barrera prepares a third raid against the English in the Laguna de Términos. He secures, at his own expense, half-ownership in his 24-gun prize and supplements it with two brigantines and six piraguas bearing 200 mulatto militia from Mérida de Yucatán, 70 regulars and 16 gunners from Campeche's garrison, plus 240 volunteers. His officers include the corsair captains Pedro de Castro and Juan Corso.

The expedition bursts into the Laguna by 17 April, seizing more than 38 craft along with 163 Baymen (among them George Rivers; *see* 7 March 1677); he also releases many Spanish hostages and slaves. De la Barrera then learns of 240 buccaneers who have departed in seven vessels to waylay the annual cocoa harvest in Tabasco; he sends a detachment in pursuit. His prisoners and prizes are carried back into Campeche, but de la Barrera does not arrive. Ironically, he becomes separated from his expedition and is captured by English stragglers, being conveyed to London and allegedly detained in the tower; eventually he is released, reaching Madrid by January 1682.

Meanwhile the Jamaicans raise strong objections to de la Barrera's Laguna incursions, feeling they violate the truce prevailing in the Caribbean.

15 APRIL 1680. ***First Pacific Incursions.*** At 6:00 A.M. on this Monday, 332 buccaneers disembark on the northeast coast of Panama's Golden Island, having hidden their ships in a small cove. Capts. John Coxon, Robert Allison, Edmund Cooke, Peter Harris (the Elder), Thomas Sawkins, and Bartholomew Sharpe have combined forces and secured native guides to march across the isthmus and raid the Spaniards in a more vulnerable theater. Ten days later they come upon the Spanish mining camp of Santa María el Real at the confluence of the Chucunaque and Tuira Rivers. Sawkins and two or three buccaneers rush the palisades at dawn, working their way inside and admitting the main force. A massacre ensues, 70 of the 200 Spanish residents being killed outright, the rest being murdered later by local Indians.

The buccaneers then press on into the Pacific, coasting west in riverboats until one night they capture an anchored Spanish bark, Sharpe taking command with 135 men. Next night Harris comes upon a second Spanish bark and seizes it; soon the privateers have a small flotilla, with which they bear down upon Panama City. The Spaniards send out a hastily mustered force to do battle, but the raiders overwhelm it in a three-hour fight, Harris receiving a mortal wound.

LATE APRIL 1680. In South Carolina, the short-lived Westo War commences. English traders and slave-catchers ally themselves with Savannah Indians—a migrating group of Shawnees—to defeat the bellicose Westo tribe farther inland (most likely Ricahericans who were expelled from Virginia in 1656). Three years later, not 50 remain.

5 MAY 1680. After the buccaneers' victory off Panama, Coxon is voted out as admiral; he retraces his

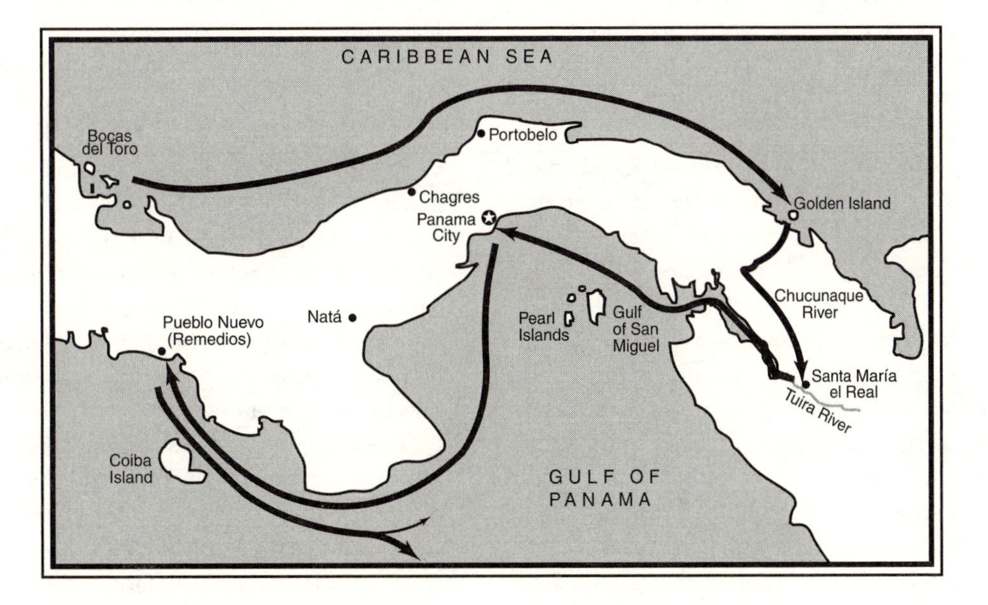

First wave of buccaneer incursions into the Pacific

steps across the isthmus to Golden Island with 70 loyal hands. Sawkins becomes chief commander aboard the captured *Santísima Trinidad* while Cooke commands an 80-ton bark and Sharpe a slightly smaller one. Next day a large ship is intercepted arriving from Lima; it becomes Sharpe's new command. The flotilla then roams west past Coiba Island, where Sawkins goes aboard Cooke's bark with 60 men two days later to attempt a landing at Remedios (then Pueblo Nuevo). During the disembarkation he is killed, Cooke bringing off the survivors. Upon quitting the river's mouth by 11 May (1 May 1680 [O.S.]), the pirates seize a Spanish bark, into which Cooke transfers (he renames it *Mayflower*).

Rejoining the main body, he finds Sawkins's death has created an upheaval, 60 of the latter's followers abandoning the enterprise altogether to sail away in Cooke's former bark for the Caribbean. Sharpe is now promoted commander aboard *Trinidad,* whereas Cooke is turned out of *Mayflower* by the crew.

EARLY JUNE 1680. Sharpe's 186 buccaneers lay in a southeasterly course from Coiba Island, reaching Gorgona Island more than a month later to replenish supplies.

26 JUNE 1680. This night the French *flibustier* chieftain Grammont mounts an exceptionally daring assault against La Guaira. Slipping ashore with only 47 followers, he infiltrates the city, whose citizens awaken to find it occupied and the garrison commander and 150 soldiers seized without a struggle. Grammont and his *flibustiers* quickly fall to looting before any relief force can arrive from nearby Caracas.

A small Spanish company under Capt. Juan de Laya Mujica escapes capture, marching around to Peñón de Maiquetía (just outside the port) to rally outlying defenders. When word of the freebooter attack reaches Caracas that same morning, there is such widespread concern that mule trains immediately begin traveling inland with the royal treasure and other valuables. Meanwhile every able-bodied militiaman falls in and sets off toward La Guaira under Gov. Francisco de Alberró. Before they arrive, however, Captain de Laya launches his own counterattack, encouraged by the small number of *flibustiers* visible in daylight. Grammont is forced to make a fighting retreat to the beach, during which nine buccaneers are killed and several others wounded—including the commander himself (he is slashed across the neck with a machete).

Even though it is thus repulsed, the raid produces plentiful booty and hostages for the *flibustiers*—and shakes Spanish morale. Grammont's stock soars among the Brethren of the Coast, although it is somewhat diminished when he subsequently loses most of the captives and profits in a shipwreck off Petit Goâve during a hurricane.

7 AUGUST 1680. ***Colônia do Sacramento.*** After massing 480 Argentine troops and 3,000 native auxiliaries around the newly installed Portuguese outpost of Colônia do Sacramento (*see* 20 January 1680), *Maestre de Campo* Antonio de Vera Múxica launches a surprise attack at 2:00 A.M. The attackers succeed in overrunning the outnumbered garrison after four hours' fighting, during which 116 defenders die and the rest are captured, compared to 34 dead and 96 wounded among the Hispano-Indian ranks.

After the captives have been transported into Buenos Aires, a Portuguese relief force of 150 soldiers appears offshore on 20 September aboard the ship of Capt. João Gomes de Sousa. By this time Colônia do Sacramento has already been razed, and the imprisoned Governor Lobo eventually dies of disease on 7 January 1683.

9 AUGUST 1680. ***Pueblo Revolt.*** In Santa Fé (New Mexico), Gov. Antonio de Otermín receives word from three separate village priests that a native uprising has been ordained for Tuesday, 13 August, by the Taos medicine man Popé. This date proves to be false, however, being planted deliberately; Popé's attacks in fact begin at dawn on Sunday, 11 August, when a panic-stricken soldier rides into Santa Fé with word that Indians at nearby Tesuque have donned war paint, killed their priest and a trader, and marched to join the San Juan natives.

De Otermín musters his 50-man garrison, sends out reconnaissance patrols, and distributes arms to every one of Santa Fé's 1,000 able-bodied residents. Over the next three days reports stream in of Spanish ranchers found dead in their fields and of revolts exterminating major settlements. Finally, on Wednesday, 14 August, news arrives of 500 warriors advancing upon Santa Fé, small groups being seen the next day moving through its cornfields. Soon they infiltrate the abandoned dwellings along the city's outskirts, hurling insults from the rooftops.

The governor attempts to parley, but he is rebuffed. He leads a dawn sally on 16 August that drives the Indians back after a furious, day-long fight. The besiegers are then joined by Popé himself, who brings in a large contingent from San Juan, Taos, and Picuries at nightfall. He allows his army's strength to build up over the next two days, launching an all-out assault with 2,500 natives at sunrise on 19 August. By midday the Indians drive the Spaniards back into the governor's palace, away from the water supply. Next day the defenders fight desperately to regain this ground but watch helplessly as Santa Fé burns to the ground during the night.

At dawn on 21 August de Otermín leads a counterattack that pushes Popé's army out of the smoldering ruins, leaving behind 300 dead Indians and 47 prisoners. The Spanish use the respite to quickly evacuate Santa Fé (after hanging the captives), hoping to find sanctuary farther south. They are not safe until they gain El Paso (Texas), their losses reaching 400—including 21 of 33 Franciscan friars.

3 NOVEMBER 1680. Sharpe's buccaneers attempt a landing at Ilo (Peru) and then at Arica the next day, being foiled on both occasions by high seas. Finally, on 6 November he gets 48 men ashore by canoe at Ilo; they easily brush aside the 60 militia riders and infantry sent to challenge them, thus obtaining fresh water and provisions. From the occupied town, Sharpe next probes inland and discovers a small sugar mill, which the locals beg him to spare in exchange for 80 cattle. Sharpe agrees but, five days later, learns that the Spaniards have used the interval to gather 300 riders from the outlying district to drive him and his forces out. He is obliged to retire to his ships the next day—but not before setting fire to the sugar works.

13 DECEMBER 1680. About 35 of Sharpe's freebooters land at Coquimbo (Chile), only to be confronted by 150 Spaniards. The buccaneer commander rushes reinforcements ashore to disperse them, afterwards overrunning the town of La Serena. Following four days of wanton pillaging, the residents offer to raise 95,000 pesos if the raiders leave the buildings intact when they withdraw. Sharpe agrees but finds that the truce had been used by the locals to marshal greater strength. He and his men have to fight hard simply to regain the sea, further discovering that an Indian swam out one night with a combustible raft in an attempt to destroy their anchored ships during their absence.

Sharpe next proceeds to the Juan Fernández Islands, intending to restock *Trinidad* to round the Strait of Magellan and regain the West Indies. His buccaneers, however, wish to continue roving the Pacific, so early in January 1681 they vote him out of office and replace him with John Watling.

30 DECEMBER 1680. Four Dutch frigates—the flagship being the 32-gun *Kurprinz*—and a two-gun fire ship arrive at Port Royal (Jamaica) escorting three small Spanish prizes. Commo. Cornelis Reers bears a commission from Friedrich Wilhelm, elector of Brandenburg, authorizing his 500-man squadron to conduct reprisals in the West Indies for Madrid's unpaid war debts. After remaining at anchor until early February 1681, Reers sets sail on another sweep; he returns to Europe by May.

8 FEBRUARY 1681. Watling leads 90 buccaneers ashore during the night to make another attempt upon Arica (Peru). The raiders draw near at 8:00 A.M. on Sunday (9 February), Watling hoping to subdue the town with one column while Sharpe directs another—armed with grenades—to storm the fortress. The Spaniards are caught sleeping, and Arica is easily penetrated—except for the fort. Nevertheless, the town and its outlying district prove too big, 600–700 militia rallying under *Maestre de Campo* Gaspar de Oviedo. Once recuperated from the initial shock, the Spaniards press the invaders back.

After four hours of intense fighting Watling is killed; 47 buccaneers stagger back aboard ship, having inflicted 24 dead and 60 injured among the Spanish. The buccaneer wounded—all have been left behind in a ransacked church—are slaughtered by the victors (except for two surgeons), and Watling's head is stuck on a pole and paraded grotesquely through the streets of Arica.

The decimated buccaneers restore Sharpe as their commander. After the force touches at Huasco and Ilo for fresh supplies in March, another faction of 50 buccaneers parts company to recross the isthmus of Panama under John Cooke. Sharpe and his remaining 70 hands, aboard *Trinidad,* at last see their luck change, capturing two valuable prizes in July and August.

NOVEMBER 1681. Sharpe attempts to sail out of the Pacific via the Strait of Magellan but, failing to find its entrance in heavy weather, continues as far south as 58 degrees before veering east. He thus becomes the first Englishman to round Cape Horn from the west. Skillfully navigating up the Atlantic out of sight of land, he makes his landfall at Barbados on 7 February 1682, later proceeding to Saint Thomas in the Danish Virgin Islands to dispose of *Trinidad.*

LATE DECEMBER 1681. A 46-man Spanish coastguard piragua boards a foreign interloper off the Laguna de Términos (Mexico), being repelled.

EARLY MAY 1682. In Virginia, the Plant-Cutter Riots erupt, requiring Dep. Gov. Sir Henry Chicheley to call out the militia. Farmers in Gloucester, Middlesex, and New Kent Counties, frustrated over depressed tobacco prices—a problem the local assembly cannot address because of the prolonged absence in England of Gov. Thomas, Lord Culpeper—begin destroying crops (their own and others') in order to drive up prices. Chicheley swiftly arrests a number of ringleaders, eventually executing two of them.

JULY 1682. The 240-ton frigate *Princesa* of Spain's West Indian squadron (the Armada de Barlovento) stands into the Mona Passage out of the northwest, bound from Havana under Capt. Manuel Delgado to deliver 120,000 pesos in Peruvian silver as *situados,* or payrolls, for the Puerto Rico and Santo Domingo garrisons. *Princesa,* its decks cluttered in anticipation of making landfall at Aguada, is surprised by *Tigre* of buccaneer chieftain Laurens de Graaf; 50 of the 250-man Spanish crew are killed or wounded in the ensuing battle. The 140 rovers (mostly French *boucaniers*) repair to Samaná Bay with their prize, releasing the Spanish prisoners toward Cuba aboard a pink while retaining *Princesa* as de Graaf's new flagship.

AUGUST 1682. The French buccaneer Capt. Jean Foccard raids Tampico (Mexico), seizing 30 Spanish captives and slaughtering a large number of cattle before departing.

NOVEMBER 1682. Outraged by the loss of their payrolls (*see* July 1682), the Spaniards of Santo Domingo retaliate by expropriating a consignment of slaves brought in by Nikolaas van Hoorn, another Dutch adventurer with French ties. Furious, van Hoorn escapes three months later with only 20 crewmen remaining aboard his ship *Sint Nicolaas.*

FEBRUARY 1683. The Dutch slaver van Hoorn obtains a letter of reprisal from Jacques Nepveu, sieur de Pouançay and governor of French Saint Domingue (Haiti), to exact vengeance for the expropriation of his slaves by the Spaniards. In order to recruit freebooters for the venture, van Hoorn is put in touch with the veteran *flibustier* Grammont, who comes aboard *Sint Nicolaas* with 300 men. The rovers depart Petit Goâve, steering toward Central America to find de Graaf and his Dutch confederate Michiel Andrieszoon, who are reputedly lying there with two ships, a bark, a sloop, and 500 men.

In the Bay of Honduras, two large Spanish merchantmen—*Nuestra Señora de Consolación* and *Nuestra Señora de Regla*—are seized at anchor while a huge pirate gathering is then celebrated at Roatán on 7 April to discuss a joint assault upon Veracruz. De Graaf and his followers agree on a plan, the privateer fleet shifting to nearby Guanaja Island for further reinforcements; it then scurries north around Yucatán before word of their design can reach Spanish ears. De Graaf leads the way in the captured *Regla,* accompanied by Dutch-born Jan Willems in another Spanish prize; three corsair ships and eight sloops trail astern, out of sight.

MARCH 1683. A French *flibustier* captain named Bréhal, seconded by the English mercenaries John Markham of New York, Thomas Paine, and Conway Wooley—plus Dutch-born Jan Corneliszoon, also of New York—sail from the Bahamas to raid Saint Augustine. They land while flying French colors, only to find the garrison has been forewarned. They withdraw after releasing some Spanish captives they have brought and looting the countryside.

MAY 1683. Two Cuban corsair captains, Gaspar de Acosta and Tomás Uraburru, lead 200 men from Havana toward the Bahamas, attacking the capital of Charles Town (New Providence) with a single piragua and the galliot *Nuestra Señora del Rosario.*

17 MAY 1683. ***Sack of Veracruz.*** This afternoon, de Graaf and Willems approach the Mexican port of Veracruz aboard two Spanish prizes, breaking off after closing within ten miles and determining that the annual plate fleet has not yet arrived. Veracruz's lookouts raise no alarm because they assume them to be a pair

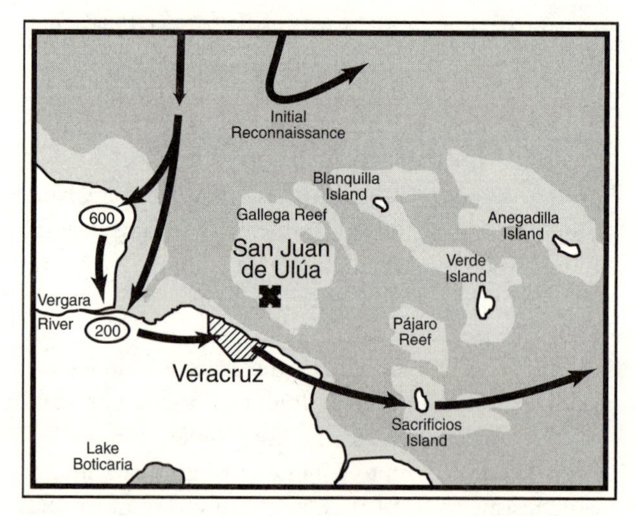

Sack of Veracruz

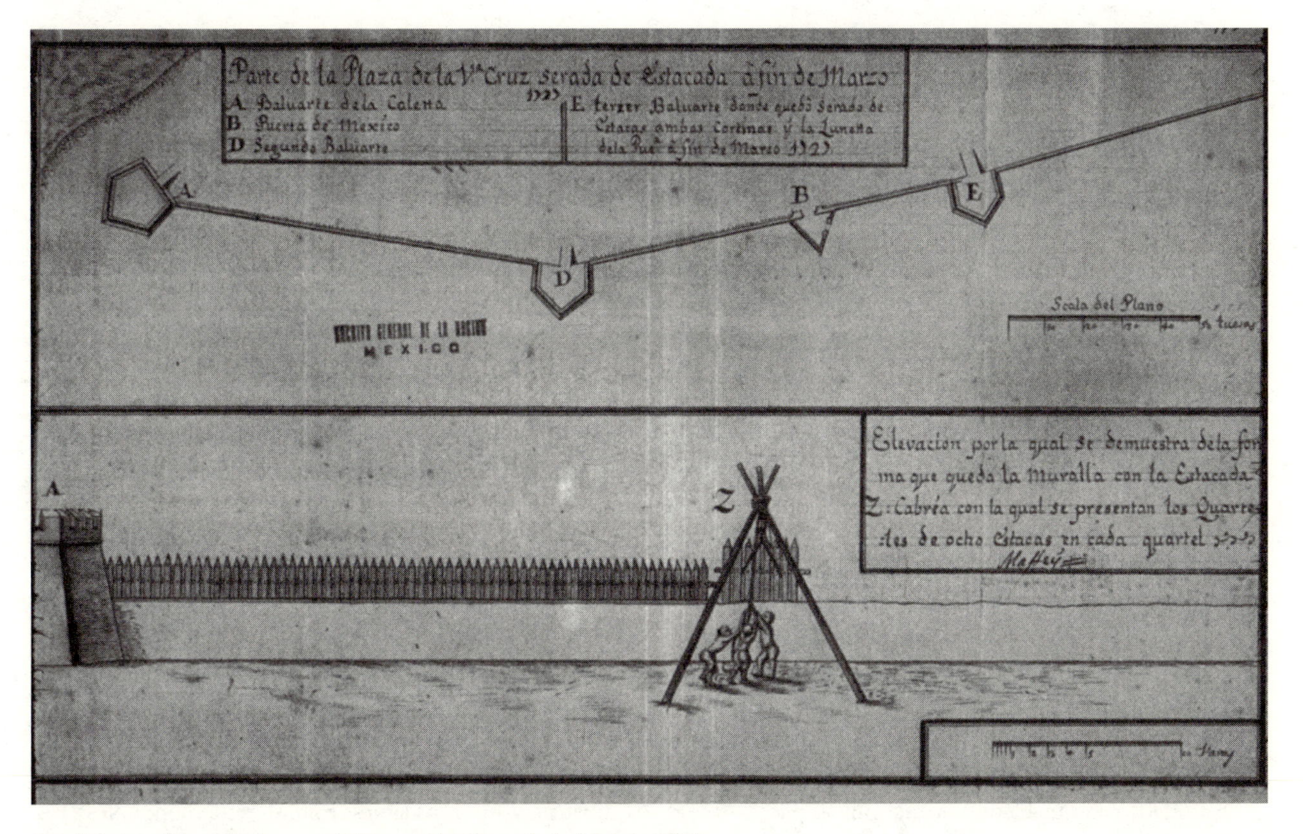

Detailed view of the palisades around Veracruz, plus the method of their installation

of Spanish merchantmen fearful of chancing the shoals after dark. But during the night de Graaf pilots his two vessels close inshore and lands 200 volunteers. While de Graaf leads a reconnaissance of the sleeping city, colleagues Grammont and van Hoorn bring another 600 buccaneers ashore farther away and stealthily march to join him. Veracruz has 6,000 inhabitants; there are 300 regular troops and another 400 civilian militia, with an additional 300 soldiers on the outlying island fortress of San Juan de Ulúa. But Veracruz's landward palisades are low and neglected, with sand dunes drifted up against them; the pirates steal over them and enter the city.

At dawn on 18 May they attack, firing indiscriminately so as to stampede the unprepared Spanish defenders. Within half an hour Veracruz is theirs, several thousand half-dressed captives being herded into the principal church. The city is ransacked during the next four days, and numerous prisoners are tortured to reveal their treasures. De Graaf and Grammont then drive the bulk of their captives down the coast and transfer two miles offshore to Sacrificios Island, beyond rescue. Here the raiders begin loading their booty while waiting for payment of a final ransom out of Mexico's interior.

Shortly after the ransom is received, the *flibustiers* herd 1,500 blacks and mulattos aboard as slaves and weigh. They encounter the annual plate fleet just as they are standing out from the coast, but its admiral, Diego Fernández de Zaldívar, defers combat, allowing the raiders to escape unmolested. The buccaneers pause at Coatzacoalcos to take on water before shouldering their way around Yucatán to Isla Mujeres, where they divide their spoils by late June and disperse.

4 AUGUST 1683. Adm. Andrés de Ochoa y Zárate, commander of Spain's West Indian squadron (Armada de Barlovento), touches at Little Cayman with his 650-ton flagship *Santo Cristo de Burgos;* the 550-ton vice-flag *Nuestra Señora de la Concepción;* the 450-ton *San José, Santa Rosa María y San Pedro de Alcántara;* and the 350-ton *Nuestra Señora de la Soledad.* They seize the tiny French privateer *Prophète Daniel* of Antoine Bernard and *Dauphin* of Pierre d'Orange, thereby learning of the massive assault on Veracruz. The Spanish prize *Nuestra Señora de Regla* is also recuperated, despite having been set ablaze by its captors with 90 slaves on board (who extinguish its flames). Ochoa arrives at Veracruz by 22 August to find it in ruins; a few of his pirate captives are executed on 22 November.

8 AUGUST 1683. At 3:00 P.M., Royal Navy Capt. Charles Carlile passes before Saint Thomas (Char-

lotte Amalie, Danish Virgin Islands) with HMS *Francis,* seeing a large ship inside masquerading as an English man-of-war. Carlile's pilot confirms it to be Jean Hamlin's *Trompeuse,* a 32-gun pirate frigate. *Francis* stands into port, but the pirate ship and the batteries open fire, obliging the frigate to retreat. Carlile sends a letter ashore requesting cooperation from the Danish governor, Adolf Esmit, but that is not secured. The English captain therefore takes *Francis*'s pinnace and another boat into the harbor after nightfall on 9 August with 14 men, who exchange shots with *Trompeuse*'s anchor watch (most of its pirates having already quit Hamlin's service). They flee ashore, leaving the Royal Navy boarders to set fire to *Trompeuse* before withdrawing. It blows up, thereby kindling another large privateer nearby, which also burns to the waterline (Bartholomew Sharpe's *Santísima Trinidad,* abandoned the previous year after his return from the South Seas; *see* November 1681).

With both wrecks smoldering, *Francis* tacks about a league eastward the next morning before sighting a grounded 300-ton Flemish vessel full of pirate stores. Carlile's men cut down its masts and set it ablaze and then return to blockade Saint Thomas; the weather changes a few days later and he is forced to retire to Nevis.

LATE NOVEMBER 1683. The buccaneer chieftain de Graaf and cohorts—Michiel Andrieszoon, Jan Willems, François Le Sage, and several others—arrive near Cartagena to prey upon coastal traffic. When Gov. Juan de Pando Estrada learns the pirates are before his harbor he commandeers the private slavers *San Francisco* of 40 guns, *Paz* of 34, and a 28-gun galliot to chase them away. The trio exits on 23 December manned by 800 soldiers and sailors under a 26-year-old naval captain named Andrés de Pez y Malzarraga.

The seven smaller pirate craft do not flee but instead swarm the Spanish vessels. In the confusion *San Francisco* runs aground, *Paz* strikes after four hours, and Willems takes the galliot. Ninety Spaniards and 20 pirates are killed during the fight. De Graaf refloats *San Francisco* and claims it as his new flagship, renaming it *Fortune* (later *Neptune*); Andrieszoon receives *Paz,* calling it *Mutine;* Willems is given de Graaf's old *Princesa.* On 25 December the triumphant buccaneers deposit their prisoners ashore, along with a message thanking Governor de Pando for the Christmas presents. De Graaf then blockades the port for the next three weeks before standing away northwest toward Roatán and Saint Domingue (Haiti).

19 JANUARY 1684 (O.S.). ***Destruction of New Providence.*** The Cuban corsair Juan de Larco stealthily approaches New Providence (Bahamas) with a pair of *barcos luengos* bearing 200 men. The Spaniards earlier captured a woodcutting sloop off Andros Island and now compel its captain, William Bell, to pilot in via the eastern channel. At daybreak de Larco disembarks 150 men a half-mile outside Charles Town (later Nassau), sending the remainder to board six vessels in the harbor.

The former governor, Robert Clarke, is wounded and captured while leading an English counterattack; his successor, Robert Lilburne, flees the Wheel of Fortune Inn toward the jungle along with most of the other residents. The ten-gun New England frigate *Good Intent,* of Capt. William Warren, and another vessel flee across the bar, leaving the Spaniards to pillage the four remaining vessels while killing three sailors. The attackers then ransack the town, loading their plunder aboard their largest prize while torching the rest of the vessels before sailing away that evening. De Larco hastens to northern Eleuthera, visiting a like treatment upon its largest English settlement before returning to Charles Town soon after to complete his work. This time, most of its buildings are burned, and the Bahamas are left depopulated. Some 200 colonists seek refuge on Jamaica while another 50 from northern Eleuthera temporarily resettle in Casco (Maine), leaving the Bahamas devoid of Englishmen until 1686.

EARLY FEBRUARY 1684. ***Pacific Incursions (Second Wave).*** The 36-gun, 70-man *Bachelor's Delight* of English renegade John Cooke rounds Cape Horn, entering the South Pacific one month later to inaugurate a new round of buccaneer depredations. On 19 March he pursues a sail near Valdivia (Chile), which proves to be yet another interloper: the ship *Nicholas* out of London, commanded by John Eaton. Although intended as a trade mission, Eaton's expedition has quickly taken to plundering, leaving a swathe of destruction down the Brazilian coast (and also raiding the River Plate and capturing a Portuguese prize, subsequently lost in a storm). At the entrance to the strait Eaton has also encountered the 16-gun *Cygnet* of Charles Swan, likewise out of London and bent upon having commerce with South America. Both ships rounded Cape Horn in company then became separated by bad weather.

The piratical Cooke and the dishonest Eaton decide to combine forces, repairing to the Juan Fernández Islands for fresh supplies before heading north on 8 April in hopes of surprising Peruvian coastal traffic.

When they seize a vessel on 3 May bearing timber from Guayaquil to Lima they learn that their presence has been disclosed. (*Cygnet* having entered Valdivia to trade, there Swan warns the Spaniards about other, more hostile Englishmen off their coast. Once their surprise wears off, Valdivia's authorities close the port, killing two of Swan's men and capturing several others.)

Withdrawing to the Lobos de Afuera Islands on 9 February to careen and to revise plans, Cooke and Eaton can only muster 108 men between them. Sighting three sail, they overhaul them the next day; they prove to be Spanish supply ships bearing flour and provisions for Panama. The buccaneers divert them to the remote Galapagos Islands on 31 May, unloading these cargos as a reserve supply.

SPRING 1684. In Europe, Spain declares war against France in retaliation for Louis XIV's continual pressure in the Spanish Netherlands and for the buccaneering raid on Veracruz. However, Madrid's power is so eroded that it cannot launch any major offensives, and Louis has no interest in fighting the Spaniards at this time. Thus, after six months the conflict ends—along with other European tensions—with the August 1684 signing of the 20-year Truce of Ratisbon (Regensburg).

12 JUNE 1684. The English buccaneers Cooke and Eaton proceed north toward New Spain, hoping news of their Pacific depredations has not yet penetrated this far. As they approach the Gulf of Nicoya (Costa Rica) to forage for beef Cooke dies; he is succeeded in command of *Bachelor's Delight* by first mate Edward Davis, who reverses course.

Meanwhile Swan also reaches the Gulf of Nicoya, where on 3 August he meets a small party of West Indian freebooters under Peter Harris (nephew to Coxon's former confederate; *see* 15 April 1680). Harris has sortied from Jamaica on a straightforward raid, crossing the isthmus of Panama via his uncle's old route, sacking Santa María el Real before gaining the ocean, and defeating a Spanish flotilla off Panama's Pearl Islands. Swan's disgruntled crew, tired of his attempts to establish trade with South America, insists on joining Harris's buccaneers in "roving on the account." The luckless merchant captain accedes but insists that *Cygnet*'s owners receive a full share of any prize money. Both commanders steer south.

AUTUMN 1684. Some 100 Scottish Covenanters under Henry Erskine, Lord Cardross, arrive at Port Royal (South Carolina) aboard *Carolina Merchant* to escape persecution in Britain. The region has been depopulated of Spanish natives due to crossborder Indians raids instigated by the English farther north at Charleston. The Scots institute a similar policy—thus antagonizing the Spaniards at Saint Augustine—while also quarreling with their English neighbors over trade questions.

EARLY OCTOBER 1684. Swan and Harris reach Isla de la Plata (Ecuador), encountering Davis's *Bachelor's Delight* and Eaton's *Nicholas.* All four muster nearly 200 men and therefore sail for the South American mainland to attack.

3 NOVEMBER 1684. Davis, Eaton, Harris, and Swan assault Paita (Peru) this morning. Although their landing force overruns it with little difficulty, the raiders find scant booty among the buildings; they put them to the torch. The Lobos de Afuera Islands are visited next; a second abortive raid against Guayaquil follows in December. A few small Spanish vessels are also intercepted, but Davis and company feel their strength is insufficient for any greater enterprise and so veer north toward Panama in hopes of dispatching messages across the isthmus and persuading other buccaneers to join them.

8 JANUARY 1685. Davis's buccaneers intercept the 90-ton *Santa Rosa* before repairing to Panama's Pearl Islands to careen and await reinforcements. On 14 February 200 French *flibustiers* and 80 English buccaneers reach them in canoes under Capt. François Grogniet (alias Chasse-Marée) and another named Lescuyer. Davis offers *Santa Rosa* to the *flibustiers;* the English buccaneers are incorporated into his own *Bachelor's Delight* and Swan's *Cygnet.* Grogniet in turn presents the English commanders with blank privateering commissions from the French governor of Saint Domingue (Haiti). He also informs them that more freebooters are on the way across the isthmus, so that a party can be sent to meet them in the Gulf of San Miguel.

On 3 March a search party meets up with Capt. Francis Townley and 180 more men (mostly English), who are sailing two captured Spanish barks. A few days later another bark bearing about a dozen Englishmen enters the Gulf of Panama from the west, having become separated from yet another interloper—Capt. William Knight—off the coast of New Spain.

11 APRIL 1685. Three French *flibustier* captains—Jean Rose, Pierre Le Picard, and Mathurin Desmarais—

join the buccaneer rendezvous off Isla del Rey (Pearl Islands) with 264 men, having left their ships at Golden Island. The freebooter fleet—now with six vessels and almost 1,000 men—settles down to blockade Panama, hoping to intercept the anticipated treasure fleet out of Peru.

3 JUNE 1685. The Peruvian silver fleet of Lt. Gen. Tomás Palavacino arrives in Panama City, having slipped past the blockaders. His force consists of the 825-ton flagship *San José*—its armament increased from 24 to 40 cannons for this expedition—with a crew of 405 under the veteran Santiago Pontejos; the 825-ton vice-flag *Nuestra Señora de Guadalupe* under Capt. Antonio de Vea, with 36 guns and 374 men; the 26-gun auxiliary *San Lorenzo* under Manuel Pantoja; and a six-gun tender. The armada is further accompanied by the private merchantmen *Nuestra Señora del Pópulo* and *Nuestra Señora del Rosario* (both mounting 20 guns) and a six-gun fire ship. The fleet bears 1,431 men plus stores and arms for Panama's garrison, along with a *situado* of 533,434 pesos and private goods. After delivering their cargo, the men-of-war sally to engage the rovers.

7 JUNE 1685. ***Isla del Rey.*** Toward noon, the Peruvian squadron emerges from a shower to find their enemy lying off Pacheca Island. The buccaneers are unprepared (particularly Grogniet, who has to delay weighing because many of his men are ashore at two small chapels). The raiders have 11 vessels, but only Davis's and Swan's mount artillery, the rest being unarmed Spanish prizes smaller than the six Peruvian men-of-war and one tender. An indecisive, long-range engagement ensues, with the rovers reluctant to close while the bigger armada vessels fear being outmaneuvered and boarded by their more nimble opponents. All afternoon both formations wheel around each other, firing until dark.

This night Palavacino extinguishes and rekindles the lights on his ships, deceiving the freebooters into believing he has shifted position. But it is the Spanish ships that are in good order next morning, whereas the privateers are scattered, the mutual pursuit resuming. The day ends with a Spanish victory, the raiders being driven off west toward Coiba Island, their Panamanian blockade ended. The buccaneers then have a falling out along national lines, each group blaming the other for the defeat.

EARLY JULY 1685. The Anglo-French buccaneer companies of Davis, Swan, and Grogniet attack Remedios (Panama), after which English and French contingents continue northwest as separate groups.

6 JULY 1685. ***Sack of Campeche.*** This afternoon six large and four small privateer ships, six sloops, and 17 piraguas under de Graaf and Grammont appear a half-dozen miles off the Mexican port of Campeche. Some 700 buccaneers begin rowing in toward shore, but four Spanish militia companies (200 men) exit the town and position themselves opposite the intended disembarkation point, prompting the invaders to put up their helms. All night they remain bobbing upon the swell, until next morning the boats begin to draw off toward their ships, which are standing in to meet them.

The rescue proves to be a feint, however, for before the defenders can react the buccaneer boats change course and come storming ashore at the outskirts of Campeche itself. Some 100 rovers form up behind Captain Rettechard as the vanguard; 200 join de Graaf and march directly toward the city center; another 200 advance under Jean Foccard along a street parallel to de Graaf; the final 200 follow Grammont in an encircling maneuver. The Spaniards fall back; out in the harbor Capt. Cristóbal Martínez de Acevedo prepares to scuttle his coast-guard frigate *Nuestra Señora de la Soledad* according to instructions. He originally intended to bore holes in the bottom, but given the speed of the invaders' advance he now directs his boatswain to run a trail of powder into the magazine, lighting the fuse from his frigate's boat. *Soledad* explodes so mightily that it collapses the defenders' morale, sending them scurrying back into their citadel, and the freebooters enter Campeche uncontested.

Over the next few days isolated strongpoints are subdued until only the citadel remains. The rovers begin bombarding the fortress at dawn on 12 July, only to be interrupted at 10:00 A.M. when two Spanish relief columns, having hastened down from Mérida de Yucatán, appear on the beach. In the past such an appearance would force smaller bands of raiders back to sea; this time, however, the freebooters stand and fight from behind Campeche's ramparts—and the first ranks of Spaniards go down to well-aimed volleys. All day the two sides battle, until Grammont circles behind the Yucatán militia and catches them between two fires. The Spanish relief force draws off in disarray, and after nightfall Campeche's disheartened garrison mutinies. By 11 P.M. the citadel is deserted, and a couple of English prisoners admit the besiegers.

Grammont organizes troops of mounted buccaneers to reconnoiter and ravage the surrounding countryside as far as 25 miles inland. But 250 rovers are defeated at Hampolol by 300 Spaniards under 44-year-old *Maestre de Campo* Juan Antonio Chacón, effectively putting an end to such forays. Nevertheless, the invaders remain in possession of Campeche for the next two months even though little plunder is obtained, as most of the wealth was withdrawn prior to the assault. Captives are threatened with death if ransoms are not forthcoming, yet Yucatán Gov. Juan Bruno Téllez de Guzmán—headquartered at Hecelchakán—prohibits any payments. Finally, on 25 August Grammont's *flibustiers* celebrate Louis XIV's feast day and the next morning begin preparations to break camp. A message is sent inland demanding 80,000 pesos and 400 cattle to leave Campeche's buildings intact; Téllez de Guzmán's rejection so infuriates Grammont that he torches the houses the next dawn; he then sends another missive inland threatening the captives.

Again he is rebuffed, so on 28 August he parades his prisoners in the main square and begins executions. De Graaf intervenes after a half-dozen deaths; after a long discussion the brutality stops and the pirates retire, pausing briefly at Sisal before rounding Yucatán for Isla Mujeres to divide their loot. The *flibustier* fleet eventually disperses, de Graaf sailing for Petit Goâve (Haiti) with his heavy-laden *Neptune,* Pierre Bot's *Nuestra Señora de Regla,* and three other vessels. Grammont's *Hardi,* a captured Spanish galliot under Nicolas Brigaut, and a sloop make for Roatán to careen.

2 AUGUST 1685. Having been advised at Cartagena of Campeche's occupation, Admiral Ochoa sorties with his flagship *Santo Cristo de Burgos;* the vice-flag *Concepción;* the 335-ton *Nuestra Señora del Honhón;* and the eight-gun sloop *Jesús, María y José* (alias *Sevillano*) to punish the raiders. The Spaniards check the Cayman Islands before touching at Trujillo (Honduras) on 17 August, then inspect Roatán shortly thereafter, finding it uninhabited. Ochoa returns to Trujillo for provisions before resuming his course north on 8 September.

EARLY AUGUST 1685. In the Pacific, Grogniet refuses to join his English colleagues Davis and Swan in raiding León (Nicaragua), so the pair proceeds independently, netting little booty. Meanwhile the French commander takes 120 men in five boats for a repeat attempt against Remedios (Panama), being repulsed. He rejoins his remaining 200 men aboard *Santa Rosa* by 3 September.

11 SEPTEMBER 1685. ***Alacrán Reef.*** At dawn, Ochoa's Spanish warships chase five sail near Isla Mujeres (Mexico). Two of them lag behind and are captured; they prove to be Pierre Bot's 22-gun prize *Nuestra Señora de Regla* and a sloop—both bearing spoils from Campeche. In their company is de Graaf's *Neptune,* which the Spaniards desperately wish to overtake. Having lost sight of that prey while securing Bot's prize and scuttling the sloop, the Spaniards spot more sails to the northwest at 2:00 P.M. the following day. Ochoa sends *Honhón* and *Sevillano* to investigate, and they recognize the largest of the vessels as de Graaf's. *Honhón* shadows the pirate chieftain while *Sevillano* returns to inform the admiral.

Honhón loses contact at nightfall and, the next morning, makes for Veracruz. *Sevillano,* however, finds Ochoa's flagship and vice-flag, leading them toward de Graaf. At 4:00 P.M. on 13 September they spot him within the Gulf of Mexico east of Alacrán Reef; both Spanish men-of-war gradually close upon the heavily laden corsair. Enjoying both the weather gauge and a two-to-one superiority, Ochoa commences fighting at dawn on 14 September despite being so infirm as to be lying under an awning upon his quarterdeck. De Graaf fights his ship brilliantly, outmaneuvering and outshooting the Spaniards until dark.

The flagship then hails Vice Adm. Antonio de Astina aboard *Concepción* to advise him that Ochoa has been given last rites—and that command of the armada is now his. Next morning de Graaf's *Neptune* is seen to windward, bearing away, and the battered Armada gives up. *Santo Cristo*'s weakened superstructure falls overboard; Ochoa dies two days later. De Astina limps back to Veracruz with his four vessels the night of 28–29 September, being court-martialled for his failure.

1 NOVEMBER 1685. Grogniet and his *boucaniers* enter Realejo (Nicaragua), finding it and its surrounding countryside devastated by an earlier English assault; they obtain little booty. Reversing course, the French then hesitate to march inland and sack Esparta (Costa Rica) on 9 December, instead pressing on into the Gulf of Chiriquí toward the end of the year.

9 JANUARY 1686. Grogniet's *flibustiers* capture Chiriquita (Panama), abandoning it a week later.

5 MARCH 1686. Grogniet's men approach Remedios (Panama) at night to forage for food and are ambushed by a small Spanish frigate, a *barco luengo,* and a piragua, suffering more than 30 casualties. They then roam west once more, anchoring off Esparta by 19 March and sighting Townley's flotilla four days later.

MARCH 1686. ***Valladolid Raid.*** From the Gulf of Honduras, de Graaf leads seven freebooter ships into Ascensión Bay (modern-day Emiliano Zapata Bay, Yucatán), disembarking 500 buccaneers who march inland against Tihosuco, which is abandoned by its terrified Spanish citizens before it can be ransacked and burned. De Graaf then penetrates deeper toward Valladolid; by the time his rovers come within a half-dozen miles, only 36 men are left to defend it. Inexplicably, de Graaf gives the order to return to the coast without attempting an assault. By April he and his followers reemerge into Ascensión Bay, soon thereafter retiring toward Roatán.

7 APRIL 1686. ***Sack of Granada.*** Despite some residual ill will, Townley's and Grogniet's groups combine for an attempt against Granada (Nicaragua), landing 345 men, who fight their way into the city three days later. Little plunder is found, for the Spaniards, forewarned, have transferred their valuables to Zapatera Island; the pirates withdraw empty-handed five days later. They weather numerous ambushes before passing Masaya and regaining their ships, after which they travel to Realejo.

Having enjoyed limited success thus far, half of Grogniet's followers vote on 9 June to join Townley in his eastward progression toward Panama. The remaining 148 *flibustiers* remain with Grogniet while he sails west; he operates for a time in the Gulf of Fonseca until a majority of his men again vote to quit his command. Those 85 sail *Santa Rosa* northwest toward New Spain and California in hopes of waylaying the Manila galleon; Grogniet retraces his course down Central America with 60 followers aboard three piraguas.

MID-APRIL 1686. Pierre, Chevalier de Troyes, departs Montréal with 70 voyageurs and 30 soldiers aboard 35 canoes to capture the English furring outposts in Hudson Bay, which are diverting trade from France's Compagnie Du Nord.

30 APRIL 1686. Grammont's 180-man *Hardi,* Brigaut's captured Spanish galliot, and a buccaneer sloop appear off Florida, bent upon attacking Saint Augustine. In order to gather intelligence, Brigaut's galliot advances alone toward Matanzas, flying false Spanish colors, while Grammont's flagship and sloop remain concealed farther south awaiting the scout's return. But Brigaut wrecks in heavy weather and fails to reappear, so Grammont sails toward Matanzas three days later only to be driven north by the same storm; the ship is lost with all hands.

LATE JUNE 1686. After an 85-day trek through 800 miles of wilderness, Pierre de Troyes's expedition arrives opposite Moose Fort (modern Moose Factory, Ontario), an English trading outpost in James Bay. Its 17 residents are caught completely by surprise and surrender, as do the inhabitants of Charles Fort on 3 July.

4 JULY 1686. Two Royal Navy frigates from Jamaica—Charles Talbot's *Falcon* and Thomas Spragge's *Drake*—catch the English renegade Joseph Bannister careening his 30-gun *Golden Fleece* near Samaná Bay, along with a small prize. The corsair has two batteries mounted ashore and fights the English frigates as they work in as close as the water will allow while beating *Golden Fleece* to pieces. *Drake* suffers 13 casualties and *Falcon* ten before they run out of ammunition. The English captains return to Port Royal by early July and are censured for not destroying both of Bannister's craft. They rearm and go back, discovering the renegade has torched *Golden Fleece* and sailed away in his prize.

6 JULY 1686. In Europe, the League of Augsburg is formed by Austria, Sweden, Spain, Bavaria, Saxony, and the Palatinate for protection against the aggressive Louis XIV of France.

22 JULY 1686. In the Pacific, Townley's buccaneers make a sudden descent upon the outskirts of Panama City, seizing merchandise reportedly worth 1.5 million pesos; it is subsequently lost thanks to a Spanish counterambush. Nonetheless, the raiders make off with 15,000 pesos in silver and 300 captives, who Townley uses to extort a truce.

After two heads are sent to the president of the *audiencia* of Panama he reluctantly agrees to supply the pirates with cattle, sheep, and flour on a daily basis. Meanwhile Townley threatens to send another 50 heads ashore if five buccaneers in Spanish hands are not released; an uneasy peace ensues.

25 JULY 1686. Using the captured English ship *Craven,* Pierre de Troyes's 25-year-old lieutenant, Pierre Le Moyne d'Iberville et d'Ardillières, attacks Albany Fort—the last remaining English outpost in Bottom of the Bay (James Bay, Ontario)—whose governor, Henry Sergeant, capitulates after a brief bombardment. The French rename it Fort Sainte Anne (Charles Fort becomes Fort Saint Jacques and Moose Fort becomes Fort Saint Louis); de Troyes installs d'Iberville as new governor with 40 followers then

withdraws to Montréal with the remainder of his forces in August.

22 AUGUST 1686. The Spaniards attempt a surprise attack against Townley's buccaneers by slipping three ships and 240 men out of Perico Island (Panama) to fall upon the raiders while they rest. The assault is fiercely beaten off; two of the Spanish ships are captured and only 65 Spaniards escape injury or death.

A furious Townley, himself wounded in the exchange, sends 20 more heads ashore to protest this violation of the truce. The Spanish promptly deliver an additional 10,000 pesos to the buccaneers on 4 September, along with a conciliatory note from the archbishop of Panama, saying all English prisoners will henceforth be considered Catholics and so enjoy protection from the church. But Townley does not have long to savor his victory, for he dies of his wounds four days later. His body is cast overboard in accordance with his wishes near Otoque Island; he is succeeded in command by George Hout (or Hutt).

AUGUST 1686. A galley and two piraguas bearing 100 Spaniards out of Saint Augustine, plus native allies and mulattoes, descend upon the new Scottish establishment at Port Royal (South Carolina). Its settlers have been reduced to 25 able-bodied men because of disease and want, so are easily overrun, the capital of Stuart's Town being destroyed.

The Spaniards then range north to the Edisto, plundering plantations (including those of English Gov. Joseph Morton and his secretary, Paul Grimball). The raiders are eventually prevented from assaulting Charleston by a hurricane, which destroys two vessels and drowns Capt. Tomás de León, obliging the remainder to retire toward Saint Augustine. The English wish to retaliate by commissioning two French privateers but are forbidden from doing so by the newly arrived Gov. James Colleton.

16 NOVEMBER 1686. An agreement is struck between James II of England and Louis XIV of France to restrict the activities of buccaneers in the New World. Three days later they also sign the so-called Neutrality Pact to settle their conflicting claims over Hudson Bay (Canada).

LATE NOVEMBER 1686. A squadron of Biscayan privateers—known collectively as the Vizcaíno or Guipúzcoa squadron—arrives in the West Indies under Commo. Francisco de Aguirre, their recruitment having been approved by Madrid to supplement the ineffectual patrols of the Armada de Barlovento:

Ship	*Guns*	*Tons*	*Men*	*Commander*
Nuestra Señora del Rosario y las Animas (flag)	34	250	180	José de Leoz y Echalar
San Nicolás de Bari (vice-flag)	24	200	142	Martín Pérez de Landeche
Nuestra Señora de la Concepción	?	140	66	Sebastián Pisón
San Antonio	?	60	36	Silvestre Soler
Santiago (32-oar galliot)	?	30	53	Fermín de Salaberría

Unfortunately, the activities of this formation also prove disappointing; no pirates and only a few foreign merchantmen are detained during their four-year service.

23 JANUARY 1687. Grogniet rediscovers Townley's contingent (now commanded by Hout) in the Gulf of Nicoya; after ravaging the area for a month they weigh together for a surprise attack against Guayaquil.

7 FEBRUARY 1687. Capt. Thomas Spragge enters Port Royal (Jamaica) with the English renegade Joseph Bannister and his accomplices—captured on the Mosquito Coast—dangling from HMS *Drake*'s yardarms.

9 MARCH 1687. Governor de Cussy of Saint Domingue (Haiti) issues a decree commanding all French *flibustiers* to cease their depredations against Spanish targets in the New World.

MAY 1687. In Veracruz, the crews of Spain's West Indian squadron (Armada de Barlovento) riot over back pay, idleness, and the arrival of competing Biscayan privateers. Some 200 Armada sailors and marines desert en masse, the rest being put down with three fatalities.

17 JUNE 1687. Gov. Jacques Denonville of New France departs Montréal to lead an expedition of 800 soldiers, 1,100 militia, and 400 native allies against the Seneca Indians. After they ravage this territory throughout July—so as to prevent the Iroquois and English from taking control of its lucrative fur trade—Fort Niagara is erected on Seneca land, only to be abandoned and demolished by 15 September 1688 because of Iroquois threats.

3 NOVEMBER 1687. A raid by 100–200 Iroquois warriors is repelled by the French garrison at Fort Chambly (Quebec).

2 JANUARY 1688. After skirmishing with some Peruvian privateers in the Gulf of Fonseca, the French rover Picard scuttles his ships and leads 260 *flibustiers* inland to regain the Caribbean. They brush aside weak Spanish-American resistance, proceeding into the central highlands and constructing rafts at the Coco River's headwaters to glide downstream; they emerge at Cape Gracias a Dios by 9 March.

28 JULY 1688. Some 60 Dutch soldiers mutiny at Fort Zeelandia (Suriname), killing the hated 41-year-old Gov. Cornelis Aerssen van Sommelsdijk with more than 50 shots. The number of mutineers soon swells to 140–150; the disgruntled men elect their own leaders, disarm the local militia, and seize two ships in the roadstead in anticipation of sailing away. Unity collapses and eventually they are compelled to surrender.

KING WILLIAM'S WAR (1688–1697)

IN EUROPE, MEGALOMANIACAL LOUIS XIV OF FRANCE invades contested areas of the Palatinate in September 1688, escalating tensions on the Continent. In England, the Protestant Dutch rulers William, Prince of Orange, and his wife, Mary Stuart, land on 15 November, overthrowing the unpopular pro-Catholic James II in a bloodless coup known as the Glorious Revolution. Come December Louis declares war against Holland; the following April he declares war against Spain as well.

On 12 May 1689, England and the Netherlands join other members of the League of Augsburg to form the so-called Grand Alliance against France; within six weeks fighting breaks out between Louis and William, a conflict that takes nine years to run its course. (For these reasons, the hostilities become known to history as King William's War, the War of the League of Augsburg, the War of the Grand Alliance, or the Nine Years War.)

SUMMER 1688. The English adventurer Thomas Hewetson attempts to beat his way through the Strait of Magellan with his 50-gun flagship *Lion* and two other vessels to found a settlement on the Pacific Coast of South America. He is eventually forced to retreat and, months later, limps into Tobago.

AUGUST 1688. A buccaneer sloop and piragua anchor off Barra de Dos Bocas (Tabasco, Mexico), sending 20 men up the Seco River to raid Chontalpa; they are defeated while retiring.

SEPTEMBER 1688. The private English frigates *Churchill* of 18 guns and *Yonge,* bearing 85 men under Adm. William Bond and Capt. John Marsh, arrive to reconquer the fur-trading outposts in Hudson Bay (*see* 25 July 1686). They blockade Le Moyne d'Iberville's 16-man frigate *Soleil d'Afrique* inside the Albany River; all then become icebound. Over the coming winter the French starve their opponents into submission; 25 Englishmen die from scurvy and exposure, another three due to combat.

NOVEMBER 1688. A junior French naval captain—the 42-year-old Huguenot and former slaver Jean Baptiste Ducasse—leads a volunteer force from Cayenne in an unsuccessful assault against Dutch Suriname. The latter defend Fort Zeelandia with 69 soldiers, 84 Jewish volunteers, and 78 Dutch militia under the newly installed Gov. Johan van Scharphuysen, compelling the attackers to withdraw out to sea.

28 JANUARY 1689. A French expedition departs Trois Rivières (Quebec) to attack British settlements along the borders with New England.

7 MARCH 1689. Louis's declaration of war against Holland is promulgated on Martinique and is enthusiastically endorsed by *flibustiers* and colonists alike.

28 MARCH 1689. Three French ships, a brigantine, a bark, and three lesser vessels quit Martinique under Governor-General de Blénac and Intendant Dumaitz de Goimpy, pausing at Guadeloupe to add another ship, then another three barks and three brigantines at Saint Kitts. His strength eventually raised to 17 sail and 1,200 men, Blénac steers toward Sint Eustatius to fall upon that Dutch colony by surprise.

3 APRIL 1689. ***Destruction of Sint Eustatius.*** Governor-General de Blénac appears off the island of Sint Eustatius, catching its tiny Dutch garrison completely unprepared. A couple of ships manage to flee out to sea with valuables, but otherwise the outnumbered defenders under Gov. Lucas Schorer can only watch the French approach. De Blénac, Col. François de Collart, and Pierre Du Buc bring one contingent ashore at Interlopers Cove (facing Saint Kitts) while

François Le Vassor circles round to the windward side and lands an even larger detachment at Pointe Blanche. The Dutch contest de Blénac's disembarkation from the cliff tops, wounding both the colonel and Du Buc before being outflanked and chased back into Fort Orange in the evening, leaving 20 dead and wounded upon the field.

Early next morning Le Vassor's small army arrives overland and joins de Blénac's detachment, after which siege guns are landed at de Goimpy's behest to be used against the Dutch citadel. The French call upon Schorer to surrender, and he agrees. In the articles of capitulation, de Blénac orders Sint Eustatius evacuated, sending its colonists toward Nevis; all shore establishments on Sint Eustatius are destroyed, booty is gathered, and a tiny 40-man French garrison is installed under Joseph d'Honon de Gallifet. (Schorer, however, proceeds only as far as Sabá, awaiting relief.)

17 MAY 1689. In Europe, William III of England officially declares war against France.

27 JULY 1689. ***Capture of Saint Kitts.*** Having learned of the outbreak of Anglo-French hostilities thanks to a swift transatlantic crossing by the dispatch vessel *Perle* under Captain Chevalier d'Arbouville, Governor-General de Blénac sails from Martinique with the recently arrived warships *Hasardeux, Émerillon, Loire, Dauphine,* and *Cheval Marin* plus 14 merchantmen and 23 sloops. He appears off Basseterre (capital of the French half of Saint Kitts) to lead its residents in a preemptive strike against their English neighbors. His army dashes ashore and quickly overruns the southern part of the island, driving the English governor, Col. Thomas Hill, and 400–500 defenders inside Fort Charles at Old Road Town. The structure, although built of stone on a high cliff, is old and not very formidable, having few guns, no moat, and gently sloping walls. Nevertheless, Blénac institutes a formal siege, digging an approach trench while his ten-gun land battery and warships patiently bombard the gate, expending more than 1,000 heavy rounds to little effect.

After two weeks of fruitless firing, the naval officer Ducasse—in command of 120 *flibustiers*—convinces de Blénac that another battery should be installed atop an adjacent hill that overlooks the fort's interior. The governor-general finally accedes, and during the night of 14–15 August Ducasse's men drag six heavy pieces to the summit. Next morning they open fire, and the besieged surrender once they find their counterfire cannot reach the peak. All English colonists are ordered evacuated to Nevis; their Irish-Catholic vassals are given their freedom, and Charles de Peychpeyrou Comminge, Chevalier de Guitaud is installed as governor of Saint Kitts. Ten days later de Blénac sails toward Martinique, leaving de Goimpy to wind up affairs.

5 AUGUST 1689. The town of Lachine (near Montréal, Canada) is surprised and overrun by 1,500 Iroquois warriors—allies of the English—who kill two dozen residents and carry off another 90 into captivity.

24 AUGUST 1689. Sir Timothy Thornhill reaches Antigua from England with a regiment of 800 men.

13 NOVEMBER 1689. The town of La Chènage (near Montréal, Canada) is attacked by an Iroquois war party; several settlers are killed.

EARLY DECEMBER 1689. Laurens de Graaf sorties from Saint Domingue (Haiti) with a *flibustier* flotilla to descend on Jamaica. Eight to ten English sloops are taken off the northern shore, and disembarkations are made to plunder plantations. Port Royal's trade is consequently embargoed, and Capt. Thomas Spragge's HMS *Drake* is sent with some auxiliaries to drive the intruders away. The embargo is not lifted until late May 1690.

DECEMBER 1689. ***Leisler's Revolt.*** In New York City, a 54-year-old German-born trader named Jacob Leisler—inspired by the deposition of James II of England—leads a group of rebels who seize Fort James and vow to hold it until a new governor arrives, appointed by William and Mary. For the next several months, Leisler assumes the mantle of governor, even convening an intercolonial congress in May 1690 to plan concerted action against the French and Indians.

26 DECEMBER 1689. ***Thornhill's Counteroffensive.*** On orders from Sir Christopher Codrington (new governor-general for the English Leeward Islands), Thornhill sets sail to attack the French on Saint Martin and Saint Barthélemy and thereby secure the meat supply for beleaguered Nevis. The first island proves too difficult to assault, but Saint Barthélemy is easily overrun, with 600–700 prisoners taken.

EARLY 1690. Captain Martín de Rivas departs Veracruz with 190 men aboard two Spanish galliots (being reinforced off Coatzacoalcos by another 110 men aboard a pair of piraguas from Tabasco and Campeche) to attack the foreign logwood cutters in the Laguna de

Términos. His operation begins promisingly, two sloops being captured six miles from its entrance. But other Baymen resist vigorously from behind tree barricades when the Spaniards come ashore in the afternoon, compelling them to withdraw the next day; de Rivas is mortally wounded.

9 JANUARY 1690. The English rover Hewetson (*see* summer 1688) arrives off Marie Galante with three ships, two sloops, and more than 400 men, armed with a privateering commission from Governor-General Codrington. Among Hewetson's captains is the Scottish-born William Kidd, who commands the 20-gun *Blessed William* with 80–90 men. The English plunder the tiny French outpost over the next five days before returning to Nevis.

MID-JANUARY 1690. On Saint Barthélemy, Thornhill—encouraged by his easy success in conquering and holding this place for three weeks—decides to make a second attempt against Saint Martin. Arriving off that island, he detaches some men under Capt. Walter Hamilton to disembark on the windward side and distract the 300 defenders while he brings the main body ashore to leeward and marches across to take the enemy from the rear.

About two miles inland Thornhill encounters a two-gun French breastwork where the defenders make a stand. It takes a couple of days for the English to dislodge them (they bring artillery across the island from their ships to demolish this position). The French then retreat into a tiny, six-gun fort, only to be quickly driven out and dispersed into the jungle. Two to three days of fighting ensue. When French resolve is about to collapse, Ducasse appears offshore with a relief force of three ships, a brigantine, and a sloop, bearing 700 men.

Thornhill now finds the roles reversed, his own forces scrambling to fend off the French disembarkation. Ducasse scatters the anchored English vessels, captures one, and next midday lands several hundred men and guns. The reinvigorated French defense recaptures the little fort and crowds Thornhill's small army into a defensive position. Three days later a further trio of French ships appears from Saint Kitts with 500 men, seriously complicating Thornhill's predicament.

JANUARY 1690. ***Hewetson's Rescue.*** Having returned to Nevis after ransacking Marie Galante, Hewetson's privateers are hurried out again by Governor-General Codrington to rescue Thornhill's expedition on Saint Martin. Hewetson recaptures an English sloop en route, gaining valuable intelligence as to French dispositions. Arriving off Saint Martin at daybreak, Hewetson's 50-gun *Lion,* Kidd's 20-gun *Blessed William,* and another English ship are immediately challenged by Ducasse's five men-of-war, which slip their cables and stand out to engage. Both squadrons pass each other at least twice in line-of-battle formation, exchanging broadsides before Hewetson closes and attempts to board. Ducasse sheers off, allowing his opponents to contact Thornhill ashore; they urge the English general to gather his troops for reembarkation. Before that can be accomplished, however, Ducasse returns, outmaneuvering the English squadron and anchoring opposite their chosen embarkation point.

Next morning Hewetson's force bears down to fight again, but Ducasse retires northwest toward Anguilla, leaving Thornhill's men and artillery to be freely evacuated and restored to Nevis the following day. Despite the successful operation, the English freebooters are unhappy at being used in a set-piece battle—at high risk and no profit. When Kidd goes ashore on 12 February his crew makes off with *Blessed William.* Hewetson soon thereafter quits the crown service as well, transferring to Barbados.

LATE JANUARY 1690. Stung by criticisms of his conduct of West Indian affairs by de Goimpy, Ducasse, Guitaud, and Gémosat, Governor-General de Blénac resigns his office and returns to France aboard *Pont d'Or* seeking vindication. He is temporarily replaced by François d'Alesso, Marquis d'Eragny, who is appointed in Paris on 1 May.

18 FEBRUARY 1690. Around midnight, 114 Canadian militia and 96 Indian allies under Nicolas d'Ailleboust, sieur de Manthet, and Jacques Le Moyne de Sainte Hélène slip into the English settlement of Corlaer (Schenectady, New York), attacking two hours before dawn. Some 60 inhabitants are slaughtered, another 25 captured; 50 are spared. The victors withdraw the same day with 50 horses loaded with plunder but are overtaken almost within sight of Montréal by Mohawk warriors, losing 18 stragglers.

20 FEBRUARY 1690. The private English salvor John Strong enters the Strait of Magellan with his 270-ton ship *Welfare,* of 40 guns and 90 men, supposedly to trade with South America. Actually he hopes to work the wreck of the 900-ton *Jesús María de la Limpia Concepción* (the flagship of Peru's Armada del Mar del Sur that went down off Puná Island the

night of 26 October 1654 with millions of silver pesos aboard). Despite Britain's alliance with Spain, Strong's first contacts prove hostile. By 20 August *Welfare* reaches Puná, where Strong learns the location of the wreck; he anchors over the spot by 7 September. However, he is unable to find any trace of remains and so stands away toward the Juan Fernández Islands, where on 21 October he rescues four English buccaneers marooned three years earlier. *Welfare* then continues down Chile, suffering 11 killed when one of Strong's landing parties is slaughtered in the surf by Spanish lancers. The English eventually return through the strait, heading north toward the Caribbean.

28 MARCH 1690. Two months after departing Trois Rivières (Quebec) under Joseph François Hertel de La Fresnière, a party of 25 French-Canadian militia, 20 Sokoki, and five Algonquian warriors mounts a three-pronged dawn attack against Fort Rollinsford and its adjacent English settlement of Salmon Falls (near modern-day Portsmouth, New Hampshire). At a cost of two killed and one captured, the raiders slay 30 residents and capture 54 within the next two hours before razing all its buildings and departing with much booty.

While retiring toward Canada, Hertel finds himself pursued by more than 100 English militia, so he ambushes them at a narrow bridge over the Wooster River, slaying another score.

MARCH 1690. The deposed James II lands in Ireland at the head of a French army, hoping to reclaim his throne from William and Mary. The action gives heart to his adherents in the New World—a distinct minority—but also spreads unease among England's American colonies. Eventually, Londonderry withstands a prolonged siege by James's army. William defeats him on 11 July at the Battle of the Boyne, and James is forced back to France.

3 MAY 1690. ***Acadian Campaign.*** New England's 40-year-old provost marshal, Sir William Phips, acting on his own responsibility, impresses the private vessels *Six Friends, Swan, Mary, Porcupine, Union, Mary Ann, Lark,* and *Bachelor* for a raid against French Acadia (Nova Scotia). Approximately 500 draftees are taken aboard the vessels at Nantasket, raising total strength to 700 men; they put to sea again five days later.

On 10 May the expedition anchors off Mount Desert and, the next day, attempts to bear down upon the French within Penobscot Fort, only to see the wind die away. It is not until the following day that the New Englanders get ashore; upon attacking the fort at dawn on 14 May, they find it deserted. Reinforcements from Salem and Ipswich subsequently join Phips's expedition; together they plunder the settlement of Passamequoddy on 16 May. Three days later they capture Port Royal (modern-day Annapolis Royal) without resistance. Phips returns to Boston by 30 May (O.S.).

21 MAY 1690. Commo. Lawrence Wright reaches Barbados, escorting a large merchant convoy with his 62-gun flagship *Mary;* the 54-gun *Foresight;* the 48-gun *Assistance, Bristol,* and *Jersey;* the 46-gun *Antelope, Hampshire,* and *Tiger;* the 28-gun frigates *Guernsey* and *Swan;* the ten-gun fire ships *Saint Paul* and *Richard & John;* plus the ketch *Quaker.* His crews are very sick, so Wright cannot join Governor-General Codrington at Antigua until 10 June.

An expedition is then marshaled at Nevis over the next couple of weeks from all surrounding English islands, eventually comprising 700 men from the Duke of Bolton's Regiment, 500 from Thornhill's, 400 from Antigua, 300 from Montserrat, 600 from Nevis, 400 marines, plus 100 of Codrington's "captain general's guard." This force is delegated to recover Saint Kitts, so that by evening of 29 June ten men-of-war, two Royal Navy fire ships, and 20 island brigantines and sloops get under way.

EARLY JUNE 1690. In the Caymans, Laurens de Graaf captures a coast-guard sloop out of Jamaica, learning that the English are contemplating a joint operation with the Spaniards of Santo Domingo against French Saint Domingue (Haiti). De Graaf immediately carries warning to Governor de Cussy, arriving before mid-June.

29 JUNE 1690. On Saint Domingue, Governor de Cussy leads 400 militia cavalry, 450 buccaneers, and 150 blacks through the Plains of Artibonite toward the Spanish frontier town of Santiago de los Caballeros. After a lengthy march through the jungle the French are ambushed on 5 July within a mile and a half of the objective, the rearguard suffering more than 40 killed before the Spaniards can be driven off. Santiago is occupied the next day but is found empty; Cussy burns it to the ground and retires by 7 July. He reaches Artibonite on 14 July and disbands his army the next day.

30 JUNE 1690. ***Reconquest of Saint Kitts.*** At 1:00 A.M., a large expedition appears before Frigate Bay,

south of the island's French capital of Basseterre. Governor de Guitaud has been forewarned of the English plan, so he deploys 1,000 troops in trenches opposite the beach to dispute Codrington's disembarkation. At sunrise, the English governor-general orders his troops to remain aboard while a naval bombardment is made. It is unable to dislodge the defense—Capt. Richard Kegwin of HMS *Assistance* dies during the action—so toward evening Codrington alters tactics; overnight he stealthily sets 600 men ashore south of Frigate Bay at Petite Saline, under Thornhill and Gov. Nathaniel Blakiston of Montserrat. The governor-general assists this flanking maneuver by sending his frigates in a diversionary attack north against Basseterre, drawing off 300 French defenders.

On the morning of 1 July Thornhill's men march down a hill upon the French rear while Codrington lands 600 men in Frigate Bay. Caught between two fires, de Guitaud's followers break and flee, allowing the entire English army ashore at a cost of only ten killed and 30 wounded. Codrington immediately strikes out along the beach toward Basseterre at the head of the Duke of Bolton's Regiment; Thornhill parallels his advance inland. About a mile from Frigate Bay 1,100 French defenders make a stand; after half an hour of desperate fighting they are defeated and stream into the interior.

Codrington occupies deserted Basseterre and lands artillery from his ships. Next day the English advance and reoccupy their former capital of Old Road Town; on the morning of 3 July they encircle the last remaining French stronghold—the 20-gun Fort Charles at Cleverley Point (just north of Brimstone Hill, near Mount Misery). De Guitaud has sought refuge inside the rectangular stone fort with 150 soldiers, 250 planters, and 80 others. Codrington's gunners manhandle two large siege pieces atop Brimstone Hill and by 10 July open fire, supported by the fleet offshore. Approach trenches are dug, and at least two dozen more artillery pieces are installed over the next fortnight; the French finally sue for terms on 22 July. The surrender is finalized four days later, the French being obliged to evacuate their half of Saint Kitts for Saint Domingue (Haiti).

SUMMER 1690. The Spaniards send a second expedition from Veracruz against the logging establishments in the Laguna de Términos, this time surprising the Baymen, burning 80 vessels and destroying their camps.

22 JULY 1690. The veteran French rover Pierre Le Picard leads a flotilla against Rhode Island in retaliation for the Phips and Leisler strikes against Canada. These raiders disembark at Block Island, which they plunder. News of the attack reaches the mainland, and a reconnaissance sloop sets out from Newport the next day. The following night Picard attempts to penetrate Newport itself, drawing off when his forces are discovered. Three days later (27 July), Rhode Island's Gov. John Easton commandeers the ten-gun sloop *Loyal Stede* in Newport's roads, placing it and 60 men under the retired privateer Thomas Paine. The latter sorties on 30 July, accompanied by a smaller consort under Capt. John Godfrey, with numerous soldiers on board.

Picard has meanwhile moved off to attempt New London, so Paine and Godfrey gain Block Island without sighting the French. Next afternoon the two New England sloops see Picard's large bark and two sloops bearing down on them. Paine retreats into a defensive position in Block Island's shallows in order to concentrate his gunners upon a single side. The French, mistaking these two vessels for coastal traders, hurry a piragua before them, but Paine's gunner opens fire too soon, missing the advance boat and warning Picard that his opponents are armed. The French piragua retreats and Picard's ships bear down together. A brisk firefight begins at 5:00 P.M. and lasts until nightfall, during which the French suffer 14 killed, including Picard's second-in-command. Paine has one dead and six wounded; Picard makes off the next morning with both New England sloops in hot pursuit, compelling the raiders to scuttle their merchant prize.

29 JULY 1690. After Saint Kitts falls, Governor-General Codrington detaches Thornhill to attack the isolated French garrison on Sint Eustatius. That force arrives and calls upon the 60 defenders to surrender. They refuse, so Thornhill disembarks 350 men the next morning, but while advancing upon Fort Orange he perceives Dutch flags in some nearby woods. The former Gov. Lucas Schorer (*see* 3 April 1689) has arrived earlier from Sabá with 100 men on a foraging

expedition—but now withdraws rather than join his English allies in the forthcoming siege.

Five days later the French garrison surrenders, without losses on either side, and is transported to Saint Domingue (Haiti). The English retain Sint Eustatius until 1693, when they are obliged to restore it to Dutch rule by William III.

19 AUGUST 1690. ***Quebec Campaign.*** In Massachusetts, Phips sails northeast from Hull with 32 vessels and 2,000 men, determined to assault Quebec City on his own and thereby secure New England's borders from French raids (despite the fact the campaigning season is far advanced and expected arms and ammunition have not yet arrived from England). Another large force of militia and Indians is to advance up the Hudson River and threaten Montréal.

Eleven days later Phips's expedition sights Cape Breton, and on 31 August (O.S.) a French fishing boat is captured near Île Percé, where Phips also disembarks and burns some houses. A few more prizes are taken as the fleet gropes its way up the Saint Lawrence seaway, soundings being taken in the lead, as the New Englanders lack knowledgeable pilots. Tadoussac is not reached until 23 September (O.S.); Quebec City is not reached until 15 October.

Four Massachusetts colonial militiamen, ca. 1690, clustered around a red-and-white flag of St. George; watercolor by David Rickman

They find the garrison—less than 200 men and 12 guns under 70-year-old Gov. Louis de Buade, Comte de Frontenac et Palluau—recently reinforced by troops from Montréal (which is no longer threatened, as the Americans' Hudson River advance has reached no closer than Lake George before turning back due to desertions and indiscipline). His own ships now suffer from smallpox and the increasing cold, so Phips anchors three miles below Quebec City on 16 October and sends an officer to demand surrender, which Frontenac refuses.

Next morning Phips advances upriver with four ships to create a diversion by bombarding the battlements while 1,300 New Englanders are disembarked at Beauport under Maj. John Walley. A one-sided duel ensues between Phips's wooden ships and Frontenac's stone ramparts until Phips is obliged to cut his cables and drift out of range. Walley fares no better, his poorly supplied troops suffering bitterly from the elements and failing to puncture the French defenses. By 22 October their plight is so desperate that Walley reembarks.

Phips hopes for a second chance but is left with no other choice than retreat when heavy gales blow up a few days later. After pausing off northern Île d'Orléans to repair the most damaged vessels—and fortuitously intercepting the French bark *Nôtre Dame de la Conception* as it arrives from La Rochelle with pork, flour, and salt—the New Englanders are remorselessly swept out to sea. Three other French merchantmen are chased a few days after but disappear into a blinding snowstorm. During the return passage toward Massachusetts Capt. John Rainsford's *Mary* is wrecked on Anticosti Island with 60 men; Phips limps into Boston at the end of November missing six ships (all but three eventually reappear).

23 AUGUST 1690. Commodore Wright returns to the Barbados with his fleet in anticipation of the hurricane season.

LATE AUGUST 1690. D'Iberville appears off York Fort (Hudson Bay) with three small French ships bearing 30 guns and 80 men, only to be driven off by a 36-gun English frigate. He then attacks the outpost at New Severn, 250 miles southeast; the commander, Thomas Walsh, blows it up and flees without resisting.

OCTOBER 1690. Wright's fleet rejoins Governor-General Codrington at Saint Kitts to assault Guadeloupe but is then ordered home to England. Wright therefore clears for Barbados again, arriving by 9 January 1691 to prepare for his transatlantic crossing.

9 NOVEMBER 1690. Spain's West Indian squadron—the 300-ton flagship *San José* (alias *Marabuto*) of Adm. Jacinto Lope Gijón; the 250-ton vice-flag *San Francisco Xavier* of Francisco López de Gómara; the 300-ton *San Nicolás* of Bartolomé de Villar y Aguirre; plus the auxiliary *Santo Cristo de San Román*—reaches Santo Domingo with the 16-gun, 140-ton French prize *Saint Joseph* (soon renamed *Nuestra Señora de la Concepción y San José* and placed under the admiral's son, Sebastián Gijón).

This squadron finds Santo Domingo's inhabitants alarmed by the recent French incursion against Santiago de los Caballeros (*see* 29 June 1690). Some 2,600 militia having already mustered at the capital, they now troop aboard the Spanish warships, swelling the complement of 827 sailors and marines. The expedition departs on 21 December, circling east around the island while another 700 Spanish cavalry advance overland under Gov. Francisco de Segura Sandoval y Castilla to reoccupy Santiago and meet the first contingent on the north coast.

Both units rendezvous near Manzanillo Bay by 14 January 1691, pressing farther west to the French frontline town of Cap-François (modern-day Cap-Haïtien).

21 JANUARY 1691. ***La Limonade.*** When news of the Spanish invasion reaches Governor de Cussy, he rushes forth to give battle with local forces instead of waiting for reinforcements from the rest of Saint Domingue. Completely underestimating the Spaniards' abilities and resolve, the defenders make a stand at Savane de la Limonade (Lemonade Plain) outside Cap-François, relying on their superior musketry—despite being outnumbered 3,000 to 1,000.

The invaders crush the buccaneers in a 90-minute confrontation during the morning of 21 January—springing 300 hidden lancers from tall grass at the battle's height while the French companies are reloading—to achieve a close-quarters melee; they kill the French governor and more than 400 followers (versus 47 Spanish dead). The attackers rampage through Cap-François and its outlying district the next day, eventually making off with 130 slaves and the 22-gun, 300-ton Saint-Malo vessels *Saint Thomas* and *Triomphant,* renaming them *Nuestra Señora de Atocha* and *Nuestra Señora de la Concepción,* respectively.

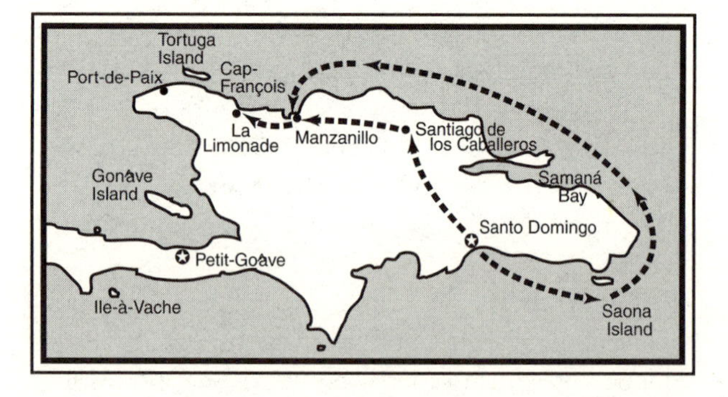

Spanish sweeps through the buccaneer strongholds of Santo Domingo and Haiti

EARLY FEBRUARY 1691. The Marquis d'Eragny, new governor-general for the French West Indies (*see* late January 1690), reaches Fort Royal (modern-day Fort de France, Martinique) with 14 men-of-war and other reinforcements.

MID-FEBRUARY 1691. Commodore Wright, having received counterorders against returning to England from Barbados, rejoins Governor-General Codrington at Antigua. The two leaders quarrel over Codrington's proposed invasion of Guadeloupe, as Wright's crews remain understrength and sickly. Nevertheless, a large expedition gathers, at Codrington's insistence, to be escorted by Wright's *Mary* (flag), *Tiger, Assistance, Bristol, Antelope, Hampshire,* and *Jersey;* the frigates *Guernsey* and *Swan;* the fire ship *Saint Paul;* the ketch *Quaker;* and the hired merchantmen *Success, Princess Ann, Wolf, Experiment,* and *Dumbarton.* Three Brandenburg privateers with 400 men also join the enterprise, bringing total numbers to 3,000. The fleet gets under way by 31 March, intending to occupy Marie Galante en route.

MARCH 1691. In New York City, troops under Maj. Richard Ingoldsby having arrived from England in January, begin restoring crown rule from the self-appointed Jacob Leisler, who refuses to vacate Fort James. He thus provokes an armed confrontation on 17 March (O.S.) in which two soldiers are killed and several others wounded. Two days later the new royal governor-designate, Col. Henry Sloughter, arrives; Leisler hastily surrenders his fort. Having created many enemies during his year-and-a-half reign, Leisler and his son-in-law, Jacob Milborne, are subsequently tried for treason and executed on 16 May (O.S.)—although their estates are later restored to their families and the convictions reversed.

6 APRIL 1691. Governor-General Codrington and Commodore Wright materialize before Marie Galante. Next day the Duke of Bolton's Regiment disembarks under Maj. Edward Nott to subdue the 240-man French garrison under Gov. Charles Auger while Wright's squadron circles northwest to reconnoiter

Guadeloupe. After a week's skirmishing, Nott rounds up all of Auger's followers, deporting them to Martinique. The entire English expedition then steers toward Guadeloupe.

1 MAY 1691. ***Defense of Guadeloupe.*** Appearing off the west of Guadeloupe, Codrington and Wright's fleet bombards the town of Le Baillif in passing (four miles north of the capital of Basse-Terre) before proceeding toward Anse à la Barque to disembark. French Gov. Pierre Hencelin, sick in bed, misconstrues the maneuver as a feint and so detaches his aide, one de Bordenave, with only 25 riders to shadow. However, Codrington leads his army ashore two to three miles south of the Anse and sends Major Nott ahead with 500–600 men to secure its heights. De Bordenave ambushes that unit from above, checking its advance for three hours before finally being outflanked and killed, his riders scattering.

Next day Codrington's main body encounters 500 Frenchmen drawn up behind a barricade at Rivière des Vieux-Habitants under Major Le Cler. Distracting the defenders with a 250-man frontal assault, Codrington sends Col. Rowland Williams in an encircling maneuver, which surprises the French that evening and sends them fleeing toward Le Baillif. At 10:00 A.M. on 3 May the English encounter another barricade at Duplessis River, carrying it after four hours' heavy fighting. The demoralized French then stream back past Fort La Madeleine, Le Baillif, and Basse-Terre without making another stand.

Nathaniel Blakiston enters the abandoned capital with 400 men by 4 May, and Codrington orders it set ablaze, making his headquarters outside. He then initiates a protracted siege against the last remaining French stronghold—Fort Saint Charles. By 23 May, with sick lists grown alarmingly long, Codrington receives word from HMS *Antelope* that a French squadron has appeared off the coast with reinforcements for the defense. They prove to be the royal warships *Hasardeux* of Jean-Baptiste Ducasse; *Mignon* of the Chevalier d'Arbouville; *Émerillon;* and *Cheval Marin*—accompanied by three 20-gun hired merchantmen and four lesser craft, bearing two infantry companies and 600 *flibustiers* from Martinique. Having passed to windward of Dominica, Ducasse has freed Marie Galante from English occupation during his passage; he then stealthily begins depositing reinforcements at Gosier (Grande-Terre section of Guadeloupe) by the evening of 23 May.

Next morning Wright removes his sailors from Codrington's siege operation and, after viewing Ducasse's squadron from a distance, suggests that the governor-general reembark his army and forsake the conquest of Guadeloupe. Codrington's staff—their morale sapped by disease and torrential rain—concur, obliging the governor-general to comply. By 25 May his expedition stands away from Guadeloupe in defeat, Wright's squadron now being reduced to *Mary, Assistance, Jersey, Antelope, Hampshire, Tiger,* and the fire ship *Saint Paul.* After two days' beating about the Saintes, Codrington sails toward Antigua with his remaining transports, escorted by *Antelope* and *Jersey,* while Wright steers toward Barbados with the remainder of the squadron. (After delegating command to his flag captain, Robert Arthur, and returning to England, Wright is severely criticized for his actions at Guadeloupe and is never again employed afloat—although he serves many more years as a commissioner of the Royal Navy.)

Ducasse proceeds back to Martinique then transfers his ships to Saint Croix on 2 August to avoid a yellow fever outbreak that kills French Governor-General d'Eragny and many others in the Windward Islands. By 7 August Ducasse sails again for Port de Paix (Haiti), where his two warships and single corvette lose 250 men before the disease finally abates. On 1 October a letter reaches him from Paris appointing him governor of Saint Domingue in succession to de Cussy.

11 AUGUST 1691. The 34-year-old Maj. Peter Schuyler with 300 New York militia and Iroquois warriors fails to carry the French outpost at Fort Laprairie (Quebec), although inflicting heavy casualties on its garrison. While retiring south, these attackers are overtaken by 700 pursuers, who kill 83 of the invaders before Schuyler's survivors can win free.

25 JANUARY 1692 (O.S.). A band of Penobscot and Kennebec Indians—incited by Gov. Joseph Robinau de Villebon of French Acadia—make a surprise winter raid against the English frontier outpost of York (Maine), killing or capturing about half its people before withdrawing.

27 FEBRUARY 1692 (O.S.). In Nassau (Bahamas), a mob of "desperate rogues, pirates, and others" free rough-hewn Col. Cadwallader Jones from prison, restoring him to office as governor.

2 MARCH 1692. A Jamaica-bound merchant convoy appears between Guadeloupe and Désirade, escorted by Commo. Ralph Wrenn, new commander in chief at Barbados (having arrived 26 January in succession to

Wright). Wrenn has earlier made one sweep searching in vain for enemy ships then detached two of his vessels to cruise independently against the French before quitting Barbados on 27 February with his 48-gun flagship *Norwich;* the 62-gun *Mary* under acting Capt. Richard Wyatt; the 48-gun *Diamond* of Clinton (or Christopher?) Maund; the 46-gun *Mordaunt* of Henry Boteler and *Antelope* of Henry Wickham; the hired frigate *England* of Captain Stubbs; plus an unnamed merchantman.

In light weather, the English sight the Comte de Blénac—restored to office as French governor-general for the West Indies following the death of d'Eragny—barring their path with his 62-gun flagship *Vermandois* as well as Vaudricourt's *Vaillant,* Contré-Blénac's *Léger,* Pontac's *François,* de La Flocelière's *Émerillon,* Sainte-Marie's *Faucon,* Vieuxpont's *Droite,* Roussel's *Basque* (or *Brusque?*), Valbelle Saint-Symphorien's *Chasseur,* Pradine's *Solide,* Julien's *Bouffone,* Du Buisson's *Jersey* (English prize), La Caffinière's *Neptune,* and five lesser craft. Heavily outnumbered, the English edge away to leeward, hoping to protect their convoy.

Next day, Blénac bears down and engages at 8:00 A.M. Mistaking *Mary* for Wrenn's flagship, the French commander assaults it with four men-of-war while *Mordaunt* and the frigate *England* also become hard-pressed. Through skillful handling, Wrenn works his convoy free by noon then stands away south, regaining Barbados three days later without losing a single vessel. The English commodore, like many other new arrivees, subsequently dies of illness on 26 March (O.S.).

30 JUNE 1692. Seven corsair vessels appear off Campeche, dropping anchor 18 miles northeast to occupy the smaller port of Jaina for 19 days.

29 AUGUST 1692 (O.S.). A Hudson's Bay Company captain, 52-year-old James Knight, reaches York Fort (Ontario) with *Royal Hudson's Bay, Dering, Pery,* and *Prosperous,* bearing 213 men.

16 OCTOBER 1692. In the Windward Islands, the 48-gun HMS *Norwich* of Capt. Richard Pugh explodes at anchor, going down with all hands.

28 JANUARY 1693. In upper New York State, a force of Caughnawagas led by the Frenchman Nicolas d'Ailleboust de Manthet captures 300 Mohawks during a raid against their villages, until forced to withdraw by the appearance of a relief column under Schuyler (*see* 11 August 1691).

10 MARCH 1693. The 37-year-old Sir Francis Wheler, recently promoted rear admiral of the Blue, reaches Barbados from England with his 68-gun flagship *Resolution;* the 52-gun *Dunkirk* of James Ward; the 42-gun *Advice* of Charles Hawkins, *Chester* of Thomas Heath, *Ruby* of Robert Deane, and *Tiger* of Thomas Sherman; the 40-gun *Dragon* of William Vickars; the 36-gun frigate *Falcon* of Nathaniel Browne; the 32-gun frigates *Experiment* of James Greenaway, *Mermaid* of William Harman, and *Pembroke* of George Warren; the hired merchantman *London* of William Orton; the storeship *Canterbury* of Robert Leonard; the ten-gun ketch *Quaker* of John Anderson; an unnamed bomb vessel; plus three fire ships. (HMSS *Diamond* and *Mordaunt* are still on this station, along with the 28-gun frigate *Guernsey* of Edward Oakley and the 24-gun *Henry Prize* under Richard Finch.)

Wheler's fleet is accompanied by 28 troop transports bearing Gen. John Foulke and Colonel Godwin's regiments in order to eliminate the last enemy holdings in the Lesser Antilles, unite with the Spaniards to drive the French out of Saint Domingue (Haiti), and continue north to New England to aid the colonials in assaulting Canada.

Gov. James Kendall immediately begins raising 900 volunteers on Barbados and sends a sloop to Antigua to advise Governor-General Codrington of the expedition's arrival. It is then agreed among the leaders to attack Martinique, for which purpose *Chester* and *Mermaid* are detached from Barbados to escort Codrington's contingent toward a rendezvous.

9 APRIL 1693. ***Repulse at Martinique.*** The Wheler-Foulke expedition departs Barbados, augmented by ten island sloops bearing 900 volunteers (bringing total strength to 32 ships of various sizes, nine barks, three brigantines, two ketches, and a galliot). Two days later the formation circles north around Martinique and heads down the western shore, shadowed by French militia cavalry under Col. François de Collart. Governor Gabaret concentrates his forces at Fort Saint Pierre, but much to his surprise the English then sweep past Pointe d'Arlet, Pointe Du Diamant, and stand into Cul-de-Sac Marin, where there are no defenses and scarcely 60 militia under Capt. Charles Auger.

Next morning (12 April) Foulke disembarks 1,000 troops at nearby Anse de Sainte-Anne; another 1,300 soldiers and 1,500 sailors follow before sunset. The English intend to get their land forces safely ashore and approach the island defenses from the rear. Wheler and

Foulke begin doing just that on the morning of 13 April, sending 30 boats, supported by a galliot and two barks, to overrun the Rivière Pilote settlement. Briefly checked by 60 reinforcements hurried down from Saint Pierre under Capt. Henri de Saint-Amour, the invaders ravage the surrounding countryside. At noon on 15 April the English use five barks, three brigantines, and 28 boats to leapfrog farther west and devastate more plantations.

By 19 April Governor-General Codrington arrives from the Leeward Islands with another four English ships, four brigantines, and two barks, bringing 1,300 volunteers under Rowland Williams, Nathaniel Blakiston, and Godfrey Lloyd. Foulke's army is already becoming sickly, so the English decide to abandon their land strategy and reembark their troops by 22 April. After failing to find any safe disembarkation points near Cul-de-Sac à Vaches, Wheler proceeds farther north on 27 April, throwing his marines ashore at Canouville (just north of Fort Saint Pierre) on 29 April. They try to expand the landing zone by advancing south but are checked by Collart's cavalry and militia hastening up under François Le Vassor and Giraud Du Poyet. More French reinforcements arrive overnight under Governor-General de Blénac, whose 100-man contingents under Saint-Amour, Christophe Renaudot, and Lefebvre de Méricourt foil another marine breakout attempt the next morning. Codrington's men then try probing south, only to be thrown back by Collart and Auger.

Defeated at every turn, the English eventually reembark by the evening of 30 April, abandoning Martinique. The operation costs them 800 killed, wounded, or captured, and many others remain ill. Codrington hopes to salvage something from the debacle by attacking Guadeloupe, but Wheler refuses once his fleet staggers into Dominica, citing orders against remaining in the Caribbean later than the end of May. The volunteers disperse, and Wheler escorts Codrington back to Saint Kitts, dismissing the notion of uniting with the Spaniards to attack Saint Domingue; instead he proceeds directly toward New England.

22 JUNE 1693. Wheler arrives in Boston from the West Indies with a sickly fleet, intending to cooperate in a venture against Quebec. However, disease is rife among his ships, and no colonial contingent is assembled. Thus, after a series of consultations with Governor Phips and other members of the council it is decided to forego an invasion.

2 JULY 1693. Capt. James Knight attacks Fort Sainte Anne (formerly Albany Fort, James Bay, Ontario) with *Royal Hudson's Bay, Pery,* and *Prosperous,* taking it with little opposition.

13 AUGUST 1693. Wheler's squadron exits Boston, continuing northeast to overrun the tiny French island of Saint Pierre off Newfoundland. However, his strength is by now so enfeebled that the French positions in Placentia Bay cannot be assaulted; he must circle to the eastern side to replenish supplies before striking out into the North Atlantic by 22 September (O.S.).

30 SEPTEMBER 1693. In the West Indies, the 48-gun HMS *Diamond* of Capt. Henry Wickham is captured by the French. (Wickham is subsequently court-martialled and sentenced to life imprisonment; he is released on the accession of Princess Anne in March 1702 although never reinstated to service in the Royal Navy.)

1 DECEMBER 1693. In the Lesser Antilles, the 46-gun HMS *Mordaunt* of Capt. Francis Maynard is lost with all hands.

16 JANUARY 1694. French missionaries Louis Pierre Thury and Sébastien de Billie lead 230 Indians in an attack on Oyster Bay (Maine), killing 100 English settlers.

APRIL 1694. Off Dominica, the 42-gun HMS *Chester* of Capt. William Julius drives ashore an 18-gun French privateer, which takes fire and explodes.

LATE APRIL 1694. The French privateer Charles François Le Vasseur de Beauregard departs Saint Domingue (Haiti) with 400–500 *flibustiers* aboard six small vessels to probe eastern Jamaica. He takes a New England ship, but the next day he is sighted by the 36-gun coast-guard frigate HMS *Falcon* and chased until he loses the new prize. When Beauregard reenters Petit Goâve shortly thereafter, he finds the royal warships *Téméraire* of 54 guns, *Envieux,* and *Solide,* recently arrived with a merchant convoy from France. Governor Ducasse decides to employ them against the English, dispatching the powerful trio into *Falcon*'s patrol area to seize the Royal Navy vessel—despite its stout resistance—then marshals all his forces for a surprise invasion.

EARLY JUNE 1694. Ducasse sorties from Petit Goâve aboard *Téméraire* under the flag captain, the Chevalier

Du Rollon, accompanied by men-of-war *Hasardeux* and *Envieux*. Off Cape Tiburón (southwestern Haiti) he gathers a fleet totaling 22 sail and 3,164 men to steer west toward Jamaica.

27 JUNE 1694. ***Assault on Jamaica.*** Ducasse's expedition appears off the eastern tip of Jamaica in a fresh morning gale. Eight of his vessels remain off Port Morant while the 14 others anchor in Cow Bay (15 miles east of Port Royal). Here the French learn that the English have been forewarned of their invasion scheme by the escaped privateer Capt. Stephen Elliott. Therefore, Ducasse's plan of storming directly into Port Royal must be altered, as Du Rollon refuses to risk the king's ships in such a hazardous undertaking. Consequently, 800 men are landed under Beauregard to march east, plundering and destroying everything in their path. Boats are also sent around from Port Morant to ravage the northeastern shores; the English under 58-year-old Gov. Sir William Beeston are reluctant to sally for fear of dividing their smaller force with the enemy host to windward.

On 1 July *Téméraire* drags its anchors, being carried downwind to Bluefields Bay along with another French vessel. Ducasse is encamped ashore and so continues directing land operations until 27 July, when he musters the bulk of his fleet in Cow Bay, threatening Port Royal. Beeston sorties to counteract the maneuver; Ducasse quickly reembarks his men under cover of darkness and sends all but the three largest ships with his deputy, de Graaf, to assault Carlisle Bay (35 miles farther west). That contingent anchors by the afternoon of 28 July, landing 1,400–1,500 *flibustiers* during the night. Next morning they assail a 250-man English garrison under Col. Thomas Sutton, with Beauregard commanding the vanguard while de Graaf directs the main body. After the French drive the defenders back, foraging parties are sent out to scour the countryside. When Ducasse joins a few days later, booty is transferred aboard his flotilla. The French weigh on 3 August, and by 14 August they are back in Petit Goâve.

31 AUGUST 1694. Seven French ships are defeated off Ferryland (Newfoundland) by the English ships *William* and *Mary*.

24 SEPTEMBER 1694. D'Iberville appears off Hayes River (Hudson Bay, Canada) with the private ship *Poli*, accompanied by the vessel *Salamandre*, under his brother Joseph, sieur de Sérigny. They besiege the English fur-trading outpost of York Fort; Gov. Thomas Walsh surrenders along with 56 men by 14 October.

LATE SEPTEMBER 1694. Governor Beeston sends the only three Royal Navy warships at Jamaica—the 42-gun *Advice* of Capt. William Harman, the 46-gun *Hampshire*, and the 32-gun *Experiment*, plus a fire ship and two barks—beating upwind toward Saint Domingue to exact some small measure of vengeance for Ducasse's raid. The village of L'Esterre near Léogâne is bombarded between 8:00 A.M. and 3:00 P.M. on 11 October, during which Harman is wounded; the formation then bears down on Petit Goâve, only to sheer off when it realizes that Beauregard is prepared to receive them. A few huts are burned on Île-à-Vache (southwestern Haiti) before the Jamaicans disappear back over the horizon; Harman dies by 16 October.

10 APRIL 1695. An expedition begins arriving at Saint Kitts under Commo. Robert Wilmot: the 60-gun warships *Dunkirk* (flag) and *Winchester;* the 48-gun *Ruby* and *Reserve;* the frigate *Swan;* the fire ships *Terrible* and *Firebrand;* 14 transports; a storeship; a hospital ship; and three hired merchantmen. The fleet bears more than 1,200 soldiers under Col. Luke Lillingston and has rushed across the Atlantic in response to Ducasse's descent against Jamaica (*see* 27 June 1694).

During the crossing Wilmot has detached *Swan* to call upon the president of the *audiencia* (high court) of Santo Domingo and propose a joint Anglo-Spanish assault against the French half of that island. Meanwhile Lillingston's small army disembarks at Saint Kitts to recuperate; 130 have already died and another 400 are ill, leaving 700 effectives. After arguing over strategy, Wilmot and Lillingston reembark and continue their voyage by 8 May, making toward Saona to receive the Spaniards' reply. *Swan* is awaiting them off that island, along with the 46-gun HMS *Hampshire*, which earlier conveyed Col. Peter Beckford from Jamaica to visit the Spanish and also suggest a coordinated operation.

The Spaniards have accepted, and Wilmot and Lillingston travel to Santo Domingo's capital aboard three men-of-war and a fire ship to confer with their new allies while the main English fleet circles north through the Mona Passage to Samaná Bay. An agreement is struck with Gov. Gil Correoso Catalán, whereby he will lead 1,500 Spanish troops across the island to rendezvous with the English expedition at Manzanillo by 12 May.

10 MAY 1695. Having departed the capital of Santo Domingo, Wilmot and Lillingston sail west out of Samaná Bay to unite with the Spaniards. *Swan* takes soundings in the lead, and two days later *Hampshire, Reserve,* and *Terrible* are sent ahead to blockade Cap-François (modern-day Cap-Haïtien), where some French ships are believed to lie. The main English expedition, meanwhile, anchors off Monte Cristi and, a day or so later, contacts Correoso's Spaniards at Bayahá. Wilmot proceeds there to disembark Lillingston's troops while joining Spain's West Indian squadron (Armada de Barlovento) under Commo. Francisco Cortés. The armada comprises only the decrepit 450-ton flagship *Santo Cristo de Maracaibo,* the 300-ton frigate *San Nicolás,* and the auxiliary *Nuestra Señora de Guadalupe* (alias *Tocoluta*).

24 MAY 1695. ***Invasion of Saint Domingue.*** The combined Anglo-Spanish force crosses the border, shouldering aside 300 heavily outnumbered French defenders under *flibustier* chieftain—and *lieutenant du roi* (king's deputy)—Laurens de Graaf. Two frigates and two fire ships meanwhile occupy deserted Cap-François (Cap-Haïtien) on 29 May. When the allied army arrives overland it finds the buildings already pillaged; they continue along the coast, wreaking destruction upon plantations.

Wilmot's warships—reinforced by two Jamaican privateers and a galliot—keep pace by weighing on 10 June, pausing at Baie de la Cul (six miles west of Cap-François) before blockading Port de Paix by 13 June. Wishing to beset the defenders before they can organize, Wilmot sets 400–500 men ashore at nearby Saint Louis, driving the enemy inside the walls until the combined army arrives overland on 25 June. The French remain besieged under 47-year-old Maj. Jean Bernanos; eventually they attempt a breakout two hours before dawn on 15 July. However, the attempted evacuation is betrayed to the foe, who ambushes the heavy-laden French column—hampered by 150 terrified women and children—and massacres many in the dark, including Bernanos.

Having thus secured Port de Paix, the victorious commanders fall out over the division of spoils, marking an end to the joint enterprise. When Wilmot suggests resuming the offensive farther south, against Léogâne and Petit Goâve, Lillingston seconds the Spaniards' refusal. Disappointed, and with sickness thinning the ranks, the allies part company on 27 July. The English head toward Jamaica to refit while the three Spanish warships touch at Santo Domingo before proceeding to Cuba.

13 SEPTEMBER 1695. After recuperating at Port Royal (Jamaica) and delegating four warships to remain behind, Wilmot decides to return to England with the remnants of his sickly squadron. He encounters dreadful weather and dies at sea on 25 September. Nine days later the 60-gun HMS *Winchester* of Capt. John Soule becomes separated and wrecks on Florida. The rest of the squadron eventually reaches home, escorting a merchant convoy.

MID-FEBRUARY 1696. A private expedition under the naval officer Jean Baptiste Gennes staggers through the Strait of Magellan to raid the Spaniards in the Pacific. Upon its departure from La Rochelle on 3 June 1695 the squadron consisted of a half-dozen ships bearing 720 men; now reduced by diseases contracted in Africa, the French shortly quit the South Seas, returning to Europe via Ilha Grande (Brazil) and the West Indies.

LATE MAY–EARLY JUNE 1696. The 44-year-old French inspector general and engineer, Bernard Renau d'Elissagaray—better known as Petit-Renau—reaches the West Indies with the ships *Intrépide* (flag), *Phénix, Gaillard,* and *Pontchartrain,* plus the frigates *Inconnu* and *Renau. Gaillard,* under Henri Louis, Marquis de Chavagnac, captures a rich, 36-gun Cartagena merchantman on 29 June after a hard-fought, five-hour sea battle 50 miles outside Havana. In suffering 30 casualties, it disables a third of the Spaniard's 260-man crew. But aside from this isolated victory—and a couple of English prizes that are taken—Petit-Renau's mission remains to assess France's military fortifications in the Caribbean, and he returns home this summer without participating in any further offensive operations.

SUMMER 1696. Capt. William Allen recaptures Fort Bourbon (originally York Fort, Hudson Bay) with five vessels and 400 men.

14 JULY 1696. D'Iberville and naval Capt. Simon de Bonaventure arrive from France with two frigates, capturing the English frigate *Newport* near Saint John's (Newfoundland).

EARLY AUGUST 1696. D'Iberville relieves French Acadia, lifting the blockade of Fort La Tour at the mouth of the Saint John River (Portland Point, New Brunswick) by capturing an English frigate and driving off two others.

15 AUGUST 1696. D'Iberville besieges the English garrison at Fort William Henry (Pemaquid) with 25

Acadian regulars and 240 Abenakis under 44-year-old Jean Vincent d'Abbadie, Baron de Saint Castin. The English commander, Capt. Pascoe Chubb, surrenders almost as soon as the French set up their batteries; he and his 92 followers are restored to Boston, and Fort William Henry is destroyed.

3 OCTOBER 1696. The French *Bon, Bourbon, Aigle, Favori, Badine,* and *Loire* arrive in the West Indies under Commodore Chevalier Des Augiers, slipping into the roadstead at La Guaira on 26 October guided by the renegade English privateer John Philip Beare, or Bell, while masquerading as Spain's West Indian squadron (Armada de Barlovento). They capture the 40-gun Spanish ship used to resupply nearby Margarita Island, cutting it out before the batteries can react.

29 OCTOBER 1696. ***Newfoundland Offensive.*** Gov. Jacques François de Mombeton de Brouillan departs Placentia Bay with three ships to destroy the English settlements farther northeast in cooperation with Pierre Le Moyne d'Iberville, who departs overland with another contingent on 1 November. Both units rendezvous at Ferryland, 50 miles south of Saint John's, advancing on the English capital while destroying its coastal fisheries.

Saint John's surrenders on 30 November after a brief siege and is put to the torch while d'Iberville's subordinate, Capt. Jacques Testard de Montigny, continues obliterating fishing settlements. By the end of winter (late March 1697), only Bonavista and Carbonear remain in British hands. The French kill 200 Englishmen, capture 700 more, and destroy three dozen villages during the campaign.

6 JANUARY 1697. This morning, Spain's West Indian squadron (the *Armada de Barlovento*)—Adm. Andrés de Pez's 56-gun, 350-man flagship *Santísima Trinidad y Nuestra Señora de Atocha;* Irish-born Vice Adm. Guillermo Murphy's 46-gun, 250-man *Santo Cristo de Maracaibo;* the 42-gun, 240-man *Nuestra Señora del Rosario y Santiago;* the 26-gun, 130-man *Nuestra Señora de Guadalupe;* and the 22-gun, 100-man *Jesús, María y José*—raises Caucedo Point off Santo Domingo after delivering the annual payrolls (*situados*) to Puerto Rico.

Four large sail are sighted, so the armada bears down to investigate. The strangers hoist English and Dutch colors (Spain's allies against France) and claim to be sailing from Jamaica to Barbuda. After sending a Spanish officer across to make a cursory inspection, Pez continues west, little realizing he has been duped and that they are actually the Chevalier Des Augiers's French royal warships *Bourbon* (flag) of 58 guns, *Bon* of 52, *Favori* of 36, and *Badine* of 24 retiring toward Saint Domingue (Haiti).

Having thus secured the weather gauge, the French steal down upon the unwary Spaniards this same moonlit night, engaging the startled armada. Pez's flagship runs before the wind toward Cuba while Murphy's *Maracaibo* is dismasted and captured by Captain de Patoulet's *Bon; Guadalupe* and *Jesús María* flee inshore toward Santo Domingo; Capt. Francisco Buitrón's *Rosario* eventually gains Santa Marta (Colombia). Augiers sails into Saint Domingue on 3 February with his prize, standing away shortly thereafter for the Bay of Honduras before striking out into the North Atlantic toward France. Pez reenters Veracruz by 5 April, having become separated from his command and failing to deliver his *situados.* He is subsequently court-martialled along with Murphy in August 1699.

EARLY MARCH 1697. The 52-year-old French Adm. Bernard Jean Louis de Saint Jean, Baron de Pointis, appears off Cap-François (modern-day Cap-Haïtien) with his 84-gun flagship *Sceptre;* 64-gun vice-flag *Saint Louis* of de Lévi Mirepoix; the 70-gun "rear admiral" *Fort* of the Chevalier de Coëtlogon; the 60-gun *Vermandois* of Du Buisson de Varenne; the 56-gun *Apollon* of Gombault, *Furieux* of La Motte-Michel, and *Saint Michel* of Marolles; the 34-gun frigate *Mutine* of de Massiac; the 30-gun frigate *Avenant* of Francine; the 28-gun frigate *Marin* of Saint-Wandrille; the bomb vessel *Éclatant* of de Mons; the corvette *Providence* of de Lescoët; plus transports *Dieppoise* and *Ville d'Amsterdam.*

Over and above their regular complements of 2,300 sailors, these ships carry 1,750 soldiers and a large siege train for a projected assault against Cartagena. Although it is late in the war, the venture has been authorized with the aim of securing a major prize before peace can be concluded. France's bankrupt royal government has provided Pointis's warships and men, but his financing has been raised by private investors, who expect to be reimbursed out of his booty. The fleet is to be augmented by a contingent of *flibustiers,* but when Pointis's flagship arrives before Petit Goâve on 16 March he is infuriated to learn only a few hundred await him, the rest having dispersed because of his delay in departing Europe. Relations worsen a day later when a French naval officer arrests an unruly *boucanier* ashore, touching off a riot in which two or three others are killed. Only the personal intervention of Governor Ducasse succeeds in calming the mob.

The freebooters are offended to learn of the secondary role being offered in the enterprise; the question of their shares is kept especially vague and Ducasse is excluded from command. Nevertheless, they enlist in good numbers once Pointis publishes a proclamation stating they will participate "man for man" with his royal crews; for his part, Ducasse offers to go as an individual ship captain with his 40-gun *Pontchartrain,* commanding only his island contingent. Pointis therefore sails on 19 March to rejoin his fleet (which has meanwhile entered the Gulf de la Gonâve), as Ducasse prepares his followers to meet at the agreed rendezvous off Cape Tiburón.

Some 170 soldiers, 110 colonial volunteers under Joseph d'Honon de Gallifet, 180 free blacks under Jean Joseph de Paty, and 650 buccaneers are raised, sailing aboard the 20-gun *Gracieuse;* the 18-gun *Cerf Volant, Saint Louis,* and *Serpente;* the 16-gun *Dorade; Pembroke* (English prize); *Marie; Françoise* of Captain La Villeauglamats from Saint-Malo; plus other vessels (among the latter apparently the former HMS *Jersey* and Augiers's prize *Christe*—formerly the Spanish *Santo Cristo de Maracaibo; see* 6 January 1697). After weathering a brief storm, the contingent joins the main French fleet off Cape Tiburón by 28 March; on 8 April the combined force sights the Spanish Main.

13 April 1697. ***Siege of Cartagena.*** The French expedition arrives, and the buccaneers propose an immediate disembarkation at Playa Grande, near Hicacos Point (northeast of Cartagena); it is canceled once Ducasse and Pointis personally reconnoiter the shoreline, finding it lined with dangerous reefs. The attackers therefore decide to force Bocachica's harbor entrance farther south, and on the afternoon of 15 April Ducasse and Pointis go ashore at Los Hornos with 1,700 troops and 1,100 buccaneers. While preparing their siege against Bocachica's 33-gun, 150-man Fort San Luis (only 15 of the defenders are regulars under Capt. Sancho Jimeno de Orozco), the buccaneers capture a coaster arriving from Portobelo and drive off Spanish reinforcements stealing down from Cartagena in boats. San Luis surrenders after being stormed on 16 April; six French soldiers and seven buccaneers die during the assault and another 22 are wounded (including Ducasse, his *flibustiers* passing temporarily under the orders of his second-in-command, Honon de Gallifet).

Pointis installs 170 men into Fort San Luis, works his fleet into the bay, then continues to drive north by land and sea toward Cartagena, finding the next redoubt—Fort Santa Cruz, also called Castillo Grande—

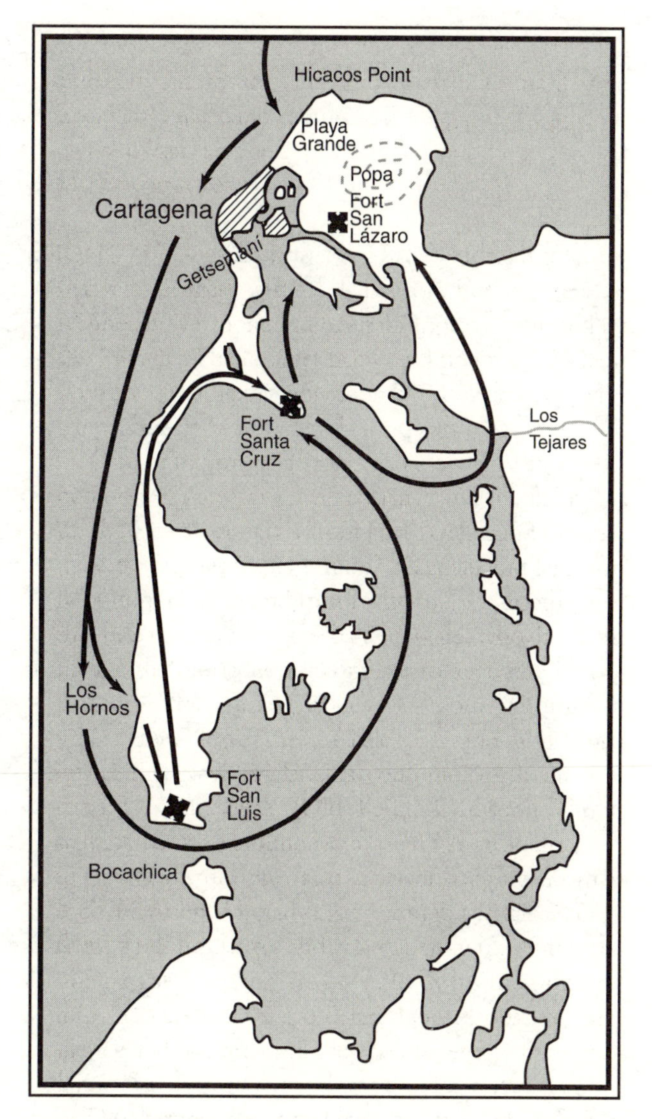

French assault on Cartagena

abandoned by the Spaniards. (Gov. Diego de los Rios y Quesada commands only 750 regulars to defend the city proper.) At this point the French admiral orders his buccaneers to traverse the bay and circle behind Spanish lines to seize the Nuestra Señora de la Popa high ground while his 2,000-man army advances overland. The buccaneers occupy the heights unopposed, and Fort San Lázaro is outflanked and stormed by Pointis and his rear admiral, de Coëtlogon; the two French contingents reunite by 20 April and institute siege proceedings against Cartagena's Getsemaní suburb, which is defended by the aged, gout-ridden Capt. Francisco Santarén with 700 men.

Approach trenches are dug and artillery landed from the French fleet; Pointis, being wounded in the leg by a sharpshooter's round, supervises from a litter. On 28 April bombardment begins against Getsemaní's walls, and during a lull on 30 April Ducasse

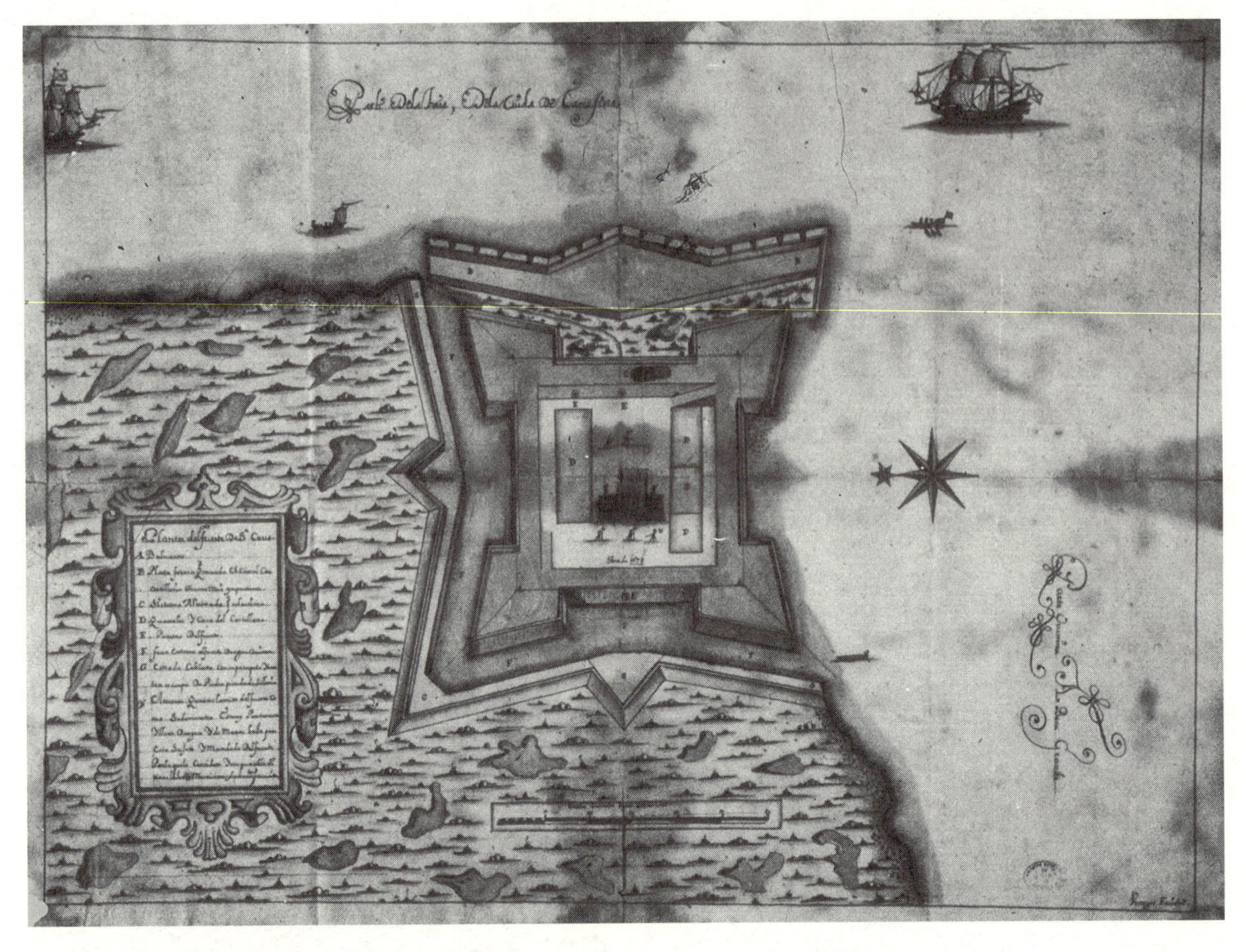

Contemporary drawing of Santa Cruz Fort, outside Cartagena

(now recuperated from his own injury) visits a Spanish officer at the gate and notices a breach has been made. At his urging Pointis orders a general assault for 4:00 P.M.; French grenadiers and buccaneers fight their way to the edge of Cartagena. The defenders' morale collapses, and by the evening of 2 May white flags are hoisted upon the walls. While finalizing terms, Pointis learns that a 1,000-man Spanish relief column is approaching, so he sends Ducasse's buccaneers with several hundred soldiers to oppose it.

The column never appears, and Pointis occupies Cartagena on 4 May. By the time Ducasse and his men return, they find the gates closed, and they are billeted in the impoverished, devastated suburb of Getsemaní. The French commander in chief fears that unruly buccaneers will violate his carefully arranged capitulation terms, so he keeps them outside the walls—and away from where the booty is being tallied. The few surviving Spanish inhabitants are obliged to surrender most of their riches, and the plunder eventually totals 8 million French crowns. The buccaneers expect one-quarter but become outraged on 25 May when they learn their share is a paltry 40,000 crowns. They have not been aware that the crews aboard Pointis's royal warships are serving for only a small percentage, and that is why the admiral deceitfully offered them shares "man for man." But by now the plunder is aboard his men-of-war, ready to depart.

Furious at being duped, the buccaneers argue for several days and then swarm into Cartagena on 30 May—despite Ducasse's protests—and round up every Spaniard they can, inflicting tortures until they extort an additional 1,000 crowns per buccaneer. Pointis meanwhile quits the scene on 1 June with his heavy-laden fleet; the buccaneers return aboard ship on 3 June and weigh by 7 June.

6 JUNE 1697. Five days after leaving Cartagena, Pointis's ten warships and two auxiliaries are sighted at sundown by an Anglo-Dutch battle fleet under Vice Adm. John Neville, who has been sent into the West Indies specifically to counter the French expedition. After rendezvousing with Commo. George Mees's squadron and eight Dutch ships under Com-

modore Hoogenhoeck at Barbados on 27 April, Neville's fleet has prowled as far west as Jamaica searching for the French admiral. Departing Port Royal on 4 June, he at last spots the quarry and next morning (7 June) gives chase. The allied fleet totals almost 30 sail, among them *Monmouth* of 66 guns; *Rupert* of 64; *Pembroke* (under Capt. James Studley, later John Litcott) and *Sunderland* (under Capt. Roger Bellwood) of 60 apiece; *Trident* of 54; *Newcastle* of 52; *Colchester, Lincoln* (under Capt. Nicholas Dyer), and *Warwick* of 50 each; *Bristol* of 48; the hired ships *Princess Anne, Gosport,* and *Virgin;* as well as Hoogenhoeck's 72-gun *Hollandia,* four fire ships, and the bomb ketch *Lightning.*

Pointis's vessels—outnumbered, overburdened, and with much of the crews dead or diseased following Cartagena—are in no condition to fight; he reverses course and runs. HMS *Warwick* of Capt. Anthony Tollet gets near enough to exchange shots with the rearmost French ship and takes a small auxiliary laden with slaves and booty. Pointis eventually forms line of battle expecting a full engagement but only duels with Capt. Stephen Elliott's *Bristol* before pulling away. For the next two days the French succeed in outrunning their pursuers; Pointis then figures he is only 60 miles from Cartagena and so steers due west during the night. By dawn on 10 June he has eluded his enemies, the only loss being a Spanish prize that lags behind and is recaptured by *Princess Anne* under Capt. William Wakelin and Hoogenhoeck's *Hollandia.*

The chase has carried Neville so near Cartagena that he visits it before roaming northeast again; on 25 June he sights Ducasse anchored with eight buccaneer vessels off Sambay. The English and Dutch pursue once more, capturing *Gracieuse* and the 50-gun *Christe* (former Spanish *Santo Cristo de Maracaibo*) and driving *Saint Louis* of Capitaine Charles hard aground; he and his crew escaping ashore—only to be hunted down by the Spaniards, captured, and put to work rebuilding Cartagena's defenses. Meanwhile Neville detaches four men-of-war to pursue Ducasse's remaining vessels, which scatter for Saint Domingue (Haiti). The 40-gun *Cerf Volant* of Capitaine Macary is driven onto the coast by Royal Navy Capt. Thomas Dilkes, but the rest of the French raiders arrive safely—complaining bitterly of Pointis's deceitfulness. (A prolonged litigation ensues, eventually resulting in slightly larger shares being paid by Pointis's backers to the defrauded buccaneers.)

29 JUNE 1697. After chasing Ducasse, Neville visits Spanish Santo Domingo to regroup.

3 JULY 1697. From Santo Domingo, Neville detaches Commodore Mees with nine vessels to raid the French half of the island. Before daybreak on 8 July, Mees disembarks several hundred men one mile east of Petit Goâve, advancing with support of a pair of smaller craft and numerous boats offshore; he takes it by surprise. Their approach proves so effective that Governor Ducasse barely manages to escape, bolting from bed through a window and directly into the jungle. The French capital is overrun and looted, the raiders causing considerable damage before their men become inebriated; they are obliged to repair back aboard ship when a French relief column appears.

Mees sails away to rejoin Neville a few days later and, after touching briefly at Jamaica, the reunited English fleet proceeds toward Havana to escort the Spanish treasure convoy across the Atlantic. Mees dies aboard his flagship *Breda* on 30 July, two days before the Cuban capital is reached. Its Spanish governor indicates there is no need for Royal Navy protection, so Neville continues to Virginia, where he too succumbs. Eventually Dilkes conducts the surviving vessels home.

JULY 1697. The 37-year-old Commo. John Norris reaches Saint John's (Newfoundland) from England aboard his 70-gun flagship *Content*—captured from the French in January 1695—accompanied by four fourth rates (50–60 guns), four frigates, two bomb ketches, and two fire ships plus 2,000 troops under 60-year-old Scottish Gen. Sir John Gibsone. The expedition is intended to recover the English fisheries that were destroyed by the French in the autumn of 1696. But on 2 August a report arrives that five French ships of the line are in nearby Conception Bay under 57-year-old Vice Adm. André, Marquis de Nesmond. This prompts the local authorities—over Norris's objections—to order the expedition to remain inside while defenses are strengthened. The English commodore is therefore unable to fulfill his mission; he sails home for England in October.

4 SEPTEMBER 1697. D'Iberville appears off the mouth of the Hayes River (Hudson Bay, Canada) with his 44-gun frigate *Pélican,* having become separated from three other French consorts. Next day he is attacked by the 56-gun HMS *Hampshire* of Capt. John Fletcher, the 36-gun private frigate *Dering,* and the 32-gun *Royal Hudson's Bay;* he engages them for four hours. The Royal Navy ship strikes a shoal and sinks with all hands, and *Royal Hudson's Bay* surrenders, only to be driven aground by a sudden storm, along with *Pélican.* Eighteen of d'Iberville's men drown while swimming through the icy waters; Capt. Michael Grimington's *Dering* escapes.

D'Iberville's three consorts appear by 8 September; five days later Gov. Henry Baley surrenders York Fort. The French leader installs his brother Joseph, sieur de Sérigny, as new governor then departs later this month before winter can set in.

9 SEPTEMBER 1697. The 39-year-old Maj. John March repulses a war party of 200 Indians and several Frenchmen on the banks of the Damariscotta River, thus preventing their descent upon eastern Maine.

20 SEPTEMBER 1697. In Europe, Britain and France sign the Treaty of Rijswijk, bringing an end to the war. By its terms, both countries largely agree to restore each other's possessions in the New World, although Newfoundland and Hudson Bay are generally conceded to England, Acadia to France.

THE DARIEN DISASTER (1698–1699)

ON 11 OCTOBER 1698, THE SCOTTISH SHIP *UNICORN* and its tender, *Dolphin,* anchor at Saint Thomas in the Danish Virgin Islands. They are part of a larger flotilla conducting 1,200 people to establish a Scottish commercial settlement at Darien. Robert Pennecuik, Robert and Thomas Drummond, William Paterson, and other leaders of this ill-conceived venture are so unfamiliar with the Spanish Main that they must hire retired privateer Robert Allison (*see* 15 April 1680) to pilot them on to their destination. Both ships rejoin the main body off Vieques Island, where Allison goes aboard the flagship *Saint Andrew* to direct its helmsmen, getting under way by 18 October.

10 NOVEMBER 1698. The Scots sight Golden Island (Panama) at dusk and begin exploring the nearby mainland the next day. After establishing friendly relations with the natives the flotilla enters a harbor on 15 November to erect a settlement, renaming the place Caledonia Bay (later New Edinburgh). Disease is already thinning the ranks, and the Scots build their first fort on a sandy promontory too deep within the bay, and they are compelled to resite it two months later. Conditions are extremely difficult, with no trade appearing, and by mid-December rumors of a Spanish counterexpedition reach them.

16 JANUARY 1699. Andrés de Pez, commander of Spain's West Indian squadron (Armada de Barlovento), reaches Portobelo from Cartagena with *Trinidad, Rosario, Guadalupe,* and the six-gun sloop *San José y las Animas* to eradicate the new Scottish settlement near the Gulf of Darien. Convinced his four warships are inadequate for a seaborne assault, he proposes to the president of the *audiencia* of Panama, Conde de Canillas, that 500 seamen march across the isthmus and be reinforced for an attack against the Scots' rear. The president agrees and contributes two companies of regulars.

Pez and his men leave Panama by 9 March, gathering volunteers as they advance. But the jungle trails grow increasingly difficult, particularly when seasonal rains set in, thus bringing progress to a halt six miles short of the objective. Pez is obliged to retreat, hurried by rumors of an English squadron bearing down upon Portobelo, where only anchor watches lie careening his vessels. That threat never materializes, but Pez nonetheless loses 90 men through desertion during the campaign, another 80 due to illness. Despite orders from Canillas to remain at anchor off Portobelo, Pez sails toward Cartagena this summer, arriving in late July. News comes that the Scots have abandoned Darien because of disease, internal strife, and lack of profits.

17 JANUARY 1699. Rear Adm. John Benbow arrives in Carlisle Bay (Barbados) with a small squadron from

England to conduct peacetime patrols and diplomatic overtures with the Spanish at Portobelo and the Danes on Saint Thomas. His crews suffer heavy mortality rates from disease before returning home.

24 JUNE 1699. The private ships *Maurepas* of 50 guns and 180 men and *Phélypeaux* of 44 guns and 150 men—both commanded by Jacques Gouin de Beauchesne—reach the tip of South America to penetrate the Strait of Magellan and trade along the Pacific Coast. For the next year and a half, Beauchesne will conduct business in these forbidden waters, at times resorting to force, thereby establishing a precedent for other French imitators.

Part 5: High Tide of Empire (1700–1777)

One must admit that we have been very unfortunate;
just when we could hope to see the campaign
end with glory, everything turned against us.
—The Chevalier de Lévis, following the fall of Quebec (1759)

Queen Anne's War (1702–1713)

In Europe, Charles II of Spain dies on 30 November 1700, leaving Archduke Charles of Austria and France's 16-year-old Prince Philip of Anjou—grandson to expansionist Louis XIV of France—as nearest claimants to the throne. Rather than see Spain's vast overseas territories added to the French empire, other European powers position themselves to contest this succession, by championing the archduke's claim.

Anglo-French tensions are further exacerbated a year later when the exiled James II dies at Saint Germain outside Paris on 17 September 1701, Louis recognizing his son James Edward as new king of Great Britain, despite angry protests from London. The English ambassador duly departs, and matters become more complicated in March 1702, when the 51-year-old William III of England breaks his collarbone while trying out a new horse, catches a chill, then dies shortly thereafter. As William's wife Mary has already predeceased him, he is succeeded by his 37-year-old sister-in-law, Princess Anne—so that the hostilities which erupt this coming summer, called the War of the Spanish Succession in Britain and on the Continent, becomes known in England's New World colonies as "Queen Anne's War."

18 June 1701. Spain and Portugal sign the Alfonza Treaty, whereby Sacramento (Uruguay) is restored to Portugal.

October 1701. Governor Elias Haskett of the Bahamas is deposed by a mob for having arrested his popular predecessor, the mulatto privateer Read Elding.

14 November 1701. In anticipation of European frictions spreading to the West Indies, 48-year-old John Benbow (now Vice Admiral of the Blue) returns to Barbados with ten Royal Navy warships, then visits Martinique, Dominica, and Nevis before anchoring in Port Royal (Jamaica) on 16 December to winter.

2 January 1702. In response to Benbow's deployment, 64-year-old Vice Adm. François Louis Rousselet, Comte de Château Renault and knight grand cross of the Order of Saint Louis, and his subordinate Marquis de Nesmond, knight of the Order of Malta, arrive at Fort Royal (modern-day Fort de France, Martinique) with:

Ship	*Guns*	*Men*	*Commander*
Merveilleux (flag)	98	720	de Combes
Monarque (vice-flag)	88	620	Félix de Beaussier
Vainqueur (rear admiral)	84	600	Commo. Marie Hyacinthe, Marquis de Rosmadec
Superbe	68	450	Commodore de la Harteloire
Orgueilleux	88	650	Dreux de Rousselet, Marquis de Château Renault (the admiral's nephew)
Prompt	76	500	de Beaujeu
Constant	70	450	de Machault
Fort	70	420	Baron de Pallières
Invincible	64	450	Comte de Sébeville
Bizarre	68	400	Chevalier de Villars
Ferme	66	450	Chevalier de Digoins
Espérance	64	420	Roland Barrin, Marquis de la Galissonnière de Saint Aubin
Bourbon	64	400	Comte de Blénac
Henri	64	400	Du Coudray
Oriflamme	64	380	de Pallas
Assuré	60	380	Philippe d'Aligre
Saint Louis	60	380	Du Quesne Mosnier (Abraham Louis Duquesne Monnier?)
Eole	62	380	Comte de Ferrière
Sirenne	66	380	de la Roche Vezançay
Prudent	60	380	de Grandpré
Capable	58	350	de la Roque Persin
Excellent	60	350	des Herbiers
Trident	60	350	Chevalier de Beaujeu
Hasardeux	50	350	Marquis de Château Morant
Modéré	52	300	de Montbault
Solide	50	330	des Nos Champmesslin
Juste	60	300	de Rochallar

These ships of the line are accompanied by the 40-gun frigates *Dauphine* of 230 men under the Chevalier Du Plessis Liancourt, and *Triton* of 250 under Claude Élisée Court de la Bruyère; the 36-gun, 220-man *Volontaire* of the Chevalier de Lannion; 50-man fireships *Éveillé* of Halis de l'Escalette, *Indiscret* of Jolibert Guay, and *Favori* of the Chevalier de la Pomarède; 40-man *Fourbe* of the Chevalier de Gabaret, and *Zeripsé* of des Moulières; plus the 45-man transports *Portefaix* of Ensign Cholence, and *Bienvenu* of Lt. Herpin Desmarais.

Paris and Madrid fear that Benbow's West Indian foray is intended to capture a Spanish-American treasure convoy and thus inaugurate hostilities with a preemptive coup. They have therefore furnished Château Renault with a Spanish commission—in addition to his French one—to defend these silver shipments. After three weeks at Martinique the French admiral is instructed to attack Barbados. Feeling such an enterprise

Stern view of the 36-gun French royal frigate Volontaire, *by a contemporary naval architect*

beyond his fleet's capabilities—his 2,200 troops being one-third of English strength at Barbados—Château Renault instead decides to sail toward Havana to escort the Mexican plate fleet across to Spain.

13 JANUARY 1702. An expedition of 235 Spaniards aboard nine coastal vessels returns to Campeche, having attempted to sweep the English logwood establishments from the Laguna de Términos; their commander—coast-guard Capt. Francisco Fernández—has been wounded in the shoulder.

22 FEBRUARY 1702. Château Renault gets under way from Martinique, his flag transferred aboard *Fort.* Upon reaching western Puerto Rico ten days later he detaches his weakest ships—*Merveilleux, Invincible, Monarque, Orgueilleux, Capable, Juste, Vainqueur, Fourbe, Constant, Bizarre, Saint Louis,* and *Trident*—to France under de La Harteloire while leading the remaining 15 ships of the line, five frigates, and ten smaller craft into Léogâne (Haiti) by next evening.

(While at Martinique, his expedition has been augmented by the frigates *Naiade* of Captain Belleville, and *Nieuport* of Captain d'Aubigny; the corvettes *Choquante* of de Rochambault, and *Émeraude* of de Sainte Osmanne; the transport *Mercure* of Comte d'Hautefort; and the dispatch vessel *Cheval Marin* of Du Dresnay.)

After corresponding with the Spaniards in Cuba and Mexico for a month, Château Renault puts to sea again on 19 March, seizing a New York sloop and two English brigantines in the Old Bahama Channel on 23 March, reaching Havana by 9 April. Leaving his main body there under Nesmond, the French admiral exits on 25 April with *Bourbon* (flag), four of the line, a frigate, and a fire ship to traverse the Gulf of Mexico and meet the outward-bound Mexican convoy under its commander in chief, Luis Manuel de Velasco, Vice Adm. José Chacón, and Rear Adm. Fernando Chacón. The French contingent reaches Veracruz by 5 May and departs again with the 14-ship Spanish formation on 10–11 June.

Upon reentering Havana on 7 July Château Renault finds his main force decimated by death, disease, and desertion—Nesmond, Rosmadec, Pallas, and Château Morant numbering among the dead—but nevertheless sets sail by 23 July with 18 of the line, six frigates, and a half-dozen smaller vessels, escorting 27 Spanish merchantmen across the Atlantic. (These ships are eventually trapped in Vigo Bay, Spain, by an Anglo-Dutch fleet under Adm. Sir George Rooke in October 1702.)

MARCH 1702. Zambo and English raiders from the Mosquito Coast ravage Spanish settlements in the Matina Valley (Costa Rica).

1 APRIL 1702. An expedition of 128 Spaniards departs Villahermosa (Mexico) to attack the logwood settlements in the nearby Laguna de Términos, guided by a renegade Irish Bayman named Archibald Macdonell. They return 18 days later with numerous captives after successfully sweeping the region.

SPRING 1702. Spanish troops in Chile mutiny for eight years of back pay but are repressed by Gov. Francisco Ibáñez de Peralta, knight of the Order of Malta.

15 MAY 1702. In Europe, England and Holland officially declare war against the Franco-Spanish union, which reciprocates in July.

LATE MAY 1702. Between Spanish Florida and English Carolina, a Creek war party—armed and abetted by English traders—exterminates the Timucuan mission of Santa Fé de Toloco. Saint Augustine's Gov. José de Zúñiga y la Cerda retaliates by dispatching 800 Apalaches into Creek territory later this summer under Capt. Francisco Romo de Uriza. Anthony Dodsworth and other Carolina traders get wind of the plan at Coweta and quickly marshal 500 Creeks, who ambush the Spanish column on the Flint River, inflicting heavy casualties.

14 JULY 1702. ***Conquest of Saint Kitts.*** Learning of the outbreak of hostilities, the new governor-general for the English Leeward Islands—Christopher Codrington, son of the prior governor-general who passed away on 30 July 1698—descends upon the shared island of Saint Kitts with 1,200 men from Antigua and Nevis, disembarking south of the French capital of Basseterre. The French colonists have only recently resettled their half of the island following expulsion during King William's War (*see* 30 June 1690 in Part 4). Their new governor, Jean Baptiste, Comte de Gennes, can muster barely 160 men in the southern quarter, with another 240 under his subordinate, de Courpon, in the north around Pointe de Sable. Their English neighbors already have 1,300 volunteers under arms and assault the Ravine Guillon north of Basseterre while Codrington's army closes in from the south and 24 British ships anchor offshore. De Gennes capitulates, and the French are once more expelled.

22 JULY 1702. Benbow sorties from Port Royal (Jamaica) with part of his fleet to commence hostilities against the nearby French base of Léogâne (Haiti). Arriving 16 days later, he drives the 46-gun French troop transport *Gironde* aground, burns two large merchantmen, and captures another two along with a brigantine and a sloop. After cruising offshore for several days the British learn of a French squadron reputedly bound for Cartagena and Portobelo under Ducasse; they set sail south to intercept on 21 August.

4 AUGUST 1702. The privateer Captain Brown quits Jamaica with his ten-gun *Blessing* and 79 men—including the famous Edward Davis (*see* 12 June 1684 in Part 4)—to attack Tolú (Colombia). The town is apparently plundered, but Brown is killed with a shot through the head; he is succeeded by Captain Christian.

8 AUGUST 1702. The 56-year-old French Commo. Jean Baptiste Ducasse (former governor of Saint Domingue; *see* Part 4) reaches Puerto Rico from Spain with a half-dozen ships of the line. Like Château Renault, Ducasse has been promoted and given a Spanish commission in addition to his French one, being ordered to escort the Mexican viceroy-designate and eight Spanish transports bearing 2,000 troops across the Atlantic.

After pausing at Puerto Rico, Ducasse detaches two men-of-war toward Mexico with the viceroy while touching at Santo Domingo to deposit the Spanish troops and collect important passengers. His next port of call is to be Santa Marta (Colombia), followed by Cartagena and Portobelo. He sets sail on 28 August with his 68-gun, 450-man flagship *Heureux* under Captain Bennet; 50-gun, 350-man *Agréable* of the Chevalier de Rency (or Roussy); 60-gun, 350-man *Phénix* under the Chevalier de Poudens; 50-gun, 300-man *Apollon* of de Muin; 30-gun transport *Prince de Frise* of Lieutenant de Saint André; fireship *Marin* of Cauvet; merchant frigate *Auguste* of Saint Marc; English prize galley *Anne;* plus two other consorts.

30 AUGUST 1702. ***Benbow's Last Fight.*** This morning Ducasse's ten sail are sighted off Santa Marta (just east of the Magdalena River, Colombia), by an English squadron: *Defiance* of 64 guns and 445 men under Richard Kirkby; *Pendennis* (48/230) under Thomas Hudson; *Windsor* (60/340) under John Constable; flagship *Breda* (70/460) under Christopher Fogg; *Greenwich* (54/280) under Cooper Wade; *Ruby* (48/230) under George Walton; and *Falmouth* (48/230) under Samuel Vincent. Benbow's strength is much superior to that of the French, who try to avoid action. By 4:00 P.M. the lead English ships overtake the French *Apollon* and *Prince de Frise,* opening fire briefly before *Defiance* and *Windsor* luff out of line. During the next few days the low-born English admiral will discover that Captains Kirkby, Hudson, Constable, and Wade are reluctant to obey his orders, thus hampering his efforts to overwhelm Ducasse's force.

Both formations steer west during the night, Benbow reforming his line and giving instructions for all ships to close next dawn. But again, only *Breda* and *Ruby* join the fighting at sunrise, the latter soon having to be towed off, badly cut up. Some broadsides are also exchanged this afternoon, the English flagship sustaining considerable damage aloft before night falls. The other captains still show little resolve on 1 September, when the French gain a favorable wind, allowing Ducasse to run with his lighter vessels in the van, *Phénix* and *Agréable* protecting his rear. Benbow pursues alone and fights the rearmost pair from 11:00

A.M. until 2:30 P.M. Nothing much occurs on 2 September, but at 10:00 A.M. on 3 September *Breda* and *Falmouth* overhaul Ducasse's squadron—which meanwhile has detached *Prince de Frise*—and about noon recapture the English galley *Anne.*

But the French commodore persists on his southeasterly heading, now coming within 50 miles of Cartagena. This prompts Benbow to once more overtake and fight a night action with *Apollon;* his right leg is smashed by a French chain shot at 3:00 A.M. on 4 September. Although carried below, Benbow returns to his quarterdeck to continue directing the action from a cot. Dawn reveals *Apollon* dismasted and in danger of being boarded, thus obliging Ducasse to turn back to its rescue. *Defiance, Windsor, Pendennis,* and *Greenwich* again refuse to fight, sheering off to leeward after a token broadside. Only *Breda* makes a stand, being severely mauled while *Apollon* is towed off.

Ducasse enters Cartagena triumphantly on 5 September, leaving a badly injured Benbow to limp back to Jamaica and court-martial his officers. Kirkby and Wade are condemned to death, Constable is cashiered and imprisoned, and Hudson dies on 25 September (O.S.). The admiral's leg is amputated, but he succumbs on 15 November. Capt. William Whetstone assumes temporary command of the Jamaica station until Vice Adm. John Graydon can come out from England. As for the French, *Agréable*'s commander, Louis de La Rochefoucauld Roye, Chevalier de Roussy, is elevated to lieutenant general and Marquis de Roye in December 1703—largely because he is the brother-in-law of France's navy minister.

6–7 SEPTEMBER 1702. The 46-year-old Commo. John Leake arrives at Bay Bulls (Newfoundland), escorting an English convoy with his 60-gun flagship *Exeter,* four other ships of 50–60 guns, two galleys of 32, and a sloop. He soon learns there are two French ships loading at nearby Trepassey Bay and another pair of enemy warships lying at Plaisance (Placentia) Bay.

Shortly thereafter four sail are sighted, and the commodore detaches his 60-gun *Montague* and 50-gun *Lichfield* in pursuit; they overhaul three of the French ships. Meanwhile Leake and the rest of his fleet proceed to Trepassey, where landing parties are set ashore on 9 September; they drive out the French and burn their structures before blockading the coast and returning to Saint John's by 30 September.

7 OCTOBER 1702. The 60-gun HMS *Assistance* and another warship appear off Saint Pierre Island (south of Newfoundland), disembarking a force that burns the church and two houses. The 45-year-old Gov. Sébastien Le Gouès, sieur de Sourdeval, drives the attackers off with a cannon, but next day the English land several hundred men who besiege the French within their tiny keep. Sourdeval surrenders and his colony is stripped bare, the English further dumping 52 French prisoners ashore before sailing away to rejoin Leake at Saint John's.

Once reassembled, the squadron departs for England, leaving Saint John's with a temporary boom and other improvements. During Leake's tenure his ships have sunk or captured 51 French vessels and leveled several settlements; he is promoted to admiral upon his return.

12 OCTOBER 1702. The French frigate *Auguste,* detached from Ducasse's squadron, sustains a vigorous encounter with a Jamaican privateer in the West Indies before winning free and continuing to France with dispatches.

27 OCTOBER 1702. Approximately 580 English militia and 370 Yamasee warriors set sail aboard 14 vessels from Port Royal (Carolina) under Gov. James Moore and Col. Robert Daniel, coming ashore in Guale (the Spanish name for eastern Georgia) a few days later. At midnight on 3 November they surprise the guardhouse at San Pedro de Tupiqui (on the northern extremity of Santa María or Amelia Island), killing its two sentries.

The English then rampage unchecked through the advance Spanish settlements, overrunning San Juan del Puerto by 5 November without resistance from Lt. Gov. Francisco Fuentes de Galarza. Moore subsequently sails with his flotilla to fall upon Saint Augustine from out at sea while Daniel takes the military contingent by boat up the Saint Johns River to approach overland.

4 NOVEMBER 1702. The Jamaican privateer Charles Gant disembarks 300 men at Casilda (south-central Cuba), marching upon the nearby town of Trinidad, whose Spanish inhabitants flee. The buccaneers ransack the empty buildings and withdraw next day with more than 100 black slaves plus considerable booty.

7 NOVEMBER 1702. ***Repulse at Saint Augustine.*** At 8:00 A.M. Spanish lookouts sight three English vessels heading south. Gov. José de Zúñiga has already learned of the Moore-Daniel attack farther to the north and braces for an assault. Next morning 13 English sail are seen

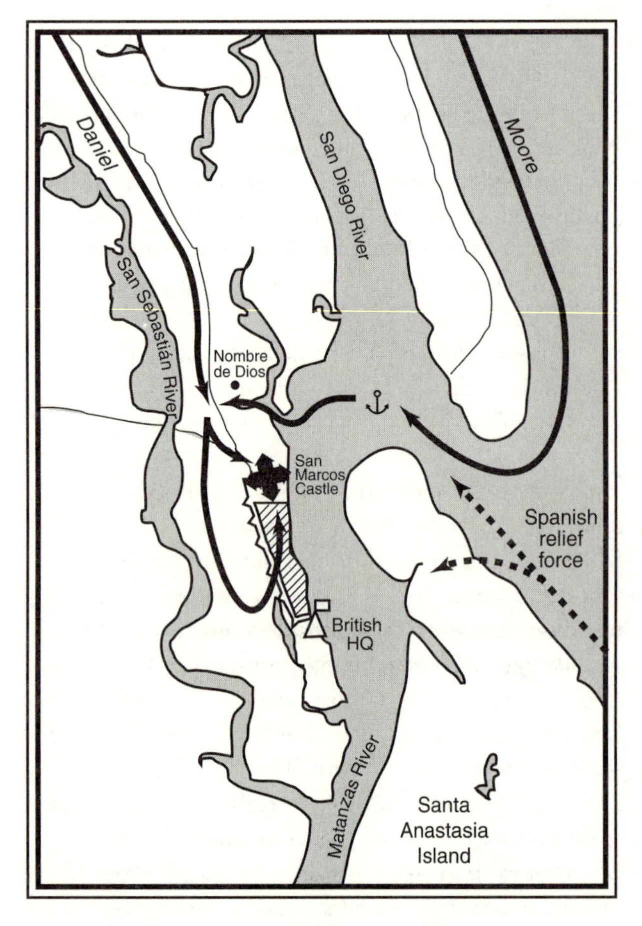

Failed Anglo-American assault on St. Augustine, Florida

bearing down on Saint Augustine's bar, prompting Capt. Luis Alfonso to remove his 16-man anchor watch from the royal frigate *Nuestra Señora de la Piedad y el Niño Jesús,* which he scuttles to prevent capture. The 400 Spanish defenders under elderly *Sargento Mayor* (Garrison Commander) Enrique Primo de Rivera also stand to their arms; this evening the smaller frigate *Gloria* slips downriver toward the Matanzas exit, hoping to carry word to Havana. On 9 November de Zúñiga learns from two Apalache scouts that another English force is approaching overland under Daniel and so orders all inhabitants into Saint Augustine's main citadel, San Marcos Castle.

The English army appears on 10 November and occupies the deserted town, establishing headquarters in its Franciscan mission; but they are unable to carry the citadel, which shelters 1,500 people plus several hundred cattle and animals. San Marcos's artillery bombards the English until one of its pieces bursts, killing three Spaniards and wounding five others. Moore and Daniel meanwhile institute a loose siege, prompting de Zúñiga to raze many buildings around his fort to provide a clear field of fire. Unable to damage San Marcos's ramparts with his light pieces, Moore detaches Daniel to Jamaica to secure siege artillery.

A lengthy respite ensues, during which the Carolinians dig emplacements and trenches while exchanging desultory bombardments with the fort. By 19 December approach lines are so close that 58 Spanish troops sally at midday, smashing numerous gabions before being driven back with one dead and several wounded. During the afternoon of 24 December a British brigantine and sloop arrive, disembarking fresh supplies next day. Morale within the beleaguered citadel begins to sag but is revived two days later when a pair of Spanish ships and two frigates are sighted offshore during the afternoon, led by Estéban de Berroa's flagship *Aguila Negra.*

They have been dispatched by Havana's Gov. Pedro Nicolás Benítez de Lugo and bear 212 troops under Capt. Lope de Solloso. The smaller English vessels now find themselves blockaded within Saint Augustine's harbor, compelling Moore to order its buildings set ablaze, his flotilla abandoned, and an overland retreat begun at dawn on 30 December from Vilano Beach. About 500 Englishmen march north toward the mouth of the Salamoto River, where they are eventually rescued by their remaining vessels and conveyed back to Charleston. Losses prove light on both sides, the Spaniards retaining three Carolina sloops, a brigantine, and materiel.

JANUARY 1703. Six English warships reach Barbados under 37-year-old Commo. Hovenden Walker, escorting ten transports bearing 4,000 soldiers, who are to subdue French strongholds in the West Indies then sail north to assail Placentia Bay (Newfoundland). Six weeks later—after a quarter of his men have died, deserted, or fallen ill—Walker proceeds to Antigua to join Governor-General Codrington, arriving early in March. Codrington has raised 14 companies of militia among the Leeward Islands, thus replacing Walker's losses.

16 MARCH 1703. At 5:00 P.M. Walker and Codrington quit Antigua with 18 armed merchantmen and 17 smaller vessels bearing 4,000 troops, escorted by the 80-gun HMSS *Boyne* (flag), *Chichester,* and *Cumberland;* the 70-gun *Burford, Edgar,* and *Yarmouth;* the 60-gun *Sunderland;* the 50-gun *Anglesea;* the frigate *Maidstone;* and the auxiliary *James and Sarah.* Two days later

most of these have rendezvoused off Marie Galante; next dawn they steer northwest to attack Guadeloupe.

19 MARCH 1703. ***Failure at Guadeloupe.*** This morning the Walker-Codrington expedition is sighted, French Gov. Charles Auger and his second-in-command, Hémon Coinard de La Malmaison, alerting their 1,400 militia. The invaders pause briefly off the Saintes before rounding the southern tip of Guadeloupe and striking north toward the capital of Basse-Terre. The English heave-to, splitting into two divisions around noon, with warships threatening Fort La Madeleine at the Baillif River while troop transports proceed six miles farther north. After a couple of days probing defenses, Walker disembarks 400–500 men at 3:00 P.M. on 21 March opposite the Goyaves Islands, only to be driven off by a French counterattack. An English frigate then accidentally drifts under the guns of Val de Lorge next day; 37 crewmen are killed before it can be rescued.

Prior to sunup on 23 March Walker and Codrington disembark 4,000 troops at three places—Gros François Cove (north of Fort La Madeleine), Val de Lorge, and Vieux Habitants Inlet—overrunning the outnumbered defenders in heavy fighting. The French make an orderly retreat through Basse-Terre, digging in behind the 370-man garrison of Fort Saint Charles on the south shores of Gallions River. Codrington meanwhile occupies the French capital then spends nine days installing an 11-gun siege battery, which opens fire on Fort Saint Charles by 2 April. Next day three French warships and 12 lesser vessels arrive at the port of Sainte Marie north of Capesterre, bearing 820 men from Martinique in 12 companies—two marines, four militia, and six buccaneers—under Jean Gabaret, recently promoted to lieutenant general for the French West Indies, plus subordinates Governor de Boisfermé of Marie Galante; Louis Gaston Caqueray de Valmenière; Jean Clair Dyel Du Parquet; François de Collart; and Jean Du Buc.

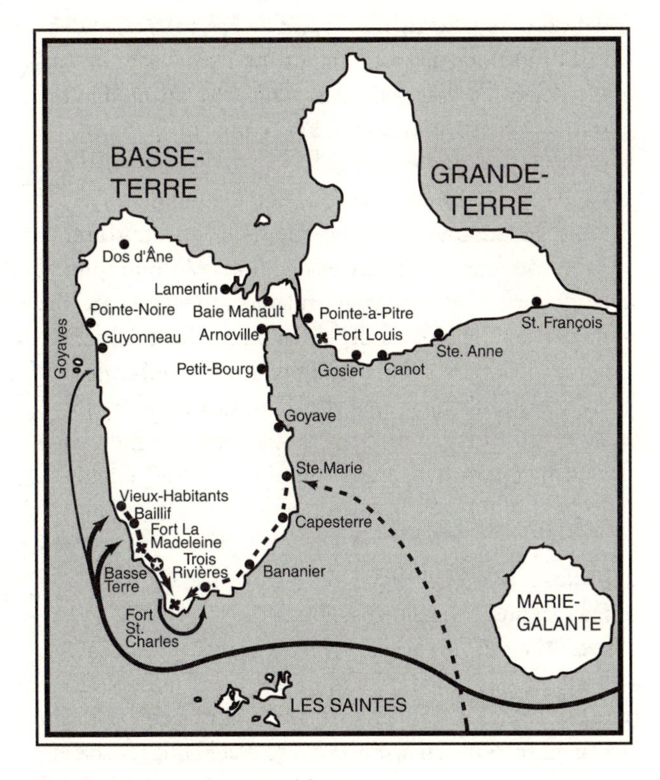

Failed English assault on Guadeloupe

This relief force marches into Fort Saint Charles with banners flying and trumpets blaring, hoping to demoralize the surprised English besiegers. Gabaret reorganizes the defenses and launches a flanking attack on 6 April, engaging the bulk of Codrington's army throughout much of the morning before retiring in the afternoon. Yet the French are compelled to abandon Fort Saint Charles two hours before dawn on 14 April; they blow its magazine and are pressed farther east.

On the morning of 27 April a large flotilla of English boats circles around the southern tip of Guadeloupe and attempts to capture Trois Rivières but is hampered by heavy seas. Disease and hunger are now sapping the attackers' resolve, and Codrington himself falls ill and sails away to Nevis to recuperate. By 5 May the remaining English commanders agree to evacuate Guadeloupe, and over the next fortnight 2,277 troops are reembarked. On the evening of 15 May Basse-Terre is set ablaze and Walker's fleet departs. Although the invasion leaves behind enormous damage, only 27 Frenchmen have been killed and 50 wounded.

EARLY APRIL 1703. English buccaneers disembark at Tonalá (Mexico), occupying nearby Tancochapa. A Spanish brigantine, sloop, and launch with 100 men from Veracruz surprise the raiders while they are ashore, capturing 42 Englishmen, four black slaves, a sloop, and two piraguas.

LATE APRIL 1703. Some 120 English raiders land at Chiltepec Bar (Mexico), plundering the countryside before retiring aboard their ships.

MAY 1703. In Louisiana, neighboring Alabama Indians inaugurate a series of attacks encouraged by English traders out of Carolina. The 23-year-old French Gov. Jean Baptiste Le Moyne de Bienville (younger brother to Pierre Le Moyne d'Iberville) leads a number of counterraids out of Fort Saint Louis at Mobile starting in December.

17 MAY 1703. Three English privateer sloops and eight piraguas anchor off the Tecoluta River (Mexico), sending a column inland to plunder Jalpa. While ransacking, the buccaneers are surprised by 80 Spanish cavalry who have made the three-hour ride from Villahermosa under Capt. Tomás Laureano de Alarcón to reinforce Jalpa's 60 defenders. Together they besiege the raiders inside the church for 24 hours until Jerónimo Alvarez del Valle can arrive with Villahermosa's main infantry force and two field pieces. After twice attempting to cut their way out, 108 Englishmen surrender; another eight are captured when their piraguas are taken offshore (the three sloops escaping).

15 JUNE 1703. The 37-year-old John Graydon, recently promoted to Vice Admiral of the White, arrives at Port Royal (Jamaica) with his 70-gun flagship *Resolution* under Capt. Thomas Lyell; the 60-gun *Montague* of William Cleveland; plus the 50-gun warships *Blackwall* of Thomas Day and *Nonsuch* under Robert Thompson. Seventeen days later—having incorporated Commodore Whetstone's vessels into his squadron—Graydon takes on water at Bluefields Bay then sails north to attack the French in Newfoundland.

After peering into Havana on 20 July, Graydon and Whetstone arrive off Newfoundland by 13 August and hold council aboard the 80-gun HMS *Boyne* in Saint Mary's Bay with Saint John's garrison commander, Capt. Michael Richards. Already feeling insufficiently strong to attack the French within Placentia Bay, the fleet is dispersed by fog and does not reassemble until one month later, the season by then being far advanced. The English therefore agree to return to England without attempting action; Graydon is subsequently cashiered from the service.

JULY 1703. A force of 600 French buccaneers descend upon the Dutch half of Sint Maarten, forcing many island inhabitants to emigrate.

21 AUGUST 1703. The 37-year-old French-Canadian naval Capt. Alexandre Leneuf de La Vallière de Beaubassin surprises the English settlement at Wells (Maine) with an Abenaki war party, laying waste a vast swathe of territory and killing or capturing more than 300 persons. The main English stronghold at Casco (Fort Loyal, Falmouth; near modern-day Portland) is able to resist thanks to Maj. John March, who is wounded and loses most of his property during the attack; he also loses his veteran subordinate, Capt. Cyprian Southack.

OCTOBER 1703. ***Destruction of Nassau.*** A privately raised Franco-Spanish expedition reaches the Bahamas from Santiago de Cuba, comprising 150 soldiers and a large number of *boucaniers* aboard two frigates commanded by Blas Moreno Mondragón and Claude Le Chesnaye. They surprise the 250 English settlers at the capital of New Providence (Nassau), slaughtering more than 100, seizing 22 guns, throwing down fortifications, then returning to Santiago a few days later with 13 prizes and 80–100 captives—among them Acting Gov. Ellis Lightwood.

25 JANUARY 1704. ***Ayubale Massacre.*** Having failed to conquer Saint Augustine, Governor Moore of Carolina marshals 50 whites and 1,500 Creeks at Okmulgee by December 1703 to assail Spanish Apalache. His column reaches the main fortified mission of Ayubale by 25 January and assaults the wooden stockade, only to be repelled by Franciscan Father Angel de Miranda and his flock. After a nine-hour siege the priest emerges under flag of truce, telling Moore that the defenders have no more ammunition; they must throw themselves upon the invaders' mercy. Miranda is murdered by the Yamasee and his congregation cruelly butchered while the mission burns.

Next day a Spanish relief column of 30 riders and 400 Indian auxiliaries arrive under Capt. Juan Ruíz Mexía, commander of Fort San Luis (24 miles farther southwest) and Father Juan de Parga. They are in turn defeated by Moore, Ruíz Mexía losing five soldiers killed and another eight captured, plus 168 Indians slaughtered, compared to about a half-dozen English and 100 Yamasee casualties. Parga dies and Ruíz Mexía is wounded and captured, after which the Anglo-Creek raiders rampage unchecked throughout most of the region. Some 325 Apalache men are carried off as slaves along with their families, another 1,300 agree to emigrate to Savannah, and many others flee into the wilderness. Spain's hold is broken—Fort San Luis being abandoned by mid-July—in a campaign that costs Moore four militia and 15 Indian dead. Such an easy victory encourages other incursions, which soon win the territory for English traders.

28 FEBRUARY 1704. A Franco-Indian war party led by Jean Baptiste Hertel de Rouville raids Deerfield (Massachusetts), killing 54 English settlers and capturing 120.

FEBRUARY 1704. The former buccaneer William Dampier rounds Cape Horn and reaches the Juan Fernández Islands with the privateers *Saint George* and

Cinque Ports. After patrolling up the Pacific Coast with little success they part company in the Bay of Panama, *Cinque Ports* returning to the Juan Fernández Islands under Capt. William Stradling (who quarrels with his 26-year-old Scottish first mate, Alexander Selkirk, and maroons him). *Cinque Ports* eventually becomes stranded, and Stradling surrenders to the Spaniards.

Dampier meanwhile is deserted by 22 men under his first mate, John Clipperton, and again in December 1704 by another 34 under his steward, William Funnel, who sails back to England. The old rover is finally compelled to abandon his rotten *Saint George* at the Lobos de Afuera Islands (Peru) and strike out across the Pacific in a brigantine prize.

30 APRIL 1704. Spain declares war against Portugal.

20 JUNE 1704. In retaliation for the Deerfield raid (*see* 28 February 1704) an Anglo-American band led by Benjamin Church captures a number of French Acadian settlements around Truro and Chignecto Bay (Nova Scotia).

16 JULY 1704. Coast-guard Captain Fernández departs Campeche with 62 soldiers under Capt. Antonio de Alcalá, and 122 volunteers, aboard 13 small craft to raid the English logwood establishments in the Laguna de Términos. On the afternoon of 18 July they come ashore at Puerto Escondido (a mile and a half from the Laguna's entrance), advancing by land and sea to capture the bar the next day. Two guard sloops, a ketch, and 25 prisoners are taken by the evening of 20 July; 30–40 Englishmen escape into the jungle.

Having thus secured the Laguna's entrance, Fernández and Alcalá request reinforcements from Yucatán's interim Gov. Alvaro de Rivaguda Enciso y Luyando, who dispatches a frigate with 80 men that arrives by 24 July. The Spaniards then use their increased strength to sweep the bay's interior, capturing another 110 interlopers, nine more ships, three sloops, two brigantines, two ketches, and 50 lesser craft before retiring.

4 AUGUST 1704. In the West Indies, the 50-gun, 670-ton HMS *Coventry* is captured by the French.

18 AUGUST 1704. A Franco-Indian war party destroys the English settlements at Bonavista (Newfoundland).

2 OCTOBER 1704. ***Sacramento Occupation.*** A Spanish expedition quits Buenos Aires, dispatched by Gov. Alonso Juan de Valdés Inclán to attack the Portuguese Colónia do Sacramento (modern-day Colonia del Sacramento, Uruguay), which for 25 years has been a point of contention between the two nations. Gen. Baltasar García Ros leads 800 Spanish regulars, 600 militia, and 300 native auxiliaries to be joined by another 4,000 Guaraní tribesmen once he crosses the River Plate. After marching north through marshy bayous the host closes in on the Portuguese settlement on 1 January 1705, laying siege to the outnumbered defenders.

A seaborne relief force appears on 5 March consisting of a 44-gun Portuguese ship, a pair of merchantmen (of 30 and 20 guns), and an eight-gun auxiliary. Capt. José de Ibarra sorties from the Spanish besiegers' anchorage with the 36-gun merchantman *Nuestra Señora del Rosario,* the 16-gun *Santa Teresa* (a Portuguese prize), and a fireship to attempt to dispute the relief force's entry. After a four-hour gun duel the Portuguese squadron gains Sacramento, only to find the garrison on its last legs. Sacramento is therefore abandoned by Gov. Veita Cabral, who sails away with his followers aboard the four Portuguese ships on 14 March.

8 JANUARY 1705. In bitter cold, a 450-man Franco-Indian expedition quits Placentia (Newfoundland) under Gov. Daniel d'Auger de Subercasse, Captain de Beaucourt, Jacques Testard de Montigny, and Jacques l'Hermitte, to march overland and attack the English settlement at Saint John's. A brigantine carrying a mortar and ammunition simultaneously sets sail to rendezvous with the small army at Bay Bulls.

That place is overrun along with Petty Harbor, and by 31 January the French are within three miles of their larger objective; they decide to attempt a surprise attack next dawn. Snow and other problems hamper their approach, and only the advance guard arrives within sight of Fort William, which opens a heavy counterfire under its commander, Lt. John Moody, along with the South battery (or South Castle) under Robert Latham. Auger is obliged to fall back to Saint John's waterfront and houses, besieging the English citadels for 33 days yet unable to storm them because the brigantine carrying his ordnance fails to arrive.

After trying an assault in vain on 6 March the French withdraw from Saint John's next day; Auger detaches Testard de Montigny with 70 men to ravage the English settlements farther north in Conception and Trinity Bays. Eventually, all English outposts (except Carbonear) are destroyed as far as Bonavista. During the three-month campaign Auger's expedition spikes or destroys 40 cannons, burns a ship, several hundred boats, and 200 wagons, and captures 1,200 Englishmen (releasing all but 80 for lack of provisions).

MARCH 1705. Recently knighted and promoted rear admiral, Whetstone returns to the West Indies with his flag aboard the 70-gun *Suffolk* to assume command at Jamaica. His flagship accidentally explodes at anchor this same autumn, killing almost 100 crewmembers.

19 APRIL 1705. Martial law is proclaimed at Havana amid fears of a popular uprising against growing French influence over Spanish affairs.

AUTUMN 1705. An army of 3,000–4,000 Carolina Indians under English leaders cuts a path of destruction through Choctaw territory, carrying away many captives. Survivors retreat to French Mobile, thus extending English influence inland from the Atlantic seaboard.

LATE JANUARY 1706. ***Chavagnac's Campaign.*** The Comte de Chavagnac, a veteran, 42-year-old commodore, arrives at Martinique with *Glorieux* (flag), *Apollon, Brillant, Fidèle, Ludlow* (English prize), and *Nymphe.* While waiting for his superior, d'Iberville, to come out from France, Chavagnac recruits 400 Martinican volunteers under Jean Du Buc—plus 300 buccaneers under François de Collart—for an attempt against English Saint Kitts, to which Gov.-Gen. Charles François de Machault, sieur de Bellemont contributes another four companies of Martinican militia.

Late on the afternoon of 4 February Chavagnac sets sail for Guadeloupe, detaching *Nymphe* to maintain watch upon Barbados. An additional 300 volunteers under Major Poullain join the expedition at Guadeloupe's capital of Basse-Terre; by the time the French finally put to sea again, on 16 February, their five warships are accompanied by two merchantmen and 24 buccaneer craft bearing a landing force some 1,200 strong.

Contrary winds prevent the force from assaulting Antigua, and by the time the French veer round and anchor three miles off Nevis's capital of Charlestown, it is already evening on 16 February. Next morning Chavagnac orders his boats inshore, but the surf is running high, and the English defenders under Col. Richard Abbott are prepared to repel the invasion. Therefore, the attackers sail away four days later to Saint Kitts.

This same afternoon—21 February—the attackers are sighted, although the garrison under Gov. Walter Hamilton is already alerted. Chavagnac's flotilla nonetheless anchors opposite Basseterre, except for a half-dozen vessels that drop down to Palmetto Point and open fire upon the fortifications. Past midnight Chavagnac disembarks his troops in Frigate Bay, and at dawn on 22 February they make for Basseterre. Poullain and his 300 Guadeloupans simultaneously circle by sea to disembark at the northern outpost of Pointe de Sable, advancing east toward Cayonne while laying waste the countryside. They are opposed by 200 English colonists, who are quickly driven back upon Col. Stephen Payne's regular garrison at Fort Charles, which checks the northern incursion.

Chavagnac meanwhile presses on toward Basseterre with subordinates Du Buc, Collart, and Jean Clair Du Parquet, scattering Hamilton's 300 infantry and 100 cavalry. Retreating through the capital, the English governor decides to make a stand at Palmetto Point. On 23 February Poullain bypasses Payne's defenses at Fort Charles to raid as far south as Goodwin's Gut. Chavagnac does the same in his area, pillaging the English plantations for several days while avoiding heavily armed citadels. On 26 February the French begin their withdrawal, loading 300 black slaves and considerable booty. At the cost of 20 casualties Chavagnac has devastated Saint Kitts and retires to Martinique.

EARLY MARCH 1706. In Alabama, a Chickasaw war party makes a nocturnal descent upon a Choctaw village, carrying off more than 150 captives to be sold as slaves in South Carolina. The French governor, Bienville, is subsequently obliged to support his Choctaw allies in a war against the English-backed Chickasaw.

7 MARCH 1706. ***D'Iberville Overruns Nevis.*** Le Moyne d'Iberville reaches Martinique with *Juste* (flag), *Prince, Aigle,* and *Sphere* to find subordinate Chavagnac recently returned from ravaging Saint Kitts. Both squadrons total a dozen men-of-war and two dozen buccaneer craft, bearing 2,000 soldiers and freebooters. They depart within two weeks, touching at Guadeloupe to gather even greater strength before proceeding north on 31 March to assault Nevis.

Steering between Montserrat and Antigua, d'Iberville materializes before that island during the afternoon of 2 April, catching Nevis's Governor Abbott completely off guard. (Following Chavagnac's earlier raid—*see* late January 1706—only 35 English regular soldiers plus 430 militia remain on the island.) Dividing their fleet into two, the French bear down upon the northern and western shores simultaneously, thus splitting the defenders' strength. Chavagnac disembarks unopposed at Green Bay, just above the capital of Charlestown, while d'Iberville anchors his contingent at Nevis's southernmost extremity (modern-day French Bay, named for this invasion), bringing his men ashore before sunrise on 3 April.

Some 25 anchored merchantmen are seized in Charlestown Roads while the panic-stricken English fall back on a small hilltop fort behind the capital. Seeing the throng of buccaneers that d'Iberville deploys to assault the frail stronghold, Abbott capitulates by 4 April. The French leader departs 17 days later, carrying away 3,187 black slaves—another 1,400 are to follow later—plus countless other booty. He returns to Martinique by 26 April and, shortly thereafter, transfers to Saint Domingue (Haiti) in hopes of organizing another such venture; he dies of disease in Havana on 8 July.

JULY 1706. Commo. William Kerr arrives at Port Royal (Jamaica) to succeed Admiral Whetstone as commander in chief. After they cruise together briefly, Whetstone sails to England while Kerr leads an unsuccessful operation against Saint Domingue (Haiti). Eventually Kerr goes home as well next year, only to be accused of accepting bribes for protecting contraband trade and sparing enemy properties; he is cashiered.

16 AUGUST 1706. Six French privateers under Capt. Jacques Lefebvre (subordinate of the deceased d'Iberville; *see* 7 March 1706) depart Havana with 200 Cuban troops and two field pieces under de Berroa to sail northwest to Saint Augustine for a combined venture against Charleston (South Carolina).

When the expedition arrives, Florida's Gov. Francisco de Córcoles y Martínez furnishes Lefebvre with an additional pair of canoes, a demigalley, 30 regular infantry, and a few Indian volunteers; thus enlarged, the expedition sets sail again by 31 August. Shortly thereafter a Dutch sloop separates the 72-gun *Brillante*—bearing the French land Commander Arbousset and 200 of his best troops—from Lefebvre's squadron; the rest of the formation presses on to its objective.

7 SEPTEMBER 1706. ***Defense of Charleston.*** The Franco-Spanish expedition of Lefebvre and Berroa arrives off South Carolina's capital and is sighted by lookouts on Sullivan's Island who put up smoke signals. Despite a yellow fever epidemic raging within the city proper, militia rally from throughout the district. Lefebvre's ships anchor off Sullivan's Island this evening and, next morning, send a surrender demand inshore. Gov. Nathaniel Johnson rejects it, and on the morning of 9 September the invasion commences.

One party lands on James Island and sets fire to a house but is driven back to their demigalley by a counterattack of Carolina militia and Indians. Another 160 Spanish soldiers disembark on a narrow stretch of land between the Wando River and the Atlantic, burning two small launches and a storehouse. They encamp overnight, only to be surprised while eating chickens by 100 English militia who kill a dozen Spaniards, capture 60, and drown six or seven as the survivors attempt to swim back to their craft. On 11 September Johnson orders six small launches and a fireship under Col. William Rhett to bear down on the five enemy vessels anchored off Sullivan's Island, scattering them farther out to sea and thereby finally convincing Lefebvre and Berroa to retire to Saint Augustine.

No sooner has the Franco-Spanish expedition sailed over the horizon when the separated *Brillante* appears, disembarking Arbousset and 200 soldiers east of Charleston. Unaware that the defenders are already fully roused, the contingent is intercepted near Holybush Plantation by a body of Carolina militia and is soundly defeated. At the same time, another group of British defenders rows out to *Brillante* and secures it. Thus, in four days of action, Johnson's garrison kills 30 invaders and captures another 320.

6 JUNE 1707. Some 23 New England sloops and transports appear off Port Royal (modern-day Annapolis Royal, Nova Scotia), escorted by the 50-gun, 669-ton HMS *Deptford* of Captain Stukely. Its military contingent is led by 49-year-old veteran Indian fighter Col. John March of Casco Bay (Portland, Maine), with Lt. Cols. Francis Wainwright and Winthrop Hilton serving as regimental commanders. From a total strength of 1,100 men, March disembarks 750 Massachusetts and Rhode Island militia on the south side, below Port Royal's French fort (which is under the command of d'Auger de Subercasse). The latter has only a 260-man garrison, so an English victory seems imminent—but March hesitates after advancing to the very gates of the outnumbered and surprised French outpost.

Following a few days of desultory, long-range exchanges, a party of Abenaki natives arrives under Bernard Anselme d'Abbadie de Saint Castin to bolster Port Royal's defenses. The French and Indians offer up a spirited resistance, and after a series of gloomy consultations the New Englanders reembark on 15 June. March retires to Casco; the bulk of his troops return to Boston, where they are accused of cowardice.

SUMMER 1707. Several hundred Talapoosa Indians, led by a few Englishmen out of Carolina, surprise Pensacola (Santa María de Galve, Florida). Its houses are burned and pillaged right up to the Spanish fort, which the attackers penetrate before the garrison can rally and expel them. Eleven Spaniards are killed and 15 captured; a dozen slaves are carried away.

13 AUGUST 1707. The 21-year-old French privateer Capt. Pierre Morpain arrives at Port Royal (Annapolis Royal, Nova Scotia) from Saint Domingue with *Intrépide,* bringing in a captured English slaver and a merchant frigate loaded with food. The refreshment is especially welcome to Governor Subercasse and his small garrison, having recently undergone an English siege.

One week later 1,600 New England troops under Colonel March make a second attempt to overrun the French outpost. Again the attack becomes bogged down, with March falling ill and turning over command to his subordinate, Wainwright. Subercasse, Saint Castin, and Morpain put up a stout fight, eventually forcing the New Englanders to withdraw. The failure of this second expedition convinces the Anglo-American authorities to pressure London for more direct support of future ventures, in the form of regular troops and warships out of England.

LATE SUMMER 1707. The 41-year-old Commo. Charles Wager arrives in Jamaica with a small squadron and convoy to assume command over the station. Shortly thereafter he conceives the plan of attacking the Spanish treasure convoy, which is to depart Portobelo and cross into Cartagena. In mid-January 1708 Wager sorties to hunt for the Panamanian galleons, but after two months of cruising he retires to Port Royal (Jamaica), hoping to lull the Spaniards into believing the danger has passed. The English commodore sets sail again on 25 April and, despite a heavy storm, maintains a stealthy watch over Cartagena for more than a month.

LATE NOVEMBER 1707. An English vessel attacks Saint Pierre Island (south of Newfoundland), obliging Governor Sourdeval and a few settlers to seek shelter in the woods. After one of his landing parties is ambushed, the English commander further threatens to burn everything in sight but instead sails away after setting a few prisoners ashore.

In the Gulf of Mexico, Spanish Pensacola is once more besieged by 1,500 Indians and Carolina frontiersmen. Dissensions soon arise, however, and three-quarters of the attackers disperse without attempting an assault. By the time French Governor Bienville arrives on 8 December with a contingent from Mobile to relieve his Spanish allies, the remaining 13 Englishmen and 350 Indians retire.

18 JANUARY 1708. Four privateer vessels under a commander nicknamed Barbillas or Bigotes—Spanish for "Little Whiskers" or "Moustache"—sack and burn the town of Lerma, near Campeche (Mexico).

8 JUNE 1708. ***Wager Versus the Spanish Galleons.*** At daybreak the English squadron prowling off Baru Island sights two sail standing in toward Cartagena. By noon the entire 17-ship silver convoy of Adm. José Fernández de Santillán, Conde de Casa Alegre, is within view of Wager's warships.

Although Casa Alegre's ships are numerous, only the 64-gun, 600-man flagship *San José* and the 64-gun, 500-man vice-flagship *San Joaquín* are actually men-of-war. The remaining Spanish vessels consist of a 44-gun hired merchantman serving as the third-in-command's flagship (referred to as a *gobierno;* in this case it bears 400 men under naval Capt. Nicolás de la Rosa, Conde de Vega Florida); a 40-gun merchantman; plus eight lesser craft. Casa Alegre is also accompanied by the 36-gun French privateer *Saint Esprit* of Capt. Claude Raoul out of Saint Malo and another 24-gun French ship, two sloops, and a brigantine.

To oppose them, Wager has his 70-gun flagship *Expedition* under Capt. Henry Long, 60-gun *Kingston* of Timothy Bridges, 50-gun *Portland* of Edward Windsor, and fireship *Vulture* under Cmdr. Caesar Brooks. The English realize they can concentrate on the three Spanish capital ships and ignore the rest. Wager orders *Portland* to attack the Spanish man-of-war in the van; *Kingston* to seek battle with *San Joaquín* toward the rear; while he himself closes upon Casa Alegre's flagship in the center.

The afternoon proves fine, with a brisk north-northeast wind; *Expedition* gradually gains on *San José* while the entire Hispano-French convoy attempts to escape north around Baru Island to Cartagena. At sunset Casa Alegre opens fire on Wager's flagship,

The Spanish flagship San José *exploding while engaged against Wager's HMS* Expedition *near Cartagena*

which replies half an hour later. Ninety minutes of hard fighting ensues, ending abruptly when Casa Alegre's *San José* explodes and goes down with almost all hands. Less than a dozen survivors are plucked from the water by English boats, only five of them living very long.

Toward 10:00 P.M. *Expedition* overhauls the Spanish rear admiral and cripples it with a broadside through its stern windows, obliging de la Rosa to strike by 2:00 A.M. on 9 June, just as the moon begins to rise. Next dawn Wager sends *Kingston* and *Portland* in pursuit of the Spanish vice-flag *San Joaquín,* which outstrips them as the afternoon wears on and finally wins free by running through the dangerous Salmedina channel, where the English dare not follow.

When Captains Bridges and Windsor rejoin Commodore Wager on 10 June, he detaches them along with *Vulture* to probe behind Baru Island, where the 40-gun Spanish merchantman is hiding. Upon seeing the Royal Navy trio draw near, the Spaniards beach their ship and set it ablaze before escaping ashore. Thus Wager returns to Port Royal (Jamaica) on 19 July, angry at obtaining only a single prize because of his subordinates' lackluster performance. Fifteen days later both Bridges and Windsor are court-martialled and cashiered.

20 JULY 1708. Commo. Andrés de Arriola's *Nuestra Señora de Guadalupe y San Antonio,* flagship for Spain's West Indian squadron, intercepts a 12-ship English convoy off Cape San Antonio (western Cuba), carrying half of them into Veracruz by 3 August.

26 JULY 1708. Capts. Jean Baptiste Hertel de Rouville and Jean Baptiste de Saint Ours Deschaillons depart Montréal with 200 men, to mount a Franco-Indian attack one month later—on 29 August—against Haverhill (Massachusetts). These raiders slay 15 of its English settlers and destroy this village, but are then ambushed as they retire by 60 pursuers under Captain Ayer, suffering ten killed and 19 wounded before regaining Canada.

29 OCTOBER 1708. Off Saint Domingue (Haiti), the 24-gun *Dunkirk's Prize* of Capt. George Purvis runs aground while in pursuit of a 14-gun French vessel; nevertheless, he seizes it and uses it to return safely to Jamaica.

25 NOVEMBER 1708. Dorset Capt. Woodes Rogers arrives off Brazil, anchoring five days later in Baía da Ilha Grande to replenish supplies for a raid into the South Pacific via the Strait of Magellan. His expedition

consists of 183 men aboard his 30-gun, 320-ton frigate *Duke* and 150 aboard Capt. Stephen Courtney' 26-gun, 260-ton *Duchess* (piloted by the veteran rover Dampier and accompanied by 48-year-old physician Thomas Dover, who has no medical charge during the cruise but is a major shareholder).

1 JANUARY 1709. After an investment lasting several days, the English settlement at Saint John's (Newfoundland) surrenders to a contingent of 170 French soldiers, Canadian militia, and Indian warriors under Capt. Joseph de Saint Ovide, dispatched by Placentia's Gov. Philippe de Costebelle.

MID-JANUARY 1709. ***Rogers's Pacific Incursion.*** The English privateers *Duke* and *Duchess* round Cape Horn in heavy weather, clawing their way to the Juan Fernández Islands by 12 February. Here they find Scottish Master Alexander Selkirk, who has been left behind four years and four months earlier by Captain Stradling (*see* February 1704). Upon his return to England two years later, Selkirk's account will inspire Daniel Defoe to write *Robinson Crusoe.* After recuperating, Rogers's expedition advances north toward Peru.

12 MARCH 1709. The 40-gun *Adventure* of Capt. Robert Clark is taken in the West Indies and its commander killed.

26 APRIL 1709. After Capt. Stephen Hutchins of the 50-gun HMS *Portland* reaches the smuggling port of Bastimentos (northern Panama) with an English trading convoy, he learns four large enemy vessels are anchored ten miles southeast at Portobelo. One week later, having reconnoitered Portobelo, Hutchins is informed by a scout that two of the ships have sailed; the remaining pair are the 50-gun former HMS *Coventry* (captured by the French almost five years previously; *see* 4 August 1704) and the 40-gun *Mignon*.

On 12 May Hutchins learns that the latter two have also sailed the previous evening and so weighs from Bastimentos in pursuit. He sights them two days later at 8:00 A.M., becoming engaged by both *Coventry* and *Mignon* that afternoon at extremely long range. *Portland* continues chasing until noon on 17 May, when *Coventry*'s mainmast falls overboard and *Mignon* makes off. *Portland*'s victory costs nine killed and 12 wounded out of a crew of 232; French casualties are estimated at 70.

4 MAY 1709. Rogers's *Duke* and *Duchess* fall upon Guayaquil, easily overrunning its surprised defenders under Gov. Jerónimo Boza y Solís. (Afterward, the English allegedly store their plunder in Guayaquil's churches, where they also sleep, despite the stench of recently buried plague victims. Upon returning aboard ship, 180 rovers fall ill within 48 hours, Doctor Dover instructing the surgeons to bleed all in both arms. He then gives them "dilute sulphuric acid to drink"; only eight die—either from the disease or its remarkable cure.)

Rogers's raiders retire offshore to Puná Island by 8 May to recover and await payment of a 30,000-peso ransom for sparing Guayaquil's buildings. The sum cannot be raised, so the English sail away with their hostages, Capts. Manuel Jiménez and Manuel de la Puente. They also intercept the French *Marquis*—which Rogers incorporates into his flotilla—and Spanish *San Dimas* out of Panama, which is stripped and sunk. The rovers subsequently spend two months careening on Gorgona Island before proceeding north-northwest toward Mexico.

LATE JULY 1709. Veteran 53-year-old militia Col. Francis Nicholson leads an expedition of Connecticut, New York, and New Jersey colonials up the Hudson River, deploying his troops in stockaded forts from Stillwater (north of Albany) to the foot of Lake Champlain, thus threatening Montréal. Colleague Samuel Vetch is to lead a similar force of volunteers around by sea from Boston into the Saint Lawrence seaway, although the arrangement is eventually canceled.

Learning of Nicholson's encroachment, Canada's Gov.-Gen. Pierre de Rigaud de Vaudreuil dispatches a reconnaissance force south under Claude de Ramezay, who skirmishes with the colonials off Scalping Point (opposite Crown Point, New York). Fatigue, short supplies, and disease prove to be Nicholson's greatest enemies, so demoralizing his army that within a few weeks troops abandon their outposts and stream home. Still determined to persist with this strategy, Nicholson subsequently sails for England to press its ministers for support of future ventures.

1 JANUARY 1710. After almost two months' wait off Cabo San Lucas (Baja California) for the Manila galleons, Rogers's *Duke, Duchess,* and the French prize *Marquis* sight a sail 20 miles out at sea. *Duke* intercepts next morning, engaging the 20-gun Spanish ship, which soon strikes and is revealed as *Nuestra Señora de la Encarnación* (alias *Desengaño*) under French Cmdr. Jean Presberty. Nine Spaniards lie dead and ten are wounded out of 193 aboard, compared to only one se-

rious injury among the English—Rogers himself, whose upper jaw is shot away.

Encarnación has sailed from the Philippines as consort to the much larger and wealthier *Nuestra Señora de Begonia,* but they become separated during the crossing. Rogers therefore stations *Duchess* and *Marquis* to keep watch while anchoring inshore to begin looting his prize. Some 142 of its passengers and crew are released aboard a captive coastal trader to continue to Acapulco, only the pilot and about 40 Filipino sailors being retained.

Three days later (Christmas Day 1709 [O.S.]), Rogers's lookout signals from high atop a hill that *Duchess* and *Marquis* are pursuing another sail, which they delay until Rogers's *Duke* can join after midnight. Dawn of 6 January reveals the 900-ton *Begonia,* manned by 450 men under Capt. Fernando de Angulo and pierced for 60 guns (although mounting only 40). Its immensely stout bulwarks resist the English shot, and Rogers's men hesitate to board. After having their rigging cut up, the English break off action.

Encarnación is subsequently renamed *Bachelor,* Dover being appointed captain and Selkirk first mate, then sails for England along with the rest of Rogers's squadron by way of Guam and the Cape of Good Hope.

26 July 1710. After visiting London, Colonel Nicholson returns to Boston with the 50-gun, 700-ton ships *Dragon* (flag) of Commo. George Martin, *Falmouth* of Walter Riddell, and *Chester* of Thomas Mathews plus the bomb vessel *Star* under Cmdr. Thomas Rochfort. A couple of months later they are joined by the 36-gun frigate *Feversham* of Capt. Robert Paston and the 32-gun frigate *Lowestoft* of George Gordon, having escorted a merchant convoy to New York. The force boasts 400 marines above complement.

Although the season is far advanced and rumors of peace negotiations back in Europe are widespread, New England nonetheless musters a large expedition to assault the nearby French outpost of Port Royal (Annapolis Royal, Nova Scotia). An expected army of English regulars under Maj. Gen. Viscount Shannon fails to appear, but by September Nicholson is still able to fill 31 transports with 3,500 troops, divided into two regiments from Massachusetts plus one each from Connecticut, New Hampshire, and Rhode Island.

16 August 1710. ***Du Clerc at Rio de Janeiro.*** A privately financed squadron of six French ships, a frigate, and a galliot appears outside Rio de Janeiro

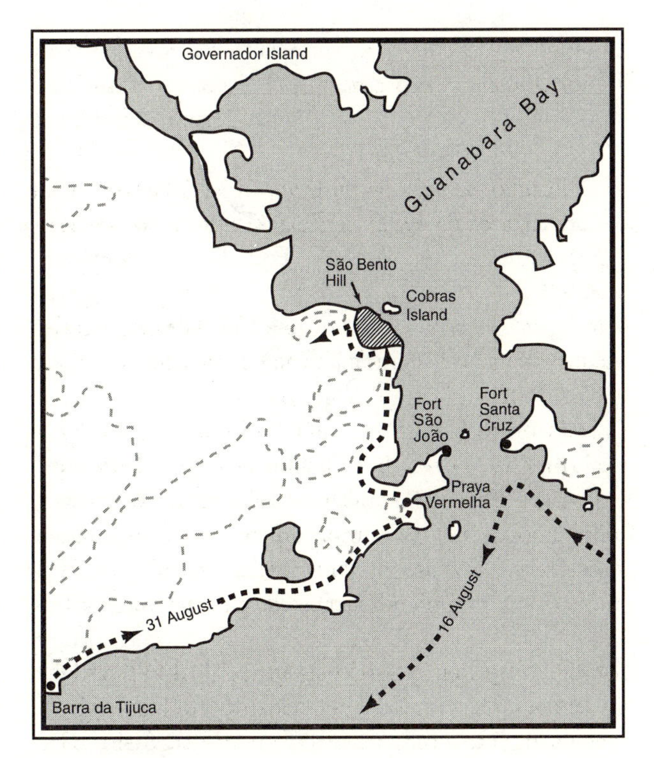

Du Clerc's failed invasion of Rio de Janeiro

under Jean François Du Clerc, recently promoted *capitaine de frégate* in France's royal navy and knight of the Order of Saint Louis, intent upon conquering the place. Although flying false English colors—England is Portugal's ally—his vessels are fired upon by Fort Santa Cruz as they attempt to stand into Rio's harbor and so continue farther west and anchor in Ilha Grande Bay.

After a few desultory disembarkations in the region of Guaratinguetá on 27 August, Du Clerc returns east and, four days later, lands 1,200 men at Barra da Tijuca (six miles west of Rio), hoping to circle inland through the Orgãos Range. Fighting through Praya Vermelha, his small army attempts to storm the capital by 18 September, only to be thrown back by Gov. Francisco de Castro de Morais's militia hordes—spearheaded by Bento do Amaral's student company—plus artillery fire from Fort São Sebastião on nearby Cobras Island. Having lost 380 men, the French next try to occupy São Bento Hill (called La Bénédictine by the invaders), only to again be repulsed and forced to seek shelter in a sugar plantation. Cornered, outnumbered, and threatened with being burned alive, Du Clerc has no choice but to surrender his army's remnants and face imprisonment.

Three of his warships materialize outside Rio on 21 September and open fire but desist when the captive French commander sends them a message advising of his fate. They sail away, and shortly thereafter Du Clerc is murdered by an enraged Brazilian mob while his senior commanders are manhandled. (Word of the mistreatment helps fuel René Duguay Trouin's subsequent strike; *see* 12 September 1711.)

21 SEPTEMBER 1710. HMS *Chester* sets sail from Massachusetts to blockade Port Royal (Annapolis Royal, Nova Scotia) in advance of 31 New England transports and a half-dozen men-of-war under Nicholson and Martin, which quit Nantasket eight days later.

4 OCTOBER 1710. ***Nicholson at Annapolis Royal.*** Having arrived outside Port Royal (Nova Scotia) and surprised its 300 French defenders under Governor Subercasse, the expedition of Nicholson and Adjutant Gen. Samuel Vetch lands in two divisions next day. They close on Port Royal's works by 6 October, installing batteries within 100 yards of the French ramparts, which open fire that night. Without hope of relief, Subercasse offers to surrender on 13 October, the actual capitulation being finalized two days later. Nicholson renames the town Annapolis Royal in honor of the English queen, leaving Vetch as garrison commander on 30 October with 500 troops so that he may return to Boston one week later with Martin. Nicholson eventually sails to London to persuade the British government that yet another, larger military effort should be mounted against French Canada.

12 NOVEMBER 1710. In the West Indies, the 34-gun frigate *Scarborough* of Capt. Edward Holland is taken by the French. (Next year it will be recaptured by the 50-gun, 620-ton HMS *Anglesea* of Capt. Thomas Legge and the 40-gun *Fowey* of Robert Chadwick.)

17 APRIL 1711. In Europe, the 32-year-old Holy Roman Emperor Joseph I dies of smallpox, being succeeded by his younger brother, Archduke Charles of Austria (whom Britain and the Netherlands have been attempting to install upon Spain's throne). However, such a prospective Austro-Spanish amalgamation is scarcely more palatable to the maritime powers than the Franco-Spanish union they are currently fighting; tentative peace feelers are therefore begun, with plenipotentiaries being delegated to meet in Utrecht as early as January 1712.

LATE APRIL 1711. A 200-man Spanish expedition sweeps through the English logwood establishments in the Laguna de Términos, returning to Campeche with an 18- and a 14-gun English frigate, a storeship, two sloops, and a brigantine.

5–6 MAY 1711. This night the 44-gun *Thétis* of Jean François de Choiseul, compte de Beaupré and former governor of Saint Domingue (Haiti), is intercepted three miles outside Havana by the 60-gun HMS *Windsor* of Capt. George Paddon and the 48-gun *Weymouth* of Richard Lestock. They batter their French opponent into submission, killing or wounding 65 of 180 crewmembers. Captives are set ashore at the Cuban capital, including the wounded Choiseul, who expires shortly thereafter.

19 JUNE 1711. Nicholson returns to New England from London, having convinced the English government to dispatch an expedition to spearhead the colonists' attempt against French Canada. That force appears two and a half weeks later, comprising 11 Royal Navy warships and 51 troop transports under Sir Hovenden Walker, recently promoted Rear Admiral of the White. His convoy bears seven regiments of foot—five of them veteran units from the Duke of Marlborough's victorious continental army—under Brig. Gen. John "Jack" Hill. New England will furnish an additional 1,300 militia, supplementing the 5,300 soldiers and 6,000 seamen and marines brought from England.

JUNE 1711. The French freebooter Du Buc descends on English Montserrat with his 36-gun *Roland* and other consorts, overrunning a battery before his men are ambushed and obliged to retreat.

21 JUNE 1711. Off Martinique the 50-gun HMS *Newcastle* of Capt. Sampson Bourne engages a 36-gun French ship, a 24-gun auxiliary, nine privateer sloops, and two other vessels, driving them into Saint Pierre's harbor and ending a filibuster expedition against Antigua and Montserrat. (Most likely this engagement involves the same French craft as the preceding entry.)

26 JULY 1711. Commo. James Littleton sorties from Port Royal (Jamaica) with five two-deckers and a sloop, having learned that the homeward-bound Spanish plate fleet is soon expected from Portobelo at Cartagena. He arrives off the latter place 11 days later, chasing five large vessels, which run in through its Bocachica entrance. Next morning, 7 August, another four sail are pursued, the 50-gun HMS *Salisbury* of Capt. Francis Hosier and the 50-gun *Salisbury Prize* (formerly the French *Heureux*) of Robert Harland

overtaking the 60-gun Spanish vice-flagship and engaging it until Littleton can join. This Spanish vessel is then secured at a cost of one British seaman killed and six wounded; a second is captured by Edward Vernon's 60-gun *Jersey*. Littleton subsequently blockades Cartagena, being obliged to withdraw a few weeks later and thus allow the remaining Spanish galleons to exit for Havana, escorted by Ducasse's French warships.

10 AUGUST 1711. Early this morning, Walker and Hill get under way from Boston to assault Canada, their 67 transports and auxiliaries being escorted by the 70-gun, 440-man flagship *Edgar* of Capt. Joseph Soanes; 80-gun, 520-man *Humber* of Richard Culliford, and *Devonshire* of John Cooper; 70-gun, 400-man *Swiftsure* of John Cooper, and *Monmouth* of John Mitchell; 60-gun, 365-man *Windsor* of Robert Arris, *Montague* of George Walton, *Sunderland* of Henry Gore, and *Dunkirk* of Captain Butler; plus the bomb vessels *Basilisk* and *Granada*. This convoy is manned by 4,500 sailors and marines, and bears 7,500 troops under Hill's lieutenant general, William Seymour, with Cols. Peircy Kirk, Jasper Clayton, Richard Kane, William Windress, Henry Disney, and Samuel Vetch as regimental commanders. One month after the expedition sets sail another 2,300 volunteers—mostly Palatine Germans and Indian warriors—march north from Albany under Colonel Nicholson to advance up the Hudson River and threaten Montréal.

23–24 AUGUST 1711 (O.S.). ***Walker's Shipwreck.*** After anchoring in Gaspé Bay on 18 August (O.S.) then gingerly probing into the Saint Lawrence seaway, Walker's expedition sails too far north. Strong currents confuse the English pilots, so that at 10:30 P.M. on 23 August (O.S.) his fleet blunders onto the breakers surrounding Île aux Œufs (near modern-day Baie Trinité, Québec). Next dawn, the following transports are reported lost:

Ship	*Men Lost*	*Men Saved*	*Commander*
Isabella Anne Katharine	192	7–8	Richard Bayley (drowned)
Smyrna Merchant	200	30	Henry Vernon (drowned)
Samuel and Anne	142	7–8	Thomas Walkup (drowned)
Nathaniel and Elizabeth	10	188	Magnus Howson
Marlborough	130	30	James Taylor
Chatham	60	40	John Alexander
Colchester	150	180	Joseph Henning
Content (Boston victualler)	—	15	William Hutton

After rescuing a few more survivors, Walker and Hill confer on 25 August (O.S.), opting to abandon their attempt against Quebec. The 40-gun frigate *Sapphire* of Capt. Augustin Rouse is sent toward Boston with a dispatch recalling Nicholson's army from its Hudson River advance, while Walker's unwieldly formation retreats into Spanish River Road (Sydney, Nova Scotia) by 25 September, to consider seizing the French fisheries in nearby Placentia Bay (Newfoundland). Even this is judged too risky, however, so after four days Walker and Hill decide to give up their North American campaign altogether and return to England. Aside from sending a colonial detachment to relieve the Annapolis Royal garrison, nothing else is achieved.

(For political reasons, neither Walker nor Hill is held responsible upon their return to London for the failure, blame being heaped instead on ineffective colonial cooperation. It is not until the government changes following the accession of the Hanoverian George I in September 1714 that both officers are cashiered.)

AUTUMN 1711. In northern Florida, frontier Capt. Theophilus Hastings and chief Brims of Coweta lead 1,300 Creeks on a destructive rampage through Choctaw territory, killing 80 and capturing 130. Another 200 Chickasaw under the Carolina frontiersman Thomas Welch visit destruction upon Spain's native allies throughout the region.

12 SEPTEMBER 1711. ***Duguay Trouin at Rio.*** The Saint Malo privateer René Trouin, sieur Du Guay, appears off Brazil with:

Ship	*Guns*	*Men*	*Commander*
Lys (flag)	74	678	Duguay Trouin
Magnanime	74	673	Chevalier de Coursérac
Mars	74	480	Joseph Danycan
Brillant	66	520	Chevalier de Goyon Beaufort
Achille	66	559	Chevalier de Beauve
Glorieux	66	552	De la Jaille
Fidèle	58	486	Miniac de la Moinerie
Aigle (royal frigate)	40	238	De la Marre de Caen
Chancelier (privateer frigate)	40	246	Du Rocher Danycan
Argonaute (royal frigate)	44	336	Emmanuel Auguste de Cahideuc, Chevalier Dubois de la Motte
Glorieuse (privateer frigate)	34	227	De la Perche
Amazone (royal frigate)	36	318	Lefer des Chesnais Le Fer
Concorde (royal frigate, victualler)	20	300	Daniel de Pradel
Astrée (royal frigate)	22	160	Rogon de Kertanguy
Bellone (galliot)	36	229	De Kerguélen

Although most of the fleet has been furnished by the French crown, its financing comes from private sources. Now 38 years old, its commander has been

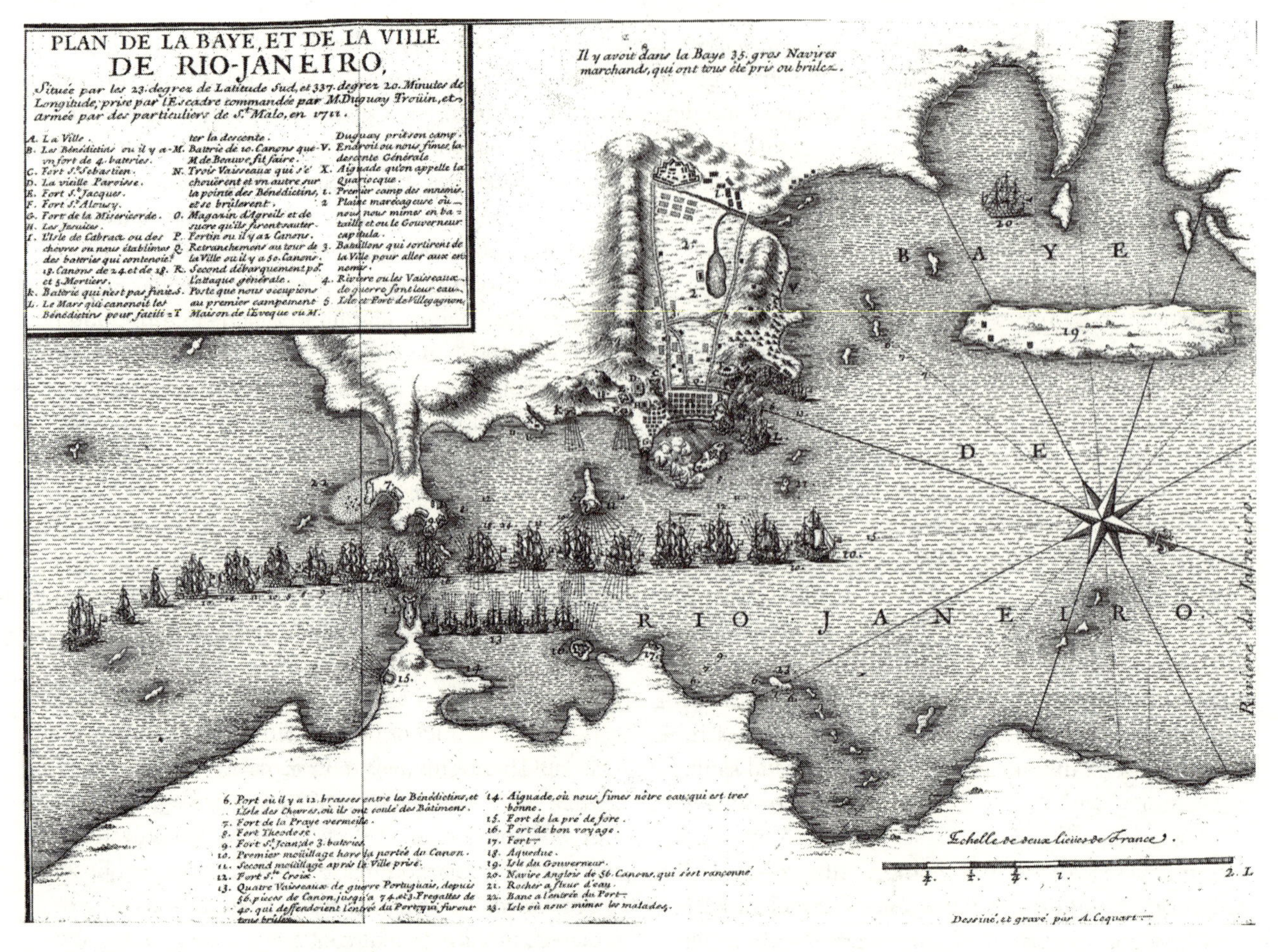

Duguay-Trouin's fleet shooting its way into Rio de Janeiro; north is to the right

ennobled two years previously for his brilliant successes as a commerce raider.

His current expedition being masked by mists and propelled by a favorable wind, Duguay decides to burst directly into Rio's harbor despite the formidable batteries covering the narrow entrance: the 44-gun Fort Santa Cruz on the eastern shore plus the 48 guns of Fort São João and Praya Vermelha on the western side. Fighting in behind Coursérac (who is familiar with the roadstead), the French encounter four Portuguese warships and two frigates inside under Commo. Gaspar da Costa, who cuts cables and grounds his ships beneath Rio's ramparts. At a cost of 300 total casualties, Duguay has penetrated the enemy harbor.

Next dawn, the Chevalier de Goyon occupies Cobras Island, where a battery of 18 guns and five mortars is quickly installed. Duguay meanwhile circles Rio on 14 September, and—supported by covering fire from *Mars*—disembarks more than 2,800 soldiers and sailors within a half-mile of its walls. Before sunrise on 15 September his encampment is struck by 1,500 Portuguese militia counterattackers, who are driven off after a sharp exchange. On 19 September Duguay calls upon Rio's Gov. Francisco de Castro de Morais to surrender; rejected, he begins a bombardment with his siege batteries and warships.

At 1:00 A.M. on 21 September a French prisoner slips out of Rio to advise the besiegers that the Portuguese have abandoned the city. Duguay occupies Rio, freeing 360 survivors from Du Clerc's failed expedition of 1710. His second-in-command, Major General de Beauville, accepts the capitulation of the Portuguese harbor batteries while Governor Castro withdraws five miles inland in vain hope of being reinforced by Brazil's Capt. Gen. António de Albuquerque. The French demand a ransom to spare Rio's buildings, which the Portuguese reluctantly pay on 10 October—only 610,000 cruzados, far less than Duguay expects.

The French depart on 13 November having incorporated the 56-gun, 550-ton *Nossa Senhora da Encarnacão* and the 44-gun *Reinha dos Anjos* into their fleet. At a cost of 500 invaders' lives, Duguay has devastated the city and burned more than 60 Portuguese vessels—but profits prove meager. During his return passage the heavily ladened *Magnanime* and *Fidèle* are lost with all hands, and *Aigle* succumbs at anchor off

Cayenne, prompting Duguay's shareholders to complain bitterly once he regains Brest on 8 February 1712.

22 SEPTEMBER (O.S.) 1711. ***Tuscarora War.*** Inland from Cape Hatteras in North Carolina, a native war party under Chief Hancock suddenly attacks Baron de Graffenried's colony of Swiss and Palatine Germans on the banks of the Trent and Neuce Rivers, slaughtering 130 men, women, and children—among them the historian John Lawson—plus another 70 in isolated homesteads nearer the Pamlico. The heretofore peaceful Tuscarora have been provoked by repeated encroachments into their territory and especially by the practice of certain white traders of selling Indian women and children into slavery whenever the Tuscaroras fail to pay their debts.

Frightened settlers now crowd into stockades, where many succumb to yellow fever, as a force of militia and Yamasee auxiliaries under Col. John Barnwell marches against Hancock's village of Cotechney. This place is destroyed but few casualties inflicted, after which a standoff occurs, resulting in an uneasy peace arrangement; but when the selling of Tuscaroras into bondage resumes next year, a new round of fighting erupts in autumn 1712.

Col. James Moore of South Carolina then leads a small body of militia and 900 Yamasee warriors against the principal Tuscarora stronghold of Neoheroka, leveling this palisaded town by March 1713 while killing or capturing 950 of its inhabitants—these prisoners being sold at ten pounds sterling each to help offset this expedition's costs. Their spirits broken by this crushing defeat, the surviving Indians migrate north beyond the mountains of the Roanoke River's headwaters, eventually joining their distant Iroquois-speaking cousins in New York as the Sixth Nation of the Seneca confederacy.

APRIL 1712. In eastern New York City, 25 black slaves and two Indian slaves arm themselves and set fire to a building, killing nine whites and wounding seven others who rush to extinguish the flames. Gov. Robert Hunter sends regular troops to aid the local militia in quelling the uprising, driving the rebels into nearby woods on Manhattan Island, where some commit suicide and others eventually surrender to face execution. About 70 more slaves are also jailed—at least 21 being executed—in a subsequent hysterical outburst.

22 MAY 1712. ***Tzeltal Rebellion.*** After five months of secret planning, the Tzeltal Indians of Chiapas (southern Mexico) rise in revolt under their chosen leader Juan García against Spanish oppression. This uprising begins with a sudden assault upon the congregants at Chiilum, who are surprised while at Sunday prayers inside their church and all beheaded. García then leads a march through the neighboring towns of Ocosingo and Cuira, slaughtering every opponent in his path. When the natives of Simojovel refuse to join the insurrectionists, their village too is burned.

García eventually comes to command 15,000 poorly armed adherents and is finally halted at Huitzan in November by a small army under *alcalde mayor* Pedro Gutiérrez. Next month the Spaniards are reinforced by troops out of Guatemala under Capt. Gen. Toribio Cosío, who reaches Chiapas's capital of Ciudad Real (modern-day San Cristóbal de las Casas) by December. The rebels are then defeated in a series of clashes and driven within their principal stronghold of Cahancú, surrendering shortly thereafter to face mass executions and imprisonment. Cosío returns into Guatemala by March 1713, his campaign concluded.

MAY 1712. When a large band of Fox or Mesquakie Indians advances out of their western Wisconsin and Illinois homeland to resettle amid their Mascouten allies near Fort Pontchartrain (modern-day Detroit, Michigan), fighting soon erupts for control of its fur trade. Governor Dubuisson besieges this camp for 19 days with 20 French soldiers, plus numerous Ottawa and Illinois allies, then pursues the fleeing Foxes and finally overwhelms them after a fierce, four-day battle. Mesquakie losses total 1,000 men, women, and children slain or captured.

JUNE 1712. ***Cassard's Campaign.*** The 32-year-old Nantes privateer Jacques Cassard—veteran of many European cruises and recently promoted captain in France's royal navy—arrives before Suriname with the warships *Neptune, Téméraire,* and *Rubis;* the frigates *Parfaite, Vestale, Méduse, Prince de Frise,* and *Allègre;* and the ketches *Anne* and *Marine.* Louis XIV has furnished these ships and crews; private subscribers provide the financing.

Cassard ventures up the Suriname River until checked by the Dutch batteries guarding the approaches to the capital of Paramaribo. He reverses course and stands back out into the Atlantic, steering northwest toward Martinique.

JUNE 1712. In Europe, a general armistice is proclaimed at Utrecht until final peace terms can be arranged.

JULY 1712. Cassard arrives at Martinique, requesting that militia Cols. François de Collart, Jean Du Buc, and Louis Du Prey augment his squadron's strength by supplying him with men. Within three days they raise 1,500 volunteers, who accompany the expedition aboard 30 of their own craft when it departs north to attack English Antigua. Cassard drops anchor in Willoughby Bay by 16 July, that night trying a disembarkation that is foiled by high wind and surf. Having lost the element of surprise, the French veer southwest toward Montserrat.

Cassard bears down upon Carr's Bay first then launches an assault against the island capital of Plymouth on 20 July. By hurrying men and artillery ashore to overwhelm the unprepared defenders, he secures an immense booty—including 1,200 slaves and four rich merchantmen—before a quartet of English ships can appear with 600 reinforcements from Antigua, obliging his engorged expedition to scatter in the general direction of Basse-Terre (Guadeloupe).

10 OCTOBER 1712. Having refreshed his followers, Cassard beats southeast to attack Suriname again. Disembarking 1,100 men, the French advance up the river by land and sea until they encounter the Dutch defenses before Paramaribo. Finding it too tough to breach, the frigate *Méduse* of Ensign d'Héricourt nonetheless slips past and into Suriname's unprotected hinterland, supported by troops under Beaudinard and Nicolas Hercule, Marquis d'Espinay Beaugroult. This threat to properties compels the Dutch to sue for terms, and although Paramaribo itself does not surrender its defenders—in order to spare the plantations—hand over sugar worth 700,000 florins as well as 730 slaves and some cash.

A French detachment under Baron de Moans de Grasse visits a like treatment upon neighboring Berbice (farther west, in modern Guyana), extorting another 100,000 florins. Cassard's expedition departs in December, retiring to Martinique.

25 JANUARY 1713. Cassard—supported by six Martinican freebooter vessels under Collart plus another three from Guadeloupe—descends upon Sint Eustatius, scattering the Dutch inhabitants into the jungle. He obtains a meager ransom before veering southwest toward Curaçao.

6 FEBRUARY 1713. Cassard's expedition parades before Curaçao's Fort Amsterdam, discovering that its Dutch defenders are forewarned of his approach. His flagship *Neptune* then strikes a reef, taking a considerable portion of the French siege train (1,000 mortar shells and 17 field pieces) to the bottom while *Rubis* is carried farther west by wind and currents.

It is not until 12 days later that Cassard and Collart can finally bring their troops ashore at Santa Cruz Bay (western Curaçao), suffering approximately 50 casualties from Dutch opposition—including the French commodore himself, who is wounded in the foot and cedes command to *Téméraire*'s captain, Anne Henry de Bandeville de Saint Périer. The attackers number 560 soldiers, 320 buccaneers, and 180 sailors versus 800 Dutch troops and militia under Gov. Jeremias van Collen. Few of the Dutch are regulars, however, so resistance remains perfunctory, confined to actions intended to delay any French penetration inland.

The invaders press forward, and on 22 February fight a pitched battle against a Dutch company entrenched atop a hill. The French Captain Rutty drives against the center, supported by Collart on the left, until d'Espinay can outflank the defenders and send them reeling into their capital, Willemstad. Bandeville occupies Otrobanda, installing three small mortars, but is otherwise powerless to menace Willemstad's major citadel (which is further protected by three large ships anchored out in the harbor). Although the French cannot inflict much damage on this Dutch stronghold, they wreak untold destruction on the island's unguarded plantations; when Bandeville sends an emissary under flag of truce to propose terms, van Collen haggles for several days before agreeing to a truce on 3 March whereby the French evacuate Curaçao without pillaging it, in exchange for 115,000 Spanish pesos.

11 APRIL 1713. The Treaty of Utrecht is finally signed, ending 11 years of hostilities. By its terms, France surrenders all claims to Hudson's Bay, Acadia, and Newfoundland plus its half of Saint Kitts while retaining New France (Quebec), Ile Saint Jean (Prince Edward Island), and Ile Royal (Cape Breton Island). Although relatively little territory changes hands, Britain's star is now beginning to ascend as France's star wanes.

Minor Incidents (1713–1719)

Despite the official cessation of hostilities in Europe, localized frictions persist in the New World. Increasing population bases and the growing prosperity of many American colonies leads to gradual expansion, not only bringing residents into conflict with surrounding tribes but also marking an end to the toleration of indiscriminate buccaneering.

April 1713. Buccaneers occupy Cozumel Island (Mexico).

5 August 1713. Buccaneers sack Chubulná (Yucatán Peninsula, Mexico).

April 1714. A dozen Englishmen lead 2,000 Alabama, Abinkha, Talapoosa, and Chickasaw warriors in a descent on the remnants of Spain's and France's Choctaw allies in northern Florida, peacefully persuading them to switch allegiance to England. The few who refuse seek shelter at Fort Saint Louis (Mobile).

23 April 1715. ***Yamasee War.*** Two English traders—William Bray among the Yamasee and Samuel Warner among the Palachacola—hasten to Charleston (South Carolina) to warn Gov. Charles Craven that a native uprising is imminent. It explodes three days later—daybreak on Good Friday, 15 April (O.S.)—when fighters in red and black warpaint surprise the veteran frontiersman Thomas Nairne and numerous other residents of Pocotaglio, slowly torturing them to death while ransacking the town.

Angry at having been victimized by dishonest Carolina traders during recent years and by encroachments upon tribal lands, the Yamasee set out to exterminate all interlopers in their midst. More than 300 terrified English residents flee onto a ship anchored off Port Royal (South Carolina), watching in horror as their homes are destroyed and their neighbors are slaughtered. Farther northeast another Indian war party sweeps through the scattered plantations between the Combahee and Edisto Rivers, claiming a further 100 lives.

Craven learns of the attacks while traveling overland to Savannah in hopes of parleying with the chiefs; he immediately orders out his militia. An assault upon his camp is repelled, after which Col. John Barnwell and Capt. Alexander Mackay are sent by sea to relieve Pocotaglio. In the week after Easter, Craven advances into rebel territory with 250 militia and settlement Indians, coming upon a Yamasee concentration near the head of the Combahee. Although outnumbered, he nonetheless defeats and disperses the natives into the swamps in an encounter known as the Sadkeche Fight.

Although the Yamasee onslaught is temporarily checked, many other tribes rise, and numerous traders are killed or robbed. Defensive measures are taken 30 miles around Charleston, and frontiersmen begin bringing in numerous captives. In mid-June the Santee border is attacked by another native group, and a relief column of 90 riders under one Captain Barker is ambushed by Congarees, who kill the officer along with about a third of his command. Schenkingh's Cowpen is also overrun when its commander, one Redwood, foolishly admits an Indian party that proposes peace but tomahawks the defenders. But a "brave and bold" officer ironically named Capt. George Chicken marches north from the Ponds with 120 Goose Creek militia to inflict a punishing reverse upon the raiders by 24 June.

In late July Craven marches north with 100 militia plus 100 black fighters and Indians to join the North Carolina forces of Cols. Maurice Moore and Theophilus Hastings in a campaign against the Saraws and other hostiles. But no sooner has South Carolina's governor crossed the Santee than word overtakes him of 500–700 Apalaches slipping through the Edisto defensive perimeter from the south to plunder its plantations, obliging him to hasten back to Charleston's defense. Halted short of Stono Island, the raider band retreats, burning Pon Pon (Jackson's) Bridge. Shortly thereafter HMS *Valour,* guard ship for Virginia, reaches Charleston with 160 muskets and other supplies, greatly easing the colonists' fears.

South Carolina's militia is then reorganized, and the situation stabilizes. By autumn Lt. Gov. Robert Daniel can lead a considerable expedition against the Indian town of Huspaw (near the northern mouth of the Altamaha River), finding it deserted. A large Cherokee delegation arrives at the end of October, promising to join the English at Savannah one month later for a combined operation against the Creeks. Those warriors fail to keep the rendezvous, however, so Moore marches into their territory with 300 frontiersmen in an attempt to persuade them to join the English cause. He eventually succeeds, and the rebel Creeks emigrate southwest by late January 1716 to seek shelter amid the Spanish and French. Only a few minor skirmishes ensue during the coming spring, and a peace treaty is concluded by 1717.

EARLY JULY 1716. The Jamaican rover Henry Jennings raids a Spanish encampment at Cape Canaveral (Florida), setting 300 buccaneers ashore from two brigantines and three *barcos luengos* to plunder its tents once the 50 defenders have been dispersed. This is the base for Havana's *sargento mayor* (garrison commander), Juan del Hoyo Solorzano, who has been salvaging the remains of Adm. Juan Estéban de Ubilla's treasure fleet, wrecked among the Palmar de Aiz Keys during a storm on 19 February.

Del Hoyo and most of his men being absent at the wreck sites with their frigate *Soledad* (flag) plus the auxiliaries *Paquita, Smith* (an English prize), *Santa Rita, Jesús Nazareno, Animas,* and galley *Perfecta,* the raiders are easily able to secure 350,000 pesos' worth of salvaged coin before sailing away. Cuban authorities later retaliate by issuing letters of reprisal against British vessels, thus heightening Anglo-Spanish tensions.

AUGUST 1716. Capt. Louis La Porte de Louvigny, with 225 French soldiers and Canadian *coureurs de bois* or backwoodsmen, plus 400 Indian allies, lays siege to the main Fox village at Butte des Morts (near modern-day Green Bay, Wisconsin). Its defenders surrender three days later, agreeing to cede their lands to the French Crown, as well as to hunt to repay for this campaign's costs.

7 DECEMBER 1716. ***Bay of Campeche.*** *Sargento Mayor* Alonso Felipe de Andrade exits Campeche with 100 soldiers and numerous volunteers under privateer Capt. Sebastián García, sailing aboard the hired frigate *Nuestra Señora de la Soledad,* two other frigates, a sloop, two coast-guard galliots under Capt. José de León, and a pair of piraguas to eliminate the English logwood establishments in the nearby Laguna de Términos. En route they are joined by another sloop and two piraguas from Tabasco bearing an additional 220 men.

A few days later the Spaniards capture a Dutch pink outside the Laguna entrance then cross its bar between 3:00 and 4:00 P.M. on 11 December, forcing the surrender of another 18 foreign frigates and sloops inside next day. Only an English captain named Thomas Porter continues to resist, melting into the jungle with 150 followers; the rest of the poachers submit and are allowed to leave—for the Spaniards, unlike previous raids, intend to stay this time. On 15 December de Andrade begins bringing ashore materiel to erect a redoubt covering the Laguna entrance, thus preventing future access.

EARLY APRIL 1717. Carpenter, one of Jennings's lieutenants, is captured aboard his frigate outside Havana by an 80-man Cuban coast-guard galliot.

MID-JULY 1717. ***El Carmen.*** Three buccaneer sloops anchor north of Tris Island (Laguna de Términos, Mexico), disembarking 335 men to dislodge the newly installed Spanish garrison. After calling upon Governor de Andrade to capitulate (without result), the English on 15 July storm the eastern ramparts under cover of darkness. Ens. Juan Muñoz's detachment is driven back and the buccaneers gain the building's interior, only to be expelled by an unexpected 42-man sally from the Santa Isabel battery, led by de Andrade himself. The Spanish commander falls, mortally wounded, yet his men drive the English back to their ships, never to return. As this victory has been won on 16 July—feast day of Our Lady of El Carmen—the Spaniards later rename the fort and island Isla del Carmen.

4 AUGUST 1717. This afternoon the veteran Woodes Rogers (*see* 25 November 1708) arrives outside New Providence as governor-designate for the Bahamas, accompanied by 250 colonists aboard the 460-ton former Indiaman *Delicia,* the frigates HMSS *Milford* and *Rose,* and the naval sloops *Buck* and *Shark.* Until now these islands have been run by a private company; under its absentee rule numerous renegade buccaneers have taken up residence. Rogers's commission calls for an end to their piratical depredations, so many—including Edward Teach, better known as Blackbeard—have already forsaken the Bahamas rather than submit to royal government.

However, the pirate Charles Vane's flagship remains defiantly at anchor; after nightfall Rogers sends *Rose* and *Shark* to take soundings in the harbor, prompting Vane to respond with a recently captured French prize fitted out as a fireship. The Royal Navy frigate and sloop retreat out to sea, and next dawn the pirates get under way, evading Rogers's attempted interception.

With this threat removed, Rogers comes ashore the morning of 7 August to be greeted by an honor guard of 300 boozy buccaneers who have remained behind under Capts. Benjamin Hornigold, Thomas Burgess, and others to swear fealty to the crown.

24 AUGUST 1717. After four and a half months of simmering unrest following the proclamation of a crown monopoly on tobacco, Gov. Vicente Raja—in office little more than a year—is compelled to resign and flee to Spain when Havana's garrison refuses to support him during a popular uprising.

AUTUMN 1717. The French mercenary Jean Nicolas Martinet rounds Cape Horn into the Pacific, having been hired by the Spanish crown to rid the South American coastline of smugglers with his purchased ships *Príncipe de Asturias* (former *Conquérant*) of 700 tons, 64 guns, and 500 men; *Triunfante* (former *Grand Saint Esprit*) of 600 tons, 50 guns, and 400 men, commanded by Captain de La Jonquières; plus the storeship *Princesse de Valois* of Capt. Garnier Du Fougerai. They have been joined off Cadiz by the 60-gun Spanish *Pembroke* of Capt. Bartolomé de Urdinzú and *Peregrino* (formerly the French *Pèlerin*) of Blas de Lezo.

Off Arica (Chile) five French vessels are seized and carried into Callao, their crews eventually being returned to Europe aboard two Spanish vessels. After a few weeks *Pembroke* circles back into the Atlantic, seizing two more Saint Malo ships off the River Plate before it wrecks in 1718. Martinet's ships return shortly thereafter to Brest and Lorient via Cadiz while Lezo remains alone in the Pacific, amassing a tidy fortune in prize money.

11 FEBRUARY 1718. José Rocher de la Peña, *gobernador de tercio* (third-in-command) of Spain's West Indian squadron, quits San Juan de Puerto Rico with his 160-man royal frigate *San Juan Bautista;* two privateer sloops belonging to Miguel Enríquez; a pair of coast-guard sloops from Santo Domingo; plus one sloop each from Cumaná and Trinidad Island to proceed southeast against English-occupied Vieques Island.

Rocher calls upon the trespassers to surrender, which their leader agrees to do—but when the Spaniards then come ashore the settlers flee into the jungle, obliging Rocher's men to spend the next ten days hunting down as many as possible while burning their dwellings. Eventually he departs with four prize sloops, 92 black slaves, and a number of English captives, who are carried into Veracruz by July.

SPRING 1718. The renegade English privateer Teach (the notorious Blackbeard)—having been driven out of the Caribbean and the Bahamas by the spread of English crown rule—blockades Charleston (South Carolina), extorting a small ransom.

Typical French man-of-war

EARLY SEPTEMBER 1718. Manuel Miralles departs Havana with the sloops *Santa Rita* of Capt. José Cordero; *Animas* of Juan Ramón Gutiérrez; *Regla* of Andrés González; *Ave María* of Juan Bustillos; *Santa Cruz* of Miguel del Manzano; *Begonia* of Ignacio Olavarría; and the brigantine *Jesús Nazareno* of Domingo Coimbra. Miralles's commission is to drive off the foreign salvors working the Palmar de Aiz shipwreck sites (*see* early July 1716), which Spain regards as its property. He returns to Havana by 25 September with five captive British sloops, 86 prisoners, 98 black slaves, and 80,000 pesos in specie. Another 70 Englishmen are believed to have fled ashore. Miralles leaves behind a 140-man, four-gun Spanish garrison under Cordero, supported by three sloops plus Coimbra's brigantine, to guard the anchorages.

21 NOVEMBER 1718 (O.S.). Toward evening Lt. Robert Maynard of HMS *Pearl* arrives opposite Ocracoke Inlet (North Carolina) with two hired Virginia sloops bearing 60 seamen. They trap the pirate Blackbeard's *Adventure* inside; next morning they take it, slaying Blackbeard and ten of his crew while wounding the other nine. The Royal Navy suffers ten killed and 24 injured during the affray.

15 MAY 1719. Off southern Cuba the Jamaican rover Jennings arrives to make a retaliatory raid for the salvors driven away from the Palmar de Aiz shipwreck sites by Miralles's flotilla. Some 200 men disembark at

the hamlet of Casilda and advance upon the neighboring town of Trinidad, only to find its garrison alerted. Frustrated in his design, Jennings instead destroys several Casilda fishing boats before departing.

SEPTEMBER 1719. The pirate Bartholomew Roberts reaches Bahia (Brazil) from Africa with his 32-gun *Royal Rover,* plundering a 42-ship Portuguese convoy preparing to depart for Lisbon.

WAR OF THE QUADRUPLE ALLIANCE (1718–1720)

THIS CONFLICT DOES NOT ERUPT OVERTLY but rather starts as a police action in Europe intended to curb Spain's activities in the Mediterranean. Madrid, never having concluded peace with Austria following the War of the Spanish Succession (because of territories lost in Italy to Emperor Charles VI), now hopes to regain those principalities through a recourse to arms. To that end a Spanish expedition invades Sardinia in August 1717 and Sicily one year later.

The Spanish aggression is opposed by France, Britain, and Holland, who have banded into a war-weary Triple Alliance to preserve the Treaty of Utrecht. Austria becomes a fourth coalition member in early August 1718, and a Royal Navy fleet destroys the Spanish expeditionary force off Cape Passaro (Sicily) on 11 August—without any official declaration of war.

The beleaguered Spanish government subsequently informs its American officials of these developments on 14 September 1718, then severs relations with Britain two days later, ordering that reprisals be taken in the New World. London declares war on 26 December 1718; hostilities spread when France sends an army to invade northern Spain via the Pyrennes in March 1719.

14 MAY 1719. ***French Occupation of Pensacola.*** Having learned before his Spanish counterparts of the outbreak of hostilities, Louisiana's 39-year-old Gov. Jean Baptiste Le Moyne de Bienville dispatches his 49-year-old subordinate (and brother), Joseph Le Moyne de Sérigny et de Loire, with four warships and 600 men to fall upon neighboring Pensacola. The expedition arrives by 14 May, calling upon its governor—Col. Juan Pedro Matamoros—to surrender. He refuses, but after a token, three-day resistance his 200-man garrison sues for terms because Pensacola's fortifications are incomplete and because there are insufficient stores for his defenders and 800 noncombatants to withstand a protracted siege.

De Sérigny offers French citizenship to all inhabitants who elect to remain then assigns the 22-gun frigate *Comte de Toulouse* and the 20-gun *Maréchal de Villars* to transport the governor and defeated Spaniards across the Gulf of Mexico to Havana. On 4 July, as the pair of vessels approaches Cuba, they are captured (notwithstanding their flags of truce) and carried into Havana by 14 Spanish privateer vessels, which are exiting to raid Louisiana under Lt. Col. Alfonso Carrascosa de la Torre.

Hearing of Pensacola's fate, the Spanish expedition—consisting of 900 volunteers and two companies of Havana regulars under *Sargento Mayor* Estéban de Berroa—instead sets sail again on 29 July to reconquer their West Florida outpost. They disembark, and by 24 August they subdue the 400 Frenchmen left as a garrison in Pensacola under Capt. Antoine Le Moyne de Châteauguay, appropriating two vessels and 160 black slaves as part of their booty. De Berroa and a Cuban coast-guard captain named Mendieta then attempt an attack upon Louisiana but are discouraged by the high state of alert maintained by Governor de Bienville.

2 SEPTEMBER 1719. ***Destruction of Pensacola.*** Commo. Marquis Desnots de Champmeslin reaches Louisiana from Saint Domingue (Haiti) with five warships and almost 2,000 men. Gathering further strength from Governor de Bienville—plus a column of native auxiliaries who are to march overland—the French expedition soon after invests the 800-man Spanish garrison within reconquered Pensacola. A two-hour assault against a couple of its weakest points persuades the defenders to capitulate by 17 September, 600 defenders being repatriated to Havana with Mendieta while Matamoros, Carrascosa, Berroa, and their two companies of Spanish regulars are carried off as prisoners of war. Not wishing to reinstall a French garrison, Champmeslin razes the site before sailing to France.

NOVEMBER 1719. In South Carolina, the local assembly revolts against the private London company that rules the colony, installing James Moore as acting

Spanish drawing from 1720 of proposed reconstruction of Pensacola

"royal" governor. The crown eventually accedes to the change in government, appointing its own representative one year later.

13 DECEMBER 1719. A few hundred English buccaneers disembark at Tavabacoa Beach (Cuba), marching inland to assault the town of Sancti Spíritus. A Spaniard early at work in the fields sights the invaders and warns the residents; militia repels the attack at Sabana de las Minas with several deaths on both sides.

27 JANUARY 1720. In Europe, Spain temporarily patches up its differences with France by signing a truce. Terms are not finalized for another year, and the actual treaty is concluded on 27 March 1721.

8 FEBRUARY 1720. The Royal Navy frigate *Happy* arrives at Casilda (Cuba) from Jamaica under Captain Laws, who lodges a protest with the authorities at the inland town of Trinidad over the privateering activities of Christopher Winter and Nicholas Brown, two English Catholic rovers serving Spain. Specifically, they are charged with stealing slaves from Jamaica, which Gov. Gerónimo de Fuentes denies; he commands Laws to depart.

FEBRUARY 1720. ***Spanish Attempt against the Bahamas.*** Three frigates under privateers Francisco Cornejo and José Cordero—plus nine sloops and brigantines bearing a combined total of 1,200–1,300 Cubans—appear outside New Providence (Nassau) to launch a surprise assault. Reluctant to steer directly across the bar because of the presence inside of Governor Rogers's flagship *Delicia* and the 24-gun frigate HMS *Flamborough,* the Spaniards instead try a disembarkation farther east. Three columns push ashore under Capts. Fernando Castro, Francisco de León, and Julián Barroso, causing considerable material damage before being repelled by Rogers's 500 militia. The Spanish remain offshore, eventually making off with 100 slaves and considerable booty.

15 MAY 1720. Having rounded Cape Horn—touching at Chiloe then plundering Paita (Peru)—former Royal Navy Lt. George Shelvocke's 24-gun, 160-man

privateer *Speedwell* is wrecked off the Juan Fernández Islands, losing two-thirds of its complement.

(This ship originally cleared Plymouth on 24 February 1719 accompanied by the 36-gun, 180-man *Success* of veteran privateer John Clipperton; *see* February 1704. Both are to have sailed in company, armed with Austrian commissions obtained at Oostende and named *Starhemberg* and *Prinz Eugen;* upon Britain's entry into this war, however, their owners instead obtained English papers. Before quitting England, Shelvocke has also been demoted from the larger to the smaller ship, so that soon after sailing he quarrels with Clipperton and separates. While rounding Cape Horn Shelvocke's first mate, Simon Hately, kills an albatross, furnishing the inspiration for the poem "The Rime of the Ancient Mariner" by Samuel Taylor Coleridge.)

JUNE 1720. The pirate Roberts ransacks a 22-ship British convoy in Trepassey Bay (Newfoundland) then seizes a half-dozen French vessels shortly thereafter off the Grand Banks, choosing one of 28 guns as his new flagship, renaming it *Royal Fortune.* He subsequently intercepts a string of prizes off New England in August before returning to the West Indies by September.

11 SEPTEMBER 1720. Cornejo's crewmembers mutiny in Havana Bay, approximately 100 privateers landing at Luyanó Beach to march on Jesús del Monte Monastery—south of the city—and lodge a heated protest regarding lack of pay. Gov. Gregorio Guazo Calderón surrounds the sanctuary with two companies of troops (thus incurring the wrath of the local bishop) before the rebels retreat aboard ship. Three days later Guazo hangs the ringleaders.

16 OCTOBER 1720. Having constructed a 20-ton vessel called *Recovery* from *Speedwell*'s remains, Shelvocke and 46 survivors strike out from the Juan Fernández Islands toward the South American mainland, eventually capturing the 200-ton Spanish merchantman *Jesús María* near Pisco, renaming it *Happy Return.* While subsequently sailing it Shelvocke is boarded off Quibo by Clipperton, but the two Englishmen again part company, proceeding northwest separately.

Shelvocke then captures the 300-ton *Sacra Familia* off Guatemala, and on 24 March 1721 he meets Clipperton yet again. Both captains try to patch up their differences for a concerted attempt against the galleon *Santo Cristo de Burgos,* which is about to depart Acapulco for Manila, but they argue bitterly over prize shares. Clipperton therefore slips away one night in May 1721, heading across the Pacific alone in hopes of intercepting the galleon off the Philippines. Shelvocke withdraws his watch outside Acapulco a few days later, reaching Puerto Seguro (near Cabo San Lucas, Baja California) by 22 August 1721, where he rests before departing west.

OCTOBER 1720. Bartholomew Roberts stations himself on Saint Lucia, intercepting numerous English and French merchantmen visiting Barbados and Martinique; he finally quits the theater for Africa in the spring of 1721.

1720–1721. In Europe, Spain is overwhelmed by the Quadruple Alliance, accepting its terms. But it is not until late March 1721 that Madrid instructs its Spanish-American officials to restore confiscated British properties, thus perpetuating local resentments.

TURMOIL (1721–1724)

ONCE AGAIN, THE RESTORATION OF PEACEFUL RELATIONS in Europe does not bring a halt to all fighting in the Americas. Numerous New World colonies continue to suffer from minor upheavals, especially in Spanish America.

4 APRIL 1721. Capt. Antonio, marqués de San Miguel de Aguayo, arrives in San Antonio (Texas) with a Mexican expedition to bolster Spain's claim over this region against French encroachments out of Louisiana. On 1 August he strikes a bargain with his French counterpart, Louis de Saint Denis, establishing a new boundary between both territories.

17 JANUARY 1722. In western Mexico, a Spanish expedition under Capt. Juan Flores de San Pedro penetrates the Mesa del Tonati Plateau (Nayarit) in two pincer movements, overwhelming the Cora defenders and bringing them under government rule.

23 AUGUST 1722. Two English smuggling sloops arrive at Mariel (Cuba), escorted by a man-of-war. Havana's Governor Guazo sends two Spanish coast-guard vessels and two piraguas under Captain Mendieta, plus two companies of regulars and another of militia overland, to detain the interlopers. The English are attacked

on 25 August, the Royal Navy warship fighting its way clear after two hours, but its consorts are captured with nine dead and 22 wounded, compared to seven Spanish fatalities.

LATE 1722. The Spanish corsair Esteban de la Barca departs Yucatán with 40 men aboard a galliot and a piragua, capturing a small English buccaneer vessel off Isla Mujeres then an interloper brigantine and a sloop off Belize before ravaging the latter's logwood camps.

18 FEBRUARY 1723. An uprising occurs in Cuba against the crown's proposed new tobacco monopoly. Learning that some 500 armed protesters are marching upon Havana, Governor Guazo sends cavalry Capt. Ignacio Barrutia with two companies of mounted infantry to disperse the mob at 9:00 P.M. on 20 February. Next dawn he falls upon them outside the town of Santiago, receiving a volley that kills a horse and wounds a trooper before he scatters the rebels with a charge. One rioter is killed and several others are wounded; 12 captured rebels are promptly hanged at Jesús del Monte as a warning to others.

SPRING 1723. ***Araucano Independence.*** In Chile, natives near Purén rise against Spanish rule, sparking a general revolt throughout the realm. The 58-year-old governor, Gabriel Cano de Aponte, knight of the Order of Santiago, calls out his militia and places it under the command of nephew Manuel de Salamanca. In August, de Salamanca defeats a rebel concentration under chief Vilumilla on the banks of the Duqueco River, but the Spaniards are too few to hold the entire territory and so abandon their outposts south of Biobío River. Eventually, they sign a peace treaty with 130 chieftains in February 1726 granting autonomy within native lands.

19 JANUARY 1724. The governor of Buenos Aires, Bruno Mauricio de Zabala, knight of the Order of Calatrava, and Commo. Salvador García Pose lead a combined land-sea expedition into Uruguay to compel a group of 300 Portuguese settlers to evacuate Montevideo (where they earlier arrived aboard a 50-gun ship and three smaller consorts). The Spaniards subsequently found their own city upon the same site.

16 MARCH 1724. Two Spanish coast-guard vessels and an auxiliary depart Cartagena and shortly thereafter stumble upon four Dutch merchantmen who are conducting clandestine trade off Tolú. The interlopers—mounting 36, 32, 22, and 20 guns, respectively—are pursued out to sea, where they turn to fight. The Spaniards succeed in capturing the 22-gun smuggler at a cost of ten dead and 30 wounded, but the remaining Dutch frigates escape.

SPRING 1724. ***Dummer's War.*** Hostilities erupt between English settlers living on the frontiers of Maine and Vermont and Abenaki Indians instigated by the French. (The conflict becomes known for William Dummer, the acting governor of Massachusetts who exercises jurisdiction over the outposts.)

One of the major actions is a carefully planned expedition of more than 200 colonial soldiers that heads up the Kennebec River from Fort Richmond (Maine) in August under Capts. Johnson Harman and Jeremiah Moulton. They intend to surprise the encampment of the French missionary Sébastien Rale, who has long incited the Norridgewock Indians to resist English expansion. After pausing briefly at Ticonic (Winslow), where they leave their whaleboats and a 40-man guard, the New Englanders continue north on foot toward Narantsouak (Old Point, Madison). Within striking distance around noon on 12 August, the raiding party divides into two units of roughly 80 men each. Harmon, who advances through the tribal cornfields, finds no natives and consequently misses the ensuing fight. Moulton, however, leads his men directly into the village, having ordered them to observe strict silence and not fire until the enemies empty their own guns.

Discovering the attackers, some 50–60 warriors rush out of their homes, firing wildly and receiving a heavy countervolley. The natives retreat to cover the escape of their women and children but are pursued by most of Moulton's men, who cut them down in the river and surrounding forest. Meanwhile the old Norridgewock chieftain Mog and Father Rale continue to hold out in the village. Rale is killed as he fires from a cabin by Lt. Richard Jaques, Harmon's son-in-law (against the direct orders of Moulton, who wishes the Frenchman to be taken alive). The village is then looted and burned; the dead are scalped.

Another encounter occurs at Pigwacket (Fryeburg, Maine) on Sunday, 9 May 1725 (O.S.), when Capt. John Lovewell is ambushed during a scalping expedition with 33 volunteers. A band of 80 warriors fells a dozen Englishmen—including Lovewell—with their opening volley. One volunteer runs away, leaving 21 others dug in under Ens. Seth Wyman, the sole surviving officer. Nonetheless, the English hold a strong position with a pond at their backs and two large fallen pines for breastworks. Toward nightfall, seeing the Indians making camp, Wyman sneaks across and kills their leader, effectively ending the fight. Eventually, 18 of his men return home before peace is reestablished with the natives.

11 APRIL 1724. A Spanish expedition departs Ascensión Bay (modern-day Emiliano Zapata Bay, Yucatán) under Nicolás Rodríguez with the corsairs José Aguirre, José Marqués de Valenzuela, Juan Rodríguez de Raya, Esteban de la Barca, Baltasar de Alcázar, and Juan de Ulloa as subordinates. Upon approaching Belize, Nicolás Rodríguez is to lead the main body inside the chain of reefs while Marqués circles outside, catching any interlopers in between.

But Marqués's galliot is shipwrecked, delaying the flotilla at Aguada Key until 28 April, when it proceeds to blockade Belize. As two Royal Navy schooners under one Captain Peyton are protecting the poachers inside, the Englishmen are allowed to exit unmolested on 1 May before the Spaniards disembark.

AUGUST 1724. ***Comunero War (Paraguay).*** An army of Guaraní Mission Indians led by Baltasar García Ros, lieutenant governor of Buenos Aires, is defeated on the banks of the Tebicuary River by 3,000 Paraguayans under 31-year-old Dr. José de Antequera y Castro, renegade governor for the province.

Three years previously, Antequera has been sent to Asunción as a special prosecutor *(fiscal)* by the acting Peruvian viceroy—Archbishop Diego Morcillo—to investigate complaints against then governor Diego de los Reyes y Balmaceda. Antequera duly imprisoned Reyes, but in so doing he alienated the Jesuits, who control much of Paraguay. They help the captive to escape to Corrientes in 1722; from there he threatens to gain reinstatement. Antequera meanwhile is proclaimed governor by the local legislature *(audiencia)*, receiving support from Paraguayan landowners anxious to exploit the native labor and territories—policies that the Jesuits have steadfastly opposed.

In 1724 the new Peruvian viceroy, José de Armendáriz, marqués de Castelfuerte, seeks to end the impasse by dispatching García Ros's Jesuit-trained army, but it is defeated by Antequera. Despite winning, the victory renders Antequera's position untenable, as it unites both crown and church officials against him. Support falls away, so that by 1725 he is forced to flee to Córdoba upon the approach of another Argentine army under Governor de Zabala; he is sheltered by some Franciscans before moving on to Charcas. Martín de Barúa (or Barcia) enters Asunción as new royal governor; Antequera is finally arrested in 1726 and conveyed to Lima to stand trial.

His confinement in the viceregal palace proves so mild, however, that Antequera is able to dispatch confederate Fernando de Mompóx y Zayas back into Paraguay to organize a second uprising (unlike the first—which entailed a dispute between aristocratic leaders—the new uprising involves the common people or *comuneros*). Even the new governor, de Barúa, joins in, venting his wrath against the Jesuits. For months the *comuneros* rule in and around Asunción, and when de Barúa steps down in 1730 they set up their own republican form of government; the leader, José Luis Barreyro, is proclaimed president of the province. This in turn provokes Viceroy de Armendáriz to eventually find Antequera and his lieutenant, Juan de Mena, guilty of heresy and treason in Lima; he orders their executions. The sentence proves unpopular enough to cause riots; the viceroy's troops shoot Antequera on his way to the gallows on 3 July 1731.

The Paraguayan revolt meanwhile plays itself out, Barreyro arresting Mompóx, who escapes his guards while being conveyed toward Lima and flees into Brazil. *Comunero* sentiment spreads as far as Corrientes, where Gov. Ruylobo Calderón is killed; Bishop Juan Arregui of Buenos Aires is elected to succeed him. Eventually the rebellion is suppressed when the retiring Governor de Zabala leads another Guaraní army from the River Plate into Paraguay, defeating the rebels at Tapabuy then entering Asunción on 30 May 1735 to execute the last remaining leaders.

ANGLO-SPANISH FRICTIONS (1725–1729)

IN APRIL 1725 MADRID CONFOUNDS EUROPE by allying with its former archenemy, Austria. Fearing the new alignment might threaten Britain's already limited access to Spanish American markets and lend added weight to Madrid's claims for the restoration of Gibraltar and Minorca, London forges a new coalition of its own in September with France, Hanover, and Prussia (later joined by Holland, Sweden, and Denmark). Russia allies with Austria, and the Spanish government orders its American officials to begin confiscating English goods at the end of

March 1726, fearing that war is imminent. However, a formal declaration never materializes, as allies of Spain and Britain do not wish to plunge into a general conflagration on account of the two belligerent nations.

12 MARCH 1726. The 36-year-old Commo. Rodrigo de Torres y Morales, knight of the Orders of San Juan and Calatrava, arrives off Cozumel (Yucatán) after delivering the annual *situados* (payrolls) to the Spanish Main. With 600 men aboard his frigates *San Juan* (flag) and *Nuestra Señora de Begonia* (alias *Holandesa*) and some lesser consorts, his orders are to rendezvous with another seven vessels bearing 300 men from Campeche led by the Cuban sloop *Aguila* of José Antonio de Herrera—and sweep the English logwood cutters from Belize. (While waiting for the contingent to appear Lt. Tomás Varela's English prize *Hamilton* also captures the Boston sloop *George* of Richard Randall on 22 March.)

By the time the Campeche reinforcements finally arrive on 10 April, Torres instead opts to retire to Veracruz to refresh his capital ships, leaving de Herrera to proceed against the English with only *Aguila* and two smaller auxiliaries. The Spanish commodore is reprimanded for dereliction of duty upon entering Veracruz on 30 April.

16 JUNE 1726. ***Hosier's Ill-Fated Campaign.*** In order to exert pressure upon Madrid, Francis Hosier—now a 53-year-old Vice Admiral of the Blue—appears off Bastimentos (Panama) with the 70-gun ships *Breda* (flag), *Berwick,* and *Lennox;* the 64-gun *Superb* (former French *Superbe*); the 60-gun *Dunkirk, Nottingham,* and *Rippon;* the 50-gun *Leopard, Tiger, Dragon,* and *Portland;* the frigate *Diamond;* the sloops *Greyhound* and *Winchelsea;* and the snow *Happy.* As a Spanish treasure fleet is loading in nearby Portobelo, its governor inquires the reason for Hosier's presence. The English admiral replies he has come to escort the South Sea Company ship *Royal George,* but even after that vessel clears port the blockaders remain, prompting the Spaniards to cancel their convoy's departure. Hosier then prevents vessels from using Portobelo until mid-December, when he sails to Jamaica, his crews ravaged by disease. Some vessels are so understrength that they experience difficulty working into Port Royal on 14 December (O.S.).

13 AUGUST 1726. Adm. Antonio Gaztañeta y de Iturribálzaga reaches Havana from Spain with 2,000 troops under the command of that city's former governor, Gregorio Guazo, who dies 16 days later of yellow fever. He is succeeded by Brig. Gen. Juan de Andía, marqués de Villahermosa.

FEBRUARY 1727. Having replenished his crews, Hosier leads his fleet from Jamaica to Havana, arriving outside by 2 April. He then circles around the Caribbean to blockade Cartagena and prevent Spain's treasure galleons from departing. The Spanish government retaliates by besieging Gibraltar back in Europe, although neither country actually declares war.

Again, sickness breaks out among the English crews in the West Indies, claiming Hosier's life on 23 August or 25 August (O.S.). His body is conveyed back to England aboard *Happy* under Cmdr. Henry Fowkes, and Capt. Edward St. Loe of *Superb* assumes temporary command over the fleet.

Vice Adm. Edward Hopsonn then comes out from England to replace Hosier, reaching Jamaica by 29 January 1728 (O.S.); however, Hopsonn also dies of illness by 18 May, followed by St. Loe on 22 April 1729 (O.S.) as the fleet continues to suffer a horrific toll in lives. It is estimated that more than 4,000 of 4,750 officers and men succumb during the three-year tour, with ships being maintained thanks to fresh crews out of Jamaica.

SPRING 1727. An expedition of English logwood cutters and native auxiliaries quits Belize, sailing north to Ascensión Bay (modern-day Emiliano Zapata Bay) to march inland and sack Chunhuhub and Telá. The governor of Yucatán, Antonio de Figueroa y Silva, leads a relief force out of Mérida, which drives the raiders back to their ships.

APRIL 1727. At Quiebra Hacha mill in the interior of Cuba, 300 black slaves revolt, the rebellion soon spreading to other properties. All are quickly put down by the mill owner, José Bayona y Chacón, who heads two mounted militia companies.

31 MAY 1727. In Paris, a truce is signed between Britain and Spain, but it does not fully resolve their disputes.

FEBRUARY 1728. ***Palmer's Raid.*** Angered by Spanish support of Yamasee forays, South Carolina decides to send a punitive expedition of 100 militia and 200 native allies into Florida under veteran Indian fighter and member of the Commons House of Assembly, Col. John Palmer. The group departs Charleston in small boats, moving south down the coastal channel without opposition. The dugouts are beached at San Juan Island (at the mouth of the Saint Johns River) in early March, and Palmer's company proceeds afoot.

During the march overland the raiders are spotted by a Spanish scout, who carries warning to the Indian villages farther south. The Yamasee concentrate at Nombre de Dios, their best fortified village, a short distance outside Saint Augustine. Despite having lost the element of surprise, Palmer's small army wins a decisive victory by overrunning the place on 9 March, slaying 30 Yamasee and capturing 15 while wounding many more and scattering the survivors into the Spaniards' Fort San Marcos. Unable to storm or besiege that powerful citadel, Palmer rests in Nombre de Dios until 13 March, stripping and torching it before retracing his steps to South Carolina.

AUGUST 1728. In Wisconsin, the French—fearful of an alliance between the Fox with their Sauk (or Sac), Mascouten, Kickapoo, Winnebago, and Dakota neighbors—dispatch Constant Le Marchand de Lignery with 400 men and 800 native allies from La Baie to make a punitive sweep through enemy territory. This force burns numerous empty villages but otherwise inflicts few casualties before retiring to the vicinity of modern-day Oshkosh.

SUMMER 1729. Governor de Figueroa of Yucatán sends a retaliatory expedition under nephew Alonso de Figueroa against the English logwood cutters in Belize.

Upon retiring from that incursion the Spaniards choose the site for a strategic new frontier outpost—San Felipe de Bacalar.

19 NOVEMBER 1729. In Europe, the Treaty of Seville is signed, settling many of the commercial and territorial grievances straining relations between Britain, Spain, France, and Holland.

INTERWAR YEARS (1730–1738)

DESPITE THE PROMULGATION OF THE TREATY OF SEVILLE back in Europe, the continuing spread of major mainland colonies into the interior of the New World leads to increasingly serious frontier flareups. Clashes between English settlers pushing south out of Georgia into Spanish Florida, as well as the traditional Hispano-Portuguese conflict centering around what is today Uruguay, soon threaten to drag in their respective home governments.

SPRING 1730. A force of 600 French soldiers and native allies under Capt. Paul Marin besieges the main Fox village at Butte des Morts (Wisconsin) for five days, convincing many tribesmen to seek refuge among the Iroquois south of Lake Ontario.

10 AUGUST 1730. A French expedition from Fort Vincennes in Upper Louisiana besieges 900 Fox Indians in an extemporized stronghold. Further reinforcements arrive one week later, until the besiegers number 200 Frenchmen and 1,200 native allies. Eventually the Fox attempt to escape under cover of darkness on 9 September, only to be overtaken and trapped; 500 are ruthlessly massacred, the rest enslaved.

AUGUST 1732. Fears of a Creek invasion grip the southern frontier of the Carolinas, prompting Col. Alexander Glover to marshal his colonial forces at Palachacola (Fort Prince George). One month later the rumors prove false, and the alert is canceled.

12 FEBRUARY 1733. More than 110 English colonists land at Yamacraw Bluff (Savannah) under 37-year-old James Edward Oglethorpe to establish a new colony, named Georgia in honor of the king, between the Carolinas and Spanish Florida. The Spaniards resent the expansion and react with hostility.

21 FEBRUARY 1733. A Spanish expedition assaults the English logwood establishments in Belize by sea and land. While a flotilla of Campeche privateers appears from Chetumal to threaten the harbor front and distract the inhabitants, troops under Yucatán's Governor de Figueroa arrive overland from Bacalar to surprise them from the rear, inflicting numerous casualties. De Figueroa remains in Belize for several weeks, destroying numerous encampments before retiring.

(Returning toward Mérida, he dies of sickness at Chunhuhub on 10 August.)

OCTOBER 1734. Baja California's Pericue Indians rise in rebellion, destroying the Santiago and San José settlements and slaying the Jesuit missionaries. When the galleon *San Cristóbal* subsequently arrives from Manila, it is unable to resupply with fresh water and provisions following its transpacific crossing, so the authorities in Mexico City organize an expedition to reconquer the outposts. Santiago is reoccupied by April 1736, San José in February 1737, after which numerous natives are herded onto reservations; most fall sick and die.

OCTOBER 1735. Because of continuous frictions with Portuguese settlers pushing southwest out of Brazil, Gov. Miguel Salcedo of Buenos Aires sends Guaraní contingents into the disputed borderlands between the nations along with a flotilla under Francisco de Alzaibar. A series of skirmishes ensues, which persists until a truce can be arranged with the Portuguese governor of Sacramento in September 1737.

JANUARY 1736. More than 170 Scottish settlers arrive at Savannah (Georgia), establishing a new town farther south called Darien on the Altamaha River. They are joined one month later by more than 250 Londoners, who venture even farther south with the sloop *Midnight* and scout boat *Carolina* to establish Fort Frederica, thus pushing back the Spanish borderlands.

26 MARCH 1736. At 8:00 P.M. 40 poorly treated soldiers mutiny at Fort Nassau (Bahamas), firing upon Gov. Richard Fitzwilliam when he attempts to intervene. The rebels free a jailed French pilot, nail up the fort's seaward guns, board a large sloop, and set sail toward Havana by 3:00 A.M. on 27 March. Unskilled sailors, they are overtaken next daybreak by Thomas Walker's sloop. He arrests them without a fight and returns them to stand trial. Their leader, George Collins, and 11 others are hanged; the remainder are flogged and transported.

18–19 APRIL 1736. The scout boats *Carolina* of Capt. William Ferguson and *Georgia* of John Ray, accompanied by a piragua from Darien (Georgia) with 30 Highlanders and ten rangers under Capt. Hugh Mackay—plus 40 Yamacraw warriors in canoes under their *mico* (chieftain) Tomochichi—disembark on the northwestern tip of Cumberland Island to begin constructing star-shaped Fort Saint Andrews.

LATE MAY 1736. Georgia militia under Capt. Christian Hermsdorf begin constructing Fort Saint George, directly opposite the Spaniards' northernmost lookout station on the Saint Johns River (modern-day Fort George Island, near Jacksonville, Florida). Work is briefly interrupted by fears of possible Spanish retaliation but resumes once Highlander reinforcements arrive aboard the scout boat *Georgia* and a yawl.

25 JUNE 1736. In retaliation for the Spanish siege of Colónia do Sacramento (Uruguay)—although still without any official declaration of war by either Lisbon or Madrid—Portuguese Commo. Luiz de Abreu Prego departs Rio de Janeiro with the 74-gun ships of the line *Nossa Senhora da Victória* (flag) and *Nossa Senhora da Conceição* of Capt. João Pereira dos Santos; the frigate *Nossa Senhora da Alampadosa* of José de Vasconcelos, knight of Malta; the galley *Santanna;* brigantine *Nossa Senhora da Piedade* (alias *Bichacadella*); a royal sloop or yacht; plus two hired merchantmen bearing 600 troops under Brig. Gen. José da Silva Paes.

Intended to reinforce Brazil's southwestern frontier, this expedition first rendezvouses off Santa Catarina Island on 21–22 July with the galley *Corta Nabos* and the transport *Rosa,* bearing an additional 250 troops from Colónia do Sacramento. All weigh together by 1 August, encountering stormy weather and skirmishing with the Spanish frigates *Hermiona* and *San Sebastián*—recently arrived from Cadiz—on 18, 20, and 26 July.

19 SEPTEMBER 1736. The frigates *Hermiona* and *San Sebastián* appear off Colónia do Sacramento (Uruguay), disembarking 110 dragoons as reinforcements for its Spanish besiegers before continuing west to Buenos Aires next day.

26 SEPTEMBER 1736. Abreu Prego and Silva Paes's expedition reaches Colónia do Sacramento (Uruguay), reinforcing its Portuguese garrison and making a sally with 800 men in three columns before dawn on 4 October to drive back the Spanish besiegers. Numerous supply dumps are burned, obliging the Spaniards to retire beyond the San Juan River.

OCTOBER 1736. After heated protests from Gov. Francisco del Moral Sánchez at Saint Augustine, Governor Oglethorpe of Georgia agrees to withdraw Fort Saint George from the mouth of the Saint Johns River and allow the border dispute to be resolved by Madrid and London. The Spanish governor is soon dismissed from office; Oglethorpe instructs his followers to build Fort Amelia at the mouth of the Saint Marys River.

LATE NOVEMBER 1736. As further reinforcements for Colónia do Sacramento (Uruguay), the Portuguese warship *Nossa Senhora da Arrabida* of Capt. Luiz Antônio Berderod quits Rio de Janeiro, accompanied by the 30-gun *Santhiago,* the eight-gun *Fangueiro,* and the hired transport *Centeno,* bearing 350 soldiers.

9 DECEMBER 1736. Capt. Antônio Rodrigues Figueira slips out of Colónia do Sacramento (Uruguay) at dawn with 180 Portuguese troops aboard three brigantines and seven boats to raid a Spanish supply dump three miles up the San Juan River. The base is surprised and burned, but the attackers' retreat is cut off, Rodrigues Figueira's survivors suffering ten killed, 37 wounded, and 87 captured before winning free.

24 DECEMBER 1736. ***Montevideo Blockade.*** Brig. Gen. Silva Paes departs Colónia do Sacramento (Uruguay) with 720 Portuguese troops aboard the galleys *Leão Dourado* and *Santana do Pôrto,* the brigantine *Piedade,* the corvette *São Francisco Xavier,* and the royal sloop *Nossa Senhora da Conceição,* appearing before Montevideo five days later in hopes of disembarking. However, even after rendezvousing on 31 December with Abreu Prego's 500-man squadron, the attackers do not muster sufficient strength to overwhelm 800 Spanish defenders, backed by batteries and a 42-gun frigate in the roads. Silva Paes therefore continues farther east on 13 January 1737, landing at Punta del Este to establish a new 130-man Portuguese outpost at Maldonado under *Maestre de Campo* André Ribeiro Coutinho, then sailing to Brazil.

15 MARCH 1737. Two additional Spanish warships reach Ensenada de Barragán (east of Buenos Aires), bringing in reinforcements and five Portuguese prizes intercepted off Brazil.

16 MARCH 1737. In Paris, Portuguese and Spanish plenipotentiaries sign an armistice.

SPRING 1737. At Guaymas (Mexico), the long pacified Pimas Bajos natives rise against the Spaniards, inspired by their medicine man. Capt. Juan Bautista de Anza puts down the rebellion, hanging its leader on 1 June.

15 MAY 1737. Salcedo returns from Buenos Aires and materializes off Colónia do Sacramento (Uruguay) with four Spanish frigates, two corvettes, and a boat flotilla to reinvigorate its besiegers. Nonetheless, his strength is insufficient to subdue the 1,000-man Portuguese garrison under Vasconcelos, supported by the brigantines *Tavares, Sereia, Bigodes, Latino,* and *Caramujo* in the roads. Both squadrons skirmish over the next few weeks without achieving significant advantage.

SUMMER 1737. A Spanish expedition departs Campeche and attacks the English logwood establishments at Belize.

15 AUGUST 1737. The royal Portuguese frigate *Nossa Senhora da Boa Viagem* of Capt. Duarte Pereira reaches Maldonado (Uruguay) with news of the cessation of Hispano-Portuguese hostilities.

MAY 1738. Three transports arrive at Savannah bearing the first contingent of 629 soldiers of the 42nd Regiment of Foot, which Oglethorpe has raised in England to defend Georgia. He arrives himself by mid-September with the remaining troops aboard five transports.

WAR OF JENKINS'S EAR, LATER KING GEORGE'S WAR (1739–1748)

BRITAIN, THE WORLD'S RISING MARITIME POWER, resents Spain's efforts to exclude its merchants from Central and South America. The friction is exemplified by an incident that occurs on 20 April 1731, when the Glasgow brig *Rebecca* of Capt. Robert Jenkins—homeward-bound from Jamaica—is intercepted and ransacked before Havana by the Cuban coast-guard vessel *San Antonio* (alias *Isabela*) of Capt. Juan de León Fandino. Jenkins is mistreated and his ear is allegedly cut off "to carry it to his majesty King George."

The struggle between British smugglers and Spanish patrols eventually climaxes in March 1738, when George II announces that all British subjects with unsatisfied claims against Spain's *guardacostas* can apply for a letter of reprisal to fit out as privateers and seize Spanish vessels by way of compensation. No licenses are applied for, such work properly belonging to the Royal Navy. Diplomatic complaints fare little better, as the Spaniards lodge counterprotests against British activities. War is narrowly averted this year but finally explodes in earnest in the spring of 1739.

(When France eventually joins Spain in 1744—impelled by the eruption of the War of the Austrian Succession in central Europe—the expanded conflict becomes known in Britain's North American colonies as King George's War.)

JUNE 1739. The British government—dissatisfied with negotiations in Madrid—decides to authorize limited strikes against Spanish shipping without officially declaring war. As a result, fleets are sent to intercept the treasure convoys; Commo. Charles Brown's Jamaica squadron is alerted; and Edward Vernon, a 54-year-old Vice Admiral of the Blue known as "Old Grog" because of the grogram waistcoat he commonly wears, is delegated to lead a squadron into the West Indies.

20 AUGUST 1739. In response to Britain's deployments, Madrid authorizes its American officials to take reprisals against British citizens and properties.

25 AUGUST 1739. Brown sorties from Port Royal (Jamaica) with *Hampton Court* (flag), *Falmouth, Diamond, Torrington, Windsor, Drake,* and *Shoreham* to cruise around Cuba. On 14 September 34-year-old Capt. Charles Knowles of *Diamond* pursues a Spanish sail and fails to rejoin, instead returning directly to Jamaica with two valuable prizes. Capt. Edward Boscawen of *Shoreham* meanwhile reconnoiters the approaches to Havana, destroying two Spanish sloops and capturing a third before landing at Puerto María on 26 September to burn a mass of lumber, despite opposition from two demigalleys and a sloop.

10 SEPTEMBER 1739. A dozen Spanish ships of the line and several auxiliaries arrive off Saint Barthélemy under the veteran Admiral de Torres, bearing 2,000 reinforcements for Spain's American garrisons. During its crossing the expedition snapped up five English merchantmen and endured a storm that damaged the 70-gun *Santa Ana* and 60-gun *Santiago,* killing 60 and incapacitating more than 1,000 men.

Three days later, steering west toward Puerto Rico, de Torres's fleet is struck by a hurricane and staggers into the small Puerto Rican port of San Francisco by 15 September with yet greater damage—the 60-gun *Nuestra Señora de Guadalupe* or *Fuerte* being obliged to continue alone to Havana (eventually entering on 11 October).

Meanwhile the 70-gun *Reina* has captured an English privateer, after which the Spanish admiral transfers his flag aboard *Nueva España,* sets some of his casualties ashore at San Francisco, and departs on 6 October to Cartagena. He arrives by 23 October, disembarking his crews to recuperate.

LATE SEPTEMBER 1739. An Angola-led slave insurrection occurs at Stono (South Carolina), during which 23 whites are killed. Panic grips the English colonies; local militias are mustered, soon cornering the rebels and killing about 40 while scattering the remainder into the swamps. Uneasy British settlers remain convinced that the uprising has been instigated by the Spaniards out of Saint Augustine (Florida).

2 OCTOBER 1739. Gov. Juan Francisco de Güemes y Horcasitas confiscates all English properties in Havana.

8 OCTOBER 1739. Governor Oglethorpe of Georgia receives official notification of the breakdown of negotiations with Madrid and orders to "annoy the subjects of Spain, and put the colonies of Carolina and Georgia in the best posture of defense."

9 OCTOBER 1739. Vernon arrives at Antigua with his 70-gun, 500-man flagship *Burford* under Capt. Thomas Watson; the 60-gun, 400-man *Princess Louisa* of Thomas Waterhouse, *Strafford* of Thomas Trevor, and *Worcester* of Perry Mayne; plus the 50-gun, 300-man *Norwich* of Richard Herbert. After refreshing supplies he proceeds to Saint Kitts then detaches Waterhouse to cruise the Spanish Main between La Guaira and Puerto Cabello with *Princess Louisa, Strafford,* and *Norwich* before rejoining Vernon's main body at Jamaica.

11 OCTOBER 1739. Commodore Brown maintains his blockade of Havana, his foraging parties being fired upon as they attempt to go ashore at Bacuranao, Jaruco, and Bahía Honda.

22 OCTOBER 1739. Waterhouse bombards La Guaira (Venezuela) for three hours with HMSS *Princess Louisa, Strafford,* and *Norwich* before standing away west.

23 OCTOBER 1739. Vernon's squadron reaches Port Royal (Jamaica).

30 OCTOBER 1739. In Europe, Britain officially declares war against Spain, which reciprocates on 26 November.

16 NOVEMBER 1739. After being rejoined at Port Royal (Jamaica) by Waterhouse's detachment and Commodore Brown's 70-gun flagship *Hampton Court*—which returned on 8 November after leaving *Windsor* and *Falmouth* to maintain the blockade of Havana—Vernon decides that no Spanish treasure convoys will likely sortie and so instead opts to attack Portobelo. Embarking 200 troops under Capt. William Newton, the British admiral quits Port Royal with HMSS *Burford, Hampton Court, Princess Louisa, Strafford, Worcester,* and *Norwich* and the 20-gun *Sheerness* of Capt. Edward Stapleton, heading southeast. *Sheerness* is detached during the crossing to maintain watch on Cartagena.

24 NOVEMBER 1739. At dawn outside Fort Amelia (Georgia), a dozen Yamasee warriors—allies of the Spanish—ambush a pair of Highlanders emerging for firewood, killing both and carrying their scalps into Saint Augustine.

1 DECEMBER 1739. ***Portobelo.*** Vernon anchors about eight miles to windward of the Panamanian harbor of Portobelo, issuing final instructions for attack. At 6:00 A.M. next day his half-dozen warships and two tenders get under way, led by Brown's *Hampton Court,* which weathers the Salmedina group by 2:00 P.M. then stands directly toward Portobelo in a faint wind.

Shortly thereafter the Royal Navy squadron opens fire on the San Felipe or Todo Fierro harbor fort (Iron Castle to the English), catching the Spanish garrison almost totally unprepared. Some 55 marines are rushed across from the city under naval Capt. Juan Francisco Garganta to raise its strength to 90 men, yet only nine of San Felipe's 32 guns are serviceable—quickly reduced to four by the British bombardment. By 4:30 P.M., when Brown sends boat parties inshore, scarcely five Spanish officers and 35 men remain to surrender, the rest having fled. At 8:00 P.M. the English shift their fire against Santiago Fortress (Castle Gloria) guarding Portobelo proper, sinking a Spanish sloop in the roads and doing other damage before their bombardment ceases at nightfall.

At 5:30 A.M. on 3 December Vernon's squadron works deeper into the harbor, only to be approached

British boat parties move to occupy the battered San Felipe harbor castle before Vernon's fleet continues against Portobelo in the distance; oil painting by George Chambers Sr.

soon after by a launch requesting terms from Acting Gov. Francisco Javier Martínez de la Vega y Retes. Vernon deems the overture unsatisfactory and gives Martínez until 3:00 P.M. to accept his conditions while continuing to warp into the roadstead. The Spaniards capitulate that afternoon, at which time the half-empty town is occupied without resistance, English casualties totaling three dead and five wounded aboard HMSS *Burford* and *Worcester,* with another seriously injured aboard *Hampton Court.*

Vernon forbids plundering and reassures the few remaining inhabitants that Britain's fight is against the Spanish crown, not the Portobelans themselves. In keeping with London's policies, he then orders Captains Knowles and Boscawen to throw down its defenses in order to leave the port "an open and defenseless bay." Upon withdrawing to Jamaica on 24 December with his three Spanish prizes—two 20-gun ships and the newly renamed snow *Triumph*—Vernon leaves behind no occupying garrison, instead announcing that Portobelo will henceforth be treated as a neutral port so long as its Spanish authorities and *guardacostas* permit free trade.

12 DECEMBER 1739. Governor Oglethorpe departs Frederica (Georgia) with 200 men aboard 14 boats, coasting south as far as the Saint Johns River (Florida) to probe Spanish preparations. Finding them weak, he reinstalls a small frontline garrison at Fort Saint George (*see* October 1736) before retiring to Frederica by 29 December.

14 JANUARY 1740. Oglethorpe returns to Fort Saint George (near modern-day Jacksonville, Florida) with 180 men, being joined by an English privateer sloop. Three days later this small expedition sails up the Saint Johns River to attack the Spanish outposts at Forts Picolata and San Francisco de Pupo. Arriving five miles north of the former at 4:00 P.M., Oglethorpe's company disembarks and creeps up at 2:00 A.M. on 18 January, finding it abandoned. The Spanish garrison at San Francisco de Pupo opposite spots Oglethorpe's native auxiliaries and—mistaking them for Yamasee allies—sends a ferry across, which narrowly escapes capture.

During the confusion Oglethorpe lands his British regulars a mile north of Pupo and marches upon it with four field pieces. The artillery is hastily sited by artillery Ens. Sanford Mace, who opens fire just before sunset. Pupo's 12-man Spanish garrison capitulates after the second salvo, allowing Oglethorpe to leave behind 50 men to hold the place under Capt. Hugh Mackay Jr., reversing course for the coast and Frederica on 22 January.

6 MARCH 1740. After wintering at Port Royal (Jamaica), Vernon sorties with his squadron, detaching the 50-gun *Greenwich* to watch Santa Marta before appearing off Cartagena on 13 March with his main body to take soundings.

On 17 March Vernon orders his recently joined bomb vessels *Alderney* of Cmdr. James Scott and *Terrible* of Cmdr. Edward Allen to begin shelling the city. The galling fire persists until the morning of 20 March, without the Spanish squadron sallying to challenge under 51-year-old Vice Adm. Blas de Lezo—a grizzled veteran already missing his left leg, right arm, and left eye (*see* autumn 1717). Vernon then leaves HMSS *Windsor* of Capt. George Berkeley and *Greenwich* of Charles Wyndham to continue the blockade, steering toward the north coast of Panama with the remainder of the squadron on 21 March.

3 APRIL 1740. ***Chagres.*** After watering at Portobelo on 25 March Vernon appears off Chagres with HMSS *Strafford* (flag), *Princess Louisa, Falmouth,* and *Norwich;* the fireships *Cumberland, Eleanor,* and *Success;* the bomb vessels *Alderney* and *Terrible;* the tenders *Goodly* and *Pompey;* plus a Cuban prize brig and sloop. They bombard Chagres's tiny 11-gun Spanish keep from 3:00–10:00 P.M., forcing the 30-man garrison under Capt. Juan Carlos Gutiérrez Cevallos to capitulate by 11:00 A.M. the next day. The English level the fortifications and strip the site bare, sailing away for Portobelo and Cartagena by 11 April. Vernon eventually returns to Port Royal (Jamaica) by 14 May.

19 MAY 1740. Oglethorpe returns from Georgia to the south bank of the Saint Johns River, disembarking an advance body of 100 men near what is modern-day Mayport (Florida) to secure the beachhead for a larger group of British colonials coming behind. Next dawn his Cherokee skirmishers chase some Spaniards toward Fort Diego, the northernmost Spanish fortification; 220 regulars of the 42nd Regiment and 125 provincials of the South Carolina Regiment under the Dutch-born Col. Alexander van der Dussen reach him that afternoon.

On 21 May Oglethorpe leaves 45 men to hold his base camp, pushing almost 20 miles with the remaining 400 and a four-pounder in hopes of overrunning Fort Diego (about a mile and a half south-southeast of modern-day Palm Valley), which is defended by 50 Spaniards under plantation owner Diego Espinosa. A surprise British assault is repulsed at dawn, but Espinosa surrenders when Oglethorpe's main body appears around midday on 22 May. A 50-man British garrison is installed under Capt. Lt. George Dunbar while the main column retires to the Saint Johns camp, where further reinforcements continue to appear.

27 MAY 1740. Oglethorpe's small army approaches captured Fort Diego this morning with fresh supplies, but one unit is ambushed by Yamasee warriors, who kill and behead a ranger. They are pursued for several miles by the British general himself, who has a horse shot out from under him before finally turning back.

29 MAY 1740. Oglethorpe returns to his Saint Johns base camp, where more Carolina reinforcements have arrived with Commo. Vincent Pearse's Royal Navy warships. Next morning the general finalizes plans for a land-sea assault against Saint Augustine. After receiving a false report at 2:00 A.M. on 31 May that Fort Diego is under attack he marches in relief, establishing a new base camp beneath its walls.

11 JUNE 1740. ***Saint Augustine.*** Having reconnoitered the approaches to the Spanish stronghold at Saint Augustine, Oglethorpe marches south from Fort Diego with 300 regulars and 400 South Carolinians. Two days later his forces occupy Fort Mosa, a deserted earthen fortification north of Saint Augustine, in hopes that 57-year-old Gov. Manuel de Montiano y Luyando might be lured out of his main citadel to fight. Instead the Spanish defenses are found to be so exceptionally strong—recently augmented by 200 men aboard two sloops and six demigalleys from Havana—that Oglethorpe retreats to his Fort Diego base camp on 14 June.

On 17 June the British—now 1,500 strong—resume their offensive when Colonel van der Dussen's 500-man South Carolina Regiment disembarks and digs in at the mouth of Saint Augustine's harbor (Point Quartell). Five days later a column of 137 rangers, Highlanders, and Indians under Col. John Palmer reoccupy Fort Mosa; on 23 June Oglethorpe lands unopposed on Anastasia Island with 200 men of his 42nd Regiment plus 200 seamen and a like number of Indians. He intends to cut off the beleaguered Spaniards then launch a general assault.

However, just before dawn on Sunday, 26 June, 300 Spaniards under Capt. Antonio Salgado surprise the English garrison in Fort Mosa from three directions.

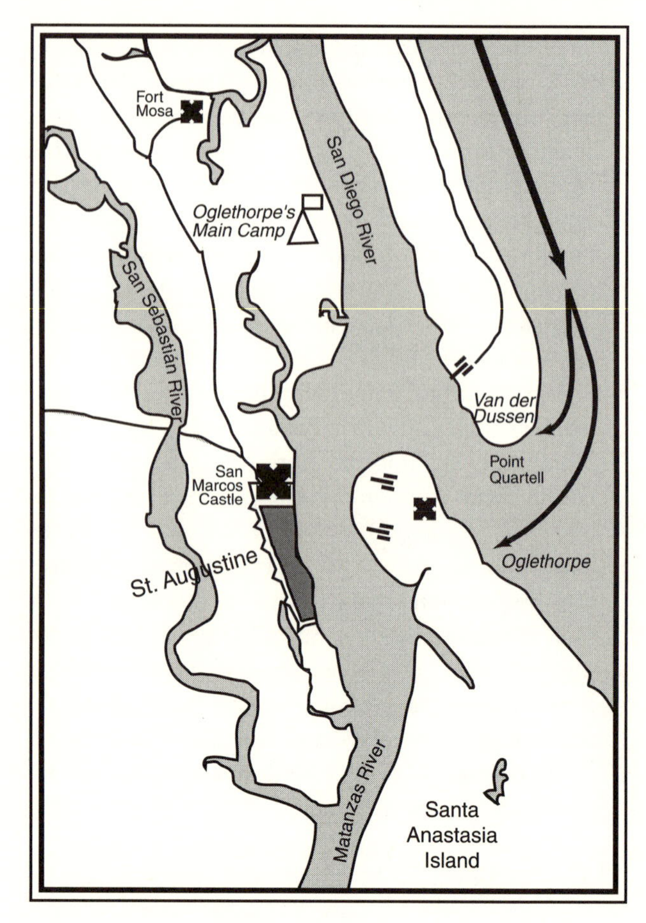

Oglethorpe's siege of St. Augustine

Although repelled twice, the Spaniards fight their way inside and overwhelm the defenders at a cost of ten dead, slaughtering 63 besiegers—including Palmer—before marching two score prisoners back to Saint Augustine. Spanish morale soars; when Oglethorpe calls upon de Montiano to surrender four days later he is refused.

On 5 July van der Dussen shifts his South Carolinians to Anastasia Island; two days later Oglethorpe transfers his own 42nd Regiment into a new camp near Fort Mosa. That afternoon (7 July) a storm threatens, so Commodore Pearse stands out to sea with: *Flamborough* (flag) of 20 guns under Vincent Pearse; *Hector* (44) under Sir Yelverton Peyton; *Squirrel* (20) under Peter Warren; *Phoenix* (20) under Charles Fanshaw; *Tartar* (22) under Hon. George Townshend; *Spence* (sloop) (6) under William Laws; *Wolf* (sloop) (8) under William Dandrige; and *Pearl* (provincial schooner) under Warren Tyrrell. Before they can resume the blockade a large Cuban sloop, two schooners, and four supply boats slip into the Matanzas River entrance 13 miles south, delivering 300 men and much-needed relief to Saint Augustine by 14 July.

Discouraged, Oglethorpe orders the siege lifted on 15 July, all save two of Pearse's warships sailing away the next day. Van der Dussen's regiment returns to Point Quartell from Anastasia Island on 20 July, retreating north to rejoin Oglethorpe at Fort Diego by 26 July. The British general, learning that a schooner with more South Carolinians is about to meet him, proposes a quick return to surprise Saint Augustine, but his weary troops refuse. The campaign has cost 122 British dead, 16 prisoners, and 14 deserters, the last invaders quitting Florida by 6 August.

13 JUNE 1740. Zambos from the Mosquito Coast attack the Spanish fortification at Matina (Costa Rica).

17 JUNE 1740. Learning that Spanish reinforcements are on their way from Europe, Vernon sorties from Port Royal (Jamaica) with seven of the line and a fireship. *Worcester* and *Falmouth* are detached into the Gulf of Mexico to await a transport bearing the viceroy-designate for New Spain, Pedro de Castro Figueroa y Salazar, duque de la Conquista and marqués de Gracia Real. Vernon meanwhile proceeds with his remaining ships to blockade Cartagena. After awaiting the Spaniards' arrival in vain, the English admiral returns to Jamaica aboard his flagship *Burford* on 2 July, having left *Hampton Court* to watch Cartagena.

During his absence the other pair of warships under Captains Mayne and Douglas have intercepted the large Dutch merchantman *Vogel Phenix* between Capes Corrientes and San Antonio at the western tip of Cuba. The new Mexican viceroy—who is traveling aboard as a passenger—escapes on a fast accompanying Puerto Rican sloop under privateer Capt. Diego de Morales but leaves behind all his papers, thereby providing the English with valuable intelligence.

13 OCTOBER 1740. A large contingent of Virginia troops sets sail for Jamaica, escorted by the ten-gun privateer sloop *Wolf* of William Dandridge (of King William County and brother to Martha Dandridge—later Martha Custis, who one day will marry George Washington; Washington's elder half-brother Lawrence also commands one of four militia companies on the expedition and will be so impressed by Jamaica's naval commander in chief that upon returning he renames the Hunting Creek Plantation into the famed Mount Vernon). Britain's North American colonies eventually supply 3,600 men from Massachusetts, Rhode Island, Connecticut, New York, New Jersey, Pennsylvania, Maryland, Virginia, and North Carolina toward Vernon's West Indian campaign.

21 OCTOBER 1740. The 30-year-old French Vice Adm. Antoine François de Pardaillan de Gondrin, Marquis d'Antin, reaches Martinique with ten ships of the line, joining three already on station. (The marquis originally departed Brest on 25 August with 14 of the line and five frigates but detached four one week later to cruise off Spain under 75-year-old Commodore Jacques, Comte de Roquefeuil.) D'Antin is being followed across the Atlantic by another eight of the line under Adm. La Roche Alart, and upon uniting the fleet is to attack English interests throughout the Caribbean in support of Spain—without any formal declaration of war by Paris.

After pausing briefly to refresh supplies and take on 1,200 militia at Martinique, d'Antin proceeds west to Port Saint Louis (Les Cayes, Haiti), arriving by 7 November. However, while still awaiting La Roche Alart and contacting Spanish authorities in this theater, d'Antin's crews begin falling ill at an alarming rate. By the time La Roche Alart arrives on 18 December, and Roquefeuil by 8 January 1741, all French complements are considerably depleted.

28 DECEMBER 1740. The 43-year-old English commodore George Anson arrives off Brazil (latitude 27 degrees 30 minutes south) with:

Ship	*Guns*	*Tons*	*Men*	*Commander*
Centurion (flag)	60	1,005	521	George Anson
Gloucester	50	866	396	Matthew Mitchell
Severn	48	683	384	Hon. Edward Legge
Pearl	42	559	299	Daniel "Dandy" Kidd
Wager	24	559	243	Hon. George Murray
Trial (sloop)	14	201	96	Lt. David Cheap
Anna (victualler pink)	—	400	16	Mr. Gerrard

His orders are to round Cape Horn and "annoy and distress" the Spaniards in the South Seas, attempt to link up with British expeditionary forces advancing across the isthmus of Panama, and hunt the Acapulco-Manila galleons.

30 DECEMBER 1740. Some 25 British warships—scattered by an Atlantic storm—begin arriving at Prince Rupert's Bay (Dominica) under Rear Adm. Sir Chaloner Ogle and Commo. Richard Lestock, escorting 100 transports bearing 8,000 soldiers under Maj. Gen. Charles, Lord Cathcart. The latter dies of dysentery on 1 January 1741, being succeeded by his second-in-command, Brig. Gen. Thomas Wentworth, before Ogle's vessels (except the detached 80-gun *Cumberland*) can reassemble and set sail for Jamaica on 7 January 1741.

16 JANUARY 1741. Spanish Commo. José Alonso Pizarro, knight of the Order of San Juan, arrives off Punta del Este (Uruguay) with the 64-gun, 700-man *Asia* (flag, official name *Nuestra Señora de Loreto*) and *Guipúzcoa* (vice-flag); the 54-gun, 500-man *Hermiona;* the 50-gun, 450-man *Esperanza;* the 40-gun, 350-man *San Esteban;* and a 20-gun auxiliary to counter Anson's venture (*see* 28 December 1740) by rounding Cape Horn first with a regiment of 500 Spanish infantry. Pizarro immediately sends to Buenos Aires for provisions and news of English movements.

18 JANUARY 1741. ***Cape Tiburón.*** This morning, as the Ogle-Wentworth expedition passes 20 miles south of Cape Tiburón (southwestern Haiti), four sail are sighted closer inshore. The British admiral detaches Capt. Lord Aubrey Beauclerk to investigate with the 70-gun *Prince Frederick* and *Orford* plus the 60-gun *Lion, Weymouth, Rippon,* and *Dunkirk.*

The unidentified foursome is the French 64-gun *Ardent* of 66-year-old Commo. Nicolas Hercule, Marquis d'Espinay Beaugroult; the 54-gun *Mercure* of Capt. Henri François Desherbiers, Marquis de Letanduère; the 50-gun *Diamant* of Captain de Poisins; and the 44-gun *Parfaite* of Captain d'Estournel returning to Admiral d'Antin's anchorage at Port Saint Louis (Les Cayes, Haiti) from visiting Petit Goâve. Suspecting they might be Spanish men-of-war, the six Royal Navy warships aggressively chase them into the night, persuading the outnumbered French that war may have already been declared back in Europe between London and Paris. Knowles's *Weymouth* even hails one of the French ships at 10:00 P.M. but receives no reply.

Beauclerk eventually fires a warning shot across one of the Frenchmen's bows, which responds with a full broadside, precipitating a round of inconclusive exchanges until dawn. At daylight on 19 January Knowles convinces Beauclerk that the encounter has been a mistake; after exchanging compliments with d'Espinay's ships the Royal Navy squadron stands away to rejoin the main body (which has since begun reaching Jamaica). D'Espinay meanwhile reports to d'Antin, who is greatly discouraged by the arrival of the huge British reinforcement in the West Indies and therefore decides to abandon the theater. He quits Port Saint Louis for France by 7 February, leaving only seven of the line at Petit Goâve under Roquefeuil.

2–8 FEBRUARY 1741. Vernon works his way out of Port Royal (Jamaica) with:

Ship	*Guns*	*Tons*	*Men*	*Commander*
Princess Carolina (flag; ex-*Ranelagh*)	80	1,353	620	Thomas Watson
Russell (Ogle's vice-flag)	80	1,350	615	Harry Norris
Boyne (Lestock's rear admiral)	80	1,390	600	Charles Colby
Chichester	80	1,278	600	Robert Trevor
Norfolk	80	1,393	600	Thomas Graves
Princess Amelia (ex-*Humber*)	80	1,352	600	John Hemington
Shrewsbury	80	1,314	600	Isaac Townsend
Torbay	80	1,296	600	Gascoigne
Burford	70	1,147	480	Thomas Griffin
Hampton Court	70	1,137	480	Digby Dent
Prince Frederick	70	1,225	480	Lord Aubrey Beauclerk
Orford	70	1,098	480	Lord Augustus Fitzroy
Suffolk	70	1,224	480	Thomas Davers
Defiance	66	949	400	John Trevor
Augusta	60	1,067	400	Dennison
Deptford	60	951	400	Savage Mostyn
Dunkirk	60	966	400	T. Cooper
Jersey	60	1,065	400	Peter Lawrence
Lion	60	1,068	400	Charles Cotterel
Montague	60	920	400	William Chambers
Princess Louisa	60	?	400	Edward Stapleton
Rippon	60	1,021	400	Thomas Jolly
Strafford	60	1,067	400	Thomas Trevor
Tilbury	60	962	400	Robert Long
Weymouth	60	1,065	400	Charles Knowles
Windsor	60	951	400	George Berkeley
Worcester	60	1,061	400	Perry Mayne
York	60	?	400	Thomas Cotes
Falmouth	50	760	300	W. Douglas
Litchfield	50	?	300	William Cleland

These are accompanied by the 40-gun frigate *Ludlow Castle* of James Cusack; 20-gun sloops *Experiment* of Capt. James Rentone, *Seahorse* of T. Limeburner, *Sheerness* of Captain Maynard, *Shoreham* of Thomas Broderick, and *Squirrel* of Peter Warren; 20-gun storeship *Astrea* (prize taken at Portobelo; see 1 December 1739) under Captain Scott; fireships *Cumberland, Eleanor, Etna, Firebrand, Phaeton, Strombolo, Success, Vesuvius,* and *Vulcan;* bomb vessels *Alderney* and *Terrible;* privateer sloop *Wolf* of William Dandridge; ordnance tender *Virgin Queen;* tenders *Goodly* and *Pompey;* plus a brig tender under Lieutenant Dampier.

Augusta is obliged to turn back shortly thereafter, having been damaged while exiting. The formation is escorting 85 troop transports, but Vernon's first aim is to beat upwind toward southwestern Haiti and confront d'Antin's French fleet within Port Saint Louis (Les Cayes) before venturing against a Spanish American target.

3 FEBRUARY 1741. At Maldonado Bay (Uruguay), Pizarro's squadron gets under way without awaiting

fresh provisions from Buenos Aires, as the Spanish commodore has learned from Portuguese sources that Anson's force lies only 500 miles northeast at Ilha de Santa Catarina (Brazil), threatening to precede him into the Pacific. The five Spanish warships—their 20-gun consort being abandoned at Maldonado—stand south in increasingly heavy weather, briefly spotting HMS *Pearl* before attempting to double Cape Horn early in March. Fierce snowstorms disperse the formation, *Hermiona* being lost with all hands. Eventually, Pizarro's *Asia* limps back to Montevideo with half its 700-man crew dead; *San Esteban* suffers proportionally before regaining Barragán Bay (Argentina); *Guipúzcoa* drifts helplessly onto Ilha de Santa Catarina and is wrecked; *Esperanza* is left with merely 58 crewmembers.

11 FEBRUARY 1741. Admiral de Torres departs Cartagena with 14 Spanish warships, continuing his voyage to Havana.

23 FEBRUARY 1741. After assembling his huge expedition outside Port Saint Louis (Les Cayes, Haiti), Vernon prepares to attack next morning, only to discover that d'Antin's fleet has already sailed for France. Replenishing provisions, Vernon and Wentworth therefore decide to assault Cartagena instead, weighing anchor on 8 March.

13 MARCH 1741. ***Siege of Cartagena.*** Two English warships and an auxiliary anchor off Canoas Point north of Cartagena. Next day a French sloop runs past, bringing warning from Charles Brunier, Marquis de Larnage and governor of Saint Domingue (Haiti) about the intended British invasion. During the afternoon of 15 March advance elements of the 176 ships under Vernon and Wentworth come up over the horizon, anchoring the following afternoon between Canoas Point and Grande Beach. Smaller English ships then feint a disembarkation north of the city while *Weymouth, Dunkirk, Experiment,* and the sloop *Spence* reconnoiter the shoreline farther south near Boca Grande. Heavy swells preclude easy landing, so the invaders opt for an attack upon Boca Chica farther south.

The Spaniards use the respite to good advantage. The 27-year-old Sebastián de Eslava, knight of the Order of Santiago and viceroy of New Granada (Colombia), has been in office less than a year, his city boasting a garrison of 1,100 regulars from the Aragón, España, and de la Plaza Regiments; 300 militia; two 100-man free black companies; plus 600 native archers, raised by Col. Melchor de Navarrete. In the harbor ride the 70-gun ships of the line *Galicia* (flag) and *San Felipe* (although all the Spanish men-of-war mount considerably less than their full allotment); *San Carlos* of 66 guns; *Africa* (officially designated *San José*) and *Dragón* (also called *Santa Rosa de Lima*) of 64; plus *Conquistador* of 62. Their commander is Vice Admiral de Lezo, who transfers his four largest ships to cover the Boca Chica entrance while sending many of his 600 sailors and 400 marines ashore to stretch its log boom, and generally bolster the defenses. The Spaniards muster perhaps 4,000 men in total.

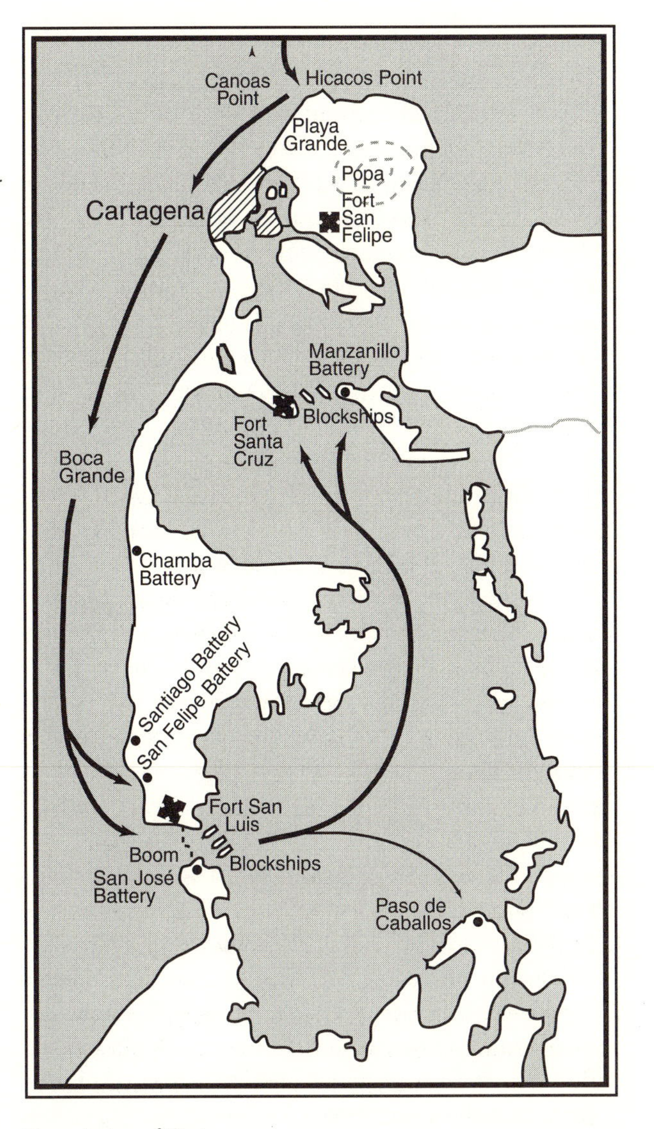

Vernon's siege of Cartagena

At 9:00 A.M. on 20 March the 80-gun HMSS *Norfolk, Shrewsbury,* and *Russell* move inshore to open fire against the Santiago and San Felipe Batteries; while the 80-gun *Princess Amelia* and smaller *Litchfield* engage the Chamba battery, bomb vessels rain shells upon Fort San Luis, and Commodore Lestock's division menaces Cartagena. *Shrewsbury*'s cable is cut by a chance Spanish round, setting it adrift under the main enemy batteries, which inflict 60 casualties before it can crawl out of danger; but otherwise the British succeed in silencing the batteries by noon, allowing Wentworth's disembarkation to begin at 2:00 P.M. north of Fort San Luis. However, the 8,000-strong English army comes ashore very slowly, some contingents not landing until next day, failing to install the first mortar battery before San Luis until three days later and heavy siege artillery not until 2 April. The sluggish pace threatens the entire enterprise, for sickness is already spreading throughout the ranks.

At dawn on 1 April 300 British sailors and 200 soldiers come ashore a mile from the 15-gun Abanicos battery under naval Captains Watson, Norris, Colby, Boscawen, Laws, and Cotes, as well as military Capts. James Murray and Lawrence Washington. Despite being ambushed by a hidden five-gun battery at Varadero, they succeed in overrunning and temporarily spiking the guns of the intended target, although the Spanish battery commander—naval Lt. José Campuzano—soon succeeds in unspiking several and resuming fire.

At first light on 3 April Lestock ventures inshore with *Boyne, Princess Amelia, Prince Frederick, Hampton Court, Tilbury,* and *Suffolk* to commence a two-day bombardment against Fort San Luis and the nearby San José battery, eventually retiring with numerous casualties (including Captain Beauclerk, who is killed). Both senior Spanish commanders, Eslava and de Lezo, are wounded during the exchange by shell fragments from a round that strikes *Galicia* on 4 April, although neither is seriously incapacitated. The Spaniards have already resolved to abandon San Luis, so when Wentworth orders it stormed at 5:30 P.M. on 5 April the 500 surviving defenders hang out a white flag and beat for a parley. Unable to see or hear the display because of the smoke and din, the British grenadiers under Brig. Gen. William Blakeney press home the attack while the exhausted Spanish garrison—fearing the onslaught means no quarter will be given—flee out the far side of San Luis. The men-of-war *San Carlos, San Felipe,* and *Africa* are scuttled shortly thereafter to block the channel.

Knowles meanwhile lands a party of seamen on the southern bank and storms the San José battery, securing that abandoned position by 10:00 P.M. He rows out into the darkness to the Spanish flagship *Galicia,* finding it manned by only 60 men and capturing it intact. He also cuts the log boom, so that next morning Vernon's fleet can begin working past the scuttled Spanish ships, gaining the safety of the lower harbor by the evening of 7 April. The British admiral then presses north against the inner Spanish defenses, using *Burford* and *Orford* to stem the upper harbor while Knowles's *Weymouth* and a sloop destroy the Paso de Caballos batteries by 8 April. So confident is Vernon that he dispatches Laws's sloop *Spence* toward England, announcing Cartagena's imminent fall.

But the Spaniards resist, scuttling their last two warships—*Dragón* and *Conquistador*—along with the rest of their merchant shipping on 10 April to block the Manzanillo Channel into the upper harbor while preparing to evacuate their 60-gun Santa Cruz fortress *(Castillo Grande)* after nightfall. Knowles notices the movement and so sails *Weymouth* directly beneath the walls, opening fire and finding the fortress empty. Its seizure allows the English greater ease in clearing the blockships, Knowles being installed as garrison commander with 100 soldiers from Lord James Cavendish's regiment. By 12 April the first bomb vessels are shelling Cartagena proper, and on the night of 16 April a large-scale disembarkation is made by Blakeney at Tejar de Gracias (three miles south of La Popa) to cut off the city from its hinterland. Encirclement is completed the following noon, when North American colonial militia occupy La Popa Heights unopposed.

Nevertheless, Wentworth closes upon Cartagena's ramparts very sluggishly, disease sapping his army. The 24-gun San Felipe de Barajas Fortress, manned by 250 Spanish marines and soldiers from the Aragón and España Regiments under military engineer Carlos Desnaux, checks his advance. Their presence prompts an assault at 3:00 A.M. on 20 April with 1,500 English troops under Brig. Gen. John Guise and Colonels Wynyard and Grant, who suffer 645 killed, wounded, or captured. Disheartened, Wentworth announces a few days later that Cartagena cannot be carried with his remaining strength—only 3,569 of his original 8,000 soldiers being left. A bitter dispute then erupts with his naval counterpart as the English expedition prepares to withdraw.

At 5:00 A.M. on 27 April the captured *Galicia*—now transformed into a floating battery—approaches Cartagena's walls under Capt. Daniel Hore, exchanging broadsides with the defenders for seven hours until it finally sinks. Six of *Galicia*'s 300-plus English crewmembers are killed and another 56 are wounded, but under cover of this action the diseased English army strikes camp and marches off to reembark. The transports set sail for Jamaica this same day, leaving Vernon and his men-of-war behind to destroy the Spaniards' shipping and fortifications while loading stores, equipment, booty, and the like. Vernon eventually quits Cartagena's lower harbor by 17 May, followed next day by Ogle's division and on 20 may by Lestock, returning to Port Royal (Jamaica) by 30 May. The Spaniards have endured some 600 deaths during the invasion plus many others wounded or lost yet exult at their success. De Lezo dies of his wounds on 7 September, being posthumously ennobled as marqués de Ovieco; Eslava is created marqués de la Real Defensa.

29 MARCH 1741. A large party of Yamasee warriors raids Governor Oglethorpe's Hermitage Plantation (also called Carr's Fort, Georgia) during his absence, killing four servants and wounding several others before retiring south with plunder. The governor dispatches scout boats in pursuit, which overtake the marauders before they can regain Spanish Florida.

19 JUNE 1741. ***Anson in the Pacific.*** At daybreak HMS *Centurion* sights the Juan Fernández Islands, anchoring three days later after a grueling passage around Cape Horn. This same day (22 June) it is rejoined by the sloop *Trial;* on 8 July by *Gloucester;* and on 28 August by the storeship *Anna.* Of more than 1,000 original crewmembers and troops, only a third are still alive (*Severn* and *Pearl* have turned back into the Atlantic; *Wager* lies wrecked on the Patagonian coast).

The British are in fact fortunate, for three days prior to Anson's arrival Peruvian Commo. Jacinto de Segurola has quit these islands for Callao with his 50-gun flagship *Concepción;* the 40-gun *San Fermín* and *Sacramento;* plus the 24-gun *Sacramento,* convinced that the long-delayed enemy incursion has been canceled.

30 JUNE 1741. In Havana, Admiral Torres's 70-gun flagship *Invencible* (officially designated *San Ignacio*) is struck by lightning at 3:00 P.M., catching fire and exploding about an hour later. The accident not only claims 16 lives and injures 21 but also damages the squadron's remaining warships: the 70-gun *Glorioso, León, Príncipe,* and *Reina;* the 62-gun *San Isidro;* the 60-gun *Fuerte, Hércules, Nueva España,* and *Real Familia.*

11 JULY 1741. ***Guantánamo.*** Vernon quits Port Royal (Jamaica) to attack Santiago de Cuba with his 80-gun flagship *Boyne* and Ogle's vice-flag *Cumberland;* the 70-gun *Grafton* and *Kent;* the 60-gun *Montague, Tilbury,* and *Worcester;* the 50-gun *Chester* and *Tiger;* the 20-gun sloops *Experiment, Sheerness,* and *Shoreham;* bomb vessel *Alderney;* fireships *Phaeton, Strombolo,* and *Vesuvius;* the sloops *Bonetta* and *Triton;* hospital ships *Princess Royal* and *Scarborough;* plus the tender *Pompey.* The fleet is further escorting 40 transports bearing 3,400 troops under Wentworth.

After rendezvousing 18 days later between Guantánamo Point and Caimanera (rechristened Walthenham Bay or Cumberland Bay by the British), Vernon dispatches eight warships on 31 July to cruise off Santiago. Judging that place impervious to sea assault, the redcoats are disembarked at three different beaches in Guantánamo Bay on the night of 4–5 August, marching against the nearby village of Catalina. (The novelist Tobias Smollett, aboard one of the English ships, later describes the landings in *The Adventures of Roderick Random.*) However, the invaders, being 65 miles short of their objective, slow down three days later because of Wentworth's growing trepidations.

Santiago's Gov. Francisco Caxigal de la Vega, *sargento mayor* (garrison commander) Carlos Riva Agüero, and local militia Capt. Pedro Guerrero have only 350 regulars and 600 militia and so retreat before the British host. Nevertheless, Wentworth's army becomes paralyzed by fatigue and disease, spending the next four months encamped, being sporadically raided by Cuban guerrillas. Vernon, disgusted at his colleague's inactivity, sends warships to cruise independently until Wentworth's sick list grows so long—2,260 soldiers being struck with fever by 5 December—that the expedition is reembarked, setting sail at dawn on 9 December to return to Port Royal ten days later. It is estimated that 3,000 Englishmen may have been incapacitated during this futile exercise.

20 JULY 1741. After suffering many years from intermittent attack, Panama's Gov. Dionisio Martínez de la Vega signs a peace treaty with the Indian chieftains Felipe de Uriñaquicha and Juan Sauni, greatly reducing anti-Spanish warfare throughout the Darien region.

20 SEPTEMBER 1741. After breaking up his storeship *Anna,* Anson resumes his Pacific penetration by departing the Juan Fernández Islands with *Centurion, Gloucester,* and *Trial.*

24 SEPTEMBER 1741. Anson's trio of warships captures the three-gun, 450-ton Spanish merchantman *Nuestra Señora del Monte Carmelo* of Master Manuel de Zamora, bound from Lima to Valparaíso. It is renamed *Carmila* and incorporated into the British squadron, bearing eight more guns.

On 6 October the 600-ton *Nuestra Señora de Aranzazu* is also intercepted, being armed with 20 guns to replace *Trial,* which is scuttled on 15 October. Pressing farther north, Anson then seizes Bartolomé Urrunaga's 300-ton, 45-man *Santa Teresa de Jesús* on 17 October and the 270-ton, 43-man *Nuestra Señora del Carmen* of Marcos Moreno on 21 November.

24 NOVEMBER 1741. At 10:00 P.M. Anson sends a 58-man boat party toward the unsuspecting town of Paita (Peru) under Lts. Percy Breitt and Augustus von Keppel, following three hours later with the larger ships. The advance force surprises the Spaniards at 2:00 A.M. on 25 November, carrying Paita with the loss of a single man and another wounded. Next morning *Centurion* and *Carmila* stem the entrance, anchoring at 2:00 P.M. to begin the process of plundering Paita's buildings. The ship *Soledad* is seized as a prize, and two snows, a bark, and a pair of demigalleys are scuttled; the town put to the torch once Anson releases all his captives and withdraws on the afternoon of 27 November.

23 JANUARY 1742. Capt. Edward Herbert's 50-gun HMS *Tiger* is lost on a key near Florida's Tortuga Bank, its crew managing to build a camp ashore, defended by 20 raised guns. The 60-gun Spanish warship *Fuerte* is sent from Havana to capture the survivors but also becomes lost. *Tiger's* men, after two months on their island, take a wayward sloop with their boats with which they reach Jamaica.

26 JANUARY 1742. Some 2,000 troops reach Jamaica from England aboard a convoy escorted by the 50-gun *Greenwich* and *Saint Albans* and the 20-gun *Fox*. Many soldiers soon fall ill, precluding their use in any immediate operation.

9 FEBRUARY 1742. After burning several prizes and releasing more prisoners off South America, Anson arrives near Colima (Mexico) with *Centurion, Gloucester,* and three Spanish ships in hopes of intercepting the annual Manila galleon. Two weeks later he takes up station outside Acapulco, waiting in vain for *Nuestra Señora de Covadonga*—which already lies inside, having entered on 6 January.

MID-FEBRUARY 1742. Santiago de Cuba is reinforced by 1,500 men of the Portugal Regiment and Almansa Dragoons under Cols. Francisco Villavicencio and Alonso de Arcos Moreno, having been transported from Spain by a Guipúzcoan convoy.

16 MARCH 1742. Vernon quits Port Royal (Jamaica) with *Boyne* (flag), *Montague, Worcester, Defiance,* and two smaller auxiliaries in hopes of intercepting six Spanish vessels rumored to be sailing from La Guaira to Cartagena. He leaves instructions for his second-in-command, Ogle, to follow with the remainder of the squadron, convoying Wentworth's 40 transports to a rendezvous off the Spanish Main. From there the combined force will descend upon northern Panama in an attempt to march across the isthmus and seize the capital.

The latter contingent sets sail from Port Royal on 19–20 March with 3,000 troops, meeting up with Vernon before Cartagena on 5 April. The expected Spanish squadron fails to materialize, so the admiral veers toward Nombre de Dios.

8 APRIL 1742. ***Portobelo Fiasco.*** According to the strategy proposed by veteran West Indian rover George Lowther—now breveted as a Royal Navy lieutenant and commanding the sloop *Triton*—Vernon and Wentworth are to first land 500–600 men at Nombre de Dios, hastening them inland to cut off the Portobelo-Panama Road to prevent news of the main body's subsequent disembarkation at Portobelo from reaching the other side of the isthmus. Instead, Vernon stands directly into Portobelo at 4:30 P.M., allowing Spanish Gov. Juan José Colomo ample time to assemble 80 regulars and 300 militia and decamp into the interior. Thus, when the English come ashore they find the Portobelo garrison already retired into the jungle, causing the invaders to lose heart. Almost 1,000 redcoats are already sick, leaving only 2,000 to march inland.

Word then arrives that Panama City's 450 defenders have been supplemented on 22 March by five warships and 1,400 men from Peru, leading the English army commanders to abandon the project altogether and sail for Jamaica aboard the transports by 20 April. Vernon follows five days later with eight of the line and three lesser craft, peering into Cartagena before running downwind to Jamaica; he reaches Bluefields Bay by 23 May.

23 APRIL 1742. The 40-gun Royal Navy frigate *Eltham* of Capt. Edward Smith and the 20-gun sloop *Lively* of Cmdr. Henry Stewart intercept three hired Spanish ships bearing reinforcements for Puerto Rico, mauling them before nightfall brings an end to action.

17 MAY 1742. Disappointed by the Manila galleon's failure to emerge from Acapulco, Anson waters at Zi-

huatanejo and scuttles his last three Spanish prizes before striking out westward across the Pacific with his two remaining warships.

1 JUNE 1742. Ten Spanish vessels quit Havana bearing the first contingent of an expedition intended to reinforce Saint Augustine, then fall upon the advance British outpost of Saint Simons (Georgia). One week later they encounter HMS *Flamborough* off Florida, which drives two of the Spanish galleys and a sloop aground before retiring to carry warning to Charleston (South Carolina). Meanwhile the main body of 25 Cuban vessels departs Havana on 6 June escorted by a royal frigate under Capt. Antonio Castañeda, straggling into Saint Augustine by 15 June after being dispersed by a storm.

Governor de Montiano quickly marshals 52 craft bearing 1,950 men, including two battalions of regular infantry, a regiment of dragoons (without mounts), gunners, numerous militia companies—some composed of runaway South Carolina slaves—and 60 Indian scouts. Finally, at 7:00 A.M. on 1 July the host sets sail from Saint Augustine, Col. Miguel de Rivas Rocafull being left in charge of the 300-man garrison.

15 JUNE 1742. Off the Bahamas, Capt. Thomas Frankland's *Rose* attacks a four-ship Spanish convoy, capturing the largest vessel—a ten-gun, 80-man snow commanded by Juan de León Fandino—after a fierce two-hour fight. (This is the privateer who allegedly cut off Jenkins's ear, precipitating the larger conflict.)

2 JULY 1742. ***Spanish Invasion of Georgia.*** This afternoon, four Spanish demigalleys, two schooners, and nine piraguas—separated from de Montiano's larger fleet by heavy west-northwesterly seas—attempt to shelter in Cumberland Sound but are fired upon by Fort Prince William and the schooner *Walker.* After an hour's exchange the Spaniards veer toward the north end of Cumberland Island, anchoring at the entrance to Saint Andrews Sound beyond range of the British artillery. A report reaches Oglethorpe next morning at Frederica (ten miles farther north), who immediately calls out his provincials—less than 1,000—to repel a Spanish invasion.

By 4 July the first British reinforcements reach Cumberland Island; Capt. William Horton leads a grenadier company and Indian band across from Jekyll Island. When Oglethorpe follows with two companies of regulars aboard three scout boats, however, he is intercepted in Saint Andrews Sound by the four Cuban demigalleys, fighting his way through with two craft

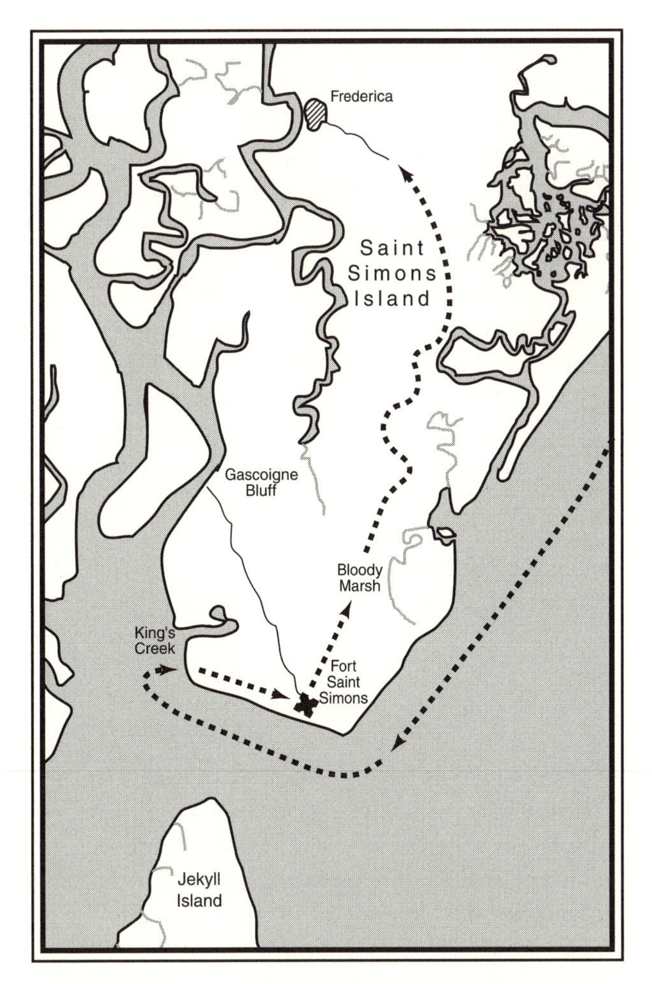

Spanish invasion of Georgia

(the third turns back, erroneously announcing that the British commander has been lost). Upon gaining Fort Saint Andrews, Oglethorpe orders it abandoned so as to concentrate his forces upon Fort Prince William. Next day he watches as the Spanish flotilla stands away from Cumberland Island toward Saint Augustine before it can be hit with an English counterattack.

Oglethorpe returns to Saint Simons Island aboard *Walker,* but on 9 July the main Spanish fleet of 36 sail comes up over the horizon, anchoring about 12 miles northeast of Fort Saint Simon by the next afternoon. Once the wind abates, on 12 July, de Montiano attempts a disembarkation on the southeastern side of the island but demurs when a sudden squall blows up. The Spaniards then shift to within five or six miles of the entrance to Saint Simons Sound on the afternoon of 15 July and, after reconnoitering approaches next morning with a galley and two demigalleys, stand in at 4:00 P.M. The British batteries open fire, backed by *Walker,* the guard sloop *Faulcon,* and the merchant frigate *Success* of Capt. William Thompson, anchored west of Fort Saint Simons. The lead Spanish warships reply effectively, sending *Faulcon* to the bottom and fighting their way to the mouth of Frederica River by 5:30 P.M., suffering only five fatalities.

Thirty minutes later de Montiano's flagship hoists a red pennant, signaling his troops to disembark at a dry marsh just below Kings Creek, a mile and a half from Fort Saint Simons. Lt. Col. Antonio Salgado brings the first 500 Spanish regulars ashore at 7:00 P.M. under covering fire from a galley, two demigalleys, and a packet that scatters the few Georgia rangers and native warriors lining the beach. By morning as many as 1,500 Spanish troops are ashore under de Montiano; meanwhile, Oglethorpe has abandoned Fort Saint Simons and concentrated 500 men in Frederica, simultaneously ordering *Walker, Success,* and a large South Carolina merchant sloop to flee out to sea. The Spaniards occupy the vacant fort the next day and, on 18 July, send a 115-man reconnaissance unit north under Capt. Sebastián Sánchez to probe the six-mile road leading to Frederica.

A mile and a half short of their destination, the Spaniards are set upon by a column of Georgia rangers, Highlanders, Chickasaw, Yamacraw, and Creek warriors—all under Oglethorpe's personal direction—who succeed in killing or capturing 36 invaders (including Sánchez and his second-in-command, Capt. Nicolás Hernández). The British commander then digs in some of his companies while returning to Frederica for greater numbers. At 3:00 P.M. 150–200 Spanish grenadiers appear under Capt. Antonio Barba, having marched from Fort Saint Simons to cover their defeated colleagues' retreat. Despite a steady drizzle, they engage the British in a heated firefight, during which most of Capt. Raymond Demere's company of 42nd regulars flees. Nonetheless, Lt. Charles Mackay's Highlanders hold, along with some rangers and other troops, obliging the Spaniards to retire at 4:00 P.M. (this engagement being known as the Battle of Bloody Marsh).

On 19 July Horton's grenadier company, two foot companies, and Fort Saint Andrews's garrison reach Frederica, bringing Oglethorpe's total strength to 700–800 men. The Spaniards remain ensconced within Fort Saint Simons, each side gingerly probing the other's defenses during the next few days but shying from any direct confrontation. Five British sail arrive from South Carolina at noon on 25 July, prompting de Montiano to order an immediate withdrawal. By nightfall Fort Saint Simons has been razed and the larger Spanish warships are standing out to sea; de Montiano's army has been ferried across to Jekyll Island to destroy Forts Saint Andrews and Prince William during the retreat to Saint Augustine.

26 JULY 1742. Retiring toward Florida, the remnants of de Montiano's expedition burns vacant Fort Saint Andrews on Cumberland Island (Georgia). Next day the Spanish commander detaches his schooners, sloops, and other sea craft to sail directly to Saint Augustine while he uses four demigalleys and his flotilla of piraguas—now rejoined after becoming separated—to proceed down the Cumberland River against Fort Prince William.

29 JULY 1742. This morning, de Montiano reaches the southern end of Cumberland Island, which he attempts to storm with 200 troops to overwhelm tiny Fort Prince William, held by only 60 regulars and a ranger detachment under Lt. Alexander Stewart. But the defenders have been forewarned of the Spaniards' approach and know Oglethorpe is marching to their relief; they send eight snipers to fire upon the Spanish boats. This persuades de Montiano to forego attack; he instead steers for Saint Augustine with his boats while the Cuban demigalleys bombard Fort Prince William's ramparts for an hour before following in his wake.

6 AUGUST 1742. A South Carolina relief force of 1,092 men arrives off Saint Simons Island (Georgia) aboard four Royal Navy warships and eight armed provincial vessels to find de Montiano's Spanish expedition already gone. Four days later Capt. Charles Hardy takes his flagship *Rye* and all other vessels back to Charleston (except the two provincial galleys) on the unfounded fear of a Spanish assault against South Carolina during his absence.

24 AUGUST 1742. A small expedition quits Port Royal (Jamaica) escorted by Cusack's 50-gun *Litchfield* and the four-gun sloop *Bonetta* of Cmdr. William Lea to sail west and establish an English presence on Roatán Island (Honduras). The convoy is accompanied by William Pitt, a well-known figure along the Mosquito Coast who ensures a hearty welcome from the local residents.

7 SEPTEMBER 1742. Oglethorpe appears off Saint Augustine with six Royal Navy warships, six armed provincial vessels, and a flotilla of scout boats. Two days later they attempt to force the entrance to destroy the half-dozen Cuban demigalleys lying inside but are repelled. On 10 September the British shift south to Matanzas Inlet, from where they try to assault a large, partially built stone blockhouse on an island (present-day Fort Matanzas Monument); again they are driven

off. When the wind rises on 11 September Oglethorpe sails for Georgia, returning safely soon thereafter.

2 October 1742. Capt. Peter Lawrence's 60-gun HMS *Tilbury* catches fire accidentally and sinks off Hispaniola, taking down 100 crewmembers.

4 OCTOBER 1742. Rear Admiral Ogle is instructed to relieve Vernon as commander in chief at Jamaica. His fleet consists of the 80-gun *Cumberland;* the 70-gun *Kent* and *Grafton;* the 60-gun *Lion, Montague, Rippon,* and *York;* the 50-gun *Assistance, Saint Albans,* and *Litchfield;* the 40-gun frigates *Adventure, Eltham, Fowey,* and *Ludlow Castle;* the 20-gun sloops *Astrea, Experiment, Seahorse,* and *Shoreham;* the six-gun sloop *Spy;* the four-gun sloop *Bonetta;* the fireships *Strombolo* and *Vulcan;* and the bomb vessels *Basilisk, Blast,* and *Thunder.* At Barbados are the 50-gun *Advice* and *Norwich* and the 20-gun sloop *Scarborough.* In the Leeward Islands are the 40-gun frigates *Gosport* and *Launceston;* the 20-gun *Lively;* and Pembroke's *Prize.*

30 OCTOBER 1742. Discouraged and at odds with one another, Vernon and Wentworth quit Jamaica for England.

18 NOVEMBER 1742. Yamasee raiders launch a dawn attack against the Mount Venture trading outpost (near the Altamaha River, Georgia), exterminating the five-man garrison before retiring to Saint Augustine.

22 FEBRUARY 1743. Having returned into the West Indies the previous month after a brief sojourn in England, during which he has been promoted commodore, 37-year-old Charles Knowles sets sail from Antigua for Saint Kitts with his 70-gun, 380-man flagship *Suffolk* and *Burford* of Franklin Lushington; 50-gun, 250-man *Norwich* of Thomas Gregory, *Advice* of Elliot Smith, and *Assistance* of Smith Callis; 40-gun, 210-man frigate *Eltham* of acting captain Richard Watkins; 20-gun, 120-man sloops *Lively* of acting captain Henry Stewart and *Scarborough* of Lachlin Leslie; 14-gun, 45-man sloop *Otter* of Cmdr. John Gage; plus eight-gun, 40-man bomb vessel *Comet* of Richard Tyrrell.

He takes on 400 militia from Colonel Dalzell's regiment aboard two transports then heads southwest on 23 February with the intent of attacking La Guaira. Knowles believes this base will prove an easy target, but the Spaniards have been forewarned of his plan, and La Guaira is heavily reinforced by the Caracas governor, 47-year-old Gen. Gabriel José de Zuloaga. Touching at Tortuga Island on 27 February, the English expedition approaches La Guaira three days later.

2 MARCH 1743. ***La Guaira.*** At first light, Knowles's squadron lies 15 miles east of the port of La Guaira, *Otter* being sent ahead to reconnoiter the inner harbor. Spanish lookouts light signal fires at 6:30 A.M., warning both La Guaira and Caracas and bringing Governor de Zuloaga galloping 25 miles down to the coast with a large body of militia. Garrison Cmdr. Mateo Gual and Capt. José Iturriaga brace for an impending assault. About midday HMS *Burford* stands into the roadstead, followed by *Eltham, Norwich, Suffolk, Advice,* and *Assistance.* Despite the hail of rounds from six batteries—some firing heated shot—the English men-of-war anchor in a double line by 1:00 P.M. and begin a furious exchange. The Spanish counterfire proves unexpectedly heavy and accurate, a heavy swell further preventing any British disembarkation.

After three and a half hours, *Burford* cuts its cable to move out of range; the frigate *Eltham* is also in distress. Both accidentally drift afoul of *Norwich,* forcing it out of action as well, thus slackening Knowles's overall effort. Shooting ceases at sundown (8:00 P.M.), with the battered *Burford* seeking shelter to leeward, escorted by *Norwich, Otter,* and *Assistance*—which cannot anchor. The English bombardment resumes rather desultorily next dawn with the bomb vessel *Comet.* De Zuloaga is obliged to return to his capital on 4 March to reassure an uneasy populace that the enemy has not come ashore. At 3:00 A.M. on 5 March Knowles sends boat parties into La Guaira's roadstead; they board a French merchantman before being discovered and driven off.

Having suffered 92 killed and 308 wounded over three days, Knowles decides to retire west before sunup on 6 March and assail nearby Puerto Cabello. Despite instructing his captains to rendezvous at Borburata Keys (four miles east of Puerto Cabello), the detached *Burford, Norwich, Assistance,* and *Otter* proceed to Curaçao, compelling the commodore to angrily follow them in. On 28 March he sends his smaller ships to cruise off Puerto Cabello, and once his main body is refitted, ventures to sea again on 31 March, only to then struggle against contrary winds and currents for two weeks before finally diverting to the eastern tip of Santo Domingo by 19 April.

15 MARCH 1743. At noon Oglethorpe quits Cumberland Sound (Georgia) with an expedition of regulars, rangers, and Indians to conduct a reprisal raid

against Spanish Florida. Two days later his advance units establish a base on the southern banks of the Saint Johns River (near Mayport, Florida), from which a Creek war party steals upon Saint Augustine and ambushes a Spanish piragua bearing 40 members of a labor battalion. Five are killed and scalped before the natives are obliged to retire by the guns of nearby Fort San Marcos. After the warriors return to Oglethorpe's camp on the afternoon of 22 March and hold a celebration they disperse, leaving the British general with only 200–300 regulars and provincials to march south three days later, hoping to lure the Spanish garrison of Saint Augustine into the open.

Oglethorpe arrives three miles north of that place at 8:00 P.M. on 27 March, but after the English conceal their columns a deserter from the 42nd Regiment—a soldier named Eels—reveals the attackers' presence to Governor de Montiano. The British immediately withdraw, returning to their Saint Johns base by afternoon on 29 March. Two separate bands of Indian allies then attempt a raid on the outskirts of Saint Augustine without result, after which Oglethorpe materializes off Anastasia Island on the afternoon of 8 April with 80 troops aboard the schooner *Walker* of Capt. Caleb Davis and a pair of scout boats escorted by the provincial frigate *Success* of William Thompson. High seas prevent any disembarkation, so the British sail away a few days later for Georgia.

26 APRIL 1743. ***Puerto Cabello.*** This afternoon Knowles arrives four miles northeast of the Venezuelan port of Puerto Cabello, sending the bomb vessel *Comet* to take up station inshore while preparing the remainder of his expedition for an assault. Next day the 50-gun *Norwich,* the 40-gun *Eltham,* and the 20-gun *Lively* move in to bombard two small Spanish batteries—one mounting 15 pieces and the other eight—north of Puerto Cabello's main harbor castle of San Felipe. This attack is intended to weary the batteries' defenders, after which a large force will be disembarked nearby under cover of darkness to overwhelm the isolated outposts and turn the artillery against the main Spanish keep.

Knowles's operation starts well, with this trio pounding the batteries until 7:00 P.M., after which 1,100–1,200 Englishmen are landed unseen under Major Lucas at 10:30 P.M. But, upon advancing, the troops stumble into a 40-man Spanish company,

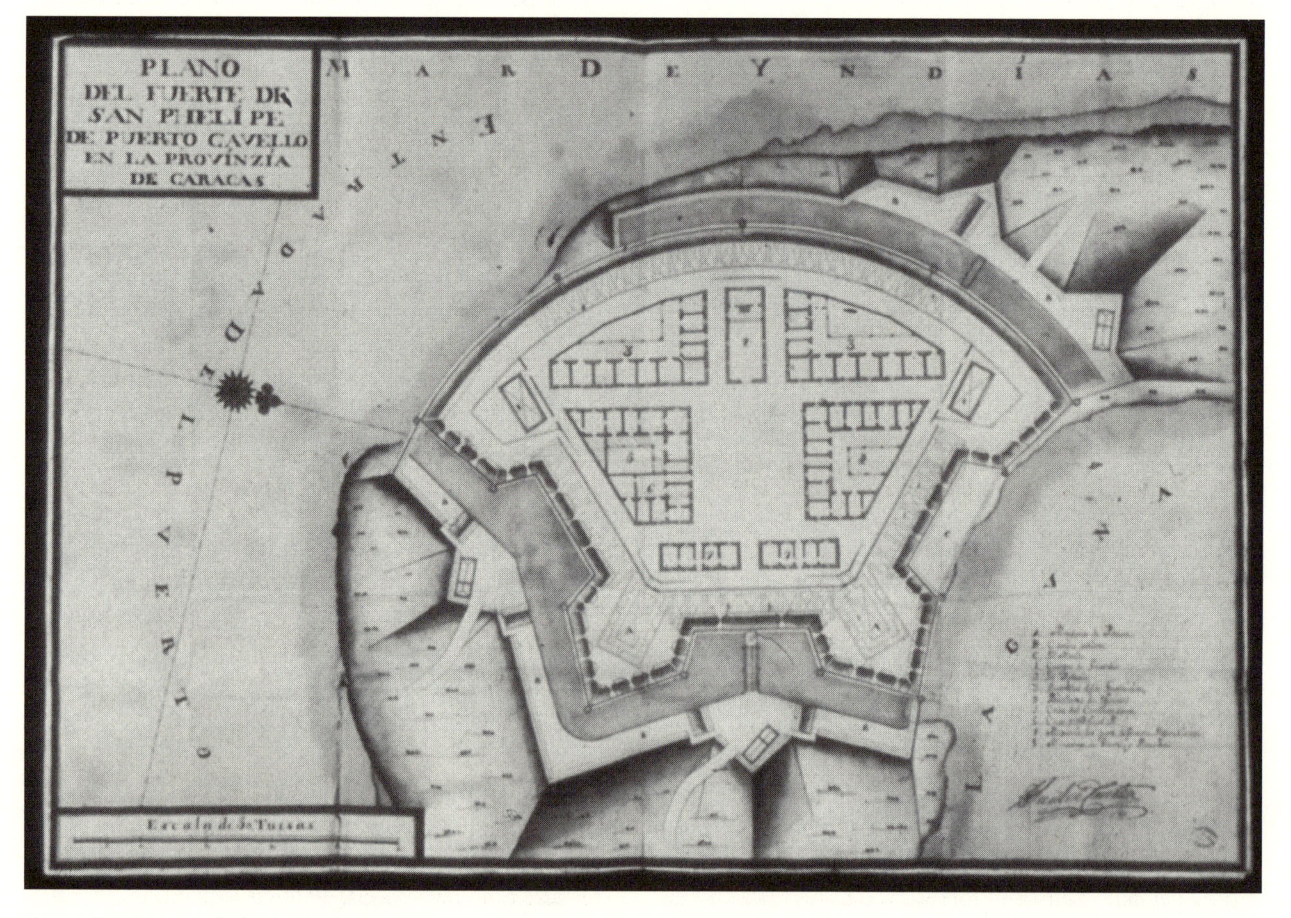

Puerto Cabello's main harbor castle of San Felipe

which falls back and turns two small artillery pieces inland, firing volleys of grape. The English troops panic, blazing wildly in all directions and eventually becoming so confused that they shoot into their own ranks, precipitating a general stampede back to the boats.

On 28 April the three Royal Navy warships resume their offshore bombardment to little effect. On 2 May Caracas's Governor de Zuloaga arrives overland with reinforcements for the Spanish garrison (normal complement is three companies of regulars and 300–400 militia). Next day de Zuloaga is wounded in the leg after inspecting the Punta Brava battery.

By now running low on ammunition and provisions, Knowles decides to attempt a general assault on 4 April (23 April [O.S.]—Saint George's Day). However, the breeze dies away before his squadron can get under way at 1:00 P.M., so the operation is postponed until 5 May. Knowles weighs at 11:00 A.M., prompting the Spaniards to man their defenses. *Assistance, Burford, Suffolk,* and *Norwich* are to batter San Felipe Castle while *Scarborough, Lively,* and *Eltham* engage the fascine batteries farther north. The battle begins shortly after 1:00 P.M. on 5 May, the warships anchoring so close to San Felipe that only 11 of its guns can be depressed. At 4:00 P.M. the wind rises, and de Zuloaga fears the English will charge the harbor mouth; he therefore orders the anchored blockship scuttled. Seeing the channel closing, Knowles gives the signal to retire two and a half hours later, only to see his formation become becalmed. The English suffer heavily before eventually warping out of range by 9:00 P.M.

Having endured 90–100 casualties during this desperate gamble—plus another 100 during previous tries—Knowles orders his most crippled ships to retire to the Borburata Keys on the morning of 7 May (*Burford* and *Assistance* are barely able to move) while still shelling the inner harbor with his lone bomb vessel. The English commodore eventually offers a prisoner exchange and, after being allowed to water by the begrudging de Zuloaga a few days later, sails away in two divisions on 11 and 13 May to Jamaica.

25 OCTOBER 1743. French and Spanish diplomats formalize a "family compact" by signing a treaty at Fontainebleu.

15 DECEMBER 1743. Because of growing fears of a rupture between England and France, Knowles reaches Barbados with the 60-gun *Superbe,* the 20-gun *Biddeford,* and the bomb vessel *Comet* to assume joint command over the station with 39-year-old Commo. Peter Warren. The latter arrives from North America on 2 January 1744, going on a cruise with *Superbe* while Knowles attends to the reconstruction of the Barbados defenses.

15 MARCH 1744. In Europe, France officially declares war against Great Britain, which reciprocates on 9 April.

LATE MARCH 1744. A 43-man Yamasee war party raids Capt. Mark Carr's Hermitage Plantation (also called Carr's Fort, Georgia), capturing five marines who are cutting logs. They are carried off to Florida, pursued by Carr's soldiers and a band of Yamacraw warriors under chief Toonahowi. The raiders are overtaken next day on the north side of the Saint Johns River; five are killed, and the captives are released. Toonahowi succumbs during the fight.

3 MAY 1744. Elderly Jean Baptiste Louis Le Prévost, seigneur Du Quesnel and governor of French Île Royale (Cape Breton, Canada), learns of France's declaration of war while at his stronghold of Louisbourg and begins organizing an expedition to reconquer some of his country's lost territories.

23 MAY 1744. Boston learns of the outbreak of Anglo-French hostilities back in Europe. Farther northeast, a French expedition quits Louisbourg under 37-year-old Capt. Joseph François Du Pont Duvivier, consisting of 139 soldiers and 212 sailors aboard the privateer *Succès* of 58-year-old Pierre Morpain (now *capitaine de brûlot* [fireship captain] in France's royal navy), another sloop under Captain Doloboratz, a supply sloop, and 14 fishing smacks. They intend to eradicate the English frontier outpost of Canso (Nova Scotia).

Duvivier arrives in Canso's fog-shrouded roadstead the next dawn, catching the English garrison—four incomplete companies of Lt. Gen. Richard Phillip's 40th Regiment (87 ill-trained soldiers in all under Capt. Patrick Heron)—completely off guard. The French bombard Canso's blockhouse, and Heron immediately surrenders; Lieutenant Ryall's Royal Navy sloop resists a bit longer out in the harbor before striking. The fortifications are demolished and Canso's buildings are set ablaze before Duvivier retires to Louisbourg with more than 100 prisoners.

2 JUNE 1744. News of the war with France reaches Antigua, prompting numerous Royal Navy warships and English privateers to put to sea for prizes. Dispatches are also sent to Jamaica, arriving eight days later.

11 JULY 1744. At the urging of Governor Du Quesnel in Louisbourg, 37-year-old French missionary Abbé Jean Louis Le Loutre convinces the Micmac Indians to rise against the English outpost of Annapolis Royal (Nova Scotia). Its 60-year-old lieutenant governor, garrison commander, and former Huguenot refugee, Paul Mascarene, discovers 300 natives six miles from his walls poised to attack. He musters 75 effectives (out of approximately 100 soldiers) and, next morning, repels the Micmac assault. The warriors remain outside his ramparts until 16 July, when they withdraw to Minas upon the arrival of the 14-gun Massachusetts provincial snow *Prince of Orange* under 61-year-old Capt. Edward Tyng bearing 70 reinforcements.

2 AUGUST 1744. The English merchant Capt. William Kinghill appears off Portobelo to demand the return of one of his ships; when satisfaction is not forthcoming, he batters the Panamanian port with a prolonged bombardment.

AUGUST 1744. Rioting occurs in Puebla (Mexico).

8 SEPTEMBER 1744. Duvivier appears off Annapolis Royal from Louisbourg with 50 French troops, 160 Micmac warriors, and 70 Malecite warriors, having approached overland via Chignecto and Minas. The English garrison has meanwhile been further augmented from Massachusetts and now numbers 250 well-armed troops. Duvivier therefore masks his army's small numbers, deceiving Mascarene into believing he is besieged by a much larger force while hoping that the French 64-gun warship *Ardent*—which has reached Louisbourg on 16 August with a damaged bowsprit—can be repaired in time to lead a seaborne pincer movement against Annapolis Royal.

Unable to effect anything more against his entrenched foes, Duvivier opens negotiations with Mascarene on 15 September, supposedly arranging terms for the forthcoming capitulation. But the truce is canceled on 23 September—and the garrison's morale is lifted—when a New England brigantine and sloop arrive in Annapolis Basin on 26 September, bringing 50 Pigwacket allies under 35-year-old Capt. John Gorham. Duvivier is informed on 2 October that *Ardent* will not join him, so he reluctantly lifts his siege and retires toward Minas a few days later.

12 OCTOBER 1744. Off Martinique, Commodore Knowles's blockading squadron drives a 24-gun French ship ashore under the Artois batteries, setting it ablaze.

28 OCTOBER 1744. In Boston, 49-year-old Gov. William Shirley declares war against the Micmac and Malecite tribes for having aided Duvivier in his assault on Annapolis Royal.

LATE OCTOBER 1744. Spanish Admiral de Torres departs Havana with four of the line and a frigate, transporting 8 million pesos in bullion to Spain by 2 January 1745. Three weeks later Philip V ennobles him as marqués de Matallana de Val Madrigal and promotes him commander in chief of Spain's Mediterranean fleet for having successfully run the Royal Navy's blockade with the treasure.

26–28 DECEMBER 1744. Louisbourg's 400-man garrison—many of them Swiss mercenaries of the Karrer Regiment—mutiny against back pay and other injustices; the mutineers are appeased by the new acting governor, 66-year-old Louis Du Pont, sieur Duchambon (his predecessor, Du Quesnel, died on 9 October).

24 MARCH 1745. Reacting to Duvivier's Nova Scotia offensives during the summer of 1744, Governor Shirley of Massachusetts has spent the ensuing winter raising financing for a counterexpedition against the main French stronghold of Louisbourg. Having assembled a sizable force, Shirley dispatches the provincial armed vessels *Prince of Orange* of 14 guns, *Boston Packet* of 12, and *Fame* of 24 by 24 March to prowl off Cape Breton in anticipation of an impending attack. The hired vessels *Molineux* of 24 guns, *Caesar* of 14, and the 400-ton provincial frigate *Massachusetts* of 22 follow on 27 March; next day the ten-gun *Resolute* and six-gun *Bonetta* also depart for Canso, where the expedition is to rendezvous.

4 APRIL 1745. At 4:00 P.M. on this Sunday afternoon 2,800 New England volunteers under 50-year-old militia Lt. Gen. William Pepperrell—a merchant originally from Kittery, Maine—and militia Brig. Gen.

Samuel Waldo set sail aboard 51 transports from Boston escorted by the 24-gun *Shirley* to launch a counterstrike against French Louisbourg. They are followed by a second contingent of 200 more New Englanders two days later.

6 APRIL 1745. French reinforcements begin arriving at Martinique under the new governor-general for the West Indies, 47-year-old Charles de Tubières, Chevalier de Caylus. His convoy takes six days to enter, being escorted by the 76-gun *Espérance;* the 64-gun *Northumberland* (recently captured from Britain), *Trident,* and *Sérieux;* the 56-gun *Diamant;* the 50-gun *Aquilon;* two or three frigates of 36–30 guns; two bomb vessels; and a pair of fireships.

11–21 APRIL 1745. Pepperrell's New England expedition straggles into Canso (Nova Scotia) after being scattered by a storm, disembarking on 15 April to drill while awaiting Commodore Warren from the West Indies; once combined, the forces will then proceed against Louisbourg.

3 MAY 1745. Captain Philip Durell's 40-gun HMS *Eltham* reaches Canso, augmenting Pepperrell's expedition.

This same morning the 32-gun French frigate *Renommée* of 42-year-old Capt. Guy François de Coëtnempren, Comte de Kersaint—unable to approach Louisbourg's harbor four days earlier because of dangerous ice—appears off Pope's Harbour, chasing the Rhode Island guard sloop *Tartar.* Next day, the galley *Shirley* of Capt. John Rouse, the snow *Prince of Wales,* and a privateer are detached from the main English body to assist *Tartar,* although the sloop successfully eludes its larger French opponent and returns by 25 April (O.S.). *Renommée* meanwhile retreats back out into the Atlantic for France.

4 MAY 1745. Warren reaches Canso from Antigua with the 60-gun HMS *Superbe* under Flag Capt. Thomas Somers, the 44-gun *Launceston* of Warwick Calmady, and the 44-gun *Mermaid* of James Douglas to assist in Pepperrell's forthcoming campaign against French Acadia. Without wasting time going ashore to visit his old friend Pepperrell, Warren instructs his men-of-war to proceed directly to Louisbourg and institute a blockade.

7 MAY 1745. The 18-gun French privateer *Saint Jean de Luz* of Capt. Janson Dufoure picks its way through ice floes into Louisbourg, reporting it has been chased the previous day by a trio of New England vessels. This report is Governor Duchambon's first inkling of an impending enemy assault. Next day the city's warning gun is fired and militia companies fall in when English blockaders begin intercepting incoming coasters—among them the 14-gun, 160-ton provision ship *Marie de Grace* of Capt. La Perrelle Du Gauran, taken on 10 May by Molineux.

10 MAY 1745. Before 6:00 A.M. Pepperrell and militia Maj. Gen. Roger Wolcott's 100 sail get under way from Canso, standing northeast escorted by *Massachusetts,* the brig *Boston Packet,* and the eight-gun provincial snow *Lord Montague.* A separate contingent of 270 New Hampshire volunteers has already departed some days earlier under veteran Col. Jeremiah Moulton (*see* spring 1724) to seize the advance French outpost of Port Toulouse (modern-day Saint Peter's, Nova Scotia), then rejoin the main force before Louisbourg. Two companies of colonials also remain at Canso under Ammi Cutter.

11 MAY 1745. ***Louisbourg.*** By 8:00 A.M. Pepperrell's expedition begins rendezvousing with Warren's blockading squadron off Gabarus Bay; three hours later the 7th Massachusetts Regiment's lieutenant colonel, John Gorham, leads a company of Indian rangers in an attempted disembarkation at Flat Point Cove. He is repelled by 20 French soldiers, obliging the invaders to land two miles farther west at Anse de la Coromandière (modern-day Kennington Cove). Rattled, Governor Duchambon belatedly sends 80 French volunteers out of Louisbourg, their leader, Morpain, being unable to contain the hundreds of New Englanders now streaming ashore. His force suffers a half-dozen killed and a like number captured—including Morpain's second-in-command, the veteran An-

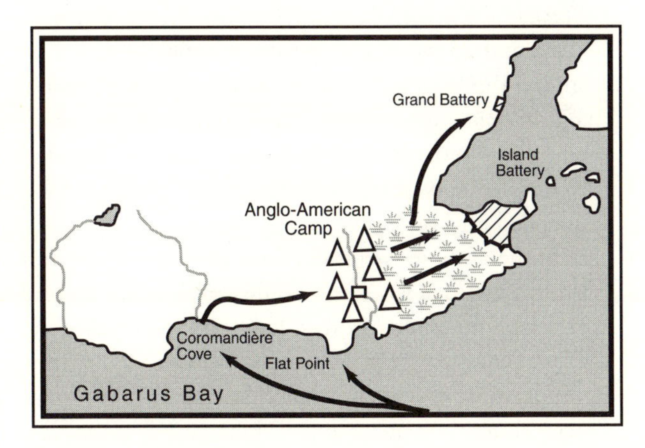

Anglo-American siege of Louisbourg

toine Le Poupet de La Boularderie—without checking the enemy. By early afternoon the first of 2,000 English colonials arrive within a mile and a quarter of Louisbourg's western ramparts and are fired upon by the batteries. Duchambon orders his gates closed at 4:00 P.M., and his city becomes besieged.

That night 200 French troops and civilians abandon the detached Grand battery, retiring undetected into Louisbourg. Pepperrell himself comes ashore with more soldiers during the morning of 12 May, and this same night—upon advice from Lt. Col. John Bradstreet of the 1st Massachusetts—sends Col. William Vaughan with 400–500 men to probe the French defenses along the waterfront. Encountering no opposition, they burn valuable warehouses and stores before retiring to their camps for the night. Vaughan, however, remains behind with a dozen men; next dawn he discovers that the Grand battery is empty. He occupies it at 9:00 A.M. on 13 May and then beats off a feeble French sally; by 14 May the New Englanders begin using its artillery to fire on Louisbourg.

A somewhat loose siege is then imposed, Duchambon being asked on 18 May to capitulate. He refuses, still having 600 regulars and 900 militia; the New England irregulars refuse to storm Louisbourg's walls, and so a protracted operation ensues—over Warren's strenuous objections. After a fortnight of artillery duels, the Rhode Island sloop *Tartar* of Capt. Daniel Fones captures a small French brigantine on Saturday, 29 May, learning that a relief convoy is expected from France. On the afternoon of 30 May Douglas's 44-gun HMS *Mermaid* sights the approaching 64-gun French *Vigilant,* commanded by Capt. Alexandre de La Maisonfort Du Boisdecourt, Marquis de La Maisonfort and knight of the Order of Saint Louis. Douglas lures the vessel toward the main British fleet, and by 9:00 P.M. the lone French man-of-war is overwhelmed by the combined broadsides of *Superbe, Launceston, Mermaid, Eltham, Shirley,* and *Massachusetts.* The French suffer 35 killed and 26 wounded opposed to only six casualties among the English and colonial vessels. Due to heavy fog *Vigilant* cannot be boarded until next morning, when its captors find more than 500 men on board as well as 1,000 barrels of powder, 40 cannons, and food intended for Louisbourg.

Some 400 New England volunteers under Captain Brooks attempt to storm Louisbourg's island battery just after midnight on 6–7 June but are repelled by Capt. Louis d'Aillebout with 60 killed and 116 captured. British morale is restored by the arrival of more siege equipment on 13 and 17 June as well as the capture of four French blockade runners. On 19 June the besiegers reveal *Vigilant's* capture to the garrison, dashing French hopes for relief; just before sunset on 26 June—amid English preparations for a massive land-sea assault next dawn—Duchambon sends out an officer requesting terms.

Louisbourg surrenders by the afternoon of 28 June, the siege having cost the defenders 53 killed, compared to 101 New Englanders. Despite sending more than 1,200 volunteers back to New England by mid-September, Pepperrell is still left with a garrison of 2,250–2,600 men throughout the coming winter.

24 MAY 1745. Commo. Fitzroy Henry Lee arrives at Barbados with a merchant convoy to assume command over the station. His flag flying aboard the 70-gun *Suffolk,* he is accompanied by another ship of the line.

1 JUNE 1745. Two French royal frigates of 36 and 30 guns under Captain Fouché, plus three privateers, make a descent upon the West Indian island of Anguilla but are repulsed by militia with 35 killed and 65 wounded.

JULY 1745. In Europe, the exiled Stuart prince, Charles Edward—also known as Bonnie Prince Charlie or the Young Pretender—lands in Scotland from France to raise the Highlands in revolt. Over the coming year, he will wage a protracted campaign to regain his title, taking Edinburgh by September 1745 and invading northern England in early December, only to have his hopes dashed when greater numbers do not rally to his side.

10 SEPTEMBER 1745. The 60-year-old veteran Isaac Townsend (*see* 2–8 February 1741) arrives at Barbados, now promoted vice admiral and commanding the 80-gun *Dorsetshire* (flag); the 70-gun *Ipswich, Lennox,* and *Princesa* (captured five years earlier from Spain); the 60-gun *Kingston, Pembroke,* and *Worcester;* plus the 50-gun *Hampshire.* Hoping to use local forces to invest French Saint Lucia, he finds, upon reaching Antigua on 2 October, that the English governors do not wish to lend troops for such a venture. Townsend therefore sorties on 14 October to blockade Guadeloupe, Dominica, and Martinique.

11 NOVEMBER 1745. At 7:00 A.M. Townsend's *Lennox, Ipswich,* the 60-gun *Dreadnought,* the sloop *Hind,* and other lesser consorts intercept a 43-ship French convoy approaching Martinique under escort by 53-year-old Commo. Hilarion Josselin, Comte

Duguay's 74-gun flagship *Magnanime,* and the smaller ship of the line *Rubis.* The convoy scatters, 14 members being captured by the English auxiliaries while the ships of the line fight an inconclusive, long-range gun duel until the next morning, when Townsend stands away toward Antigua with his prizes.

The English admiral subsequently learns that a second, 80-ship convoy has parted company earlier from Duguay, sailing directly to Saint Domingue (Haiti) with 55-year-old Commo. Jean Baptiste Macnemara's *Invincible, Jason,* and *Atalante* (sometimes mistaken as *Galante* in English reports). Consequently, Townsend detaches some of his men-of-war to reinforce Jamaica.

29 NOVEMBER 1745. Lt. Paul Marin de La Malgue, with 400 French-Canadian militiamen plus 200 Abenaki and Micmac allies, destroys Saratoga (New York), capturing 100 prisoners.

26 DECEMBER 1745. At sunrise a 32-ship convoy 18 days out of Port Royal (Jamaica)—bound for England escorted by Capt. Cornelius Mitchell's 60-gun HMSS *Strafford* and *Plymouth* plus the 20-gun sloop *Lyme*—sights a 23-ship French convoy 30 miles west of Cape Saint Nicholas Mole (Cap du Môle, Haiti). The latter are making for France with two ships of 74 and 64 guns plus the 36-gun frigate of Commodore Macnemara. All the merchantmen scatter, leaving both naval squadrons to clash at 4:00 P.M. Mitchell engages at long range until evening then breaks off and steers north before reversing course to Jamaica; Macnemara returns to Saint Domingue. *Strafford* suffers five killed and eight wounded during the encounter, *Plymouth* eight and 14. (Two years later Mitchell is court-martialled for not having attempted more during this particular affair but is acquitted; *see* 8 August 1746.)

APRIL 1746. In Scotland, the Stuart pretender Bonnie Prince Charlie is defeated at Culloden (near Inverness) by an English army; he flees back to France in September, never to return.

MID-JUNE 1746. The 56-year-old French Commo. Hubert de Brienne, Comte de Conflans and knight of the Order of Saint Louis, reaches Martinique with a 214-ship merchant convoy escorted by his 74-gun flagship *Terrible,* the 58-gun *Neptune,* the 50-gun *Alcyon,* and the 46-gun *Gloire.* Commodore Lee appears belatedly to blockade the French island, retiring empty-handed by 3 July. Conflans sails again the same day, guiding a significant portion of his charges to Saint Domingue (Haiti).

JULY 1746. A force of 680 French-Canadian militiamen arrives near Beaubassin (northeast of the Bay of Fundy, Nova Scotia), occupying the Isthmus of Chignecto in conjunction with their native allies. A Massachusetts regiment under Colonel Noble counters by taking up position at Grand Pré.

8 AUGUST 1746. The 14-gun English sloop *Drake* of Cmdr. Edward Clark sights Conflans's four French warships off southwestern Saint Domingue beginning the homeward leg with 93 West Indiamen. *Drake* hastens north and four days later advises Commodore Mitchell, who is cruising off Cape Saint Nicholas Mole (Cap du Môle, Haiti) with his 60-gun *Strafford* (flag), *Lennox* of Peter Lawrence, *Plymouth* of Digby Dent, and *Worcester* of Thomas Andrews as well as the 24-gun frigate *Seahorse.* (The 44-gun *Milford* of Capt. Edward Rich joins shortly thereafter.)

Mitchell steers toward the French, coming within sight of Conflans's host by 3:00 P.M. on 14 August in faint breezes. Unable to overtake, the English commodore stands away north, apparently to prevent the French convoy from slipping past and exiting the Windward Passage in darkness. But, next day, Mitchell continues to maneuver for the weather gauge rather than bear down, thus allowing Conflans further respite. The English commodore still shows shy on 16 August and eventually allows the French to regain Cap-François (modern-day Cap-Haïtien), losing only a single merchantman to *Drake.*

When Mitchell returns to Port Royal (Jamaica) on 30 August he is greeted by a storm of protest and, a few weeks later, is court-martialled and cashiered. Conflans has meanwhile departed Cap-François after only a fortnight's stay, conducting his convoy safely into Brest by October—capturing the 50-gun HMS *Severn* en route.

10–17 SEPTEMBER 1746. ***French Counterstrike.*** The 37-year-old Adm. Jean Baptiste Louis de La Rochefoucauld de Roye, duc d'Anville, arrives off Nova Scotia with *Northumberland* (flag); the 64-gun *Trident* (vice-flag), *Ardent, Mars, Léopard,* and *Alcide;* the 60-gun *Caubon* and *Tigre;* the 56-gun *Mercure* and *Diamant;* the 50-gun *Borée;* the 30-gun frigate *Mégare;* the 26-gun frigates *Argonaute* and *Prince d'Orange;* three bomb vessels; plus approximately 60 transports bearing 3,500 troops. His orders are to free Louisbourg, drive the English invaders from Acadia, then ravage the New England coastline as far as Boston.

However, his fleet has been badly battered by storms during the two-and-a-half-month passage, and in the first two weeks after arriving 2,300 of his soldiers and sailors die from scurvy and smallpox while anchored in Chebucto Bay (modern-day Halifax). D'Anville himself succumbs on 27 September, being replaced by 55-year-old Commo. Constantin Louis d'Estourmel, knight of the Orders of Malta and Saint Louis (and commanding *Trident*), who, because of sickness and an attempted suicide, is himself quickly superseded by 61-year-old Commo. Pierre Jacques Taffanel de La Jonquière, d'Anville's original flag captain aboard *Northumberland.*

Faced with such complications, de La Jonquière detaches four warships to circle into the Bay of Fundy and attack the small English garrison at Annapolis Royal, but that squadron is struck by a storm and obliged to retreat to Chebucto without sighting its objective. De La Jonquière therefore lands his remaining troops and steers his shattered expedition back to Brest by early November.

AUTUMN 1746. The Mohawk chieftain Theyanoguin (also known as White Head or Hendrick) visits French Gov. Charles de Beauharnois at Montréal, receiving presents to remain neutral in the war. Nevertheless, Theyanoguin and his warriors attack some French carpenters at Isle La Motte (Vermont) upon their journey homeward, so next spring a raiding party is sent to kidnap him. The Mohawk leader preempts that attempt with a large war party, which strikes at various points along the Saint Lawrence seaway near Montréal before being dispersed by French forces under Louis de La Corne and Jacques Legardeur de Saint Pierre.

29 NOVEMBER 1746. Lee's blockading squadron sights a recently arrived French convoy north of Martinique, sailing west toward Saint Domingue escorted by 63-year-old Commo. Emmanuel Auguste de Cahideuc, Comte Dubois de La Motte and knight of the Order of Saint Louis, with his 74-gun flagship *Magnanime* and the 48-gun frigate *Étoile.* HMSS *Suffolk, Dreadnought,* the 50-gun *Sutherland,* and the 44-gun *Gosport* give chase, skirmishing with the French escorts and snapping up six merchantmen while the rest of the convoy scatters into the night. Dubois de La Motte eventually reaches Cap-François (modern-day Cap-Haïtien) with his surviving charges.

12 FEBRUARY 1747. At 3:00 A.M., the Massachusetts militia garrison at Grand Pré (Nova Scotia) is surprised and overwhelmed by 236 French-Canadian raiders and 50 Micmac warriors, the survivors being repatriated to Annapolis Royal.

5 APRIL 1747. While cruising 20 miles northwest of Cape Saint Nicholas Mole (Cap du Môle, Haiti), Commo. Digby Dent's 60-gun *Lennox, Plymouth,* and *Worcester* pursue a French convoy heading south into the Bight of Léogâne. Its naval escort, under Dubois de La Motte—the 74-gun flagship *Magnanime,* the 64-gun *Alcide,* and the 54-gun *Arc-en-Ciel*—turns to give battle, leaving the merchantmen protected by the frigate *Étoile.*

Action erupts shortly past noon, both formations criss-crossing repeatedly throughout the afternoon, firing when courses intersect. At 4:00 P.M. *Lennox's* foremast topples, compelling it to bring to and halting the engagement when Dubois de La Motte retires toward his convoy. *Plymouth* has suffered two killed and nine wounded; *Lennox* 11 and 25; *Worcester* four and five—allowing the French convoy to escape. Dent returns to Port Royal (Jamaica) on 10 April to refit and reprovision.

25 APRIL 1747. Commo. Edward Legge arrives at Barbados with the 70-gun *Captain,* plus the 60-gun *Dragon* and *Sunderland,* escorting a 44-ship English convoy. A few days later he proceeds to Antigua, relieving Lee as commander in chief.

13 AUGUST 1747. Zambos and English Baymen from the Mosquito Coast capture the Spanish fortification at Matina (Costa Rica).

8 JANUARY 1748. Knowles—recently promoted rear admiral and designated to command the Jamaica station—returns to Barbados from Boston with HMSS *Canterbury, Norwich, Lark,* and *Fowey* and the sloop *Achilles,* escorting a merchant convoy. After cruising briefly with Capt. George Pocock (acting commodore in the Lesser Antilles following the death of Legge on 29 September 1747), Knowles reaches Port Royal by 7 February.

LATE JANUARY 1748. The Spanish corsair Felipe López de la Flor departs Honduras to raid the English establishments at Roatán, Belize, and Yucatán.

17 FEBRUARY 1748. Knowles quits Port Royal with 240 of Governor Trelawney's Jamaican troops aboard:

Ship	*Guns*	*Tons*	*Men*	*Commander*
Cornwall (flag)	80	1,350	600	Richard Chadwick
Plymouth	60	954	400	Digby Dent
Elizabeth	70	1,224	480	Polycarpus Taylor

Ship	*Guns*	*Tons*	*Men*	*Commander*
Canterbury	58	1,117	400	David Brodie
Strafford	60	1,067	400	James Rentone
Warwick	60	951	400	Thomas Innes
Worcester	60	1,061	400	Thomas Andrews
Oxford	50	767	300	Edmund Toll

They are accompanied by the six-gun, 100-man sloops *Merlin* and *Weazel.* The expedition intends to attack Santiago de Cuba, but contrary winds prevent Knowles's ships from beating north, so instead he steers for Port Saint Louis (modern-day Les Cayes, Haiti). After watering in Tiburón Bay on 9 March, then pausing at Île-à-Vache to reorganize the landing forces, the English are prepared for battle.

22 MARCH 1748. ***Port Saint Louis.*** Shortly before midday HMS *Elizabeth* leads Knowles's squadron into the Haitian harbor of Port Saint Louis, completely surprising its defenders. An imposing 78-gun island castle guards the roadstead, manned by 310 troops and a company of black gunners under Gov. Étienne Cochard de Chastenoye behind 24-foot-high stone walls. The first French guns open fire at 12:05 P.M., but Knowles's ships remain silent until all anchor beneath the ramparts, letting fly with broadsides simultaneously. A heated exchange ensues for the next three hours, during which the defenders send a fireship down from the inner roads, compelling *Elizabeth* to cut its cable and warp out of danger.

The remaining Royal Navy ships maintain such fierce pressure, however, that Chastenoye sends an officer out at 3:00 P.M. to suggest terms. Knowles makes a counteroffer, and half an hour later the French commander accepts. His garrison has suffered 160 casualties, compared to 19 killed and 60 wounded among the British warships. Port Saint Louis's castle is dismantled and blown; Knowles stands away on 30 March, again hoping to assault Santiago de Cuba.

He pauses in Tiburón Bay to take on water once more before continuing north on 5 April.

8 APRIL 1748. ***Santiago de Cuba.*** This afternoon Knowles sights Cuba with *Plymouth, Cornwall, Canterbury* (flag), *Elizabeth, Strafford, Warwick, Worcester, Lennox,* plus smaller consorts *Vainqueur, Vulture,* and *Sharp* (tender). Dent's *Plymouth,* which has been selected to lead the attack, has earlier reconnoitered Santiago's entrance, but faint winds prevent the En-

Knowles's warships pound the harbor castle guarding Port Saint Louis.

glish from rushing its mouth the next morning, leaving them becalmed within view of the Spaniards. The governor, Brig. Gen. Arcos Moreno, immediately orders a 200-ton ship warped out of the inner bay to support a ten-inch cable stretched from shore to shore.

When a breeze finally springs up that afternoon, *Plymouth* guides the squadron toward the entrance, only to sheer off when a chain is sighted in addition to the cable. Next day (10 April) Knowles gives up, shifting his flag back aboard *Cornwall,* detaching vessels on independent cruises, then leading the remainder back to Jamaica, where he prefers charges against Dent for not having burst the boom (he is exonerated).

10 JULY 1748. News of the recently concluded cessation of Anglo-French hostilities in Europe reaches Knowles at Jamaica, determining him to lead his squadron into the Gulf of Mexico to take up station off Florida's Tortuga Bank in hopes of intercepting a Spanish treasure fleet between Veracruz and Havana before peace is concluded with Spain as well.

JULY 1748. A second raid by the Honduran corsair Felipe López de la Flor against the English logwood establishments in Belize ends badly when his vessel is ambushed from a cliff top; he suffers three killed, 11 wounded, and one captured.

LATE AUGUST 1748. Knowles quits Port Royal (Jamaica) with the flagship *Cornwall* and *Canterbury, Tilbury, Strafford, Oxford,* and a sloop tender to await Mexican treasure ships off the Tortuga Bank.

2 OCTOBER 1748. Learning of Knowles's presence off Florida, 56-year-old Spanish Vice Adm. Andrés Reggio Branciforte Saladino y Colonna, knight grand cross of the Order of San Genaro and commander in chief at Havana, reluctantly puts to sea with his 74-gun, 710-man flagship *Africa* (officially designated *San Francisco de Asis*) under Juan Antonio de la Colina and vice-flagship *Invencible* (also called *San José*) under Rear Adm. Benito de Spínola or Espínola; the 64-gun, 610-man *Conquistador* (official name *Jesús, María y José*) under Tomás de San Justo, *Dragón* under Manuel de Paz, *Nueva España* under Fernando Varela, and *Real Familia* under Marcos Forestal; plus the 36-gun, 300-man privateer frigate *Galga* under Pedro de Garaycoechea. His crews have been supplemented by a military regiment and numerous conscripts, the squadron further accompanied by a brigantine and xebec.

Reggio edges away from Cuba, patrols sweeping the horizon before him, until they capture a British sloop on 4 October, revealing Knowles now has nine of the line with him rather than five. This information causes the Spaniards to retreat to Havana, arriving by 6 October and remaining hove-to a dozen miles offshore.

11 OCTOBER 1748. At dawn Reggio's squadron sights a mass of sails coming up over the western horizon. By noon a frigate signals that it is a homeward-bound English convoy out of Jamaica, consisting of several score merchantmen protected by a large and a small Royal Navy escort. Reggio orders a general chase; warships and prey scatter in every direction. The convoy commander is Capt. Charles Holmes, whose flagship *Lennox* is so old and decrepit it has had 18 of its 74 guns removed. He tries in vain to protect his charges, even exchanging a few shots with *Galga* before turning northwest to advise Knowles that the Spaniards are at sea.

Coming upon the admiral this same evening off the Tortuga Keys, Holmes's report prompts Knowles to immediately begin beating upwind toward Havana with his 80-gun, 600-man flagship *Cornwall* under Captain Taylor; the 60-gun, 400-man *Strafford* under David Brodie and *Warwick* under Thomas Innes; the 58-gun, 400-man *Tilbury* under Charles Powlett and *Canterbury* under Captain Clarke; the 56-gun, 400-man *Lennox* under Charles Holmes; and the 50-gun, 300-man *Oxford* under Edmund Toll.

12 October 1748. ***Knowles's Action.*** Just before dawn the squadrons sight one another east of the Cuban capital on converging courses. Reggio's formation is regrouping after pursuing the Jamaican convoy the previous day (during which it captured the merchantmen *Julius Caesar, Mary, Gloucester,* and *Queen of Hungary*). Upon spotting his enemy, Knowles orders his warships to wear around and form line-of-battle; Reggio mistakes this evolution as more merchantmen fleeing from his squadron and so races north. Sunrise reveals the heavy English two-deckers, so at 7:00 A.M. the startled Spanish admiral orders his lead ships—*Africa, Invencible, Conquistador,* and *Galga*—to wear around and unite with *Dragón, Nueva España,* and *Real Familia* coming up from astern.

Knowles signals his own squadron to tack toward the Spaniards, who remain clumped together, sailing away under easy canvas while the English experience difficulty closing the six miles or so due to light winds. Through faulty signal reading their line becomes disjointed, *Warwick, Oxford,* and *Canterbury* lagging two miles behind

While engaged against the Spaniards, Knowles's Cornwall *(center) loses its topmast.*

Knowles's flagship while *Tilbury* and *Strafford* surge a mile ahead. Thus, rather than bearing down upon the Spaniards en masse, the English approach piecemeal.

When the Spanish commander in chief orders the privateer *Galga* out of his line, Knowles does the same with *Oxford* in order to have a reserve to aid any English warship that becomes hard-pressed. Between 1:00 P.M. and 2:00 P.M. the wind picks up; the Royal Navy squadron gains. As *Tilbury* creeps three-quarters of a mile off the Spanish line, shots ring out from Reggio's center. The range is too great for accuracy and no hits are scored, but when some of *Tilbury's* guns respond, Knowles grudgingly signals his two van vessels to open fire while steering directly toward the enemy flagship accompanied by *Lennox.*

Cornwall holds its fire until shortly after 4:00 P.M., when it comes within pistol range and crashes its opening broadside into Reggio's *Africa.* Ahead, *Strafford* pours salvos into *Conquistador* while *Lennox* joins the action from astern. Within less than an hour *Conquistador* is battered out of the Spanish line, its captain and two lieutenants lying dead before striking to *Strafford*—which then plunges into the smoke searching for another opponent. The British flagship also sheers out of the line, its main topmast head felled by a round from *Africa;* it is quickly replaced in the British line by *Canterbury* coming up from astern.

Warwick finally appears ready to overtake by 5:30 P.M., and Spanish resolve collapses. Low on ammunition, every Spanish ship attempts to save itself, *Strafford* and *Canterbury* clinging to the huge *Africa* while *Tilbury* and *Oxford* pursue the vice-flag *Invencible* (the other Spanish warships having limped off into the night, with *Lennox* and *Warwick* lagging far astern). By 9:00 P.M. *Invencible* appears silenced, but its English attackers are too weak to prevent its escape. The same occurs with the Spanish flagship: *Strafford* and *Canterbury* pound *Africa* until its main- and mizzenmasts fall, but the pair of Royal Navy vessels is too crippled to maneuver and so break off at 11:00 P.M. to begin setting up jury rigging and claw back out to sea. Casualties aboard the five surviving Spanish ships are more than 150 dead and a like number seriously wounded.

Next morning, the victors reassemble before Havana with their prize *Conquistador.* Most Royal Navy vessels have sustained some damage, so the day is spent effecting repairs. Early the following day (14 October), Knowles takes part of his squadron to windward, searching for the crippled *Africa,* which he finds at 4:00 P.M. on 15 October, dismasted and helpless in a small unguarded bay 25 miles east of Havana. When the Spaniards perceive the English warships standing in they cut *Africa's* cables and set it afire, sending it drifting ashore to blow up one hour later.

Knowles returns before Havana, preparing to follow up his victory by waylaying the Mexican treasure ships. But on 16 October a sloop approaches out of the west, bearing news from Cadiz that peace preliminaries have been signed between London and Madrid back in Europe. Disappointed, Knowles deposits his prisoners ashore then makes for Port Royal with *Conquistador.* (Bitter recriminations eventually lead to court-martials and even duels when the squadron regains England the next year. The Spaniards, in contrast, exonerate Reggio after an inquiry in July 1749, investing him knight grand cross in the Order of San Juan de Jerusalem and giving him command of the Cadiz fleet, where he remains until his death 31 years later.)

Late in October 1748, the small Spanish frigate *Industria* of Ens. Antonio José Posadas reaches Cartagena with copies of the official peace, thus marking an end to the War of Jenkins's Ear.

Spanish-American Disturbances (1748–1754)

Despite the general peace achieved in Europe, localized frictions continue to persist in Spain's New World colonies, especially in the remote hinterlands of South America.

December 1748. Capt. José de Escandón quits Querétaro (Mexico) with 750 troops and 2,000 colonists to establish a new Spanish colony amid the nomadic Tamaulipa Indians. After following a route through Los Pozos, San Luis de la Paz, Santa María del Río, San Luis Potosí, and Tula his expedition enters Tamaulipa territory and sets down new settlements. De Escandón returns to Querétaro next year; he is ennobled conde de la Sierra Gorda and created knight of the Order of Santiago for his privately financed effort.

19 April 1749. At Panaquire (Venezuela) the wealthy *hacendado* (landowner) Juan Francisco de León leads a popular uprising against Biscayan Company influence. Marching on Caracas with several thousand adherents, he enters the capital the next day, compelling Gov. Luis de Castellano to flee toward La Guaira two days later disguised as a friar. When no further action results, de León leads a second march upon the capital on 1 August that again produces nothing. Two years later, Felipe Ricardos arrives as Venezuela's new governor backed by 1,200 troops. He deports de León to Spain aboard the man-of-war *Santa Bárbara* and razes his Caracas home.

13 January 1750. Spain and Portugal sign the Treaty of Permuta, tentatively fixing the boundaries of their American empires. Specifically, Sacramento is to pass under Spanish control; seven Jesuit "reductions," or missions, in the Ibicuy territory (a wedge several hundred miles wide east of the Uruguay River) are to pass to Portugal. Many Spanish Americans are dissatisfied with the arrangement, feeling sold out by their Portuguese-born queen, María Bárbara of Braganza.

Spring 1751. The Spanish corsair José Antonio de Palma leads an expedition from Yucatán against the English logwood establishments at Belize, capturing 43 interloper vessels off Río Hondo before scattering another 57 further upriver.

November 1751. An expedition of English logwood cutters, Zambos, and Mosquito Indians attacks the Spanish garrison at San Felipe de Bacalar (Yucatán).

This same month in northern Mexico Pima Indians rise in revolt against the Spaniards; they are put down in 1752.

December 1752. The Spanish corsair Alberto José Rendón is killed in a confrontation with several English interlopers off Belize.

February 1753. ***Guaraní War.*** Sepé Tiarayú, a Guaraní corregidor at the Jesuit missions east of the Uruguay River, meets with Spanish and Portuguese commissioners but refuses to accept transfer of his people to Portuguese rule as specified by the Treaty of Permuta (see 13 January 1750). Although he initially commands only 68 men, his European opponents withdraw rather than provoke needless bloodshed, unwittingly persuading Madrid and Lisbon that this is cowardice in the face of Jesuit machinations. Both governments therefore order brutal countermeasures; the Guaraní in turn besiege the small Portuguese fort at Santo Amaro by February 1754, capturing it after a month.

July 1754. A combined army of 2,000 Spaniards and 1,000 Portuguese advance from two directions to capture San Borja, cutting off the flow of Guaraní supplies from missions west of the Uruguay. After four months of resistance several chieftains surrender to the Portuguese commander, Gomes Freire, but Sepé responds by forging an alliance with the savage Charrúa warriors. In late 1755 another joint Hispano-Portuguese expedition is mounted to exterminate the remaining 1,500–1,600

Indian fighters. Sepé is killed around this time in a minor skirmish, succeeded by the less charismatic Nicolás Ñeenguirú. Finally, on 10 February 1756 the Guaraní are trapped at Caaybaté in the hill country south of the Yacuí River. Despite Nicolás's last-minute attempts to negotiate terms, his followers are slaughtered in little more than an hour of vicious hand-to-hand combat; three Spaniards and two Portuguese are killed, another 30 wounded. The few Indians who flee into the jungle continue Guaraní resistance for several more weeks, but the war is effectively ended.

8 SEPTEMBER 1754. A Spanish privateering expedition under José Antonio de Palma attacks the English logwood establishments at Belize, seizing numerous prizes and captives and burning many properties.

FRENCH AND INDIAN WAR (1754–1763)

AS EARLY AS 1752 THE CENTURY-AND-A-HALF-LONG rivalry between French and English interests in North America provokes renewed fighting around Pickawillany on the upper Great Miami River followed by a sweep through the upper Ohio Valley by French Canadians and their native allies, who capture or kill every English-speaking trader they find. Consternation grips Pennsylvania and Virginia, whose citizens consider these wildernesses vital to their western expansion from the tidewater region—especially when it is subsequently learned the French are building forts at the headwaters of the Allegheny River to contain future English encroachments.

On 31 October 1753 a 21-year-old Virginia militia major named George Washington is dispatched to Fort Le Boeuf (near modern-day Waterford, Pennsylvania) by Gov. Robert Dinwiddie to demand that the French garrison evacuate the territory. The ultimatum is refused, and Virginia retaliates by obtaining a special grant from the English crown to build a rival fort at the confluence of the Allegheny and Monongahela Rivers (modern-day Pittsburgh). But as English workmen are completing the emplacement, in April 1754, 500 French troops descend the Allegheny and occupy the site, renaming it Fort Duquesne. Virginia appeals to London for assistance and prepares to dispatch troops into the interior.

Although war is not yet officially declared back in Europe, this North American friction is symptomatic of other disputes developing between the French and British empires throughout the world. Hostilities soon begin to escalate and gradually evolve into a "great war for empire"; two years later it becomes intermingled with the Seven Years War, a separate conflict erupting in central Germany in 1756 over completely unrelated issues.

MAY 1754. Having been promoted to lieutenant colonel and returned up the Allegheny with 350 Virginia militia and backwoodsmen, Washington erects a temporary log fortification—dubbed Fort Necessity—at Great Meadows (near Farmington, or Confluence, Pennsylvania), 40 miles south of the French stronghold of Fort Duquesne. From this base, the young officer presses north with 40 men and at dawn on 28 May surprises a 30-man French outfit, killing its commander—35-year-old Ens. Joseph Coulon de Villiers de Jumonville—along with nine others and capturing all but one of the remainder and withdrawing.

26 JUNE 1754. Jumonville's older brother, 43-year-old Louis Coulon de Villiers, reaches Fort Duquesne with 600 French-Canadian troops and 100 native allies to learn of his sibling's death. Two days later garrison Cmdr. Claude Pierre Pécaudy de Contrecœur delegates Coulon de Villiers on a retaliatory strike against Washington's position.

3 JULY 1754. Coulon de Villiers's expedition drives Washington's troops—now reinforced by two independent companies under Captain McKay—back inside Fort Necessity, which proves to be in a poorly situated defensive position. After a nine-hour siege in heavy rain, the 400 defenders surrender at nightfall and are obliged to withdraw into their own country, promising not to build another fort upon the Ohio for a year. French casualties are three killed and 17 wounded.

FEBRUARY 1755. The 59-year-old Scottish-born Edward Braddock—recently promoted major general—arrives in Hampton Roads (Virginia) from England with a convoy escorted by the 50-gun *Centurion* of Capt. Augustus Keppel and *Norwich* of Samuel Barrington, bearing 1,000 infantrymen of the 44th and 48th Regiments.

14 APRIL 1755. The British decide upon a four-pronged offensive against the French in North Amer-

ica: Braddock's regulars are to march inland and recapture Fort Duquesne (Pittsburgh); Governor Shirley of Massachusetts is to reoccupy Oswego with colonial forces and drive toward Niagara; Commissioner William Johnson is to advance up the Hudson and take Crown Point; acting Brig. Gen. Robert Monckton is to invade French Acadia (modern Nova Scotia and New Brunswick).

MAY 1755. Braddock reaches Fort Cumberland with his two brigades: Lt. Col. Sir Peter Halkett commands the 44th Foot—now 700 strong—plus 230 Virginia, New York, and Maryland rangers and a New York independent company; Col. Thomas Dunbar leads 650 men of his 48th Regiment, 230 rangers from Virginia and the Carolinas, and another New York independent company. Both units have 14 field pieces and 15 mortars.

3 JUNE 1755. ***Bay of Fundy Campaign.*** After sailing northeast from Massachusetts, 2,000 Anglo-American colonials under brevet Brig. Gen. Robert Monckton and Col. John Winslow disembark under cover of Fort Lawrence (near modern-day Amherst, Nova Scotia) to advance across the Missaguash River and attack the principal French stronghold for the Acadia region: Fort Beauséjour (near modern-day Sackville, New Brunswick). Its defenders total 160 regulars under the corrupt and unpopular governor, 41-year-old Capt. Louis Du Pont Duchambon de Vergor, knight of the Order of Saint Louis, plus 1,200–1,500 reluctant militia scattered throughout the district.

Neither side is eager for battle; the British gingerly approach Fort Beauséjour, seizing a nearby ridge by 13 June and opening fire with mortars upon its crowded interior. The defenders' morale soon collapses and—faced with an Acadian mutiny—Duchambon de Vergor is compelled to capitulate to the invaders by 16 June. His subordinate Benjamin Rouer de Villeray surrenders smaller Fort Gaspereau (near modern-day Port Elgin, New Brunswick) without a fight shortly thereafter. Determined to forever eradicate French influence from this disputed border region, the victors detain most Acadians who do not escape into the wilderness north of the Isthmus of Chignecto, expelling them down the Atlantic seaboard as far as Louisiana.

6 JUNE 1755. In a further escalation of hostilities, 11 English ships of the line, a frigate, and a sloop under 43-year-old Vice Adm. Edward Boscawen sight four French ships of the line groping past fog-shrouded Newfoundland with reinforcements for Quebec. The chase is resumed two days later, and on 10–11 June the 74-gun French *Alcide* of Captain Hocquart and *Lys* of Captain de Lorgeril—the latter's armament reduced to only 22 guns to accommodate more troops—are overtaken. HMSS *Torbay* of Flag Capt. Charles Colby and *Dunkirk* of Richard Howe subdue the former while *Defiance* of Thomas Andrews and *Fougueux* of Richard Spry capture the latter.

Still, the transport *Dauphin Royal* eludes Boscawen's cruisers and, along with another dozen ships from a scattered French convoy, reaches its destination 11 days later protected by 72-year-old Rear Admiral Dubois de La Motte's 74-gun flagship *Entreprenant* and *Bizarre.* They deposit several battalions of regulars plus the 54-year-old Saxon-born Maj. Gen. Jean Armand, Baron de Dieskau, who is to assume overall command of Canada's defenses. The English admiral meanwhile retires to Halifax by 9 July after detaching Rear Adm. Francis Holburne to blockade Louisbourg, his fleet very sickly. (By the time Boscawen regains Britain, in early November, almost 2,000 of his sailors and marines are dead.)

25 JUNE 1755. Braddock's weary army begins reaching Little Meadows, deciding after a brief stopover to advance upon Fort Duquesne with a 1,200-man vanguard while leaving Dunbar behind to guard the baggage train.

8 JULY 1755. Contrecœur, commander of the 1,600 French and Indians holding Fort Duquesne, delegates Capt. Daniel Hyacinthe Marie Liénard de Beaujeu to sortie with 250 French irregulars and 650 Indians to ambush Braddock's approaching army at the Monongahela River crossing eight miles away.

9 JULY 1755. ***Braddock's Defeat.*** Lt. Col. Thomas Gage leads the British advance guard across the Monongahela, followed closely by Braddock with his redcoats in two columns, grenadiers on the flanks, and Virginia provincials (including Washington) bringing up the rear. Suddenly, Capt. Liénard de Beaujeu rises from a nearby woods, waving his hat as a signal for his men to open fire. The French officer is killed almost instantly by the opening volleys, and many of his Canadian followers take to their heels, but the native contingent under Capts. Dumas and Charles Laglande steadily fires into the British ranks from hiding places.

The bewildered redcoats attempt to maintain battlefield formation, paying heavily: 63 of Braddock's 86 officers are killed or wounded; the commander himself finally falls, pierced through an arm and lung after having five horses shot from under him. Out of 1,200–1,300 men, 914 become casualties, compared to 44 total killed or wounded among the French and Indians. Washington leads Braddock's survivors back to Gist's Plantation, where Dunbar orders the supply train destroyed to facilitate the army's retirement toward Fort Cumberland. Braddock dies of his wound on 13 July during the retreat and is buried at Great Meadows. His baggage falls into French hands, including all of the plans for British offensives throughout North America.

8 AUGUST 1755. A Franco-Indian war party ambushes a contingent of Anglo-American troops near Fort Edward (New York).

15 AUGUST 1755. Dubois de La Motte's fleet departs Canada, eluding British blockaders by daringly sailing through the Belle Isle Strait, thereby regaining France without mishap.

1 SEPTEMBER 1755. When Acting Maj. Gen. William Johnson marches north from Albany with 3,000 Anglo-American colonials and 300 Mohawks (mostly from Caughnawaga, Quebec, under the elderly chieftain Theyanoguin), threatening to ally himself with native friends throughout the region and destroy Fort Saint Frédéric and ravage Franco-Canadian settlements as far as Montréal, Dieskau is sent to check him. The French general leaves part of his army at Fort Frontenac while traveling down the Richelieu River and marshaling 1,500 regulars, 1,000 Canadian militia, and 500–600 Indians near the head of Lake George (future site of Fort Carillon—modern-day Ticonderoga, New York).

At Johnson's base on Lac du Saint Sacrament (Fort Edward) at the southern end of the portage to the Hudson River, the English commander learns of Dieskau's deployment and decides to send a contingent 14 miles northwest to construct a fort to contain the French concentration. Dieskau learns of the countermove on 3 September and furthermore believes—mistakenly—that Johnson is left with only 500 men at Fort Edward; he thus advances to engage the colonials' camp with a select corps of 200 French regulars, 600 Canadian militia, and about 700 Indians. But when he reaches Wood Creek on the Hudson by 7 September Dieskau learns his native allies will not storm Fort Edward's ramparts; instead he diverts the attack against the contingent at the head of Lake George.

8 SEPTEMBER 1755. ***Crown Point.*** Dieskau's small army advances toward the English concentration at Crown Point, regulars marching along a wagon road while militia and Indians serve as flank guards in the woods. Nearing their objective, the French learn that Johnson has detached 1,000 men under Col. Ephraim Williams and the Mohawk chieftain Theyanoguin (alias Hendrick) to hurry back and relieve Fort Edward, which the English commander in chief fears will be assaulted during his absence. Dieskau draws his regulars up in the road and places his militia and natives in ambush along both flanks in the forest. The trap is sprung prematurely yet sends Williams's column reeling back toward the main English army. The colonel is killed, and the elderly, corpulent Theyanoguin has his horse shot out from under him; he is easily run down, stabbed, and scalped. The defeated Anglo-Americans stream back to the safety of Johnson's army while Dieskau pursues.

But when the principal English position is confronted French fortunes falter. The French bravely assault Johnson's extemporized barricade of carts, tree trunks, overturned boats, and cannons for several hours, yet the battle ends in a stalemate. Dieskau is wounded three times in his legs and is left propped against a tree by his second-in-command, Pierre André de Montreuil; he falls prisoner when the French retreat. Johnson claims a major victory, but in fact his thrust against Canada is halted, and his invaders are left to erect Fort William Henry near this spot—which the French counter by constructing Fort Carillon.

FEBRUARY 1756. Some 360 Canadians and Indians under Gaspard Joseph Chaussegros de Léry are sent to harass English communications between Fort Oswego (eastern Lake Ontario) and Schenectady. They take Fort Bull (on Oneida Lake, New York), massacring the garrison and leveling the walls while maintaining a steady pressure on isolated Oswego throughout the spring and early summer.

11 MARCH 1756. At daybreak the 60-gun HMS *Warwick* of Capt. Molyneux Shuldham is pursued off Martinique by the 74-gun *Prudent* of 58-year-old Capt. Charles Alexandre de Morell, Comte d'Aubigny. The latter ship is fresh out of France and is accompanied by the 34-gun frigate *Atalante* of 48-year-old Capt. Louis Charles, Comte Duchaffault de Besné, and the frigate *Zéphyr.* With less than 300 crewmembers fit for duty, Shuldham attempts to flee in heavy seas, only to be overtaken and engaged off his weather quarter by *Atalante.*

Warwick's rigging is soon so cut up that when the wind suddenly veers in a hard squall it is half-swamped, and *Prudent* overhauls. After half an hour of one-sided shooting, Shuldham hauls down his flag. Duchaffault eventually sails *Warwick* back to Brest, where Shuldham is incarcerated for the next two years (he will later be released, court-martialled in England, and exonerated for the loss of his ship).

27 MARCH 1756. Fort Bull (New York) falls to a Franco-Indian contingent.

8 MAY 1756. The 44-year-old Maj. Gen. Louis Joseph, Marquis de Montcalm and knight of the Order of Saint Louis, arrives in the Saint Lawrence seaway from France with two battalions (1,200 men) of the La Sarre and Royal Roussillon Regiments. His second-in-command is 36-year-old Brig. Gen. François Gaston, Chevalier (later duc) de Lévis; other aides include Cols. Louis Antoine de Bougainville and Bourlamaque. After traveling overland to Quebec City on 13 May, Montcalm proceeds toward Montréal to report to his superior, Gov.-Gen. Pierre de Rigaud de Vaudreuil.

18 MAY 1756. Britain officially declares war against France after learning of the French invasion of its Mediterranean base at Minorca.

2 JULY 1756. At Matina the interim Costa Rican governor, Francisco Fernández de la Pastora, is surprised on the beach by Zambos, who carry him off toward Moin to be killed.

JULY 1756. Commo. Charles Holmes, commanding the Royal Navy squadron in Nova Scotia, cruises off Louisbourg with HMSS *Grafton, Nottingham, Hornet,* and *Jamaica,* skirmishing with smaller enemy flotillas.

MID-JULY 1756. James Campbell, Earl of Loudoun, reaches Massachusetts to replace Shirley as governor; he is accompanied by the 35th and 42nd Infantry Regiments.

29 JULY 1756. ***Oswego.*** Montcalm joins 3,000 men already massed at Fort Frontenac (Kingston, Ontario), leading them south against the frontline English outpost at Oswego (New York). A few minor attacks are brushed off as the French drive a road for their artillery; otherwise, little resistance is encountered from Oswego's isolated and demoralized defenders. After the French invest the place on 10 August, inaugurate a siege bombardment, and press close to the ramparts with Canadian and Indian irregulars under François Pierre de Rigaud de Vaudreuil (governor of Montréal and brother of New France's governor-general), the English under Colonel Mercer capitulate by 14 August. French casualties total 40 men, English, 50; 1,700 prisoners are taken along with more than 100 guns, after which Oswego is stripped bare and burned to the ground.

16 MARCH 1757. The 50-gun HMS *Greenwich* of Capt. Robert Roddam is cruising off Cape Cabrón (near Samaná Bay, Santo Domingo) when it sights eight large sail approaching to windward. It is a squadron coming from France under 42-year-old Commo. Joseph de Bauffremont, Prince de Listenois and knight of the Order of Malta, his flag flying aboard *Tonnant. Greenwich* is pursued and overhauled two days later by the 74-gun *Diadème,* the 64-gun *Eveillé,* and a frigate. Outnumbered and outgunned, Roddam surrenders and is carried into Saint Domingue (Haiti).

MARCH 1757. François Pierre de Rigaud de Vaudreuil leads 1,200 French-Canadian troops and native allies on a successful series of raids near the British base of Fort William Henry on Lake George (New York).

25 MAY 1757. In New York 3,500 English colonials go aboard 90 transports under the Earl of Loudonn to travel north to Halifax for a joint assault on the French fortress of Louisbourg. They are to be escorted by the 50-gun privateer *Sutherland* (flag) of Capt. Edward Falkingham; the 20-gun *Nightingale* of James Campbell and *Kennington* of Dudley Digges; the 16-gun *Vulture* of Sampson Salt; and the 14-gun sloop *Ferret* of Arthur Upton—all under the command of Gov. and Rear Adm. Sir Charles Hardy. Departure is delayed by rumors of five French ships of the line and a frigate off Halifax, which compel Hardy to send two sloops ahead to reconnoiter.

5 JUNE 1757. At Louisbourg, five French ships of the line and a frigate enter from Saint Domingue (Haiti) under Commodore de Bauffremont to help bolster the garrison's defenses. Inside he finds four of the line and two frigates already arrived from Toulon under Joseph François de Noble Du Revest.

This same day, Loudonn and Hardy—reassured no French squadron is hovering off Nova Scotia—quit New York City with their troop convoy, reaching Halifax a few days later and disembarking their forces to unite with three infantry regiments and one artillery company already exercising ashore. The English army totals approximately 11,000.

19 JUNE 1757. The 74-year-old French Adm. Dubois de La Motte reaches Louisbourg with nine of the line and two frigates from Brest bearing reinforcements that raise the garrison to 7,000 effectives. Naval strength on the station is now 18 of the line and five frigates, yet despite such powerful forces Dubois de La Motte does not sortie to fall upon the weaker English squadrons at Halifax, instead obeying instructions to hold Louisbourg at all costs without hazarding any sea engagements.

7 JULY 1757. After lengthy delays, Vice Adm. Francis Holburne reaches Halifax from Ireland with a troop convoy to participate in the forthcoming campaign against Louisbourg.

13 JULY 1757. On the Spanish half of Hispaniola, 180 members of Santo Domingo's garrison run riot, protesting arrears in pay.

1–2 AUGUST 1757. After detaching the 20-gun *Winchelsea* of veteran Capt. John Rous and other frigates to reconnoiter the French concentration at Louisbourg, Admiral Holburne and Lord Loudonn load their forces aboard ship to proceed toward Gabarus Bay (6 miles west of Louisbourg) and initiate an offensive. The English learn en route the true strength of French preparations and decide to abandon the project. Some troops are left in Halifax while others are deposited in the Bay of Fundy to reinforce Fort Cumberland and Annapolis Royal; the rest return to New York City with Loudonn, who suffers great public disapproval for his retreat.

3 AUGUST 1757. ***Siege of Fort William Henry.*** At the southern tip of Lake George (New York), 6,200 French regulars and Canadian militia under General Montcalm, backed by 1,800 Indian allies, arrive to besiege Lt. Col. George Monro's 2,500 men within the 44-gun Fort William Henry (also called Fort George). After his initial call for capitulation is rebuffed, Montcalm institutes formal siege proceedings, building a road, entrenchments, and gun emplacements. Eight French cannons open fire on 6 August, and three days later Monro requests terms. The surrender is quickly arranged, the English being allowed to retire with honors of war and their baggage while agreeing not to serve again for another 18 months; in addition, all French prisoners in Anglo-American hands are to be restored to Canada.

But during evacuation the British are attacked by the Indians, who kill at least 80 and drag 500–600 off to their camps. Montcalm and his officers attempt to intervene and recover about 400; Governor-General Vaudreuil later ransoms most of the rest—but not before several score more are killed or otherwise mistreated. Because of this, the English generals, Daniel Webb and Lord Loudoun, refuse to recognize the articles of capitulation; Fort William Henry's survivors soon return to English service, and no French prisoners are sent to Canada. Moreover, Montcalm fails to follow up his victory by attacking the 1,200-man garrison under Webb at Fort Edward—15 miles farther south—even though he has orders to do so.

16 AUGUST 1757. Admiral Holburne quits Halifax with part of his fleet and, four days later, appears off Louisbourg to probe its defenses. Adm. Dubois de La Motte signals his larger fleet to unmoor, upon which the English ships bear away, disappearing by nightfall.

24 SEPTEMBER 1757. Having returned to blockade Louisbourg with 19 ships of the line, two 50-gunners, and several frigates, Holburne's fleet is suddenly struck by a gale toward evening. Come next morning, the 60-gun *Tilbury* of Capt. Henry Barnsley (or Barnsby) and the 14-gun sloop *Ferret* of Cmdr. Arthur Upton are both lost with almost all hands; Commo. Charles Holmes's 70-gun *Grafton* is lucky to survive striking, and more than a dozen other vessels lie dismasted. Detaching the most damaged vessels directly toward England under Sir Charles Hardy and Holmes, Holburne leads his remaining ships back to Halifax.

Eventually, he follows his first contingent across the Atlantic, leaving the 40-year-old Commo. Alexander, Baron Colville of Culross, to winter at the station with the 70-gun *Northumberland* and a handful of other vessels. The French Adm. Dubois de La Motte also quits Louisbourg by 30 October, escorting a large convoy home to Brest, arriving on 23 November with 5,000 men sick from typhus.

21 OCTOBER 1757. This morning Commo. Arthur Forrest appears off northern Saint Domingue (Haiti) with his 60-gun flagship *Augusta* and the 60-gun *Dreadnought* of Maurice Suckling and the 64-gun *Edinburgh* of William Langdon, having been detached from Jamaica by Rear Adm. Thomas Cotes to intercept a homeward-bound French convoy. The French, under Kersaint, having recently been reinforced, exit Cap-François (modern Cap-Haïtien) with their 70-gun flagship *Intrépide* and *Sceptre* of Captain Clavel (its armament reduced, having served as a transport); the 64-gun *Opiniâtre* of Captain Mollieu; the 50-gun *Greenwich* under Captain Foucault (recently captured

from the English by Bauffremont; *see* 16 March 1757); the 44-gun *Outarde;* and the 32-gun frigates *Sauvage* and *Licorne.*

Despite inferior strength the English steer into action with Suckling in the van, Forrest in the center, and Langdon bringing up the rear. Fighting erupts about 3:20 P.M., lasting two and a half hours until Kersaint signals a frigate to tow his damaged *Intrépide* out of the line. Other French ships then quit the engagement, their squadron eventually making off. The English suffer 23 killed and 89 wounded—although without securing any prizes and being obliged to retire to Jamaica. Kersaint, despite being wounded, meanwhile conducts his convoy to France—although near home *Opiniâtre, Greenwich,* and *Outarde* are driven aground by a storm and wrecked.

22 MARCH 1758. Admiral Hardy returns to Halifax from New York, assuming command of the station from Commodore Colville.

5 APRIL 1758. Hardy's squadron sails from Halifax, to blockade Louisbourg.

12 MAY 1758. Admiral Boscawen reaches Halifax with a large convoy from England, drilling the troops ashore while waiting for 41-year-old Maj. Gen. Jeffery Amherst to arrive from New York with another large contingent of colonials.

29 MAY 1758. Boscawen puts to sea from Halifax to launch an initial strike against Louisbourg, sighting HMS *Dublin* (bringing Amherst) while he is clearing harbor. After a brief shipboard conference, the New England and British contingents unite. Their land forces now total 13,000 regulars, divided into 14 infantry regiments plus four American ranger companies and a large siege train. Amherst's brigadiers are: 64-year-old Edward Whitmore (colonel of the 22nd Foot and veteran of Walker's failed effort; *see* 23–24 August [O.S.] 1711), who directs the 17th, 47th, 48th, and 58th Regiments, 1st Royals, and 3rd Battalion of the Royal Americans; 49-year-old Nova Scotia Gov. Charles Lawrence, who commands the 13th, 22nd, 35th, and 45th Foot plus 2nd Battalion of the Royal Americans; and 31-year-old James Wolfe, who leads the grenadiers and light infantry plus the 42nd Regiment (Black Watch). Boscawen's fleet consists of 23 ships of the line, 16 lesser warships, and 118 transports and auxiliaries manned by 14,000 sailors and marines.

Another large Anglo-American army is to advance up Lake Champlain under Maj. Gen. James Abercromby while Brig. Gen. John Forbes leads another 6,000 men against Fort Duquesne (Pittsburgh).

2 JUNE 1758. ***Fall of Louisbourg.*** Lawrence and Wolfe's divisions reach Gabarus Bay, reconnoitering the shore with Amherst and deciding to disembark on the western side of the French stronghold of Louisbourg rather than east. Bad weather sets in, however, postponing action until Whitmore's division can also stagger into the bay by 6 June.

The wind dies down on 7 June, allowing Amherst to land one regiment under Royal Navy bombardment and send it east around Black Point to establish a small base at Lorembec. At 2:00 A.M. on 8 June the main British force heads inshore to disembark in the teeth of strong French opposition. Louisbourg's governor—56-year-old naval officer Augustine de Boschenry de Drucour, knight of the Order of Saint Louis—has sortied with 2,000 soldiers to oppose any landing. (His total garrison consists of 3,500 troops divided into four regiments of regulars and 24 companies of marines; 4,000 sailors and militia; plus 4,000 civilians.) Under covering fire from the frigate *Kennington* and the snow *Halifax,* Wolfe's division moves toward Anse à la Coromandière (modern-day Kennington Cove), followed by Lawrence and Whitmore. The first boats are repelled, but three others slip behind a rocky headland, their men gaining shore in Freshwater Cove. Lawrence's division distracts the defenders by making a feint farther east at Simon's Point while Whitmore leads a pretended approach even closer to town.

Wolfe's division is already marching around the French left by the time Lawrence and Whitmore move to Anse à la Coromandière and disembark. Drucour's columns retreat inside Louisbourg, pursued by three British regiments, who take 70 prisoners until halted by artillery fire from the ramparts. By 11 June Amherst is able to bring his light artillery ashore (mainly six-pounders at Lorembec), although the seas remain too high to manhandle 24- or 32-pounders. Boscawen blockades the Island battery at the harbor entrance while Amherst takes 1,200 of Wolfe's light troops and

While the grounded warship Prudent *erupts in flames, British boarding parties sail the* Bienfaisant *out of the harbor at Louisbourg.*

some field pieces on a long march around the inner shoreline, occupying Lighthouse Point at its far end. Meanwhile Whitmore directs the siege works, their efforts proceeding mostly at night to avoid drawing French fire. Good weather returns by 16 June, when Amherst lands and begins installing his heavy artillery. Inside the citadel, Drucour persuades his naval counterpart, Jean Antoine Charry Desgouttes, to scuttle four of his ships to block the channel, thus leaving only five French ships of the line and a frigate afloat.

Over the next few weeks the invaders patiently labor on their siege lines, drawing ever closer to the walls. A sortie by 725 French troops briefly overruns Black Point; an English officer is killed and 34 men are captured, but otherwise the sortie fails to halt the siege's progress. At noon on 21 July a heated ball from one of Amherst's batteries strikes Desgouttes's 74-gun flagship *Entreprenant,* igniting its magazine. The resulting explosion spreads fire to *Capricieux* and *Célèbre* nearby, and both are consumed by 4:00 P.M. During the night of 25 July the British send 50 small boats loaded with troops into the harbor, occupying the devastated Island battery and stealing upon the 74-gun *Prudent.* Finding it hard aground, the boarders set it ablaze then cut out the 64-gun *Bienfaisant* despite the presence of 152 crewmembers still aboard. This raid costs the English only seven killed and nine wounded; next morning Drucour requests terms. The actual surrender takes place on 27 July, Boscawen transporting 5,000 prisoners to England while Amherst repairs Louisbourg and installs Whitmore as governor with a sizable garrison before departing to New York.

5 JULY 1758. ***Fort Carillon.*** While Amherst has been subduing Louisbourg, a second powerful British force is threatening French Canada from the south. At the bottom of Lake George (New York), 52-year-old Major General Abercromby marches north with 6,000 British regulars and 9,000 colonials. His aim is to capture Fort Carillon—Ticonderoga, as the English call it—thus opening up a passage to the Saint Lawrence seaway and Montréal. Montcalm, Carillon's commander, feverishly strengthens its defenses, even contemplating blowing it up and retreating to Fort Saint Frédéric (Crown Point). But the English advance is delayed when George Augustus Howe, a popular and able brigadier and Abercromby's second-in-command, is killed in a skirmish on 6 July during a portage. That allows Montcalm more time for construction, and on the evening of 7 July he is joined by his subordinate,

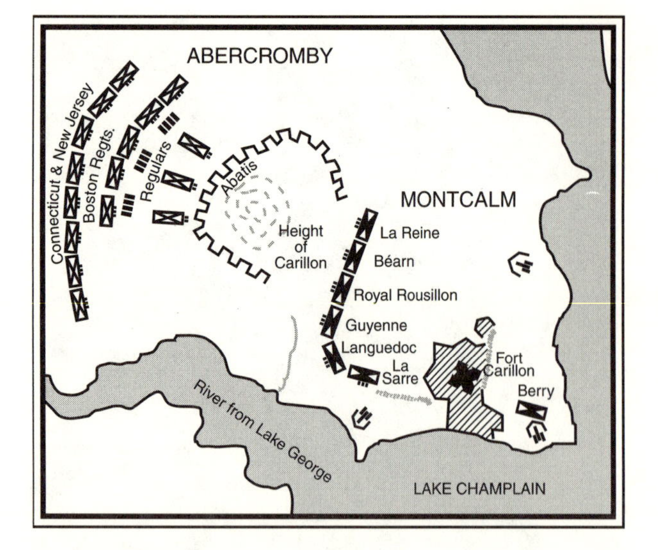

Assault on Fort Carillon

Lévis, who brings in 400 troops, thereby raising Carillon's strength to more than 3,600 men, mostly French regulars.

When Abercromby arrives next day, he is under the mistaken belief that another 3,000-man relief column is about to reach Montcalm and so launches a precipitate frontal assault without waiting for his guns to come up (also failing to note that Carillon is more easily assaulted from the rear). Shortly after noon on 8 July his regulars form up into four columns, with colonial skirmishers between, and the attack commences. The English formations quickly disintegrate as they scramble through felled trees and then are shot to pieces by steady French musket fire from behind an abatis. The British bravely reform and attack throughout the afternoon but finally give up by 7:00 P.M. At this point the French vault over their log barricades and drive off the remaining colonial skirmishers. The Anglo-American army disintegrates and flees in wild disorder into the night, abandoning arms, equipment, and their wounded comrades, suffering 1,944 casualties—1,610 of them regulars—compared to 377 among the French.

14 AUGUST 1758. ***Fort Frontenac.*** The 44-year-old Nova Scotia-born Lt. Col. John Bradstreet sets out from Fort Stanwix (modern-day Rome, New York) with 157 regulars of the 60th Foot (Royal Americans), 2,100 colonials and native scouts, and 200 New Englanders to man his flotilla of boats. After pausing at Oswego on 21 August for more craft, the expedition strikes north across Lake Ontario, disembarking west of Fort Frontenac (Kingston, Ontario) by 25 August.

Overnight 30-year-old French Commo. René Hypolite Pépin—better known as La Force—warns infirm 68-year-old Gov. Pierre Jacques Payen de Noyan et de Chavoy that redcoats and their Indian allies are ashore. Next day, Bradstreet's gunners build a battery overlooking the fort from the west, and at dusk they open fire. On Sunday morning (27 August) La Force attempts to escape with his flagship *Marquise de Vaudreuil,* the snow *Montcalm* (former British *Halifax*), and the brigantine *Georges* (formerly the British *London*); but they run aground and are abandoned, being lost to the British along with six smaller vessels in the harbor as de Noyan capitulates to Bradstreet. The French governor is allowed to retire to Montréal with noncombatants, but his garrison of 50 regulars and 60 militia is marched to Albany as prisoners of war, and Fort Frontenac destroyed. Although La Force and his men have rowed to La Présentation (modern-day Ogdensburg, New York), communication between Quebec and Louisiana is effectively severed; control over Lake Ontario passes to the British.

2 SEPTEMBER 1758. This morning, off Port au Prince, the 60-gun HMS *Dreadnought* of Capt. Maurice Suckling and the 50-gun *Assistance* of Robert Wellard chance upon the 74-gun French *Palmier,* which has previously taken the ten-gun English *Stork.* When the Royal Navy pair closes in the wind dies, leaving *Dreadnought* engaged alone against *Palmier,* which disables the English ship before escaping.

SEPTEMBER 1758. Brig. Gen. John Forbes—Scottish-born soldier and colonel of the 17th Foot—advances upon Fort Duquesne with 1,600 men (including Montgomery's Highlanders, a battalion of Royal Americans under Swiss-born Henri Bouquet, numerous Virginians under Washington, as well as other provincials and Indians). Conditions prove difficult—a road must be tediously cut through the woods—and Forbes himself falls ill from dysentery.

Upon approaching the objective in early November, Maj. James Grant—commanding 800 Highlanders and Virginians—gets permission from Bouquet to attempt a nocturnal assault against Fort Duquesne. But the attackers become lost, although they are within a mile of their target, and suffer 300 casualties from a French countersally on 14 November. Driven back into Bouquet's camp, the Anglo-Americans endure cold and rain for a fortnight before learning that the 200-man French garrison is retiring. On 25 November Forbes occupies the abandoned remains, renaming the place "Pittsborough" and installing Bouquet as governor before returning to Philadelphia (where Forbes soon dies).

20 OCTOBER 1758. Montcalm is promoted lieutenant general, thus gaining seniority over his former superior, Canada's Governor-General Vaudreuil.

3 NOVEMBER 1758. This afternoon the 70-gun HMS *Buckingham* of Capt. Richard Tyrrell and the 14-gun *Weazel* encounter a French convoy off Sint Eustatius being escorted homeward from Martinique by the 74-gun *Florissant,* the 38-gun frigate *Aigrette,* and the 28-gun frigate *Atalante.* The two ships of the line fight each other from 3:00 P.M. until nightfall, both becoming disabled. *Buckingham* suffers seven killed and 46 wounded, including Tyrrell, who is thus powerless to prevent the Frenchmen's escape.

3 JANUARY 1759. An English expedition reaches Barbados under Commo. Robert Hughes, bringing total naval strength on this station—headed by 40-year-old Commo. John Moore—to the 80-gun flagship *Cambridge* of Capt. Thomas Burnett; 90-gun *Saint George* of Clarke Gayton; 74-gun *Norfolk* of Hughes; 70-gun *Buckingham* of Richard Tyrrell (later Lachlin Leslie) and *Burford* of James Gambier; 64-gun *Berwick* of William Harman; 60-gun *Lion* of Sir William Trelawney, *Rippon* of Edward Jekyll, and *Panther* of Molyneux Shuldham; 50-gun *Winchester* of Edward Le Cras and *Bristol* of Lachlin Leslie (later Peter Parker); 44-gun frigates *Woolwich* of Peter Parker (later Daniel Dering) and *Roebuck* of Thomas Lynn; 40-gun *Ludlow Castle* of Edward Clarke; 32-gun *Renown* of George Mackenzie; 26-gun *Amazon* of William Norton; 20-gun *Rye* of Daniel Dering; 14-gun sloop *Bonetta* of Richard King and *Weazel* of John Boles; 13-gun *Antigua* of Weston Varlo; ten-gun *Spy* of William Bayne; eight-gun bomb vessels *Falcon* of Mark Robinson, *Grenado* of Samuel Uvedale, *Infernal* of James Mackenzie, and *Kingfisher* of Sabine Deacon. (The 66-gun *Lancaster* of Capt. Robert Mann joins later, along with the 28-gun frigates *Emerald* and *Griffin.*)

Hughes's squadron is convoying 60 troop transports with 3,700–3,800 soldiers under Maj. Gen. Peregrine Thomas Hopson: 3rd Old Buffs (East Kent or Howard's) Regiment under Lt. Col. (breveted brigadier) Cyrus Trapaud; 4th (Royal Lancashire or Duroure's) of Lt. Col. Byam Crump; 61st (Elliott's) of Lt. Col. John Barlow; 63rd (Manchester or Watson's) of Lt. Col. Peter Debrissay; 64th (North Staffordshire or Barrington's) of Maj. Thomas Ball; plus 65th (York and Lancaster, or Armiger's) of Col. Robert Armiger. The Second Battalion of the 42nd Regiment (Black Watch) is also to join, plus units from 38th (South Staffordshire or Ross's), already serving at Antigua. Their intended target is Martinique, which Moore and Hopson set sail to attack on the morning of 13 January.

15 JANUARY 1759. ***Defense of Martinique.*** After passing between Saint Lucia and Martinique, the 100-ship English expedition of Moore and Hopson arrives off Martinique's southern coast this afternoon, attacking the French batteries at 7:30 A.M. the next morning. HMSS *Bristol* and *Rippon* silence and briefly occupy a fort on Negro Point while *Winchester, Woolwich,* and *Roebuck* cannonade the batteries in Cas des Navires Bay in anticipation of a disembarkation. This is effected starting at about 4:00 P.M. within Cas des Navires Bay; by morning of 17 January almost 4,400 British troops are ashore. However, their numbers are apparently insufficient against the sizable militia concentrations marshaling under French Gov.-Gen. François de Beaumont, Comte de Beauharnois. The British are also too far from any significant strong point and without food or water, toiling ineffectually through dense underbrush while being galled by sniper fire.

Such slow progress prompts an aged and infirm Hopson to ask Moore whether a combined attack might be attempted closer to the capital of Fort Royal (modern-day Fort de France); this idea is rejected after a hasty conference among the naval officers. Hopson therefore orders a stealthy reembarkation, ordering his sappers to continue digging trenches until nightfall on 17 January to deceive the French into believing he is staying; his redcoats are extricated by moonlight in a few hours. The abortive landing has cost 22 killed, 49 wounded, and four captured; one Irishman deserted. In fact, however, the French defenses are much weaker than Hopson realizes, with Beauharnois having slightly less than 600 demoralized regulars to defend Fort Royal.

18 JANUARY 1759. After withdrawing, Moore and Hopson probe northwest to the vicinity of Martinique's principal harbor, Saint Pierre. At dawn on 19 January HMS *Panther* is sent in to sound the entrance while *Rippon* and two Royal Navy bomb vessels provide covering fire. They engage the batteries until 6:30 P.M., but the British fleet stands away 90 minutes later without attempting a disembarkation, its commanders preferring to instead steer toward Guadeloupe.

21 JANUARY 1759. Beauharnois sends two large privateer vessels, crammed with 400 Martinican volunteers, to warn his compatriots on Guadeloupe of the approaching Moore-Hopson expedition.

22 JANUARY 1759. ***Capture of Guadeloupe.*** At noon the British fleet comes within sight of the southwestern tip of Guadeloupe, spending the rest of the day reconnoitering its capital, Basse-Terre. By 10:00 A.M. the next day, HMSS *Lion, Saint George, Norfolk, Cambridge, Panther, Burford, Berwick,* and *Rippon* bear down upon diverse French batteries and open fire. Moore directs the action from aboard the frigate *Woolwich* while bomb vessels prepare to lob shells from farther out at sea. In a day-long exchange the Royal Navy succeeds in silencing most of the defenders' guns; only *Rippon* suffers extensive damage from French counterfire after running aground.

At 5:00 P.M. Moore directs his landing craft to board the troops, but Hopson countermands the order, feeling the day is too far advanced. Basse-Terre—largely abandoned by its inhabitants—burns to the ground during the night and, at 11:00 A.M. on 24 January, the British fleet anchors in the roadstead, setting men ashore just north of the smoldering ruins by early afternoon. The French, with only 100 regulars and a horde of undisciplined militia under Gov. Charles François Emmanuel Nadau Du Treil, have fled north to Dos d'Âne after haphazardly spiking their guns and failing to blow their citadel. The invaders occupy Basse-Terre but then begin succumbing to disease; 1,500 fall sick by 30 January. After vainly calling upon Nadau to surrender, the British venture inland, fighting a major skirmish on 4 February at Madame Ducharmey's plantation (4 miles northeast of Basse-Terre), which she defends tenaciously with her retainers, inflicting a dozen deaths and 30 injuries among Maj. Robert Melville's column.

On 14 February, after six hours of bombardment by HMSS *Berwick* and *Panther,* the frigates *Roebuck, Renown,* and *Woolwich,* the bomb vessel *Bonetta,* and other lesser consorts, a force of Royal Marines and Highlanders under Colonel Rycaut is set ashore on the eastern part of Guadeloupe (Grande-Terre). Moore has detached the contingent with naval Captain Harman to establish another British foothold; Fort Louis's wall is breached and overrun at bayonet point, thereby wresting it from its French garrison under Joseph de Beaulés. Moore visits the captured bastion on 22 February, returning to the main British camp three days later.

Hopson dies of disease at 1:00 A.M. on 27 February and is succeeded in command of the land forces by Maj. Gen. John Barrington. Given that only 2,796 redcoats remain fit for duty, that Basse-Terre is laid to waste, and that French forces are dug in a strong defensive position at Dos d'Âne, he decides to shift operations to the Fort Louis foothold. British casualties thus far total 55 killed, 140 wounded, and 1,649 sick (several hundred more already having been evacuated to Antigua). Early on 6 March, after installing 500 men under Colonel Debrissay to hold Basse-Terre—supported by HMSS *Saint George* and *Buckingham*—Barrington leads the remainder aboard the transports and straggles into Fort Louis from 7–12 March due to difficult winds.

Moore learns of the arrival at Martinique on 8 March of eight French ships of the line (led by flagship *Défenseur*) and three frigates under 60-year-old Commo. Maximin de Bompar—former governor-general of the French West Indies—plus troop reinforcements. The British commodore therefore sails the bulk of his squadron to Prince Rupert's Bay (northern coast of Dominica) on 14 March, arriving two days later to keep Bompar in check while leaving only *Woolwich* at Fort Louis to guard Barrington's transports. Barrington meanwhile sends a flotilla of boats east on Guadeloupe to attack the towns of Sainte Anne and Saint François by 25 March, disembarking between the two with 600 men under Lieutenant Colonels Crump and Barlow. The assault not only overruns both places at the cost of only one British death and two wounded but further draws off a 300-man French relief column from Gosier (2 miles east of Fort Louis). Barrington avails himself of the opportunity by sending Maj. Charles Teesdale with 300 men to raid Gosier from the sea; they destroy it on 30 March. Teesdale then advances upon the rear of the French besiegers surrounding Fort Louis while Barrington leads a separate sally. Between them these two columns scatter the last organized French resistance on the eastern half of Guadeloupe.

After Barrington falls ill, Brig. Gen. John Clavering begins the process of subduing the island's west-central region, disembarking 1,450 men near Arnoville on 12 April under *Woolwich*'s covering fire. The French fall back behind their Coin River defenses, only to have the invaders fight their way across at the cost of 14 dead and 54 wounded (seizing 70 prisoners and six guns). The French retreat pell-mell through the fortified town of Petit Bourg, which the British occupy by 14 April. Next day Clavering sends Crump north with 700 men to destroy the vital French supply port of Baie Mahault; another contingent of 100 redcoats marches south to eradicate the seven-gun battery at

Goyave. On 20 April Clavering leaves a 250-man garrison in Petit Bourg and resumes the advance south, pressing the French into the island's southernmost corner. Next day the islanders request terms; they surrender on 1 May. A relief force of 600 volunteers from Martinique under Governor-General Beauharnois, aboard 18 coasters escorted by two of Bompar's frigates, reaches Sainte Anne on 27 April—too late to affect the outcome; it withdraws two days later.

EARLY MAY 1759. Twenty French supply ships reach Quebec bearing 350 recruits under Bougainville.

14 MAY 1759. HMSS *Berwick, Bristol,* and *Ludlow Castle* and two bomb vessels set sail from Guadeloupe to subdue the neighboring island of Marie Galante. The French inhabitants surrender without a fight, and Major Ball of the 64th Regiment is installed as governor.

6 JUNE 1759. Wolfe (recently promoted major general) and Vice Adm. Sir Charles Saunders set sail from Louisbourg with 8,500 soldiers of the 15th, 28th, 35th, 43rd, 47th, 48th, and 58th Regiments—as well as Fraser's battalion of Highlanders (the 78th) and the 2nd and 3rd Battalions of the 60th (Royal Americans)—traveling aboard 119 transports to invest the French within Quebec City. Wolfe's brigadiers are Robert Monckton, George Murray, and George Townshend. His quartermaster general is Guy Carleton; chief engineer is Patrick Mackellar, once held prisoner at Quebec. Although without cavalry, the British expedition boasts three artillery companies and six American ranger companies.

23 JUNE 1759. A troop convoy sails from Guadeloupe for New York escorted by HMS *Rye* and bearing 693 men of the 3rd, 61st, and 64th Regiments and 507 Highlanders for Wolfe's army.

26 JUNE 1759. ***Fall of Quebec.*** Wolfe's expedition reaches Île d'Orléans, four miles below Quebec City, immediately detaching Brigadier General Monckton to occupy Point Lévis on the southern bank of the Saint Lawrence River as an advance base.

Two days later the French send fireships downstream in an attempt to scatter Saunders's fleet, but the attack proves ineffectual as the vessels were lit too soon. The British therefore anchor safely in the lee of Point Lévis, installing artillery two miles west of there a few days later to bombard Quebec's citadel. On 9 July Wolfe probes east of Montmorenci Falls with a column of troops, trying in vain to lure Montcalm's garrison out from behind its defenses. On 27 July the French launch a second fireship attack, which also proves unsuccessful.

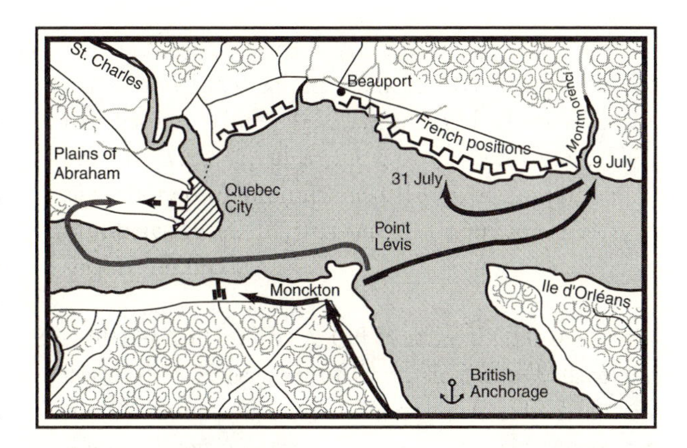

Battle of the Plains of Abraham

On 31 July Wolfe launches a combined assault directly against Montcalm's main position—the Beauport Lines, which stretch eight miles east of the city. The disembarkation is hampered by a hidden rocky ledge close inshore that slows the pace of the landing so much that the redcoats storm into battle piecemeal rather than in a single wave. The British grenadiers in particular suffer heavy casualties while climbing up the slope beyond; eventually a downpour soaks the ammunition on both sides, and Wolfe orders a withdrawal. British losses total some 500 officers and men.

The besiegers consequently attempt to break the defenders' morale by firing all nearby settlements and sending troops upstream to sever communications with Montréal. A lengthy stalemate ensues, punctuated by occasional bombardments and sallies. Wolfe falls ill in late August and, by early September, decides to land a column of troops at a cove called Anse au Foulon above Quebec City to surprise Montcalm from the rear. News that French provision ships will soon attempt to relieve Quebec's beleaguered garrison prompts the British general to act; at 1:00 A.M. on 13 September he sets forth with 1,700 troops aboard 30 boats. They will scale the 175-foot cliffs and secure passage onto the Plains of Abraham beyond; once ashore they are to be followed by a second wave of 1,900. A diversionary attack by British warships meanwhile diverts Montcalm's attention in the direction of Beauport.

At 4:00 A.M. Wolfe's vanguard, under Capt. William Howe, disembarks and picks its way up a dark path, overwhelming the sentry post above. Having achieved a breakout the British continue to ferry troops across the river during the next couple of hours until Wolfe

The death of Wolfe; a nineteenth-century rendering

has 4,500 redcoats arrayed for battle. Montcalm initially believes only a small party has landed, but upon galloping across to view the scene, at 6:30 A.M., he realizes he is confronted by the main British effort and summons out his own forces. Within three hours he has massed 4,250 troops, with the Béarn and La Sarre Regiments on the right, the Guyenne and Languedoc Regiments on the left.

Montcalm attacks at 10 A.M. without waiting for reinforcements approaching out of the west under Bougainville. But the French general underestimates the discipline of the British disembarkment, believing he can dislodge Wolfe before he becomes too firmly entrenched. The French charge is greeted by long lines of redcoats rising out of the grass, where they have been lying prone to avoid the galling fire from Indian and French-Canadian skirmishers. British artillery also opens fire, having been hoisted up to the cliff tops by hard-working naval parties. At 40 yards the French assault is stopped dead in its tracks by a crashing volley and is then rolled up by a redcoat counterattack with bayonets. Montcalm's army disintegrates and suffers 500 killed along with 350 captured before scattering back into Quebec City and its surrounding countryside. British losses total 58 killed—including the commander in chief himself, who suffers three wounds—plus 600 injured.

Bougainville appears on the battlefield but is too late, so he retires west toward Montréal after witnessing the French flight. Montcalm is carried back into Quebec City, where he expires from a wound on 14 September. Townshend assumes overall command of the British land forces, continues the siege, and accepts the final capitulation of Quebec City on 18 September.

9 JULY 1759. Colonel Johnson—having succeeded the deceased British General Prideaux—arrives with an Anglo-American army to besiege the French garrison

under 47-year-old François Pouchot inside Fort Niagara (New York). On 24 July the British and their native allies crush a French relief column approaching out of Ohio in the so-called Battle of La Belle Famille, prompting Pouchot's demoralized survivors to capitulate next day.

AUGUST 1759. A joint expedition of Zambos and English Baymen—the latter aboard three sloops—is ambushed near Matina (Costa Rica) by Spanish Lt. José Galiano, who kills 60 of the invaders and scatters the rest.

FEBRUARY 1760. A small French force attempts to recapture Point Lévis opposite British-held Quebec City, but General Murray sends troops out of their winter billets and across the frozen Saint Lawrence River to drive them away.

26 APRIL 1760. Ice on the Saint Lawrence River having broken, General Lévis travels downstream from Montréal with six frigates, assembling 7,000 troops at Saint Augustin to march upon the British captors of Quebec City, 15 miles distant.

28 APRIL 1760. ***Lévis's Countersiege.*** Murray exits Quebec City with 2,500 redcoats to erect defensive works on the Plains of Abraham against Lévis's anticipated arrival. Before they can be completed, however, the first French troops appear on the road from Sainte Foy. The British immediately attack, driving back the surprised French, who then regroup and press their outnumbered opponents back inside Quebec City; the British abandon 20 field pieces.

Lévis institutes a formal siege, shelling the ruined city; both sides anxiously maintain watch northeastward—up the Saint Lawrence toward the open ocean—to see whether it will be British or French ships that arrive first from across the Atlantic to bring relief after the debilitating Canadian winter. On 9 May the frigate HMS *Lowestoft* appears, cheering Murray's beleaguered garrison. The French redouble their bombardment, but by 15 May the first of Commodore Colville's five ships of the line appears below Île d'Orléans, bearing two fresh British regiments from Louisbourg. Next day two more English frigates arrive, sailing upstream and driving Lévis's six smaller frigates aground. Faced with a rapidly worsening situation, the French have no choice but to lift their siege and retreat toward Montréal.

8 JULY 1760. After a lengthy pursuit, five British men-of-war under Capt. John Byron capture the French frigate *Machault* of Lt. François Chenard de La Giraudais and four cargo vessels off Restigouche (Quebec).

14 JULY 1760. Murray departs Quebec City with 2,500 redcoats to advance up the Saint Lawrence and bottle Lévis's army at Montréal in conjunction with two other British offensives: Amherst will approach Canada out of the west via Hudson-Mohawk-Oswego–Lake Ontario with 10,000 men; and Lt. Col. William Haviland will lead 3,400 troops north from Crown Point (New York) and up Lake Champlain.

7 AUGUST 1760. Murray's army circles past the French battery at Trois Rivières (Quebec), his boats hugging the south shore of the Saint Lawrence River.

Meanwhile farther southwest Amherst's vanguard—Capt. Joshua Loring's snows *Mohawk* and *Onondaga*—quit Oswego, chasing away some French scout vessels near Lost Channel in the Thousand Islands.

10 AUGUST 1760. Amherst's main flotilla—more than 900 armed galleys and whaleboats bearing 10,000 men and 100 siege guns—departs Oswego (New York) to proceed down the Saint Lawrence River.

16 AUGUST 1760. This evening Amherst's expedition approaches deserted Pointe au Baril (modern Maitland, Ontario) to erect a battery ashore. Next day the 13-gun, brigantine-rigged corvette *Outaouaise* of Capt. Pierre Boucher de Labroquerie fires a signal gun to warn Gov. Pierre Pouchot at nearby La Présentation (modern-day Ogdensburg, New York), then weighs to engage the enemy. Col. George Williamson's five armed galleys meet the challenge, hammering *Outaouaise* into submission after a three-hour struggle.

20 AUGUST 1760. After marshaling his strength, Amherst resumes the advance up both banks of the Saint Lawrence against the French stronghold of Fort Lévis on Île Royal (modern-day Chimney Island, New York). The log fort is defended by 200 French militia and five guns under Capt. Pierre Bouchot; the 12-gun, 160-ton, 100-man corvette *Iroquoise* of Commo. René La Force is beached offshore. The English bombard for three days, losing the prize *Outaouaise* (pressed into service as *Williamson*) and the snows *Onondaga* and *Mohawk* to Bouchot's counterfire. The French exhaust their ammunition by 24 August; the wounded Bouchot is obliged to surrender next day.

27 AUGUST 1760. Murray's army reaches Varennes, close to the east end of Île de Montréal, digging in to await the arrival of Amherst's and Haviland's contingents. Many disheartened French-Canadian militia surrender to his forces, reducing Lévis's strength within Montréal to 2,500 men.

5 SEPTEMBER 1760. Haviland's army arrives on the south shore of the Saint Lawrence opposite Montréal.

6 SEPTEMBER 1760. ***Surrender of Montréal.*** Amherst's 6,500-man army appears nine miles west of Montréal, bringing total British strength to 17,000 men and thus collapsing the morale of the outnumbered and beleaguered French garrison. Lévis requests terms and capitulates two days later, surrendering on 9 September; he and his regulars are transported to New York as prisoners of war. The remaining portions of Canada quickly pass under English control.

10 OCTOBER 1760. Commodore Colville's squadron sails toward its winter quarters at Halifax, arriving by 24 October.

17 OCTOBER 1760. At dawn the 50-gun HMS *Hampshire* of Capt. Coningsby Norbury, the 28-gun frigate *Boreas* of Samuel Uvedale, and the 20-gun sloop *Lively* of Frederick Lewis Maitland intercept a French merchant convoy one day out of Cap-François (modern-day Cap-Haïtien)—the latter escorted by the 32-gun frigates *Sirène, Duc de Choiseul, Prince Edward,* and *Fleur de Lys* and the 20-gun sloop *Valeur.* Due to faint breezes the British pursuit is hampered until evening, when the wind freshens.

At midnight *Boreas* engages *Sirène* but is damaged aloft and forced to fall astern until 2:00 P.M. on 18 October, when the French frigate is once more overhauled off the eastern tip of Cuba. Nearly three hours later *Sirène* strikes, having suffered 80 casualties as opposed to one killed and another wounded aboard the Royal Navy opponent. Lively meanwhile uses its sweeps to get alongside *Valeur* at daybreak, pounding it into submission after 90 minutes with 38 killed and 25 injured aboard the French sloop. *Hampshire* gets between *Duc de Choiseul* and *Prince Edward* around 3:30 P.M., forcing the latter to be run aground and burned by its crew. *Duc de Choiseul* escapes into Port au Paix, but *Fleur de Lys* is found in an unprotected bay to leeward on 19 October and so is scuttled to prevent capture by *Hampshire* and *Lively.*

12 FEBRUARY 1761. Charles III of Spain issues the so-called Pardo Declaration, whereby he rejects the Permuta Treaty's redrawn boundaries between the Spanish and Portuguese spheres of influence in South America (*see* 13 January 1750). Shortly thereafter Brazilian colonists begin settling in the Viamont and Yacuy territories.

MARCH 1761. Indian raiders destroy Cabagna (Costa Rica).

3 JUNE 1761. ***Dominica.*** Having been scattered by stormy weather during their month-long passage from New York, the transports bearing four battalions of regulars, several companies of American rangers, and an artillery train under 57-year-old Scottish-born Lt. Col. (brevet brigadier) Andrew, Lord Rollo—escorted by the 64-gun *Stirling Castle* of Michael Everitt; 50-gun *Norwich* of William McCleverty, *Falkland* of Francis Samuel Drake, and *Sutherland* of Julian Legge; 44-gun frigate *Penzance* of acting Capt. John Boyd; 32-gun *Repulse* of John Carter Allen; plus 28-gun *Lizard* of James Doake—fail to appear together at Guadeloupe.

Undaunted, the English commander decides to launch an immediate strike against the French garrison on Dominica with his early arrivals before the enemy should learn of his presence. Having been reinforced by 300 West Indian militiamen under Colonel Melville, the expedition departs Basse-Terre by 4 June, accompanied by Commo. Sir James Douglas's *Dublin* (flag), *Belliqueux, Montague* and *Sutherland,* plus a few frigates.

Two days later they materialize three miles off Dominica's principal town of Roseau, sending a pair of emissaries ashore at noon to call upon the 2,000 island residents to surrender. After some confusion the French Governor de Lamprie prepares to resist but is powerless to prevent an English disembarkation at 5:00 P.M. Melville quickly outflanks the defenses with the grenadier companies of the 4th and 22nd Regiments while Rollo leads the main English force against de Lamprie's headquarters, snuffing out all resistance by nightfall. The invaders' losses total eight killed and wounded.

5 JUNE 1761. The 74-gun *Centaur* of Capt. Arthur Forrest captures the armed French merchantman *Sainte Anne,* pierced for 64 guns but only mounting 40.

15 AUGUST 1761. Spain signs a secret "family compact" with France, whereby it agrees to join the war against Great Britain by 1 May 1762.

NOVEMBER 1761. At the town of Cisteil (Yucatán, Mexico), an Indian baker known as Jacinto to the Spaniards—Canek among his own people—leads a native uprising. When troops from the nearby Sotuta garrison under Capt. Tiburcio Cosgaya attempt to put down the rebellion they are defeated, half their number being slaughtered. Provincial Gov. José Crespo y Honorato is obliged to send a sizable contingent under Cristóbal Calderón de Helguera to deal with the situation. The Spaniards fight their way to Cisteil, but Canek wins free, eventually being captured at the Huntulchac Hacienda. He is conducted into Mérida de Yucatán and broken alive upon a wheel in the main square on 7 December.

22 NOVEMBER 1761. Rear Admiral Rodney arrives alone at Carlisle Bay (Barbados), his squadron having been scattered during the transatlantic crossing. He is to assume command of the Leeward Islands station from Douglas and marshal an expedition against Martinique. Immediately upon arriving, Rodney detaches Douglas's ships to blockade Saint Pierre (Martinique) and bombard its batteries.

9 DECEMBER 1761. Rodney's three missing ships of the line, two frigates, and three bomb vessels reach Barbados.

14 DECEMBER 1761. A convoy of British transports arrives at Barbados from Belleisle (France), escorted by HMS *Téméraire* and a frigate, bearing a large contingent of troops.

24 DECEMBER 1761. Maj. Gen. Robert Monckton reaches Barbados with a troop convoy from British North America escorted by three ships of the line and a 40-gun frigate.

5 JANUARY 1762. ***Martinique Overrun.*** Rodney and Monckton set sail from Barbados with 13,000 troops and 1,000 auxiliaries, escorted by the 70-gun flagship *Marlborough* of Capt. John Hollwell; Commodore Douglas's 74-gun vice-flagship *Dublin* under Capt. Edward Gascoigne; 84-gun *Foudroyant* of Robert Duff; 74-gun *Dragon* of Augustus John Hervey, and *Téméraire* of Matthew Barton; 70-gun *Temple* of Lucius O'Brien, and *Vanguard* of Robert Swanton; 64-gun *Modeste* of Robert Boyle Walsingham, *Stirling Castle* of Michael Everitt, *Devonshire* of George Darby, *Raisonable* of Molyneux Shuldham, and *Alcide* of Thomas Hankerson; 60-gun *Nottingham* of Samuel Marshall; 50-gun *Rochester* of Thomas Burnett, *Sutherland* of Julian Legge, *Norwich* of William McCleverty, and *Falkland* of Francis Samuel Drake; 44-gun frigates *Woolwich* of William Bayne, and *Penzance* of John Boyd; 40-gun *Dover* of Chaloner Ogle; 32-gun *Echo* of John Laforey, *Stag* of Henry Angell, and *Repulse* of John Carter Allen; 28-gun *Actaeon* of Paul Henry Ourry, *Crescent* of Thomas Collingwood, *Lizard* of James Doake, *Levant* of William Tucker, and *Nightingale* of James Campbell; 20-gun sloops *Fowey* of Joseph Mead, *Greyhound* of Thomas Francis, and *Rose* of Francis Banks; 16-gun *Ferret* of Cmdr. James Alms; ten-gun *Antigua* of John Neale Pleydell Nott, and *Barbados* of Cmdr. Stair Douglas; 12-gun *Virgin,* and *Zephyr* of Cmdr. John Botterell; eight-gun bomb vessels *Basilisk* of Cmdr. Robert Brice, *Thunder* of Lt. Robert Haswell, *Grenado* of Lt. James Hawker, and *Infernal* of Cmdr. James Mackenzie.

This expedition joins Douglas's advance squadron off Martinique two days later, anchoring in Saint Pierre's Bay by 8 January. A unit is then detached under Commodore Swanton to reconnoiter Petite Anse d'Arlet farther south near Fort Royal (modern-day Fort de France) while five frigates make a feint against La Trinité. Masked by these distractions, the initial British disembarkation takes place at Saint Luce in Sainte Anne's Bay on 10 January, under covering fire from Douglas's squadron (which has earlier lost *Raisonable* on a reef). But the distance to the island capital proves too great and difficult, so the British army blows up Saint Anne's works and reembarks, proceeding by sea toward Fort Royal on 14 January.

Early on the morning of 16 January the Royal Navy ships enter adjacent Cas des Navires Bay and open fire upon the French batteries, silencing them by noon and thereby allowing troops to be landed. By sunset two-thirds of the army is ashore, followed next day by the rest plus 900 marines. The invaders establish a fortified camp while bluejackets land artillery to clear the nearest French heights—Morne Tortensson and Morne Garnier.

By 24 January the British have their field pieces in place and launch a dawn assault against Morne Tortensson. Colonel Rufane's brigade and the marines on the right, supported by 1,000 seamen in boats offshore, overrun battery after battery. Meanwhile the massed grenadier companies—plus Lord Rollo's brigade—slowly drive back the defenders in the center thanks to a flanking maneuver by Scott's light infantry. Morne Tortensson is won by 9:00 A.M.; the British then come up against the still higher Morne Garnier. Brig. Gen. William Haviland secures a foothold on the left and while digging batteries, is struck by a counterattack on the evening of 27 January. His troops not only repulse it but capture all the French batteries on the lower slopes of Morne Garnier, and by midnight steal to its summit. Defeated, French Gov.-Gen. Louis Charles Le Vassor de La Touche leaves 1,000 men to hold Fort Royal and retires with the bulk of his forces toward Saint Pierre.

The invaders drive on through difficult terrain, establishing a new battery atop Morne Capuchin, which compels Fort Royal's citadel to beat for terms by evening of 3 February. Next day 800 defenders surrender along with 170 guns while Ramiers Island and 14 privateer vessels capitulate to Rodney out in the harbor. Hervey is then dispatched with a small squadron to support the frigates at La Trinité, disembarking 500 seamen and marines that seize this port. By 16 February the remaining parts of Martinique capitulate; the campaign has cost the British 500 casualties. Captain Darby of *Devonshire* and Major Horatio Gates (later an American hero during the Revolutionary War) are delegated to convey dispatches announcing this victory to London, each being rewarded with £500 from the king.

24 FEBRUARY 1762. After the fall of Martinique, Hervey is detached to blockade Saint Lucia with *Dragon, Norwich, Penzance, Dover,* and *Basilisk.* He calls upon the French governor, de Longueville, to surrender; rebuffed, Hervey attacks the next day. Seeing his warships approaching the harbor mouth, the outnumbered defenders capitulate.

3 MARCH 1762. Commodore Swanton's blockading squadron is joined off Grenada by British troops, which force the surrender of the island and the adjoining Grenadines by 5 March.

7 MARCH 1762. This Sunday afternoon the French Rear Adm. Charles, Comte de Blénac Courbon (grandson to the seventeenth-century West Indian governor-general; *see* 3 October 1677 in Part 4) arrives off southeastern Martinique with his 80-gun flagship *Duc de Bourgogne;* the 74-gun ships *Hector* of the Comte de Sanzay, *Diadème* of the Chevalier Fouquet, and *Défenseur* of Louis Armand Constantin, Prince de Rohan Montbazon; the 64-gun *Protée* of Pierre Claude Hocdenau, Comte de Breugnon, *Dragon* of the Chevalier Des Roches, and *Brillant* of Etienne Pierre, Vicomte de Rochechouart; the 32-gun frigates *Diligente* of Bory and *Zéphyre* of the Chevalier de Grasse de Barre (perhaps François Joseph, Comte de Grasse Tilly); and the 26-gun frigates *Opale* of the Chevalier Doisy and *Calypse* of Duchilleau. They are bearing 3,000 regulars from the Juercy, Foix, and Boulognois Regiments to bolster France's Caribbean garrisons.

The following evening Blénac bears down on Presqu'île de la Caravelle and detaches *Calypse* to reconnoiter the coastal town of La Trinité, learning that Martinique is entirely in English hands. At 8:00 A.M. the next day his squadron briefly pursues the 44-gun English frigate *Woolwich* and the 28-gun *Aquilon,* which flee north to advise Rodney. On 10 March Blénac continues northwest toward Saint Domingue (Haiti), standing into Cap-François (modern-day Cap-Haïtien) one week later—*Dragon* striking a hidden reef while entering and going down with 50 hands.

4 APRIL 1762. This evening the French frigate *Calypse* enters Havana, Captain Duchilleau presenting dispatches from Admiral de Blénac the next day to the Spanish Gov. Juan de Prado proposing a joint operation against Jamaica. The Spaniard demurs, preferring to husband his resources for other duties, and Duchilleau departs the Cuban capital on 10 April to begin the two-week beat back to Cap François (Cap-Haïtien).

20 APRIL 1762. The Pocock-Albemarle expedition reaches Carlisle Bay (Barbados) from England with four regiments for the forthcoming campaign against Havana. Three days later the fleet sails for Cas des Navires Bay on Martinique, arriving by 26 April to be further augmented by the victorious forces of Rodney and Monckton. On Thursday, 6 May, Pocock and Albemarle get under way once more, heading northwest (being joined next day by a trade convoy out of Saint Kitts) to rendezvous with other English contingents off Cape Saint Nicholas Mole (Cap du Môle, Haiti).

3 MAY 1762. In Europe, a Spanish division crosses the Portuguese frontier—after several weeks of diplomatic threats but no official declaration of war—because of Portugal's friendliness toward England, thereby dragging another belligerent into the hostilities. Britain supports Lisbon with an expeditionary force.

27 MAY 1762. Having been further reinforced by a squadron from Jamaica under Commodore Douglas, the Pocock-Albemarle expedition clears Cape Saint Nicholas Mole with the 90-gun flagship *Namur* under Capt. John Harrison; 80-gun *Cambridge* of William Goostrey; 74-gun vice-flagship *Valiant* of Adam Duncan, *Culloden* of John Barker, *Dragon* of Augustus Hervey, *Dublin* of Edward Gascoigne and *Temeraire* of Matthew Barton; 70-gun *Temple* of Julian Legge; 68-gun *Marlborough* of Thomas Burnett; 66-gun *Devonshire* of Samuel Marshall and *Orford* of Marriot Arbuthnot; 64-gun *Belleisle* of Joseph Knight, *Hampton Court* of Alexander

Innes and *Stirling Castle* of James Campbell; 60-gun *Defiance* of George Mackenzie, *Edgar* of Francis William Drake, *Nottingham* of Thomas Collingwood, *Pembroke* of John Wheelock and *Rippon* of Edward Jekyll; 50-gun *Deptford* of Dudley Digges, *Hampshire* of Arthur Usher and *Sutherland* of Michael Everett; 44-gun frigate *Dover* of Chaloner Ogle; 40-gun *Penzance* of Philip Boteler; 38-gun *Alarm* of James Alms; 32-gun *Richmond* of John Elphinston; 28-gun *Cerberus* of Charles Webber and *Trent* of John Lindsay; 22-gun *Echo* of John Lendrick and *Mercury* of Samuel Granston Goodall; 20-gun *Glasgow* of Richard Carteret, *Port Mahon* of Richard Bickerton and *Rose* of John N. P. Nott; 18-gun sloop *Cygnet* of Charles Napier; 16-gun *Bonetta* of Lancelot Holmes; 14-gun *Ferret* of Peter Clarke and *Viper* of Nathaniel Davies; bomb vessels *Basilisk* of William Lowfield, *Grenado* of Stair Douglas and *Thunder* of Robert Haswell; plus the eight-gun cutter *Lurcher* of James Walker.

These warships are manned by slightly more than 14,000 men plus another 3,000 hired sailors working the 160 accompanying transports, victuallers, ordinance, and hospital ships to convey Albemarle's 12,000-man army: 314 soldiers of 1st Saint Clair's Regiment, 229 of 4th Duroure's, 952 of 9th Whitmore's, 416 of 15th Amherst's, 519 of 17th Monckton's, 579 of 22nd, 522 of 27th Warburton's, 464 of 28th Townshend's, 957 of 32nd Lord Cavendish's, 454 of 35th Otway's, 362 of 40th Armiger's, 558 of 42nd Lord John Murray's Highlanders, 562 of 42nd Highlanders (the Black Watch, later 43rd Highlanders; 2nd Battalion only), 357 of 43rd Talbot's, 518 of 48th Webb's, 960 of 56th Keppel's, 591 of 60th (3rd Battalion), 101 of 65th Lord Malpas's, 959 of 72nd Duke of Richmond's, 587 of 77th Colonel Montgomery's Highlanders, 422 of 90th Lieutenant Colonel Morgan, 618 of 95th Colonel Burton, and 218 of Major Freron's Corps. There are also 380 gunners in the British artillery train and more than 600 black slave laborers.

2 JUNE 1762. At 9:00 A.M. the 22-gun frigate *Mercury*—advance scout of Pocock's expedition—spots five unidentified sail approaching out of the west. They prove to be the 22-gun Spanish frigate *Tétis* and the 18-gun armed storeship *Fénix,* which are escorting a hired Spanish brig and two private schooners from Havana toward Sagua to pick up a cargo of timber. Despite faint winds, the 38-gun frigate *Alarm* chases the two Spanish men-of-war into the shallows by 2:00 P.M., engaging them in a one-hour gun duel before compelling both to strike. The other three Spanish craft seek refuge closer inshore, thus allowing the British fleet to press on toward unsuspecting Havana.

6 JUNE 1762. ***Siege of Havana.*** At dawn, lookouts atop Havana's harbor castle (or *morro*) espy a huge mass of

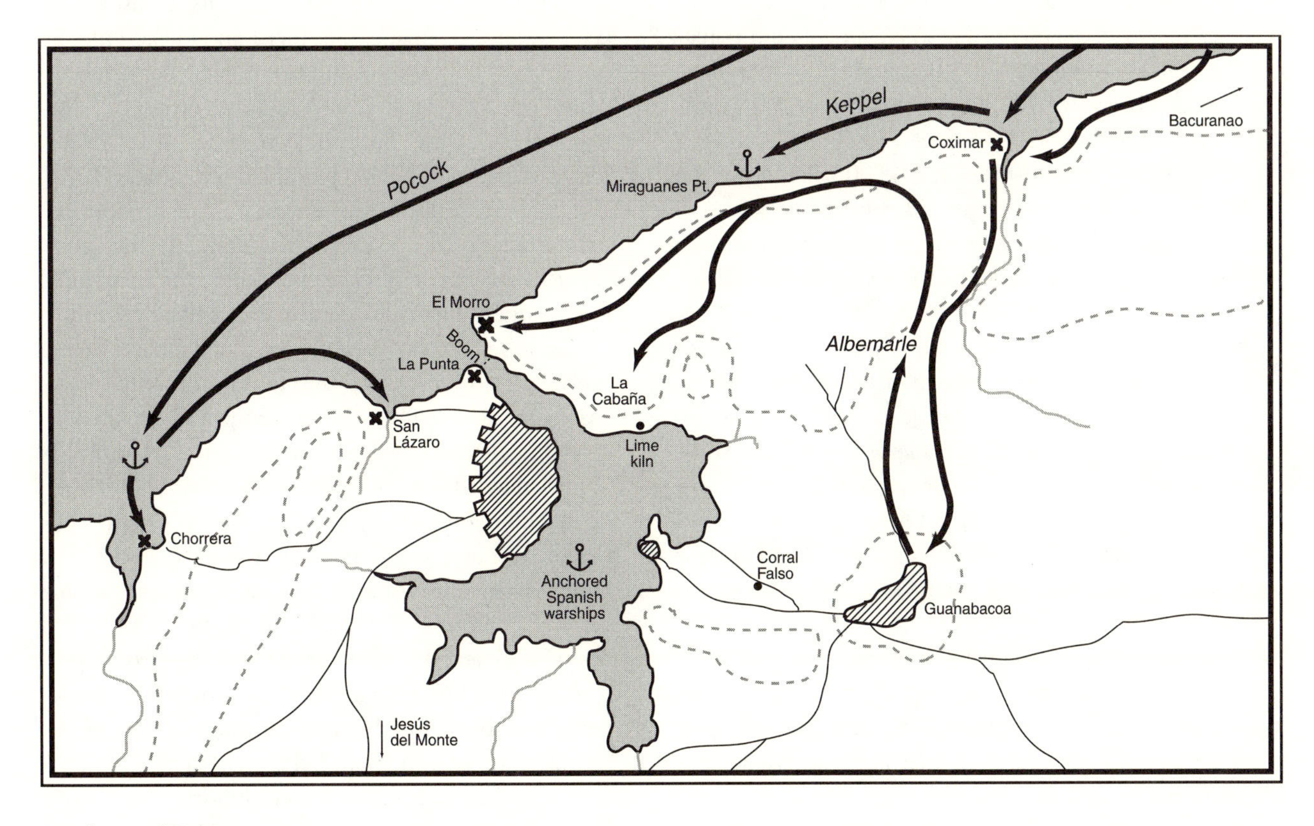

British siege of Havana

El Morro harbor castle. The channel leading into Havana's inner bay is further protected by guard boats, a log boom, floating batteries, and scuttled blockships.

shipping 20 miles east and by 8:00 A.M. sound the alarm. After a perfunctory telescopic examination, Governor de Prado dismisses them as an England-bound Jamaican convoy, so the city garrison stands down. At 1:00 P.M.—after the English expedition has drawn considerably closer—the Spaniards are at last fully roused, their nominal strength consisting of 3,500 foot soldiers of the Havana Infantry Regiment, Aragón Regiment (2nd Battalion), España Regiment (2nd Battalion), plus city militia. Cavalry consists of 100 Havana Dragoons, 200 Edimburgo Dragoons without mounts, plus 70 artillerymen.

A further 1,000 marines and 4,000 sailors serve the Marqués del Real Transporte's 70-gun flagship *Tigre* (official name: *San Lorenzo*) under Capt. Juan Ignacio de Madariaga; *Aquilón* (*San Damaso*) of Vicente González y Bassecourt, Marqués González; *Infante* (*San Luis Gonzaga*) of Francisco de Medina; *Neptuno* (*San Justo*) of Pedro Ignacio Bermúdez; *Reina* of Luis Vicente de Velasco; *Soberano* (*San Gregorio*) of Juan García del Postigo; 60-gun *América* (*Nuestra Señora de Belén*) of Juan Antonio de la Colina; *Asia* of Juan Francisco Garganta; *Europa* (*Nuestra Señora del Pilar*) of José Díaz de San Vicente; and 58-gun *Conquistador* of Pedro Castejón. Another four militia regiments—2,800 men, 700 of them mounted lancers (albeit poorly trained and equipped)—can be raised from Havana's outlying districts.

The Spaniards spend the ensuing night dispatching their best soldiers (grenadier companies and pickets of the Aragón, España, and Havana Regiments plus 200 marines) to meet Pocock's threat—but fail to reinforce the tiny outposts at Bacuranao and Coximar, where Albemarle actually intends coming ashore. The storm blows itself out, and at 6:00 A.M. the next day redcoats begin boarding their landing craft, standing in toward Bacuranao three hours later under covering fire from the frigates *Mercury, Richmond,* and *Trent,* the sloop *Bonetta,* and the bomb vessel *Basilisk*. The redoubt's few defenders flee, and by 10:30 A.M. the first British troops wade ashore. Albemarle joins them, and by 3:00 P.M. he has amassed several thousand troops, who subsequently march upon the square, ten-gun stone fortress of Coximar, where some Spanish companies have rallied. *Dragon* along with *Bonetta* plus the bomb vessels *Basilisk* and *Thunder* work close inshore to provide support fire, again putting the Spaniards to flight. At this point *Dragon* sends across its marines to secure the abandoned fortress until Albemarle's regulars can arrive overland.

The English army encamps for the night and on the morning of 8 June strikes directly south toward Guanabacoa in three columns, believing the Spanish are concentrating here. But only 600 troops (with 120 hastily acquired mounts) confront them under Col. Carlos Caro of the Edimburgo Regiment, the Spanish high command's attention still being distracted by Pocock's feint farther west. Caro awaits Col. Guy Carleton's leading column a half-mile north of Guanabacoa, but his rattled troops break and flee after a brief long-range exchange.

Albemarle and his staff therefore enter the town at noon and by 4:00 P.M. witness the scuttling of the Spanish *Neptuno* in Havana's channel as a block ship. At 8:00 P.M. the untried defenders holding La Cabaña Heights begin firing at shadows, further drawing heavy artillery fire from *Aquilón* and *Conquistador* out in the harbor. This confused two-hour exchange not only results in 20 Spanish casualties—no English soldiers being anywhere near—but, more importantly, convinces Governor de Prado to order that high ground abandoned without a fight.

At 8:00 A.M. on 9 June the Spanish scuttle *Asia* astern of *Neptuno,* despite the fact that Havana's log boom is at last installed. The English land commander meanwhile changes his line of advance, choosing to veer northwest against Havana's eastern headland and El Morro, notwithstanding its imposing natural obstacles—plus indications that a quick strike might carry the less-well-defended city. Col. William Howe's scouts report that El Morro's promontory is set upon solid rock, making it impossible to dig approach trenches, and that it is also protected by a trench 100 feet wide and 60 deep, invisible from out at sea.

Albemarle nevertheless leaves a flank guard in Guanabacoa under his second-in-command, George Eliott, then retraces his steps to Coximar with the main body to march along the shoreline toward La Cabaña and El Morro. This maneuver allows the Spaniards time to recuperate from their initial shock and bolster El Morro's defenses. *Reina*'s 51-year-old Capt. Luis de Velasco is sent across with 400 seamen as artillerymen—thus raising the garrison's strength to more than 1,000 men—while on the night of 9–10 June *Europa* is further scuttled out in the channel.

Pocock anchors off Chorrera Inlet three miles west of Havana while Albemarle establishes his supply beachhead at Miraguanes Point, two miles east of El Morro. Mounted Cuban irregulars under Capt. Diego Ruiz clash on the afternoon of 10 June with Eliott's advance guard at Corral Falso, killing and capturing a few redcoats before being driven off by an English counterattack that claims Ruiz's life. Toward evening Pocock sends the 64-gun *Belleisle* inshore (backed by *Cerberus, Echo, Bonetta,* and *Lurcher*) to bombard the ancient six-gun Spanish redoubt at Chorrera, a feint to distract the defenders from Colonel Carleton's stealthy advance through the eastern underbrush to occupy La Cabaña Heights.

At 1:00 A.M. on Friday, 11 June, the colonel's men overrun the Spanish position just as a rainstorm bursts, *Tigre, Aquilón, Soberano,* and *Conquistador* subsequently opening up a desultory counterfire from out in the harbor. At dawn the 30-gun private merchantman *Perla* is also warped into the channel by naval Lt. Francisco del Corral to shoot at the English atop La Cabaña from closer range. Pocock meanwhile resumes his bombardment at Chorrera with such intensity that Col. Luis de Aguiar's militia abandon that outpost by 11:00 A.M., thereby allowing it to fall to a marine landing party around noon. Pocock then shifts his bomb vessels *Basilisk* and *Thunder* toward the San Lázaro Inlet to commence a galling fire against Havana's walls.

Albemarle's sappers and sailors struggle amid torrential downpours to drag their siege train into position atop the eastern headland while Cuban guerrillas cut off several score English foragers and seriously alarm the invaders' encampments—where disease is also beginning to spread. It is not until 22 June that the first British siege mortars open fire against El Morro (killing 43 and wounding 243 of the garrison over the next week). At dawn on 23 June a pair of English howitzers also opens up from La Cabaña, obliging the Spanish ships *Infante, Soberano, Tigre,* and *Aquilón* to withdraw deeper into the harbor two days later.

On Sunday, 27 June, Pocock detaches *Defiance* and *Hampton Court* with nine lesser craft to probe west along the coast in search of a suitable anchorage in case of storms. Next dawn they fight their way in past two scuttled ships blocking the mouth of Mariel (25 miles west of Havana), seizing the 24-gun Spanish frigate *Venganza* of Capt. Diego Argote and the 18-gun storeship *Marte* of Domingo Bonachea and occupying that port.

During the night of 28–29 June 720 troops under Col. Alejandro de Arroyo slip out of Havana aboard darkened boats, gliding across to El Cabrestante, from where they ascend El Morro's eastern headland to fall upon Albemarle's main siege works. Another 500 men under Lt. Col. Ignacio Moreno support this attack with a flanking maneuver while 400 men under naval Lts. Francisco del Corral and Juan de Lombardón advance on an English battery being installed at an abandoned lime kiln at the foot of La Cabaña. All these contingents attack at sunup on 29 June but encounter stiff resistance, Arroyo and Moreno's force suffering 38 killed, 70 wounded, and more than 100 captured, compared to ten British casualties and 17 prisoners; del Corral's sally is beaten off with 37 casualties and a large number of captives, the naval lieutenant himself being badly wounded.

The besiegers now hope to panic El Morro's demoralized garrison by simultaneously bombarding the eastern ramparts with two recently completed batteries of a dozen 24-pounders and four 13-inch mortars and the seaward face with a Royal Navy squadron. At first light on Thursday, 1 July, the new batteries open fire, and at 8:00 A.M. HMSS *Dragon, Cambridge, Marlborough,* and *Stirling Castle* bear down to join in, accompanied by the frigate *Trent. Stirling Castle* refuses to close, but the other three ships of the line drop anchor a couple of hundred yards off El Morro's northern face between 9:00 and 9:30 A.M. and pound it for the next five hours. But de Velasco's defenders refuse to yield, and the battered English men-of-war eventually withdraw, having suffered 44 dead and 148 wounded. El Morro endures 130 casualties and numerous dismounted guns but remains unbowed.

Over the next fortnight almost 500 Spaniards are killed or injured within the citadel by continuous English shelling, although they are replaced every night from Havana—while the besiegers' sick lists soar to more than 3,500. On Sunday, 11 July, Commodore Douglas's 50-gun *Centurion* appears out of the west escorting a 160-ship Jamaican convoy toward London. Pocock and Albemarle commandeer cotton bales out of the merchantmen, dragging them onto El Morro's stark headland to be extemporized into fascines. Eliott also retreats from his flanking position at Guanabacoa, adding his contingent to Albemarle's dwindling ranks.

Before dawn on 18 July Pocock's San Lázaro battery is overrun by 300 Cuban militia, who make off with 18 English prisoners after spiking three guns. This same afternoon Douglas's Jamaican convoy departs, but within the next two days its bales allow the siege engineers to drive their lines to the very edge of El Morro's moat, from where a party of sappers dart across the northern walkway to begin mining the northeastern corner. In order to retard that operation 1,500 Cuban militia slip out of Havana and assault the English encampments before sunrise on 22 July, their initial approach being checked by 30 men of the 90th Regiment under Lt. Col. James Stuart. The green Cuban recruits do not press home the attack and are driven off within the hour by the 3rd Battalion of the 60th Foot (Royal Americans), who pursue the attackers down to the water's edge, killing, wounding, or capturing 250 as opposed to 50 English casualties. Another 60 Spaniards are also slain or injured within El Morro while supporting the sally. El Morro appears doomed, so on 24 July de Velasco—who a fortnight earlier has been conveyed, wounded, into Havana to convalesce—returns, relieving *Infante*'s Francisco de Medina.

At first light on 28 July seven transports materialize out of the east bearing 1,700 troops from New York. They disembark at Chorrera this evening to recuperate from their voyage, being the first portion of a much larger contingent that quit New York in two units: 16 transports setting out on 9 June escorted by the 60-gun *Intrepid* of Capt. John Hale and smaller *Chesterfield* with the 46th Regiment of Foot (668 men); New York City Independent Companies (335); New Jersey Provincials (222); Rhode Island Provincials (217); New York Provincials (90); Connecticut Provincials (904). Another 14 transports departed on 30 June escorted by the 40-gun frigate *Enterprise* of Capt. John Houlton, the 28-gun frigate *Lizard* of Francis Banks, and the 16-gun sloop *Porcupine* of Harry Harmood with the 58th Regiment of Foot (590); Gorham's Rangers (253); and New York Provincials (477).

On the morning of 21 July the transports *Juno* and *Masquerade* of the first convoy ran aground north of Cuba, only the latter being refloated (although all of *Juno*'s complement are later saved). This same afternoon the second convoy blunders into the Chevalier Fouquet's 74-gun *Diadème,* 64-gun *Brillant,* and 36-gun frigate *Opale* near the Caicos, having its transports *Britannia, Pelling, Betsy and Sally, Nathaniel and John,* and *Hopewell* seized with 488 soldiers on board. Before dawn on 24 July Hale's first convoy again comes to grief when his consort *Chesterfield* and transports *Industry, Smiling Nancy, Swallow,* and *Masquerade* strike on Cayo Confites, near Cayo Romano. The surviving passengers and crews remain behind until Hale can send craft from Havana to their rescue.

During the night of 29–30 July a pair of Spanish schooners tow a floating battery out of Havana's harbor and around the El Morro headland to open fire on the English sappers, who suffer few casualties, the Spanish vessels being driven off. At sunrise de Velasco's beleaguered garrison prepares to repel an English assault, retiring into subterranean quarters at midday to eat and rest. At 1:00 P.M. that day (30 July) English charges are detonated—and El Morro's northeastern bastion explodes. Col. William Keppel and military engineer Lt. Col. Patrick Mackellar send the 1st Royal Regiment of Foot (later Royal Scots) scrambling into the breach, followed by the 90th Foot and 35th Foot. Although numbering only 650 men, the assault force overwhelms the 800 stunned Spaniards inside El Morro at bayonet point. Both de Velasco and his 40-year-old second-in-command, *Aquilón*'s Marqués González, fall mortally wounded along with 341 defenders; 37 more are wounded and 326 are captured, little more than 100 Spaniards reaching Havana alive.

Artillery fire now rains down upon the city from both La Cabaña and El Morro while 2,000 New Englanders advance from their San Lázaro encampment to occupy Jesús del Monte; on 2 August the frigate *Echo* brings in seven more transports from the second New York convoy (which have escaped de Fouquet's squadron). After transferring the bulk of his troops to the eastern peninsula and installing more batteries to encircle Havana, Albemarle sends a message to Governor de Prado on 10 August calling for surrender. Rebuffed, the English general orders his artillery to pound the city the next day, prompting La Punta's panic-stricken garrison to abandon their fortress.

De Prado requests terms that afternoon, which are agreed upon by 13 August; next day 936 Spanish regulars march out of Havana to capitulate along with a large naval contingent. Another 2,000 Spaniards remain injured or sick within hospital, 3,800 having died during the siege. The British report 2,764 casualties due to death, wounds, desertion, or capture, with many others still being diseased. The surrender of Governor de Prado's command not only includes the city but the western third of Cuba from Cape San Antonio to Sagua 160 miles farther east. Detachments of redcoats are therefore sent out to occupy those towns.

12 JUNE 1762. Spain officially declares war against Portugal, more than a month after invading it (*see* 3 May 1762).

JUNE 1762. Zambos raid the Matina Valley (Costa Rica).

MID-JUNE 1762. ***Newfoundland Campaign.*** The 39-year-old French Commo. Charles Henri Louis d'Arsac, Chevalier de Ternay, materializes off Bay Bulls with his 74-gun flagship *Robuste;* the 64-gun *Éveillé* under François Aymar, Baron de Monteille; the 30-gun frigate *Licorne* under Sillark de Surville; and the 26-gun transports *Biche* under Dupuy and *Garonne* under "Clonard"—actually an Irishman named Sutton. They carry 600 troops under marine Colonel Comte d'Haussonville plus 160 Irish Catholics led by Sutton, intending to spearhead a revolt of their fellow countrymen against English rule.

On 24 June the expedition enters Saint John's Harbor and takes the town. Capt. Thomas Graves—the British governor for Newfoundland, who is lying at Placentia with his 50-gun *Antelope* and 24-gun *Siren*—immediately requests aid from Commodore Colville at Halifax. The latter sails to join him on 10 August with his 70-gun flagship *Northumberland,* John Jervis's 40-gun frigate *Gosport,* and the 20-gun Massachusetts sloop *King George.* By 25 August both contingents are blockading de Ternay within Saint John's.

On 11 September 1,300 New York troops arrive via Louisbourg under Lt. Col. William Amherst and, two days later, are disembarked at Torbay, its French occupiers being easily driven back; but on the foggy night of 15–16 September de Ternay's squadron slips its cables and escapes out into the Atlantic. D'Haussonville's garrison is compelled to surrender by 18 September.

27 JULY 1762. Having been notified three months earlier by the royal frigate *Victoria* of Spain's impending declaration of war against Portugal, the River Plate's Gov. Pedro de Ceballos (or Cevallos) Cortés y Calderón has been secretly marshalling an expedition. Getting wind of these preparations on 27 July, the Portuguese authorities at Colónia do Sacramento (Uruguay; *see* 2 October 1704) brace to receive an assault.

3 SEPTEMBER 1762. A Spanish force sets sail from Buenos Aires under Governor de Ceballos: the 26-gun royal frigate *Victoria* of Lt. Carlos José de Sarria; private merchantman *Santa Cruz* of the Mendineata Co.; three dispatch vessels; 12 gunboats; and 15 troop transports bearing 700 regulars, 200 dragoons, 1,800 militia, and numerous native laborers. Another 1,200 Jesuit-led Indians depart the mission district around this same time while a 113-wagon Spanish siege train travels overland from Montevideo.

Starting on 7 September, de Ceballos's expedition takes a week to disembark in Uruguay. From this advance staging area, he intends to attack the nearby Portuguese settlement of Colónia do Sacramento as soon as he receives final authorization from Madrid. On 28 September a tartan arrives from Cadiz with word that war has officially been declared as of 12 June (*see* 3 May 1762); de Ceballos's host advances on 1 October.

7 SEPTEMBER 1762. French Admiral de Blénac sails from Cap-François (modern-day Cap-Haïtien) with five ships of the line and two frigates, bearing 600 regulars of the Murcia and Granada Infantry Regiments who have marched across from Santo Domingo as belated reinforcements for Cuba. Two days later de Blénac deposits them at Santiago de Cuba and learns that Havana surrendered four weeks earlier; he proceeds to the Bight of Léogâne to rendezvous with a homeward-bound French merchant convoy. Eventually he wins his way clear of the Caribbean, losing one merchantman in the Windward Passage to the 22-gun English frigate *Echo* of Capt. John Lendrick and another pair to privateers operating out of New Providence (Nassau, Bahamas).

24 SEPTEMBER 1762. The 400 Portuguese infantry, 40 troopers, 32 gunners, 230 militia, and assorted crewmembers of ten small vessels defending Colónia do Sacramento (Uruguay) are reinforced from Rio de Janeiro by a ten-ship convoy escorted by the frigate *Nossa Senhora da Estrêla* of Capt. João da Costa de Ataíde and the brigantine *São Pedro e São Paulo.* Although conveying only 65 soldiers, the expedition brings in abundant ammunition and supplies.

1 OCTOBER 1762. ***Sacramento Capture.*** De Ceballos's expedition appears a half-mile outside Colónia do Sacramento (Uruguay), proclaiming their intent to attack the Portuguese outpost and erecting a siege camp. Saplines are begun, the garrison shooting their first rounds on 5 October, after these draw close to their walls. The Spaniards respond by firing heated rounds into the settlement and then calling upon the defenders to surrender on 6 October; the demand is rejected. The besiegers maintain only a poor naval blockade, however, de Sarria's squadron allowing Portuguese vessels to slip in and out with resupplies. By 11 October two batteries of 24- and 18-pounders commence battering a breach while mortars drop shells behind the Portuguese ramparts.

A pair of gaps appear by 20 October, but de Ceballos prefers to renew negotiations one week later with the wounded garrison commander—Brig. Gen. Vicente da Silva da Fonseca—rather than storm the walls, finally hammering out capitulation terms by 30 October. Three days later the gates swing open and 2,355 Portuguese soldiers and sailors surrender with full honors of war, along with 1,600 civilians. Spanish casualties during the campaign total 12 dead and 200 wounded; booty includes 87 artillery pieces and 26 vessels anchored in the roads—most of them British.

2 NOVEMBER 1762. ***River Plate Campaign.*** An Anglo-Portuguese expedition arrives at Rio de Janeiro, spearheaded by the private English vessels *Lord Clive* (formerly HMS *Kingston*) of 50 guns and the 28-gun frigate *Ambuscade.* Both were purchased from the Royal Navy by a group of London investors to be led by Capts. John Macnamara—an ex–East India Company officer—and William Roberts in a surprise raid against the River Plate before word can precede them of the latest outbreak with Portugal. During a stopover at Lisbon the two were joined by a pair of Portuguese transports bearing 500 troops under Lt. Col. Vasco Fernandes Pinto Alpoim, plus five storeships; all nine set sail on 3 August 1762 toward Rio de Janeiro.

Accompanied by the 38-gun Portuguese frigate *Glória,* McNamara departs Rio on 21 November for the River Plate but is disappointed to find the Spanish defenders fully alerted; he thus steers toward the recently conquered Colónia de Sacramento in hopes of retaking it. On 6 January 1763 Macnamara anchors close offshore with his two English and one Portuguese men-of-war while the transports await farther out to sea. After a three-hour bombardment of Sacramento's defenses, smoke can be seen rising from *Lord Clive,* which explodes, taking down 272 of 350 crewmembers—including Macnamara. The badly mauled *Ambuscade,* with 105 dead and 40 wounded, leads the remainder of the expedition back to Rio de Janeiro.

3 NOVEMBER 1762. As of this date, a triumphant England has signed peace preliminaries with French and Spanish representatives at Fontainebleu, marking an effective end to hostilities. By the terms Britain will retain Canada and all of France's North American possessions east of the Mississippi River (except the islands of Saint Pierre and Miquelon off Newfoundland), plus Spanish Florida, which Madrid agrees to cede in exchange for Havana's return. To compensate Spain for its loss Louis XV agrees to give Louisiana to Charles III. In the Caribbean, Britain is to retain possession of Grenada, Dominica, Saint Vincent, and Tobago, whereas Martinique, Saint Lucia, Guadeloupe, and Marie Galante are to be restored to French rule. The victorious British also secure vast new territories in Africa and India, thereby establishing the first global empire.

JANUARY 1763. Having refurbished Sacramento, Governor de Ceballos leads two columns east in a coastal sweep through what is today northeastern Uruguay to eliminate other Portuguese outposts. Forts San Miguel and Santa Teresa east of Negra Lagoon are taken—the latter on 19 February—and another stronghold is encountered at the Chuy Narrows, whose defenders sally with 400 men. This sortie being defeated, its garrison melts away, leaving only 25 officers and 280 troops to surrender to the advancing Spaniards. Rio Grande (Brazil) is then occupied, and de Ceballos is advised of the cessation of hostilities in Europe by 8 April, thus concluding his campaign.

BOUNDARY DISPUTES (1763–1774)

THE CONCLUSION OF THE SEVEN YEARS WAR FINDS the European powers spent; no conflict will erupt for another generation. Nevertheless, minor frictions persist in the New World, some the direct result of the recently realigned borders. One example occurs in the Ohio Valley and the Great Lakes region of North America, where the erstwhile Indian allies of France are now expected to switch loyalties to the British. Native opposition runs deep, especially against Lord Amherst, who has offended and alienated many with his contemptuous attitude. Therefore, throughout the winter of 1762–1763 the Ottawa chieftain Pontiac forges a confederacy with the Chippewa, Huron, Delaware, Mingo, Kickapoo, Muscoatin, Seneca, Shawnee, and nine other tribes to drive the British out. When spring arrives isolated British garrisons become easy prey to surprise attacks by some 10,000 warriors.

23 FEBRUARY 1763. At Magdalenenburg Plantation on the Canje River in Berbice (Guyana), slaves revolt against brutal Dutch masters, sparking a general uprising throughout the region. By 8 March Gov. Simon van Hoogenheim abandons Fort Nassau, sailing down the Berbice River with the terrified white populace crammed aboard three large merchantmen, the slaver *Adriana Petronella,* and a few sloops. Some 2,000 black rebels take over the evacuated district under their leader, Coffy.

On 28 March the hired English brigantine *Betsy* reaches van Hoogenheim's isolated refugee camp at Fort Andries, bringing 100 Dutch reinforcements from Suriname. After an initial probe up the Canje is repelled at Fredericksburg Plantation by black rebels under Fortuyn, the Dutch troops recapture Dageraad by 31 March. On 2 April hundreds of blacks under Accara attack that outpost from different directions, suffering heavy losses.

After five weeks of uneasy negotiations, Coffy attempts another all-out assault on 13 May, storming Dageraad's ramparts with three columns of 500–600 men apiece. They are decimated by the accurate counterfire from entrenched troops and the ten-gun Sint Eustatius bark *Zeven Provinciën* out in the river; after five hours the poorly armed rebels withdraw with considerable loss (the Dutch suffer a dozen dead and ten wounded).

A stalemate ensues until Capt. Maarten Haringman's warship *Sint Maartensdijk* arrives from Holland on 28 October bearing 150 soldiers—the first contingent of a much larger expedition organized by the States General to restore order under Lt. Col. Jan Marius de Salve. By this time the disgraced Coffy has already committed suicide; the rebels have also fallen out along tribal lines. On 19 December van Hoogenheim pushes upriver from Dageraad, encountering little opposition. De Salve eventually appears on 1 January 1764 with 600 troops aboard a half-dozen vessels, but only mop-up operations remain—in addition to scores of vicious executions.

9 MAY 1763. ***Pontiac's War.*** Warned by a squaw of an impending native attack, Col. Henry Gladwyn—commanding officer at Detroit—refuses to admit Pontiac and his braves into his fort when they appear for a conference and dance. The Indians immediately institute a siege, launching coordinated assaults against all other outlying British outposts: Fort Sandusky (Ohio) falls on 16 May, Fort Saint Joseph (Michigan) on 25 May, Fort Miami (Indiana) on 27 May, Fort Ligonier (Pennsylvania) on 28 May, Fort Ouiatenon on the Wabash (Indiana) by 1 June, and Fort Michilimackinac (Mackinac, at the junction of Lakes Michigan and Huron) by 2 June. (Fort Michilimackinac is captured when warriors stage a friendly lacrosse game against the garrison and deliberately throw the ball over the ramparts to rush unchecked through the gates—slaughtering every man, woman, and child inside.)

Within little more than a month the only British garrisons remaining in the western district are Detroit and Fort Pitt (Pittsburgh). The former is resupplied by ships crossing the lakes; in July a relief column sets out from southwestern Pennsylvania under Col. Henri Bouquet to bring succor to Fort Pitt. His strength consists of his own battalion of Royal Americans, a contingent of Black Watch Highlanders (42nd Foot), and some militia, totaling just over 500 men. Pontiac prepares an ambush with some 1,000 warriors at Bushy Run (modern-day Bloody Run, west of Carlisle, near Harrisburg, Pennsylvania). Bouquet has anticipated such a development; when the trap is sprung on 4 August 1763 his troops form up in a circle around the baggage train. His light forces, trailing behind, act as a mobile reserve. When the frustrated Indians attack Bouquet's camp the next morning they are repulsed with heavy casualties; they are broken on 6 August when the British light forces catch them from the rear.

Both sides suffer comparatively heavy losses, but Bouquet is able to march the remaining 150 miles and relieve Fort Pitt one week later. Native hopes that France might resume its role in North America fade, and the more sympathetic actions of Gen. Thomas Gage (Amherst's successor) win over a number of tribes, causing dissension among the rest. The rebellion loses momentum, and Pontiac lifts his Detroit siege. In the spring of 1765 he accepts British rule, but his change of heart creates enemies among his own people. Four years later he is murdered by a Peoria warrior.

JUNE 1763. A band of Zambos under chiefs Alanar and Quiantales raid the Matina Valley (Costa Rica).

EARLY 1764. The veteran French adventurer Bougainville (*see* 8 May 1756) reaches the uninhabited islands 300 miles east of the Strait of Magellan with his private ships *Aigle* and *Sphinx* to establish a permanent settlement. These South Atlantic islands—

two large and 200 small ones—have been known to sailors since the late sixteenth century; when the English salvor John Strong sailed through them in January 1690 he named them the Falkland Islands in honor of Lucius Carey, Viscount Falkland (*see* 20 February 1690 in Part 4). French sailors out of Saint Malo also came to know about the island group, dubbing it the Malouines (*see* 24 June 1699 in Part 4). That name became transcribed into Spanish as Maluinas and then evolved into Malvinas (u and v being interchangeable in eighteenth-century script).

Bougainville's colony at Port Louis on the large eastern island is its first establishment; from there, exploratory cruises are made to the nearby straits and Patagonia. In January 1765 the 40-year-old English circumnavigator John Byron visits the western (Saunders) Island with HMS *Dolphin* of 24 guns and 150 men and the 14-gun *Tamar* under Cmdr. Patrick Mowat, leaving a small party behind at Port Egmont before striking out into the Pacific. When he regains London in May 1766 Byron reports upon the strategic value of the island group; the British government thus sends out Capt. John Macbride with the 32-gun frigate *Jason* and three lesser consorts to maintain Britain's claim.

Meanwhile the Spanish government has lodged a protest with Paris about Bougainville's original colony, which the French agree to withdraw on condition the explorer is indemnified for his expenses. Bougainville duly makes a second voyage out to Buenos Aires, where he is joined by the Spanish naval Capt. Felipe Ruiz Puente and continues on to Port Louis, which is renamed Soledad and given over to Spanish rule by 1 April 1767. When the French depart Ruiz begins corresponding with the English settlers at nearby Port Egmont, insisting they too must leave. Cmdr. Anthony Hunt therefore departs for England for instructions aboard the 14-gun *Tamar.*

JUNE 1764. The newly appointed French governor-general at Saint Domingue (Haiti)—34-year-old Vice Adm. Charles Henri, Comte d'Estaing—lays claim to the Turks and Caicos Islands, provoking heated diplomatic recriminations from London. Eventually the French are obliged to retire, and the island groups are annexed to Bahamian authority.

5 MARCH 1766. The 50-year-old naval Capt. Antonio de Ulloa y de la Torre Guiral arrives at New Orleans with 90 troops to assume office as Louisiana's first Spanish governor. Many French residents resent the transfer to Spanish rule, which complicates de Ulloa's task.

22 MAY 1766. At 7:00 P.M. rioting breaks out in Quito to protest the introduction of new taxes. The authorities are powerless to resist, but the disorders eventually die out.

DECEMBER 1766. After reoccupying Concepción (Chile) following 40 years of truce with its Araucano Indians (*see* spring 1723) the Spaniards again face a major native uprising. It takes more than seven years to restore peace (by the 1784 Treaty of Santiago de Tapihuc).

30 MAY 1767. At dawn throughout much of Spanish America soldiers arrest Jesuit friars, expel them from the realm, and seize their property for the crown. (In parts of South America these arrests take place in August.)

27 OCTOBER 1768. In New Orleans a French mob—after fruitless attempts to rescind Louisiana's transfer to Madrid—spike the city's guns. The next afternoon they swarm through the streets, prompting the Spanish Governor de Ulloa to seek refuge aboard the frigate *Volante* out in the harbor. De Ulloa sets sail for Havana on 1 November, after which the Creole leaders offer allegiance to the English at nearby Pensacola and even contemplate independence.

17 AUGUST 1769. ***Spanish Louisiana.*** Alejandro O'Reilly y McDowell, the 45-year-old, Irish-born inspector general and knight of the Order of Alcántara, reaches New Orleans this afternoon from Havana with 2,000 Spanish troops aboard a frigate and 23 lesser consorts to reimpose rule over the 5,500 inhabitants of this onetime French colony. He proceeds mildly, peaceably proclaiming Spanish rule on 18 August; the 12 ringleaders of creole independence are arrested during a breakfast on 21 August (half are later executed; the others are transported to Cuba). O'Reilly departs in early March 1770, leaving Luis de Unzaga y Amézaga as interim governor.

10 JUNE 1770. ***The Falklands.*** Capt. Juan Ignacio de Madariaga's frigates *Industria, Santa Bárbara, Santa Catalina,* and *Santa Rosa,* plus the xebec *Andaluz,* surprise the English settlement at Port Egmont. The squadron has been dispatched by Francisco Bucareli, the governor of Buenos Aires, to expunge the British and bears an additional 1,400 soldiers and a siege train under Col. Antonio Gutiérrez. Although the English have erected a wooden blockhouse and an eight-gun battery of 12-pounders, they prove no match against the Spanish force. The Spaniards wade ashore and, after a token exchange of

shot, Royal Navy Cmdrs. William Maltby and George Farmer sue for terms. They and other settlers are detained for 20 days then permitted to sail for England aboard their sole remaining vessel (the 16-gun *Favourite*); the new occupiers rename the town Cruzada and take over ownership.

When news reaches Britain it produces a public outcry. Paris refuses to back Madrid in its predicament, so the Spaniards are eventually obliged to back down on 22 January 1771, alleging the seizure has been done without Charles III's authorization; they offer to restore Port Egmont as it existed before being captured. By April the 32-gun frigate *Juno* of Capt. John Stott arrives to resume British rule, accompanied by the 14-gun *Hound* and the storeship *Florida*. (Three years later Britain abandons the Falklands because of the costs of maintaining such a remote garrison.)

16 MAY 1771. ***Regulator Revolt.*** After prolonged resentment against southeastern residents of the Carolinas who control government and commerce, certain Irish-Scottish settlers in the northwestern corner—calling themselves Regulators—refuse, in the spring of 1771, to have anything more to do with the government. Gov. William Tryon raises 1,018 militia and 30 light cavalry to put down the rebellion; they march west and burn many farms and homes.

On 16 May his army confronts 2,000 half-armed Regulators at Alamance Creek (20 miles west of Hillsboro, North Carolina), defeating them in a two-hour battle in which he suffers nine killed and 61 wounded. Some 20 Regulators die, 50 are injured, and a dozen are captured; ten prisoners are later hanged, effectively ending the insurrection.

LATE DECEMBER 1772. Holland dispatches 800 soldiers—plus the gunboats *Charon* and *Cerberus*—to Suriname under Swiss-born Col. Louis Henry Fourgeoud to subdue several thousand runaway slaves, or "maroons," settled along the upper Cottica River. Despite repeated campaigns over the next few years, Fourgeoud is unable to bring the elusive maroons to battle.

LATE 1773. After repeated complaints of Portuguese crossborder cattle raids out of Rio Grande do Sul Province, the Spanish governor of Buenos Aires—Juan José de Vértiz—leads more than 1,000 men north from Montevideo, erecting the large fort of Santa Tecla at the confluence of the Negro and Piraí Rivers near modern Bagé in January 1774. Brazilian guerrillas respond by ambushing a couple of supply columns.

10 OCTOBER 1774. ***Point Pleasant.*** In Kentucky, the inland expansion of English settlers following the collapse of French influence produces a series of skirmishes with local Shawnee, Delaware, Wyandotte, and Mingo (western Iroquois) natives. This becomes known as Lord Dunmore's War, after Virginia Gov. John Murray, Earl of Dunmore.

In the autumn Dunmore links up with 1,100 Virginia militia under Col. Andrew Lewis at the confluence of the Kanawha and Ohio Rivers. On the night of 9 October a Shawnee army under chief Cornstalk crosses the Ohio; he attacks the colonials at dawn. In a fierce, day-long fight the Virginians hold their position, and by evening the Indians withdraw with heavy casualties. The militia endure 50 killed and 100 wounded, but native power in the Ohio Valley is broken.

UNDECLARED HISPANO-PORTUGUESE CONFLICT (1776–1777)

IN SOUTH AMERICA, THE EXPANSION OF BOTH Spanish and Portuguese territories creates competition, which eventually explodes into open hostility—although due to the reluctance of each belligerent's European allies the campaigns are never endorsed by any official declaration of war.

OCTOBER 1775. Along the undefined border among Guyana, Venezuela, and Brazil a Spanish expedition under Antonio López explores and claims the Parima District (headwaters to the Orinoco River), only to be ambushed while retiring into Venezuela's plains by a sizable Portuguese contingent that has recently founded a new settlement at the mouth of the Mao River.

19 FEBRUARY 1776. The Spanish brig *Santiago,* the auxiliaries *Misericordia* and *San Francisco,* the schooner *Pastoriza,* and the corvette *Dolores,* at anchor off Rio Grande (Brazil) under Capt. Francisco Javier de Morales, are attacked by two Portuguese frigates, two storeships, a sloop, and four armed boats under Irish-born Commo. William Robert MacDouall. Although

expecting to be backed by a simultaneous land assault from the 4,500-man Portuguese army of Gen. Johann Heinrich Böhm—an Austrian mercenary—MacDouall's warships are left unsupported, suffering heavy losses. His attack is repelled after a three-hour firefight, during which the Spanish suffer 15 killed and 25 wounded while sinking the Portuguese sloop and burning another beached vessel the next day.

5 MARCH 1776. ***Lagoa dos Patos.*** Despite MacDouall's defeat, the Portuguese return to contest the new Spanish establishment at Rio Grande (Brazil), laying siege to its principal stronghold. After a 27-day encirclement 1,500 grenadiers rout a Spanish force in Lagoa dos Patos on 1 April, prompting the fortress and other outlying batteries to surrender shortly thereafter. Of four small Spanish men-of-war anchored in Rio Grande's roads, only the flagship *Santiago* escapes, the others being beached and burned.

When news of this unexpected Portuguese victory reaches Europe, it brings a halt to diplomatic negotiations between both belligerents; Madrid prepares to retaliate.

23 MARCH 1776. Brazilian irregulars under the guerrilla chieftain Rafael Bandeira capture the advance Spanish outpost of Fort Santa Tecla (near Bagé).

20 JUNE 1776. A sergeant and 12 Spanish soldiers sent into the Mao District (the Venezuela-Brazil border) are attacked by 200 Portuguese troops and 500 native auxiliaries who have been rushed up the Amazon River by the governor of Pará (Belém).

22 OCTOBER 1776. A popular uprising occurs in Urubamba (Peru), followed by disturbances in Arequipa, which are eventually put down by a series of executions in Cuzco.

6–7 FEBRUARY 1777. A 116-ship, 19,000-man Spanish expedition appears off Brazil, spearheaded by the 74-gun ships of the line *Poderoso* of Flag Capt. Juan de Lángara, *San Dámaso* of Francisco de Borja, *Santiago la América* of Antonio Asorio y Herreras, *San José* of José Bauzes, and *Monarca* of Antonio Osorio y Funco; 64-gun *Septentrión;* frigates *Santa Ana, Santa Clara, Vénus, Santa Florentina, Santa Teresa, Santa Margarita, Santa Rosa,* and *Liebre; chambequín Andaluz;* bomb vessels *Santa Casilda* and *Santa Eulalia;* plus three lesser consorts. These intercept a trio of Portuguese merchantmen bound from Rio de Janeiro toward Europe—although this formation's actual purpose is to retaliate on a much grander scale for recent clashes. Some 8,600 infantry, 640 dragoons, and 150 gunners are aboard 96 transports under veteran Lt. Gen. Pedro de Ceballos (*see* 3 September 1762), knight of the Orders of Santiago and San Genaro, and now also viceroy-designate for Buenos Aires.

Originally directed to assault the Portuguese Colônia do Sacramento (Uruguay), de Ceballos decides to assail Brazil's Santa Catarina Island in passing, over the objections of his naval counterpart Vice Adm. Francisco Javier Everardo, Marqués de Casa Tilly and knight of the Order of Santiago. While coasting southwest toward this destination, the huge Spanish fleet further brushes aside MacDouall's four Portuguese ships of the line, four frigates, and four auxiliaries, which it finds anchored at Garupas on 17 February.

20 FEBRUARY 1777. ***Santa Catarina.*** De Ceballos and the Marqués de Casa Tilly materialize outside the Brazilian base of Santa Catarina, filing into Canavieiras Bay at the northern end of the island to probe for a landing point. The entrances on either side of Ratones Island are covered by Forts São José and Santa Cruz, so the attackers disembark at nearby São Francisco Beach the night of 22–23 February without opposition.

De Ceballos aims to take Fort São José from the rear while shelling it from out at sea with his 60-gun ship of the line *Septentrión,* frigate *Liebre,* and two bomb vessels; but the 2,900 unprepared Portuguese defenders under Gen. Antônio Carlos Furtado de Mendoça abandon all their citadels without a fight, mostly retreating to the mainland by boat then deserting en masse while being marched to reinforce Rio Grande. Both of Santa Catarina's forts fall into Spanish hands by 25 February along with 195 artillery pieces; 3,816 surviving Portuguese troops and residents gradually give themselves up by 5 March rather than face starvation in the jungle.

25 MARCH 1777. After installing a garrison on Santa Catarina Island under Col. William Vaughan of Hibernia Regiment, de Ceballos sails south with the bulk of his forces, intending to disembark at Lagoa dos Patos—again, over Admiral Tilly's protests—and attack the Portuguese concentration at Rio Grande in conjunction with a northeasterly movement out of Uruguay by a Spanish army under Vértiz. Instead, his expedition encounters such heavy weather that de Ceballos is obliged to stagger into Maldonado by 18 April without seeing action. He then detaches his heavier ships of the line on 10 May to cruise in search

of MacDouall's Portuguese squadron while retaining his lighter craft to conduct his army to Sacramento.

9 APRIL 1777. Antonio Barreto, newly designated governor of the Upper Orinoco, departs Santo Tomé de Guayana (Venezuela) with 50 soldiers aboard nine small vessels to sail upriver; he will be reinforced by an additional 50 soldiers farther inland and probe the Portuguese defenses on the Negro River.

21 APRIL 1777. The 74-gun Spanish ship of the line *San Agustín* of Capt. José Techaín and the smaller auxiliary *Santa Ana*—having arrived too late from Europe to overtake the de Ceballos–Tilly expedition, then becoming separated from their 74-gun consort *Serio* and the frigate *Magdalena*—are captured near the mouth of the River Plate by MacDouall's Portuguese squadron.

22 MAY 1777. ***Sacramento.*** *Mariscal de Campo* Victorio de Navia disembarks the vanguard of de Ceballos's 4,500 troops at El Molino, three miles from Sacramento, being joined next day by the commander in chief despite heavy rains. This expedition is further reinforced from Buenos Aires and begins digging its first siege works by 30 May, consisting of a mortar battery, another of eight-pounders to fire heated shot, plus a pair of heavy pieces and other lighter ones to protect its flanks. The surprised 1,000-man Portuguese garrison under Col. Francisco José de Rocha—already half-starved because of a prolonged Spanish blockade—quickly sues for terms and surrenders by the afternoon of 4 June. The Spaniards' booty includes 700 prisoners, 141 artillery pieces, and 2,300 muskets.

De Ceballos spends the next two months demolishing the fortifications at Sacramento and the twin batteries on adjacent San Gabriel Island with explosives before finally scuttling blockships to close up its entrance then reembarking his troops to sail east toward Maldonado on 4 August. His intent is to launch another offensive against Rio Grande, but this is cancelled once news reaches him on 27 August of the restoration of relations between Madrid and Lisbon back in Europe.

9 JULY 1777. Tilly sets sail from Santa Catarina Island with seven ships of the line and five frigates, steering toward Rio Grande. However, bad weather hampers his progress, compelling him to stand into the River Plate by 26 July. Approaching harbor after nightfall, the frigate *Santa Clara* is wrecked on the Banco Inglés and goes down with 120 hands.

The death of José I of Portugal on 23 February 1777 has produced a reversal in Lisbon's policies, as he is succeeded by Spanish-born Queen María Victoria, who brings an end to the disputes by a preliminary treaty signed at San Ildefonso on 1 October. The Portuguese give up all claims to Sacramento and Uruguay, further agreeing to restore the ship *San Agustín* to Spain; Madrid returns Santa Catarina Island and agrees to recognize Rio Grande as falling within Brazilian territory. The pact is finalized at El Pardo on 24 March 1778; one month later Tilly's expedition quits the River Plate.

Part 6: Independence (1775–1825)

Oh God! It is all over!
—Prime Minister Lord North,
upon learning of the British
defeat at Yorktown in 1781

American Revolutionary War (1775–1783)

With the collapse of France's New World empire, Britain's North American subjects no longer need the protection of the home country. Long-simmering political, economic, and social grievances therefore come to the fore, leading to a transatlantic split. Tensions finally come to a boil in Virginia on 23 March 1775, when its provincial convention calls for a "posture of defense," prompting Governor Dunmore to retaliate by seizing the powder supply at Williamsburg.

On 14 April, Maj. Gen. Sir Thomas Gage, British commander in chief at Boston—under mounting pressure to take action against spreading American sedition—decides to destroy the military supplies stored at nearby Concord and arrest any delegates heading for the Continental Congress. Consequently, Lt. Col. Francis Smith is delegated to march 800 men through Lexington, a deployment the colonial militia vows to oppose.

Paul Revere and William Dawes carry warnings of the sortie a few days later, so that Samuel Adams and John Hancock—both staying in Lexington while en route to attend the congress in Philadelphia—escape the night of 18 April. Around midnight, a Lexington militia captain named Parker draws up his 130 "minutemen," dismissing them with instructions to assemble again upon the beat of a drum.

19 April 1775. ***Lexington and Concord.*** At dawn Smith's vanguard—six companies of light infantry under Maj. John Pitcairn (200 redcoats in all)—reaches Lexington, six miles short of Concord. Parker's minutemen are summoned, but because of insufficient weapons only 70 muster upon the green, the rest running to the arsenal. Pitcairn's regulars meanwhile advance in three lines, intending to surround and disarm the Americans, who give way. Although both sides are under orders not to fire, a shot rings out in the gloom, and ragged shooting commences, resulting in eight American dead and ten wounded. Only one redcoat receives a wound, in the leg, and Pitcairn's horse is struck twice; but the skirmish rouses American resistance.

By the time Smith's regiment approaches Concord a few hours later 150 minutemen are drawn up on a ridge behind the North Bridge under militia Col. James Barrett. British Capt. Walter Laurie advances with three companies while Barrett's farm and Concord are searched for hidden war stores. At this point Laurie's men are driven back with some losses, until Smith can bring up reinforcements and eventually break off the engagement.

Having accomplished their immediate objective, the redcoats begin the return march to Boston around noon through country now in a fury. From Meriam's Corner, one mile outside Concord, they are harassed by sniper fire, unsuccessfully rallying at Fiske's Hill, where Pitcairn loses his horse and pistols and Smith is wounded. At Lexington the British are reinforced by Brig. Gen. Lord Hugh Percy with 1,400 men and two six-pounders, fighting their way until under the safety of naval guns at Charlestown Neck. Of 3,765 Americans involved, 50 are killed, 40 are wounded, and five are missing; British casualties total 250 men plus 26 deserters. Within a week minutemen lay siege to Boston, and the Revolutionary War is joined.

2 May 1775. In Virginia, Maj. Patrick Henry leads a rebel force to retrieve the powder seized by Governor Dunmore at Williamsburg, who further agrees to pay £330 by way of compensation.

9 May 1775. In order to obtain military stores for the patriot cause, Maj. Benedict Arnold suggests seizing Fort Ticonderoga, an isolated outpost on Lake Champlain. He is breveted colonel and raises 400 men for the venture, joining another 200 on 9 May already at Castleton (Vermont) under 36-year-old Maj. Ethan Allen. Before dawn of 10 May 300 colonials assemble at Hand's Cove, and Arnold ferries across immediately to Ticonderoga with 83 men rather than await the rest.

The gamble pays off when the garrison of two English officers and 48 soldiers (mostly invalids) is taken completely by surprise, Capt. William Delaplace surrendering without resistance. Patriot Maj. Seth Warner subsequently marches ten miles farther north and occupies Crown Point as well, capturing another nine Englishmen along with ten women and children. In this fashion the revolutionaries obtain 78 guns, six mortars, three howitzers, thousands of cannonballs, and 30,000 flints. Ticonderoga and Crown Point are then held by 1,400 men under Col. Benjamin Hinman.

25 May 1775. Gage's beleaguered English garrison within Boston is joined by other contingents under Maj. Gens. John "Gentleman Johnny" Burgoyne, William Howe, and Henry Clinton, bringing combined strength to 6,500. By early June some 15,000

colonials are encamped outside, although they are short of ammunition and accouterments.

12 JUNE 1775. In Boston, Gage offers a royal pardon to all insurgents except Samuel Adams and John Hancock, a proposal that is ignored by his American besiegers who next day learn that the British intend to occupy adjacent Charleston Peninsula on 18 June. The Americans counter by sending Col. William Prescott with 1,600 men at 9:00 P.M. on 16 June to hold the position, digging in on Breed's Hill (rather than the higher Bunker Hill) and preparing for the British disembarkation.

17 JUNE 1775. ***Bunker Hill.*** At dawn HMSS *Glasgow, Lively, Somerset,* and *Falcon* open fire on the American redoubts in anticipation of the English army's sally out of Boston. At noon General Howe lands with 2,400 heavily burdened redcoats, who are twice repulsed as they attempt to advance upon the colonial lines. Joined by an additional 400 troops under General Clinton, and with the Americans running low on ammunition, Howe's third attack succeeds in driving the provincials from their redoubts and, eventually, off Breed's Hill as well as Bunker Hill. The Americans retreat toward Cambridge, Howe halting his pursuit at the neck of the Charleston Peninsula.

Although the British have won the day and remain in possession of the field, their casualties total 1,050 men as opposed to 100 colonials killed and 270 wounded. More importantly, the naval bombardment of Charleston creates increased animosity against the loyalist cause, and Gage is obliged to abandon his plans for marching on Cambridge by way of Dorchester.

2 JULY 1775. George Washington assumes command of the 17,000 Continental troops besieging Boston. Many enlistments are due to expire in the new year, thus necessitating the recruitment of a more professional army.

17 AUGUST 1775. Because of a bout of rheumatic gout, 41-year-old American Maj. Gen. Philip John Schuyler temporarily cedes command of his 1,200 troops—gathering at Crown Point (New York) for a projected campaign against British Canada—to 39-year-old Irish-born Brig. Gen. Richard Montgomery. Learning that two 12-gun, 60-foot boats are nearing completion at the British base of Saint Jean (20 miles south of Montréal), Montgomery disembarks with 1,500 men on Ile aux Noix (Richelieu River) by 30 August, thus preventing them from reaching Lake Champlain—an action that Schuyler fully endorses upon reassuming command on 4 September.

5 SEPTEMBER 1775. ***Invasion of Canada.*** Schuyler's American army approaches the British base at Saint Jean (Quebec), which consists of a barracks fortified by two redoubts defended by 200 regulars, an Indian contingent, and several cannons under Maj. Charles Preston. Disembarking a half-mile away, the invaders are ambushed by an Indian party under British Captain Tice, suffering 16 killed. Schuyler then judges Saint Jean too difficult to storm and so returns to Ile aux Noix with his force.

After being reinforced by another 500 New Yorkers under Col. Rudolph Ritzema, the Americans again invest Saint Jean on 10 September but are repelled despite three assaults led by the colonel in person. On 16 September Montgomery reassumes command over the American army and receives 270 additional reinforcements. However, by this time British Maj. Gen. Sir Guy Carleton has increased Saint Jean's garrison to 500 men, with another 90 stationed at nearby Chambly, thereby frustrating the invaders' plans.

Farther east, however, Col. Benedict Arnold has set out from Cambridge (Massachusetts) on 12 September with an additional 1,100–1,200 American volunteers to

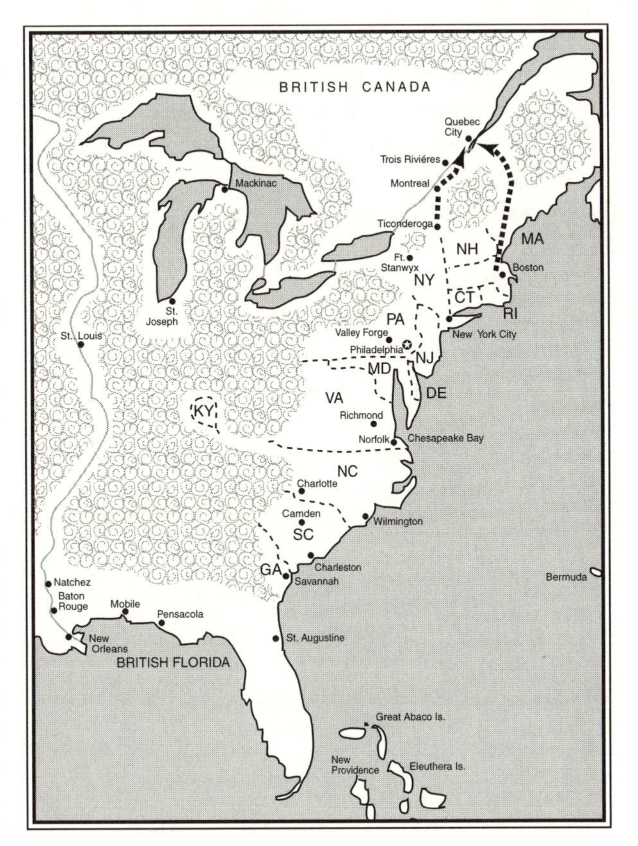

Two-pronged American offensive into Canada

advance up the Kennebec River, then down the Chaudière River, to attack the British stronghold at Quebec City.

24 SEPTEMBER 1775. Having been detached from Montgomery's main American army before Saint Jean (Quebec), Col. Ethan Allen tonight crosses the Saint Lawrence River, disembarking below Montréal with 110 men while Col. John Brown is to lead another 200 ashore above. Brown fails to appear, however, so dawn finds Allen's contingent alone, facing 35 British regulars and 200 Canadian volunteers under Carleton. Allen and 40 of his men surrender; they are held prisoner for the next two and a half years.

10 OCTOBER 1775. Sir William Howe succeeds Gage as commander in chief of the British armed forces in North America.

18 OCTOBER 1775. The British outpost at Chambly (Quebec) surrenders to Montgomery's army, heartening the Americans while tightening the siege around the larger British base at nearby Saint Jean.

24 OCTOBER 1775. Virginia's heavy-handed royal governor, Lord Dunmore—upon learning of Gage's offer to pardon all except two insurgents (*see* 12 June 1775)—flees onto a British warship and sends Capt. John Squire with six tenders into Hampton Creek to bombard the town. A party that lands to set fire to the place is driven back by American riflemen; overnight Col. William Woodford arrives with 100 colonial militia to defend Hampton against a second attack.

At sunrise on 25 October the British open fire again and move in, only to be repelled by heavy counterfire. Two British sloops are beached and captured, five ships are sunk, and one is captured with seven sailors aboard. There are no American casualties, but—as at Boston—the loyalist aggression helps stiffen colonial resolve.

30 OCTOBER 1775. Carleton vainly tries to relieve Montgomery's siege of Saint Jean (Quebec) by crossing at nearby Longueuil, only to be repelled. Three days later—2 November—the isolated, half-starved forward outpost finally surrenders to the Americans, opening the road to Montréal.

OCTOBER 1775. General Gage is recalled to England; command of military operations within Boston devolves to General Howe.

11 NOVEMBER 1775. Montgomery disembarks above Montréal with a strong American force; Carleton has only 150 British regulars and a few militia to defend the town. Next day his garrison evacuates aboard 11 ships as the invaders enter. While attempting to escape down the Saint Lawrence River into Quebec City the retreating British are intercepted off Sorel, capitulating by 19 November (although Carleton and a few officers escape ashore in a small boat).

13 NOVEMBER 1775. ***Quebec.*** Having arrived four days previously at Point Lévis—opposite Quebec City—with 600–650 half-starved survivors from his 230-mile wilderness trek from Massachusetts, American Col. Benedict Arnold crosses the Saint Lawrence River then attempts to invest the British garrison of 50-year-old Lt. Col. Allan Maclean from the Plains of Abraham. Unable to breach the fortifications without a siege train, however, the invaders must remain encamped outside until 19 November, when they retire west to Pointe aux Trembles to await the arrival of another American contingent from Montréal under Montgomery.

He appears the evening of 2 December and is joined the next day by 600 of his troops with some artillery. However, the Americans still cannot fully besiege Quebec City's 1,700-man garrison (now under General Carleton) so instead decide to storm it from two directions in the early hours of 31 December, their approach being muffled by a blizzard. Montgomery leads 500 men by a southerly route toward Près de Ville, reaching it by 4:00 A.M., only to be suddenly killed—along with two dozen of his men—by a pair of British three-pounders. His second-in-command, Col. Donald Campbell, quickly orders retreat.

Arnold meanwhile approaches from Saint Roch by a northern route with another 700 men, drawing fire that wounds him in the knee. His second-in-command—6-foot 4-inch Kentucky Col. Daniel Morgan—instead pushes forward into the alerted lower town, only to become trapped in Sault au Matelot; he is obliged to surrender at 9:00 A.M. along with his 425 followers. Total American casualties are 30 killed and 42 wounded, compared to five dead and 13 injured among the defenders.

9 DECEMBER 1775. Virginia's royal governor, Lord Dunmore, attempts to halt the advance on Norfolk by Colonel Woodford and 390 rebels, choosing to make a stand at Great Bridge (nine miles outside the town) by fortifying one end of the causeway, which is otherwise surrounded by impenetrable swamps. Woodford arrives and builds a redoubt at the opposite end, leaving Lieutenant Travis with 90 men to hold the emplacement while taking his remainder to a hill several hundred yards farther back.

Dunmore impetuously orders Captain Fordyce to charge across the 40-yard bridge supported by Capt. Samuel Leslie's 230 men. Fordyce's first attack is driven back, so he brings up two cannons for a second attempt. The Americans deceive the British officer into thinking their redoubt is abandoned, holding fire until the assault column has advanced to within point-blank range. A ferocious volley kills Fordyce and sends his men reeling back in defeat. Although the whole action takes only 25 minutes, the British suffer 62 casualties and lose both cannons, whereas only one American is wounded in the hand. More importantly, a way into Norfolk is now open.

5 FEBRUARY 1776. Brig. Gen. Donald McDonald and Col. Donald McLeod reach Cross Creek (Fayetteville, North Carolina) with a small British contingent to restore royalist rule. Although they quickly raise several hundred local loyalists and Scots, American Cols. James Moore, Alexander Lillington, and John Ashe begin to press the force back to the coast.

18 FEBRUARY 1776. This morning, 57-year-old American Commo. Esek Hopkins sets sail from Delaware with the 24-gun frigates *Alfred* (flag) and *Columbus;* the 14-gun brigs *Andrew Doria* and *Cabot;* 12-gun sloop *Providence;* the ten-gun sloop *Hornet;* and the eight-gun schooners *Wasp* and *Fly* to attack Lord Dunmore's loyalist squadron in Chesapeake Bay—or any other target of convenience.

26 FEBRUARY 1776. ***Moore's Creek.*** Brigadier General McDonald and Colonel McLeod retreat with 1,800 Anglo-loyalists to North Carolina's coast, but their route is barred at Moore's Creek bridge (near Wilmington) by 1,000 American militia under Colonels Lillington, Ashe, and Richard Caswell. After camping six miles west, the British resume their march at 1:00 A.M. on 27 February, reaching the partially demolished bridge by dawn and believing it to be abandoned.

But the Americans are entrenched on the far side and shoot down the British vanguard when it draws near, killing Scottish Capt. John Campbell and 30 of his 80 men with the opening volleys. The defenders then storm across to attack McLeod's main body while American Lt. Ezekiel Slocum belabors the British rear. Panicked, the British suffer 30 killed and 850 captured, including McLeod. American losses are one killed and another wounded.

3 MARCH 1776. ***Bahamian Raid.*** American Commodore Hopkins bears down upon New Providence (Nassau) with *Alfred, Columbus, Andrew Doria, Cabot, Providence, Wasp,* and two Bahamian sloops captured off Great Abaco (50 miles away). Ignoring the long-range fire from New Providence's British batteries, Hopkins disembarks 200 marines and 50 sailors under Capt. Samuel Nicholas on the opposite end of the island; they then advance from the landward side and compel the defenders under Gov. Montfort Browne to surrender. More than 100 field pieces and a considerable amount of materiel are captured, taking the Americans two weeks to load.

17 MARCH 1776. The Americans' 11-month siege of Boston finally ends when General Howe orders Castle William blown up and evacuates the last of his 12,000 redcoats to pursue a campaign in New York. The colonials jubilantly occupy the city, retrieving 69 usable cannons and other valuable stores. Massachusetts remains free of British forces for the remainder of the war.

6 MAY 1776. The British ship *Surprise* reaches Quebec City with supplies, effectively putting an end to the winter-long siege by the survivors of the Montgomery-Arnold expeditions. A sally soon after by the British garrison under Carleton and Maclean chases the Americans away.

20 MAY 1776. An Anglo-Canadian force under Capt. George Forster descends the Saint Lawrence River from Fort Oswegatchie (Ogdensburg, New York), capturing 400 Americans at the nearby Cedars.

1 JUNE 1776. British generals Burgoyne and Friedrich, Baron von Riedesel reach Quebec City with an Anglo-Hessian army.

6 JUNE 1776. ***Trois Rivières.*** Mistakenly believing that the advance Canadian outpost of Trois Rivières is held by only 300 British troops, Brig. Gen. William Thompson is sent forward by Maj. Gen. John Sullivan to occupy it with 2,000 Americans

from Sorel (Quebec). Sailing up the Saint Lawrence River, Thompson disembarks seven miles above Trois Rivières at 3:00 A.M. on 8 June then strikes inland while leaving 250 men to guard his boats. His main body comprises the regiments of Cols. Arthur St. Clair, William Irvine, William Maxwell, and "Mad Anthony" Wayne.

A Canadian guide deliberately leads the invaders into a swamp, and so they do not confront the British until dawn—who are in much greater numbers than anticipated: Lt. Col. Simon Fraser having recently reinforced Trois Rivières with the British 24th Regiment and four other fresh battalions. Wayne's 200-man vanguard immediately attacks; the assault is initially successful, but the defenders soon drive the Americans back into the swamp from their line of trenches, killing or wounding 400 and taking another 236 prisoner—including Thompson. British losses are only eight killed and nine wounded.

The American survivors return to Sorel by 11 June, much discouraged; joined by Arnold's garrison—driven out of Montréal by the approach of Carleton and Maclean with 4,000 redcoats—they then retreat to Fort Ticonderoga (New York) by late July.

8 JUNE 1776. Three days after appearing off Sullivan's Island (South Carolina), Commo. Peter Parker's 55-vessel British fleet crosses its bar and deposits General Clinton's army on Long Island, in anticipation of securing nearby Charleston as a regional base of operations. American Maj. Gen. Charles Lee meanwhile feverishly fortifies this city, while Col. William Moultrie prepares Sullivan's Island's 25-gun, 1,200-man garrison to resist the British incursion. Parker and Clinton delay for almost three weeks before advancing, giving the Americans ample time to strengthen defenses.

14 JUNE 1776. Carleton reaches Trois Rivières (Quebec) with the Burgoyne–von Riedesel expeditionary force, creating a British concentration of 8,000 troops.

17 JUNE 1776. Carleton's army reoccupies Montréal.

28 JUNE 1776. ***Sullivan's Island.*** This morning Parker's Royal Navy warships bear down to bombard the earth-and-palmetto log ramparts of the American fort on Sullivan's Island (South Carolina) then press upchannel against Charleston. The British simultaneously launch a 100-man diversionary attack from nearby Long Island, which is quickly repelled by Colonel Moultrie's defenders, leaving the bulk of the subsequent fighting to Parker's men-of-war.

The British bomb vessel *Thunder* opens fire from a mile and a half away while the 50-gun HMSS *Bristol* and *Experiment* cover the approach to within 400 yards of the frigates *Active* and *Solebay* plus the smaller consorts *Syren, Actaeon,* and *Sphinx*. A ferocious, day-long exchange ensues, with the attackers suffering heavy casualties while being totally unable to discomfit the well-protected Americans. During the afternoon *Actaeon* and *Sphinx* collide then run aground along with *Syren*. By 9:30 P.M. Parker draws off in defeat, his vessels having suffered 420 casualties as opposed to negligible losses among the defenders. The British abandon their project of capturing Charleston and retire north to join General Howe's forces investing New York.

22 AUGUST 1776. An American outpost on Long Island (New York) reports signs of General Howe's massive British concentration on adjacent Staten Island preparing to cross from that marshaling area and attack New York City. A few days later the British army begins to disembark—covered by the fleet of Howe's brother, Adm. Richard "Black Dick" Howe—then moves north toward the Brooklyn defenses with Colonel Grant commanding 5,000 redcoats on the left, Gen. Philip von Heister leading 5,000 Hessians in the center, and Generals Howe, Clinton, and Cornwallis bringing up another 10,000 British troops on the right. Awaiting them are 6,500 American defenders along the Brooklyn defenses under Maj. Gen. Israel Putnam with another 3,500 out in front, holding the Guian Heights.

24 AUGUST 1776. Following his withdrawal from Canada, Arnold realizes that naval control over Lake Champlain will become important and so departs Crown Point (New York) for Windmill Point—near the Canadian border—with a small flotilla.

27 AUGUST 1776. ***Long Island.*** Howe's 20,000-man army bears down on the ridge called Guian Heights, its four passes being strongly held by 3,500 Americans. At 9:00 A.M. the British general orders a frontal assault by his 5,000 Hessians in the center, followed shortly thereafter by an advance of Colonel Grant's 5,000 redcoats on the left. Howe aims to draw General Putnam's American reserves over to the left and then outflank the defenses with a massive movement by his right.

Grant encounters stiff opposition and is killed, his left wing having to be reinforced by 2,000 more British troops from Staten Island. Nevertheless, the effort draws the American reserves, allowing Howe to then move his remaining 10,000 men—supported by 28 guns—around behind the American left. The defenders' line along Guian Heights finally disintegrates, American Maj. Gen. John Sullivan being routed and captured in the center while Brig. Gen. William Alexander fights a brave delaying action before eventually surrendering to Heister—thereby allowing 2,000 men to safely retreat behind the Brooklyn defenses. Still, American losses total more than 1,400 killed, wounded, and captured compared to 380 Anglo-Hessian casualties.

Howe presses on against the Brooklyn defenses, which the Americans abandon on the night of 29–30 August; New York City becomes besieged.

6 SEPTEMBER 1776. In an attempt to blow up the 64-gun HMS *Eagle,* flagship of Admiral Howe's blockading fleet off New York, a one-man American submersible called *Turtle* (designed by David Bushnell of Westbrook, Connecticut) is released after dark by two whaleboats. Its sole crewmember, Sgt. Ezra Lee, eventually reaches his target by patiently working the hand cranks but cannot attach his "torpedo"—a cask filled with 150 pounds of powder plus a timer—against the barnacle-encrusted hull. At daybreak he narrowly avoids capture while retiring behind Governor's Island, his mine exploding harmlessly in the water.

15 SEPTEMBER 1776. ***Fall of New York.*** After a two-week wait, Howe resumes his drive to capture New York City despite the relief efforts being organized by the American commander in chief, George Washington. This morning five British warships take up station 200 yards off Kip's Bay, being followed at 10:00 A.M. by a fleet of transports bearing 4,000 redcoats out of Newton Creek (Long Island). The Royal Navy's bombardment commences at 11:00 A.M., and the British troops disembark on both sides of Kip's Bay by 1:00 P.M.; its defenders flee without offering opposition.

American Major General Putnam, realizing that the invaders cannot be contained in their new bridgehead, gallops south to bring as many troops and artillery out of doomed New York City as possible. Leading them north along Post Road (now Lexington Avenue), he succeeds in evading the rapidly closing British, who have now been joined atop Onclenberg (Murray) Hill by 4,000 more redcoats under Clinton. General Howe arrives by 2:00 P.M. and has his army ashore three hours later, advancing south and west toward the Hudson River and northwest toward Harlem Heights. Washington extemporizes a three-line defense at Harlem Heights; by evening the British have penetrated three-quarters of a mile, establishing their own line from Horn's Hook to Bloomingdale (East 90th Street).

Next morning a 150-man reconnaissance company under American Lt. Col. Archibald Crary contacts the advance British troops—two infantry battalions and some men of the Black Watch under Brig. Gen. Alexander Leslie—near present-day East 105th Street, fighting a sharp engagement that soon attracts attention. The British are driven back when Lt. Col. Thomas Knowlton and Maj. Andrew Leitch attempt to encircle them from the right with 230 American rangers, although both American lieutenant colonels are then slain along with 28 of their men; 100 more are wounded or missing compared to 14 dead and 150 injured among the British ranks.

Eventually the redcoats return at 2:00 P.M. with 5,000 men, effectively ending resistance around New York as Washington draws off with his army. Nevertheless, Howe has failed to destroy the force, thus he must spend the next month fortifying New York to secure it as base of operations.

11 OCTOBER 1776. After withdrawing into the half-mile channel between Valcour Island and Cumberland Head (northwest corner of Lake Champlain, Quebec), Arnold's American flotilla is attacked by a superior British force advancing down from Saint Jean under Carleton. The 12-gun British schooner *Carleton* leads the charge, a general engagement erupting shortly after noon. Although the attackers withdraw by dusk, most of the American ships have nonetheless become crippled and so attempt to escape into the lake during the night.

Next dawn Carleton sails in pursuit and overtakes the Americans by 11:00 A.M. on 13 October off Split Rock—28 miles short of the American base at Crown Point, New York. The 110-man *Washington* of Brigadier General Waterbury surrenders and *Lee* runs ashore; Arnold's other vessels are beached on the Vermont shore and set ablaze. Of 15 original American ships, only *Trumbull, Enterprise, Revenge,* and *Liberty* reach Crown Point safely, the British retaining temporary control of Lake Champlain.

13 OCTOBER 1776. After four weeks spent fortifying New York, General Howe traverses to the mainland at Pell's Point with 13,000 redcoats to hunt for Washington's 6,000-man army. A fortnight later the American commander in chief falls back to White Plains to await the enemy.

28 OCTOBER 1776. ***White Plains.*** At dawn Howe's army bears down on the outnumbered Americans, also being in a position to outflank them. Belatedly recognizing his danger, Washington immediately fortifies 180-foot Chatterton's Hill on his right with 1,600 men and two guns under Brig. Gen. Alexander McDougall, sending out Maj. Gen. Joseph Spencer to fight a delaying action. Spencer skirmishes with the approaching redcoats for an hour before finally retreating to rejoin the main body at 9:30 A.M. to avoid being cut off.

Three Hessian regiments under Maj. Gen. Wilhelm, Baron von Knyphausen, are meanwhile building a bridge over the Hudson River while Brigadier General Leslie fords it farther south with two regiments. Eventually, the bulk of Howe's 13,000-man army works its way across and engages Washington's main body. The Massachusetts Militia—facing British dragoons on the American right—are the first to flee; Washington's center gradually gives way after a stubborn resistance. Defenders' casualties total 150, just under half that suffered among the Anglo-Hessians.

Howe prepares to finish off the 6,000-man American army the next morning but is prevented by a heavy storm. Washington thereby escapes with his main force once more, this time to Connecticut.

15 NOVEMBER 1776. Howe's British army closes in on Fort Washington—a crude pentagonal earthwork atop 200-foot Mount Washington (modern-day Harlem Heights, northern tip of Manhattan Island, New York)—calling on its garrison to surrender this afternoon. When that is rejected 7,000 Anglo-Hessians prepare a three-pronged assault for next day while American Maj. Gens. Putnam and 34-year-old Nathanael Greene visit its 2,900 defenders under Col. Robert Magaw, reassuring themselves as to its strength. (Unbeknownst to the Americans, however, the spy William Demont has already revealed Fort Washington's weaknesses to its attackers.)

16 NOVEMBER 1776. ***Fort Washington.*** Before dawn General von Knyphausen advances from King's Bridge with 3,000 Hessians aboard 30 flatboats and crosses the Hudson upriver to attack Harlem Heights on its weak northern side; Brig. Gen. Lord Hugh Percy leads another 2,000 redcoats up from the south to dislodge 800 Americans under Lt. Col. John Cadwallader who are holding the rise one and a half miles below Fort Washington. Brig. Gen. Edward Mathew's 2,000 men are then to cross the Harlem River from the east at midday, followed by Cornwallis's reserves, to complete the Americans' rout.

Von Knyphausen's troops, supported by heavy artillery fire from British batteries and the frigate *Pearl,* push Fort Washington's outlying defenders back after stubborn hand-to-hand combat; Percy—subsequently supported by Mathew, Cornwallis, and two more battalions under Colonel Sterling—drives the Americans up Harlem Heights, securing 170 prisoners. Magaw is once more called upon to surrender overcrowded Fort Washington by this same afternoon and agrees at 3:00 P.M. American losses total 59 killed, 96 wounded, 2,837 prisoners, plus nearly 150 cannons and 2,800 muskets, compared to 136 dead and 646 injured among the Anglo-Hessians.

18 NOVEMBER 1776. After the fall of Fort Washington the Americans must evacuate the 2,000-man garrison from Fort Lee on the opposite bank of the Hudson River (New York). Cornwallis does not cross until two days later, bringing 4,500 redcoats ashore six miles north of the fort on the morning of 20 November, only to find that Washington's army has already escaped into New Jersey. Only 150 American stragglers are detained; valuable supplies are also taken.

11 DECEMBER 1776. Washington's retreating army crosses the Delaware River into Pennsylvania, causing the Continental Congress to abandon its headquarters at Philadelphia; the British pursuers under Cornwallis go into winter quarters shortly thereafter.

13 DECEMBER 1776. American Major General Lee is captured by a British patrol in New Jersey, Sullivan assuming command over his troops and continuing the march to rejoin Washington.

26 DECEMBER 1776. ***Trenton.*** Hoping to rejuvenate his demoralized army's fortunes, Washington halts his retreat into Pennsylvania long enough to launch a surprise counterattack back across the Delaware River against the 1,400-man Hessian garrison now quartered in Trenton (New Jersey).

Col. Johann Rall, the Hessians' commander—although forewarned of an imminent American assault—still dismisses the possibility as a mere foraging probe and is carried to bed after a drunken Christmas party. Next day at 8:00 A.M., 2,400 American troops emerge out of a fierce snowstorm with 18 guns, marching directly into Trenton from the north (under General Greene) and west (under Sullivan), brushing aside the few pickets. The unprepared Hessians of the Lossberg

Regiments are driven east into open fields, where Rall is killed and 105 of his men are shot dead or wounded before 920 survivors surrender. American losses amount to two wounded.

Despite the wholesale victory, however, Washington again retires beyond the Delaware, secondary attacks—with 2,000 men under Cadwallader against Bordenton and 1,000 under Brig. Gen. James Ewing against Trenton Ferry—having been unable to go forward to wholly secure his position.

30 DECEMBER 1776. Encouraged by his Trenton success, Washington recrosses the Delaware with 2,000 men, only to encounter a superior British force advancing from Princeton (New Jersey) under Cornwallis. Fighting a delaying action until nightfall, the American general then leaves 400 men with their campfires burning as a diversion, slipping east toward Princeton with the rest.

3 JANUARY 1777. ***Princeton.*** At dawn, British Lt. Col. Charles Mawhood sets out from Princeton with two of his three garrison regiments—1,200 men—to join Brigadier General Leslie on the Trenton road. Upon reaching Clark's Orchard, though, Mawhood is confronted by 350 Americans under Brig. Gen. Hugh Mercer; a skirmish ensues in which the latter are pushed back and Mercer killed.

At this point, Washington catches up to the British formation with his main body, dispersing it while inflicting 65 casualties and capturing 35 prisoners. The Americans then march on to Princeton, where the remaining garrison fortifies its college building, only to be flushed out by artillery. A further 200 redcoats are seized, Cornwallis's reinforcements arriving after Washington has already left.

5–6 JANUARY 1777. Washington's exhausted 1,600-man army retreats into winter quarters at Morristown (New Jersey).

23 MARCH 1777. A force of 500 redcoats disembarks with four light guns from a Royal Navy frigate and some transports, destroying the American depot at Peekskill (New York), which its small patriot garrison under Brigadier General McDougall is powerless to defend.

23 APRIL 1777. ***Danbury Raid.*** Inspired by the success of his Peekskill foray, General Howe dispatches Brig. Gen. William Tryon with 2,000 Anglo-Hessian troops to destroy another American depot—this time at Danbury (Connecticut). The raiders depart Long Island (New York) on 23 April, landing near Fairfield two evenings later. On 26 April, the British march 23 miles across country into Danbury, arriving by 3:00 P.M. to chase away its 150-man American garrison and burn a vast quantity of supplies.

Tryon then returns toward the coast via Ridgefield, 15 miles farther south, while American Gen. Benedict Arnold scrapes together 600 men and a six-pounder to oppose him on some high ground beside the Saugatuck River. The redcoats outflank this position, but Arnold is then joined by a further 100 Americans under Brig. Gen. David Wooster, attacking the British rearguard on 28 April. This assault is driven off by 400 redcoats under Brig. Gen. William Erskine, enabling Tryon's expedition to reembark without any greater loss. British casualties during this campaign total 150 killed and wounded compared to 100 American—the latter including Wooster and Col. John Lamb.

26 JUNE 1777. Brigadier General Fraser departs Crown Point (New York) with the vanguard of Burgoyne's 9,500-man army. It is the British commander's intent to push south from Canada, down Lake Champlain and the Upper Hudson River until reaching Albany to meet Howe's army, which meanwhile will be sweeping through Pennsylvania.

2 JULY 1777. Fraser's British vanguard overruns Mount Hope (New York), being joined by Burgoyne's main body next day.

4 JULY 1777. ***Ticonderoga.*** After posting von Riedesel's Hessians on the east side of Lake Champlain to attack the Americans holding Mount Independence, Burgoyne installs his artillery atop Mount Defiance on its west side to cover the approaches into Fort Ticonderoga. Realizing this twin deployment will soon doom his 2,500-man garrison, American Major General St. Clair decides to evacuate, preceding this with a heavy artillery exchange. Under cover of darkness, 500 of his men leave by boat shortly after midnight on 5–6 July, sailing south toward Skenesborough; the rest march out stealthily across Ticonderoga's boat

bridge at 2:00 A.M., hastening southeast toward Castleton (Vermont).

Burgoyne sets off in pursuit next morning by water, delegating Brigadier General Fraser to chase the retreating Americans overland. This same day (6 July), the British commander in chief gains Skenesborough and next day his vanguard unit—the 9th British Regiment under Lt. Col. John Hill—overtakes Col. Pierce Long's 150-man patriot rearguard outside Fort Anne, reinforced by 400 New York militia under Col. Henry van Rensselaer. Not expecting to encounter this much resistance, Hill's redcoats are chased up a 500-foot ridge by the Americans, holding out for two hours. Finally an Indian war whoop farther north heralds the appearance of Burgoyne's main body, convincing Long and van Rensselaer to break off this delaying action, set Fort Anne ablaze, then retreat 13 miles farther south to rejoin General Schuyler's army at Fort Edward.

Meanwhile Fraser has also caught up with part of St. Clair's contingent by evening of 6 July: specifically, 1,000 men under American Col. Seth Warner—the latter's own Vermont regiment, plus Cols. Turbott Francis and Nathan Hale's regiments—which the American general has detached to make a stand at Hubbardton (New York) to cover his rearguard's escape while his main body continues toward Castleton. After halting three miles short of Warner's camp, Fraser advances with 750 men at 4:30 A.M. of 7 July, surprising and routing Hale's regiment; but Warner and Francis's troops rally, checking the British charge with a heavy volley. Fraser then attempts to outflank the American left atop Zion Hill, but the Americans swivel back to contain this threat while menacing Fraser's left.

At this point von Riedesel arrives, immediately attacking the American right while sending his grenadiers in a flanking movement. Colonel Francis is killed and his regiment pulls back, leaving Warner's Vermonters to face a bayonet charge alone, in which they are overwhelmed. Two hours of heavy fighting has left the Americans with 80 casualties plus 320 captured; the Anglo-Hessians suffer 35 killed and 150 wounded. Nevertheless, the bulk of St. Clair's army escapes intact; Burgoyne must leave behind 1,000 men to garrison Ticonderoga.

25 JULY 1777. British Lt. Col. Barry St. Leger departs Fort Oswego (New York) with 350 redcoats, plus 1,650 Canadian and loyalist militia and native allies, to advance east-southeast up the Mohawk River and threaten Albany in conjunction with Burgoyne's drive out of Canada.

29 JULY 1777. Burgoyne's army overruns both Fort Edward and Fort George, although his drive south is now slowing because of his lengthening supply lines out of Canada plus the lack of the anticipated loyalist support in central New York.

31 JULY 1777. Schuyler's American army retreats south across the Upper Hudson River into Stilwater, 30 miles above Albany (New York).

2 AUGUST 1777. ***Fort Stanwyx.*** St. Leger arrives outside the American outpost of Fort Stanwyx—also spelled Stanwix—on the Mohawk River near Rome (New York), stationing his 350 regulars a quarter-mile northeast of its fort while dividing his Canadian and loyalist militia between two outposts on the west bank of this river and Wood Creek, with Indian allies patrolling the forests between. The 550-man patriot garrison under Col. Peter Gansevoort finds itself besieged, although word arrives on 5 August of an 800-man relief column approaching under American Maj. Gen. Nicholas Herkimer.

St. Leger detaches 400 loyalists, Canadians, and Indians eastward under chief Joseph Brand and Maj. John Butler to ambush this column ten miles away at Oriskany. The site is a ravine 200 yards wide, heavily wooded on both sides, which the mile-long American column enters without its 60 Oneida scouts perceiving any danger. At 10:00 A.M. on 6 August the shooting begins, Lt. Col. Richard Vischer's 200-man patriot rearguard instantly fleeing. Herkimer is wounded but nonetheless directs his remaining 600 men to high ground, where hand-to-hand fighting rages for another 45 minutes before being interrupted by a heavy downpour. During this hour-long pause, Maj. Stephen Watts arrives with further British reinforcements, and fighting resumes until early evening, when the attackers withdraw. Herkimer's column is so decimated as to be unable to continue, having suffered 140 casualties, double the ambushers' numbers.

Gansevoort's garrison meanwhile attempts a few sallies against the depleted British siegelines this same morning, after which a three-day truce is arranged around Fort Stanwyx. The patriots are subsequently able to get a message through to General Schuyler, who dispatches another 800-man relief column under

Gen. Arnold on 10 August. By the time this contingent approaches, Indian morale has declined so precipitously that St. Leger must raise his siege by 22 August and retreat west to Lake Oneida. Arnold quickly rebuilds Fort Stanwyx's strength to 700 men then returns east with 1,200 men to swell the American numbers closing in on Burgoyne around Saratoga.

15 AUGUST 1777. ***Bennington.*** Having been detached southeast from Burgoyne's main army to raid the American depot at Bennington (Vermont), Hessian Lt. Col. Friedrich Baum's 800-man contingent is encamped at Cambridge this morning when he learns of a superior patriot force gathered farther northeast at Manchester. Baum calls for reinforcements from Burgoyne before pressing on, and the British general sends an additional 640 men and two six-pounders in support under Lt. Col. Heinrich Breymann.

Patriot Brig. Gen. John Stark meanwhile closes in on Baum with 1,500 members of the Green Mountain militia, followed out of Manchester by another 300 Americans under Colonel Warner. Heavy rains slow progress on both sides, but by the afternoon of 16 August Baum's Anglo-Hessians are drawn up on the Walloomsac River, where they are attacked by a double American envelopment: Col. Moses Nichols leads 200 patriots on the right flank while Col. Samuel Herrick takes 300 to attack the enemy rear. At the same time, Cols. David Hobart and Thomas Stickney deliver a small pincer attack against the loyalist redoubt on the left bank, routing its defenders after a single volley and thus seizing two more Hessian positions. Baum makes a stand atop a hill on the right bank but—his men's ammunition running low—is mortally wounded when a reserve dump explodes.

Breymann's relief column reaches Sancoick's Mill by 4:30 P.M., pushing on the remaining four miles to rescue Baum in the mistaken belief he is still able to resist. Instead Breymann encounters Warner's fresh contingent at Walloomsac, which defeats the Hessians after a hard-fought struggle, the latter running out of powder and fleeing into the night. Anglo-Hessian casualties total 205 plus another 700 captured compared to 60 Americans killed or wounded.

19 AUGUST 1777. The 49-year-old, British-born Maj. Gen. Horatio Gates replaces Schuyler as commander in chief of the patriot forces confronting Burgoyne's offensive in New York State.

24 AUGUST 1777. Howe's 15,000-man British army reaches Elk River—a few miles from Delaware Bay—intending to overrun Philadelphia in twin columns before eventually striking north to relieve Burgoyne.

3 SEPTEMBER 1777. At 9:00 A.M., Brigadier General Maxwell's patriot forces fire upon the vanguard of General Cornwallis's Grand Division, as the latter attempts to cross the Christiana River at Cooch's Bridge (Delaware). From the British left, Hessian Lieutenant Colonel Wurmb leads an attack that envelopes the American right, driving the defenders back at bayonet point.

Maxwell only retires a short distance, however, quickly reforming his troops and continuing this delaying action. When British light infantry come up in support, the patriots finally withdraw to rejoin Washington's main body at White Clay Creek. British casualties from these skirmishes are 25 killed or wounded compared to 30 Americans.

11 SEPTEMBER 1777. ***Brandywine.*** In order to check Howe's drive northeast against Philadelphia—the patriot capital—Washington decides to make a stand with 10,500 troops at Brandywine (Pennsylvania), centering his defense upon Major General Greene's division and Brigadier General Wayne's brigade at Chadd's Ford. On their left, Brig. Gen. John Armstrong is guarding Pyle's Ford, while Major General Sullivan on the right is responsible for all other northern crossings. As reserves, Major General Alexander waits behind the American right while Maj. Gen. Adam Stephen is to support the defenders at Chadd's Ford.

At 10:30 A.M., Major General von Knyphausen opens fire against this latter position and advances with 5,000 Hessians, launching a diversionary attack while Howe and Cornwallis circle left with 7,500 redcoats in a wide movement intended to turn the American right. An hour later Washington learns of Cornwallis's approach toward Taylor's and Jeffrey's Fords farther north, so he directs Alexander and Stephen to march their reserves to Birmingham Meeting House and cut off this threat. Instead, confused patriot communications halt this redeployment and at 2:00 P.M. two British divisions are sighted atop Osborne Hill, two miles north of Sullivan's flank.

Alexander and Stephen belatedly resume their march toward Birmingham, but after being joined by Sullivan they are attacked southwest of this place by Cornwallis. By 5:30 P.M., as Washington reaches this battlefield, Sullivan's left is already crumbling, although his right is temporarily shored up by Brig. Gen. George Weedon's brigade. Ultimately Sullivan's wing collapses, and the defeated Americans stream back toward Chester. At this point Knyphausen's Hessians increase their bombardment and drive across Chadd's Ford, forcing back Wayne and Maxwell and linking up with Cornwallis by 7:00 P.M. Patriot losses total 1,200 killed, wounded, or captured compared to 580 Anglo-Hessians. Despite his victory, Howe—who establishes his headquarters at nearby Dilworth—has been unable to crush Washington's army.

13 SEPTEMBER 1777. In New York State, Burgoyne's increasingly isolated 5,600-man British army crosses the Hudson River, probing cautiously down its western bank in hopes of finding General Clinton's reinforcements already awaiting them, in or near Albany.

19 SEPTEMBER 1777. ***Freeman's Farm (or First Battle of Saratoga).*** Having discovered a 12,000-man patriot army under Major General Gates barring his advance four miles ahead at Bemis Heights (New York), Burgoyne probes forward in three columns: Brigadier General Fraser leading 2,200 redcoats on the right in a wide sweep toward Freeman's Farm; Burgoyne taking a 2,600-man central column south then west to meet Fraser; while General von Riedesel and Maj. Gen. William Phillips follow the Hudson River road with another 800, guarding the British supply boats.

Brig. Gen. Arnold persuades the American commander to allow him to sally with 3,000 men of Brigadier General Morgan and Col. Henry Dearborn's units to maul the British vanguard. The Americans attack Burgoyne's contingent at Freeman's Farm by 12:45 P.M. while the British commander is still waiting for Fraser to appear. The British recoil and form up along the northern edge of this clearing, fighting back and forth against the patriots—who occupy its southern edge—for the next four hours.

Von Riedesel eventually sends 500 troops and two artillery pieces to reinforce Burgoyne, allowing the Anglo-Hessians to drive off the Americans with a heavy counterattack at nightfall. Nevertheless their casualties total 600 killed and wounded, double the patriots' numbers.

21 SEPTEMBER 1777. ***Paoli.*** In order to cover Washington's withdrawal north following his Brandywine setback, American Brigadier General Wayne conceals 1,500 troops and four guns two miles southwest of Paoli Tavern on the west bank of Pennsylvania's Schuylkill River to ambush passing British forces. Instead General Howe gets wind of this plan and detaches Maj. Gen. Charles Grey to surprise this force with two British regiments and a light infantry battalion.

The British attack shortly after midnight, producing chaos in the patriot camp. Wayne succeeds in extricating his artillery and numerous survivors by daybreak but suffers 150 killed, wounded, or captured during this action compared to six dead and 22 injured among the British. Wayne is subsequently court-martialled for inattention but is honorably acquitted.

24 SEPTEMBER 1777. British Lt. Gen. Sir Henry Clinton is reinforced at New York City, bringing his strength up to 2,700 redcoats and 4,200 Hessians. He now feels sufficiently strong to attempt a relief effort into the interior to ease pressure on Burgoyne's beleaguered expedition; he sets out nine days later with 3,000 troops in three divisions.

26 SEPTEMBER 1777. The British enter Philadelphia, Cornwallis being installed as garrison commander while Howe's main body encamps five miles away at Germantown.

3 OCTOBER 1777. ***Germantown.*** Two days after reaching Center Point (Pennsylvania), Washington's retreating 11,000-man American army reverses at 7:00 P.M. to return under cover of darkness and attack Howe's British encampment outside Philadelphia. The patriots know that their enemies are dispersed, with 3,000 redcoats guarding the overland supply routes from Delaware Bay, another contingent acting as Cornwallis's garrison inside Philadelphia; only 9,000 remain with Howe at Germantown.

At dawn on 4 October, the American vanguard crests Chestnut Hill—southwest of Germantown's main British encampment—Washington's intent being for Major General Sullivan and Brigadier General Alexander to continue advancing along Shippack Road while Major General Greene leads a wide encircling movement against the British right. Instead the first patriot units are driven back from Airy Hill by Capt. Allen McLane's light horse before Greene can even begin to deploy.

Sullivan consequently orders Brigadier General Wayne to cover his left and two other regiments his right before advancing against the British lines. This American approach—through dense fog—is further delayed at Chad House on the British left by Lt. Col. Thomas Musgrave's 40th Regiment, which makes a brave stand against heavy odds for 30 minutes. Greene eventually pushes forward to begin encircling the

British right, but by this time its units have already been strengthened, and he in turn must veer south to avoid being cut off.

Washington is about to order a general assault when Major General Stephen's troops sight Wayne's line in the gloom and mistakenly commence exchanging volleys with one another. Although order is restored within a few minutes, the American commander by now believes his plan has so miscarried that a retirement must be made. (Stephen is subsequently court-martialled and dismissed from the service.) The patriots withdraw in good order, without any vigorous pursuit by the British; only Cornwallis emerges from Philadelphia with three fresh battalions to follow Washington for five miles, soon giving up this chase. American casualties total 675 killed or wounded plus 400 captured compared to 540 dead or injured Anglo-Hessians and 14 prisoners.

Despite being repulsed, Washington's surprise attack proves that the patriot cause is still alive and well and his army dangerous. Howe remains in Philadelphia while the Americans withdraw northwest into grim winter quarters at Valley Forge.

5 OCTOBER 1777. ***Fort Clinton.*** This evening British Lieutenant General Clinton disembarks on the east side of the Hudson opposite Stony Point (New York), routing a small American outpost in a diversionary move. Patriot Major General Putnam immediately withdraws four miles into its surrounding hills, calling for reinforcements from Forts Montgomery and Clinton on the west side—which are Clinton's true objectives. To further deceive his opponent, the British general then leaves 1,000 redcoats at Verplancks Point, slipping the remaining 2,000 across the Hudson in heavy fog and occupying Stony Point by next morning.

Leading his soldiers up through 850-foot-high Timp Pass and down into Doodletown, two and a half miles from Fort Clinton, Clinton drives off an American patrol at 10:00 A.M. then detaches 900 redcoats to circle around Bear Mountain and attack Fort Montgomery from the west. Meanwhile he guides the rest in an encircling movement, and by 4:30 P.M. he is in position to storm Fort Clinton from the south. Although the former stronghold is carried without much difficulty, the latter presents greater problems, its defenses being protected by an abatis and ten cannons.

Having no siege guns and little room to maneuver, Clinton's troops must mount a frontal assault, supported by a single regiment circling Hessian Lake to attack from the northwest. The redcoats suffer 300 casualties overwhelming this garrison compared to 250 American losses under Brig. Gen. James Clinton. Next day (7 October), the British break the boom across the Hudson and also rout the patriot garrison within Fort Constitution.

7 OCTOBER 1777. ***Bemis Heights (or Second Battle of Saratoga).*** At 11:00 A.M., an increasingly isolated Burgoyne advances from his camp deep in New York State to make a second reconnaissance in force against Gates's 20,000-man American army, awaiting atop Bemis Heights. This redcoat thrust—1,500 men and ten guns—is led by Capt. Edward Fraser's Rangers and other auxiliaries in some woods on the very far right; Lieutenant Colonel the Earl of Balcarres's Light Infantry on the right; Major General von Riedesel's Hessians in the center; plus Maj. John Ackland's grenadiers on the left.

Gates instantly dispatches Brigadier General Morgan to attack the British right and Brig. Gen. Enoch Poor to fall upon their left. The latter's 800 patriots strike first, shattering Ackland's bayonet charge with a heavy volley, which mortally wounds this officer along with many of his men. Meanwhile Morgan defeats Fraser's rangers in the woods then wheels around to catch Balcarres's light infantry in their flank and rear. When the latter turn to meet this threat, they are routed by Colonel Dearborn's force bearing down upon their exposed left.

Burgoyne orders a retreat as more and more American units continue to appear—eventually 7,000 are committed to this battle—but his message goes astray, obliging von Riedesel to eventually make a fighting retirement on his own initiative into Balcarres's redoubt. British Maj. Gen. Simon Fraser then attempts to mount a delaying action with the surviving light infantry but is killed, so that after only 52 minutes the Anglo-Hessians are withdrawing in considerable disarray. American Major General Arnold follows up this success by launching two fierce assaults upon the British entrenchments, failing to carry Balcarres's redoubt but overrunning Lieutenant Colonel Breymann's (who is shot by one of his own men in the heat of battle).

This operation costs the British 600 killed or wounded plus another 200 captured, along with ten guns; American casualties total 150 dead or injured. Next day Burgoyne orders a general retreat, but his diminished army is soon surrounded by Gates at nearby Saratoga. On 12 October, the British officers vote unanimously to open negotiations toward a surrender, which begin two days later and conclude on 17 October with the capitulation of Burgoyne's entire army.

21 OCTOBER 1777. Col. Carl von Donop is detached with 2,000 Hessians and two field pieces from Howe's occupying forces at Philadelphia to attack American-held Fort Mercer on the Delaware River (New Jersey), which along with Fort Mifflin opposite on Mud Island (Pennsylvania) prevent seaborne supplies from reaching his army. Von Donop's contingent camps overnight at Haddonfield then sets out at 3:00 A.M. on 22 October toward Fort Mercer.

22 OCTOBER 1777. ***Forts Mercer and Mifflin.*** At noon, von Donop's 2,000 Hessians arrive outside Fort Mercer—an unprepossessing earthenwork located on Red Bank (New Jersey)—calling upon its 400-man garrison under Lt. Col. Christopher Greene to surrender. The patriots refuse, so the besiegers confidently prepare for an assault.

At 4:30 P.M. two grenadier battalions and the von Mirbach Regiment advance from the north while more Hessian units approach out of the west and von Lengerke's Battalion and a company of Jägers are held in reserve. Fort Mercer's outer defense on its northern side is only a brush abatis, which the defenders promptly abandon, giving the impression of great weakness; however, the French military engineer Du Plessis has reinforced its interior with a stone wall lined with some of the Americans' 14 guns. As the Hessians attempt to cut their way through the branches, they are decimated by a withering counterfire, which causes them to break and flee. A second assault is personally directed by von Donop but also fails, costing him his life. Hessian casualties total 400 killed, wounded, or captured compared to 40 dead or injured Americans. The British support ships *Augusta* and *Merlin* are also blown up out in the Delaware during this second attack.

The remaining Hessians settle in for a loose siege and a fortnight later are joined by a British contingent that arrives to bombard Fort Mifflin on the opposite or Pennsylvania bank of the river. This latter stronghold boasts 18 ten-pounders and four blockhouses of four guns apiece, manned by 450 patriots under Lt. Col. Samuel Smith. Rather than directly assault this island redoubt, the Royal Navy commences a long-range bombardment on 10 November with five land batteries located on Province Island plus a floating battery of 22 24-pounders upstream. These are reinforced on 14 November by ten warships from Admiral Howe's battle fleet, eventually compelling the American defenders to retreat across the Delaware into Fort Mercer on the night of 15–16 November after sustaining 250 casualties compared to seven British killed and five wounded.

Without its counterpart, this latter place cannot long hold out, so the patriots evacuate Fort Mercer too on 20 November, opening up the Delaware as far as the British encampments at Philadelphia.

6 FEBRUARY 1778. In Paris, French ministers sign a treaty of "commerce and amity" with American plenipotentiaries; they also sign a secret accord promising a military alliance.

7 MARCH 1778. Off Barbados, the 64-gun HMS *Yarmouth* of Capt. Nicholas Vincent chases a squadron of American ships, overhauling the 32-gun frigate USS *Randolph* of Capt. Nicholas Biddle. During the subsequent running fight, the American frigate suddenly explodes and goes down with all 315 hands (except four who are rescued five days later by the British, clinging to wreckage). *Yarmouth*'s losses total five killed and 12 wounded.

9 MARCH 1778. In the West Indies, the 24-gun *Ariadne* of British Capt. Thomas Pringle and the 18-gun *Ceres* of Cmdr. James Richard Dacres compel the 20-gun, 180-man warship *Alfred* of American Capt. Elisha Hinman to strike while the 32-gun consort *Raleigh* flees.

15 MARCH 1778. Having learned two days earlier of the treaties signed between France and the United States, Britain withdraws its ambassador from the court at Versailles.

22 JUNE 1778. The British decide to abandon Philadelphia, withdrawing to New York closely pursued by an American force, taking eight days to reach safety at Middleton.

8 JULY 1778. Having departed Brest on 13 April, the 48-year-old French Vice Adm. Charles Henri, Comte d'Estaing, arrives off the Delaware River with:

Ship	*Guns*	*Commander*
Languedoc (flag)	90	de Boulainvilliers
Tonnant (vice-flag)	80	de Broves; (flag captain) de Bruyères
César (rear admiral)	74	Pierre Claude Hocdenau, Comte de Bruegnon; (flag captain) de Raymondis
Hector	74	Moriès Castellet
Zélé	74	Louis Jacques, Comte de Barras Saint Laurent
Guerrier	74	Louis Antoine, Comte de Bougainville

Ship	*Guns*	*Commander*
Marseillais	74	Lapoype Vertrieux
Protecteur	74	d'Apchon
Vaillant	64	Joseph Bernard, Marquis de Chabert Cogolin
Provence	64	de Champorcin
Fantasque	64	Pierre André de Suffren
Sagittaire	50	François Hector, Comte d'Albert de Rions

Although he has captured a number of English vessels during his transatlantic crossing, d'Estaing's real mission is to furnish aid to the American forces. After detaching the advice ship *Chimère* toward Philadelphia he sails to Sandy Hook (New York), arriving two days later.

2 AUGUST 1778. France declares war against Great Britain.

17 AUGUST 1778. The French frigate *Concorde* reaches Martinique with orders from Paris to begin reprisals against the English. The West Indian governor-general, Claude François Amour, Marquis de Bouillé du Chariol, decides to launch a surprise attack against neighboring Dominica, for which he issues a call for volunteers.

Five days later the 32-gun *Concorde*—having proceeded on its voyage—surprises the like-sized HMS *Minerva,* capturing it after a two-and-a-half-hour engagement in which Capt. John Stott and his first mate are killed.

6 SEPTEMBER 1778. After sunset, 1,200 French troops and 1,000 volunteers depart Martinique aboard the frigates *Tourterelle, Diligente,* and *Amphitrite,* the corvette *Étourdie,* plus numerous lesser vessels. They slip ashore on Dominica next dawn, obliging the outnumbered English garrison to surrender without a shot being fired.

26 SEPTEMBER 1778. Off Boston, the 50-gun, 345-man HMS *Experiment* of Capt. Sir James Wallace and the 28-gun, 198-man *Unicorn* of Cmdr. Matthew Squire intercept the 32-gun, 235-man American frigate *Raleigh* of Capt. John Barry as it returns from commerce raiding. Although the American vessel is able to avoid capture for the moment, next morning it is crippled, beached, and taken.

25 NOVEMBER 1778. Cruisers from Admiral d'Estaing's fleet intercept three English transports and learn they are part of a much larger convoy bringing out several thousand reinforcements for the British West Indies escorted by three 64s and two 50s under Commodore Hotham. D'Estaing hovers indecisively off Désirade for the next two days before finally leading his entire force into Fort Royal (modern-day Fort de France) to strengthen Martinique's defenses.

11 DECEMBER 1778. ***Saint Lucia Campaign.*** One day after Hotham's convoy has reached Barbados, Rear Adm. Sir Samuel Barrington sets sail from

D'Estaing fleet exchanges broadsides with Barrington's anchored warships in Cul de Sac Bay, Saint Lucia.

the island with seven ships of the line and a troop convoy bearing 4,000 soldiers under Maj. Gen. Sir William Meadows. Two days later they fall upon Saint Lucia, disembarking a sizable contingent near Cul de Sac Bay, which quickly secures the anchorage. Next day the invaders march upon the capital of Morne Fortuné, which is evacuated without a fight by Gov. Claude Anne Guy de Micoud. The French retire into the jungle, allowing Meadows and his subordinate, Grant, to occupy the other major anchorage—the Carénage, three miles north of Cul de Sac—without losses by the evening of 14 December.

Meanwhile an American privateer has carried news of this activity to d'Estaing, at Martinique, who sorties with his fleet accompanied by numerous auxiliaries under Governor-General de Bouillé. They arrive off Saint Lucia during the evening of 14 December and, next dawn, attempt to disembark at the Carénage, believing it still in French hands. Counterfire from shore convinces d'Estaing otherwise, so he steers his squadron into Cul de Sac Bay, where Barrington has anchored his men-of-war in a line across the mouth, screening the English transports inside (still holding a good portion of Meadows's army). After a couple of passes, during which broadsides are exchanged at long range, the French admiral retires into Choc Bay and disembarks his own soldiers.

On 18 December the French army advances inland in three columns, led by d'Estaing, Bouillé, and the Comte de Lowendal. At the foot of Morne de la Vierge they encounter the English land forces drawn up in a defensive position; they repel these attackers with considerable losses after heavy fighting. D'Estaing's army suffers 840 casualties and withdraws out of range, leaving the admiral to contemplate another naval assault. But when the frigate *Iphigénie* signals that the wind is favorable for another such attempt on the morning of 24 December, the French squadron takes until 3:00 P.M. to work into position, at which point a discouraged d'Estaing calls off the operation. When word then arrives that Vice Adm. John "Foul Weather Jack" Byron is soon expected in the West Indies—having departed Rhode Island on 14 December with *Princess Royal* (flag), *Royal Oak, Conqueror, Fame, Grafton, Cornwall, Sultan, Albion, Monmouth, Trident, Diamond,* and *Star*—the French reembark their troops during the night of 28–29 December and return to Martinique by 30 December.

23 DECEMBER 1778. ***Georgia Counteroffensive.*** With the campaign season in the north halted by winter, 3,500 English and loyalist soldiers under Lt. Col. Archibald Campbell appear off Tybee Island at the mouth of the Savannah River escorted by a Royal Navy squadron under Commo. Hyde Parker. The British commander in chief, Clinton, has dispatched the army from New York almost a month earlier to mount a concerted pincer campaign with the forces of Gen. Augustine Prevost, who is to advance and meet up with Campbell, farther south in East Florida.

Georgia is defended by 1,050 Americans under Maj. Gen. Robert Howe, stationed at Sunbury (30 miles south of Savannah). In order to hold the capital, Howe enters Savannah on Christmas Day with 850 men, finding its fortifications in such disrepair that he establishes himself a half-mile southeast on the road leading toward the British beachhead. Here the Americans dig a defensive trench after destroying a causeway over a marshy stream with swamps on either side. Col. Samuel Elbert commands the colonials' left, Col. Isaac Huger the right, and Col. George Walton the extreme right. Howe has one gun on each flank plus two in his center.

On 28 December Hyde Parker's advance ships arrive at Giradeau's Plantation, two miles below Savannah, and wait for the tide after driving off a pair of American galleys. The invaders push back a small company under Capt. John Smith, establishing a disembarkation point from which a line of English skirmishers advance to within 800 yards of Howe's trench. Recognizing that the American general is expecting an assault on his left flank, Campbell sends a battalion of light infantry as a feint while sneaking Baird's Light Infantry and Turnbull's New York Volunteers by a secret path through the swamps to fall on the American right. Walton's unit is wiped out in a sudden descent from the rear on 29 December, creating such turmoil within the American ranks that Campbell runs his guns forward and orders his English infantry to charge.

Howe's army disintegrates and attempts to escape across the Musgrove Swamp Causeway, only to be overtaken by the onrushing British units. Some of the American right and center get through, but Elbert's militia is either captured or drowns in the swamp. The British suffer three killed and ten wounded; the colonials suffer 180 dead and 450 prisoners while losing three ships, three brigs, eight smaller craft, 48 cannons, 23 mortars, and their supply depot when Savannah falls. Despite the victory, Campbell does not pursue, allowing Howe to camp for the night eight miles away at Cherokee Hill before the American general retires to join Maj. Gen. Benjamin Lincoln at Purysburg.

6 JANUARY 1779. Byron's fleet anchors off Saint Lucia with several ships damaged by storms (particularly the 64-gun *Trident*) and missing both the frigate *Diamond* and the 74-gun *Fame,* which do not limp into harbor until 8 and 16 January, respectively. Disease also infects the British crews; a month later more than 1,200 are ill.

11 JANUARY 1779. D'Estaing sorties from Fort Royal (Fort de France, Martinique) to reconnoiter Saint Lucia next day, confirming that Byron and Barrington have effected a juncture when he sights their 15 ships of the line anchored within the main harbor. The British sally with 13 of the line and three frigates, obliging the French admiral to retire into port.

3 FEBRUARY 1779. After the victory at Savannah and taking of Fort Augusta, General Prevost decides to avail himself of British naval supremacy in the region to make an attempt on the patriot island-fortress of Port Royal (South Carolina). He disembarks Major Gardiner with 200 soldiers and one gun to try to carry the place by surprise; it is defended by 320 Americans under Brig. Gen. William Moultrie with three guns.

The British attack lasts three-quarters of an hour, their gun being disabled early on, but they enjoy the advantage of occupying woodland while the rebels fight on open terrain. After an indecisive exchange both sides run out of ammunition and retire simultaneously, although Moultrie sends his mounted troops in pursuit of the retreating British, harrying them back to their boats. Gardiner's attackers suffer some 50 casualties as opposed to 30 Americans. This setback discourages the British from attempting any further seaborne ventures until the fall of Charleston in May 1780.

10 FEBRUARY 1779. The fall of Savannah stirs embers of loyalist counterrevolution in Georgia's backcountry, where Lt. Col. John Hamilton is dispatched with 200 mounted troops to raise recruits. Another loyalist force attempts to join him from North Carolina under Colonel Boyd, soon swelling to 700 men. The patriots are concerned with preventing the juncture of this sizable column with Hamilton's company, which after bloodying a rebel contingent, has retired into Fort Carr.

Col. Andrew Pickens assumes command of the 350 Americans remaining in the sector, crossing the Savannah River at Cowen's Ferry on 10 February then recrossing near Fort Charlotte when he locates Boyd's approaching North Carolinians, who attempt to fight their way across at Cherokee Ford. They are stopped by a two-gun outpost manned by eight rebels and so move five miles upstream and traverse on rafts, continuing their march to Fort Augusta. Pickens shadows from the Georgia side, observing as Boyd's loyalists cross the Broad River on 13 February and encamp near Kettle Creek.

Next morning the outnumbered patriots surprise the North Carolinians—whose horses are grazing and cattle are being slaughtered. Col. John Dooley commands the rebel right, Pickens the center, and Col. Elijah Clarke the left. The loyalist pickets open fire upon perceiving the Americans' advance and fall back into camp, where Boyd manages to resist for about an hour before being mortally wounded; his army is routed. The patriots suffer 30 casualties as opposed to 40 among the North Carolinians, but they also capture 70 prisoners (five are hanged). This puts an end to the loyalist uprising in Georgia's backcountry for the moment, but 300 men among Boyd's defeated force are able to reach the concentration at Fort Augusta.

19 FEBRUARY 1779. The 56-year-old Adm. François Joseph Paul, Comte de Grasse Tilly, arrives at Martinique from Brest with the ships of the line *Dauphin Royal, Magnifique, Robuste,* and *Vengeur,* bearing troops. Despite such reinforcement, his superior, d'Estaing, decides to remain on the defensive at Fort Royal with 16 of the line and two frigates.

27 FEBRUARY 1779. ***Briar Creek.*** In Georgia, 2,600 American militia under Brig. Gen. John Ashe, plus 100 regulars under Colonel Elbert, are advancing down the Savannah River to break the British stranglehold on the coast. General Prevost, the English commander in chief for this theater, has countered by detaching units to repel the rebel offensive—in particular, 900 troops under Lt. Col. Mark Prevost, who are circling far west to surprise the Americans from the rear.

On 27 February Ashe's army reaches Briar Creek, pausing to rebuild a bridge and construct a road to link with the patriots under Brig. Gen. Griffith Rutherford at Mathew's Bluff, five miles east. Opposite Ashe, on the south side of Briar Creek, is Maj. John Macpherson with a battalion of British troops and some loyalist militia. On 3 March Colonel Prevost's 900-man flanking column takes Ashe utterly by surprise, trapping his army with a three-mile-wide swamp behind it, the bridge as yet unfinished. The American commander desperately attempts to regroup his army in three columns, only to have the British smash through his ranks, compelling the Halifax Regiment to flee. Patriot casualties total 200 (many drowning in the swamp) plus 170 prisoners, including Elbert. The British suffer only five killed and 11 wounded.

Ashe is subsequently court-martialed and censured for "want of sufficient vigilance"; only 450 of his militia rejoin the American army.

12 APRIL 1779. In Europe, French and Spanish plenipotentiaries sign an alliance against England.

26 APRIL 1779. The 55-year-old Commo. Louis Philippe Rigaud, Marquis de Vaudreuil, reaches Martinique with the ships of the line *Fendant* and *Sphinx,* having seized several English slaving stations in West Africa during his outward passage. Notwithstanding the arrival of this pair—plus the 50-gun *Fier* bringing in a convoy—Admiral d'Estaing still refuses to quit the safety of Fort Royal with his 19 ships of the line.

10 MAY 1779. Commo. Sir George Collier descends on Portsmouth (Virginia) with his 64-gun flagship *Raisonnable,* 44-gun frigate *Rainbow,* 14-gun sloops *Otter* and *Harlem,* plus the eight-gun galley *Cornwallis,* bearing 2,500 troops under Major General Matthew. The patriot base goes up in flames, *Elizabeth* and *Chesapeake* being secured as prizes. By the time Collier returns to New York on 28 May he is able to report the capture or destruction of 130 American vessels.

18 MAY 1779. Madrid secretly advises its Spanish American officials that war will soon erupt against Britain.

1 JUNE 1779. British columns push out of New York and take the fort at Stony Point as well as Fort Lafayette at Verplanck's Point on the far side of the Hudson River. Guarding the nearest ferry into New York City, these strongholds are of importance to the Americans' east-west lines of communication. Washington thus instructs Brig. Gen. Wayne to study the possibility of retaking Stony Point (*see* 15 July 1779).

5 JUNE 1779. After blockading Martinique for several months, Admiral Byron's fleet bears away south toward Grenada to escort a large merchant convoy north to Saint Kitts and then England. His Royal Navy warships reach the Saint Kitts capital of Basseterre by 10 June and remain five days to reprovision and effect repairs before exiting; he beats back upwind to resume station off Martinique by 30 June.

9 JUNE 1779. ***Seizure of Saint Vincent.*** Availing himself of Byron's absence, French Admiral d'Estaing detaches 35-year-old Lt. Charles Marie, Chevalier de Trolong du Romain and commander of the corvette *Lively,* to sortie in the opposite direction and attack Saint Vincent. Trolong du Romain quits Fort Royal (modern-day Fort de France) with three corvettes and two sloops bearing 400–450 troops, progressing slowly south because of scanty winds and strong countercurrents. On 16 June his expedition sights two English vessels, which he captures; next day he raises Saint Vincent.

The Martinican militia officer, Laroque Perein, has already infiltrated the island and primed its Carib inhabitants to rise against the English. As soon as Trolong du Romain's troops come ashore on 17 June and occupy the high ground above the capital of Kingstown, the English garrison of 464 men of the 60th (Royal American) Foot under Lieutenant Colonel Etherington surrenders without a fight, the capitulation being signed by Gov. Valentine Morris.

15 JUNE 1779. Near Charleston (South Carolina), General Prevost—the British commander in chief out of Georgia—decides to halt his invasion northeastward when he learns that General Lincoln is marching to the capital's relief. To cover his retreat Prevost leaves a 900-man rearguard under Lt. Col. John Maitland at Stono Ferry on James Island, which boasts three strong redoubts, an abatis, and a boat bridge across to Johns Island. By 15 June Maitland is ready to withdraw as soon as ships can be made available; five days later, before they arrive, he is set upon by 1,200 Americans from the Charleston garrison under Brigadier General Moultrie.

Having crossed the Ashley River, Moultrie marches eight miles until he arrives within 300 yards of the foremost British defenses at Stono Ferry, his presence screened by the woods. With Brig. Gen. Jethro Sumner commanding the right and recently promoted Brig. Gen. Huger commanding the left, the American attack commences on 20 June, catching Maitland completely off guard. After one hour of heavy fighting his Highland Corps suffers comparatively heavy losses; his Hessians begin to retreat. However, with the Americans already on the abatis, the British commander rallies the Hessians and throws in his reserves from Johns Island. This counterattack compels the attackers to withdraw with 150 casualties and another 150 men missing. Maitland's losses are 130 killed or wounded plus one missing, and he is able to successfully evacuate his command on 23 June, sailing to Beaufort on Port Royal Island (South Carolina).

21 JUNE 1779. In Europe, Spain officially declares war against Great Britain.

27 JUNE 1779. The 58-year-old Commo. Toussaint Guillaume Picquet de La Motte (better known as Comte de Lamotte Picquet) reaches Martinique with the ships *Annibal, Diadème, Réfléchi, Artésien,* and *Amphion* plus the frigates *Blanche, Amazone,* and *Fortunée* escorting a 60-vessel troop convoy. Admiral d'Estaing finally decides to use this strength to attack one of the major British West Indian bases, sortieing on 31 June with 25 ships of the line and numerous auxiliaries in hopes of falling upon Barbados.

Next morning, 1 July, Admiral Byron returns to Saint Lucia from his digression to Saint Kitts and learns that the French have occupied Saint Vincent during his absence. Meanwhile contrary winds prevent d'Estaing from reaching his original destination, so his fleet instead veers toward Grenada, coming within sight of that island next day.

2 JULY 1779. ***Capture of Grenada.*** D'Estaing anchors off Beauséjour Point, near the capital of Georgetown, and leads his 2,500-man army ashore. The English, under Gov. Lord Macartney, adopt a defensive posture, entrenching atop the Hospital Hill strong point with several hundred men and field artillery. The French advance this evening in three columns under Cols. Arthur Dillon, Édouard Dillon, and de Noailles while d'Estaing's ships launch a diversionary attack from out at sea. By 11:00 P.M. the assault columns come into contact with the defenders, driving them off Hospital Hill in confusion; by next morning the heights are in French hands. On 4 July Macartney sues for terms, Grenada's capitulation netting d'Estaing several hundred prisoners, 118 artillery pieces, and 30 merchantmen lying offshore.

During the night of 5–6 July the French admiral learns of the approach of a large British fleet. Byron has quit Saint Kitts on 3 July with 21 ships of the line, the frigate *Ariadne,* and 28 troop transports to recoup Saint Vincent from the French (*see* 9 June 1779). En route he is informed that Grenada is also under attack and sails to its rescue. Not realizing that d'Estaing has been forewarned, Byron makes the signal for a general chase once he sights the French fleet assembling off Georgetown at sunup of 6 July, believing he has caught them unprepared. The lead English ships open fire on the French vanguard by 7:30 A.M. yet are badly mauled, Barrington's vice-flag *Prince of Wales,* Captain Sawyer's *Boyne,* Gardner's *Sultan,* Collingwood's *Grafton,* Edwards's *Cornwall,* Cornwallis's *Lion,* and Fanshaw's *Monmouth* receiving the brunt of the concentrated French fire.

Byron regroups his scattered fleet, and by 9:00 A.M. he proceeds to Georgetown's harbor but again is surprised when the batteries hoist French flags and open fire. Reversing course, the English engage d'Estaing's fleet once more as they exit, then break off action and stand back out to sea by noon. The English have suffered 183 killed and 346 wounded, the French 190 dead and 759 injured; but only a single vessel has actually changed hands—an English transport bearing 150 soldiers.

HMS *Monmouth* is then detached from Byron's fleet to proceed toward Antigua and effect repairs while other Royal Navy vessels report considerable damage—notably *Lion, Cornwall,* and *Grafton*—as they limp toward Saint Kitts. On the French side, Capts. de Champorcin of *Provence,* Ferron du Quengo of *Amphion,* and de Montault of *Fier Rodrigue* are dead. Nonetheless, d'Estaing is able to dispatch the corvette *Diligente* to France with news of Grenada's conquest and Byron's retreat, after which Suffren occupies the Grenadines. The victorious French fleet retires from the region by 15 July (the same day Byron reaches Saint Kitts; *Monmouth* follows next day, and *Lion* seeks shelter at Sabá.)

After touching at Guadeloupe on 19 July, d'Estaing continues for Cap-François (modern-day Cap-Haïtien) with a merchant convoy, passing before Saint Kitts on 21–22 July and reaching Saint Domingue by the last day of the month. Here he receives word that the English have made great gains against the Americans in both Georgia and the Carolinas and so sets sail north with the entire fleet on 16 August.

15 JULY 1779. At Sandy Beach (near Fort Montgomery, New York), General Wayne begins a march at around noon with 1,200 patriots and two field guns to attempt to retake the fort at Stony Point from 625 British defenders under Col. Henry Johnson. By 8:00 P.M. the Americans have approached within a mile and a half of their objective and maintain strict silence as they subdivide into two columns to launch a simultaneous surprise attack from north and south. Each will be preceded by a party of 20 men to kill the sentries and hack through the abatis; two 150-man storming parties will follow them inside. A company of light horse under Major Murfree is also to create a diversion in the center, the company containing the only troopers authorized to open fire.

Shortly after midnight the attacking columns ford the marsh around the fort and commence their assault.

Colonel Johnson is deceived by Murfree's noisy feint, leading half his garrison down the hill, where they are cut off and captured. After 15 minutes of turmoil the British begin surrendering in isolated groups; they suffer 470 captives plus 95 killed or wounded. The Americans suffer 100 casualties during this bold stroke, which proves a great boost to the revolutionaries' morale. Nonetheless, the victors are obliged to evacuate Stony Point on 18 July, as Clinton quickly reinforces nearby Fort Lafayette so that it cannot be carried by Brig. Gen. Robert Howe's subsequent attack. Unable to remain in this untenable position, Wayne's garrison therefore withdraws, in the process losing the 12 British guns they have captured and shipped to West Point aboard an American galley.

14 AUGUST 1779. Commodore Collier breaks the American blockade of Penobscot (Maine) with his 64-gun flagship *Raisonnable,* the 32-gun frigates *Blonde* and *Virginia,* and the 20-gun sloops *Greyhound, Camilla,* and *Galatea.*

18 AUGUST 1779. At 10:30 A.M. 23-year-old Maj. Henry Lee—a 1773 graduate of Princeton better known as "Light Horse Harry"—sets out from Paramus (New Jersey) with two companies and some wagons as if on a foraging expedition. But at New Bridge, four miles away, he is joined by the rest of his irregulars, bringing total strength to 300 men and, at 4:30 P.M., strikes south toward Bergen. Under cover of darkness Lee intends to surprise the 200 British and Hessians under Maj. William Sutherland garrisoning the fort at Paulus Hook, a low point of land protruding into the Hudson River one and a half miles opposite New York City. Capturing this stronghold might help solve Washington's communications problems.

Lee's subordinate, Capt. Allen McLane, earlier reconnoitered the fort, finding it protected on its landward side by a salt marsh, tidal moat, and Harsimus Creek. The Americans decide to launch their attack just past midnight, before the moat can become filled by high tide at 2:00 A.M. Boats for a retreat are to await on the Hackensack River, west of Bergen. However, a guide misdirects Lee, and that detour costs his assault columns three hours. As they reach the marsh, Major Clark reports half his Virginia troops still missing; by now the ditch is also almost full, but Lee nonetheless chooses to press home his attack, reorganizing his force into two contingents under Clark and Captain Forsyth, with a reserve under Capt. Levin Handy.

The Americans wade through the marsh with muskets unprimed; the defense is not alerted until Lee's men enter the ditch. They then rush it, find an opening in the main work, and capture a blockhouse and redoubt, with Handy feeding men into the fight from his reserve. A number of British and Hessian troops are captured in 30 minutes of battle, although Captain Schaller is able to hold out in the fort's round redoubt. With dawn approaching, and the alarm being sounded in New York across the river, Lee orders a retreat with his 150 prisoners, most of the remaining 50 defenders having been killed or wounded (one of the few exceptions being the commanding officer, Major Sutherland, who has taken refuge in a blockhouse). Upon retiring Lee finds that the boats on the Hackensack have been withdrawn on the assumption that the raid has been called off and so faces a long march back along the Bergen route. Fortunately for the Americans, reinforcements arrive just before they are attacked by Lieutenant Colonel van Buskirk and his loyalists, who are driven away.

Although failing to hold the fort on Paulus Hook, Lee's venture nevertheless fires American morale; Lee and Wayne receive gold medals from a grateful Continental Congress.

27 AUGUST 1779. Gov. Bernardo de Gálvez departs New Orleans with a mixed force of 667 soldiers, recruiting another 800 as he presses northeastward to attack the advance British outpost of Fort Manchac (near modern-day Baton Rouge, Louisiana).

31 AUGUST 1779. ***Defense of Savannah.*** D'Estaing drops anchor off South Carolina's coast, setting a military officer named de Fontanges ashore to consult with American officials at Charleston about a combined effort against the English in neighboring Georgia. On 2 September five French men-of-war—including the flagship *Languedoc*—are damaged by an unexpected gale, yet d'Estaing's strength remains sufficiently impressive that the mere appearance of his 39 vessels creates a sensation off Charleston next day. (Even as far north as New York, the British high command shows some concern at the French expedition's sudden materialization, rescinding Cornwallis's orders to sail to Jamaica and recalling the Rhode Island garrison into New York; Washington, for his part, is equally irritated by d'Estaing's failure to support him directly.)

On 6 September the first French troops begin disembarking on Tybee Island at the mouth of the Savannah River, from which a British outpost hastily withdraws. General Prevost, commanding the English forces in Georgia, orders Lt. Col. John Cruger to march from Fort Sunbury and join him in the capital;

Spanish Gen. Bernardo de Gálvez

Lieutenant Colonel Maitland is to do the same from Port Royal. On 11–12 September d'Estaing lands his main body at Beaulieu (13–14 miles south of Savannah); when joined with American units under Brig. Gens. Lachlan McIntosh and Casimir Pulaski on 15 September, allied numbers rise to 6,000. Next day d'Estaing demands the surrender of Savannah, and Prevost asks 24 hours in which to reply. During this time Maitland arrives with another 800 men, raising the defenders' strength to 3,200, so the offer is rejected.

On 16 September General Lincoln arrives to assume command of the American contingent, and siege preparations begin (over the objections of Brig. Gen. William Moultrie, who calls for an immediate assault). Bad weather retards the arrival of siege ordinance until 24 September and bombardment does not commence until 3 October. Already d'Estaing is under pressure from his naval captains to withdraw because of the impending hurricane season, so on 8 October it is decided to attempt an assault next dawn. The main Franco-American thrust is aimed against Spring Hill, with diversionary actions on both flanks under Gen. Théobald Dillon and Brig. Gen. Isaac Huger. Both flanking attacks are driven back by heavy fire, and the principal assault proves poorly coordinated, the French arriving at their positions late then attacking early.

D'Estaing's troops suffer severely while covering 500 yards of open ground toward the English abatis, the only success being scored by Lt. Col. Francis Marion—the fabled "Swamp Fox"—who breaks through the southwestern abatis to take the Spring Hill redoubt. He is soon driven back by an English counterattack, and Pulaski's cavalry suffers heavily (their commander being mortally wounded), and McIntosh's force is misdirected into a swamp and fired upon from the river by the Royal Navy brig *Germain*. After the American and French assault columns withdraw, a heavy fog prevents any English pursuit. Franco-American casualties total 800 (of which 650 are French, including an injured d'Estaing) plus 120 prisoners; the British sustain 60 killed or wounded.

The attackers lift their siege on 18 October and go their separate ways: Lincoln retires toward Charleston while the French admiral prepares to regain France, first subdividing his command. The frigates *Fortunée, Blanche, Cérès,* and *Boudeuse,* along with the corvette *Ellis,* are to carry reinforcements to Grenada and Saint Vincent; troops belonging to Saint Domingue (Haiti) are to be returned aboard Lamotte Picquet's division; de Grasse's squadron is to reprovision at Chesapeake Bay before making for Martinique. The latter sets sail on 26 October with *Robuste, Fendant, Diadème,* and *Sphinx,* followed shortly thereafter by *Vengeur, Dauphin Royal,* and *Artésien.* On 28 October bad weather parts *Languedoc, Provence,* and *Tonnant*'s cables off Georgia, obliging d'Estaing to sail alone for France, followed four days later by his subordinate, de Broves, with *César, Hector, Guerrier, Protecteur, Vaillant, Zélé, Marseillais, Sagittaire,* and *Fantasque* and the 50-gun English prize *Experiment* (captured by d'Albert de Rions on 24 September; *Amazone* has also taken the 26-gun British frigate *Ariel* of Capt. Thomas Mackenzie on 10 October).

EARLY SEPTEMBER 1779. Lt. Col. José Rosado leads 800 Spanish troops out of Bacalar (Yucatán), attacking the English logwood establishments in neighboring Río Hondo (Belize). Capturing two sloops, a schooner, and numerous lesser prizes, he arms them with swivels and 300 men to sail farther south and attack the main English concentration around Cayo Cocinas (Saint George's Key).

6 SEPTEMBER 1779. ***Spain's Mississippi Campaign.*** Governor de Gálvez's expedition, now reduced to less than 1,000 effectives, comes within sight of Fort Manchac. Its English commander, Lt. Col. Alexander Dickson, decides to make a stand at nearby

Baton Rouge, so next dawn the Franco-Spanish militia under Gilberto Antonio de San Maxent storm Fort Manchac, killing one English soldier and capturing 20; the remaining six escape.

After resting his small army for a few days, de Gálvez presses on to Baton Rouge, where 400 British regulars and 150 auxiliaries have erected an earthen redoubt on the Watts-Flowers Plantation, defended by 13 cannons and a ditch 18 feet wide by nine deep. On the night of 20 September the Spanish commander sends a work detail into some nearby woods to draw the defenders' fire with their noise, stealthily installing ten siege guns on the opposite side. When the cannons open fire next day they pound the British fortification into submission by 3:30 P.M., Dickson surrendering not only his own stronghold but Fort Panmure (Natchez) as well. Some 375 English regulars are taken at Baton Rouge; another 80 are taken when Capt. Juan de la Villanueva reaches Natchez by 5 October with 50 Spanish soldiers to accept its capitulation.

15 SEPTEMBER 1779. ***Belize.*** At dawn Rosado's 300-man Spanish expedition appears off Saint George's Key (Belize), having slipped landing parties ashore the previous night to surprise the English settlements from both sides. Many logwood cutters are captured, their are dwellings burned, and slaves and vessels are seized at a cost of four Spanish dead and five wounded.

While the Spaniards are gathering booty, two Royal Navy frigates and a brigantine arrive off the coast on 20 September under Commo. John Luttrell. Their presence compels Rosado to retire to Yucatán, carrying away prisoners and destroying every settlement in his path.

23 SEPTEMBER 1779. In retaliation for the Spanish descent against Belize, Luttrell appears in the Honduran Gulf of Omoa with his 44-gun flagship *Charon,* the 32-gun *Lowestoft* of Capt. Christopher Parker, the 28-gun *Pomona* of Capt. Charles Edmund Nugent, the 20-gun sloop *Porcupine* of Cmdr. John Pakenham, the schooner *Racehorse,* and a number of lesser consorts. They bear a company of the Royal Irish Regiment under Maj. William Dalrymple, another from the 79th Regiment, and numerous Jamaican volunteers.

16 OCTOBER 1779. ***Omoa.*** Having probed the approaches to the Honduran port of Omoa but finding the San Fernando harbor castle too formidable, Luttrell and Dalrymple tonight disembark their Irish troops, many Royal Navy marines and sailors, plus 250 Baymen on nearby Puerto Cabello Peninsula (modern-day Puerto Cortés), to march nine miles into Omoa proper under cover of darkness and surprise its 200-man citadel under Capt. Simón Desnaux from the landward side. Progress proves impossible because of dense mangroves; dawn of 17 October reveals the English six miles short of their destination, so that it is not until midafternoon that they storm the town, easily scattering 50–60 defenders stationed outside Fort San Fernando. However, that citadel continues to hold out, even when *Charon* and *Lowestoft* bear down to open fire. (The latter soon runs aground, being badly mauled before it can be refloated and towed out of range.)

As a result, some of *Pomona*'s guns are landed and manhandled into position as a siege battery by 18 October, after which the besiegers launch another diversionary attack from sea the night of 19–20 October. With Desnaux's garrison distracted by this demonstration, four British storming parties slip over the walls, carrying the building before its defenders can react, at a cost of five English fatalities. Out in the roadstead the Spanish galleon *San Carlos* and another ship are seized, bearing approximately 3 million pesos in treasure. Dalrymple installs English troops to hold San Fernando then sails away toward Roatán and Jamaica with Luttrell. (On 28 November this new garrison is obliged to evacuate when a 500-man Spanish relief column arrives from the interior under Guatemalan Gov. Matías de Gálvez.)

28 OCTOBER 1779. Lt. Col. Francisco Pineiro sallies from San Felipe de Bacalar (Yucatán) with 390 troops aboard five captured English sloops, ten piraguas, and eight dories to again assault Saint George's Key (Belize) and its surrounding district. A second Spanish expedition of 120 men under Capt. José Urrutia sets sail aboard nine piraguas and four dories by 2 November to raze other English settlements in this territory.

EARLY DECEMBER 1779. Lamotte Picquet reaches Martinique from North America with *Annibal, Réfléchi, Vengeur, Magnifique, Diadème, Dauphin Royal,* and *Artésien,* his squadron so worn that the latter four vessels immediately undergo extensive repairs.

18 DECEMBER 1779. Parker's squadron intercepts a 26-vessel French convoy approaching Martinique escorted by the frigate *Aurore.* Lamotte Picquet sorties from Fort Royal with the only ships available to him—*Annibal, Réfléchi,* and *Vengeur*—but is powerless

to prevent the English from capturing ten merchantmen and driving another four aground.

21 DECEMBER 1779. Rear Adm. Joshua Rowley's 74-gun ships *Magnificent, Suffolk,* and *Vengeance,* plus the 64-gun *Stirling Castle,* intercept the 32-gun French frigates *Fortunée* and *Blanche* and the 28-gun *Elise* off Guadeloupe, capturing all three by next morning.

26 DECEMBER 1779. Clinton decides to leave 10,000 troops under von Knyphausen in winter quarters at Sandy Hook (New York) to keep an eye on Washington while taking a large contingent to campaign farther south in the Carolinas. Quitting New York the day after Christmas with 7,550 troops aboard 90 transports, he is escorted by Vice Adm. Marriot Arbuthnot's fleet: 74-gun *Russell* of Commo. Francis Samuel Drake and *Robust* of Phillips Cosby; 64-gun *Europa* (flag) of William Swiney, *Defiance* of Maxwell Jacobs, and *Raisonnable* of Thomas Fitzherbert; the 50-gun *Renown* of George Dawson; 44-gun frigates *Roebuck* of Sir Andrew Snape Hammond and *Romulus* of George Gayton; 32-gun frigates *Richmond* of Charles Hudson, *Blonde* (French prize) of Andrew Barkley, and *Raleigh* (American prize) of James Gambier; 28-gun frigate *Virginia* of John Orde; the 20-gun sloops *Perseus* of George Keith Elphinstone and *Camilla* of John Collins; plus the armed ships *Sandwich* and *Germaine.*

The expedition endures such a rough passage that it does not reach Tybee Island (Georgia) until the end of January 1780, many horses and much of the artillery having been lost. This delays the start of Clinton's southern campaign, as he must summon reinforcements and equipment from New York and Savannah.

11 JANUARY 1780. ***De Gálvez at Mobile.*** Governor de Gálvez departs New Orleans with 43 regulars of the 2nd Battalion of the *España* Regiment, 50 of the Havana Regiment, 141 of the Louisiana Regiment, 14 artillerymen, 26 *carabineros* (riflemen), 323 white and 107 mulatto or black militia, 26 American auxiliaries, plus two dozen slaves. They are traveling aboard the royal frigate *Volante;* the merchant frigate *Misericordia;* the galleys *San Vicente de Ferrer, San Francisco de Paula, Merced,* and another unnamed; the packet *Rosario* (hospital ship); the brigantines *San Salvador de Orta, Gálvez,* and another unknown; the galliot *Valenzuela;* and the royal brig *Kaulicán.*

After pausing at the mouth of the Mississippi River, they strike east on 6 February, working into Mobile Bay four days later in foul weather. Six vessels ground on its bar, so that de Gálvez experiences difficulty assembling his army ashore, although he is then reinforced on 20 February by 549 soldiers of the Navarra Regiment arriving from Havana aboard the 22-gun frigate *Caimán* of Cmdr. Miguel Goicoechea, 18-gun storeship *San Pío* of Lt. Pedro Obregón, 14-gun brigantine *Santa Teresa* of Lt. Manuel Bilbao, the 18-gun brigantine *Renombrado* of Lt. José María Chacón, plus an unnamed Catalan galley. They are accompanied by the American sloop *Terrible* of Capt. Joseph Calvert.

On 24 February the Spaniards move from Mobile Point to Dog River (nine miles below Mobile); three days later they begin probing the British outer perimeter. Fort Charlotte is invested by 29 February, de Gálvez calling on its commander—Capt. Elias Durnford—to surrender next day; he is rebuffed. After an 11-day siege, during which a heavy Spanish battery is emplaced within point-blank range, Durnford sues for terms by sundown of 12 March. The capitulation occurs two days later, when 300 prisoners are taken. A 500-man British relief column with three guns, approaching from Pensacola under Col. John Campbell, turns back upon learning of Mobile's fate.

3 FEBRUARY 1780. The 21-year-old Capt. Horatio Nelson quits Port Royal (Jamaica) with his frigate *Hinchinbroke,* escorting the transport *Penelope,* two brigs, three sloops, and the tender *Royal George,* bearing 100 regulars of the 60th Royal American Regiment under acting Lt. Col. John Polson; 140 of the 79th Liverpool Blues under Capt. Richard Bulkeley; 240 Royal Jamaica volunteers under Maj. James Macdonald; 250 members of the Jamaica Legion; 125 of the Royal Batteaux Corps; plus an unspecified number of black volunteers.

The expedition intends to cross to the Mosquito Coast, be reinforced by several hundred logwood cutters and Indians under militia Maj. James Lawrie, then advance up Nicaragua's San Juan River to attack the Spaniards. On 9 February Nelson and Polson pause at Providencia Island to secure a Central American pilot before continuing toward Cape Gracias a Dios to rendezvous with Lawrie's contingent.

10 February 1780. Having refurbished his army, Clinton sails for the Edisto River and Saint Johns Island (near Charleston) to march overland toward the Ashley River and eventually invest South Carolina's capital.

7 MARCH 1780. A Spanish fleet departs Havana:

Ship	*Guns*	*Men*	*Commander*
San Gabriel (flag)	70	600	Joaquín de Cañaveral
San Juan Nepomuceno	70	551	José Perea
San Ramón	64	577	José Calvo de Irrazábal
Nuestra Señora de la O (frigate)	42	284	Gabriel de Aristizábal
Santa Matilde (frigate)	36	265	Cmdr. Miguel de Alderete
Santa Marta (frigate)	36	271	Cmdr. Andrés Valderrama
San Francisco Xavier (brigantine)	10	24	Master Juan Vicente Carta
San Juan Bautista (brigantine)	10	24	Master Pedro Imán
Santo Peregrino (galley)	14	44	Lt. Juan de Herrera
Nuestra Señora del Carmen (sloop)	14	88	Lt. Miguel de Sapiáin

They are ecorting 26 transports with 2,150 troops under Lt. Gen. Juan Bautista Bonet to unite with De Gálvez's force at Mobile, and attack the English at Pensacola.

On 27 March this expedition inadvertently sights Pensacola, provoking panic among its English defenders, who spike their cannons and retreat inside Fort George in anticipation of an invasion. Instead, Cañaveral and Bonet steer toward Mobile, straggling in by 30–31 March. After lengthy consultations, the Spaniards decide not to attack Pensacola this spring; their fleet returns to Havana by 20 May.

13 MARCH 1780. Lamotte Picquet's squadron quits Martinique to reinforce Saint Domingue (Haiti).

22 MARCH 1780. While cruising along northern Saint Domingue, Lamotte Picquet's *Annibal* (flag) of 74 guns, *Diadème* of 70, *Réfléchi* of 64, and *Amphion* of 50 chase three large sail. They prove to be Commo. Sir William Cornwallis's *Lion* of 64 guns, *Bristol* of 50, and *Janus* of 40, who flee before the superior French force. Due to scanty winds only *Annibal* can overtake, fighting the English trio this evening and next morning until the latter makes good its escape and a wounded Lamotte Picquet puts into Cap-François (modern-day Cap-Haïtien).

23 MARCH 1780. The 67-year-old Vice Adm. Luc Urbain du Bouexic, Comte de Guichen, reaches Martinique with a squadron, incorporating de Grasse's division into his command.

24 MARCH 1780. ***San Juan River.*** After lengthy delays awaiting the arrival of Lawrie's irregulars—who fail to appear—Nelson and Polson drop anchor off San Juan del Norte (also known as Greytown or Saint John's) to begin their offensive into Nicaragua. All

Nelson at 19 years of age. The portraitist, John Rigaud, later added the depiction of Nicaragua's Fort San Juan in the background.

1,500 of Polson's troops are assembled aboard boats by 27 March, advancing upriver in two contingents. On 8 April Nelson overruns a small Spanish battery on Bartola Island; two days later British scouts come within sight of the 20-gun Inmaculada Concepción Fort—called San Juan Castle by the invaders (modern-day El Castillo, Nicaragua)—which bars their progress.

On 11 April Polson and Nelson's boats approach the stronghold, disgorging their army and four small four-pounders. Nelson opens fire by 13 April to little effect because of his guns' light caliber. Nevertheless, after two weeks' close siege the Spanish garrison commander, Juan de Ayessa, requests terms; next afternoon (29 April) he surrenders his 160 men (60 being Spanish regulars). Yet just as British colors are being hoisted over the fort a 500-man relief column appears on the far bank under Guatemala's governor, Matías de Gálvez, who promptly withdraws. Disease is already decimating the British ranks, however, so they do not pursue, satisfied with possession of their prize; they subsequently perish by the hundreds and evacuate six months later.

29 MARCH 1780. ***Siege of Charleston.*** Clinton's 11,200-man army slips across South Carolina's Ashley River, four miles farther north than the outnumbered American defenders expect. By next day the first

British columns are within 800 yards of Charleston's defenses, driving 5,600 patriots inside its walls and instituting a full investment within a fortnight. On 10 April Clinton calls for Lincoln's capitulation, which the American commander refuses; three days later the invaders detach loyalist Lt. Col. Banastre Tarleton with his so-called British Legion to attack the vital American supply depot at Monck's Corner (30 miles north).

Capturing a messenger en route, Tarleton learns of General Huger's dispositions, so he falls upon Monck's Corner at 3:00 A.M. on 14 April, taking the patriot defenders by surprise. The 300 American cavalry before Biggins's Bridge are routed and the militia guard scattered; only three men and five mounts are killed or wounded among the British as opposed to 20 American casualties and 67 prisoners. Tarleton's stroke not only nets 42 loaded wagons and 185 horses but, more importantly, cuts off the last important American supply route into Charleston—and the only avenue of retreat.

Before the beleaguered capital, Maj. James Moncrieff accelerates British siege operations by using prefabricated mantelets; by 19 April lines have advanced within 250 yards of the American ramparts. Lincoln offers to surrender two days later, but his demand for full honors of war is rejected by Clinton. At dawn of 24 April Lieutenant Colonel Henderson of the British right overruns Charleston's outer line of works. Some 75 miles farther northwest, Tarleton also continues to be active, checking the movements of a mixed patriot force under Col. Anthony White, which crosses the Santee River at Dupuis's Ferry on 5 May, capturing a loyalist officer and 17 men. Knowing that another 350-man American force is waiting nearby at Lenud's (or Lanneau's) Ferry under Col. Abraham Buford, Tarleton cunningly circles southeast and falls upon that place at 3:00 P.M. on 6 May with 150 British Legion dragoons, just as White is joining Buford. Without suffering a single casualty, the loyalists disperse both American contingents, inflicting 40 casualties and capturing 65.

Tarleton returns to the siege camps around Charleston with his prisoners and a large number of horses, raising British morale while deflating that of the defenders. After suffering heavy bombardments from land and river, the city council (which until now has opposed surrendering) decides to give up on 11 May; next day 5,500 Americans—including seven generals—march out of Charleston to capitulate. Patriot casualties total 230 compared to 270 British. Clinton prepares to return to New York with one-third of his army for spring campaigning while leaving 41-year-old Lt. Gen. Charles, Marquis Cornwallis, in command of South Carolina.

11 APRIL 1780. Two British sloops and nine merchantmen carry supplies into Pensacola from Jamaica.

13 APRIL 1780. De Guichen's fleet quits Martinique, covering the departure of a merchant convoy bound for Saint Domingue (Haiti) escorted by the 50-gun *Fier* and the frigate *Boudeuse.* The French admiral then intends to descend upon Barbados accompanied by transports bearing 3,000 troops under the Marquis de Bouillé. On 16 April, as the expedition stems the Martinique Passage opposite Dominica, it sights the battle fleet of 62-year-old Adm. Sir George Brydges Rodney, which closes to engage.

17 APRIL 1780. ***Encounter off Martinique.*** During this morning, Rodney's fleet maneuvers in three divisions to overtake the French, his van comprising Carkett's 64-gun *Stirling Castle;* 74-gun *Ajax* under Uvedale and *Elizabeth* of Maitland; Hyde Parker's 90-gun vice flagship *Princess Royal* under Hammond; 74-gun *Albion* of Bowyer and *Terrible* of Douglas; plus 64-gun *Trident* under P. Molloy. The center is made up of Collingwood's 74-gun *Grafton;* Bateman's 64-gun *Yarmouth;* Edwards's 74-gun *Cornwall;* Rodney's 90-gun flagship *Sandwich* under Young; Crespin's 74-gun *Suffolk;* Cotton's 68-gun *Boyne;* Home's 64-gun *Vigilant;* plus Hotham's 74-gun *Vengeance.* In the rear are the 60-gun *Medway* of Edmond Affleck; Joshua Rowley's 74-gun *Montague* under Houlton; 74-gun *Conqueror* of Watson; 64-gun *Intrepid* of Saint John; 74-gun *Magnificent* of Elphinstone; and 64-gun *Centurion.*

The English vessels do not sail as well as their opponents, so it takes some time to close upon de Guichen, whose van contains the 74-gun *Destin* of François Louis, Comte Dumaitz de Goimpy Feiquières; 64-gun *Vengeur* of de Betz; 60-gun *Saint Michel* of d'Aymar; 74-gun *Pluton* of Lamarthonie; Hippolyte Augustin, Comte de Sade's 80-gun vice-flagship *Triomphant* under de Gras Préville; 74-gun *Souverain* of Jean Baptiste de Glandevès; plus 64-gun *Solitaire* of de Cicé Champion. The center is de Nieuil's 74-gun *Citoyen;* de Framond's 64-gun *Caton;* 74-gun *Victoire* of d'Albert Saint Hippolyte and *Fendant* of Commodore de Vaudreuil; de Guichen's 80-gun flagship *Couronne* under Pierre Louis François Buor de La Charoulière; 74-gun *Palmier* of Commo. François Aymar, Baron de Monteil; 64-gun *Indien* of de Balleroy, and *Actionnaire* of de Larchantel. Bringing up the rear are Duplessis Parfeau's 74-gun *Intrépide;* Brun de Boades's 64-gun

Triton; plus the 74-gun *Magnifique* of de Brach; *Robuste* of Rear Admiral de Grasse; *Sphinx* of de Soulanges; *Artésien* of de Peynier; and *Hercule* of Claude François Renart de Fuch Samberg, Marquis d'Amblimont.

Having formed into roughly parallel battle lines and overhauled the French rear and center, Rodney at 11:50 A.M. signals his men-of-war to bear down on their opposite numbers; unfortunately, this hoist is misinterpreted by some to mean their literal opposite number—that is, sixth British ship versus sixth French ship—so that his fleet disintegrates into a straggling mass while attempting to carry out this unintended command.

The French open fire at 1:00 P.M. as Rodney's flagship veers down and tries to burst through their line, accompanied by a few consorts. He eventually succeeds after *Actionnaire* staggers out of the battle, only to be enveloped by numerous French warships as de Guichen gives the signal for his fleet to haul their wind. Both formations drift apart at 4:30 P.M., ceasing fire. The English suffer 120 killed and 354 wounded during this indecisive exchange, the French 222 and 537. Rodney is obliged to transfer aboard *Conqueror* because of extensive punishment absorbed by *Sandwich* then draws off to berate his captains. De Guichen claims a victory but must abandon his Barbados plan, instead retiring into Basse-Terre (Guadeloupe) to refit.

9 MAY 1780. While de Guichen's expedition is preparing to invade Saint Lucia, Rodney's fleet materializes off Guadeloupe, drawing the French out to sea. During the next fortnight both fleets circle warily, seeking an advantage. Fighting erupts on the evening of 15 May and again on the afternoon of 19 May, neither producing a decision. Rodney stands away and de Guichen retires into Fort Royal (modern-day Fort de France, Martinique) by 22 May.

18 MAY 1780. Cornwallis leads 2,500 British troops inland to stamp out the last vestiges of revolutionary resistance in South Carolina—specifically Colonel Buford's 350 survivors from the Lenud's Ferry disaster (*see* 29 March 1780) who are retiring north at Huger's prompting. It soon becomes apparent that Cornwallis's cumbersome army cannot overtake the nimble foe, so the British general detaches loyalist Colonel Tarleton with 40 dragoons, 130 cavalry, and 100 infantry (mounted double with his riders) to press ahead of the main body.

Tarleton covers 105 miles in 54 hours, catching up with Buford shortly after noon on 29 May at Waxhaw (North Carolina). The loyalist sends an officer forward under flag of truce to call for surrender; the patriots refuse, after which the British vanguard mauls the American rearguard under Lieutenant Pearson at 3:00 P.M. Buford halts his retreat and draws his remaining 250 men up in a single line under cover of an open wood; Tarleton deploys his attackers 300 yards away in three columns: 30 under himself on the left, 50 infantry and 60 dragoons under Major Cochrane on his right, plus another 60 in the center. (His other 70 men are to form up on a small hill to the rear as they arrive as a reserve.) The Americans hold their fire too long as Tarleton's men charge across the field and are broken by the impact. The British commander's horse goes down, leading his men to assume he is dead, thus precipitating a slaughter of the surviving patriots. The Americans lose 113 men killed and 203 captured, 150 too badly wounded to be moved; British casualties total 19 men and 31 horses dead or injured.

26 MAY 1780. Capt. Emmanuel Hesse descends the Mississippi River from Mackinac (Michigan) with 1,000 Anglo-Indian fighters to assault the Franco-Spanish forces at Saint Louis (Missouri). The fort is defended by 25 regulars, 289 colonists, and 20 cannons under Capt. Fernando de Leyba, who two and a half weeks earlier has received warning of the enemy's approach. Finding the defense well primed, the English and their native allies retire.

EARLY JUNE 1780. A Spanish frigate enters Fort Royal (Martinique), bringing word that Adm. José Solano y Bote is arriving in the West Indies with *San Luis* of 90 guns; *San Nicolás* of 80; *Gallardo* (officially designated *San Juan de Sahagún*), *Guerrero* (also called *San Raymundo*), *San Agustín, San Francisco de Asis, San*

The 74-gun Spanish ship of the line San Genaro; *modern drawing by Berenguer*

Francisco de Paula, San Genaro, and *Velasco* of 74; *Arrogante* of 68; *Astuto* (official name *San Eustaquio*), and *Dragón* of 60; frigates *Santa Cecilia* and *Santa Rosalía;* the former English sloop *Duque de Cornwallis;* xebec *Andaluz;* and storeship *San Gil.* This fleet is escorting 62 transports with 12,400 soldiers under Lt. Gen. Victorio de Navía Osorio, 38 merchantmen, and seven privateers.

De Guichen sorties with 15 French ships of the line, meeting the Spanish armada by 8 June; next day he persuades its commander to put into Martinique with the main body and convoy into Guadeloupe. Despite the offensive possibilities available, both admirals cannot agree on a concerted plan of action against the English, and disease begins to spread aboard the crowded transports. Eventually, both fleets sail together—but simply to deliver reinforcements to Puerto Rico. Solano then proceeds to Havana (arriving in early August with 1,200 sick), while de Guichen visits Saint Domingue (Haiti).

20 JUNE 1780. The veteran French Admiral de Ternay appears southwest of Bermuda with *Duc de Bourgogne* (flag) of 80 guns; *Neptune* and *Conquérant* of 74; *Provence, Éveillé, Jason,* and *Ardent* (English prize) of 64; plus the frigates *Surveillante* and *Amazone.* They are escorting 30 transports bearing 6,000 troops under 54-year-old Lt. Gen. Jean Baptiste Donatien de Vimeur, Comte de Rochambeau, to bolster the Americans.

Six sail approach out of the northeast, proving to be Commodore Cornwallis's 74-gun *Hector* and *Sultan,* 64-gun *Lion* and *Ruby,* 50-gun *Bristol,* and 32-gun frigate *Niger,* returning to the West Indies after escorting a British convoy north. Mistaking the French expedition for a lightly protected merchant convoy, *Ruby* charges ahead but is nearly cut off by de Ternay's *Neptune, Jason,* and *Duc de Bourgogne.* After exchanging several broadsides, the squadrons continue on opposing courses. Cornwallis does not wish to engage a superior force, while de Ternay is reluctant to expose his troop convoy to unnecessary dangers.

4 JULY 1780. The de Ternay–Rochambeau expedition appears off Chesapeake Bay near sundown, sighting about a dozen sail inside, which they fear might be a British fleet. The French therefore stand out into the Atlantic. Next morning they sail to Rhode Island, anchoring at Newport between 10 and 12 July (one transport becomes separated and enters Boston on 8 July). Rochambeau's army remains inactive for a year, reluctant to abandon de Ternay's fleet, which is blockaded inside Narragansett Bay by the British under Arbuthnot and Graves starting on 21 July, when they appear with 11 of the line.

12 JULY 1780. A half-mile outside Williamson's Plantation (now Brattonville, South Carolina), a 400-man loyalist camp under British Captain Huck—including some of Tarleton's cavalry—is surprised by 90 American partisans under Colonels Bratton and McClure. The British are pinned down between two wooden-rail fences and are quickly routed at point-blank range, suffering 90 casualties (including Huck himself, who is killed) compared to one American death.

25 JULY 1780. American Maj. Gen. Horatio Gates arrives at Coxe's Mill, assuming command of patriot forces throughout the south and incorporating Maj. Gen. Johann Kalb's 1,200 men into his army. Refusing to support Cols. William Washington and Anthony White, who are trying to build up a cavalry force for partisan raids against British lines, Gates orders his troops to immediately march on the advance enemy base of Camden (South Carolina). Two days later—27 July—he directs his army to take a shortcut through barren country rather than advance by the longer route around Salisbury and Charlotte.

30 JULY 1780. In an effort to further hamper British movements in South Carolina, 600 patriots set out under Brig. Gen. Thomas "the Carolina Gamecock" Sumter to attack the English outpost at Rocky Mount on the vital Charleston-Camden Road. Arriving on 1 August the Americans find three log cabins, protected by a ditch and abatis and manned by 150 British soldiers under Lt. Col. George Turnbull. Sumter calls upon the defenders to surrender; they refuse, sparking a general assault. Patriot Lt. Col. Thomas Neal breaks through the abatis, only to be killed with five of his men. Switching tactics, Sumter's men set fire to the buildings with burning wagons, and a white flag is hoisted—but promptly withdrawn when a sudden shower extinguishes the flames. After eight hours Sumter breaks off and withdraws to the Catawba River, a dozen men being killed or wounded on both sides.

3 AUGUST 1780. Gates's advancing American army is joined by 100 South Carolina patriots under Colonel Marion and Lt. Col. Charles Porterfield. Despised by regulars, these Carolina guerrillas are dispatched into the interior to watch and report on British movements, furnishing valuable intelligence.

5 AUGUST 1780. American partisans under Maj. William Davie attack a loyalist band under Col. Morgan Bryan, lodged in a farmhouse near Hanging Rock (South Carolina). This encounter, in which the patriots capture 60 horses and 100 muskets, escalates next day into a much larger clash when Sumter's contingent arrives from assaulting Rocky Mount (*see* 30 July 1780).

Sumter forms three columns and attacks Bryan and Col. Thomas Brown's loyalist forces, driving them in on the British center. Loyalist Major Carden attempts a counterattack from the right but is defeated by accurate patriot fire. At this point Carden seems to lose his nerve, resigning command to Captain Rousselet. Some 40 mounted infantry of the British Legion join in the fight, only to be driven back by Davie. While Sumter's men plunder the loyalist camp Carden pulls himself together and forms his men into a square; supported by a pair of guns, he holds out for the remainder of the engagement. By the time the Americans melt into the woods, the British have suffered 190 killed or wounded as opposed to 50 patriot casualties.

6 AUGUST 1780. Gates's army is joined by 2,100 militia under Maj. Gen. Richard Caswell, continuing to drive toward the British base at Camden (South Carolina).

13 AUGUST 1780. Cornwallis arrives at Camden with 2,120 British troops to reinforce the garrison under Lt. Col. Lord Rawdon, who has advanced 15 miles northeast in a vain attempt to check Gates's approaching American army at Lynches Creek.

15 AUGUST 1780. An American militia regiment under Col. Thomas Taylor surprises Fort Carey, a small fortification protected by a redoubt west of Wateree Ferry (South Carolina). The patriots overrun the outpost and capture its commander, Col. Isaac Carey, along with 30 men plus 36 wagonloads of provisions. The Americans subsequently take another 56 wagons and 700 cattle and sheep, being driven from nearby Fort Ninety-Six before retreating upriver to avoid an approaching British relief column.

16 AUGUST 1780. ***Camden.*** At 2:30 A.M. Gates's patriot vanguard under Colonel Armand clashes with 40 British Legion irregulars from Cornwallis's royalist forces at Parker's Old Field (northeast of Camden, South Carolina). Although 4,000 strong, Gates's army is ravaged by dysentery, yet retreat is now impossible given the proximity to the enemy. At sunrise the Americans discover Cornwallis's 2,100 men drawn up with light infantry on his extreme right, the whole British right wing being under Lt. Col. James Webster, the left under Lord Rawdon. Gates places his militia on his left flank, opposite the British regulars; his right is commanded by General Kalb. Six American guns are in the center, with the commanding general stationed 600 yards farther back.

Action commences when Webster attacks the American left, the patriot militia throwing down their unfired weapons and fleeing in disarray. Tarleton pursues the throng while Webster wheels on the American main body. American Generals Gates, Caswell, and William Smallwood, are swept away in this stampede; only Kalb's right wing mounts any sort of effective resistance. Although wounded, Kalb leads a brief counterattack before being mortally injured. The battle ends when Tarleton returns from chasing the broken militia and Webster drives the last American reserves from the field. Patriot losses total 800 killed plus 1,000 captured compared to 324 British dead and wounded. Cornwallis subsequently advances toward Rugeley's Mill and prepares to invade North Carolina, whereas Gates retreats 200 miles into Hillsborough by 19 August, eventually being succeeded by 38-year-old Maj. Gen. Nathanael Greene.

This same day, 16 August, the French Admiral de Guichen quits Cap-François (modern-day Cap-Haïtien) to escort a Spanish merchant convoy toward Europe, leaving Commodore de Monteil in command of the ten remaining French warships at Saint Domingue.

17 AUGUST 1780. Following his Camden victory, Cornwallis detaches Lieutenant Colonel Tarleton with 350 British Legionnaires and a cannon to fall upon Sumter's retreating partisans (*see* 5 August 1780). Advancing up the Wateree River's eastern bank, Tarleton sights patriot encampments on the opposite side this evening, bivouacking his own men without fires in hopes that the Americans will attempt to cross. But next morning Sumter continues north; still undetected, Tarleton follows to Fishing Creek.

By this time the loyalist foot soldiers are exhausted, so Tarleton uses 100 dragoons and 60 infantry to make a surprise descent. Catching Sumter's men resting, the loyalists charge. Sumter leaps coatless onto an unsaddled horse and flees (arriving at Maj. Davie's camp two days later); some of his men put up a fight from behind wagons, and Capt. Charles Campbell is killed. The British suffer 16 killed or wounded during the assault as opposed to 150 American dead and 300 captured. Almost 100 British prisoners are also liberated, as are 44 wagonloads of supplies.

7 SEPTEMBER 1780. Cornwallis takes Charlotte and prepares to penetrate deeper into North Carolina.

23 SEPTEMBER 1780. Resentful at his failure to be fully exonerated eight months earlier on some petty misconduct charges, Maj. Gen. Arnold—commander of the key American stronghold of West Point, in New York's Hudson Valley—defects from the patriot to the loyalist cause when his treasonous secret correspondence with British Maj. John André is discovered.

LATE SEPTEMBER 1780. The British believe that revolutionary ardor is winding down in the Carolinas, yet 1,000 patriots muster from both sides of the Blue Mountains to meet several hundred South Carolinians and march under Col. William Campbell to the enemy base at Gilbert Town. Loyalist Maj. Patrick Ferguson sends for reinforcements and makes his stand on 6 October at King's Mountain (South Carolina).

7 OCTOBER 1780. ***King's Mountain.*** Atop a rocky ridge with wooded and boulder-strewn slopes, Ferguson becomes overconfident, detaching 200 of his 1,100 men to forage while maintaining such poor watch that he does not notice eight patriot columns bearing down until Colonel Shelby's force arrives within a quarter-mile. Ferguson compounds his error by ordering bayonet counterattacks each time the 900 Americans storm the slopes, thus needlessly exposing his men to partisan counterfire. Eventually the loyalists are pushed back and surrounded in their camp at the east end of the ridge. Ferguson is killed along with 156 of his men (Capt. Abraham de Peyster assuming command). Another 163 are severely wounded, 698 captured; American losses total 90. The event compels Cornwallis to postpone his North Carolina offensive for another three months; American morale soars.

16 OCTOBER 1780. Bernardo de Gálvez, Spanish victor at Mobile (*see* 11 January 1780), departs Havana with 3,800 troops aboard 49 transports escorted by seven warships, five frigates, a storeship, a brig, and an armed lugger. Two days later, however, the convoy is struck by a hurricane, compelling it to turn back.

9 NOVEMBER 1780. Learning that Sumter is at Moore's Hill (South Carolina) with 300 Americans, Cornwallis sends Maj. James Wemyss with 100 mounted infantry and 40 cavalry from the British Legion to disperse these patriots. The English encounter Sumter's outposts at 1:00 A.M. on 9 November five miles south of Moore's Hill. Wemyss is wounded in the arm and knee, after which Lt. John Stark leads a cavalry charge directly into Sumter's camp at Fishdam Ford. But the attackers are silhouetted against the American campfires and suffer such heavy casualties that they are compelled to withdraw. Sumter also manages to escape, hiding near the Broad River until the British retire.

19 NOVEMBER 1780. Advised that Sumter is marshaling 1,000 patriots for an attack against Col. James Kirkland's loyalist outpost on Little River (15 miles from Fort Ninety-Six), Cornwallis sends Tarleton to drive the partisans away. Sumter retreats, and in order to overtake him Tarleton pushes forward with 190 dragoons and 80 cavalry, leaving his infantry and a three-pounder to follow. As the Americans reach the Tyger River, by 20 November, the loyalists catch up with their rearguard; Sumter turns to fight at Blackstocks, the American left anchored on a hill with five log-houses held by Col. Wade Hampton. Sumter also posts troops on a wooded hill on the right; Col. Richard Winn's men are held in reserve.

Tarleton perceives the strength of the patriot dispositions, so waits for his infantry to join. At the start of the battle Sumter orders Col. Elijah Clarke to turn Tarleton's right, while himself attacking the British center with 400 men. Both assaults are driven back, as is a subsequent try by Col. William Lacey against Tarleton's left. Sumter is seriously wounded in the shoulder and spine, after which Tarleton leads an unsuccessful cavalry charge. Both sides then withdraw, British Legion losses totaling 50 killed or wounded as opposed to three patriots killed and five wounded. Nonetheless, Tarleton resumes pursuit the next two days, as far as the Pacolet River and Fishdam Ford before Sumter's force eventually disperses. The loyalists return to Brierley's Ford by 1 December, while Sumter recuperates quickly from his injuries.

12 DECEMBER 1780. Britain withdraws its ambassador from The Hague to protest support being offered to the Americans by Dutch commercial houses. Britain officially declares war against the Netherlands eight days later.

5 JANUARY 1781. Turncoat Brig. Gen. Arnold appears before Richmond (Virginia), having reached Hampton Roads in December 1780 with Clinton's orders to destroy American depots throughout the theater; obstruct the passage of patriot reinforcements to Greene in North Carolina; and encourage loyalists to rise against the Revolution. Although a major

American supply center and the seat of Virginia's legislature, Richmond has only 200 troops under Thomas Jefferson and so cannot mount much resistance to Arnold's advance. Lt. Col. John Simcoe's loyalist rangers drive the defenders back from Richmond Hill, and Arnold offers to spare the town if British ships can come up the James River and remove tobacco from the warehouses. Jefferson refuses, and Arnold's army enters Richmond at 1:00 P.M. on 7 January, burning its buildings before leaving the same day.

7 JANUARY 1781. This Sunday morning Hessian Col. Johann Ludwig Wilhelm von Hanxleden attacks the 150 Spaniards holding Mobile Village (on the eastern shores of Mobile Bay) under Lt. Ramón del Castro. The raiding force, out of Pensacola, consists of 60 soldiers from the Waldeck Regiment, 100 from Britain's 60th (Royal American) Regiment, 200–250 Pennsylvania and Maryland loyalists, 300 Choctaw Indians, and 11 militia cavalrymen. Despite inferior numbers and lack of any warning, del Castro repels the assault, his garrison suffering 14 killed and 23 wounded.

16 JANUARY 1781. In South Carolina, Tarleton emerges from the rough country between Fort Ninety-Six and King's Mountain with 1,100 British Legionnaires, intending, in conjunction with a pincer movement by Cornwallis's main body, to fall upon the 1,050 Americans who have been disrupting the British rear under Brig. Gen. Dan "the Old Waggonner" Morgan. Arriving five miles behind the American encampment, Tarleton finds Morgan forewarned and preparing to make a stand on the Cowpens high ground. The patriot general is joined this evening by Col. Andrew Pickens's 70 men and posts a forward line of 150 concealed riflemen with instructions to fire on the British once they come within 50 yards then withdraw to Pickens's line, drawn up on the first crest of high ground 150 yards behind. Again, this combined force is to fall back under loyalist pressure to the left flank of a third formation, entrenched 150 yards up the hill and commanded by Maj. John Howard, with Captains Triplett and Tate on his left and right, respectively, and Captain Beale on the extreme right. A reserve awaits a half-mile farther back. In this way, Tarleton's men are to be lured into a succession of prearranged defensive positions.

17 JANUARY 1781. ***Cowpens.*** At 3:00 A.M. Tarleton's loyalist army sets out on a four-mile march toward Cowpens. As soon as cavalry patrols make contact, Captain Ogilvie is sent out to reinforce them and probe the American positions. Tarleton draws up his main force 400 yards from Morgan's forward line and orders Ogilvie's 50 dragoons to drive in the enemy skirmishers. Accurate counterfire quickly empties 15 British saddles, but the patriots retreat nonetheless. Unaware that the patriot retirement is a trap, the loyalists advance at 7:00 A.M., only to be checked by Pickens's line and suffer many casualties. Again the Americans withdraw, although this time prematurely. Nevertheless, when the British dragoons attempt a charge on the right they are checked by Triplett's riflemen then driven back by a counterattack from patriot Capts. William Washington and James McCall. A second assault launched at 7:15 A.M. by Tarleton in person is slowed but not entirely halted by Howard's third American line. At 7:30 A.M. the loyalist commander rides back and orders Maj. Archibald McArthur to envelop the American right.

The patriots, in refusing their flank, suffer momentary disorder, and a general flight begins but is promptly controlled by Howard. Still, the British follow the patriots down the hill's reverse slope, only to be repelled when the Americans turn and fire a volley at 50 yards, followed by a bayonet charge. Simultaneously, Washington and McCall hit the British flank and rear, obliging Maj. Timothy Newmarsh's regiment to surrender. The loyalist right tries to escape to the rear but is rounded up by American cavalry. On the left the Highlanders continue to engage Howard's entire line until Pickens's militia joins the fight from the other flank, compelling McArthur to surrender as well. Tarleton, notwithstanding these reverses, rides back to order his British Legion reserve to charge into the dispersed American forces, only to see them turn and flee. With the British facing defeat 50 men rally around the loyalist leader, who rushes to save his guns, arriving too late and seeing all of his gunners slain.

Tarleton retires, pursued by Washington, whom he turns and mauls before riding from the field and recrossing the Broad River with 200 dragoons, regaining camp by 18 January. Behind him lie 100 British dead, 230 wounded, and 600 captured; the Americans have only suffered a dozen killed and 60 wounded. This defeat proves a serious hindrance to Cornwallis's strategy, and a boost to American morale.

MID-JANUARY 1781. In order to counteract Arnold's activities (*see* 5 January 1781) and because a storm has driven Admiral Arbuthnot's blockading squadron off station, Capt. Armand Le Gardeur de Tilly sorties from Rhode Island with the ship of the line *Éveillé,* frigates

Gentille and *Surveillante,* and cutter *Guêpe.* These take a few English prizes, including the 44-gun *Romulus,* but otherwise accomplish little before being recalled.

30 JANUARY 1781. ***Sweep of the Dutch Antilles.*** Rodney quits Saint Lucia with 3,000 soldiers under Gen. John Vaughan to occupy Dutch possessions throughout the West Indies. After detaching a squadron under Rear Adm. Drake to maintain watch over four French ships of the line in Fort Royal (modern-day Fort de France, Martinique), the main body proceeds to Sint Eustatius, arriving by 3 February.

Seven English men-of-war stand into the principal harbor of Orange Bay under Rear Adm. Samuel Hood, followed closely by the main force under Rodney, fanning out to prevent escape. Fourteen English ships of the line, three frigates, and several lesser consorts are already inside by the time the startled captain of the lone guardship—the 38-gun Dutch frigate *Mars*—sends an officer out to inquire about the intruders' intentions. Before this emissary can arrive, a British officer comes aboard *Mars* to demand the Dutchman's surrender. The latter refuses to give up while his guns are still loaded and so opens fire, only to strike after a token exchange of shot.

Meanwhile Rodney sends another messenger ashore to demand the surrender of the entire island within an hour. Gov. Johannes de Graaff—with only 60 soldiers under his command—has no choice but to comply, the only resistance coming from a handful of American merchantmen in the roads who are quickly subdued. Rodney then detaches Hood in pursuit of a 24-ship Dutch convoy, which has departed Sint Eustatius a few days earlier escorted by a 60-gun warship under Rear Adm. Willem Crul. It is overtaken and captured on 4 February along with 23 of 24 charges. Rodney increases his haul by leaving the Dutch flag flying over Orange Bay for another month, luring many other ships—including a convoy out of Guadeloupe—into port to be seized. Altogether, 150 vessels are taken, 60 of them American-owned, plus 2,000 American sailors.

On 4 February four of Rodney's warships occupy nearby Sint Maarten and Sabá, commandeering another 40 ships. Smaller contingents occupy Essequibo, Demerara, and Berbice in the Guianas by late February, although Curaçao is not attacked, its Fort Amsterdam being considered impregnable.

1 FEBRUARY 1781. Advancing across the Catawba River at Cowan's Ford into North Carolina, Cornwallis sends Tarleton with some British dragoons to attack an American militia band at nearby Tarrant's Tavern. These smash into the unwary patriots, rout them, and narrowly fail to capture General Greene. The American commander is able to reunite with Brigadier General Morgan and retreat from Cornwallis as far as the River Dan before the British in turn are eventually forced to turn back south with a larger American army in pursuit. Although outnumbered, Cornwallis hopes to bring the rebels to battle.

12 FEBRUARY 1781. This morning a small Hispano-Indian expedition out of Saint Louis (Missouri) surprises the English garrison at Saint Joseph (Michigan), plundering and destroying it.

18 FEBRUARY 1781. Greene detaches recently promoted Brigadier General Pickens and Lieutenant Colonel Lee across the Dan River to break up a loyalist insurrection in North Carolina's interior. Hearing that several hundred men are marching to join the British at Hillsborough, Lee awaits them at the Haw River, Pickens's force hiding in a nearby woods. On 25 February loyalist Col. John Pyle arrives with 300 men, mistaking Lee's troops for members of the British Legion. Posing as Tarleton, the patriot commander convinces Pyle to pull his followers to one side of the road to allow his own soldiers to pass. Lee advances with his column and is in the very act of shaking Pyle's hand when the loyalist left observes Pickens's force in the woods and opens fire. In a one-sided fusillade, the loyalists suffer 90 killed, and the rest are wounded; Lee and Pickens suffer no losses.

28 FEBRUARY 1781. Bernardo de Gálvez quits Havana with the 74-gun, 410-man flagship *San Ramón* of Capt. José Calvo de Irrazábal; 36-gun, 290-man frigates *Santa Clara* of Cmdr. Miguel de Alderete and *Santa Cecilia* of Cmdr. Miguel de Goicoechea; 20-gun, 154-man frigate *Caimán* of Cmdr. José Serrato; and 18-gun, 110-man storeship *San Pío* of Lt. José María Chacón. They are escorting 28 transports bearing more than 1,500 soldiers of the Rey, Príncipe, España, Navarra, Soria, Guadalajara, Hibernia, Aragón, and Flandes Regiments for an assault on the British stronghold at Pensacola. Spanish dispatch vessels are also detached to New Orleans and Mobile to request additional support.

8 MARCH 1781. The 53-year-old Commo. Charles René Sochet, Chevalier Destouches, quits Rhode Island at sundown with his 80-gun flagship, two 74-gun ships, four 64s, the 44-gun English prize *Romulus,* and

Infantryman and cavalry trooper from Mexico's Príncipe Regiment, which took part in the capture of Pensacola

a 32-gun frigate to escort troop transports to Virginia. The convoy is carrying American reinforcements under 23-year-old Maj. Gen. Marie Joseph Paul Yves Roch Gilbert du Motier, Marquis de La Fayette, and 50-year-old, Prussian-born Maj. Gen. Friedrich Wilhelm Augustus Heinrich Ferdinand, Baron von Steuben. Next morning, Destouches's squadron finds itself alone upon the sea and so proceeds to its Delaware Bay rendezvous.

9 MARCH 1781. ***Pensacola.*** At 6:00 A.M. de Gálvez's expedition appears off Santa Rosa Island, disembarking its grenadier and light infantry companies this night six miles east of Punta Sigüenza battery, without opposition. When Col. Francisco Longoria's column approaches next morning, this English redoubt is found abandoned, although some fire is drawn from the anchored frigates HMSS *Mentor* of Capt. Robert Deans and *Port Royal,* as well as Red Cliffs Fort. De Gálvez responds by bringing two 24-pounders ashore and replying on the afternoon of 11 March, obliging the English frigates to retire out of range.

Shortly thereafter the Spanish fleet tries to cross Pensacola's bar, but Capt. Calvo de Irrazábal's flagship *San Ramón* draws too much water, so this attempt is deferred; supplies are instead offloaded on Santa Rosa Island. Unsuccessfully imploring the Spanish commodore to make a second attempt, de Gálvez boards his private brig *Gálveztown,* and with the sloop *Valenzuela* and two armed launches, dashes past Red Cliffs on 18 March. Shamed by this example, the entire fleet except *San Ramón* enters between 2:00 and 3:00 P.M. of 19 March, Calvo's heavy flagship standing away toward Havana.

At 9:30 A.M. on 22 March 905 Spanish reinforcements under Col. José de Ezpeleta reach de Gálvez overland from Mobile, followed next afternoon by 1,348 more sailing from New Orleans aboard 14 vessels, thus raising total strength to 3,553 men. Such numbers allow the army to ferry across from Santa Rosa Island on 24 March, landing on the mainland behind Barrancas. Meanwhile, British Gov. Peter Chester and the garrison commander, Col. John Campbell, have abandoned Pensacola in favor of defenses around Fort George. Indian allies of the British harry the Spaniards when they march from Tartar Point (Punta Agüero) during the evening of 26 March, to circle round Moore's Lagoon and en-

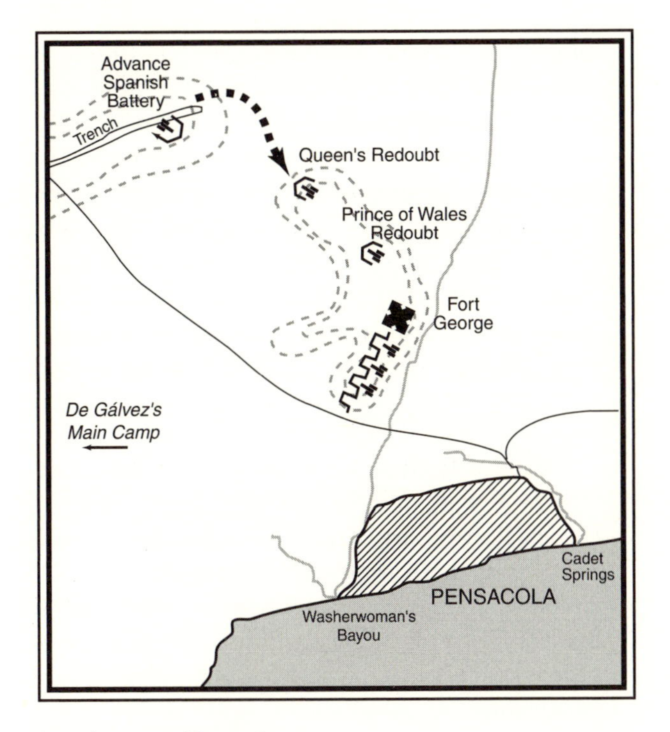

Spanish capture of Pensacola

camp southwest of Sutton's Lagoon. Another Spanish advance occurs on 30 March, when they move their base still closer to the British citadel.

De Gálvez, however, does not attempt a close siege of Fort George until after 19 April, when Admiral Solano materializes from Havana with the warships *San Luis* (flag), *Astuto, San Nicolás, Asis, Paula, Magnánimo, Guerrero, Gallardo, San Gabriel, Dragón,* and *Arrogante;* frigates *Nuestra Señora de la O* and *Mexicana* (hospital ship); plus the brigantines *Pájaro* and *Renombrado.* These are accompanied by 55-year-old French Commodore François Aymar, Baron de Monteil with the 74-gun *Palmier* (flag) under the Chevalier de Monteil, *Destin* of Dumaitz de Goimpy, and *Intrépide* of Duplessis Parfeau; 64-gun *Triton* of Deidier de Pierrefeu; 40-gun frigate *Andromaque* of the Chevalier de Ravenel; 22-gun frigate *Licorne* of Saint Urse(?); brigantine *Levrette;* and cutter *Serpent* under Lalone. Some 1,600 Spanish and 725 French soldiers are travelling aboard under *Mariscal de Campo* (Field Marshal) Juan Manuel de Caxigal, and Brigs. Gerónimo Girón and Manuel de Pineda. Admiral Solano further contributes 1,350 of his crewmembers, swelling de Gálvez's host to more than 7,400.

On 28 April, Spanish engineers commence digging a covered trench or tunnel toward a small hill that commands Fort George's advance outpost, Queen's Redoubt. This trench is completed three days later, allowing the besiegers to install a battery of six 24-pounders by 1 May while continuing their trench toward Pine Hill. The English destroy this new branch of the trench with a sudden sally which kills 18 Spanish soldiers, wounds 16, captures others, and spikes four field pieces. The besiegers' operations press on regardless, and on 8 May a chance round detonates the Queen Redount's magazine, leveling it with a blast that claims 76 lives, and wounds two dozen other Englishmen. Spanish light troops under Girón and de Ezpeleta immediately occupy these ruins, installing a new siege battery within point-blank range, which compels Chester and Campbell to request terms by 3:00 P.M.

The actual capitulation occurs two days later on the afternoon of 10 May, when 1,113 Englishmen surrender with 193 artillery pieces, 2,100 muskets, and other booty. This campaign has cost the Spanish 74 dead and 198 wounded. Prisoners set sail for Havana on 1 June, eventually being repatriated into New York by 12 July. De Gálvez meanwhile names Arturo O'Neill as Pensacola's new governor before departing.

15 MARCH 1781. ***Guildford Courthouse.*** In North Carolina, Cornwallis's 1,900 British troops turn and engage the pursuing 4,300 Americans under Greene. After a 12-mile march the loyalist vanguard under Lieutenant Colonel Tarleton clashes, at 7:15 A.M., with a patriot force under Brig. Gen. William Campbell and "Light Horse Harry" Lee. Tarleton distinguishes himself during the fight despite a seriously injured right hand. Meanwhile Cornwallis uses the distraction to draw together his other ten columns, to fall upon the enemy. The Americans deploy in three defensive lines, although they are not close enough to effectively support one another. Their front consists of a militia screen under Brigs. John Butler and Pinketham Eaton, who are behind a rail fence with their flanks supported by infantry and riflemen; the second line consists of 1,200 irregulars drawn up in a woods under Brigs. Edward Stevens and Robert Lawson; the third is 550 yards farther to the rear, commanded by Brigs. Otho Williams and Isaac Huger. There is no reserve.

After an ineffectual artillery exchange the British advance at 2:00 P.M., the American front line fleeing after a pair of volleys. The second patriot line holds better, momentarily encouraged by a counterattack by Col. William Washington; but when Lawson is wounded on the left their will wavers. British Col. James Walker's first assault on the third line is repelled by accurate musketry, which is followed by a bayonet charge. Finally, on the British right, Lieutenant Colonel Stuart makes the decisive attack, driving back

Washington's and Capt. Robert Kirkwood's men after some fierce fighting; by 3:30 P.M. Greene orders a general retreat. The American commander retires three miles to await stragglers, then withdraws into Speedwell Ironworks at Troublesome Creek; Cornwallis remains at the Guildford battlefield until 18 March before drawing back to Wilmington. The mauling proves a Pyrrhic victory, however, for the English general's smaller army sustains 532 total casualties as opposed to 78 killed and 183 wounded among the Americans.

This same day in the West Indies—15 March—a small English squadron under Cmdr. Lawrence Graeme of the 18-gun *Sylph* is detached from Sint Eustatius by Admiral Rodney to occupy French Saint Barthélemy two days later.

16 MARCH 1781. Commodore Destouches's French squadron sights Vice Admiral Arbuthnot's 90-gun flagship *London* in fog off the Delaware Capes; accompanied by two Royal Navy ships of 74 guns, four 64s, a 50-gunner, and three frigates. The formations close, running past each other and exchanging broadsides before separating at nightfall. Three British ships sustain considerable damage, and Arbuthnot retires south into Chesapeake Bay. The French *Conquérant* of Captain de La Grandière and *Ardent* of Capt. Charles René Louis Bernard, Vicomte de Marigny, are also crippled, suffering the bulk of the 72 killed and 112 wounded among Destouches's squadron. After a hasty conference aboard his flagship *Duc de Bourgogne,* he is obliged to retrace his course north to Newport (Rhode Island).

20 APRIL 1781. While Cornwallis's army is driving northeast through the Carolinas his subordinate, Lt. Col. Lord Rawdon, has remained behind to fend off partisan thrusts by Greene. In response, the American general has detached Brigadier Marion and Lieutenant Colonel Lee to operate in the east, while himself marching 140 miles toward Camden, the principal British stronghold in South Carolina.

Learning that Rawdon is prepared to receive him here, Greene by 20 April retires with his 1,550 men to Hobkirk's Hill to await reinforcement and resupply. After some desultory maneuvering, the British commander decides to assault this position with 800 troops, finding the main American force drawn up on a hill with Capt. Robert Kirkwood's regiment to the southeast, covered by a pair of outposts under Capts. Perry Benson and Simon Morgan. Greene has kept his dragoons and North Carolina militia in reserve.

Rawdon approaches from the southeast on the morning of 25 April, Greene countering with an attempted double-flanking movement. The British are temporarily checked by close-range fire from three guns, but as soon as the American line advances, Rawdon moves up his second line while extending his first. Thus Greene is in danger of being outflanked, especially when Capt. John Gunby's regiment collapses on the left. The latter withdraws and tries to reform his troops, but the British right seizes this opportunity and breaks the entire American left. The 5th Virginia Regiment holds at right-center, probably saving Greene's army from annihilation. A general retreat is followed by a gallant rescue of the three patriot guns.

Next day the American army moves back to Rugeley's Mill, with their artillery and supply train. Although Rawdon has achieved a victory, his losses almost equal the patriots'—38 British dead and 220 wounded, as opposed to 18 Americans killed and 248 injured. His smaller English force is therefore compelled to evacuate Camden, and retire toward Charleston.

22 APRIL 1781. Some 200 English settlers and Indians under John Blommart at Natchez, disgruntled by Fort Panmure's tame surrender to the Spaniards (*see* 6 September 1779), rise against their occupiers. Although forewarned, Captain de la Villanueva and his 76-man garrison surrenders next day after repelling the opening assault.

25 APRIL 1781. Baffled by Greene's resistance in the Carolinas and convinced that Virginia must also be reduced in order to put down the rebellion, Cornwallis strikes north out of Wilmington (North Carolina) with his remaining 1,400 redcoats.

28 APRIL 1781. Twenty ships of the line and three frigates arrive off Martinique from Brest under veteran Admiral de Grasse accompanying a French convoy. Shortly before sundown they learn that Fort Royal (Fort de France) is blockaded by 18 English warships under Hood, so they pause off Salines Point until they can gather greater intelligence from an officer set ashore at Sainte Anne. The French expedition resumes its course next morning, sighting Hood's formation at 8:00 A.M., which bears down to attack. De Grasse adopts a defensive posture while 74-gun *Victoire* and 64-gun *Caton, Solitaire,* and *Réfléchi* sortie from Fort Royal in support.

Broadsides are exchanged by 11:00 A.M., just as de Grasse's convoy safely enters port. Despite his numerical superiority, the French admiral is satisfied to hug Martinique's coast and fight a delaying action. At 6:30 P.M.

Hood draws off, his 74-gun *Russell* and *Centaur,* as well as 64-gun *Intrepid,* enduring the heaviest damage. Both sides suffer some 300 casualties, and no prizes are taken. On the evening of 30 April the British retire to Saint Kitts, pursued briefly by de Grasse before returning to Fort Royal by 6 May.

29 APRIL 1781. The Marquis de La Fayette reaches Richmond (Virginia) by sea with reinforcements, superseding General von Steuben as commander in chief for the theater.

8 MAY 1781. The French 74-gun *Pluton* under veteran Capt. d'Albert de Rions, accompanied by the 50-gun *Expériment* and several frigates, quits Fort Royal (Martinique) with 1,300 troops under Col. Philibert François Rouxel de Blanchelande to conquer Tobago. This same day, another French squadron probes the eastern side of Saint Lucia, disembarking 1,200 men after nightfall under the governor-general Marquis de Bouillé, who makes a brief reconnaissance before retiring with 100 English prisoners, and regaining Fort Royal by 15 May.

10 MAY 1781. The 61-year-old Commo. Louis Jacques, Comte de Barras de Saint Laurent, arrives at Newport (Rhode Island) aboard the frigate *Concorde* to supersede Destouches.

20 MAY 1781. Cornwallis reaches Petersburg (Virginia) from North Carolina, joining his troops with those under William Phillips and Benedict Arnold; further reinforcements from New York bring his total strength to more than 7,000 men.

George Washington meets Rochambeau at Wethersfield (near Hartford, Connecticut) to devise a Franco-American strategy to destroy this British concentration before Clinton can react from New York.

22 MAY 1781. Admiral de Grasse learns that Hood has put to sea from Saint Kitts, so dispatches a fast frigate to warn d'Albert de Rions and Blanchelande at Tobago while simultaneously preparing to sail in support of the expedition with his fleet and troops under the Marquis de Bouillé.

24 MAY 1781. ***French Occupation of Tobago.*** The expedition of d'Albert de Rions and Blanchelande disembarks at Scarborough, compelling British Governor-General Ferguson to retire to a defensive position atop Concordia Hill with 400 troops, 500 militia, ten guns, and many noncombatants. Meanwhile Rodney rejoins Hood at Barbados with his 90-gun flagship *Sandwich* and 74-gun *Triumph,* learning on the evening of 26 May that Tobago has been attacked; he therefore orders Rear Admiral Drake to sail immediately to its relief with six of the line.

Such strength proves inadequate, though, as more French forces are concentrating offcoast under Admiral de Grasse and Governor-General de Bouillé. English and French squadrons meet and circle warily; on Tobago proper, Blanchelande feels he has lost the element of surprise, so reembarks his army the night of 30–31 May. (This same night, the French ship of the line *Hector* loses its bowsprit in a collision with *César* and is obliged to retire to Grenada.) However, by noon of 31 May de Bouillé arrives overland with an additional 1,200 men to take Ferguson from the rear. The French governor-general sends his subordinate, Comte de Dillon, to call on the British to surrender; morale collapses, leading to the desertion of redcoat regulars, and final capitulation by 2 June. Meanwhile Drake has rejoined Rodney at Barbados and informed him of the increased French presence off Tobago. The admiral sorties with 21 sail, coming within sight of de Grasse's anchored 23 sail on 4 June. After observing the French from a distance throughout the next day, Rodney retires into his base.

LATE MAY 1781. In South Carolina, 1,000 Americans under Greene close in on Fort Ninety-Six, a key garrison held by 550 loyalists under Col. John Cruger; it is protected by a star-shaped redoubt with stockade and abatis to the east, and smaller Fort Holmes (for protection of watering parties) to the west. The patriots institute a formal siege under 35-year-old, Polish-born military engineer Col. Tadeusz Andrzej Bonawentura Kosciuszko, whose initial effort starts too close—70 yards—and is promptly wiped out by a sally. The Americans begin afresh 400 yards away and, by 3 June, are close enough to the star redoubt to demand its surrender, which is refused. The besiegers bring a tower into action, but Cruger counters by raising the rampart height; flaming arrows are also fired into the fort, but the loyalists strip the buildings of roofs.

On 8 June Lieutenant Colonel Lee arrives with some British prisoners from Fort Augusta and attempts to open new siege operations to the west, only to be repelled by yet another sally. At this point Greene receives word that British reinforcements are on the march from Charleston; he therefore orders Brigadier Generals Sumter, Pickens, and Marion to delay their advance. Meanwhile he launches a coordinated attack on Fort Holmes and the star redoubt by Lee and Col.

Richard Campbell, respectively; both are repulsed. On 19 June Greene begins withdrawing to Charlotte (North Carolina); two days later the British relief column under Lt. Col. Lord Rawdon reaches Fort Ninety-Six. American casualties during the siege are 185 men as opposed to 85 loyalists.

22 JUNE 1781. Natchez is reoccupied without opposition by a French force out of New Orleans under Etienne Robert de La Morandiere.

5 JULY 1781. Having returned to Martinique from conquering Tobago, Admiral de Grasse's fleet sets sail, escorting a 200-ship convoy as far as Cap-François (modern-day Cap-Haïtien), arriving three days later. Here he finds messages from the combined Franco-American leadership in North America requesting that he strengthen that theater. De Grasse duly takes aboard 3,200 troops furnished by Saint Domingue's Gov. Jean Baptiste de Tastes de Lillancourt, plus a small siege train, then sets sail on 5 August. He is pursued by 14 English ships under Admiral Hood.

6 JULY 1781. In Virginia, Cornwallis decides to discontinue his northern move, retiring south of the James River from Williamsburg to dispatch reinforcements toward New York. Aware he is being shadowed by an American army under La Fayette, the British commander tricks his opponent into believing that his main body is already across by afternoon of 6 July; in reality only Lieutenant Colonel John Simcoe's rangers have traversed with the baggage train, leaving 7,000 redcoats concealed for a mile along the wood-lined Williamsburg-Jamestown road.

American Brig. Gen. Wayne's 500-man vanguard gradually drives back Lieutenant Colonel Tarleton's rearguard, little realizing that he is being lured into a trap near Jamestown Ford. Reinforcements join Wayne at 5:00 P.M., but just as he closes in on the British position La Fayette—at last grown suspicious—holds back some reserve troops, leaving Wayne only 900 men and three guns. The Marquis then makes a personal reconnaissance from the riverbank and sends Wayne a belated warning. At this moment the trap is sprung; finding himself confronted by the entire British army, Wayne charges through a hail of grape and musket fire, desperately holding off the enemy host for 15 minutes until his army can retreat in fair order to Green Spring. From there he is able to extricate his column under cover of darkness, having suffered only 130 casualties as opposed to 75 killed or wounded among the British.

14 JULY 1781. Threatened by American partisan forces under Brigadier Gen. Francis Marion and Col. Lee, British Col. John Crates withdraws his 19th Regiment and a company of mounted rangers from their outpost at Monck's Corner (South Carolina) into Biggin Church by 14 July. He then retires 18 miles farther, reaching Quinby Bridge on the Cooper River by 17 July. After loosening the planks over this bridge, Crates waits for his rearguard to cross, only to be overtaken by Lee.

Captain Armstrong and Lieutenant Carrington lead an immediate American cavalry charge across, driving the English back; but the bridge's boards are so loosened that Captain O'Neal's troops are unable to join; the patriots are compelled to retreat. When Marion arrives he agrees with Lee that the British position is too strong, but Brigadier Gen. Sumter appears at 5:00 P.M. and overrules them.

The British form a square with their front covered by a howitzer, and their flanks by buildings and fences on Capt. Thomas Shubrick's plantation. The Americans deploy with Marion's infantry on the left, Col. Thomas Taylor's militia in the center, and Colonel Horry's cavalry on the right. Taylor renews the action by attacking across a field but is driven back by accurate counterfire. Marion charges diagonally, but after suffering 50 casualties and running low on ammunition, he too must withdraw. The American assault finally falters as a result of Sumter's failure to bring up his artillery, leaving Taylor to swear that he will never serve under this brigadier again. Marion and Lee retire with their dead and wounded, and Sumter draws off too when he learns of 700 British reinforcements approaching.

21 JULY 1781. While patrolling off Cape Breton (Canada) with the 32-gun frigates *Astrée* and *Hermione* the veteran 39-year-old French campaigner Jean François de Galaup, Comte de Lapérouse and knight of the Order of Saint Louis, intercepts a British convoy escorted by the 28-gun frigate *Charleston* (formerly the American *Boston*) of Capt. Henry Francis Evans; 16-gun sloops *Allegiance* of Cmdr. David Phips and *Vulture* of Cmdr. Rupert George; plus the 14-gun armed ships *Vernon* and *Jack*. After a long chase Lapérouse's pair engages the British escorts between 7:00 and 8:00 P.M., eventually compelling *Jack* and another vessel to strike. The French put into Boston with their prizes to refit.

19 AUGUST 1781. After feigning an attack against New York to keep its British defenders occupied, Washington and Rochambeau begin wheeling the

bulk of their armies south to crush Cornwallis's red-coats before Clinton can react.

25 AUGUST 1781. Barras quits Newport (Rhode Island) with eight ships of the line, four frigates, ten transports, and eight American consorts to sail to Chesapeake Bay.

27 AUGUST 1781. Hood appears off Chesapeake Bay; seeing no sign of de Grasse's expeditionary force (which he has unwittingly passed during his voyage), the British admiral sails to New York next day, anchoring off Sandy Hook with his 14 ships of the line and four frigates by evening of 28 August.

30 AUGUST 1781. De Grasse's fleet arrives off Cape Henry at the mouth of Chesapeake Bay. He finds Washington and Rochambeau hastening their armies south from New York to reinforce La Fayette and von Steuben, and attack Cornwallis before Clinton or the Royal Navy can intervene. The French admiral duly disembarks his troops under the Marquis de Saint Simon to travel upriver toward Jamestown and join La Fayette's 1,800 men, who are waiting at Williamsburg. Both contingents begin coming together on 7 September, and eventually hem in Cornwallis at Yorktown.

31 AUGUST 1781. Having been joined by Hood, Adm. Thomas Graves sets sail from New York with 19 ships of the line and seven frigates for Chesapeake Bay to prevent any juncture between the French fleets under Barras (sailing from Newport, Rhode Island) and de Grasse.

5 SEPTEMBER 1781. ***Virginia Capes.*** This morning, Graves comes within sight of Chesapeake Bay, his fleet in three divisions. In the van are Robinson's 74-gun *Shrewsbury;* Molloy's 64-gun *Intrepid;* Charles Thompson's 74-gun *Alcide;* Drake's 70-gun vice-flagship *Princessa* under Charles Knatchbull; the 74s *Ajax* under Charrington, and *Terrible* under Finch; plus Child's 64-gun *Europa.* In the center are the 74s *Montague* of George Bolven, and *Royal Oak* of Ardesoif(?); 90-gun flagship *London;* the 74s *Bedford* under Graves, and *Resolution* of Lord Robert Manners; Samuel Thompson's 64-gun *America;* plus John Inglefield's 74-gun *Centaur.* The rear comprises Francis Reynolds's 74-gun *Monarch;* Hood's 90-gun *Barfleur* under John Knight; 74-gun *Invincible* under Saxton; 64-gun *Belliqueux* under Brine; William Bague's 74-gun *Alfred;* plus the 60-gun hired ship *Adamant* under Johnstone, and 64-gun *Solebay.* The British admiral is further accompanied by seven frigates, and becomes greatly surprised to discover a superior French force already anchored inside.

De Grasse immediately gives the order for all his ships save *Experiment, Triton, Glorieux,* and *Vaillant* to exit, beginning this operation around noon. Contrary north-northeast winds hamper his sally, and Graves misses a golden opportunity to destroy the enemy fleet as it emerges piecemeal, unformed into any cohesive line of battle. Instead, overawed by de Grasse's vast numbers, he reverses course out to sea and tightens his own formation for the impending clash.

Gradually the French exit on an easterly heading, their van composed of the 74-gun *Pluton* of d'Albert de Rions, *Marseillais* of de Castellane Masjastre, *Bourgogne* of de Charitte, and *Réfléchi* of Cillart de Suville; Commodore de Bougainville's 80-gun vice-flagship *Auguste* under Castellan; de Monteclerc's 74-gun *Diadème;* de Chabert's 80-gun *Saint Esprit;* plus de Framond's 74-gun *Caton.* In the center are the 74s *César* of Coriolis d'Espinouse, and *Destin* of Dumaitz de Goimpy; de Grasse's 104-gun flagship *Ville de Paris* under de Sainte Césaire; 74-gun *Victoire* of d'Albert Saint Hyppolite; 80-gun *Sceptre* of de Vaudreuil; 74s *Northumberland* of de Briqueville, and *Palmier* of d'Arros d'Argelos; plus de Cicé Champion's 64-gun *Solitaire.* The rear consists of the 74s *Citoyen* of d'Ethy, *Scipion* of de Clavel, *Magnanime* of Le Bègue, and *Hercule* of de Turpin de Breuil; Commodore de Monteil's 80-gun *Languedoc* under Duplessis Parscau; plus the 74s *Zélé* of de Gras Préville, *Hector* of Renaud d'Aleins, and *Souverain* of de Glandevès.

By afternoon Graves edges downwind and both vans converge, opening fire around 4:00 P.M. At this point the wind dies away, leaving both fleets only partially engaged, yet a furious fight nonetheless ensues between the two advance divisions over the next couple of hours, HMSS *Terrible, Montague, Shrewsbury, Intrepid,* and *Ajax* receiving considerable damage (the former being set afire and abandoned five days later). The British suffer 79 killed and 230 wounded; the French 220 casualties.

But it is Graves who breaks off this action and retires, hovering in the middle distance over the next three days in hopes of gaining some advantage. Despite repeated maneuverings, the British are unable to find any significant opening, and by evening of 9 September Graves retreats toward New York (which he reaches on 20 September), leaving Cornwallis's army isolated in Virginia. On 10 September, the French fleet is joined by Barras's squadron from Newport, and on

11 September the British frigates *Isis* and *Richmond* are captured by de Grasse while attempting to reach the beleaguered British soldiers ashore, after which the French admiral returns to anchor.

8 SEPTEMBER 1781. ***Eutaw Springs.*** In South Carolina, General Greene's patriot army—now 2,200 strong—resumes its offensive, determined to surprise the last major British concentration in this theater: Lt. Col. Alexander Stuart's 1,800 men at Eutaw Springs. This British commander has learned of Greene's approach when one of his foraging parties brings in two North Carolina deserters. Stuart sends out a morning reconnoitering party under loyalist Capt. John Coffin, who is lured into an ambush four miles outside camp, losing five men killed and 40 captured. Nevertheless, he manages to return and warn Stuart, who draws his troops up for battle. Maj. John Marjoribanks is posted on the British right in a blackjack thicket to protect against cavalry charges, Coffin's foot and horse are held in reserve on the left, while Major Sheridan is placed in the right rear to hold a brick plantation house. Stuart assembles the remainder of his forces facing south, at right angles to the Santee River.

At the onset Stuart seeks merely to hold his ground, but his left wing inadvertently advances, driving back the American militia. Greene plugs this gap with Brig. Gen. Jethro Sumner's North Carolina troops, who repel the British, only to in turn be broken by Stuart's reserves. Greene then commits his main body, and in fierce hand-to-hand fighting the British left-center are driven back among their tents. However, Marjoribanks's flank holds, and patriot assaults by Cols. William Washington and Wade Hampton are badly mauled. The American center meanwhile disintegrates into drunken rioting as it swarms over the British encampment, while on the right Lieutenant Colonel Lee hopes to link up with Maj. Joseph Egleston and defeat Coffin, only to find that Egleston has already been driven from the field.

The battle finally centers around the brick house, where Marjoribanks counterattacks against the Americans, first capturing their guns, then driving them back toward the woods despite being mortally wounded. Although obliged to retreat, Greene is better able to absorb his 520 casualties than Stuart is to replace 690 killed, wounded, or missing. The British must therefore withdraw into Charleston, leaving South Carolina's interior once more in rebel hands.

26 SEPTEMBER 1781. ***Yorktown.*** A huge force of 20,000 American and French troops gradually begins coming together under Washington and Rochambeau—a large portion being transported down Chesapeake Bay by water—to begin investing Cornwallis's 9,750 British and Hessians, already cornered upon the Yorktown Peninsula by La Fayette, von Steuben, and Wayne. Aware of his plight, the British commander detaches Lt. Cols. Tarleton and Tom Dundas to hold Gloucester across the York River, while using his main forces to dig defensive works close to Yorktown proper (not having enough troops to fully man a perimeter longer than 1,000 yards).

Eventually, Yorktown's inner line of defenses sprouts 14 batteries, 65 guns, and ten redoubts, its principal strong point being the "Horn Work" to the south. Ahead of this are outworks to dispute the flat ground; to the west—covering the Williamsburg Road—is the Fusilier Redoubt, with Redoubts Nine and Ten on its opposite flank. A French force under Brigadier General de Choisy bottles up the British troops within Gloucester while the main army begins its investment of Yorktown on 6 October by commencing a 2,000-yard parallel. On 9 October the besiegers' bombardment starts, and work gets under way on a second parallel. At this point it becomes necessary to reduce Redoubts Nine and Ten, the former being attacked by a French force under Col. Guillaume Deuxponts, the latter by a mixed force under Lt. Col. Alexander Hamilton. (Simultaneous diversionary attacks are also mounted against the Fusilier Redoubt and Gloucester.) The British defenders of Redoubt Nine, under Lieutenant Colonel McPherson, inflict heavy casualties as the French penetrate their abatis but surrender after a bayonet charge; Hamilton's assault on Redoubt Ten is carried out successfully, with few casualties.

There is no British counterattack, but the defense trains all available guns on its lost redoubts. The completion of the second parallel allows Franco-American siege batteries to be installed perilously close to the fortifications. A sally by British Lt. Col. Robert Abercrombie's men is made at 4:00 A.M. on 16 October but proves only partially successful; Cornwallis's desperate attempt to ferry his army across to Gloucester that night is thwarted by a sudden storm and lack of boats. On the morning of 17 October 100 Franco-American pieces begin an even fiercer bombardment, and by 10:00 A.M. the British commander requests a truce to discuss terms. The capitulation is signed at noon on 20 October, the Americans and French having sustained 400 casualties during the brief siege as opposed to 600 British and Hessians—although 8,080 are subsequently marched into captivity, effectively ending Britain's hopes of suppressing the American Revolution by dint of arms.

19 OCTOBER 1781. Admiral Graves's fleet, reinforced by the arrival of six more Royal Navy ships at the beginning of the month, quits New York for Virginia with a troop convoy bearing 7,000 reinforcements under Clinton.

27 OCTOBER 1781. Clinton arrives off Chesapeake Bay too late to save Cornwallis, who has surrendered one week earlier.

5 NOVEMBER 1781. Admiral de Grasse's fleet sets sail from Chesapeake Bay for Martinique, save for *Romulus* and two frigates, which are left in Virginia. *Victoire, Vaillant, Provence, Triton,* and the frigates *Gentille* and *Railleuse* are detached during the voyage to Saint Domingue to escort a merchant convoy home to France.

16 NOVEMBER 1781. ***French Reconquest of Dutch Antilles.*** A 1,200-man expedition sets sail from Martinique under Governor-General de Bouillé aboard the frigates *Amazone* and *Galathée,* corvette *Aigle,* and several privateer craft to wrest Sint Eustatius back from the English (*see* 30 January 1781). Because of contrary winds the island is not raised until evening of 25 November; by 3:00 A.M. next day only 400 Frenchmen have managed to struggle ashore through high surf.

De Bouillé nonetheless leads a march to Sint Eustatius's capital, arriving by 6:00 A.M. as part of the British garrison exercises on the beach. Mistaking the red tunics of an Irish contingent at the head of de Bouillé's column for friendly forces, the English are mowed down by an unexpected volley at point-blank range. The English governor is then seized as he returns from a morning ride; 200 French troops under the Comte de Dillon quickly overrun the barracks, and 100 under Major de Frène capture the citadel. Soon 700 prisoners are rounded up, after which de Bouillé sends detachments to reoccupy neighboring Sint Maarten and Sabá before returning to Martinique.

26 NOVEMBER 1781. Admiral de Grasse reaches Fort Royal (modern-day Fort de France, Martinique) from Virginia.

5 JANUARY 1782. ***Saint Kitts Offensive.*** De Grasse and Governor-General de Bouillé set sail from Martinique with 26 ships of the line and a troop convoy, reaching Salines Bay (just south of Basseterre, on the western coast of Saint Kitts) by 11 January. The British have already retired into their Brimstone Hill stronghold under General Frazer, so the French landing forces disembark without opposition and institute a siege.

Hood's anchored warships prevent de Grasse's fleet (left) from disrupting the British troop disembarkation in Frigate Bay, Saint Kitts.

On 24 January 22 English warships under Admiral Hood are sighted near Nevis, evidently intending to reinforce Saint Kitts with troops from Barbados and Antigua. De Grasse exits to intercept, but by next dawn Hood has veered toward Montserrat and contrary east-southeast winds impede the French from reaching the British before they circle north around Nevis and drop anchor in Frigate Bay, off Basseterre. De Grasse attacks the anchored British expedition on both the morning and afternoon of 26 January but is beaten off, their disembarkation proceeding apace. During these naval engagements the French suffer 107 killed and 207 wounded, compared to 72 dead and 244 injured among the British.

On 28 January the 1,500-man British vanguard advances against the town of Basseterre under General Prescott while its French occupiers fight a delaying action under Colonel de Fléchin until the Marquis de Bouillé can hasten reinforcements across the island. Prescott's drive is eventually repelled, but otherwise French efforts continue to be hampered by the loss of their field artillery in a wreck while approaching Saint Kitts and the capture of an ammunition ship by one of Hood's frigates. *Caton*'s 24-pounders are therefore disembarked and used by de Bouillé to batter Brimstone Hill into submission by 12 February. Next day de Grasse ventures to Nevis to meet an arriving convoy of French victuallers; Hood avails himself of the opportunity to escape in the opposite direction on the morning of 14 February.

With Saint Kitts now in French hands, de Grasse and de Bouillé install a garrison and return to Martinique by 26 February.

22 JANUARY 1782. The former Dutch colony of Demerara is recaptured by the French naval Capt. Armand Guy Simon de Coëtnempren, Comte de Kersaint, with his 32-gun flagship *Iphigénie* and four lesser consorts, followed by Berbice on 5 February and Essequibo on 8 February. Five Royal Navy auxiliaries are seized during this operation: the 20-gun *Orinoque* of Cmdr. William Tahourdin, 16-gun *Barbuda* of Cmdr. Francis Pender, 18-gun *Sylph* of Cmdr. Lawrence Graeme, 16-gun *Stormont* of Cmdr. Christmas Paul, and 16-gun brig *Rodney* of Lt. John Douglas Brisbane.

22 FEBRUARY 1782. The English island of Montserrat surrenders to a French squadron under Admiral de Barras.

LATE FEBRUARY 1782. Admiral Rodney reaches the Lesser Antilles with 17 ships of the line to reinforce Hood against an anticipated Franco-Spanish junction. Assuming overall command of the combined force, Rodney spreads his fleet between La Désirade in the north to Saint Vincent in the south to check vessels arriving by the trade winds across the Atlantic.

14 MARCH 1782. Spanish Commo. Enrique Macdonell sets sail from Trujillo (Honduras) with the royal frigates *Santa Matilde* and *Santa Cecilia;* privateer frigate *Nuestra Señora de la Concepción;* four gunboats; and 16 troop transports bearing 1,000 soldiers. The force falls upon Roatán, bombarding its three main batteries before storming ashore and exterminating the British outpost.

20 MARCH 1782. A French convoy escorted by Capt. Mithon de Genouilly reaches Fort Royal (modern-day Fort de France, Martinique), having eluded Rodney's blockade by circling north of La Désirade and hugging the coastlines of Guadeloupe and Dominica. This evasion prompts the British admiral to regroup his fleet off Saint Lucia.

8 APRIL 1782. At dawn a 123-ship French convoy sorties from Martinique escorted by the ships *Experiment* and *Sagittaire* plus the frigates *Railleuse, Engageante,* and *Richmond* (an English prize). A few hours later Admiral de Grasse stands out to sea with 33 ships of the line to protect these merchantmen against Rodney's pursuit. The British admiral immediately sorties from nearby Saint Lucia with a similar-sized force, after his spotting frigates advise him of de Grasse's departure. Both fleets sail slowly up Dominica, becoming becalmed in its lee overnight.

Next daybreak Hood's van uses a faint breeze to overhaul the French rear, so de Grasse signals his whole battle fleet to turn and fight. Only eight British and 15 French ships become engaged in the ensuing melee before this wind too dies away, *Zélé, Auguste, Northumberland, Sceptre,* and *Citoyen* bearing the brunt for the French, in which both HMSS *Royal Oak* and *Montague* are also dismasted. But when another breeze springs up after several hours—so that Rodney's main body can begin to close—the French break off and return to guard their convoy. The British maintain pursuit for the next two days in faint east-northeast winds until de Grasse notices *Magnanime* and *Zélé* lagging astern at nightfall on 11 April near the Saintes Island grouping (between Dominica and Guadeloupe). Reversing course to provide cover, de Grasse's flagship *Ville de Paris* collides with *Zélé* at 2:00 A.M. on 12 April, destroying its bowsprit and mizzenmast and obliging the French admiral to delegate his frigate *Astrée* to tow *Zélé* toward Guadeloupe.

12 APRIL 1782. ***Les Saintes.*** At first light the French fleet finds itself scattered, with the damaged *Zélé* lagging astern in plain view of the pursuing British. De Grasse, fearful this ship will fall easy prey, at 5:45 A.M. signals his fleet to reverse course, form line of battle, and intercept the approaching enemy. Learning of this maneuver from his scouting frigates, Rodney gives the order to close his own column for the impeding encounter, while clearing Point Jacques on Dominica.

Because of gentle easterly breezes, it takes the French an hour and a half to assemble, not steering south until 7:15 A.M.:

Van

Ship	*Guns*	*Commander*
Hercule	74	Jean Isaac Chadeau de la Clochetterie
Souverain	74	Jean Baptiste de Glandevès
Palmier	74	Joseph Jacques François de Martelli Chautard
Northumberland	74	de Sainte Césaire
Neptune	74	Laurent Emmanuel de Renaud d'Aleins
Auguste (rear admiral)	80	Commodore Louis Antoine, Comte de Bougainville; (flag captain) Pierre Joseph de Castellan
Ardent	64	Jean Guillaume Michel de Gouzillon
Scipion	74	Pierre Antoine de Clavel
Brave	74	Claude François Renart de Fuch Samberg, Marquis d'Amblimont
Citoyen	74	Alexandre d'Ethy

Center

Ship	*Guns*	*Commander*
Hector	74	de la Vicomté
César	74	Charles René Louis Bernard, Vicomte de Marigny
Dauphin Royal	70	Pierre Antoine de Montpéroux, Chevalier de Roquefeuil
Languedoc	80	Jean François d'Argelos, Baron d'Arros
Ville de Paris (flag)	104	Admiral François Joseph Paul, Comte de Grasse Tilly; (flag captain) Jean Baptiste François de Lavilléon
Couronne	80	Claude de Mithon, Chevalier de Genouilly
Éveillé	64	Armand Le Gardeur de Tilly
Sceptre	74	Commodore Louis de Rigaud, Comte de Vaudreuil
Glorieux	74	Baron d'Escars

Rear

Ship	*Guns*	*Commander*
Diadème	74	Louis Augustin de Monteclerc
Destin	74	François Louis, Comte Dumaitz de Goimpy Feiquières
Magnanime	74	Jean Antoine Le Bègue
Réfléchi	74	Charles de Médine
Conquérant	74	Charles Marie de la Grandière
Magnifique	74	Jean Baptiste de Macarty Macteigne
Triomphant (vice-flag)	80	Commodore Louis Philippe de Rigaud, Marquis de Vaudreuil; (flag captain) Jean François Du Cheyron, Chevalier Du Pavillon
Bourgogne	74	Charles de Charitte
Duc de Bourgogne	80	Commodore Charles Régis Coriolis d'Espinouse; (flag captain) Pierre Joseph François Samson de Champmartin
Marseillais	74	Henri César de Castellane Majastre
Pluton	74	François Hector, Comte d'Albert de Rions

These are accompanied by the frigates *Aimable* of Lt. Jean Baptiste François de Suzannet, *Amazone* of Ens. Charles Elzéar Bourgarel de Martignan (acting captain in place of De Montguyot, killed earlier), *Galathée* of Lt. Joachim de Roquart, and *Richmond* of Lt. Vicomte de Mortemart; corvette *Cérès* of Lt. Louis Jean Marie, Baron de Paroy; plus cutter *Clairvoyant* of Ens. François Robert, Vicomte Daché.

Forging north to meet them is another ten-mile-long column of warships under Rodney:

Van

Ship	*Guns*	*Commander*
Marlborough	74	Taylor Penny
Arrogant	74	Samuel Cornish
Alcide	74	Charles Thompson
Nonesuch	64	William Truscott
Conqueror	74	George Balfour
Princessa (rear admiral)	70	Francis Samuel Drake; (flag captain) Charles Knatchbull
Prince George	90	James Williams
Torbay	74	John Lewis Gidoin
Anson	64	William Blair
Fame	74	Robert Barber
Russell	74	James Saumarez

Center

Ship	*Guns*	*Commander*
America	64	Samuel Thompson
Hercules	74	Henry Savage
Prothée (French prize)	64	Charles Buckner
Resolution	74	Robert Manners
Agamemnon	64	Benjamin Caldwell
Duke	98	Allen Gardner
Formidable (flag)	90	Rodney; (flag captain) Charles Douglas
Namur	90	Cranston Inglis
Saint Albans	64	William Cornwallis
Canada	74	Thomas Demarest
Repulse	64	Charrington
Ajax	74	Robert Fanshaw

Center

Ship	*Guns*	*Commander*
Bedford	74	Commodore Affleck

Rear

Ship	*Guns*	*Commander*
Prince William	64	George Wilkinson
Magnificent	74	Robert Linzee
Centaur	74	John Inglefield
Belliqueux	64	Alexander Sutherland
Warrior	74	James Wallace
Monarch	74	Francis Reynolds
Barfleur (vice-flag)	90	Hood; (flag captain) John Knight
Valiant	74	S.G. Goodall
Yarmouth	60	Anthony Parry
Montague (under jury rig)	74	George Bowen
Alfred	74	(none, Capt. Bayne having been killed on 9 April)
Royal Oak (under jury rig)	74	Thomas Burnett

Shortly before 8:00 A.M., HMS *Marlborough* and the French *Hercule* arrive opposite each other and open fire. Travelling at two miles an hour, each fleet then creeps past one another within 100 yards, exchanging broadsides. Soon after 9:00 A.M. the wind begins shifting around to the southeast, bringing several French ships up short and causing gaps in their line, while not affecting the British. Rodney immediately takes advantage by leading his flagship *Formidable* through an opening astern of *Glorieux,* followed by HMSS *Duke, Namur,* and *Canada.* He also signals Drake to attempt the same in the van, but it is Hood who pierces de Grasse's line a second time, astern of *César.* A confused melee ensues, in which the Royal Navy ships—many armed with powerful carronades—pound their opponents at close quarters for the next several hours.

By 3:30 P.M. *Glorieux, Hector, César,* and *Ardent* have struck, and de Grasse's *Ville de Paris* is surrounded by British warships, who finally compel the French flagship to surrender by 6:15 P.M., with almost 400 dead aboard. The Royal Navy suffers 237 killed (including Captains Blair and Manners) and 766 wounded, but lose no ships; French casualties are estimated at more than 3,000, mostly prisoners aboard their five captured vessels, although also including Captains de Sainte Césaire of *Northumberland,* Du Pavillon of *Triomphant,* and de la Clochetterie of *Hercule.*

A wounded Marquis de Vaudreuil assumes command of the remaining French ships, detaching *Conquérant* to carry word of this defeat to Cap-François

British warships surround de Grasse's Ville de Paris *in the latter stages of the Battle of the Saintes.*

(modern Cap-Haïtien), while following by 25 April with *Triomphant, Bourgogne, Réfléchi, Magnanime, Destin, Diadème, Sceptre, Languedoc, Dauphin Royal, Citoyen, Brave, Scipion, Northumberland, Palmier, Souverain,* and *Neptune.* (*Duc de Bourgogne, Couronne,* and *Magnifique* are already at anchor, along with the convoy.) Meanwhile, Bougainville's *Auguste* puts into Curaçao along with *Éveillé, Hercule, Marseillais,* and *Pluton* to effect repairs, rejoining Vaudreuil's main body one month later. The victorious Rodney remains off the Saintes for three days refurbishing his vessels, before detaching Hood with ten ships to precede his fleet into Jamaica.

19 APRIL 1782. While stemming the Mona Passage, Hood's ten ships sight five sail running before the wind, which prove to be the French 64-gun ships *Caton* and *Jason,* frigates *Astrée* and *Aimable,* and the corvette *Cérès,* fleeing Guadeloupe. All save *Astrée* surrender to the British.

22 APRIL 1782. ***Fall of the Bahamas.*** A Hispano-American expedition begins standing out of Havana comprising 59 vessels (12 American) escorted by the 40-gun frigate *South Carolina* of Commo. Alexander Gillon. They bear 1,500 sailors and a small Spanish army under Lt. Gen. Juan Manuel de Caxigal, governor of Havana: 668 regulars of the Guadalajara Regiment, 594 of España, 326 from Mexico's Corona Regiment, 140 artillerymen and support staff, 50 light infantry, plus 202 black militia. It takes the convoy a week to clear port, Matanzas not being sighted until 30 April, Bimini on 2 May, then Nassau by evening of 5 May.

Next afternoon a surrender demand is sent ashore, which Gov. John Maxwell accepts by 7 May, the actual British capitulation being signed on 8 May. Although the defenders number more than 1,400—274 regulars, 338 militia, 800 sailors—wealthy plantation owners fear seeing their properties destroyed in an all-out battle and distrust the loyalty of many of their followers. Thus, without a single casualty, the Spaniards gain 153 artillery pieces and the 77 prizes in the roadstead.

A disgruntled Gillon quits the venture at this point, preferring to sail directly toward Philadelphia on 14 May rather than escort the Spanish expedition back into Havana or Haiti as promised. Caxigal departs Nassau a few days later, leaving behind a 300-man garrison under Capt. Antonio Claraco y Sanz and seven small Spanish men-of-war crewed by 150 sailors under Capt. Raymundo Andrés.

31 MAY 1782. The veteran Captain Lapérouse sets sail from Cap-François (modern-day Cap-Haïtien) with his new command *Sceptre,* plus the frigates *Astrée* and *Engageante* under Lieutenants de Langle and de La Jaille respectively, with 250 soldiers, 40 artillerymen, four field pieces, and two mortars to campaign against the British in Hudson's Bay (Canada).

4 JULY 1782. The Marquis de Vaudreuil quits Cap-François (modern-day Cap-Haïtien) with 13 ships of the line, escorting a Spanish contingent as far as Havana before steering north up the Atlantic seaboard.

8 AUGUST 1782. Lapérouse, having circled into Hudson's Bay (Canada) by mid-July with his ship of the line *Sceptre* and the frigates *Astrée* and *Engageante,* arrives within sight of the entrance to Churchill River (Manitoba). Next day he disembarks his few hundred troops and calls upon the chief English factor for this outpost, Samuel Hearne, to surrender. Hearne immediately complies, and Fort Prince of Wales is partially destroyed, its supplies and furs taken. Nearby York Factory is successfully attacked on 24 August, after which Lapérouse—now pressed by bad weather—departs toward Europe, having carried out his commission without losing a single man (and treating his captives with great kindness).

10 AUGUST 1782. Vaudreuil's French fleet anchors off Boston for repair and resupply, except *Magnifique,* which is wrecked while being piloted into Nantasket Bay. A grateful Continental Congress will offer to replace their ally's loss with the brand new, 74-gun USS *America.*

4 SEPTEMBER 1782. The 60-year-old British Adm. Hugh Pigot reaches New York from the West Indies, having followed Vaudreuil north.

17 OCTOBER 1782. Commodore James Kempthorne is cruising off Saint Domingue (Haiti) with his 90-gun, 743-man flagship HMS *London;* 82-gun, 594-man *Torbay* of Capt. John Lewis Gidoin; and 14-gun sloop *Badger* when two sail approach. These prove to be the 74-gun, 734-man *Scipion* of 39-year-old Capt. Nicolas René Henri, Comte de Grimouard, and 32-gun, 275-man frigate *Sibylle.* After a prolonged chase, the French pair succeeds in crippling the larger British pursuers, although *Scipion* then strikes a rock and sinks while attempting to anchor in Samaná Bay on 20 October.

6 DECEMBER 1782. British Rear Adm. Sir Richard Hughes intercepts a small French convoy off Mar-

tinique. During this action the 72-gun HMS *Ruby* of Capt. John Collins captures the 64-gun, 1,521-ton *Solitaire* of 49-year-old Jean Charles de Borda, killing 35 and wounding 55 of its crewmembers.

20 DECEMBER 1782. The 54-gun, 297-man, 891-ton HMS *Diomede* of Capt. Thomas Lennox Frederick, supported by the 40-gun, 217-man, 699-ton frigate *Quebec,* sights the 40-gun, 450-man *South Carolina* of Capt. John Joyner off the Delaware River, chasing it for 18 hours. The American vessel eventually surrenders following a two-hour fight.

20 JANUARY 1783. The preliminaries to the Treaty of Versailles are signed between French and British plenipotentiaries, coming into effect one month later in Europe, two months later in the Americas.

2 MARCH 1783. The 44-gun Royal Navy frigate *Resistance* of Capt. James King and 14-gun sloop *Duguay Trouin* of John Fish capture the 28-gun French frigate *Coquette* of Capt. Marquis de Grasse Briançon. From prisoners King learns that French forces have recently occupied Turk's Island north of Santo Domingo, so informs his colleague, Horatio Nelson.

Although hostilities are plainly winding down, Nelson sails to that objective with his 28-gun frigate *Albemarle,* Cmdr. Charles Dixon's 14-gun sloop *Drake,* and one other vessel, arriving by 7 March. After sending an officer inshore with a surrender demand—which is refused—Nelson bombards the island overnight then sends Dixon to disembark with 167 men next dawn. The 150 well-entrenched defenders easily repulse the assault, wounding eight Englishmen and obliging Nelson to reembark his men by the morning of 9 March.

30 MARCH 1783. ***Bahamian Reconquest.*** A 24-year-old loyalist militia colonel named Andrew Deveaux—exiled from Beaufort, South Carolina, because of the patriots' victory—sorties from Saint Augustine with 70 followers to be joined at sea two days later by the 26-gun privateer brigantine *Perseverance* of Thomas Dow and 16-gun, 120-man brigantine *Whitby Warrior* of Daniel Wheeler. The expedition anchors off Harbour and Eleuthera Islands on 6 April, recruiting another 170 volunteers for an attempt against the Spanish garrison at New Providence (Nassau). Four days later the sloop *Flor de Mayo* reaches the Bahamian capital with a message from the new governor of Havana, Luis de Unzaga, saying that peace preliminaries have been signed back in Europe and that the Bahamas are to be restored to British rule in exchange for Florida.

Therefore, when Deveaux's flotilla draws near to New Providence on 13 April, Spanish commander Claraco mistakes it for mere smugglers. His customs patrols are surprised next dawn to find a heavily armed landing party storming ashore to occupy Fort Montague and three guardboats. Claraco retreats into his citadel and a brief truce is arranged; Deveaux rescinds it next day. The Spaniards scuttle their remaining warships on 16 April and huddle within their main fort until they decide to give up two days later, being repatriated to Cuba.

LESSER HOSTILITIES (1780–1790)

4 NOVEMBER 1780. ***Tupac Amaru Rebellion.*** While returning to Tinta (Peru) from a banquet celebrating the King's feast day, 38-year-old José Gabriel de Condorcanqui, Marqués de Oropesa—an Inca better known as Tupac Amaru, chief of Tungasuca—captures the cruel Spanish *Corregidor* Antonio de Arriaga and executes him in Tungarica six days later. A popular uprising immediately explodes, and Tupac Amaru leads 20,000 Indians and 300 mestizo followers on an invasion of Quispicanchi Province, slaughtering the hastily assembled forces of *Corregidor* Fernando Cabrera at Sangarará. Viceroy Agustín de Jáuregui y Aldecoa attempts to placate the rebels from his distant capital of Lima, banning forced native labor on 7 December while dispatching 200 troop reinforcements into the Andes.

The insurrection sweeps on toward Cuzco, which is defended by 3,200 men under Cols. Manuel Villalta and Gabriel de Avilés y del Fierro. Although having few trained soldiers, an advance unit under *Sargento Mayor* (garrison commander) Joaquín Valcarce inflicts some 300 casualties on Tupac Amaru's host in January 1781 when it hesitates six miles outside Cuzco. Additional crown reinforcements arrive on 23 February under *Mariscal de Campo* (field marshal) José del Valle y Torres, who sets about reorganizing Cuzco's militias until the district has more than 15,000 royalist defenders. Going over to the offensive on 9 March, del Valle's army is attacked at dawn on 22 March by Tupac Amaru after a heavy snowfall, which dampens the Spaniards' powder. No decision is reached until Friday, 6 April, when the rebels are defeated and del

Valle occupies their headquarters at Tinta. Tupac Amaru flees to Langui, only to be betrayed to the Spaniards, who draw and quarter him on 18 May along with his wife, Micaela Bastidas, one son, and other adherents.

The rebellion continues under Tupac Amaru's brother, Diego Cristóbal, and surviving son Mariano. Chucuito is overrun and Puno is hard-pressed, although a royalist force under Lt. Col. José Reseguín defeats the mestizo rebel Luis Laso de la Vega at Tupiza. The final campaign is launched by Diego Cristóbal, who attacks Sorata and lays siege to La Paz (Bolivia) with perhaps as many as 40,000 Indians. After 109 days the city is relieved by a royalist column in June 1781; when Diego Cristóbal attempts a second siege his forces are scattered by 7,000 reinforcements from Oruro, under Reseguín. The Inca leader finally accepts the general amnesty offered by the Spaniards on 10 September and surrenders.

When Felipe Velasco—better known as Tupac Inca Yupanqui—mounts another short-lived uprising at Huarochirí (near Lima) a year and a half later, he is quickly arrested and hanged on 7 July 1783. Twelve days later Diego Cristóbal and other past rebel leaders are also executed, their tongues being cut out before they are drawn and quartered.

16 MARCH 1781. ***Comunero Revolt.*** After growing discontent throughout Nueva Granada (Colombia) on account of increased royal taxes imposed by Inspector Gen. Juan Francisco Gutiérrez de Piñeres, plus the precedent of Tupac Amaru's rebellion in Peru farther to the south, a mob led by José Delgadillo runs riot in Socorro. Other towns quickly follow suit, and by April some 6,000 *comuneros* (commoners) have gathered at Socorro, electing Juan Francisco Berbeo as their leader. Inspector General Gutiérrez sends a company of troops under Captain Barrera to put down the mutiny, but it is defeated at Puente Real outside Vélez, further inflaming the uprising. Berbeo next marches on the distant capital of Santa Fe de Bogotá, gathering more adherents at every step, and prompting Gutiérrez to flee into Honda on 13 May. At the end of the month the *comuneros* are joined by the Zipa Indian chieftain Ambrosio Pisco, who is proclaimed lord of Chía and prince of Bogotá.

On 4 June the rebels present their demands—Gutiérrez's dismissal, repeal of all taxes, and greater creole participation in government—to the remaining viceregal authorities, who accede and sign the so-called Zipaquirá Pact three days later. Berbeo's tens of thousands of followers disperse, but another leader, named José Antonio Galán, persists with the revolt north of Bogotá; the royal Gov. Policarpo Fernández is slain at Neiva. Meanwhile 500 regular troops reinforce Bogotá on 15 August, and Viceroy Manuel Antonio Flores declares the Zipaquirá Pact null and void. The natives of Nemocon rise and kill their overseer, provoking military reprisals, and the revolt collapses. Galán is forsaken by his last few adherents and escapes to Chagonuete, only to be captured by soldiers and executed on 1 February 1782. Many other executions and arrests follow, marking an end to the insurrection.

17 JULY 1781. In northern Mexico, Yuma Indians rise against Spanish rule, eradicating the newly established outposts of Colorado, Purísima Concepción, and San Pedro y San Pablo de Bicuñer. The setback effectively halts Spanish expansion into the territory.

11 JUNE 1784. A Spanish expedition quits Havana under Brig. Gen. Vicente de Céspedes, escorting several thousand settlers who are to repopulate Saint Augustine.

JANUARY 1786. A major Spanish expedition quits Cartagena under *Mariscal de Campo* Antonio de Arévalo to pacify the untamed shoreline of the Gulf of Urabá and northeastern Panama. The effort proves successful, the new town of Caimán being established; Forts San Rafael and San Gabriel are erected in April and May to protect the newly created settlements of San Elías (Mandinga) and Nuestra Señora de la Concepción in the Gulf of San Blas. By August the Spaniards reach Caledonia Bay (formerly occupied by the Scots; *see* The Darien Disaster in Part 4), where they found Carolina del Darien and later build Príncipe Fort at the Sabana River mouth on the Pacific Coast.

23 FEBRUARY 1786. Now promoted rear admiral, Lapérouse reaches Concepción (Chile) with the frigates *Astrolabe* and *Boussole,* having rounded Cape Horn. This peacetime expedition is funded by the French government and the Académie des Sciences to explore the Pacific. By 9 April he reaches Easter Island, Maui (Hawaii) in May. On 23 June *Astrolabe* and *Boussole* raise Mount Saint Elias (modern-day border between Alaska and Canada) before veering down the West Coast of America, taking surveys. By 14 September they reach Monterey, refreshing before Lapérouse strikes out into the Pacific; he is lost with all hands in June 1788.

21 JULY 1787. With help from the Englishman Henry Hooper, the Spanish authorities in Colombia sign a peace treaty with the natives in the Gulf of Urabá.

SUMMER 1790. ***Britain's "Spanish Armament."*** In retaliation for the Spanish expedition sent to Vancouver to eject a new English trading settlement, the British government authorizes a massive naval buildup to pressure Madrid; it becomes known as the Spanish Armament. Eventually swelling to 29 ships of the line, nine frigates, two sloops, four cutters, and two fireships under Admiral Richard, Lord Howe, the fleet puts to sea during August and September 1790—without any declaration of war—while Rear Adm. Samuel Cornish sails to the West Indies with six of the line in October. The Spanish government finally bows to Britain's terms on 28 October, agreeing to restore Nootka Sound and compensate the dispossessed English settlers.

DISCORD IN THE EARLY AMERICAN REPUBLIC AND THE OLD NORTHWEST INDIAN WARS (1786–1795)

IN THE IMMEDIATE AFTERMATH OF U.S. INDEPENDENCE from Great Britain there ensues a period of economic hardship for the new republic because of lost export markets, felt especially severely in New England. Against a backdrop of monetary collapse and depression, bankrupt state governments impose a heavy tax burden, provoking a brief flurry of armed protest.

A more protracted struggle ensues in the inland wilderness, where 250,000 square miles west of the Alleghenies and north of the Ohio River (modern-day Indiana, Illinois, Wisconsin, Michigan, Ohio, and part of Minnesota) pass under American control from the British in July 1787. A confederacy of Miami, Shawnee, Pottawatomie, and Chippewa tribes resists the transfer, disputing American settlement in the Northwest Territory.

LATE AUGUST 1786. In an attempt to prevent any more foreclosures, forfeitures, or imprisonments for debt, a mob of 1,500 armed men closes the courthouse at Northampton (Massachusetts). During the next few weeks, similar actions are carried out in neighboring Middlesex, Bristol, and Worcester Counties while antigovernment sentiment also spreads into Rhode Island, Vermont, and New Hampshire. Gov. James Bowdoin is powerless to control these self-styled Massachusetts "regulators"—their name derived from an earlier Carolinian revolt; *see* 16 May 1771 in Part 5—so he raises a regiment of state militia under Major General Lincoln.

NOVEMBER 1786. Capt. Job Shattuck of Groton (Connecticut) attempts to close the courthouse in Middlesex County, being defeated, wounded, and imprisoned in Boston along with his two lieutenants by Massachusetts state militia; his rebel followers disperse westward.

EARLY DECEMBER 1786. ***Shays's Rebellion.*** After closing the supreme court at Worcester, a Regulator mob is reinforced by 350 men under 39-year-old Daniel Shays of Pelham, a Revolutionary War veteran risen from the ranks and now a retired captain of 5th Massachusetts Regiment. He petitions the state legislature with a list of grievances then disperses his following.

In late January 1787 Shays again marches from Wilbraham with 1,200 rebels, this time to prevent the Hampshire County court from opening in nearby Springfield. Approaching out of the southeast on the afternoon of 25 January, he hopes to carry its 1,100 militia defenders under Gen. William Shepard with the support of another 400 Regulators out of West Springfield, led by a former major named Luke Day. However, the latter fails to appear, so Shays is confronted by Shepard's full strength. Two warning shots are fired by the militia cannons; the third round smashes into the insurgent ranks, killing four and causing the rest to flee.

Lincoln then arrives and pursues the demoralized throng northeast into Petersham, surprising the Regulators at dawn on Sunday, 4 February, after an all-night march through a snowstorm. Some 150 rebels are captured to stand trial; Shays escapes north. The militia army subsequently moves across the Connecticut River to disperse seditious nests in the Berkshires, so that by the end of the month only scattered resistance remains. Most Regulators—including Shays—are eventually pardoned; Governor Bowdoin is voted out of office in favor of John Hancock.

LATE SUMMER 1790. The 37-year-old Gen. Josiah Harmar departs Fort Washington (Cincinnati, Ohio) with 320 U.S. regulars and 800 militia to crush the dissident Indians who—encouraged by the British—are refusing to allow American settlers into their territory.

18 OCTOBER 1790. ***Miami River.*** Harmar's 1,100 men come upon 2,500 Indians under the

Miami chief Little Turtle in Ohio and are defeated in a sharply contested fight. Four days later the U.S. forces are beaten again, having to retreat into Fort Washington with the loss of 200 men. In both engagements the militia runs away, leaving the regulars to be slaughtered.

OCTOBER 1791. The newly appointed governor for the Northwest Territory, Gen. Arthur St. Clair, departs Fort Washington with 500–600 U.S. regulars and 1,500 militia.

3 NOVEMBER 1791. ***St. Clair's Defeat.*** After marching 100 miles north and suffering numerous desertions, St. Clair's army arrives on the banks of the Wabash River, camping 40 miles southwest of modern-day Lima (near Fort Recovery, Ohio). Next dawn the Americans are surprised by 2,200 Indians under Little Turtle, most of the ill-trained militia fleeing as the regulars are overwhelmed. Approximately 900 men and women are slaughtered by the exultant warriors; St. Clair and his surviving followers escape to Fort Jefferson, 22 miles away, before eventually regaining Fort Washington. Next year the general resigns his commission.

JULY 1794. After having been promoted major general and given command of the western army two years previously—then failing to sway the Indians by a diplomatic mission in 1793—"Mad Anthony" Wayne's 2,000 regulars are joined at Greenville (Ohio) by 1,600 Kentucky militia, advancing north to Fort Defiance on the Miami River. Wayne makes a final effort to reach an accord with the Indians; when rebuffed he advances with the army.

20 AUGUST 1794. ***Fallen Timbers.*** Overtaken during their retreat, 1,300 Indians make a stand on the banks of the Maumee River (near modern-day Toledo, Ohio) behind a barricade of trees felled by a storm. Wayne pins them down with his infantry while sending cavalry to circle their flanks. The warriors are

Undated lithograph of St. Clair's defeat

routed, with several hundred being killed or wounded; American casualties total 33 dead and 100 injured. (This action takes place within sight of a British garrison still illegally upon American soil; some members of the garrison allegedly fight alongside the Indians.)

AUGUST 1795. The American victory at Fallen Timbers effectively ends native resistance. Hostilities conclude with the signing of the Treaty of Greenville on 3 August 1795, which permits American settlers to occupy the Northwest Territory in peace.

HAITIAN REVOLUTION (1790–1803)

THE 1789 UPHEAVALS IN EUROPE HAVE A PROFOUND IMPACT on France's overseas colonies, especially Saint Domingue. Many of its elite whites (*grand blancs*) already feel alienated by their lack of political and economic influence in Paris—although its radical new government soon frightens them even worse. Bourgeois whites (40,000 *petit blancs*) and 28,000 free *affranchis* (creoles, mulattoes, and blacks) selectively embrace egalitarian ideals in hopes of personal advancement—yet ignore the needs of a half-million slaves. The result will be a dozen years of chaotic civil war in which each side is torn between monarchism, republicanism, patriotism, racism, and a desire for liberty.

21 OCTOBER 1790. ***Ogé's Insurrection.*** The 35-year-old mulatto coffee merchant and minor plantation owner Jacques Vicente Ogé, backed by colleague Jean Baptiste Chavannes, land a small contingent to raise a mulatto revolt. (Ogé has been in Paris during the French Revolution and requested funds from the national assembly for his cause. When these were denied he arranged financing from the British abolitionist Thomas Clarkson, buying arms and ammunition in the United States.)

His attempt is repressed, obliging Ogé and Chavannes to flee to Santo Domingo, from where they are extradited by unsympathetic Spanish authorities.

24 JANUARY 1791. Some 200 black slaves arm themselves around Port Salut (near Les Cayes); they are quickly dispersed, their leaders hanged.

25 FEBRUARY 1791. Ogé and Chavannes are broken alive on the wheel, yet resistance in the south continues to smolder under the 30-year-old mulatto goldsmith and militia officer André Rigaud, who wins a provisional understanding from whites that they will not oppose acts from the Parisian national assembly on behalf of freemen.

EARLY MARCH 1791. A French squadron arrives at Port au Prince, depositing the revolutionary Artois and Normandie Regiments. On 4 March the 110th Port au Prince Colonial Regiment mutinies, killing its colonel and parading his head about on a spike.

14 AUGUST 1791. ***Bois Caïman.*** After several weeks of clandestine meetings, 200 blacks gather secretly at Lenormand de Mézy Plantation in Morne Rouge (north-central Haiti) under their leaders, "Zamba" Boukman Dutty, Jeannot Bullet, Jean François, and Georges Biassou. They hold a voodoo ceremony in nearby Bois Caïman at which they decide to rise against their masters by 22 August.

16 AUGUST 1791. Some slaves in the Limbé District begin their uprising prematurely, being arrested while setting fire to Chabaud Estate.

22 AUGUST 1791. At 10:00 P.M. slaves gather at the Clément Plantation under Boukman, destroying the nearby Tremes Estate and the Noé, Molines, and Flaville Plantations by sunup, thereby sparking a general insurrection on Saint Domingue's north-central plain. Boukman marches west from Acul on 23 August, his numbers swelling to 2,000 upon entering the Limbé District. Whites and loyal blacks are slaughtered, and equipment and buildings burned. Port Margot is attacked early on the evening of 24 August, and armed resistance is encountered next day at Plaisance, where French militia scatter the rebels, who fortify themselves within Champagne Ravine.

Despite this lone setback, the rebellion is too widespread, whites too few and isolated. Within a few days, Governor-General Blanchelande recalls his militia and noncombatants into Le-Cap (modern-day Cap-Haïtien), which is threatened on 30–31 August by Boukman with 15,000 followers. They are unable to penetrate and so content themselves with leveling the surrounding 50 miles of countryside. By mid-September 200 sugar and 1,200 coffee plantations are

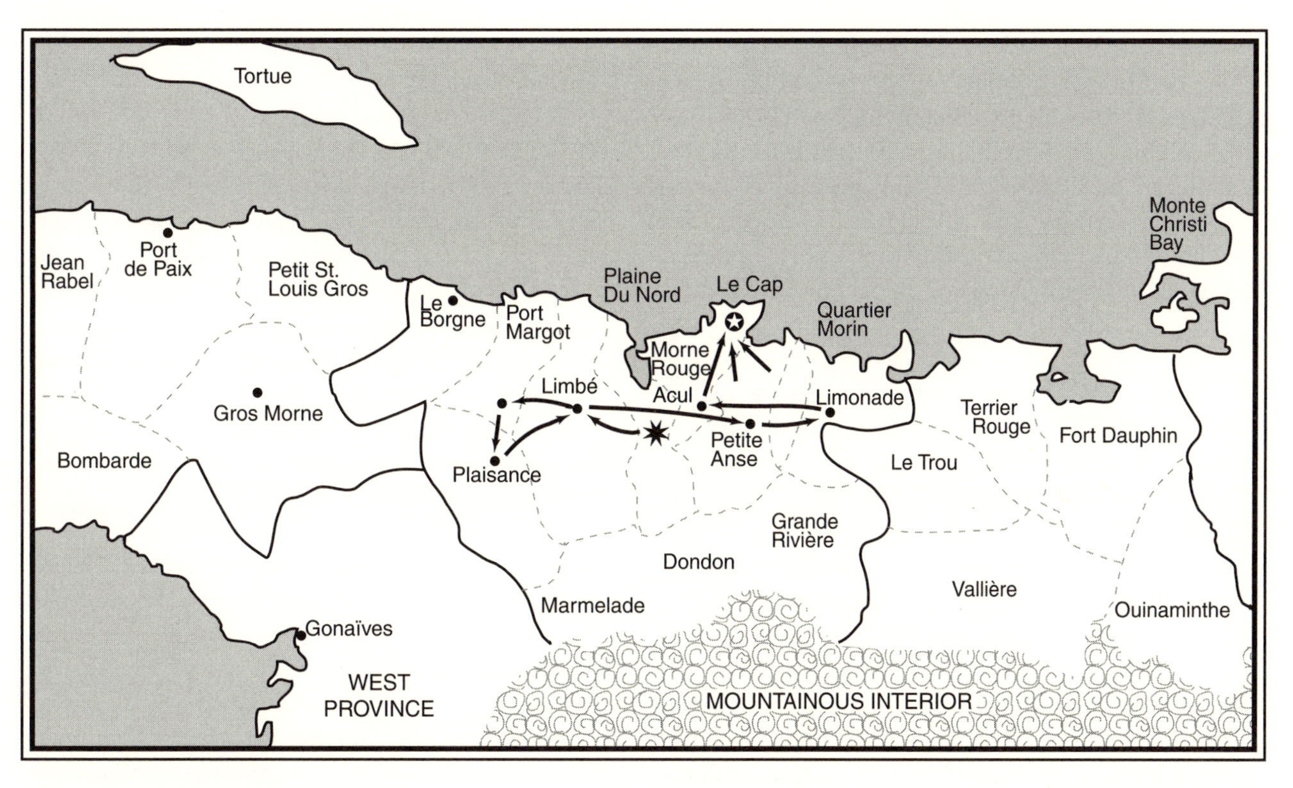

First successful Haitian uprising

destroyed, and 40,000 of northern Haiti's 170,000 blacks are in open rebellion.

2 SEPTEMBER 1791. In southwestern Saint Domingue, after several minor clashes between whites and mulattoes—the latter seeking greater rights—a militia column with a few cannons sets out from the capital, Port au Prince, to disperse a mulatto concentration in the nearby Charbonnière Mountains under Bauvais, Pinchinat, Lambert, and Rigaud. The latter attempt to shift camp but, when intercepted near Croix des Bouquets, defeat the white militia.

At this point the local royalist leader, Hamus de Jumécourt, offers the mulattoes an alliance against the radical French representatives in Port au Prince; an agreement is signed by 7 September. Four days later those same French representatives make the mulattoes a counteroffer, and a multifaceted struggle ensues, with mulattoes shifting allegiance between whites and blacks, royalists and republicans, as expediency demands. (Outside sources also begin playing a role: the British on Jamaica, fearful of France's spreading revolution, quietly support Saint Domingue's monarchists against the republicans as well as their efforts to suppress the slave revolt. The Spaniards of Santo Domingo, in contrast, openly encourage this second uprising in hopes of weakening the French hold over half of the island.)

OCTOBER 1791. At Jérémie, whites disarm all mulattoes and free blacks, herding them aboard smallpox-infested ships, where most die.

MID-NOVEMBER 1791. Civil commissioners arrive from revolutionary France, opening up dialogues with local black rebel leaders. Around the same time, Boukman is killed in a minor skirmish; the insurrection survives its leader.

22 NOVEMBER 1791. After several weeks of white attempts to crush mulatto and black aspirations, Port au Prince erupts in flames at dawn; it burns for two days as rioting rages in the streets. This produces a backlash in the surrounding district, where further uprisings occur; a few weeks later black leader Romaine La Prophétesse occupies Jacmel with 1,300 followers.

15 JANUARY 1792. Giving up on negotiations, Jean François's band recaptures the Ouinaminthe District.

22–23 JANUARY 1792. A rebel army under Biassou attacks Le Cap to secure ammunition and replenish diminished resources.

4 MARCH 1792. France's assembly issues a decree recognizing the equality of mulattoes with whites, creating a stir on Saint Domingue.

22 MARCH 1792. ***Croix des Bouquets.*** The Marquis de Caradeux marches out of Port au Prince into Cul de Sac Plain to put down its mulatto-black-royalist combination. Instead, he is defeated at Croix des Bouquets by 10,000–15,000 untrained black insurgents, inspired by 22-year-old voodoo leader Hyacinthe. This setback precipitates more uprisings around Mirebalais, Arcahaye, Petite Rivière, Verettes, and Saint Marc.

MID-JULY 1792. While visiting the Platons region (southwestern Haiti), Governor Blanchelande attempts to placate 2,000 black rebels operating around Les Cayes under Armand and Martial. During a sudden storm on 29 July, however, the rebels attack Bérault Plantation—one of the white colonists' major military camps—destroying it. They then rampage through the Torbeck region and gain hundreds more adherents.

4 AUGUST 1792. Blanchelande advances into the Platons's southwestern hills in three columns, searching for Armand and Martial, who confuse and ambush his forces piecemeal. Blanchelande is therefore obliged to retreat back into Les Cayes four days later, having suffered 200 killed and two lost artillery pieces. By 10 August he sets sail for Le Cap, later being deported to France.

SEPTEMBER 1792. The 28-year-old Jacobin commissioner, Léger Félicité Sonthonax, reaches Saint Domingue with 6,000 soldiers, bearing instructions to reimpose governmental order. At first he favors the mulattoes, making no concessions to rebellious slaves or disgruntled whites (whom he suspects of being royalists). The slave rebellion persists in the north.

9 JANUARY 1793. ***Platons.*** Republican Colonel Harty of the Aube Regiment marches out of Les Cayes with nearly 2,000 troops—including 200 armed blacks under former slave Jean Kina—to exterminate the Armand-Martial rebel encampment at Platons. The latter resist desperately but are powerless to prevent four columns from closing in on their hideout three days later. Some 3,000 black insurgents disperse higher into the mountains at Macaya while a few hundred noncombatants—women, children, aged, and infirm—are left behind and brutally massacred by the French on 13 January.

21 JANUARY 1793. France's execution of Louis XVI and its declaration of war against England and Spain add confusing new undercurrents to the Haitian insurrection.

LATE JANUARY 1793. Independent maroons of Bahoruco rise in revolt, descending upon the area of Fond Parisien while Jean Pineau leads another insurrection in the Crochus region, just outside Cul de Sac Plain. Both risings are secretly incited by Hyacinthe.

EARLY APRIL 1793. The French commissioners Sonthonax and Étienne Polverel march on Port au Prince, besieging it to prevent the seditious antirepublican machinations of Auguste Borel. The capital eventually surrenders, Borel fleeing to Jamaica.

SUMMER 1793. A joint army of rebellious blacks under Gens. Jean François and Georges Biassou—plus Spanish militia out of Santo Domingo—invade northern Saint Domingue.

20 JUNE 1793. ***Le Cap Revolt.*** Political prisoners held aboard ships off Le Cap (modern-day Cap-Haïtien) rise against the republican commissioners, being joined by almost 2,000 sailors. They make an armed disembarkation, capture the main arsenal, and next day compel Sonthonax and Polverel to flee for the protection of Bréda Plantation outside the city. Behind them, fierce fighting rages in the streets as prisons are opened and thousands of slaves become embroiled in the carnage.

Desperate to regain control, Sonthonax and Polverel promise freedom and full French citizenship to any slaves willing to fight for the republican government. A 3,000-man contingent under the maroon leader Pierrot, part of the Hispano-black invasion force encamped in the hills beyond Le Cap, responds to this call; on 22 June—after pledging allegiance to France—he fights his way into the burning city. The commissioners return by 27 June, only to find many blacks skeptical of their offer. Although some abandon their Spanish allies, major leaders such as Biassou refuse to be swayed, because black noncombatants will remain slaves.

AUGUST 1793. The Hispano-black forces reach Le Cap.

29 AUGUST 1793. In a desperate bid to reestablish republican control, Sonthonax proclaims the total abolition of slavery throughout northern Saint Domingue. Although this tactic wins some additional black support—former slaves forming so-called legions of equality—it

also alienates many whites and mulattoes when it is announced in the west on 21 September.

9 SEPTEMBER 1793. ***British Intervention.*** Commo. John Ford quits Port Royal (Jamaica) with his 64-gun flagship HMS *Europa* of Capt. George Gregory, 14-gun sloop *Goéland* (French prize) of Cmdr. Thomas Wolley, and schooner *Flying Fish* to conduct 36-year-old Lt. Col. John Whitelocke's 13th Foot across to Jérémie to support its white French monarchists. The English force arrives ten days later to a peaceful reception, Whitelocke going ashore with 700 men to take possession of the port in the name of the French crown.

On 21 September he and Ford continue north to Cap du Môle, which is gripped with fear at a possible attack by black rebels. The English induce its garrison—largely the 87th (former *Dillon* Irish) Regiment—to switch sides and admit them by 22 September.

4 OCTOBER 1793. Whitelocke and Ford attempt to seize Cape Tiburón, but the promised cooperation by white French landowners fails to appear, so the English are repulsed.

2 JANUARY 1794. Ford detaches the 32-gun frigate *Penelope* of Capt. Bartholomew Samuel Rowley to offer capitulation terms to Port au Prince, which are refused; he therefore blockades its harbor.

2 FEBRUARY 1794. Having been reinforced with 800 men from Jamaica, Whitelocke and Ford again make an attempt on Cape Tiburón; this time they are successful and after slight resistance, install a small garrison next day, under Lt. George Bradford of the 23rd (Royal Welsh) Fusiliers.

4 FEBRUARY 1794. In Paris, the national convention officially abolishes slavery throughout France's overseas colonies.

11 FEBRUARY 1794. Whitelocke and Ford advance against Fort Acul, carrying it by storm on 19 February.

LATE MARCH 1794. The African-born Alaou joins Sonthonax's republican cause at Port au Prince but is assassinated shortly thereafter along with 200 of his followers by the rival mulatto chieftain Bauvais. The black leader Hyacinthe is also murdered by mulattoes around this time.

19 MAY 1794. Brigadier General Whyte arrives off Saint Domingue with three regiments, superseding

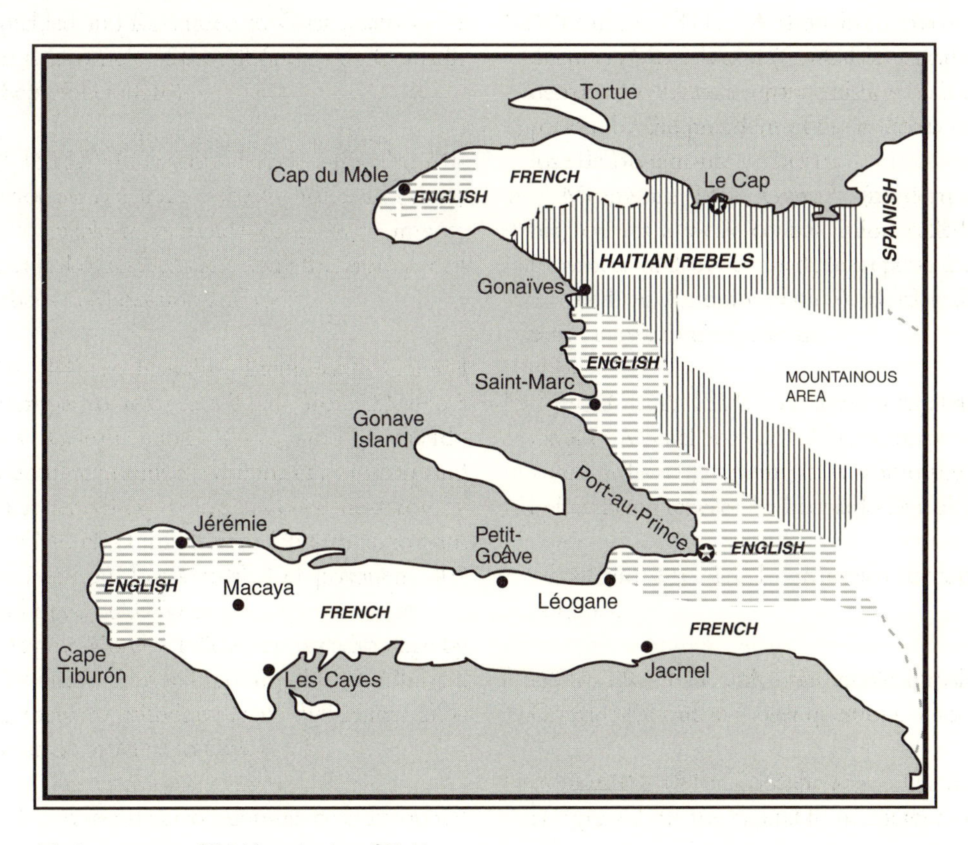

Maximum extent of British occupation of Haiti

Whitelocke as commander in chief of the theater. Together with French royalists they overrun Camp Bizo then advance on the island capital.

31 MAY 1794. ***Port au Prince Assault.*** Ford bears down on Saint Domingue's capital with his 64-gun flagship *Europa,* 74-gun *Irresistible* of Capt. John Henry, 64-gun *Belliqueux* of James Brine and *Sceptre* of James Richard Dacres, three frigates, and three sloops, bearing 1,465 soldiers under Brigadier General Whyte. The soldiers are disembarked next afternoon while *Belliqueux, Sceptre,* and frigate *Penelope* engage nearby Fort Brissoton. That operation is interrupted at 6:00 P.M. by a heavy downpour, but the attackers nevertheless carry the fort at bayonet point.

On 3 June the 32-gun frigates *Hermione* of Capt. John Hills and *Iphigenia* of Patrick Sinclair create a diversion by bombarding the French works at Bernadou, allowing Whyte's troops to advance. Next day Port au Prince is overrun in a brave assault spearheaded by Whitelocke, who is sent home with the dispatches announcing victory. Commissioner Sonthonax retreats to Jacmel, but within a month he is driven into British hands and is returned to France.

25 JUNE 1794. Having previously withdrawn his 4,000 soldiers from the combined Hispano-rebel army in the north, Brig. Gen. Toussaint l'Ouverture (born 51 years earlier as a household slave named François Dominique Toussaint) joins embattled French Gen. Etienne Laveaux in his efforts against the English and Spanish invasions and monarchist and mulatto resistance. L'Ouverture's switch is motivated by Sonthonax's 1793 abolition of slavery—which an English, Spanish, white, or mulatto victory will in all likelihood void. Guerrilla skirmishes persist, but little active campaigning is conducted, as both the British and Spanish forces are decimated by disease, while island factions concentrate on holding individual territories.

Toussaint l'Ouverture

25 DECEMBER 1794. At dawn a French force from Les Cayes attacks the small English garrison at Cape Tiburón, sinking the armed transport *King George* and obliging the invaders to retire to Cape Doña María.

JULY 1795. In Europe, Spain withdraws from the coalition against France, signing the Treaty of Basle that—among other things—cedes all of Santo Domingo to the French in exchange for the return of other conquered territories. Paris insists that the Spanish half of Santo Domingo must be surrendered to a French army rather than to l'Ouverture's black forces, so the actual transaction is deferred a few years.

OCTOBER 1795. News of Santo Domingo's transfer to French rule reaches the island, provoking massive Spanish emigration.

20 MARCH 1796. In Le Cap (modern-day Cap-Haïtien), a mulatto faction arrests French General Laveaux, feeling he is too closely aligned with the interests of former black slaves. Laveaux is rescued by Toussaint, who marches from Gonaïves at the head of

his 10,000-man army, and is thus rewarded with the deputy governorship.

21 MARCH 1796. British occupying forces under Major General Forbes attempt to advance from Port au Prince and recapture Léogâne, supported by 74-gun *Leviathan* of John Thomas Duckworth and *Swiftsure* of Robert Parker; 64-gun *Africa* of Roddam Home; 32-gun frigates *Ceres* of James Newman and *Iphigenia* of Francis Farrington Gardner; 18-gun sloop *Cormorant* of Cmdr. Francis Collingwood; plus 16-gun sloops *Lark* of Cmdr. William Ogilby and *Sirène* (French prize) of Cmdr. Daniel Guerin.

Léogâne proves more strongly defended than anticipated, the British being forced to retreat, with *Leviathan* and *Africa* considerably damaged.

MAY 1796. Sonthonax and other commissioners return to Saint Domingue from France, openly backing its black factions. When the mulatto General Rigaud is unwillingly compelled to attack the English at Cape Tiburón later this summer with his legion of equality—four columns of 1,200 troops apiece—he is defeated, and the French blame his leadership. Some of his lieutenants are subsequently arrested at Les Cayes, provoking widespread rioting, with blacks and mulattoes fighting each other, and the few remaining whites being massacred. Rigaud returns from his base camp near Cape Tiburón to put down the fighting with 3,000–4,000 mulatto followers, then deposes the commissioners in his district. Soon after Toussaint l'Ouverture does the same to Sonthonax in his northern region, returning him to France.

MID-MARCH 1798. After losing 25,000 British troops in five years—mostly due to disease—Brig. Gen. Thomas Maitland enters into negotiations with Toussaint l'Ouverture for the evacuation of his forces from Saint Domingue.

29 MARCH 1798. A new commissioner, Gen. Thomas Hédouville, reaches Le Cap from France. Whereas previous commissioners have favored blacks over mulattoes, Hédouville reverses this policy because of the growing power of Toussaint l'Ouverture's black army. The latter resists by forming a united front with the mulatto leader Rigaud in the south.

EARLY MAY 1798. ***British Withdrawal.*** In a bargain struck with l'Ouverture, Maitland's expeditionary force evacuates Port au Prince, Saint Marc, and Les Cayes—carrying away any French or mulatto inhabitants who wish to accompany them. All are conveyed to Cape Saint Nicholas Mole by Royal Navy warships for eventual emigration.

SUMMER 1798. Hédouville presses his anti-Toussaint machinations by ordering the arrest of the black leader's adopted nephew, Moïse, who resists and is shot at while escaping. Infuriated, l'Ouverture orders his brutal 40-year-old Gen. Jean Jacques Dessalines—originally a slave born Jean Jacques Duclos, now nicknamed "the Tiger"—to march on Le Cap (modern-day Cap-Haïtien) and crush the French commissioner, who flees the island.

FEBRUARY 1799. ***War of the Knives.*** Mulatto General Rigaud announces he is reassuming command over Léogâne and Jacmel in southern Saint Domingue from Toussaint l'Ouverture's appointees, and two of his mulatto subordinates precipitously attack Petit Goâve, sparking an uprising against l'Ouverture's northern black rule. This struggle subsequently becomes known as the War of the Knives. At first Rigaud's mulatto army does well, capturing Grand Goâve and Jacmel; soon, however, it is confronted by more numerous armies from the north, tacitly backed by Anglo-American support and black sentiment.

16 JUNE 1799. Col. Henry Christophe (born a slave 32 years earlier on Grenada) arrives under l'Ouverture's direction to besiege Rigaud's followers within Jacmel, while the black general himself campaigns throughout the rest of this southern territory with Dessalines. Jacmel resists for five months until starvation obliges its garrison to evacuate across enemy lines. The mulatto army disintegrates, waiting in vain for a relief force from France.

AUGUST 1800. After being pressed back on Les Cayes by Dessalines's triumphal advance, Rigaud flees into exile in France, leaving l'Ouverture to appoint Dessalines as occupational governor for southern Saint Domingue. The latter cruelly slaughters hundreds of mulattoes in revenge for their opposition and suppresses black laborers.

26 JANUARY 1801. ***Santo Domingo Coup.*** Learning that First Director Napoleon Bonaparte is contemplating the dispatch of an army from France to occupy the Spanish half of Santo Domingo (*see* July 1795), Toussaint l'Ouverture steals a march by sending 10,000 black troops across its border from Le Cap under Moïse; l'Ouverture appears before the Spanish capital

on 26 January with his own forces—much to the consternation of its inhabitants and numerous French refugees. After assuming overlordship of the territory, abolishing slavery, and appointing brother Paul as governor, the "black Spartacus" returns to the western half of Saint Domingue to continue his reconstruction work. The operation goads Bonaparte into mustering a full-bore expedition to reestablish French control over the entire island.

LATE OCTOBER 1801. L'Ouverture, Dessalines, and Christophe suppress a rebellion by black laborers backed by General Moïse in Le Cap District. The latter is executed in mid-November along with scores of ringleaders.

29 JANUARY 1802. ***Leclerc's Campaign.*** The 29-year-old Gen. Charles Victor Emmanuel Leclerc arrives at Samaná Bay, accompanied by his wife—Bonaparte's youngest sister, Pauline—and a 20,000-man military expedition to reassert France's grip over Saint Domingue. He appears before Le Cap (modern-day Cap-Haïtien) with part of the force four days later, and on 3 February threatens to come ashore with 5,000 soldiers. Christophe, in command of the garrison, requests 48 hours to consult with Toussaint l'Ouverture, but the French general refuses. Christophe therefore evacuates Le Cap, putting it to the torch before retiring into the interior.

Meanwhile other French contingents are disembarked at different points around the island to begin its reconquest. One column marches directly on the Spanish city of Santo Domingo, capturing it with little difficulty (its inhabitants regarding the French as liberators); another under Gen. Jean Boudet seizes Port au Prince, and the mulatto commander Laplume surrenders most of its surrounding district. Dommage prepares to resist at Jérémie but is betrayed; his stronghold is overrun, effectively ending resistance in the south by mid-February. Toussaint and Christophe continue to hold out with some 10,000 black troops dispersed throughout the north; in the west 1,500 black guerrillas under Dessalines occupy Crête à Pierrot. Leclerc sends a large army to besiege them, both of which are bloodily repulsed twice before Dessalines cuts his way out and vanishes into the hills.

Resistance quickly erodes, however, Christophe giving himself up to the French with 1,200 men and his artillery train by 26 April, followed by l'Ouverture on 6 May and Dessalines shortly thereafter. Saint Domingue's revolutionary fortunes appear to be waning, as Leclerc—his own forces now reduced by more than a third because of disease—treacherously orders l'Ouverture seized on 7 June by General Brunet (despite promises of clemency) and begins the process of disarming the entire black populace.

LATE JULY 1802. Reports reach Saint Domingue that the French government has officially restored slavery on Guadeloupe and reopened the transatlantic slave trade, also denying persons of color the title "citizen."

AUGUST 1802. Black resistance on Saint Domingue flares anew, despite Leclerc's attempts to crush it through fearsome massacres and gruesome executions (e.g., by crucifixions and dog attacks). L'Ouverture is deported to France (where he will die of pneumonia in the Alpine fortress of Joux); Christophe—after serving briefly with the French—rejoins the insurrection in October, along with Dessalines and the 32-year-old mulatto exile Alexandre Sabès Pétion. Yellow fever rages through the French ranks, killing Leclerc himself at Le Cap by the night of 2 November. The 47-year-old Gen. Donatien Marie Joseph de Vimeur de Rochambeau (son of the Count of Rochambeau; *see* 20 June 1780) succeeds him as governor and commander in chief.

16 JANUARY 1803. After pressing French troops back inside their garrisons, Dessalines's subordinate Nicolas Geffard briefly occupies the southern port of Anse à Veau, followed shortly thereafter by a successful assault on Cape Tiburón by 2,000 guerrillas out of its hills under the combined leadership of Gilles Bénech, Nicolas Régnier, and Goman. When Colonel Berger subsequently assembles the Port Salut mulatto militia to march to Tiburon's relief early in February, the latter troops also rise in rebellion against French command.

5 MARCH 1803. Geffard's northern army joins Férou's guerrillas at Plaine des Cayes, besieging Berger's French forces within Les Cayes. A relief convoy of 1,200 troops freshly arrived from France under General Sarrazin pauses at Cape Tiburón during the passage to reconquer that place. Instead, he suffers 300 killed before staggering into Les Cayes.

MAY 1803. England renews its war against France, blockading French ports on Saint Domingue as early as June.

AUGUST 1803. Surrounded by insurrection on all sides, cut off at sea, and ravaged by disease, the French forces abandon Jérémie.

3 SEPTEMBER 1803. Facing massacre at the hands of Dessalines, French General d'Henin's 850-man Saint Marc garrison surrenders to Capt. James Walker of HMS *Vanguard,* being evacuated aboard three prizes to Cape Saint Nicholas Mole.

MID-SEPTEMBER 1803. Dessalines, emerging as victor in the struggle against the French, proclaims himself governor-general of the island for life.

21 SEPTEMBER 1803. French General Brunette requests that the Royal Navy evacuate his surviving troops from Les Cayes.

17 OCTOBER 1803. The mulatto General Geffard takes possession of Les Cayes.

LATE NOVEMBER 1803. ***French Evacuation.*** More than 50,000 of 58,000 troops transferred to Saint Domingue within the past two years having died—mostly due to disease—France's cause is lost. A massive flight of white residents occurs from Le Cap (modern-day Cap-Haïtien), effectively ending French rule. Governor Rochambeau's ship is intercepted by the Royal Navy while its leaves, and he is imprisoned for eight years.

1 JANUARY 1804. Dessalines proclaims the new Republic of Haiti (its ancient Arawak name) and orders a convention to be celebrated at Gonaïves to draft a new constitution. The island population has been reduced to about half of its 1790 total by more than a dozen years of genocidal warfare.

FRENCH REVOLUTIONARY WARS (1793–1802)

IN EUROPE, THE OPENING ROUND OF HOSTILITIES between France and an Austro-Prussian coalition in 1792 spreads when the radical new French rulers execute Louis XVI on 21 January 1793 then declare war against Great Britain, Spain, and the Netherlands. Given England's maritime might, plus the purging of royalist elements from France's navy and lack of any significant territorial holdings in the New World, most of the subsequent fighting is confined to European waters. Nevertheless, certain expeditions are dispatched to the Americas, especially to vie for control over the rich sugar islands of the Caribbean.

1 FEBRUARY 1793. Britain officially declares war against revolutionary France.

12 APRIL 1793. At Bridgetown (Barbados), British troops go aboard Vice Adm. Sir John Laforey's 50-gun flagship HMS *Trusty* of Captain John Drew, 16-gun sloop *Nautilus* of Cmdr. Lord Henry Paulet, armed schooner *Hind,* and the hired merchantman *Hero* to attack French Tobago. Arriving off the coast two days later, they call upon the governor to surrender; he refuses. Therefore, at 1:00 P.M. on 15 April Scarborough Fort is carried by assault, the English suffering three killed and 25 wounded, after which the entire island capitulates.

This is followed by an attempt (in conjunction with some French loyalists) against the much larger Martinique, which proves unsuccessful. Naval support consists of Rear Adm. Alan Gardner's 98-gun *Queen* under flag captain John Hutt, 98-gun *Duke* of Capt. George Murray, 74-gun *Hector* of George Montagu, and 74-gun *Monarch* of Sir James Wallace, bearing a large contingent of troops from Barbados under Major General Bruce. This attack miscarries, and many of the French monarchists are left to their fate.

7 MAY 1793. A small British force is embarked at Halifax (Canada) to proceed to the nearby French islands of Saint Pierre and Miquelon, escorted by the 28-gun frigate *Alligator* of Capt. William Affleck and armed schooner *Diligente.* They capture the French outposts without resistance on 14 May.

LATE JANUARY 1794. A British expedition under Vice Adm. Sir John Jervis and 64-year-old Lt. Gen. Sir Charles Grey reaches Barbados from England to spearhead a renewed offensive against French possessions in the West Indies.

2 FEBRUARY 1794. ***Jervis's Sweep.*** The British admiral departs Barbados with his 98-gun flagship *Boyne* under George Grey; Commo. Charles Thompson's 74-gun vice-flagship *Vengeance* under Lord Henry Paulet, and *Irresistible* of John Henry; 64-gun *Asia* of John Brown, and *Veteran* of Charles Edmund Nugent; 40-gun frigate *Beaulieu* of John Salisbury (later Edward Riou); 36-gun frigate *Santa Margarita* of Eliab Harvey; 32-gun frigates *Blonde* of John Markham, *Ceres* of Richard Incleton, *Quebec* of Josiah Rogers, *Solebay* of William Hancock Kelly, and *Winchelsea* of Viscount

Faulknor captures Fort Louis, Martinique, under covering fire from his 16-gun sloop, Zebra; *oil painting by William Anderson*

Garlies; 28-gun frigate *Rose* of Edward Riou (later Matthew Henry Scott); 16-gun sloops *Avenger* of Cmdr. James Milne (later William Henry Bayntun), *Nautilus* of Cmdr. James Carpenter, *Rattlesnake* of Cmdr. Matthew Henry Scott, and *Zebra* of Cmdr. Robert Faulknor (later Richard Bowen); eight-gun bomb vessel *Vesuvius* of Charles Sawyer; 44-gun storeship *Woolwich* of John Parker; and 24-gun storeship *Dromedary* of Sandford Tatham. These are escorting transports bearing 6,100 troops under General Grey.

This expedition arrives off Martinique by 5 February, finding only the 32-gun French frigate *Bienvenue* anchored before Fort Royal (modern-day Fort de France) and an 18-gun corvette at Saint Pierre. The troops are therefore disembarked at three different places, with little opposition. By 16 March they have General Rochambeau's 600 defenders besieged within Forts Louis and Bourbon, the rest of this island being in English hands at a cost of 71 redcoats killed, and 196 wounded or missing. The capital's main citadel of Fort Louis is stormed by 20 March, Commander Faulknor's sloop *Zebra* working in so close during the bombardment that he leaps ashore with a landing party and carries a crucial part of its works. Once this stronghold falls, Rochambeau surrenders Fort Bourbon on 22 March, and Martinique passes entirely into British hands. (*Bienvenue* is incorporated into the Royal Navy as *Undaunted,* Faulknor being promoted its new captain.)

By 31 March most of the British army is reembarked, Jervis and Grey striking out toward Saint Lucia. Arriving next day, they again disembark their forces at three different places toward evening, obliging General Ricard to surrender by 4 April. The greater part of the troops then return to Martinique next day, gathering strength for an assault against Guadeloupe. Reinforcements continually swell the British fleet, including the 44-gun frigates *Assurance* of Velters Cornwall Berkeley, and *Roebuck* of Alexander Christie; 44-gun storeships *Experiment* of Cmdr. Simon Miller, and *Ulysses* of Cmdr. Richard Morice; 32-gun frigates *Blanche* of Christopher Parker (later Faulknor), and *Terpsichore* of Sampson Edwards; 28-gun frigate *Resource* under its acting captain, Cmdr. Charles Herbert; 16-gun sloop *Inspector* of Cmdr. Wyndham Bryer; 14-gun sloop *Bulldog* of Edward Browne; 14-gun cutter *Seaflower* of Lt. William Pierrepoint; plus the gunboats *Spiteful* of John Hindes Sparkes, *Teaser* of J. Hope, *Tickler* of Lt. Henry Wray, *Tormentor* of William Wells, *Vernon* of Lt. Thomas Henry Wilson, and *Vexer* of R. Smith.

On 8 April Jervis sets sail toward Guadeloupe, detaching the frigates *Quebec, Ceres,* and *Rose,* plus a sloop, to occupy the adjoining Saintes two days later. This same evening of 10 April, the first contingent of Jervis's main fleet anchors in Guadeloupe's Gosier Bay, some troops disembarking next day under covering fire from the frigate *Winchelsea.* The transports arrive by 12 April, Fleur d'Epée being taken by Major General Dundas and Captain Faulknor. Shortly thereafter Fort Saint Louis, Point à Pitre, and Islot à Cochon battery are abandoned by the French, so that Grande Terre passes entirely into British hands. The army reembarks and circles west to Petit Bourg (Basse-Terre) on 14 April, again landing without opposition and compelling Gen. Georges Henri Victor Collot to surrender the entire island by 20 April. Dundas is installed as governor, after which the Jervis-Grey expedition withdraws.

2 JUNE 1794. ***Hugues's Counteroffensive.*** A nine-ship squadron arrives from France to recuperate Guadeloupe, disgorging 1,100 troops in Gosier Bay on the afternoon of 4 June under Commissioner Jean Baptiste Victor Hugues and General Aubert. The 21-year-old British commander for its Basse-Terre region, Lt. Col. Gordon Drummond, is obliged to retreat by boat to Grande-Terre. News of this French counteroffensive reaches Jervis and Grey at Saint Kitts by 5 June, who immediately sail to Guadeloupe's relief with what forces they can muster, arriving on 7 June. Grey disembarks while Jervis proceeds to Point à Pitre with HMSS *Boyne, Vanguard, Vengeance,* and *Veteran.*

Neither side is sufficiently strong to drive the other off this island, so several months' desultory campaigning ensues. On 19 June two battalions of British seamen under *Veteran's* Capt. Lewis Robertson are landed at Anse à Canot (Grande-Terre), but after several minor skirmishes they reembark on 3 July, having suffered seven killed—including Robertson—29 wounded, and 16 missing.

Finally, on 27 September, after receiving additional reinforcements from France, Hugues disembarks contingents at Basse-Terre's Goyanne and Lamentin to attack the main British encampment at Berville. Its 2,000 defenders hold out until 6 October, when they surrender and are deported (their 400 French royalist allies being executed). Only Fort Mathilde remains in British hands, and is evacuated after two months' siege by Capt. Richard Bowen of *Terpsichore* during the night of 10 December, leaving Guadeloupe once more entirely in French hands.

NOVEMBER 1794. Jervis returns home to England, being relieved in the Lesser Antilles by Vice Adm. Benjamin Caldwell.

5 JANUARY 1795. Off Désirade, 74-gun *Bellona* of Capt. George Wilson and 32-gun frigate *Alarm* of Charles Carpenter intercept a French troop convoy being escorted toward Guadeloupe by 50-gun *Hercule,* 36-gun frigate *Astrée,* two corvettes, and some armed ships. The Royal Navy pair is only able to capture the 20-gun *Duras,* thus allowing 3,000 reinforcements to reach General Hugues at Point à Pitre next day.

MID-JANUARY 1795. In Europe, French revolutionary armies overrun the Netherlands, helping install a satellite government known as the Batavian Republic.

JANUARY 1795. French forces raid the British island of Saint Vincent.

3 MAY 1795. HMS *Zebra* arrives at Stabroek (Essequibo, Guiana), bearing a letter from the exiled Prince of Orange, directing its Dutch colonial authorities to recognize England as Holland's ally. Gov. Albertus Backer is willing to comply, but the settlers demur, and the vessel retires.

Toward the end of the month, however, nine British warships appear off the mouth of the Demerara River to renew the offer, which is also refused.

19 JUNE 1795. After being invaded the previous day by French forces from Guadeloupe, the tiny English garrison on Saint Lucia is evacuated by the armed storeship *Experiment* of Lt. John Barrett and a transport. Similar French attempts against Dominica, Grenada, and Saint Vincent prove unsuccessful.

22 JULY 1795. In Europe, Spain and Prussia cease hostilities against the French.

10 OCTOBER 1795. The French campaign against Grenada is hampered when Capt. Henry Warre's 32-gun frigate *Mermaid* intercepts the ten-gun sloop *Brutus,* followed four days later by the 18-gun *Républicaine,* which are bearing a French general and troops toward this embattled island.

21 APRIL 1796. The 48-year-old Rear Adm. Sir Hugh Cloberry Christian, recently invested with a Knighthood of the Bath, reaches Carlisle Bay (Barbados) with two ships of the line and five lesser men-of-war. From there, he escorts the remnants of

a convoy—scattered by a storm—with a large contingent of troops under 61-year-old Lt. Gen. Sir Ralph Abercromby. After uniting with Vice Adm. Sir John Laforey, commander in chief of the Leeward Islands, the fleet proceeds next day to Marin Bay (Martinique), where it anchors on 23 April. Laforey subsequently resigns his command to Christian by 24 April and sails for England aboard 74-gun HMS *Majestic.*

23 APRIL 1796. Commodore Thomas Parr appears off the Dutch colonies of Demerara and Essequibo with his 54-gun flagship *Malabar;* 64-gun *Scipio* of Francis Laforey; 40-gun frigates *Undaunted* of Henry Roberts and *Pique* of David Milne; plus the auxiliary *Babet* of William Granville Lobb.

These have been detached eight days earlier by Vice Admiral Laforey to convey a contingent of troops under Maj. Gen. John Whyte to occupy the Dutch possessions. This they easily accomplish, further seizing Berbice by 2 May along with the 24-gun frigate *Thetis* and the 12-gun sloop *Zeemeeuw* plus several richly laden merchantmen.

26 APRIL 1796. ***Britain's Windward Isles Triumph.*** Christian and Abercromby depart Martinique with the 74-gun *Thunderer* of flag Capt. James Bowen, *Canada* of George Bowen, *Vengeance* of Thomas Macnamara Russell, *Minotaur* of Thomas Louis, *Ganges* of Robert McDowall, and *Alfred* of Thomas Durry; 54-gun *Hindustan* of Thomas Bertie, *Madras* of J. Dilkes, and *Abergavenny* of Edward T. Smith; 44-gun frigate *Charon* of J. Stevenson; 40-gun *Beaulieu* of L. Skinner; 38-gun *Arethusa* of Thomas Woolley, and *Hebe* of M. H. Scott; 36-gun *Undaunted* of H. Roberts; 32-gun *Astrea* of R. Lane; and 28-gun *Laurel* of Robert Rolles; 16-gun brigs *Fury* of H. Evans, *Bulldog* of G. F. Ryves, *Pelican* of John Clarke Searle, and *Victorieuse* of Jemmett Mainwaring; 44-gun storeship *Woolwich* of Daniel Dobree; 20-gun *Tourterelle* of Edward Fellowes; 16-gun *Beaver* of S. G. Warren; plus eight-gun bomb vessel *Terror* of D. Douglas.

Next morning these arrive off French-held Saint Lucia with a large number of transports, a disembarkation being immediately effected in Longueville Bay under covering fire from *Ganges* and *Pelican.* Another landing is made at 10:30 A.M. of 28 April in Choc Bay—the same day on which Morne Chabot is carried—while a third disembarkation is completed in Anse La Raye by 29 April. The French nonetheless resist vigorously, repelling an attack against some of their advance batteries on 3 May, then against Vigie on 17 May, with heavy losses to the invaders. After being driven into Morne Fortunée, however, 2,000 Frenchmen have no choice but to offer to surrender by 24 May, this entire island capitulating at noon two days later.

A similarly stout resistance is met when Christian and Abercromby subsequently detach *Arethusa, Hebe,* the 32-gun frigate *Mermaid* of Capt. Robert Waller Otway, *Pelican,* and 16-gun *Beaver* of Cmdr. S. G. Warner with a contingent of troops to subdue Saint Vincent. This round of fighting ends by 11 June, after which nearby Grenada also surrenders a few days later. (In late June Christian is relieved by Rear Adm. Henry Harvey, so returns to England in October aboard *Beaulieu.*)

18 AUGUST 1796. France and Spain sign an alliance at Madrid that is ratified in Paris on 12 September. Immediately thereafter Britain places an embargo on Spanish shipping.

28 AUGUST 1796. The 38-year-old French Rear Adm. (and former nobleman) Joseph de Richery arrives unexpectedly off Newfoundland with a squadron, finding only Capt. Thomas Graves's 32-gun frigate *Venus* inside Saint John's. The British brace for an assault, but Richery instead bears away south, entering Bay Bulls on 4 September to destroy its fishing camps. Next day he detaches 34-year-old Rear Adm. Zacharie Jacques Théodore, Comte Allemand, to raid the Bay of Castles (Labrador) with *Duquesne, Censeur,* and *Friponne* while Richery himself proceeds to Saint Pierre and Miquelon with his main body to visit a like treatment upon its shore establishments. Because of contrary winds, Allemand does not gain Labrador until 22 September, burning its largely deserted fishing bases. Both French contingents then recross the Atlantic safely.

6 OCTOBER 1796. Spain declares war against England.

OCTOBER 1796. Revolutionary France, angry at U.S. ratification of John Jay's treaty with Great Britain (contrary to Paris's insistence that the 18-year-old Franco-American alliance is still in effect), begins harassing American shipping. Within eight months 316 American vessels are seized on the high seas.

25 NOVEMBER 1796. The 28-gun British frigate *Lapwing* of Capt. Robert Barton hastens out of Saint Kitts, having been summoned to help repel a French disembarkation on nearby Anguilla. Next day it arrives, obliging the invaders to retire aboard their 20-gun

sloop *Décius* and ten-gun *Vaillante*. The former is captured after a one-hour firefight in which 120 of 336 men aboard are either killed or wounded; the latter is beached and destroyed by *Lapwing*'s guns.

12 FEBRUARY 1797. ***Trinidad.*** Admiral Harvey sails south from Fort Royal (modern-day Fort de France, Martinique), being reinforced off Carriacou Island two days later, so as to bring his strength up to 98-gun flagship *Prince of Wales* of Capt. John Harvey; 74-gun *Bellona* of George Wilson, *Vengeance* of Thomas Macnamara Russell, and *Invincible* of George William Cayley; 64-gun *Scipio* of Charles Sydney Davers; 38-gun frigate *Arethusa* of Thomas Wolley; 32-gun frigate *Alarm* of Edward Fellowes; 16-gun sloops *Favourite* of Cmdr. James Atholl Wood, *Zebra,* and *Thorn* of Cmdr. John Hamstead; 12-gun sloop *Victorieuse* of Cmdr. Edward Stirling Dickson; plus eight-gun bomb vessel *Terror* of Cmdr. Joseph Westbeach. The fleet is escorting 40 transports bearing 6,750 soldiers under General Abercromby, who has returned from a visit to England for an attempt against the Spanish sugar island of Trinidad.

The British sight their objective early on 16 February, steering for the Gulf of Paria by way of Boca Grande. At 3:30 P.M., as the expedition clears the channel, they discover Spanish Rear Adm. Sebastián Ruiz de Apodaca anchored inside Chaguaramas Bay with his 80-gun flagship *San Vicente* of Commo. Jerónimo González de Mendoza; 74-gun *Gallardo* (official name *San Juan de Sahagún*) of Gabriel Sorondo and *San Dámaso* of José Jordán; 68-gun *Arrogante* of Rafael Benazar; 34-gun frigate *Santa Cecilia* (alias *Concha*) of Manuel Urtizabal; plus the brigantine *Galgo.* The Spanish squadron has recently arrived in reply to Gov. José María Chacón's request for reinforcements, but the crews have been so decimated by disease—suffering more than 700 deaths—that *Gallardo* and *Arrogante* have been unable to continue toward Cartagena as planned.

Batteries on Gaspar Grande Island cover both entrances of the bay with 20 guns and two mortars, so Harvey anchors offshore while directing Abercromby's transports to find a berth about five miles from the island capital of Puerto España (Port of Spain), and detaching *Arethusa, Thorn,* and *Zebra* to patrol overnight. The outnumbered Spaniards are so demoralized by their enemies' sudden materialization that Ruiz de Apodaca orders his batteries spiked and

The British observe Ruiz de Apodaca's burning Spanish warships inside Chaguaramas Bay, Trinidad, during the night of 16–17 February 1797.

warships scuttled during the night before retreating inland to join Governor Chacón.

The British are surprised to see the Spanish men-of-war burst into flames at 2:00 A.M. on 17 February, managing to save only *San Dámaso* next morning, and incorporating it into the Royal Navy. Meanwhile Abercromby disembarks three miles outside Port of Spain without opposition from Chacón's 600 troops. The capital is occupied that evening, the entire island capitulating ten days later. Losses total seven Spaniards killed and one Briton wounded; for their feeble resistance both Chacón and Ruiz de Apodaca are cashiered upon their return to Spain.

8 APRIL 1797. ***Puerto Rico.*** After being reinforced by the 74-gun *Alfred* of Capt. Thomas Totty, 38-gun frigate *Tamer* of Thomas Byam Martin, plus several lesser craft, Harvey's fleet steers for Puerto Rico with Abercromby's transports. The 60 vessels arrive on 17 April and probe San Juan's shoreline before anchoring off Cangrejos Beach that evening, disembarking numerous troops under Abercromby next morning against slight opposition.

The Spanish governor, Brig. Gen. Ramón de Castro—although commanding only 200 regulars—mounts a vigorous defense based on the capital's natural impregnability. San Antonio Bridge is fortified as are the city's other major defenses, and a half-dozen floating batteries are launched in the harbor under frigate Capt. Francisco de Paula Castro. Even 100 French privateers under Captains Barron and Paris are pressed into service ashore.

After reconnoitering San Juan's defenses, Abercromby institutes formal siege proceedings but is unable to make any headway against the garrison. Castro leads a sally with 800 militia and two troops of cavalry on the night of 29–30 April, finally compelling the British to break camp and lift the siege next day. They sail away by 2 May after suffering 31 killed, 70 wounded, and 124 captured or missing.

OCTOBER 1797. American commissioners arrive in Paris to patch up strained relations with its revolutionary directory. Three agents of French Foreign Minister Charles Maurice de Talleyrand Périgord—identified only as "X," "Y," and "Z"—request a bribe and are angrily rejected.

20 MAY 1798. A Spanish squadron reluctantly quits Campeche to sail toward Cozumel—except Capt. Sancho de Luna's 40-gun royal frigate *Minerva* (flag), which turns back—then detaches the eight-gun sloop *Feliz* of Sr. Lt. Francisco de Fuentes Bocanegra and brigantine *Príncipe de la Paz* of Jr. Lt. Pedro Grajales to proceed into Chetumal with a troop convoy by 28 July and attack the English logwood establishments in Belize.

3 JUNE 1798. Spanish Gov. Arturo O'Neill de Tyrone marches out of Mérida de Yucatán with four militia companies plus two half-companies of black troops to reinforce San Felipe de Bacalar and launch an offensive into Belize.

9 JULY 1798. ***Quasi-War with France.*** As a result of continuous maritime frictions, the United States declares war against France. Because of the distance separating the belligerents it will prove to be a commercial war, with American warships protecting traffic from French commerce raiders.

31 AUGUST 1798. ***Belize.*** O'Neill's 2,000-strong army advances from Bacalar (Yucatán), skirmishing into Belize, which is defended by detachments of the 63rd and 6th West Indian Regiments under Lt. Col. Thomas Barrow. The Spanish expedition is soon reinforced by its flotilla offshore, the only Royal Navy warship in these waters being the 16-gun sloop *Merlin* of Cmdr. John Ralph Moss—although the colony also boasts the gunboats *Tickler, Towzer,* and *Mermaid,* the schooners *Teaser* and *Swinger,* plus eight lesser craft. They prove sufficient to repel attacks off Montego Key on 3, 4, and 5 September and off Saint George's Key on 6 September.

By 10 September O'Neill orders Lieutenant de Fuentes to lead his flotilla into battle against the English vessels anchored off Saint George's Key, but this senior officer refuses. The governor therefore delegates de Fuentes to command the transports while personally leading the attack of four Spanish gunboats, a sloop, three schooners, and two launches. The force advances at 2:00 P.M., passing between Saint George's Key and Cocina Key to open fire on a portion of the British flotilla. When *Merlin* and others weigh to join the action the second-in-command, Grajales, hoists the withdrawal signal after an hour's fighting, the attackers retreating until nightfall.

The Spaniards then remain off Chapel Key until 15 September, when their land contingent retires to Bacalar and Fuentes's flotilla returns to Campeche.

DECEMBER 1798. Having driven French raiders out of American waters, 21 U.S. Navy ships are assigned to rid the West Indies of privateers; the American ships operate out of British bases.

9 FEBRUARY 1799. Thomas Truxtun's 36-gun *Constellation* captures the 40-gun *Insurgente* of "citizen" Barreaut off Nevis, inflicting 70 casualties. The American frigate suffers one killed and two wounded.

31 JULY 1799. Vice Adm. Lord Hugh Seymour sets sail from Fort Royal (Fort de France, Martinique) with his 98-gun flagship *Prince of Wales* under Capt. Adrian Renou; 74-gun *Invincible* of George William Cayley; 38-gun frigates *Tamer* of Thomas Western and *Unité* (French prize) of John Poo Beresford; 32-gun *Siren* of Thomas Le Marchant Gosselin; 28-gun frigates *Lapwing* of Thomas Harvey and *Amphitrite* of Charles Ekins; 20-gun sloop *Daphne* of Richard Matson; and 12-gun sloop *Requin* (French prize) of Lt. William Wood Senhouse. They carry numerous troops under Lt. Gen. Thomas Trigge for an operation against the last remaining Dutch colony in South America, Suriname.

11 AUGUST 1799. Seymour and Trigge arrive off Suriname, convincing its Dutch governor to capitulate on 20 August, Fort Amsterdam's garrison marching out next day with full honors of war. By 22 August all important points in Suriname—including the capital, Paramaribo—are occupied, and 16-gun brig-sloop *Kemphaan* and 20-gun French *Hussard* are seized, both being incorporated into the Royal Navy.

1 FEBRUARY 1800. This evening Thomas Truxtun's 36-gun *Constellation* brings the 54-gun *Vengeance* to action off Guadeloupe, killing 28 and wounding 40 French crewmembers before the frigate limps into Curaçao. The American ship suffers 14 dead and 25 injured and loses its mainmast.

30 SEPTEMBER 1800. America's quasi-war with France ends after seven months of negotiations with First Consul Napoleon Bonaparte. The French give up their insistence that the 1778 treaty of alliance is still in force (having hoped thereby to prevent the United States from dealing with Britain); the Americans drop their demand for $20 million compensation. Public displeasure in the U.S. proves so profound that incumbent John Adams loses the presidential election to Thomas Jefferson this autumn.

EARLY 1801. In Europe, Britain reacts against the League of Armed Neutrality, organized the previous winter by Russia's Tsar Paul I as a countermeasure to the Royal Navy's blockade of France. Consequently, the English take action against Russia, Denmark, Sweden, and Prussia.

20 MARCH 1801. On instructions from London, an expedition under 53-year-old Rear Adm. John Thomas Duckworth, veteran commander of the Leeward Islands station (*see* 21 March 1796), and General Trigge occupy the tiny Swedish colony of Saint Bartholomew, then Saint Martin four days later. The Danish outposts of Saint Thomas and Saint John (Virgin Islands) are seized by 29 March, and Saint Croix capitulates to the English two days later.

16 APRIL 1801. The French are obliged to evacuate the islands of their Dutch allies, Sint Eustatius and Sabá, which are then seized by Capt. John Perkins of 20-gun sloop *Arab* with a few troops under Colonel Blunt of 3rd Buffs. (Perkins is apparently a mulatto naval officer commissioned in the West Indies, known as "Jack Punch" because one of his earliest commands was the schooner *Punch*.)

MAY 1801. Rear Adm. Jean Baptiste Raymond Lacrosse reaches Guadeloupe with 400 French troops, and one month later, begins to reorganize its 4,100 defenders. Numerous black officers and troops have been raised during this island's lengthy blockade who resent Lacrosse's wholesale dismissal of their services. They therefore mutiny under Col. Magloire Pélage and drive the admiral from office as governor.

12 OCTOBER 1801. In Europe, Britain and France agree to a temporary cessation of hostilities.

MAY 1802. Gen. Antoine Richepanse reaches Guadeloupe with 3,500 soldiers to restore French rule to the island and disarm its black troops. A sharp, one-month campaign crushes most opposition, slavery being reintroduced shortly thereafter. (On 3 September this general dies of yellow fever.)

1802–1803. In Europe, the Treaty of Amiens is signed on 27 March 1802, marking a temporary halt to hostilities. By its terms, Saint Pierre, Miquelon, Tobago, Martinique, and Saint Lucia are to be restored to France; the Netherlands will receive Demerara, Essequibo, Berbice, Suriname, and Curaçao. The tiny Swedish and Danish colonies in the Virgin Islands are also to be returned by Great Britain—which thus only retains Trinidad for its efforts.

The truce will last less than 14 months before fighting flares anew.

Napoleonic Wars (1803–1810)

Hostilities between Britain and France resume on 16 May 1803—the Netherlands (Batavian Republic) joining their French allies on 25 June—so that the Royal Navy reimposes its blockade on continental ports.

17 June 1803. Late this evening, 41-year-old Commodore Samuel Hood (a cousin of Admiral Lord Hood; *see* 30 January, 1781) reaches Barbados with an English squadron to escort Lt. Gen. William Grinfield's expeditionary force against objectives in the West Indies. The commodore immediately detaches Capt. James O'Bryen of the 36-gun frigate *Emerald* with some consorts to blockade French Saint Lucia while Grinfield's troops are embarked.

20 June 1803. ***Saint Lucia.*** Hood sets sail from Barbados with HMSS *Centaur* (flag), *Courageux, Argo, Chichester, Hornet,* and the 18-gun sloop *Cyane,* escorting Grinfield's troop convoy to Saint Lucia. HMSS *Emerald* and *Osprey* join next morning, bearing Maj. Gen. George Prevost (governor of Dominica); the whole British flotilla anchors in Choc Bay by 11:00 A.M.

The 2nd Battalion of the Royals are landed by 2:00 P.M. on 21 June under Brigadier General Brereton along with two field pieces, followed by Grinfield with the rest of his small army; a contingent of marines meanwhile occupies nearby Gros Islet. After calling on the French to surrender and being rebuffed, the British general carries the Morne Fortunée stronghold by storm at 4:30 A.M. on 22 June, leading to a capitulation of the entire island.

31 June 1803. British forces capture Tobago.

24 July 1803. At 6:00 P.M. on this squally Sunday, the French 74s *Duquesne* and *Duguay Trouin* slip out of Cap-François (modern-day Cap-Haïtien) with the frigate *Guerrière* in an attempt to elude Capt. John Loring's blockading squadron. The 74-gun HMS *Elephant* of Captain Dundas pursues the trio westward, along with the frigates *Æolus* and *Tartar;* the English 74s *Theseus* and *Vanguard* lag behind.

During the night, Captain Kerrangel's *Duquesne* doubles back east and surrenders at 3:30 P.M. next day to *Theseus* and *Vanguard* after a token exchange of shot. Loring's squadron also snaps up Lieutenant Druault's 16-gun, 60-man French schooner *Oiseau* during the pursuit, between Tortuga and Saint Domingue.

31 August 1803. ***Capture of Demerara.*** Having learned at Barbados of the month-old rupture in Anglo-Batavian relations, General Grinfield leads a small army aboard Hood's *Centaur* (flag), *Chichester, Alligator,* transport *Brilliant,* auxiliaries *Heureux* and *Netley,* plus several smaller storeships to set sail next morning and attack the Dutch settlements on the Wild Coast.

The British expedition arrives off Demerara's roads by evening on 16 September, Lieutenant Lawrence's *Netley* probing the shoreline and capturing 24 boats to disembark the troops. A surrender demand is also sent ashore to Gov.-Gen. A. Meerteks, who requests terms next morning. *Hornet* and *Netley* then sail upriver by evening on 19 September, taking possession of Fort Willem Frederick, the 18-gun Batavian corvette *Hippomenes,* and a dozen prizes, the actual capitulation of Demerara and Essequibo being formalized next day.

Immediately, Capt. Loftus Otway Bland of *Heureux* departs to obtain the surrender of Berbice as well, with a detachment of troops and marines under Lieutenant Colonel Nicholson aboard *Alligator, Netley,* and *Brilliant.*

19 October 1803. Spain signs a secret alliance with France, which is to be made public once its treasure ships arrive safely from the Americas. (Among the treaty's terms: Madrid cedes Santo Domingo and Louisiana to France; Napoleon promptly sells the latter to the United States on 20 December.)

6 January 1804. ***Diamond Rock.*** This evening Hood's 74-gun flagship HMS *Centaur* under Capt. Murray Maxwell anchors off Diamond Rock—a small strategic islet a mile southwest of Martinique—and next morning sends a party of British seamen to occupy it, installing heavy batteries to hold it against enemy counterattack. By 3 February a 120-man garrison is in place, and for administrative purposes the British commission this outpost "His Majesty's sloop of war *Fort Diamond*" (later changed to *Diamond Rock*). Martinique's governor—56-year-old Vice Adm. Louis Thomas, Comte Villaret de Joyeuse—is unable to muster effective countermeasures.

March 1804. Fearful of a possible invasion of Haiti by France—which has not yet relinquished claims to the island—Governor-General Dessalines massacres nearly every remaining white and many mulattoes.

5 APRIL 1804. Commodore Hood departs Barbados with HMSS *Centaur* (flag), 44-gun frigate *Pandour, Serapis, Alligator, Drake,* sloops *Hippomenes* and *Guachapin,* plus the schooner *Unique,* escorting a convoy bearing 2,000 troops under Maj. Gen. Sir Charles Green to attack Dutch Suriname. Captain O'Bryen's HMS *Emerald* joins en route.

25 APRIL 1804. ***Suriname.*** Hood and Green arrive off the Dutch colony, a division of 700 men under Brigadier General Maitland being immediately disembarked at Warapa Creek. Next evening HMSS *Emerald, Pandour,* and *Drake* cross the bar and bombard the seven-gun Dutch battery at Braam Point, allowing Brigadier General Hughes's division to wade ashore and capture its 43-man garrison (three of whom are wounded). On the morning of 27 April Hood and Green transfer from *Centaur* aboard *Emerald* and proceed to the Suriname River mouth to call upon the authorities—inland at Paramaribo—to surrender. Gov. P. Berranger, Lt. Col. B. A. Batenburg, and Commo. H. O. Bloys van Treslong next day refuse, so the English squadron slowly forges upstream.

Hughes's division also presses overland, overrunning Leyden Redoubt the morning of 30 April after being disembarked at Resolution Plantation by a Royal Navy boat party. The Dutch garrison fire the magazine and withdraw, inflicting numerous casualties when the British unwarily enter and it detonates. Meanwhile Maitland closes in from the west, and Hood's shallow-draft warships arrive off Fort New Amsterdam by evening on 5 May. Batenburg has already requested terms the previous evening, and on 6 May the Dutch capitulate, surrendering their colony along with the 32-gun frigate *Proserpine,* the 18-gun corvette *Pylades* (captured from the English earlier in the war), three merchantmen, the ten-gun sloop *George,* and seven gunboats.

5 OCTOBER 1804. Captain Graham Moore, with the Royal Navy frigates *Amphion, Lively, Medusa,* and *Indefatigable,* intercepts the Spanish frigates *Medea, Clara, Mercedes,* and *Fama* as they approach Spain from the Americas under Brig. Gen. José Bustamante y Guerra, governor of Montevideo. The latter are bearing treasure from Manila, Callao, and the River Plate, which Moore demands they surrender. When the Spaniards resist the English open fire; *Mercedes* explodes before the other three give up.

8 OCTOBER 1804. Dessalines proclaims himself Emperor Jacques I of Haiti.

2 DECEMBER 1804. In Paris, First Consul Bonaparte crowns himself Emperor Napoleon I.

12 DECEMBER 1804. Spain officially declares war against Britain.

20 FEBRUARY 1805. The 48-year-old French Rear Adm. Edouard Thomas de Burgues, Comte de Missiessy, appears off Martinique, entering two days later with five ships of the line, three frigates, two brigs, and a schooner bearing 3,300 men, having eluded the British blockading squadron off Rochefort.

22 FEBRUARY 1805. French forces raid the British island of Dominica, departing five days later.

LATE FEBRUARY 1805. ***Haitian Offensive.*** In order to attack French Gen. Jean Louis Ferrand, still holding out in Santo Domingo, black Emperor Jacques I (formerly Dessalines) advances along both the northern and southern shores of the island toward the Spanish capital. Santo Domingo is reached on 8 March by 21,000 Haitian troops and besieged for three weeks. Only the chance appearance of Missiessy's small squadron on 26 February breaks the encirclement, as Jacques fears it portends a French invasion of Haiti during his absence. (Actually, Missiessy is homeward-bound to France, having quit Martinique on 22 February; he exits the Caribbean by 28 March.)

The Haitians raise their siege and fall back through the interior, laying waste to Monte Plata, Cotui, and La Vega, as well as slaughtering the inhabitants of Moca and Santiago.

MARCH 1805. Local French forces launch raids against Saint Kitts, Nevis, and Montserrat.

3 APRIL 1805. Rear Adm. Sir Alexander Forrester Inglis Cochrane (knight of the Bath and uncle to Thomas, Lord Cochrane; *see* 28 November 1818) reaches Barbados with the 74-gun HMS *Northumberland* and four other British ships of the line, having traversed the Atlantic in pursuit of Missiessy. Within two days he incorporates another ship and four frigates into his command and stands away to Santo Domingo. Finding his foe already gone, Cochrane proceeds to Jamaica to reinforce Rear Adm. James Dacres.

25 April 1805. Cochrane quits Port Royal (Jamaica) with his squadron to take up station in the Leeward Islands.

14 May 1805. ***Villeneuve Versus Nelson.*** The 41-year-old French Vice Adm. Pierre Charles Silvestre de Villeneuve, and his 34-year-old second-in-command Rear Adm. Pierre Étienne René, Comte Dumanoir Le Pelley, arrive from across the Atlantic at Fort de France (Martinique) with the 80-gun flagship *Bucentaure, Neptune, Formidable,* and *Indomptable;* 74s *Pluton, Mont Blanc, Berwick, Atlas, Swift-sure, Scipion,* and *Intrépide;* 40-gun frigates *Cornélie, Rhin, Hortense, Hermione, Sirène,* and *Thémis;* plus two gun brigs and the British sloop *Cyane* (captured 150 miles to windward of Barbados). Their crews are fleshed out with several hundred soldiers, and carry a separate force of 3,332 troops under Gen. Jacques Lauriston. This fleet is also accompanied by Spanish Adm. Federico Carlos Gravina's ships of the line *Argonauta* (flag), *Terrible, América, España, San Rafael,* and *Firme,* with 1,930 soldiers over and above their usual complements.

This combined formation's objective is to lure a major British battle fleet across the ocean in its wake, then immediately return to Europe and gain a temporary advantage in the Channel for an invasion of England. Over the next two weeks, Villeneuve remains at anchor in Fort de France, blockading its offshore English base of Diamond Rock while awaiting the arrival of an additional fleet from Brest under 49-year-old Vice Adm. Honoré Joseph Antoine, Comte Ganteaume.

29 May 1805. ***Reclamation of Diamond Rock.*** At 5:30 p.m. the French *Pluton* of 43-year-old Commo. Julien Marie, Baron Cosmao Kerjulien; *Berwick* of Captain Carmas; frigate *Sirène* of Captain Chabert; brig *Argus* of Captain Taillard; and schooner *Fine* of Captain Meynard tow 11 gunboats out of Fort de France (Martinique), bearing 240 troops under Major Boyer to attack Diamond Rock. After circling out to sea, the French squadron closes at 7:00 a.m. on 31 May, opening fire an hour later. Capt. James Wilkes Maurice offers a spirited resistance with his 128-man garrison, destroying three gunboats and continuing to shell the French troops once they wade ashore. Finally, although having suffered only two killed and one wounded, the exhausted British magazines oblige the defenders to request terms at 4:30

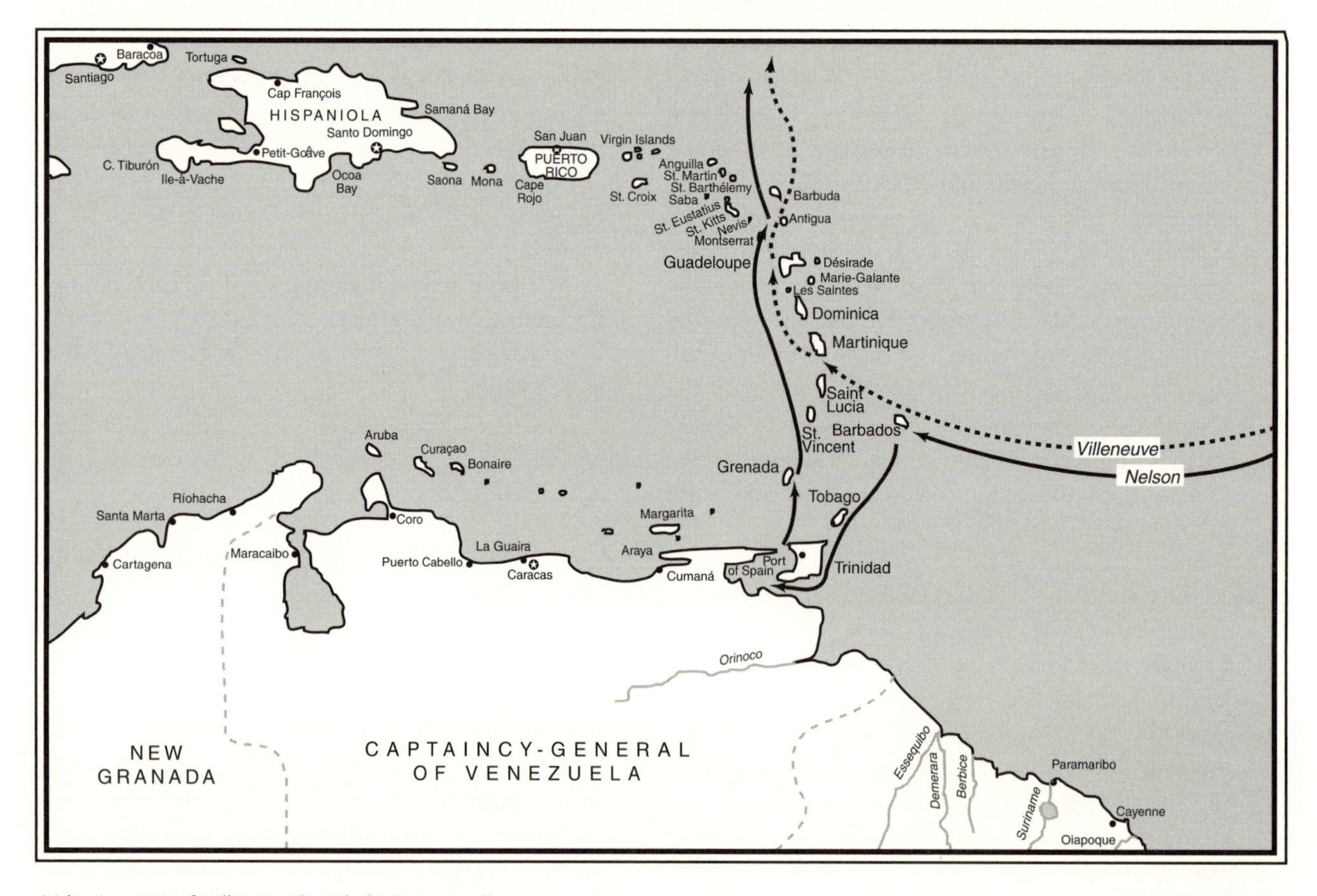

Nelson's pursuit of Villeneuve through the Lesser Antilles

P.M. on 2 June, capitulating next day and being repatriated to Barbados by 6 June.

Meanwhile the French frigate *Didon* has reached Martinique on 30 May with new orders from Napoleon instructing Villeneuve to land his troops as reinforcements for the West Indian garrisons, ravage the British colonies as a diversion, then steer quickly to Europe. On 4 June the French 74s *Algésiras* and *Achille* also arrive under 41-year-old Rear Adm. Charles René Magon de Médine, having escaped from Rochefort; at 4:00 A.M. next day the combined fleet weighs for Guadeloupe. Several hundred local troops are taken on board here on the afternoon of 6 June before the expedition presses on to Antigua.

8 JUNE 1805. At 10:00 A.M., while rounding Antigua, the combined Franco-Spanish fleet spots 15 British merchantmen setting sail for Europe. They are easily captured, but upon interrogating some crewmembers Villeneuve learns that Nelson's fleet arrived at Carlisle Bay (Barbados) four days earlier. Assuming the British admiral has brought 12–14 ships of the line—rather than ten plus three frigates—the French commander fears they will be added to Cochrane's six in the Windward Islands to produce a force equal to his own. Villeneuve therefore holds a hurried conference with Gravina; both agree to abandon the diversion and return to Europe forthwith. The colonial volunteers are rapidly disembarked, no regular troops are landed, prizes are dispatched to Martinique, and the Franco-Spanish fleet (now including the ship of the line *Aigle*) disappears into the Atlantic by 11 June.

Nelson meanwhile has incorporated Cochrane's two ships of the line at Barbados—plus 2,000 local troops—into his force, but through faulty intelligence he steers southwest to Trinidad under the impression he will find his enemy here. Dawn on 8 June reveals his mistake, and it is not until next afternoon, when he calls at Grenada, that the British admiral finally discovers the combined fleet's true heading. Racing north, he arrives off Antigua by 12 June, only to learn a few days later that Villeneuve and Gravina have forsaken the West Indies altogether. Nelson disembarks his own colonial forces and refreshes supplies before sailing in Villeneuve's wake.

21 JANUARY 1806. Duckworth—now a vice admiral and knight of the Bath—arrives at Saint Kitts with a Royal Navy squadron, having chased a small French force across the Atlantic. He is joined by Cochrane with two more ships, and on 1 February learns that the enemy is off the coast of French-held Santo Domingo; he sails to overtake. After passing through the Mona Passage, Duckworth is joined on the afternoon of 5 February by the frigate *Magicienne,* bearing intelligence.

6 FEBRUARY 1806. ***Duckworth's Action.*** At dawn British scouts sight a French squadron anchored off Santo Domingo, so stand in to engage in two columns: Duckworth's weather division consists of his 74-gun flagship *Superb* under Captain Keats, Cochrane's vice-flag *Northumberland,* and the Hon. Robert Stopford's *Spencer,* plus the 64-gun *Agamemnon* under Sir Edward Berry. The lee division comprises Rear Admiral Louis's 84-gun *Canopus* (ex-French *Franklin*), as well as the 74s *Donegal* (ex-French *Hoche*), and *Atlas* under Pym. These are accompanied by the frigates *Acasta* of Dunn, *Magicienne* of McKenzie, *Kingfisher* of Nathaniel Day Cochrane, and *Epervier.*

Surprised and outnumbered, the 47-year-old French Vice Adm. Corentin de Leissègues orders his ships to slip their cables and run west before the wind past Point Nisao to shelter under the Ocoa Bay batteries. French strength consists of the 120-gun flagship *Impérial* (ex-*Vengeur*) of Captain Le Pigot; 84s *Alexandre* of Garreau, and *Diomede* of Henri; plus the 74s *Brave* of Condé, and *Jupitre* of Laignel. Closer inshore are the frigates *Felicité* and *Comète,* plus corvette *Diligence.*

Shortly after 10:00 A.M. *Superb* overhauls the lead French ship *Alexandre,* and the battle is joined. After an hour and a half of fighting, Leissègues steers his flagship—only its foremast still standing—in toward land, deliberately running aground by 11:40 A.M. *Diomede* soon follows, *Brave, Alexandre,* and *Jupitre* having already struck to the British, after suffering 760 total casualties. Duckworth sustains 74 killed and 264 wounded, then detaches Stopford to sail toward Jamaica with *Spencer, Donegal, Atlas,* and his three prizes. Cochrane meanwhile returns toward the Leeward Islands with a jury-rigged *Northumberland* and also *Agamemnon.*

27 APRIL 1806. ***Miranda's Landing.*** The wealthy, 51-year-old, Caracas-born revolutionary Francisco de Miranda arrives west of Puerto Cabello (Venezuela) aboard Captain Lewis's *Leander,* hired in New York with the help of American backers Col. W. S. Smith and S. G. Ogden, and two schooners chartered at Santo Domingo. It is Miranda's dream to raise a revolt against Spanish rule in his homeland, but when he attempts to disembark at Puerto Cabello with 150 followers they are repelled by the local garrison, with two vessels and 60 men lost. Miranda therefore retires

Leissègues's flagship Impérial *(center) losing its mainmast as his squadron is defeated by Duckworth off Santo Domingo*

to Barbados to ask for help from British Rear Admiral Cochrane.

8 JUNE 1806. ***River Plate.*** The 43-year-old English Commo. Sir Home Riggs Popham arrives off Cape Santa María (Uruguay) with the 32-gun frigate HMS *Narcissus* to reconnoiter the approaches to Buenos Aires for an impending assault. Having earlier helped conquer the Cape of Good Hope from the Dutch, Popham has heard from Capt. T. Wayne of the American slaver *Elizabeth* that the River Plate's residents are resentful of Spanish rule, so he has persuaded Gen. Sir David Baird to lend him a contingent for an independent campaign.

One week later Popham's main body joins him near Montevideo, consisting of HMSS *Diadem* (flag) and *Raisonnable* of 64 guns; *Diomede* of 50; 38-gun frigate *Leda;* and brig *Encounter,* escorting the transports *Triton, Melantha, Willington,* and *Walker,* bearing 1,200 soldiers under 37-year-old Brig. Gen. William Carr Beresford. The army consists mostly of the 1st Battalion, 71st Highland Light Infantry Regiment under 34-year-old Lt. Col. Dennis Pack, plus a dragoon squadron, artillery company, and others. (The expedition is further accompanied by the merchantman *Justina.*)

Popham convinces Beresford that in order to take advantage of the element of surprise, Buenos Aires should be assaulted first, so he transfers all marines and troops aboard the lighter vessels by 16 June. Detaching *Raisonnable* and *Diomede* to blockade Maldonado (Uruguay) and *Diadem* to do the same off Montevideo, he advances deeper into the fog-shrouded River Plate.

During the evening of 24 June the Buenos Aires viceroy—Rafael, Marqués de Sobremonte—is summoned from the theater by the arrival of pilot José de la Peña from Montevideo with news that an English expedition is about to invade. Next morning the militia is mustered; in the distance, the small English army is already coming ashore at Quilmes, bolstered by 340 marines, 100 sailors, 16 horses, and eight field pieces. Beresford marches quickly on Buenos Aires, brushing aside the ill-equipped contingents sent to bar his path. During the morning of Sunday, 27 June, he easily crosses the Riachuelo River despite the presence of 400 Spaniards manning a six-gun battery under the military engineer, Lieutenant Colonel Gianini.

The very swiftness of the English approach unmans Sobremonte, who exits Buenos Aires with his remaining 600 troops—allegedly to attack the English from the rear

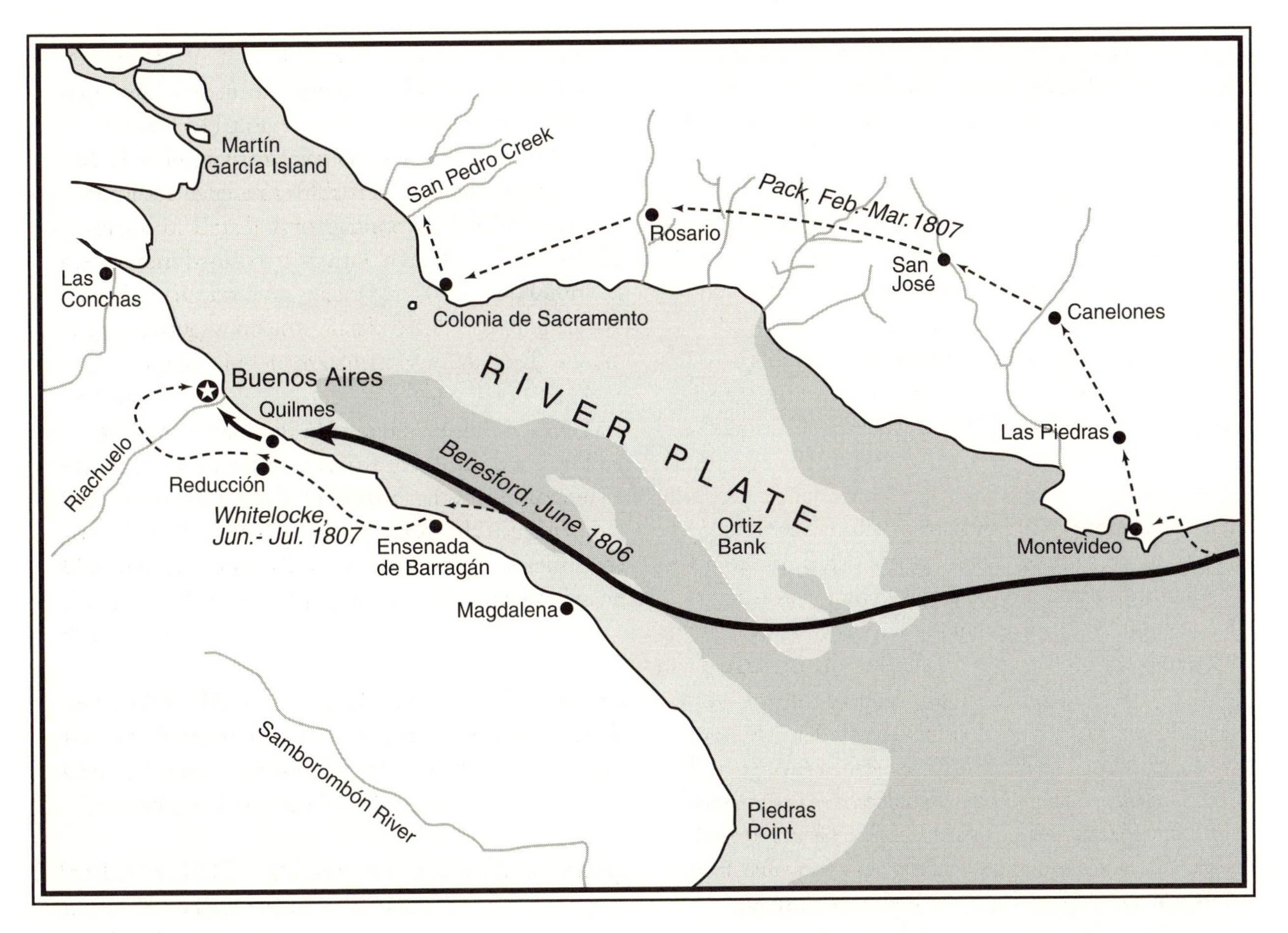

British invasions of the River Plate estuary

but actually to flee inland to Córdoba. Command is left to Brig. Gen. José Ignacio de la Quintana, who surrenders to Beresford this afternoon. At 4:00 P.M. on 27 June English troops peacefully occupy strong points throughout the city in a driving rainstorm, seizing more than 90 guns, 7,000 firearms, and other goods. The official capitulation is signed by 2 July, and two weeks later an exultant Popham dispatches *Narcissus* to England with glowing accounts, plus more than 1 million pesos in booty.

2 JULY 1806. French raiders strike the West Indian island of Montserrat.

1 AUGUST 1806. Having perceived the weakness of the English forces occupying Buenos Aires, Spaniards from outlying districts begin mustering outside the city to expel the invaders. Warned of this plan after returning from the theater, Beresford sallies at 1:30 A.M. with 550 soldiers under Pack and six field pieces, defeating a force under 30-year-old Juan Martín de Pueyrredón at Perdriel Manor (outside Buenos Aires) at 8:00 A.M.

3 AUGUST 1806. Reinforced with British contingents from Barbados and Trinidad, the revolutionary Francisco Miranda returns to Coro (Venezuela) with ten vessels and 500 men, disembarking 300–400 and occupying the port as defenders flee inland. His call for a South American revolt falls on deaf ears, however, it being perceived as a British stratagem. Ten days later, after being attacked by Coro's regional militias, Miranda is forced to retire to Aruba.

4 AUGUST 1806. ***Argentine Reconquest.*** The 53-year-old, French-born naval captain and commander of the Ensenada de Barragán Garrison—Santiago de Liniers y Bremond, knight of the Order of Malta—disembarks at Las Conchas (20 miles outside Buenos Aires) with another Spanish relief force from Montevideo (transported by a flotilla under Juan Gutiérrez de la Concha); and once ashore he joins de Pueyrredón's defeated contingent. Together they muster 2,500 troops, with which de Liniers marches against Buenos Aires through a cold rain. On 11 August de Liniers encounters Beresford's defenders at Retiro and installs his Spanish siege artillery while throwing up a cavalry screen around the city.

Next day, in a sharp, two-hour fight during which the Spaniards suffer 205 casualties (as opposed to 157

British), they fight their way into Buenos Aires, pressing back the outnumbered English. By 3:00 P.M. on 12 August Beresford and his 1,300 men have no choice but to surrender, eventually being interned at Luján in Argentina's interior. Popham's vessels retire from the roadstead; because of the Spanish victory de Liniers is popularly acclaimed acting viceroy of Buenos Aires in place of the disgraced Sobremonte.

12 OCTOBER 1806. ***Maldonado.*** A belated English relief convoy appears off the River Plate from the Cape of Good Hope under Lieutenant Colonel Backhouse: 913 soldiers from the 38th Infantry Regiment, 770 from the 47th, 116 (one company) of the 54th, two squadrons (215 troopers) of the 20th Dragoons, 158 troopers from 21st Dragoons, plus six gunners. Their four transports are escorted by HMS *Lancaster* of 64 guns, 32-gun frigate *Medusa,* the sloop *Howe,* brig *Protector,* and *Rolla* (a detained American brig). Popham advises this force that Buenos Aires has fallen and persuades Backhouse to attempt an assault on the smaller Montevideo. The English *Triton, Hero, Royal Charlotte, Columbine, Fanny, Encounter, Protector, Leda, Medusa, Diomede,* and *Lancaster* approach the harbor by morning on 28 October, but finding its waters too shallow to silence its batteries, withdraw following a three-hour bombardment.

Popham next steers to Maldonado (Uruguay), setting 400 soldiers of the 38th Regiment ashore southeast of there under Lieutenant Colonel Vassal on 29 October backed by a company of marines and sailors. At a cost of two dead and four wounded they overwhelm Captain Borras's 230 militia defenders, inflicting more than 50 casualties and capturing two of the Spaniards' four guns. Vassal then overruns the 12-gun battery at Punta del Este by 30 October; Popham seizes the 20-gun battery on Gorriti Island. Thus, the English secure a defensible encampment at Maldonado to await further reinforcements.

Some time later the Spanish naval Lieutenant Abreu is sent from Montevideo with 400 riders to invest the British base, only to be defeated and killed near San Carlos. Lt. Col. José M. Moreno then inaugurates harassing raids with gaucho cavalry, preventing the invaders from foraging inland.

4 DECEMBER 1806. Rear Adm. Charles Stirling reaches Maldonado from England with HMS *Sampson* of 64 guns, the Indiamen *Earl Spencer* and *Sir Stephen Lushington,* and some victuallers, relieving Popham, who returns to England to stand trial for his unauthorized campaign into the theater (eventually being "severely reprimanded," although without affecting either his popularity or subsequent career).

1 JANUARY 1807. In a bold raid, Royal Navy Captain Brisbane captures the strongly defended Dutch island of Curaçao with four frigates.

5 JANUARY 1807. British reinforcements arrive off Maldonado (Uruguay): 3,600 troops under 50-year-old Brig. Gen. Sir Samuel Auchmuty (a New York–born American loyalist) escorted by 64-gun HMS *Ardent,* 32-frigate *Unicorn,* and sloop *Cherwell.* His army consists of 706 troopers of the 17th Dragoons; 215 of the 20th; 158 of the 21st; 1,125 infantrymen from the 40th Regiment of Foot; 901 from the 87th; 116 from the 54th; 258 (three companies) from the 95th Rifles; plus 131 artillerymen with six field pieces.

Finding Colonel Backhouse's Maldonado base camp hard-pressed by gaucho guerrillas, Auchmuty orders it evacuated by 13 January, leaving only a small garrison to hold Gorriti Island offshore, with support from *Lancaster* and *Diomede.* Escorted by Stirling's *Diadem* (flag), *Raisonnable, Ardent,* and *Lancaster;* frigates *Leda, Unicorn, Medusa,* and *Daphne;* sloops *Pheasant* (of 16 guns), *Howe,* and *Cherwell;* and brigs *Encounter, Protector, Staunch,* and *Rolla,* the main English body then veers west to attack Montevideo.

16 JANUARY 1807. ***Montevideo.*** Around noon, Auchmuty disembarks his troops at Mulata or Verde Beach between Manzo Point and Gorda Point six miles east of the Uruguayan capital (population 10,000). Viceroy Sobremonte detaches Colonel Allende with 800 lancers and six field pieces to bolster the few defenders resisting atop Carretas Point, but they are unable to affect much. During the next two days the British bring their entire 5,500-man army ashore, plus six guns and 800 marines and sailors. Opposing them are 3,500 troops inside Montevideo under Gov. Pascual Ruiz Huidobro, consisting of four companies of regulars, a militia battalion, four volunteer battalions (three called *Carlos IV,* under Maj. Nicolás de Vedia), Catalan irregulars, three squadrons of Buenos Aires dragoons, Mordeille's hussars—from the French privateers *Reine Louise* and *Orient* out in the harbor—180 regular gunners, a battalion of militia artillerymen, plus numerous seamen. Outside the city another 2,500 Uruguayan riders muster under Sobremonte.

By 19 January Auchmuty strikes toward Montevideo in three columns. Sobremonte, with 1,300 troops, falls on the English vanguard, supported by Allende's cavalry on both flanks. Lieutenant Colonel Brownrigg drives off the attack with a brilliant countermaneuver that captures a piece and compels the Spaniards to retire inside the city with 100 casualties as opposed to 25 British (Auchmuty having a horse shot out from under him). The skirmish allows the invaders to gain Tres Cruces Heights, overlooking the city, by afternoon.

Next dawn, Ruiz Huidobro sends out 270 Buenos Aires foot, 260 dragoons, 650 volunteer infantry, 422 artillerymen, 300 hussars, 200 militia, 60 chasseurs, and 200 seamen under Brig. Gen. Bernardo Lecoq to launch an assault on the English in conjunction with 1,700 riders under Sobremonte, who are to attack from inland in a pincer movement intended to cut Auchmuty off from the sea. The Spanish infantry collide with the British left flank at Cristo del Cordón, their trailing columns hurrying toward that objective as Auchmuty deploys his light brigade and 95th Rifles in cornfields along the line of march, ambushing the Spaniards in a crossfire. Lecoq's troops flee toward Montevideo, having suffered 200 killed, 400 wounded, plus 200 men and a gun captured, compared to 149 English casualties. Sobremonte's cavalry—viewing the action from a safe distance—retire to Las Piedras encampment without engaging; many subsequently desert.

That afternoon (20 January) the British seize the Aguada Wells outside Montevideo and begin constructing siege works. Without sufficient strength to entirely surround the city or equipment to dig through the flinty subsoil, Auchmuty hopes to batter Montevideo into submission. Stirling sends hundreds of sailors ashore to install and man heavy batteries, the first of which opens fire on 23 January. On 2 February more than 500 Spanish reinforcements slip into the city from Buenos Aires under Brig. Gen. Pedro de Arce.

Seeing that an 11 yard–wide breach has been pounded along the southern ramparts, Auchmuty decides to storm it next dawn. The assault commences at 3:30 A.M. on 3 February, Ruiz Huidobro and Arce being captured after fierce hand-to-hand combat in which 800 Spaniards are killed and 500 wounded. The entire garrison capitulates by 5:20 A.M., with 2,000 Spanish troops surrendering. British losses total 121 dead and 276 wounded. The 22-gun Spanish frigates *San Francisco de Paula* and *Fuerte,* 10-gun brigs *Héroe, Dolores,* and *Paz,* and another 52 vessels are seized by Stirling; a 28-gun frigate and three armed launches also lie scuttled in the harbor. Military booty includes 345 guns, 2,500 muskets, and much ammunition.

6 FEBRUARY 1807. Auchmuty is reinforced at Montevideo by another 711 troopers of the 9th Dragoons who arrive from Cape Verde (West Africa) aboard four transports and three hired merchantmen, escorted by the frigate HMS *Nereide.*

10 FEBRUARY 1807. Because of his ineffectual action outside Montevideo, Sobremonte is deposed as viceroy of the River Plate.

25 FEBRUARY 1807. Beresford and his staff reach Montevideo, having escaped from imprisonment in the interior.

26 FEBRUARY 1807. Auchmuty dispatches Lieutenant Colonel Pack west from Montevideo with six companies of the 40th Foot, four companies of light infantry, three companies of the 95th Rifles, and a squadron of 9th Dragoons to seize Colonia (Uruguay) and impede any possible Spanish counterattack from Buenos Aires. Pack succeeds, overwhelming Colonia's 2,800 inhabitants without opposition.

FEBRUARY 1807. A mulatto-dominated assembly at Port au Prince results in divided rule, President Christophe governing the "state of Haiti" in the north while Pétion and a mulatto faction hold sway in the "Republic of Haiti" in the south.

22 APRIL 1807. At 1:00 A.M. Col. Francisco Javier de Elío—recently arrived from Spain with fresh troops—attempts a surprise attack with 1,500 men against Pack's garrison inside Colonia (Uruguay). The English repel the assault after suffering one dead and three wounded, as opposed to eight Spaniards killed and eight injured. Elío's retreating columns are pursued as far as Real de San Carlos.

10 MAY 1807. The veteran Lt. Gen. John Whitelocke (*see* 9 September 1793) and his second-in-command, Maj. Gen. John Leveson-Gower, reach Montevideo from England aboard the frigate HMS *Thisbe,* superseding Auchmuty in command of all British forces in this theater next day.

7 JUNE 1807. At 3:00 A.M. on this Sunday Pack steals out of Colonia (Uruguay) with 541 infantry of the 40th Regiment, 225 of the 95th, 278 skirmishers, 61 troopers of the 9th Dragoons, 34 gunners, and two field pieces to surprise Colonel Elío's encampment at San Pedro. The British arrive four hours later to find 2,000 Spaniards drawn up in battle array with 16 guns.

Without pause Pack drives straight into Elío's army, scattering it while losing only five English dead and 40 wounded. Spanish casualties total 120 killed, numerous wounded, and 105 captives; eight guns and 250 muskets are also taken.

15 JUNE 1807. The 43-year-old Brig. Gen. Robert Craufurd (having been diverted from an expedition against Chile) reaches Montevideo with 940 soldiers of the 5th Infantry Regiment, 925 of the 36th, 956 of the 45th, 898 of the 88th (Connaught Rangers), 410 (five companies) of the 95th Rifles, 336 troopers of the 6th Dragoons, 273 gunners, and 18 field pieces. They are traveling aboard 33 transports escorted by 48-year-old Rear Adm. George Murray's 64-gun *Polyphemus* (flag) and *Africa;* 36-gun frigate *Nereide;* 16-gun sloop *Saracen;* brig *Haughty;* schooner *Flying Fish;* and storeship *Camel.* The frigates *Medusa, Unicorn,* and *Daphne* are awaiting them at Montevideo.

General Whitelocke, having decided to attack Buenos Aires immediately upon the arrival of these reinforcements, does not allow them to disembark but rather leaves 1,500 men to garrison Montevideo under Colonel Dean of the 38th Foot—the 47th Regiment, two companies from the 38th, part of the 20th and 21st Dragoons, and a company of marines—while going aboard ship with another 4,000 soldiers by 21 June to steer toward his objective.

22 JUNE 1807. Off Chesapeake Bay, 50-gun HMS *Leopard* intercepts 39-year-old American Commo. James Barron's 40-gun frigate USS *Chesapeake,* firing three heavy broadsides and compelling it to strike 15 minutes later for refusing to allow a party aboard to search for Royal Navy deserters. Three Americans are killed and 18 wounded, the incident provoking a downturn in Anglo-American relations.

26 JUNE 1807. Colonel Pack's garrison abandons Colonia (Uruguay), joining Whitelocke's expedition against Buenos Aires.

28 JUNE 1807. ***Buenos Aires.*** On this Sunday, Whitelocke disembarks 9,000 men, 350 horses, and 16 field pieces at Ensenada de Barragán (30 miles southeast of Buenos Aires). From here the English initiate a march, leaving behind five field pieces and many horses mired in muddy terrain. Leveson-Gower's vanguard reaches Reducción de Quilmes by 1 July in a steady rain, finding its Spanish battery already withdrawn. While Whitelocke's main body and rearguard rest, Leveson-Gower advances from Bernal and fords the Riachuelo River next day at 9:30 A.M., with 2,600 men and four field pieces.

South of the river at Barracas lies de Liniers with 6,900 men and 53 field pieces, having sortied from Buenos Aires to give battle. Realizing Leveson-Gower is now between him and his capital, the Spanish commander rushes his vanguard to Misere Ranch to prevent an immediate assault on Buenos Aires. His men dig in with 11 pieces by 5:00 P.M., only to be displaced by Craufurd, the Spaniards suffering 60 casualties, 80 prisoners, and the loss of all their artillery. The English suffer 14 dead and 30 wounded.

However, the English vanguard—not realizing Buenos Aires now lies defenseless—remains encamped at Misere, awaiting the arrival of the main body. This gives de Liniers time to recall his own troops and organize resistance behind the capital's barricaded streets. By 3 February the English have gathered 6,900 men in the western suburbs, probing its defenses, then calling upon the Spaniards to surrender next day.

This is rebuffed, so at 6:30 A.M. on 5 July Whitelocke sends eight battalions (5,800 men) into the streets in 13 columns. The invaders estimate the Spanish garrison to be 6,000 (actually it is more than 7,000), and the total Buenos Aires population at 70,000 (in reality 42,000). Their hope is to avoid its central core around the citadel and great square, instead panicking the Spaniards into abandoning the city. The British right gets possession of Hospicio de la Residencia, and the left takes the bullring, but the 88th Regiment and Light Brigade under Craufurd then meet stout resistance in the city center from Spanish regulars and militia firing from the rooftops. Gradually the column becomes surrounded and surrenders; the day costs Whitelocke 311 killed, 679 wounded, 208 missing, and 1,600 prisoners. The defenders suffer 600 casualties with 700 prisoners.

That evening de Liniers proposes a cessation of hostilities and mutual restoration of captives if the defeated British will evacuate the River Plate—including Montevideo—within two months. Whitelocke accepts after consulting with Leveson-Gower and Auchmuty, convinced his remaining strength is insufficient to subdue Buenos Aires and its outlying provinces. His army gathers at Retiro and begins reembarking by 9 July, sailing away on 12 July—much to the disgust of its rank-and-file, who take to toasting, "Success to gray hairs, but bad luck to white locks."

24 JULY 1807. General Ackland reaches Montevideo with more than 1,800 British troops (1,125 from the 89th Foot), but in light of the debacle before Buenos

Aires they are dispatched directly to India one week later along with Whitelocke's 47th and 87th.

27 JULY 1807. A small British squadron appears before Baracoa (Cuba), hoping to take the port by surprise. However, its garrison commander, Capt. José Repilado—with only 20 Spanish regulars, 70 militia, and 100 French allies plus six cannons in Punta and Matanchín Forts—has been forewarned of the enemy approach and ambushes them on the beach. A dozen raiders are slain and another 84 captured, the rest retiring out to sea.

8 AUGUST 1807. The 88th (Connaught Rangers) and 95th Rifles evacuate Montevideo for England.

LATE AUGUST 1807. In Europe, a British fleet opens hostilities against Denmark for having once more joined the "continental system" against English commerce.

9 SEPTEMBER 1807. Whitelocke evacuates Montevideo with his remaining 6,500 men, returning to England with the defeated army by 7 November; he is court-martialled and cashiered.

17 OCTOBER 1807. The hated Jacques I—formerly General Dessalines—is murdered at sunrise by mutinous troops at Pont Rouge (Haiti), his body being defiled.

15 DECEMBER 1807. Early this Tuesday morning the British sloop of war *Fawn* reaches Barbados with dispatches announcing the official declaration of war against Denmark. Next day Rear Admiral Cochrane has Gen. Henry Bowyer's final troops embark—the expedition having been preparing for some weeks—and orders other contingents to assemble off Danish Saint Thomas from Saint Kitts, Antigua, and Grenada; he sets sail on 16 December with his 74-gun flagship *Belleisle* and consorts.

21 DECEMBER 1807. ***Danish Virgin Islands.*** After touching at Sandy Point (Saint Kitts), Cochrane and Bowyer arrive off Saint Thomas, sending Brig. Gen. Sir Charles Shipley and naval Capt. William Charles Fahie close inshore with HMS *Ethalion* to call on Gov. W. von Scholten to capitulate. The Dane does so the next day, terms being agreed upon in negotiations with Maj. Gen. Frederick Maitland and *Ramillies*'s Capt. Francis Pickmore. A 300-man garrison from the 70th Regiment is installed under Brigadier General Maclean, and 67 prizes are seized in the roads; the British expedition then steers toward nearby Saint Croix by evening on 23 December, repeating the process and occupying that island by Christmas Day, gaining another 21 vessels at Christiansted.

EARLY MARCH 1808. The French island of Marie Galante is captured by the British, followed by La Désirade.

4 JULY 1808. The British schooners *Subtle, Balahou,* and *Elizabeth* plus the sloop *Wanderer* make an abortive 135-man disembarkation on the French West Indian island of Saint Martin, being repelled with heavy losses.

10 NOVEMBER 1808. Capt. C. Dashwood of the Royal Navy frigate *Franchise,* having chanced to unite with British frigates *Aurora* and *Dædalus* plus brigs *Reindeer* and *Pert,* uses them to make a surprise descent next morning against the French privateering base at Samaná Bay (northern Dominican Republic). Its 900 startled inhabitants offer scant resistance, instead streaming aboard the 100-ton schooner *Échange* and 90-ton *Guerrier* to attempt to row away. They are intercepted by four boatloads of British sailors and boarded; the harbor castle and three other prizes are also seized. Dashwood hands over the port to a Spanish force under Diego de Lira and sails to Port Royal (Jamaica) a couple of weeks later with his captures.

DECEMBER 1808. An Anglo-Portuguese expedition led by Rear Adm. Sir William Sidney Smith's subordinate, Capt. James Lucas Yeo of HMS *Confiance,* and artillery Lt. Col. Manoel Marques occupy Oiapoque in the border region between French Guiana and Brazil.

6 JANUARY 1809. This morning Yeo and Marques appear outside the roadstead of Cayenne (French Guiana) with 550 Portuguese troops and 80 British marines and sailors crammed aboard the brigs *Voador* and *Infante,* cutters *Lion* and *Venganza,* plus several smaller boats. Pushing upchannel under cover of darkness, they surprise two French batteries at Grande Cane and Fort Diamant next dawn, carrying them by storm along with another pair of batteries a mile away that afternoon.

Meanwhile Brig. Gen. Victor Hugues, France's governor for this colony, sorties from Cayenne—a dozen miles upriver—with several hundred defenders but is unable to recuperate his lost batteries despite a three-hour firefight this afternoon. On the morning of 8

January the invaders overrun Hugues's fortified plantation then press on toward the town of Cayenne proper, arriving outside next day. The French request terms and agree to capitulate by 12 January, Yeo and Marques entering the gates on 14 January as 400 French regulars, 600 militia, and 200 black auxiliaries lay down their arms.

On 13 January the 48-gun, 330-man frigate *Topaze* of Captain Lahalle appears offshore with 100 troops as belated reinforcements from France, only to be chased away. The vessel is intercepted nine days later south of Pointe Noire, Guadeloupe, and captured by HMSS *Cleopatra, Jason,* and *Hazard* under Capt. Samuel John Pechell, suffering 12 killed and 14 wounded. British losses are only two dead and one injured.

28 JANUARY 1809. ***Martinique.*** At noon Rear Admiral Cochrane departs Barbados with the ships of the line *Neptune* (flag), *Pompée, Belleisle, York, Captain,* and *Intrepid;* frigates *Acasta, Penelope, Ethalion, Æolus, Circe, Ulysses,* and *Eurydice;* and lesser warships *Gorée, Wolverine, Cherub, Stork, Amaranthe, Haughty, Express, Swinger, Forrester, Recruit, Star, Eclair, Ringdove,* and *Frolic.* They are escorting a troop convoy bearing the army of Lt. Gen. George Beckwith to attempt the conquest of Martinique.

On the morning of 30 January Capt. Philip Beaver of *Acasta* leads the principal British contingent into Cul de Sac Bay, dropping anchor and disembarking 4,500 redcoats by sunset. The rest of the main body under Beckwith and Maj. Gen. Sir George Prevost comes ashore next morning; a second unit under Major General Maitland is landed at Sainte Luce under the supervision of Captain Fahie of *Belleisle.* As both columns push inland 600 men disembark from HMS *York* under Major Henderson of the Royal York Rangers to secure the French batteries on Salomon Point and Pigeon Island, so that the invasion fleet might anchor in safety.

On 1 February Beckwith—advancing on the commanding Surirey Heights—defeats a French concentration under Capt. Gen. Villaret de Joyeuse, thus gaining the strategic high ground and compelling the defenders to evacuate Fort de France in favor of Fort Bourbon. Meanwhile Maitland encounters no resistance and reaches Lamantin by 2 February, effecting a juncture with Beckwith's main body. Brigadier Generals Shipley and Edward Stehelin simultaneously besiege the isolated, 136-man French garrison on Pigeon Island, obliging them to surrender by sunrise of 4 February thanks to the fire of two five-gun naval batteries installed by Commo. George Cockburn of *Pompée.*

Beckwith subsequently institutes a formal siege against Villaret de Joyeuse's 2,250 defenders inside Fort Bourbon (their backbone being the 26th and 82nd Regiments); heavy rains slow the British deployment, and the first four batteries open fire from the western side at 4:30 P.M. on 19 February. Over the next three days Capts. Robert Barton and Christopher J. W. Nesham employ 400 seamen and marines from HMSS *York* and *Intrepid* to manhandle another four 24-pounders and four mortars atop Mount Surirey, on its eastern side. Before they can join the general bombardment, Villaret de Joyeuse requests terms on 23 February, the capitulation being arranged next day. The French lay down their arms on 25 February, Martinique passing under British control at a cost of more than 400 casualties plus 435 sick. For this success, Beckwith is created a knight of the Bath; Cochrane is promoted to vice admiral.

12 APRIL 1809. ***The Saintes.*** Three French ships of the line and two frigates having been intercepted bringing reinforcements out from Lorient, then blockaded at the Saintes by Cochrane's fleet, a British expedition departs Fort Royal (modern-day Fort de France) on occupied Martinique to subdue the outpost. The invasion force consists of 2,000–3,000 men of the 3rd and 8th West Indian, 15th, 60th, and 64th Regiments, Royal York Rangers, York Light Infantry Volunteers, plus an artillery train, all under the command of Major General Maitland. Their convoy is led by Captain Beaver of *Acasta,* who, after examining the shoreline on 13 April and being scattered by a brief storm, disembarks the redcoats—virtually unopposed—at 10:00 A.M. on 14 April in Bois Joli Bay, under covering fire from HMSS *Intrepid, Gloire, Acasta, Narcissus, Circe,* and *Dolphin.*

The army easily pushes its way up 800-foot Mount Russel, gaining a commanding view of the three small French forts and of the harbor. Two British eight-inch howitzers commence a galling fire against the French squadron that evening; the three French ships of the line weigh at 10:00 P.M. and stand out in the west channel, followed next morning by the two frigates via the eastern exit—all hoping to elude Cochrane's blockaders. On 15 April Maitland reembarks part of his army and disgorges the troops in Vanovre Bay to outflank the French defenders under Col. M. Madier. By 16 April the British have the island's 700–800 defenders bottled up inside Forts Napoléon and Morelle; Madier requests terms at noon on 17 April. Next day his garrison surrenders, Maitland having suffered six killed and 68 wounded during the campaign.

Meanwhile Cochrane pursues the three fleeing French ships as far as Puerto Rico's Cape Rojo, bringing the sternmost—the brand-new, 74-gun *D'Hautpoult* of Capt. Amand Leduc, knight of the Légion d'Honneur—to battle at 3:30 A.M. on 17 April. The vessel is battered into submission within less than two hours by Captain Fahie's 80-gun HMS *Pompée* and Commander Roberts's sloop *Castor,* inflicting 80–90 casualties among the 680-man crew. British losses total 11 killed and 41 wounded; the other two ships escape.

7 JUNE 1809. ***Santo Domingo.*** Maj. Gen. Hugh Lyle Carmichael quits Jamaica with the 2nd West Indian, 54th, 55th, and Royal Irish Regiments to aid Britain's newfound Spanish allies in reducing the isolated French garrison besieged in southeastern Hispaniola (*see* 7 November 1808 under Latin American Insurgencies section). His convoy is escorted by Capt. William Price Cumby's HMSS *Polyphemus* (flag), *Aurora, Tweed, Sparrow, Thrush, Griffin, Lark, Moselle, Fleur de la Mer,* and *Pike.*

Carmichael disembarks at Polingue (30 miles west of Santo Domingo) on 28 June, hastening ahead of his army to confer with his Spanish counterpart—one General Sánchez, commander of a Puerto Rican regiment and numerous local guerrillas—who for the past eight months has been investing the 1,200-man French garrison of Brig. Gen. J. Barquier. Four hundred of 600 Spanish regulars are sick, yet they advance on 30 June at Carmichael's behest to seize San Carlos Church on the outskirts of the capital and cut off communication between Santo Domingo and Fort San Jerónimo two miles west, while simultaneously securing a beach for Cumby's supporting squadron.

The demoralized French defenders have already requested an armistice and been rebuffed, repeating the suggestion on 1 July as the first British troops arrive overland (hampered by torrential rains). As negotiations progress Carmichael maintains pressure by installing heavy siege batteries around the city and massing his forces for an assault. On 6 July the capitulation is finalized, Barquier pointedly surrendering to the British rather than to the Spaniards. Next day redcoats occupy the city and Fort San Jerónimo, the French defenders being transported directly to Port Royal (Jamaica) without loss of life on either side.

22 JANUARY 1810. ***Guadeloupe.*** Beckwith and Cochrane quit Fort Royal (modern-day Fort de France, Martinique) with units from the 3rd, 4th, 6th, and 8th West Indian Regiments plus the 13th, 15th, 25th, 63rd, and 90th Foot, Royal York Rangers, York Light Infantry Volunteers, 300 artillerymen, and a siege train to conquer the last major enemy outpost in the West Indies: Guadeloupe, blockaded for the past several weeks by the Royal Navy. After rendezvousing with additional contingents in Prince Rupert's Bay (Dominica) on 24 January, the British move against the main objective two days later in a pair of divisions: Brig. Gen. George William Richard Harcourt and Commodore Ballard of HMS *Sceptre* leading one 2,450-soldier convoy to the nearby Saintes Islands to await the French defenders' reaction; Beckwith and Cochrane sailing their 3,700-man main army directly against Guadeloupe.

At noon on 27 January the flagship HMS *Pompée* drops anchor off Gosier; next dawn Major General Hislop leads the first wave of redcoats ashore at the village of Sainte Marie, landing without resistance. That afternoon the 3rd Brigade strikes south toward Capesterre; the 4th drives north on Grande Rivière while the British reserve protects the beachhead. Bananiers River is forded by 29 January, and next day Trou au Chien Pass is breached by the invaders, who thus threaten the main town of Trois Rivières.

The previous afternoon Cochrane has directed Ballard's squadron to make a feint against the far side of that place before depositing Harcourt's division nine miles north of the town of Basse-Terre at dawn on 30 January. The outnumbered French subsequently abandon Trois Rivières without a fight, leaving behind some artillery. Beckwith resumes his advance on 2 February after resupplying, the strategic Palmiste and d'Olot Heights being occupied uncontested by his twin columns; Morne Hoüel is also taken, by Brig. Gen. C. Wale's vanguard at 8:00 P.M. Everywhere the French defenses are found empty, their guns spiked.

Under cover of darkness Wale turns the French left flank in the heights above Matouba during the evening of 3 February, suffering 40 casualties. Basse-Terre is occupied by Commodore Fahie with a detachment of marines from his fleet offshore. As a result of these swift penetrations, Capt. Gen. Manuel Louis Jean Baptiste Ernouf requests terms next morning, so that by 8:00 A.M. on Monday, 6 February, all resistance ceases and 3,500 defenders lay down their arms. The British win control over the entire island; they also claim the imperial eagle of the French 66th Regiment among their booty.

14 FEBRUARY 1810. Following the fall of Guadeloupe, Brigadier General Harcourt appears off the island of Saint Martin with a large detachment of redcoats, con-

voyed by Fahie's HMSS *Abercrombie* (flag), *Vimeira, Snap, Morne Fortunée, Frolic, Surinam, Superieure,* and *Ringdove.* A company of the 25th Regiment under Captain Beattie is disembarked in Marigot Bay by Captain Scobell's brig *Vimeira* to demand the surrender of the 18-man French garrison—which surrenders forthwith.

A similar disembarkation in Little Cool Bay persuades the 76 soldiers on the Dutch half of the island to capitulate two days later, just as Harcourt is closing in on the principal town of Phillipsburgh. After securing the island Fahie weighs at dawn on 21 February for nearby Sint Eustatius, arriving at midday and demanding the surrender of its Dutch garrison. They comply at 9:00 A.M. next day, Maj. J. N. Karesboom's 56 soldiers laying down arms as the 25th Regiment's grenadier company occupies the lone fort.

Although Napoleon will not be crushed and sent into exile at Elba until the spring of 1814, the Royal Navy's dominance precludes further hostilities in the New World for the remaining four years of this Anglo-French conflict. Upon the ascension of Louis XVIII to France's throne, most overseas colonies are restored by Britain. When the emperor subsequently escapes from confinement and briefly regains power in March 1815, only Guadeloupe rises in support in the Americas, replacing the Bourbon white fleur-de-lis with the tricolor flag on 17 June. The next day, Napoleon is defeated at Waterloo; he abdicates by 22 June.

A British envoy eventually reaches Guadeloupe on 3 August, calling for the island's resubmission to the French king. Colonel Boyer refuses to comply, but a strong British force disembarks on 9 August, and, after some skirmishes—with few losses on either side—the disheartened defenders capitulate by 10 August.

Latin American Insurgencies (1808–1826)

In early November 1807 a 23,000-man French army marches through Spain under Gen. Andoche Junot to attack Portugal, which has refused to implement Napoleon's "continental system" by closing its ports to English vessels. The ensuing winter witnesses a series of pivotal events for Central and South American history, as Lisbon is occupied by 1 December—the royal family fleeing to Brazil two days earlier—while Marshal Joachim Murat brings another massive French army into Spain by March 1808, overrunning its major cities and capturing its monarchs (who wait until the very last moment before attempting flight).

On 19 March Spain's Charles IV abdicates in favor of his son Ferdinand VII, but both Bourbon rulers are soon imprisoned in France—prompting a brief uprising in Madrid on 2 May—and Joseph Bonaparte is installed as the new Spanish king on 7 June. Although this crude usurpation of power is initially resisted by most Spanish Americans, it will eventually lead to a weakening of the bonds between the home government and its empire.

For many years Spanish American citizens have been growing disenchanted with Madrid's rule, typified by self-serving dictates that not only thwart commercial development but routinely deny positions of influence to creoles (those of mixed heritage) in favor of peninsular-born Spaniards. Nevertheless, there is little sentiment at first in favor of New World independence; instead there is support for the liberal *junta* (council) formed at Aranjuez on 25 September 1808 to spearhead resistance against the French and uphold the Bourbon cause. Out of the ensuing years of uncertainty and turmoil, however, emerges a new will for freedom.

22 January 1808. The Portuguese prince regent, João (later João VI), arrives at Bahia (Brazil) to a warm reception, having fled Lisbon aboard his flagship *Principe Real* accompanied by eight other Portuguese warships, eight lesser men-of-war, and 30 merchantmen—all escorted by four English Royal Navy vessels under Rear Adm. Sir Sidney Smith. Virtually the entire court, government, treasury, as well as 1,600 marines are aboard the Portuguese expedition, which totals 10,000–15,000 people. After a few weeks João continues to the Brazilian capital of Rio de Janeiro, arriving 7 March to install his imperial government.

The transfer of Portugal's ruler to the New World has a profound effect not only on Brazil but also on its surrounding region, for he is accompanied by his Spanish-born wife, Carlota Joaquina—sister to the imprisoned Ferdinand VII. She offers to rule Spanish America on behalf of her brother, adding to the

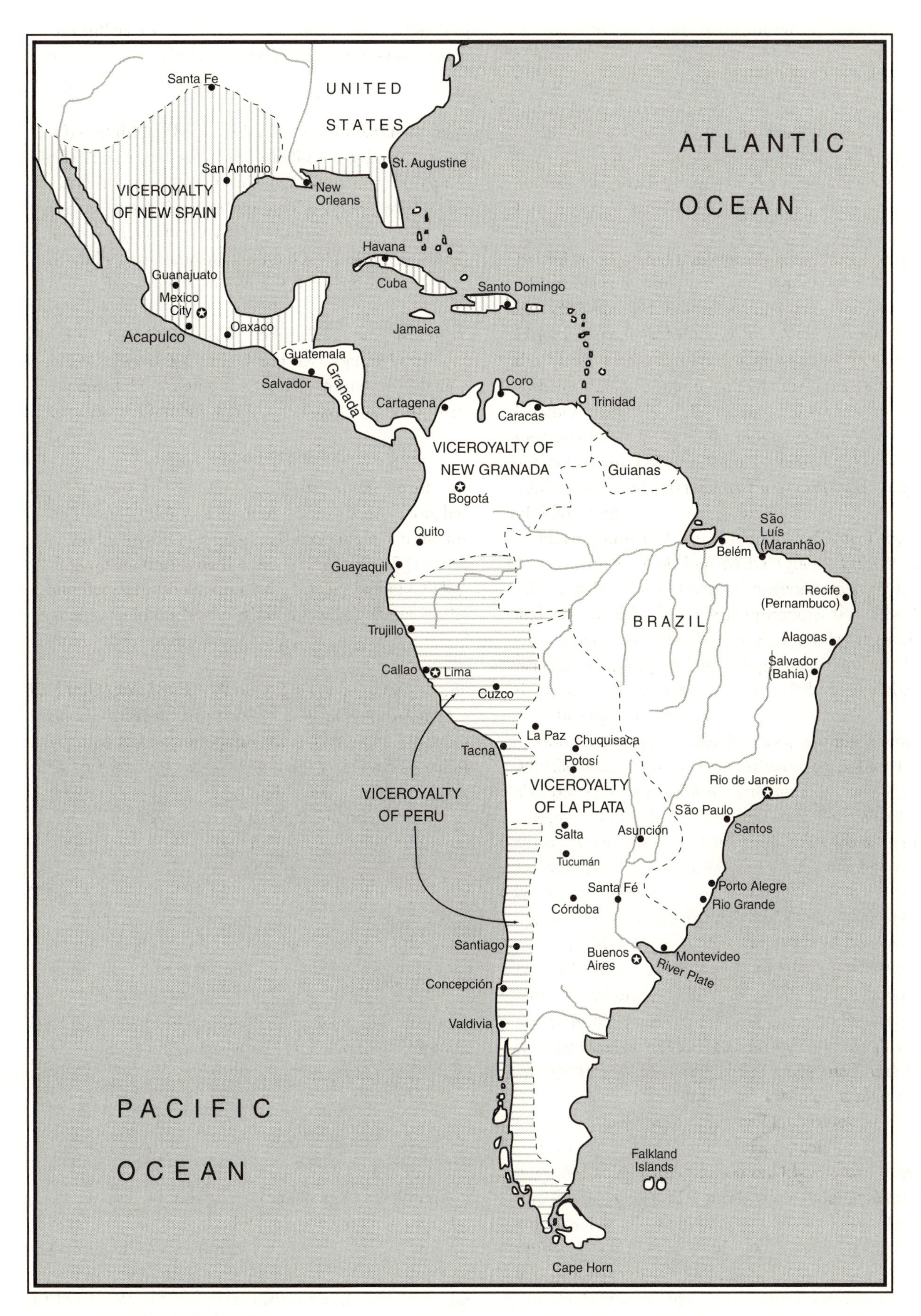

Latin America on the eve of independence

confusion already gripping its authorities. Soon, Spanish officers in the River Plate also become concerned by Brazilian designs upon the Banda Oriental (the Eastern Band—Uruguay).

15–16 SEPTEMBER 1808. In Mexico City, 300 armed peninsular Spaniards led by conservative merchant Gabriel de Yermo penetrate the palace at night and depose Viceroy José de Iturrigaray, fearful he is about to declare total independence from Madrid. A retired octogenarian field marshal (*mariscal de campo*), Pedro de Garibay, is temporarily substituted; the peninsulars then shift Mexico's financial and logistical support behind the Spanish factions already opposing France.

21 SEPTEMBER 1808. An ultraloyalist junta is established at Montevideo by Spanish officer Francisco Javier de Elío, who not only upholds the rule of Ferdinand VII but further doubts the loyalty of Buenos Aires's acting viceroy—French-born Santiago de Liniers—simply on account of his birth (and for having been approached by a Bonapartist agent the previous month). When the trusted Adm. Baltasar Hidalgo de Cisneros y Latorre (a veteran of Trafalgar) is sent out from Seville some months later to replace de Liniers, the junta is dissolved.

7 NOVEMBER 1808. ***Dominican Reconquest.*** Led by the rich *hacendado* (landowner) Juan Sánchez Ramírez, the Spanish residents of Santo Domingo rise against their French occupiers after four months of careful planning. At Sabana de Palo Hincado (or Seybo to the French), 2,000 Dominican insurgents confront 600 French soldiers, annihilating the force and compelling its leader, Governor Ferrand, to commit suicide.

Sánchez Ramírez marches on the capital, but its remaining French defenders mount a desperate resistance under Brigadier General Barquier that the Dominicans—without siege artillery—cannot overcome. An eight-month encirclement ensues, supported by a Royal Navy blockade out of Jamaica. (This campaign becomes known as Santo Domingo's *Guerra de la Reconquista*—the War of Reconquest.)

NOVEMBER 1808. Prominent Caracan citizens propose establishing a Venezuelan junta—similar to the one spearheading resistance in Spain—only to be arrested by acting Gov. Juan de Casas.

DECEMBER 1808. Spain's supreme junta is driven out of Aranjuez by the French and forced to relocate in Seville, from where it continues to send instructions to the American empire.

1 JANUARY 1809. A coup against Viceroy de Liniers is attempted in Buenos Aires but easily put down.

25 MAY 1809. A provisional junta is established at Chuquisaca, the provincial capital of so-called Upper Peru (modern-day Bolivia), under the leadership of agitators such as Argentine-born Bernardo de Monteagudo.

7 JULY 1809. Santo Domingo's exhausted French garrison surrenders to British blockaders rather than to their Dominican besiegers (*see* 7 June 1809 in previous section). The Dominicans become annoyed when they subsequently learn that they will have to pay the English in order to reoccupy their capital.

16 JULY 1809. The intendant and bishop of La Paz (Bolivia) are deposed, and a junta founded eight days later by Pedro Domingo Murillo. Its membership—although recognizing the legitimacy of Ferdinand VII—nonetheless wishes for greater self-government.

10 AUGUST 1809. The Conde de Ruiz de Castilla, head of the *audiencia* of Quito, is deposed and a junta established by Juan Pío María de Montúfar y Larrea, Marqués de Selva Negra, whose desire to exercise regional power in the name of Ferdinand VII prompts the Peruvian viceroy, José Fernando de Abascal y Sousa, to dispatch troops to suppress it (as well as Murillo's junta in La Paz, Bolivia). The Quito assembly soon dissolves amid much bickering, Ruiz de Castilla reassuming his office.

OCTOBER 1809. José Manuel de Goyeneche, president of the *audiencia* of Cuzco, approaches La Paz with a small but disciplined army, obliging its outlaw junta to collapse. Numerous ringleaders are captured and punished.

14 FEBRUARY 1810. Spain's supreme junta having been driven offshore to León Island (near Cádiz), a general legislative assembly (*cortes*) is convened from throughout the overseas empire. The process of electing delegates reinforces creole desire for full independence.

19 APRIL 1810. Leading Caracan creoles—desperate because of the imminent collapse of Spain's junta before Bonaparte's armies—depose royal Gov. Vicente Emparan and establish their own junta, vowing loyalty

to the captive Ferdinand VII—but also resolving to act independently of the mother country until such time as he can be set free. Most of Venezuela follows suit, with only Coro and Maracaibo remaining loyal to the Spanish junta in Cádiz.

22 MAY 1810. A three-man junta is formed at Cartagena (Colombia).

22 MAY 1810. Bowing to popular demand, Viceroy Hidalgo de Cisneros authorizes the establishment of a creole junta at Buenos Aires, himself acting as its president. This is consecrated two days later. On 25 May, however, he is deposed; control passes to militia Col. Cornelio Saavedra and the radical politician Mariano Moreno in the so-called May Revolution.

9 JULY 1810. Some 1,500 Argentine volunteers depart Buenos Aires under Col. Francisco Ortiz de Ocampo and Lt. Col. Antonio González Balcarce to spread revolutionary authority into the country's interior.

20 JULY 1810. A junta is set up at Bogotá (Colombia) initially including New Granada's viceroy, Antonio Amar y Borbón, but dispensing with his services five days later.

AUGUST 1810. A loyalist counterrevolutionary conspiracy is discovered at Córdoba (Argentina), centered around the former viceroy, de Liniers. The radical Buenos Aires junta orders its ringleaders shot—including de Liniers—on 26 August at Cabeza de Tigre. González Balcarce succeeds Ortiz de Ocampo in command of the patriot Army of the Andes, which presses into Upper Peru (Bolivia).

10 SEPTEMBER 1810. In Querétaro (Mexico), a seven-month-old creole conspiracy for an uprising leading to independence—hatched by 57-year-old Miguel Hidalgo y Costilla, village priest at Dolores—is revealed to the authorities by one of its members, Capt. Joaquín Arias, and confirmed three days later at Guanajuato. The Spanish intendant for the province, Juan Antonio Riaño y Bárcena, orders Hidalgo arrested.

16 SEPTEMBER 1810. ***Hidalgo's Uprising.*** Learning the previous night through Lt. Juan Aldama that his insurrectionist plans have been discovered, Hidalgo rouses his followers at Sunday dawn by pealing Dolores's church bells and calling for Mexico's independence (becoming known as *El Grito de Independencia*—The Cry of Independence). Numerous local monarchists are arrested, and by 11:00 A.M. 400 riders and 400 men on foot have formed up under 41-year-old Capt. José Ignacio María de Allende y Unzaga to march with Hidalgo to nearby San Miguel el Grande. The insurgents encounter no resistance and are in fact joined by hundreds of followers as they advance.

18 SEPTEMBER 1810. An independent Chilean junta is established at Santiago.

19 SEPTEMBER 1810. Hidalgo's throng departs San Miguel el Grande, occupying Celaya next day. From here he calls on Intendant Riaño to surrender the provincial capital of Guanajuato, which the latter rejects.

22 SEPTEMBER 1810. A second junta is founded at Quito (*see* 10 August 1809).

23 SEPTEMBER 1810. Hidalgo's followers quit Celaya, overrunning Salamanca, Irapuato, and Silao as they advance on Guanajuato. Four days later they reach Burras Hacienda, again calling on Riaño to surrender.

28 SEPTEMBER 1810. ***Alhóndiga de Granaditas.*** After advancing through the towns of Venta de la Purísima, Santiaguillo, Puentecillas, Estanco del Pulque, Retiro, and Marfil, Hidalgo's 20,000–25,000 poorly armed adherents circle around Cuarto and San Miguel Hills to fall upon the city of Guanajuato by 1:00 P.M. As the insurgents storm down Nuestra Señora de Guanajuato Avenue, Intendant Riaño seeks shelter inside the recently completed granary—a formidable stone building called the Alhóndiga de Granaditas—with a few loyal troops and Guanajuato's peninsular-born Spaniards.

After desperate resistance they are overwhelmed when a young miner named Juan José María Martínez (alias Pípila) crawls through a hail of bullets with a stone slab tied to his back, setting the wooden doors ablaze with a torch. As evening falls, the insurgents fight their way inside and slaughter every monarchist by dawn of 29 September. The massacre stains the rebels' reputation and alienates many segments of Mexican society.

8 OCTOBER 1810. After returning to Dolores, Hidalgo learns that the Spanish authorities in neighboring Michoacán have been detained at Acámbaro on orders of the insurgent, María Catalina Gómez de Larrondo; he therefore sends José Mariano Jiménez in her support with 3,000 men.

Interior view of the Alhóndiga de Granaditas in Guanajuato

Hidalgo soon follows with his own main body and occupies the capital of Valladolid (modern-day Morelia) by 17 October without a struggle. After remaining a day he continues to Zinapécuaro with 80,000 poorly armed and disciplined adherents. En route he is joined by 45-year-old José María Morelos y Pavón—a former seminary pupil, now village priest at Curácuaro—who he delegates to spread rebellion in the south.

Meanwhile Hidalgo enters Maravatío by 23 October and decides to lead his unwieldy host to Mexico City. Toluca is reached by 28 October, then Tianguistenco.

29 OCTOBER 1810. ***Cotagaita.*** In Upper Peru (Bolivia), González Balcarce's 1,500 Argentine invaders encounter 2,000 royalists under Gen. José de Córdoba at Cotagaita 240 miles north of San Salvador de Jujuy. The royalists put up a stubborn resistance, compelling the revolutionaries to retire south. After a few days' rest de Córdoba sets off in pursuit of the retreating rebels.

30 OCTOBER 1810. ***Monte de las Cruces.*** In a mountain pass leading from Toluca to Mexico City, Hidalgo and Allende's 80,000 insurgents—the so-called Army of America—find their path barred by 7,000 loyalists under Lt. Col. Torcuato Trujillo and 27-year-old artillery Capt. Agustín de Iturbide. The outnumbered defenders offer stiff resistance, inflicting 5,000 casualties among the rebel ranks while suffering 1,000.

After six hours of heavy fighting the loyalists are forced back through sheer weight of numbers. Although victorious, Hidalgo's bloodied army advances no farther than Cuajimalpa before veering northwest on 2 November, unwilling to risk a direct assault on the viceregal capital's defenses. Instead, Hidalgo opts to continue propagating insurrection throughout the provinces.

LATE OCTOBER 1810. An Argentine revolutionary army of 950 men and six field pieces marches out of Bajada del Paraná into Paraguay to attempt to spread the cause of independence under 39-year-old Gen. Manuel Belgrano.

EARLY NOVEMBER 1810. Morelos arrives near Acapulco with a few hundred followers to raise the

Hidalgo celebrating mass before the Battle of Monte de las Cruces

banner of revolt. After driving Capt. Juan Antonio Fuentes's royalist company out of Tecpan on 7 November he is joined by contingents under brothers José and Antonio Galeana, then roams through El Zanjón, Coyuca, and Aguacatillo gathering further strength. With Indian allies from Atoyac, Morelos invests Acapulco on 9 November, leaving 600 of them to harry the defenders while visiting nearby Veladero with his main body.

7 NOVEMBER 1810. ***Aculco.*** Advancing northwest from the Valley of Mexico to Querétaro, the 55,000 followers of Hidalgo and Allende blunder into 15,000 loyalists under 55-year-old Gen. Félix María Calleja del Rey, heading in the opposite direction. Calleja quickly divides his army into five columns, smashing into the undisciplined insurgent throng and wreaking fearful havoc; rebels flee in utter confusion, suffering 12,000 casualties, compared to 1,000 among Calleja's ranks.

Routed, Hidalgo retires with a portion of his survivors via Villa del Carbón, San Pablo, Arroyo Zarco, Amealco, Coroneo, and Celaya, heading to Valladolid. Meanwhile Allende leads another contingent back through Maravatío and Acámbaro to Guanajuato.

7 NOVEMBER 1810. ***Suipacha.*** After retreating from their Cotagaita (Bolivia) setback, González Balcarce's 600 revolutionaries, with two field pieces, are overtaken at Suipacha by de Córdoba's 800 royalists with four cannon. This time, the Argentines triumph, and de Córdoba is executed following the battle, as are two royalist governors, Nieto of Chuquisaca and Paula Sanz of Potosí.

The revolutionaries resume their drive north, entering the immensely rich silver-mining town of Potosí shortly thereafter. At first the rebels are greeted as liberators, but Argentine political commissar Juan José Castelli and his radical associates soon offend local citizens with their haughty behavior, severity toward defeated royalists, and extremist ideology.

17 NOVEMBER 1810. Having learned three days earlier that Guadalajara—Mexico's second-largest city—

Spanish Gen. Félix María Calleja del Rey

has fallen to insurgents José Antonio Torres and Miguel Gómez Portugal, Hidalgo departs Valladolid with 7,000 riders to establish a new headquarters and revive his cause. However, while Hidalgo is busy promulgating decrees and naming new officials (as well as executing 400 royalists), Calleja's monarchist army fights its way through the central highlands, reversing many earlier insurgent gains and reconquering Guanajuato from Allende by 25 November.

1 DECEMBER 1810. Morelos's 3,000 guerrillas clash with the royalist defenders of Acapulco and are scattered, suffering minor losses on both sides.

6 DECEMBER 1810. Allende rejoins Hidalgo in Guadalajara, having evacuated Guanajuato on 24 November because of Calleja's royalist advance.

11 DECEMBER 1810. Exiled revolutionary Miranda (*see* 27 April 1806) returns to Venezuela from England aboard the vessel *Avon*.

13 DECEMBER 1810. At Paso Real de la Sabana (Guerrero, Mexico), Morelos's subordinate, Julián de Avila, ambushes a royalist relief column approaching Acapulco under Capt. Francisco Paris, commander of the 3rd Oaxaca Militia.

19 DECEMBER 1810. In Paraguay, Belgrano's small revolutionary army crosses the Paraná River from Candelaria into Campichuelo at dawn, defeating a 500-man Paraguayan force under Commander Thompson.

28 DECEMBER 1810. Royalist Brig. Gen. José de la Cruz reoccupies Valladolid (modern-day Morelia, Mexico) and takes reprisals against its insurgent sympathizers.

4–5 JANUARY 1811. ***Tres Palos.*** Tonight more than 1,000 insurgents under Morelos and the Galeana brothers assault 3,000 royalists under Captain Paris, encamped at Tres Palos (near Acapulco). The attack results in 400 royalist casualties and 700 prisoners in addition to 700 muskets, five artillery pieces, ammunition, and supplies. Mexican losses total 200 killed and wounded.

12 JANUARY 1811. ***Calderón Bridge.*** In Guadalajara (Jalisco), Hidalgo learns that Calleja's monarchist forces—after a six-week respite following their capture of Guanajuato—have now pressed into nearby San Juan de los Lagos. Over objections from Allende, the insurgent leader decides to give battle at Calderón Bridge 20 miles outside Guadalajara; Hidalgo orders it fortified, arriving by 15 January with many of his followers. Allende appears next day with his own forces, bringing total insurgent strength to 35,000 men (only 1,200 actually bearing muskets) plus a few field pieces.

On 17 January Calleja's 14,000 royalists begin a series of assaults against the rebel positions, suffering considerable losses before an insurgent grenade accidentally detonates one of their own ammunition wagons, creating widespread panic. The monarchists take advantage with a heavy cavalry charge. Despite being driven from the field after six hours' fighting with 3,000 casualties, Hidalgo and Allende retire in good order. Calleja, on the other hand—despite having had only 400 men killed or wounded—is slow to pursue, occupying Guadalajara four days later. Still, his victory is a serious reverse for the insurgency and earns him the title Conde de Calderón.

19 JANUARY 1811. ***Paraguary.*** Belgrano's 700 Argentine revolutionaries, with six field pieces, encounter 6,000 Paraguayans with 16 cannons under General Velasco, entrenched on the far side of Yuquery Creek in front of the town of Paraguary. Despite the heavy odds

Belgrano launches a dawn attack, only to be worn down after four hours' heavy fighting, during which he loses one-fifth of his men.

22 JANUARY 1811. Texas's royalist governor, Manuel María de Salcedo is deposed and confined at San Antonio by militia Capt. Juan Bautista de las Casas.

LATE JANUARY 1811. Hidalgo, Allende, and other defeated insurgents meet at Pabellón Hacienda outside Zacatecas, where Hidalgo is stripped of military command in favor of Allende.

31 JANUARY 1811. A small insurgent force is defeated at San Blas (Mexico).

EARLY FEBRUARY 1811. Allende and Hidalgo retreat north from Zacatecas with the remnants of their army, reaching Saltillo one month later.

8 FEBRUARY 1811. Alejo García Conde, royalist governor of Sonora (Mexico), defeats an insurgent force under José María González Hermosillo at San Ignacio Piaxtla.

This same day, Morelos's guerrillas attempt an assault on Fort San Diego at Acapulco, believing they have successfully bribed royalist gunner José Gago to cripple the artillery. Instead they are received with grapeshot, suffering 14 deaths before retreating out of range.

17 FEBRUARY 1811. Royalist Cmdr. Manuel Ochoa reoccupies the city of Zacatecas (Mexico).

20 FEBRUARY 1811. The royalist Regimiento de las Tres Villas (Regiment of Three Towns) under Capt. Juan Bautista de la Torre attempts to reconquer Zitácuaro (Mexico) from insurgents under Benedicto López, only to be repelled.

28 FEBRUARY 1811. The wealthy, 46-year-old José Gervasio Artigas and other Uruguayan patriots raise the banner of revolt at Asencio; they are soon supported by Argentine troops under Belgrano.

2 MARCH 1811. In Texas, a dawn countercoup deposes de las Casas at San Antonio and restores royalist rule.

Off San Nicolás (Uruguay), Spanish naval forces defeat an Argentine flotilla under Azopardo, consisting of the brigantine *25 de Mayo,* sloop *Invencible,* and schooner *América.*

5 MARCH 1811. Calleja's monarchist army reconquers San Luis Potosí (Mexico) from the insurgents.

13 MARCH 1811. Royalist Col. Joaquín de Arredondo y Muñiz quits Veracruz with 500 troops aboard the brigantine *Regencia* and the schooners *San Pablo* and *San Cayetano* to help put down Mexican insurgents and American settlers who have combined to rise in southern Texas and Tamaulipas.

MID-MARCH 1811. Royalist forces under *Sargento Mayor* (adjutant) Nicolás Cosío and Lieutenant Colonel Fuentes resume their sallies from Acapulco against Morelos's guerrillas.

16 MARCH 1811. Leaving 4,000 men to garrison Saltillo under 37-year-old Ignacio López Rayón (who will eventually fight his way south into Michoacán), Allende and Hidalgo retire north with another 1,300 insurgents, hoping to gain support in the United States.

Next day 30-year-old Col. José Bernardo Gutiérrez de Lara is detached to ride to Washington, D.C., where he will eventually meet with Secretary of State James Monroe yet refuse to agree to any concessions in exchange for American aid.

19 MARCH 1811. ***Tacuari.*** While encamped north of the confluence of the Tacuari and Paraná Rivers (Paraguay), Belgrano's 400 Argentine revolutionaries, with six field pieces, are surprised by 500 Paraguayans and a river flotilla attacking from the west. They prove to be a diversion, however, for 2,000 men under General Cabañas burst out of the jungle from the north, annihilating Belgrano's flank guard under his second-in-command, Machain.

Nevertheless, Belgrano is able to throw back both assaults then negotiate a truce with Cabañas before withdrawing south into Argentina. Although defeated twice during his incursion, Belgrano's actions spark the establishment of an independent local junta in Paraguay.

20 MARCH 1811. Mexican insurgents under Juan B. de la Torre gain a small victory at Zitácuaro.

21 MARCH 1811. After riding two days with retired militia Capt. Francisco Ignacio Elizondo's 342 followers, Allende, Hidalgo, and other rebel leaders are treacherously arrested at Acatita de Baján (Coahuila) and conveyed to Monclova next day to be surrendered to Governor de Salcedo in exchange for a royalist reward.

4 APRIL 1811. Royalist Lieutenant Colonel Fuentes defeats some of Morelos's guerrillas at Las Cruces Point, outside Acapulco.

MID-APRIL 1811. A creole plot to kidnap Viceroy Francisco Javier Venegas and exchange him for Hidalgo is uncovered in Mexico City.

30 APRIL 1811. An assault by royalist *Sargento Mayor* Cosío against Morelos's positions at La Sabana (near Acapulco) is repelled. A second attempt next day is also defeated, costing the royalist his command.

10 MAY 1811. This morning, royalist Colonel Arredondo clashes with a force of Tamaulipas insurgents under Villerías.

16 MAY 1811. After penetrating as far as Huaqui (modern-day Guaqui) and encamping on the shores of the Desaguadero River—the traditional boundary between the viceroyalties of Buenos Aires and Peru—Argentine political commissar Castelli and royalist Commander Goyeneche sign a 40-day truce.

18 MAY 1811. ***Las Piedras.*** The Uruguayan insurgent Artigas's 1,100 men defeat 1,200 royalists under José de Posadas at Las Piedras Mill 12 miles north of Montevideo. The victors suffer 70 deaths compared to 100 killed, 60 wounded, and 500 captured among the royalists.

This rebel victory allows 38-year-old Argentine revolutionary Gen. José Rondeau to lay siege to Montevideo by 1 June, although its garrison still continues to be sustained from the sea.

21 MAY 1811. Morelos subordinate Hermenegildo Galeana aids the Bravo family—Leonardo, Miguel, Víctor, Máximo, and Nicolás—at their hometown of Chichihualco (Mexico), in defeating a royalist contingent under Garrote. This victory nets 100 muskets and allows the insurgents to occupy nearby Chilpancingo unopposed, being joined there on 24 May by their main body.

22 MAY 1811. Royalist Capt. Juan Bautista de la Torre is defeated and captured by insurgent forces at Tuzantla (Mexico). He is subsequently killed while being transported to Túxpan.

26 MAY 1811. ***Tixtla.*** Morelos's army overruns Tixtla (modern-day Ciudad Guerrero, Mexico), where *Sargento Mayor* Cosío and wealthy landowner Joaquín de Guevara have dug in with 1,500 royalists. The insurgent victory nets 600 prisoners, 200 muskets, and eight field pieces.

20 JUNE 1811. ***Huaqui.*** Eight days before his truce is scheduled to expire, royalist General Goyeneche advances at dawn with 6,500 troops in three columns along the shores of Lake Titicaca (Bolivia) to surprise González Balcarce's 5,000 Argentine invaders and several thousand Indian auxiliaries. Although Goyeneche's column is at first repelled, Brig. Gen. Domingo Pío Tristán's central column gains control of Yauricoragua Ravine, taking the revolutionaries in the flank and preventing communication with the other half of their army under General Viamonte.

The latter is eventually defeated by Brigadier General Ramírez, the rest of the patriots being annihilated. Continuously harassed during their retreat and having left a small contingent to guard Suipacha Ford, only 800 revolutionaries reach Salta (Argentina), where Pueyrredón assumes command of the shattered remnant and continues their retirement as far as Tucumán.

22 JUNE 1811. The insurgent General López Rayón captures Zitácuaro, which becomes the capital of Mexico's new national congress.

JUNE 1811. A minor uprising occurs at Tacna (southern Peru), in part inspired by the presence of Argentine

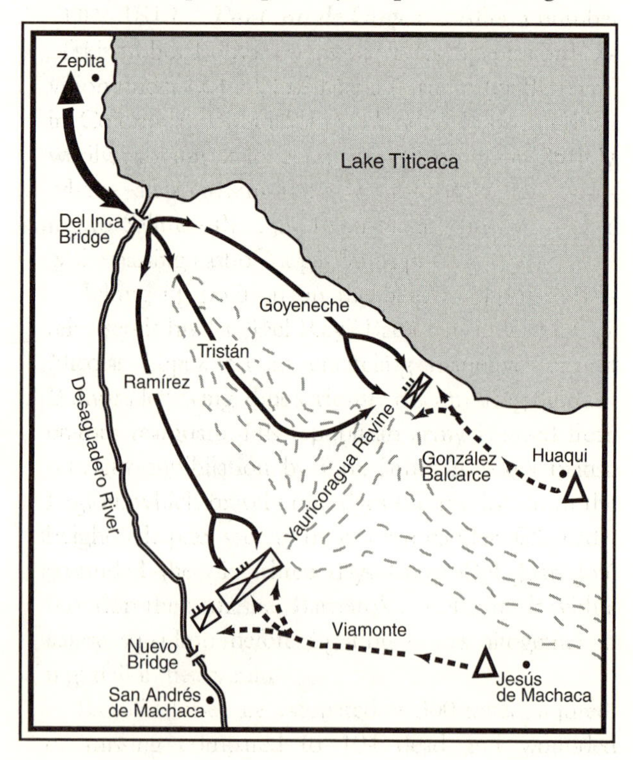

Battle of Huaqui

forces in nearby Bolivia (*see* 7 November 1810). This revolt is quickly suppressed.

5 JULY 1811. ***The First Republic.*** Venezuela officially proclaims independence and becomes a republic. A serious counterrevolution soon develops at Valencia, however, supported from Coro. Later this month a patriot division marches from Caracas under Francisco Rodríguez, Marqués del Toro, but is repulsed with slight losses and is obliged to retire to Maracay. Miranda is selected by the patriot government to succeed him.

17 JULY 1811. At the invitation of Buenos Aires's Spanish Viceroy-Designate Francisco Javier de Elío, a 5,000-man Portuguese army under 56-year-old Gen. Diogo de Sousa, governor of Brazil's Rio Grande do Sul Province, enters the *Banda Oriental* (Uruguay) as a temporary occupying force against insurgency. De Elío—without loyal formations of his own to contain spreading revolutionary fervor throughout his jurisdiction—has resorted to this desperate expedient of calling on Spain's traditional rival for help in this long-disputed territory.

30 JULY 1811. In Chihuahua City, Hidalgo is executed by firing squad five days after his subordinates Allende, Jiménez, Aldama, and numerous others. Their heads are pickled and forwarded to Guanajuato, to be exposed on the corners of the Alhóndiga de Granaditas (*see* 28 September 1810).

12 AUGUST 1811. After considerable difficulty, Miranda's patriot army subdues loyalist Valencia (Venezuela), but is unable to persuade congress to impose centralized rule. Loyalist resistance will therefore persist at such hotbeds as Maracaibo and Coro.

15 AUGUST 1811. Royalist Lieutenant Colonel Fuentes attempts to recapture Tixtla from Morelos's subordinates Galeana and 47-year-old Leonardo Bravo. His assault columns are caught in a crossfire and repelled, their retirement being hastened next day by the arrival of Morelos himself from Chilpancingo with 300 riders. Fuentes's losses total 400 prisoners, 400 muskets, and three field pieces.

On 18 August Morelos follows up his advantage by attacking Fuentes's demoralized royalists at Chilapa, compelling them to withdraw from the theater altogether and retreat to Mexico City.

AUGUST 1811. A second creole conspiracy is discovered in Mexico City, resulting in a number of executions.

21 OCTOBER 1811. In Uruguay, Argentine revolutionaries come to terms with Spanish Viceroy-Designate de Elío, agreeing to evacuate the territory if he withdraws his Portuguese allies (*see* 17 July 1811). Local Uruguayan leader Artigas feels betrayed by this arrangement, as royalists will be left in undisputed possession of his district. Angry, he retires inland to the confluence of the Paraná and Ayuí Rivers (north of Concordia) with 16,000 followers in the so-called Exodo Oriental (Exodus of the Easterners). This intransigence furnishes Portuguese General de Sousa with an excuse to delay his own troop withdrawal.

EARLY NOVEMBER 1811. Having secured most of the land that today comprises the state of Guerrero, Mexico, Morelos launches a three-pronged offensive inland: Miguel Bravo leads one column to Oaxaca; Hermenegildo Galeana takes another to Taxco; Morelos marches at the head of two companies of insurgents and 800 Indian archers to Izúcar, overrunning it without opposition by 10 December. (He installs 29-year-old Capt. Vicente Ramón Guerrero Saldaña as garrison commander.)

11 NOVEMBER 1811. Cartagena (Colombia) declares outright independence from Spain.

NOVEMBER 1811. A short-lived creole insurrection occurs in San Salvador (Central America), starting with demands to create a separate bishopric. It is quickly repressed by the president of the *audiencia* of Guatemala, José de Bustamante y Guerra.

Meanwhile New Granada (modern-day Colombia) creates a weak central union called the United Provinces of New Granada (excepting Bogotá, which is ruled by Antonio Nariño). Border disputes soon erupt between the factions.

18 DECEMBER 1811. At dawn a royalist force under naval Lt. Miguel Soto de la Maceda surprises Morelos at Izúcar (Mexico), fighting its way into the main square before being repelled by Leonardo Bravo's division.

25 DECEMBER 1811. Morelos occupies Cuautla Amilpas.

DECEMBER 1811. A brief creole uprising occurs at Granada (Nicaragua) over questions of local misrule.

1 JANUARY 1812. ***Zitácuaro.*** Mexico's national congress shifts the capital from Zitácuaro to Sultepec when Calleja's 5,000-strong royalist army ap-

proaches. Gen. López Rayón meanwhile prepares to defend Zitácuaro with 20,000 poorly armed, ill-trained insurgents.

Next day Calleja's columns push inside after heavy fighting, inflicting 7,000 casualties among the defenders while suffering 2,000 of their own. In order to punish Zitácuaro's disloyalty to Spain the victors then sack and burn the town.

22 JANUARY 1812. Morelos falls upon the royalist Porlier at Tenancingo, forcing him to retire to Toluca without artillery.

25 JANUARY 1812. Learning that the victorious royalist army of General Calleja is approaching after destroying Zitácuaro, Morelos retreats to Cuautla Amilpas by 9 February, occupying Cuernavaca along the way.

29 JANUARY 1812. The royalist Commander Paris defeats 400 insurgents at Omotepec (Mexico) under Miguel Bravo, Valerio Trujano, and Julián Ayala.

17 FEBRUARY 1812. ***Siege of Cuautla.*** Calleja's 7,000 royalists encamp at Pasulco two and a half miles outside Cuautla, having cornered Morelos inside with 2,000 riders, 1,000 infantry, and 1,300 auxiliaries under his subordinates, Cols. Hermenegildo Galeana, Miguel Bravo, and 41-year-old Mariano Matamoros (originally a village priest from Jantetelco). Next day the royalists advance to probe Cuautla's defenses, only to have Morelos launch a surprise cavalry charge against their rear. In heavy fighting, the insurgent leader is almost captured before being rescued by Galeana.

At dawn on 19 February Calleja launches a four-pronged attack against Cuautla's San Diego Convent, which is defended by Galeana. The insurgents wait until the royalists draw within 100 yards then lay down a withering fire. Despite heavy losses, Calleja's men overrun the city's northeastern trench system, only to be blown off the northern parapets by a heroic, 12-year-old gunner named Narciso Mendoza, stationed at the Encanto Street battery. After six hours of close combat the royalists retreat, leaving behind 200 dead (including Cols. Conde de Casa Rul and Juan N. Oviedo). Having thus been bloodily repulsed in a direct assault, Calleja opts to impose a siege.

In late February he is reinforced by 5,000 troops from the Puebla Division under Ciriaco de Llano. Royalist batteries open fire on Cuautla from Zacatepec and Calvario Hills by 4 March, and siege lines are begun from north and south next day. Over the next few weeks Calleja cuts off the city's water supply, the insurgents responding by recapturing Juchitengo Dam, holding it against all royalist counterattacks. On 21 April Matamoros leads a desperate, ten-dragoon sally from Santa Inés Gate that contacts an insurgent relief column bringing food under Miguel Bravo at Tlayacac Ravine (Barranca Hediohonda); Bravo is unable to escort the succor back to Cuautla, however, instead being ambushed at Amazingo by Llano's cavalry and compelled to flee to Tlacalaque (where Matamoros is eventually defeated by Mateo Nieto).

By 28 April provisions within the beleaguered city are exhausted, and at 2:00 A.M. on 2 May Morelos leads a dash to freedom. The starved insurgents quietly wend their way down the Cuautla River bank until encountering the royalist picket lines, at which point they charge and fight their way through. Losses are heavy on both sides, some of Calleja's divisions mistakenly firing on one another in the gloom. Morelos escapes to Ocuituco, but his insurgent army is broken and dispersed, units being chased for many miles by royalist cavalry while Cuautla is given over to the sack.

MARCH 1812. Máximo Bravo flees to the coast from Cuautla, helping keep Mexico's insurgency alive by joining forces with Galeana, Ayala, and Father Mariano de Tapia to skirmish with the royalists around Petaquillas, Citlala, and Tlapa.

Meanwhile in Cadiz the legislative assembly (*cortes*) promulgates Spain's first-ever constitution, a liberal document that generates much enthusiasm throughout large segments of the empire because of its promises of limited self-rule and other reforms.

10 MARCH 1812. ***Monteverde's Counteroffensive.*** After being reinforced from Spanish-held Puerto Rico, 230 loyalists begin moving east from Coro (Venezuela) under the Canarian naval Capt. Juan Domingo de Monteverde, who is joined at Siquisique by Indian chief Juan de los Reyes Vargas.

Before they can resume their march, an earthquake destroys much of Caracas and other republican-held cities on the afternoon of 26 March—Holy Thursday—while leaving the monarchist regions largely untouched. Demoralized and disorganized, the patriots are subsequently powerless to halt the expedition's advance, Monteverde pressing ahead and occupying Barquisimeto without resistance. His numbers soon swell to 1,000 followers, and he penetrates ever deeper into patriot territory despite being cautioned by Gov. José Ceballos (or Cevallos) at Coro.

5 APRIL 1812. This Sunday, royalist Lt. Col. Francisco Caldelas appears before Huajuapan (Oaxaca, Mexico) with more than 2,000 men and 14 field pieces to besiege its insurgent garrison under Col. Valerio Trujano. After the initial assault is repelled Caldelas institutes a formal siege, camping north of the town on Calvario Heights; subordinate Gabriel Esperón occupies the western side, Juan de la Vega the southern, and José María Régules the eastern bank of the Huajuapan River with his *Batallón de la Mermelada* (Marmalade Battalion, so called because of its purple uniforms). Siege batteries are installed by 10 April, opening fire on Trujano's defenders, who have no artillery. Opposing trenches encircle the town, and royalists settle in to starve the garrison into submission.

23 APRIL 1812. In a desperate bid to stem Monteverde's incursion, the Venezuelan congress grants Miranda dictatorial powers, although the gesture proves to be too little too late. The creole rulers have already alienated many blacks by failing to implement the touted abolition of slavery, further drafting legislation aimed at extending private ownership over the rangelands (*llanos*), thus reducing the status of tough plainsmen (*llaneros*) to indentured servants.

Both groups now provide formidable guerrilla contingents for the royalists, the former rising east of Caracas and the latter in the Calabozo Plains; two days later Monteverde defeats the patriot garrison at San Carlos.

3 MAY 1812. Monteverde's royalist troops occupy Valencia (Venezuela) without opposition but soon slow their advance, intimidated by the large numbers of patriots rallying around Miranda.

6 MAY 1812. Leonardo Bravo is captured with two dozen insurgent followers while sleeping at San Gabriel Hacienda (Morelos), being conveyed to Mexico City to face execution on 13 September.

17 MAY 1812. A hastily assembled insurgent force under Fathers Sánchez and Tapia approaches Huajuapan from Tehuacán (Mexico) to lift the royalist siege. The relief column is ambushed near Chilapilla by black royalist troopers under Lieutenant Colonel Caldelas, being scattered and compelled to abandon nine field pieces and the supply train.

19 MAY 1812. Belgrano reaches Jujuy (Argentina) with 1,500 sickly revolutionary troops to support the Cochabamba (Bolivia) uprising and reverse other royalist gains.

23 MAY 1812. The Mexican insurgent leader Torres, captured by loyalists, is hanged, drawn, and quartered.

30 MAY 1812. Ceballos reaches Valencia from Coro (Venezuela) with reinforcements for Monteverde's royalist army. Shortly thereafter Miranda attempts a couple of assaults against the city but is obliged to retire to La Cabrera, on the road leading toward Caracas.

Monteverde then launches three unsuccessful assaults against the patriot defenses guarding Guaica Pass before outflanking the position and compelling Miranda to retreat to Victoria. Here some 5,000 patriots make a stand; the outnumbered royalists must retire to Maracay to regroup.

4 JUNE 1812. Having recruited 800 new adherents following his Cuautla disaster, Morelos defeats the royalist Cerro at Citlala (Mexico).

30 JUNE 1812. Prominent monarchist captives imprisoned at Puerto Cabello (Venezuela)—its garrison commanded by Ramón Aymerich but political governorship exercised by a 28-year-old wealthy creole militia colonel named Simón Bolívar—rise and seize the citadel, holding on until loyalist forces can arrive to help besiege this city from outside. After six days of resistance Bolívar and Aymerich flee aboard a brig, reaching La Guaira by 7 July.

13 JULY 1812. After lengthy delays and diplomatic threats from Britain, de Sousa's Portuguese army evacuates Uruguay (*see* 21 October 1811). The general is nonetheless rewarded for his efforts during the campaign, being invested as knight grand cross of the Order of Cristo five months later, then made first conde de Rio Pardo in 1815.

MID-JULY 1812. Heartened by the Venezuelan patriots' evident disarray, Monteverde resumes his advance. Miranda is compelled to surrender Caracas by 25 July (and is prevented from leaving the country by Bolívar and other disgruntled subordinates, who suspect treason in the capitulation). Miranda is therefore handed over to the loyalists and eventually sent to Cádiz in chains, where he dies four years later. Bolívar meanwhile is allowed to flee to Curaçao on 27 August, and the First Republic dies. Through lack of skill, however, Monteverde fails to successfully reintroduce royalist rule.

22 JULY 1812. ***Siege of Huajuapan.*** The first division of Morelos's army appears southwest of Huajuapan

under Miguel Bravo in hopes of raising the extended royalist siege (*see* 5 April 1812). Caldelas scatters this relief column with a sharp sally, obliging Bravo to abandon two small field pieces.

Next day, however, Morelos and Galeana arrive from Tlapa with 1,800 additional men to reinforce Bravo. The latter attacks Esperón's camp west of Huajuapan while Galeana assaults Caldelas's positions farther north; meanwhile the beleaguered garrison emerges east out of Huajuapan to distract Régules.

The divided royalists are quickly overwhelmed, Caldelas being killed along with 400 of his men; another 200 are captured along with 14 guns, more than 1,000 muskets, and considerable materiel. Morelos remains here two weeks before marching to Tehuacán de las Granadas, which he enters triumphantly on 10 August.

11 AUGUST 1812. ***Texas Incursion.*** Insurgent Colonel Gutiérrez de Lara (*see* 16 March 1811) recrosses the Sabine River into east Texas with 400 American volunteers raised at New Orleans and Natchez—helped by former U.S. Army Lt. Augustus William Magee, now promoted lieutenant colonel for the expedition. The so-called Republican Army of the North seizes undefended Nacogdoches on 11 August as royalist support collapses throughout the eastern part of the province. Trinidad is easily overrun by mid-September; the invaders encamp there for more than a month.

On 2 November royalist Gov. Manuel de Salcedo and Col. Simón de Herrera sally east from San Antonio with 1,500 troops, deploying along the Guadalupe River. Learning of this move, Gutiérrez de Lara and Magee's army (now numbering 800 men) slide south-southwest, overwhelming the tiny Spanish coastal keep at Bahía del Espíritu Santo on 7 November.

De Salcedo pursues and traps the outnumbered insurgents inside, bombarding its ramparts with 14 field pieces; after three failed assaults a protracted siege ensues. Magee dies of disease on 6 February 1813; two additional royalist attempts to storm the walls cost 300 casualties, so de Salcedo and Herrera commence a disorderly withdrawal back to San Antonio on 19 February. Two days later Gutiérrez de Lara's survivors emerge from Espíritu Santo and follow.

20 AUGUST 1812. At the head of 200 insurgent guerrillas, Nicolás Bravo (26-year-old son of Leonardo and nephew to Miguel, Víctor, Máximo, and Nicolás) ambushes a royalist mule train at San Agustín del Palmar bound from Veracruz to Puebla. Most of the 360-man royalist escort under Lt. Col. Juan Labaqui are slaughtered; 300 muskets and three field pieces are captured.

23 AUGUST 1812. Belgrano's revolutionary army is obliged to evacuate Jujuy (Argentina), retreating south to Tucumán because of the approach of superior royalist forces out of the north under General Tristán.

3 SEPTEMBER 1812. While retiring south Belgrano makes a brief stand on the bank of the Piedras River, bloodying a 600-man royalist cavalry patrol under Colonels Llano and Huici, who have been hounding his rearguard (commanded by Argentine Brig. Gen. José Miguel Díaz Vélez). The pursuers suffer 20 killed and 25 captured, allowing the revolutionaries to resume their retreat undisturbed.

23 SEPTEMBER 1812. ***Tucumán.*** Belgrano learns his loyalist pursuers have reached Nogales (ten miles north of Tucumán); determined to halt his retreat—despite orders from the Argentine junta to continue retiring as far south as Córdoba—he decides to give battle. His 1,000 cavalry and 800 infantry take up a defensive position just north of Tucumán, only to be surprised next day by the approach out of the southwest of Tristán's 1,000 cavalry, 2,000 infantry, and 13 field pieces (the royalists having circled around the city).

Shifting across to Carreras Field, Belgrano meets Tristán's opening assault head-on, his cavalry on the right flank dispersing the loyalist Tarija Cavalry Regiment, thereby allowing the patriot infantry to defeat the Abancay, Cotabamba, and Real Lima Battalions. On the Argentine left, however, its black battalion and the Santiago del Estero militia cavalry regiment are defeated by the loyalist Paruro, Chichas, and Fernando VII Battalions, leading Belgrano to believe all is lost.

The patriot general therefore gathers some 200 stragglers around him by evening at El Rincón (nine miles south of Tucumán) in anticipation of resuming the retirement south. Instead, his other patriot formations have won a victory, subordinate Díaz Vélez reentering Tucumán with most of his infantry and artillery plus 687 captive royalists and five field pieces. Tristán has also lost 450 dead, compared to 80 killed and 200 wounded among the revolutionaries.

Next day—25 September—Belgrano realizes his good fortune and advances on the royalist survivors with 500 men, calling for surrender. Tristán refuses and retires north to Salta; that night Belgrano mistakenly sends his cavalry toward Manantiales, thereby inadvertently losing contact with the enemy.

8 OCTOBER 1812. Buenos Aires's patriot government—known as the First Triumvirate—is overthrown in favor of a Second Triumvirate.

20 OCTOBER 1812. The vanguard of Gen. Manuel de Sarratea's Argentine army reaches the outskirts of Montevideo (Uruguay) and joins 350 local volunteers under José Culta to lay siege to its royalist garrison.

29 OCTOBER 1812. Morelos raids the royalist stronghold at Orizaba (Mexico), overwhelming the garrison under Col. José Antonio Andrade and burning a valuable shipment of tobacco. Two days later, while retiring to his encampment, the insurgent leader defeats a smaller royalist force on the Acultzingo Heights.

EARLY NOVEMBER 1812. Nicolás Bravo captures the Port of Alvarado (Veracruz, Mexico), then attacks Jalapa while marching inland.

10 NOVEMBER 1812. After being joined at Tehuacán (Mexico) by Matamoros and Nicolás Bravo—each bringing 2,000 new recruits—Morelos marches to Oaxaca with 5,000 men.

24 NOVEMBER 1812. ***Oaxaca.*** Morelos's 5,000-man army arrives at Etla and calls on the 2,000-man, 36-gun royalist garrison within nearby Oaxaca City to surrender; he is rejected.

At 11:00 A.M. next day his insurgent columns mount an assault, Eugenio Montaño leading a cavalry charge past Xochimilco that cuts off the road to Tehuantepec and enters the city via La Merced. Ramón Sesma meanwhile storms the Soledad Fortress with his San Lorenzo Battalion under covering fire from Manuel de Mier y Terán's artillery. Matamoros—now a *mariscal de campo* (field marshal)—assaults the fortified Carmen Convent, while Hermenegildo Galeana carries the Santo Domingo Convent.

When Morelos enters the devastated city at 2:00 P.M. he orders the execution of its monarchist commanders—Régules, Saravia, Bonavia, Aristi, and many others.

MID-DECEMBER 1812. Having fled to New Granada (Colombia) from Venezuela (*see* mid-July 1812) and accepted a command in its patriot army, Bolívar advances from Barranca with 200 men up the Magdalena River, dislodging the loyalist garrison at Tenerife. Mompós (or Mompóx) is overrun by 27 December; after being reinforced by numerous local volunteers Bolívar occupies El Banco and defeats a Spanish force at Chiriguaná on 1 January 1813.

Tamalameque, Puerto Real, and Ocaña fall shortly thereafter, opening the Upper Magdalena region to insurgent control. Ramón Correa, royalist commander at Maracaibo, responds by occupying Cúcuta, thereby threatening the patriot outposts at Pamplona and Ocaña.

31 DECEMBER 1812. ***El Cerrito.*** At dawn 2,300 royalists under the viceroy-designate, Gaspar Vigodet, sally from Montevideo (Uruguay) with three field pieces, surprising Rondeau's Argentine besiegers. Advancing in three columns, the loyalists scatter outlying patriot units before the revolutionary general makes a stand at El Cerrito with his 4th and 6th Infantry Regiments and Patria Dragoons.

The central royalist column under Brigadier General Muesas then succeeds in breaking the black infantrymen of the 6th Infantry Regiment, but Rondeau gathers sufficient stragglers to mount a counterattack and thus throws back Vigodet's entire force. The royalists withdraw to Montevideo after suffering 100 dead, 146 wounded, and 30 prisoners; Argentine losses total 90 casualties and 40 prisoners.

Shortly thereafter Argentine commander in chief de Sarratea joins Rondeau, closely shadowed by a rival Uruguayan force under Artigas. The latter sends 28-year-old Cmdr. Fructuoso Rivera to steal Sarratea's herd of horses, prompting the Argentine leader to return alone to Buenos Aires, leaving Rondeau in command before Montevideo.

12 JANUARY 1813. Belgrano marches north from Tucumán (Argentina) to attack Tristán's royalist army at Salta.

13 JANUARY 1813. The 24-year-old aristocratic revolutionary Santiago Mariño and 45 companions (including 18-year-old Antonio José de Sucre Alcalá)—having earlier sought refuge on the British island of Trinidad—now make a dawn landing at Güiria in eastern Venezuela, quickly establishing a patriot foothold in the Gulf of Paria.

28 JANUARY 1813. The 34-year-old revolutionary officer José Francisco de San Martín departs Retiro (Argentina) with 125 troopers, shadowing the movements of a royalist flotilla foraging up the Paraná River. San Martín closes in on their anchorage the night of 2 February, uniting stealthily at San Lorenzo Monastery with another 50 patriots under Celedonio Escalada.

Next dawn 250 royalists come ashore with two field pieces to pillage that place, only to be surprised by twin columns of insurgents emerging from behind the building under San Martín and Captain Bermúdez. The raiders are repelled, suffering 40 killed and 14 wounded as opposed to six dead and 22 injured among the revolutionaries.

7 FEBRUARY 1813. Morelos's army exits the city of Oaxaca, slowly wending west to Acapulco.

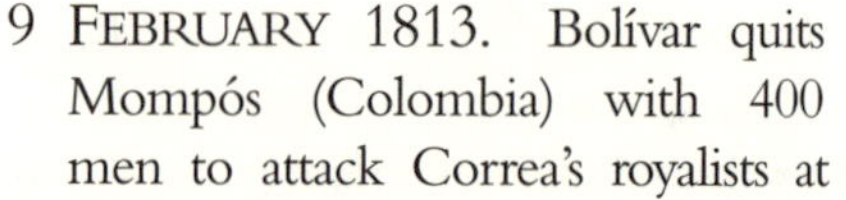

9 FEBRUARY 1813. Bolívar quits Mompós (Colombia) with 400 men to attack Correa's royalists at Cúcuta (Venezuela). After reaching San Cayetano and being reinforced by 100 patriots from Pamplona, Bolívar crosses the Zulia River at dawn on 28 February and encounters Correa at San José, driving him back to San Antonio after a four-hour struggle.

18 FEBRUARY 1813. ***Salta.*** Learning that Belgrano is marching on Salta through the rainy season, General Tristán takes up a defensive position to the southeast with 3,400 royalists and ten field pieces. The Argentine commander sends his vanguard under Brig. Gen. Díaz Vélez to mount a diversionary attack at Portezuelos while leading the bulk of his 3,700-man, 12-gun army on an encircling maneuver through Chachapolas Ravine that night. By dawn of 19 February the main revolutionary force emerges at Castañares Hacienda (three miles north of Salta), prompting Tristán to hastily redeploy along the Tagarete de Tineo Ditch.

After a heavy downpour Belgrano's army assaults at midday on 20 February, the cavalry on the patriot right dispersing their opponents then chasing them into the streets of Salta itself along with the royalist infantry. Tristán's line disintegrates, only a small unit resisting atop San Bernardo Hill, which is overwhelmed when Belgrano throws in his reserves. Salta is consequently taken, patriot losses totaling 103 dead and 433 wounded. Tristán's army is annihilated, suffering 480 dead and 114 wounded; virtually everyone else is taken prisoner then paroled.

26 FEBRUARY 1813. Uruguayan guerrillas under Artigas join Rondeau's Argentine revolutionary army in besieging the royalist garrison at Montevideo.

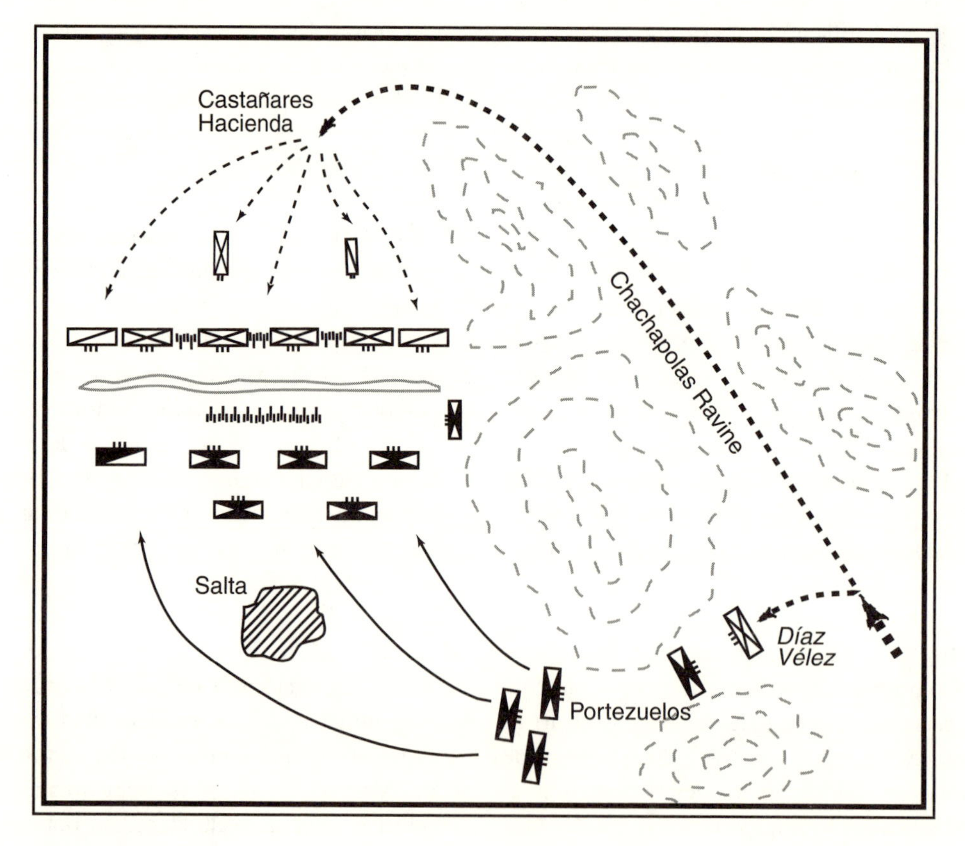

Battle of Salta

The Battle of Salta, by Aristene Papi

4 MARCH 1813. Calleja is appointed viceroy of New Spain (Mexico) in recognition of his military successes.

28 MARCH 1813. ***Rosillo.*** In Texas, insurgent Colonel Gutiérrez de Lara drives on the capital of San Antonio from Bahía del Espíritu Santo, his army having been reinforced by fresh American volunteers and Indian warriors. Royalist Colonel de Herrera challenges at Rosillo (nine miles southeast of San Antonio, on a ridge along the banks of Salado Creek) with 1,500 regulars, 1,000 militia, and 12 artillery pieces. The Americans, using their Indian allies to charge directly into the Spanish cavalry, quickly outflank the royalist infantry and defeat them in 15–20 minutes, inflicting 330 deaths and capturing 60 prisoners. Republican losses total six killed and 26 wounded.

On 1 April Governor de Salcedo sends out terms for San Antonio's capitulation to the victorious Gutiérrez de Lara at Concepción Mission; he refuses and even detains the emissaries. Next morning the capital is occupied, and on 3 April captives de Salcedo and Herrera are murdered along with a dozen other royalists at Rosillo by their insurgent escort under Antonio Delgado. The República del Norte (Northern Republic) is proclaimed three days later, symbolized by a green flag.

6 APRIL 1813. ***Fall of Acapulco.*** Morelos occupies Iguanas and Mira Heights outside Acapulco with 1,500 men, bombarding its buildings for six days with his few field pieces. This obliges the royalists to evacuate Casamata and their Hospital bulwark, withdrawing inside 90-gun Fort San Diego under garrison Cmdr. Pedro Vélez.

The insurgents settle in for a lengthy siege, seizing Roqueta Island offshore by 9 June. It is not until they tighten their siege lines around Fort San Diego on 17 August, however, that enough hardship is exerted to force the defenders to capitulate three days later. The victory proves hollow, for it threatens no major royalist interest, although it does allow Morelos to address the Mexican constitutional congress at Chilpancingo from a position of greater political strength on 13 September.

MID-APRIL 1813. Belgrano leads an Argentine army north from Salta into Upper Peru (Bolivia), occupying Potosí on 21 June.

19 ABRIL 1813. An insurgent force under Matamoros defeats royalist Servando Dombrini at Tonalá (Mexico).

23 APRIL 1813. Colombian patriot Col. Manuel del Castillo advances against La Grita (Venezuela), defeating its royalist garrison under Correa.

17 MAY 1813. ***The "Admirable Campaign."*** Having been promoted brigadier in the Colombian

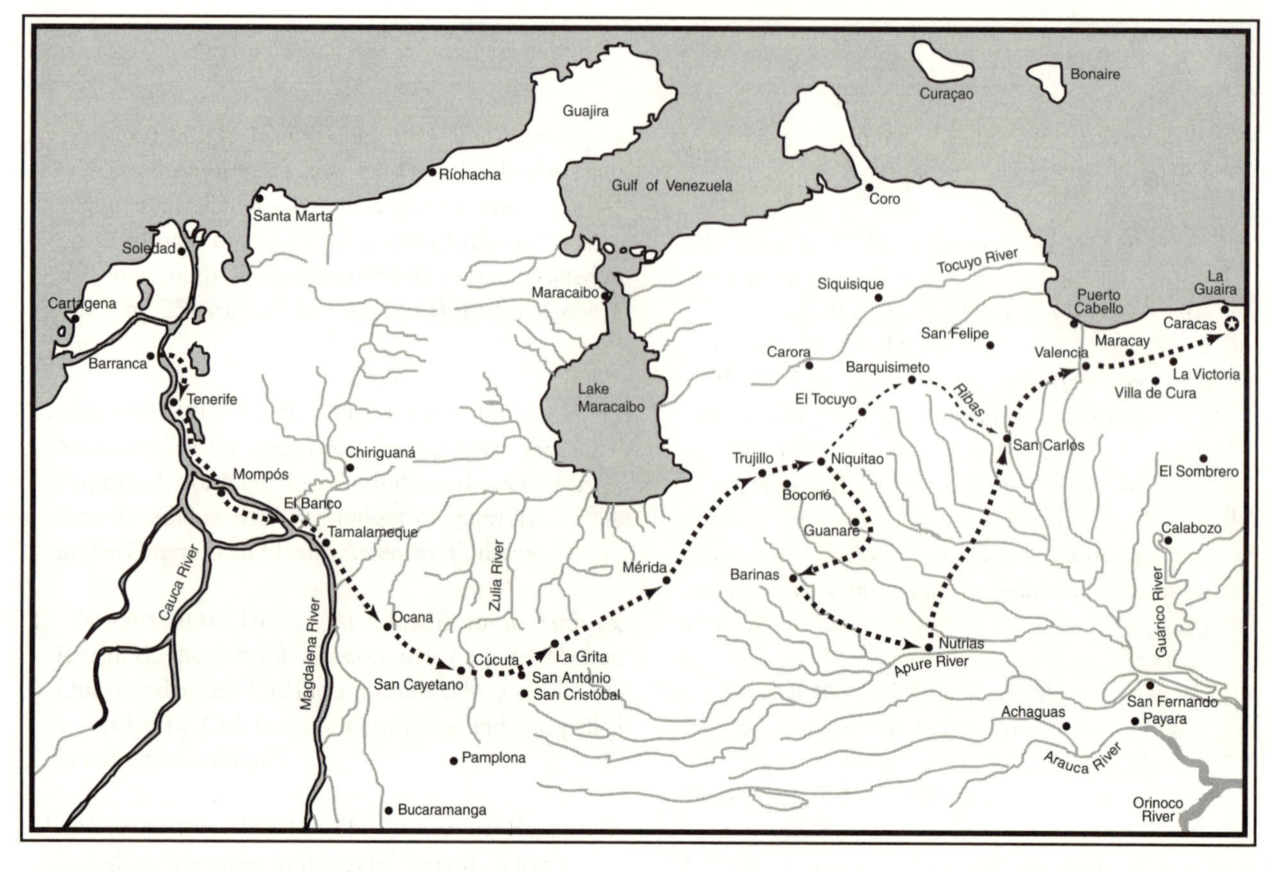

Bolívar's "Admirable Campaign"

army, Bolívar departs La Grita to reconquer Venezuela from the west. He enters Mérida triumphantly on 23 May, and on 8 June—after learning of the execution of his friend, Col. Antonio Nicolás Briceño, and other patriot martyrs—calls for a "war to the death" against all peninsular Spaniards. Including noncombatants in his decree will lead to an increasingly vicious cycle of reprisals on both sides, individual executions soon escalating into outright massacres.

Bolívar gains Trujillo by 14 June, departing toward the end of the month to march against the royalist forces gathered at Barinas under Lt. Col. Antonio Tizcar. The sudden appearance of Bolívar's army surprises Tizcar, precipitating a sudden evacuation that disintegrates into chaos when the royalists attempt to recross the Apure River, only to have the citizens of Nutria rise against them. Tizcar reaches San Fernando virtually alone; his subordinate José Martí is also defeated at Niquitao Heights around the same time by patriot Col. José Félix Ribas, all Spanish captives being put to the sword. Ribas then occupies El Tocuyo by 18 July, marching on Barquisimeto and destroying the royalist forces stationed at Los Horcones under Col. Francisco Oberto. Without pausing, Ribas crosses El Altar Mountain and rejoins Bolívar at San Carlos by 30 July.

Next day the combined patriot contingents destroy a royalist army under Col. Julián Izquierdo on Taguanes Plain, slaughtering all its infantry. Upon receiving this grim news Monteverde flees Valencia to Puerto Cabello, leaving the road to Caracas open. Bolívar enters Valencia triumphantly on 2 August, detaching Col. Atanasio Girardot to watch Monteverde's movements while he drives to the capital. Its royalist governor, Brig. Gen. Antonio Fierro, offers to capitulate, and the victorious patriots enter on 6 August amid scenes of cruel reprisals. Bolívar's whirlwind offensive becomes known to history as the *campaña admirable* (admirable campaign); Bolívar himself is called El Libertador, although once in power he does not restore republican government, instead maintaining a military dictatorship under the guise of a second republic.

EARLY JUNE 1813. ***Alazán.*** Royalist Lt. Col. Francisco Ignacio Elizondo invades Texas with 3,000 badly trained Mexican conscripts to avenge insurgent Gutiérrez de Lara's deposal and murder of Governor de Salcedo. Although under orders from Colonel Arredondo to advance no farther north than Frío River, Elizondo progresses to the very outskirts of San

Antonio, camping on the banks of Alazán Creek by 16 June and challenging the republican army to battle.

Although outnumbered, the new American leader, Henry Perry, leads the republican force out after nightfall, charging across the Alazán next dawn with the sun behind him to crush the royalists in a four-hour fight. Elizondo sustains 400 casualties and flees into Laredo, where he is superseded by Arredondo.

A month and a half later the unpopular Gutiérrez de Lara is overthrown as insurgent leader by his Cuban rival José María Alvarez de Toledo with support from American William Shaler.

3 AUGUST 1813. The patriot leader Mariño captures Cumaná, establishing himself as virtual ruler of eastern Venezuela one month later.

15 AUGUST 1813. ***Atascoso.*** Alvarez de Toledo's 850 American troops and 600 Cochate Indian allies march out of San Antonio (Texas), taking up a defensive position on the Medina River two days later to contest another royalist invasion from the south. They encounter a 180-man cavalry patrol under Elizondo, who engages and retreats across the Medina, drawing the republicans toward Arredondo's main body.

At Atascoso the pursuers encounter 1,200 royalist riders and 700 infantry drawn up with their artillery. A four-hour battle ensues in which Arredondo crushes the insurgents; he then brutally overruns San Antonio on the afternoon of 18 August. Alvarez de Toledo, Perry, and other republican leaders flee to Louisiana, effectively putting an end to the rebellion in Texas.

16 AUGUST 1813. Matamoros's insurgents maul the royalist Asturias Battalion at San Agustín del Palmar (Mexico), executing its commander, Cándano.

MID-SEPTEMBER 1813. Having been reinforced from Spain by a 1,300-man division under Col. José Miguel Salomón, Monteverde's loyalists sortie from Puerto Cabello (Venezuela) to attack Girardot's patriot besiegers, already retreating to Valencia.

On 30 September the pursuers collide at Bárbula with a relief column arriving under Bolívar, being mauled and driven back to the protection of Salomón's regulars at Las Trincheras. Monteverde is wounded there on 3 October, and the Spaniards are driven back into Puerto Cabello, which is once again encircled by patriot Col. Patricio de Elhuyar (successor to Girardot, who was killed at Bárbula). Monteverde—his jaw shattered in the fighting—renounces his command on 28 October in favor of Juan Manuel Cajigal (or Cagigal).

SEPTEMBER 1813. In order to dispute a loyalist occupation of Popayán (north of Pasto, in southwest Colombia), the insurgent Nariño—having forged a temporary alliance with neighboring New Granada—marches out of Bogotá at the head of a small army. He retakes Popayán, but after winning small victories at Palacé and Calbío, is captured while advancing on Pasto and shipped to Spain.

1 OCTOBER 1813. ***Vilcapugio.*** Argentine General Belgrano—having gained Vilcapugio Plain (Bolivia) four days earlier—is awaiting the arrival of 1,200 insurgent troops from Cochabamba under Colonel Zelaya plus 2,000 Indian auxiliaries from Chayanta under chief Cárdenas. The latter, however, has been defeated at Ancacato by a royalist force under Castro; moreover, revolutionary plans are laid before the theater's new commander in chief, Peruvian Viceroy Joaquín de la Pezuela y Sanchez.

Determined to destroy the insurgent factions before they can unite, de la Pezuela leads 4,000 loyalists and 12 field pieces out of the Condo Condo Range at dawn on 1 October to attack Belgrano's 3,500 men and 14 cannons, resting below on Vilcapugio (or Vilcapujio) Plain. The revolutionaries quickly form ranks, dispersing the cavalry on the royalist left as soon as this battle is joined. Shortly thereafter the royalist infantry also breaks and flees, abandoning their artillery; Belgrano senses victory.

At this moment, however, Castro's royalist cavalry materializes out of the north, catching the patriots in the flank and rolling up their line. The defeated insurgents divide into two, one contingent fleeing down the Potosí road under Díaz Vélez, the other to Macha under Belgrano.

7 NOVEMBER 1813. Morelos marches northwest out of Chilpancingo, hoping to conquer Valladolid (modern-day Morelia, Mexico) and make it the capital of his new republican government.

10 NOVEMBER 1813. Bolívar reinforces Col. Rafael Urdaneta's patriot division with a small contingent but is repulsed near Barquisimeto by Ceballos's royalist forces; he is then obliged to retire to San Carlos before rebuilding his army and driving the enemy from Vigirima Heights.

13 NOVEMBER 1813. ***Ayohuma.*** Having recuperated from his Vilcapugio defeat, Argentine General Belgrano marches north from Macha (Bolivia) on 9 November with 3,400 revolutionaries and

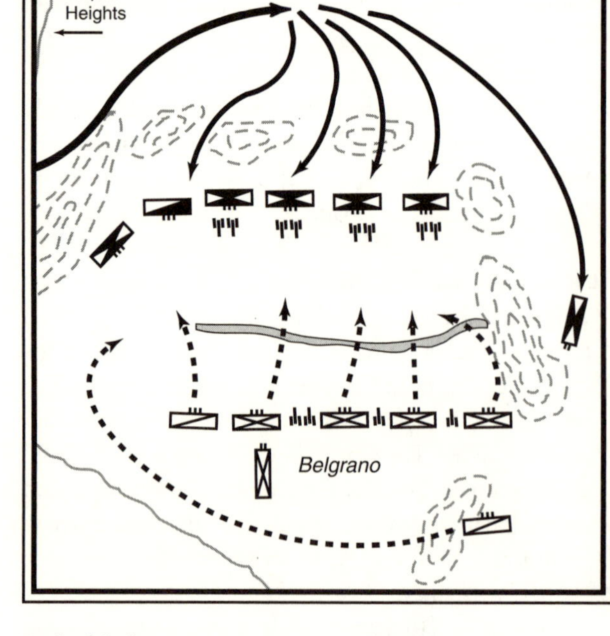

Battle of Ayohuma

eight cannons, establishing himself in Ayohuma Plain. Four days later de la Pezuela appears on the Taquirí high ground with 3,500 royalists and 18 guns, descending into the valley to give battle next day.

After a brief opening bombardment, the royalists repel Belgrano's cavalry and infantry assaults. They destroy the insurgent army in three hours of brutal fighting, which costs de la Pezuela 500 casualties. Belgrano's army is virtually annihilated by sundown on 14 November, only 400 men leaving the field with their defeated general.

Belgrano quickly retreats south, unsuccessfully attempting to blow up the Potosí Mint during his retirement to Argentina. De la Pezuela follows up his advantage, reoccupying the cities of Jujuy and Salta early next year. On 30 January 1814, at Tucumán, the disgraced Belgrano is succeeded in command of the revolutionary Army of the Andes by San Martín.

5 DECEMBER 1813. Ceballos's royalist forces are joined by Col. José Yáñez and engaged at the town of Araure (Venezuela) by Bolívar, who defeats them after a hard-fought struggle.

11 DECEMBER 1813. In Europe—Napoleon's armies having been driven out of Spain by Wellington—peace is restored between the Emperor and Spain via the Treaty of Valençay, which also promises to restore Ferdinand VII to the throne.

22 DECEMBER 1813. ***Valladolid-Puruarán.*** Morelos appears at the Valladolid suburb of Santa María with 5,000 men and 30 artillery pieces. Next day subordinates Galeana and Bravo attempt to seize the Zapote Gate to prevent the entry of royalist reinforcements. That assault fails, however, and the city's garrison is strengthened the morning of 24 December by the Toluca and Guanajuato Divisions under Llano and Col. Agustín de Iturbide.

That evening Iturbide slips out of Valladolid with 190 cavalry and an infantry company, stealing upon the unwary insurgent camp as darkness falls. In a brilliant stroke, Iturbide launches a nocturnal attack that startles the insurgents, who fire on their own ranks and eventually dissolve in panic.

Morelos flees to Chupío with a handful of followers, hoping to regroup his army at Puruarán. Instead, the disorganized insurgents are once again surprised during the night of 4–5 January 1814 by Llano's cavalry, being utterly routed and losing 25 guns, 1,000 muskets, and additional materiel. Among the prisoners is Matamoros, caught while attempting to cross the Puruarán River; he is conveyed to Valladolid to be executed on 3 February.

A royalist column under Gabriel Armijo continues to Chilpancingo and defeats the troops of Victor and Miguel Bravo, thereby crushing any insurgent hopes of resuming an offensive.

DECEMBER 1813. A creole conspiracy, centered around the Bethelemite religious order, is discovered in Guatemala City.

JANUARY 1814. Manuel José de Arce leads a second creole uprising at San Salvador (Central America).

EARLY FEBRUARY 1814. Having failed to placate Venezuela's blacks and *llaneros* following the restoration of creole rule, Bolívar's republican government is beset by royalist guerrilla raids—the most effective being those organized by 31-year-old José Tomás Boves, a onetime peninsular merchant and smuggler who proves an inspired leader of these tough nomads.

After numerous skirmishes, Boves manages to crush patriot Cmdr. Vicente Campo Elías's army at La Puerta (southwest of Caracas). His 7,000–8,000 followers then drive Bolívar from his San Mateo Hacienda—in the process slaying Campo Elías—while Ceballos's royalists threaten Valencia and Francisco Rosete closes in on Caracas from the east, destroying patriot Gen. Juan Bautista Arismendi's smaller force before finally being checked by Ribas.

Bolívar staves off disaster by compelling Ceballos to raise the siege of Valencia; Ribas halts Boves's drive by winning a victory at La Victoria on 12 February. Nevertheless, the frightened republicans execute at least 800 monarchist captives between 14 and 16 February.

23 FEBRUARY 1814. His following reduced to 900 demoralized men after the twin disasters at Valladolid and Puruarán, Morelos departs Tlacotepec (Mexico), only to be overtaken next day by a royalist column and nearly captured as his troops scatter. The insurgent leader eventually straggles into Acapulco by early March with only 100 men.

11 MARCH 1814. Patriot naval officer William "Guillermo" Brown—born 36 years earlier in Foxford, Ireland, and raised in Philadelphia—attacks a royalist flotilla under Jacinto Romarate, anchored off Martín García Island in the River Plate. Brown deploys virtually the entire fledgling Argentine navy: corvettes *Hércules* (flag) and *Cefir;* sloops *Julia* and *Fortuna;* the *sumanca Trinidad;* gunboat *América;* auxiliaries *San Martín* and *San Luis;* plus the schooner *Carmen.* He is repelled after his flagship runs aground.

Four days later Brown returns and conquers the island, occupied by loyalists for the past four months. Romarate's flotilla flees up the Uruguay River, pursued by a patriot squadron under Notter. The latter is checked at Arroyo de la China on 28 March yet keeps the royalist vessels bottled up.

22 MARCH 1814. Ferdinand VII returns to Spain. During the ensuing weeks he and his absolutist followers heavy-handedly abolish the liberal constitution of March 1812 and restore many trappings of their past regime.

31 MARCH 1814. The royalist Boves encounters Mariño at Bocachica (Venezuela) as the latter marches to Bolívar's relief at San Mateo. Both sides suffer heavy casualties during the engagement, Mariño retiring to La Victoria while Boves withdraws to Valencia.

9 APRIL 1814. Learning that royalist forces under Armijo are closing in on his Acapulco stronghold, Morelos burns the place, hangs more than 100 royalist prisoners, and disappears into the Atijo Mountains one week later with a handful of loyal adherents. Monarchists reoccupy the now devastated Acapulco on 14 April.

20 APRIL 1814. ***Fall of Montevideo.*** Following his conquest of Martín García Island, Brown blockades the royalist stronghold of Montevideo with seven Argentine warships, complementing the as yet ineffective land siege of 4,000 revolutionaries under General Rondeau.

Faced with this new threat, 13 royalist vessels sortie on 14 May under Miguel Sierra, pursuing Brown, who turns and defeats them near El Buceo in a three-day running fight. Brown reimposes his blockade, and Rondeau is soon reinforced by 1,500 Argentine troops under Carlos María de Alvear.

On 20 June Spanish Governor Vigodet at last requests terms, and three days later Montevideo surrenders. The Argentine patriots seize 500 guns, 9,000 muskets, 100 ships, and 7,000 prisoners (most of whom are repatriated to Spain). However, the occupation creates friction with the local Uruguayan leader, Artigas.

EARLY MAY 1814. Chile's patriot leader Bernardo O'Higgins arranges a shaky truce with loyalist forces invading from Peru.

28 MAY 1814. Bolívar defeats a royalist army under Cajigal and Ceballos on the Plains of Carabobo as it advances against Caracas.

15 JUNE 1814. ***First Battle of La Puerta.*** Boves's *llanero* cavalry crushes the combined forces of Bolívar and Mariño at La Puerta (southwest of Caracas), compelling the patriots to retire inside their capital with only 800–1,000 troops. Boves's main body turns to subdue the last republican stronghold at Valencia (under Col. Juan Escalona), one division being detached to occupy Caracas.

25 JUNE 1814. An Uruguayan militia company reaches Las Piedras under Colonel Ortogués, requesting that Argentine General Alvear give them possession of recently conquered Montevideo. Alvear not only refuses but dispatches 800 riders during the night to disperse the rival formation, capturing 200 Uruguayans with artillery and baggage.

6 JULY 1814. Believing the royalist division approaching Caracas to be weak, Bolívar sorties from his capital to give battle. He is defeated with heavy losses, however, and the republicans abandon Caracas by the thousands to Barcelona, fearing monarchist vengeance.

9 JULY 1814. Valencia surrenders to Boves, a number of executions being carried out.

31 JULY 1814. Argentina's guerrilla leader Güemes reoccupies Salta, abandoned by de la Pezuela's royalists when they retired north to Jujuy.

2 AUGUST 1814. ***Pumacahua Rebellion.*** Following nearly a year of disputes, the liberal creole councilors (*cabildo*) of Cuzco escape confinement by the more conservative *oidores* (justices); they arrest many peninsular Spaniards and call for the full implementation of Spain's March 1812 constitution. The rebels are led by middle-class citizens—José and Vicente Angulo and Gabriel Béjar—although the insurrection becomes known for one of its military leaders, the elderly *curaca* (local Indian official) Mateo García Pumacahua.

Tens of thousands of poorly armed peasants advance quickly against Huamanga and Huancavelica in the north and La Paz and Arequipa in the south. They also ally with Argentine insurgents besieging Upper Peru (Bolivia); when the latter are defeated toward the end of this year Pumacahua's followers are brutally repressed.

3 AUGUST 1814. Jujuy (Argentina) is reoccupied by revolutionary forces as de la Pezuela's royalists withdraw to Cotagaita (Bolivia).

17 AUGUST 1814. Royalist Col. Francisco Tomás Morales—Boves's second-in-command—overtakes Bolívar's fleeing republican army at Aragua (eastern Venezuela), inflicting stinging losses and compelling the Liberator to continue through Barcelona to Cumaná, where he escapes by sea with Mariño by 25 August.

AUGUST 1814. The Italian mercenary Giuseppe Bianchi—commissioned as a republican privateer—makes off with three Colombian ships and much silver plate from Caracas.

12 SEPTEMBER 1814. Republican Gen. José Francisco Bermúdez halts Morales's royalist drive through eastern Venezuela at Maturín, prompting Boves to march to his subordinate's aid. Along the way he defeats Bermúdez in an hour-long fight at Magueyes, then combines forces with Morales to bear down upon Maturín.

LATE SEPTEMBER 1814. Bolívar and Mariño reach Cartagena safely.

1 OCTOBER 1814. ***Rancagua.*** Weakened by internal fighting between O'Higgins and José Miguel Carrera, Chile's patriots suffer a crushing defeat at the hands of a loyalist army in the two-day Battle of Rancagua (50 miles south of Santiago). Many insurgents are subsequently obliged to flee to Argentina; those who remain suffer harsh repression by monarchists.

6 OCTOBER 1814. In Uruguay, Argentine General Alvear detaches 27-year-old Col. Manuel Dorrego with 600 men to disperse the 1,000 Uruguayan militia gathered at Marmarajá (18 miles northeast of Montevideo). The Uruguayans are surprised and defeated, suffering 70 deaths plus the loss of artillery and baggage trains.

5 DECEMBER 1814. ***Urica.*** Rather than await Boves at Maturín (eastern Venezuela), Commanders Ribas and Bermúdez sortie with 3,000 republican troops to seek engagement. They come upon 5,500 royalists encamped at Urica, join battle, and are almost totally annihilated. Ribas and Bermúdez stagger back to Maturín with a few hundred survivors; however, Boves is slain in the fighting and succeeded by Morales.

8 DECEMBER 1814. Having been given command of Urdaneta's division in New Granada (Colombia), Bolívar arrives outside Bogotá to subdue the rival republican government under the elderly Manuel Bernardo Alvarez (Nariño's successor; *see* September 1813). Surrender is refused, so Bolívar attacks on 10 December, pushing the defenders into the main square next day; he accepts capitulation by 12 December.

11 DECEMBER 1814. Morales overruns Maturín (eastern Venezuela) in a four-hour fight, defeating 300–400 defending infantry under Bermúdez and Ribas. The latter is taken prisoner and executed along with most of the town's residents.

10 JANUARY 1815. ***Guayabos.*** Argentine Colonel Dorrego, with 800 men (including 200 former royalists) and one small gun, are defeated by 1,200 Uruguayan troops and a single cannon under Bernabé Rivera. Dorrego suffers 200 casualties, plus 400 prisoners or deserters, the few survivors escaping in the night. Dorrego retires inland to Entre Ríos while the remaining Argentine forces in Uruguay fall back to Montevideo. Unable to maintain a garrison, Buenos Aires agrees to cede the city to

the patriot leader Artigas, and Montevideo is evacuated on 15 February 1815.

24 JANUARY 1815. Bolívar departs Bogotá in hopes of raising an expedition to invade western Venezuela and reassert republican rule. The project is abandoned due to the absence of any support from the divided Colombian government.

26 JANUARY 1815. At El Tejar (Bolivia), royalist riders surprise Argentine Col. Martín Rodríguez resting with 40 of his men, capturing all except Capt. Mariano Necochea.

27 MARCH 1815. Bolívar's division occupies the Popa high ground outside Cartagena to besiege its ruling faction under Brig. Gen. Manuel del Castillo. Civil war divides the republican camp—at a time when royalist fortunes are reviving.

EARLY APRIL 1815. ***Royalist Resurgence.*** In Europe, Napoleon's fall and the return of stable government allows Spain to concentrate on the rebellion in its American colonies. An expedition of 10,500 conscripted soldiers reaches eastern Venezuela aboard 18 warships and 42 transports at the beginning of April under an experienced, 36-year-old general named Pablo Morillo y Morillo—dubbed *pacificador de Tierra Firme* (pacifier of the Spanish Main); he is also to become its governor and intends to use the province as a staging area for subsequent attacks against strategic theaters.

Finding that the insurgents under Arismendi and Bermúdez have transformed Margarita Island into a patriot outpost, Morillo takes 3,000 loyalists aboard under Morales and subdues it by 11 April (only Bermúdez and a few followers escaping). When progress resumes, though, the 74-gun flagship *San Pedro de Alcántara* accidentally explodes, killing 900 and costing the expedition much of its money, artillery, weapons, and provisions. Reaching Caracas on 11 May, Morillo restores Madrid rule but alienates many black royalists and sets up a virtual military dictatorship to secure provisions and funding for his army.

15 APRIL 1815. In Buenos Aires, "supreme director" Alvear is overthrown by Rondeau.

17 APRIL 1815. At Puesto del Marqués (Bolivia), a 500-man Argentine cavalry patrol under Col. Fernández de la Cruz surprises 300 royalist riders.

9 MAY 1815. Bolívar quits the fratricidal struggle among rival republican factions within New Granada (Colombia), sailing for Jamaica aboard an English warship, arriving four days later.

2 JUNE 1815. Morillo quits Caracas for Puerto Cabello (Venezuela) with his main royalist army, leaving Brig. Gen. Salvador Moxó in command of the Venezuelan capital.

13 JULY 1815. Morillo departs Puerto Cabello with his 5,000 regulars, entering New Granada (Colombia) via Santa Marta. From there he dispatches two columns to clear the Magdalena River by reinforcing the royalist garrison at Mompós and occupying Ocaña and Antioquía. Meanwhile Morales advances overland against Cartagena, where Morillo joins him on 1 September by landing unopposed; together they besiege the rebel defenders.

25 SEPTEMBER 1815. Zacatlán (Mexico) falls to the royalists.

29 SEPTEMBER 1815. Guerrilla leaders Morelos, Nicolás Bravo, Páez, Father Carvajal, and Irrigaray exit Uruapan, escorting Mexico's national congress east to the safety of Tehuacán. Royalists get wind of the plan and send cavalry units to intercept. They fail to prevent the congressional caravan under Guerrero from crossing the Mezcala River at Tenango on 3 November, but two days later Lt. Col. Manuel de la Concha's cavalry overtakes an insurgent contingent at Tezmalaca. The latter are defeated; among 29 prisoners being Morelos himself. He is conveyed to Mexico City, stripped of his religious orders, interrogated, tortured, and executed at San Cristóbal Ecatepec on 22 December. The demoralized congressional congress disbands before the year is out.

17 OCTOBER 1815. Insurgent Commander Castillo is deposed as governor of beleaguered Cartagena, and succeeded by Bermúdez. Morillo's siege is so tight that eventually its residents are starved into submission; they flee in great numbers by early December. On 6 December the Spanish general enters the streets triumphantly; Morales conducts wholesale executions at nearby Bocachica Fortress.

20 OCTOBER 1815. An Argentine striking force of 350 infantrymen and 200 riders under Col. Martín Rodríguez (who has been exchanged; *see* 26 January 1815) attempts to surprise a 300-man royalist force at

Venta y Media (12 miles north of Chayanta, Bolivia), only to be discovered and repelled.

23 OCTOBER 1815. The 28-gun, 200-man Argentine frigate *Hércules* departs Montevideo under Capt. Guillermo Brown, accompanied by the brig *Trinidad* under younger brother Miguel to round Cape Horn and attack the Spaniards in the Pacific.

27 NOVEMBER 1815. ***Sipe Sipe.*** With 5,100 men and 23 field pieces, royalist General de la Pezuela intercepts Rondeau's 3,000–3,500 Argentine rebels and nine guns as they attempt to gain Cochabamba (Bolivia). Descending into the plain from Viluma Heights, de la Pezuela spends the next two days maneuvering around Rondeau's right flank before launching his attack on 29 November. The royalists shatter the revolutionary army, killing, wounding, and capturing 1,000 invaders (along with all artillery and 1,500 firearms); survivors flee down the road to Potosí, eventually being joined by 1,000 Argentine reinforcements under Col. Domingo French. Royalist losses total 32 dead and 198 injured.

30 NOVEMBER 1815. Royalist militia Col. Sebastián de la Calzada, after advancing inland with the 5th Division, defeats the patriot General Urdaneta at Chitaga (Colombia).

15 DECEMBER 1815. Guerrero forces the surrender of the royalist garrison under Antonio Flon, Conde de la Cadena, at Acatlán (Mexico). Shortly thereafter, monarchist reinforcements arrive under General Lamadrid, who puts Guerrero's company to flight.

16 DECEMBER 1815. Prince Regent João—rather than return to Portugal following Napoleon's fall—instead proclaims Brazil a kingdom and decides to remain in the New World. (Three months later, upon the death of his deranged mother, Maria, he becomes ruler of Portugal's global empire.)

20 JANUARY 1816. Having been joined off Chile by the 16-gun, 130-man patriot corvette *Halcón* of Capt. Hipólito Bouchard—born 32 years earlier in France—Brown's Argentine raiders *Hércules* and *Trinidad* blockade Callao (Peru). Action ensues for two days and two nights, resulting in the sinking of the Spanish merchant frigate *Fuente Hermosa* and other damage. On 23 January the royalist frigate *Consecuencia* is intercepted while approaching and is renamed *Argentina*. On the night of 24–25 January another boat raid is attempted; Brown eventually lifts his blockade on 30 Janaury, having suffered 30 losses.

31 JANUARY 1816. Retreating before de la Pezuela's victorious royalists, Argentine General Lamadrid fights a delaying action at Culpina (Bolivia), followed by another at Uturango on 2 February and another on the banks of the San Juan River ten days later, as the revolutionaries continue to retire to their ultimate destination—Tucumán.

EARLY FEBRUARY 1816. The three patriot raiders under Brown and Bouchard enter the Gulf of Guayaquil with seven prizes, sailing up the Guayas River with the shallow-draft *Trinidad* and a boat party. Despite overrunning a small keep and battery near Guayaquil during a nocturnal assault, Brown and his men suffer 50 casualties and are taken prisoner when *Trinidad* runs aground. They are then exchanged on 16 February when *Hércules* and *Halcón* appear off the city.

22 FEBRUARY 1816. ***Cachirí.*** This morning Spanish Colonel de la Calzada—reinforced by a contingent sent by Col. Miguel de la Torre—pulverizes a 3,000-man patriot division under Gen. Custodio García Robira at Cachirí, which is attempting to bar his advance into Colombia's central highlands. The Spaniards take no prisoners, and the road to the insurgent capital lays open.

21 APRIL 1816. In Mexico, the insurgent Commander Osorio is beaten at Venta de Cruz by Manuel de la Concha and again two days later at San Felipe.

2 MAY 1816. Bolívar returns to Margarita Island (eastern Venezuela) from Haiti with 250 followers aboard a brig, six schooners, and a Spanish prize. Sighting a royal brig and schooner off Los Frailes, he captures them and kills Spanish Capt. Rafael Iglesias before dropping anchor in Juan Griego Harbor next day. Here the Liberator is greeted by patriot General Arismendi, who has already partially thrown off royalist rule. Although the Spaniards evacuate their capital, Asunción, Bolívar is unable to storm the Pampatar stronghold under Brig. Gen. Juan Bautista Pardo. He therefore continues his voyage on 25 May, leaving that operation to Arismendi.

5 MAY 1816. De la Torre's Spanish division occupies Bogotá and is joined three weeks later by Morillo. Many patriots are arrested and executed, others fleeing into exile in the eastern *llanos*. By the end of the year

virtually all of New Granada (Colombia) is once again in royalist hands, including Quito.

26 MAY 1816. De la Torre scatters the remnants of Col. Manuel Roergas de Serviez's defeated patriot division from Cáqueza (eastern Colombia).

31 MAY 1816. Bolívar's small company disembarks at Carúpano (eastern Venezuela), occupying its tiny royalist keep and seizing a brig and schooner from the roads. The Liberator then dispatches mulatto colleagues Mariño and Manuel Piar inland to recruit followers at Güiria and Maturín.

19 JUNE 1816. Spanish Brig. Gen. Tomás de Cires, advancing from Cumaná (eastern Venezuela) to engage Bolívar's beachhead at Carúpano, attacks patriot Col. Francisco de Paula Alcántara's outpost at Esmeralda, forcing it back. Realizing the royalists are closing in on his position, the Liberator sets sail on 1 July with 700 followers, shifting operations farther west.

5 JULY 1816. Bolívar's 700-man army lands unopposed at Ocumare (Venezuela), 20 miles east of Puerto Cabello. Two days later he detaches Lt. Col. Carlos Soublette with 300 men to occupy La Cabrera and raise rebellion in the Aragua Valley. The detachment is attacked by Morales, marching out of Valencia, and driven back to Los Aguacates Hill. From there Soublette calls for help; Bolívar sets out with 200 reinforcements.

9 JULY 1816. The United Provinces of the River Plate (Argentina) officially proclaims independence from Spain.

12 JULY 1816. ***Santa Fe Campaign.*** Buenos Aires's supremacy is challenged by a rival republican government at the inland city of Santa Fe. Gen. Díaz Vélez is dispatched up the Paraná River, occupying the mostly deserted city with 1,500 troops by 4 August. The enemy refuses to deal, however, so the invaders retreat downriver by 31 August.

13 JULY 1816. At dawn Morales's loyalists attack Bolívar's and Soublette's defenses at Los Aguacates (Venezuela). Although outnumbered two-to-one, they defeat the patriots and drive them back to Ocumare, while killing, wounding, or capturing one-third of Bolivar's insurgents. Believing his hopes are now dashed, the Liberator goes aboard the armed brig *Indio Libre* that evening and sails to Bonaire, abandoning his followers.

Command of the survivors is offered next day to Gregor MacGregor—a tough Scottish mercenary, former captain in the British army, and veteran of Miranda's campaign—who instantly marches to the Aragua Valley, skirmishing with royalist forces until chancing upon a patriot cavalry detachment under Col. Leonardo Infante, part of Pedro Zaraza's larger guerrilla band.

EARLY AUGUST 1816. In Brazil, the Portuguese avail themselves of the collapse of royalist rule and fratricidal rifts between republicans in Argentina, Uruguay, and Paraguay to launch an offensive—allegedly to restore peace throughout the region but actually to extend their own western borders. The 52-year-old Lt. Gen. Carlos Frederico Lecor, barão de Laguna and knight grand cross of the Order of Torre e Espada, launches a two-pronged offensive by marching southwest from Rio Grande do Sul along the coast with his main body; a second army penetrates west from Porto Alegre to the headwaters of the Uruguay River. The invaders' total strength is some 10,000 troops, half of them Portuguese regulars.

10 AUGUST 1816. ***MacGregor's March.*** Col. Juan Nepomuceno Quero's loyalist division overtakes MacGregor's smaller insurgent company at Quebrada Honda (Venezuela), only to be thrashed. This victory allows the Scottish mercenary to continue his progress; he is reinforced at San Diego de Cabrutica by 300–400 men under Zaraza plus José Tadeo Monagas's guerrillas.

MacGregor seizes Barcelona, and 27-year-old José Antonio Anzoátegui occupies the nearby port of Píritu. At this point General Piar's division joins MacGregor, and together they sally and defeat Morales's 3,000 loyalists at El Juncal, scarcely a tenth of the latter surviving the engagement.

16 AUGUST 1816. Bolívar returns to Güiria (Gulf of Paria, eastern Venezuela), only to have Mariño and Bermúdez disavow his authority because of his unseemly flight from Ocumare. Chased down to the beach by Bermúdez, who is brandishing a sword, the Liberator is constrained to sail to Haiti.

13 SEPTEMBER 1816. Royalist forces reoccupy Janitzio Island in Lake Pátzcuaro (Michoacán, Mexico).

18 SEPTEMBER 1816. Lecor's Brazilian army occupies Maldonado (Uruguay) with little opposition.

25 SEPTEMBER 1816. Brown reaches Antigua Island (British West Indies) with only 53 men remaining

aboard his Argentine privateer *Hércules,* which is auctioned after its raid into the Pacific. Brown then travels to Britain, returning to the River Plate in November 1818.

EARLY OCTOBER 1816. Piar marches out of Barcelona (Venezuela) with 1,500 men to cross the Orinoco River and subdue Guayana.

3 OCTOBER 1816. The 23-man schooner of American mercenary Isaiah Homer—armed with a Colombian privateering commission—is brought to Santiago de Cuba as a prize by the corsair José Cepeda.

5 OCTOBER 1816. ***San Borja.*** Two days earlier the Uruguayan patriot and Indian chief Andresito, with 2,000 followers, has besieged 200 Brazilian invaders under Brig. Gen. (and military engineer) Francisco das Chagas Santos inside San Borja, opposite Santo Tomé at the headwaters of the Uruguay River. When advised that Portuguese Gen. José de Abreu is approaching with a 600-man relief column, Andresito detaches 800 riders while maintaining his siege. The Uruguayan militia detachment is unable to check the Brazilian advance, however, and Abreu kills 500 of Andresito's followers and scatters the rest.

19 OCTOBER 1816. Portuguese Brig. Gen. Menna Barreto's 500 men and two field pieces ambush 600 Uruguayan militia under Verdún on the eastern shores of Ibiracahy Creek, killing 150 and dispersing the remainder.

27 OCTOBER 1816. ***Carumbé.*** With 500 infantry and 700 cavalry, Uruguayan leader Artigas makes a stand on Carumbé Hill, west-northwest of Santana do Livramento, against 800 Portuguese invaders under 39-year-old acting Brig. Gen. Joaquim António de Oliveira Alvares (originally a naval officer, and graduate of Coimbra University). The patriots are soundly defeated, Artigas losing approximately half his men.

7 NOVEMBER 1816. Royalist forces reconquer Fort Monte Blanco, next to Córdoba (Mexico).

14 NOVEMBER 1816. In northern Argentina, a 3,000-man royalist army presses south under Gen. José de la Serna, its vanguard under Brigadier General Marquiegui surprising 600 revolutionary troops under General Campero at Yavi on 15 November. Having seized the Argentine mounts with the opening assault, the royalists gain an easy victory when they storm from two directions, capturing Campero with half of his command.

19 NOVEMBER 1816. ***India Muerta.*** In an unavailing attempt to check the Brazilian invasion of Uruguay, patriot Gen. Fructuoso Rivera's 1,000 followers attack Portuguese Brig. Gen. Pinto de Araújo's 900-man column on the western shores of India Muerta Creek, suffering a resounding defeat. Coupled with other setbacks, this prompts the Uruguayans to request aid from their political rivals in Buenos Aires.

25 NOVEMBER 1816. In Mexico, the royalists recover Mezcala Island (in Lake Chapala) from the insurgents.

NOVEMBER 1816. Mexican guerrilla leader Guerrero is driven into Los Naranjos Canyon by royalist Carlos Moya.

10 DECEMBER 1816. Mexican royalists reoccupy Cuiristarán Fort.

This same day in Santiago del Estero (Argentina), Cmdr. Juan Francisco Borges revolts against Pueyrredón's four-month-old republican administration in Buenos Aires. The federalist uprising is quickly quelled by a contingent from Belgrano's *Ejército del Norte* (Northern Army), Colonel Lamadrid surprising Borges's followers on 27 December and executing the leader four days later.

28 DECEMBER 1816. Recalled from Haiti, Bolívar returns to Margarita Island (eastern Venezuela) to find that the Spanish garrison has abandoned Pampatar and that General Arismendi has proceeded to the mainland with 300 troops. Three days later the Liberator enters Barcelona to a warm reception from his followers.

DECEMBER 1816. Morillo's regular army reenters Venezuela to reassert the royalists' increasingly shaky hold over this country.

LATE 1816. The Argentine privateer *Potosí,* commanded by an English mercenary named John Chase, captures the Mexican merchant frigate *Ciencia* off northern Cuba.

3 JANUARY 1817. Portuguese General Abreu, with 600 men and two field pieces, surprises the Uruguayan leader Artigas with 400 followers on a hill north of the Arapey River (60 miles east of Belén), killing 80 patriots and scattering the rest.

4 JANUARY 1817. ***Catalán Creek.*** This morning—after a nocturnal approach—an Uruguayan army under General Latorre attacks 3,000 Portuguese troops and 11 field pieces under Lt. Gen. Luiz Telez da Silva Caminha e Meneses, fifth marquês de Alegrete and governor of Brazil's Rio Grande do Sul Province, on the western banks of Catalán Creek (headwaters of the Guareim River). A brutal, six-hour engagement erupts, during which the attackers suffer 900 killed and 100 wounded before retiring; Portuguese losses are 230 dead.

Alegrete remains in place after this victory, detaching flying columns to exterminate Spanish towns that have been established in this disputed territory—La Cruz, Yapeyú, Santo Angel de la Guarda, Santo Tomé, Concepción, Santa María, and Mártires. It is estimated that more than 3,900 people are slaughtered during this campaign.

4 JANUARY 1817. The *llanero* guerrilla chieftain Ramón Nonato Pérez leads a descent against de la Calzada's advancing royalist contingent at Guasdualito (Venezuela), only to be bloodily repulsed.

5 JANUARY 1817. Bolívar and Arismendi, advancing out of Barcelona (Venezuela) with only 700 men, are repulsed by the loyalist garrison at Clarines.

6 JANUARY 1817. Royalist forces under Pedro Antonio de Olañeta occupy Jujuy (northern Argentina) without opposition but remain bogged down in the district by *gaucho* guerrilla warfare.

7 JANUARY 1817. The insurgent garrison within Fort San Pedro Cóporo, outside Jungapeo (Michoacán, Mexico), surrenders to the royalists.

18 JANUARY 1817. After six months' preparation and psychological warfare (*guerra de zapa*—sapper's war), 38-year-old revolutionary Gen. José Francisco de San Martín's advance units quit Plumerillo (Argentina), followed next day from Mendoza by his small but well-trained expedition, intending to free Chile from Spanish rule. His 4,000-man Army of the Andes—plus more than 1,000 militia and auxiliaries—can manufacture their own armaments and ammunition and are accompanied by such prominent Chilean refugees as Bernardo O'Higgins. Six Andean passes have been surveyed in advance by military engineers, and San Martín strikes out along the Los Patos route with his main body to descend into Putaendo Valley (Aconcagua Province).

This same day in Venezuela, Piar launches an unsuccessful assault against the loyalist stronghold of Angostura, being repulsed. He then proceeds to occupy the rich Capuchin Missions on the Caroní River.

19 JANUARY 1817. Mariño attacks the loyalist garrison of Cumaná (eastern Venezuela), only to be repulsed, retreating first to Cautaro then to Cumanacoa.

In northern Uruguay, the patriot leader Andresito's 500 followers are ambushed on the banks of the Aguapey River by 600 Portuguese troops and five field pieces under Brigadier General Chagas, being totally routed.

20 JANUARY 1817. Portuguese Lieutenant General Lecor occupies Montevideo with his 8,000-man army—spearheaded by the Voluntários Reais de El Rei Division (Royal Volunteers of the King)—while Uruguay's defeated patriots can do little more than harass foraging parties in the outlying countryside. Soon the port of Colonia de Sacramento surrenders to the Portuguese without a struggle, and several of patriot leader Artigas's lieutenants either take up service with their political rivals in Argentina or are captured by the Portuguese occupiers.

This same day, the Mexican insurgent Mier y Terán surrenders to royalists at Cerro Colorado, near Tehuacán.

28 JANUARY 1817. ***Mucuritas.*** After reuniting with Calzada, royalist General de la Torre marches northeast along the south bank of the Apure River toward Nutrias, with 1,500 infantry in three columns screened by 800 irregular cavalry on his flanks under Remigio Ramos. At 9:00 A.M. the royalist force is surprised to find 1,300 *llanero* lancers barring their path at Mucuritas (Venezuela) under 26-year-old patriot chieftain José Antonio Páez.

Despite having no infantry or artillery—and precious few firearms—Páez scatters the royalist cavalry with his opening charge then sets the grassland ablaze around the infantry. Over the next several hours de la Torre struggles to retreat three miles through blinding smoke to Frío Ford on the Apure while enduring repeated patriot attacks. By 4:00 P.M. Páez's riders draw off, having inflicted numerous casualties and captured 300 packhorses.

Next day Morillo's main army overtakes de la Torre, and the *llaneros* disappear.

8 FEBRUARY 1817. ***Siege of Barcelona.*** This morning royalist militia Gens. Pascual Real and

Morales attack Bolívar's 600-man garrison inside Barcelona (Venezuela) with 4,500 followers. The town is occupied without opposition, the Liberator preferring to hold out in the fortified San Francisco Convent to await relief from Mariño. At nightfall the attackers withdraw to El Pilar, and as a result patriot reinforcements are able to join Bolívar three days later.

Shortly thereafter a small Spanish squadron seizes Barcelona's harbor castle, only to be dispossessed by an insurgent counterattack. The royalists then withdraw, both Real and Morales being stripped of command for their failures.

9 FEBRUARY 1817. Royalist forces wrest San Juan Coscomatepec (Veracruz, Mexico) from the insurgents.

12 FEBRUARY 1817. ***Chacabuco.*** After swiftly traversing the Patos and Uspallata Passes, San Martín's insurgent Army of the Andes has already defeated unwary Spanish outposts at Salala, Copiapó, and Vega del Campeo (Chile). After reuniting at San Felipe, they encounter advance elements of Brig. Gen. Rafael Maroto's 2,500 royalists on 11 February; they are in the process of occupying the hills north of Chacabuco with five field pieces, thus blocking the road to the Chilean capital of Santiago. The defenders' strength is: Valdivia Infantry Battalion under Maroto; Talavera Infantry Battalion under Major (acting lieutenant colonel) Marqueli; Chiloé Infantry Battalion under Lieutenant Colonel Elorreaga; Abascal Carabineers (two companies) under Lieutenant Colonel Quintanilla; and Concordia Hussars (one company) under Lieutenant Colonel Bananco.

At 2:00 A.M. on 12 February the 3,600-man rebel army advances from Manantiales in two divisions, O'Higgins being on the left to distract the enemy with the 7th Infantry Battalion (fusilier companies only) under Lieutenant Colonel Crámer; the 8th Infantry Battalion (fusilier companies only) under Lieutenant Colonel Conde; horse grenadiers (three squadrons) under Colonel Zapiola; and two cannons. Meanwhile Brig. Gen. Miguel Estanislao Soler is to circle behind Maroto on the right to assault the Spaniards from the rear with the 11th Infantry Battalion under Colonel Las Heras; Andean Chasseur Regiment under Lieutenant Colonel Alvarado; horse grenadiers (one squadron) under Lieutenant Colonel Necochea; and seven guns under Captain Frutos.

Instead, O'Higgins rashly charges without waiting for Soler, yet—supported by effective cavalry charges from Zapiola and Lt. Col. Mariano Necochea—he destroys the royalist squadrons. When Soler finally attacks from the flank, Maroto's army is routed, suffering 600 fatalities before streaming off in defeat, leaving behind the artillery, the ammunition train, 1,000 muskets, and 550 prisoners. Patriot casualties are 11 killed and 110 wounded. Two days later San Martín enters Santiago without opposition from royalist Field Mar-

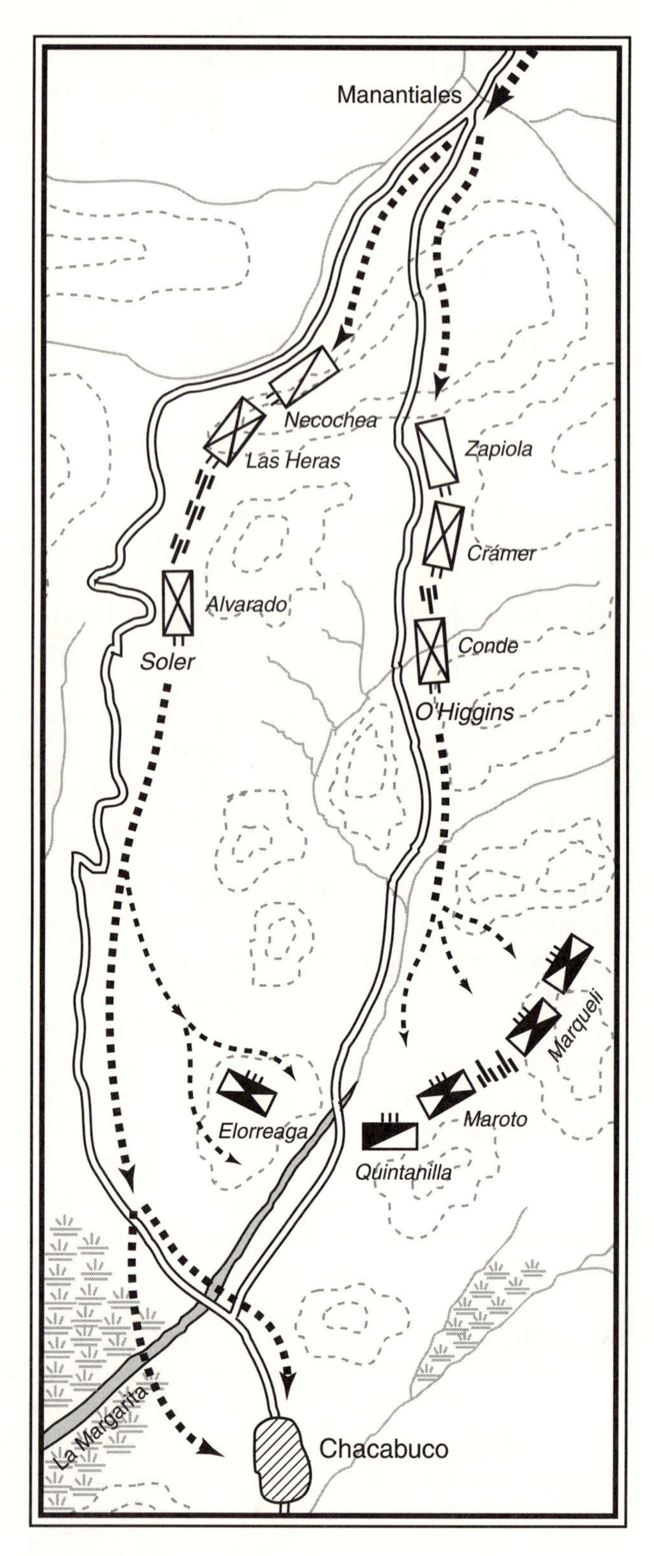

Battle of Chacabuco

San Martín watching his troops march into the Battle of Chacabuco; lithograph from an oil painting by Pedro Subercaseaux

shal Francisco Casimiro Marcó del Pont, handing the governorship of Chile to O'Higgins.

17 FEBRUARY 1817. Huatusco (Mexico) is reconquered by royalists.

1 MARCH 1817. Patriot Col. Manuel Eduardo Arias surprises the 130-man, seven-gun royalist garrison under La Roza in Humahuaca (northern Argentina) by a descent with 150 *gauchos* on a rainy night. The defenders suffer 24 killed and 92 captured before Arias disappears into the mountains.

3 MARCH 1817. Patriot Colonel Lamadrid departs Tucumán with 250 cavalry, 150 infantrymen on mules, and two small field pieces to bedevil the royalist army occupying northern Argentina. On 15 March he obliges the 294-man garrison of Tarifa to surrender, then evades royalist columns until 12 June, when his troops are ambushed and badly defeated, compelling him to retreat.

6 MARCH 1817. ***Pernambuco Rebellion.*** At the port of Olinda (Brazil), Gov. Caetano Pinto de Miranda Montenegro orders the arrest at dawn of several local conspirators who have been plotting to overthrow Portuguese rule in favor of Brazilian independence. One of them—a sexuagenarian militia veteran named José de Barros Lima—kills the officer sent to detain him then leads an immediate uprising that drives Governor Pinto into hiding within Brum Harbor Castle.

Some 800 rebels (a mixed brigade of white and mulatto militia plus half an artillery regiment) quickly release their captive leaders, seize the bridges leading off Santo Antônio Island, and overrun Pernambuco's mainland capital of Recife by sunrise on 7 March. Cut off, Pinto arranges safe passage to Rio de Janeiro on 12 March—only to be incarcerated on Cobras Island upon his arrival at King João VI's behest, for having reached an accommodation with the rebels. The monarch then begins raising an army to reconquer the northern province.

10 MARCH 1817. The fortified pass of Mesa de los Caballos, near San Felipe (Guanajuato, Mexico) is recaptured from the insurgents.

29 MARCH 1817. The American mercenary Thomas Taylor, whose corvette *Zephyr* and more than a dozen other privateers arrive bearing Argentine commissions, attempts a dawn disembarkation in Guantánamo Bay (Cuba), only to be repelled.

LATE MARCH 1817. The Conde dos Arcos, Portuguese governor of Bahia (Brazil), sends two corvettes and a schooner to blockade the rebel city of Recife. Adm. Rodrigo Lobo follows on 2 April with more warships; one month later four Portuguese regiments set off for the mutinous province under Luiz do Rego, Pernambuco's governor-designate, recently arrived from Lisbon.

3 APRIL 1817. With San Martín absent in Argentina, his subordinate Col. Juan Gregorio de Las Heras has led a 1,300-man army (*División del Sur*) in a campaign to eliminate the last royalist stronghold in Chile: 1,000 men under Col. José Ordóñez occupying the coastal keep of Talcahuano on the narrow Tumbes Peninsula.

On 3 April Las Heras reaches Curapaligüe Hacienda (ten miles east of Concepción); at 1:30 A.M. on 5 April royalist *Sargento Mayor* José Campillo slips out of Talcahuano with 600 infantry, 109 cavalry, and two field pieces to surprise the sleeping insurgents. His plan miscarries in the darkness, only four patriots being killed and seven wounded; Campillo retires with similar casualties. Las Heras follows up the royalists' retreat and this same day occupies deserted Concepción, where he pauses to await 800 Chilean troops and two field pieces under O'Higgins.

5 APRIL 1817. Loyalist Col. Juan Aldama occupies the town of Barcelona (Venezuela) without opposition and two days later overwhelms its citadel—the fortified convent of San Francisco—slaughtering every patriot inside.

8 APRIL 1817. ***San Félix.*** Learning that Angostura (Venezuela)'s royalist Gov. Nicolás María Cerruti and militia Cmdr. Miguel de la Torre have gone down the Orinoco River with most of the garrison, Piar establishes headquarters at San Félix and waits for the enemy.

De la Torre appears on the afternoon of 11 April with 1,350 royalist infantry and 150 cavalry (mostly dismounted). Piar commands 700 patriot fusiliers, 900 cavalry (300 on foot), plus 200 native archers. At 4:00 P.M. the loyalists advance in three columns, firing volleys. Anzoátegui and Pedro León Torres hold the patriot center while Piar circles behind the assault columns with a company of mounted carabiniers and Pedro Hernández's *llaneros* worry the Spaniards' flanks.

After half an hour de la Torre's ranks break and head for the hills two miles away. They are pitilessly hunted down until nightfall, suffering 593 deaths; of 497 captured 160 (all peninsular Spaniards) are subsequently executed by decapitation, including Cerruti. De la Torre is among the 260 survivors to escape. Patriot losses total 31 killed and 65 injured.

13 APRIL 1817. At San Antonio (Venezuela), Jacinto Perera's 300-man royalist garrison repels repeated attacks by 500 *llanero* lancers under Páez, who retires after suffering 132 men killed.

This same day, royalist General La Serna departs Jujuy (northern Argentina) with 2,500 men, occupying Salta two days later. However, after two and a half weeks of occupation he retires north on 4 May because of San Martín's invasion of Chile and other local patriot successes. Jujuy is also abandoned by 21 May.

15 APRIL 1817. ***Mina's Intervention.*** Weathering a brief storm in the Gulf of Mexico, the 27-year-old Spanish adventurer Francisco Javier Mina y Larrea disembarks unopposed at Soto la Marina (state of Veracruz) with 500 foreign mercenaries to bolster the Mexican insurgency's flagging fortunes. An avowed antimonarchist, he has recruited Spanish, Italian, English, and American followers during a cruise from Liverpool to Norfolk (Virginia), Baltimore, Saint Thomas (Virgin Islands), Port au Prince, Galveston, and New Orleans, sailing aboard the hired American ships *Cleopatra, Neptuno,* and *Congreso Mexicano.* He erects a fort on the eastern side of Soto la Marina's plaza, armed with artillery from his ships.

On 17 May the Spanish frigate *Sabina* appears from Veracruz and sinks one of Mina's ships, drives another aground, and forces the third to flee. Cut off from the sea, the intruder consequently decides to strike inland one week later with 300 men to join forces with other insurgents while leaving behind a 200-man garrison under Major Sardá.

16 APRIL 1817. Portuguese Admiral Lobo calls on the Brazilian insurgents holding Recife (Pernambuco Province) to surrender or face summary execution, but they refuse to capitulate; he therefore tightens the blockade.

23 APRIL 1817. De la Torre returns to Angostura (Venezuela) with 300 royalists following his devastating defeat at San Félix. He is closely pursued by Piar, who—heartened by the recent victory—attempts to storm Angostura again at 2:00 A.M. on 25 April, only to be repelled after a stiff, four-hour encounter in which his men suffer 85 casualties. Next day a Spanish river squadron appears; Piar subsequently institutes a loose siege.

1 MAY 1817. Colonel Ordóñez's royalist garrison at Talcahuano (Chile) is reinforced by four ships bearing 1,600 troops who fled Valparaíso following San Martín's victory at Chacabuco, only to be turned back by the Peruvian viceroy upon reaching Callao.

5 MAY 1817. ***Gavilán.*** Determined to defeat Las Heras's 1,300-man Argentine army before O'Higgins can join with his Chilean forces (*see* 3 April 1817), Ordóñez sorties from Talcahuano to assault the rebel redoubt on Gavilán Hill (northwest of Concepción, Chile). The royalists intend to attack in twin columns: 600 men and two field pieces coming down Penco road under Colonel Morgado while Ordóñez drives from Chepe with another 800 and three guns.

Action begins at 6:45 A.M., when nine royalist gunboats open fire on the insurgents within Concepción. Ordóñez appears and immediately assaults Las Heras's left without waiting for Morgado, who arrives an hour and a half late. By this time Ordóñez's column has been decimated storming the rebel lines; the same fate befalls Morgado. The royalists are irretrievably broken when two companies of Chilean insurgents appear on the battlefield, heralding the imminent arrival of O'Higgins's army. Ordóñez retreats behind his Talcahuano trenches, having lost 118 killed, 80 wounded, four guns, and 200 muskets. Patriot casualties are six dead and 62 injured, O'Higgins arriving by nightfall to assume command over the siege operations.

15 MAY 1817. Argentine Lt. Col. Ramón Freyre is detached with 300 men from the insurgent siege works at Concepción (Chile) to capture isolated royalist keeps south of the Bío Bío River, thereby preventing refreshments from reaching the beleaguered garrison within Talcahuano. He returns by 11 July, having succeeded in his sweep.

17 MAY 1817. The Brazilian insurgent leader Domingos José Martins, having marched south from his rebel stronghold at Recife (Pernambuco Province), is defeated and captured at Serinhão by 800 loyalist militia from Bahia, who call themselves "Scipios" after the famous Roman general.

19 MAY 1817. The Brazilian rebel chieftain Domingos Teotônio Jorge evacuates Recife with two infantry regiments, straggling inland as Portuguese Admiral Lobo reoccupies the port. The insurgents eventually disband at Engenho Paulista, many being hunted down and executed over the next few months.

30 MAY 1817. The 34-year-old Curaçao-born patriot Commo. Philippus Ludovicus Brion—in Spanish, Felipe Luis Brion—sets sail east from Margarita Island (Venezuela) with the brigs *Terror, Tártaro, América Libre, Conquistador,* and *Indio Libre* and the schooners *Diana* (under the French privateer Vincent Dubouille), *Guayaneja,* and *Conejo.* He is supposed to stem the Orinoco River and wrest royalist control over this important waterway.

8 JUNE 1817. After seizing 700 horses at Cojo Hacienda, fording the Tamesí River, and emerging into the Valle del Maíz (central Mexico), the intruder Mina defeats a force of 400 royalists under Captain Villaseñor.

11 JUNE 1817. The royalist Commander Arredondo arrives from Veracruz to besiege Mina's garrison under Major Sardá at Soto la Marina, compelling it to surrender five days later. The prisoners are conducted to San Juan de Ulúa and the fortress at Perote (near Jalapa).

15 JUNE 1817. While continuing his march to San Luis Potosí (Mexico) the adventurer Mina defeats 2,000 royalists drawn up at Peotillos Hacienda under Col. Benito Armiñán.

19 JUNE 1817. Mina's small army occupies Real de Pinos (Zacatecas, Mexico).

22 JUNE 1817. Mina links up with some Mexican insurgents, reaching Fort Sombrero in the Comanja Range (modern-day Guanajuato) two days later to join forces with guerrilla chieftains Pedro Moreno and Encarnación Ortiz.

29 JUNE 1817. Mina and Moreno sortie from Fort Sombrero (Mexico), mauling a royalist force under Ordoñez at Ferrero Ranch on the San Juan de los Llanos Hacienda, killing the commander and capturing 152 of his men.

7 JULY 1817. Mina and Moreno attack the Jaral Hacienda, seizing 300,000 pesos in silver bars.

14 JULY 1817. ***Margarita Counteroffensive.*** After being reinforced at Barcelona (Venezuela) by Aldama's division and off Cumaná by 2,600–2,700 regulars from Spain under Gen. José de Canterac in late March, Morillo has detached contingents to attack minor patriot garrisons at Cariaco, Cumanacoa, and Carúpano under Cmdr. Francisco Jiménez. Taking them with ease, the Spaniards fortify the coastline and proceed against Güiria; Morillo himself sails from Cumaná with 3,000 men aboard 22 ships to personally reconquer Margarita Island, reaching the port of Guamacho by 14 July.

Col. Francisco Esteban Gómez, the island's patriot commander, falls back before Morillo's advance inland, harassing his outriders. Pampatar and Porlamar are occupied without resistance on 24 and 31 July, but a royalist attack on the capital of Asunción is repulsed with considerable loss. Marching to the island's northern tip, the invaders take the port of Juan Griego by 8 August but evacuate Margarita nine days later because of news of Bolívar's successful patriot offensive up the Orinoco; Morillo returns to Caracas by early September.

17 JULY 1817. Tonight de la Torre—his 2,000-man royalist garrison starving inside Angostura (Venezuela) because of the recent arrival of Brion's patriot flotilla up the Orinoco from the sea—decides to evacuate the isolated outpost. Boarding 30 boats along with 1,800 noncombatants, he retreats west to the last remaining loyalist stronghold on the river (Guayana la Vieja), arriving by the evening of 19 July. The previous dawn Angostura had been occupied by Bermúdez's jubilant land forces.

1 AUGUST 1817. After unsuccessfully attacking León (Guanajuato, Mexico), Mina and Moreno are besieged within their Fort Sombrero base camp by royalist forces under *Mariscal de Campo* (field marshal) Pascual Liñán. The latter storm Fort Sombrero's defenses on 4 August, only to be repelled; the insurgents in turn fail to cut their way out on 7 August.

Next night Mina and Moreno slip out with part of their small army and attempt to rescue their colleagues by attacking Liñán's positions from the rear on

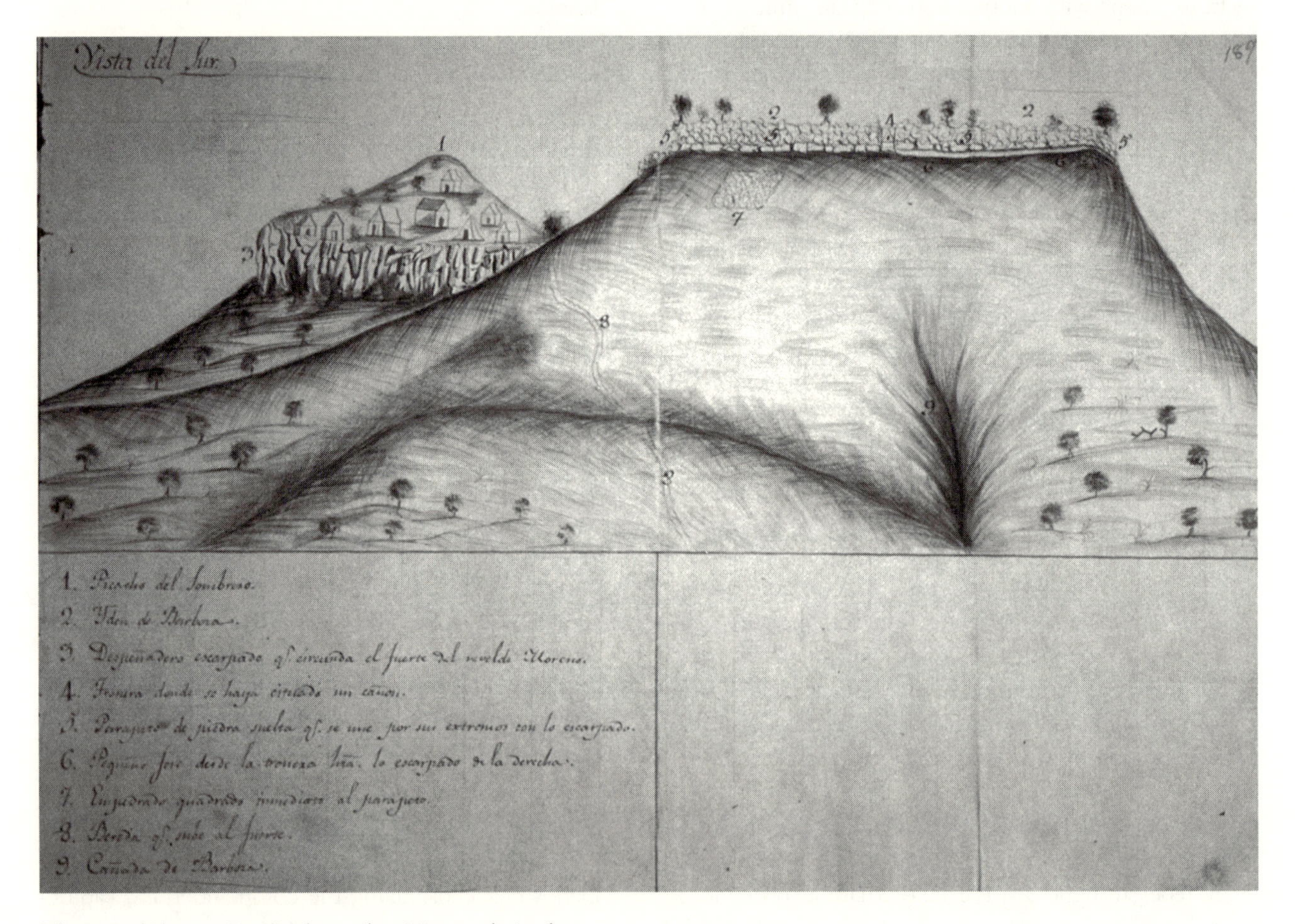

The patriot hideout at Fort Sombrero, where Mina was besieged

12 August. When that fails Mina and Moreno withdraw five days later to install themselves at Remedios Fort (near Pénjamo); their beleaguered associates surrender to the royalists by 19 August.

2 AUGUST 1817. ***Cabrián.*** After waiting in vain for the arrival of a Spanish relief force, de la Torre's 2,600 desperate royalists in Guayana la Vieja (Venezuela) decide to abandon this overcrowded outpost and flee east down the Orinoco into the open Atlantic—despite Brion's patriot flotilla anchored off Cabrián. Perceiving the preparations for this flight, Anzoátegui's besiegers storm Guayana's palisades this same evening, but are checked by de la Torre.

Next morning the Spaniards are ready to sail under naval Capt. Fernando Lizarza:

Ship	*Guns*	*Sailors*	*Soldiers*	*Commander*
Merced (corvette, flag)	14	23	70	(flag captain) Costa y Mur
Carmen (schooner, vice-flag)	12	37	61	Lt. Francisco Sales de Echeverría
Monteverde (schooner)	12	20	60	?
Dolores (schooner)	6	22	20	?
Carmen (poleacre)	10	32	59	Manuel López
Vigilante (brigantine)	12	19	69	F. A. Casanueva
Pancha (schooner)	4	30	57	José Elorriaga
Isabel (schooner)	3	15	69	?
María (*guayro*)	6	28	42	J. A. Pérez
Reina Luisa (sloop)	1	14	20	Burguera
Malagueña (bomb)	6	16	30	José Bonet
Guadalupe (schooner)	2	14	20	?
Guayanesa (schooner)	2	18	25	?
Rapelo (schooner)	2	26	40	?

These are accompanied by half-a-dozen gunboats, four large native canoes, plus a dozen transports bearing an additional 930 sailors and 800 soldiers.

This royalist flotilla dashes downriver through a hail of fire from patriot encampments ashore, until forming into a double column to engage Brion's squadron before Cabrián. Having a favorable westerly wind behind him, Lizarza instantly attacks to give his consorts time to escape, but is wounded in both legs by an early patriot salvo. The action degenerates into a general pursuit, as darkness falls and a storm blows up. The fleeing loyalists are hunted down in the channels and byways, 14 ships and many smaller vessels being captured over the next three days. Their casualties are 280 killed, a similar amount wounded, and 1,731 taken prisoner. De la Torre is among the few to escape, reaching the Antillan island of Grenada by 9 August with *Merced* and the poleacre *Carmen,* then proceeding toward Cumaná and La Guaira. Brion's losses total 32 killed and 31 injured, his annihilation of royalist sympathizers ensuring that Bolívar now enjoys undisputed control over the entire length of the Orinoco.

14 AUGUST 1817. Páez makes a surprise raid on the royalist stronghold of Barinas (Venezuela) with 1,000 *llanero* guerrillas, seizing much valuable booty.

15 AUGUST 1817. Some 1,000 royalists under Olañeta and Marquiegui capture Humahuaca (northern Argentina) but endure increasing *gaucho* attacks as they press farther south; finally they retire to Yavi on 3 January 1818.

27 AUGUST 1817. Spanish Lt. Col. Francisco Jiménez crosses the Paria Peninsula (Venezuela) from the Caribe River with 800 regulars of the Clarínes and Reina Isabel battalions plus royalist guerrillas under Nacario Martínez to capture the port of Yaguaraparo. Its patriot defenders, under Col. José María Hermoso, leave 250 casualties on the field before fleeing into the surrounding hills.

Three days later Jiménez retakes Güiria, killing Hermoso and inflicting 140 patriot casualties; survivors scatter inland or out to sea aboard the schooner *Tigre.*

12 SEPTEMBER 1817. Royalist forces assault the 150-man insurgent garrison within the coastal keep of Arauco (Chile), thus diverting O'Higgins's attention from the siege of nearby Talcahuano.

25 SEPTEMBER 1817. To counteract the effects of Morillo's offensive (*see* 14 July 1817), Bolívar sends Bermúdez to reorganize the patriot units on Cumaná (Venezuela) while Monagas does the same at Barcelona.

27 SEPTEMBER 1817. Acting on Bolívar's orders, Gen. Manuel Sedeño and Capt. Remigio Femayor arrest Piar at 4:00 A.M. at Aragua de Maturín (Venezuela) to stand trial for treason.

10 OCTOBER 1817. While returning to base camp at Fort Remedios (near Pénjamo, central Mexico) after raiding San Luis de la Paz, Mina and Moreno are defeated in a clash at the Caja Hacienda by royalists under Colonel Orrantia.

16 OCTOBER 1817. Bolívar—who brooks no rivals—tricks his brilliant mulatto commander, Piar, into camp, where he is executed for "insubordination."

25 OCTOBER 1817. Mina, Moreno, and other insurgent leaders attack the royalist garrison within the Mexican city of Guanajuato with 1,400 men, only to be repulsed. Two days later, while sleeping at Venadito Ranch, the two leaders and their aides are surprised by a monarchist column under Orrantia; all are slain except Mina, who is carried into Liñán's encampment near Fort Remedios and shot on 11 November atop Bellaco Hill. (Because of this royalist triumph, the Mexican viceroy, Juan Ruiz de Apodaca, is subsequently rewarded from Madrid with the title conde de Venadito.)

27 NOVEMBER 1817. Because of the large number of British veterans flocking to join the patriot cause (*see* 16 January 1818), London is compelled—following diplomatic complaints by Madrid—to issue a proclamation forbidding its subjects from taking sides in this Spanish American dispute.

2 DECEMBER 1817. ***Hogaza.*** After a four-day forced march from Calvario (Venezuela), de la Torre's 900 loyalist infantry and 300 cavalry surprise patriot General Zaraza at La Hogaza—three miles from Murianga Ford on the banks of the Manapitre—who is resting with 1,000 troopers and 1,100 infantry, in anticipation of soon joining Bolívar's army at Santa María de Ipire.

Despite his men's weariness, de la Torre quickly deploys them on a hill overlooking the patriot camp, with the 1st Castilla and 2nd Navarra Infantry Battalions in the center, single squadrons of the 1st and 2nd Fernando VII Hussars on his flanks, plus another of Calabozo Lancers as his reserve. Perceiving the weakness of the enemy, the insurgents move forward to meet de la Torre's advance a few minutes later, only to have the patriot cavalry on the right flank suddenly break and flee before the royalists.

Seeing this, the patriot infantrymen under Pedro León Torres take to their heels and are nearly completely wiped out as they attempt to escape the battlefield. Patriot casualties are calculated at 350 plus a like number captured, compared to 11 dead and 86 wounded among the loyalists. Dry grass catches fire from the discharges, provoking a general conflagration that burns many of the wounded and destroys much materiel. Satisfied with his triumph, de la Torre returns to Calvario and Calabozo with his royalists, leaving the shaken patriot survivors to reassemble.

6 DECEMBER 1817. ***Talcahuano.*** After a seven-month siege O'Higgins's 3,700 Chileo-Argentine troops assault Ordóñez's 1,700 royalists entrenched at Talcahuano (Chile). The defenders enjoy considerable advantages, having 70 cannons and several warships to protect the swampy, half-mile-wide isthmus leading out to Tumbes Peninsula.

At 2:45 A.M. Las Heras storms the easternmost bastion of El Morro with four battalions, carrying it despite heavy losses. His subsequent attempt to drive northwest and overrun Cura Hill fails, though, obliging him to retire at dawn. A diversionary attack by insurgent Cmdr. Pedro Conde against San Vicente Castle (at the opposite end of the royalist line), is also repulsed with considerable casualties. Altogether, the attackers suffer 156 killed and 280 wounded; the defenders, 300 casualties. Less than one month later O'Higgins lifts the siege.

9 DECEMBER 1817. Royalist Gen. Mariano Osorio quits Callao with 3,276 troops and ten field pieces, sailing south to Talcahuano (Chile) aboard ten vessels.

15 DECEMBER 1817. Argentine Colonel Montes de Oca departs Buenos Aires with 600 troops, traveling up the Uruguay River to Ibicuy to impose republican rule over that breakaway district. On Christmas Day he is defeated at Ceballos Creek (north of Gualeguaychú) by a 31-year-old local leader, Francisco Ramírez,

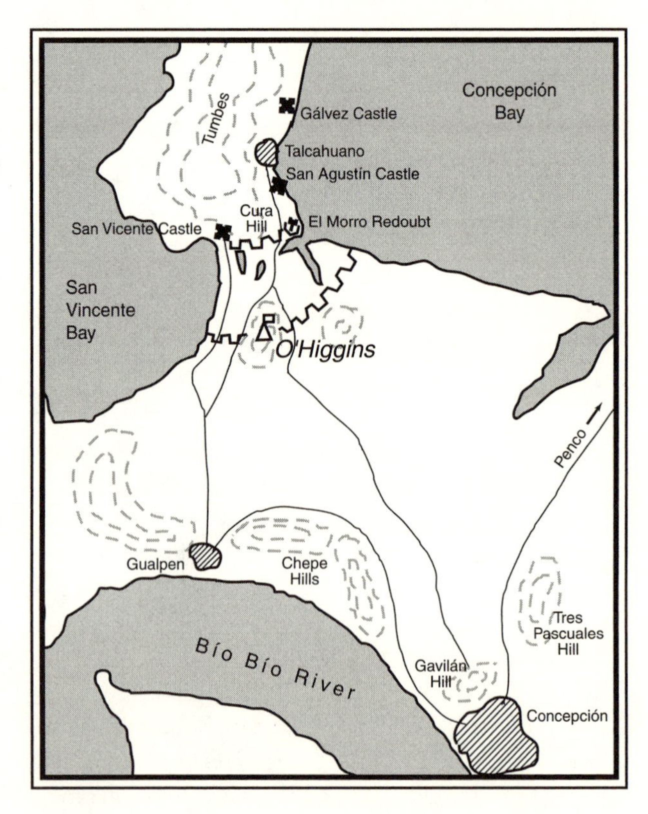

Insurgent siege of Talcahuano

and suffers a second reverse at Santa Bárbara ranch—south of Gato Creek (near the same city)—on 4 January 1818.

17 DECEMBER 1817. Under cover of darkness guerrilla chief Páez probes the royalist Castellano and San Casimiro redoubts outside San Fernando de Apure (Venezuela). When he repeats the operation the following night, however, his *llaneros* are ambushed at dawn by two companies of the Unión and Barinas Infantry Battalions, who inflict 100 casualties.

21 DECEMBER 1817. The Mexican insurgent Nicolás Bravo is captured and his Cóporo Fort is reoccupied by royalist forces. Transferred to Mexico City on 9 October 1818, he is pardoned two years later.

1 JANUARY 1818. O'Higgins lifts his siege of Talcahuano (Chile), retiring north from Concepción, harassed by royalist pursuers. A clash occurs when the insurgents are traversing the Nuble River on 15 January; another skirmish occurs on 19 January before O'Higgins passes into safety north of the Maule River by the end of the month.

11 JANUARY 1818. A new, 2,400-man royalist army under Olañeta surprises Huacalera (northern Argentina), fighting into Jujuy three days later against feeble patriot opposition. The countryside rises against the invaders, however, so the Spanish commander abandons his prize on 16 January, suffering 300 casualties while struggling back to Yavi.

MID-JANUARY 1818. Osorio's 3,300-man royalist expedition from Peru reinforces Talcahuano (Chile), then initiates its campaign by blockading Valparaíso by sea while the army marches north.

16 JANUARY 1818. The first of four English vessels—*Britain, Esmeralda, Dawson,* and *Prince* (*Indian* having succumbed in an Atlantic storm)—reaches Gustavia on the Antillan island of Saint Barthélemy, bearing 800 mercenaries contracted in London by the Venezuelan agent Luis López Méndez to serve the patriot cause. Many of the veterans balk at their conditions of service; after transferring south to Georgetown (Grenada) by 27 February only 150 actually continue up the Orinoco River to join Bolívar.

30 JANUARY 1818. Having advanced west from the Orinoco with his army, Bolívar joins forces with Páez at Payara to attack the Spaniards farther north at San Fernando and Calabozo (central Venezuela).

6 FEBRUARY 1818. ***Calabozo.*** Bolívar materializes at the Apure River's Diamante Ford, just east of San Fernando in central Venezuela, with 600 men of Valdés's Brigade (Barlovento and Angostura Infantry Battalions); 635 of Torres's Brigade (1st Barcelona and Valerosos Cazadores Infantry Battalions); Monagas's Brigade (353 of 2nd Barcelona Infantry Battalion, plus 342 troopers in three cavalry squadrons); 726 men in the chasseur and fusilier infantry battalions of the Honor Guard; Sedeño's Division (310 troopers in three cavalry squadrons of Lara's Brigade, plus another 294 in three squadrons of Martín's Brigade); and Sánchez's Brigade (632 of the Bajo Orinoco and Guayana Infantry Battalions, plus 87 troopers in a cavalry squadron). These are further augmented by Páez's 1,000 *llaneros* and 300 infantry for a combined strength of 5,200 men.

Having surprised San Fernando's 650-man royalist garrison under Col. José María Quero, Bolívar and Páez quickly throw their contingents across its river and cut off this city's communications from the far side, leaving its defenders bottled up by detaching Sánchez Brigade's to begin siege preparations, while the main body speeds north toward their true objective: the city of Calabozo.

Soon learning of this invasion, Spanish General Morillo hastens from the northwest to bolster Calabozo's 650-man garrison with an additional 1,800 troops, entering this city during the evening of 10 February. Yet he is caught unprepared two days later by Bolívar's rapid appearance out of the west, 4,200 patriots advancing at dawn of 12 February to cut off the Spanish outpost lying beyond the city defenses at Trinidad Mission (also known as *Misión de abajo,* or Lower Mission). This royalist detachment—Castilla Infantry Battalion, two companies of the Navarra Battalion, plus three hussar squadrons—desperately attempts to regain Calabozo, but is cut off and forms a square in an open field. It is quickly overwhelmed and destroyed, suffering 320 killed and a like number captured, as opposed to 200 insurgent casualties.

Lacking a siege train, Bolívar marches his main body ten miles north at noon on 13 February to pasture his horses at El Rastro, while hoping Morillo emerges from behind his walls. The patriots' Apure Hussar Regiment under Col. Guillermo Iribarren is left to watch Calabozo, but the following day at 11:00 P.M. the Spaniards slip out undetected, heading toward La Uriosa on the west bank of the Guárico River in hopes of reaching El Sombrero, 20 miles away on the Caracas road.

When Iribarren discovers Calabozo empty the morning of 14 February he informs Bolívar, and the patriots set off in pursuit. Yet Morillo's 1,700–1,800 royalist troops and 7,000–8,000 noncombatants are not found until 4:00 P.M., a couple of hundred stragglers being slain before the Spanish general takes up a defensive position at El Sombrero by next morning. The Liberator then loses 100 men storming the royalist lines, before finally allowing Morillo's army to resume its march uncontested on 16 February, escaping northeast.

This chastened but unbeaten Spanish force enters Comatagua by 18 February and San Sebastián de los Reyes on 21 February, where it is reinforced by de la Torre and Aldama's Divisions. Meanwhile Páez—having fallen out with Bolívar over this bungled chase—parts company to return south with his own followers and press the siege of San Fernando de Apure. The Liberator, despite this defection and his reduced numbers, continues north toward Caracas.

12 FEBRUARY 1818. O'Higgins and San Martín proclaim the independence of Chile then sally from Santiago to engage Osorio's royalist army, approaching from the south.

6 MARCH 1818. The insurgent stronghold of Fort Jaujilla (on an island in Zacapu Lake, central Mexico), surrenders to the royalists.

14 MARCH 1818. ***Maracay.*** At dawn a large detachment from Bolívar's army—1,200 cavalry and 370 infantry delegated to occupy the town of Maracay (Venezuela)—are surprised by a sudden cavalry charge by two Spanish squadrons of Unión Dragoons and one of Guías del General, which immediately fight their way into the town's main square.

Although initially contained by the patriot Angostura Infantry Battalion and Monagas's cavalry, the Spanish units are quickly joined by royalist chasseurs under Col. Matías Escuté and the Barinas Infantry Battalion under Col. Juan Tello. It soon becomes apparent that the attack is part of a much larger Spanish counteroffensive spearheaded by General Morales's entire division; the patriots hastily abandon Maracay for La Victoria, arriving this evening through torrential rains after suffering 80 casualties and 220 missing.

14 MARCH 1818. Royalist Cmdr. Francisco Jiménez, after a swift march west from Güiria (eastern Venezuela), falls upon 400 patriots who have recently reoccupied Cariaco under Mariño. The patriots are ejected, leaving behind 96 dead and many wounded, although Jiménez is killed during the action.

15 MARCH 1818. ***La Puerta (or Semen Valley).*** Belatedly realizing that royalist columns under Morillo, Morales, and de la Torre are closing in on his 2,200 remaining troops from three different directions, Bolívar hastily retraces his route south, only to be overtaken and compelled to make a stand near La Puerta, in Semen Valley. Action commences at 6:00 A.M. on 16 March, when the royalist vanguard of 1,000 infantry and 500 cavalry under Morales charges.

After three hours of confused fighting, Morillo's main body arrives from six miles away; 1,500 of his Spanish infantry immediately join. (De la Torre's 900 troops are too distant yet to become engaged.) Insurgent lines begin to waver and finally break, leading to a crushing defeat for the infantry. Patriot losses are estimated at 300 killed, 400 wounded, and 350 captured compared to 500–600 royalist casualties. A crestfallen Bolívar leaves the field by noon; Spanish counterpart Morillo is badly wounded in the final charge, being transfixed by a lance—which doctors will eventually have to pull out through his back.

Correa temporarily assumes command of the royalist forces and continues to pursue the fleeing insurgents as far as San Juan de los Morros, inflicting heavy punishment. In addition to most of the infantry and war materiel, the Liberator and his staff lose all their personal papers; Generals Urdaneta, Valdés, Torres, and Anzoátegui suffer body wounds. Retreating by way of Ortiz and El Rastro, the patriot survivors reenter Calabozo four days later.

19 MARCH 1818. ***Cancha Rayada.*** At dawn San Martín and O'Higgins—having learned at Quechereguas (Chile) that 4,600 royalists and 14 cannons under Osorio and Ordóñez are advancing from Camarico to Talca—make a forced march down Tres Montes Road with 8,000 Argentino-Chilean troops and 33 guns to intercept. However, the insurgents arrive too late this afternoon to prevent the invaders from gaining Talca and deploy a mile and a half northeast, at Cancha Rayada.

Unexpectedly confronted with a superior force, Ordóñez suggests to Osorio that the royalists launch a surprise nocturnal assault, when lesser numbers will not be such a handicap. The latter agrees, and at 9:00 P.M. Ordóñez leads three columns toward the revolutionaries, who are in the process of repositioning for the night. The attack hits O'Higgins's Chilean contingent, creating widespread panic among the ranks; only Col. Rudecindo Alvarado's Andean chasseurs reach Las Heras's Argentine division intact. The 3rd Chilean Battalion disintegrates altogether, O'Higgins is wounded in the elbow, and insurgent units fire wildly upon each other in the darkness. By midnight the disconcerted rebels are fleeing north in jumbled masses, having lost 120 killed, 26 artillery pieces, and hundreds of deserters or prisoners. Royalist casualties are approximately 300; five days later Osorio resumes his march on the capital of Santiago.

25 MARCH 1818. ***Saucecito.*** In northeastern Argentina, the 2,400-man army of Buenos Aires Gen. Marcos Balcarce is attacked by a slightly smaller local force under rival republican leader Ramírez. The latter combines a frontal assault with a dual enveloping movement, inflicting 1,000 losses on Balcarce and obliging him to depart hastily down the Uruguay River aboard his flotilla.

26 MARCH 1818. ***Ortiz.*** Having been hastily reinforced by divisions under Sedeño (or Cedeño) and Páez following his stinging La Puerta defeat, Bolívar unexpectedly turns on his royalist pursuers with 2,660 troops. At dawn on 26 March he catches de la Torre resting his 1,100 weary infantry—mostly the Unión and Castilla Battalions under Lt. Cols. Manuel Bausá and Tomás García—at Ortiz (Venezuela); the royalist leader has also dispersed another 1,400 troops to forage throughout neighboring districts.

Both sides skirmish warily for possession of La Cuesta Heights until 5:00 P.M., when the patriots retire after suffering 12 killed and 30 injured, compared to 37 dead and 50 wounded among the royalists—who immediately commence retiring north before their more numerous opponents return.

3 APRIL 1818. At San Carlos, in northeastern Corrientes Province (Uruguay), Portuguese General Chagas again defeats patriot Indian leader Andresito.

5 APRIL 1818. ***Maipú.*** Quickly regrouping after his Cancha Rayada setback (*see* 19 March 1818), San Martín sallies from Santiago on 1 April with 5,300 Chileo-Argentine troops, taking up position six miles south on Blanca Hill to intercept Osorio's approaching royalists with:

Colonel Las Heras's Division: 11th Infantry Battalion under Major Guerrero; Coquimbo Chasseurs under Major Thompson; Patria Infantry Battalion of Lieutenant Colonel Bustamante; four squadrons of horse grenadiers under Colonel Zapiola; plus eight guns under Lieutenant Colonel Blanco Encalada.

Colonel Alvarado's Division: 2nd Chilean Infantry Battalion of Lieutenant Colonel Cáceres; 8th "Los Andes" Infantry Battalion of Lieutenant Colonel Martínez; Andean Infantry Chasseurs of Major Sequeira; four squadrons of "Los Andes" Chasseurs under Major Arellano; plus nine artillery pieces under Lieutenant Colonel Burgoyne.

Colonel de la Quintana's Reserve Division: 1st Chilean Infantry Battalion of Lieutenant Colonel Rivera; 3rd "Los Andes" Infantry Battalion of Lieutenant Colonel Conde; two squadrons of San Martín's escort under Colonel Freire; plus four cannons under Lieutenant Colonel Plaza.

Osorio hopes to capture Valparaíso first, but after reaching Lo Espejo Hacienda by 4 April, discovers his insurgent enemy to be very close, so prepares his 4,900 royalist troops to give battle next day. Colonel Ordóñez's 1st Brigade consists of the Concepción Infantry Battalion under Major Navia; "Infante don Carlos" Infantry Battalion of Lieutenant Colonel de la Torre; a company of royal sappers under Captain Casacana; "Del Rey" Lancers of Lieutenant Colonel J. Rodríguez; Arequipa Dragoons of Lieutenant Colonel A. Rodríguez; plus four guns. Colonel Morla's 2nd Brigade comprises the Arequipa Infantry Battalion under Lieutenant Colonel Rodil; 2nd Burgos Infantry Battalion of Morla; a Chillán cavalry squadron under Lieutenant Colonel Palma; the second squadron of the Frontera Dragoons under Colonel Mongado; plus four artillery pieces. Colonel de Rivera's 3rd or Reserve Brigade is made up of mixed grenadier and *cazador* companies from the Burgos, Concepción, Infante, and Arequipa battalions, plus four cannons.

After both armies march into position near Maipó (today spelled Maipú), San Martín orders a general advance by his entire line at noon. The patriot cavalry are victorious on both flanks, while Las Heras's division defeats Primo de Rivera's royalist left. However, Alvarado's 2nd and 8th Battalions are initially repelled by Ordóñez's Division, retreating across the field until a counterattack by the Andean Chasseurs and San Martín's reserve stabilizes this situation. Meanwhile Osorio's loyalist left collapses, and flees back toward Lo Espejo. Ordóñez fights a delaying action, but after a fierce six-hour struggle the royalists are annihilated. The patriots sustain about 1,000 casualties, compared to 2,000 dead and 2,400 prisoners (including 1,000 wounded) among the Spaniards, who also lose all their artillery and 3,800 muskets. Only Osorio manages to

O'Higgins and San Martín greeting each other after their victory at Maipú; lithograph from oil painting by Pedro Subercaseaux

escape this disaster toward Talcahuano with less than 600 men, leaving Ordóñez to surrender.

16 APRIL 1818. This night Bolívar is nearly assassinated at his Rincón de los Toros (Venezuela) headquarters, when a young royalist captain named Tomás de Renovales—armed with the patriot password—penetrates the Liberator's sleeping camp with eight chasseurs from the Burgos Battalion and fires into his tent.

The Liberator flees on horseback, and next dawn his 400 leaderless infantry and 400-man cavalry escort are attacked by Col. Rafael López's flying column of 500 royalist riders and 360 infantry. After a sharp skirmish Zaraza's patriot troopers are dispersed and the insurgent infantry is massacred suffering 200 casualties plus 150 prisoners (most of whom are executed). López suffers eight dead and 26 wounded; Bolívar reenters Calabozo next day unscathed.

18 APRIL 1818. Having been detached by the victorious San Martín, insurgent Colonel Zapiola battles the royalists in and around Talca (Chile) with a flying column of 250 mounted grenadiers.

23 APRIL 1818. Despite Bolívar's absence, Páez assaults the town of San Carlos (Venezuela) with his *llanero* contingent alone. The royalist garrison emerges under de la Torre to give battle, but each side confronts the other from a distance without clashing; the patriots withdraw five days later.

2 MAY 1818. ***Cojedes.*** Royalist General Correa having united two days earlier with de la Torre at San Carlos (Venezuela), both commanders sally with 370 men of the 1st Unión Infantry Battalion; 320 of 2nd Castilla Infantry Battalion; 350 of Barinas Infantry Battalion; 380 of Burgos Infantry Battalion; 380 of "Infante" Infantry Battalion; two companies (150 men) of Victoria Infantry Battalion; 225 black infantrymen in three companies of the Pardos de Valencia Battalion; 105 militia (two companies) of Aragua Infantry Battalion; plus 800 troopers in eight cavalry squadrons. These 3,080 men advance west into the Cojedes (or Cogedes) Plain, searching for Páez's slightly smaller *llanero* army—composed largely of cavalry.

While resting at Seyba, the royalists are provoked by a charge by Páez's vanguard, which disperses three of their cavalry squadrons. When the Spanish main body then advances to offer battle, they are lured out to a preselected site on Cojedes Plain, where the patriot riders can have greater play. The royalists find their enemy drawn up before the town of Cojedes: Anzoástegui's 700 infantry of the "Guardia de Honor del Jefe Supremo" and Barcelona battalions in the center, in ranks three-deep; plus 1,900 cavalry on both flanks and the rear.

The Spanish columns march relentlessly toward the insurgent lines, being greeted at 4:00 P.M. by massed volleys at a range of 50 yards. Páez then leads a wild cavalry charge that sweeps away the outnumbered royalist left and descends on de la Torre's rear—but without inflicting a crippling blow. The patriot infantry is meanwhile destroyed by the Spaniards, even though de la Torre has a foot badly mangled by a shot, requiring his replacement by Correa. By evening the royalists have slain 300 patriots, wounded 400, and captured several hundred more, along with 1,500 packhorses and all their supplies. Spanish losses total 91 dead, 130 injured, and 76 missing.

Both sides claim victory, Páez remaining on this field with his *llaneros* when the Spaniards retire toward San Carlos next morning. However, he soon withdraws to Apure to reorganize his forces, reentering San Fernando by 21 May.

10 MAY 1818. The patriot Mariño seizes Cariaco (northeastern Venezuela) and defeats a royalist column at Cautaro two weeks later.

15 MAY 1818. Royalist Lieutenant Colonel Reyes Vargas, after advancing with 400 men from Barinas (Venezuela), wrests Nutrias from its patriot garrison, inflicting heavy casualties.

16 MAY 1818. Bermúdez besieges the royalist garrison within Cumaná (Venezuela) with 500 patriot infantry, 200 cavalry, and a pair of field pieces. On the night of 19–20 May and during daylight on 21 May he attempts to carry it by storm, only to be repelled on both occasions.

Discouraged, Bermúdez digs in with his small army three miles away at the port of Madera, hoping to be joined by Brion's patriot squadron, bringing reinforcements from Margarita Island. But Spanish Governor de Cires sorties from Cumaná with 700 infantry of the Granada, Barbastro, and Reina Battalions, driving the patriots south with heavy losses.

17 MAY 1818. Venezuelan Commodore Brion is lying at Gustavia on Saint Barthélemy with his corvette *Victoria* (flag), five brigs, and three schooners—having just received partial delivery of a shipment of British arms—when Spanish naval Capt. José María Chacón arrives outside with eight men-of-war and 1,400 crewmembers to institute a brief blockade. The patriot vessels are eventually allowed to depart unchallenged.

19 MAY 1818. ***Los Patos.*** After abandoning Calabozo (Venezuela) and allowing it to be reoccupied by Spaniards under Morales and Col. Antonio Plá, patriot General Sedeño decides to make a stand with 1,200 cavalry and 300 fusiliers in the hill country to the southwest—beside Los Patos Lagoon, near Chinea.

Morales approaches with 250 infantry of the Navarra, Corona, and Aragua (militia) Battalions; 650 lancers of the "Del Rey" Cavalry Regiment; plus 150 troopers from the Sombrero, Tiznados, and Calvario Militia Regiments. Awaiting them are Pedro León Torres, commanding the patriot infantry in the center; Col. Francisco Aramendi with the Apure, Guayabal, and Camaguán Cavalry Squadrons on the right; Jacinto Lara with the Calabozo, Rastro, and Tiznados Squadrons on the left; and four patriot squadrons in reserve under Juan Antonio Mina and Remigio Ramos, former royalist.

The encounter proves disastrous for Sedeño, his demoralized forces being unwilling to engage. Aramendi refuses to charge on the right, while Lara's troopers on the left melt away as the royalists advance. The patriot infantry is consequently left alone on the field, losing two-thirds of its numbers before escaping. By the time Sedeño resumes his retreat to Guayabal only 500 men remain with him.

30 MAY 1818. After throwing back Bermúdez's assault on the outskirts of Cumaná (Venezuela), its royalist defenders sally and rout him at the port of Madera, obliging the patriots to fall back to Cumanacoa then Angostura.

4 JULY 1818. On the banks of the Queguay Chico River (Uruguay), patriot leader Artigas is defeated by a Portuguese contingent that is in turn bested by Artigas's subordinate Fructuoso Rivera shortly thereafter.

MID-JULY 1818. San Martín subordinate Zapiola—now commanding a regiment of mounted grenadiers, the Coquimbo Battalion, and two field pieces—is bloodily repulsed by the 500-man royalist garrison at Chillán (Chile).

23 AUGUST 1818. Bermúdez and Brion unite to assault the royalist stronghold of Güiria (facing the Gulf of Paria, eastern Venezuela), their English naval subordinate Captain Hill losing the brig *Colombia* to a Spanish boarding party during the opening action.

Next dawn Bermúdez and Sucre disembark at nearby Cauranta but become pinned down in Chachá Ravine when the garrison sallies in a counterattack. Finally, the patriot naval Capt. Antonio Díaz recaptures *Colombia,* and along with Brion, bombards Güiria sufficiently for its divided defenders to panic and flee west to Río Caribe.

15 SEPTEMBER 1818. Mexican guerrilla leader Guerrero defeats his royalist pursuer Armijo at Tamo, wresting sufficient arms and ammunition to supply 1,800 men.

SEPTEMBER 1818. Royalist General Osorio strips the defenses at Talcahuano (Chile) of 35 guns and sets sail for Peru with his remaining 700 troops.

13 OCTOBER 1818. Repelled in an earlier attempt to seize Carúpano (northeastern Venezuela), Bermúdez retreats and instead captures the royalist outpost of Río Caribe on 13 October.

Two days later, however, the victorious patriots are surprised by a flying royalist column under commander Ramón Añés, who inflicts 60 casualties and drives the startled survivors out to sea.

31 OCTOBER 1818. ***Cariaco.*** Patriot General Mariño advances on the royalist outpost of Cariaco (Venezuela) with 1,140 infantry, 340 cavalry, and 40 gunners for his two field pieces. Rather than wait to be invested, however, a portion of the 900-man garrison—after an ineffectual opening assault by the patriot vanguard under Col. Domingo Montes—unexpectedly sallies under Spanish Cmdr. Agustín Nogueras and sows terror among the disorganized patriot army. Mariño must quickly retreat to Catuaro, suffering 400 killed or wounded.

1 NOVEMBER 1818. Patriot General Sedeño destroys Hilario Torrealva's royalist stronghold at Quebrada Honda (Venezuela).

8 NOVEMBER 1818. The Argentine federalist leader Estanislao López of Santa Fe surprises a rival republican army from Buenos Aires under Gen. Juan Bautista Bustos at Fraile Muerto (modern-day Bell Ville, on the Tercero River). López steals many of Bustos's mounts, but the republicans press into his territory regardless.

MID-NOVEMBER 1818. Patriot General Balcarce advances on Concepción (Chile) with 3,400 men and eight field pieces, obliging royalist Colonel Sánchez's smaller force to retire inland to Los Angeles.

20 NOVEMBER 1818. At Araya (Venezuela), Spanish Capt. José Guerrero—his squadron reinforced by troops from the Granada Infantry Battalion—surprises and defeats a patriot flotilla from Margarita Island under Commander Gutiérrez, taking five gunboats as prizes.

27 NOVEMBER 1818. ***Aguirre Ford.*** Republican Gen. Juan Ramón Balcarce of Buenos Aires attacks the outer defenses of Estanislao López's rival federalist capital of Santa Fe (Argentina). A direct assault is made against Aguirre Ford, masking a republican enveloping movement around a nearby hill that outflanks López and compels him to retreat with heavy losses. Santa Fe is occupied, but next day a 600-man republican pursuit column under Colonel Hortiguera is massacred at Aguiar Creek (north of the city), only its commander and a handful of troopers surviving. This disaster, coupled with fatigues brought on by lack of supplies and reinforcements, convinces Balcarce to evacuate his prize on 4 December; he therefore retires down the Paraná River to Rosario.

28 NOVEMBER 1818. The 42-year-old Scottish-born naval officer Thomas Alexander, Lord Cochrane (later Earl of Dundonald; also nephew to Rear Adm. Sir Alexander Cochrane), arrives in Valparaíso at the invitation of the newly independent Chilean government to assume command of its fledgling navy from 28-year-old Adm. Manuel Blanco Encalada. Strength consists of the captured 50-gun frigate *O'Higgins* (formerly the Spanish *María Isabel*), the ex-Indiamen *San Martín* of 56 guns and *Lautaro* of 44, 18-gun sloop *Galvarino* (formerly the British *Hecate*), plus the smaller *Chacabuco, Aracauno,* and *Pueyrredón.*

16 JANUARY 1819. A contingent of Balcarce's retreating republican army under Col. Francisco Pico is overtaken and defeated at Pergamino (Argentina) by 600 rival federalist troops—mostly Indians—from Santa Fe under the Irish-born Pedro Campbell.

17 JANUARY 1819. After being reinforced at the mouth of the Pao River (Venezuela) by a squadron of

English cavalry under Col. James Rooke and 459 infantry under Monagas, Bolívar merges with Cedeño's division and other reinforcements from Araguaquén, marching to join Páez at San Juan de Payara. This gives the patriots some 1,000 cavalry and 3,400 infantry—far less than the 7,000 royalists assembling at Calabozo under de la Torre. Learning that more English mercenaries are arriving at Angostura under Cols. George Elsom and James T. English, the Liberator proceeds there to incorporate them into his Army of the West.

19 JANUARY 1819. On the banks of the Bío Bío River (Chile), patriot forces mop up the remnants of royalist resistance in the region, capturing 70 men and five field pieces.

24 JANUARY 1819. Morillo crosses the Apure River at San Fernando (Venezuela) with 4,700 infantry and 1,500 cavalry, erecting a small fort before advancing without opposition and occupying the vacated patriot headquarters at San Juan de Payara. Páez shadows his movements with *llanero* cavalry, watching as the Spaniards traverse the Arauca River and seize deserted El Caujaral by 5 February.

Resuming his march four days later, Morillo reaches as far as Cunaviche before retracing his steps and recrossing the Arauca on 25 February. After reinforcing San Juan de Payara and San Fernando he occupies Achaguas (capital of Apure province) on 8 March.

JANUARY 1819. After sailing north from Valparaíso with *O'Higgins* (flag), *Lautaro, San Martín,* and *Chacabuco,* Cochrane attempts to surprise Callao with the first two vessels only, flying American colors. He is thwarted by dense fog and fired on when it clears; he therefore blockades Peru for the next five months. Cochrane makes many captures, both on land (Huacho and Patavilca) and at sea, before finally returning triumphantly to Valparaíso on 16 June.

5 FEBRUARY 1819. ***San Nicolás de los Arroyos.*** Estanislao López's federalist advance down the Paraná River from Santa Fe (Argentina) is at last halted at San Nicolás de los Arroyos, when his 700 troops are repelled by 2,400 republicans marching north out of Buenos Aires under General Viamonte. His rear threatened by Bustos, López retires west.

16 FEBRUARY 1819. Bolívar is elected president of the Venezuelan congress at Angostura.

Royalist artilleryman clad in a blue coat with red trim, brass buttons, black hat, and white crossbelts and trousers

18 FEBRUARY 1819. Republican General Bustos, holding a defensive position at La Herradura on the Tercero River (Argentina) with 700 troops, is attacked by federalist commander López. The defenders respond to the initial probes with a feeble fire but then break a federalist cavalry charge with heavy volleys, allowing José María Paz and Lamadrid's troopers to launch countercharges. Fighting continues next day, before López breaks off action to deal with Viamonte, approaching his rear.

10 MARCH 1819. Advancing west from Rosario (Argentina) republican General Viamonte's 400-man cavalry vanguard under Colonel Hortiguera is annihilated by federalist Estanislao López at Las Barrancas (18 miles southeast of Fraile Muerto on the Tercero River). The disaster compels Viamonte to retreat to Rosario, where he is besieged by the federalists. Eventually he will agree to the San Lorenzo Armistice, signed on 12 April.

11 MARCH 1819. Brion sorties from Margarita Island (Venezuela) with nine patriot vessels manned by

1,300 crewmembers to challenge a Spanish flotilla recently sighted off the coast: the Cuban-built corvette *Ninfa* (flag), a brigantine, two schooners, and 14 smaller consorts. The Spaniards flee under the protection of the batteries at Cumaná next day, leaving Brion to sweep up a number of prizes.

26 MARCH 1819. A small royalist army under Olañeta and Vigil briefly occupies Jujuy (northern Argentina), retreating soon after for fear of being besieged by *gaucho* guerrillas.

27 MARCH 1819. This morning, while approaching Morillo's army as it rests inside Achaguas (Venezuela), Bolívar attacks a 364-man Spanish outpost at Gamarra Ranch, 15 miles outside the city. The outnumbered loyalist defenders slip across the Apure River and carry warning to Morillo. When the Liberator nears Achaguas next day the Spaniards advance in battle array; the armies then camp opposite one another on the banks of the Arauca.

On 2 April Páez fords the river with 150 riders for a reconnaissance in strength, luring Morillo's cavalry into the open before turning on it at Queseras del Medio, inflicting scores of casualties. Two days later Morillo retires to Achaguas; Bolívar departs to forage.

10 APRIL 1819. Patriot Col. Antonio Rangel's cavalry regiment attacks 300 Spanish soldiers at Alejo Mill (six miles outside Nutrias, Venezuela), mauling the formation before retiring.

1 MAY 1819. Morillo's Spanish army recrosses the Apure River (Venezuela), abandoning Achaguas with the advent of the rainy season.

26 MAY 1819. Bolívar also quits the Apure region (Venezuela), leading 800 troopers in three cavalry squadrons and 1,300 men in four infantry battalions from El Mantecal to campaign farther west in New Granada (Colombia). On 4 June they cross the Arauca River, entering Casanare Province and reaching the patriot stronghold of Tame by 11 June.

12 JUNE 1819. ***Cantaura.*** Patriot General Mariño's 900 fusiliers and 400 *llanero* lancers collide with Cmdr. Eugenio de Arana's 700 Spanish infantry—mostly from the Reina Battalion—and 110 cavalry at Cantaura Ranch south of Barcelona (Venezuela). In a 15-mile pursuit north up the banks of the Unare River, the loyalists suffer 250 killed, wounded, captured, or missing compared to 24 dead and 47 injured among the patriot ranks.

15 JUNE 1819. At Itacurupí Ford on the Camacuán River north of San Borja (Uruguay), the patriot leader Andresito is annihilated along with his force by Portuguese General Abreu.

27 JUNE 1819. Entering the Andes, Bolívar's army disperses 300 royalists guarding the town of Paya (Colombia). After resting five days they then press on to Pisba Plain.

17 JULY 1819. Patriot General Urdaneta occupies the evacuated town of Barcelona (Venezuela), having disembarked nearby a few days earlier with 1,200 troops—mostly British mercenaries with some Germans under Major Freudenthal and Venezuelans under Commander Cala. The English contingent proves highly obstinate, refusing to help subdue Barcelona's harbor castle due to disillusionment over service conditions. Instead, Brion's patriot marines must carry the royalist garrison.

Next day the Spanish corvettes *Ninfa* and *Descubierta,* brig *Morillo,* the schooner *Conejito,* and two falouches appear outside Barcelona but are chased east-northeast back to Cumaná by Brion's 12 small men-of-war.

20 JULY 1819. ***Pantano de Vargas.*** After a number of skirmishes, Bolívar's army meets the Spanish 3rd Division under Lt. Col. José María Barreiro (or Barreyro) in Colombia's Bonza Plains. They circle one another warily, probing at long range until noon on 25 July, when—after crossing the Sogamoso River and heading to Salitre—the 2,500 patriots are finally checked while passing east of Vargas Swamp.

Taking up position on the heights opposite, Barreiro sends his 1st "Del Rey" Battalion under Lt. Col. Nicolás López on an encircling maneuver against Bolívar's left wing, thus seriously discomfiting the Liberator's rearguard. His republican army is saved from outright annihilation by Col. James Rooke's British Legion, which bravely dislodges the royalists from the heights despite seeing their commander fall, badly wounded (he dies three days later); Col. Juan José Rondón then smashes Barreiro's counterattack with a *llanero* squadron before fighting ceases altogether at nightfall in heavy rain.

Royalist losses are estimated at 300 killed, injured, or missing compared to 104 dead and wounded among the patriots. Neither side wishes to renew action next day, the Spaniards retiring to the town of Paipa and the patriots to the Bonza corrals. Eventually, Bolívar's army is allowed to advance one week later without further challenge; Paipa is occupied by the patriots on 3 August, Tunja two days later.

21 JULY 1819. Hoping to surprise the Spanish garrison at Guanare (Venezuela), Páez's 700 *llaneros* instead stumble on a 200-man detachment from the Barinas Battalion under Captain Durán, stationed at La Cruz—30 miles northwest of Nutrias. A furious battle erupts in which the patriots suffer 25 killed and 96 wounded, as opposed to 45 dead and 85 wounded among the outnumbered loyalists, who nevertheless manage a fighting retreat.

26 JULY 1819. American Commo. Oliver Hazard Perry reaches Angostura (Venezuela) on an official visit to protest Admiral Brion's detention of the merchant vessels *Tiger* and *Liberty*. As his USS *John Adams* draws too much water, Perry has left it at Trinidad and ventured up the Orinoco aboard his consort, the schooner *Nonsuch*. After contacting the Venezuelan vice president, Francisco Antonio Zea, the commodore reverses course, only to die of yellow fever at the mouth of the Orinoco on 23 August.

1 AUGUST 1819. Urdaneta abandons Barcelona (Venezuela) with his 1,200 recalcitrant English mercenaries, sailing east-northeast aboard Brion's patriot squadron to invest the royalist stronghold at nearby Cumaná. Disembarking at Bordones next day, his men unsuccessfully storm its walls on 5 August; after three days of bloody repulses they retire southeast to Maturín.

6 AUGUST 1819. Five days after patriot General Urdaneta has quit Barcelona (Venezuela) it is occupied by another insurgent contingent under Bermúdez.

7 AUGUST 1819. ***Boyacá.*** After two weeks of feinting against Bolívar's army, Barreiro is retiring southwest toward Bogotá (Colombia) in two divisions. Col. Francisco Jiménez commands the royalist vanguard—500 men of 2nd Numancia Infantry Battalion under Lt. Col. Juan Tolrá, 350 of 3rd Numancia Infantry Battalion under Lt. Col. Juan Loño, plus 160 dragoons under Lieutenant Colonel Salazar—while Barreiro's main body consists of 640 men of 1st "Del Rey" Infantry Battalion under Lt. Col. Nicolás López; 400 of 2nd "Del Rey" Infantry Battalion under Major Figueroa; 480 Tambo Chasseurs under Lt. Col. Esteban Díaz; 320 Granada Dragoons under Lt. Col. Victor Sierra; plus 90 gunners under Lieutenant Coletes for two howitzers and a field piece.

Learning of this retirement, Bolívar intercepts the royalists at 2:00 P.M. when they are about to recross the Boyacá River bridge. Gen. Francisco de Paula Santander commands the patriots' Colombian vanguard: 400 men of Col. Joaquín París's *Cazador* Battalion, 410 of Lt. Col. Antonio Obando's 1st Line Battalion, plus the 1st Squadron (200 troopers) of Capt. Diego Ibarra's Apure Guides. General Anzoátegui's center division consists of 220 men of Lt. Col. Arthur Sandes's Rifle Battalion; 120 British Legionnaires under Major Mackintosh; 300 infantrymen of Col. Ambrosio Plaza's Barcelona Battalion; 300 of Colonel Cruz's "Bravos de Páez" Battalion; plus the 2nd Squadron (100 troopers) of Apure Guides under Colonel Mujica. Bolívar brings up the rear with 500 militiamen of the Tunja Battalion under Cmdr. José Gabriel Lugo; 300 of Socorro Battalion under Commander Soler; 300 lancers of the *Llano-arriba* (Upper Plains) Regiment under Col. Juan José Rondón; plus 90 carabineers of Capt. Juan Mellado's 3rd Squadron.

After Santander gains the high ground, this battle starts with some light cavalry skirmishes. Colonel Jiménez's royalist chasseurs succeed in crossing the bridge and forming a defensive line, but Barreiro orders his main body to concentrate about three-quarters of a mile away, thereby allowing the insurgents to come between both royalist contingents. Santander immediately storms the bridge, while Anzoátegui attacks Barreiro's right and center with his lancers. The right flank of the Spanish infantry is encircled and their artillery captured, as the patriot rifle battalion assaults its front. Meanwhile the royalist cavalry are cut up and flees, abandoning Barreiro to his fate.

Exposed and without guns or cavalry, the Spanish general surrenders by 4:30 P.M. along with his 1,600 infantry and entire supply train. Lieutenant Colonels Loño and Díaz lead the few royalist survivors off toward Chiquinquirá. Next morning the Liberator rides toward Bogotá with his *Llano-arriba* Regiment, eventually taking control of 12 provinces as a result of this victory.

9 AUGUST 1819. This morning Viceroy Juan Sámano abandons the capital of Bogotá (Colombia), allowing Bolívar to enter triumphantly next afternoon. After spending a month and a half installing a new administration, the Liberator travels to Venezuela, where a coup by Arismendi has challenged his title as president.

11 AUGUST 1819. Bermúdez's 1,300-man patriot army is driven out of Barcelona (Venezuela) by the approach of the 2nd Navarra and 2nd Valencey Infantry Battalions under Spanish Col. José Pereira.

23 SEPTEMBER 1819. Patriot General Soublette—marching east through the Andes after Bolívar's triumph at Boyacá—clashes with 800 royalists under de la Torre, who is attempting to bar his path at Alto de las Cruces near Cúcuta (Colombia). Neither side gains any advantage after several hours of combat, in which 60–65 casualties are suffered by each side. The outnumbered Spaniards eventually retire northeast to Mérida de la Grita, temporarily granting the insurgents passage into northwestern Venezuela.

30 SEPTEMBER 1819. Patriot naval Capt. Antonio Díaz—operating far up the Apure with a river squadron—captures 30 loyalist vessels from Nutrias (Venezuela) opposite the town of San Antonio; he also destroys a flotilla from San Fernando at the mouth of the Portuguesa River, leaving both cities isolated.

SEPTEMBER 1819. Cochrane's insurgent squadron returns to blockade the Peruvian port of Callao.

11 OCTOBER 1819. In Bogotá (Colombia), Santander orders the execution by firing squad of Barreiro and 38 other captive Spanish officers.

MID-OCTOBER 1819. The Spaniards abandon San Fernando, Nutrias, and Barinas (Venezuela), retiring north.

OCTOBER 1819. Exasperated by a week-long sack of Ríohacha (Colombia) by 300 British occupiers under MacGregor, the residents rise and slaughter 250 patriot troops and restore royalist rule.

11 NOVEMBER 1819. Tucumán (Argentina) proclaims itself an independent republic with Gen. Bernabé Aráoz as "supreme director."

15 NOVEMBER 1819. Thirty-year-old patriot General Anzoátegui dies at Pamplona (Colombia).

14 DECEMBER 1819. In a desperate bid to free his country from Portuguese occupation, Uruguayan leader Artigas invades southwestern Brazil with a small army, defeating a contingent under Abreu outside Santa Maria (Rio Grande do Sul Province). This victory prompts 3,000 Portuguese troops to enter the area, annihilating Artigas's vanguard at Belarmino Ravine a few days later and scattering his followers back into Uruguay.

17 DECEMBER 1819. Páez occupies Barinas (Venezuela)—abandoned by its Spanish garrison—with 1,200 *llaneros* and 1,900 infantry of the Colombian Tiradores and Boyacá Battalions, "Bravos de Apure," and an English contingent.

23 DECEMBER 1819. A royalist contingent under Col. Manuel Lorenzo advances east from Carúpano (Venezuela) and reoccupies Yaguaraparo.

1 JANUARY 1820. At the town of Cabezas de San Juan near Seville (Spain), Col. Rafael del Riego of the 2nd Battalion of the Asturias Regiment—rather than take ship with his men for the Americas—mutinies against Ferdinand VII, calling for the restoration of the liberal constitution of March 1812. His example is followed by other contingents of the 14,000-man expeditionary force preparing under Calleja to reconquer the River Plate. Popular support will compel the king to accept the resolution by 9 March, its effects soon spreading to the New World.

8 JANUARY 1820. Civil war having resumed a month and a half earlier between republican Buenos Aires and federalist Santa Fe, a contingent of Argentine troops under Bustos—marching to join Supreme Director Rondeau at San Nicolás—mutinies and withdraws to Córdoba rather than proceed with the antifederalist campaign, Bustos being acclaimed city governor. Next day Capt. Mariano Mendizábal's 1st Battalion of Cazadores de los Andes (Andean Chasseurs) does the same at San Juan, rising and proclaiming Mendizábal governor of the town—although he is soon deposed by Lieutenant Corro.

18 JANUARY 1820. Cochrane appears outside Valdivia—the last loyalist stronghold in southern Chile—masquerading his flagship *O'Higgins* as the royal frigate *Prueba* (expected daily by the Spaniards from around Cape Horn). Capturing Valdivia's pilot boat, he learns that the 18-gun sloop *Potrillo* is also anticipated with the garrison's *situado* (payroll); he intercepts it a few days later. After calling at Concepción for 250 Chilean troops under French mercenary Major Beauchef, Cochrane puts out to sea on 25 January, bound for Valdivia.

22 JANUARY 1820. ***Tacuarembó Chico.*** Some 2,000 Uruguayan patriots under General Latorre are

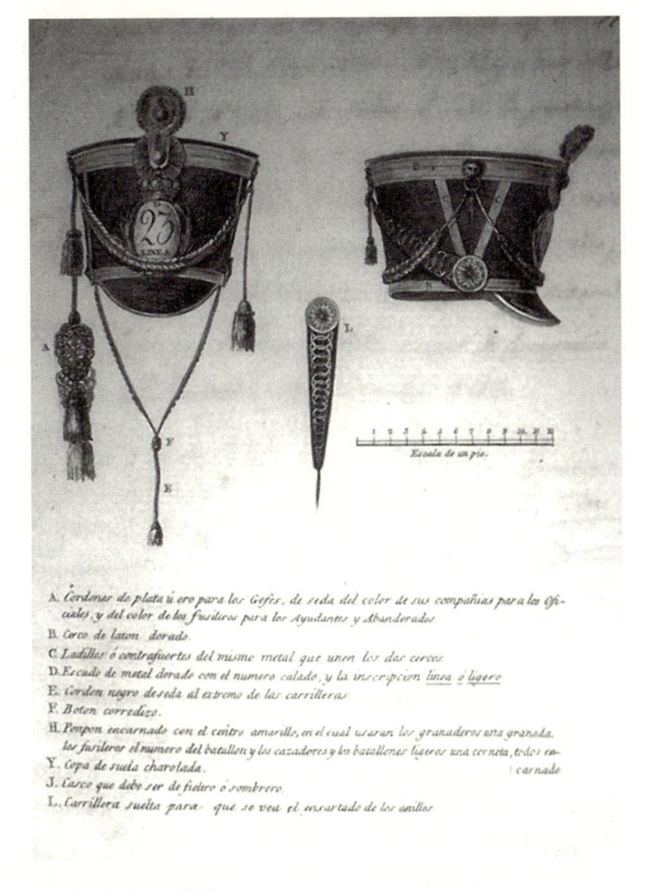

Escala de un pie.
A. Cordones de plata ú oro para los Gefes, de seda del color de sus compañias para los Oficiales, y del color de los fusileros para los Ayudantes y Abanderados.
B. Cerco de laton dorado.
C. Ladillos ó contrafuertes del mismo metal que unen los dos cercos.
D. Escudo de metal dorado con el numero calado, y la inscripcion linea ó ligero.
E. Cordon negro de seda al extremo de las carrilleras.
F. Boton corredizo.
H. Pompon encarnado con el centro amarillo, en el cual usaran los granaderos una granada, los fusileros el numero del batallon y los cazadores y los batallones ligeros una corneta, todos encarnado
Y. Copa de suela charolada.
J. Casco que debe ser de fieltro ó sombrero.
L. Carrillera suelta para que se vea el ensartado de los anillos

Royalist shakos, 1820

annihilated on the western banks of the Tacuarembó River by 3,000 Portuguese troops under Gen. Gaspar de Sousa Filgueiras, effectively ending organized opposition to Brazilian occupation. (On 18 July 1821, Uruguay is annexed into the Portuguese empire as the Cisplatine Province; it remains so until 1825.)

23 JANUARY 1820. At Barbacoas Cliff on the Magdalena River, below the Carare confluence (Colombia), a 26-vessel patriot river squadron of 100 sailors and 127 soldiers under Lt. Col. José Antonio Mayz y Alcalá confronts 11 Spanish gunboats manned by 300 sailors under naval Captain Mier and 153 soldiers under Lt. Col. Isidro Barradas. After a lengthy struggle, in which Barradas's troops are defeated on land and four Spanish vessels are captured by the patriots (along with 87 prisoners), a badly wounded Mayz wins control over the Magdalena.

24 JANUARY 1820. At dawn Calzada's 1,000 royalists—including the Quito and Patía Infantry Battalions—surprise 600 patriots under Col. Antonio Obando stationed at Popayán (Colombia), utterly routing the garrison.

1 FEBRUARY 1820. ***Cepeda.*** Buenos Aires Supreme Director Rondeau's 2,000 demoralized men are attacked on the banks of Cepeda Creek (southwest of San Nicolás) by 1,600 federalists under Estanislao López and Brigadier General Ramírez, who circle behind and scatter the host. Shortly thereafter Rondeau retreats to San Nicolás with only 900 effectives, resigning as supreme director on 10 February. Two weeks later the Argentine civil war ends with the signing of the Treaty of Pilar—although Uruguayan leader Artigas refuses to acknowledge its validity, thereby placing himself at odds with his former ally Ramírez.

3 FEBRUARY 1820. ***Fall of Valdivia.*** Cochrane materializes at Aguada del Inglés outside the loyalist base of Valdivia, his brig *Intrépido* and schooner *Moctezuma* disguised as Spanish vessels. Suspicious gunners open fire from Fort Inglés; despite this, mercenary Maj. William Miller leads 44 Chilean marines ashore in two launches, securing a foothold. During the night Forts Inglés, San Carlos, and Amargos are abandoned in rapid succession as Cochrane's forces circle behind them, inflicting casualties and capturing scores of Spanish prisoners.

Next dawn Colonel Hoyos surrenders Fort Corral, leaving Cochrane in possession of Valdivia's western peninsula at a cost of seven dead and 19 wounded. *Intrépido* and *Moctezuma* enter the roads as *O'Higgins* appears offshore, causing the demoralized Spanish defenders to flee inland. When Cochrane proceeds upriver on 6 February to assault the city proper, the few remaining inhabitants capitulate. Insurgent booty includes the ship *Dolores,* 128 cannons, and much ammunition.

27 FEBRUARY 1820. Cochrane returns into Valparaíso after conquering Valdivia.

6 MARCH 1820. A popular uprising in Buenos Aires deposes the interim governor, Sarratea, in favor of Gen. Juan Ramón Balcarce. Six days later Sarratea is reinstalled in office by the federalist army under Estanislao López and Brigadier General Ramírez.

12 MARCH 1820. Patriot Admiral Brion appears before Ríohacha (Colombia) with ten small warships and six transports from Margarita Island (Venezuela), bearing Col. Mariano Montilla's contingent—mostly 700 disgruntled Irish mercenaries, brought from Europe by Lt. Col. John d'Evereux—to reoccupy the port following an uprising against MacGregor (*see* October 1819). The few Spanish defenders under Gov.

José Solís flee west to Santa Marta that night, allowing the patriots to disembark and enter the empty town unopposed next day.

MID-APRIL 1820. Spanish General Morillo receives orders from Madrid to promulgate the liberal constitution of 1812. After considerable hesitation, he contacts Bolívar to attempt to arrange a truce toward that end, although realizing that its articles sap the royalist cause. Desertions to the patriots increase throughout the year.

28 APRIL 1820. Patriot Col. José Mires—having been detached from Gen. Manuel Valdés's division at Bogotá and marched southwest with the Albión and Guías de Carvajal Battalions—perceives a 310-man royalist unit under Captain Domínguez approaching La Plata (Colombia), which he instantly attacks and outflanks. The Spaniards are routed, suffering 80 casualties and 100 prisoners, as opposed to 28 killed or wounded and 19 missing among the patriots. This small victory opens the way to Cauca Valley.

6 MAY 1820. In light of the political upheaval in Spain, royalist General Morillo unilaterally declares a 40-day truce in Venezuela and Colombia to which all insurgents adhere.

18 MAY 1820. ***Laguna Salada.*** After being forced to the defensive and compelled to retire to Ríohacha (Colombia) by the approach of 1,200 loyalists from Santa Marta under Col. Vicente Sánchez Lima, patriot Colonel Montilla learns that his 700 Irish mercenaries under d'Evereux refuse to serve the insurgent cause any longer because of their lack of pay and food. Notwithstanding the mutiny, the defenders are able to repel a royalist assault against Ríohacha two days later, although the Irishmen refuse to sally and chase the enemy away.

Montilla must sortie on 25 May with only 380 marines and local militia, two field pieces, and 200 loyal Irish lancers under Lt. Col. Francis Burdett O'Connor to give battle against Sánchez Lima's host, which is waiting at nearby Laguna Salada. Despite being outnumbered, the patriots drive the loyalists back then smash them at Sabana del Patrón, precipitating a headlong flight to Santa Marta. Montilla returns to Ríohacha and, with some difficulty, disarms his obstinate Irish mutineers, deporting them to Jamaica on 4 June.

24 MAY 1820. The merchants of Veracruz organize a battalion called the Fernando VII Volunteers and compel the garrison commander, José Dávila, to proclaim the 1812 liberal constitution. Similar demonstrations occur at Jalapa and other Mexican towns.

28 MAY 1820. A 4,000-man royalist army under General Ramírez Orozco—with Canterac, Olañeta, José María Valdéz, Marquiegui, Agustín Gamarra, and Vigil serving as colonels—occupies Jujuy (northern Argentina) and Salta three days later. Their southerly progress slows, however, as *gaucho* opposition stiffens.

5 JUNE 1820. After the departure of his Irish mutineers patriot Colonel Montilla is compelled to abandon a shaky foothold at Ríohacha (Colombia), sailing southwest with Brion to Sabinilla—at the mouth of the Magdalena River—by 11 June; he proceeds upriver and joins Lt. Col. José María Córdova's forces, who capture Mompós by 20 June.

6 JUNE 1820. ***Pitayó.*** Patriot Generals Valdés and Mires, advancing south down the Cauca Valley (Colombia) with more than 2,000 troops to put down resistance around Popayán, collide with a loyalist contingent barring the Las Moras Moor approach route at Pitayó. They consist of 1,100 troops of the Cazadores and Patía Battalions under veteran Lt. Col. Nicolás López. (Royalist General Calzada is meanwhile guarding the Guanacas Moor approach farther east—at Piendamó—with 500 men of the Aragón Infantry Regiment plus 100 cavalry.)

Without waiting for Mires's rearguard to join from Páramo, Valdés storms López's lines with his vanguard at noon, only to be repelled. The royalists counterattack, but over the next three hours wear down; at last a charge by the patriot Albión Battalion and Juan Carvajal's Guías break the defenders' will. López's army flees to Guambia, leaving behind 133 casualties and 150 prisoners compared to 30 dead and 62 wounded among the attackers. (This victory will soon compel the outnumbered royalists to evacuate Popayán without a fight, Valdés entering it triumphantly—after uniting with Concha at Cali—at the head of 2,400 men. However, the patriot general's subsequent harshness blunts the welcome extended by the inhabitants, so royalist resistance continues to smolder.)

8 JUNE 1820. ***Cuesta de la Pedrera.*** At dawn a large patriot guerrilla force under Colonels Zerda and Zabala attacks a 2,000-man royalist column southeast of Salta (Argentina), bedeviling it until midafternoon, when the royalists regain the city defenses. Shortly thereafter they begin a general retirement north, their

rearguard being overtaken six days later at Yala and suffering 60 killed and 200 wounded.

15 JUNE 1820. ***Guachas.*** In the Entre Ríos District, south of Tala on the western banks of the Gualeguay River, the Uruguayan patriot Artigas's 2,200 men defeat 500–600 Argentine federalists under Brigadier General Ramírez, heavy casualties being sustained on both sides.

Ramírez retreats downriver, hard-pressed by Artigas. Nine days later, at Avalos, Ramírez takes up a strong defensive position with 900 men and pulverizes his pursuers. Artigas is obliged to make a fighting retreat to Paraguay, which he reaches by 23 September. He is then kept a virtual prisoner by its dictator, Dr. José Gaspar Rodríguez de Francia, for the next 30 years.

22 JUNE 1820. Patriot Colonel Lara and Lt. Col. Francisco Carmona advance from Tamalameque (northeastern Colombia) with 1,500 troops, coming upon Sánchez Lima's 1,100 loyalists two days later at Chiriguaná, scattering them back to Santa Marta and opening the way for an offensive against Maracaibo.

25 JUNE 1820. At dawn, a 100-man patriot river squadron under Lieutenant Colonel Córdova and Cmdr. Hermógenes Maza surprise their Spanish counterparts at Tenerife (Colombia). Approaching in seven boats—after first depositing Córdova's troops ashore—Maza captures nine of the 11 Spanish craft and slaughters the crews. Loyalist commander Vicente Villa blows himself up with his flagship rather than surrender. Of 300 Spaniards present, only 27 are captured alive; 70 grenadiers of the León Regiment (stationed ashore under commander Esteban Díaz) manage to escape. The victory gives the patriots total control over the Magdalena River.

28 JUNE 1820. ***Cañada de la Cruz.*** In Argentina's renewed civil war, federalist Estanislao López and Chilean-born Brig. Gen. José Miguel Carrera march on Buenos Aires with slightly more than 1,500 troops to restore their ally, Alvear, as its governor. At Cañada de la Cruz (12 miles southwest of Campana), they are confronted by 1,750 soldiers under the rival governor, Soler, with French and Pagola as his brigadiers.

While advancing to give battle, French's right wing unwittingly marches into a swamp, compelling the entire unit to surrender without firing a shot. Soler's main body sustains some 200 killed, obliging him to retreat and resign as governor a few days later. The federalists are unable to gain the capital, however; Dorrego is thus named Soler's successor, and Alvear becomes governor of Luján as a consolation.

1 JULY 1820. Patriot Colonel Montilla establishes his 700 troops at Turbaco (Colombia), supported by Admiral Brion's squadron offshore to harass the royalist lines of communication leading to Cartagena, only 12 miles away. Its 1,150-man Spanish garrison is rent by dissension because of the recent political turmoil in Spain (*see* 1 January 1820); it does not react. Instead, Viceroy Sámano and other officials are deposed by a coup led by Brig. Gen. Gabriel Torres.

18 JULY 1820. ***Dorrego's Offensive.*** The new Buenos Aires governor, Dorrego, sallies with a small army to drive away the rival Argentine federalist force under López. Two weeks later (2 August), Dorrego makes a rapid nocturnal march to fall upon 700 unsuspecting federalists at San Nicolás under Col. José M. Benavente. At a cost of seven dead and 42 wounded Dorrego destroys the unit, killing 60 and capturing 450. The governor then achieves a second victory ten days later when he crosses Pavón Creek with 1,500 riders and disperses 500 troopers encamped on its north bank under López himself.

At Gamonal (Pavón Creek headwaters), however, Dorrego's luck runs out; on 2 September he overtakes the fleeing López with 600 riders and a field piece, unaware that his opponent has been reinforced and now commands 1,000 cavalry. The armies collide in a frontal charge that sees Dorrego enveloped; he is forced to surrender after suffering 320 killed and 100 captured.

20 AUGUST 1820. At Valparaíso, San Martín leads 2,400 Argentine and 2,000 Chilean troops aboard the transports *Dolores, Gaditana, Consecuencia, Emprendedora, Santa Rosa, Aguila, Mackenna, Perla, Jerezana, Peruana, Golondrina, Minerva, Libertad, Argentina, Hércules,* and *Potrillo* to invade royalist Peru. His Argentine contingent consists of 457 men of Seventh Infantry Battalion under Colonel Conde; 478 of Eighth Infantry Battalion under Colonel Martínez; 583 of 11th Infantry Battalion under Major Deheza; 213 gunners under Major Luna; 418 horse grenadiers under Colonel Alvarado; plus 283 chasseurs under Colonel Necocheta. The Chileans are 630 men of Colonel Aldunate's Second Infantry Battalion; 678 of Lieutenant Colonel Sánchez's Fourth Infantry Battalion; 343 of Colonel Larrazabal's Fifth Infantry Battalion; 52 of Colonel Campino's Sixth Infantry Battalion; 230 gunners under Lieutenant

Colonel Borgono; 30 troopers of Lieutenant Colonel Guzmán's Second Dragoon Regiment; plus 53 sappers. They are further accompanied by 35 field pieces.

They set sail north next morning, escorted by Cochrane's:

Ship	*Guns*	*Tons*
San Martín (flag; formerly British *Cumberland*)	64	1,300
O'Higgins (frigate; formerly Spanish *María Isabel*)	44	1,220
Lautaro (frigate; formerly British *Windham*)	46	850
Independencia (frigate; formerly American *Curiosity*)	28	380
Galvarino (brigantine; formerly *Lucy*)	18	398
Araucano (brigantine; formerly American *Columbus*)	16	270
Pueyrredón (brigantine; formerly Spanish *Aguila*)	16	220
Montezuma (sloop; Spanish prize)	7	200

This squadron is manned by 1,600 sailors, approximately 600 of them British.

22 AUGUST 1820. In Mexico City, a general pardon is issued to all insurgents.

1–2 SEPTEMBER 1820. Spanish Colonel Balbuena leads a midnight sally out of Cartagena (Colombia) with 420 soldiers of the León Regiment and 60 gunners to attack Montilla's patriot siege lines near Turbaco. They disembark at Cospique and, at 6:00 A.M., surprise the 1,000-man patriot garrison under Col. Ramón Ayala at Bellavista, consisting of the Magdalena and Bajo Magdalena Chasseur Battalions plus a Soledad cavalry squadron. The startled defenders begin fleeing in disarray, suffering 125 killed and 50 wounded before they spike the guns and retire.

7 SEPTEMBER 1820. ***San Martín's Peruvian Campaign.*** The Chilean-Argentine expedition of San Martín anchors in Paracas Bay, where Las Heras disembarks with the 11th Reinforced Battalion and marches nine miles north to seize Pisco. Its 600-man royalist garrison under Colonel Quimper withdraws rather than resist; four days later the insurgent fleet enters the roadstead, and San Martín's main army goes ashore. Outnumbered by the loyalist forces remaining in Peru, his aim is to avoid battle while winning over the inhabitants. A brief truce is arranged with Viceroy de la Pezuela between 26 September and 4 October, after which hostilities resume.

26 SEPTEMBER 1820. Because of Dorrego's capture (*see* 18 July 1820), Gen. Martín Rodríguez proclaims himself governor of Buenos Aires. Five days later Brigadier General Pagola rises against him, his faction being put down after two days' heavy fighting in the streets. The 5th "Colorados del Monte" Militia Cavalry Regiment proves crucial in supporting Rodríguez, winning its 27-year-old commander Juan Manuel de Rosas promotion to colonel.

SEPTEMBER 1820. Royalist commander Vicente Benavídez receives a Peruvian armaments shipment in southern Chile, which he uses to mount a short-lived offensive north of the Bío Bío River, eventually being repulsed when he assaults Freyre's patriot garrison at Talcahuano.

This same month, royalist Capt. Juan Manuel Silva leads a revolt in Venezuela against Morillo's command, being promoted lieutenant colonel upon joining the patriot cause.

1 OCTOBER 1820. Bolívar enters Mérida (Venezuela) with his staff only, the royalist garrison having fled the previous day.

4 OCTOBER 1820. San Martín subordinate Arenales marches inland from Pisco (Peru) with 2,500 men in two battalions, a half-squadron of cavalry, and two field pieces to raise insurrection in the Andes. Three days later two companies of Quimper's royalist troops, rather than resist, switch allegiances and join Arenales's army at Palpa.

9 OCTOBER 1820. A popular uprising against Spanish rule occurs at Guayaquil, this district proclaiming its independence.

15 OCTOBER 1820. Arenales's subordinate, Lt. Col. Manuel Rojas, leads 80 patriot cavalry and 80 mounted grenadiers in a surprise attack against Colonel Quimper's royalist base at Nazca (Peru), killing 41 and capturing 86. Next day the loyalists' ammunition train is also seized at Acari by Lt. Vicente Suárez with 30 chasseurs. By 21 October Arenales's insurgent army strikes into the Andean foothills.

28 OCTOBER 1820. Leaving a small patriot garrison at Pisco (Peru), San Martín's Chilean-Argentine expedition reembarks and sails northwest, appearing before Callao next day then disembarking 30 miles northwest of Lima at Ancón by 30 October. Again, San Martín pursues a nonconfrontational policy, sowing revolutionary sedition while avoiding major battles.

This same day, the 500-man British Legion mutinies at Achaguas (Venezuela), killing or wounding several officers before being put down by Páez.

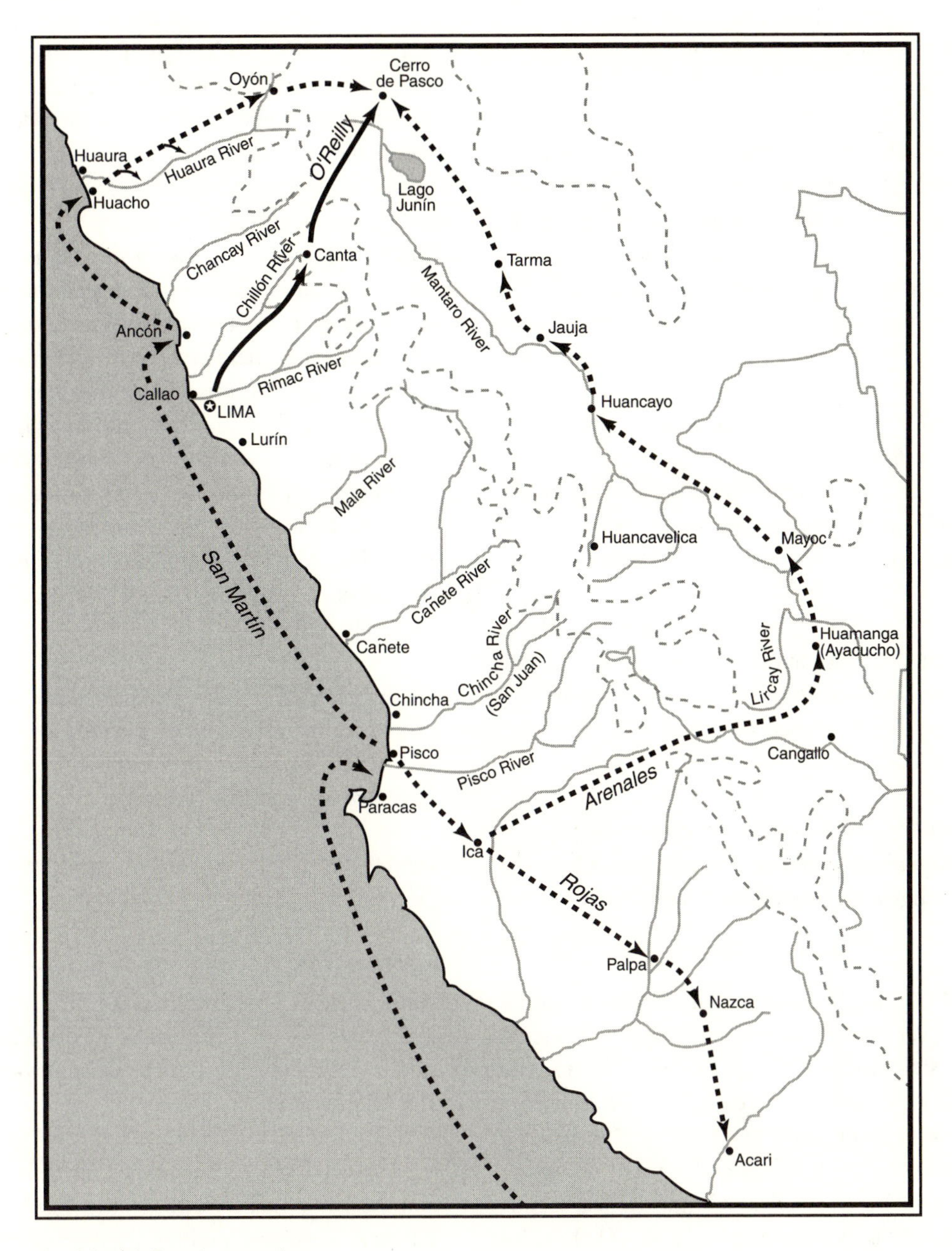

San Martín's Peruvian campaign

3 NOVEMBER 1820. Cochrane arrives outside Callao with *O'Higgins, Lautaro,* and the 28-gun corvette *Independencia;* two nights later he leads 14 boats bearing 160 seamen and 80 marines past its boom—as well as the anchored USS *Macedonian* and 42-gun HMS *Hyperion* of Capt. Thomas Searle—to board the 44-gun Spanish frigate *Esmeralda* of Captain Coig. At a cost of 11 dead and 30 wounded the insurgents storm the vessel, inflicting 160 casualties among the sleeping crew within 15 minutes before sailing it out with 200 prisoners aboard; they eventually rename it *Valdivia.*

9 NOVEMBER 1820. San Martín's Chilean-Argentine expedition quits Ancón (Peru), sailing farther north to disembark three days later at Huacho and take up defensive positions beyond the Huaura River. In response, Viceroy de la Pezuela orders royalist Colonel Valdéz to advance with 2,000 troops to check the invasion force.

This same day, a patriot division from Guayaquil—while marching inland to liberate Quito—defeats a royalist contingent under Gen. Melchor Aymerich, president of the *audiencia.*

11 NOVEMBER 1820. In the Andes, royalist Brigadier General Montenegro digs in with 600 men and two cannons to oppose Arenales's passage of the Mantaro River. The patriots nonetheless fight their

way across at Mayoc Bridge, obliging Montenegro to retire to Jauja.

MID-NOVEMBER 1820. Patriot General Valdés is ordered by Bolívar to advance on Pasto (Colombia) and secure it at all costs before a general truce can be arranged with the Spaniards. Instead, Valdés is defeated at Genoy, south of the Juanambú River, and recalled in favor of 25-year-old Venezuelan Brigadier General Sucre.

16 NOVEMBER 1820. The royalist Iturbide quits Mexico City for Teloloapan, having been appointed commander of New Spain's southern district with orders to subdue the last vestiges of guerrilla activity under Guerrero and Pedro Ascencio Alquisiras.

22 NOVEMBER 1820. At Huachi (near Ambato, Ecuador), the patriot division marching to liberate Quito under Luis Urdaneta is crushed by a royalist division led by Col. Francisco González and compelled to retire to Guayaquil.

24 NOVEMBER 1820. The Treaty of Benegas is signed in Argentina, in hopes of bringing a halt to the fratricidal struggle among Buenos Aires, Santa Fe, and Córdoba.

26 NOVEMBER 1820. After four days of meetings at Trujillo (Venezuela), patriot and royalist delegates arrange a six-month truce between Bolívar's and Morillo's forces. Shortly thereafter—3 December—Morillo turns over command of his remaining 10,000 troops to de la Torre and returns to Spain, where he will be invested as Conde de Cartagena and Marqués de la Puerta (*see* 15 March 1818) for his New World services.

29 NOVEMBER 1820. A large contingent of Indian rebels is slaughtered at Huamanga (Peru) by royalist General Ricafort; a similarly lopsided encounter occurs at Cangallo three days later.

2 DECEMBER 1820. General Carrera, dissatisfied with the terms of the Treaty of Benegas, sacks and burns the town of Salto near Buenos Aires with the aid of allied Indian warriors, then retires south. He is pursued two weeks later by General Ramírez in the so-called *Expedición al Desierto* (Expedition into the Desert), which fails to catch the renegade. After capturing San Luis and laying siege to Córdoba in March, Carrera is defeated.

2–3 DECEMBER 1820. In Peru, the 675-man Numancia Battalion—originally recruited in Venezuela—mutinies and switches allegiance, abandoning the royalist cause to join San Martín's army. During the ensuing weeks its strength builds back to a full 1,000.

6 DECEMBER 1820. ***Cerro de Pasco.*** High in the Peruvian Andes, Arenales's insurgent army is checked at Cerro de Pasco by 1,200 royalist infantry, 180 cavalry, and two field pieces under Gen. Alejandro O'Reilly. Early on this snowy morning a company of patriots drags four cannons onto its commanding hill, opening fire when three patriot attack columns finally advance after the weather clears. Once outflanked the royalists break and flee, suffering 58 killed, 18 wounded, and 380 captured; numerous survivors are subsequently captured in the following days, including O'Reilly himself.

29 DECEMBER 1820. More than 5,000 poorly armed Indian rebels under patriot Colonel Bermúdez and Maj. Félix Aldao are massacred by royalist General Ricafort at Huancayo (Peru).

2 JANUARY 1821. Guerrero defeats a small loyalist contingent at Zapotepec (Mexico).

5 JANUARY 1821. The Mexican guerrilla leader Ascencio defeats a royalist force at Tlatlaya.

Meanwhile at Tanizahua (Ecuador) a patriot band under Colonel García is surprised and routed by a royalist contingent.

8 JANUARY 1821. Arenales's insurgent army rejoins San Martín's main body at the headwaters of the Chancay River, high within the Peruvian Andes.

10 JANUARY 1821. Iturbide contacts his insurgent leader (and enemy) Guerrero to propose they join forces to forge a new alliance for Mexico's independence based on Spain's liberal constitution of 1812.

18 JANUARY 1821. A group of Maracaibo's leading citizens conspires against Spanish rule, allowing patriot General Urdaneta to close off its lagoon and blockade the royalist garrison inside. On 26 January Urdaneta advances with a battalion of troops to the very edge of the lagoon; by evening of 28 January he sends a column under Cuban-born Lt. Col. José Rafael de las Heras to support a "revolution" within—a clear violation of the six-month truce arranged two months earlier. Spanish General de la

Torre complains to Bolívar about the breach of the peace, to no avail.

29 JANUARY 1821. Following a mutiny by the Spanish Generals Canterac and Valdés at Asnapuqio (near Lima), Peru's Viceroy de la Pezuela is deposed in favor of royalist General de la Serna.

30 JANUARY 1821. Cochrane arrives before Callao with 650 insurgent troops under English mercenary Lt. Col. William Miller to accept the prearranged surrender of its shore defenses. This capitulation fails to take place, so the patriot expedition returns to Huacho.

24 FEBRUARY 1821. Iturbide, Guerrero, and other Mexican insurgent leaders announce the so-called Plan of Iguala, whereby Mexico would proclaim independence from Spain subject to three conditions, or "guarantees": the predominance of the Catholic faith, total independence (although under the continuing symbolic rule of Spain's royal family), and a union or reconciliation between Mexico's embittered creoles and peninsulars. Viceroy Ruiz de Apodaca rejects the arrangement and declares Iturbide an outlaw on 14 March.

10 MARCH 1821. At a conference held at Acatempan (near Teloloapan, Mexico), Guerrero agrees to merge his insurgent forces with Iturbide's loyalists, thus creating the patriotic *Ejército de las Tres Garantías* (Army of the Three Guarantees—Catholicism, independence, union) better known as the *Ejército Trigarante.*

This same day, in Venezuela, Bolívar informs Spanish General de la Torre that because of disputes over certain territories the six-month truce arranged in November 1820 will be rescinded by the patriots within 40 days.

13 MARCH 1821. Cochrane departs Huacho (Peru) with three ships bearing 500 patriot infantry and 100 cavalry under Lieutenant Colonel Miller. They disembark one week later at Pisco, being observed from a distance by royalist Lieutenant Colonel García Camba's 200 troopers in Chincha Valley. Neither side campaigns vigorously due to a malaria outbreak.

23 MARCH 1821. The 27-year-old loyalist Antonio López de Santa Anna Pérez de Lebrón arrives at Orizaba (Mexico) with 200 troopers, arresting Cristóbal Ballesteros for suspected disloyalty. Ballesteros attempts to persuade Santa Anna to join Iturbide and Guerrero's *Ejército Trigarante,* but the young officer resists; he is later defeated and accepts appointment as a lieutenant colonel under insurrectionist Gen. José Joaquín de Herrera. Together they overrun Córdoba; Herrera then marches to Puebla while Santa Anna subdues Topete at Alvarado (Veracruz).

24 MARCH 1821. Insurrectionist Mexican Gens. Luis de Cortazar and Anastasio Bustamante capture the city of Guanajuato.

2 APRIL 1821. Cochrane blockades Callao for three days.

10 APRIL 1821. High in the Peruvian Andes at Ataura (near Jauja), a royalist army under Ricafort slaughters 500 of 3,000 poorly armed Indian rebels; his own ranks suffer one minor injury.

15 APRIL 1821. One month after crossing Argentina's northern frontier, Olañeta's royalist army passes through Jujuy, heading south. On 23 April, however, his 500-man vanguard under Marquiegui is annihilated at León (seven miles north of Yala) by 600 patriots under Gen. José Ignacio de Gorriti. This defeat prompts Olañeta to retire toward Mojos while leaving a small garrison at Yalvi under Lieutenant Colonel Valdéz.

21 APRIL 1821. Patriot General Arenales departs Huaura (Peru) with 2,500 men in three battalions and a cavalry squadron plus four field pieces to once more campaign against the royalists in the Andes.

This same day, farther south at Pisco, 180 of Miller's sick patriot troops are reembarked for return to Huacho aboard two of Cochrane's vessels; the third vessel—flagship *San Martín*—sets sail southwest with the remaining 400 troops and 100 black Peruvian recruits to attack Arica (Chile).

25 APRIL 1821. Insurrectionist Mexican General Herrera is defeated at Tepeaca by loyalist Col. Francisco Hevia. However, after being reinforced by Santa Anna, Herrera drives off Cols. Juan Horbegoso and Flores and gains Jalapa.

28 APRIL 1821. This morning, hostilities resume between Venezuela's patriots and loyalists when a cavalry detachment crosses the Santo Domingo River and routs a royalist outpost at Boconó. Patriot Col. Ambrosio Plaza's Guardia Division then follows this up by entering Guanare and marching on San Carlos, which is

evacuated by the loyalists and taken by Bolívar for his headquarters.

APRIL 1821. The Argentine town of Dolores is destroyed by an Indian invasion from the south, prompting a counterexpedition two years later by Gen. Martín Rodríguez, who builds Fort Independencia on the banks of Tandil Creek.

1 MAY 1821. Iturbide's *Ejército Trigarante* enters León (Mexico), having marched uncontested from Teloloapan via Tlalchapa, Cutzamala, Tusantla, Zitácuaro, and Acámbaro. Field Marshal Liñán refuses to stir forth from his Cuernavaca headquarters with the loyalist southern army.

3 MAY 1821. ***Argentine Civil War.*** Fighting resumes when General Ramírez—deploring Buenos Aires' refusal to declare war against the Portuguese invaders of Uruguay—fords across the Paraná from Bajada del Paraná with 1,200 riders, and advances on Santa Fe. Three days later López repels Ramírez's 960 men and four field pieces before his capital, obliging the latter to retreat to Rosario. On 8 May Ramírez meets a similar-size cavalry force under Lamadrid just north of Rosario that he defeats and pushes back to Medio Creek.

4 MAY 1821. Cochrane's *San Martín* bombards Arica (Chile) then disembarks Colonel Miller's small regiment at nearby Sama. A detachment under Major Soler occupies Arica one week later; Miller's larger company takes Tacna on 14 May with little opposition.

11 MAY 1821. Patriot General Urdaneta occupies Coro (Venezuela), installing Col. Juan de Escalona as governor while chasing its fleeing loyalists as far as San Juan del Tocuyo.

12 MAY 1821. ***Guatire.*** The Venezuelan patriot General Bermúdez—after arriving from Cumaná with 1,200 men—defeats a matching loyalist force under Col. José María Hernández Monagas at Ibarra Mill (near Guatire), suffering seven dead and eight wounded compared to 50 killed, 60 injured, and 100 captured among his opponents.

Two days later Bermúdez occupies Caracas at 5:00 P.M.; its loyalist residents flee to Puerto Cabello and Curaçao aboard 70 vessels escorted by the Spanish frigate *Ligera*. Bermúdez then empties the arsenal at La Guaira, raises a host of volunteers, and proceeds to the Aragua Valleys by 18 May.

MID-MAY 1821. Sucre reaches Guayaquil, which has recently proclaimed independence, with 700 troops.

19 MAY 1821. At Lagunetas (Venezuela), Bermúdez's patriot army chases off some loyalist skirmishers; next day he defeats 700 men under Governor Correa at Consejo, finding Spanish Brig. Gen. Tomás de Cires among the captives. When the patriots occupy Victoria the beaten loyalists fall back to Valencia.

News of Bermúdez's successful sweep persuades Spanish General de la Torre to leave his 1st and 5th Divisions (1,700 men) at Araure to watch Bolívar while countermarching to San Carlos with 2,800 infantry to challenge Bermúdez and reconquer Caracas.

20 MAY 1821. Valladolid (modern-day Morelia, Mexico) surrenders to Iturbide.

22 MAY 1821. Learning that three royalist columns are converging from Oruro, Puno, and Arequipa (Peru) to contest his invasion of northern Chile, patriot Lieutenant Colonel Miller surprises the first of them—Lieutenant Colonel La Hera's 250 soldiers—at Mirave with 310 insurgent infantry, 70 cavalry, and 60 *montoneros* (guerrillas). The royalists suffer 44 killed and 106 captured as opposed to 25 deaths among Miller's ranks.

As the engagement ends, royalist Lieutenant Colonel Rivero arrives with an additional 250 troops, only to immediately retire and be pursued. Two days later another 30 monarchists are killed at Moquegua, and Rivero's company finally collapses with the insurgent approach to Calera on 26 May; most are captured or voluntarily join the rebel ranks.

23 MAY 1821. Peruvian Viceroy de la Serna signs a brief truce with San Martín, known as the Punchauca Armistice (ending 30 June).

24 MAY 1821. ***Coronda.*** Despite his 8 May setback near Rosario, Buenos Aires, General Lamadrid is reinforced and rides with 1,500 troopers to join López in defense of his capital of Santa Fe (Argentina); 24 miles south-southwest of there Lamadrid chances upon Ramírez with 700 cavalry at Coronda and attacks in hopes of cutting the renegade off from the Paraná River. Instead, Lamadrid is outflanked and defeated, leaving Ramírez in possession of the battlefield.

Two days later, however, López—who has been riding with 700 troopers to meet Lamadrid—incorporates 300 of his stragglers into the latter's ranks and surprises Ramírez at Coronda. The renegade retreats to Desmochados, hoping to unite with Carrera.

24 MAY 1821. ***Márquez.*** Brigadier General Morales's 2,800 loyalists attack Bermúdez's 1,500 patriots, dug in at Márquez between Las Lajas and Las Cocuizas (near Caracas). The patriots repulse the attackers throughout the day, but after nightfall, retire from the field; they then evacuate Caracas by 26 May, continuing the retreat to Guatire while pursued by the 2nd Valencey Battalion under Spanish Brigadier General Pereira.

5 JUNE 1821. Patriot leader Reyes Vargas advances on San Felipe (Venezuela) with 100 cavalry and 500 infantry, being defeated at Cocorote—southeast of the city—by loyalist Colonel Lorenzo. The patriots leave 80 dead and a like number wounded on the field.

Three days later Reyes Vargas materializes at Tinajas, north of San Felipe, only to again be beaten by Lorenzo at La Candelaria; he then withdraws south.

7–11 JUNE 1821. Páez joins Bolívar at San Carlos (Venezuela) with 1,000 infantry and 1,500 cavalry. When Urdaneta arrives on 16 June with another 2,000 troops, patriot strength reaches 6,500 soldiers in three divisions.

8 JUNE 1821. Royalist Lieutenant Colonel Valdéz slips into Salta (northern Argentina) at dawn with 400 riders, capturing the city and patriot General Güemes. Two weeks later royalist General Olañeta arrives with 1,200 troops; by 14 July he comes to terms with local patriots and retires to Bolivia.

14 JUNE 1821. Bermúdez—after a rapid march—surprises Lucas González's 550 loyalists at Macuto promontory near Santa Lucía (Venezuela) and destroys the force. The loyalist commander is killed, and his men suffer 148 casualties and 200 prisoners; only 260 manage to escape. Patriot loses are 73 dead and wounded.

16 JUNE 1821. The renegade Generals Ramírez and Carrera join forces, their 700 troopers falling upon 200 Argentine republican cavalry, 300 infantry, and four field pieces under Bustos at Cruz Alta (west of Rosario). Unable to overwhelm the position, the attackers withdraw to Fraile Muerto upon learning of Lamadrid's approach with a relief column. Ramírez then retires north of Córdoba with some 200 followers; Carrera proceeds to the Cuarto River with 700 men, hoping to regain his Chilean homeland.

19 JUNE 1821. Patriot Lt. Col. Laurencio Silva's cavalry squadron overruns a Spanish picket force at Tinaquillo (near Carabobo, Venezuela).

22 JUNE 1821. Colonel Carrillo's 1,000 patriots enter San Felipe (Venezuela); the loyalist garrison, under Lorenzo, are compelled to evacuate because of a threatened encirclement.

23 JUNE 1821. ***Calvario.*** On Calvario Hill, just west of Caracas, Brigadier General Pereira makes a stand behind Caruata Creek with 1,200 loyalists against Bermúdez's similar-size patriot force. The latter attacks ferociously in twin columns; by this afternoon his small army is annihilated, however, having suffered 500 casualties plus another 500 lost as prisoners or deserters. Bermúdez retreats to Guarenas with his 200 survivors and is followed briefly by the victorious Pereira.

24 JUNE 1821. ***Carabobo.*** This morning, while advancing northeast against Valencia (Venezuela), Bolívar crests Buena Vista Heights with General Páez's 1st Division in the van: "Bravos de Apure" Battalion under Colonel Torres; *Cazadores Británicos* (British Legion) under Col. Thomas Farriar; "Honor" Infantry Regiment under Colonel Muñóz; Páez's hussars under Colonel Iribarren; *Regimiento de la Muerte* (Death Regiment) under Colonel Borrás; "Honor" Lancer Regiment under Colonel Farfán; *Cazadores Valientes* (Brave Chasseurs) under Lieutenant Colonel Gómez; Venganza Regiment under Major Escalona; plus a reserve under Colonel Rosales. General Sedeño's 2nd Division consists of the Vargas Battalion of Lieutenant Colonel Gravete; Boyacá Battalion of Lieutenant Colonel Flegel; "Tiradores" Battalion of Lieutenant Colonel de las Heras; and Sagrado Cavalry Squadron of Colonel Aramendi. General Plaza's 3rd Division brings up the rear:

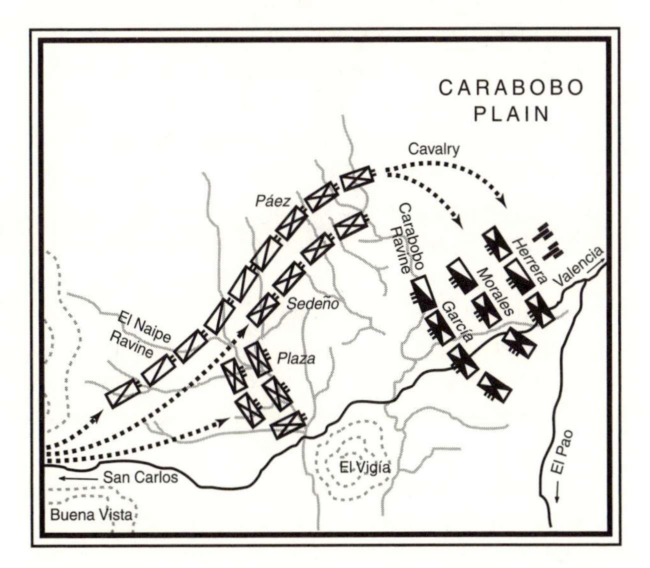

Battle of Carabobo

Anzoátegui Battalion under Colonel Arguindegui; "Vencedor en Boyacá" Battalion under Col. Johann von Uslar; Grenadier Battalion of Col. Francisco de Paula Vélez (under its acting commander, Manrique); Rifle Battalion under Lieutenant Colonel Sandes; "Primero de la Guardia" Cavalry Regiment under Colonel Rondón; a dragoon squadron under Lt. Col. Julián Mellado; and a hussar squadron under Col. Fernando Figueredo.

These 6,400 patriots sight 5,100 royalists awaiting them three miles away on the Carabobo Plain and its surrounding hills, under General de la Torre: Col. Tomás García's 1st Loyalist Division comprises the 1st Valencey Battalion under Lieutenant Colonel Riesco; Barbastro Light Infantry Battalion under Lieutenant Colonel Montero; Hostalrich Light Infantry Battalion under Lieutenant Colonel Illas; and "Fernando VII" Hussar Regiment under Lieutenant Colonel Calderón. General Morales's Vanguard Division includes the 2nd Burgos Battalion of Lieutenant Colonel Dalmar; "Infante don Francisco de Paula" Light Infantry Battalion of Lieutenant Colonel Sicilia; plus "Del Rey" Lancer Regiment of Lieutenant Colonel Renovales. Colonel Herrera's 5th Division consists of the "Príncipe" Light Infantry Battalion under Lieutenant Colonel de Castro; "Leales a Fernando VII" Dragoon Regiment under Lieutenant Colonel Morales; de la Torre's own regiment under Lieutenant Colonel López; plus 62 horse artillerymen under Capt. Vicente Mercadillo, for two pieces.

The Liberator sends Páez's division down a track running off to the left of the San Carlos road, passing through a narrow defile in hopes of outflanking its defenders. The patriots' Apure Battalion, backed by the British Legion and several companies of the "Tiradores" Battalion, manage to fight through after fifteen minutes of bloody exchanges, in which they lose a third of their number. At this point the insurgent cavalry charges onto the plain, putting the royalist riders to flight and rolling up their infantry, which surrenders in large numbers. Within an hour de la Torre abandons his artillery to begin an orderly retreat with his reserves and part of his cavalry toward Valencia, 20 miles distant, closely pursued by Páez's *llaneros,* plus the grenadier and rifle battalions under Bolívar. When overtaken, the Spanish general cuts his way through, although only the royalist Valencey battalion actually reaches this city intact.

Loyalist losses are estimated at 1,000 dead or wounded, plus another 1,500 captured. Patriot losses total 200 killed, mostly among the British mercenaries, and an unknown number of injuries. Generals Sedeño and Plaza, plus Colonels Farriar and Mellado, are among the dead.

25 JUNE 1821. At dawn patriot Colonel Montilla launches a surprise attack on Cartagena's beleaguered loyalist garrison in conjunction with the naval squadron under Commo. José Padilla—which has gained the inner roads thanks to the defenders' earlier retreat from Bocachica Fortress. The royalists mass all their strength to oppose a feint against their landward defenses by Col. Friedrich de Adlercreutz (a Swedish count serving the republican cause), thereby allowing Padilla to make off with 11 ships.

28 JUNE 1821. This evening Bolívar enters Caracas to a tumultuous reception and, next day, detaches Lt. Col. Diego Ibarra to occupy the nearby port of La Guaira. Ibarra is at first thwarted by the intervention of Pereira's loyalist column, which retreats when the main republican army appears.

1 JULY 1821. Bravo besieges the Mexican city of Puebla.

2 JULY 1821. Surrounded by patriot forces, loyalist commander Pereira retreats to La Guaira (Venezuela), surrendering his 700 men next day before sailing with 200 followers to Puerto Cabello aboard a French vessel; he dies shortly thereafter of yellow fever.

5 JULY 1821. Most of New Spain having joined Iturbide's call for independence, artillery Gen. Francisco Novella mutinies at the head of a group of royalist officers in Mexico City, deporting the seemingly ineffectual viceroy, Ruiz de Apodaca, toward Spain. Some 5,000 soldiers are then mustered to defend the capital.

6 JULY 1821. Peruvian Viceroy de la Serna evacuates the capital of Lima because of starvation and disease, leaving behind only 1,000 troops that are too sick to march. The insurgents arrive three days later, proclaiming independence on 28 July.

7 JULY 1821. Santa Anna storms loyalist Veracruz in a failed assault that costs him half his men, then imposes a tight siege.

10 JULY 1821. Renegade Argentine General Ramírez is overtaken at San Francisco del Chañar (110 miles north of Córdoba) by 400 republican cavalry under acting Governor Bedoya, who defeats and slays him.

11 JULY 1821. After leading a loyalist revolt in Coro (Venezuela), Spanish Lt. Col. Pedro Luis Inchauspe sorties with 800 men and attacks patriot Governor Escalona at the port of Cumarebo; he is repulsed with considerable losses.

17 JULY 1821. A group of royalists rebel at Guayaquil (Ecuador), seizing the corvette *Alejandro* and bombarding the city wharf until driven out to sea several hours later by the shore batteries under Commander Reina. The loyalists are then pursued by the patriot brig *Sacramento* and two schooners under Commander Luzarraga, who recaptures the boats.

19 JULY 1821. Patriot commander Nicolás López mutinies with his infantry battalion at Babahoyo (northeast of Guayaquil, Ecuador), marching east into the Andes to join the royalist General Aymerich at Guaranda. However, López is overtaken at Palo Largo by several of Sucre's dragoon squadrons; he fights through, but with only 170 survivors.

22 JULY 1821. Patriot Lieutenant Colonel Miller evacuates Arica (Chile), his small regiment traveling aboard two brigantines.

30 JULY 1821. The new viceroy-designate of New Spain, Lt. Gen. Juan O'Donojú, arrives to find only three cities remaining loyal to Madrid—Mexico City, Acapulco, and Veracruz—the rest having joined Iturbide's cause. Bowing to the inevitable, O'Donojú obtains safe conduct from Veracruz's besieger, Santa Anna, to travel inland. Three weeks later he signs the Treaty of Córdoba, recognizing Mexico's independence as a limited constitutional monarchy governed by a three-member regency. (The Spanish government later refuses to ratify this agreement.)

3 AUGUST 1821. Arenales's patriot army enters Lima from its Andean campaign.

4 AUGUST 1821. The armies of royalist Generals de la Serna and Canterac—4,000 sickly troops—unite at Jauja (Peru) for a last stand.

8 AUGUST 1821. Loyalist commander Inchauspe having been reinforced at Coro (Venezuela) by 500 Spanish troops from Puerto Cabello under Colonel Tello, both contingents—1,250 men—advance to attack patriot Governor Escalona at Cumarebo. However, the latter has been joined by 500 cavalry under Col. Juan Gómez, so his combined force of 800 men successfully repels the assault.

12 AUGUST 1821. ***Yaguachi.*** Sucre's 1,200-man patriot army waits on Palo Largo Plain (Ecuador) for General Aymerich's 700 royalist cavalry and 1,200 infantry, advancing from Guaranda. The latter soon appears but refuses to attack, expecting the further arrival of Colonel González's 1,000-man "Constitución" Battalion from Cuenca, to catch the patriots in a pincer.

Learning on 17 August that these loyalist reinforcements are near, Sucre retires swiftly to Yaguachi (alternately spelled Yahuachi), reconnoitering through its surrounding woods next day for González's column. On 19 August he detects it nine miles away at Cone, so brings up his main body to check its progress, while launching a surprise attack with his vanguard: Mires's Santander Battalion and a dragoon squadron. González's startled loyalists form a square in a clearing, only to be pulverized by a cavalry charge, then chased from this field by the "Albión" and Guayaquil Battalions. Spanish losses total 152 dead, 88 wounded, and 600 captured, compared to 18 killed and 22 injured among the patriots. Gónzalez escapes back across Río Nuevo with scarcely 120 followers.

Sucre then retraces his steps on 22 August toward Babahoyo, prompting Aymerich to retreat northeast into the Andes a few days later.

14 AUGUST 1821. ***Siege of Callao.*** A month after the occupation of Lima, patriot General Las Heras assaults the Pacific port of Callao with 1,200 men, only to be repelled by the 2,000-man royalist garrison under Gen. José de la Mar.

On 10 September another 3,200 royalists under Canterac slip past the 5,900 patriots guarding Lima and help themselves to Callao's huge cache of military stores. With the sickly insurgent forces powerless to intervene, Canterac then emerges six days later and marches north into Chillón Valley with his booty, trailed at a discreet distance by 800 patriot riders under Miller.

De la Mar eventually offers on 19 September to switch allegiances and surrender an empty Callao, his terms being accepted by the patriots two days later.

25 AUGUST 1821. Inchauspe surrenders to patriot Colonel Rangel at Pedregal (Venezuela), thus bringing an end to the brief loyalist insurrection at Coro.

31 AUGUST 1821. After defeating republican Gen. Bruno Morón on the banks of the Cuarto River,

Chilean-born renegade Carrera is intercepted at Médano Point on the north shore of Guanacache Lake (Argentina), while marching around Mendoza to San Juan. His contingent is overtaken by Col. José Albino Gutiérrez's cavalry and annihilated; Carrera is executed in Mendoza four days later.

EARLY SEPTEMBER 1821. Mexican forces under Isidro Montes de Oca and 31-year-old Juan N. Alvarez besiege the royalist garrison within Fort San Diego at Acapulco while Santa Anna takes Perote (near Jalapa, Veracruz).

12 SEPTEMBER 1821. ***Huachi (or Ambato).*** Having advanced northeast into the Andes following his victory at Yaguachi (Ecuador), Sucre's 100 patriot cavalry and 900 infantry are cornered at Huachi—near the town of Ambato—by 500 loyalist cavalry and 1,200 infantry under Aymerich. Hoping to fight a defensive battle from behind fences and hedges, Sucre is let down by his second-in-command, Mires, who leads the Guayaquil Battalion into the open during a heated counterattack.

Compelled to support this unit or watch it be destroyed, Sucre orders the other contingents to sally; they are defeated after five hours' heavy fighting by a two-pronged loyalist infantry assault, preceded by a heavy cavalry charge led by Spanish Col. José Moles. The patriot army is devastated, suffering more than 300 casualties and 500 captives—including Mires and many other officers. Sucre is lucky to escape with 100 men.

13 SEPTEMBER 1821. At a meeting held between Iturbide, O'Donojú, and Novella at the Pateza Hacienda near Mexico City, the latter agrees to surrender the royalist capital without a struggle.

27 SEPTEMBER 1821. Insurgent Admiral Brion dies in Amsterdam.

27 SEPTEMBER 1821. The 9,000 infantry and 7,000 cavalry of Iturbide's *Ejército Trigarante* occupy Mexico City on his birthday, effectively ending Spanish rule and marking the country's full independence. Next day Nicaragua also declares independence, followed on 29 September by El Salvador.

1 OCTOBER 1821. Loyalist Brig. Gen. Gabriel de Torres surrenders the city of Cartagena (Colombia) to 2,500 patriot besiegers under Montilla. By the terms of capitulation more than 700 Spanish officers and men are allowed to sail to Cuba.

6 OCTOBER 1821. Cochrane departs Callao, angered by the back pay owed his squadron.

15 OCTOBER 1821. In Mexico, Alvarez officially accepts the surrender of royalist Fort San Diego (Acapulco).

16 OCTOBER 1821. The Spaniards formally surrender the city of Cumaná (Venezuela) to patriot General Bermúdez, who arranges for the 800-man garrison under Caturla to be transported to Puerto Rico aboard Colombian ships.

25 OCTOBER 1821. General Dávila, still loyal to Spain's Ferdinand VII, retires offshore from Veracruz to occupy the island fortress of San Juan de Ulúa.

26 OCTOBER 1821. Spanish Gen. Juan de la Cruz Mourgeon departs Panama with 800 regulars to reinforce South America, reaching Quito (Ecuador) the day before Christmas.

6 NOVEMBER 1821. The loyalist commander Carrera besieges Col. Juan Gómez's patriot garrison within Coro (Venezuela). On the third day of the siege patriot Cmdr. León Pérez fights his way inside with a relief column; next day the combined forces scatter the besiegers.

12 NOVEMBER 1821. Learning that Chiapas has declared independence and wishes to become incorporated into Mexico, Iturbide dispatches 5,000 soldiers under the Conde de la Cadena to ensure it is accomplished peacefully.

19 NOVEMBER 1821. At Babahoyo (Ecuador), Sucre signs a temporary armistice with Aymerich's representative, Col. Carlos Tolrá, whereby the royalists agree to retire into the Andes around Riobamba while the patriots remain at their coastal stronghold of Guayaquil.

22 NOVEMBER 1821. Juan Lindo, insurgent leader at Comayagua (Honduras), announces his country's incorporation into Mexico.

28 NOVEMBER 1821. Panama declares independence from Spain and opts to become part of Colombia.

7 DECEMBER 1821. Royalist Colonel Lórida defeats 300 badly armed insurgent militia and 5,000 Indians at Cerro de Pasco (Peru).

17 DECEMBER 1821. Royalist Colonel Carratalá torches the rebel town of Cangallo (Peru).

29 DECEMBER 1821. Certain factions in Guatemala City and Quezaltenango request to become incorporated into Mexico.

9 JANUARY 1822. The former Spanish captain general of Guatemala, Gabino Gaínza, announces the union of Central America.

11 JANUARY 1822. The Spanish frigates *Venganza* and *Prueba* contact Sucre at Guayaquil, offering to switch allegiance and join the insurgent cause in return for payments to their crews. Four days later they receive 80,000 pesos and become incorporated into Peru's navy under orders from San Martín.

12 JANUARY 1822. ***Brazilian Schism.*** At Rio de Janeiro, 23-year-old Prince Pedro refuses to acknowledge the Portuguese *Cortes*'s recall to Lisbon and its peremptory relegation of Brazil to secondary status within the empire. However, Lt. Gen. Jorge Avilez's d'El Rei Regiment—2,000 Portuguese regulars recently returned from service at Montevideo—then proclaims its intention of embarking this evening for Europe, taking the prince.

Thousands of Brazilian militia, black Henriques guerrillas, and Indian units mass to contest this threat, prompting Avilez to call for their disbandment. Pedro refuses, attempts to replace the general, then on 14 January orders his regiment off the commanding Flagstaff Hill into Praia Grande, across Rio's bay. A lengthy standoff ensues; Pedro finally addresses Avilez through a speaking trumpet from the frigate *União* on 9 February, commanding his men to depart, which the Portuguese general grudgingly obeys by 15 February. As he sails away, Brazil prepares to assume full independence—with Pedro as its emperor.

29 JANUARY 1822. Cochrane appears outside Acapulco, hunting for the Spanish frigates *Venganza* and *Prueba*. Learning three days later that they are at Guayaquil, he steers southeast.

9 FEBRUARY 1822. Sucre reaches Saraguro (Ecuador) with 1,200 patriot troops, who are to be reinforced by two infantry battalions and two cavalry squadrons sent by San Martín under Bolivian-born Col. Andrés Santa Cruz. With his strength thus raised to 3,000 men, Sucre is to then advance north into the Andes and eliminate the royalist defenders under Aymerich.

19 FEBRUARY 1822. Portuguese Gen. Inacio Luiz Madeira de Melo seizes control of the port city of Salvador (Brazil) at a cost of 100 killed, holding it in Lisbon's name against the rising tide of Brazilian nationalism.

25 FEBRUARY 1822. Bolívar's 3,000 troops begin marching out of Popayán (Colombia) to help push back the royalists in the southwestern theater.

2 APRIL 1822. Spanish Lt. Col. Francisco Buceli rises against Mexican rule at Juchi but is put down next day.

7 APRIL 1822. ***Bomboná.*** While circling around Galeras Volcano to approach the royalist stronghold of Pasto (Colombia) from the south, Bolívar's army is confronted by Col. Basilio García's 2,000 men from the 1st Aragón, 2nd Cataluña, and Pasto Battalions plus two field pieces and some irregulars, which are dug in atop the Cariaco Heights. The patriot vanguard—Vargas and Bogotá Battalions under Gen. Pedro León Torres—makes a belated attack against the defenders' center-left at noon, only to be repulsed and Torres himself mortally wounded. Col. Luis Carvajal then leads a second republican assault, which is also repelled, the colonel being injured.

Meanwhile Gen. Manuel Valdés is leading the patriots' Rifles Battalion in a flanking maneuver around the Yusepe Heights to fall upon García's right. When Bolívar sees Valdés gain the summit he orders a third frontal assault, by José Ignacio Pulido's Vencedor Battalion. Caught in a crossfire, the royalist right breaks, leading to a wholesale retreat by García's division. Nevertheless, the 250 royalist casualties are much less than the republican losses—116 dead and 341 wounded; the Liberator is therefore forced to retrace his steps across the Juanambú River and await reinforcements from Popayán.

7 APRIL 1822. ***Macacona.*** Learning of a 2,000-man royalist army under Canterac advancing west from Mantaro Valley (Peru) and a 500-man contingent under Valdéz approaching from Arequipa, rebel General Tristán—once a staunch monarchist (*see* 20 June 1811 and subsequent entries)—evacuates Ica on 6 April with his own 2,000 troops. At Macacona (north of Ica), he is ambushed at 1:00 A.M. next day by Canterac, who captures 1,000 rebels and scatters the rest.

21 APRIL 1822. High in the Andes, the cavalry under Lavalle—vanguard of Sucre's 2,400-man patriot army—scatters the screen of royalist defenders around Riobamba (Ecuador), killing 52 and wounding 40.

8 MAY 1822. The United States recognizes the independence of Argentina, Chile, Colombia, Mexico, and Peru.

23 MAY 1822. ***Pichincha.*** This evening Sucre arrives before the royalist stronghold of Quito (Ecuador) with 500 infantrymen of the Trujillo battalion; 400 of Piura Battalion; 260 of Yaguachi Battalion; 600 of Paya Battalion; 200 of "Albión" Battalion; plus 200 of Magdalena Battalion. His cavalry consists of 100 mounted grenadiers, 100 dragoons, and 200 others. Forty gunners man two field pieces.

Circling west as night falls to cut off reinforcement from the north, the patriots oblige General Aymerich to redeploy his own 1,700 defenders toward the base of Mount Pichincha, and reluctantly prepare for battle.

Next day Sucre defeats the royalists in several hours' fighting, killing 400 and wounding 200, while suffering 200 dead and 140 injured among his own ranks. Realizing further resistance is futile, Aymerich capitulates by 25 August, surrendering his 1,260 survivors, 14 cannons, 1,700 muskets, and all the ammunition and supplies within Quito.

7 JUNE 1822. Spanish General Morales sorties from Puerto Cabello and defeats a patriot force under Soublette at Dabajuro (Venezuela).

8 JUNE 1822. At 5:00 P.M. Bolívar's 2,000-man army enters Pasto (Colombia) unopposed, the loyalist garrison agreeing to capitulate because of Sucre's recent conquest of Quito.

14 JULY 1822. San Martín departs Callao aboard the sloop *Macedonia* to meet Bolívar at Guayaquil.

25 JULY 1822. Bolívar and San Martín meet at Guayaquil to discuss the future of South America. Generally speaking, San Martín favors a constitutional monarchy, whereas Bolívar favors republican forms of government. San Martín asks Bolívar to help eliminate the last royalist strongholds high in the Andes, but the latter refuses.

12 AUGUST 1822. Spanish General Morales is defeated at Naguanagua (Venezuela) by Páez while marching from Puerto Cabello to Valencia at the head of 1,800 loyalists.

27 AUGUST 1822. A trio of Portuguese warships arrives off Salvador, evading the ineffectual blockade of Brazilian Commo. Rodrigo Lamare and disembarking 600 troops to reinforce the loyalist garrison under General Madeira. Prince Pedro, returning to São Paulo from Santos, learns of this escalation of hostilities 11 days later and proclaims Brazil's full independence from Portugal.

7 SEPTEMBER 1822. After sailing with a royalist expedition from Puerto Cabello, Morales disembarks on the Guajira Peninsula and defeats patriot General Clemente at Salina Rica (Venezuela), occupying nearby Maracaibo the next day.

20 SEPTEMBER 1822. San Martín resigns as "protector of Peru," and next day sets sail from Callao to Chile aboard the brigantine *Belgrano* to retire at his small farm near Mendoza (Argentina).

17 OCTOBER 1822. Patriot General Alvarado sets sail from Callao to attack the royalist stronghold of Arica (Chile).

LATE OCTOBER 1822. Led by the royalist Benito Boves, Pasto (Colombia) rises against insurgent rule.

6 NOVEMBER 1822. Portuguese Commo. Félix de Campos brings another 1,200 reinforcements into the loyalist stronghold at Salvador (Brazil), aboard the 74-gun ship *Dom João VI* and frigate *Perola*.

1 DECEMBER 1822. Throwing off all allegiance to Portugal, Pedro I is proclaimed emperor of Brazil.

6 DECEMBER 1822. A 4,300-man, ten-gun patriot expedition under Alvarado disembarks at Arica (Chile) without opposition, remaining 20 days while gathering mounts to press north against royalist forces.

23 DECEMBER 1822. ***Fall of Pasto.*** After many skirmishes, Sucre's 1,500-man patriot army fights its way across Guáitara Bridge and advances to Taindala to put down Boves's loyalist insurrection at Pasto (Colombia). The latter attempts a brief stand at Yacuanquer but is brushed aside by Sandes's rifle battalion.

Next day the 2,000-man Pasto garrison requests terms, but Sucre ignores the overture and instead launches a two-pronged offensive at noon intended to seize the commanding heights and Santiago Church. After a desperate struggle the defenders break and flee to Sebondoy or Juanambú, leaving behind 300 dead. Sucre's losses total eight dead and 32 injured; after three days of looting he proclaims a general amnesty.

Brazilian Emperor Pedro I

29 DECEMBER 1822. The vanguard of Alvarado's patriot army—1,000 men under General Martínez—advances north from Arica and occupies Tacna (Peru). Three days later royalist commander Valdéz attempts a surprise dawn attack; but after becoming lost in the darkness his 800 troops arrive well past sunup, so Valdéz instead prudently withdraws to Moquegua by 10 January 1823.

14 JANUARY 1823. A royalist detachment under Colonel Ameller fails to prevent Alvarado's large patriot army from crossing the Locumba River (southern Peru).

19 JANUARY 1823. ***Torata-Moquegua.*** After being driven out of Moquegua (or Moquehua, southern Peru) by Alvarado's advance, Valdéz's 1,000 outnumbered royalists make a stand at nearby Torata, hoping to be joined by two approaching infantry battalions and four cavalry squadrons under Canterac. Alvarado engages and seems on the verge of achieving victory when Canterac's cavalry suddenly materializes and puts the patriots to flight. Alvarado suffers 500 casualties—double the royalist number.

Two days later Canterac and Valdéz storm the disorganized patriot army within Moquegua, engaging it with a frontal assault and winning the day by driving in Alvarado's right flank. More than 1,000 patriots are subsequently taken prisoner—including 60 senior officers—while the survivors flee to the coast. Lavalle's division of Andean grenadiers is one of the few patriot formations to maintain cohesion, repeatedly fighting rearguard actions. Alvarado goes aboard ship at Ilo with only 500 men, escaping north to Callao.

28 JANUARY 1823. Surrounded by mutinies and surly resistance, Chile's dictator, O'Higgins, resigns.

13 MARCH 1823. Cochrane, having quit the Chilean service amid complaints about official corruption, reaches Rio de Janeiro and agrees to assume command of Brazil's newly independent navy: 74-gun *Pedro Primeiro;* 62-gun frigates *Piranga, Real Carolina* of 44, and *Niterói* of 38; corvettes *Maria da Gloria* of 26, *Liberal* and *Maceio* of 20; brigs *Caboclo* of 18, *Cacique* of 16, *Real Pedro* and *Guaraní* of 14; plus the ten-gun brigantines *Real, Atlanta,* and *Rio de Plata.*

18 MARCH 1823. In order to repair Alvarado's disastrous losses in southern Peru, patriot General Valdés leads 2,400 troops aboard the transports *Proserpina, Cornelia, San Juan, Bomboná, Flecha, Sacramento, Sofía,* and *Chimborazo.* The bulk of the expedition is composed of Jacinto Lara's brigade ("Vencedor en Boyacá," Voltíjeros, and Pichincha Battalions).

20 MARCH 1823. Gen. Gregorio Tagle leads a dawn uprising in Buenos Aires against the anti-ecclesiastical reforms promulgated by Argentina's republican government on 18 November 1822. His 200 followers, including Colonels Bauzá and Viera, are quickly crushed.

1 APRIL 1823. Cochrane sets sail from Rio de Janeiro with the Brazilian *Pedro Primeiro* (flag), *Piranga, Maria de Gloria,* and *Liberal* to blockade the Portuguese garrison holding Salvador (*see* 19 February 1822).

12 APRIL 1823. Sandes departs Guayaquil with 1,250 men of the Bomboná Rifles and 1st de la Guardia Bat-

talions aboard the transports *Rosa, Perla, Dolores,* and *Mirlo* to take part in a second patriot expedition under Generals Santa Cruz and Gamarra against royalist forces in southern Peru. The frigate *O'Higgins* follows a few days later with another 300 troops; 582 more arrive on 18 April aboard three other transports.

4 MAY 1823. Cochrane's Brazilian squadron skirmishes inconclusively with de Campos's Portuguese warships outside beleaguered Salvador, neither side being able to gain any decisive advantage because of their green and disaffected crews. When the Portuguese commodore withdraws inside the inner roads of Baía de Todos os Santos, Cochrane retires 30 miles south to São Paulo Fortress and concentrates all his veteran British and American sailors aboard *Pedro Primeiro* (flag) and *Maria da Gloria,* so as to provide at least two reliable vessels. By the end of the month he is joined off Salvador by Capt. James Thompson's *Real Carolina,* plus *Niterói* and the brig *Bahia* toward the end of June.

11 MAY 1823. Col. León Galindo departs Guayaquil with 668 men of his Bogotá Battalion aboard the brig *Balcarce,* sloop *Armonia,* and another transport to take part in the Santa Cruz–Gamarra expedition to subdue royalist forces in southern Peru. Galindo's contingent is followed three days later by another 250 men aboard the frigate *Brown* plus 200 recruits from Pasto and Chocó aboard the English brig *Romeo.* (The latter mutiny off Muerto Island, kill some of their officers, then compel the English master to deposit them at Esmeraldas on the Atacames coast.) On 15 May the brig *Chimborazo* sails with 250 Venezuelan Hussars and mounted grenadiers, the entire division being commanded by Col. Luis Urdaneta.

Eventually, Santa Cruz's expedition swells to 5,100 men and eight field pieces; he disembarks at Ilo in mid-June with the main body while detaching subordinate Gamarra to Arica with another contingent. Gamarra establishes his base of operations at Tacna; Santa Cruz chooses Moquegua.

2 JUNE 1823. Having gathered 9,000 troops and 14 field pieces at Huancayo (Peru), royalist Generals Canterac and Valdéz descend from the Andes to drive on Lima during the absence of the main patriot armies farther south.

12 JUNE 1823. Patriot Col. Juan José Flores sorties from Pasto (Colombia) to subdue yet another local insurrection. Instead, 600 rebels fall upon his column three miles south of there—at Catambuco—killing 300 and capturing 200 of his troops in ferocious hand-to-hand combat.

18 JUNE 1823. ***Royalist Seizure of Lima.*** Canterac and Valdéz surprise and occupy Lima with 9,000 loyalists, while Sucre's 5,000 patriots must retire behind Callao's coastal defenses. Despite their easy victory the invaders are unable to remain inside the capital for want of provisions; they therefore begin an evacuation to Jauja and Huancavelica by 1 July, completing it two weeks later.

2 JULY 1823. ***Fall of Salvador.*** After more than a year's siege and blockade, General Madeira and Commodore de Campos decide to evacuate Bahia as their supplies have become exhausted, and Cochrane is threatening a fireship attack with his Brazilian squadron. Some 13 Portuguese warships therefore exit this harbor, escorting 60–70 troop transports with 2,000 soldiers and many noncombatants. Behind them, jubilant Brazilian irregulars surge into the now empty streets.

Cochrane's five warships then pursue this fleeing Portuguese convoy north to prevent it from reinforcing the last loyalist holdouts in Maranhão Province. Due to an insufficiency of skilled seamen, the chasing squadron must cripple many of its prizes by cutting down their masts or staving in water casks, obliging them to return into Bahia to be secured. The frigate *Niterói* of Capt. John Taylor (a 30-year-old Royal Navy deserter, former first lieutenant of Sir Thomas Hardy's flagship HMS *Doris*) even pursues some vessels as far as Portugal, burning four within sight of Lisbon itself. Altogether, 16 ships bearing 1,000 troops are taken.

13 JULY 1823. Sucre sends patriot General Alvarado by ship from Callao with 2,000 soldiers of Lara's brigade to reinforce Santa Cruz. They are followed by 1,200 more under Gen. Francisco Antonio Pinto, consisting of the 2nd and 4th Chilean Battalions plus two cavalry squadrons and four field pieces.

17 JULY 1823. ***Ibarra.*** In order to crush the recurrent Pasto (Colombia) rebellions, Bolívar marches swiftly north from San Pablo with 1,500 men to attack 2,000 rebels gathered at Ibarra (Ecuador) under Agustín Agualongo. He attacks their right flank by 2:00 P.M., quickly driving the rebels across Tahoando Creek and up Aluburo Hill. Agualongo's troops finally break and flee, leaving behind 600 dead compared to 13 killed and eight wounded among Bolívar's ranks.

20 JULY 1823. Sucre sails from Callao to Arequipa with 3,000 troops, to join Santa Cruz in subduing the royalist resistance in Upper Peru (Bolivia).

23 JULY 1823. Santa Cruz marches inland from Moquegua (Peru); while his subordinate Gamarra does the same from Tacna. Their objective is to ascend the Andes and occupy the royalist stronghold of La Paz (Bolivia), which Santa Cruz reaches by 8 August. Next day Gamarra appears 20 miles south, at Viacha, turning on 12 August to pursue the outnumbered royalist army under Olañeta, which is retiring to Oruro.

26 JULY 1823. Hastening past the defeated Portuguese troop convoy that has evacuated Bahia (*see* 2 July 1823), Cochrane enters the loyalist stronghold of São Luis—capital of Maranhão Province—with false colors flying from his 74-gun Brazilian flagship *Pedro Primeiro.* Once anchored in a commanding position Cochrane bluffs Gov. Agostinho António de Faria into surrendering; for this feat, Brazil's emperor ennobles the admiral as marques de Maranhão.

2 AUGUST 1823. Sucre's expedition reaches Chala, steering to Arequipa upon receiving news of Santa Cruz's movements.

3 AUGUST 1823. Besieged within Maracaibo by both land and sea, Spanish General Morales surrenders to the patriots.

10 AUGUST 1823. Cochrane's flag lieutenant, John Pascoe Grenfell, enters the loyalist port of Belém (eastern mouth of the Amazon River), his Brazilian brig *Maranhão* flying false Portuguese colors until safely at anchor. He compels the cowed civic leaders to declare independence.

Five days later rioters begin looting the warehouses of Portuguese merchants, only to have Grenfell's crewmembers intervene; they arrest 261 participants, shoot five ringleaders, and incarcerate the remaining 256 aboard a ship out in the harbor. During the ensuing night 255 die in the stifling hold, the guards misinterpreting their agitation as a prelude to a rising.

25 AUGUST 1823. ***Zepita.*** After falling back from Carratalá three days earlier, Valdéz's 1,900 royalists are overtaken at the town of Zepita (southwestern shore of Lake Titicaca) by Santa Cruz's 2,500 patriots. Both sides fight an indecisive battle with minor casualties, before retiring after nightfall. Patriot losses total 28 dead and 84 wounded; Valdéz suffers 100 killed and 184 captured.

31 AUGUST 1823. Sucre lands and occupies Arequipa (Peru), contacting Santa Cruz inland to propose a joint operation against the royalists in Upper Peru (modern-day Bolivia), which is refused.

1 SEPTEMBER 1823. Bolívar reaches Callao aboard the frigate *Chimborazo;* a fortnight later he assumes office as Peru's governor.

8 SEPTEMBER 1823. ***Santa Cruz's Flight.*** The patriot armies under Santa Cruz and Gamarra reunite at Panduro (some 20 miles north of Oruro, Bolivia), marching south 4,500 strong. Four days later a 4,000-man royalist army circles east of Sora Sora under Viceroy de la Serna and General Valdéz; on 14 September it joins Olañeta's contingent approaching from Potosí, thereby giving a combined strength of 6,500 men.

Learning of this formidable host, Santa Cruz and Gamarra hastily retreat northwest, hoping to find Sucre near Lake Titicaca. The patriots are overtaken by royalist pursuers near Ayo Ayo on 17 September, and Santa Cruz contemplates making a stand. However, when informed his artillery has not yet arrived he renews the retreat, which quickly degenerates into a rout. His troops—now desperate to flee the highlands—fall easy prey to the enemy. Some 2,000 are taken prisoner along with all the patriot guns and the artillery and supply trains (captured at Desaguadero Ford on 20 September). Santa Cruz reenters Moquegua by 24 September with 900 weary survivors, immediately continuing on to Ilo to sail away.

27 SEPTEMBER 1823. Sucre is 24 miles northeast of Arequipa (Peru) when informed of Santa Cruz's rout. The patriot general retraces his route back to the coast and sails off with his army by 12 October.

8 NOVEMBER 1823. The loyalist garrison at Puerto Cabello (Venezuela) capitulates to the insurgents.

11 NOVEMBER 1823. Bolívar departs northwest from Lima with 4,800 troops to put down the mutinous patriot José de la Riva Agüero, headquartered around Huaráz and Trujillo (Peru). Two weeks later Riva Agüero is arrested at dawn by one of his subordinates—Col. Antonio Gutiérrez de la Fuente—who believes the rebel and his ministers are about to strike a pact with the Spanish loyalists at Jauja.

12 NOVEMBER 1823. Brazil's Emperor Pedro I uses troops to dissolve the legislature; many delegates are arrested.

10 DECEMBER 1823. Spanish Brig. Gen. Juan Loriga occupies Cerro de Pasco (Peru) with 350 loyalist cavalry and 300 infantry, only to retire to Jauja shortly thereafter upon receiving word of Riva Agüero's arrest.

5 FEBRUARY 1824. ***Callao Mutiny.*** The unpaid Argentine Río de la Plata Regiment—performing garrison duty in the Peruvian port of Callao—rises in rebellion and detains Col. Ramón Estomba and the fortress commander, Rudecindo Alvarado. The mutineers are joined next day by Callao's 11th Infantry Battalion and artillery companies; when threatened with harsh reprisals they place themselves under the royalist Colonel Casariego (who has been confined in one of the fort's dungeons), offering to surrender the place to the loyalists.

When the mounted Grenadiers of the Andes Regiment is ordered to ride from Cañete on 14 February to help put down the insurrection, it too mutinies at Lurín, arresting officers and professing loyalty to the crown.

After first suspecting a trap, royalist General Canterac at last dispatches a column under Brig. Gen. Juan Antonio Monet from Jauja in the central highlands to secure this prize. Monet arrives after a two-day march from Lurín on 29 February, his approach prompting Bolívar's weak and divided government to evacuate Lima in favor of Pativilca. The capital is thus briefly reoccupied by the royalists, who forsake it again on 18 March—although Callao remains under Brig. Gen. José Ramón Rodil for the next two years.

8 APRIL 1824. Having been dispatched by Brazilian Emperor Pedro I to put down a republican election at Recife (Pernambuco Province), Captain Taylor attempts to persuade Gov. Manoel de Carvalho País de Andrade to install a royalist candidate; when that is refused he institutes a blockade with the frigates *Niterói* and *Piranha.*

20 JUNE 1824. Royalist General Olañeta refuses to obey Viceroy de la Serna's orders in Upper Peru (Bolivia); Valdéz is therefore sent to deal with the rebellious officer.

28 JUNE 1824. Taylor lifts his blockade of Recife (Brazil) in order to rejoin Admiral Cochrane, who is concentrating his forces against a threatened invasion from Portugal.

2 JULY 1824. Carvalho declares Pernambuco to be an independent republic then sends two vessels under John Mitrovich (a Maltese deserter from the Royal Navy) to invest Barra Grande. The vessels are captured on 25 July by an imperial Brazilian schooner.

2 AUGUST 1824. Cochrane sails from Rio de Janeiro with his squadron, transporting 1,200 Brazilian troops to put down the separatist republican regime in Pernambuco. He deposits the royalist contingent at Alagoas (80 miles short of Recife) by 10 August, arriving off the latter port on 18 August to institute a blockade. After failing to come to terms with its leader, Carvalho, the admiral shells Recife with his schooner *Leopoldina;* the overland arrival of Pedro's 1,200 troops effectively ends the insurrection by mid-September. A few executions ensue, Carvalho fleeing into exile aboard HMS *Tweed.*

5 AUGUST 1824. ***Junín.*** Two days after departing Cerro de Pasco (Peru), Bolívar's 9,600 patriots reach

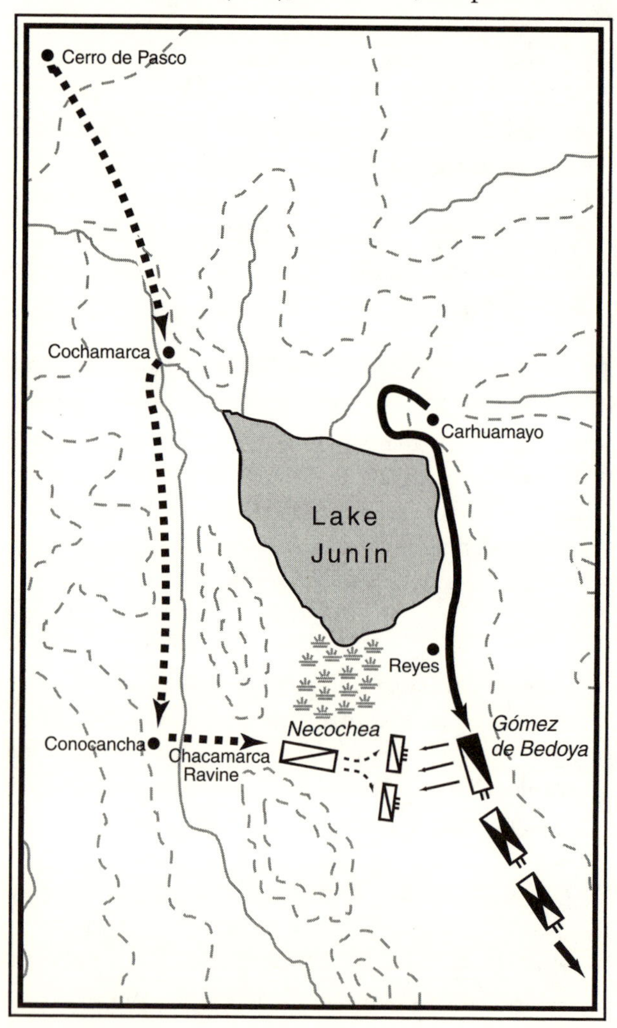

Battle of Junín

Conocancha, only to discover that Canterac's 7,000–8,000 royalists have been circling around the far side of Lake Junín toward their previous base. The Liberator therefore turns east, while his opponent Canterac—surprised to learn at Carhuamayo that the patriots have already sallied—now hastily retraces his steps, hoping to avoid a flank attack.

On 6 August the patriot army begins to advance through Chacamarca Ravine with Necochea's 900 cavalry six miles in advance of Bolívar's main body. Upon disgorging into Junín Plain, Necochea is attacked by 1,300 royalist troopers under Ramón Gómez de Bedoya who are screening Canterac's retirement. The six squadrons overwhelm the two squadrons of mounted Colombian grenadiers in the patriot vanguard then drive the remainder back through the ravine's narrow confines. However, the charging royalist troopers are in turn surprised by a flank attack from Lt. Col. Isidoro Suárez's Peruvian Hussars, who chase Bedoya's men back through the ravine toward the fleeing royalist army. Neither side engages with their infantry or artillery, only cavalry charges being involved, and losses are light on both sides: 248 royalist troopers dead, wounded, and missing, as opposed to a comparable number of patriots.

Nevertheless, Canterac's precipitate flight shatters the morale of his followers, some 3,000 dropping out by the time he recrosses the Apurimac River. Bolívar meanwhile proceeds to Chalhuanca then, in early October, turns over command of his army to Sucre to travel to Lima.

17 AUGUST 1824. Spanish General Valdéz's 3,000-man army defeats a column from Olañeta's rebellious royalist faction at Lava (Bolivia) then is recalled to Cuzco by Viceroy de la Serna to prepare for a forthcoming campaign against Sucre.

6 OCTOBER 1824. At Callao, the loyalist corvette *Ica,* plus brigs *Pezuela, Constante,* and *Moyano*—having been reinforced from Europe by the 64-gun Spanish ship of the line *Asia* and brig *Aquiles* of Commo. Roque Guruceta—are challenged by Rear Adm. Martín Jorge Guise with the insurgent frigate *Protector,* corvette *Pichincha,* brig *Chimborazo,* and sloops *Macedonia* and *Guayaquileña.* This Colombian-Peruvian squadron drops anchor off San Lorenzo Island, provoking the Spaniards into emerging next day and engaging in an inconclusive exchange of long-range salvos. Both sides then observe each other until 22 October, when they withdraw—the patriots north toward Guayaquil, the two Spanish warships south.

(A month and a half later, after Sucre's victory at Ayacucho, *Asia* and *Constante* attempt to cross the Pacific to the Philippines; their crews mutiny in the Marianas, however, and Guruceta's flagship is eventually handed over to the Mexican authorities at Acapulco. *Aquiles*'s crew also rises against its captain, surrendering later to the Chileans.)

10 OCTOBER 1824. Valdéz rejoins Viceroy de la Serna at Cuzco with 3,000 men of the 1st and 2nd Gerona Battalions, Imperial Alejandro Battalion, 1st Cuzco Regiment, 2nd Fernando VII Regiment, plus four squadrons of the de la Guardia mounted grenadiers and another of Peruvian dragoons. The concentration gives the royalists a numerical superiority over Sucre's approaching patriot army.

22 OCTOBER 1824. De la Serna and Valdéz quit Paruro with 11,200 royalists, leaving behind another 1,800 to garrison nearby Cuzco, then cross the Apumirac River at Agcha and advance against Sucre. Detecting the approach of this host ten days later, Sucre retires north to Andahuaylas Province.

3 NOVEMBER 1824. After Urdaneta reoccupies Lima a patriot contingent advancing on the nearby seaport of Callao is ambushed and scattered at La Legua by two royalist cavalry squadrons and four infantry companies. Bolívar appears shortly thereafter, however, and with 3,000 patriot troops reimposes a siege against the isolated 2,700-man royalist garrison inside Callao—comprising two infantry battalions, a cavalry squadron, artillery brigade, and some irregulars.

9 NOVEMBER 1824. Cochrane intervenes in the civil strife at Maranão (Brazil), deposing Miguel Bruce in favor of Manuel Lobo, to little effect.

20 NOVEMBER 1824. Discovering de la Serna's larger royalist army has swung southwest behind him, Sucre turns his own 6,000 men around and digs in on Bombón Heights. Through clever maneuvering, de la Serna is able to trick the patriot general into believing he is about to be attacked from the rear; the latter therefore forsakes his strong position four days later and slowly retires farther west.

3 DECEMBER 1824. In Collpahuayco Ravine (Peru), Valdéz's royalist cavalry defeats a patriot rifle battalion from Lara's brigade, part of Sucre's rearguard. The patriots suffer 300 casualties and lose a field piece.

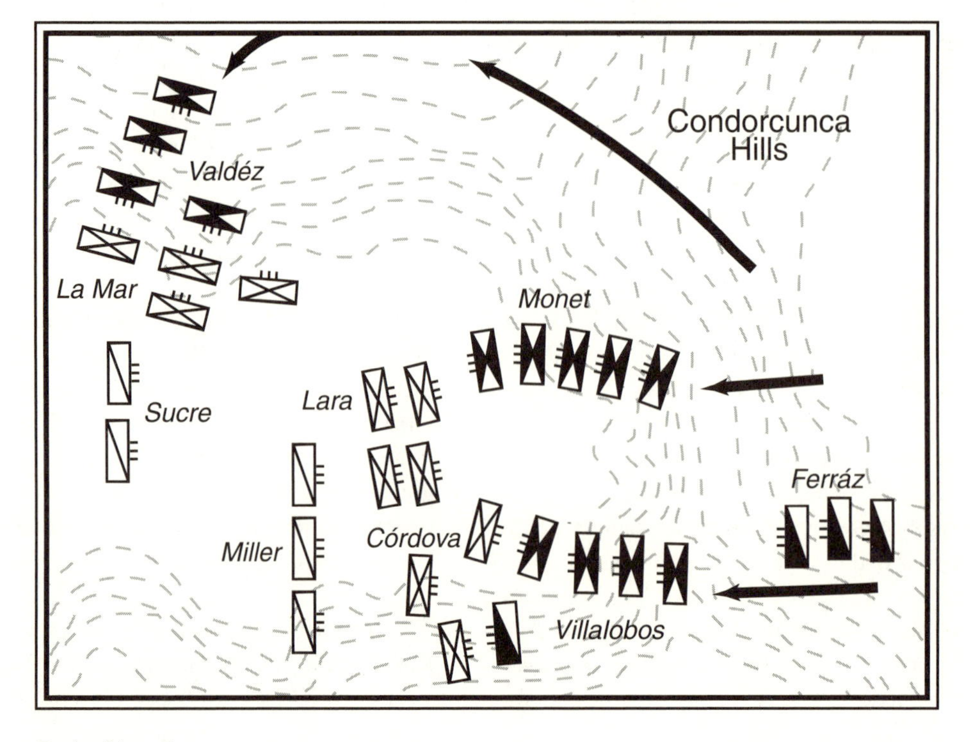

Battle of Ayacucho

6 DECEMBER 1824. ***Ayacucho.*** Sucre's 5,800 retreating patriots and single field piece reach Quinua Plain—called Ayacucho by local Indians—seven miles from Huamanga (modern-day Ayacucho, Peru) and take up defensive positions: Marshal de la Mar's Peruvian Infantry Legion under Colonel Plaza, 1st Infantry Battalion of Lieutenant Colonel Bermúdez, 2nd Infantry Battalion of Lieutenant Colonel González, and 3rd Infantry Battalion of Lieutenant Colonel Benavides; Colombian General Lara's "Vencedor en Boyacá" Infantry Battalion under Col. Ignacio Luque, Vargas Infantry Battalion of Col. José Trinidad Morán, plus Sandes's Rifle Battalion; Colombian Gen. José María Córdova's Bogotá Infantry Battalion under Colonel Galindo, Pichincha Infantry Battalion of Col. José Leal, *Voltíjeros* Battalion of Colonel Guas(?), and Caracas Infantry Battalion of Col. Manuel León. General Miller's cavalry division consists of two squadrons of Colombian hussars under Colonel Silva, two of Colombian horse grenadiers under Col. Lucas Carvajal, two of Junín Hussars under Lieutenant Colonel Suárez, plus one of Argentine horse grenadiers under Lieutenant Colonel Bogado.

Two days later, their 9,300 royalist pursuers and eleven cannons approach out of the northeast under Viceroy de la Serna to encamp on Condorcunca Hills. On 9 December, the royalists drive across Ayacucho Plain in three columns: General Valdéz's vanguard division, consisting of 1st "Imperial Alejandro," 1st Castro, 1st Centro, and 1st Cantabria Infantry Battalions; Marshal Monet's first division, being 2nd "Primer Regimiento de Cuzco," 2nd Burgos, 2nd Guías (Tacnena Legion), 2nd "Victoria," and 2nd "Infante" Infantry Battalions; plus Marshal Alejandro Villalobos's second division, comprising 1st Gerona, 1st "Primer Regimiento de Cuzco," 2nd "Imperial Alejandro," and "Fernando VII" Infantry Battalions. These are supported by Brig. Gen. Valentín Ferráz's cavalry division—two squadrons of mounted Grenadiers of the Guard, three of "Fernando VII" Hussars, three of *Dragones de la Unión,* two of Peruvian dragoons, plus one each of the San Carlos Cavalry Regiment and Viceregal Halberdiers—as well as an artillery battalion under General Cacho and engineering battalion under General Atero.

As this battle becomes joined, Villalobos's division on the left is repelled by Córdova's Colombians; the same occurs to Monet's royalists in the center when counterattacked by Suárez's Junín Hussars and Bruix's mounted grenadiers. Only Valdéz's division on the royalist right does well initially, driving back de la Mar's Peruvians. However, the patriot cavalry soon bests their royalist counterpart, so that when de la Serna commits his reserves—the Fernando VII battalion—these are also defeated, and the wounded viceroy captured. Seeing this, Valdéz's division begins a disorganized retirement, and the royalists flee back into the hills, having suffered 1,800 killed and 700 wounded, compared to 310 dead and 609 injured among the patriots.

A caricature of the insurgent triumph over the royalist cause

This night Canterac assumes command of de la Serna's defeated survivors and attempts to order the royalists to march back toward Cuzco. Instead his demoralized forces mutiny; next day the remaining 1,000 royalists surrender to Sucre, bringing organized resistance to Spanish American independence to a virtual end.

12 DECEMBER 1824. After a brief pause Sucre inaugurates a campaign into Bolivia to stamp out the last sparks of royalist resistance. He encounters no opposition, General Alvarez tamely surrendering the 1,700-man royalist garrison at Cuzco to Gamarra two weeks later. The same occurs at Arequipa, where the self-proclaimed viceroy, Domingo Pío Tristán, capitulates with 700 troops, followed shortly thereafter by Brigadier General Echeverría at Puno with another 480. Only Olañeta continues to pose a threat, with 5,900 troops concentrated around La Paz.

10 JANUARY 1825. The republican frigate *O'Higgins* appears off Callao and is eventually joined by *Pichincha, Chimborazo, Moctezuma, Limeña, Macedonia,* and *Congreso del Perú* to blockade the last remaining royalist outpost.

14 JANUARY 1825. Olañeta's garrison commander at Cochabamba (Bolivia)—Col. A. S. Sánchez—throws off Olañeta's rule and proclaims himself in favor of republicanism.

1 FEBRUARY 1825. Republican guerrilla chief José Miguel Lanza occupies La Paz (Bolivia), obliging Olañeta to fall back to Potosí.

7 FEBRUARY 1825. Sucre reaches La Paz.

12 FEBRUARY 1825. Olañeta's garrison in Valle Grande (Bolivia) mutinies and detains General Aguilera.

16 FEBRUARY 1825. Gen. Bartolomé Salom's patriot besiegers defeat a sally by Rodil's garrison out of Callao, inflicting 200 casualties.

22 FEBRUARY 1825. Olañeta's subordinate, Col. Francisco López, mutinies at Chuquisaca (Bolivia) with a squadron of Charcas Dragoons, proclaiming himself governor. This brings the number of soldiers

who have switched allegiance from Olañeta's royalist cause to 1,800.

1 APRIL 1825. Royalist General Olañeta is mortally wounded at Tumusla (Bolivia) while attempting to put down a mutiny by a chasseur battalion under Colonel Medina Celi.

18 MAY 1825. Cochrane deserts the Brazilian service, sailing from São Luis with the frigate *Piranha;* he reaches Spithead (England) by 26 June.

23 JANUARY 1826. After nearly two years' resistance, royalist General Rodil finally surrenders his isolated garrison at Callao to the Peruvian authorities; this same month Chile's last loyalist holdouts surrender in remote Chiloé Archipelago, thus marking an end to Spanish America's 18-year struggle for independence. Ominously, the last few years have been marred by internal bickering among republican ranks—a portent of the bitter civil wars to follow.

Part 7: Nationhood (1812–1897)

Remember our maxim:
it is better to do well late, than never.
—Sam Houston (1835)

WAR OF 1812 (1812–1815)

ALTHOUGH THE UNITED STATES (population 7.5 million) had previously fought a limited "quasi-war" against France—*see* French Revolutionary Wars in Part 6—the War of 1812 has the distinction of being the first full-scale conflict conducted by an independent New World government against an international foe.

For several years, neutral American shipping has been harassed by England's Royal Navy in its attempts to throttle Napoleonic France and its satellites. Settlers in the American South and West further complain of British trade restrictions creating economic depressions throughout their regions, and Indian resistance to American expansion inland—especially under the 43-year-old Shawnee chief Tecumseh, whose confederacy encompasses the Great Lakes—is suspected of being fomented out of Canada (population 135,000). The Americans also have designs on Florida, owned by Spain, one of England's European allies.

In the autumn of 1811, after fruitless negotiations, the American governor of the so-called Indiana Territory—38-year-old William Henry Harrison—advances with a mixed force of 900 regulars and militia against Tecumseh's home village of Tippecanoe (near modern-day Lafayette, Indiana). Arriving by 7 November, he repulses a dawn counterattack by Tecumseh's brother, Lolawauchika, known as the Prophet. Harrison's forces slay at least 38 natives before advancing and burning the deserted town to the ground. Next spring the absent Tecumseh requests aid from the British at Amherstburg (Ontario), as tensions escalate.

Finally, on 1 June 1812 Pres. James Madison succumbs to pressure from "war hawks" in the U.S. government—their rallying cry being "Free trade and sailors' rights!"—and requests that Congress declare war against London because of British impressment of American sailors; interference with neutral trade; and intrigues involving North American tribes. Although New England and the mid-Atlantic states are reluctant, a measure passes the House of Representatives three days later by a 79–49 vote and—after two weeks' bickering—by a 19–13 vote in the Senate. Hostilities commence on 19 June.

22 JUNE 1812. Commodores John Rodgers and Stephen Decatur depart New York with the 44-gun frigates USS *President* and *United States,* the 38-gun *Congress,* plus the sloop *Hornet* and brig *Argus* of 16 guns apiece, to protect homeward-bound American shipping. Two days later they intercept a British convoy sailing from Jamaica for England but fail to capture its 36-gun escort HMS *Belvidera* or any prizes despite a lengthy transatlantic pursuit.

24 JUNE 1812. Rumors of war reach Montréal, followed five days later at Halifax.

8 JULY 1812. Capt. Charles Roberts—British garrison commander at the island fortress of St. Joseph in the St. Mary's River, southeast of Sault Sainte Marie (Ontario)—is ordered to surprise the nearby American outpost of Fort Michilimackinac (Upper Michigan).

12 JULY 1812. The 61-year-old U.S. Brig. Gen. William Hull—governor of the Michigan Territory and uncle to naval Capt. Isaac Hull—crosses the Detroit River with 1,200 troops and 1,000 auxiliaries, occupying the village of Sandwich (western Windsor, Ontario) unopposed, as Lt. Col. Thomas Bligh St. George falls back with 300 British regulars of the 41st Foot, Royal Artillery, and the Royal Newfoundland Fencibles plus 400 Indian allies. Rather than continue south against the main British stronghold of Fort Malden (Amherstburg), however, Hull remains immobile, and his volunteer army soon begins to dissipate.

16 JULY 1812. This morning Roberts departs Fort St. Joseph with 45 British regulars of the 10th (Royal Veterans), 180 Canadian militia, and 400 Indian warriors aboard the North West Company schooner *Caledonia* and a boat flotilla, sailing 50 miles southwest across Lake Huron to surprise the Americans at Fort Michilimackinac. His expedition disembarks at 3:00 A.M. next day, dragging a six-pounder atop a nearby hill, then calling upon Lt. Porter Hanks to surrender his log fort at the southeastern tip of Mackinac Island by sunup. The unprepared 61-man U.S. garrison surrenders and is paroled.

17 JULY 1812. At dawn the 54-gun, 460-man frigate USS *Constitution* of Capt. Isaac Hull—proceeding from Baltimore to join Rodgers at New York—is pursued off New Jersey by the 64-gun HMS *Africa* and frigates *Belvidera, Guerrière, Shannon,* and *Aeolus,* escaping into Boston ten days later.

19 JULY 1812. A British lake squadron out of Kingston (Ontario) attempts to bombard Sackets Harbor (New York) but is driven off.

1 AUGUST 1812. A British ship reaches Quebec City from Halifax with news that London has belatedly agreed to stop interfering with neutral American shipping. This report is forwarded to 61-year-old Maj. Gen. Henry Dearborn's headquarters at Greenbush (across the Hudson from Albany, New York), producing a brief local truce.

2 AUGUST 1812. Michilimackinac's paroled American garrison reaches Hull at Detroit, the same day the local Wyandotte Indians switch allegiance and cross over into Amherstburg (Ontario) to join the British. Three days later Tecumseh leads two dozen warriors against an American supply train approaching from Ohio, provoking Hull into contemplating an assault on Fort Malden.

8 AUGUST 1812. Reversing his decision to attack Fort Malden (because of the rumored approach of a British relief column under 42-year-old Maj. Gen. Isaac Brock, commander in chief for Upper Canada), Hull recrosses the Detroit River with most of his army.

Next day he sends 600 men to protect an American supply train arriving from the Raisin River; the escort is ambushed early this afternoon near the Indian village of Maguaga by 150 British regulars and Canadian militia under Capt. Adam Muir plus a number of Tecumseh's warriors. The Americans repel the attack, suffering 18 killed and 64 wounded compared to six killed, 21 injured, and two captured among the enemy. While retiring into Detroit next day the Americans are shelled by the brig *Queen Charlotte* and schooner *General Hunter.*

11 AUGUST 1812. Hull orders the last of his troops to evacuate Sandwich (Ontario) and return to Detroit, prompting disgusted subordinates to circulate petitions demanding his recall.

13 AUGUST 1812. Shortly before midnight Brock reinforces 25-year-old Col. Henry A. Procter's garrison at Fort Malden with 50 British regulars, 250 Canadian militia, and a six-pounder. Two days later he calls on Hull to surrender Fort Detroit but is rebuffed; he therefore opens fire with a three-gun battery and two mortars installed at Sandwich under Capt. M. C. Dixon.

15 AUGUST 1812. This morning—having previously been ordered by Hull to evacuate Fort Dearborn (modern-day Chicago)—Capt. Nathan Heald's garrison of 54 U.S. regulars, 12 militia, and 27 noncombatants begin retiring toward Fort Wayne (Indiana); 400 Pottawatomie warriors under chief Blackbird attack and massacre 26 soldiers, all the militia, two women, and a dozen children while capturing the rest and torching the empty building. Soon the 70-man garrison at Fort Wayne is also besieged.

16 AUGUST 1812. ***Detroit.*** Some 600 warriors under acting Lt. Col. Matthew Elliott of the British Indian Department having disembarked the previous night at Spring Wells (three miles below Detroit), they are joined this morning by 700 redcoats and Canadian militia under Brock, supported by *Queen Charlotte* and *General Hunter* offshore.

With 400 of his best Ohio volunteers absent under Cols. Lewis Cass and Duncan McArthur—and with the Michigan militia deserting to their homes—Hull decides he cannot resist. Detroit surrenders, the U.S. commander and 582 regulars being marched off to captivity at Quebec City; 1,600 Ohio volunteers are paroled. Brock—later created knight of the Bath for this success—also gains 33 cannons, 2,500 muskets, and the 14-gun brig *Adams* (renamed *Detroit*).

19 AUGUST 1812. Four hundred miles south of Newfoundland, Hull's *Constitution* defeats the 48-gun, 244-man frigate HMS *Guerrière* of Capt. James Richard Dacres in a two-and-a-half-hour duel starting around 5:00 P.M. British casualties total 15 killed and 63 wounded, compared to seven American dead and seven injured.

4 SEPTEMBER 1812. After duly ending the truce of 1 August, Dearborn resumes offensive operations.

5 SEPTEMBER 1812. In Indiana Territory, Fort Harrison is attacked by hostile warriors but is successfully defended by 27-year-old Capt. Zachary Taylor.

12 SEPTEMBER 1812. Governor Harrison—now a major general in the Kentucky state militia—relieves the U.S. garrison trapped in Fort Wayne (Indiana) without opposition from Indian besiegers.

16 SEPTEMBER 1812. An American boat party attacks a British supply convoy opposite Toussaint Island (below Prescott, Ontario, on the Saint Lawrence River), only to be repelled by a military escort.

Aftermath of the battle between the USS Constitution *and HMS* Guerrière

21 SEPTEMBER 1812. Availing themselves of the absence of part of the Canadian garrison at Gananoque (17 miles below Kingston, Ontario), Capt. Benjamin Forsyth's gray-clad company of U.S. regulars and 30 New York militia traverse the Saint Lawrence River from Cape Vincent, disembarking west of the village to overrun it. At a cost of one American killed and another wounded, the raiders wound four Leeds militia and capture eight before withdrawing.

25 SEPTEMBER 1812. With 500 redcoats and a like number of native allies, Muir—now brevet major—discovers 2,500 Americans under elderly Brig. Gen. James Winchester advancing northeast up the Maumee River (Ohio). Both sides dig in for a defensive struggle then withdraw in opposite directions when neither presses home an attack.

4 OCTOBER 1812. Elderly British Col. Robert Lethbridge assembles two companies of green-clad Glengarry Light Infantry Fencibles and 600 other Canadian militia at Prescott to strike across the Saint Lawrence against Ogdensburg (New York). His flotilla is checked midriver by American shore batteries under 37-year-old militia Brig. Gen. Jacob "Potash" Brown. Lethbridge is recalled to Montréal as a result of the fiasco and replaced by Lt. Col. Thomas Pearson.

6 OCTOBER 1812. Forty-year-old U.S. Commo. Isaac Chauncey arrives at Sackets Harbor (New York) to create a naval counterweight to the British squadron at Kingston (Ontario).

9 OCTOBER 1812. An American boat party under 31-year-old naval Lt. Jesse Duncan Elliott cuts the British brigs *Caledonia* and *Detroit* out from under the guns at Fort Erie (Ontario), burning the latter when it runs aground.

10–11 OCTOBER 1812. ***Queenston Heights.*** After an abortive nocturnal attempt to invade Ontario across the Niagara River from Lewiston, Maj. Gen. Stephen van Rensselaer of the New York state militia makes a second try at 3:00 A.M. on 13 October, sending across 300 U.S. regulars under Lt. Col. John Chrystie of the 13th Infantry plus 300 volunteers under Lt. Col.

Romanticized view of the battle of Queenston Heights

Solomon van Rensselaer aboard 13 boats. Most land a bit above Queenston, being pinned down by the British 49th (Hertfordshire or Green Tigers) Regimental Grenadier Company until Capt. John E. Wool leads a company from the 13th up a winding path to the top of Queenston's 350-foot heights.

Here the Americans overrun a single-gun redan then slay Brock when he leads an unsuccessful counterattack with 100 redcoats of 49th Regiment plus 100 Lincoln militia. His successor and aide—Lt. Col. John Macdonell—is also wounded and driven back into Vrooman's Point after launching a second failed counterattack with two York Volunteer companies. Wool, badly injured, is reinforced and superseded by 26-year-old American Lt. Col. Winfield Scott.

By midmorning 1,300 invaders have ferried across into Queenston, although many others refuse to leave New York. Only 350 U.S. regulars and 250 militia are actively engaged against the defenders atop Queenston Heights when British Maj. Gen. Roger Hale Sheaffe—born 49 years earlier in Boston—arrives at noon with reinforcements: 300 redcoats of the 41st Foot, a horse-drawn field battery, and 250 Canadian militia (Niagara Light Dragoons, Capt. Robert Runchey's "Company of Coloured Men," plus more Lincoln and York militia and Mohawk warriors). Sheaffe leads these forces and some Indians in a flanking maneuver, gathering en route an additional 100 regulars, 150 militia, and 300 Six Nations warriors under chief John Brant.

At 3:00 P.M. he takes the Americans completely by surprise out of the west, obliging Scott to surrender with 958 men. The invaders have suffered 300 casualties compared to only 14 Anglo-Canadian dead, 77 wounded, and 21 missing (plus 14 casualties among native allies). Van Rensselaer retires across the border and resigns his command to the regular Brig. Gen. Alexander Smyth at nearby Buffalo. Sheaffe is knighted for his timely action.

23 OCTOBER 1812. At dawn American militia from French Mills (New York) surprise 31 Franco-Canadian militia *voyageurs* at St. Regis, killing eight and capturing the rest.

27 OCTOBER 1812. The 32-gun frigate USS *Essex* of Capt. David Porter slips out of Boston, followed three days later by Commo. William Bainbridge's *Constitution* and *Hornet* for a raid against British shipping in the South Pacific.

8 NOVEMBER 1812. Chauncey sorties from Sackets Harbor (New York) with his 18-gun brig *Oneida* (flag) and a half-dozen armed schooners, chasing the 22-gun British corvette *Royal George* and schooners *Prince Regent* and *Duke of Gloucester* into Kingston (Ontario) two days later. Although checked by shore batteries, the Americans mount a blockade. Anglo-Canadian losses are one dead and a few injuries compared to two killed and eight wounded among Chauncey's crews.

20 NOVEMBER 1812. ***Stillborn Invasion.*** At dawn advance elements of Dearborn's 3,000 U.S. regulars and 3,000 militia break the border near Champlain (New York), in a long-anticipated northern offensive. A screen of gray-clad voltigeurs—French-Canadian light infantry—and 300 Caughnawaga warriors, stationed at Lacolle (Quebec) under Maj. Charles Michel d'Irumberry de Salaberry, engage in the darkness. Some American units fire on each other in the melee, after which the Vermont and New York militia refuse to leave the United States, prompting Dearborn to order a general retirement. Three days later his troops withdraw into winter quarters at Plattsburgh.

23 NOVEMBER 1812. British Capt. Andrew Gray leads 70 redcoats and some Cornwall and Glengarry militia companies in a descent on the American outpost on the Salmon River (near French Mills, New York).

28 NOVEMBER 1812. ***Smyth's Offensive.*** Before dawn American Brig. Gen. Alexander Smyth pushes twin assault columns under Col. William Henry Winder and Lt. Col. Charles G. Boerstler of the 14th U.S. Infantry across the Niagara River from Black Rock (New York), disembarking two and a half miles below Fort Erie (Ontario). The invaders establish a beachhead by overrunning a small British battery, having 1,200 men ashore by midday. However, after being counterattacked by British regulars and Canadian militia under Lt. Col. Cecil Bisshopp—their numbers quickly swell to 1,100—Smyth cancels the operation and retreats back across the river. Redcoat losses total 17 killed, 47 wounded, and 35 captured or missing.

Two nights later the American brigadier attempts a second invasion, embarking 1,500 troops, but abandons the operation at daylight on 30 November.

29 DECEMBER 1812. *Constitution* is 30 miles off São Salvador (Brazil), awaiting its consort *Hornet*—which has ventured inshore searching for the missing *Essex*—when Bainbridge sights the 38-gun frigate HMS *Java* of Capt. Henry Lambert towing the American prize

William. The Royal Navy warship casts off its tow and bears down on *Constitution,* which maneuvers away, using its heavier artillery at long range starting at 2:00 P.M. Once *Java* is crippled, Bainbridge closes and compels the British to strike after two hours, the latter suffering 22 dead (including Lambert) and 102 wounded. American losses are 12 killed and 22 injured.

18 JANUARY 1813. ***Frenchtown.*** On Winchester's initiative, 660 Kentucky militia under Lt. Cols. William Lewis and John Allen advance northeast up the Maumee River to surprise the 50 Essex militia and 100 Indian warriors garrisoning the outpost at Frenchtown (Monroe, Michigan). After several hours' fighting, the Canadians are driven toward Brownstown—20 miles away—Winchester joining the Frenchtown victors two days later with an additional 300 U.S. regulars under Col. Samuel Wells.

In reaction, Procter crosses the ice from Fort Malden (Amherstburg, Ontario) with 273 redcoats, 275 Canadian militia, 600 Shawnee warriors under Wyandotte chief Roundhead, 28 sailors, plus sleigh-drawn three-pounders. They fall upon the unwary Americans before dawn on 22 January, quickly breaking their militia contingent (of whom only 30–40 escape through the deep snow). The U.S. regulars resist bravely until called upon to surrender by the captive Winchester—still clad in nightclothes—who fears an Indian bloodbath. Anglo-Canadian casualties total 185 compared to 400 Americans killed and 500 captured. Some 30 captives are murdered by drunken Shawnee, the battle thus being remembered by Americans as the River Raisin Massacre; Procter is dubbed "the Butcher."

The defeat prompts Harrison to burn his stores at the nearby Maumee Rapids (kept for an anticipated advance against Detroit) and retire south. Procter is promoted brigadier by Canada's governor-general (45-year-old Lt. Gen. Sir George Prevost, himself a veteran West Indian campaigner; *see* 20 June 1803 under Napoleonic Wars in Part 6).

7 FEBRUARY 1813. At dawn Forsyth's 200 troops surprise the Canadian militia outpost at Brockville (formerly Elizabethtown, Ontario), returning across the icy Saint Lawrence into Ogdensburg (New York) with 52 prisoners—most soon paroled; he is promoted major for this exploit.

MID-FEBRUARY 1813. A 45-year-old militia major general and former U.S. senator, Andrew "Old Hickory" Jackson, reaches Natchez after a monthlong trek from Nashville with 2,000 western Tennessee volunteers. His force is intended to occupy Spanish Florida but is instead recalled at the last minute by Madison.

Only the disputed borderland between Louisiana and western Florida is to be seized, the operation being carried out by 55-year-old Maj. Gen. James Wilkinson, who leads a contingent from New Orleans to displace the Spanish garrison at Fort Charlotte (Mobile, Alabama) by 15 April. The outnumbered Spaniards retire into Pensacola without bloodshed.

22 FEBRUARY 1813. At 7:00 A.M. recently promoted Lt. Col. "Red George" Macdonell and Capt. John Jenkins of the Glengarry Light Infantry launch a two-pronged strike from Prescott (Ontario) across the frozen Saint Lawrence with 120 regulars of the 8th (King's) Foot, 30 Royal Newfoundland fencibles, 350 Canadian militia, and sleigh-drawn guns, storming into Ogdensburg (New York) before its defenders are fully alert. After 90 minutes of fighting Forsyth's garrison retreats southwest toward Black Lake, having killed seven Anglo-Canadians and wounded 48—including Macdonell and Jenkins. American losses are 20 dead and 70 captured (mostly wounded); their icebound gunboats are torched and Ogdensburg looted before the raiders retire.

Fearing this event presages a larger winter offensive, Dearborn hastily reinforces Sackets Harbor with 800 U.S. regulars from Plattsburgh under 33-year-old Col. Zebulon Montgomery Pike and 400 militia out of Greenbush.

17 MARCH 1813. American artillery at Black Rock (New York) bombard Fort Erie (Ontario), apparently marking Saint Patrick's Day.

25 APRIL 1813. ***Little York.*** Chauncey exits Sackets Harbor (New York) with the 24-gun American corvette *Madison,* brig *Oneida,* schooner *Julia,* and a dozen lesser consorts, conveying Dearborn's army across Lake Ontario to attack Little York (modern-day Toronto). They bear 1,700 troops (mostly regulars from the 6th, 15th, and 16th U.S. Infantry Regiments); detachments from the 14th and 21st; two companies of light artillery; Forsyth's rifle corps; plus some volunteers.

Next afternoon their vessels are spotted off Scarborough Bluffs, and Sheaffe's 750-man British garrison stands to arms: two companies of the 8th Foot; another pair from the Royal Newfoundland Regiment; a company of Glengarry Light Infantry Fencibles; flank companies of the 3rd York Militia; 50–100 Mississauga, Chippewa, and Ojibway warriors; plus assorted dockyard workers. Around 8:00 A.M. on 27 April the Americans disembark west of York at Sunnyside, Forsyth brushing aside opposition from native snipers and Capt. Neale McNeale's 8th Grenadier Company (whose commander dies during an American bayonet charge that secures the beachhead).

By 10:00 A.M. most of Pike's contingent are ashore; Chauncey's dozen armed schooners commence bombarding the two-gun Western battery. One of its magazines explodes accidentally an hour later, killing 20 defenders and wounding many others, compelling the Canadians to fall back once the small American army—now bolstered by its field artillery—pushes east. Briefly checked at 12:30 P.M. by the two 12-pounders of Half Moon battery, the Americans soon subdue it with their cannons; Sheaffe (having suffered 62 dead and 94 wounded) thus orders a general retirement to Kingston.

However, the defenders delay the invaders by leaving Half Moon's flag flying; they also ignite their main magazine upon departing. The resultant explosion kills 38 Americans and injures 222, Pike being among those mortally wounded. The Americans hold York for four days, setting many of its buildings ablaze between 30 April and 1 May, when they depart for Niagara.

28 APRIL 1813. ***Fort Meigs.*** Procter arrives from Amherstburg at the mouth of the Maumee River with 550 redcoats, 61 fencibles, and 464 Canadian militia aboard a half-dozen vessels, two gunboats, and a boat flotilla. Quickly erecting batteries on both banks, he is joined by 1,200 Indians under Tecumseh then advances six miles upriver to invest Harrison's newly constructed Fort Meigs by 1 May (just below the Maumee Rapids and named for Ohio's governor, Return J. Meigs). The attackers cannot completely encircle the stockaded stronghold, so Harrison contacts 1,200 Kentucky militia moving northeast to his support under Brig. Gen. Green Clay.

On the morning of 5 May 900 Kentuckians disembark under Col. William Dudley and rush the British siege batteries on the north bank while Harrison launches a sally against the southern bank. Three companies of the British 41st Foot and some Canadian militia under Muir check the first attack, allowing Tecumseh's warriors to close in behind the Kentuckians, killing or capturing almost all. A second disembarkation by Clay overwhelms the southern British battery, after which he and Harrison retire into the fort, arranging a two-day truce. American losses total 400 dead and 600 captured; Procter suffers 15 killed, 46 injured, and 40 captured.

Despite the victory Procter cannot carry Fort Meigs, and his weary militia insist upon planting their spring crops. The British general is thus compelled to abandon his siege by 9 May.

8 MAY 1813. After destroying York and heading south across Lake Ontario, the Dearborn-Chauncey expedition appears outside Fort George (Niagara-on-the-Lake, Ontario). His men being "sickly and depressed" because of foul weather, he sails back east instead, toward Sackets Harbor.

15 MAY 1813. The 31-year-old veteran Commo. Sir James Lucas Yeo (*see* December 1808 under Napoleonic Wars in Part 6) arrives at Kingston (Ontario) with 150 British seamen, soon joined by another 300, to help man the newly launched 23-gun *Wolfe;* 21-gun *Royal George;* 14-gun brig *Earl of Moira;* plus 14-gun schooner *Prince Regent* (soon renamed *Lord Beresford*) and 12-gun schooner *Sir Sidney Smith.*

This same day, on the Atlantic seaboard, a British naval force disembarks to sack Havre de Grace (Maryland).

25 MAY 1813. ***Fort George.*** This morning Chauncey's American lake squadron begins bombarding Fort George (Niagara-on-the-Lake, Ontario), quickly setting all its log buildings ablaze. Two days later Colonel Scott (having been exchanged the preceding winter [*see* 10–11 October 1812] and now substituting for the indisposed Dearborn) disembarks his vanguard, followed by contingents under Brigs. John Parker Boyd, Winder, and John Chandler.

To oppose the 4,000 Americans, British Brig. Gen. John Vincent has 1,000 men of the 8th and 49th Foot; Royal Newfoundland Fencibles; Glengarry Light Infantry Fencibles; plus 300 Canadian militia. Unable to contain Scott's beachhead, and having suffered 52 killed and 306 wounded or missing, the British commander spikes Fort George's guns then retreats southwest to Beaver Dam (Thorold). Scott thus secures the strategic outpost at a cost of 40 American dead and 120 injured.

Around that time, American Lt. Col. James P. Preston pushes across the Niagara from Black Rock and occupies deserted Fort Erie (Ontario).

27 MAY 1813. ***Sackets Harbor.*** Availing themselves of Chauncey's absence at the west end of Lake Ontario, Prevost and Yeo slip southeast out of Kingston (Ontario) with a 750-man assault force aboard *Wolfe, Royal George, Earl of Moira,* two armed schooners, two gunboats, and 30 lesser craft. Col. Edward Baynes brings a grenadier company of the 100th (County of Dublin) Foot; a section of the 1st (Royal Scots); two companies of the 8th, four of the 104th (former New Brunswick Fencibles), one of the Glengarry Light Infantry, and two of Canadian voltigeurs; plus a pair of six-pounders.

Next morning the expedition appears off Sackets Harbor (New York) but is unable to close because of contrary winds. The 400 U.S. defenders under militia Maj. General Brown are reinforced by several hundred hastily assembled local militia. Shortly after daylight of 29 May Baynes fights his way onto Horse Island (one mile west-southwest), scattering 500 American defenders but being checked in the outskirts of Sackets Harbor by U.S. regulars at Fort Tompkins. Fighting bogs down until Brown slips a militia contingent behind the British right, persuading Prevost and Bayne to withdraw three hours later.

The Anglo-Canadians set sail for Kingston that night having suffered 47 killed (including Captain Gray), 194 wounded, and 16 missing. American losses are 21 dead, 85 injured, and 154 captured; three six-pounders are also taken from them. Brown is promoted brigadier in the regular U.S. army for the defense.

1 JUNE 1813. The 38-gun frigate USS *Chesapeake* of Capt. James Lawrence emerges from Boston, being engaged 20 miles out at 5:50 P.M. by Capt. Philip Bowes Vere Broke's 38-gun frigate HMS *Shannon.* Within 15 minutes the American vessel is pounded into submission, suffering 61 dead (including Lawrence, who falls mortally wounded but crying, "Don't give up the ship!") and 85 wounded, compared to 24 killed and 59 injured aboard *Shannon. Chesapeake* is sailed to Halifax by its captors.

2 JUNE 1813. This evening 30-year-old U.S. Lt. Thomas Macdonough's armed schooners *Growler* and *Eagle* anchor at Rouses Point (north end of Lake Champlain, New York). Next morning they penetrate the Richelieu River to attack the British garrison at Île aux Noix (later Fort Lennox, Quebec), only to be surprised by a mist-shrouded boat counter-sortie. Both American men-of-war are captured, suffering one killed, 19 wounded, and more than 90 captured. The defenders' losses are only three injured; the prizes are renamed *Shannon* and *Broke.*

3 JUNE 1813. Yeo's British squadron sails west across Lake Ontario bearing 220 redcoats of the 8th Foot, ammunition, and stores to relieve Vincent.

5 JUNE 1813. ***Stoney Creek.*** Having observed American Brigadier Generals Winder and Chandler's 3,500 men and four field pieces bivouac for the night at Stoney Creek (Ontario), Vincent detaches a nocturnal raid of 700 redcoats of the 8th and 49th Foot under Lt. Col. John Harvey to check the invaders' westward progress toward Burlington. Armed with their password, the British column silently penetrates the U.S. encampment at 2:00 A.M. on 6 June, surprising their enemy.

Although startled the Americans react well, ejecting Harvey's outnumbered force by dawn; the redcoats suffer 23 killed, 134 wounded, and five missing. U.S. casualties total 55 with another 100 missing, but among the latter are both American generals, who have been carried off as prisoners. Command therefore devolves upon Col. James Burn of the 2nd Dragoons, who opts to retreat to Forty Mile Creek (Grimsby).

The American depot there is attacked from offshore by Yeo's squadron during the afternoon of 7 June. He seizes 16 boatloads of supplies, thereby forcing Burn to withdraw as far as Fort George (Niagara-on-the-Lake, Ontario) by 8 June.

13 JUNE 1813. British naval forces sack Hampton (Virginia); nine days later they suffer a heavy repulse off Craney Island.

22 JUNE 1813. This evening Mrs. Laura Ingersoll Secord—a Canadian housewife from Queenston (Ontario)—reaches Lt. James Fitzgibbon's detachment of 49th Foot at Beaver Dam to warn of an American column advancing southwest from Fort George.

The attackers appear two mornings later, consisting of 575 cavalry and infantry under Lieutenant Colonel Boerstler plus two field pieces. At 9:00 A.M. the American rear is attacked by 300 Caughnawaga warriors under Capt. Dominique Ducharme of the British Indian Department, soon joined by 100 Mohawks under Capt. William Johnson Kerr and chief John Brant. By the time Fitzgibbon arrives at noon with 50 redcoats, the wounded Boerstler is already so discouraged that he surrenders his entire command. The Caughnawaga suffer 15 killed and 25 wounded. Some 462 U.S. regulars are marched off in captivity; their militia contingent—mounted partisans under Cyrenius Chapin of Buffalo (New York), better known as the Forty Thieves—are paroled.

5 JULY 1813. An Anglo-Canadian party under Lt. Col. Thomas Clark crosses the Niagara River and raids an American depot at Fort Schlosser (New York), capturing a six-pounder and numerous other stores.

11 JULY 1813. Bisshopp raids the American depot at Black Rock (New York) with 250 British regulars and Canadian militia. While retiring he is overtaken by Tuscarora warriors and mortally wounded. Redcoat losses total 13 killed and 25 wounded.

18 JULY 1813. Two American gunboats capture 15 British supply boats near Rockport (Ontario) then repel a rescue mission out of Kingston at Goose Creek (New York).

20 JULY 1813. Having traversed Lake Erie from Amherstburg (Ontario) with 300 redcoats and 3,000 warriors, Procter invests Fort Meigs (Ohio), withdrawing eight days later when the American garrison under Clay refuses to be lured into an open fight.

21 JULY 1813. Chauncey sorties west from Sackets Harbor (New York) with his new 26-gun corvette *General Pike,* accompanied by another warship, a brig, and ten schooners. They embark a troop contingent at Fort Niagara before probing Vincent's defenses at Burlington (Ontario).

27 JULY 1813. ***Creek War.*** In Alabama, American settlers under militia Col. James Caller attack 300 Lower Creek warriors under chief Peter McQueen, returning home after obtaining arms at Spanish Pensacola. Although the tribe is contemplating hostilities against the Upper Creek—already at war against the Americans near the Coosa and Tallapoosa Rivers—Caller's men are convinced that the visit to hostile Pensacola portends treachery. The so-called Battle of Burnt Corn Creek ends inconclusively but drives the Lower Creek to join their brethren in hostilities against the settlers.

29 JULY 1813. ***Plattsburgh Raid.*** This morning British Lt. Col. John Murray departs Île aux Noix (Quebec) with 950 troops of the 13th, 100th, 103rd, and Canadian Fencibles plus two dozen gunners (for a pair of three-pounders) and 35 militia. They travel aboard 47 boats escorted by a trio of gunboats and the captured American schooners *Broke* and *Shannon*—now under Cmdr. Thomas Everard of HMS *Wasp* and Lt. Daniel Pring.

Pushing south into Lake Champlain, the expedition overruns Chazy then surprises the American depot at Plattsburgh next dawn, disembarking without opposition from its few militia defenders—Hampton being absent at Burlington (Vermont) with his main army and squadron. Storehouses here and at Swanton are destroyed, after which Everard continues to Burlington with his schooners and a gunboat, capturing four American vessels. Murray retires north into Canada.

31 JULY 1813. Chauncey's squadron returns to York (Toronto). Finding no British troops, the Americans pillage and fire its storehouses before departing two days later to Fort Niagara (New York).

1 AUGUST 1813. Early this morning, after retreating from Fort Meigs (*see* 20 July 1813), Procter disembarks 300 redcoats and a like number of Indian allies near the mouth of the Sandusky River (Ohio) to invest smaller Fort Stephenson. After a preliminary bombardment the British attackers launch an assault at 4:30 P.M., which the garrison stoutly resists. Although earlier ordered by Harrison—whose large American army is nearby—to evacuate, the 160 U.S. regulars under Maj. George Croghan (with a single six-pounder) break Procter's columns and oblige him to reembark next day with 96 casualties.

7 AUGUST 1813. With two British ships, a pair of brigs, and two schooners, Yeo confronts Chauncey's larger squadron off Fort Niagara; both commanders circle warily. Two American schooners capsize in a squall that night; two more become separated and are captured in the early hours of 11 August before Yeo retires.

25 AUGUST 1813. The 28-year-old American Commo. Oliver Hazard Perry appears outside Fort Malden (Amherstburg, Ontario) with his new 20-gun brigs *Lawrence* (flag) and *Niagara* plus lesser vessels *Ariel, Caledonia, Ohio, Scorpion, Somers, Tigress, Porcupine,* and *Trippe* (mounting 15 guns between them). The 490-man squadron has earlier ventured west from Presque Isle (Erie, Pennsylvania) to establish a base at Put-in-Bay (Ohio). The one-armed 28-year-old acting British commodore, Robert Heriot Barclay, has insufficient strength to sortie.

29 AUGUST 1813. ***Fort Mims.*** A black slave reports hostile Indians approaching Fort Mims (40 miles north of Mobile on the eastern bank of the Alabama River) but is flogged for lying.

At noon next day 800–1,000 "Red Stick" warriors steal upon the outpost's open gates under chiefs William Weatherford and Josiah Francis, surprising the garrison of 100 Mississippi volunteers and 400 noncombatants. After a lengthy struggle the attackers overrun the now blazing structure, massacring 247 people and carrying off most of the rest as captives. This not only spreads terror throughout the American settlements but also provokes an all-out military countereffort from neighboring Tennessee and Georgia.

1 SEPTEMBER 1813. Perry's American squadron again shows itself off Amherstburg (Ontario), increasing pressure on Barclay to sortie because of disruptions to British lake traffic.

7 SEPTEMBER 1813. Chauncey's American squadron sights Yeo's weaker force off the mouth of the Niagara River, chasing it across Lake Ontario for five days until the British shelter in a fortified bay five miles west of Kingston, having suffered four killed and seven wounded.

9 SEPTEMBER 1813. ***Lake Erie.*** This morning Barclay sallies from Amherstburg (Ontario) with his new 19-gun flagship *Detroit,* 17-gun *Queen Charlotte* under Lt. Robert Finnis, the ten-gun *Hunter,* and *Chippawa, Lady Prevost,* and *Little Belt* (with 19 guns between them) to beat southeast and surprise Perry's more powerful American squadron, which is at anchor ten miles southwest of Pelee Island.

Because of contrary winds Perry can see the British slowly approaching next morning; he sorties with virtually his entire strength—nine vessels in a straggling line (*Ohio* being absent on a cruise). Barclay opens fire around noon from long range, yet the Americans, enjoying the weather gauge, close with the 103-man *Lawrence* in the van so that their carronades might bear. By 2:00 P.M. both flagships are incapacitated and Barclay is severely wounded. Thirty minutes later the American commodore transfers a half-mile from his devastated *Lawrence* aboard Elliott's undamaged vice flagship *Niagara* then sails through the British line, splitting it asunder. Barclay's *Detroit* and two other battered British schooners are put out of action, and by 3:00 P.M. Finnis is dead, the attackers' entire fleet being crippled.

Eventually, all British vessels strike, with casualties totaling 41 killed and 94 wounded as opposed to 27 dead and 96 injured among Perry's vessels—83 losses aboard *Lawrence* alone. (Upon taking possession of his prizes the American commodore makes a famous report to Harrison: "We have met the enemy, and they are ours: two ships, two brigs, one schooner, and one sloop.")

19 SEPTEMBER 1813. The 59-year-old U.S. Maj. Gen. Wade Hampton pushes across the Canadian border near Odelltown (Quebec) to divert attention from a larger American buildup at Sackets Harbor (New York). Next day Hampton retires back across the border into Chazy.

24 SEPTEMBER 1813. Following Barclay's defeat, Procter torches his supply dump within Detroit then retreats crossriver into Fort Malden (Amherstburg, Ontario).

26 SEPTEMBER 1813. As Perry's victorious warships enter the Detroit River from the south, Procter destroys Fort Malden then begins slowly retiring east into Ontario next morning with 800 redcoats—mostly 41st Infantry—plus 1,000 Indian allies under Tecumseh.

This same day, Harrison arrives with 4,500 U.S. regular and militia infantry, occupying Amherstburg, Sandwich, and Detroit. On 28 September he sets out in pursuit of the retreating British with 3,000 troops.

28 SEPTEMBER 1813. Chauncey's American squadron—despite suffering considerable damage—chases Yeo's warships into Burlington Bay (Ontario), killing five and wounding 13 British seamen.

1 OCTOBER 1813. Harrison's column is reinforced by 500 mounted Kentucky Rifles under 32-year-old Lt. Col. (and congressman) Richard Mentor Johnson, thereby giving his army greater mobility. Late next day they rendezvous with Perry's gunboats at the mouth of the Thames River (eastern Lake Saint Clair), pressing upstream together on 3 October in pursuit of the retreating Procter and Tecumseh.

5 OCTOBER 1813. ***Thames (or Moraviantown).*** On the north bank of the Thames River, five miles southwest of Moraviantown (modern-day New Fairfield, Ontario), Procter's and Tecumseh's retreating columns make a stand against their American pursuers. A rearguard of 500 British troops form two lines across the road into some woods while 500 Shawnee and allied warriors hide in a nearby swamp. They possess a single six-pounder without ammunition.

Upon contacting the deployment with his 3,000-man army, Harrison refuses to be drawn into a flanking attempt, instead following Johnson's suggestion of a direct frontal charge by his 500 mounted Kentuckians at midafternoon. They scatter the demoralized redcoats within ten minutes, after which the Americans dismount to attack the Shawnee farther north in the swamp; they hold their ground for an hour until Tecumseh is mortally wounded, then break and flee, leaving behind 33 dead. British casualties total 18 killed, 22 wounded, and 477 captured as opposed to 15 dead and 30 injured among the Americans (including Johnson, who receives five wounds but survives).

Procter reaches Burlington with 250 survivors; the American cavalry retires into Detroit four days later, followed by the infantry.

11 OCTOBER 1813. In a diversionary move, American Col. Isaac Clark enters Missisquoi Bay (Quebec) with 200 militia, surprising the tiny Canadian garrison at Philipsburg.

12 OCTOBER 1813. After dispatching his kinsman—42-year-old militia Maj. Gen. John Coffee—south with a cavalry vanguard for Huntsville (Alabama), Jackson departs Fayetteville (Tennessee) with his 2,500-man main body to invade Creek territory.

14 OCTOBER 1813. After signing an armistice with the Pottawatomie, Wyandotte, Miami, and Chippewa Indians at Detroit, receiving numerous hostages, then appointing Brigadier General Cass as his successor, Harrison departs triumphantly for Washington. (He is eventually elected ninth president of the United States but dies in office after serving only a single month; his subordinate, Johnson, becomes ninth vice president under Van Buren—campaigning under the slogan "Rumpsey, dumpsey, Johnson killed Tecumseh.")

17 OCTOBER 1813. This evening Wilkinson departs Henderson's Bay (west of Sackets Harbor, New York) with 8,000 American troops—14 infantry regiments, two of dragoons, plus three artillery companies—to join Hampton's army farther northeast for a drive against Montréal. Wilkinson's expedition sails aboard 300 craft escorted by a dozen gunboats but is struck by a storm before reaching Grenadier Island (at the mouth of the Saint Lawrence River) and further decimated by cold weather and poor supplies. Wilkinson, now quite ill, does not resume the advance until two weeks later.

21 OCTOBER 1813. This morning Hampton crosses the Quebec border from Four Corners (New York) with 4,000 American infantry, 200 dragoons, and ten field pieces—1,400 New York militia refusing to march out of state—to push up the Châteauguay River, join Wilkinson on the Saint Lawrence, and threaten Montréal.

25 OCTOBER 1813. ***Châteauguay River.*** After moving north to within 14 miles of Montréal, Hampton's scouts early this afternoon detect 50 Canadian fencibles, 150 voltigeurs, 100 militia, and 50 native allies under Lieutenant Colonel de Salaberry, occupying a defensive line on the western side of the Châteauguay. Without awaiting Wilkinson—whom he dislikes—Hampton decides to brush aside the formation with a two-pronged assault next morning and so detaches Col. Robert Purdy's 1,500-man 1st Infantry Brigade over to the eastern bank for a flanking maneuver, little realizing that another 1,300 Canadian troops are dug in upriver under Swiss-born Maj. Gen. Louis de Watteville.

Purdy's column becomes slowed and disoriented overnight, not arriving opposite de Salaberry's position until noon on 26 October. When the main American body moves forward under Brig. Gen. George Izard at 2:00 P.M. it draws fire from as yet undetected Canadian militia companies, after which Purdy is struck by a counterattack led by Capts. Joseph Bernard Bruyère and Charles Daly. Surprised by this unexpected strength, the 4,000 invaders—having suffered only 50 casualties—withdraw as far south as Chateaugay (New York) without informing Wilkinson. De Salaberry's losses are two dead, 16 wounded, and seven missing.

2 NOVEMBER 1813. This evening Coffee fords the Coosa River at Fish Dams with 900 cavalry, attacking the Creek village of Tallushatchee (near Jacksonville, Alabama) an hour after sunrise on 3 November, killing 186 natives and capturing 84—of whom only 40 are marched back into Jackson's main camp. American losses total five dead and 41 wounded.

6 NOVEMBER 1813. This evening British Maj. Gen. Francis, Baron de Rottenburg, detaches Lt. Col. Joseph W. Morrison—born 30 years earlier in New York City—from Kingston (Ontario) to pursue Wilkinson with 450 regulars (nine companies) of the 89th Foot; 160 of the 49th; plus 20 gunners for two six-pounders. They sail aboard Cmdr. William Howe Mulcaster's schooners *Lord Beresford* and *Sir Sydney Smith* plus seven gunboats and numerous lesser craft.

7 NOVEMBER 1813. Wilkinson disembarks at Morristown (opposite Brockville, Ontario) to work his empty boats past Fort Wellington—farther down the Saint Lawrence at Prescott—under cover of darkness. Once past the British defenses, American Brig. Gen. Leonard Covington is set ashore next morning at Iroquois with 1,200 troops to clear its northern shoreline of snipers; he is joined on 9 November by Brown's 2,500 men and some field pieces to drive on Cornwall (Ontario). Although Wilkinson continues to press his advance he remains worried about his rear, as Morrison's counterexpedition has also reached Prescott that morning (9 November).

8 NOVEMBER 1813. ***Talladega.*** This evening—after a forced 30-mile march from the Coosa River—Jackson's 2,000 troops arrive within six miles of a village of 160 friendly Creeks at Talladega (east of modern-day Birmingham, Alabama), who are being besieged by 1,000 hostile Red Sticks. Next dawn the Americans advance with cavalry on both wings, their vanguard luring the Creek warriors into a counterattack, during which they are enveloped. Hostile casualties total at least 299 dead compared to 17 killed and 80 wounded among Jackson's ranks. Notwithstanding this victory, the Americans are obliged to retire north into Fort Schlosser at Ten Islands due to a lack of supplies.

10 NOVEMBER 1813. ***Crysler's Farm.*** On a rainy afternoon, Morrison's 900 redcoats and three six-pounders overtake the rear of Wilkinson's much larger American army as it prepares to drive through Cornwall to Montréal. Headquartered at John Crysler's farm, the British commander probes the U.S. rearguard next morning, provoking a minor exchange that goads Wilkinson into ordering Brigadier Generals Covington, Boyd, and Robert Swartout to swing about their 2,000 troops and march in three columns to drive off the pursuers.

The American counterattack begins well, easily pushing back a line of three Canadian voltigeur companies. By 2:00 P.M., however, the Americans are checked by Morrison's main body, which they cannot outflank. Boyd suffers heavy casualties charging the British lines in piecemeal fashion, eventually drawing off in disarray. His losses total 102 dead (including Covington), 237 wounded, more than 100 captured, plus a lost field piece. The Anglo-Canadians suffer 22 killed, 148 wounded, and nine missing.

On the morning of 12 November Wilkinson learns that Hampton has withdrawn into New York, so cancels his own operation. His army veers south two days later to recross the Saint Lawrence and enter winter quarters on the Salmon River banks at French Mills (renamed Fort Covington).

18 NOVEMBER 1813. Militia Brig. Gen. James White—a subordinate of Jackson's bitter East Tennessee rival, Maj. Gen. John Cocke—attacks the Hillabee (or Hillibee) towns of the Upper Creek along the Tallapoosa River headwaters, little realizing that the tribes have already asked Jackson for peace. Over the next couple of days White slaughters more than 60 Indians and captures 250 without suffering a single loss, thus unwittingly goading the Upper Creek into renewing hostilities.

28 NOVEMBER 1813. This evening Brig. Gen. John Floyd's 950 Georgia militiamen bivouac within a few miles of the Upper Creek village of Auttose (20 miles from the Tallapoosa-Coosa confluence in Alabama). Next dawn their surprise attack kills an estimated 200 Indians compared to 11 American dead and 54 wounded.

30 NOVEMBER 1813. The 26-gun sloop HMS *Racoon* of Cmdr. William Black reaches the American fur-trading outpost of Fort Astoria (Oregon), finding it already flying the Union Jack. Two weeks later it is renamed Fort George in a formal ceremony ashore.

10 DECEMBER 1813. With only 100 men left to garrison Fort George (Niagara-on-the-Lake, Ontario), American Brig. Gen. George McClure turns 400 Canadian civilians out into the snow then torches the structure along with the villages of Newark and Queenston before retreating across the Niagara River into New York.

19 DECEMBER 1813. ***Riall's Winter Forays.*** Before dawn Murray slips across the Niagara River with 550 redcoats, disembarking three miles beyond the U.S. garrison at Fort Niagara (New York). A bayonet charge slays 67 of its surprised defenders and wounds 11—only 20 Americans escaping—thus securing the fort at a cost of five British dead and three injured.

Murray is followed by the recently arrived 38-year-old Irish-born Maj. Gen. Phineas Riall with 500 men of Royal Scots and the 41st Foot plus 500 Indian auxiliaries, destroying the villages of Youngstown, Lewiston, Tuscarora, Fort Schlosser, and Manchester in retaliation for the burning of Fort George. The raiders halt at Tonawanda Creek—10 miles north of Buffalo—having secured 422 prisoners, 27 cannons, 3,000 firearms, and copious stores.

Ten days later Riall recrosses the Niagara under cover of darkness, this time disembarking beyond the falls with 1,000 redcoats and 400 natives. Lt. Col. James Ogilvie of the 8th Foot leads the vanguard two miles toward Black Rock (New York), securing the bridge over Scajaquada Creek at dawn on 30 December so that Lt. Col. John Gordon can charge through the village at sunrise, fighting his way into neighboring Buffalo. Despite resistance from Maj. Gen. Amos Hall's 1,200-man American garrison, the British torch both places, along with four armed schooners and large supply dumps, before retiring into Ontario. The attackers' casualties total 112; the defenders suffer 30 killed, 40 wounded, and 69 captured.

23 DECEMBER 1813. After a ten-day 100-mile march north from Fort Caroline (Alabama), Brig. Gen. Ferdinand L. Claiborne's 1,000 U.S. regulars, Mississippi militia, volunteers, and Choctaw allies fall upon chief Weatherford's village of Econochaca, killing 30 residents and scattering the rest. American casualties are one dead and six wounded.

30 DECEMBER 1813. The British ship *Bramble* reaches Annapolis (Maryland) with news of Napoleon's defeat at Leipzig as well as a proposal from Foreign Minister Lord Castlereagh to open peace negotiations between London and Washington. Madison accepts ten days later.

17 JANUARY 1814. ***Jackson's Reverse.*** His previous army of West Tennesseans having demobilized when their enlistments expired, Jackson is reinforced at Fort Strother by 800 new recruits, setting out with 930 men and a six-pounder to fall upon a Creek concentration at Emuckfaw Creek (a tributary of the Tallapoosa River in Alabama). En route his army is bolstered by 200–300 friendly Creeks and Cherokees.

On 22 January hostiles ambush Jackson's column, forcing a retreat, then deliver a second deadly attack two days later at Enotachopco. Many recruits panic and flee, the rearguard being saved only with difficulty. American losses total two dozen dead and 71 wounded compared to 72 slain Creeks.

Andrew Jackson

27 JANUARY 1814. ***Calibee Creeks.*** After a nine-day 50-mile march from Fort Mitchell on the Chattahoochee River (south of Columbus, Georgia) to attack the Upper Creek village of Tuckaubatchee, Floyd's 1,200 volunteers and 400 Indian allies suffer a dawn attack ten miles short of their destination. After a bitter engagement around the Calibee Creeks the warriors draw off, leaving behind 37 fallen comrades. Floyd's losses are 22 killed and 147 wounded, prompting a retreat.

1 FEBRUARY 1814. Wilkinson evacuates French Mills (New York), detaching Brown to Sackets Harbor with 2,000 men while leading the remainder southeast to Plattsburgh.

6 FEBRUARY 1814. Royal marines and Canadian militia cross the Saint Lawrence from Cornwall (Ontario), plundering Madrid (New York).

8 FEBRUARY 1814. After a yearlong Pacific cruise—during which he has captured dozens of British prizes—Porter's USS *Essex* is blockaded within Valparaíso (Chile) by Capt. James Hillyar's 36-gun frigate HMS *Phoebe* and Cmdr. Tudor Tucker's 26-gun sloop

Cherub. Porter exits on 28 March, being dismasted by a squall and defeated three miles down the coast.

5 March 1814. This evening a 165-man foraging party under Capt. A. H. Holmes of the 24th U.S. infantry is attacked near Longwood (Ontario) by 240 redcoats, Canadian militia, and Indian warriors under Capt. James Basden of the 89th Foot. The Americans are dug in, so the three-pronged British attack through deep snow fares badly, resulting in 14 dead and 52 wounded. Holmes's casualties are only seven, allowing him to retire unmolested into Detroit.

27 March 1814. ***Horseshoe Bend.*** After being reinforced by the 39th U.S. Infantry Regiment and making a two-week advance south from Fort Strother, Jackson's 3,000 regulars, militia, and native allies (among them 21-year-old Maj. Sam Houston of the 39th) come upon 1,200 Creek warriors this morning, ensconced with their families on a 90-acre peninsula called Tohopeka on a horseshoe bend in the Tallapoosa River. The neck of the peninsula is protected by a log breastwork; canoes are beached at its far end to facilitate escape.

The American commander orders Coffee's riders, plus the Cherokee and Creek allies, to take up position opposite the bend to impede flight. Meanwhile Jackson's two field pieces bombard the breastwork until he learns Coffee's force has attacked the Creeks from the rear. At this point the 39th launches a frontal assault, and the attackers fight their way into the compound from both directions.

By nightfall 557 Creeks are dead and another 350—mostly women and children—are taken prisoner, several hundred others being drowned or shot while attempting to swim away. American casualties total 26 dead and 106 wounded; Cherokee, 18 and 36; friendly Creeks, five and 11.

30 March 1814. ***Wilkinson's Last Gasp.*** After advancing up Lake Champlain with 4,000 troops in three brigades plus a pair of 12-pounders, Wilkinson breaks the Canadian border and occupies Odelltown (Quebec). But upon proceeding farther north against the 180-man garrison of Maj. Richard B. Handcock at the Lacolle River Ford (10 miles west of Île aux Noix), his army becomes bogged down by heavy snow then fails to carry the thick stone mill serving as Handcock's blockhouse. Rocket artillery fired by a detachment of Royal Marines inflicts considerable punishment, obliging the discouraged Americans to retire south to Plattsburgh (New York).

Wilkinson requests a court of inquiry, so is replaced on 1 May by newly promoted 37-year-old Maj. Gen. George Izard.

31 March 1814. In Europe, allied armies enter Paris. Ten days later Arthur, Duke of Wellington, wins the Battle of Toulouse, compelling Napoleon to abdicate next day at Fontainebleu. As the emperor goes into exile on Elba Island, Britain will begin diverting troops to the North American theater.

7 April 1814. A half-dozen British barges ascend eight miles up the Connecticut River, destroying 20 American vessels.

14 April 1814. At Kingston (Ontario), Yeo launches the 58-gun HMS *Prince Regent* and 40-gun *Princess Charlotte,* which become the most powerful warships on Lake Ontario.

5 May 1814. At noon Yeo materializes off Fort Oswego (New York), his squadron bearing a British raiding force under the recently arrived 41-year-old veteran Lt. Gen. Gordon Drummond (*see* 2 June 1794 in Part 6). Because of a heavy northwesterly gale, Swiss-born Lt. Col. Victor Fischer cannot disembark until next morning with 140 redcoats, 400 marines, and 200 seamen, but the 290 American defenders—mostly artillerymen—quickly retire into the interior, having suffered six killed, 38 wounded, and 25 missing. British casualties are 18 dead and 73 injured, after which the raiders strip Fort Oswego of its stores, departing by 7 May.

10 May 1814. Capt. Hugh Pigot of the brigs HMS *Orpheus* and *Shelburne* reaches the Apalachicola River mouth (western Florida) to recruit Creek and Choctaws against the Americans.

14 May 1814. This afternoon 800 American raiders descend on Port Dover (Ontario), torching it next afternoon. The worst excesses are committed by Canadian turncoats under Maj. Abraham Markle.

19 May 1814. A small American raiding party destroys Port Talbot (Ontario).

20 May 1814. In order to prevent heavy American artillery pieces out of Oswego Falls from reaching Sackets Harbor (New York) to be installed aboard the recently launched 62-gun USS *Superior,* Yeo institutes a close blockade.

30 MAY 1814. Soon after daylight British naval Cmdrs. Stephen Popham and Francis B. Spilsbury sight 18 American boats hiding up Sandy Creek under Master Commandant Melancthon T. Woolsey—friend of James Fenimore Cooper—waiting to dash eight miles into Sackets Harbor (New York). Popham moves his three gunboats and four lesser craft, manned by 200 sailors, inshore to steal upon the flotilla—little realizing that it is escorted by brevet Maj. Daniel Appling's 130 U.S. regulars, 120 Oneida warriors, plus a strong contingent of troops out of Sackets Harbor. A half-mile from his objective Popham is ambushed, suffering 14 killed and 28 wounded before surrendering.

6 JUNE 1814. Having failed to impede American guns from reaching the new U.S. warship *Superior,* Yeo lifts his blockade of Sackets Harbor (New York) and retires into Kingston (Ontario).

21 JUNE 1814. A small British expedition under Capt. Robert Barrie captures the American outposts of Thomaston and St. George, west of Penobscot Bay (Maine).

3 JULY 1814. Early on this rainy morning Brigadier General Scott disembarks 1,300 New England troops below Fort Erie (near Niagara Falls, Ontario), while Brig. Gen. Eleazer Wheelock Ripley brings another 1,000 U.S. regulars ashore above the stronghold, prompting the isolated garrison of two British companies (137 men) under Maj. Thomas Buck to surrender. Brown—now promoted major general—then arrives with 325 gunners and 600 Pennsylvania volunteers under Brig. Gen. Peter B. Porter (a New York congressman) plus 500–600 Six Nation warriors.

Next day Scott pushes north to Street's Creek and by evening spots 1,500 British troops and 300 natives concentrating south of the Chippawa (modern-day Welland) River under Riall. The Americans bring up reinforcements and prepare to fight on 5 July.

5 JULY 1814. ***Chippawa River.*** Riall, unaware that Fort Erie has already fallen—and that he is thus confronting the bulk of Brown's invasion force—advances across open fields toward the American positions south of Street's Creek. The British commander is also oblivious to the fact that the host contains a large percentage of U.S. regulars rather than undisciplined frontier militia.

At 5:00 P.M. Brown orders Scott to move his three battalions out and meet the British challenge head on. After a brief exchange of long-range artillery salvos, Riall sends the 8th Foot to assault the American left while the 1st and 100th Regiments drive against the center. The steady counterfire and unwavering U.S. ranks reveal the true nature of the opposition—but too late, for by the time Riall signals the recall 148 of his men have been killed and 321 wounded with 46 missing, as opposed to 60 dead and 268 injured among the American ranks. The British retire north behind the Chippawa River, having destroyed its lone remaining bridge.

7 JULY 1814. Brown crosses the Chippawa River at two places, prompting Riall to retreat to Fort George (Niagara-on-the-Lake, Ontario), forestalling any potential encirclement. The Americans follow, occupying Queenston and fortifying its strategic heights while waiting for siege artillery and reinforcements to arrive from Sackets Harbor (New York) aboard Chauncey's squadron.

11 JULY 1814. At 3:00 P.M. British Lt. Col. Andrew Pilkington's 102nd Regiment—recently arrived at Halifax from Bermuda—is deposited by Commo. Thomas Hardy's 74-gun *Ramillies* and several transports on Moose Island (Passamaquoddy Bay, New Brunswick), subduing the 88-man American outpost under Maj. Perley Putnam at Eastport without resistance.

MID-JULY 1814. The recently arrived veteran Vice Adm. Sir Alexander Cochrane (*see* 3 April 1805 in Part 6) detaches Capt. William Henry Percy with 28-gun frigate *Hermes,* sloop *Carron,* and two other Royal Navy warships—plus 100 marines, two howitzers, and a field piece under acting Lt. Col. Edward Nicholls—to the Apalachicola River (western Florida) to take aboard Creek and Choctaw warriors and convey them to Spanish Pensacola for a forthcoming assault against American Fort Bowyer (South Mobile Bay, Alabama). Percy eventually recruits 600 warriors for this purpose.

17 JULY 1814. A retired Canadian fur trader named William McKay—temporarily appointed militia

lieutenant colonel—reaches Prairie du Chien (Fort Shelby, Wisconsin) with 120 volunteers, 530 Indian allies, and a three-pounder, obliging the garrison of 66 U.S. regulars and five guns under Lt. Joseph Perkins to surrender after three days of desultory exchanges on condition that they be paroled into American territory. Total casualties are three wounded warriors.

About 400 Sauk, Fox, and Kickapoo Indians pursue the escaping 14-gun U.S. gunboat *Governor Clark* down the Mississippi, overtaking it at Rock Island Rapids along with some other craft. A hard-fought battle ensues in which 35 Americans are killed or wounded before the flotilla retires into St. Louis.

22 JULY 1814. By the Treaty of Greenville the Creek, Delaware, Miami, Seneca, Shawnee, and Wyandotte Indians make an alliance with the United States, declaring war against Great Britain.

24 JULY 1814. Learning that no reinforcements will reach him from Sackets Harbor (New York), and with his army outside Queenston (Ontario) now depleted to 2,644 effectives because of disease and desertion, Brown withdraws south of the Chippawa River. He is pursued by 1,000 redcoats under Pearson out of Fort George (Niagara-on-the-Lake), followed by another 600 under Riall dragging four field pieces: two 24-pounders plus two six-pounders.

25 JULY 1814. ***Lundy's Lane.*** This morning Drummond reinforces Fort George from York (Toronto), sending Morrison's 89th Foot south to join Riall while detaching another 500 redcoats and Indians out of Fort Niagara under Lt. Col. J. G. P. Tucker to threaten Lewiston (New York). Learning of this two-pronged menace, Brown orders Scott to advance north at 5:00 P.M. with the 1,070 survivors of his brigade and launch a diversionary strike against Riall's vanguard at Lundy's Lane (a mile from Niagara Falls).

At 6:00 P.M. Scott smashes into the 1,600-man British formation, Maj. Thomas Jesup's 25th U.S. Infantry Regiment driving back Riall's left while Drummond fends off the American 11th and 22nd in the center. Riall is badly wounded and then captured when his stretcher-bearers mistakenly enter American lines. By 8:30 P.M. Scott's brigade has been reduced to 600 effectives when he is joined by Brown with Ripley's and Porter's brigades. They push back Drummond and seize some British guns, only to have 1,200 redcoats of Lt. Col. Hercules Scott's 103rd Regiment and assorted Canadian militia with two six-pounders arrive at 10:00 P.M. from Twelve Mile Creek (St. Catharines) and swing the advantage back to the defenders. By midnight—Brown and Scott being wounded—Ripley orders a withdrawal to Chippawa, the Anglo-Canadians being too exhausted to pursue.

American casualties total 173 dead, 571 wounded, and 117 missing; British losses are 84 killed, 559 injured (including Drummond and Riall), and 193 missing among their regulars, plus a further 162 casualties among the Canadian militia. Next morning the invaders destroy the Chippawa's lone bridge and their baggage train before retiring southeast to Fort Erie.

26 JULY 1814. More than three weeks after quitting Detroit to sail up Lake Huron aboard five small U.S. vessels, Croghan—now a lieutenant colonel—appears off British-held Michilimackinac with 700 American regulars (five companies) and Ohio militia. Judging its fortifications too strong for direct assault, he disembarks at the other end of the island on 4 August, moving inland to take its defenders from the rear.

Lt. Col. Robert McDouall of the Royal Newfoundland Regiment—commanding only 140 redcoats plus 280 Canadian militia and Indian warriors—emerges from his lines to await the Americans behind a low breastwork in a woodland clearing. When Croghan drives against the position he suffers 13 killed and 51 wounded; he reembarks next day and departs, leaving behind a pair of blockading vessels.

(While returning to Detroit this American expedition destroys the British schooner *Nancy* of Lt. Miller Worsley near the mouth of the Nottawasaga River, although its commander and crew escape to Michilimackinac by canoe.)

2 AUGUST 1814. ***Fort Erie Siege.*** Having recuperated from their encounter at Lundy's Lane, advance elements of Drummond's army arrive outside Fort Erie (opposite Buffalo, New York) to find 2,200 American defenders completing a newly fortified camp. Brig. Gen. Edmund Pendleton Gaines has also traveled from Sackets Harbor to assume command over the U.S. garrison for the wounded Brown.

The British commander appears next day with his main body but, realizing that 3,500 redcoats are insufficient to storm the defenses, settles down to await his siege train. On 5 August Chauncey's squadron materializes out of Lake Ontario, detaching several U.S. warships to support the defenders ashore and restrict British lake traffic. On 12 August the American men-of-war *Somers* and *Ohio* are captured by Cmdr. Alexander Dobbs's *Charwell;* next day Drummond opens fire on Fort Erie's ramparts with six siege guns. Two hours before daylight on 15 August he sends five columns of redcoats to assault Gaines's lines; the attempt proves premature and is repulsed with heavy losses (especially when an advance British magazine blows up). All told, the attackers suffer 57 dead, 309 wounded, plus 539 captured or missing, as opposed to 84 Americans killed or injured.

Following this repulse Drummond is reinforced by two fresh regiments—1,200 men—so maintains his siege. On 29 August a British shell explodes in Gaines's quarters, wounding him so severely that the convalescent Brown must reassume command. On 15 September the besiegers complete a third battery, compelling the Americans (now reinforced by 1,000 New York militia) to contemplate a sally. At 3:00 P.M. on 17 September, during a heavy downpour, Porter emerges with 1,600 U.S. regulars and militia, catching the British by surprise. Their No. 3 battery and protective blockhouse are quickly overrun—guns are spiked and magazines blown—before Porter proceeds against No. 2 battery supported by 400 of Scott's men. That position is overwhelmed before Royal Scots, the 6th (1st Warwickshire), 82nd (Prince of Wales Volunteers), and 89th Regiments contain the breakout and drive the Americans back inside Fort Erie. The besiegers sustain 115 killed, 176 wounded, 315 missing, and three guns destroyed compared to 79 American dead plus 432 injured or missing.

Disheartened, Drummond raises his siege four days later, retiring toward the Chippawa River at 8:00 P.M. on 21 September. Brown does not pursue, instead entering winter quarters at Buffalo.

9 AUGUST 1814. Four months after erecting a fort at the confluence of the Coosa and Talapoosa Rivers, Jackson—now a brevet major general in the regular U.S. army—dictates terms to the defeated Creeks, compelling them to cede two-thirds of their lands to the United States and shift their villages out of the settlers' path into southwestern Alabama.

This same day, Hardy's Royal Navy squadron bombards Stonington (Connecticut) and is repulsed.

16 AUGUST 1814. A British expedition escorted by the 80-gun HMS *Tonnant* (flag) and nine other ships of the line sweeps through the Virginia Capes and up Chesapeake Bay under Cochrane, bearing 4,000 regulars—the 4th (King's Own; 1st Battalion), 21st (Royal North British or Royal Scots Fusiliers), 44th (East Essex), 85th (Bucks Volunteers) Light Infantry, plus the 3rd Royal Marine Battalion and an artillery company—freshly arrived from England and Bermuda under Maj. Gen. Robert Ross.

19 AUGUST 1814. Ross's troops disembark at Benedict (Maryland), advancing north up the Patuxent River next day supported by a light naval division under Rear Adm. George Cockburn—Cochrane's second-in-command—to trap Commo. Joshua Barney's flotilla of American gunboats 40 miles upstream.

22 AUGUST 1814. Threatened by the approach of Ross's redcoats, Barney scuttles his gunboats and leads his 400 men overland to Washington. The British veer west next day, driving for the capital.

24 AUGUST 1814. ***Bladensburg.*** At dawn Washington authorities learn Ross is nearing Bladensburg (Maryland), prompting President Madison to exit northeast with more than 3,000 hastily assembled militia and join a similar force already gathered at the town. Eventually, Brigadier General Winder scrapes together almost 7,000 American troops—mostly raw recruits, no match for Ross's 4,000 disciplined veterans.

Shortly after midday a British column under Col. William Thornton easily drives the defenders from the lone bridge across the Potomac then panics the entire American army with a steady advance. Only Barney's naval gunners stand and fight, eventually being obliged to retreat when their leader is wounded and captured. So many American volunteers run that the redcoats dub this battle the "Bladensburg Races." Defensive casualties total 26 killed, 51 wounded, plus 100 captured compared to 64 dead and 185 injured among the British.

The road into Washington now lies open, and 1,500 British troops (after resting for several hours) enter unopposed that evening, finding that the president and Mrs. Dolly Madison have fled west into Virginia via Georgetown along with most of the capital's residents. Snipers fire on Ross's party out of the gloom, provoking exchanges throughout the night. U.S. naval Capt. Thomas Tingey also sets the nearby Washington navy yard ablaze, destroying the new 44-gun frigate *Columbia* and 18-gun sloop *Argus.*

Next day (25 August), British parties burn the presidential residence, capitol, and numerous other buildings—allegedly in revenge for the torching of towns in Canada (*see* 25 April 1813 and following entries)—then exit that night, returning to Benedict to reembark by 30 August. (When the Americans subsequently reoccupy Washington they whitewash the burn marks

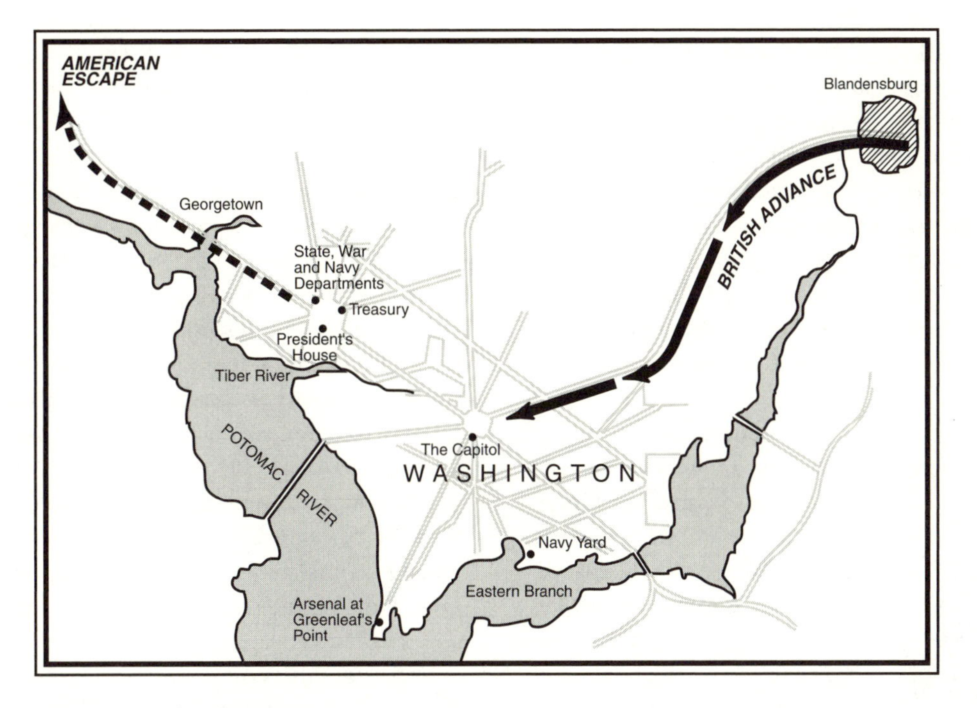

British capture of Washington, D.C.

on the presidential mansion, thereby transforming it into the White House.)

1 SEPTEMBER 1814. ***Maine Offensive.*** This morning British Rear Adm. Edward Griffith appears off Castine (Maine) with ten warships and ten transports, depositing Lt. Gen. Sir John Coape Sherbrooke's 2,000 redcoats: the 29th (Worcestershire), 62nd (Wiltshire), and 98th Regiments of Foot plus two companies of the 7th Battalion of 60th (Royal Americans) and an artillery detachment. Its 140 American defenders detonate the magazine, abandon the fort, and retreat north up the Penobscot River while Maj. Gen. Gerard Gosselin crosses to occupy Belfast opposite with 600 troops aboard HMS *Bacchante.*

Two mornings later Barrie's pair of pursuing British sloops, one transport, and boat flotilla materialize at Bald Head Cove (3 miles below Hampden), disembarking seven companies—700 regulars—and a five-and-a-half-inch howitzer under Lt. Col. Henry John. The veterans easily brush aside 600 American militia under Maj. Gen. John Blake, suffering only one killed, eight wounded, and another missing while overrunning the town by 5:00 P.M. (compared to 13 defender casualties and 81 prisoners). The anchored frigate USS *Adams* is torched by its captain, Charles Morris, so as not to fall into enemy hands, but 20 of its cannons are seized in a battery ashore, after which John and Barrie push on to accept the surrender of Bangor.

On 9 September Pilkington sets sail from Castine with several more British companies, circling east to land in Bucks Harbor (10 miles south of Machias) by next evening. At sunrise on 10 September the invaders occupy Fort O'Brien—5 miles away in Sanborn Cove—without a struggle; they take Machias an hour later. The entire state of Maine capitulates by 13 September.

2 SEPTEMBER 1814. At sunset naval Lieutenant Worsley slips out of Michilimackinac (Michigan) with four boatloads of Canadian militia under Lt. W. Andrew Bulger of the Royal Newfoundland Fencibles to surprise the American blockading schooner *Tigress* anchored six miles off Drummond Island. Next evening the boarders row out, rush the vessel at 9:00 P.M., and carry it with a loss of two killed and several wounded.

Worsley and Bulger leave its American colors flying until *Tigress*'s consort, *Scorpion,* arrives two evenings later, anchoring two miles away. Early next morning the British slip their cable and surprise the second warship as well, suffering only eight injured.

3 SEPTEMBER 1814. Capt. Nicholas Lockyer of the sloop HMS *Sophia* contacts Jean Lafitte at Grande Terre (Barataria Bay, south of New Orleans), requesting freebooters' help in the forthcoming British campaign against Louisiana. Despite the facts that his brother Pierre is jailed in New Orleans and that U.S. authorities are contemplating destroying Barataria as a smugglers' nest, Lafitte—while assuring the British of his cooperation—reveals the plan to the Americans two days later.

5 SEPTEMBER 1814. While advancing up the Mississippi from St. Louis to reclaim Prairie du Chien (renamed Fort McKay, Wisconsin), 350 U.S. regulars and Illinois militia under Taylor are ambushed near Rock Island Rapids early this morning by Winnebago, Sioux, and Sauk warriors under chief Black Hawk, supported by a three-pounder under Royal Artillery Sgt. James Keating. The Americans retreat downriver, pausing at the mouth of the Des Moines River to erect a small fort, which they abandon shortly.

6 SEPTEMBER 1814. This evening, after five days' march south from Quebec along the western shores of Lake Champlain, Canadian Governor-General Prevost invests Plattsburgh (New York) with 10,350 redcoats in three brigades: Maj. Gen. Frederick P. Robinson's 27th (Inniskilling, 3rd Battalion), 39th (Dorsetshire), 76th, and 88th (Connaught Rangers) Regiments; Maj. Gen. Thomas Brisbane's 8th (2nd Battalion), 13th (1st Somersetshire), and 49th, plus the Swiss de Meuron (Neuchâtel), Regiments, Canadian voltigeurs, and Canadian chasseurs; as well as Maj. Gen. Manley Powers's 3rd (East Kent or Buffs), 5th (Northumberland), 27th (1st Battalion), and 58th (Rutlandshire) Regiments.

The motley, 3,300-man American garrison—less than half being effective troops, Izard having departed west on 29 August with the 4,000 best regulars—retreats across the Saranac River and digs in under Brig. Gen. Alexander Macomb. Rather than storm Plattsburgh's fortifications Prevost deploys his siege train; two days later he orders Commo. George Downie to sail 12 miles south from nearby Chazy with his small British squadron to destroy Commodore Macdonough's U.S. squadron anchored offshore. The respite allows many New York and Vermont militia contingents to rally in Plattsburgh.

10 SEPTEMBER 1814. After resting for a fortnight the Cochrane-Ross expedition, with 50 British ships, sweeps up Chesapeake Bay to attack Baltimore. Next afternoon it reaches the Patapco River and prepares to disembark troops.

11 SEPTEMBER 1814. ***Lake Champlain.*** This Sunday at 8:30 A.M., Downie rounds Cumberland head to enter Plattsburgh Bay with the 37-gun frigate *Confiance* (flag), 16-gun brig *Linnet,* sloops *Chubb* and *Finch,* plus 11 gunboats, manned by 800 Anglo-Canadian seamen. Macdonough's 850 American sailors wait aboard their newly built 26-gun corvette *Saratoga* (flag) and 20-gun brig *Eagle,* plus the seven-gun *Ticonderoga* and *Preble,* and ten oared gunboats mounting 16 guns between them.

After struggling upwind for half an hour Downie's flagship anchors 400 yards away and opens fire on *Saratoga.* The British commodore is killed within the first 15 minutes, and over the next couple of hours *Chubb* drifts helplessly into the American lines and strikes, and *Finch* runs aground on Crab Island. Only four British gunboats engage, while the American gunners completely outfight their opponents—some even swinging their warships around midbattle to present their undamaged broadsides.

Although losses on both sides are comparable—57 dead and 72 wounded British, 52 killed and 58 injured Americans—all four attacking ships surrender; their gunboats escape back out into Lake Champlain under oars. Prevost, who made no attempt to storm Plattsburgh's fortifications while the naval battle rages, inexplicably orders a general retreat north that rainy night. Total casualties from his army's campaign are 35 dead, 47 wounded, 72 captured, and 234 missing; American losses on land are 37 dead and 62 injured. (Next spring Prevost is relieved of command because of faint-heartedness.)

12 SEPTEMBER 1814. ***Fort McHenry.*** At 3:00 A.M. Ross's 4,000 redcoats—joined by 700 marines and sailors under Cockburn—begin disembarking at North Point (Maryland), assembling ashore before striking northwest four hours later to circle 12 miles inland and invest Baltimore. Their task proves daunting, for not only does Maj. Gen. (and senator) Samuel Smith have 16,400 men to defend the city and its approaches but shortly thereafter the British general is killed by American skirmishers, so that command devolves upon Col. Arthur Brooke of the 4th Regiment.

The latter encounters a detached American contingent of 3,200 militia under Brig. Gen. John Stricker near Bread and Cheese Creek, pushing them back after two hours' fighting, then camping for the night. The assault costs the redcoats 46 dead and 273 wounded, as opposed to 24 Americans killed, 139 injured, and 50 captured. Meanwhile Cochrane sails 16 of his Royal Navy frigates and lighter warships up the Patapco, dropping anchor by midafternoon on 12 September a few miles south of Fort McHenry to offer covering fire against its 1,000-man garrison under U.S. Maj. George Armistead.

At 5:00 A.M. next day the bomb vessels *Volcano* and *Meteor* plus the rocket ship *Erebus* creep within two miles of the American stronghold and commence a bombardment in anticipation of the assault by Brooke's redcoats ashore. (The sight of the rockets' "red glare" bursting against Fort McHenry's 30- by 42-foot flag inspire Francis Scott Key—held eight miles downriver aboard a waiting American truce vessel—to compose "The Star Spangled Banner.") The bomb ships *Terror, Devastation,* and *Ætna* soon join in, the outranged American artillery being unable to reply—although no land attack then occurs. At 3:00 P.M. Cochrane's ships close the range, only to retreat precipitately when they come under accurate counterfire.

This evening a discouraged Brooke orders his army to retreat next morning, and his troops reembark from North Point on 15 September having suffered 346 total casualties. Soon after, Cochrane and Brooke part company, the admiral proceeding to Halifax while the colonel leads his expedition to Jamaica.

15 SEPTEMBER 1814. After disembarking from Percy's squadron three days earlier at Mobile Point (Alabama), Nicholls advances with 730 royal marines and Indian allies to invest the 130-man garrison of U.S. regulars holding Fort Bowyer under Maj. William Lawrence. The British squadron appears offshore to help bombard the ramparts, but the Americans repel the combined assault, killing 162 and wounding 72 attackers while suffering only four dead and four injured. Percy's flagship *Hermes* runs aground opposite the American batteries and is abandoned and destroyed. The British retire 60 miles east to Spanish Pensacola.

16 SEPTEMBER 1814. This morning Lafitte's illegal base at Barataria is raided by 70 American soldiers under Commo. Daniel Todd Patterson of the 14-gun schooner USS *Carolina,* escorted from New Orleans by six gunboats under naval Lt. Thomas ap Catesby "Tac" Jones. They capture 80 freebooters, along with six schooners and eight lesser vessels, and destroy many buildings without suffering casualties.

15 OCTOBER 1814. ***Last Ontario Invasion.*** After crossing the Niagara River into Upper Canada Izard probes the British defenses at Chippawa (Ontario) with 5,500 U.S. regulars and 800 militia, finding the fortifications stronger than anticipated. Next day he learns that Chauncey's squadron has retired into Sackets Harbor (New York) for fear of an attack by the new 112-gun HMS *Saint Lawrence* out of Kingston. Without naval support in the rear the American general hesitates to penetrate deeper.

On 19 October Brig. Gen. Daniel Bissell's U.S. regulars defeat a small British force at Cook's Mills on Lyon's Creek, but next day Yeo's squadron arrives off Fort George (Niagara-on-the-Lake) with *Saint Lawrence*—a warship that so dwarfs American vessels on Lake Ontario that Izard cancels his projected campaign into Upper Canada.

4 NOVEMBER 1814. American Brigadier General McArthur reaches Oxford (Ontario) with 800 troops, having been sent from Detroit on a foraging raid throughout Upper Canada. British Lt. Col. Henry Bostwick is powerless to resist, merely shadowing the invaders' movements with 400 Canadian militia until McArthur returns west one week later.

5 NOVEMBER 1814. After Izard and Brown retire across the Niagara River—the former into winter quarters in Buffalo, the latter to Sackets Harbor (New York)—American engineers blow up Fort Erie (Ontario).

6 NOVEMBER 1814. ***Pensacola.*** Irate at the British use of Spanish Pensacola as an advance base—despite Madrid's neutrality in the ongoing Anglo-American hostilities—Jackson appears outside its walls with 2,000 mounted Tennesseans under Coffee, 700 U.S. regulars, a detachment of Mississippi dragoons under Maj. Thomas Hind, plus other auxiliaries.

Major Henry D. Peire of the U.S. 44th Regiment is sent forward under flag of truce to demand that Pensacola's two principal forts—San Miguel and Barrancas, now manned by British garrisons—be surrendered by Spanish Gov. Mateo González Manrique. Instead, Peire's party is fired upon by redcoats, prompting Jackson to storm the town. Its only battery is carried at bayonet point, resistance melting away with almost no blood shed. Percy's Royal Navy warships conduct a brief bombardment from out in the harbor before the British destroy Fort Barrancas (6 miles farther west) and withdraw.

Jackson then installs an American garrison and returns to Mobile, where he delegates two U.S. regiments and some militia to hold the coast between Pensacola and Mobile under Winchester before Jackson continues overland to New Orleans on 21 November.

25 NOVEMBER 1814. Cochrane's *Tonnant* weighs from Negril (Jamaica), followed next day by Rear Adm. Pulteney Malcolm's 74-gun *Royal Oak* (vice flag), *Norge, Bedford, Ramillies,* and *Asia;* 64-gun Dictator; frigates *Diomede, Gorgon, Alceste, Hydra, Weaver, Traave,* and *Belle Poule;* plus numerous brigs and schooners. They are escorting more than two dozen transports bearing 8,000 troops under Maj. Gen. John Keane: the 4th, 21st, 44th, 85th Light Infantry, the 93rd (Argyll and Sutherland Highlanders), the 95th Rifle Corps, the 1st and 5th West Indian Regiments, plus two squadrons of the 14th (Duchess of York) Light Dragoons. They are to rendezvous in the Gulf of Mexico with another contingent arriving from England and capture New Orleans.

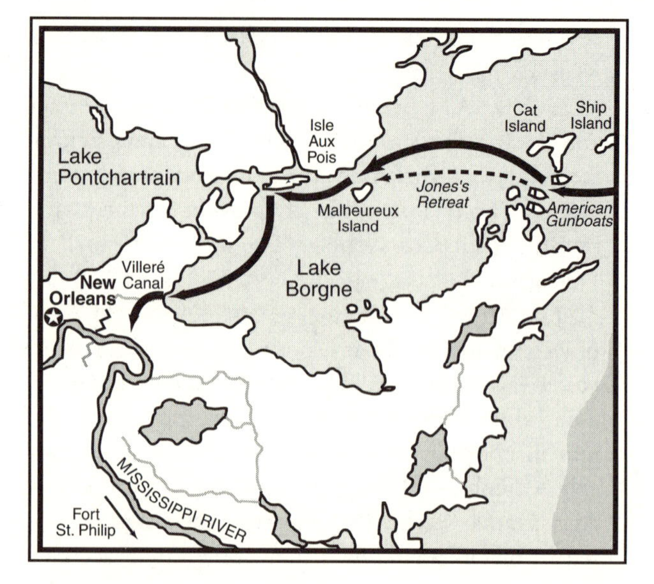

British advance against New Orleans

1 DECEMBER 1814. Jackson reaches New Orleans (population 10,000) and begins preparing for an anticipated British attack.

8 DECEMBER 1814. The 50-ship Cochrane-Keane expedition departs Pensacola, rendezvousing with Percy's squadron two days later near Mobile. On 12 December they anchor north of the Chandeleur Islands (Louisiana) to transfer Keane's troops west across shallow Lake Borgne.

The lake's mouth, however, is barred by five American gunboats plus the tenders *Sea Horse* and *Alligator* manned by 200 sailors under Lt. "Tac" Jones. Next day Lockyer leads 1,500 British sailors and marines aboard 45 boats against the flotilla. Jones falls back, but his vessels run aground between Malhereux Island and the mainland, being overwhelmed at dawn on 14 December after a two-hour fight in which he suffers ten killed and 35 wounded, the rest being captured. British casualties are 17 dead and 77 injured.

By 15 December Cochrane begins ferrying Keane's army to Isle aux Pois, taking five days to complete the operation.

17 DECEMBER 1814. Within New Orleans, Jackson offers a full pardon to Lafitte and his Baratarians, who join the American cause.

22 DECEMBER 1814. This evening Keane's vanguard—1,800 soldiers of the 85th, 95th, and 4th Regiments—disembark east of New Orleans. At 7:30 P.M. the next day they are struck by 1,800 Americans under Jackson and Coffee plus schooner *Carolina* of Capt. John Henley. After two hours' confused fighting the attack breaks off, the Americans suffering 24 killed, 115 wounded, and 74 missing. British losses are 46 dead, 167 injured, and 64 missing. Nevertheless, Keane's army continues to be reinforced and so presses on.

24 DECEMBER 1814. The Treaty of Ghent is signed in Europe, needing only ratification in London and Washington to bring an end to hostilities.

25 DECEMBER 1814. This afternoon 37-year-old Gen. Sir Edward Michael Pakenham (Wellington's brother-in-law) reaches the British camp near New Orleans, having hurried out from England aboard the frigate *Statira* to supplant Keane. He is being followed from Jamaica by an additional 2,700 redcoats of 42-year-old Gen. John Lambert's 3rd Division: the 7th (Royal "Fuzileers"), 40th (2nd Somersetshire), and 43rd (Monmouthshire) Regiments.

27 DECEMBER 1814. A five-gun British battery east of New Orleans destroys *Carolina* with red-hot shot then compels Lt. Charles Thompson's 16-gun *Louisiana*—a mile farther up the Mississippi—to be towed out of range.

28 DECEMBER 1814. At 8:00 A.M. Pakenham probes Jackson's line east of New Orleans, ordering a recall after suffering 60 casualties, as opposed to 16 American casualties.

1 JANUARY 1815. Having stealthily installed 17 heavy naval guns in two batteries, the British besiegers open fire on Jackson's line of earthen ramparts. American counterfire—especially from the two-gun

Baratarian battery of Dominique You and Renato Beluché—proves so accurate that the British guns are silenced and Pakenham's assault columns restrained from advancing.

4 JANUARY 1815. New Orleans is reinforced by 2,300 Kentucky militia under Brig. Gen. John Adair (although only 700 are armed). Two days later Lambert reaches Villeré with 1,700 redcoats of the 7th and 43rd Regiments, bringing Pakenham's strength up to 8,000 by 7 January. The British commander, unable to conceive of a maneuver around Jackson's line, now prepares to storm straight at it.

8 JANUARY 1815. ***New Orleans.*** Despite the failure of Thornton to shift 1,400 redcoats overnight to the Mississippi's western bank—thereby outflanking the American defenses—two columns of British troops march directly against Jackson's line at 4:00 A.M. this Sunday: the 4th, 21st, and 44th Regiments on the left and one company each of the 7th and 43rd, plus the 93rd and 5th West Indian Regiments on the right.

Awaiting them on the riverbank are the 7th U.S. Infantry with Thomas Beale's Orleans Riflemen next inland; then Maj. Jean Baptiste Plauché's Louisiana carabinière militia, two battalions of black troops under Majs. Pierre Robin Lacoste and Daquin, and the 44th U.S. infantry, the whole western half being under regular Col. George T. Ross. The remaining Americans are commanded by Coffee, their center being manned by Maj. Gen. William Carroll's Tennessee Rifles with Adair's Kentuckians farther east and a screen of 60 Choctaw warriors under Pierre Jugeat in the cypress swamps beyond. Jackson thus has 4,000 men on his firing line protected by a ten-foot earthen rampart and eight batteries.

In the growing light the redcoats march bravely into a hail of fire, only to be remorselessly mowed down. When his first assault wave falters Pakenham personally intervenes to rally his troops, receiving three mortal wounds. His 6,500-man army eventually retires under Lambert after absorbing 858 dead, 2,468 injured, and 500 captured in contrast to 13 killed and 39 wounded among Jackson's ranks.

Thornton belatedly reaches the western bank of the Mississippi with 450 redcoats, royal marines, and sailors, easily scattering Brig. Gen. David B. Morgan's 1,200 American defenders: the 1st and 2nd Louisiana Militia, Col. Alexandre Declouet's conscripts, plus a company of Kentucky volunteers under Col. John Davis, supported by three field pieces. Although suffering only three killed and 30 wounded, Thornton's victory cannot possibly offset the devastation of the main British body, so he retires this evening. Next day a local truce is arranged so Lambert's survivors might gather the fallen.

9 JANUARY 1815. This afternoon Cochrane's squadron approaches Fort St. Philip (45 miles southeast of New Orleans), deploying the sloops *Herald, Nymph,* and *Thistle;* schooner *Pigmy;* plus bomb vessels *Ætna* and *Meteor* close inshore to commence a bombardment by 3:00 P.M. The fort's 366-man American garrison, under Maj. Walter H. Overton—some 7th U.S. Infantry regulars, a Louisiana volunteer battalion, a company of free blacks, plus 120 gunners under English-born artillery Capt. Charles Wollstonecraft—endure nine days of continuous fire, suffering two killed, before the British withdraw on the morning of 18 January.

15 JANUARY 1815. Decatur's USS *President* sorties from New York during a snowstorm, is damaged by grounding, then is pursued next dawn by HMSS *Majestic,* of 56 guns, and *Endymion.* The latter—a 48-gun frigate commanded by Capt. Henry Hope—eventually overtakes *President* this evening off Connecticut, inflicting 75 casualties before the Royal Navy warships *Pomone* and *Tenedos* also join, compelling Decatur to strike after a one-sided exchange.

18 JANUARY 1815. After a fortnight of paralyzed inactivity before Jackson's line outside New Orleans, Lambert stealthily withdraws his shattered British survivors this evening toward Lake Borgne and begins to reembark Cochrane's transports off Cat Island next morning. The Americans do little to hamper the retirement; by 26 January the invaders depart east toward Dauphine Island (Alabama).

7 FEBRUARY 1815. ***Fort Bowyer.*** Having been reinforced by two fresh regiments out of England, Lambert disembarks 1,200 redcoats and 450 gunners for 16 heavy naval guns, plus numerous sappers and Royal Marines, behind Fort Bowyer on Mobile Point. They quickly invest the 360-man garrison under Major Lawrence, compelling him to surrender under easy terms by sundown on 11 February. Victory celebrations are cut short by the arrival of a Royal Navy frigate bearing news of the official cessation of hostilities.

14 FEBRUARY 1815. President Madison receives his copy of the Treaty of Ghent, which is ratified by the

U.S. Congress three days later. Despite the last-minute victory at New Orleans, the War of 1812 ends badly for the Americans: their capital burned, no new territories won (except some Creek lands), and exports reduced from more than $108 million in 1807 to $7 million by 1814.

U.S. Expansion through Eastern Tribelands (1816–1842)

As American settlers push inland from the Atlantic seaboard, Great Lakes region, and Mississippi delta, they encroach upon the territories of their seminomadic Indian neighbors, resulting in clashes because of each side's differing philosophy regarding landownership. The pioneers are also quick to call upon state and federal authorities for support whenever they perceive a threat.

One of the earliest conflicts develops with the Creek and Seminole residents of northern Florida, who are squeezed between homesteaders migrating south out of Georgia and east out of Alabama. Although Florida remains nominally under Spanish control, Madrid is too distracted by the ongoing wars of independence in Latin America to defend these isolated, sparsely populated imperial outposts. Armed Americans therefore begin crossing Florida's border with impunity, especially in pursuit of runaway slaves who seek sanctuary amid its Spanish missions.

July 1816. ***Fort Negro.*** Incensed at having a U.S. supply ship that earlier attempted to ascend the Apalachicola River toward Fort Scott fired upon by the black and Seminole garrison at Fort Negro, Brigadier Gaines dispatches an American land and naval force under 29-year-old, 250-pound Lt. Col. Duncan L. Clinch to deal with this obstacle. Clinch penetrates 60 miles into Spanish territory and invests this stronghold. On 24 July a lucky round from one of his blockading gunboats scores a direct hit on the fort's magazine, killing 270 of its 300 defenders and wounding the rest. After the Americans raze Fort Negro and regain their own territory, Spain protests this violation of its sovereignty, to no avail.

20 November 1817. ***First Seminole War.*** After months of increasing frictions, Chief Neamathla of the Mikasuki Seminoles at Fowltown and Chief Bowlegs of the neighboring Alachua warn Gaines not to send any more formations from Fort Scott across the Flint River (southwestern Georgia). Deeming this to be U.S. rather than Indian or Spanish territory, Gaines responds angrily by dispatching Maj. David E. Twiggs with 250 troops to arrest Neamathla. Next day, the soldiers engage in an indecisive firefight near Fowltown, thus inaugurating open hostilities.

The conflict soon escalates when the Seminoles ambush 40 regulars under Lt. Richard W. Scott of 7th U.S. Infantry who are advancing up the Apalachicola River to reinforce Fort Scott. This force is almost totally annihilated, with 34 soldiers killed, plus seven soldiers' wives. As a result, President Monroe authorizes Gaines on 16 December to pursue hostiles deep into Spanish territory, so that on 4 January 1818 the general advances upon Fowltown and—finding it deserted—burns it to the ground.

The war then multiplies exponentially when the highly aggressive westerner Jackson reaches Fort Scott in early March 1818 to assume overall command. Soon he strikes south with 500 regulars, 1,000 Tennessee militia, and 2,000 Creek allies. Outnumbered and outgunned, the Seminoles scatter, their only opposition being made by 200 to 300 black warriors who fight delaying actions west of the Suwannee River. Determined to eradicate such nuisance raiders once and for all, Jackson presses ahead and seizes the Spanish outpost of San Marcos de Apalache by early April, hanging two British subjects on 29 April as agents provocateurs. The American general then proceeds to occupy Spanish Pensacola and directs Gaines to capture Saint Augustine as well one month later.

Jackson returns toward Tennessee by 30 May, finding that while his high-handed actions are cheered by the public, they meet with disapproval in official circles. This August, Monroe offers to restore Florida to Spain—which soon proposes selling this indefensible province back to the United States for several million dollars. On 31 October 1818, almost as an afterthought, the First Seminole War is declared ended.

August 1823. ***Arikara War.*** A semisedentary Pawnee tribe (a northern offshoot of the Caddoans), the Arikara live in earth-covered lodges with their Mandan and Hidatsa Sioux neighbors in what is today South Dakota, planting corn and hunting buffalo for their subsistence. In the summer of 1823, their warriors resist the ascent up the Missouri River of a swelling number of American traders, eventually resulting in a pitched battle. When news of this encounter reaches 40-year-old Col. Henry Leavenworth 600 miles downstream at Fort Atkinson (Kansas), he swiftly leads a small force of U.S. regulars, trappers, traders, and Indian allies upstream to the mouth of Grand River, where he defeats the Arikara.

SPRING 1832. ***Black Hawk War.*** Having been driven onto the western shores of the Mississippi River this previous year by white encroachments, Sauk and Fox planters return to Rock Island (Illinois) to sow new crops. Panicky American militia shoot down an Indian carrying a flag of truce, prompting the 65-year-old Chief Ma'katawimesheka'ka ("Black Sparrow Hawk") to authorize a series of cross-border raids. Eventually his overmatched tribesmen are defeated at Wisconsin Heights on 20–21 July by a volunteer army under Col. Henry Dodge and James D. Henry. Black Hawk flees west with his own small band, which is subsequently massacred on the banks of the Bad Axe River. The chieftain is captured and confined in Fort Monroe (Virginia).

21 OCTOBER 1834. Retired Maj. Gen. Wiley Thompson of the Georgia militia, now an Indian agent at Fort King on the southern banks of the Alachua River (north-central Florida), informs its Seminole chieftains of President Jackson's decision to transplant their 5,000 tribesmen onto reservations west of the Mississippi. During the forthcoming year, native opposition coalesces around the 34-year-old war leader Asi Yaholo ("black drink singer"; mispronounced "Osceola" by whites, who also refer to him as "Powell").

28 DECEMBER 1835. ***Second Seminole War.*** On this cold, drizzly morning, 108 U.S. regulars under 43-year-old Brevet Maj. Francis Langhorn Dade are ambushed a few miles north of the Little Withlacoochee River while marching from Fort Brooke (Tampa Bay) as reinforcements for Fort King, 30 miles deeper into central Florida. Their attackers are 160 Seminole warriors and black allies under Chiefs Micanopy, Abraham, Jumper, and Alligator, who despite being briefly checked by Dade's 6-pounder cannon eventually massacre this entire command (only two badly wounded survivors escaping with their lives). This same afternoon, another 40 warriors under Osceola attack the outskirts of Fort King proper, killing seven whites—including the fort's Indian agent, Thompson—then retiring south to join Micanopy's band.

This outbreak marks the culmination of several months' increasing volatility throughout this region, as natives protest Washington's plan to expel them into Arkansas. Three days later, brevet Brigadier Clinch leads a second column into hostile Seminole territory, consisting of 250 regulars under one-armed brevet Lt. Col. Alexander C. W. Fanning and 500 Florida volunteers under militia Brig. Richard Keith Call. While fording the Withlacoochee River they are ambushed by 230 Seminole and 30 black warriors under Osceola, who—despite being injured—obliges these invaders to withdraw by late afternoon after suffering four dead and 59 wounded.

The federal government in Washington responds to these two unexpected setbacks by dispatching Gen. Winfield Scott to Picolata with orders to marshal a large body of regulars and militia and stifle all resistance. In the marshy wilds of central Florida, meanwhile, Osceola's followers expand their revolt by attacking plantations and freeing slaves while simultaneously preparing to wage a protracted guerrilla struggle.

13 FEBRUARY 1836. Having arrived four days previously at Tampa Bay from New Orleans with a relief force, Major General Gaines strikes inland with 1,000 men and a 6-pounder to reinforce Clinch in central Florida. After departing Fort King on 26 February, however, Gaines is pinned down next day by Osceola's warriors while attempting to ford the Withlacoochee River. Although suffering only four soldiers killed and 38 wounded, his half-starved army nevertheless cannot be extricated by Clinch until 6 March.

25 MARCH 1836. Scott orders three columns of more than 1,000 troops apiece to advance into Seminole territory: Col. William Lindsay's force from Tampa Bay, brevet Brig. Abraham Eustis's from Volusia, plus Clinch's from Fort Drane. After repeatedly drawing fire from native snipers, these contingents meet at Fort Brooke by 4–8 April, having slain only 60 of their elusive foes during this advance. Osceola's followers further begin attacking isolated American outposts in the rear, plus harassing Scott's supply lines.

27 APRIL 1836. While marching to the relief of Fort Alabama, Col. William Chisholm's 600 militia volunteers are ambushed, suffering five killed and 24 wounded.

29 SEPTEMBER 1836. Call—now Florida's governor—crosses the Suwannee River with some U.S. regulars, local militia, and 1,500 Tennessee volunteers, driving toward Fort Drane. Though they are reinforced by 200 more regulars and 750 Creek auxiliaries under Col. John F. Lane, little is accomplished during

Call's subsequent two-month campaign beyond surprising a few unwary Seminole bands.

Finally Wahoo Swamp is approached by 21 November, but Call fails to press home his attack, instead retiring toward Volusia after suffering 55 casualties—little realizing that 600 native and black warriors have been trapped nearby, protecting their families. By early December, Call is relieved of military command in favor of U.S. Quartermaster General Jesup.

22 JANUARY 1837. Jesup departs Fort Armstrong with approximately 2,000 U.S. regulars, marines, Alabama and Georgia militia, plus Creek auxiliaries, choosing to pursue elusive Seminole bands with flying detachments rather than his cumbersome main force. This change of tactics produces a series of small victories near Lake Apopka, Hatcheelustee Creek, and Big Cypress Swamp, obliging Chiefs Micanopy, Abraham, and Jumper to request terms by 3 February.

Eventually a treaty is signed on 6 March whereby 1,000 Seminoles gather at Tampa Bay in mid-May to be transported west of the Mississippi by sea. However, Jesup's arrangements founder amid public criticism of his clemency, plus the lack of any amnesty for the natives' black allies (who are to be enslaved). On the night of 2 June, therefore, when Osceola and Sam Jones appear outside this unhappy Indian encampment with 200 warriors, their comrades join them in resuming hostilities.

EARLY SEPTEMBER 1837. Once Florida's summer heat has abated, Jesup resumes his campaign by deploying 3,700 troops in four columns: one moving along the St. Johns River, another patrolling Mosquito Inlet, a third advancing down the Kissimmee River from Tampa, the fourth going up the Caloosahatchee. These sweeps result in a number of important captures, culminating on 27 October when Osceola and 94 followers are treacherously seized near Fort Payton by 250 troops under Brig. Joseph M. Hernandez—despite having been asked to a parley and displaying a white flag. American public opinion deplores this act of perfidy, and Osceola is lionized upon being transferred into Fort Moultrie outside Charleston (South Carolina), where he subsequently dies of malaria on 30 January 1838.

2 DECEMBER 1837. Jesup launches a winter offensive by sending seven small armies roaming into the interior of Florida, denying any respite to its recalcitrant Seminole bands.

25 DECEMBER 1837. ***Lake Okeechobee.*** About midmorning, approximately 1,000 men of 1st, 4th, and 6th U.S. Infantry Regts., 1st Missouri Volunteers, plus Delaware and Shawnee scouts—all under Col. Zachary Taylor—capture a man who promises to guide them toward a Seminole encampment atop a rise bordering Lake Okeechobee. Expecting to encounter only minimal resistance, Taylor launches a frontal assault by 12:30 P.M. across half a mile of sawgrass swamp.

His front ranks are riddled by accurate counterfire from three bodies of waiting warriors: 250 on the right under Sam Jones, 120 in the center under Alligator, plus 80 on the left under King Philip's son Coacoochee (called "Wildcat" by the Americans). After the 180 Missouri volunteers of Col. Richard Gentry break and run, 6th U.S. Infantry of Col. Ramsey Thompson also retreats, so that by the time Taylor's reserves begin a flanking maneuver at 3:00 P.M. the Seminoles are able to escape eastward. American losses total 26 dead (including Gentry and Thompson) plus 112 wounded, as opposed to 11 fallen warriors and 14 injured.

24 JANUARY 1838. At noon a company of U.S. dragoons under Capt. William M. Fulton—vanguard for Jesup's main army—are fired upon by 200 to 300 Seminole and black warriors who are occupying the high ground near Locksahatchee. Despite making a rapid advance, the Americans are unable to prevent their opponents' flight and suffer seven killed and 32 wounded (including Jesup, who is slightly injured).

7 FEBRUARY 1838. Jesup meets Chief Tuskegee and over the next few days persuades him to bring his emaciated followers to Fort Jupiter, on the understanding that these Seminoles will not be obliged to abandon Florida. Some 500 Indians and blacks soon are encamped within a mile of this outpost, but when Washington rejects Jesup's terms on 17 March, the general sends the 2nd U.S. Dragoons to surround and imprison this band, thus violating his promise.

15 MAY 1838. Jesup relinquishes command of the 1,800 U.S. regulars and 500 militia remaining in Florida to brevet Brigadier Taylor, to return toward Washington. By now, Seminole activity consists of feeble hit-and-run raids against mostly civilian targets.

1838–1842. Over the next four years, American forces fight a protracted brush war against Seminole bands hiding throughout the Everglades, gradually hunting these into extinction while deporting hundreds of captives.

Disgusted U.S. regulars refer to this inglorious struggle as a "dirty little war of aggression," many resigning from the service. On 14 August 1842, their 48-year-old, lame commander—Col. William Jenkins Worth—at last announces an end to the Second Seminole War, which has cost 1,466 American soldiers their lives (328 in battle).

Mexican Turbulence (1822–1834)

For many emerging Latin American nations, independence from Spain does not bring an end to strife; rather, there ensues bitter wrangling as to how best to replace the vanished imperial apparatus. Many innovations are proposed, ranging from radical republicanism to constitutional monarchies—all backed by a ready resort to arms now seemingly justified after the recent struggle for liberty. As a result a nation such as Mexico endures countless military coups and countercoups during the next dozen years.

18 May 1822. After learning two weeks earlier that Spain has refused to recognize Mexico's independence, as defined by the Plan of Iguala (*see* 24 February 1821 in Part 6), troopers from the 1st Cavalry Regiment abandon their San Hipólito barracks in Mexico City at 8:00 P.M. and—in a contrived gesture spearheaded by a sergeant named Pío Marcha—urge the insurgent hero Iturbide to become emperor. Next morning congress is bullied into ratifying this arrangement, and Agustín I is proclaimed.

June 1822. A small army under the 37-year-old Italian-born Brig. Gen. Vicente Filisola arrives in Guatemala with orders from Iturbide to secure Central America for Mexico.

26 August 1822. Numerous military officers are arrested throughout Mexico on suspicion of plotting to depose Agustín I in favor of a republic.

Mid-September 1822. Emperor Iturbide dispatches Brig. Gen. Zenón Fernández from San Luis Potosí to put down a republican mutiny in Tamaulipas led by Brig. Gen. Felipe de la Garza.

26 October 1822. In Veracruz, Gen. Santa Anna fails to wrest its island fortress of San Juan de Ulúa from the last loyalist Spanish holdout, Gen. José Dávila. Because of this setback and other secret complaints regarding his conversations with the prorepublican American ambassador, Joel R. Poinsett, the emperor on 16 November orders Santa Anna to return to Mexico City.

31 October 1822. In Mexico City, Agustín I dissolves congress with the help of Gen. Luis de Cortazar's troops.

2 December 1822. Threatened with demotion as Iturbide's governor at Veracruz, Santa Anna mutinies with 400 soldiers of the 8th Infantry Regiment. Four days later he promulgates a republic and braces for Iturbide's counteroffensive, which is encharged to Generals Echávarri, Cortazar, and Lobato.

Nicolás Bravo and Vicente Guerrero also rise against the Mexican emperor, prompting the further dispatch of Gen. Gabriel Armijo's army.

23 January 1823. Armijo's subordinate, Epitacio Sánchez, comes into contact with the Bravo-Guerrero rebel contingents at Almolonga (Veracruz), defeating them over the next two days in a series of clashes that costs Sánchez his life.

January 1823. Unaware of the Mexican emperor's growing predicament, Filisola's army subdues patriotic unrest in El Salvador (Central America).

1 February 1823. After briefly besieging Veracruz, Generals Echávarri and Armijo agree to join rebels Santa Anna and Bravo against Iturbide, formalizing the agreement with the Plan of Casamata. Mutiny quickly spreads to most other Mexican army units.

9–12 February 1823. Virtually all imperial troops in Mexico City mutiny against Iturbide, obliging the emperor to shift his headquarters to Ixtapalucan while imprisoned congressmen are released.

19 March 1823. With rebel Generals Echávarri, Marqués de Vivanco, Bravo, and Miguel Barragán marching on Mexico City, Iturbide abdicates. In order to avoid further bloodshed, Gen. Manuel Gómez Pedraza arranges a safe conduct for the fallen emperor, who is escorted to Antigua (Veracruz) under Bravo's protection then deported on 11 May aboard the frigate *Rawlins.*

29 March 1823. Upon learning of Iturbide's fall, Filisola convenes a constitutional congress in Guatemala

City to decide Central America's fate before departing with his Mexican army. On 1 July this body opts for full independence, only Chiapas choosing to remain as part of Mexico.

31 MARCH 1823. The Mexican congress decides a triumvirate of Bravo, Guadalupe Victoria (originally born Manuel Félix Fernández), and Pedro Celestino Negrete will rule the country until a republican constitution can be drafted. Debate soon splinters into two contending factions: those favoring a strong central authority (known as *escoceses*, or "Scots"), opposed by those wishing for a looser federal system (*yorkinos*, or "Yorkists").

5 JUNE 1823. In San Luis Potosí, Santa Anna issues a demand for a federal system of government; he is recalled to Mexico City and briefly incarcerated for his temerity.

JUNE 1823. Bravo marches into Jalisco at the head of 2,000 men to calm that state's disturbances.

31 JANUARY 1824. Mexico's new constitution is promulgated, establishing a republican form of government.

JUNE 1824. Bravo marches into Jalisco with 4,000 men due to continued political unrest.

JULY 1824. After a year's sojourn in Italy and England former emperor Iturbide returns to Mexico, only to be taken prisoner and executed in Tamaulipas.

10 OCTOBER 1824. The 36-year-old insurgent hero Guadalupe Victoria is sworn into office as Mexico's first elected president.

23 DECEMBER 1827. Col. Manuel Montaño leads an uprising at Otumba (Mexico), which is soon joined at Tulancingo by Vice President Bravo, who assumes overall command of the rebel forces.

7 JANUARY 1828. Guerrero defeats Bravo's following, the latter being exiled to Ecuador (although pardoned next year).

1 SEPTEMBER 1828. After a tightly contested presidential campaign, the electoral college proclaims moderate Gen. Gómez Pedraza as winner; Guerrero—the second-place finisher—becomes Mexico's vice president. Eleven days later Santa Anna revolts at the fortress of Perote (Veracruz), calling for the annulment of these results—and Guerrero's elevation to president. The uprising is quickly put down, and Santa Anna retreats to Oaxaca.

Around this same time, President Gomez Pedraza uses the Mexican army to eject the liberal governor of the state of Mexico, 40-year-old Dr. Lorenzo de Zavala.

30 NOVEMBER 1828. The Acordada garrison in Mexico City mutinies in favor of Guerrero, and fighting erupts in the streets two days later. Pres. Gómez Pedraza eventually flees on 3 December for exile in France, leaving power in the hands of Guerrero.

20 MARCH 1829. Guerrero orders all Spaniards expelled from Mexico.

1 APRIL 1829. Guerrero officially assumes office as president, with 58-year-old Gen. Anastasio Bustamante as vice president and Santa Anna as governor of Veracruz.

7 JULY 1829. ***Spanish Invasion.*** A 15-ship expedition departs Havana under veteran Brig. Gen. Isidro Barradas (*see* 23 January 1820 in Part 6) to attempt a Spanish reconquest of Mexico—presumably with the aid of local sympathizers now disillusioned by republican rule.

By 27 July the force sights Cape Rojo (Veracruz), and its 3,500 troops disembark. The first actual clash occurs on 31 July while Barradas's invaders are attempting to traverse Corchos Pass, after which they skirt the burning, abandoned fortress at La Barra before occupying Tampico without resistance on 6 August. Two days earlier Santa Anna lands farther south at Tuxpan with a 3,750-troop counterexpedition from Veracruz, proceeding northwest on foot. Tampico's small garrison meanwhile withdraws north into the village of Altamira, where it is joined on 8 August by another 1,800 Mexican soldiers under General de la Garza.

Learning of this latter concentration, Barradas leaves his subordinate, Colonel Salomón, to hold Tampico with a small garrison while advancing a week later against de la Garza with his main body. The Mexicans brace to receive the Spaniards at Altamira, being reinforced from Matamoros on 15 August by 40-year-old Gen. José Manuel Rafael Simón de Mier y Terán. Following a brief exchange of long-range fire on 17 August the defenders abandon Altamira to Barradas.

Having meanwhile circled the Pánuco River, Santa Anna joins Mier y Terán and de la Garza by 20 August then slips a contingent across by boat that

Lithograph by Carlos Paris, showing Santa Anna directing operations against Barradas's Spanish invasion at Tampico

night to attack Salomón at dawn on 21 August within Tampico. He is unable to carry that town by storm, however, so retires to Pueblo Viejo once Barradas returns to rescue his subordinate. Still, the Spanish incursion has been checked, and after a further buildup of Mexican strength action resumes.

On 3 September Col. Carlos Beneski captures a Spanish schooner offshore; on 7 September Mier y Terán blocks Doña Cecilia Pass (the last remaining road inland); at 1:45 P.M. on 10 September he assaults the Spanish contingent at La Barra with 900 men, carrying it next day. Barradas therefore decides to come to terms with Santa Anna on 11 September, being allowed to reembark along with his 1,800 demoralized survivors. (In retaliation for the invasion the Mexican government soon commissions Gen. José Ignacio Basadre to travel to Haiti and recruit black guerrillas to infiltrate Cuba, raising a slave revolt against Spanish rule.)

6 NOVEMBER 1829. Yucatán rebels against Guerrero's government.

4 DECEMBER 1829. ***Bustamante's Uprising.*** Still in command of the large army raised in the wake of Barradas's Spanish invasion, Vice President Bustamante mutinies at Jalapa (Veracruz) against President Guerrero. The latter quickly finds himself without supporters—Bravo defeating his troops at Chilpancingo, then occupying Acapulco—so the president flees his capital on 18 December and establishes a tenacious guerrilla campaign in southern Mexico. His rival Bustamante assumes office as president on 1 January 1830 and sends General Armijo to fight Guerrero.

15 JANUARY 1831. After a year of successful guerrilla forays, Guerrero is lured aboard the Genoese brigantine *Colombo* at Acapulco, its Capt. Francesco Picaluga having been offered a 50,000-peso bounty by President Bustamante to kidnap his intransigent predecessor. Instead of the anticipated lunch, Guerrero is sailed to Huatulco (Oaxaca) and handed over to Capt. Miguel González, who shoots him the morning of 14 February at Cuilapan.

2 JANUARY 1832. ***Santa Anna's Insurrection.*** Santa Anna rises in revolt against Bustamante with the Veracruz military garrison, calling for the restoration of the exiled president, Gómez Pedraza (*see* 30 Novem-

ber 1828). Despite a difficult start, this rebellion gradually spreads throughout central Mexico.

19 MARCH 1832. Gov. Francisco Vital Fernández of Tamaulipas revolts against the Mexico City authorities but flees upon the approach of Mier y Terán's loyal troops.

8 JULY 1832. Mier y Terán, humiliated by his inability to put down another revolt in Tamaulipas—this time by the Tampico garrison under General Moctezuma—commits suicide by falling upon his sword at Padilla.

14 AUGUST 1832. Bustamante is obliged to march out of Mexico City at the head of his army to battle the spreading antigovernment revolt in central Mexico.

AUGUST 1832. In the state of Guerrero, Gen. Juan Alvarez rises against Bustamante, supporting the exiled Gómez Pedraza.

17 SEPTEMBER 1832. Bustamante defeats a rebel concentration at Gallinero Pass (near Dolores Hidalgo, Guanajuato) but must then retrace his steps to Puebla in order to intercept Santa Anna's army, which is advancing inland from Veracruz.

5 OCTOBER 1832. Former president Gómez Pedraza reaches Veracruz from exile in France, becoming the figurehead for Santa Anna's movement.

21 DECEMBER 1832. Santa Anna's army clashes with Bustamante near Puebla; two days later an armistice is signed at Zavaleta Hacienda, whereby Bustamante resigns as president in favor of Gómez Pedraza.

3 JANUARY 1833. Gómez Pedraza and Santa Anna enter Mexico City in triumph, the former temporarily reoccupying his presidency, although little more than a puppet of the victorious general. When elections are held a couple of months later Santa Anna becomes president (51-year-old liberal politician Dr. Valentín Gómez Farías is his vice president), officially taking office on 1 April.

2 JUNE 1833. Santa Anna marches out of Mexico City at the head of his army to put down a minor insurrection by Gen. Gabriel Durán.

5 MARCH 1834. Gen. Juan Alvarez defeats Bravo's conservative followers at Chilapa.

9 NOVEMBER 1834. General Juan Alvarez rises in revolt against Santa Anna's rule at Tecpan, eventually besieging Acapulco and clashing with Bravo.

During this 12-year period not a single Mexican president completes his term in office, military force becoming a regular feature of political life.

CISPLATINE WAR (1825–1828)

SOUTH AMERICA'S INDEPENDENCE DOES NOT BRING an end to the traditional Hispano-Portuguese rivalry regarding the territory later known as Uruguay. On 19 April 1825, 33 Uruguayans under Juan Antonio Lavalleja set sail aboard two boats from San Isidro (Argentina), landing at Rincón de la Agraciada to raise the banner of revolt against the Brazilian occupiers of their homeland.

Many local troops and gauchos quickly rise in Lavalleja's support while the Brazilian emperor vainly files protests with Bernardino Rivadavia's Argentine government at Buenos Aires. They are ignored, for on 25 August Lavalleja's interim Uruguayan government has voted to unite with Argentina.

4 SEPTEMBER 1825. At Aguila Creek (southeast of Mercedes), Uruguayan Cmdr. Fructuoso Rivera is defeated when he attacks 800 Brazilian troops under Bento Manuel Riveiro.

24 SEPTEMBER 1825. At Rincón de las Gallinas, Rivera with 700 men seizes 800 mounts from a Brazilian unit under Colonel Jardim and then defeats him.

8 OCTOBER 1825. Argentine Gen. Carlos de Alvear and diplomat Dr. José Miguel Díaz Vélez visit the famous liberator Bolívar in Potosí (Bolivia), proposing an alliance against Brazil. The latter demurs.

12 OCTOBER 1825. ***Sarandí.*** Lavalleja's 2,000 Uruguayan troops defeat 2,200 Brazilians under Gens. Riveiro and Bento Manuel Gonzalves at Sarandí,

killing more than half the enemy. Brazil's hold over Uruguay is reduced to a few isolated garrisons.

24 OCTOBER 1825. Argentina recognizes Lavalleja's request to incorporate Uruguay into the union, advising Rio de Janeiro of this fact.

NOVEMBER 1825. Sent to recruit troops in Tucumán for the forthcoming hostilities against Brazil, Argentine General Lamadrid deposes the local governor, Javier López, and assumes office. Soon he forms a centralist union with Salta and Catamarca, provoking the hostility of other Argentine provinces.

10 DECEMBER 1825. Brazil officially declares war against Argentina, which responds in kind on 1 January 1826. Neither country is prepared for extended hostilities.

21 DECEMBER 1825. A Brazilian squadron arrives to blockade the River Plate.

9 FEBRUARY 1826. Off Colares Point, Argentine Adm. Guillermo Brown's 28-gun frigate *25 de Mayo* (flag); brigantines *Belgrano, Balcarce, Congreso Nacional,* and *República Argentina;* sloop *Sarandí;* and hospital vessel *Pepa* clash with the Brazilian squadron, retiring into Los Pozos naval base near Buenos Aires with 26 casualties.

26 FEBRUARY 1826. Brown's squadron attacks the Brazilian garrison occupying Colonia de Sacramento (Uruguay) and is repelled, retiring to San Gabriel Island, where *Belgrano* sinks.

28 FEBRUARY 1826. Brown makes a second attempt against Colonia de Sacramento (Uruguay), boarding and firing the 18-gun brigantine *Real Pedro* in its roads; he suffers 200 losses when three of his gun launches are destroyed.

11 APRIL 1826. A mile off El Cerro (Uruguay), Brown's flagship *25 de Mayo* battles the 42-gun Brazilian frigate *Nichteroy* until nightfall, suffering 13 killed.

27 APRIL 1826. Brown attempts to cut the 52-gun Brazilian ship *Imperatriz* out of Montevideo's harbor but fails.

3 MAY 1826. Brown fights a second inconclusive duel with the Brazilian *Nichteroy* and smaller *Maceió* off Ortiz Bank (between Argentina and Uruguay in the River Plate), being hampered by the shallow waters.

25 MAY 1826. The 63-year-old Brazilian Adm. Rodrigo Pinto Guedes, having moved his squadron close to Buenos Aires, fights a prolonged action with Brown off Balizas Exteriores, which ends with the former's withdrawal.

11 JUNE 1826. A Brazilian squadron under 37-year-old Adm. James Norton attacks the Argentine naval base at Los Pozos near Buenos Aires, although shallow water prevents his seven largest vessels from coming within range. Brown launches a counterattack that drives off the scattered Brazilian formation.

29 JULY 1826. Brown encounters Norton's superior Brazilian squadron—*Nichteroy* under flag Capt. G. Parker; corvettes *Maria da Gloria* of Théodore de Beaurepaire, *Maceió* of J. I. Maze, and *Itaparica* of G. Eyre; brigantines *Caboclo* of John Pascal Grenfell and *29 de Agosto* of Raphael de Carvalho; gunboat *Leal Paulistana* of Sena Pereira; plus other lesser vessels—off Lara Point near Quilmes (east-southeast of Buenos Aires). The Argentine flagship *25 de Mayo* and Captain Rosales's schooner *Río* become hard-pressed next day, eventually being rescued by consorts *Sarandí, Oriental Argentino, Balcarce, Piraja, República Argentina, Congreso,* and *Liberal.* The damaged *25 de Mayo* subsequently sinks while being towed to Los Pozos.

9 OCTOBER 1826. Argentine federalists under Capt. Pantaleón Argañaraz from La Rioja defeat unitarian Governor Gutiérrez of Catamarca at Coneta (a dozen miles southwest of the provincial capital). The latter is replaced by Colonel Figueroa but soon returns with reinforcements recruited at Tucumán to reassume office.

25 OCTOBER 1826. Colonel Rauch advances south from Toldos Viejos (near Dolores, Argentina) with 800 men to ravage Indian settlements in La Ventana Range. One month later he leads a second punitive expedition, this of 1,200 troops.

26 OCTOBER 1826. Brown departs the River Plate with *Sarandí* and *Chacabuco* (purchased from Chile) to prey on Brazilian shipping off Rio de Janeiro. He returns two months later with few captures.

27 OCTOBER 1826. ***Tala.*** Federalist Gov. Juan Facundo Quiroga of La Rioja invades the rival Argentine province of Catamarca with 1,000 men, clashing with a

similar-sized unitarian army at Tala under Lamadrid, who is badly wounded. Quiroga briefly occupies the capital Tucumán, before retreating at the approach of another unitarian army from Salta under Colonel Bedoya.

26–28 DECEMBER 1826. An Uruguayo-Argentine army departs Arroyo Grande for the Negro River valley in three divisions—under Lavalleja, Alvear, and Soler—to invade the southern Brazilian province of Rio Grande do Sul.

31 DECEMBER 1826. Unitarian Argentine Colonel Bedoya occupies rival Santiago del Estero for five days before retiring to Tucumán.

26 JANUARY 1827. The Brazilian town of Bagé is occupied by Lavalleja and Alvear. The local Brazilian commander—Filisberto Caldeira Brant Pontes, Marqués de Barbacena—falls back before the more numerous Uruguayo-Argentine cavalry, taking shelter in the Camacuá Range until reinforcements can reach him from Rio Grande.

7 FEBRUARY 1827. While marching to the relief of Governor Arenales of Salta, unitarian Colonel Bedoya's entire command is massacred at Chicoana (30 miles south-southwest of this city) by a rebel force under Francisco Gorriti, better known as "Pachi."

8 FEBRUARY 1827. This afternoon south of Juncal Island (mouth of the Paraná Guazú River), Brown's Argentine squadron intercepts 17 Brazilian riverboats descending the Uruguay River from Paysandú under Cmdr. Sena Pereira. After two hours' inconclusive fight a gale blows up, but Brown ends this action next day by destroying ten enemy vessels and capturing another five off Gualeguaychú.

12 FEBRUARY 1827. The Alvear-Lavalleja army enters São Gabriel (Brazil), continuing west to the Santa Maria River next day. On the western banks of the Vacacaí River they encounter 1,100 troopers of the 22nd and 23rd Brazilian Cavalry Regiments under Gen. Riveiro on 13 February. The latter suffers 30 casualties, as opposed to seven killed and six wounded among the Argentine and Uruguayan invaders. However, intelligence gathered as to Riviero's plans allows General Barbacena to begin marshaling his main body across their intended path.

On 14 February Alvear detaches Brigadier General Mansilla with 350 troopers to drive off Riveiro, who overtakes his opponent next day while traversing the Ibicuy River at Ombú Ford. The Brazilians suffer some 40 casualties, as opposed to ten Argentine dead and 12 wounded; but by 17 February Barbacena's main army is taking up position near Rosario Ford on the Santa Maria River to await Alvear. The invaders arrive by afternoon on 19 February and prepare for battle north of Ituzaingó Creek the next day.

20 FEBRUARY 1827. ***Ituzaingó.*** At 2:00 A.M. this moonlit night Barbacena orders his 2,300 Brazilian in-

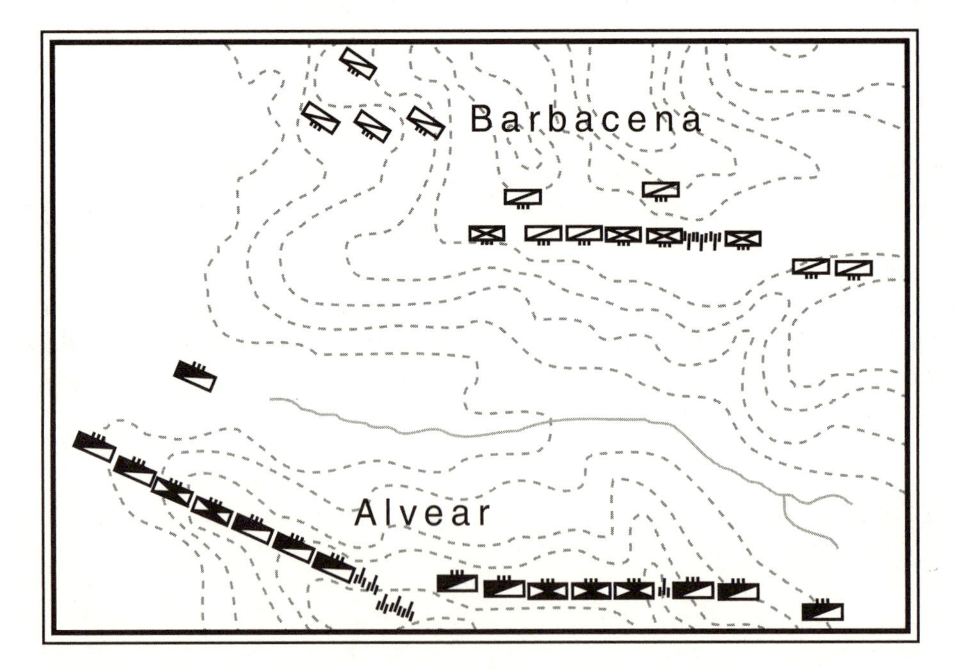

Battle of Ituzaingó

fantry, 3,700 cavalry, and 12 field pieces (with 300 gunners) to advance on the enemy vanguard under Olazábal. Alvear perceives this movement at dawn, so he in turn commands Olazábal to hang on at all costs while hastening his own army into action: 1,800 infantry, 5,400 troopers (including 2,000 Uruguayan *gauchos*), and 500 artillerymen manning 16 cannons. Brigadier General Laguna's cavalry are sent to hold the Argentine left, and in the process collide with Brigadier Brown's onrushing Brazilian infantry, that forms into squares after receiving three full cavalry charges.

Brown's division is gradually pressed back, at which point Lavalleja's cavalry disperses Abreu's Brazilian troopers on the southern flank; they find refuge behind their own 2nd Infantry Division. A second Argentine charge by Olavarría's 16th and Zufriategui's 18th Cavalry Regiments force back the Brazilian left while 29-year-old Juan Galo Lavalle's 4th Regiment and the Colorados do the same farther north. Brown's Brazilian infantry once more begins to advance but is gradually halted by successive charges by Federico de Brandzen's 1st Regiment, José María Paz's 2nd Cavalry, and the Calado Regiment.

After six hours of confusion Barbacena orders his army to retreat north toward Cacequí, having suffered 200 killed and 150 captured. Argentino-Uruguayan losses total 147 dead and 256 injured; although they remain in possession of Rosario Ford the invaders prefer to retrace their steps to São Gabriel by 26 February.

24 FEBRUARY 1827. Brown's Argentine squadron—returning to Buenos Aires from Martín García Island—is sighted by a Brazilian squadron anchored off Quilmes. After an inconclusive engagement a Brazilian schooner explodes, killing all but three of the 120-man crew, thus bringing the action to an end. Argentine casualties total 17 men.

28 FEBRUARY 1827. The Brazilian ships *Duquesa de Goyaz, Itaparica, Escudeiro,* and *Constanza*—commanded by the English mercenary Capt. James Shepherd—fight their way in past Argentina's Negro River battery; five days later (*Duquesa* having run aground) they disembark 350 men to march inland and destroy Carmen de Patagones, 15 miles from the sea. Instead, the raiders are defeated at Caballada Hill on 7 March by local irregulars, Shepherd being killed and his men and ships surrendering.

1 MARCH 1827. The Alvear-Lavalleja expeditionary force quits São Gabriel (Brazil) to return to Uruguay at Minas de Corrales, 50 miles south of Santana do Livramento.

6 APRIL 1827. Brown slips out of the Buenos Aires naval base of Los Pozos with the brigantines *República Argentina* (flag) and *Independencia,* bark *Congreso,* and sloop *Sarandí,* hoping to evade the Brazilian blockaders and unite with the prizes seized on the Negro River (*see* 28 February 1827) to make a privateering cruise against Rio de Janeiro.

Instead, next dawn his vessels are sighted by the Brazilian corvette *Maceió* and run aground on Monte Santiago Bank while attempting to escape to sea, *Congreso* being obliged to turn back for repairs. Norton's flagship *D. Paulo* and other Brazilian warships overtake the squadron and exchange long-range volleys by 4:00 P.M. in bad weather. On 8 April 19 Brazilian ships close in and annihilate the Argentine trio: *República Argentina* suffering three killed and 14 wounded (including Brown) before striking; *Independencia* loses 49 killed (among them Captain Drummond) and 69 injured or captured before surrendering. Only *Sarandí* escapes, with 17 casualties.

13 APRIL 1827. Alvear's 4,000 Argentine troops march north once more from Minas de Corrales—this time unaccompanied by Uruguayan allies—to again invade the Brazilian province of Rio Grande do Sul in a desperate bid to win better terms from the ongoing peace talks. After five days' progress through steady rain Bagé is reoccupied without opposition.

23 APRIL 1827. ***Camacuá.*** Twenty miles north of Bagé—on the banks of the Camacuá Chico River—1,600 Brazilian troopers are almost surprised by the nocturnal approach of 2,500 Argentine cavalry. Instead, the former are able to make good their escape, suffering only 50 casualties.

7 MAY 1827. Alvear's Argentine army quits Bagé, proceeding south to encamp two days later on the western banks of Yaguarón River (Jaguarão in Portuguese). On 16 May he detaches Brigadier General Lavalle with the 4th and 6th Cavalry Regiments to raid deeper into Brazil. The latter reaches Erval by 21 May, and four days later turns to attack 400 Brazilian guerrillas under chief Yuca Teodoro, who have been hounding his tracks.

Despite the token incursion Alvear decides to take the rest of his demoralized army into barracks at Cerro Largo (modern-day Melo, Uruguay) on 9 June, effectively ending all active campaigning for the year. Argentina's defeated government teeters on the verge of collapse.

6 JULY 1827. At Rincón (also called Manantial, six miles outside Tucumán), the reinstated unitarian gov-

ernor, Lamadrid, is crushed by Argentine rival Quiroga and must flee north to Bolivia.

7 DECEMBER 1827. Norton sights the 20-gun Argentine brigantine *Congreso* of Cmdr. César Fournier with the captive Brazilian merchantman *Harmonia dos Anjos,* chasing them aground near Lara Point. Next day the Brazilian admiral's gunboat *Grenfell* of flag Capt. Isidoro Nery, schooners *D. Paulo* of Thomas Read and *Bella Maria* of G. Parker, plus the gunboats *Esperada, 1 de Dezembro,* and *Victória da Colonia* attack and burn the pair; their Argentine crews escape ashore.

21 FEBRUARY 1828. Having assumed command of the combined Uruguayo-Argentine army at Melo, Lavalleja leads a cavalry raid against Padre Filiberto Ranch—15 miles north of Jaguarão—to secure mounts. Although successful, he is pursued back into Uruguay by Brazilian units.

15 APRIL 1828. ***Las Cañas.*** Brazil's Marshal Brown crosses the Yaguarón River with three infantry battalions and three cavalry regiments, surprising and utterly routing the Uruguayo-Argentine troops bivouacked north of Las Cañas Creek under Brigadier General Laguna.

16 JUNE 1828. The Argentine brigantine *General Brandzen* (manned by an Anglo-American privateer crew under George C. Kay) is chased aground near Lara Point and burned by Norton's Brazilian squadron. Kay and his men escape ashore, Norton losing an arm during the fighting.

AUTUMN 1828. Exhausted by its efforts, the Argentine government ends the war; its Brazilian opponents are left in scarcely better shape.

UNITARIAN-FEDERALIST WAR (1828–1831)

INTERNAL STRIFE PERSISTS WITHIN ARGENTINA as its interior provinces struggle against the primacy of Buenos Aires and other coastal territories in the aftermath of this nation's defeat at the hands of Brazil.

26 NOVEMBER 1828. The first defeated Argentine contingents return to Buenos Aires from Uruguay, having lost the war against Brazil. Embittered and frustrated, five days later General Lavalle leads a dawn revolt that deposes Pres. Manuel Dorrego.

6 DECEMBER 1828. Learning that Dorrego has united with the influential 35-year-old landowner Juan Manuel de Rosas and is marching toward Santa Fe with 2,000 men for more help, Lavalle leaves Admiral Brown as interim governor of Buenos Aires and sallies in pursuit.

9 DECEMBER 1828. ***Navarro.*** Lavalle's 1,500 troops overtake and defeat the poorly armed militia under Dorrego and Rosas at Navarro. Rosas retreats to Santa Fe; Dorrego is captured near Areco and shot four days later. (His execution will incite numerous counterrevolutions against Lavalle's unitarian rule.)

17 FEBRUARY 1829. The federalist leader Molina is defeated and executed at Palmitas Lagoon (near Junín) by unitarian Col. Isidoro Suárez.

12 APRIL 1829. Unitarian General Paz enters Córdoba, where he raises his army to 1,000 men and marches west to confront federalist General Bustos.

22 APRIL 1829. ***San Roque.*** At this hacienda on the banks of the Primero River (30 miles west of Córdoba), Paz's 1,000 unitarians engage Bustos's 1,600 federalists. The former delegates Colonel Deheza to distract Bustos by a frontal assault with the 5th Battalion and Lamadrid's cavalry while circling swiftly around the federalists' northern flank with the 2nd Battalion and 2nd Cavalry Regiment. Bustos's army disintegrates under the speed of this attack, fleeing to La Rioja and leaving behind 30–40 dead, 200 captives, eight guns, and their entire ammunition train.

26 APRIL 1829. ***Puente de Márquez.*** Lavalle's 1,900 unitarian troops and four guns fight an indecisive action at Márquez Bridge over the Reconquista River against more than 2,000 federalists under Rosas and Estanislao López. Although undefeated, a beleaguered Lavalle retires to Altolaguirre (a dozen miles outside Buenos Aires), where he enters into protracted negotiations with Rosas.

8 MAY 1829. La Rioja's federalist Governor Quiroga invades Córdoba Province at Serrezuela, slowly driving upon its capital, from whence unitarian General Paz sallies to give battle. One month later Quiroga eludes Paz and occupies Córdoba, bracing for Paz's inevitable counterassault.

22 JUNE 1829. ***La Tablada.*** As Paz's 1,650 unitarian cavalry, 720 infantry, and 12 field pieces (with 80 gunners) approach Córdoba they find Quiroga's 4,000–5,000 federalists massed east of the city at La Tablada. The unitarians advance in three columns, and a seesaw battle erupts. Charges and countercharges are launched until Quiroga finally attempts to smash the unitarian left with 1,500 riders, only to be checked by Paz's 2nd Cavalry Regiment and Lamadrid's troopers then routed by a counterattack by the unitarian 5th Battalion, supported by two guns.

Both armies retreat at nightfall, Paz's troops recuperating at nearby González Ranch before resuming the advance on Córdoba next day. Upon entering its streets the unitarian Tucumán militia and a squadron of "Argentine volunteer" cavalry is blasted by two cannons, setting off another round of fighting before the federalists are at last driven out in defeat. Over these two days Quiroga's army suffers 1,000 killed and 500 captured, his losses being considerably higher than Paz's unitarians.

EARLY JANUARY 1830. Quiroga departs Mendoza to again invade Córdoba Province, this time via San Luis and Salto. Upon reaching Oncativo (or Laguna Larga, 24 miles southeast of the capital) one month later, he pauses for Gen. Benito Villafañe, advancing from the northern provinces of La Rioja and Catamarca with another 1,500 federalists. But before they can unite Paz sallies from Anisacate on 18 February to attack Quiroga's smaller army.

24 FEBRUARY 1830. ***Oncativo.*** Paz approaches Quiroga with 3,000 unitarian cavalry, 1,000 infantry, and 70 gunners, rejecting a last-minute mediation offer from Rosas. The federalists dig in their eight artillery pieces on the fringe of a small copse and brace for Paz's assault.

Next day the unitarians charge in three columns, Paz concentrating most of his efforts against Quiroga's left flank. Lamadrid's 1st Division attacks first, only to be driven back. Nevertheless, continued pressure obliges the federalist cavalry to shift to the left wing, where it is smashed by a charge of unitarian Colonel Pedernera's 2nd Cavalry Regiment and "Republican Lancers." The rout is completed by Colonel Vilela's 2nd and 5th Battalions, which leaves the federalist infantry in the copse without cavalry protection.

Quiroga's army disintegrates, the general himself fleeing to Buenos Aires while his cavalry is hunted down and most of his infantry surrenders.

5 JULY 1830. Inspired by Paz's victory at Oncativo, the inland provinces of La Rioja, San Juan, Mendoza, San Luis, Santiago del Estero, Tucumán, Catamarca, Salta, Jujuy, and Córdoba form the *Liga Unitaria* (Unitarian League, also known as the *Liga del Interior,* or Interior League).

4 JANUARY 1831. In response to the formation of the Unitarian League federalist Buenos Aires, Corrientes, Santa Fe, and Entre Ríos sign the Pacto Federal, thus creating the so-called Liga del Litoral (Shoreline League).

4 FEBRUARY 1831. Federalist Gen. Estanislao López marches on the unitarian city of Córdoba.

5 FEBRUARY 1831. Federalist Col. Angel Pacheco surprises and defeats unitarian Colonel Pedernera's 2nd Cavalry and other militia units at Fraile Muerto (modern-day Bell Ville).

1 MARCH 1831. ***Calchines.*** Paz advances from Pilar with 5,000 unitarian troops; at Calchines (50 miles east-southeast of Córdoba) he checks the invasion by López's 2,000 federalists, compelling them to withdraw.

5 MARCH 1831. Federalist General Quiroga carries the city of Río Cuarto by storm, accepting the surrender of its 400-man garrison under Colonel Echevarría. The unitarian cavalry under Colonel Pringles has meanwhile escaped north; it is run down 13 days later at Río Quinto by federalist Col. José Ruiz Huidobro and annihilated.

28 MARCH 1831. ***Rodeo de Chacón.*** After occupying San Luis, Quiroga's 1,000 federalists confront a slightly larger unitarian army under Col. Videla Castillo at Rodeo de Chacón (Mendoza Province). The latter are so demoralized that the San Juan cuirassiers—all mounted on mules—join the federalist side at the beginning of action. Nevertheless, the unitarian infantry resist stubbornly for three hours before finally being dispersed by repeated cavalry charges.

10 MAY 1831. Paz is captured by federalist forces and succeeded as unitarian leader by Lamadrid at Córdoba.

4 NOVEMBER 1831. ***Ciudadela de Tucumán.*** Quiroga's 1,200 federalist cavalry and 450 infantry confront Lamadrid's 1,200 unitarian troopers and 750 foot soldiers at Tucumán, smashing both wings with cavalry charges. After a fierce struggle the federalists seize their opponents' ten guns and annihilate the infantry. At least 33 unitarian officers are executed following this bloody victory.

Quiroga's federalist triumph effectively ends the war, although passions linger. Little more than three years later he is assassinated at Barranca Yaco by brothers José Vicente, and Guillermo Reinafé with Capt. Santos Pérez. As late as January 1836 a unitarian revolt is led by Gen. Javier López, who is defeated and executed on the banks of the Famaillá River by the federalist governor of Tucumán, General Heredia.

Minor Disputes (1830–1837)

Although few major international confrontations ensue immediately after the War of 1812 and the Latin American struggle for independence, a number of lesser regional campaigns erupt during this eight-year interlude.

APRIL 1830. ***Lircay.*** A small *pipiolo* (greenhorn) army under the 42-year-old liberal Chilean former president, Ramón Freire Serrano, is defeated near the Lircay River by *pelucón* (bigwig) forces under conservative Gen. Joaquín Prieto, when the former attempts to oppose the seizure of power by the centralist, traditionalist, landowning wealthy classes and Catholic Church. After the battle Freire is deported to Peru and Prieto is installed as nominal president, although power actually rests in the hands of 37-year-old policymaker Diego Portales.

22 AUGUST 1831. Before dawn this Monday morning the 31-year-old black preacher Nat Turner launches a slave revolt in Southampton County (southeastern Virginia) by slaughtering several white families in their beds. His 60 followers are defeated and scattered next day by state militia, most being killed, while Turner escapes into hiding. Hysteria grips the South, hundreds of innocent blacks being killed or imprisoned until Turner is finally captured on 30 October; he is hanged 11 days later in Jerusalem.

10 JANUARY 1832. ***Bulnes's Sweep.*** Argentine Col. Manuel Bulnes marches into southern Mendoza Province with 2,000 troops to destroy the lairs of a band of Chilean brothers named the Pincheiras. He makes four individual forays, executing José Antonio Pincheira and destroying numerous Indian camps along the banks of the Atuel and Salado Rivers.

10 OCTOBER 1832. Pinedo, commander of the Argentine warship *Sarandí,* occupies the Falkland Islands.

LATE DECEMBER 1832. ***Falklands Encounter.*** Cmdr. John James Onslow's 18-gun HMS *Clio* arrives at Port Egmont (Falklands), sent by Rear Adm. Sir Thomas Baker to reclaim the islands for Britain. An Argentine garrison found at Port Louis on the main eastern island under Pinedo is ejected on 1 January 1833 aboard the schooner *Sarandí.*

NOVEMBER 1834. Jujuy Province rises and—covertly supported by Bolivia—declares itself independent from the rest of Argentina. Shortly thereafter Gen. Alejandro Heredia (governor of Tucumán Province) also invades neighboring Salta, and in conjunction with troops from Jujuy plus a Bolivian contingent under Lt. Col. Fernando Campero he defeats the Argentine governor, Latorre, who is captured and murdered in prison.

20 SEPTEMBER 1835. ***Farroupilha Revolt.*** In Brazil, the constitutional chaos created by regency rule in name of the future emperor, Pedro II, fosters widespread political and economic dissatisfaction. Rio Grande do Sul Province consequently explodes in rebellion, led by rancher Bento Gonçalves da Silva, whose irregulars soon capture the provincial capital of Pôrto Alegre. It is retaken by imperial forces in June 1836, after which the rebels are driven deep into the interior, creating an independent republic of their own at the town of Piratini that September.

Despite deriding their opponents as *farrapos* (ragamuffins) because of the fringed leather garb they typically wear, the imperial commanders are unable to completely stamp out the rebellion because of chronic troop shortages, conflicting fields of authority, and inadequate logistical support. The rebels in turn are maintained by small amounts of arms and money from the Uruguayan leader Rivera, who dreams of uniting his country with Rio Grande do Sul and the Argentine provinces of Entre Ríos and Corrientes to form a vast new republic.

In 1839 a rebel expedition crosses the northeastern border into neighboring Santa Catarina Province, helping its residents establish a second independent republic, which is put down by imperial forces four months later. The rebellion then collapses into factionalism, but it is not until 39-year-old Gen. Luís Alves de Lima e Silva, barão de Caxias, assumes overall command of the imperial forces in 1842 that this weakness can be exploited on the battlefield. After victories at Caçapava, Bagé, and Alegrete the general offers generous peace terms—including freedom for rebel slave soldiers—thus resolving this conflict by February 1845.

10 NOVEMBER 1837. ***Lower Canada Rebellion.*** After six months of growing turmoil and political repression, a column of mounted Anglo-Tory militia arrives south of Montreal at Saint Jean in l'Acadie region (Quebec) to arrest leaders of its rural French-Canadian *patriote* movement. Dr. Cyrille H. O. Côté and Lucien Gagnon contemplate resisting with 200–300 followers but demur when a company of British regulars also arrives next day. On the morning of 17 November, however, 150 *patriote* militia under Bonaventure Viger intercept 20 troopers of the Montreal cavalry as they pass through Longueuil with a pair of prisoners. The riders are fired upon, receiving numerous wounds before losing their captives, which success galvanizes many other *patriotes* into taking up arms throughout this district.

Gen. Sir John Colborne, British commander-in-chief for Lower Canada, responds by dispatching two columns to crush this insurgency, the first—300 troops and a 12-pound howitzer—reaching Saint Denis early on 23 November after marching overnight through a heavy snowstorm. They are met by 800 *patriotes* under Dr. Wolfred Nelson (only 200 bearing arms), who resist and are reinforced throughout this day, eventually obliging the British to withdraw by 3:00 P.M. after suffering six dead, 10 wounded, six missing, plus the loss of their field piece. *Patriote* casualties total 12 killed and seven injured.

On 25 November a second British column of 406 regulars, 20 militia riders, and two cannons under Lt. Col. George Augustus Wetherall reaches the main southern *patriote* stronghold at Saint Charles from Chambly. Of more than 1,000 *patriotes* gathered here under Thomas Storrow Brown, only 200–250 stand and fight from behind a low wall, being overrun within the hour amid great slaughter. Between 50 and 150 are slain and the rest scattered, after which the victors—having lost only three of their own number—retire toward Pointe Olivier and Montreal with 28 prisoners.

Colborne then masses 1,280 British regulars, 220 Canadian volunteers, and five field pieces to strike north against Saint Eustache where another 800–900 *patriotes* are concentrated under Amury Girod. The Anglo-Canadian vanguard arrives opposite this town at 11:00 A.M. of 14 December, prompting 300 overconfident defenders to sally across its frozen river—who break and flee when the main British army suddenly materializes behind them. Only 200–250 *patriotes* remain to defend Saint Eustache, 70 being killed in its subsequent bombardment and assault. Colborne further destroys the neighboring town of Saint Benoit next day, effectively bringing an end to armed *patriote* resistance.

17 NOVEMBER 1837. ***Sabinada.*** In Salvador—Brazil's second largest city and capital of Bahia Province—the 3rd Artillery Battalion, which is garrisoning Fort São Pedro, mutinies and joins the separatist movement of medical doctor and radical newspaper editor Francisco Sabino Álvares da Rocha Vieira (more commonly known as "Sabino," the rebellion carrying his name). Within hours they are joined by the 3rd Infantry Battalion; only the city's marines and part of its national guard militia remain loyal to the imperial government at Rio de Janeiro.

While a newly independent republic is thus being proclaimed many loyalists flee into the surrounding sugar-producing region called Recôncavo and begin organizing a counterrevolutionary force, the so-called Restorationist army. By the end of the month 1,900 Restorationists (mostly national guardsmen) are besieging the rebels inside Salvador while imperial warships join them offshore. By December hunger is experienced inside the city; the besiegers' numbers gradually swell to 5,000.

On 12 March 1838 the Restorationists mount an all-out assault to retake debilitated Salvador, inflicting hundreds of casualties in two days of heavy fighting. Final surrender comes on 16 March; Sabino is captured a week later and exiled to remote Goiás after a lengthy trial. Thousands of mulatto and black rebels are also condemned to hard labor on Fernando de Noronha Island.

4 DECEMBER 1837. ***Upper Canada Rebellion.*** After months of political protest against patronage appointments and other restrictive practices, 150 men gather this Monday at John Montgomery's tavern on Yonge St. north of Toronto (population 12,000) to spearhead an insurrection under the direction of the Scottish-born reformist newspaper editor and former Mayor William Lyon Mackenzie. Alarmed at this mutinous assemblage, militia Lt. Col. James FitzGibbon calls out loyalist volunteers this same night, and sends scouts to investigate—two men being killed, and numerous others captured in nocturnal skirmishes with rebel pickets.

Next day Mackenzie advances down Yonge St., his followers soon swelling to 1,000 and wearing white armbands for identification. After burning the houses of several prominent citizens, the rebels are scattered north toward evening by a volley from 27 loyalist pickets under Sheriff William Botsford Jarvis. After both sides are reinforced by contingents from the countryside on 6 December, FitzGibbon marches up Yonge St. on 7 December with 1,000 men in three columns, supported by two 6-pounders. Brushing aside 200 insurgent pickets at Paul Pry Inn between Mount Pleasant Cemetery and modern Davisville Ave., the loyalists then rout the few hundred disheartened insurgents remaining at Montgomery's tavern, killing two before torching this building. Mackenzie escapes to Buffalo (New York), his revolt ending in scores of arrests and the eventual execution of two of his lieutenants.

On 13 December, loyalist Col. Allan MacNab's 800 militia further scatter another 400 rebels at Scotland (Ontario), raised by the Connecticut-born medical doctor and reformer Charles Duncombe, who also flees across the border into the United States.

14 DECEMBER 1837. Mackenzie occupies Navy Island in the Niagara River east of Chippawa (Ontario), backed by the American adventurer Rensselaer van Rensselaer and two dozen supporters. Over the next couple of weeks, more than 425 republican volunteers reinforce this outpost, using their single cannon to fire upon 2,500 Canadian militia assembled opposite under MacNab.

Noting that the 26-ton American steamer *Caroline* is used to ferry supplies from Niagara Falls (New York), ex-Royal Navy Capt. Andrew Drew leads a 50-man boat party across to destroy this vessel. Failing to discover it anchored off the Canadian island, Drew instead boards *Caroline* before dawn of 30 December at Fort Schlosser, killing one of its crew members and wounding others before setting it ablaze and towing it out into the river to sink. American public opinion is incensed by this attack in U.S. territorial waters, but Gen. Winfield Scott arrives to stifle local hostilities, while MacNab and Drew are replaced on the British side by more professional officers.

Mackenzie and Van Rensselaer eventually abandon Navy Island by 13 January 1838; it is reoccupied by the Upper Canada militia two days later.

8 JANUARY 1838. The Irish-born, self-proclaimed "Brigadier" Edward Theller departs Gibraltar—20 miles below Detroit, Michigan—with 200 Canadian rebels and American sympathizers to occupy Bois Blanc Island opposite Amherstburg (Ontario). The 41-year-old lawyer and militia Lt. Col. John Prince of 3rd Essex responds by massing volunteers on the Canadian shoreline, including a company of ex-American slaves from Windsor under Rev. Josiah Henson (later to become the inspiration for Harriet Beecher Stowe's *Uncle Tom's Cabin*). After gaining this island, Theller bears down upon the mainland on 9 December with his schooner *Anne* and sloop *George Strong,* bombarding loyalist concentrations. At 7:00 P.M., however, his 21-man flagship *Anne* runs aground and is captured by the British, who discover one dead and eight wounded aboard—including Theller. Left leaderless, his followers subsequently retire to Sugar Island on the American side.

21 FEBRUARY 1838. Mackenzie and Van Rensselaer, having hoped to lead a republican army across the frozen Saint Lawrence River from Grindstone Island (New York) to Hickory Island (Ontario) and assail the 1,900-man garrison at Kingston, instead abandon this enterprise when only 300 volunteers are mustered.

23 FEBRUARY 1838. Despite efforts by the U.S. authorities to curb cross-border ventures, Duncombe slips out of Detroit with a small contingent of Canadian rebels and American republicans aboard the steamer *Erie* to occupy Fighting Island below Sandwich (Ontario). Next day he is joined by another company out of Cleveland under "Major General" Donald McLeod—an ex-sergeant in the British army—bringing total strength to 150 men and a 6-pounder. Having been warned of this encroachment by Gen. Hugh Brady of the U.S. regular army, British Maj. Henry Dive Townshend of the 24th (Warwickshire) Regt. sallies from Fort Malden (Amherstburg) with two companies of redcoats, 400 militia, and a field piece, traversing the ice to scatter these invaders by 25 February, wounding five and capturing another in the process.

26 FEBRUARY 1838. "Colonels" H. C. Seward and E. D. Bradley lead 400 American republicans across the ice from Sandusky (Ohio), capturing Pelee Island (Ontario). At 6:00 P.M. of 2 March, Lt. Col. the Hon. John Maitland of 32nd (Cornwall) Regt. quits Fort Malden with five companies of regulars—300 men—plus a pair of field pieces and two companies of mounted militia, to drive these invaders back. Despite heavy snowdrifts and dense woods, the redcoats succeed in scattering the republicans and capturing 11, while suffering five killed and 30 wounded among their own ranks.

3–4 NOVEMBER 1838. Overnight, Robert Nelson and Dr. Côté launch a second *patriote* uprising in French Canada, marshalling 1,500 men at Napierville (Quebec) while several hundred others assemble at various points along the Richelieu River, and in the Châteauguay area. Despite carrying Beauharnois by storm, this insurgency soon falters because of factional bickering, lack of weaponry, effective loyalist opposition at Lacolle and Odelltown, plus an ill-judged *patriote* attempt to occupy the Mohawk village of Sault Saint Louis or Kahnawake, resulting in the capture of 64 of their men. By the time Colborne's redcoats march south out of Montreal a few days later, rebel sentiment is already ebbing and this insurrection ceases without further fighting.

11 NOVEMBER 1838. This Sunday, the commandeered paddle steamer *United States* departs Sackets Harbor (New York), towing the schooners *Charlotte of Oswego* and *Charlotte of Toronto* with 400 American republicans to attempt to raise a popular insurrection in British Canada. Led by "General" John Ward Birge, these invaders are dubbed "Hunters" because of the secretive "hunters' lodges" formed along the border this past summer to organize such a project.

At 2:00 A.M. of 12 November, both schooners are released and approach Prescott (Ontario), only to sheer off when its sentries open fire. Some 200 Americans then disembark a mile downriver at Windmill Point by sun-up, occupying a stone mill at New Jerusalem while electing the 31-year-old, Finnish-born ex–French Foreign Legionnaire Nils von Schoultz as their leader. However, the 25-man armed British steamer *Experiment* of Lt. William Fowell then prevents any further Hunter reinforcements from reaching this outpost out of Ogdensburg on the opposite bank, and the invaders become besieged by a host of British regulars and Canadian militia.

After repelling a direct assault on 13 November, the outnumbered and isolated Americans are finally battered into submission by evening of 16 November, 161 survivors surrendering after suffering more than 30 killed due to heavy artillery and musket fire. Eleven are eventually executed, and many others are transported to the penal colony at Van Diemen's Land (Australia).

3 DECEMBER 1838. This evening "General" Lucius V. Bierce's 250–300 republican followers commandeer the American steamer *Champlain* at Detroit, disembarking three miles above Windsor (Ontario) at 2:00 the next morning to attack 28 Canadian militia of the 2nd Essex

Soldiers of the 71st Highland Light Infantry Regiment conveying three patriote *suspects to the Montreal jail*

under Sgt. Frederick Walsh asleep in their barracks. Two defenders are killed and the building torched along with the docked steamer *Thames,* while the town is occupied.

At sunrise, five companies of Canadian militia arrive from nearby Sandwich under Colonel Prince and Capt. John Frederick Sparke, engaging the invaders until Capt. Edward Broderick can appear from Amherstburg at 11:00 A.M. with 100 regulars of 34th (Cumberland) Regt., 40–50 Indian allies, and a field piece. Together they rout the republicans, killing 21 and capturing 44, while the rest escape aboard boats toward Hog Island (modern Belle Isle). Furious at finding his friend Dr. John Hume slain, Prince orders another five captives summarily executed during the heat of battle, while six more are later hanged at London (Ontario) and 16 transported to Australia.

Texan Independence (1835–1836)

Since April 1823 Texas—a remote, arid province historically shunned by most Mexicans—has been open to American emigration out of Louisiana on the Mexican government's condition that the latter accept Mexican citizenship and the Catholic faith. Within a few years the 4,000 Mexican residents are outnumbered by 28,000 Americans, prompting Mexico City authorities to curtail their policy in April 1830 and attempt to reimpose centralist rule.

After a brief skirmish at Velasco in June 1832 the American colonists—who call themselves Texians—choose 39-year-old Stephen F. Austin as leader and attempt to persuade the Mexico City congress to elevate their region into a state within the Mexican union; another, even more radical faction led by the 39-year-old former governor of Tennessee, Samuel P. Houston, pushes for incorporation into the United States.

Tensions build until the summer of 1835, when Santa Anna crushes other rebellions against his authority in central Mexico then sends a 1,400-man army north under his 33-year-old brother-in-law, Martín Perfecto de Cós, to subdue the Texian dissidents. Late this September Col. Domingo de Ugartechea—garrison commander at San Antonio (population 2,000)—detaches an 80-man cavalry patrol under Capt. Francisco Castañeda to dispossess a group of 500 Texians of their single small cannon at the town of Gonzales.

2 October 1835. South of Gonzales, 150 Texian militia under Col. John W. Moore surprise Castañeda's bivouacked Mexican troops at dawn, killing one and scattering the rest. Austin, Houston, and other leaders shortly thereafter proceed to San Felipe to hold a Texian convention.

9 October 1835. After a brief skirmish 50 Texians under Capt. James Collingsworth compel Goliad's 40-man Mexican garrison under Capt. Francisco Sandoval to surrender.

27 October 1835. The wealthy 39-year-old adventurer James Bowie and a 31-year-old West Point dropout from Georgia named James Walker Fannin advance from Gonzales with 300 Texians and defeat a 230-man Mexican detachment at Concepción Mission (two miles south of San Antonio), killing 67 and wounding a similar number while suffering only one American killed.

Four days later the bulk of the Texian army arrives under Austin and imposes a loose siege on Cós's unhappy garrison—comprised of the regular Morelos Battalion and five conscript companies.

3 November 1835. The Texian convention at San Felipe resolves to oppose Santa Anna as loyal Mexican citizens, upholding Mexico's 1824 federal constitution while further calling on other Mexican states to resist his dictatorial ways. Austin is to be sent to the United States to raise support and recruit more volunteers; on 25 November a former Indian fighter, "Colonel" Edward Burleson, assumes overall command of the Texian army before San Antonio.

Next day Bowie leads 60 mounted volunteers to intercept a Mexican pack train a few miles south of San Antonio, escorted by 100 cavalry. A running fight ensues right up to San Antonio's gates, during which the Mexicans suffer some 50 casualties compared to two American casualties (this is later referred to as the Grass Fight).

4 December 1835. ***Cós's Surrender.*** After considerable delay Burleson orders an assault against the Mexican garrison within San Antonio, only to cancel it at the last minute and instead propose a retirement to eastern Texas. Mutiny erupts, during which "Colonel" Benjamin Rush Milam—a longtime Texas resident originally from Kentucky—assumes leadership over a band of volunteers, proposing to storm San Antonio next day.

At 3:00 A.M. on 5 December Milam's 210 attackers begin pressing into San Antonio's outer fringes while Cós's beleaguered army is distracted by a simultaneous bombardment of the Alamo. Three days of intense house-to-house fighting ensues, with Milam being killed on 8 December, just as the last Mexican defenders retreat into the Alamo. Next dawn the Mexican general sues for terms from "Colonel" Frank Johnson, Milam's successor.

Cós's capitulation is finalized on 11 December, more than 1,100 defeated Mexican troops marching south within the next few days, leaving behind 300–400 dead or deserters (as opposed to 20–30 Texians killed). Winter now having set in, many of the victorious Americans decamp in the erroneous belief that the war for Texian independence is largely ended.

7 JANUARY 1836. Santa Anna reaches Saltillo (Coahuila, northern Mexico) to begin organizing a large army to invade Texas, and reimpose his government's rule following the defeat of Cós.

Within three weeks Santa Anna heads north with one cavalry and two infantry brigades, plus a siege train to join Brig. Joaquín Ramírez y Sesma's army, already operating near the Río Grande. The Mexican order of battle for this forthcoming campaign is:

Commander-in-chief: Santa Anna
Second-in-command: Maj. Gen. Vicente Filisola
Chief-of-staff: Brig. Juan Arago
Aides-de-camp: Brigs. Manuel Fernández Castrillón, Cós, and Juan Valentín Amador; Cols. Juan Nepomuceno Almonte, Juan Bringas, and José Bates
Quartermaster: Col. (brevet brigadier) Adrián Woll
Artillery chief: Lt. Col. Tomás Requena
Chief of engineers: Capt. (brevet lieutenant colonel) Ignacio Labastida

Vanguard Brigade under Brig. Ramírez y Sesma

Unit	*Men*
Matamoros Permanent Infantry Battalion	272
Jiménez Permanent Infantry Battalion	274
San Luis Potosí Active Infantry Battalion	452
Dolores Permanent Cavalry Regiment	290
Eight artillery pieces, with 62 gunners	

1st Brigade under Col. (brevet brigadier) Antonio Gaona

Unit	*Men*
Aldama Permanent Infantry Battalion	390
1st Toluca Active Infantry Battalion	320
Querétaro Active Infantry Battalion	370
Guanajuato Active Infantry Battalion	390
Río Grande Presidial Company	60
Zapadores (Sappers) Battalion	185
Six artillery pieces, with 63 gunners	

2nd Brigade under Colonel (brevet brigadier) Eugenio Tolosa

Unit	*Men*
Morelos Permanent Infantry Battalion	300
Guerrero Permanent Infantry Battalion	400
1st México Active Infantry Battalion	350
Guadalajara Active Infantry Battalion	420
Tres Villas Active Infantry Battalion	189
Six artillery pieces, with 60 gunners	

Cavalry Brigade under Brig. Juan José Andrade

Unit	*Men*
Tampico Permanent Cavalry Regiment	250
Guanajuato Active Cavalry Regiment	180

Independent Division under Brig. Juan José Urrea

Unit	*Men*
Yucatán Active Infantry Battalion	300
Cuautla Permanent Cavalry Regiment	180
San Luis Potosí Auxiliary Cavalry Troop	40
Bajío Auxiliary Cavalry Troop	30
One artillery piece, with eight gunners	

Total: 6,050 (4,500 infantry, 1,120 cavalry, 190 artillerymen, 185 sappers, 50 staff).

3 FEBRUARY 1836. The 26-year-old William Barret Travis, newly appointed lieutenant colonel in the Texian cavalry, reaches San Antonio with 30 troopers and agrees to share command of the Alamo garrison with Bowie. Volunteers continue to trickle in, such as a 49-year-old former U.S. congressman named Davy Crockett, who arrives on 8 February with his 14 "Tennessee Mounted Volunteers."

11 FEBRUARY 1836. News is received at San Antonio of Santa Anna's advance on the Río Grande with a large army. The force is delayed two days later by a two-foot snowfall yet continues approaching swiftly.

23 FEBRUARY 1836. ***Alamo.*** At dawn, somewhat sooner than anticipated, the first elements of Santa Anna's 2,500–3,000-man main body are sighted a mile and a half outside San Antonio. The 150 surprised Texian defenders and 25 noncombatants gather inside the Alamo (east of San Antonio's River) and are invested that afternoon by the 1,500-man Mexican vanguard. A battery consisting of two eight-pounders and a seven-inch howitzer opens fire next day, a loose siege being imposed while further batteries are installed to weaken defenses, Santa Anna seemingly intent on cowing the garrison into capitulation.

Crude contemporary engraving of Davy Crockett (1786–1836) dying at the Alamo

Skirmishes occur on 25 and 27 February; just after midnight on 29 February–1 March 32 more volunteers slip into the Alamo from Gonzales, led by Lt. George Kimball (or Kimbell, originally a New York hatter). Realizing that the defenders are willing to fight to the death, Santa Anna sends 1,700 men in four columns at 5:00 A.M. on 6 March to storm the Alamo's walls: Cós leads the Aldama Battalion and three companies of the San Luis Potosí Battalion against the northwestern corner; the northeastern is attacked by Col. Francisco Duque and Brig. Gen. Fernández Castrillón's Toluca Battalion plus the balance of the San Luis Potosí troops; from the east come Col. José María Romero's Matamoros and Jiménez companies of fusiliers; the light companies of the Matamoros, Jiménez, and San Luis Potosí units advance from the south under Col. Juan Morales. In his reserve Santa Anna keeps five grenadier companies and sappers (approximately 385 men) plus 350 cavalry.

After charging through the Texian artillery fire (which kills Duque and numerous others), the Mexicans gain the outer walls and eventually scale the north side, forcing the defenders back inside their sleeping quarters—known as the Long Barracks—where the last few are slaughtered by 6:30 A.M. Mexican casualties total 70 men killed and 300 seriously wounded; 182 of the 183 Texian defenders are killed. Their courageous resolve inspires the cause of Texas independence and attracts many volunteers from the United States.

27 FEBRUARY 1836. Under cover of a rainstorm 40-year-old Mexican Brigadier General Urrea slips into San Patricio (Texas) at the head of a 100-trooper vanguard, killing 16 and capturing 24 Texian defenders while the remainder escape north under Col. Frank Johnson.

2 MARCH 1836. The reconvened Texian convention at "Washington-on-the-Brazos" declares Texas to be independent.

3 MARCH 1836. One of Urrea's cavalry patrols exterminates Col. James Grant's followers at Agua Dulce (20 miles west of San Patricio), killing 22 of 25 men.

11 MARCH 1836. Learning that the Alamo has fallen and General Ramírez y Sesma is approaching with 700 Mexican troops, Houston abandons Gonzales with his 375 followers and a large number of refugees, retreating east in what becomes known as the Runaway Scrape.

18 MARCH 1836. Fannin also falls back from Goliad but so ineptly that his 300 men and 25 cavalry are overtaken next day two miles west of the Coleto River by a detachment from General Urrea's 600-

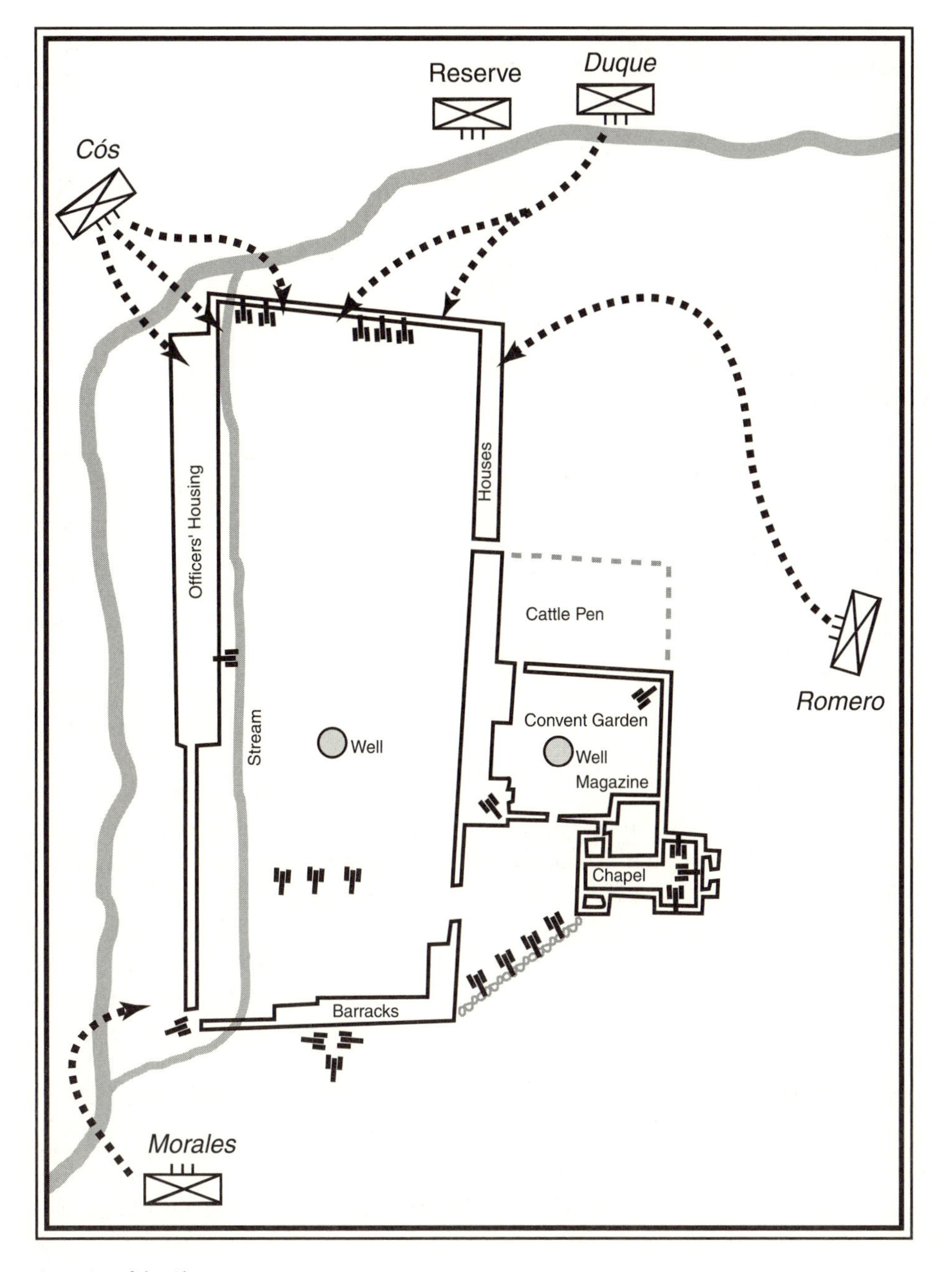

Storming of the Alamo

man division. They kill ten Texians, wound 70 (including Fannin), and compel the rest of the thirsty, tired band to surrender by 20 March.

27 MARCH 1836 (PALM SUNDAY). Santa Anna—determined to terrify Texas into submission—orders 375 American prisoners marched out of Goliad early this morning on the pretext of being paroled to New Orleans. Instead, they are shot by Urrea's troops; only 30 survive the massacre.

18 APRIL 1836. Learning that Santa Anna's army has fragmented in pursuit of different fleeing Texian contingents, Houston arrives east of Harrisburg after a two-and-a-half-day forced march, close to the unsuspecting Mexican commander in chief. Houston's own 780 untested troops are in an ugly mood after their prolonged retreat; they cross to the Harrisburg side of Buffalo Bayou next day and take up a defensive position on the wooded banks of the San Jacinto River by 20 April to await the Mexican army's approach.

21 APRIL 1836. ***San Jacinto.*** After discovering Houston's army, skirmishing briefly, then placing his own troops opposite, Santa Anna is reinforced this

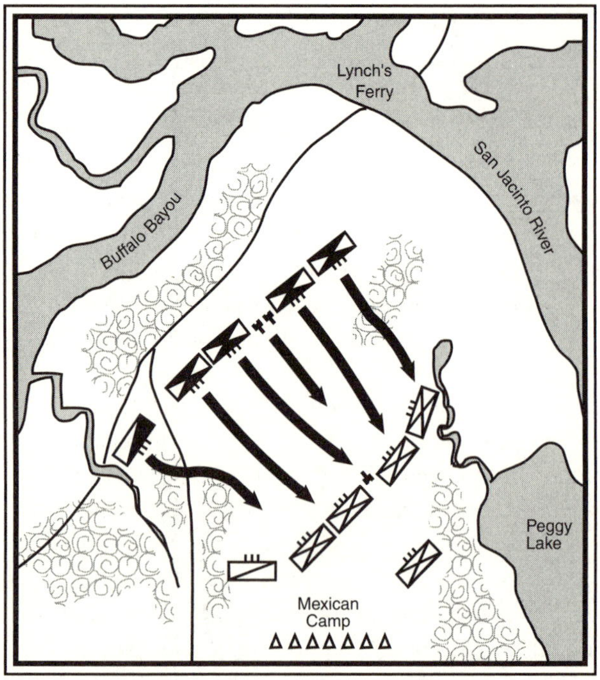

Battle of San Jacinto

morning by General Cós, bringing total Mexican strength to more than 1,300 men and a single six-pound field piece. When no action develops by noon the invaders repair to their encampments, assuming no fighting will occur until next day (dawn being the traditional time for battle in this era).

But Houston instead gives the order for his troops to trail arms and silently charge the Mexican lines at 4:30 P.M. in four columns: the 260-man 2nd Texas Volunteer Regiment of Col. Sidney Sherman; 220 men of the 1st Texas Volunteer Regiment under Col. Edward Burleson; 240 of the Texas Regular Battalion under Lt. Col. Henry Millard; plus 50 cavalry under "Colonel" Mirabeau Buonaparte Lamar. They are within 200 yards of the improvised Mexican breastworks before they are detected, two Texas six-pounders—the "twin sisters," donated by citizens of Cincinnati and manned by 31 gunners—arriving at this crucial juncture to unlimber and open fire.

Within 18 minutes, at a cost of only eight killed and 17 wounded, Houston annihilates Santa Anna's unprepared army. Shouting "Remember the Alamo!" and "Remember Goliad!" the Americans butcher 600–650 Mexican soldiers and capture another 730 (including a disguised Santa Anna next day, after having fled the field).

Santa Anna is compelled to sign an armistice in order to regain his freedom from the vengeful Texans, and his field commanders retire to Mexico upon learning of his capitulation. Eventually, the Mexican government will repudiate the arrangement, insisting it is not valid because its terms have been extorted. Yet Mexico is powerless to reimpose its will over the Republic of Texas—which is soon recognized by the United States, Britain, France, the Netherlands, and Belgium. Nine years later—in 1845—Texas becomes part of the United States.

War of the Peru-Bolivia Confederation (1836–1839)

In the years following the collapse of Spain's American empire, old jurisdictional rivalries become a source of regional disputes, such as when 43-year-old Bolivian leader Andrés de Santa Cruz imposes a confederation with Peru in 1836. This potentially powerful alignment displeases Chile, farther south, which in turn seeks its own secret accommodation with Rosas's Argentina.

Matters quickly come to a head when Santa Cruz's financially strapped Bolivian government nullifies a treaty giving Chile preferential tariff treatment; Peru—anxious to develop its own trade through Callao—also imposes a special tax on goods imported via gold-rich Valparaíso. Angered by these steps—and the fact that the renegade liberal Gen. Ramón Freire has recently used a Peruvian port in another abortive attempt to topple the Chilean government during the summer of 1836—Chile's 43-year-old de facto leader, Diego José Pedro Victor Portales Palazuelos, orders his fleet to attack Callao, where it impounds three Peruvian vessels.

Infuriated, Santa Cruz retaliates by briefly detaining Chile's ambassador, although he releases him almost immediately with an apology. But Portales uses this excuse to demand that Peru pay reparations, reduce its navy, and dissolve its confederation with Bolivia. Santa Cruz refuses, so Chile declares war on 11 November 1836—despite considerable public reluctance.

13 February 1837. Argentina, nursing its own separate grievances against Bolivia because of Santa Cruz's intervention in Andean insurrections (*see* November 1834 under Minor Disputes), severs diplomatic relations with his government.

1 MAY 1837. The Peru-Bolivia confederation is officially proclaimed, Santa Cruz being recognized as its leader by both France and Britain.

19 MAY 1837. Argentina's dictator, Rosas, declares war against Peru and Bolivia.

6 JUNE 1837. The Chilean garrison at Quillota mutinies and seizes General Portales, who is on an inspection tour. Taken to Valparaíso by the rebels, he is murdered when other garrisons refuse to join the insurrection.

28 AUGUST 1837. Two small Bolivian cavalry units invade Argentina, capturing the isolated outposts of Cochinoca and Iruya.

11 SEPTEMBER 1837. Bolivian troops occupy Humahuaca (Argentina), only to be defeated at La Herradura and driven back north next day by three cavalry squadrons and a company—400 men in total—under Gen. Felipe Heredia.

On 13 September Heredia's contingent also clashes at Santa Bárbara (two and a half miles north of Humahuaca) with a similar-sized Bolivian force under Lt. Col. Campero, driving the invaders back into their territory while killing 15 and capturing ten.

SEPTEMBER 1837. The Argentine *Cazadores de la Libertad* (Liberty Chasseurs) Battalion mutinies at Salta, but is quickly put down by loyal troops under Col. Gregorio Paz.

17 NOVEMBER 1837. ***Paucarpata.*** Shortly after disembarking in Peru, Adm. Blanco Encalada's Chilean expeditionary force is defeated and forced to surrender by Santa Cruz. The Bolivian leader imposes generous terms not only for this army's capitulation but also to end the entire war: Chile has merely to return the three Peruvian vessels it has seized and tacitly recognize the Peru-Bolivia confederation; in return the latter will pay part of its debt to Chile and allow Blanco Encalada's army to be repatriated. The captive commander—former president of Chile—agrees, signs the Treaty of Paucarpata, but once his troops are home Portales Palazuelos repudiates the arrangement, resumes the war, and court-martials Blanco Encalada.

11 DECEMBER 1837. Two small Argentine and Bolivian companies clash at Vicuñay (near Tres Cruces).

2 JANUARY 1838. Argentine Captain Gutiérrez defeats a tiny Bolivian contingent at Rincón de las Casillas then occupies the village of Negra Muerta two miles north. Learning that a large enemy force is approaching to dispute the seizure, he withdraws under cover of darkness, watching from a safe distance as his opponents fire on each other in stormy Negra Muerta.

2 FEBRUARY 1838. The Argentine Coraceros de la Muerte (Death Cuirassiers) Regiment mutinies at Humahuaca but is put down by loyal forces.

29 MARCH 1838. Argentine Colonel Carrillo leads an uprising at Santiago del Estero, his forces subsequently being defeated at La Poma by General Heredia.

27 APRIL 1838. ***Failed Argentine Offensives.*** Colonel Paz departs Humahuaca with 1,000 Argentine troopers, penetrating Bolivia and skirmishing with the garrisons at Acambuco Lagoon on 29 May, Zapatera (3 June), San Diego (3 June), and Pajonal (9 June). Upon closing within nine miles of Tarija, however, a superior Bolivian force is encountered, and Paz is compelled to retire. He is overtaken on 24 June and his rearguard annihilated before regaining the safety of Argentine territory.

Meanwhile Col. Manuel Virto marches out of San Andrés (35 miles east-northeast of Humahuaca) on 5 June to attack Iruya with more than 1,500 men, but he too is defeated and obliged to retrace his route.

21 OCTOBER 1838. A Rosist revolt occurs at Santa Fe (Argentina), led by Juan Pablo López, who deposes governor Cullen.

12 NOVEMBER 1838. Gen. Alejandro Heredia, governor of Tucumán Province, is assassinated at Lules by Col. Gabino Robles. Juan B. Bergeire briefly succeeds him before resigning.

20 NOVEMBER 1838. The garrison at Jujuy (Argentina) mutinies and deposes Gen. Pablo Alemán as governor, installing Rosist Col. José Mariano Iturbe in his place.

22 NOVEMBER 1838. Gen. Felipe Heredia, governor of Salta, flees into neighboring Tucumán before the threatened attack of Col. José Manuel Pereda and is succeeded by Manuel Solá.

20 JANUARY 1839. ***Yungay.*** After being first defeated at the Battle of Buin, Santa Cruz is routed at Yungay (in the highlands north of Lima, Peru) by 6,000 Chilean troops under 39-year-old Gen. Manuel

Bulnes Prieto and rebel Peruvian contingents under Agustín Gamarra, Antonio Gutiérrez de la Fuente, and Ramón Castilla. His rule in both Peru and Bolivia now ended, Santa Cruz flees to Ecuador aboard a British frigate and eventually dies in exile in France.

14 FEBRUARY 1839. Following Santa Cruz's flight, the Peru-Bolivian confederation is dissolved, and Bolivia's provisional president—Gen. José Miguel de Velasco—calls for a cessation of hostilities. Victorious General Bulnes uses his popularity to be elected president of Chile in 1841, serving two terms. On 8 December 1851 he defeats his cousin, José María de la Cruz, at the bloody Battle of Loncomilla, thus quelling a revolt in the southern provinces.

WAR OF THE CAKES, OR PASTRY WAR (1838–1839)

IN THE CHAOTIC YEARS FOLLOWING MEXICO'S independence from Spain, foreign traders and investors often complain to their home governments about losses suffered due to the many insurrections, military coups, and civil unrest. In 1837 France sends a special plenipotentiary—Baron Deffaudis—to demand compensation for the sacking of French businesses during such disturbances and the imposition of forced loans by rebel leaders. The Mexican government rejects the claim, arguing it is beyond the duty of any nation to protect foreign visitors from the vicissitudes even its own citizens must endure. Unsatisfied, Deffaudis quits talks on 1 January 1838 and, 15 days later, takes ship from Veracruz.

21 MARCH 1838. Deffaudis returns to Veracruz with a French squadron, anchoring off Sacrificios Island and setting an ultimatum ashore from the flagship *Herminie,* demanding 600,000 pesos to compensate for a long list of wrongs. (When the note is delivered in Mexico City popular opinion believes it to include a claim for pastries taken from the Remontel restaurant in Tacubaya by Santa Anna's troops in 1832; the subsequent hostilities therefore become derisively known among Mexicans as the Guerra de los Pasteles—War of the Cakes.)

16 APRIL 1838. ***Blockade.*** The deadline for satisfaction having elapsed on 15 April, the French squadron imposes a limited naval blockade on Veracruz next day, restricting entry for many items to deprive the Mexican government of its revenues. The 53-year-old Rear Adm. Charles Baudin is sent from France to assume command of the operation, and other nations detach men-of-war to look after their own interests.

21 OCTOBER 1838. After a six-month blockade Baudin sets another communication ashore at Veracruz, leading to a face-to-face meeting at the inland town of Jalapa on 17 November with the Mexican foreign minister, Luis G. Cuevas. The latter is willing to concede most points, but the French admiral demands an additional 200,000 pesos to compensate the French government for expeditionary costs. Cuevas refuses, and Baudin departs at 5:00 A.M. on 21 November, returning to Veracruz.

27 NOVEMBER 1838. ***Bombardment.*** At 9:00 A.M. the Mexican officers Valle and Díaz Mirón board Baudin's flagship *Néréide* with a last-minute offer from Foreign Minister Cuevas to renew negotiations, only to have the French admiral reject it several hours later. Within five minutes—while Valle and Díaz Mirón are still being rowed ashore—the frigates *Néréide, Iphigénie,* and *Gloire,* corvette *Créole,* and bomb vessels *Cyclope* and *Vulcain* open fire on Veracruz's 153-gun, 1,186-man harbor castle of San Juan de Ulúa, using the newly developed Paixhans explosive shells.

The exchange persists until 6:00 P.M., when the garrison commander, Antonio Gaona, requests a truce to attend to his wounded. During the afternoon the French squadron has suffered four killed and 39 injured; San Juan de Ulúa 224 casualties and 20 dismounted guns. Overnight the French inform Gaona his fortress will be leveled if he does not surrender, so after consulting with Gen. Manuel Rincón in Veracruz at 3:30 A.M. the garrison commander capitulates next morning along with a corvette, two sloops, and three brigs moored beneath the walls. By midday on 28 November the French are in possession of San Juan de Ulúa; Rincón—with the backing of Santa Anna, who has arrived from nearby Manga de Clavo Hacienda—agrees to a cessation of hostilities. Baudin's vessels are allowed to refresh provisions ashore, French citizens are promised compensation, and the blockade is lifted for eight months to permit a diplomatic resolution of all grievances.

30 NOVEMBER 1838. When news of Rincón and Gaona's capitulation reaches Mexico City, infuriated government officials order both officers arrested and

their agreement voided; a declaration of war against France is then passed.

3 DECEMBER 1838. This night Santa Anna is informed near Veracruz of the Mexican government's declaration of war and that he is to command the 700–800 soldiers remaining in the port—out of a nominal garrison of 1,353 men—to resist the French invaders. Next morning he informs Baudin of the rejection of the truce, and both leaders agree to refrain from local hostilities until 8:00 A.M. on 5 December.

5 DECEMBER 1838. ***Disembarkation.*** During the night the 36-year-old Gen. Mariano Arista enters Veracruz, having ridden ahead of his 871-man relief column—which he leaves encamped about eight miles away at Santa Fe—to consult with Santa Anna. The latter orders this contingent to advance on Veracruz's outlying town of Los Pocitos at dawn, and both commanders turn in at 2:00 A.M.

A few hours later they are awakened by gunfire as Baudin sweeps down on Veracruz's waterfront in a three-pronged assault. Boatloads of marines and sailors occupy the Santiago and Concepción bastions at the city's southeastern and northwestern corners, spiking the few guns; other French forces advance on the main square from the wharf. Santa Anna narrowly escapes his headquarters at Coliseo and Damas Streets, but Arista is taken, surrendering his sword to the Prince of Joinville. Baudin besieges Veracruz's garrison within the fortress-like barracks in La Merced square, vainly firing upon the doors with small artillery pieces to gain entry. After an hour the French decide to retreat, hoisting a white flag to call for a truce, which the Mexicans refuse to honor.

By 10:00 A.M. Baudin fights his way back to the wharf with his wounded and begins the reembarkation. Santa Anna arrives at 11:00 A.M. with 200 men he has hastily formed into a company, only to receive a blast from a French field piece covering the beach that kills nine of his men and blows off his left leg below the knee and one finger on his right hand. Baudin retires to his warships and continues bombarding Veracruz for another two hours, having suffered eight killed and 60 wounded during the foray. The Mexicans retreat out of their devastated city that afternoon, taking up positions in the dunes beyond.

16 DECEMBER 1838. With passions at last beginning to cool on both sides, Baudin dismisses part of the squadron blockading Veracruz.

22 DECEMBER 1838. Richard Pakenham, the 41-year-old British ambassador to Mexico, arrives at Veracruz from the capital to mediate this Franco-Mexican dispute. He is joined four days later by Vice Adm. Sir Charles Paget with the 74-gun *Cornwallis* of Flag Capt. Sir Richard Grant, and *Edinburgh* of William Honyman Henderson; 46-gun frigate *Madagascar* of Provo William Perry Wallis; 36-gun frigate *Pique* of Edward Boxer; 28-gun frigate *Andromache* of Robert Lambert Baynes; 26-gun frigate *Vestal* of Thomas Wren Carter; 18-gun sloops *Rover* of Cmdr. Thomas Matthew Charles Symonds, *Modeste* of Cmdr. Harry Eyres, and *Racehorse* of Cmdr. Henry William Craufurd; plus the 16-gun sloops *Snake* of Cmdr. Alexander Milne, and *Ringdove* of Acting Cmdr. Keith Stewart.

After consulting for a few days with Baudin, the British agree to withdraw part of this squadron, so as to leave it on a par with the French. Pakenham then departs inland on 8 January 1839 for Mexico City, eventually arranging a meeting between Baudin and the Mexican delegates Manuel Eduardo de Gorostiza and Guadalupe Victoria for 7 March.

9 MARCH 1839. Mexican and French representatives sign a peace treaty whereby the former agree to pay the 600,000-peso compensation and the latter to restore San Juan de Ulúa to Mexican control.

ROSAS'S CAMPAIGNS (1838–1852)

IN MARCH 1835 THE ARCH-CONSERVATIVE Juan Manuel de Rosas returns to the governorship of Buenos Aires, establishing a terrorist dictatorship in reaction to decades of anarchy and strife which have beset this young republic. His rule is maintained by a large standing army and a paramilitary organization called the Mazorca.

EARLY MARCH 1838. The French vice consul in Buenos Aires submits a list of diplomatic complaints to Rosas, who in turn presents him with his traveling papers to quit the country. The French representative goes only as far as Montevideo, where he boards the squadron of Admiral Leblanc.

24 MARCH 1838. ***French Blockade.*** The French vice consul reappears off Buenos Aires with Leblanc's squadron, once more submitting his government's complaints to Rosas. The latter refuses to deal, and a blockade is imposed four days later.

15 JUNE 1838. The former president of Uruguay, Fructuoso Rivera, invades his homeland from Brazil with a volunteer army (one-third being Argentine exiles) and, at El Palmar, defeats his Blanco Party rival, Manuel Oribe, forcing him back inside Montevideo.

11 OCTOBER 1838. Eight French warships from Leblanc's blockading squadron cover the disembarkation of an Uruguayan flotilla on Martín García Island; the 125-man Argentine garrison under Lt. Col. Jerónimo Costa is quickly subdued.

23 OCTOBER 1838. After a lengthy siege of Montevideo by Rivera's forces, Oribe agrees to capitulate and, two days later, sets sail for Buenos Aires. Rivera's temporary new administration—he is not officially elected president until 1 March 1839—includes many Argentine exiles who are enemies of Rosas.

31 DECEMBER 1838. In addition to his French support, Rivera also signs an alliance with Gov. Berón de Astrada of the inland province of Corrientes (Argentina).

20 JANUARY 1839. Gov. Berón de Astrada throws off Rosas's rule.

24 FEBRUARY 1839. Uruguay's president, Rivera, officially declares war against Rosas, which is seconded by Gov. Berón de Astrada four days later.

31 MARCH 1839. ***Pago Largo.*** Rebel Gov. Berón de Astrada quits his Avalos base camp (near San Roque, northwest of Goya, Argentina), heading southeast toward Mocoretá in hopes of uniting with his Uruguayan ally, Rivera. Instead, a loyal Rosist army under Governor Echagüe of Entre Ríos Province quickly marches north from Calá (east of Tala) to intercept him before the combination can be effected.

Learning of his approach, Berón de Astrada withdraws to Pago Largo (southwest of Curuzú Cuatiá), bracing his 4,500 riders, 450 infantry, and three field pieces to receive the onslaught. Echagüe attacks with 5,500 cavalry, 360 foot soldiers, and two guns, his right wing under 37-year-old Justo José de Urquiza defeating Olazábal's rebel division, then swinging behind the loyal army to help scatter Berón de Astrada's other flank, under Brig. Gen. José V. Ramírez. At a cost of 55 dead and 104 injured Echagüe's Rosist forces massacre 2,000 rebels; the huge disparity occurs because all wounded and captured are summarily executed as traitors, including Berón de Astrada.

2 JULY 1839. Rosas's rival Lavalle returns from ten years of exile in Uruguay, leading 160 volunteers ashore from a French flotilla out of Montevideo to occupy the Argentine island of Martín García.

LATE JULY 1839. Echagüe invades western Uruguay from Entre Ríos Province with 5,000 Argentine troops. Rivera warily circles the invaders from a distance with mounted irregulars.

2 SEPTEMBER 1839. Escorted by French vessels, Lavalle sails up the Uruguay River and disembarks 800 men a dozen miles south of Gualeguaychú (Argentina) to raise an anti-Rosas revolt.

12 SEPTEMBER 1839. ***Yeruá.*** Finding little anti-Rosas sentiment at Gualeguaychú, Lavalle's small army marches north to Villaguay then east toward Concordia, accompanied by a French flotilla in the Uruguay River. On the south side of Yeruá Creek his 800 men are intercepted by 1,600 Rosist militia advancing from Nogoyá under the acting provincial governor, Col. Vicente Zapata.

Lavalle advances into battle in four lines, driving into Zapata's center before fanning out right and left and thus scattering his more numerous opponents.

25 OCTOBER 1839. Lavalle safely reaches the anti-Rosist territory around Corrientes, camping at Ombú (18 miles northeast of Curuzú Cuatiá) to be joined by Brigadier General Ferré and other rebels.

29 OCTOBER 1839. A group of wealthy landowners revolts against Rosas, beginning at Dolores (southeast of Buenos Aires).

5 NOVEMBER 1839. ***Chascomús.*** Argentine rebel Pedro Castelli leads 4,000 followers north from Dolores while three loyal Rosist columns converge on his small army: Col. Vicente González from Monte, Col. Nicolás Granada from Tapalqué, and Col. Prudencio Rosas from Azul.

On 6 November Castelli camps on the northeastern shores of Chascomús Lagoon (east of the town of the same name), expecting to confront González's contingent. Instead, he is surprised next day by Prudencio Rosas's 1,300 regular troops and defeated after three hours' confused fighting. Some 500 rebels are killed or captured, Castelli being among the fallen; his head is exhibited on a pike. Another 800 succeed in escaping to Montevideo aboard French ships, where they eventually join Lavalle's anti-Rosas army.

29 DECEMBER 1839. ***Cagancha.*** After closing in on Montevideo in early November, Echagüe finally brings Rivera to battle at Cagancha, on the banks of the San José River (northwest of the capital of Cagancha). The Uruguayans muster 4,000 riders, 800 infantry, and ten field pieces to oppose slightly less than 5,000 Argentine invaders, with four cannons.

Echagüe's cavalry wings, commanded by Urquiza and Lavalleja, engage in a wide-ranging series of clashes, retreats, and pursuits, leaving the Argentine infantry to receive the brunt of Rivera's 1,500-man counterattack and be defeated. Echagüe retreats from the field, having lost 480 dead and 1,000 prisoners compared to 323 Uruguayans killed and 190 injured. Both sides also lose hundreds of strays and deserters, as the Argentines retreat toward Entre Ríos Province.

9 MARCH 1840. Lavalle returns to the Yeruá battlefield with greater numbers after his excursion into northern Argentina; one week later he strikes west-southwest in search of Rosist General Echagüe.

26 MARCH 1840. A 150-man rebel detachment from Lavalle's army under Col. Mariano Vera is annihilated at Cayastá Creek (north of Santa Fe, Argentina) by Rosist Cmdr. Juan Pablo López.

10 APRIL 1840. ***Don Cristóbal.*** Lavalle's 3,400-man, two-gun rebel army comes upon 4,500 Rosists and a half-dozen field pieces under Echagüe dug in between Don Cristóbal Creek and the Montiel Jungle (southeast of Paraná, Argentina). Preferring to commence action next day, Lavalle is attacked that afternoon by Echagüe's left wing, which is beaten back by a rebel cavalry counterattack. Darkness brings a halt to the confused fighting, and the Rosists retire during the night, a few hundred casualties having been sustained on both sides.

15 JULY 1840. ***Sauce Grande.*** Rebel commander Lavalle resumes his slow progression toward the city of Paraná (Argentina) and encounters Echagüe's 4,500 Rosists and eight field pieces again barring his path, this time at an encampment on the banks of Sauce Grande Creek, 20 miles southeast of the city. The advancing 3,400 rebels drive in Echagüe's pickets, then Lavalle uses his artillery to pound the Rosist lines until his gunners run out of shells and night falls.

Hoping to resume action at dawn on 16 July, Lavalle must instead wait until midday for heavy fog to burn off. His main effort sends 2,000 cavalry to drive in Echagüe's right wing, and although it defeats Urquiza's division, Oribe's and Gómez's cavalry shift over from the Rosist left to contain the gain. The rebel infantry makes no headway against the center, so the battle ends with 500 rebel fatalities, as opposed to 150 Rosists.

Discouraged, Lavalle veers west, reaching the port of Diamante by nightfall to begin transferring his army out to Coronda Island and rejoin the French flotilla.

5 AUGUST 1840. Having hurried down the Paraná, Lavalle's main body disembarks at San Pedro while a smaller contingent goes ahead to Baradero. His 2,700 troopers, 300 infantry, and four field pieces reunite and advance southwest into Arrecifes, commandeering mounts along the way. After a brief respite Colonel Vilela leads one rebel column through Carmen de Areco before rejoining Lavalle's main body on 19 August at Guardia de Luján to press on together against Rosas's capital of Buenos Aires.

23 AUGUST 1840. A 600-man rebel cavalry patrol under Colonel Vega drives 700–800 Rosist troopers under Commander Lorea out of Navarro, chasing them as far as Lobos before rejoining Lavalle at Guardia de Luján.

29 AUGUST 1840. Lavalle hesitates but resumes his advance on nearby Buenos Aires from Guardia de Luján, concerned by a lack of local support plus the apparent strength of Rosas's garrison (greatly exaggerated through false intelligence reports). Five days later, at Cañada de la Paja—near the Morales Creek headwaters, three miles southwest of the capital—his 400-man cavalry vanguard easily scatters 200 Rosist troopers and takes Merlo by 5 September. At this point Lavalle halts his army, convinced it is too weak to successfully storm Buenos Aires; next day he reverses direction to attack the inland city of Santa Fe.

EARLY SEPTEMBER 1840. Having learned that Corrientes has signed an alliance with the Uruguayan leader Rivera and begun to raise troops under the Argentine fugitive Paz, Rosist General Echagüe strikes

Juan Manuel de Rosas

across the Paraná with 5,000 troops. Paz resorts to a guerrilla campaign with his 3,000 followers, and Echagüe retires across the river one month later.

11 SEPTEMBER 1840. Having invaded Rioja Province to reimpose Rosist rule over the uncooperative "northern coalition"—which consists of this Argentine province plus Tucumán, Salta, Jujuy, and Catamarca—Gen. José Félix Aldao's 400-man vanguard is defeated at Pampa Redonda (also called Salinas, 90 miles south of the city of Rioja) by General Lamadrid, compelling him to retire into Cuyo.

27 SEPTEMBER 1840. Lavalle's subordinate, Gen. Tomás de Iriarte, approaches Santa Fe with a 1,000-man vanguard, clashing with 700 Rosist defenders under General Garzón. The latter capitulates two days later upon the approach of the main rebel army.

29 OCTOBER 1840. The signing of the Arana-Mackau Treaty puts an end to France's differences with Rosas, the former being granted all its demands. In exchange, the naval blockade is lifted, Martín García Island is restored to Argentina, and Uruguay and the rebels are left to fight alone.

28 NOVEMBER 1840. ***Quebracho Herrado.*** After a grueling nine-day march to Romero (Córdoba Province, Argentina), Lavalle's 4,250 rebel cavalry—1,200 on foot—350 infantry, and four field pieces are overtaken and attacked at Quebracho Herrado by 2,000 Rosist riders. They prove to be merely the vanguard of Oribe's 4,900 cavalry, 1,600 infantry, and five guns, which charge the rebel left wing repeatedly before finally breaking through and disintegrating Lavalle's line. Through logistical error, the rebel artillery only has a few rounds, so the rout goes completely unchecked. At a cost of 36 dead and 50 wounded Oribe kills 1,500 rebels and captures another 500 along with all artillery and baggage trains. Devastated, Lavalle and Lamadrid retreat northwest with 1,500 survivors.

19 JANUARY 1841. ***Sancala.*** Colonel Vilela's 1,500 rebels and two field pieces, resting at Sancala (50 miles west-northwest of Córdoba, Argentina) are surprised at dawn by Gen. Angel Pacheco's 1,100 Rosists. At least 400 rebels are killed and several dozen others captured; the survivors disperse.

20 MARCH 1841. After a successful guerrilla campaign Col. Mariano Acha's 400 rebel troopers are surprised at Machigasta (Argentina) by Gen. Nazario Benavídez's Rosist forces and dispersed.

24 MAY 1841. With the withdrawal of the French blockade, Admiral Brown sorties with an Argentine squadron from Buenos Aires to bottle up the smaller Uruguayan navy—under a hired American commodore named John H. Coe—inside Montevideo.

On 24 May Coe sorties and encounters Brown three miles south of the Uruguayan capital, engaging from 10:00 A.M. until sunset, when he returns to port. The Uruguayan flagship *Sarandí* and *Pereyra* sustain some damage; *Montevideano* is unable to regain port and is beached next morning to prevent its capture. The following night (25–26 May) the crew of the Uruguayan schooner *Palmar* also mutinies and carries the vessel into Buenos Aires.

20 JUNE 1841. Rebel Governor Brizuela is killed at Sañogasta (45 miles west of the Argentine city of Rioja), when his 600 troopers are defeated by Rosist General Benavídez.

3 AUGUST 1841. Coe's Uruguayan squadron sorties and, this afternoon, has a three-hour confrontation with Brown's Argentine warships five miles south of Montevideo. Action ends at nightfall, the Uruguayan schooner *Rivera* colliding with another vessel while reentering port and being lost.

13 AUGUST 1841. ***Angaco.*** Having captured the Argentine city of San Juan, Colonel Acha sorties with 500 troopers to confront the 2,100 Rosists approaching in diverse contingents under Aldao and Benavídez. Three days later, at Angaco (20 miles northwest of San Juan), he surprises and defeats 400 advance riders under Benavídez, prompting Aldao to lead his 600 cavalry and 700 infantry on a forced march through the desert to engage.

Although outnumbering the rebels, the Rosist general's initial cavalry charges against Acha's flanks prove too feeble to be effective, and when his infantry becomes embroiled it soon has to form a defensive square. Eventually, the attackers suffer 1,000 killed and 157 captured, as opposed to 200 dead among Acha's ranks.

Despite the brilliant feat of arms on 16 August the rebel colonel is in turn surprised two days later on the outskirts of San Juan by Benavídez, whose 700 men smash into Acha's 250, driving them to seek shelter inside nearby buildings. The colonel and his 100 survivors surrender on 22 August; Acha is executed by being ignominiously shot in the back and beheaded in San Luis Province on 15 September.

3 SEPTEMBER 1841. Having chased Benavídez out of San Juan, rebel General Lamadrid occupies the city of Mendoza (Argentina); a couple of weeks later he sorties 15 miles east to await Pacheco's approaching Rosist army at Rodeo del Medio.

12 SEPTEMBER 1841. Rosist General Echagüe marches out of Villaguay with 5,000 men to invade the rebel Corrientes Province.

18 SEPTEMBER 1841. ***Famaillá.*** After a lengthy pursuit through Tucumán Province, Lavalle's 1,300 rebel riders, 70 infantry, and three field pieces are overtaken by Rosist General Oribe's 1,700 cavalry, 700 infantry, and three cannons. Although still having the Famaillá River as a barrier between them, Lavalle this night adopts the desperate expedient of crossing upstream and positioning himself west of his opponent in hopes of gaining some advantage.

Although the initial Rosist cavalry charge against the rebel left is broken next morning, the issue is soon decided. Within an hour the rebel army crumbles, suffering 600 killed and 480 captured. Lavalle escapes into Jujuy with 200 riders.

24 SEPTEMBER 1841. ***Rodeo del Medio.*** Lamadrid's 1,200 cavalry, 400 infantry, and nine field pieces are dug in less than a mile behind a swamp with a single bridge, which Pacheco's 1,200 cavalry, 1,800 infantry, and ten guns are able to cross despite enemy artillery fire. Once in position the cavalry on Pacheco's right is driven back by Alvarez's initial rebel charge yet recovers when several Rosist squadrons are shifted over from the left to contain the development.

Meanwhile Pacheco's left outflanks the rebel opponents, after which Lamadrid's outnumbered infantry is decimated by the Rosist troops opposite in the center. Only 18 Rosists are killed and 80 wounded; the rebels suffer 400 casualties and another 300 captured before being driven from the field. Having lost all his artillery and baggage trains, Lamadrid escapes across the Andes into Chile with 100 followers.

9 OCTOBER 1841. Lavalle is killed in Jujuy by a chance round.

28 OCTOBER 1841. Echagüe's Rosist army reaches Pago Largo (southwest of Curuzú Cuatiá), prompting rebel General Paz to retire north behind the Corrientes River and dig in to cover Caaguazú Ford. The Rosists encamp opposite, six miles upstream, and both armies remain in proximity for the next month.

26 NOVEMBER 1841. ***Caaguazú.*** Determined to break the month-long stalemate with his Rosist opponent Echagüe, Paz slips across the Corrientes River after nightfall with approximately 5,000 men and a dozen

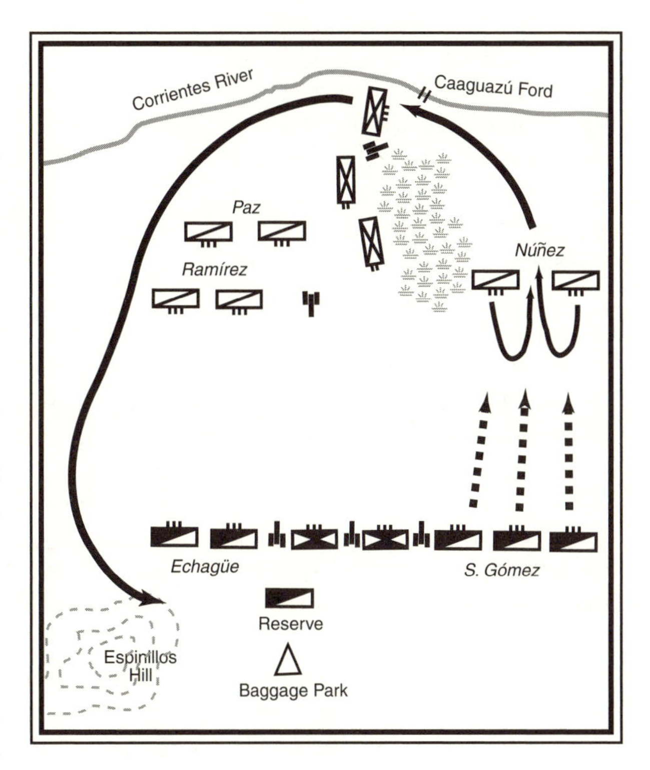

Battle of Caaguazú

field pieces. On the morning of 27 November he sends out a 500-man cavalry patrol but is discovered first by Echagüe, who deploys his own 5,000 men and 12 guns to attack the rebels, whose backs are still to the river.

On the morning of 28 November, however, the rebel left under Núñez launches an attack upon the Rosist right then deliberately retreats, drawing Gómez's counterattack into a bottleneck between the river and a nearby swamp. A carefully stationed infantry battalion and two cannons then allow the rebel cavalry to ride between them, opening up a withering fire upon their pursuers. While the Rosist right is thus being destroyed Núñez continues in a sweeping arc far to the west, gradually outflanking Echagüe's left. When this begins to crumble the Rosist center is doomed.

Echagüe's army is destroyed, suffering 1,350 casualties plus the capture of 800 men, nine guns, and all supply trains.

9 DECEMBER 1841. The Uruguayan squadron under Coe battles Brown's Argentine blockaders 15 miles south of Montevideo, the engagement ending after four hours when a storm blows up. The 12-gun, 106-man Uruguayan brigantine *Cagancha* is unable to regain port with its consorts; next day it is chased down and captured off Ortiz Bank.

15 DECEMBER 1841. Echagüe is replaced as Rosist governor of Entre Ríos Province by Urquiza.

21 DECEMBER 1841. Uruguayan and Argentine warships exchange long-range volleys between Indio Point and Montevideo, the action ending indecisively after several hours.

11 JANUARY 1842. After the Caaguazú victory, Paz's rebel army invades Entre Ríos Province.

20 JANUARY 1842. Rivera crosses the Uruguay River with 2,500 troops, threatening to trap Urquiza's remaining 600 Rosists between he and Paz. The loyal governor therefore evacuates Entre Ríos Province at Gualeguay, allowing the city of Paraná to fall into rebel hands.

MARCH 1842. Rather than pursue the advantage, rebel Governor Ferré returns to Corrientes to demobilize his army; Paz does the same.

12 APRIL 1842. Rosist General Oribe defeats Juan Pablo López—now a rebel—at Coronda. Four days later he does so again at Aguirre Ford, compelling López to retire to Corrientes.

APRIL 1842. Rosist Governor Benavídez of San Juan Province defeats the Argentine rebel Peñaloza—who has invaded from Chile—at Cuesta de Miranda (9 miles south of Sañogasta).

MAY 1842. Oribe crosses the Paraná River near the city of the same name with 7,000 Rosist troops.

26 JUNE 1842. The 34-year-old exiled Italian revolutionary Giuseppe Garibaldi—later to become his homeland's unifier but now the new commander of Rivera's navy—sweeps past Martín García Island with three small Uruguayan warships, exchanging shots with the Argentine garrison for two hours before disappearing up the Paraná River. His mission is to carry armaments to Corrientes Province and revive the rebellion against Rosas.

18 JULY 1842. The Argentine rebel Peñaloza is defeated once again by Rosist governor Benavídez, this time near Tucumán (Argentina).

19 JULY 1842. Garibaldi's squadron clashes with an Argentine flotilla under Maj. Juan F. Seguí at Bajada del Paraná, pressing upriver regardless, little damage being sustained on either side.

15 AUGUST 1842. At Costa Brava, opposite San Juan Creek (the border between Corrientes and Entre Ríos Provinces), Garibaldi's Paraná incursion is brought to an end when his flotilla is overtaken by Brown's Argentine river squadron. Outnumbered, Garibaldi ties up his vessels and entrenches ashore, only to be defeated by a disembarkation force under Brown's subordinate, Lt. Mariano Cordero. Next day, his ammunition gone, Garibaldi blows up *Constitución* and *Pereyra,* retiring north with the survivors and eventually regaining Montevideo overland.

OCTOBER 1842. At Paysandú (Argentina), Uruguayan President Rivera signs an alliance with the rebel governors Paz, Ferré, and Juan Pablo López.

6 DECEMBER 1842. ***Arroyo Grande.*** After entering Entre Ríos Province on 20 January to bolster its anti-Rosas rebellion, President Rivera's 5,500 Uruguayo-Argentine cavalry, 2,000 infantry, and 16 field pieces are confronted at Arroyo Grande—south of Concordia—by 6,500 Rosist troopers, 2,500 infantry, and 18 guns under his old political rival, Oribe (*see* 15 June 1838). Brigadier General Urquiza commands the loyalist right wing, Angel Pacheco the center, and José María Flores the left.

Their attack begins when Oribe's infantry advances on Rivera's center and smashes through, thus dividing the Uruguayo-rebel army. Flores's cavalry defeats and disperses opponents on the left; Urquiza's seesaw struggle on the right is eventually decided when the victorious Rosist infantry moves to his support, taking the enemy in the flank. Rivera is routed, suffering 2,000 killed and 1,400 prisoners while being pitilessly chased back into Uruguay. Oribe only endures 300 total casualties, the disparity in losses being the result of numerous executions carried out after the battle. Urquiza occupies the city of Corrientes with a flying cavalry column, installing Dionisio Cabral as its new Rosist governor.

LATE DECEMBER 1842. Oribe advances into Uruguay with his victorious Rosist army, leading one contingent to besiege his former capital of Montevideo while detaching another to keep Rivera in check.

3 JANUARY 1843. Brown's Argentine squadron sorties from Buenos Aires to begin blockading Montevideo in anticipation of the arrival of Oribe's besieging army.

7 JANUARY 1843. An Argentine flotilla deposits 200 troops at Paysandú (Uruguay) before reversing course and penetrating east along the Negro River to support Oribe's approaching army.

15 JANUARY 1843. Argentine rebel Peñaloza is defeated by Rosist Governor Benavídez in a clash at Illisca (100 miles south of the city of La Rioja); he is then beaten again two days later farther west at Saquilán.

29 JANUARY 1843. Some 2,500 Argentine troops disembark and seize Colonia (Uruguay).

16 FEBRUARY 1843. ***Siege of Montevideo.*** Oribe's Argentine army reaches Cerrito (three miles north of the Uruguayan capital) to institute a siege. The operation is complicated by the fact that many foreign residents within Montevideo rally to its defense: 2,000 Frenchmen under Col. Jean Thiebaut, 600 Italians under Colonel Garibaldi, plus 500 Argentine exiles under Eustaquio Díaz Vélez, swelling the garrison under General Paz to 7,000 men.

More importantly, the Royal Navy squadron of Commo. Brett Purvis—at anchor in the harbor since 7 January—refuses to allow Brown to blockade Montevideo and declares that any British-born subjects serving aboard Argentine warships (a good percentage of their skilled seamen) will be condemned as traitors if caught in action against the Union Jack. This is sufficient to cause Brown's squadron to retire into port, rendering the ensuing Argentine land siege useless.

10 MARCH 1843. Oribe's troops begin their first landward assaults against Montevideo's defenses.

LATE MARCH 1843. ***Santa Lucía.*** Having gathered 5,000 mounted irregulars on the banks of the Santa Lucía River (northwest of Montevideo), Uruguayan President Rivera is challenged by the approach of 4,000 Argentine cavalry under Urquiza, supported by small infantry and artillery contingents. Rather than give battle, the Uruguayans melt away, preferring to adopt guerrilla tactics against the invaders.

31 MARCH 1843. Joaquín Madariaga invades Corrientes Province from Rio Grande do Sul with 110 Argentine exiles, marching on its capital while gathering a host of adherents and thus deposing the Rosist governor. Col. José Miguel Galán marches in relief with 1,600 Rosist troops but is ambushed and defeated at Laguna Brava (18 miles east) by 600 of Madariaga's rebel partisans.

8 MAY 1843. Argentine rebel Peñaloza is defeated by Rosist Governor Benavídez at Leoncito (75 miles northwest of the city of San Juan), prompting him to recross the Andes into Chile.

MID-JUNE 1843. London having disavowed Purvis's threats against the Argentine navy (*see* 16 February 1843), Brown sorties from Buenos Aires and blockades Montevideo.

DECEMBER 1843. Argentine rebel Madariaga invades Entre Ríos Province from Corrientes with 4,500 troops, hoping to depose Rosist Governor Garzón and thus create difficulties in the rear of Oribe's and Urquiza's armies, which are fighting in Uruguay. On 30 December Madariaga crosses to the east side of the Uruguay River, seizing Salto—which has been abandoned during the previous night by its Rosist garrison—and presenting the prize to Rivera.

17 JANUARY 1844. Some 2,000 Argentine rebel riders from Corrientes Province endure an indecisive clash with 1,300 Rosist troops under Governor Garzón at Arroyo Grande (Entre Ríos Province); action ends at nightfall.

24 JANUARY 1844. ***Arroyo Sauce.*** After an arduous three-day ride Urquiza's Argentine cavalry column

disperses 3,000 Uruguayan irregulars gathered at Sauce Creek under Rivera.

15 FEBRUARY 1844. Two battalions sally from beleaguered Montevideo, damaging Oribe's Argentine siege works.

28 MARCH 1844. Gen. Venancio Flores succeeds in breaking the Argentine siege lines around Montevideo with 2,000 men and four field pieces.

24 APRIL 1844. ***Arroyo Pantanoso.*** Montevideo's garrison commander, Paz, attempts to break Oribe's siege, committing 7,800 troops to a surprise three-pronged assault against its lines. The plan is to cut off Pacheco's Argentine contingent opposite Cerro then annihilate Oribe's reserves near Pantanoso Creek as they hasten to the rescue. Instead, Paz's operation breaks down, the 2,000 men sent by boat to outflank Pacheco disembarking so noisily as to forewarn the enemy, after which the main body of infantry falls back into the city at the mere threat of an Argentine cavalry charge.

4 JULY 1844. General Paz resigns as Montevideo's garrison commander, emigrating to Rio de Janeiro.

27 MARCH 1845. ***India Muerta.*** After patiently stalking his opponent, Argentine General Urquiza finally surprises Rivera's 3,000 mounted irregulars at India Muerta Creek (south of Mirim Lagoon) with his slightly smaller contingent of troopers. With the first charge the attackers drive in the Uruguayan left and center; Urquiza commits his reserve against their right, thus turning this battle into a rout. Rivera suffers 400 killed and 500 captured, retiring north to the safety of Brazil's Rio Grande do Sul Province.

18 APRIL 1845. British plenipotentiary Robert Gore Ouseley and French representative Deffaudis reach Buenos Aires. They jointly pose their governments' protests before Rosas, complaining of the protracted siege of Montevideo, which affects their citizens' interests. The Argentine dictator refuses to oblige, and the diplomats withdraw.

LATE JUNE 1845. Argentine rebel Juan Pablo López invades Santa Fe Province from Corrientes with 700 troopers to raise an anti-Rosas revolt. By the time he reaches the town of Andino (north of Santa Fe), López's numbers have swelled to 1,500—including 600 Indian warriors—and he pulverizes a Rosist force that has sallied under Santa Coloma to meet the threat.

6 JULY 1845. López's Argentine rebels fight their way into the city of Santa Fe while Rosist Governor Echagüe awaits reinforcements from Argentina.

22 JULY 1845. ***Anglo-French Intervention.*** Off Montevideo, a combined British and French squadron under Commo. Sir Thomas Sabine Pasley seizes Brown's Argentine blockaders and hands over the vessels to the Uruguayans. Their prisoners are paroled by the captors on condition that they not take up arms against the Anglo-French entente.

12 AUGUST 1845. After chasing Argentine rebel López out of Santa Fe, Governor Echagüe's 3,000 Rosists overtake his army at San Jerónimo or Mal Abrigo, inflicting a stinging defeat that drives the force even farther north.

31 AUGUST 1845. ***Garibaldi's Incursion.*** Having gone aboard the three Argentine prizes seized by the Anglo-French squadron, Colonel Garibaldi sets sail from Montevideo with 700 Italian volunteers, 200 Uruguayan infantry under 35-year-old Col. Lorenzo Batlle, and 100 cavalry to reoccupy nearby Colonia de Sacramento.

6 SEPTEMBER 1845. Garibaldi's flotilla seizes the Argentine island of Martín García before proceeding up the Uruguay River.

18 SEPTEMBER 1845. The British and French announce a blockade of Argentina's shorelines along the River Plate.

20 SEPTEMBER 1845. Having advanced up the Uruguay River, Garibaldi's 1,000 Italo-Uruguayan troops disembark and sack Gualeguaychú (Argentina).

LATE OCTOBER 1845. Garibaldi seizes Salto (Uruguay), remaining for a few months with his small army while skirmishing with local Argentine units under Urquiza, Díaz, and Servando Gómez. Eventually, the Italian adventurer returns to Montevideo, where he is promoted general on 16 February 1846 for his efforts.

8 NOVEMBER 1845. ***Paraná River Offensive.*** Having been instructed by their home governments to establish free navigation up the Paraná—which Rosas has long stifled due to commercial animosity against Paraguay, and the hinterlands of Uruguay and Brazil—a shallow-draft Anglo-French expedition departs Martín

García Island to drive past the Argentine batteries at Vuelta de Obligado (literally, Obligatory Turn, about 60 miles below Rosario between San Pedro and Ramallo):

English

Ship	*Guns*	*Tons*	*Commander*
Gorgon (flag, paddle)	6	1,111	Charles Hotham
Firebrand (paddle)	6	1,190	James Hope
Philomel	8	428	Cmdr. Bartholomew James Sullivan
Comus (sloop)	18	492	Acting Cmdr. Edward Augustus Inglefield
Dolphin	3	318	Lt. Reginald Thomas Jonathan Levinge
Fanny (schooner, Argentine prize)	1	?	Lt. Astley Cooper Key

French

Ship	*Guns*	*Tons*	*Commander*
San Martin (Argentine prize)	8	200	François Thomas Tréhouart
Fulton (paddle)	2	650	Lieutenant Mazères
Expéditive (sloop)	16	?	Lieutenant Miniac
Pandour	10	?	Lieutenant Duparc
Procida (Argentine prize)	4	?	Lieutenant de la Rivière

This flotilla is carrying an additional 70 Royal Marines under Capt. Thomas Hurdle, plus three field pieces.

11 NOVEMBER 1845. The rebel Argentine province of Corrientes signs a military alliance with Paraguay.

18 NOVEMBER 1845. The Anglo-French expedition anchors two miles below the Argentine defenses at Vuelta de Obligado, Commander Sullivan and Lieutenant Mazères reconnoitering the position and finding it formidable: 24 large armed hulks held together across a half-mile by triple chains; four batteries on the west bank; and two gunboats and the schooner *Republicano* guarding the eastern bank. Mansilla, the Rosist general in charge, commands 2,500 troops—including two squadrons of cavalry, 600 infantry regulars, plus 300 volunteer militia.

On the morning of 20 November Sullivan weighs with *Philomel, Expéditive, Fanny,* and *Procida,* advancing past Tréhouart's heavier division of *San Martin, Comus, Pandour,* and *Dolphin.* (Hotham is to remain in reserve with the steamers *Gorgon, Firebrand,* and *Fulton* until the chains have been burst, as they might foul his propellers.) *Dolphin* dashes directly upstream, drawing much of the Argentine fire until being passed by Tréhouart's 100-man *San Martin,* after which all the attackers drop anchor opposite the batteries and return fire. Because of the strong current and faint breeze, most vessels struggle to reach their assigned positions. Ten Argentine fire vessels are released at 10:50 A.M., drifting harmlessly past the allies, at which Hotham and Mazères join the action.

Republicano is set fire and abandoned by its crew at 11:30 A.M., blowing up 45 minutes later. In the midst of the battle Hope of *Firebrand* leads three boatloads of men aboard the sixteenth hulk from shore, chopping its cables and thus opening a gap through which *Fulton* passes, followed by *Gorgon* and *Firebrand.* From here Hotham rakes the northern Argentine batteries, silencing them by 5:00 P.M.; one hour later he sets 180 British seamen, 145 Royal Marines, and 135 French sailors ashore. They oblige the defenders to retreat; Mansilla is wounded in the process, replaced by Col. Ramón Rodríguez. By next morning all the defenses are occupied at a cost of 24 dead and 72 wounded among the allied force. Rosist losses are at least 150 dead and 90 wounded, with several hundred deserters or stragglers.

2 JANUARY 1846. Rosist General Urquiza departs Concordia with 6,000 troops, marching north into Corrientes Province to confront Argentine rebel Paz before his 4,000-man, 14-gun army can be reinforced from Paraguay.

16 JANUARY 1846. At Las Osamentas Creek (northwest of Pago Largo), an advance contingent of Urquiza's troops surprises a rebel cavalry force after a nocturnal march and disperses them.

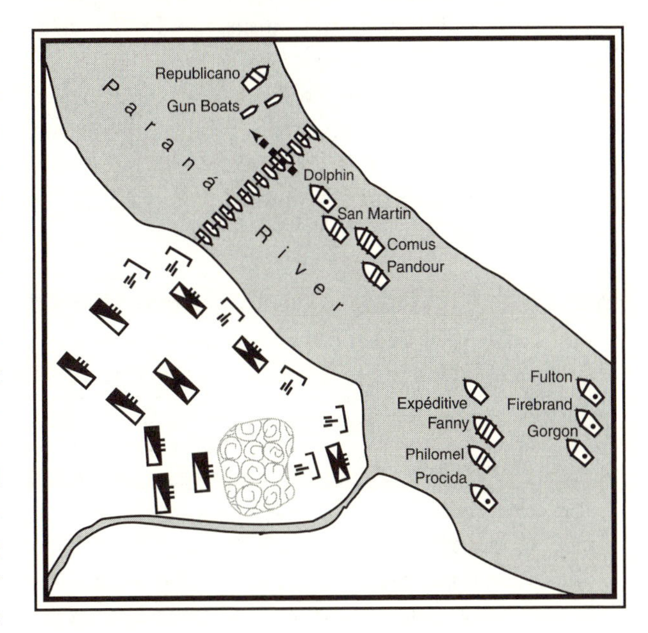

Battle of Vuelta de Obligado

20 JANUARY 1846. Part of the Anglo-French expedition reaches Corrientes on the Paraná River, from where Hotham continues as far as the Paraguayan capital, Asunción, aboard the French *Fulton*.

4 FEBRUARY 1846. A 1,200-man rebel cavalry screen is scattered at Laguna Limpia (northeast of Bella Vista) by 600 Rosist troopers riding ahead of Urquiza's army. Among their prisoners is Juan Madariaga, brother to the rebel governor of Corrientes Province, who is released next day with a peace proposal.

General Paz, however, is to be excluded from negotiations, so Urquiza continues against his defensive positions at Ubajay (north-northwest of Loreto, south of the Paraná River). They are judged so large and impregnable, that Urquiza orders a full-scale retirement back toward Entre Ríos Province by 12 February.

2 APRIL 1846. The British *Philomel* fights its way past the new Argentine batteries installed on the Paraná River at San Lorenzo.

4 APRIL 1846. Governor Madariaga removes Paz as commander of the rebel forces in Corrientes Province.

16 MAY 1846. Hotham assembles a convoy of 110 merchantmen at Bajada de Santa Fe to be escorted down the Paraná past Rosas's Argentine batteries at San Lorenzo.

4 JUNE 1846. Hotham's convoy works its way past the Argentine batteries at San Lorenzo, which are distracted by hidden rocket batteries installed on an uninhabited island out in the stream by Lt. Lauchlan Bellingham Mackinnon of *Alecto*.

(As a reward for their services in reaching Paraguay, the senior British commander Hotham is created Knight Commander of the Bath, while his French counterpart Trehouart is promoted to rear admiral in February 1847.)

JULY 1846. British plenipotentiary Thomas Samuel Hood reaches Buenos Aires to negotiate an end to Anglo-Argentine hostilities, only to be rebuffed by Rosas.

14 AUGUST 1846. Governor Madariaga signs a treaty at Alcaraz with Rosist General Urquiza, whereby the rebel Corrientes Province rejoins Rosas's rule on condition that it not have to take part in the ongoing hostilities against Uruguay, England, or France. Paraguay's independence is also recognized in this document.

MAY 1847. English and French representatives reach Buenos Aires to renew attempts to reach a diplomatic solution to their hostilities with Rosas.

15 JULY 1847. Britain lifts its blockade of Buenos Aires, leaving France to maintain this operation alone.

20 OCTOBER 1847. Rosist General Urquiza once more invades Corrientes Province, departing his Calá base camp (east of Tala) with 6,000 troops. During the advance Correntine Col. Nicanor Cáceres switches sides and joins the invaders on the border, as do commander Juan Verón at Mercedes and Col. Juan Francisco Soto at the Corrientes River.

OCTOBER 1847. President Rivera is driven out of Uruguay.

27 NOVEMBER 1847. ***Vences.*** At small Vences Ranch (deep in the jungle 50 miles east-southeast of the city of Corrientes), the provincial governor, Madariaga, digs in with 4,100 riders, 900 infantry, and 12 field pieces, but his army's morale is low. Urquiza arrives to attack with 6,000 Rosist cavalry, 500 foot soldiers, and seven cannons.

A frontal assault by two infantry battalions, a cavalry squadron, and two guns under Rosist commander Francia ties down the Correntine defenders, allowing huge flanking movements to penetrate the jungle on both sides and take Madariaga's followers by surprise. The effect of the cavalry columns pouring down on the Correntine rear, plus enfilading salvos from a five-gun battery hidden in the trees, breaks the defenders' will and causes a wholesale flight. Some 500 Correntine soldiers are killed and another 2,100 captured, the rest dispersing into the jungle.

14 DECEMBER 1847. Urquiza installs Gen. Benjamín Virasoro in the capital of Corrientes as its new Rosist governor.

15 JUNE 1848. France lifts its blockade of Buenos Aires.

24 NOVEMBER 1849. Britain signs a peace treaty with Rosas.

31 AUGUST 1850. Admiral Lapredour signs a peace treaty with Rosas on behalf of the French government.

5 APRIL 1851. Following Rosas's election to a fourth term as president—and growing fears about Buenos

Aires's domination over the rest of Argentina—Governor Urquiza of Entre Ríos Province contacts other leaders about a possible revolt.

1 MAY 1851. Urquiza proclaims Entre Ríos Province to be in open rebellion against the Rosas dictatorship.

29 MAY 1851. Urquiza signs a military alliance with Brazil and Uruguay, promising to help them in their ongoing war against Oribe's 14,000 troops, which hold most of the country (except Montevideo) thanks to support from Rosas.

26 JULY 1851. ***Uruguayan Campaign.*** Urquiza begins mustering 7,500 troops near Paysandú; two days later he crosses the Uruguay River to attack Oribe from the rear. He is soon joined by Rosist deserters and Uruguayan patriots, bringing his strength to 9,000 men.

16 AUGUST 1851. From Buenos Aires, Rosas officially declares war against Brazil for its intervention in Argentine affairs.

4 SEPTEMBER 1851. Having encountered no opposition in Uruguay, Urquiza reaches the town of Durazno while a 16,000-man Brazilian army crosses the frontier from Santana do Livramento to join him.

13 SEPTEMBER 1851. Urquiza's huge army contacts Oribe; after nearly a month of negotiations Oribe capitulates at Pantanoso on 8 October, bringing the Uruguayan civil war to a close. His Argentine followers are incorporated into Urquiza's ranks; the Uruguayans agree to serve the government in Montevideo.

17 DECEMBER 1851. An 11-vessel Brazilian river squadron under Adm. John Greenfield fights its way past General Mansilla's 1,500 Rosist defenders and 16 guns at Tonelero (northwest of San Pedro, on the Paraná River), disembarking the 1st Brazilian Division to establish a beachhead.

Shortly thereafter 5,000 of Urquiza's cavalry cross farther upriver from his base camp at Diamante to pave the way for the main body. No opposition is encountered.

28 DECEMBER 1851. Urquiza's main army begins embarking at Diamante, traveling down the Paraná River to land and reassemble at Espinillo (between Rosario and San Lorenzo) by 8 January 1852.

10 JANUARY 1852. Urquiza's Aquino Division—formerly under Oribe in Uruguay (*see* 13 September 1851)—mutinies and kills its officers at Espinillo, fleeing to Santos Lugares to rejoin Rosas.

15 JANUARY 1852. Urquiza departs Espinillo, beginning his final offensive against Buenos Aires. Three days later his army traverses Medio Creek, encountering no resistance from Rosist forces, who continue to fall back as the invaders gain Pergamino, Chivilcoy, Luján, and Márquez Bridge (over the Conchas River—the modern-day Reconquista River).

31 JANUARY 1852. A 3,000-man cavalry detachment under Juan Pablo López clashes with 3,500 Rosist troopers under Col. Hilario Lagos at Alvarez Fields (6 miles west of Márquez Bridge), killing 200 and capturing a similar number before the Rosists retire to Santos Lugares.

3 FEBRUARY 1852. ***Caseros.*** At long last, Rosas decides to make a stand at Caseros Estate (on the banks of Morón Creek, just southwest of Buenos Aires) with 12,000 cavalry, 10,000 infantry, and 1,000 gunners and auxiliaries manning 56 artillery pieces. Urquiza traverses the creek during the morning with his slightly larger army; after drawing up in battle array he launches a devastating charge with 10,000 riders on the right. This destroys Rosas's left and consumes his reserves; he vainly attempts to check the onslaught.

Although the Rosist left, Brigadier General Díaz's infantry, and Chilavert's batteries resist tenaciously, the rest of the army disintegrates, leaving Urquiza triumphant. Rosas flees the battlefield, his army having suffered 1,500 casualties and 7,000 prisoners plus the loss of all artillery, provisions, and equipment. Urquiza's losses are 600 dead and wounded; next day he designates Vicente López y Planes as governor of Buenos Aires.

Following his defeat, Rosas flees with his daughter to the British embassy in Buenos Aires, whose ambassador Robert Gore conducts him aboard the man-of-war *Centaur.* From here the fallen despot is transferred aboard *Conflict* and sails a few days later toward England, living out the remaining 25 years of his life as an exile in Southampton. His dictatorial methods and restrictive economic policies, which initially maintained his regime, in the end hasten its downfall.

Simmering Confrontations (1839–1844)

Minor outbursts continue to erupt throughout Central and South America—especially in Mexico, which is gripped by political anarchy following its recent humiliation at the hands of France. All the while Mexican authorities feebly attempt to reconquer the lost province of Texas.

18 May 1839. Centralist tendencies and increased taxation by the Mexico City government provoke a brief revolt in the state of Jalisco, which is quickly suppressed.

29 May 1839. Another anticentralist uprising erupts in Yucatán, where a leader called Santiago Imán besieges the town of Tizimín until 11 November before finally carrying the place. After a month-long occupation his followers are dispersed east into the jungles by forces loyal to the government.

17 February 1840. Rebel Col. Sebastián López de Llergo arrives outside Yucatán's capital, Mérida, and is allowed inside three days later thanks to the defection of Col. Anastasio Torrens's garrison at the San Benito barracks. The combination of López de Llergo and Torrens so emboldens the separatist cause that the state legislature soon severs relations with Mexico City.

2 April 1840. A small separatist expedition appears out of Yucatán under López de Llergo and Imán, blockading and laying siege to Campeche's centralist garrison, which requests terms by 6 June and capitulates ten days later.

15 July 1840. At 2:00 A.M. General Urrea—incarcerated in Mexico City's old Inquisitorial headquarters for abetting the French cause during the recent War of the Cakes—is broken out of confinement then leads troops from the 5th Battalion and Comercio Militia Regiment in an assault against Bustamante's palace, capturing the latter in bed and proclaiming Gómez Farías the new president. Army Chief of Staff Gabriel Valencia, however, along with Gens. Antonio Mozo and Juan Nepomuceno Almonte, leads a loyalist counterattack from the Ciudadela barracks, opening fire on the rebels with artillery.

During the night of 15–16 July Bustamante cuts his way free with 28 dragoons; a fortnight of street fighting that inflicts many civilian casualties finally compels Urrea to surrender and retire north to Durango.

8 August 1841. In a prearranged coup 44-year-old Mexican Brig. Gen. Mariano Paredes y Arrillaga—military commander at Guadalajara—rises against President Bustamante, being joined shortly thereafter by Santa Anna at Veracruz. Paredes marches on Guanajuato with 600 men and receives the defection of Brig. Gen. Pedro Cortázar. They then proceed together toward Querétaro to incorporate Gen. Julián Juvera's garrison into the ranks, thereby swelling rebel numbers to 2,200.

Santa Anna meanwhile occupies Perote with a few hundred troops while General Valencia mutinies with another 1,200 inside Mexico City proper, seizing the Ciudadela and Acordada barracks. The president fights back with 2,000 loyal troops and a dozen guns, calling for reinforcements from the countryside; civilians flee out of the line of fire. Although his following eventually numbers 3,500, Bustamante is driven out of his capital by 20 September, resigning nine days later to go into exile in Europe.

1 October 1841. Yucatán contemplates declaring independence from Mexico while signing peace and commerce treaties with the Republic of Texas (which reciprocates by sending armed gunboats to help protect Yucatán's coastline).

6 February 1842. The British brig *Jane and Sarah* and the sloop *Little William* are boarded and ransacked by five of General Carmona's Colombian warships while at anchor off Zapote (near Cartagena). The six-gun, 55-man Royal Navy brig *Charybdis* of Lt. Michael de Courcy is sent to demand satisfaction, and in an hour-long engagement seizes the Colombian flagship—a corvette—while inflicting 26 fatalities. He then sinks a brig and captures three schooners before blockading Cartagena's roadstead. De Courcy is promoted for these actions.

7 May 1842. Having failed to arrive at a reconciliation with Yucatán, Mexico's congress severs relations with the breakaway province.

22 August 1842. ***Yucatán Rebellion.*** A Mexican expedition escorted by the British-built steamers *Guadalupe, Moctezuma,* and the captured *Yucateco* arrive before the Gulf port of El Carmen to begin subduing the rebel provinces of Campeche and Yucatán. The outpost surrenders by 30 August, and a 4,000-man army

advances northeast through Champotón, Seybaplaya, and Lerma under Vicente Miñón without resistance.

At Campeche, however, the centralists meet 3,500 separatist defenders under Santiago Méndez, who compels them to settle in for a lengthy siege. Miñón is eventually recalled on 29 January 1843 because of his inactivity, being replaced by Matías de la Peña y Barragán.

AUTUMN 1842. ***Texas Incursion.*** General Adrián Woll—a former Napoleonic officer—leads a Mexican raid across the border against San Antonio. The Republic of Texas attempts to retaliate by marching on Santa Fe (New Mexico), but the entire 270-man expedition is captured at Antón Chico and Laguna Colorada and conducted south for incarceration within the fortress of El Perote.

SEPTEMBER 1842. While lying at Callao with Capt. James Armstrong's frigate *United States* and 20-gun, 200-man, 790-ton sloop *Cyane,* the veteran commander of America's Pacific squadron, Commo. Thomas ap Catesby "Tac" Jones (*see* 16 September 1814), receives seemingly reliable information as to an outbreak of hostilities between the United States and Mexico because of border frictions involving the Republic of Texas. Concerned lest California be peremptorily seized by British or French interests during the confrontation, he sets sail northwest.

19 OCTOBER 1842. ***Jones's War.*** At 2:45 P.M. Commodore Jones drops anchor in Monterey, determined to launch a preemptive strike. The few ships in this California port are consequently taken as prizes of war, and at 4:00 P.M. Armstrong is sent ashore under a flag of truce to demand the Mexican garrison's surrender. The former governor, Juan B. Alvarado, and Capt. Mariano Silva command only 29 soldiers and 25 raw recruits plus 11 nearly useless cannons within the tiny redoubt; they therefore agree to capitulate that night. Next morning Jones lands 150 men and a band, marching inland to occupy the position and renaming it Fort Catesby.

By next day, however, it becomes obvious even to Jones that there is no state of belligerency, so he restores all his captures. Notwithstanding this unwarranted action, his subsequent stay in California is not unfriendly, although he is eventually recalled by an embarrassed—yet not altogether reproving—government in Washington.

4 FEBRUARY 1843. After the newly arrived centralist Mexican General de la Peña decides to reinvigorate the Campeche siege by detaching General Andrade with 800 troops into the town of Chiná (five miles east), the force is surprised by 500 separatist troops under Lt. Col. Manuel Oliver. In a ferocious exchange some 400 men are slain on both sides and many others wounded before the separatists retreat to Campeche.

25 MARCH 1843. De la Peña disembarks 2,500 centralist troops at the tiny port of Telchac (north-central Yucatán), hoping to surprise its capital, Mérida, from the rear. Although able to overrun Motul, de la Peña is checked at Tixcocob by López de Llergo on 10 April then compelled to seek terms two weeks later at Tixpéhual. De la Peña's army reembarks at Chicxulub by 26 May, sailing away in defeat.

26 JUNE 1843. The 39-year-old Cuban-born centralist Gen. Pedro Ampudia lifts the siege of the separatist garrison within Campeche, sailing away toward El Carmen.

15 APRIL 1844. Fearing a preemptive Mexican invasion of the Republic of Texas before it can be annexed by the United States, U.S. officials order Commo. David Conner to concentrate his squadron in the Gulf of Mexico. (When the U.S. Senate subsequently rejects the treaty of annexation on 6 June the vessels are withdrawn.)

30 OCTOBER 1844. In Guadalajara, Paredes—en route to take up a new command in Sonora—agrees to spearhead a revolt against Santa Anna's regime. He is backed one week later by the Aguascalientes garrison, by that of Mazatlán on 7 November, by Zacatecas and Colima next day, then Durango and Querétaro by 10 November.

22 NOVEMBER 1844. ***Santa Anna's Overthrow.*** Santa Anna marches northwest out of Mexico City toward San Juan de los Lagos with a small army to confront the rebel Paredes, who has reached Mochiltic (Querétaro) with 4,000 troops. On 6 December the *Batallón de Reemplazos* (Reserve Battalion) also revolts in the capital's Acordada barracks, sparking a general uprising against Santa Anna's 50-year-old handpicked "interim president," Gen. Valentín Canalizo. The latter is arrested, and next day the mutineers select 52-year-old Gen. José Joaquín de Herrera as the new president of Mexico.

By early January Santa Anna gives up all hope of reclaiming power, so departs his shrunken army toward Veracruz with a small cavalry escort. En route he disguises himself as a muleteer but is nonetheless recognized upon reaching Naolinco; he is then detained in Perote Castle until banished to Cuba on 3 June 1845 aboard the gunboat *Victoria.*

MEXICAN-AMERICAN WAR (1846–1848)

WHEN THE UNITED STATES CONGRESS VOTES on 1 March 1845 to accede to American settlers' wishes and annex the Republic of Texas, Juan Nepomuceno Almonte—the 41-year-old Mexican ambassador in Washington—requests his passport five days later to depart in protest, as his nation still regards Texas as a breakaway province. Three weeks of wrangling ensue between the American and Mexican governments, but on the last day of March Mexico severs diplomatic relations.

20 MARCH 1845. Conner is ordered back into Mexican waters with the 50-gun, 480-man, 1,700-ton frigate *Potomac* of Capt. John Gwinn; 22-gun, 190-man, 700-ton sloop *Falmouth* of Cmdr. Joseph R. Jarvis; plus ten-gun, 80-man brigs *Lawrence* (364 tons) of Cmdr. Samuel Mercer and *Somers* (260 tons) of Cmdr. Duncan N. Ingraham.

18 APRIL 1845. Conner anchors off Antón Lizardo (southeast of Veracruz).

EARLY MAY 1845. The 50-year-old Commo. Robert Field Stockton arrives at Galveston (Texas) for a two-month visit with his 13-gun, 166-man, 670-ton, propeller-driven flagship *Princeton* under Cmdr. Frederick Engle, plus a small flotilla.

4 JULY 1845. Anglo-Texans accept U.S. terms for annexation.

22–23 JULY 1845. To match Mexico's military buildup near the mouth of the Río Grande—apparently threatening the peaceful annexation of Texas by the United States—61-year-old Brevet Brig. Gen. Zachary "Old Rough and Ready" Taylor departs Fort Jesup (Louisiana) with 1,500 troops of Lt. Col. Ethan Allen Hitchcock's 3rd Infantry Regiment and other auxiliaries, their transport steamer *Alabama* being escorted by the 22-gun, 210-man, 960-ton sloop *St. Mary's* of Cmdr. John L. Saunders.

25 JULY 1845. Taylor arrives at Saint Joseph's Island (Aransas Inlet) and after some difficulty disembarking camps six days later at Corpus Christi, near the mouth of the Nueces River—traditionally regarded by Mexicans as the Texas border.

24 AUGUST 1845. Taylor is joined at Corpus Christi by 300 troopers under 59-year-old Col. David E. "Old Davy" Twiggs's 2nd Dragoon Regiment, who have traveled overland from Louisiana via San Antonio. (By late October Taylor's contingent will consist of 3,500 U.S. regulars: four infantry regiments, one of dragoons, and four artillery regiments—half the peacetime army.)

30 OCTOBER 1845. Stockton departs Hampton Roads (Virginia) aboard the 54-gun, 480-man, 1,860-ton frigate *Congress* of Cmdr. Samuel F. Du Pont to round Cape Horn and become second-in-command to 64-year-old Commo. John D. Sloat in the Pacific. The latter is lying at Mazatlán (Mexico) with the 50-gun, 480-man, 1,700-ton frigate *Savannah* of Capt. James Armstrong; sloops *Cyane* of Capt. William Mervine; 22-gun, 210-man, 1,020-ton *Portsmouth* of Cmdr. John B. Montgomery; 20-gun, 200-man, 790-ton *Levant* of Cmdr. Hugh N. Page; 24-gun, 190-man, 690-ton *Warren* of Cmdr. Joseph B. Hull; 12-gun, 100-man, 200-ton schooner *Shark* of Lt. Neil M. Howison; and four-gun, 43-man, 610-ton storeship *Erie* of Lt. James M. Watson.

31 OCTOBER 1845. In order to help facilitate a reconciliation with Mexico, Conner withdraws his squadron from off Veracruz.

29 NOVEMBER 1845. Former U.S. congressman from Louisiana John C. Slidell arrives at Veracruz aboard *St. Mary's* to reopen diplomatic contacts with the Mexican government.

14 DECEMBER 1845. Frustrated in his attempts to mobilize an effective fighting force at San Luis Potosí, Paredes revolts against President Herrera, marching on Mexico City with his small army. The latter is abandoned by his troops, Paredes entering the capital uncontested on 2 January 1846 to be acclaimed president.

5 MARCH 1846. A 32-year-old explorer and brevet captain in the U.S. engineers named John Charles Frémont—already gaining fame as the "Pathfinder" and son-in-law to an influential U.S. senator from Missouri, Thomas Hart Benton (close adviser to newly inaugurated President James Knox Polk)—approaches Monterey out of the Santa Cruz Mountains with a 60-man survey party to refresh supplies. Although approved by

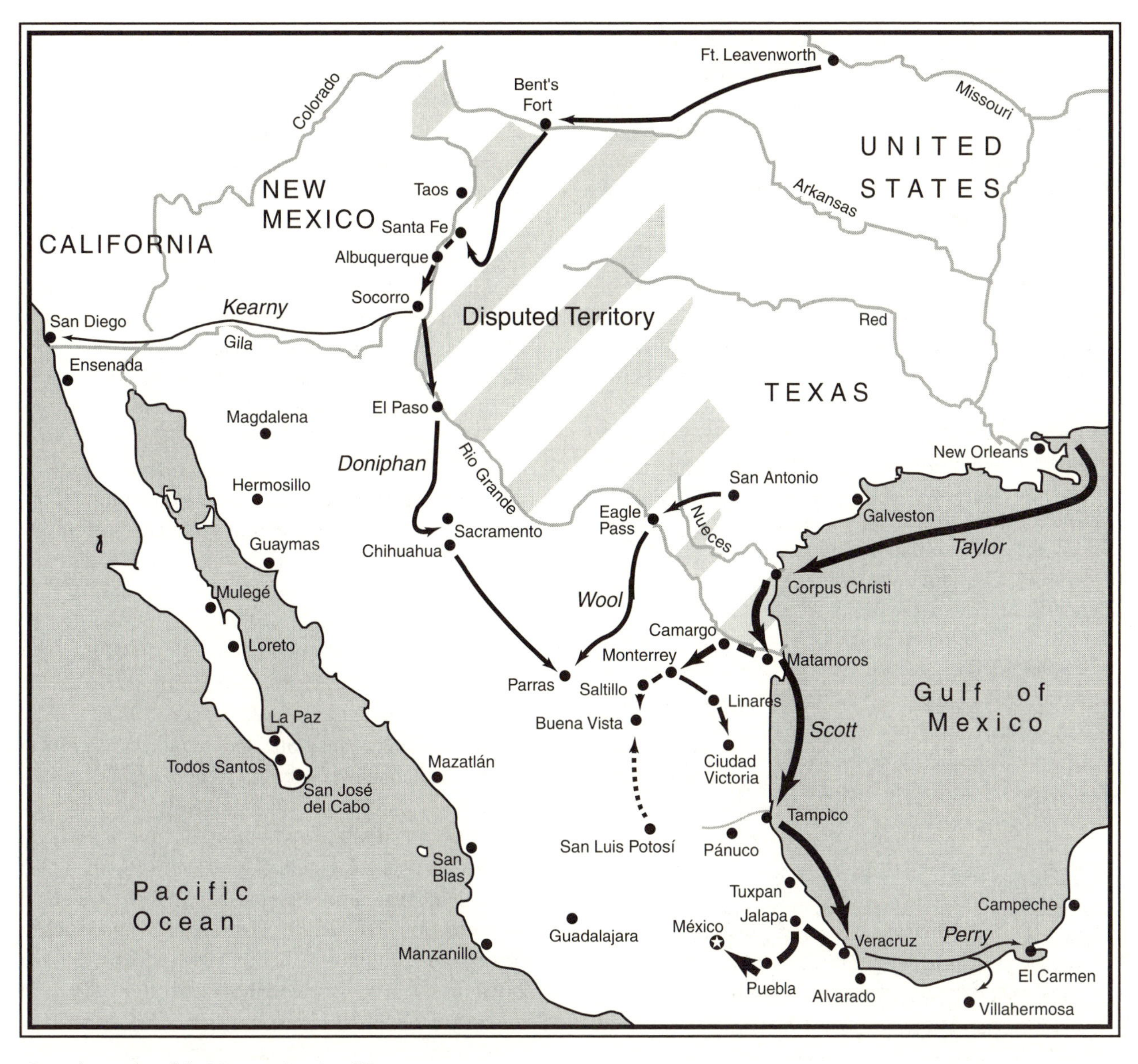

General campaign of the Mexican-American War

the Mexican authorities, Frémont's visit is canceled when he is a mere 25 miles away; he is peremptorily ordered to leave California.

Instead, he entrenches atop Gavilán (modern-day Frémont) Hill northeast of Salinas and is besieged by a 350-man force under Gen. José María Castro. After four days of bombastic exchanges the Americans withdraw north toward Oregon under cover of darkness.

8 MARCH 1846. Taylor, having been authorized to move his 3,500 troops south from Corpus Christi—deeper into disputed territory—orders his vanguard to break camp this Sunday, followed by segments of his main body over the next few days. The first American troops sight Point Santa Isabel by 24 March, finding supply ships awaiting them in the Gulf of Mexico. The town of El Frontón is found ominously burned and evacuated by its 280-man Mexican garrison.

Four days later the U.S. expedition reaches the Río Grande and receives a frosty reception from Col. Francisco Mejía, commander in Matamoros, who considers the advance an invasion of Mexican territory. Nevertheless, he is not empowered to do anything more than observe as Taylor erects a 2,200-man camp opposite named Fort Texas. (Mejía's own strength consists of the 1st and 10th Infantry, 2nd Light Infantry, and 7th Cavalry Regiments; a sapper plus several border guard companies; and a battalion of Matamoros militia—3,000 men in total plus 20 guns. Other units are soon on their way to reinforce him.)

30 MARCH 1846. Having failed to reach agreement with the Mexican government, Slidell departs Veracruz aboard the ten-gun, 260-man, 1,700-ton paddle steamer *Mississippi* of Capt. Andrew Fitzhugh.

4 APRIL 1846. Mexico's war minister, José María Tornel y Mendivil, appoints Maj. Gen. and former president Mariano Arista to organize an "Army of the North" to confront Taylor's incursion. Shortly thereafter Arista sets out from Monterrey (Nuevo León) with diverse bodies of troops, marching for Matamoros.

11 APRIL 1846. Arista's vanguard—1,000 cavalry and 1,500 infantry under Ampudia—reaches Matamoros and two days later orders Taylor to begin retiring north to Corpus Christi within 24 hours. The American general refuses and directs his warships out in the Gulf to blockade the Río Grande, cutting off seaborne supplies for the Mexican army.

17 APRIL 1846. *Lawrence* and the Texas revenue cutter *Santa Anna* turn back the schooners *Equity* and *Floridian,* which are approaching Matamoros from New Orleans with provisions for the Mexican forces. Upon learning of this action five days later Ampudia lodges a formal protest.

23 APRIL 1846. Paredes declares a "defensive war" against the American intervention and Arista orders Gen. Anastasio Torrejón to cross the Río Grande a few miles upstream of Taylor's encampment with 1,600 cavalry. The American general responds by dispatching a reconnaissance patrol of 63 dragoons under Capt. Seth Thornton. The U.S. force is ambushed at Carricitos next day by 200 Mexican troopers; 16 Americans are killed and the remainder captured.

28–29 APRIL 1846. During the night Capt. Samuel Walker's 77 volunteer "Texas Rangers" clash with Mexican irregulars, suffering ten killed.

1 MAY 1846. Fearful he is about to be encircled by a Mexican flanking maneuver, Taylor leaves the 7th Infantry (the Cotton Balers) of 58-year-old Maj. Jacob Brown and two four-gun batteries to hold Fort Texas while commencing a 30-mile forced march northeast this afternoon with his remaining 2,300 men and 300 wagons toward the detached coastal contingent at Point Santa Isabel.

This same day, Arista's army slips east-southeast out of Matamoros, hoping to cross the Río Grande at Longoreno and unite with Torrejón's cavalry behind American lines. (A lack of boats, however, slows this deployment.)

2 MAY 1846. Taylor reaches Point Santa Isabel at noon and digs in.

3 MAY 1846. At dawn Mexican artillery in Matamoros opens a heavy fire across the Río Grande against Fort Texas, being returned over the next several days. (While inspecting outposts on 5 May Brown is killed by a shell. Fort Texas is therefore renamed Fort Brown in his honor, the town that eventually springs up around it becoming known as Brownsville.)

4 MAY 1846. This morning Conner departs Veracruz for the Río Grande with his 50-gun, 480-man, 1,700-ton frigates *Cumberland* (flag) of Capt. Bladen Dulany, *Raritan* of Capt. Francis H. Gregory, and *Potomac;* 22-gun, 190-man, 700-ton sloop *John Adams* of Cmdr. William J. McCluney; plus the brig *Somers* (leaving *Falmouth* behind to maintain watch). Four days later the squadron arrives off Taylor's base camp at Brazos de Santiago, using the army steamer *Monmouth* to set 500 sailors and marines ashore and reinforce Maj. John Monroe's garrison at Fort Polk.

7 MAY 1846. ***Palo Alto.*** Learning that Fort Texas has been attacked, Taylor departs Point Santa Isabel with 2,300 men at 3:00 P.M. to relieve his beleaguered detachment. After camping overnight he encounters Arista's and Torrejón's 3,200 Mexicans on 8 May blocking the road at Palo Alto Pond in a battle line more than a mile long.

Having secured their baggage train the Americans advance early that afternoon with the 8th Infantry and Capt. James Duncan's light battery on the left; the 4th and 3rd Infantry in the center supported by heavy 18-pounders; plus the 5th Infantry and Capt. Samuel Ringgold's light artillery on the right. The Mexican guns open fire as Taylor advances, making poor execution due to weak powder and lack of high-explosive shells. The American horse-drawn "flying" light batteries wreak fearful havoc by swiftly deploying ahead of Taylor and then pouring heavy fire into the static Mexican lines.

Arista orders Torrejón's lancers to charge the American left, but the attack is broken before it can develop by Ringgold's accurate fire. Having suffered more than 400 casualties without coming to grips with the enemy, as well as being blinded by a dense brushfire raging through the chaparral, the Mexicans withdraw by evening. American losses total nine dead (among them Ringgold), 44 wounded, and two missing.

9 MAY 1846. ***Resaca de la Palma.*** At 6:00 A.M. Arista retreats into a new defensive position, redeploying four hours later in an empty lake bed called Resaca de la Palma, six miles south of Palo Alto. Taylor resumes his advance and reestablishes contact shortly after noon.

Finding Arista's army again in a long, narrow line, the American general decides to drive directly down the road at his opponent's center. The subsequent fighting is confused because of limited visibility in the heavy undergrowth, but at a cost of 39 American dead and 82 wounded Arista's artillery is overrun and his line broken. Mexican losses are estimated at 200 dead, 300 wounded, and 100 captured, their outer wings fleeing back toward Matamoros in disarray. (This evening the American garrison in Fort Brown is heartened to see defeated columns streaming back across the Río Grande.)

11 MAY 1846. In Washington on this Monday, Polk—having been informed two days previously of the Carricitos incident (*see* 23 April 1846)—asks Congress for an official declaration of war, which is passed by a 173–14 vote in the House of Representatives and by a vote of 40–2 next day in the Senate; it is signed by the president on 13 May.

17 MAY 1846. After regrouping at Fort Brown, Taylor pushes across the Río Grande despite a belated armistice offer from Arista. The Americans encounter no resistance next day upon entering Matamoros (population 4,000), which has been abandoned by the Mexican garrison, leaving behind 300 wounded.

Arista retreats southwest toward Linares (Nuevo León), losing many men in the desert. He resigns his command to Gen. José María Ortega and requests to be court-martialled in early July so as to defend his conduct.

18 MAY 1846. The eight-gun, 1,100-ton paddle steamer *Moctezuma* and six-gun, 775-ton *Guadalupe*—having been repossessed from the Mexican navy by their British builders for lack of payment—slip out of Alvarado (Veracruz) for Havana, eluding the rapidly approaching American blockade.

19 MAY 1846. *St. Mary's* arrives off Tampico, proclaiming a blockade next day.

20 MAY 1846. *Mississippi* blockades Veracruz. This same day, amid growing dissatisfaction with Paredes's handling of state affairs, a revolt occurs in Guadalajara. Both the governor and garrison commander are arrested, the former being replaced by liberal politician Juan N. Cumplido, with support from Cols. José María Yáñez, J. Guadalupe Montenegro, and Santiago Xicoténcatl.

8 JUNE 1846. Early this afternoon *St. Mary's* shells the fort on the north bank of the mouth of the Pánuco River (near Tampico) plus the anchored, single-gun, 25-man, 74-ton gunboat schooners *Unión, Isabel,* and *Poblano.* Little damage is inflicted due to the extreme long range.

This same day in the Pacific Sloat departs Mazatlán with *Savannah* to sail northwest to Monterey (California). Despite having received numerous reports over the past three weeks as to the outbreak of hostilities, he wishes to refrain from any offensive actions until advised by Washington.

10 JUNE 1846. Ezekial Merritt and five or six other American settlers seize a 150-horse herd destined for Castro's camp at Santa Clara; four days later 40 of them arrest Gen. Mariano Guadalupe Vallejo—titular Mexican commander for northern California—at his Sonoma home, along with 18 other followers, eight guns, 250 muskets, and 250 horses.

12 JUNE 1846. Already embroiled in conflict with Mexico, Washington arrives at a diplomatic compromise with Britain over territorial claims in the Pacific Northwest, agreeing to establish a boundary between the United States and Canada along the 49th parallel, with Vancouver Island being ceded to the British.

The Mexican government, for its part, experiences even worse problems, for today the first half of a 6,000-man government army arrives to besiege the liberal rebels within Guadalajara (*see* 20 May 1846). A protracted encirclement ensues, both sides firing on each other to little effect.

14 JUNE 1846. After failing to get a cutting-out expedition into Tampico's roads under cover of darkness, *St. Mary's* shells the port ineffectually at dawn before retiring.

24 JUNE 1846. The leading 50 men of Castro's 160-man column, moving north across San Francisco Bay to contain Merritt's insurrection at Sonoma (California), are easily defeated by American settlers.

1 JULY 1846. Having returned to California, Frémont leads some men across San Francisco Bay to spike the ten-gun San Joaquín battery, which is unoccupied on the southern shore.

3 JULY 1846. Sloat's *Savannah* arrives at Monterey (California), joining *Cyane* and *Levant.* The commodore hesitates to secure the Mexican port because of continuing uncertainty about the true state of hostilities.

4 JULY 1846. California's rebellious American settlers—led by former Vermonter William B. Ide—proclaim themselves independent from Mexico, dubbing their new country the "Bear Flag" Republic.

5 JULY 1846. Cmdr. Alexander Slidell Mackenzie (brother of John Slidell; *see* 29 November 1845) reaches Havana; two days later he meets the exiled Santa Anna to enumerate Polk's terms for a peace in case the Mexican strongman should ever regain power.

7 JULY 1846. At 7:30 A.M. Sloat calls on Monterey (California) to surrender, encountering no opposition as Capt. Mariano Silva has no means to resist and withdraws. Boats convey 85 marines and more than 140 sailors ashore three hours later to occupy the town.

9 JULY 1846. This morning Montgomery's *Portsmouth* sets 70 men ashore at Clark's Point (San Francisco), occupying the California town. No resistance is offered, as Mexican authorities have already been displaced by rebellious American settlers and the defenses destroyed by Frémont.

When news of the U.S. Navy's seizures of Monterey and San Francisco reach Sonoma and Sutter's Fort that afternoon, the "Bear flag" Republic is dissolved and allegiance formally proclaimed to the United States.

11 JULY 1846. The British sloop *Juno* of Capt. F. J. Blake enters San Francisco Bay, prompting Montgomery to man its defenses. The Americans suspect that rear Adm. Sir George F. Seymour's Pacific squadron—spearheaded by his 80-gun, 2,600-ton flagship HMS *Collingwood*—will attempt to appropriate portions of California during the volatile transition from Mexico's rule. *Juno* merely observes, however, departing six days later.

MID-JULY 1846. American consul John Black relays a peace feeler from the Mexican government to Washington.

16 JULY 1846. Frémont with 160 men occupies the abandoned Mexican base of San Juan Bautista (California), gaining nine cannons, 200 old muskets, and ammunition.

25 JULY 1846. Frémont departs Monterey (California) with 200 men aboard *Cyane,* disembarking four days later near San Diego to isolate the Mexican concentration around Los Angeles under Castro and Gov. Pío Pico.

28 JULY 1846. This afternoon Conner quits Antón Lizardo with the frigates *Cumberland* (flag), *Potomac,* and *Raritan* plus single-gun, 40-man, 74-ton schooners *Reefer* of Lt. Isaac Sterrett and *Petrel* of Lt. T. Darrah Shaw to proceed southeast against Alvarado. Upon passing the northwest side of Chopas Reef, however, *Cumberland* runs aground and is holed, bringing a halt to the operation.

29 JULY 1846. Two weeks after reaching Monterey (California) aboard *Congress,* Stockton replaces Sloat as commander in chief of the U.S. Pacific squadron. Old and infirm, Sloat immediately sets sail for home aboard *Levant.*

31 JULY 1846. After an arduous 650-mile westward trek from Fort Leavenworth (Kansas), the 52-year-old brevet Brig. Gen. Stephen Watts Kearny arrives nine miles outside Bent's Fort (near modern-day Animas, Colorado) with 300 of his 1st Dragoons; 860 of 1st Missouri Volunteer Mounted Infantry under his second-in-command—six-foot, six-inch 240-pound Col. Alexander William Doniphan—plus 250 gunners under Maj. Merriwether Lewis Clark. (The 2nd Missouri under Col. Sterling Price is to follow later.) This so-called Army of the West is intended to capture the Mexican outpost of Santa Fe.

4 AUGUST 1846. Taylor departs Matamoros up the Río Grande toward Camargo, having already sent most of his 12,000-man army ahead under Brig. Gen. William Jenkins Worth. Many of his latest reinforcements—inexperienced 90-day volunteers—sicken at an alarming rate (1,500 of them eventually dying).

This same day out in California, Stockton—three days after quitting Monterey with his flagship *Congress*—occupies Santa Barbara without opposition, leaving behind a 17-man garrison before proceeding to San Pedro.

5 AUGUST 1846. At dawn, just as Paredes is preparing to depart Mexico City to invigorate his besiegers outside the rebel city of Guadalajara (*see* 12 June 1846), Gen. José Mariano Salas mutinies at the capital's main citadel, or *ciudadela,* arresting and then deposing the president.

6 AUGUST 1846. Conner detaches *Falmouth* from Antón Lizardo this afternoon to join *Somers* in blockading Alvarado, then next morning follows with the frigates *Cumberland* (flag) and *Potomac;* steamers *Mississippi* and *Princeton;* schooners *Reefer, Petrel,* and *Bonita* of Lt. Timothy G. Benham; plus the British frigate HMS *Endymion* (as an observer) to yet again assail the Mexican port. The steamers tow *Cumberland* and *Potomac* along the coast then cast off to deploy before Alvarado that afternoon.

Its outer channel is guarded by the 16-gun Fort Santa Teresa plus the six-gun brig *Zempoalteca* and single-gun, 25-man, 50-ton gunboats *Guerrero, Queretana,* and *Victoria* under junior naval Capt. Pedro A. Díaz Mirón, with other lesser batteries and warships inside. The Americans open a long-range bombardment toward evening on 7 August, only to cease fire at 6:30 P.M. Overnight Conner prepares a boat party, only to cancel plans next morning when the weather turns foul. Leaving *Falmouth* on station, his squadron returns to its Antón Lizardo anchorage by noon on 8 August.

7 AUGUST 1846. A day after disembarking 360 of *Congress*'s sailors and four field pieces at San Pedro to assault nearby Los Angeles (population 1,500), Stockton receives a truce proposal from Castro's headquarters at Campo en la Mesa (now Boyle Heights). Rejecting it, the American commodore advances four days later to Rancho Los Cerritos (North Long Beach), entering Los Angeles by 13 August without opposition from the 100 defenders, who have melted away.

One hour later Frémont's small force arrives overland from the opposite direction; the remnants of Castro's army surrender by 14 August along with ten guns. A joint party of marines and Frémont's men then overtake the former governor, Alvarado, and several other prominent Mexican officials at San Luis Obispo, capturing them after a brief skirmish.

14 AUGUST 1846. Toward dusk in a heavy gale Cmdr. Edward W. Carpenter's ten-gun, 80-man, 330-ton brig *Truxtun* runs onto Tuxpan Reef, surrendering to the port's Mexican garrison under Gen. Antonio Rosas three days later. The steamer *Princeton* arrives just past midday on 20 August in a belated rescue attempt, burns *Truxtun*'s stripped remains two days later, and returns to Antón Lizardo by 23 August.

16 AUGUST 1846. Santa Anna returns to Veracruz from Cuban exile aboard the British mail packet *Arab*—which is allowed to enter Veracruz by the U.S. blockaders because Washington believes he will help conclude a peace.

18 AUGUST 1846. Kearny—after approaching Santa Fe (population 3,000) via a circuitous, southwesterly route—occupies the New Mexican capital without a fight; Gov. Manuel Armijo retires to Albuquerque with his troops.

19 AUGUST 1846. Taylor advances west out of Camargo toward Mier and Cerralvo (Nuevo León), taking all 3,200 regulars and his 3,000 best volunteers, leaving behind 4,700 of the latter as garrison troops.

2 SEPTEMBER 1846. Du Pont—now commanding *Cyane*—arrives off the Pacific port of San Blas (Nayarit), setting a landing party ashore that spikes 24 cannons and seizes the sloop *Solita* and brig *Susana.*

7 SEPTEMBER 1846. Shortly after midday Hull's *Warren* stands into the Pacific port of Mazatlán, anchoring a quarter-mile from the 12-gun, 114-ton Mexican brig *Malek Ahdel* and sending a 70-man boarding party across in four boats to secure that vessel without a fight. After exiting, the prize is commissioned under Lt. William B. Renshaw; the inbound brig *Carmelita* is taken next day.

12 SEPTEMBER 1846. Taylor's vanguard marches southwest out of Cerralvo for Monterrey (Nuevo León), followed by his main body, spread out over the next three days.

14 SEPTEMBER 1846. After rendezvousing with Hull off Mazatlán, Du Pont's *Cyane* seizes nine Mexican vessels at La Paz (Baja California) despite the neutrality agreement established with its governor, Col. Francisco Palacios Miranda.

15 SEPTEMBER 1846. Santa Anna appears outside Mexico City on the eve of Independence Day celebrations, entering next morning to a tumultuous reception while escorted by Salas's troops.

19 SEPTEMBER 1846. ***Monterrey.*** This Saturday morning Taylor's 6,645 troops come within sight of the northern Mexican city, being fired upon by its dark, formidable, eight-gun citadel, or *ciudadela*—quickly dubbed Black Fort by the Americans. Garrison commander Ampudia commands 7,000 Mexican regulars and 2,000–3,000 militia; he intends to wage a defensive struggle.

Next afternoon Worth swings west in a flanking maneuver with Col. John C. "Jack" Hays's Texas Cavalry Regiment, Lt. Col. Thomas Staniford's 1st Infantry Brigade, and Col. Persifor F. Smith's 2nd Brigade. Early

View of street fighting in Monterrey

on 21 September a mixed body of 1,500 Mexican cavalry and infantry under Lt. Col. Juan N. Nájera confronts the American column, suffering 100 casualties—including their commander—before retiring 15 minutes later, having killed or wounded only a dozen invaders. Thus, by 8:00 A.M. Worth sits astride the Saltillo Road, having cut off Monterrey's supply lines. At noon he continues east, up nearby Blanca Hill to overrun its Federación and El Soldado strongpoints by nightfall.

Taylor's main body also launches an assault on Monterrey's northeastern suburbs that day (21 September), during which Twiggs's 1st Division—temporarily commanded by Lt. Col. John Garland—and other units become enfiladed by various Mexican redoubts, suffering 394 casualties. Despite such punishment the Americans capture the 200-man Tenería (Tannery) stronghold and five Mexican artillery pieces.

While Taylor's main force recuperates in the rain on 22 September, Worth steals up Independencia Hill, surprising its defenders. Lt. Edward Deas's 50 gunners manhandle a 12-pound howitzer to the 800-foot summit by noon, opening fire on the 200 Mexican troops holding Obispado Fortress (the Bishopric or Bishop's Palace) under Lt. Col. Francisco Berra. They are overwhelmed by 4:00 P.M., prompting a discouraged Ampudia to call in all his outposts that night.

By morning on 23 September the principal American army notices the Rincón or Diablo strongpoint is abandoned and so quickly occupies it with the 1st Mississippi Rifle Regiment under Jefferson Davis, a 38-year-old colonel and U.S. congressman (also Taylor's former son-in-law and future Confederate president). Supporting units then begin fighting their way into northeastern Monterrey house by house, joined in the afternoon by a similar offensive out of the west under Worth.

By dawn on 24 September most of Monterrey is in American hands and Ampudia requests terms. The capitulation is signed next morning, Taylor agreeing to permit the Mexican army to march out with their arms and six guns over a number of days, retreating beyond Rinconada Pass, after which both sides will observe a two-month cessation of offensive operations. This conquest has cost 120 American dead and 368 wounded; the defenders suffer 700 casualties.

23 SEPTEMBER 1846. The 52-year-old Commo. Matthew Calbraith Perry (destined to open Japan seven years later) joins Conner off Veracruz as his second-in-command, arriving from New York aboard the three-gun, 50-man, 240-ton paddle steamer *Vixen* of Cmdr. Joshua Sands.

This same day out in Los Angeles marine Lt. Archibald H. Gillespie's 48-man garrison endures a dawn attack by 20 Californio guerrillas under Servulo Varela, sparking a general rising next day under paroled Mexican Capt. José María Flores. The latter's 150 followers trap Gillespie atop Fort Hill, compelling him to capitulate by 29 September. According to the surrender terms, the Americans are allowed to depart San Pedro with their arms by 4 October aboard the merchantman *Vandalia.*

25 SEPTEMBER 1846. Almost six weeks after arriving in San Antonio (population 2,000) to organize an expedition in support of Taylor's campaign, Brig. Gen. John E. "Old Fussy" Wool departs with his first 1,300 troops, proceeding southwest toward Presidio del Río Grande (modern-day Eagle Pass). One month later he is followed by another 1,200 under Col. Sylvester Churchill.

This same day Kearny quits Santa Fe (New Mexico) for California with 300 troopers of Maj. Edwin V. Sumner's 1st Dragoons.

28 SEPTEMBER 1846. Santa Anna leaves Mexico City northward with a small body of troops, arriving at San Luis Potosí by 8 October to begin the four-month process of marshaling a 21,500-man army to proceed against Taylor.

EARLY OCTOBER 1846. Having been reinforced at Santa Fe (New Mexico) by Price's 1,200-man 2nd Missouri Mounted Infantry plus the 500-man Mormon Battalion of Lt. Col. Philip St. George Cooke, Doniphan launches a seven-week mountain campaign against the Utah and Navajo tribes, who have been massacring outlying Mexican settlements.

1 OCTOBER 1846. Du Pont's *Cyane* seizes the Mexican schooners *Libertad* and *Fortuna* at Loreto, intercepting three more vessels in the Gulf of California during the next few days.

6 OCTOBER 1846. Early this morning Mervine—now commanding *Savannah*—appears off San Pedro to reverse the recent Californio revolt at Los Angeles. Next day 225 Americans come ashore and begin marching inland. After camping overnight at Rancho Dominguez (North Long Beach), they encounter 80 Mexican riders and ten soldiers under José Antonio Carrillo on 8 October, barring their path with a four-pounder. Despite three charges Mervine's sailors and marines are unable to close with their more nimble opponents and must retreat back aboard their frigate. (Four of the ten American wounded die and are subsequently buried in San Pedro Harbor, on Isla de los Muertos or Deadmen's Island.)

Also on the morning of 6 October Kearny's 300 dragoons meet 36-year-old Christopher "Kit" Carson and eight other scouts near Socorro (New Mexico), learning that California is now in American hands. Kearny therefore orders 200 of his men to return to Santa Fe, continuing westward nine days later across the mountains with only two companies—100 troopers.

7 OCTOBER 1846. A day after arriving off Guaymas (Sonora) and calling for the surrender of its single-gun schooner gunboats *Anáhuac* of 105 tons and *Sonorense* of 27, plus the merchant brig *Condor*—which is rejected by Col. Antonio Campuzano, local military commander—Du Pont's *Cyane* begins bombarding the port by midafternoon on 7 October. Both gunboats are set ablaze (possibly by their Mexican crews); a 42-man American boarding party then cuts out *Condor* despite a brisk exchange of small-arms fire with defenders ashore. The brig is subsequently found to be useless and so is scuttled.

15 OCTOBER 1846. Just after midnight, Conner and Perry quit Antón Lizardo with the paddle steamers *Vixen* (flag), *Mississippi* (vice flag), and six-gun, 370-ton revenue cutter *McLane* of Capt. William A. Howard; schooners *Reefer, Bonita,* and *Petrel;* six-gun, 150-ton revenue cutter *Forward* of Capt. H. B. Nonnes; plus captured four-gun, 122-ton Mexican schooner *Nonata* under Lt. Samuel F. Hazard to once again attack Alvarado.

Arriving offshore that dawn, the Americans find the sea too rough for immediate penetration and so content themselves with a long-range bombardment of the outer defenses. Fort Santa Teresa's 39-man garrison under Díaz, plus the Mexican warships under Commo. Tomás Marín—nine-gun, 70-man, 175-ton brig *Veracruzano Libre; Zempoalteca;* seven-gun, 40-man, 130-ton schooner *Aguila;* and two gunboats—are left largely unscathed.

Early this afternoon Conner bears down on Alvarado's bar in two columns, towing *Reefer* and *Bonita* with *Vixen* while *McLane* tows *Nonata, Petrel,* and *Forward.* Although his flagship weathers the defenders' batteries and crosses at 1:45 P.M., *McLane* runs aground 30 minutes later, obliging the Americans to retreat back to Antón Lizardo by 2:30 P.M.

16 OCTOBER 1846. Perry departs Antón Lizardo eastward with *Mississippi* (flag), *Vixen, McLane, Reefer, Bonita, Nonata, Forward,* and a 250-man landing force

under Capt. French Forrest of *Cumberland* to ascend the Grijalva River and seize San Juan Bautista de Villahermosa (Tabasco). A storm separates *Reefer* en route, but the remaining vessels rendezvous off the San Pedro y San Pablo River five days later before steering east toward the town of Frontera.

21 OCTOBER 1846. Mexican forces begin the week-long process of evacuating Tampico as part of Santa Anna's concentration of forces around the inland city of San Luis Potosí.

23 OCTOBER 1846. After transferring aboard the shallow-draft *Vixen,* Perry tows *Forward* and *Bonita* across the Grijalva River bar, followed by *McLane*—which attempts to tow *Nonata* and Forrest's boat party, only to run aground. Perry nonetheless presses on toward the nearby town of Frontera, sighting it by 3:00 P.M. and rushing ahead with *Vixen* to secure the schooner *Laura Virginia* and the paddle steamers *Petrita* and *Tabasqueña;* the schooner *Amado* escapes upriver pursued by *Bonita.*

Having occupied Frontera, the American commodore installs a small garrison under Lt. Joseph C. Walsh then transfers Forrest's boat party aboard the 200-ton prize *Petrita* to continue next morning toward Villahermosa, 72 miles farther up the Grijalva. (A short distance ahead they find *Bonita* with the captured *Amado.*)

25 OCTOBER 1846. At 8:45 A.M. Perry's 600-man expedition sights Fort Acachapan beyond Vuelta del Diablo (Devil's Bend, two miles below Villahermosa). Its tiny garrison flees, allowing the Americans to disembark a mile away and spike its guns before noon. By 1:00 P.M. Perry drops anchor before the town proper, calling for surrender one hour later. Villahermosa's governor, Lt. Col. Juan Bautista Traconis—despite commanding only 330 infantry and cavalry regulars plus a militia battalion—bids the invaders open fire whenever they choose.

Twenty-five minutes later, at 3:05 P.M., *Vixen* commences a desultory bombardment, followed by a disembarkation around 5:00 P.M.; American boat parties also board the anchored brigs *Yunaute* and *Rentville,* schooners *Tabasco* and *Alvarado,* plus the sloop *Deseada.* Notwithstanding the light resistance encountered, Perry withdraws his landing party at nightfall then retires downriver next morning with his prizes.

25 OCTOBER 1846. Late this afternoon Stockton's *Congress* reaches San Pedro (California), reinforcing *Savannah* and setting a landing party ashore at dawn on 27 October. Unable to advance on Los Angeles, the American commodore decides to shift southeast toward San Diego, setting sail with his flagship by 29 October.

31 OCTOBER 1846. Stockton sets reinforcements ashore to relieve Lt. George Minor's beleaguered American garrison at San Diego (California).

11 NOVEMBER 1846. Conner detaches *Potomac* and *Raritan* to join *St. Mary's* and 11-gun, 225-ton brig *Porpoise* of Lt. William E. Hunt off Tampico, himself following next morning with *Princeton* (flag), *Mississippi, Vixen,* and three-gun, 50-man, 240-ton paddle steamer *Spitfire* of Cmdr. Josiah Tattnall plus *Reefer, Bonita, Petrel,* and *Nonata.*

13 NOVEMBER 1846. Taylor pushes southwest out of Monterrey (Nuevo León) with a portion of his army, occupying the undefended town of Saltillo three days later.

14 NOVEMBER 1846. ***Tampico.*** At dawn Conner's squadron rendezvouses off the port of Tampico; he sends a 300-man boat party across the bar by 11:00 A.M. Ninety minutes later they spot the Stars and Stripes flying above the abandoned town, raised by Mrs. Anna McClarmonde Chase (Irish-born wife of the former American consul). The Mexican garrison of Anastasio Parrodi having already withdrawn (*see* 21 October 1846), Conner gains Tampico without a fight and claims schooners *Unión, Poblano,* and *Isabel* as prizes along with merchantmen *Mahonese* and *Hormiga.*

15 NOVEMBER 1846. Early this morning the 20-gun, 190-man, 700-ton sloop *Boston* of Cmdr. George F. Pearson is lost on Eleuthera Island in the Bahamas.

Stockton's *Congress* also runs aground at San Diego (California) and almost heels over with the ebbing tide, tempting 100 Californio guerrillas to launch an assault against its distracted garrison. The attack is repelled, and the frigate saved.

16 NOVEMBER 1846. Near San Luis Obispo, Manuel Castro's 100 Californios scatter a formation of American volunteers marching to reinforce Frémont's 400 men at Monterey.

18 NOVEMBER 1846. While preparing Tampico to receive an American garrison of 2,000–3,000 troops, Conner detaches Tattnall 25 miles upriver with *Spitfire* and *Petrel* (plus 32 extra marines and sailors) to raid the

Mexican outpost at Pánuco. It is overrun early next morning and leveled by the time the Americans withdraw two mornings later.

23 NOVEMBER 1846. Perry returns to Tampico from Brazos de Santiago (Texas), having brought 500 of Maj. Gen. Robert Patterson's soldiers to garrison the town.

26 NOVEMBER 1846. After the Mexican schooner *Criolla* runs into Veracruz, passing the blockading brig *Somers* of Lt. Raphael Semmes—later captain of the famed Civil War raider *Alabama*—eight men volunteer to cut it out from under the guns of the island fortress of San Juan de Ulúa. Despite boarding the schooner before midnight, the Americans become becalmed and must burn the prize and escape back out to sea through a hail of gunfire, taking seven prisoners. (*Criolla* subsequently proves to have been a spy ship allowed to slip into Veracruz with Conner's blessing.)

30 NOVEMBER 1846. Having failed to bring the Mexican government to the bargaining table despite occupying northern Mexico, Washington decides on a different strategy: Rather than order Taylor to march south across the desert from Monterrey into the teeth of Santa Anna's waiting army, the U.S. Navy will transport another army to Veracruz to invade nearer the enemy capital. Consequently, six-foot, five-inch, 59-year-old Maj. Gen. Winfield Scott and his staff set sail from New York for New Orleans and then Brazos de Santiago in order to organize this second expedition.

6 DECEMBER 1846. At dawn Kearny's 100 weary dragoons and Carson's 20 scouts—reinforced the day before, following their trans-Sierra hike, by 40 sailors and marines under Gillespie plus a brass four-pounder—surprise 72 Mexican riders encamped near San Pascual under Capt. Andrés Pico, brother of Gov. Pío Pico.

The American mounts are exhausted, and the outnumbered Mexicans acquit themselves well despite being driven from the field. American losses total 19 killed and 13 wounded (including Kearny and Gillespie) and one of two howitzers lost, compared to only one man captured and a dozen injured among Pico's men. The Americans limp toward San Diego, encumbered by convalescents and harassing raids, finally being relieved on 10 December by a 215-man rescue column under Lt. Andrew V. F. Gray.

On 6 December the polarized senate in Mexico City votes 11–9 to offer the presidency to Santa Anna and vice presidency to Gómez Farías. The former remains at San Luis Potosí training his army, leaving the latter to assume office alone on 23 December.

8 DECEMBER 1846. While pursuing a blockade runner off Veracruz *Somers* accidentally overturns and sinks, drowning 32 of Semmes's 76 crew members; seven others are captured by the Mexicans, the remainder being rescued by neutral British, French, and Spanish warships anchored off Sacrificios Island.

14 DECEMBER 1846. While marching from San Juan Bautista to contain the Californio revolt at Los Angeles, Frémont surprises San Luis Obispo this rainy night, capturing its commander, Jesús Pico (cousin to Pío and Andrés Pico), at nearby Wilson's Ranch along with 35 Mexicans.

16 DECEMBER 1846. Doniphan marches south out of Valverde (New Mexico) with his 850-man 1st Missouri Mounted Infantry to proceed 200 miles down the Río Grande and across the Jornada del Muerto (Dead Man's Journey) against El Paso (Texas).

17 DECEMBER 1846. In order to cut the clandestine trade entering Mexico through the neutral state of Yucatán, Perry sets sail from Antón Lizardo with *Mississippi* (flag), *Vixen, Bonita,* and *Petrel* to capture the border outpost of El Carmen.

18 DECEMBER 1846. Having returned through Monterrey with his main army to press southeast against Ciudad Victoria (Tamaulipas), Taylor instead learns that Santa Anna is moving north from San Luis Potosí to assail Worth's small garrison in Saltillo. The American commander therefore retraces his route with his regulars, leaving Brig. Gen. John A. Quitman to continue against Ciudad Victoria with an all-volunteer force.

Saltillo is reinforced on 19 December by an American unit out of Monterrey under Maj. Gen. William O. Butler and another two days later under Wool from Parras (Coahuila). Realizing the enemy is gathering in strength, Santa Anna cancels the operation.

20 DECEMBER 1846. Perry arrives off El Carmen Bar, transfers his flag aboard the shallow-draft *Vixen,* then leads *Bonita* and *Petrel* across to proceed five miles inside the bay and assail El Carmen proper. Next morning it surrenders unconditionally; Perry strips it of military stores and installs Sands as governor. Leaving *Vixen* and *Petrel* behind, the commodore rejoins *Mississippi* by 22 December aboard *Bonita* before standing away west.

23 DECEMBER 1846. Although absent from Mexico City on active duty in San Luis Potosí, Santa Anna is officially inaugurated as president, with Gómez Farías as vice president.

25 DECEMBER 1846. This afternoon Doniphan's vanguard reaches the confluence of the Brazito and Río Grande Rivers (30 miles north of El Paso), finding perhaps 1,200 Mexican irregulars under Col. Ponce de León barring their path. After rebuffing a surrender demand, the better-armed Americans easily repel an amateurish cavalry charge, inflicting 100 fatalities while suffering none among their own ranks. The city is occupied shortly thereafter without further resistance.

26 DECEMBER 1846. Taylor reaches Montemorelos (45 miles southeast of Monterrey), learning of Scott's imminent arrival to organize a second front—although not realizing that his own army is to be stripped of 8,000 regular infantry, 1,000 cavalry, and two field batteries for the new campaign. Next day Scott arrives at Brazos de Santiago (Texas) and begins issuing instructions.

28 DECEMBER 1846. ***Los Angeles.*** This morning Stockton and Kearny quit San Diego with 600 men—dismounted U.S. dragoons; two companies of the California Battalion; naval contingents from *Congress, Savannah,* and *Portsmouth;* plus a small artillery train—to march 140 miles northwest and recapture the city of Los Angeles. They do not sight the enemy until evening of 7 January 1847, when Flores is discovered waiting at La Jabonería Ford with 450 Mexicans and a few guns to dispute the Americans' passage across the San Gabriel River.

Next morning Stockton and Kearny swing right, hoping to slip across at Bartolo Ford before Flores becomes aware, but the Mexican commander checks the maneuver by redeploying his own riders opposite. The Americans form a square and push across while disregarding the feeble Mexican fire, unlimber their own artillery, then scatter the Californio riders in a 90-minute melee that causes about a dozen casualties on each side.

The Mexicans retreat, about 300 regrouping six miles away at Cañada de los Alisos on the mesa between the San Gabriel and Los Angeles Rivers (near the modern-day Union Stockyards). The Americans again approach in a square, exchanging long-range artillery salvos and weathering a halfhearted cavalry charge before Flores's army finally gives up two and a half hours later. One American and one Mexican are killed; five Americans and an unknown number of Mexicans are wounded.

Stockton and Kearny cross the river about three miles below Los Angeles that evening, waiting until next day—10 January—before making their triumphal entry into the city (the commodore establishing his headquarters in the Avila Adobe House, on modern-day Olvera Street). At a cost of 20 American casualties the campaign has subdued the last Mexican stronghold in California.

29 DECEMBER 1846. Quitman's small army approaches Ciudad Victoria, prompting 1,500 Mexican cavalry to abandon it without a fight and retire southwest toward Tula.

Also, Marine Capt. Ward Marston leaves San Francisco with 100 men and a field gun to put down a Californio insurrection. On 2 January 1847 he comes upon Francisco Sánchez and 120 rebels about seven miles from the Santa Clara Mission. They are dispersed after a brief skirmish in which four Californios are killed and five wounded compared to only two Americans injured. Four days later a local armistice is finalized.

4 JANUARY 1847. Taylor enters Ciudad Victoria, detaching Twiggs's division east toward Tampico.

5 JANUARY 1847. Frémont, with 400 men and six field pieces, disperses a small band of Californio riders at San Buenaventura Mission (modern-day Ventura) and another 60–70 again the next day.

11 JANUARY 1847. Late this evening Frémont comes upon Flores's 100 surviving troops at Rancho Los Verdugos (near San Fernando Mission), persuading them to surrender next day—although the Mexican commander escapes into Sonora.

13 JANUARY 1847. Infantry Lt. John Alexander Richey, carrying one of two sets of Scott's campaign plans to Taylor, is killed while attempting to buy provisions in the village of Villagrán (between Monterrey and Ciudad Victoria). The captured papers are forwarded to Santa Anna at San Luis Potosí.

19 JANUARY 1847. At 6:00 A.M., because of high-handed actions by unruly American occupiers, the home of the popular Gov. Charles Bent is attacked at Taos (New Mexico) by a mob of Mexicans and Indians, led by Pablo Montoya and Tomás Romero. Bent is murdered in front of his Mexican wife and sister-in-

law (Kit Carson's 17-year-old bride, Josefa Jaramillo), along with five other American residents. Seven more are killed at nearby Arroyo Hondo, and eight more at the town of Mora.

23 JANUARY 1847. Having learned three days previously of the anti-American insurrection at Taos (New Mexico), Price leads 290 of his 2nd Missouri Troopers plus 63 local volunteers under Capt. Ceran St.Vrain—all afoot—north with four field howitzers to battle the rebels. One day later, at the village of La Cañada, the column encounters some 1,500 Mexicans and Indians, driving them from their entrenchments and slaying 36. American losses are three killed and six wounded, Price being reinforced shortly thereafter by a company of 1st Dragoons under Capt. J. H. K. Burgwin and another of 2nd Missouri, bringing his total strength to 479.

24 JANUARY 1847. Patterson reaches Tampico with 4,500 men.

25 JANUARY 1847. Some 60 miles south of Saltillo a 50-man patrol of Kentucky and Arkansas riders under Majs. John P. Gaines and Solon Borland are surprised and captured at Encarnación by a large body of Mexican cavalry. A second detachment of 30 Kentuckians under Capt. William J. Heady, sent to find the first patrol, shares the same fate.

28 JANUARY 1847. Knowing of Taylor's diminished strength because of an intelligence windfall (*see* 13 January 1847), Santa Anna decides to strike north and surprise his American opponent. The vanguard—an artillery train, a sapper battalion, and the San Patricio Company of Irish-American deserters—departs San Luis Potosí, followed by Francisco Pacheco's infantry division next day, Manuel Lombardini's on 30 January, and finally Ortega's on 31 January. In all, more than 20,000 Mexican troops advance to rendezvous south of Saltillo at Encarnación.

29 JANUARY 1847. At El Embudo (New Mexico), 180 of Burgwin's and St.Vrain's troopers defeat a small rearguard of Taos rebels, killing 20 and wounding another 60 while suffering only one killed and another wounded.

2 FEBRUARY 1847. Price's small army passes through Taos (New Mexico), deploying five miles north to besiege the rebellious Mexicans and Indians within the old pueblo. After battering its adobe church throughout 3 February with their howitzers, the Americans launch a two-pronged assault next day at 11:00 A.M. that kills about 150 rebels by nightfall, ending all effective resistance. The survivors surrender next day, 17 leaders eventually being executed—including Montoya and Romero. Price's losses are seven dead (including Burgwin) and 45 wounded.

15 FEBRUARY 1847. Scott departs Brazos de Santiago, arriving at Tampico three days later and then proceeding 65 miles farther southeast to his expedition's rendezvous off Lobos Island.

17 FEBRUARY 1847. Pacheco's division reaches Encarnación, soon followed by the rest of Santa Anna's army. Only 14,000 Mexican troops and 17 guns have completed the grueling march from San Luis Potosí, the remainder having deserted or fallen by the wayside. Santa Anna nevertheless prepares to assail Taylor's encampment at nearby Agua Nueva (Coahuila).

20 FEBRUARY 1847. This evening a 400-man American reconnaissance unit under Lt. Col. Charles A. May spots Miñón's 4,000 cavalry approaching Hediona Ranch in advance of Santa Anna's main army. Riding through the night, the scouts advise Taylor of the danger next morning at Agua Nueva. (Major Benjamin McCulloch of the "Texas Rangers" brings in even more detailed information at midday, having penetrated the Mexican base at Encarnación in disguise.)

Taylor contemplates making a stand with his 4,800 troops but is instead persuaded by Wool to fall back to La Angostura—a narrow pass on Buena Vista Hacienda, six miles south of Saltillo—where his flanks cannot be turned by superior enemy numbers because of the mountains. Leaving the 1st Arkansas Cavalry Regiment of Col. Archibald Yell to break camp at Agua Nueva, the rest of the American army retires.

This same night (21 February), Santa Anna rests only six miles south, at Carnero Pass. After midnight Miñón's cavalry descends on the vacated American camp, chasing Yell's regiment—plus a Kentucky cavalry battalion and two companies of 1st Dragoons—north to rejoin Taylor and Wool by next morning.

22 FEBRUARY 1847. ***Buena Vista.*** While Taylor quickly visits Saltillo to ensure that Santa Anna has not slipped behind him, Wool digs in, facing south down the San Luis Potosí road with the 580-man 1st Illinois Infantry Regiment of Col. John J. Hardin; 573-man 2nd Illinois Infantry of Col. William H. Bissell; 571-man 2nd Kentucky Infantry of Col. William R. McKee; 628-man 2nd Indiana Infantry of Col. William A. Bowles; and 625-man 3rd Indiana Infantry of Col.

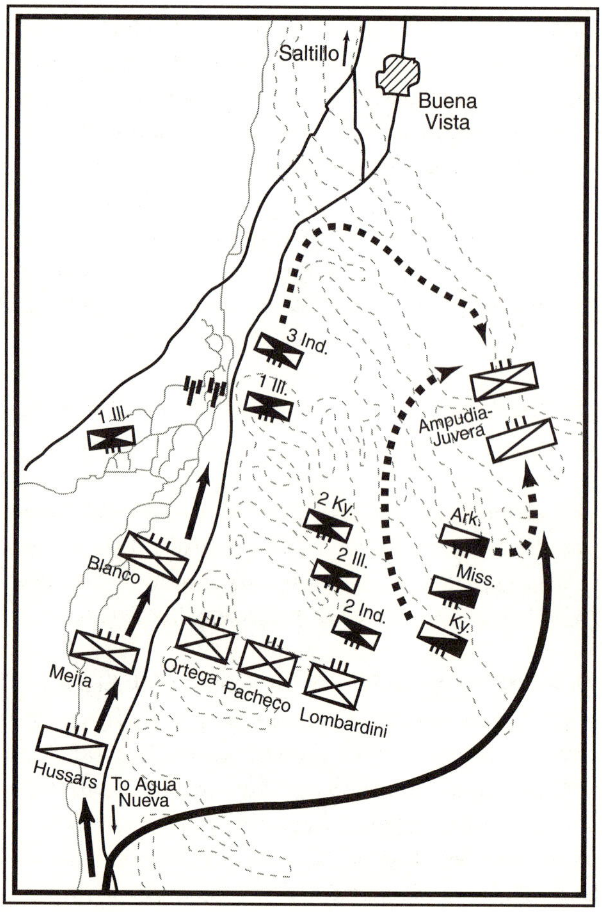

Battle of Buena Vista

James H. Lane. The American mounted contingent consists of the 368-man 1st Mississippi Rifles of Col. Jefferson Davis; 479-man 1st Arkansas Cavalry of Col. Archibald Yell; 305-man 1st Kentucky Cavalry of Col. Humphrey Marshall; 133 1st U.S. Dragoons under Capt. Enoch Steen; 76 2nd U.S. Dragoons under Lt. Col. Charles A. May; plus 88 Texas Rangers under Maj. Benjamin McCulloch. All are supported by 18 cannons manned by 150 gunners of Capt. Braxton Bragg's 3rd Artillery Battery; 150 of Capt. Thomas W. Sherman's 3rd Artillery Company; and 117 of Capt. John M. Washington's 4th Artillery Battery. Only the dragoons and gunners are regulars; of the remaining regiments, the Mississippians alone are experienced in battle.

Shortly after sunrise, Santa Anna's 18,000 troops appear, and at 11:00 A.M. the Mexican general sends a surrender demand ahead under flag of truce. Taylor, who has just returned from Saltillo, rejects it. Around noon Ampudia's light infantry brigade and Juvera's cavalry are detached to occupy the high ground east of this plateau, prompting the American commander to send his Arkansas and Kentucky Cavalry Regiments, plus a battalion of Indiana infantry, to contest this flanking maneuver. After an indecisive firefight the Americans withdraw at nightfall, the only other action being a long-range exchange between Blanco's leading Mexican division and Taylor's main battleline.

Early next morning the Mexicans resume the action, Blanco being repulsed by Washington's battery and 1st Illinois. However, Ampudia and Juvera repel a second attempt by Yell's Arkansas and Marshall's Kentucky cavalry to gain the eastern high ground, after which Pacheco's division hits Bowles's 2nd Indiana, sending it reeling out of Wool's line. By the time Taylor again returns from Saltillo around 9:00 A.M., the situation has grown precarious, but is soon rectified when 1st Mississippi and 3rd Indiana plug this hole.

As in previous encounters, the American horse-drawn artillery proves too much for the attackers, repeatedly breaking up threatened Mexican breakthroughs. Taylor's army is compressed but does not break, while Santa Anna has a horse shot out from under him. A flanking maneuver by Pacheco's division is intercepted atop a ridge at 1:00 P.M. by the Mississippians, 3rd Indiana, and Bragg's artillery, resulting in heavy Mexican losses. By nightfall, the Americans have suffered 267 killed, 456 wounded, and 1,500 desertions, but still hold the field. They are further encouraged by the arrival of two fresh regiments behind them at Saltillo under Brig. Gen. Thomas Marshall and Col. George W. Morgan.

The Mexicans, in contrast, have had enough, enduring 1,800 dead or injured, plus another 300 captured. After conferring this evening with his staff, Santa Anna orders a stealthy retreat toward Agua Nueva. The Americans awaken on the morning of 24 February to find the plain virtually empty. Satisfied with his hard-won victory, Taylor retires northeast into Monterrey shortly thereafter.

28 FEBRUARY 1847. ***Sacramento.*** After pushing south from El Paso (Texas) into the state of Chihuahua, Doniphan's 924 Missouri troopers and 300 wagonloads of auxiliaries learn that 1,200 Mexican cavalry, 1,200 infantry, 1,400 irregulars, and 300 gunners for ten brass cannons are deployed just north of the Sacramento river (15 miles above Chihuahua City) under Pedro García Conde, a 40-year-old general and senator.

At sunrise the Americans begin a wide flanking maneuver to the west, which is not discovered by the defenders until 3:00 P.M., when García Conde launches a belated 800-man cavalry charge. This counterattack is easily dispersed by Clark's artillery, after which Doniphan methodically works his way behind the static Mexican lines, rolling up García Conde's hopelessly overmatched throng. At a cost of only one

American killed and 11 wounded, Doniphan slaughters 300 opponents and wounds a similar number while capturing all ten guns and the baggage train.

Next day the Americans occupy Chihuahua City, finding it largely abandoned.

2 MARCH 1847. After marshaling his seaborne expedition off Lobos Island (southeast of Tampico), Scott's steamer *Massachusetts* gives the signal to get under way for Antón Lizardo. His 8,600-man army is aboard 40 transports, in three divisions: Worth's, consisting of Garland's 4th, Lt. Col. J. S. MacIntosh's 5th, Col. N. S. Clarke's 6th, and Maj. C. A. Waite's 8th Regular Infantry Regiments; Col. James Bankhead's 2nd and Lt. Col. F. S. Belton's 3rd Artillery Regiments; Duncan's field battery; Capt. G. H. Talcott's rocket and mountain battery; plus a sapper company under Capt. A. J. Swift.

Twiggs's 2nd Division comprises Col. William Davenport's 1st, Lt. Col. Bennett Riley's 2nd, Capt. Edmund B. Alexander's 3rd, and Lt. Col. Joseph Plympton's 7th U.S. Infantry Regiments; Col. Thomas Childs's 1st and Maj. J. L. Gardner's 4th Artillery Regiments; Col. Persifor F. Smith's mounted rifle regiment; plus Capt. Francis Taylor's field battery. Patterson's 3rd Division contains Col. P. M. Butler's South Carolina (Palmetto), Col. F. M. Wynkoop's 1st Pennsylvania, Col. J. W. Geary's 2nd Pennsylvania, Col. W. B. Campbell's 1st Tennessee, and Col. William T. Haskell's 2nd Tennessee Volunteer Regiments; plus Capt. E. J. Steptoe's field battery.

The first vessel arrives two days later, anchoring between Antón Lizardo and Salmedina Island to begin preparing for the disembarkation.

6 MARCH 1847. In order to permit Scott to view the proposed landing site at Collado Beach (three miles southeast of Veracruz), Conner takes him aboard *Petrita* along with Patterson, Brigadier Generals Worth, Twigg, and Gideon Johnston Pillow, Capts. Robert E. Lee and Joseph E. Johnston, plus Lts. Pierre G. T. Beauregard and George G. Meade. The steamer is unexpectedly shelled by the big guns at San Juan de Ulúa, compelling it to withdraw.

7 MARCH 1847. Generals Quitman, Fields, and Jesup set sail from Tampico for Veracruz, bringing more troops for Scott's army.

9 MARCH 1847. ***Veracruz.*** After a one-day delay, during which Scott's troops are transhipped from transports aboard navy vessels, Conner's men-of-war stand toward Sacrificios Island at 11:00 A.M., detaching a line of gunboats closer inshore by 3:30 PM., to provide cov-

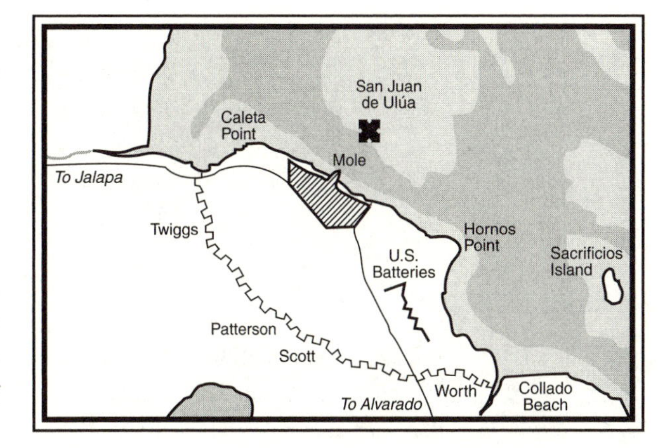

American siege of Veracruz

ering fire at Collado Beach. They open up the bombardment at 5:00 PM., an hour before Worth's 2,600-man 1st Division actually begins disembarking. The initial landing meets no opposition and is soon followed by Twiggs's 2nd Division then Patterson's 3rd Division. By nightfall all 8,600 American soldiers are ashore along with a 1,200-man naval contingent, being joined next morning by Scott and his headquarters staff.

Before sunrise on 10 March Conner directs Tattnall's *Spitfire* to mount a brief diversionary attack against San Juan de Ulúa while the American troops fan out at daylight to begin investing the city proper. Veracruz (population 15,000) is defended by 3,360 Mexicans—about two-thirds of them regulars—with 86 guns under Maj. Gen. Juan Morales; their offshore island fortress of San Juan de Ulúa boasts an additional 1,030 men and 135 artillery pieces. However, the ill-prepared defenders do not respond, preferring to wait behind their ramparts.

Shortly after midday on 13 March Twiggs reaches the sea northwest of Veracruz, thus cutting off the city. Patterson has meanwhile taken up position in the center, with Worth farther southeast, after which the Americans begin building formal siege works. By noon on 21 March their first heavy batteries are ready to open fire, Scott calling for Morales's capitulation next afternoon. Upon being rejected, a concerted bombardment commences, seconded by Perry's warships offshore. (Perry, having returned on 20 March from repairing *Mississippi* in Norfolk, Virginia, has supplanted Conner.)

The besiegers increase their rate of fire until dawn on 26 March, when Gen. José Juan Landero—the new garrison commander within Veracruz in place of the ill Morales—requests terms. The city officially capitulates by 29 March, along with San Juan de Ulúa, all defenders being paroled and officers allowed to retain sidearms, mounts, and personal effects. At a cost of 14 Americans killed and 59 wounded, Scott gains a secure base for his march inland.

American batteries pounding the city of Veracruz

21 MARCH 1847. Having led 10,500 survivors of his shattered army back from Buena Vista into San Luis Potosí, Santa Anna appears with his two best divisions at the Guadalupe suburb north of Mexico City. He ends the dispute between General Peña and Vice President Farías by deposing the latter in favor of a 51-year-old general and congressman named Pedro María Anaya.

29 MARCH 1847. Midday, Montgomery's *Portsmouth* arrives off San José del Cabo (Baja California), calling for its surrender. The Mexican authorities refuse but offer no resistance when Lt. Benjamin F. B. Hunter disembarks next day with 140 men.

30 MARCH 1847. This afternoon Scott detaches Quitman to march southeast from Veracruz along the coast with his brigade and a naval squadron offshore, to seize the port of Alvarado. When the three-gun, 60-man, 230-ton, twin-propeller steamer *Scourge* of Lt. Charles G. Hunter bombards La Vigía battery next morning, Hunter discovers Alvarado already abandoned by the Mexican garrison. He immediately occupies it and pushes upriver as far as Tlacotalpan, capturing three vessels and burning a fourth.

After a brief occupation, Quitman's brigade rejoins Scott at Veracruz, leaving the navy to garrison both Alvarado and Tlacotalpan under Capt. Isaac Mayo.

3 APRIL 1847. Santa Anna departs Mexico City, traveling east to assume command of three infantry divisions, one cavalry brigade, and 2,000 militia guarding the Veracruz highway under Canalizo.

This same day, on the Pacific Coast, Montgomery's *Portsmouth* seizes San Lucas (Baja California).

8 APRIL 1847. Scott's vanguard departs Veracruz under Twiggs, consisting of 2,600 infantry, a dragoon squadron, two light field batteries, and a dozen heavier pieces. He is to be followed up the national highway toward Jalapa by Patterson's division; Scott emerges on 11 April with the balance of his forces.

12 APRIL 1847. ***Tuxpan.*** Perry departs Sacrificios Island with a flotilla of small steamers and gunboats, rendezvousing next evening with his main fleet off Lobos Island to veer south and make a descent on land. Despite being briefly scattered by a sudden storm from the north, the Americans appear outside the mouth of the Tuxpan River by morning on 17 April with steamers *Spitfire* (flag), *Vixen,* and *Scourge;* schooners *Bonita,*

Petrel, and *Reefer;* plus 30 barges bearing a 1,500-man landing force under Capt. Samuel L. Breese of the 22-gun, 210-man, 1,040-ton sloop *Albany.*

After gingerly crossing the bar on the morning of 18 April, the raiders proceed upriver. By 2:30 P.M. Perry's advance elements are fired on by the three-gun La Peña battery, which is abandoned when a contingent of Americans disembarks nearby. The same occurs shortly thereafter at the two-gun La Palmasola water battery, after which Perry's flotilla arrives directly before Tuxpan by 3:30 P.M. The 350-man garrison under General Cós (Santa Anna's brother-in-law; *see* introduction to Texan Independence) melts into the interior, fighting a rear-guard action that kills two invaders and wounds nine.

The American commodore spends the next four days stripping Tuxpan of everything of military value before retiring to Antón Lizardo on 22 April.

13 APRIL 1847. Montgomery's *Portsmouth* occupies La Paz (Baja California).

14 APRIL 1847. ***Cerro Gordo.*** Three days after Twiggs's vanguard detects a large Mexican force dug in four miles northwest of Plan del Río (Veracruz), barring further progress up the national highway toward Jalapa—four miles beyond—Scott arrives to assume direct command over operations. Desperate to halt the American offensive before it can penetrate Mexico's fertile interior, Santa Anna has emplaced 12,000 raw troops and 43 field pieces east of the town of Cerro Gordo (its 1,000-foot prominence today called El Telégrafo). This ground being well chosen, Scott waits until Worth's division joins, bringing his strength to 8,500 effectives.

On the morning of Saturday, 17 April, Twiggs circles north of the Mexican positions with Riley's 2nd Infantry, Smith's mounted rifles (temporarily commanded by Col. William S. Harney), and Brig. Gen. James Shields's brigade (the 3rd and 4th Illinois plus the New York Regiment). Although intended only as a preliminary deployment, the column is hit around La Atalaya Hill by a Mexican counterattack, provoking the outnumbered Twiggs to push as far forward as Santa Anna's main force before withdrawing at nightfall.

Next morning the Americans move forward again from La Atalaya, and with support from a frontal assault by Scott's main army this flanking maneuver breaks the Mexican line and overruns Cerro Gordo. Fearful of being cut off from the rear, Santa Anna's panic-stricken troops flee south toward Orizaba, leaving behind more than 3,000 prisoners. His carriage and six-mule team having been riddled by American shots, the Mexican commander is compelled to join the flight, along with Ampudia and other generals. Scott's losses total 63 killed and 367 wounded.

20 APRIL 1847. Led by Patterson's division, the victorious American army enters deserted Jalapa.

21 APRIL 1847. After an exhausting cross-country ride Santa Anna reaches Orizaba and begins to reassemble 4,000 of his defeated troops. Next day Ampudia rides to Puebla with the remnants of his cavalry.

28 APRIL 1847. Doniphan quits Chihuahua City, striking southeast to join Wool at Saltillo.

6 MAY 1847. Worth's division departs Jalapa, pushing west-southwest to Puebla. En route, one of his regiments occupies the abandoned Mexican stronghold of El Perote.

This same day, seven of Scott's volunteer regiments—3,000 men of the 3rd and 4th Illinois, 1st and 2nd Tennessee, Georgia, and Alabama infantry plus Tennessee cavalry—quit Jalapa eastward under Patterson, their terms of enlistment having expired. Scott is therefore left with scarcely 3,000 troops in Jalapa.

10 MAY 1847. Perry departs Antón Lizardo southeastward with *Mississippi* (flag), *Vixen,* and the four-gun, 60-man, 340-ton paddle steamer *Scorpion* of Cmdr. Abraham Bigelow to sweep the Mexican coastline. Two days later, off Coatzacoalcos, he joins *John Adams;* 16-gun, 150-man, 566-ton sloop *Decatur* of Cmdr. Richard S. Pinckney; and 47-man, 180-ton bomb brig *Stromboli* (formerly *Howard*) of Cmdr. William S. Walker. Finding the 12-gun fort guarding the entrance abandoned and demolished by the Mexicans, Perry sends a reconnaissance party upriver on 13 May that surveys as far as Minatitlán—24 miles inland—before retiring.

11 MAY 1847. Doniphan reaches Parras (Coahuila), his vanguard rescuing a group of Mexican captives being carried off by Lipan Indians and slaying 15 of the raiders.

15 MAY 1847. Scott's army occupies the city of Puebla without opposition.

16 MAY 1847. After watering at Frontera (Tabasco), Perry's *Mississippi* (flag), *Vixen, Scorpion, John Adams,* and *Decatur* arrive off El Carmen to join the brigs *Porpoise* and single-gun *Washington* of Lt. Samuel P. Lee plus 47-man, 240-ton bomb brig *Vesuvius* (formerly *St. Mary's*) of Cmdr. George H. Magruder. Next day, in

order to once again stem clandestine traffic into Mexico (*see* 20 December 1846), Perry reoccupies the town of El Carmen with a party of sailors and marines, naming Magruder as governor.

19 MAY 1847. Returning west to Antón Lizardo from El Carmen, Perry pauses to appoint Cmdr. Gershom J. van Brunt of the 47-man, 180-ton bomb brig *Etna* (formerly *Walcott*) as military governor of Coatzacoalcos and its inland district.

28 MAY 1847. Scott rejoins Worth at Puebla, their combined forces totaling 5,820 effectives—too few to push on to Mexico City. For the next three months the Americans await reinforcements before resuming the offensive.

9 JUNE 1847. Perry departs east from Antón Lizardo aboard *Mississippi,* commanding his forces to gather at Frontera (Tabasco) for a campaign up the Grijalva River.

14 JUNE 1847. ***Tabasco.*** Early this morning Perry's steamers *Scorpion* (flag), *Scourge, Spitfire,* and *Vixen* begin towing *Washington, Stromboli, Vesuvius,* merchant schooner *Spitfire,* plus approximately 40 boats with a 1,200-man landing party across the mouth of the Grijalva River, joining *Bonita* and *Etna* already anchored off Frontera. The deep-draft *Mississippi, Raritan, John Adams, Albany, Decatur,* and 22-gun, 210-man, 940-ton sloop *Germantown* of Cmdr. Franklin Buchanan remain outside (although contributing men toward this enterprise).

After spending the first day coaling, Perry signals his expedition to proceed upriver at 5:25 P.M. At 4:00 next afternoon his advance elements are fired on by 150 Mexicans under Col. Miguel Bruno, occupying a hill at Santa Teresa (12 miles below Villahermosa). The Americans push past unscathed, weathering further sniping at Vuelta del Diablo before anchoring for the night opposite some underwater obstacles at Siete Palmas.

At 6:00 A.M. on 6 June the Mexican breastwork at La Colmena opens fire on an American reconnaissance boat, prompting Perry to disembark and lead his 1,200-man "naval brigade" in a flanking maneuver. Within a few hours he has circled far enough inland to approach Fort Acachapan out of the east, finding it defended by 300 Mexican infantry, 300 militia cavalry, and two guns under Col. Claro Hidalgo. The attackers deploy troops and artillery, scattering the garrison with a charge. Meanwhile 34-year-old Lt. David Dixon Porter—acting commander of *Spitfire*—clears the river's log obstructions then passes Perry's small army while it is still pressing southwest against Villahermosa's last lines of defense.

Shortly after 10:30 A.M. the flotilla runs past the Iturbide breastwork, raking it from behind. The Mexican gunners flee, allowing Porter to set 68 men ashore and secure the strongpoint. The vessels anchor before Villahermosa, which has been deserted by Gov. Domingo Echegaray's garrison; it surrenders at noon. Perry's brigade arrives three hours later in heavy rain. American casualties total five wounded as opposed to about 30 among the Mexican ranks.

22 JUNE 1847. Perry departs Villahermosa, having installed a small garrison under Commander van Brunt supported by *Spitfire, Scourge,* and *Etna.*

24 JUNE 1847. Mexican guerrillas launch a nocturnal attack against the American garrison in Villahermosa; they are dispersed but remain outside, harassing foraging parties.

30 JUNE 1847. Having sallied west from Villahermosa before dawn to chastise the Mexican guerrillas encircling the town, Commander Bigelow approaches their base camp at Tamulté (4 miles up the Grijalva River) with 200 men and a pair of six-pounders, accompanied by *Scourge* and *Vixen.* After a 20-minute skirmish in which one American is killed and five wounded, the raiders disperse the Mexican encampment, destroying everything of value before retiring.

8 JULY 1847. Scott is reinforced at Puebla by 4,500 American troops under Pillow, MacIntosh, and Brig. Gen. George Cadwalader.

16 JULY 1847. Mexican guerrillas launch a daylight assault against the American garrison within Villahermosa but are repelled.

19 JULY 1847. Because of increasing sickness and persistent Mexican guerrilla attacks, Perry orders Villahermosa evacuated. This is completed by the evening of 22 July, rearguard actions costing the Americans one killed and three wounded.

21 JULY 1847. The six-gun, 43-man, 690-ton storeship *Lexington* of Lt. Theodore Bailey anchors two miles outside La Paz (Baja California), depositing Lt. Col. Henry S. Burton's 110 men of the 1st New York Volunteer Regiment to act as a garrison.

27 JULY 1847. On Santa Anna's orders, Gen. Gabriel Valencia arrives at Guadalupe (north of Mexico City) from San Luis Potosí, bringing 4,000 veterans of the army defeated at Buena Vista.

Mexican counterattack against an American river squadron

6 AUGUST 1847. Franklin Pierce, the 42-year-old brigadier and former U.S. senator (and future president) reaches Scott's army at Puebla with 2,400 reinforcements. This same day, another 1,000 men of 9th Infantry begin marching inland from Veracruz under Maj. F. T. Lally, taking 13 days to reach Jalapa because of constant harassing attacks by 2,000 Mexicans under Gen. Juan Soto.

One day after Pierce arrives Scott launches his long-anticipated offensive against Mexico City, dispatching Twiggs's division west-northwest out of Puebla in advance of his main army. All told, Scott has 14,000 troops—of whom 2,500 are sick and 600 convalescent.

10 AUGUST 1847. Learning that the Americans are at last moving, Anaya's brigade marches out of Mexico City this morning to begin fortifying El Peñón Hill (10 miles east) with 7,000 troops and 30 cannons in accordance with Santa Anna's plans for defending the capital.

14 AUGUST 1847. Mexico's former president Paredes—disguised as "M. Martínez"—arrives at Veracruz from Havana aboard the British mail steamer *Teviot.* The 46-year-old Cmdr. David Glasgow Farragut of the 22-gun, 275-man, 880-ton sloop *Saratoga* fails to make an inspection, thus allowing Paredes to escape ashore.

16 AUGUST 1847. Rather than approach the main Mexican defenses at El Peñón head-on, divisions under Worth, Pillow, and Quitman veer southwest this morning, leaving Twiggs's division at Ayotla (20 miles east-southeast of Mexico City) to hold Santa Anna in check while they circle around.

18 AUGUST 1847. Scott's vanguard reaches the town of San Agustín and turns north, only to have the advance cavalry screen draw fire from a heavy battery at San Antonio, three miles south of Churubusco (which kills Seth Thornton, among others). Unable to outflank the position because of an impassable lava field called El Pedregal to the west, the Americans decide to again slip farther around, along a road reconnoitered by Captain Lee.

Meanwhile Santa Anna—now alerted to the movement around his southern flank—redeploys Valencia's 5,500 men into San Angel, Francisco Pérez's 3,500 into Coyoacán two miles farther east, and Bravo's into Churubusco; Rincón remains at El Peñón in reserve. Fearing his troops will see no action, however, Valencia disobeys and takes up station five miles southwest of his designated position in the village of Padierna.

19 AUGUST 1847. ***Contreras-Churubusco.*** This morning Twiggs sets out west from San Agustín to lead

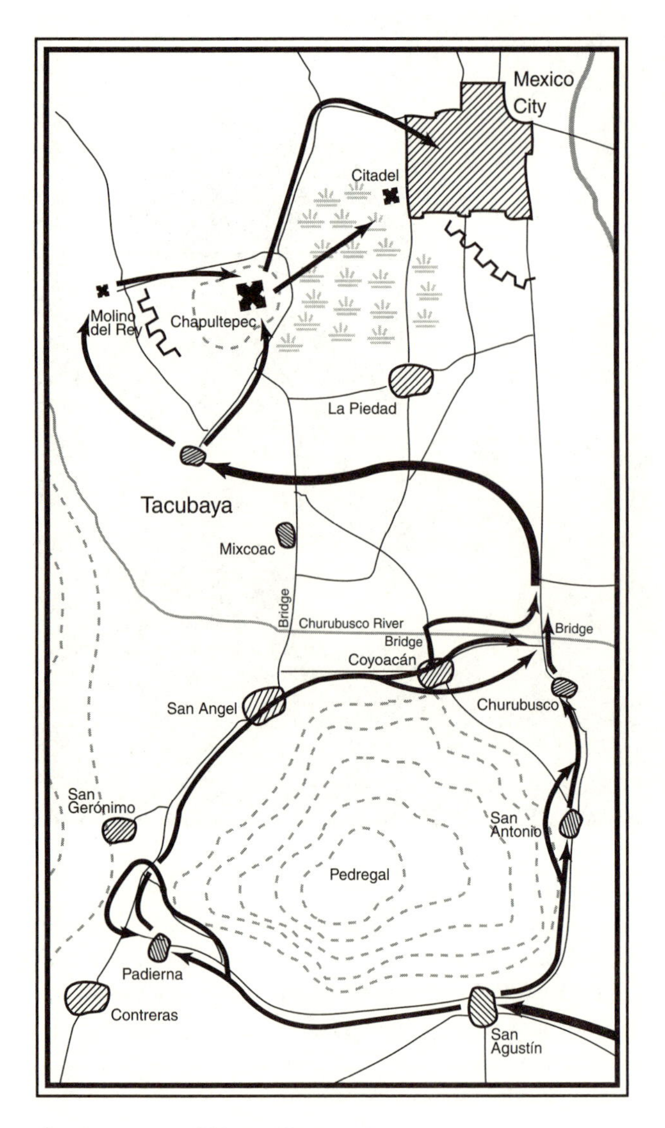

American capture of Mexico City

Pillow and Worth in the latest flanking maneuver. Early this afternoon, while approaching the San Angel-Contreras highway at its Padierna crossroads, his advance elements come under artillery fire, prompting him to deploy Capt. John Magruder's two field batteries. When it becomes evident they are dueling Valencia's 22 heavy guns and not some minor outpost, Pillow commits 3,500 men under Riley, Cadwalader, and Morgan to capture vacant San Gerónimo, hoping to thereby isolate Valencia from the Mexican main body.

Instead, late in the day Santa Anna moves southwest with another 3,500 Mexicans to extricate Valencia, in the process unwittingly threatening to crush the American thrust between two pincers. Realizing the danger, Smith follows Riley, Cadwalader, and Morgan into San Gerónimo at nightfall, directing them to leave a screen facing north against Santa Anna while continuing with him behind Valencia's positions under cover of darkness with their combined strength. Next dawn Santa Anna unexpectedly begins retiring northeast, so when Riley suddenly launches his surprise attack from Valencia's rear at 6:00 A.M. the latter's men are already feeling lost. They scatter in 17 minutes, suffering 700 killed plus 813 captured; all their artillery is lost.

The American pursuit of this broken formation carries as far northeast as San Angel and Coyoacán, spreading panic among other Mexican units. Worth takes advantage of the breakthrough to send Clarke's brigade (the 5th, 6th, and 8th Infantry) wheeling behind the San Antonio stronghold, causing the Mexican garrison to flee north to Churubusco rather than risk being cut off. Santa Anna's dispersed contingents now utterly collapse as a cohesive fighting force, every man struggling to recross the river at either Coyoacán or Churubusco. Scott directs Shields and Pierce to attack the bridgehead at Coyoacán while sending Worth and Pillow against Churubusco around noon.

After more than two hours' heavy fighting the 2,600 troops of Clarke's and Cadwalader's brigades, plus Duncan's artillery battalion, overcome the Churubusco bridgehead; Alexander's 3rd Infantry then storms its last stronghold, the fortified San Mateo Convent. The convent's defenders—renegade Irish-American deserters reformed into the so-called San Patricio Battalion—resist desperately but are eventually overwhelmed (30 of 69 survivors being later court-martialled and executed). By midafternoon on 20 August Santa Anna has fled back into his capital, his army ruined. Mexican casualties total 4,000 killed or wounded plus another 3,000 captured—including two former presidents and six generals. Scott's losses are 139 killed and more than 900 wounded or missing.

Although having Mexico City at his mercy, Scott hesitates to move against the capital next morning, instead allowing Santa Anna time to request a truce—which the Americans grant on Sunday, 22 August, hoping this will lead to a general peace.

6 SEPTEMBER 1847. After two weeks' fruitless talks, Scott informs Santa Anna that the American army will resume offensive operations next midday.

7 SEPTEMBER 1847. ***Molino del Rey.*** This afternoon Scott learns that a large body of Mexican troops has occupied the Molino del Rey, barely more than a mile from his Tacubaya headquarters. Wishing to brush back this outpost before his main army launches its final drive against Mexico City, the American commander sends 3,500 men next morning under Worth.

Expecting the Mexicans to fall back, the attackers encounter five brigades and heavy artillery, stubbornly holding both Molino del Rey and the adjacent stone Casa Mata. Twin columns under Maj. George Wright and Garland, supported by a field battery, become embroiled in a fierce two-hour battle before finally rooting the defenders out of the strongholds. American losses total 116 killed and 671 wounded.

12 SEPTEMBER 1847. ***Chapultepec.*** Having marshaled his forces, Scott orders his artillery to begin bombarding the hilltop castle of Chapultepec at 5:00 A.M. to take it before continuing against Mexico City. The 260 defenders under old General Bravo—including 50 young cadets from Mexico's military college—endure a day-long barrage, along with 600 troops stationed in surrounding woods.

At 8:00 next morning Pierce's brigade charges east from Molino del Rey, supported by Quitman's brigade on the right, to overwhelm the lower defenses in intense hand-to-hand fighting. Scaling ladders are then brought forward, and by 9:30 A.M. Col. Joseph E. Johnston's gray-coated Voltigeur Regiment unfurls the American colors atop the lofty fortress. (A half-dozen Mexican cadets fight to the death rather than surrender, one—Fernando Montes de Oca—jumping off the ramparts with the flag still clutched in his arms. All six are today immortalized as los Niños Héroes, or "Boy Heroes").

Two American columns sweep past, speeding toward the capital's western gates. By nightfall Santa Anna has suffered a total of 1,800 casualties (compared to Scott's 450), and at 1:00 A.M. he decides to evacuate Mexico City.

14 SEPTEMBER 1847. Encountering only sporadic resistance, Scott fights his way into Mexico City's main square by noon as Santa Anna and his surviving troops retreat north to Guadalupe. After a couple of days of severe rioting, some semblance of order is restored in the capital, Quitman being appointed its military governor.

15 SEPTEMBER 1847. At Guadalupe, Santa Anna resigns the presidency in favor of Chief Justice Manuel de la Peña y Peña.

20 SEPTEMBER 1847. Brig. Gen. Joseph Lane departs Veracruz with 2,500 American reinforcements, joining Lally shortly thereafter at Jalapa.

21 SEPTEMBER 1847. Santa Anna appears outside Puebla with 3,200 irregular cavalry and 2,500 militia, calling on the American garrison commander—Col. C. F. Childs—to surrender. He refuses, but the Mexicans balk at storming the walls and instead institute a halfhearted siege.

30 SEPTEMBER 1847. The 16-gun, 150-man, 566-ton sloop *Dale* of Cmdr. Thomas O. Selfridge approaches Mulegé (Baja California) under false English colors, then raises the Stars and Stripes and cuts out the schooner *Magdalena* this afternoon with a 50-man boarding party. Deemed unseaworthy, the prize is burned.

Next morning Selfridge calls on Mulegé's officials to submit to U.S. authority. Capt. Manuel Pineda—having earlier overthrown the collaborationist Palacios Miranda—refuses, prompting the Americans to disembark 17 marines and 57 sailors around 3:30 P.M. following a 90-minute bombardment by *Dale.* Although able to fight its way into town, the landing party accomplishes little before retiring at nightfall. On 2 October the U.S. sloop reverses course southeast for Loreto.

5 OCTOBER 1847. Selfridge's *Dale* disembarks a company of marines and sailors at Loreto (Baja California), seizing two brass four-pounders and other armaments.

8 OCTOBER 1847. Walker's "Texas Rangers," acting as scouts for Lane's brigade, surprise Santa Anna's pickets and chase them back to Huamantla (Puebla), where the main Mexican army lies, complete with two artillery pieces. It devastates the pursuit and kills Walker. Lane's infantry arrives, scattering Santa Anna's force and capturing his two guns before continuing west into Puebla next day.

Shortly thereafter Santa Anna is ordered by President Peña to turn over command to Rincón and prepare to stand trial for his conduct of Mexico's defense.

17 OCTOBER 1847. Captain Elie A. F. La Vallette arrives outside Guaymas (Sonora) with *Congress, Portsmouth,* and the brigantine *Argo* (a Chilean blockade runner intercepted earlier), calling on its governor—Colonel Campuzano—to surrender his 400-man garrison next afternoon. The Mexican officer refuses, so La Vallette installs a 32-pounder on Almagre Grande Island that night, covering the bay.

At 5:30 A.M. on 19 October *Portsmouth* is rowed into Guaymas's inner harbor, its commander again calling for capitulation at noon and threatening to shell the town. Campuzano rebuffs this offer as well, and so *Portsmouth* and *Congress* open fire next day at 6:30 A.M., halting an hour later when the Mexican garrison retreats four miles into Bocachicacampo. A marine company occupies Casa Blanca Hill briefly this afternoon, and on 21 October razes the Guaymas fortifications. Otherwise the Americans install no garrison, preferring to control the port by leaving a warship anchored in its roadstead.

1 NOVEMBER 1847. Patterson strikes inland from Veracruz with 3,000 reinforcements, reaching Jalapa one week later. He is followed soon after by Butler with another 4,000.

10 NOVEMBER 1847. ***Mazatlán.*** The new commander in chief of the U.S. Pacific squadron—Commo. W. Branford Shubrick—arrives this evening off Mazatlán (Sinaloa), anchoring his 56-gun, 750-man, 1,900-ton flagship *Independence* due west at Olas Altas and *Congress* northwest in Puerto Viejo. *Cyane* inches into Puerto Nuevo farther east. (The storeship *Erie* joins after dark.) With the city thus threatened on three sides, Col. Rafael Telles withdraws his 560-man garrison inland to Palos Prietos that night.

Next morning the Americans discover Mazatlán undefended and so disembark 730 men in 29 boats. After beginning repairs on the fortifications, Shubrick installs a 400-man garrison, with Captain La Vallette as military governor. Telles is satisfied to maintain cavalry patrols outside, preventing supplies from entering the city.

11 NOVEMBER 1847. In an attempt to drive the Americans out of Baja California, Pineda launches a dawn assault against the La Paz garrison with 120 men, being repulsed by artillery fire.

This same day, elections are held in the unoccupied portions of Mexico, Anaya emerging as interim president for the next two months; Peña becomes foreign minister.

17 NOVEMBER 1847. In an attempt to impose sterner American control over Guaymas, Selfridge leads 17 marines and 50 seamen ashore from *Dale,* encountering 250 Mexicans at Casa Blanca Hill. The Americans are pinned down in a brief firefight and their commander seriously wounded before the defenders disperse.

This same day, Pineda mounts a second attack against La Paz (on the far side of the Gulf of California), suffering four or five killed and a like number wounded before withdrawing six miles to La Laguna. American casualties are one killed and two wounded.

18 NOVEMBER 1847. Delegates from eight Mexican states agree to seek peace from the Americans.

19 NOVEMBER 1847. Lt. Charles Heywood's 24-man marine garrison at San José (Baja California) is called upon to surrender by 150 Mexicans under Capts. Vicente Mejía and José Matías Moreno plus naval Lt. José Antonio Mijares. The Americans refuse and, along with 20 Mexican collaborators, endure two nights of assaults within the old mission. The attackers withdraw by morning on 21 November as two approaching sail seemingly promise relief—although proving to be only the whalers *Magnolia* and *Edward.*

20 NOVEMBER 1847. Before dawn two large American boat parties push out of Mazatlán, attempting to surprise a 90-man Mexican patrol ten miles away at Urias under Swiss-born Carlos Horn. One sailor is killed and 20 others wounded after a brief encounter, which also leaves four Mexicans killed and an unknown number injured.

26 NOVEMBER 1847. The eight-gun, 43-man, 567-ton storeship *Southampton* of Lt. Robert D. Thorburn reinforces the garrison at San José (Baja California) with 26 men and two guns.

27 NOVEMBER 1847. This afternoon Pineda rushes La Paz (Baja California) with 350 men, only to be repulsed by Burton's 112 defenders.

11 JANUARY 1848. *Lexington* joins the bark *Whiton* of Lt. Frederick Chatard off San Blas (Nayarit), combining to set 47 men ashore next morning to strip the harbor castle of guns and cut out two schooners.

18 JANUARY 1848. Chatard goes ashore at Manzanillo (Colima) with a small party from *Whiton,* spiking three guns.

22 JANUARY 1848. Pineda and several hundred men capture an American foraging party outside San José (Baja California) then besiege 27 marines, 15 sailors, 20 Mexican collaborators, and 50 noncombatants inside its old mission. The defenders resist until dawn on 15 February, when *Cyane* deposits 100 men three miles away and relieves the garrison.

30 JANUARY 1848. Before sunrise 12 marines and two companies of seamen quit *Dale*—now under acting command of Lt. Edward M. Yard—to row stealthily to Cochori (8 miles east of Guaymas) and surprise a Mexican concentration. The raiders disembark three miles short of their destination and close in on it from three directions. Cochori is carried in a rush, with three Mexicans being killed, five wounded, and many

others captured before the landing party returns aboard *Dale* two hours later.

13 FEBRUARY 1848. At dawn 60 of *Dale's* seamen and marines close on the remnants of Campuzano's camp at Bocachicacampo from three directions, dispersing and destroying his camp.

22 MARCH 1848. Another company of the 1st New York Volunteer Regiment plus 115 recruits reach La Paz (Baja California). Reassured by these reinforcements, Capt. Seymour G. Steele leads a 33-man raiding party three days later against Pineda's main encampment at San Antonio, severely wounding the Mexican commander, capturing three of his men, and releasing five American captives.

31 MARCH 1848. Eight days after departing La Paz (Baja California) with three companies—217 men—of the 1st New York Volunteers, Burton surprises a Mexican concentration under Gov. Mauricio Castro at Todos Santos, killing ten and dispersing the rest. Many of the fleeing troops (including the governor) are captured 25 miles farther east at Santiago by two American detachments out of San José.

9 APRIL 1848. A small American unit disembarks in the Soldado River estuary (Sonora), marching 12 miles inland to spike three Mexican guns, suffering two men wounded during their retirement.

APRIL 1848. American garrisons at both San José and La Paz (Baja California) experience mutinies, numerous ringleaders being detained.

1848. After fitful negotiations between the American occupiers and the faction-riven rump of Mexico's government, the Treaty of Guadalupe Hidalgo is finally signed on 2 February 1848. By its terms the United States wrests away half of Mexico's territory: the largely empty provinces of California, Nevada, Utah, Colorado, Arizona, and New Mexico (in addition to recognizing its earlier acquisition of Texas).

In exchange, the American government pays Mexico $15 million in compensation for the lands while assuming responsibility for an additional $3.5 million in claims by U.S. citizens. Mexicans living in the ceded territories are to be treated as American citizens. The agreement is ratified by the U.S. Congress on 10 March and by Mexico on 19 May. Veracruz is finally restored to Mexican control by 11 June, the last of 18,300 American troops departing through there by 31 July.

FILIBUSTERISM (1852–1860)

DURING THE MID-NINETEENTH CENTURY the weakness and divisiveness of many Latin American countries encourages foreign adventurers to mount private campaigns into the region, akin to those of their seventeenth-century predecessors, the so-called filibusters (legally defined as individuals waging war without government sanction). The first country to undergo such incursions is Mexico, still reeling from its defeat by the United States.

In December 1850 a group of French investors (headed by France's ambassador in Mexico City, André Levasseur) persuade Gov. José de Aguilar and his compliant assembly in the remote northwestern state of Sonora to allow their company to develop the potentially rich mining district between the 31st parallel and the newly defined borders with California and New Mexico. Although this unauthorized arrangement fails to win ratification from the national congress in Mexico City, it nonetheless furnishes an excuse for future armed interventions, which the central authorities are powerless to resist.

1 JUNE 1852. ***Raousset's Invasion.*** Having failed to win riches during California's gold rush, a 34-year-old French soldier of fortune named Gaston Raoul Raousset, Comte de Boulbon, agrees to recruit and command an armed expedition into Sonora's interior to stake out a huge new claim in this untamed Indian territory for the Franco-Mexican Restauradora del Mineral de Arizona mining company. Having hired 600 mercenaries at San Francisco (California)—260 of them French—Raousset arrives at the port of Guaymas by 1 June, organizing his small army into six infantry companies, plus one each of cavalry and artillery, before striking north toward Hermosillo on 13 June.

21 SEPTEMBER 1852. Camped at Magdalena, Raousset receives a message from the new acting governor of Sonora, Fernando Cubillas, directing that he and his French followers either adopt Mexican citizen-

ship or leave the country. Knowing this officer and Gen. Miguel Blanco, military commander for the state, to be shareholders in a rival mining enterprise, Raousset refuses, instead proclaiming Sonora an independent country before marching south with 184 infantry, 50 dragoons, and 25 gunners (for four small field pieces) to defeat Blanco on 30 September and then occupy its capital, Hermosillo.

26 OCTOBER 1852. After almost four weeks' occupation, Raousset's isolated garrison abandons Hermosillo, retreating south to Guaymas while hounded by Mexican guerrillas under Blanco. Falling sick with dysentery, Raousset leaves his army nine miles outside Guaymas on 29 October to sail for Mazatlán and then San Francisco (California). His survivors are allowed to depart undisturbed after surrendering their artillery train to the Mexican authorities in exchange for 11,000 pesos.

15 OCTOBER 1853. ***Walker's Mexican Adventure.*** Self-proclaimed "colonel," 29-year-old William Walker departs San Francisco with 45 followers aboard the schooner *Caroline* to carve out a new country. Disembarking at La Paz (Baja California, population 1,100) on 3 November, he raises a flag with two stars—ostensibly signifying Baja California and Sonora—proclaiming the "Republic of Lower California," with himself as president. Street fighting erupts ten days later, obliging Walker and his adherents to retreat north to Ensenada (just south of Tijuana), which he designates as his new capital.

Despite receiving reinforcements from nearby California, Walker's hold soon weakens further when he comes into conflict with Ensenada's local landowner, Antonio María Meléndez. Nevertheless, the adventurer sets out east-northeast in March 1854 with 100 American filibusters, hoping to push overland into northern Sonora. After crossing the Colorado River into Sonora by 4 April he is obliged to turn back. Now harassed by local guerrillas, Walker is finally defeated by Lt. Col. Javier Castillo Negrete in a skirmish at La Grulla (near Santo Tomás Mission, southeast of Ensenada), compelling him to flee north across the California border with his 33 remaining followers by 8 May and surrender to U.S. military authorities.

Walker is subsequently tried in San Francisco (California) on a charge of violating America's neutrality laws; he is acquitted in October.

MARCH 1854. ***Raousset's Demise.*** After appealing his October 1852 expulsion from Sonora before President Santa Anna in Mexico City without success, the young adventurer Raousset returns to San Francisco (California) and recruits another 300 volunteers—mostly French. Raousset arrives near Guaymas with this force on 28 June 1854 after a 35-day passage, setting up temporary headquarters in a cave.

Having failed to persuade the local federal commander, Gen. José María Yáñez, to join the ongoing Ayutla Revolution against Santa Anna (*see* 1 March 1854 under Ayutla Revolution), Raousset's contingent is eventually defeated by this Mexican general in a three-hour fight on 31 July, suffering 100 casualties. The French leader is captured, tried before a military tribunal, and executed in Guaymas's La Mole Square at sunrise on 12 August.

4 MAY 1855. ***Walker in Nicaragua.*** The adventurer again departs San Francisco (California), this time with 57 heavily armed American followers who grandiloquently refer to themselves as The Immortals, to partake in Nicaragua's civil war. Having been contacted the previous year by this nation's liberal opposition—the Democrat Party—to raise a force of filibusters and join their struggle against the ruling conservative Legitimist Party for a promised reward of 52,000 acres of land, Walker disembarks in this country by June. His so-called *Falange Americana* immediately plunges into the fighting, abetted by the American-owned Accessory Transit Co., a corporation hoping to secure an overland monopoly from the Caribbean across Central America into the Pacific.

Forming the core of the liberal army, Colonel Walker's forces capture the capital of Granada by 13 October and, under the subsequent peace arrangement creating a coalition government, he becomes commander in chief of the Nicaraguan army. He then acquires compromising letters written by the new minister of war, Ponciano Corral—the former Legitimist army commander—soliciting intervention from other Latin American countries to oust Walker, and so gains an excuse to eliminate his most formidable rival by having Corral executed for treason.

From November 1855 to June 1856, Walker rules Nicaragua through a figurehead, Pres. Patricio Rivas. He continues to receive American volunteer reinforcements (brought in free of charge by the Accessory Transit Co.) and in a propaganda move designed to win native support is dubbed the Gray-eyed Man in local newspapers, after a Mosquito Indian legend. In May 1856 Washington recognizes Rivas's government; Walker then breaks with this figurehead, being elected president himself in a controlled vote on 29 June and installed into office by 12 July. He dreams of uniting all of Central America into a military empire, digging a canal, and fomenting agriculture by reintroducing African slavery.

However, neighboring republics such as Honduras, El Salvador, Guatemala, and Costa Rica fear he contemplates incorporating Nicaragua into the United States, so combine forces to prepare a counterinvasion—covertly backed by Great Britain, with its own separate imperialist agenda for this region. A rift then erupts within the Accessory Transit Co., prompting Walker to seize its ships and properties in Nicaragua and turn these over to one particular faction; the other is headed by the formidable capitalist Cornelius Vanderbilt, who works toward Walker's downfall.

Soon Washington withdraws its recognition and when the coalition forces finally invade Nicaragua, Walker finds himself cut off from further American reinforcements to replace those men lost to disease. Compelled to evacuate Granada, he orders his capital razed and on 1 May 1857, after being cornered inside the town of Rivas with only a handful of survivors, he surrenders to Cmdr. Charles Henry Davis of the USS *St. Mary's* to be deported home.

24 MARCH 1857. A band of 104 American filibusters under Henry A. Crabb crosses the border from San Diego (California), capturing Sonoíta (Sonora) two days later. In conjunction with his Mexican accomplice Agustín Ainza, it is Crabb's intent to create a new breakaway republic in this territory.

However, two columns of Mexican troops move to contain this incursion, one from Ures under Lt. Col. José María Girón and the other under Capt. Lorenzo Gutiérrez. Starting on 1 April near Caborca, they defeat the invaders in a series of clashes lasting four days. Crabb's main contingent has meanwhile besieged the capital of Hermosillo, whose garrison resists until relieved by Hilario Gabilondo. The American commander and 57 of his followers are then executed in Hermosillo's graveyard on 7 April; another 33 have already been shot in isolated groups elsewhere, thus ending this invasion.

NOVEMBER 1857. Eluding the U.S. federal authorities, Walker sails from Mobile (Alabama) with 150 filibusters to reclaim the office of Nicaraguan president. Defying the U.S. sloop *Saratoga,* his expedition disembarks at the Caribbean port of Greytown, only to be overtaken by the American squadron of Commo. Hiram Paulding, who throws 350 men ashore and arrests Walker without bloodshed on 8 December.

The adventurer is once more returned home, this action meeting with approval from the antislavery states of the North and disapproval in the South. Nicaragua rewards Paulding with a jeweled sword, and the administration of Pres. James Buchanan releases Walker shortly thereafter.

EARLY MARCH 1858. Gen. Julián Castro spearheads a revolt against despotic Venezuelan Pres. José Tadeo Monagas, compelling the oligarch to resign from office by 15 March, thus ending his family's stranglehold on power. Monagas is given sanctuary in the French embassy when the triumphant revolutionaries enter Caracas, prompting enraged mobs to attack foreign legations.

8 MAY 1858. British and French men-of-war enter Caracas' port of La Guaira, peremptorily demanding an apology from the new Venezuelan government for recent revolutionary excesses, which is refused.

AUGUST 1860. After evading Anglo-American naval forces by zigzagging across the Caribbean via Roatán and Cozumel, Walker appears off the Honduran coast in hopes of once again seizing power in Central America. Instead he is arrested on 3 September by Royal Navy Capt. Norvell Salmon and turned over to the Honduran authorities at Trujillo, who court-martial Walker and execute him on 12 September. The short-lived era of filibusterism is effectively ended.

BUENOS AIRES VERSUS THE ARGENTINE CONFEDERATION (1852–1863)

FOLLOWING ROSAS'S FLIGHT INTO EXILE, the triumphant Urquiza and other delegates from Argentina's interior reorganize the national government along confederate lines, thus reducing the influence of Buenos Aires. When Gov. Vicente López and other ministers resign in protest on 23 June 1852 (to allow Gen. Manuel Guillermo Pinto to succeed in office), Urquiza voids the gesture, dissolves the legislature, and compels his most vocal critics to depart the country.

A second insurrection occurs on 11 September, three days after Urquiza has quit Buenos Aires to attend the national congress at Santa Fe. His governor within the capital—Gen. José M. Galán—retires outside to San Nicolás with his outnumbered troops, allowing Pinto to become proclaimed president and the rebellion to take hold. Rather than plunge Argentina back into civil war, Urquiza sends emissaries to Buenos Aires on 18 September, recognizing its separation from the other provinces. Eventually, a rival capital is established at Paraná with Urquiza as president.

16 NOVEMBER 1852. In an effort to install a friendlier administration in neighboring Entre Ríos Province, the Buenos Aires authorities dispatch Gen. Manuel Hornos with a small invasion force, which occupies Gualeguaychú then defeats a confederate force at Calá. Soon, however, an army under Urquiza drives Hornos north into Corrientes Province, where his followers are disarmed.

20 NOVEMBER 1852. Gen. Juan Madariaga leads a small Buenos Aires force in an abortive landing near Concepción del Uruguay, reembarks, then again attempts to storm this place next day, only to be repelled by the confederate defenders. Discouraged, Madariaga returns to Buenos Aires.

1 DECEMBER 1852. Col. Hilario Lagos—campaigning on behalf of Buenos Aires in the center of the province—mutinies against its government, feeling it should join Urquiza's confederacy.

22 JANUARY 1853. Lagos defeats a Buenos Aires contingent sent to subdue him at Rincón de San Gregorio (near the mouth of the Salado River).

EARLY SPRING 1853. ***Siege of Buenos Aires.*** After failing to achieve a reconciliation with the authorities within the capital, Urquiza arrives to lay siege to the city of Buenos Aires with 12,000 troops. The noose is tightened on 17 April, when Coe's confederate naval squadron destroys its Buenos Aires counterpart under Zurowky then blockades the port.

However, Coe is bought off on 20 June, bringing his squadron into Buenos Aires in exchange for 26,000 ounces of gold. The confederate congress passes a resolution federalizing Buenos Aires, prompting numerous besieging units—including Lagos's—to switch loyalties and join the defenders. By 13 July Urquiza is obliged to lift his siege and return to Entre Ríos Province, where he retires to his residence at San José and threatens to quit public life.

10 JULY 1853. Just before raising his siege of the capital, Urquiza signs a treaty with representatives from France, England, and the United States promising free navigation up the Paraná and Uruguay Rivers. The agreement causes much resentment within Buenos Aires, which has traditionally controlled trade through the River Plate.

5 MARCH 1854. Urquiza officially takes office again as president of the Argentine confederation.

8 NOVEMBER 1854. After numerous raids into confederate territory, Gen. Jerónimo Costa's 500 Buenos Aires troopers are defeated at Tala by General Hornos and forced to seek sanctuary in Santa Fe.

20 DECEMBER 1854. Buenos Aires and the Argentine confederation sign a truce, one month later formalizing this arrangement with the so-called *pactos de convivencia* (convivial pacts).

30 MARCH 1855. ***Indian Wars.*** In order to avenge a 5,000-man Indian raid by chief Calfucurá that massacred 300 inhabitants of Azul and made off with many female captives, 33-year-old Col. Bartolomé Mitre leads 700 troops south into the Chica Range. He is defeated by chief Catriel on 30 March, suffering 16 killed and 234 wounded, before withdrawing under cover of darkness.

Next year General Hornos suffers an even more stunning setback at the hands of Calfucurá, when he quits Azul with 3,000 Argentine troops and a dozen field pieces to avenge the extermination of Lt. Col. Nicanor Otamendi's 124-man cavalry patrol (only two troopers having survived). Hornos is ambushed between the San Jacinto Range and Tapalqué Creek, suffering 270 killed and a like number of captured; he also loses the artillery train.

25 JANUARY 1856. Confederate Gen. José M. Flores violates the truce by invading Buenos Aires Province, only to be defeated at Cardozo Lagoon and driven back into Santa Fe Province. This campaign sparks a brief renewal of hostilities.

31 JANUARY 1856. General Costa sails from Montevideo and disembarks near Zárate, only to be defeated by Colonel Conesa and executed along with 125 of his followers.

29 MAY 1859. After three years of further frictions over customs duties and free passage, the confederation authorizes Urquiza to use any means necessary to bring Buenos Aires back into the nation.

7 JULY 1859. Buenos Aires sends the steamers *General Pinto* and *Buenos Aires* up the Paraná River to prevent any confederate advance. However, the marines aboard *General Pinto* mutiny, capture their commander, Col. José Muratore, kill Capt. Alejandro Muratore, and switch loyalties to the confederation.

14 OCTOBER 1859. A confederate squadron under Col. Mariano Cordero fights its way past the Buenos Aires garrison on Martín García Island to proceed up the Paraná River and aid Urquiza's advance.

22 OCTOBER 1859. ***Cepeda.*** Urquiza arrives north of Pavón Creek with 10,000 confederate troopers, 3,000 infantry, and 1,000 gunners and auxiliaries manning 32 field pieces. To the south awaits General Mitre with 4,700 Buenos Aires infantry, 4,000 cavalry, and 300 gunners for two dozen guns. A Buenos Aires cavalry force under General Hornos crosses Medio Creek and clashes near Rica Canyon with advance confederate elements, only to retire once reinforcements are rushed in.

On 23 October confederate General Virasoro drives in Mitre's skirmishers from the east bank of Medio Creek; Urquiza's main army then crosses and slowly takes up position opposite the Buenos Aires lines. The attack does not actually start until 6:00 P.M., the confederate cavalry on both flanks soon defeating their outnumbered opponents. Meanwhile the confederate infantry splits into two, trying to avoid the 16-gun battery in the Buenos Aires center. Nevertheless, Mitre is doomed, his infantry on the left flank being annihilated when ordered to redeploy toward the right.

By 11:00 P.M. the Buenos Aires survivors are streaming off in defeat, Mitre reaching San Nicolás (50 miles away) with only 2,000 men and six cannons after a 36-hour forced march. Urquiza remains in possession of 2,000 prisoners, 20 field pieces, and all baggage trains.

7 NOVEMBER 1859. Urquiza's confederate army—now swollen to 20,000 men—halts at San José de Flores; four days later Buenos Aires agrees to become reincorporated into the Argentine union.

16 NOVEMBER 1860. After a year of uneasy peace the people of San Juan Province rise against confederate rule, killing Gov. José Antonio Virasoro (brother of the general) and most of his retinue. Liberal Dr. Antonio Aberastain is installed in his place; Col. Juan Sáa—confederate governor of San Luis—is sent to deal with him.

11 JANUARY 1861. At Rinconada del Pocito, Aberastain is caught and immediately executed by confederate Cmdr. Francisco Clavero. This brutal expedient provokes such an outcry, especially in Buenos Aires, that Clavero must flee to Chile.

15 APRIL 1861. Valentín Alsida and Rufino de Elizalde, duly elected Buenos Aires delegates to the national congress, have their credentials challenged and are refused their seats. Rather than hold new elections, Mitre and his followers begin preparations for war.

5 JULY 1861. The Argentine confederation accuses Buenos Aires of violating the peace and preaching sedition and authorizes the use of force to restore order. Two days later Mitre proclaims martial law within Buenos Aires; Urquiza is then reappointed to command the confederate armies.

6 SEPTEMBER 1861. After mustering at Rojas, the main Buenos Aires army under Mitre reaches Pergamino.

16 SEPTEMBER 1861. ***Pavón.*** Mitre crosses Medio Creek and camps a mile to the north with 9,000 Buenos Aires infantry, 6,000 cavalry, and 1,000 gunners and auxiliaries to man 35 field pieces. North of nearby Pavón Creek, Urquiza is attempting to organize his 11,000 confederate troopers, 5,000 ill-disciplined foot soldiers, and 42 cannons. Despite the difficulties, Urquiza chooses to assume the offensive next day, crossing the Pavón to take up position opposite the enemy.

Around noon on 17 September Mitre launches a concentric attack with his infantry against the smaller confederate line, charging through an artillery barrage to break through. Meanwhile the more numerous confederate cavalry disperses the Buenos Aires troopers yet is unable to follow up the advantage due to the large formations of well-trained infantry guarding Mitre's rear and baggage train. Seeing his infantry and artillery succumb while his riders scatter beyond his control, a demoralized Urquiza orders a general confederate retreat to Rosario. He leaves behind 1,650 prisoners, 37 guns, 5,000 mounts, 3,000 rifles, and his supply train, vowing never to fight again in Argentina's civil wars.

4 OCTOBER 1861. ***Arroyo Manantial.*** Confederate Gen. Octaviano Navarro's 4,000 troops—marching on Santiago del Estero Province to reinstall its governor after

a liberal uprising led by the Taboada family—defeats 2,000 Tucumán rebels under Gen. José María del Campo at Manantial Creek. Despite the victory and subsequent occupation of Santiago del Estero, Navarro proves unable to reimpose confederate rule and so retires to Catamarca.

11 OCTOBER 1861. Mitre's triumphant Buenos Aires army occupies Rosario.

5 NOVEMBER 1861. Confederate Pres. Santiago Derqui resigns.

13 NOVEMBER 1861. Confederate Governor Allende is deposed at Córdoba; when Generals Sáa and Juan de Dios Videla march to reinstall him, they are dispersed and compelled to flee to Chile by the approach of 3,000 Buenos Aires troops under Gen. Wenceslao Paunero.

22 NOVEMBER 1861. ***Cañada de Gómez.*** A Buenos Aires cavalry column under Gen. Venancio Flores surprises 1,300 confederate troopers under Virasoro in Gómez Canyon. The latter launches an immediate charge, only to be lured into a trap and suffer 300 killed, 150 captured, and the dispersal of his survivors. This defeat marks the end of effective confederate resistance.

13 DECEMBER 1861. The confederate vice president, General Pedernera, dissolves his government, leaving Buenos Aires's Mitre as de facto president of all Argentina.

17 DECEMBER 1861. Liberal Gens. Antonio and Manuel Taboada easily disperse 2,400 confederates gathered at Seibal (Tucumán Province) under Gen. Celedonio Gutiérrez, slaying 40.

JANUARY 1862. Mendoza and San Juan are occupied without resistance by Buenos Aires Col. Ignacio Rivas.

10 FEBRUARY 1862. Confederate Generals Peñaloza and Gutiérrez are defeated at Monte Grande (also called Río Colorado, 20 miles south of Tucumán) by José María del Campo.

4 MARCH 1862. Confederate General Peñaloza enters the city of Rioja unopposed, its 600-man Buenos Aires garrison under Colonel Echegaray having withdrawn earlier (later deserting). One week later at Salinas de Moreno, Peñaloza is overtaken and defeated by Col. Ambrosio Sandes.

3 APRIL 1862. At Chañaral Negro (on the Quinto River banks in San Luis Province), Col. José Iseas defeats 300 confederate partisans under Fructuoso Ontiveros.

12 APRIL 1862. Confederate General Peñaloza attacks Iseas's forces at Casas Viejas (the western edge of Córdoba Province), only to be bloodily repulsed and obliged to withdraw to San Luis.

His 1,600 confederates arrive five days later and lay siege to its 300 defenders. By 21 April the garrison is willing to capitulate, but before Peñaloza can consummate this, he is compelled to flee because of the approach of Buenos Aires Colonel Iseas.

20 JUNE 1862. Peñaloza signs a truce with the Buenos Aires government.

12 OCTOBER 1862. Mitre is officially installed as president of Argentina.

31 MARCH 1863. Peñaloza having once again risen against Mitre's rule, a series of skirmishes are fought by government troops against confederate guerrillas during the next month and a half at Callecita (31 March), Punta de Agua (2 April), Villaprima (21 April), Chumbicha (22 April), Mal Paso (3 May), Santa Rosa (7 May), and Lomas Blancas (20 May).

JUNE 1863. Confederate exiles, led out of Chile by Colonel Clavero, invade southern Mendoza Province and briefly occupy Fort San Rafael before being defeated by government Cmdr. Juan Manuel Puebla.

10 JUNE 1863. ***Las Playas.*** Gov. Justiniano Pose is deposed at Córdoba and replaced by Simón Luengo, who summons Peñaloza to take office. The latter arrives three days later with 100 followers to set about organizing defenses.

Some time later Peñaloza sorties four miles south to Las Playas with 3,500 men to confront 4,000 government troops—the 1st, 2nd, and 7th Cavalry Regiments plus a force of national guards—approaching from San Luis under General Paunero. The latter defeats the defenders and drives them into Rioja Province.

21 AUGUST 1863. Ontiveros's 200 confederate partisans are defeated at San Francisco (San Luis Province), and again four days later at Río Seco.

25 AUGUST 1863. Confederate guerrilla leader Puebla is defeated on the banks of the Sauces River (San Luis Province), losing 100 of 150 men.

30 OCTOBER 1863. Some 1,000 confederate partisans under Puebla are scattered at Caucete (San Juan Province) by 150 government troopers and 80 foot soldiers under Mayor Pablo Irrazábal. Next day the retreating guerrillas are again attacked at Bajo de los Gigantes by another government force under Colonel Arredondo and routed.

12 NOVEMBER 1863. Peñaloza is surprised at the town of Olta (Rioja Province) with only 50 followers and captured by a flying column of government cavalry under Capt. Ricardo Vera. Upon Irrazábal's arrival, the confederate chieftain is executed, his head being exhibited upon a spike.

1863. Although soon distracted by the larger Paraguayan conflict (*see* War of the Triple Alliance), Argentina's political structure continues to be riven by this Buenos Aires–hinterland split.

AYUTLA REVOLUTION (1853–1855)

On 6 February 1853, the exiled Santa Anna is elected president of Mexico for the fifth and final time. His last two years in office are marked by increasing internal strife, exploding in the so-called Revolution of Ayutla, which in turn culminates a few years later with the War of the Reform and French intervention in Mexico.

7 FEBRUARY 1853. The 51-year-old Gen. Manuel María Lombardini leads a coup against Juan Bautista Ceballos, temporarily occupying the office of president until Santa Anna can arrive from exile in Turbaco (Colombia) to succeed him.

20 APRIL 1853. Santa Anna reaches Mexico City and becomes president.

SUMMER-AUTUMN 1853. Santa Anna negotiates numerous territorial disputes with U.S. Ambassador James Gadsen, creating unease in Mexico over the nature of the claims.

16 DECEMBER 1853. Santa Anna seizes dictatorial powers by abolishing all political parties, dispensing with the legislature, and choosing to be addressed as "most serene highness."

30 DECEMBER 1853. Santa Anna signs the Gadsen Treaty, whereby Mexico cedes to the United States freedom of transit for mails, merchandise, and troops across the Isthmus of Tehuantepec and readjusts the boundaries of the earlier Treaty of Guadalupe Hidalgo to give the Americans almost 30,000 more square miles in New Mexico and Arizona in exchange for $10 million. The Mexican public is outraged.

1 MARCH 1854. ***Uprising.*** Col. Florencio Villareal leads the garrison of Ayutla (Guerrero) in a mutiny against Santa Anna's rule. What makes this uprising unusual—among the numerous other insurrections then breaking out—is that Villareal proclaims the Plan de Ayutla, a program drawn up by his 63-year-old superior, former governor Juan N. Alvarez, and 54-year-old Gen. Tomás Moreno to reform Mexico's government by deposing the dictator and convening a national congress to draft a new constitution. The reformers' liberal, democratic program will gradually attract many adherents.

11 MARCH 1854. The Acapulco garrison joins the Plan de Ayutla, led by a 41-year-old former customs collector, Ignacio Comonfort. He calls upon Alvarez to assume command of the *Ejército Restaurador de la Libertad* (Restorer of Liberty Army), which is accepted on 13 March, Moreno agreeing to act as second-in-command.

16 MARCH 1854. Having ordered Gen. Luis Noriega and Col. Francisco Cosío Bahamonde to close in on Guerrero from different directions, Santa Anna marches out of Mexico City at the head of 5,000 troops to help put down the uprisings on the Pacific Coast.

30 MARCH 1854. Having shot numerous persons suspected of disloyalty and twice been attacked by Faustino Villalba's guerrillas on both banks of the Balsas River near Mezcala (Guerrero), Santa Anna's army finally reaches the mountain pass at Chilpancingo, heading down from the Sierra Madre Mountains into coastal lands.

13 APRIL 1854. Santa Anna's army fights a skirmish with rebel forces at El Coquillo (Guerrero).

20 APRIL 1854. ***Siege of Acapulco.*** Santa Anna's army arrives and attempts to surprise Comonfort's

rebel garrison within Fort San Diego. After six days' fruitless bombardment and siege, the attackers are compelled to retire because of outbreaks of disease and lack of provisions, firing numerous dwellings during their retreat.

30 APRIL 1854. Guerrilla partisans hound Santa Anna's retirement, so the general fights a rearguard action at Peregrino Hill, which sufficiently bloodies his pursuers under Diego and Encarnación Alvarez to allow his crippled army to proceed. This ignominious withdrawal from the coast, however, greatly inspires other rebellions. Comonfort, meanwhile, sets sail from Acapulco for San Francisco to raise financing in the United States.

12 JULY 1854. The 41-year-old Brig. Gen. Félix María Zuloaga—loyal to Santa Anna—defeats the guerrilla chief Villalba at Iguala, killing him.

7 DECEMBER 1854. Comonfort returns to Acapulco, from where he soon advances northwest to Michoacán to spread the revolt.

JANUARY 1855. Zuloaga's 1,000 men and five field pieces are besieged within Nuxco Hacienda (Guerrero) by rebel forces under General Alvarez, eventually agreeing to switch sides and take up arms against Santa Anna. The same happens with the garrison at Ajuchitlán under Colonel Vélez when rebels capture nearby Huétamo.

25 FEBRUARY 1855. Liberal General Alvarez marches for Chilpancingo (Guerrero) but halts two miles short at Mazatlán Hacienda, deciding against a siege.

26 FEBRUARY 1855. Liberal forces take the garrison at Chilapa (Guerrero).

4 AUGUST 1855. Santa Anna resigns from office; five days later he flees Mexico City for Veracruz, where the ship *Iturbide* carries him to Cuba and then exile at Turbaco (Colombia).

OCTOBER 1855. After triumphantly entering Mexico City, General Alvarez is provisionally elected president and convenes a constitutional congress to commence the year-long process of reforming Mexico's institutions. Although the liberals have defeated Santa Anna, they will soon encounter much more serious opposition from conservatives (*see* War of the Reform and French Intervention in Mexico).

WAR OF THE REFORM (1858–1860)

THE UNITED VICTORY OVER SANTA ANNA in August 1855 only masks the fact that ever since Mexico's independence from Spain it has become increasingly polarized between conservative, centrist forces who wish to maintain old colonial institutions largely intact—especially with respect to social status and privilege, plus predominance of the Catholic church—and liberal, federalist forces who feel the break with the mother country should also usher in a loosening of institutional structures. Both sides are diametrically opposed: Conservatives argue for a return to constitutional monarchy and hierarchical order to avoid the weakness and anarchy of republican rule, whereas liberals insist upon ever greater reforms to strengthen Mexicans' participation in their national affairs.

The liberal congress rewriting Mexico's constitution uncovers these fissures with its very first pronouncement; on 23 November 49-year-old Justice Minister Benito Juárez (former political prisoner and exile) abolishes separate tribunals for members of the military and clergy. Conservative uprisings quickly follow under the cry *"¡Religión y fueros!"* ("Religion and privileges!"), the one in Puebla early next year proving especially tenacious. The official new constitution, or *Reforma,* is unveiled on 5 February 1857, setting off an even greater wave of resentment from conservative elements. General Comonfort—interim president after Alvarez's resignation—at first refuses to even accept office as president under its aegis.

17 DECEMBER 1857. Brig. Gen. Félix María Zuloaga—now one of Comonfort's protégés (*see* 12 July 1854 under Ayutla Revolution)—leads a mutiny by the Mexico City garrison and proclaims the so-called Tacubaya Plan, whereby the liberal constitution is voided, Comonfort recognized as president, and a new congress convened to draft a more moderate document.

The president accepts these conditions two days later, and Justice Minister Juárez—legally next in the line of succession to the presidency—is jailed.

11 JANUARY 1858. After three weeks of confused indecision, conservative Gen. José de la Parra mutinies against Comonfort's rule with the Tacubaya garrison. After a brief spate of fighting around Mexico City's *ciudadela* (citadel), the president—now out of favor with conservatives and liberals alike—agrees to resign from office, fleeing the capital by 21 January and taking ship from Veracruz to New Orleans on 7 February.

Before departing, Comonfort releases Juárez from prison; he proclaims himself president and travels clandestinely to Guanajuato City to begin organizing liberal resistance to the coup. Meanwhile Zuloaga is proclaimed the rival president in Mexico City on 22 January and abolishes all liberal reforms.

19 JANUARY 1858. Juárez reaches Guanajuato and is recognized as the legitimate president of Mexico by its liberal governor, Manuel Doblado. Soon the states of Querétaro, Michoacán, Colima, Zacatecas, and Aguascalientes concur, followed later by Veracruz, Oaxaca, Nuevo León, and Guerrero.

14 FEBRUARY 1858. Threatened by the approach of 5,400 conservative regulars under Gen. Luis G. Osollo, Juárez transfers his liberal headquarters from Guanajuato to Guadalajara, arriving next day.

10 MARCH 1858. ***Salamanca.*** Hostilities officially erupt when conservative General Osollo—seconded by Brigs. Miguel Miramón, Tomás Mejía, Casanova, and José María Blancarte—leads 5,400 soldiers into battle against a liberal militia throng gathered at Salamanca (Guanajuato) under liberal Gen. Anastasio Parrodi and Brigs. Leandro Valle, Doblado, Mariano Moret, and others. The conservative force emerges victorious by 11 March, forcing the defeated liberals to fall back on Guadalajara.

13 MARCH 1858. Guadalajara's garrison mutinies under Colonel Landa; Juárez and his cabinet are paraded before a firing squad, only to be saved at the last moment by the eloquence of Minister Guillermo Prieto, who persuades the soldiers to lower their weapons and spare their lives.

20 MARCH 1858. Juárez is forced to flee Guadalajara for the Pacific Coast with 90 liberal troopers, as General Parrodi surrenders to the approaching conservative army under Osollo next day.

23 MARCH 1858. Osollo's victorious conservative army occupies Guadalajara without resistance.

11 APRIL 1858. After a close pursuit by conservative riders, Juárez is able to depart Manzanillo (Colima) aboard the American steamer *John L. Stephens,* accompanied by four cabinet ministers.

17 APRIL 1858. The 36-year-old conservative Brigadier General Miramón wins a victory over a liberal concentration at Carretas Pass (near Ahualulco de los Pinos, San Luis Potosí) under 36-year-old Gen. Juan Zuazua, Brig. Gen. José Silvestre Aramberri, and Col. Francisco Naranjo.

27 APRIL 1858. While Miramón is distracted elsewhere, liberal General Zuazua captures the conservative garrison holding the city of Zacatecas.

LATE APRIL 1858. ***First Siege of Guadalajara.*** Bespectacled General Degollado and Pedro Ogazón Rubio arrive with the 1st Liberal Division to besiege Guadalajara, which is defended by conservative Generals Casanova and Blancarte. The operation lasts until 13 June, when the attackers are obliged to raise their siege.

4 MAY 1858. After passing through Panama, Havana, and New Orleans, Juárez and his fugitive liberal cabinet reach Veracruz aboard the American steamer *Tennessee* to be greeted and installed in office by Gov. Manuel Gutiérrez Zamora.

18 JUNE 1858. Following the death of General Osollo from typhoid in San Luis Potosí, Miramón—who is at Guadalajara—and his 38-year-old rival, Leonardo Márquez Araujo (also at San Luis Potosí), vie to succeed as commander in chief of the conservatives' main *Ejército del Norte* (Northern Army). Their respective strategies are to drive off Degollado's forces, which are threatening Guadalajara; defeat the liberal army advancing south from Nuevo León and Coahuila under Gen. Santiago Vidaurri; then proceed southeast to expel Juárez's government from Veracruz.

30 JUNE 1858. Vidaurri's liberal subordinate, Zuazua, drives Márquez's conservative garrison out of the city of San Luis Potosí and occupies it.

2 JULY 1858. ***Atenquique.*** Liberal Generals Degollado, Miguel Blanco, and Valle are overtaken by conservative Generals Miramón, Francisco Vélez, and Ruelas advancing south from Sayula and fight a heavy but indecisive battle at the bottom of Atenquique Ravine (near modern-day Ciudad Guzmán, Jalisco).

The very next day other liberal forces establish a renewed siege around Guadalajara, which they maintain until compelled to lift it on 21 July—despite having fought in as far as the Hospicio—when Miramón returns from his southern foray.

21 SEPTEMBER 1858. ***Second Siege of Guadalajara.*** When Miramón is obliged to forsake the state of Jalisco in order to bolster Márquez's hard-pressed conservative forces in central Mexico, liberal General Degollado is able to defeat Casanova at Cuevitas (near Techaluta); six days later he begins to again besiege Guadalajara, seconded by Ogazón, Núñez, Sánchez Román, and Antonio Corona.

After repeated liberal assaults the conservative garrison commander, Blancarte, capitulates on 28 October, the victors entering next day amid great disorder (during which Blancarte and numerous other conservatives are executed without trial). The ensuing occupation lasts two months before the liberals evacuate.

29 SEPTEMBER 1858. ***Ahualulco de los Pinos.*** In central Mexico, conservative Generals Miramón, Márquez, Mejía, and Cobos defeat the entrenched liberal forces of Generals Vidaurri, Zuazua, Aramberri, and Naranjo at Ahualulco de los Pinos (near the capital of San Luis Potosí). Márquez leads a flanking maneuver that shakes the liberal line; Miramón finishes them off with a charge against the center. The victory greatly elevates Miramón's prestige at Márquez's expense, but the conservative army is so bankrupt that it cannot march to Guadalajara's relief.

26 OCTOBER 1858. The conservative garrison within Villahermosa de Tabasco is besieged by liberal forces out of Tabasco and Chiapas, surrendering on 7 November.

OCTOBER 1858. Liberal General Blanco leads a small army from Morelia through the Valley of Toluca to assault the very outskirts of Mexico City itself. The 25-year-old Brig. Gen. Leandro Valle fights in as far as San Antonio Abad before being wounded and replaced by Brig. Gen. José Justo Alvarez. The liberal attackers are beaten off and retreat to Michoacán.

8 DECEMBER 1858. ***Jalisco Counteroffensive.*** In a series of encounters on the banks of the Santiago River (Jalisco)—from Puente Grande near Tolotlán as far as Atequiza—conservative Generals Miramón, Márquez, and Cobos defeat liberal Generals Degollado, Ogazón, and Contreras Medellín, the final battle occurring on 14 December at San Miguel Ranch (3 miles from Poncitlán), which allows the conservative troops to reoccupy Guadalajara this same day. On 20 December Miramón again defeats Degollado in a skirmish at San Joaquín Ranch (15 miles outside the state line of Colima), hastening their retirement by 26 December.

20 DECEMBER 1858. Gen. Miguel María Echegaray revolts at Ayotla (state of Mexico), seconded three days later in the capital by Manuel Robles Pezuela, who deposes conservative President Zuloaga. Thus, both commanders briefly control Mexico City, during which time they issue the so-called *Plan de Navidad* (Christmas Plan) in hopes of ending the civil war.

Instead, they must submit because of lack of support, and the conservative presidency is offered to the victorious Miramón in Jalisco by early January 1859; he refuses. Therefore, the now thoroughly discredited Zuloaga is reinstalled but resigns on 31 January in favor of Miramón, who reaches Mexico City by 2 February and finally accepts this office.

10 JANUARY 1859. An ammunition dump in Guadalajara explodes, causing extensive damage to the municipal palace.

16 FEBRUARY 1859. ***First Siege of Veracruz.*** Miramón departs Mexico City at the head of his army, marching down from the central highlands to besiege Juárez's liberal government within Veracruz. Slowed by numerous guerrilla attacks, the conservatives do not throw up siege works until 17 March. Moreover, the operation is soon interrupted by news that Degollado is driving on Mexico City with a large liberal army, prompting Miramón to withdraw his forces by the end of the month.

18 FEBRUARY 1859. Liberal General Degollado captures the conservative garrison at León (Guanajuato).

1 MARCH 1859. Degollado seizes the city of Guanajuato, advancing through Querétaro for Mexico City.

At Calamanda Hacienda (south of the city of Querétaro), one of his liberal divisions, under Gen. José María Arteaga, chances upon conservative General Mejía's lancer corps and is badly cut up. Mejía and Callejo are hastening for the capital to bolster its conservative garrison before the liberals can arrive.

22 MARCH 1859. ***Tacubaya.*** Degollado's 6,000-plus liberal troops appear outside Mexico City, occupying the suburbs of Tacubaya and Chapultepec. However, General Corona's 4,000 defenders are well entrenched and heartened by news that Márquez is hastening to their relief. Degollado defers attacking until 2 April, when he probes the Tlaxpana and San Cosme defenses without success.

A few days later Márquez arrives with his conservative relief column, and on 10 April he goes over to the offensive. This day and the next Degollado's liberals suffer a crushing defeat around Tacubaya, which sends their survivors streaming southwest to Jalisco and Michoacán. Márquez mars the triumph by ordering every liberal captive executed—including medical personnel and civilians—thus earning the sobriquet "Tiger of Tacubaya."

After the battle Miramón belatedly regains the Valley of Mexico, annoyed to discover that his old rival Márquez has won the accolades for defeating Degollado.

1 APRIL 1859. Immediately after Miramón lifts his siege of Veracruz the American representative, Robert H. MacLane, reaches the port; five days later he recognizes the legitimacy of Juárez's government. This provokes violent criticism from conservatives, who know Washington will expect territorial and commercial concessions in exchange for assistance.

12 JULY 1859. In order to finance American aid and maintain his government, Juárez issues the first Leyes de Reforma (Reform Laws) at Veracruz, confiscating most church properties. Conservatives vehemently oppose these measures.

SEPTEMBER 1859. At San Leonel (Nayarit), the 31-year-old conservative brigand Manuel Lozada—born Manuel García González—disperses a liberal cavalry troop under Colonel Valenzuela.

2 NOVEMBER 1859. After a week of skirmishing Lozada assaults Tepic.

13 NOVEMBER 1859. ***Estancia de Vacas.*** After meeting at Calera Hacienda to attempt to resolve their differences, Miramón attacks liberal Generals Degollado, Arteaga, and Doblado's 7,000 troops at Estancia de Vacas Ranch (six miles outside the city of Querétaro). At first the battle goes well for the liberals, but Degollado is eventually obliged to retreat to prearranged defenses, at which point Miramón launches a devastating assault that collapses the liberal morale. His enemies stream off in defeat, leaving Miramón master of the field. Shortly thereafter he marches into Guadalajara, arresting his rival Márquez on a charge of theft and sending him prisoner to Mexico City.

14 DECEMBER 1859. MacLane signs a treaty with Juárez's foreign minister, Melchor Ocampo, at Veracruz, whereby the United States will provide the liberal government with $4 million in exchange for free passage for rail lines across both the Isthmus of Tehuantepec and northwestern Mexico to be guarded by American troops. (Conservatives are outraged, but the MacLane-Ocampo Treaty eventually fails to win ratification in the U.S. Senate.)

24 DECEMBER 1859. After a long pursuit, during which Miramón has defeated liberal General Ogazón at Beltrán (Jalisco), the conservative general also beats Juan Rocha at Tonila (also called Albarrada, Colima).

8 FEBRUARY 1860. ***Second Siege of Veracruz.*** Miramón marches out of Mexico City with a large army to proceed down to the Gulf Coast and once more besiege Juárez within Veracruz. Despite repeated guerrilla raids, the conservative general establishes his headquarters at Antón Lizardo (southeast of his objective) by 6 March, when secret help appears: thanks to covert financing from the Spanish government, conservative Rear Adm. Tomás Marín has been able to hire the vessels *General Miramón* and *Marqués de la Habana* at Havana to blockade Veracruz in support of Miramón's army.

However, when the ships sail menacingly past the liberals' island fortress of San Juan de Ulúa without displaying any ensign, the representatives of the Juárez government declare them to be piratical craft, thus subjecting them to capture by any vessel, domestic or foreign. Availing himself of this excuse, Commander Turner of the USS *Saratoga*—stationed in Veracruz as part of Washington's ongoing support for the liberal regime against French, Spanish, and British backing of the conservative cause—immediately sorties and captures both.

In addition to depriving Miramón of his blockaders, this action costs the conservatives two mortars and 1,000 shells (plus 4,000 rifles) that are being transported from Cuba, all winding up in Juárez's hands.

On 15 March Miramón begins his bombardment of Veracruz but soon runs out of heavy ammunition and is compelled to withdraw to Mexico City six days later.

7 APRIL 1860. Liberal "colonel"—and former brigand—Antonio Rojas defeats Lozada at Barranca Blanca (Jalisco).

APRIL 1860. Sidelined conservative President Zuloaga issues a pamphlet in Mexico City criticizing the performance of Miramón, who arrests his predecessor and takes him on his subsequent campaign northwest in May to "show him how the presidency is won."

24 MAY 1860. Liberal Gen. José López Uraga arrives before Guadalajara with 8,000 followers and calls on its conservative garrison commander—French-born veteran Adrián Woll—to surrender. He refuses, so López Uraga makes an assault, during which he is wounded and captured. The bespectacled, 31-year-old Brig. Gen. Ignacio Zaragoza assumes overall command and withdraws upon news of Miramón's approach with the main conservative army.

8 JUNE 1860. Having relieved Guadalajara, Miramón sorties with 6,000 soldiers in pursuit of Zaragoza, Valle, Plácido Vega, Rojas, and Col. Ramón Corona's 5,000 liberals. The latter dig in along Zapotlán Crest (between Ciudad Guzmán and Sayula, Jalisco), which the conservative general hesitates to assault.

15 JUNE 1860. A 38-year-old self-taught liberal general and governor, Jesús González Ortega, leads 10,000 followers in a victory over Silverio Ramírez's 3,000-man army at Peñuelas Hacienda (Aguascalientes) while the latter is marching southwest toward Guadalajara to join forces with Miramón.

This victory allows the liberals to seize control of this crucial state, prompting the conservative commander in chief to leave a 5,000-man garrison in Guadalajara on 27 June under Gen. Severo del Castillo, then hasten northeast to Lagos de Moreno (Jalisco) by 30 June to begin concentrating his forces and bar the road into Mexico City.

JULY 1860. Miramón shifts his conservative army southeast from Lagos into León (Guanajuato) at news of the approach of a liberal division under Zaragoza from his southwestern flank to reinforce González Ortega. The two liberal contingents meet at vacated Lagos and continue to press Miramón back.

10 AUGUST 1860. ***Silao.*** Now in full-blown retreat southeast from León toward Querétaro before a 10,000-man liberal buildup under Gens. González Ortega, Zaragoza, Doblado, and Felipe Berriozábal, Miramón's demoralized conservative army is overtaken at Silao (Guanajuato) and brought to battle. In a sharp three-hour engagement Mejía's conservative lancers are dispersed by Carbajal's cavalry, after which Miramón's infantry is pulverized.

Conservative morale collapses, leading to a wholesale flight toward Querétaro, during which all the artillery and baggage trains are abandoned. Miramón reaches safety with a handful of riders; González Ortega treats his prisoners magnanimously, releasing most. Zuloaga, still accompanying Miramón as a captive, escapes on 13 August and regains the capital, attempting to restore himself to office as president, only to fail because of lack of support. The liberal commander reverses his army from in front of Querétaro and marches west—at Degollado's order—to subdue Guadalajara before commencing the final push to Mexico City.

22 SEPTEMBER 1860. ***Fall of Guadalajara.*** González Ortega's liberal army arrives to besiege the garrison within the conservative stronghold of Guadalajara after a weary, rain-sodden march through central Mexico. Four days later he is joined at San Pedro Tlaquepaque by Ogazón's corps, bringing total strength to 20,000 men and 125 field pieces, which open fire by 27 September. The 5,000 defenders under Severo del Castillo put up a stout resistance until 29 October, when the populace is allowed to evacuate.

The last conservative hope for relief is extinguished when Márquez is defeated at nearby Zapotlanejo on 1 November, surrendering his 3,000 men and 18 cannons to the encircling army. Del Castillo therefore capitulates to González Ortega's subordinate Zaragoza two days later on generous terms (the liberal commander in chief having been ill throughout most of the operation).

8 DECEMBER 1860. Miramón surprises Degollado and Berriozábal at Toluca (state of Mexico), capturing both liberal generals.

21 DECEMBER 1860. ***Calpulalpan.*** All liberal armies close in on Mexico City for a final confrontation. Miramón—who is so desperately short of cash that his chief of police, Lagarde, breaks into the British legation and commandeers 630,000 pesos over the objections of Ambassador Barton—prepares to give battle at San Miguel Calpulalpan on the outskirts of the capital. Liberal Brigadier Generals Valle and Alvarez suggest a tactic to González Ortega on the very eve of battle, whereby

Miramón's main thrust will be drawn out by retreating liberal lines, only to then be engulfed by flanking attacks, thereby allowing the liberals' superior numbers to tell. The commander in chief approves, and next day (22 December) the conservatives are utterly routed.

A few diehards such as Márquez, Cobos, and Mejía withdraw to the hills to continue the struggle, but the conservative cause is essentially lost. Miramón pauses in Mexico City only long enough to release his prisoner, Berriozábal, and leave him in command before being secretly whisked down to Veracruz through the intervention of the French ambassador, Dubois de Saligny; the conservative general sets sail for Europe aboard a Spanish warship in January 1861.

25 DECEMBER 1860. González Ortega's army makes a triumphant entry into Mexico City.

5 JANUARY 1861. Juárez departs Veracruz and, six days later, officially assumes his duties as president in Mexico City, thus marking an end to the War of the Reform (also known as the Three Years War). Although Mexico's conservatives have been temporarily subdued, they quickly make a resurgence with foreign support (*see* French Intervention in Mexico).

A particular case in point is offered by the brigand Lozada, who early in 1861 is cornered in Alica Pass (Nayarit) by 3,000 liberal troops converging from three directions under Colonels Rojas, Corona, and Anacleto Herrera y Cairo. They disperse Lozada's followers after nine days' hard fighting, which earns Lozada the nickname Tigre de Alica. By May, however, he is resuming his depredations, capturing both Tepic and San Pedro Lagunillas before being checked by Ogazón.

American Civil War (1861–1865)

In the United States, as in other republics throughout the New World, the evolution from colonial monarchy to electoral democracy gradually comes to include a contest between those groups holding that each individual state is virtually independent within a loose confederation and those feeling that the federal government—representing the entire Union—must be paramount over any single member or region. This issue specifically impinges on the North's desire to enact antislavery measures into federal law (their superior population giving them a majority in Washington), against deep-seated opposition from the agriculture-based interests of the South.

By the late 1850s feelings are running so high that the dispute over whether the new Kansas territory should be admitted into the Union as a "free" or "slave" state precipitates cross-border raids between rival factions. On the night of 16 October 1859, the fanatical abolitionist John Brown further escalates tensions by seizing the arsenal at Harpers Ferry (Virginia) with 18 followers in hopes of fomenting a slave uprising. Instead he is overpowered two days later by a contingent of marines under Col. Robert E. Lee and hanged after a month-long trial.

Passions continue to build until armed secessionist units surround the Federal garrison at Fort Sumter—a pentagonal island fortress guarding the sea entrance into Charleston, South Carolina—during the winter of 1860–1861, threatening to occupy it in the name of the breakaway "Confederate States of America": Alabama, Florida, Georgia, Louisiana, Mississippi, South Carolina, and Texas (soon joined by Arkansas, North Carolina, Tennessee, and Virginia). When the newly inaugurated administration of Pres. Abraham Lincoln proposes to resupply this isolated outpost the following spring, the encircling Southerners react belligerently.

Because of the overall wealth and manufacturing might of the nation, as well as the hosts of eager volunteers willing to fight for their beliefs on native soil, the resultant hostilities will be conducted on a scale never before witnessed in the Americas. Within the first year the Federal government raises and arms 600,000 regulars and militia from its population of 23 million, the Confederates 250,000 from their 9 million (of which 3.5 million are slaves).

7 APRIL 1861. All intercourse between Fort Sumter and Charleston (South Carolina) is stopped by order of Gen. P. G. T. Beauregard. Next day Washington informs South Carolina authorities that provisions will be sent to the beleaguered outpost, by force if necessary.

11 APRIL 1861. United States troops are stationed in Washington as Confederate commissioners depart. This evening General Beauregard demands the surrender of Fort Sumter, which Maj. Robert Anderson refuses.

12 APRIL 1861. ***Fort Sumter.*** Confederate batteries at Fort Moultrie open fire on Fort Sumter at 4:00 A.M., the Union artillery not replying until three hours later. After enduring 30 hours of bombardment, Anderson's 111-man garrison surrenders on the afternoon of 13 April, being allowed to evacuate

with their sidearms and accouterments for New York next day.

15 APRIL 1861. Lincoln calls for troops to help put down the secessionist movement, being refused by North Carolina, Kentucky, Virginia, and Tennessee. Fort Macon (North Carolina) is also occupied by Confederate troops.

17 APRIL 1861. Virginia secedes from the Union, Jefferson Davis issuing commissions to Confederate privateers.

18 APRIL 1861. The U.S. arsenal at Harpers Ferry (Virginia) is destroyed by Lieutenant Jones to prevent it from falling into Confederate hands.

19 APRIL 1861. Lincoln orders a U.S. naval blockade of southern ports and calls for the recruitment of 82,000 long-term Union servicemen. Also today the 6th Massachusetts Volunteers are attacked by a mob while passing through Baltimore, three soldiers and 11 civilians being killed.

Unidentified child soldier

20 APRIL 1861. Several bridges on the Northern Pennsylvania Railroad are destroyed by Maryland Confederates to prevent the passage of troops to Washington. Also today the Gosport Navy Yard (Norfolk, Virginia) is ordered destroyed and several vessels scuttled by 68-year-old Commo. Charles S. McCauley to prevent their falling into Confederate hands (only the USS *Cumberland* being towed out; the burned remains of the screw frigate *Merrimack* are left behind)—this despite the last-minute arrival of 1,000 Marine reinforcements under Commo. Hiram Paulding. Also, the arsenal at Liberty (Missouri) is seized by Confederates.

21 APRIL 1861. Starting at 4:20 A.M. the Norfolk Navy Yard is partially destroyed by U.S. Navy personnel before they evacuate aboard the Federal steam sloop *Pawnee*. The Confederates occupy the base, which is operating again within a few weeks.

22 APRIL 1861. The U.S. arsenal at Fayetteville (North Carolina) is seized by Confederate troops.

23 APRIL 1861. Fort Smith (Arkansas) is seized by Confederates as are the U.S. officers at San Antonio (Texas). Also today Maj. Gen. Robert E. Lee is offered command of the Confederate forces in Virginia.

25 APRIL 1861. At Saluria (Texas), Major Sibley surrenders 420 U.S. troops to Confederate Col. Earl Van Dorn.

26 APRIL 1861. Maj. Gen. Joseph E. Johnston is given command of the defense of Richmond (Virginia), which becomes the Confederate capital on 6 May.

4 MAY 1861. U.S. ordnance stores are seized at Kansas City (Missouri).

10 MAY 1861. Some 800 Confederates surrender to Capt. Nathaniel Lyon at St. Louis (Missouri).

11 MAY 1861. The U.S. steamer *Niagara* arrives to blockade Charleston (South Carolina).

13 MAY 1861. Gen. George B. McClellan is given command of the Department of Ohio; Baltimore is reoccupied by U.S. troops.

24 MAY 1861. Some 13,000 Union troops cross the Potomac into Virginia, occupying Alexandria and Ar-

lington Heights to help secure Washington. Next day they destroy seven bridges and miles of railroad line between Alexandria and Leesburg.

26 MAY 1861. The U.S. sloop *Brooklyn* arrives to blockade New Orleans.

28 MAY 1861. Brig. Gen. Irwin McDowell assumes command of the Department of Northeastern Virginia.

31 MAY 1861. The Union steamers *Freeborn* and *Anacosta* bombard the Confederate batteries at Aquia Creek (Virginia).

2 JUNE 1861. Beauregard assumes command of the Confederate forces at Manassas Junction (Virginia).

4 JUNE 1861. The brig USS *Perry* captures the Confederate privateer *Savannah,* carrying it to New York 11 days later.

15 JUNE 1861. The Confederates under Johnston—threatened by Patterson's approach—evacuate Harpers Ferry, transferring its armory machinery to Richmond.

17 JUNE 1861. The Wheeling Convention unanimously declares West Virginia independent from the Confederate state of Virginia, temporarily assuming the name Kanawha.

20 JUNE 1861. McClellan personally assumes command of the Union army in West Virginia.

29 JUNE 1861. A Confederate column makes a dash toward Harpers Ferry, destroying several boats and its railway bridge.

8 JULY 1861. Confederate Brig. Gen. Henry H. Sibley is ordered to Texas to expel the Union forces in neighboring New Mexico. He eventually reaches Santa Fe in March 1862, only to be maneuvered by Edward R. S. Canby into a disastrous retreat that ends all Confederate designs on the New Mexico Territory.

11–13 JULY 1861. After crossing the Ohio River, McClellan defeats the small army sent across the Alleghenies to restore Confederate rule at Rich Mountain and Carrick's Ford (West Virginia).

16 JULY 1861. Union General McDowell advances from Alexandria with approximately 30,000 troops to drive Beauregard's 20,000 behind the Rappahannock.

21 JULY 1861. ***Bull Run (First Battle).*** After skirmishing three days previously at Blackburn's Ford (Virginia) with Beauregard, McDowell's Union army prepares to smash the Confederate defensive line at Bull Run by a direct frontal assault on its stone bridge with one division while two others circle right to cross at Sudley Ford, two miles farther northwest. On the evening of 20 July, however, General Johnston arrives with Confederate reinforcements and prepares a surprise counterattack.

The Federal troops strike first at 6:00 A.M. next day, storming the stone bridge, although their flanking movement at Sudley develops very slowly. Both armies being untried, many Confederates abandon Matthews Hill in confusion when the Union right finally attacks at 9:30 A.M. but are steadied by the sight of Gen. Thomas J. Jackson's brigade, which is standing "like a stone wall" atop neighboring Henry House Hill.

After a day of confused fighting the 18,500 Union troops break and retreat, having suffered 2,900 casualties (compared with 2,000 among the 18,000 Confederates). Their retirement turns into panic-stricken flight to the far side of the Potomac, although the Confederates are too exhausted and disorganized to pursue—instead choosing to establish themselves at Centreville.

22 JULY 1861. The three-month terms of the earliest Union volunteers come due, prompting many to return home.

25 JULY 1861. Gen. John Charles Frémont is appointed to command the Union's Western Department, headquartered at St. Louis.

26 JULY 1861. Fort Fillmore (New Mexico) is surrendered to Confederate forces by Major Lynde.

7 AUGUST 1861. Hampton (Virginia) is burned by Confederate forces.

8 AUGUST 1861. The 39-year-old Brig. Gen. Ulysses Simpson Grant assumes command of the Union district at Ironton (Missouri).

10 AUGUST 1861. ***Wilson's Creek.*** After chasing Missouri's Confederate Gov. Claiborne Jackson out of office, Union General Lyon advances with 5,800 troops and, ten miles from Springfield, confronts 12,000 Confederates drawn up at Wilson's Creek under Gen. Sterling "Pap" Price and the Mexican War veteran Ben McCulloch (*see* 20 February 1847). Lyon's German-born subordinate, Brig. Gen. Franz Sigel,

leads three volunteer St. Louis regiments in a flanking maneuver around the Federal left, which catch the Confederates from the rear but fail to break their line. Sigel's detachment is then repelled by a counterattack, Lyon is slain, and the main Union body is defeated and obliged to retreat toward Rolla.

14 AUGUST 1861. Frémont declares martial law at St. Louis.

15 AUGUST 1861. Jefferson Davis orders all Northern men to leave the South within 40 days. Next day Lincoln officially proclaims all the seceding states to be in a state of insurrection, forbidding all intercourse with them.

17 AUGUST 1861. Gen. John E. Wool assumes command at Fortress Monroe (tip of Yorktown Peninsula, Virginia).

20 AUGUST 1861. McClellan assumes command of the Army of the Potomac.

27 AUGUST 1861. Seven Union warships and two transports under Commo. Silas H. Stringham drop anchor off Hatteras Inlet (North Carolina), bombarding Forts Hatteras and Clark next dawn and prompting their garrisons to evacuate, thereby allowing 900 Union soldiers ashore under Gen. Benjamin F. Butler to occupy the coastal keeps.

30 AUGUST 1861. Frémont issues an emancipation proclamation, which is modified by Lincoln 12 days later.

1 SEPTEMBER 1861. Grant assumes command in southern Missouri.

2 SEPTEMBER 1861. The U.S. Navy dry dock at Pensacola is destroyed.

4 SEPTEMBER 1861. Kentucky—until now a neutral state—is invaded by Confederate troops under Gen. (and bishop) Leonidas Polk, who begins constructing fortifications at Hickman, Chalk Cliffs, and Columbus.

6 SEPTEMBER 1861. To counter Polk's incursion, Paducah and Smithland (Kentucky) are occupied by Union troops under Grant.

14 SEPTEMBER 1861. A descent is made on the Pensacola Navy Yard by U.S. gunboats.

18 SEPTEMBER 1861. Bowling Green (Kentucky) is occupied by Confederate forces under newly appointed Gen. Albert S. Johnston.

20 SEPTEMBER 1861. Confederate Governor Price captures Lexington, although he is soon forced to retreat to Springfield by the approach of 40,000 Union troops under Frémont.

7 OCTOBER 1861. The Confederate ironclad *Virginia*—built atop the charred hull of the screw frigate *Merrimack*—makes its first appearance off Fortress Monroe (Hampton Roads, Virginia).

8 OCTOBER 1861. The 41-year-old Brig. Gen. William Tecumseh Sherman supersedes Gen. Robert Anderson in command of the Department of the Cumberland.

11 OCTOBER 1861. The Confederate steamer *Theodore* escapes from Charleston (South Carolina), bearing diplomatic commissioners James M. Mason and John Slidell.

21 OCTOBER 1861. After four Federal regiments under Col. Edward D. Baker have been ferried across the Potomac to make a reconnaissance in strength toward Leesburg (Virginia), they are confronted on the fringe of a wood atop Balls Bluff by a superior Confederate force and driven back with the loss of 900 Union dead, wounded, or captured—more than half their numbers.

29 OCTOBER 1861. ***Port Royal.*** Commo. Samuel F. Du Pont sets sail from Fortress Monroe with 30 warships escorting 50 transports bearing 13,000 troops under Gen. Thomas W. Sherman to attempt to capture Port Royal Sound (South Carolina) as an advance Union naval base. Although his fleet is scattered by a storm, Du Pont's flagship *Wabash* leads two columns of 14 warships past Fort Beauregard (on northernmost St. Helena Island) at 9:00 A.M. on 7 November, shelling its batteries. He reverses course two miles into the sound to visit a like treatment on Fort Walker, on Hilton Head Island farther south. By nightfall both Confederate garrisons have evacuated, leaving the strongholds to be occupied and held by Union troops until the end of the war.

1 NOVEMBER 1861. Winfield Scott resigns as commander in chief of all Union forces, being replaced by McClellan.

Confederate cavalry and soldiers are pictured in this undated lithograph.

2 NOVEMBER 1861. Gen. David Hunter supersedes Frémont in command of the Department of the West.

7 NOVEMBER 1861. Grant descends the Missouri River with 3,000 men to attack Confederate General Polk's positions at Belmont (15 miles downstream from Cairo, Illinois), eventually being obliged to reembark his troops and withdraw after incurring more than 400 casualties.

15 NOVEMBER 1861. The screw sloop USS *San Jacinto* of Capt. Charles Wilkes (a former Antarctic explorer) arrives at Fortress Monroe, having removed the Confederate commissioners Mason and Slidell from the English mail steamer *Trent.* Britain protests the boarding of its neutral vessel.

20 NOVEMBER 1861. McClellan holds a review with 70,000 Union troops near Washington.

4 DECEMBER 1861. General Henry W. Halleck issues a series of punitive measures at St. Louis aimed at secessionist supporters.

18 DECEMBER 1861. Union Gen. John Pope captures 1,300 Confederates, a number of horses and wagons, plus 1,000 firearms at Milford (Missouri).

27 DECEMBER 1861. Having been illegally detained, Confederate commissioners Mason and Slidell are surrendered to the British ambassador, leaving Fort Warren for England five days later aboard the British steamer *Rinaldo.*

17 JANUARY 1862. ***Mill Springs.*** After pushing through the Cumberland Gap into Kentucky, Gen. Felix Zollicoffer's slightly less than 4,000 Confederates are attacked at Mill Springs—otherwise known as Logan's Crossroads, near Somerset—by a similar-size Union army moving out of Lebanon under 45-year-old Gen. George Henry Thomas. In the confusion Zollicoffer blunders into the Federal line and is shot, after which his army disintegrates and flees, leaving behind 11 field guns, their supply train, plus more than 1,000 horses and mules.

6 FEBRUARY 1862. ***Fort Henry.*** After 15,000 Union troops under Grant disembark two miles below Confederate Fort Henry on the Tennessee River and become bogged down in its marshlands, Commo. Andrew H. Foote bombards the flooded fort with his four Union "turtles"—flat-bottomed, stern-wheeled ironclads—and compels the defenders to evacuate for nearby Fort Donelson an hour later. The capture of Fort Henry also prompts Johnston to abandon Bowling Green with half his 24,000-man army for Nashville; he directs the other half to Fort Donelson.

8 FEBRUARY 1862. ***Roanoke Island.*** Union Gen. Ambrose E. Burnside takes six Confederate forts and 2,500 prisoners on Roanoke Island (North Carolina) and destroys all their gunboats except two vessels.

13 FEBRUARY 1862. Brig. Gen. Samuel L. Curtis takes possession of Springfield (Missouri).

14 FEBRUARY 1862. ***Fort Donelson.*** After occupying Fort Henry, Grant's army has marched ten miles across difficult terrain to invest 17,000–18,000 Confederates under Brig. Gens. Gideon Pillow and John B. Floyd inside Fort Donelson at Dover (Tennessee). During the afternoon of 14 February, Foote appears on the Cumberland River with a convoy of Union reinforcements and attempts to bombard this Confederate stronghold—located on a bluff 150 feet high—with four of his stern-wheel ironclads. This attack is repelled and Foote is compelled to retire after being wounded, with two of his vessels disabled and the others damaged.

Grant therefore institutes a siege with his 27,000 troops and next morning contains an attempted breakout, driving the defenders back into their last line of trenches. Pillow, Floyd, and the Confederate cavalry commander, Nathan Bedford Forrest, escape on the night of 15–16 February with a few of their men, leaving Brig. Gen. Simon Bolivar Buckner to request terms from the Union commander. The latter calls for "immediate and unconditional surrender"—thus earning the nickname "Unconditional Surrender" Grant throughout the North—and accepts the capitulation of its remaining 15,000 Confederates. The fort's capture prompts Johnston to abandon Nashville farther downriver.

16 FEBRUARY 1862. The Tennessee ironworks (near Dover) are destroyed by the Union gunboat *St. Louis.*

17 FEBRUARY 1862. Two regiments of Confederate Tennesseans, unaware of the capture of Fort Donelson, approach it to reinforce Floyd and Pillow, only to be captured.

22 FEBRUARY 1862. Jefferson Davis is officially inaugurated as Confederate president with Alexander Stephens as vice president.

24 FEBRUARY 1862. Nashville is occupied by Union troops under Gen. Don Carlos Buell.

5 MARCH 1862. Beauregard assumes command of the Confederate Army of the Mississippi three days after evacuating Columbus (Kentucky) and removing its armament to New Madrid and Island No. 10.

7–8 MARCH 1862. Confederate Generals Van Dorn and Price attack Curtis at Pea Ridge (Elk Horn, Arkansas), only to be routed.

8 MARCH 1862. ***Hampton Roads.*** At 12:45 P.M., after lengthy trials, the Confederate ironclad *Virginia* (former USS *Merrimack* or *Merrimac*) stands out of Norfolk under Capt. Franklin Buchanan to attack the Union naval squadron stationed in nearby Hampton Roads. Guns aboard the Union vessels are powerless to penetrate the vessel's low, sloped, greased plating, which is two inches thick. *Virginia* therefore plows through a hail of fire to ram the 24-gun sloop USS *Cumberland,* sending it to the bottom, then pounds 50-gun frigate USS *Congress* into submission, leaving it ablaze when the ironclad retires into Norfolk for the night.

At 7:00 A.M. next day *Virginia* returns to finish its panic-stricken prey, this time commanded by Lt. Catesby ap Roger Jones (nephew of Commo. Thomas ap Catesby Jones; *see* 16 September 1814 and 19 October 1842), because Buchanan has been wounded the day before by a shell fragment in the leg. Upon approaching the grounded steam frigate USS *Minnesota,* however, *Virginia* finds it accompanied by the low-slung, turreted ironclad USS *Monitor* of Capt. John L. Worden, which arrived from New York the previous evening. Designed by the inventor John Ericsson, *Monitor* is faster and more maneuverable than *Virginia,* firing 168-pound solid shots from two 11-inch Dahlgren guns.

Although *Virginia* initially fires on *Minnesota* from a mile away, it cannot close through the shallows and is soon challenged by *Monitor.* The two ironclads pound one another over the next four hours, circling as close as 50 yards before the Confederate vessel finally breaks off action and withdraws behind Sewell's Point (Norfolk). *Monitor's* presence prevents it from any further action.

11 MARCH 1862. McClellan is relieved as commander in chief of all Union armies, although retaining command of the Army of the Potomac.

12 MARCH 1862. Winchester (Virginia) is abandoned by its Confederate garrison and occupied by Union forces.

13 MARCH 1862. Lee is appointed commander in chief of all Confederate armies.

14 MARCH 1862. Union Brigadier Gen. William S. "Old Rosy" Rosencrans assumes command of the Mountain Department.

16 MARCH 1862. Union General Garfield, with 600 Ohio and Kentucky volunteers, surprises a Confederate camp at Pound Gap (Tennessee), destroying it before withdrawing.

17 MARCH 1862. ***Peninsula Campaign.*** The first regiments of McClellan's Army of the Potomac begin embarking at Alexandria (Virginia) for transfer to Fortress Monroe by 2 April; they will launch a drive toward the Confederate capital of Richmond—the long anticipated Peninsula Campaign—two days later.

After investing Yorktown on 5 April McClellan settles down to patiently construct siege works, allowing the outnumbered, ill-equipped Confederate forces throughout the region to regroup. Gen. Joseph Johnston's garrison slips away on 3 May, just as McClellan's batteries are about to open fire, then fights a sharp rearguard action at Williamsburg two days later. McClellan slowly resumes progress toward Richmond, his army now numbering more than 100,000 men in five corps.

By 20 May he reaches the Chickahominy River and splits his army to both banks, waiting to be joined by McDowell (who is being delayed in the Shenandoah Valley by Stonewall Jackson). On 31 May Johnston attacks McClellan's two corps on the right bank of the Chickahominy in the battle known as Seven Pines, but Johnston is severely wounded early on; the Confederate army is obliged to retire next day. Johnston is succeeded by Lee, who on 15 June directs Jackson to march swiftly to join him and crush McClellan before McDowell can intervene.

On 25 June McClellan is only four miles outside Richmond, but next day he is struck full-force by Lee. In the Seven Days' Battle one of his corps on the left bank of the Chickahominy is defeated by 27 June, prompting the Union commander to attempt a flank march south through White Oak Swamp toward the safety of the James River. In order to cover the passage of his trains, McClellan is compelled to stand and fight while the Confederates fall upon his rear and right flank. The critical day is 30 June, when Lee fails to break through the Federal center. After repulsing a final assault at Malvern Hill on 1 July McClellan reaches the James next day and entrenches at Harrison's Landing, refusing to budge despite his superior strength and Lee's

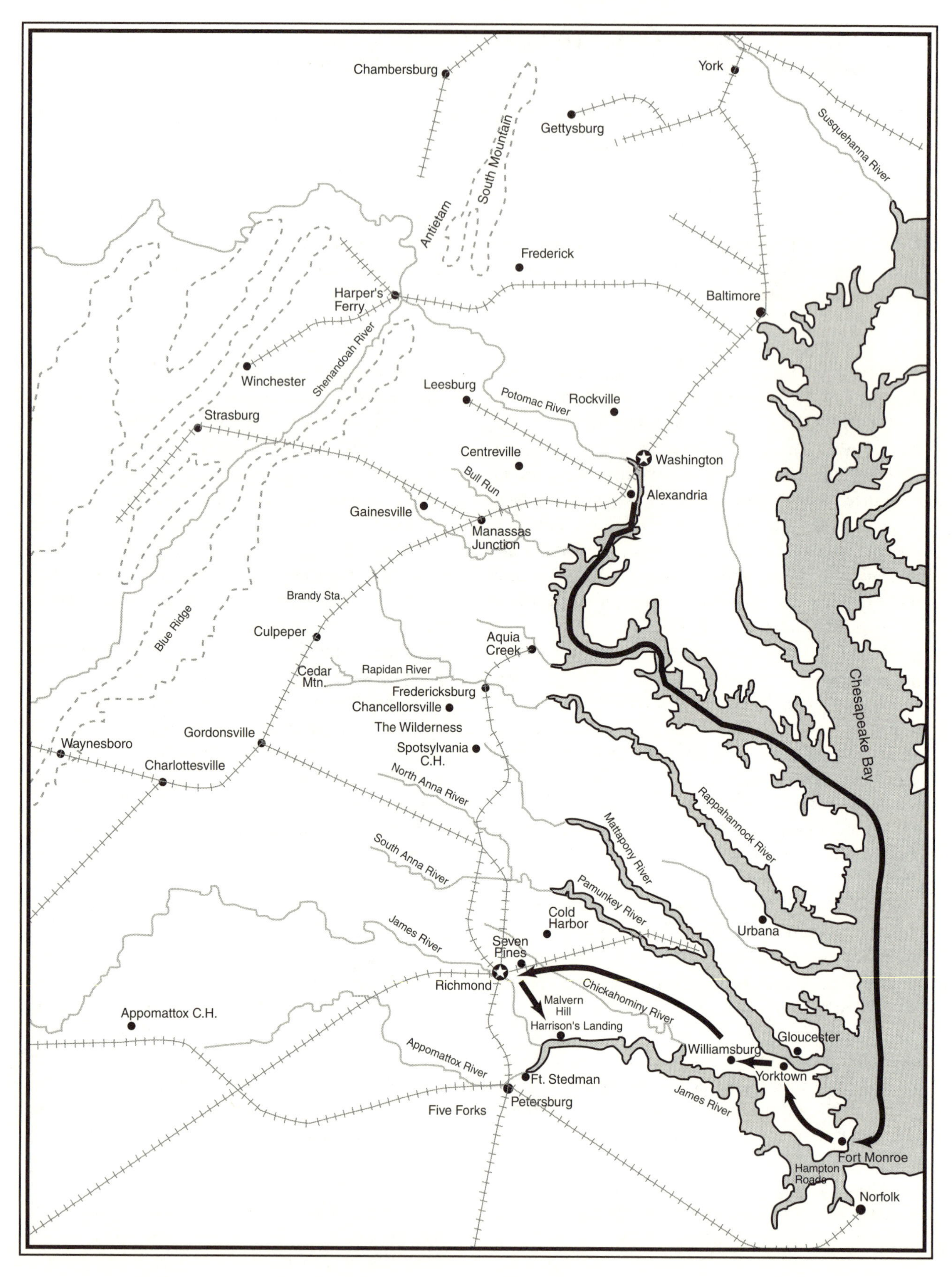

The Peninsula campaign

General Ulysses S. Grant (standing center) poses with members of his staff.

more extensive losses. The Army of the Potomac is eventually evacuated on 16 August, thereby ending the Peninsula Campaign.

6 APRIL 1862. ***Shiloh.*** After confidently ascending the Tennessee River and disembarking at Pittsburgh Landing to await Buell—who is advancing across from Nashville—Grant's 45,000-man Union army is surprised by 40,000 Confederates stealthily approaching out of Corinth (Mississippi) under Albert Johnston and Beauregard.

Their first attack erupts at 6:00 A.M. near Shiloh Church two miles inland, smashing the forward-most Union division under Brig. Gen. Benjamin Prentiss. However, the Confederate attacks become increasingly uncoordinated as they penetrate deeper into Grant's encampment, and Johnston himself is killed assaulting a strongpoint dubbed the Hornet's Nest. By 5:30 P.M. Grant is able to stiffen his shortened lines a few hundred yards from the landing, supported by artillery fire from gunboats offshore.

During the night Grant is reinforced by 25,000 fresh troops from Buell's corps plus a detached division under Gen. Lew Wallace (later the author of *Ben Hur*). At 5:00 A.M. on 7 April, therefore, the Union army goes over to the offensive, driving Beauregard from the field after hard fighting. Each side suffers some 10,000 casualties, taking several weeks to recuperate.

9 APRIL 1862. Jacksonville (Florida) is evacuated by Union forces.

18 APRIL 1862. ***New Orleans.*** Union Commo. David Glasgow Farragut arrives off Louisiana with a squadron of men-of-war (led by the flagship *Hartford*) plus 21 mortar boats under his subordinate David Dixon Porter and a fleet of transports bearing 13,000 soldiers under General Butler to capture New Orleans. Porter's mortar boats—with branches tied in their tops as camouflage—are towed into position below Forts Saint Philip and Jackson and begin dropping a steady rain of 13-inch shells upon the strongholds.

Before sunrise on 24 April Farragut dashes through a gap in the Confederate boom with 17 warships, suffering mostly minor damage despite a ferocious bombardment. His squadron defeats Commodore Mitchell's Confederate ram *Manassas* and some armed steamers before reaching New Orleans 35 miles farther upstream on the morning of 25 April, compelling the city to surrender three days later.

21 APRIL 1862. Pope, after capturing the 7,000-man Confederate garrison on the Missouri River's Island No. 10, joins Halleck and Grant.

9–12 MAY 1862. Confederate forces evacuate Pensacola, destroying its navy yard.

10 MAY 1862. Union forces retake Norfolk, which has been evacuated by the Confederates after destroying the ironclad *Merrimack* and much materiel.

30 MAY 1862. Under pressure from Halleck's slowly advancing Union army, Beauregard evacuates Corinth for Tupelo (Mississippi).

3 JUNE 1862. Confederate forces evacuate Fort Pillow (below Island No. 10) and Memphis.

6 JUNE 1862. Union Commo. Charles H. Davis's ironclads defeat a Confederate flotilla before Memphis, sinking or capturing all but one vessel after a sharp fight and wild pursuit.

18 JUNE 1862. Union troops occupy Cumberland Gap (Tennessee).

11 JULY 1862. Confederate Gen. John Hunt Morgan enters Glasgow (Kentucky).

18 JULY 1862. A band of Confederate raiders assails Newburg (Indiana), causing widespread destruction.

3 AUGUST 1862. Confederate Gen. Jeff Thompson is defeated near Memphis.

9 AUGUST 1862. With the threat against the Confederate capital of Richmond receding as McClellan prepares to evacuate the Peninsula (*see* 17 March 1862), Lee shifts operations against recently promoted Major General Pope's army in northwestern Virginia. The first major clash occurs on 9 August, when Jackson's corps strikes Union Maj. Gen. Nathaniel P. Banks's corps at Cedar Mountain. Although heavily outnumbered, the Federal troops resist for more than an hour before being routed and driven from the field at nightfall. Pope's main body comes up next day, and Jackson draws off to await Lee's Army of Northern Virginia.

19 AUGUST 1862. Pope retires from the Rapidan River with 45,000 Union troops to take up position behind the Rappahannock and await the arrival of McClellan's army, which three days earlier began a withdrawal from the Peninsula. Pope is shadowed from Gordonsville (Virginia) by 55,000 Confederates under Lee, who probes the new Rappahannock defense lines until 25 August then detaches Jackson on a long march around the Union right flank.

Jackson covers 50 miles in two days, reaching the railway at Bristoe before sunset on 26 August, capturing Manassas Junction—Pope's supply depot—by midnight. Jackson's three divisions hide in some woods 12 miles from Thoroughfare Gap while Pope—his strength now at 70,000 troops with the addition of two of McClellan's corps—orders a concentration at Manassas.

Failing to find Jackson, the Union army presses toward Centreville while Lee begins arriving through Thoroughfare Gap on the evening of 28 August with James Longstreet's troops. Not wanting Pope to withdraw behind the protection of Bull Run, Jackson deliberately reveals his position at 5:30 P.M. that day by attacking King's division of McDowell's corps near Groveton, thus luring the larger—but fragmented—Union army into battle.

29 AUGUST 1862. ***Bull Run (Second Battle).*** Having at last located Jackson, Pope attacks his strong defensive position with only Sigel's corps and Brig. Gen. John Reynolds's division, the rest of his Union contingents being scattered. Four Federal divisions arrive from Centreville by noon and are thrown into the fight but are repeatedly repelled by Gen. A. P. Hill's division on the Confederate left. Lee meanwhile appears with Longstreet's corps to reinforce Jackson; Porter and McDowell—unaware of the growing rebel strength—arrive from Manassas with their Union corps, which have been making for Gainesville.

Next morning Pope orders McDowell to pursue the Confederates, still mistakenly assuming he faces only Jackson's contingent, which is attempting to escape from Federal encirclement. McDowell soon discovers the truth; launching a heavy attack against the Confederate lines he also secures Bald and Henry House Hills to secure his flank. After heavy fighting Lee sends Longstreet's five divisions against the Federal left at 4:00 P.M., crumpling Union resistance and starting a full-scale retreat.

It is too late in the day for the Confederates to achieve a complete victory, however, and Pope is able to extricate most of his forces across Bull Run into Centreville, joining Franklin's corps from Alexandria. On 1 September Lee sends Jackson on another flanking march; Jackson fights a sharp but indecisive engagement at Chantilly with the confused Union forces. Despite being further reinforced by Gen. Edwin "Old Bull" Sumner's corps and thus considerably outnumbering Lee, a demoralized Pope decides on 2 September to retire all the way into the Federal fortifications around Washington, having suffered 14,000 casualties during five days of fighting compared to 9,000–10,000 Confederate losses.

30 AUGUST 1862. Confederate Gen. Edmund Kirby Smith's 15,000 troops brush aside an extemporized Federal force under Gen. William Nelson at Richmond (Kentucky), occupying Lexington three days later.

6 SEPTEMBER 1862. Union Colonel Lowe recaptures Clarksville (Tennessee).

7 SEPTEMBER 1862. After being reinforced from Richmond, Lee's army crosses the Potomac at Leesburg and occupies Frederick (Maryland).

10 SEPTEMBER 1862. Lee divides his 40,000-man army, sending Jackson with six divisions to seize Harpers Ferry while he retires behind South Mountain with three divisions.

13 SEPTEMBER 1862. ***Harpers Ferry.*** Jackson appears out of the west, and other Confederate divisions occupy the heights north and east of Harpers Ferry on the opposite banks of the Potomac and Shenandoah Rivers, compelling its isolated 12,500-man Union garrison to capitulate two days later.

14 SEPTEMBER 1862. Buell's Union army confronts Gen. Braxton Bragg's Confederates at Bowling Green (Kentucky); they circle each other one week later without clashing.

15 SEPTEMBER 1862. Chased by McClellan, Lee retreats behind Antietam Creek into Sharpsburg (Pennsylvania) to reunite with Jackson.

16 SEPTEMBER 1862. ***Antietam.*** Jackson rejoins Lee this morning at Sharpsburg with two Confederate divisions, followed by a third during the afternoon. By evening, 48-year-old Joseph "Fighting Joe" Hooker's I Corps—vanguard of McClellan's slowly approaching 70,000-man Federal army—collides with 31-year-old Brig. Gen. John Bell Hood's two brigades on the Confederate left; both sides brace for battle next day.

At 5:30 A.M. on 17 September Union forces assault the Confederate left under Jackson, ceasing five hours later after negligible gains. The 10:00 A.M. Federal attack on Lee's center fares somewhat better, Brig. D. H. Hill's Confederate division being enfiladed and driven out of Bloody Lane (a sunken road) after heavy fighting. Farther south the Union attackers do even better, Burnside's IX Corps fighting its way across Antietam's stone bridge by 1:00 P.M. then driving on Sharpsburg two hours later, thereby threatening to roll up Lee's entire army.

At this crucial moment Gen. A. P. Hill's Confederate division arrives after a forced march from Harpers Ferry, and at 4:00 P.M. he takes Burnside's corps in its unprotected left flank, sending the Union column reeling back across Antietam Creek. McClellan has suffered approximately 12,000 casualties this day compared to Lee's 9,000 (although with only 40,000 men to begin with, deep in enemy territory, the Confederate general can ill afford to lose many more). Lee offers to renew action next day, but McClellan demurs despite being reinforced by two more Union divisions. Instead, he allows the Confederates to retreat west across the Potomac on the night of 18 September, uncontested.

19 SEPTEMBER 1862. Rosencrans defeats Confederate General Price at Iuka.

1 OCTOBER 1862. Buell sallies from Louisville to drive Bragg's Confederate invaders out of Kentucky.

3 OCTOBER 1862. ***Corinth.*** Confederate General Van Dorn appears outside Corinth (Mississippi) with 22,000 men, hoping to recapture this key strategic town and rupture Grant's line of communications. Its 20,000 Federal defenders under Rosencrans brace for an assault, which is launched next day and eventually halted after heavy fighting around a strongpoint called Battery Robinet. By evening, Van Horn is in retreat.

7 OCTOBER 1862. ***Perryville.*** This evening, advance elements of Buell's Union army begin encamping west of Perryville (Kentucky), along a stream known as Doctor's Creek. Rearguard units from the Confederate army under Gen. Braxton Bragg, which the Federals have been pushing back from Louisville, are also in the vicinity, and soldiers on both sides start fighting over waterholes.

Next day a heavy battle erupts, the Confederates attacking the left end of Buell's line and routing the greater part of a corps, without either general planning on such an engagement. The Union commander—whose headquarters are several miles away—only learns of this action at dusk, after losing 4,000 men. Confederate casualties are comparable, and the disheartened Bragg soon resumes his retirement, abandoning the state altogether by retreating through the Cumberland Gap into Tennessee.

30 OCTOBER 1862. Buell is replaced as Union commander in Kentucky by Rosencrans.

7 NOVEMBER 1862. Because of his continued reluctance to commit the Army of the Potomac to a renewed offensive against Lee, McClellan is relieved of command and replaced by Burnside.

11 DECEMBER 1862. ***Fredericksburg.*** After establishing the Army of the Potomac's new base at Aquia Creek, Burnside's 122,000 men have spent two weeks circling southeastward of Lee's main body into the vicinity of Falmouth (Virginia), hoping to slip across the Rappahannock River at or below Fredericksburg to drive directly on the Confederate capital of Richmond 54 miles away. However, a delay in forwarding pontoons from Washington has prevented his traversing right away, affording Lee's 79,000 troops time to arrive and take up position in the heights just west of the town.

Despite having lost the element of surprise, Burnside persists with his original plan, eventually ordering pontoon bridges erected on the morning of 12 December. The Army of the Potomac pushes across in the face of considerable opposition, disgorging through Fredericksburg into a shallow open plain to the west of the town. On 13 December, Burnside orders twin columns to continue advancing and attack Lee's waiting lines in the hills beyond, being repulsed with 12,500 losses (compared to 4,200 rebel casualties). Two days after this lopsided slaughter, Burnside retreats and both armies then settle in for the winter on opposite banks of the Rappahannock.

12 DECEMBER 1862. The Federal gunboat *Cairo* sinks after striking a Confederate "torpedo" in a Mississippi River tributary, thereby becoming the first victim of mine warfare.

20 DECEMBER 1862. A Confederate cavalry raid by Van Dorn on Grant's supply depot at Holly Springs (northern Mississippi) compels him to defer his advance on Jackson (Mississippi).

29 DECEMBER 1862. Sherman's 30,000-man army is defeated by Confederate Gen. John C. Pemberton at Chickasaw Bluffs, six miles north of Vicksburg (Mississippi), and is obliged to retreat after losing 2,000 troops.

30 DECEMBER 1862. ***Murfreesboro.*** Four days after advancing out of Nashville, Rosencrans deploys his 43,000 Union troops along the banks of the Stone River, facing south toward Murfreesboro (Tennessee), which is defended by a slightly smaller Confederate army under Bragg. Next dawn four rebel brigades launch a devastating flank attack against Gen. Alexander McDowell McCook's corps on the Federal right, causing it to disintegrate. However, Thomas's two divisions hold the Union center, reinforced by Gen. Thomas L. Crittenden on the left.

The day seemingly ends with a Confederate victory, but Rosencrans refuses to retire. Instead, after a couple of days of long-range skirmishing, Bragg drives against the Union left on 2 January 1863, only to see his attacking columns smashed by Federal artillery. The rebels then abandon Murfreesboro and fall back upon Tullahoma, leaving Rosencrans triumphant despite his 13,000 casualties.

10 JANUARY 1863. ***Arkansas Post.*** In order to clear Confederate concentrations from their rear, Gens. John A. McClernand and Sherman lead 32,000 troops against Fort Hindman at Arkansas Post (40 miles from the confluence of the Arkansas and Mississippi Rivers), supported by a river squadron under Porter. After a preliminary naval bombardment the Union army invests this stronghold next day, suffering about 1,000 casualties before compelling the 5,000-man garrison to surrender.

26 JANUARY 1863. Hooker replaces Burnside in command of the Army of the Potomac.

31 JANUARY 1863. The Confederate ironclads *Palmetto State* and *Chicora* attack Du Pont's blockading squadron outside Charleston, capturing the converted merchantman *Mercedita* and crippling *Keystone State.*

14 MARCH 1863. Farragut's fleet attempts to push past the Confederate batteries at Port Hudson (Louisiana), but only some of his vessels succeed. *Mississippi* runs aground and is destroyed.

7 APRIL 1863. Shortly after noon Du Pont reluctantly leads in his Union ironclads to give battle against Charleston's Confederate batteries. Despite their invulnerability, the cumbersome vessels are able to loose off

only 139 heavy rounds by evening compared to 2,200 by the shore batteries and retire mauled (*Keokuk* sinking next day).

Shortly thereafter Du Pont is replaced by Rear Adm. John A. Dahlgren (inventor of the gun that bears his name), who gradually strangles the Confederate defenses.

15 APRIL 1863. After two and a half months assembling 45,000 Union troops at Milliken's Bend (ten miles above Vicksburg) under his corps commanders—Sherman, McClernand, and Scottish-born James B. McPherson—Grant strikes south with the latter two units along the west bank of the Mississippi toward New Carthage, hoping to circumvent Vicksburg and eventually invest this Confederate stronghold from the rear. Sherman's corps in the meantime feints toward Chickasaw Bluffs; Porter's seven ironclads, assorted gunboats, and three storeships slip past the Vicksburg batteries next night to support Grant's main body along the river.

After reaching Hard Times Plantation on 24 April, Grant crosses to the eastern bank of the Mississippi at Bruinsburg, defeats a small Confederate force a few miles inland, then occupies Grand Gulf. From here he orders Sherman to rejoin, and on 7 May Grant presses east toward the town of Jackson.

17 APRIL 1863. In a coordinated move designed by Grant to further confuse Confederate forces in Mississippi, Col. Benjamin H. Grierson departs Lagrange (near Memphis, Tennessee) with 900 troopers of 6th and 7th Illinois Cavalry plus six field guns to fight his way 600 miles down toward the Gulf of Mexico—giving the impression of being the spearhead of a much larger army. After wreaking great material damage, Grierson emerges at Baton Rouge by evening on 2 May.

18 APRIL 1863. The 2,000-man Union garrison holding Fayetteville (Arkansas) repulses an attack by 3,000 Confederate troops with four cannons.

30 APRIL 1863. ***Chancellorsville.*** Eager to launch a spring offensive against Lee, Hooker masses 60,000 Union troops near Chancellorsville (west of Fredericksburg, Virginia) while Gen. John Sedgwick pushes across the Rappahannock farther east with another 40,000. Despite being outnumbered two-to-one, Lee outfights both contingents by leaving 10,000 men to check Sedgwick while his main body swings around under Jackson to confront Hooker on 1 May.

Lee's initial attack throws the main Union army over to the defensive; next day he outflanks and rolls up Hooker's right wing with Jackson's corps. The Army of the Potomac falls back to a fresh defensive position, at which point (3 May) Lee turns on Sedgwick, who in the meantime has captured Fredericksburg's commanding heights. On 4 May the Confederates drive Sedgwick back across the river then countermarch to strike another blow against Hooker at Chancellorsville. Thoroughly outgeneralled and having suffered 17,000 casualties compared to 12,000 Confederate losses, Hooker retires across the Rappahannock by nightfall on 5 May, the only success coming when Jackson—Lee's ablest subordinate—is mortally wounded by a chance round from his own troops.

12 MAY 1863. Grant defeats a Confederate concentration at Raymond (Mississippi) and then captures nearby Jackson two days later, preventing the passage of 6,000 Confederate reinforcements to Vicksburg under Gen. Joseph E. Johnston.

16 MAY 1863. ***Siege of Vicksburg.*** After sallying 25 miles east out of Vicksburg, its garrison commander, General Pemberton, challenges Grant's approaching army at Champion Hill, suffering 2,500 Confederate casualties in a seesaw battle before retreating. Next day the rebels fight a rearguard action at a crossing of the Big Black River, being defeated again and driven back inside their Vicksburg trenches.

On 18 May Grant arrives outside, his troops quickly storming Vicksburg's defenses on 19 May. A second assault on 22 May results in 3,000 Union casualties, after which the Federal army settles down to a protracted siege. Confederate relief columns are kept at bay for the next several weeks as Grant's strength swells to 75,000 men. Eventually Pemberton requests terms on 3 July, and 31,000 defenders capitulate next day, along with 172 cannons and 60,000 small arms.

23 MAY 1863. ***Capture of Port Hudson.*** Five weeks after departing Baton Rouge northward, 14,000 Union troops under Banks besiege 7,000 Confederates inside Port Hudson (200 miles below Vicksburg on the Mississippi River). When news is received of the fall of Vicksburg, Port Hudson's half-starved Confederate garrison also capitulates on 9 July.

3 JUNE 1863. Lee strikes north from Virginia with three corps under Longstreet, Gen. Richard S. Ewell, and A. P. Hill to invade Pennsylvania.

9 JUNE 1863. Lee's cavalry clashes with Union troops at Brandy Station (Virginia), revealing to Hooker that the Army of Northern Virginia is moving over to the offensive.

13 JUNE 1863. Refused permission to advance against the Confederate capital of Richmond while Lee is absent, Hooker must instead fall back toward Manassas in hopes of intercepting the Army of Northern Virginia before it can threaten Washington.

15 JUNE 1863. Confederate General Ewell captures Winchester (northern Virginia) and crosses over into Maryland, pushing his cavalry forward into Pennsylvania.

23 JUNE 1863. After six months' inactivity near Murfreesboro, Rosencrans's 60,000-man Army of the Cumberland breaks camp and pushes south to drive Bragg's 45,000 Confederates out of central Tennessee. By sliding east around the rebel flank, Rosencrans compels Bragg to pull back into Chattanooga by 4 July.

28 JUNE 1863. Lee learns that Hooker is concentrating at Frederick (Maryland), thereby threatening the Confederate rear. Lee's flamboyant cavalry commander, J. E. B. Stuart, has left Lee without reconnaissance capabilities, preferring to raid deep into Union territory alone.

Also today Hooker is replaced by George Gordon Meade as Union commander in chief.

30 JUNE 1863. ***Gettysburg.*** A Confederate brigade—part of two corps approaching under A. P. Hill and Longstreet—bears down on Gettysburg out of the west in hopes of looting its shoe factory, only to find the small Pennsylvania town held by a Union cavalry contingent. Rather than scatter, the Federal troopers—detached from Meade's much larger concentration at Pipe Creek, farther southeast—make a stand, provoking a full-scale assault by Hill next morning.

The Confederates encounter unexpectedly stiff resistance from Gen. John Buford's Federal cavalry division, plus I Corps infantry under Gen. John F. Reynolds, until the defenders are compelled to retreat when Ewell's Confederate corps appears out of the north and sends in an assault column under Brig. Gen. Jubal Early. The Federal forces retire no farther than Cemetery Hill and brace for another battle while awaiting reinforcements.

Arriving upon the scene, Lee wishes to destroy this portion of the Army of the Potomac before it can be built up to full strength; however, due to poor communication he is unable to commit Longstreet's corps until the late afternoon of 2 July, by which time the Federals are dug in and increasing in numbers (eventually reaching 82,000 compared to 75,000 Confederates). Desperate fighting swirls around the Peach Orchard and Devil's Den, with no side gaining a decisive advantage; Lee decides to launch an all-out assault against the Union center next day.

Meade strikes first at dawn on 3 July, however, sending a division from XII Corps, which reoccupies Culp's Hill from the Confederates after four hours of intense fighting. Despite this setback Lee goes forward, opening his main attack with an extensive bombardment of the Union center by 140 Confederate guns under Col. E. P. Alexander. When the 77 Union artillery pieces fall silent near 3:00 P.M.—having been ordered by Gen. H. J. Hunt to preserve ammunition—38-year-old Gen. George Edward Pickett's fresh Confederate division emerges from the trees three-quarters of a mile away and charges the Union lines atop Cemetery Hill in the belief the defenders' guns are out of action. Instead, his regiments endure a merciless pounding from renewed artillery fire and massed musket volleys, losing 3,400 of 4,800 men before eventually retreating.

Having lost a total of about 30,000 men killed, wounded, or missing during four days of fighting, a defeated Lee retires toward Virginia by 5 July. Union casualties total 23,000, leaving Meade too drained to do much but follow.

5 JULY 1863. Confederate General Morgan captures 400 Union prisoners at Lebanon (Kentucky) and three days later crosses the Ohio River into Harrison County (Indiana) with 2,500 troopers and four artillery pieces in hopes of fomenting an insurrection by antifederalist sympathizers called Copperheads. After penetrating into Ohio, he is cornered and defeated near Pomeroy on 18 July, surrendering the remnants of his command two days later in Columbiana County.

13 JULY 1863. Anticonscription riots erupt in New York City, resulting in 150 deaths before troubles are put down by Federal troops four days later.

17 JULY 1863. Having quit occupied Vicksburg 12 days earlier with elements of three Union Army corps, Sherman drives the outnumbered Johnston out of Jackson (Mississippi). Natchez is also seized by another Federal detachment; the rebel supply depot at Grenada is destroyed one month later.

20 AUGUST 1863. At dawn, Lawrence (Kansas) is surprised by 300 irregulars under William C. Quantrill of Cass County (Missouri), who slay 191 residents and wound another 581 before burning this town to the ground. Local militia Gen. James H. Lane retaliates by raiding Grand River (Missouri), claiming 80 lives.

2 SEPTEMBER 1863. Burnside occupies Knoxville.

8 SEPTEMBER 1863. Bragg evacuates Chattanooga; Rosencrans occupies it next day.

17 SEPTEMBER 1863. Learning that Bragg is not in full retreat to Rome (Georgia) as expected but is instead holding position, Rosencrans hastily reconcentrates his three corps near Chickamauga Creek, 12 miles south of Chattanooga.

Next day Bragg begins advancing on the Union left under Crittenden at Lee Mill and Gordon's Mill, being reinforced en route by three freshly arrived Confederate brigades under Hood.

19 SEPTEMBER 1863. ***Chickamauga.*** Bragg's army approaches through dense woods, hoping to envelop Rosencrans's left then drive the 60,000 Union troops back on Lookout Mountain, without escape. However, the Federal general has already begun shifting his army to the left, and on the morning of 19 September Gen. George H. Thomas sends a division forward to reconnoiter near Chickamauga Creek, discovering dismounted Confederate cavalry. A confused series of confrontations erupts, most units being unable to see any great distance because of the landscape, thus fighting independently wherever they chance upon the enemy.

Bragg is reinforced overnight and next morning launches a two-pronged assault, most of which hits Thomas's corps. He calls for support, and Rosencrans shifts three Union divisions to the left; a fourth is mistakenly pulled out of the Union line, allowing Longstreet's recently arrived Confederate reinforcements to pour through at noon. The Federal right—now reduced to less than 7,000 men—is swept from the field, although managing to make a stand in McFarland's Gap. Rosencrans and Crittenden are carried off in the Union flight to Chattanooga, only Thomas hanging on with five divisions against the entire 60,000-man Confederate army.

They mount a desperate defense along Missionary Ridge, earning Thomas the nickname "Rock of Chickamauga." The Union survivors are pressed back around 4:00 P.M. and withdraw north, the victorious Confederates giving up their pursuit at sunset. Each side suffers approximately 16,000 casualties, Thomas retiring unmolested to Chattanooga on 21 September.

5 OCTOBER 1863. A four-man Confederate submersible under Lt. William T. Glassell slips out of Charleston (South Carolina) after night and badly damages the ironclad USS *New Ironsides* with a "torpedo" (a spar tipped with an explosive charge); the submersible also sinks from the blast.

23 OCTOBER 1863. Grant reaches Chattanooga to assume command of the remnants of Rosencrans's army, now beleaguered within under Thomas after its defeat at Chickamauga. To extricate the Army of the Cumberland from its difficulties, it has already been reinforced by XI and XII Corps (12,000 men) under Hooker from the Army of the Potomac in Virginia and is just awaiting the arrival of XV Corps under Sherman from the Army of the Tennessee in Mississippi to attempt a breakout.

17 NOVEMBER 1863. Having been detached with 15,000 troops from Bragg's victorious army, Confederate General Longstreet arrives to invest Burnside within Knoxville. After a nocturnal assault is repulsed with heavy losses, the Southerners institute a siege.

23 NOVEMBER 1863. ***Chattanooga.*** After a month of preparation, Grant's 60,000 Union troops begin to push southeast out of Chattanooga to break the siege by Bragg's 34,000 Confederates dug in along the nearby heights. In the center, Thomas's corps moves out onto the open plain and pushes back the rebel picket lines around Orchard Knob, in anticipation of a two-pronged envelopment by other Federal contingents: Hooker, who is to storm Lookout Mountain on the right, and Sherman, who is to outflank the Confederates on the left.

Next midday the Union offensive is launched, as Hooker easily carries his objective, although without threatening Bragg's main army. Sherman's corps meanwhile encounters greater resistance among the broken hills at the northeastern tip of Missionary Ridge from the Confederate division of Irish-born Gen. Pat Cleburne, and the Union drive bogs down by nightfall.

When fighting resumes on 25 November, Grant directs Thomas's corps to pressure Bragg's center with a frontal assault during the afternoon in order to relieve his wings. Against all expectations, 18,000 Union infantry surge through the lower rebel trenches at 3:30 P.M. then without orders scale the 500-foot heights of Missionary Ridge in an irresistible tide led by 32-year-old Maj. Gen. Philip Henry Sheridan. Bragg's army is broken and retreats in disorder, having suffered 8,700 killed, wounded, or captured; Grant's losses are approximately 6,000.

4 DECEMBER 1863. After helping defeat Bragg outside Chattanooga, Sherman's corps raises the Confederate siege of Knoxville.

3 FEBRUARY 1864. Sherman departs Vicksburg with XVI and XVII Corps, launching a devastating sweep through Confederate-held Mississippi. On 5 February his Union columns pass through Jackson; they level Meridian by 14–15 February before returning into their original cantonments on 27 February.

17 FEBRUARY 1864. The eight-man Confederate submersible *H.L. Hunley* (named for its deceased inventor, Horace L. Hunley) slips out of Charleston under Lt. George E. Dixon and sinks the Union steam sloop *Housatonic* by ramming it with a torpedo—which also claims the luckless submarine.

8 MARCH 1864. Grant is promoted to lieutenant general by Lincoln and next day is made commander in chief of all Union armies.

14 MARCH 1864. Federal forces under Gen. A. J. Smith capture 325 Confederates and 12 guns at Fort DeRussey on the Red River (Louisiana).

25 MARCH 1864. A cavalry raid by Confederate General Forrest levels Paducah (Kentucky).

12 APRIL 1864. Forrest surprises and destroys the Union garrison at Fort Pillow (Tennessee).

3 MAY 1864. ***The Wilderness.*** After reorganizing the Army of the Potomac and appointing Sheridan as its cavalry commander, Grant this evening departs Culpeper (Virginia) southward with 120,000 men subdivided into five corps to cross the Rapidan River at Germanna and Ely's Fords in search of Lee. Next evening the Union vanguard camps in the middle of a large forest dubbed The Wilderness in Spotsylvania County, where advance Confederate units surprise it on the morning of 5 May.

With scarcely 70,000 troops and less artillery than the Union host, Lee has opted to push his own army into this wooded area from the opposite direction and fight blind, wherever his troops become engaged; in this manner Grant's superior numbers and guns cannot easily be brought to bear. The left wing of the Confederate army therefore collides with the left-center of the Army of the Potomac shortly after daybreak, and isolated skirmishes gradually evolve into a pitched battle, as reinforcements are hastened toward the sound of gunfire by both sides. Unable to see more than 100 yards because of the dense undergrowth, many formations and batteries fire wildly throughout the night, until the brush itself catches fire.

Next day the battle regains its intensity, a threatened breakthrough by Gen. Winfield Scott Hancock's II Union Army Corps being contained by the timely arrival of Longstreet's division—who is then accidentally shot by his own troops. Long-range exchanges mark the 7 May, after which an undaunted Grant—despite having suffered almost 18,000 casualties to Lee's 11,500—resumes his advance southeastward toward Spotsylvania Court House.

8 MAY 1864. ***Spotsylvania.*** A Union column under Sheridan hastens to seize the crossroads at Spotsylvania Court House so as to get between Lee's army and the Confederate capital of Richmond, but a rebel contingent bars its path. Both armies then collide again and another ferocious, confused battle erupts over the next ten days, as Grant and Lee slowly circle one another.

On 12 May a fierce contest is fought in pelting rain from dawn to dusk, over a horseshoe-shaped arc of Confederate trenches called the Bloody Angle, guarding the principal road crossing. Union casualties total 7,000 this day compared to 4,500 for the rebels (plus another 4,000 captured). The Army of the Potomac nevertheless persists in sliding southeast, all the while maintaining contact with the Army of Northern Virginia. By 20 May, total Federal losses since the beginning of the campaign stand at 35,000; for the Confederates, 26,000.

13 MAY 1864. ***Drive on Atlanta.*** Less than a week after departing Chattanooga southeastward with 90,000 Union troops, Sherman encounters Johnston's 60,000 Confederates dug in behind Buzzard's Roost on Rocky Face Ridge, with his headquarters in nearby Dalton (Georgia). Rather than storm the heights, two Federal corps pin down the Southerners while Union General McPherson leads the 30,000-man Army of the Tennessee on a wide flanking movement to the right, passing through Snake Creek Gap to threaten Johnston's line of communications two days later at Resaca.

The Confederates fight their way free, but Sherman continues to press Johnston back toward Atlanta, outflanking the rebels whenever they make a stand. Eventually the Confederates retire into prepared positions on Kenesaw Mountain, which Sherman assaults on 27 June, suffering 3,000 casualties. Resuming their former tactic, the Federal columns again outflank Johnston, obliging him to withdraw beyond the Chattahoochee River by 9 July and into trenches around Atlanta (population 13,000) one week later.

At this point President Davis replaces Johnston with Hood, who attacks General Thomas's Union corps on

20 July as it is crossing Peachtree Creek just a few miles outside Atlanta. This assault is beaten off with considerable difficulty, and two days later Hood also mauls McPherson's detached force as it approaches out of the east after having secured Decatur. Sherman nevertheless continues to encircle Atlanta, despite another sally by Hood westward against the Union positions at Ezra Church on 28 July. Eventually a lengthy siege results, culminating in the escape northwestward of Hood's army and capitulation of the battered city by 2 September.

23 MAY 1864. Six months after escaping from imprisonment in Ohio, Gen. Morgan (*see* 5 July 1863) enters Kentucky with a body of Confederate cavalry raiders. On 11 June he threatens Frankfort but otherwise has little effect on Union activities.

3 JUNE 1864. ***Cold Harbor.*** Three days after Sheridan's cavalry have occupied this village close to the Chickahominy River (Virginia), Grant mistakenly assumes Lee's forces are overextended, so he orders a direct frontal assault on the nearby Confederate trenches for 4:30 A.M. on 3 June in hopes of achieving a breakthrough. Instead he discovers this sector to have been heavily reinforced by Lee, and the Union storm columns suffer 8,000 casualties in a half-hour.

Such brutal slaughter temporarily checks the Federal offensive, resulting in ten days of long-range exchanges. Union casualties for the preceding month total 50,000 compared to Lee's 32,000; yet Grant is able to quickly replenish his lost men and equipment, whereas Confederate resources are almost exhausted. In mid-June the Army of the Potomac again slips southeast, seeking to circle around and take Petersburg, thus threatening the rebel capital of Richmond.

15 JUNE 1864. ***Petersburg Siege.*** After stealthily crossing both the Chickahominy and James Rivers, the Army of the Potomac's vanguard under Gen. William F. "Baldy" Smith surprises the small Confederate garrison under Beauregard holding Petersburg (Virginia). Despite ample opportunity over the next five days, the Federal columns fail to carry this strategic city before Lee can hasten his main army down into its defenses. Grant then settles in for a protracted trench warfare, pinning the outnumbered Confederates in place.

Miners from the 48th Pennsylvania Regiment eventually attempt to break this stalemate by detonating an eight-ton subterranean explosive beneath a Confederate strongpoint at dawn of 30 July; although it blows a huge breach, the ensuing Union assault is botched through the incompetence of Burnside (who is subsequently cashiered). The siege of Petersburg persists for another eight months, until the very final stages of the war.

5 JULY 1864. ***Alarm at Washington.*** After defeating small Union contingents in the Shenandoah Valley, Confederate General Early has decided to move into Maryland to threaten Washington, D.C., in hopes of relieving

Robert E. Lee and his generals are depicted in this famous painting, Summertime

pressure on Lee's hard-pressed army in Virginia. Gen. Bradley T. Johnson this day crosses the Potomac River with the 3,000-man rebel vanguard, followed shortly thereafter by Early's 10,000-man main body.

By 10 July the Confederates have passed through Rockville and next morning encounter the Union fortifications at Fort Stevens (Brightwood, D.C.), which are held by the 1st and 2nd Divisions of VI Corps under Gen. Horatio G. Wright—hastily withdrawn from Grant's army around Petersburg—plus a scratch force of rear-echelon troops and convalescents. Without a siege train, Early can only test the defenses, suffering 500 casualties before retiring on 13 July toward the Shenandoah Valley via Leesburg, Snickers Gap, and Winchester. Federal losses in defending their capital are 54 killed and 319 wounded.

5 AUGUST 1864. ***Mobile Bay.*** At 5:30 A.M. Farragut—his flag flying aboard USS *Hartford*—stands in toward the Confederate defenses at Mobile Bay, his squadron consisting of the monitors *Tecumseh, Manhattan, Winnebago,* and *Chickasaw* plus 14 wooden warships (the latter lashed together in pairs for greater protection). Ninety minutes later they begin exchanging salvoes with Fort Morgan; *Tecumseh* presses close inshore to engage the waiting Confederate ironclad *Tennessee* under Rear Adm. Franklin Buchanan.

But the lead Union monitor suddenly strikes a mine or "torpedo," capsizing within minutes along with Cmdr. T. A. M. Craven and 91 of his 113-man crew. The next Union ship in line—the steam sloop USS *Brooklyn*—hesitates to follow, until Farragut bellows across the water to its commander: "Damn the torpedoes! Full speed ahead!"

The Union vessels clear the Confederate minefield without further incident, and while some dispose of three Confederate gunboats supporting the *Tennessee,* the entire squadron gives its full attention to its formidable opponent. *Monongahela, Lackawanna,* and *Hartford* all unsuccessfully attempt to ram the ironclad, which is eventually checked by the 440-pound solid shots fired by the 15-inch guns aboard *Manhattan.* Surrounded—its gunports battered shut, its steering gear shot away, and its commander seriously wounded—*Tennessee* surrenders to its tormentors at 10:00 A.M.

Despite capturing this vessel, plus Forts Morgan and Gaines ashore, the Union forces are unable to subdue the city of Mobile itself (30 miles farther north). Nevertheless, Mobile ceases to serve as a viable seaport for importing desperately needed goods from abroad.

7 AUGUST 1864. In order to win Union control in the Shenandoah Valley, Sheridan is given command of all its Federal forces. Three days later he advances out of Harpers Ferry, driving Early's Confederates back toward Strasburg.

21 AUGUST 1864. Forrest makes a hit-and-run raid against Memphis with a body of Confederate cavalry.

19 SEPTEMBER 1864. ***Winchester.*** With 8,000 Union cavalry and 23,000 infantry, Sheridan confronts Early's smaller Confederate army two miles east of Winchester (Virginia). Despite some initial confusion and a bloody repulse, the Federal commander rallies his troops, brings up reinforcements around noon, then launches an entire cavalry division in a devastating charge behind the rebel flank, which secures 1,200 captives and sends Early retreating toward Strasburg.

The Confederates regroup at Fisher's Hill between the Shenandoah River and Little North Mountain, only to be routed again three days later when their flank is once more turned. Early then retires into Port Republic on 25 September with his surviving units.

19 OCTOBER 1864. At dawn, Early's Confederate army—having been reinforced by Longstreet—surprises Sheridan's unprepared corps at Cedar Creek (Virginia), capturing 1,300 prisoners and 18 guns. The Union commander rides 20 miles from his headquarters at Winchester to rally his troops and rout Early by nightfall, seizing 23 rebel guns.

11 NOVEMBER 1864. ***March to the Sea.*** Having detached Thomas's corps back into Tennessee to keep an eye on Hood, Sherman orders his 60,000 remaining troops to burn empty Atlanta to the ground then next day begins striking out in four parallel columns toward the Atlantic on an uncontested sweep designed to underscore the South's prostrate condition. On 23 November a few thousand raw Confederate militia—mostly boys and old men—are brushed aside outside Milledgeville (then Georgia's capital), but otherwise no armed resistance is encountered.

After cutting a swathe of destruction 60 miles wide and 250 miles long, Sherman's army reaches the environs of Savannah on 10 December, first circling around to the right to gain the Ogeechee River and overwhelm the Confederate garrison at Fort McAllister so as to reestablish contact with Union warships in Ossabaw Sound. Reprovisioned from supply ships, the Federal troops then return to occupy Savannah by 21 December, its 10,000-man garrison under Gen.

William J. Hardee having withdrawn north into the Carolinas.

LATE NOVEMBER 1864. In a last-ditch effort to discomfit the North, Hood crosses the Tennessee River from northern Alabama with 40,000 Confederates, driving toward Nashville. Thomas responds by detaching Gen. John Schofield with 22,000 Union troops to check this invasion, hoping to buy time to assemble even greater strength at his base.

But Hood emerges at Spring Hill behind Schofield on 29 November, compelling the startled Union column to make an abrupt about-face and hurriedly retrace their route out of danger. Poor Confederate communications prevent any attack until next morning, when Forrest's cavalry overtakes Schofield's rearguard, only to be repelled by artillery.

30 NOVEMBER 1864. ***Franklin.*** Schofield's retreating army entrenches just south of the town of Franklin (Tennessee) while his engineers rebuild the burned bridge across to the north bank of the Harpeth River so as to regain Thomas's main defenses at Nashville 18 miles away. Shortly after noon Hood comes up, furious at having let the Federal army escape him earlier at Spring Hill.

A mass of 18,000 Confederate infantry charge the strongest portion of the Union line, only to be turned back by artillery salvos and rifle volleys. Although a few Southerners fight their way through, this assault column is shattered and flees after enduring 6,000 killed or wounded. Schofield, who has suffered 2,000 casualties of his own, completes the bridge overnight and continues his retirement into Nashville.

15 DECEMBER 1864. ***Nashville.*** Two weeks after Hood's smaller army has instituted a loose siege, Thomas emerges from behind his Nashville fortifications in full force, pinning the Confederate right with two brigades of African-American troops while a solid corps of infantry and Gen. James H. Wilson's cavalry punches through the left. The outnumbered Southerners cannot man their entire line and are driven two miles back in heavy fighting.

Next morning Hood stands and fights again, only to see his line broken once more. This time the rebel army reels away in disarray, leaving behind its artillery as Forrest's cavalry covers the retirement. Eventually Wilson's carbine-toting Union troopers hound the defeated Confederates out of Tennessee. Upon regaining Muscle Shoals (Alabama) on 29 December, Hood's army is found to be reduced to only 21,000 men.

24 DECEMBER 1864. Porter has the former blockade runner *Louisiana* towed stealthily up to the seaward face of Fort Fisher (Wilmington, North Carolina) and detonates 215 tons of powder on board at 1:40 A.M. This is to be followed by an immediate amphibious assault by 2,100 troops under General Butler, but they take almost ten hours to appear, reembarking when the weather turns foul. The latter is shortly thereafter relieved of command and replaced by Maj. Gen. Alfred H. Terry.

12 FEBRUARY 1865. Three and a half weeks after departing Savannah northeastward with 60,000 Union troops through swampy terrain along the Atlantic seaboard, Sherman crosses the South Carolina border and occupies Branchville. Confederate General Johnston is powerless to halt the Federal advance, and the Union soldiers—convinced South Carolina is the cradle of secessionism—ravage the countryside during their march, burning Columbia to the ground five days later. Charlotte is evacuated by the Confederates on 18 February.

22 FEBRUARY 1865. Having advanced east out of Tennessee with yet another Union army, Schofield occupies Wilmington (North Carolina) in anticipation of uniting with Sherman.

2 MARCH 1865. At the head of 10,000 cavalry, Sheridan runs down Early's depleted Confederate forces at Waynesboro (between Staunton and Charlottesville, Virginia), extinguishing the last rebel army in the Shenandoah Valley by capturing 1,600 prisoners plus all its baggage and artillery trains.

22 MARCH 1865. General Wilson crosses the Tennessee River into northern Alabama with 12,500 Union troopers armed with carbines, to seize the last rebel munitions center at Selma.

23 MARCH 1865. Sherman and Schofield combine their armies at Golsboro (North Carolina).

25 MARCH 1865. Desperate to break the eight-month Union stranglehold on Petersburg (Virginia)—*see* 15 June 1864—Lee orders a dawn attack against a strongpoint in the Federal siegelines called Fort Stedman. Although this objective is initially carried, the Confederate sally is beaten back within a few hours at a cost of 5,000 killed, wounded, or captured.

31 MARCH 1865. ***Appomattox.*** Southwest of Petersburg, Sheridan circles beyond the Union left with a

large body of cavalry, seizing the Five Forks crossroads until driven back into Dinwiddie Court House by three counterattacking Confederate cavalry divisions and Pickett's five infantry brigades. However, Federal infantry hold nearby White Oak Ridge despite suffering 2,000 casualties; next afternoon Union reinforcements pulverize Pickett's corps.

This collapse on the farthest Confederate flank prompts Grant to bombard all of Lee's lines overnight then launch a general assault on 2 April. Despite inflicting 1,100 casualties in 15 minutes, A. P. Hill's rebel corps is broken, and ten miles of the defenders' 37-mile perimeter eventually must be abandoned. At 3:00 P.M., Lee gives the order for his 55,000 surviving troops to evacuate both Petersburg and Richmond at nightfall, in the forlorn hope of circling west-southwest and uniting with Johnston's beleaguered army in North Carolina.

While Grant sets off in pursuit of the retreating Army of Northern Virginia on 3 April, Lincoln visits the burning capitol of Richmond. On 7 April Sheridan's cavalry and two of Meade's corps crush a fleeing rebel column at Sayler's Creek, capturing General Ewell and many prisoners. Sheridan's troopers and infantrymen from both V and XXIV Corps then get ahead of Lee's retreating army, compelling the Confederate commander in chief to surrender his remaining 28,300 troops at Appomattox Court House by 9 April (Palm Sunday), on generous terms.

2 APRIL 1865. Union General Wilson occupies Selma (Alabama).

10 APRIL 1865. Sherman advances from Golsboro (North Carolina) against Johnston's tattered 27,500 men, occupying Raleigh three days later and compelling the Confederate general to request terms by 14 April. (When Lincoln is assassinated this same evening in Washington, Johnston's capitulation cannot be consummated until 26 April at Greensboro.)

12 APRIL 1865. A Union expedition headed by General Canby captures Mobile (Alabama).

4 MAY 1865. The last Confederate forces in Alabama and Mississippi surrender to Canby.

9 MAY 1865. Newly installed Pres. Andrew Johnson issues a proclamation declaring the Civil War to be at an end, although the Union naval blockade is maintained until 22 May to impede the escape of fugitive Confederates. Jefferson Davis is arrested on the morning of 10 May near Abbeville (Georgia) by the 1st Wisconsin and 4th Michigan Volunteer Cavalry, after which the final rebel holdouts gradually give themselves up: Jeff Thompson at Chalk Bluff (Arkansas) on 11 May; Kirby Smith in Texas on 26 May; and Hood by 31 May.

FRENCH INTERVENTION IN MEXICO (1861–1867)

ON 17 JULY 1861 THE BANKRUPT, six-month-old government of Mexico's liberal president, Benito Juárez, suspends all payments on 82.2 million pesos in foreign debt for two years—70 million being owed to British interests, 9.4 million to Spanish, and 2.8 million to French. English and French ambassadors sever diplomatic relations in protest eight days later; their home governments then begin casting about for additional means of punishing the default. The most direct method is armed intervention, so by 31 October London, Paris, and Madrid sign a pact to send an expedition to occupy Veracruz and garnish customs dues until these obligations are met.

However, since the earliest days of Mexico's independence from Spain, a constitutional monarchy has been proposed as a means of stabilizing the administration. Therefore, José Manuel Hidalgo—a Mexican conservative who in September 1861 is living at Empress Eugénie's French court at Biarritz—suggests that this intervention be used to implement such a scheme, further proposing 29-year-old Archduke Ferdinand Maximilian of Austria as the ideal neutral candidate. Napoleon III agrees, and the archduke in turn is convinced to assume the mantle of emperor, should this be offered.

29 NOVEMBER 1861. ***Occupation of Veracruz.*** A Spanish squadron under Adm. Joaquín Gutiérrez de Rubalcava begins departing Havana, consisting of 13 warships, five hired merchantmen, and five horse transports, conveying 5,800 soldiers under Gen. Manuel Gasset y Mercader across the Gulf of Mexico.

They anchor off Antón Lizardo (southeast of Veracruz) by 10 December, then contact the French and British representatives aboard the anchored frigates *Foudre* and HMS *Ariadne,* proposing a joint seizure of Veracruz. The latter demur.

On 14 December the Spaniards deliver a unilateral ultimatum, calling upon the 43-year-old republican governor, Ignacio de la Llave, to surrender. He is under orders to not offer resistance, so the Mexican garrison evacuates the port, thereby allowing the Spaniards to occupy the town and the off-lying island fortress of San Juan de Ulúa by 17 December.

3 JANUARY 1862. English and French contingents having reached Havana, they continue toward Mexico under the overall command of Spanish Gen. Juan Prim. The British fleet consists of two warships, a pair of frigates, and two gunboats under Commo. Hugh Dunlop, bearing the plenipotentiary Sir Charles Lennox Wyke. The French warship and three frigates under 49-year-old Adm. Jean Pierre Edmond Jurien de la Gravière convey representative Dubois de Saligny and 2,000 troops.

7 JANUARY 1862. The allied fleet reaches Veracruz, its diplomats sending a joint offer inland to Mexico City one week later, hinting at a resolution to the crisis. The Mexican foreign minister, Manuel Doblado, responds in kind, but excessive demands by the French delegation hamper further progress.

From their beachhead, the French also secretly allow Mexican conservatives—driven out following their defeat in the War of the Reform—to return from exile and begin contacting sympathizers and foment uprisings against Juárez's republican regime.

25 JANUARY 1862. Seditious propaganda emanating out of Veracruz leads the Mexican government to declare this foreign incursion a piratical act, proclaiming the death penalty for any citizen found collaborating with the invaders.

27 JANUARY 1862. The Mexican monarchist ideologue, Father Francisco Javier Miranda, reaches Veracruz and calls on conservatives to rally around Almonte when he arrives, paving the way for the Emperor Maximilian.

2 FEBRUARY 1862. Disease having already compelled Prim to send 800 convalescents back to Havana (another 300 Frenchmen remain hospitalized at Veracruz) the Spanish general informs the Mexican authorities that his joint expedition will have to advance inland to healthier cantonments. Foreign Minister Doblado responds by reopening negotiations; on 19 February a preliminary accord is signed at Orizaba.

25 FEBRUARY 1862. Without waiting for the Orizaba accord to be ratified, the French contingent moves inland from Veracruz.

1 MARCH 1862. The Mexican conservative exile Almonte reaches Veracruz, followed by 4,500 more French troops five days later under 47-year-old Gen. Charles Ferdinand Latrille, Comte de Lorencez. Almonte—with plenary powers from Maximilian to act on his behalf—is escorted inland to Córdoba along with other returning Mexican monarchists by a French chasseur battalion, all the while calling for an uprising against Juárez.

9 APRIL 1862. After a lengthy consultation between the allied commissioners at Orizaba, the British and Spaniards dissolve their association with the French, now openly pursuing their own agenda of installing a puppet regime in Mexico. Wyke and Prim agree to withdraw their forces from Veracruz nine days later, leaving the situation solely in French hands.

19 APRIL 1862. At dawn Lorencez strikes inland from Córdoba with Mangin's 1st Battalion of Chasseurs à Pied; l'Heriller's two battalions of 99th Line Regiment; Gambier's two battalions of 2nd Zouave; Focault's 2nd Chasseurs d'Afrique; Hennique's marine regiment; plus Allegre's marine fusiliers. They are supported by 16 artillery pieces of Bernard's 9th Artillery Regiment, Mallat's marine battery, and Bruat's field battery plus a company of 2nd Engineers under Barrillon and 3rd Supply Train Squadron under Torracinta. Five miles inland the 6,600 troops skirmish at El Fortín with Mexican cavalry under Col. Félix Díaz, who in turn warns 33-year-old republican Gen. Ignacio Zaragoza to begin evacuating Orizaba.

Also today, in a coordinated move, Gen. Antonio Taboada revolts against Juárez outside Córdoba, his example soon being imitated by other conservative commanders: Márquez, Mejía, and Juan Vicario all bringing Mexican units in to join Lorencez; Ignacio Buitrón, Lamadrid, Gutiérrez, Ordóñez, López Herrán, Tovar, and Lozada rise in the interior. Their combined strength represents 8,000 Mexican soldiers.

20 APRIL 1862. The French army occupies Orizaba.

27 APRIL 1862. Lorencez continues marching inland from Orizaba with 6,000 troops, occupying the town

of Acultzingo by 9:00 next morning then finding 2,000 Mexican infantry, 200 dragoons, and 18 artillery pieces entrenched atop nearby heights under General Arteaga. In a three-hour engagement starting early this afternoon the French drive the defenders back toward El Palmar, minimal casualties being inflicted on either side.

4 MAY 1862. ***Cinco de Mayo.*** After passing uncontested through El Palmar, Quecholac, and Acatzingo, the French army enters Amozoc to await Mexican conservative reinforcements under Márquez. When they fail to appear Lorencez resumes his advance next dawn—5 May (*cinco de Mayo*)—reaching Los Alamos Hacienda by 9:00 A.M. and preparing to assault the nearby city of Puebla. It is defended by Zaragoza with 1,200 regulars of the Negrete Division; 3,100 from the Berriozábal, Díaz, and Lamadrid Brigades; plus 500 cavalry of Alvarez's division. Puebla also boasts small artillery and engineer companies plus militia contingents; noncombatants have already been withdrawn.

At 11:30 A.M. the French general orders a long-range bombardment of the Loreto and Guadalupe Hills northeast of the city then shifts troops over to his right wing for an assault. Forewarned by this movement, Zaragoza dispatches Alvarez's cavalry by a hidden route to lay in reserve behind his left flank. After 45 minutes' ineffectual shooting the French artillery falls silent and moves nearer Lorencez's headquarters at Oropeza Ranch to resume shelling; despite expending 1,000 rounds, almost half their supply, they are unable to weaken the Mexican defenses, thus compelling Lorencez to launch a direct assault against Guadalupe Hill by midafternoon.

Two columns of Zouaves advance through heavy fire, led by their commanders, Morand and Cousin. Berriozábal reinforces the threatened section, the Mexicans three times checking the French approach, killing the few who succeed in reaching the summit. Lorencez finally commits two more Zouave companies, but a sudden rainstorm makes it impossible to ascend the slippery slope, after which they are hit in the right flank by Alvarez's cavalry. The defeated attackers make an orderly retreat to Los Alamos, having suffered 117 killed and 305 wounded. Mexican losses total 83 dead and 232 injured.

8 MAY 1862. Lorencez retires east from Los Alamos, regaining Amozoc next day then retreating to Acultzingo by 11 May. Almonte and Miranda dissuade him from withdrawing all the way back to Veracruz.

17 MAY 1862. The first of 2,500 conservative Mexican troopers under Márquez reinforce Lorencez at Tecamalucan.

18 MAY 1862. ***Barranca Seca.*** This morning republican Gen. Santiago Tapia's 500 troopers discover Márquez's cavalry near Tecamalucan; after being reinforced by 1,500 infantry they storm across Barranca Seca Bridge that afternoon to attack the conservatives. Once engaged the Mexicans are suddenly surprised by two relief columns of the French 99th Line Regiment (2nd Battalion), which have marched 12 miles from Tecamalucan in three hours to rescue Márquez. These reinforcements drive in Tapia's left, killing 100 republicans, wounding 200, and capturing 1,200. Allied casualties total 214, among them only two French dead and 26 injured.

30 MAY 1862. Lozada's conservative irregulars clash with some of Corona's forces at the base of Ceboruco Hill (Nayarit).

10 JUNE 1862. After being reinforced by 6,000 conscripted troops under republican Gen. Jesús González Ortega, Zaragoza's 14,000-man army marches out of Acultzingo to attack the French in Orizaba.

13 JUNE 1862. ***Borrego.*** After stealing upon Lorencez's army in two columns, Zaragoza and González Ortega arrive outside Orizaba, the latter quietly occupying Borrego (or Tlalchichilco) Hill. Learning of this, the French commander sends a company under Captain Detrie of the 99th Line Regiment to reconnoiter; he ascends the height before sunup on 14 June and discovers sleeping sentinels from the 4th Zacatecas Battalion.

A skirmish erupts, and a second 99th company joins the nocturnal clash under Captain Leclerc. Despite heavily outnumbering their opponents, the raw Mexican troops fire on each other in the darkness, suffering 400 deaths and an even greater number of desertions before retreating. At dawn Lorencez skirmishes with Zaragoza's main body outside La Angostura Gate (leading into Orizaba), prompting the latter to withdraw to El Retiro.

28 AUGUST 1862. A French convoy arrives at Veracruz with 2,000 reinforcements under Colonel Brincourt, disembarking over the next four days.

8 SEPTEMBER 1862. Zaragoza dies of typhoid fever in Puebla, being succeeded by González Ortega.

21 SEPTEMBER 1862. The 58-year-old Gen. Elie Frédéric Forey arrives at Veracruz, having been appointed to succeed Lorencez as commander in chief of the French expeditionary force. Next day he assumes command at Orizaba, and on 23 September dissolves Almonte's provisional Mexican government.

LATE SEPTEMBER 1862. After a difficult disembarkation at Veracruz because of foul weather, Forey detaches 5,400 troops under General Berthier, who occupies Jalapa despite resistance by 2,000 Mexican guerrillas (*chinacos*) under Salvador Díaz Mirón.

7 NOVEMBER 1862. De la Llave abandons Perote Fortress at the approach of Forey's 1st Division (under the French general's 51-year-old second-in-command, François Achille Bazaine), the French brushing aside the few Mexican irregulars roaming outside under Gen. Aurelio Rivera—although not actually garrisoning the building until 9 September 1863.

23 NOVEMBER 1862. French forces disembark at Tampico, searching for mules and cattle to supply their army.

19 JANUARY 1863. Republican Gen. Juan José de la Garza recaptures Tampico with 500 troops and two cannons.

3 FEBRUARY 1863. Conservative General Taboada's cavalry brigade departs Orizaba to reconnoiter the road leading inland toward Puebla in advance of Forey's main army.

23 FEBRUARY 1863. Forey quits Orizaba, striking inland to meet up with other converging French columns under Douay and Bazaine.

8 MARCH 1863. Forey's 2nd Infantry Division captures Amozoc, paving the way for his main body to enter two days later.

15 MARCH 1863. ***Siege of Puebla.*** Advance French elements occupy Los Alamos Hacienda; next afternoon Forey's vanguard—the 1st and 2nd Infantry Divisions plus a marine battalion and several squadrons of conservative Mexican cavalry—begin encircling Puebla. Despite the presence of Gen. Ignacio Comonfort's 8,000 troops and 40 artillery pieces among the nearby Uranga Hills, the 25,000-man French army

Mexican chinacos *battling French Zouaves*

occupies San Juan Hill unopposed by midday on 18 March, thereby isolating González Ortega's 25,000-man, 180-gun garrison.

Carvajal's and Rivera's republican cavalry brigades manage to dash out of the beleaguered city on 21 March, but next day French siege lines and batteries are laid out; an intense bombardment commences by 24 March. At dawn on 28 March three French columns storm the San Javier Monastery—now strengthened and renamed Fort Iturbide—but are repelled by three battalions of the Zacatecas Regiment. The place is carried next afternoon by a second assault that costs 600 French casualties.

After many lesser skirmishes Gen. Tomás O'Horan slips out of Puebla with 2,500 republican troopers the night of 13 April to join Comonfort's army at nearby San Jerónimo. Six days later the French besiegers once again storm the southeastern portions of Puebla, Santa Inés Convent changing hands several times in fierce fighting. During the night of 20 April Rivera attempts to lead a supply column into Puebla, mistakenly clashing with the 4th Zacatecas Battalion in the darkness. At dawn on 24 April French sappers detonate mines beneath Santa Inés Convent, and next morning attempt to overrun the strongpoint; they are thrown back by Lt. Col. Lalane's Zacatecas Battalion plus the 1st Toluca and 2nd Puebla.

On 5 May Comonfort's republican army takes up position at San Lorenzo, hoping to break the siege lines at La Cruz Hill and thereby resupply Puebla. After clashing inconclusively with Márquez's conservative contingent next day, however, Comonfort's left flank is suddenly driven in at dawn on 8 May by a surprise French counterattack under Bazaine. The small Mexican army collapses, suffering 2,000 killed, wounded, or captured; demoralized survivors flee to Tlaxcala. On 9 May Forey releases many prisoners into Puebla, carrying news of the defeat.

On 16 May González Ortega requests terms, surrendering at 5:30 P.M. next day. Forey proves generous, but in one final act of defiance the Mexican defenders destroy their remaining materiel and attempt to disband their units so as not to be considered prisoners of war. Nevertheless, the French seize 1,000 officers and 16,000 troops upon occupying Puebla—5,000 of whom join the victors' ranks.

30 APRIL 1863. ***Camerone.*** At 1:00 A.M. Captain Danjou—wearing a wooden prosthesis, his left arm having been blown off ten years previously by an exploding musket—departs Chiquihuite (Veracruz) with 61 men of the 3rd Company of the 1st French Foreign Legion Battalion to reconnoiter the road leading inland from Paloverde to Puebla in advance of a scheduled payroll shipment for the main army.

While breakfasting at 8:00 A.M. his Legionnaires are surprised by 650 Mexican riders under Colonel Milán who have massed undetected at nearby La Joya. They chase Danjou's company into the hamlet of Camarón, where the desperate French fortify themselves one hour later inside its abandoned hacienda. By afternoon another 1,000 Mexicans of the Veracruz, Jalapa, and Córdoba Mounted Infantry Battalions join Milán, and this evening all overwhelm the defenders in a massive assault. Despite repeated calls for their surrender, Danjou's handful fight gallantly to the last, suffering 30 killed and 32 severely wounded while inflicting heavy casualties.

(Next day 48-year-old Colonel Jeannigros reaches the site with his main Foreign Legion column; in honor of such spirited resistance he removes Danjou's wooden arm before burial, and today it is preserved as a sacred relic at headquarters in Aubagne, France. Every 30 April the legion holds its regimental parade on Camerone Day, with Danjou's wooden arm receiving the salute after a public recitation of his brave act.)

31 MAY 1863. Feeling Mexico City to be indefensible despite a 12,000-man garrison, Juárez abandons the capital for San Luis Potosí, escorted by a division under 32-year-old Gen. José de la Cruz Porfirio Díaz Monroy.

4 JUNE 1863. Forey's vanguard—the Chasseurs de Vincennes Battalion—reaches San Lázaro, just outside Mexico City.

9 JUNE 1863. Juárez's republican government-in-exile reaches San Luis Potosí.

10 JUNE 1863. Led by Márquez's conservative contingent, Forey's army occupies Mexico City. Five days later a new government is temporarily appointed.

17 JUNE 1863. Spanish-born Col. Eduardo G. Arévalo appears before Villahermosa de Tabasco with 200 conservative troops, conquering the town next day.

5 JULY 1863. Berthier occupies Toluca (state of Mexico).

10 JULY 1863. Under Forey's guidance, the new Mexican government offers the title of emperor to Maximilian.

29 JULY 1863. Franco-conservative forces occupy Cuernavaca.

15 AUGUST 1863. Lozada openly swears loyalty to the new conservative government.

12 SEPTEMBER 1863. The French occupy Zacapoaxtla (Puebla).

1 OCTOBER 1863. As a reward for his services, Forey is promoted field marshal; succeeded as commander in chief by Bazaine, he takes ship to Europe by 21 November.

3 OCTOBER 1863. In Europe, a Mexican delegation offers the throne to Maximilian, who requests that a plebiscite be held to determine the Mexican people's will.

10 OCTOBER 1863. The 42-year-old conservative Mexican Gen. Tomás Mejía defeats a republican force at Actopan (Hidalgo) under Herrera y Cairo.

MID-OCTOBER 1863. Arévalo temporarily subdues a republican uprising in Tabasco by surprising the forces gathered at Comalcalco under Andrés Sánchez Magallanes and Gregorio Méndez.

23 OCTOBER 1863. Franco-conservative forces occupy Jalapa.

27 OCTOBER 1863. Díaz attacks the rich mining town of Taxco (Guerrero) with two battalions of Oaxaca chasseurs under Gen. José María Ballesteros (1st Infantry Brigade); two battalions of México Regiment under Col. Manuel González (2nd Infantry Brigade); three battalions of the Sinaloa Regiment under Col. Apolonio Angulo (3rd Infantry Brigade); three squadrons of the San Luis Potosí Cavalry Regiment under Gen. Mariano Escobedo; plus an artillery battery under Lt. Col. Martiniano Ruiz. These 7,000 men overwhelm the defenders next day, taking 269 prisoners.

29 OCTOBER 1863. A hastily organized republican brigade under Sánchez Magallanes and Méndez occupies Cunduacán (Tabasco), three days later defeating conservative Colonel Arévalo at Jahuactal, compelling him to retreat to Villahermosa.

LATE OCTOBER 1863. Douay marches north from Mexico City toward Querétaro with l'Heriller's 1st Brigade, Neigre's 2nd Brigade, Du Barail's cavalry brigade, plus de Maussion's reserve brigade. On 17 November the city is occupied without resistance.

12 NOVEMBER 1863. The Pacific port of Mazatlán is seized without opposition by a French squadron under Cmdr. L. Kergriss (or Kergrist), backed by a military column advancing overland next day under conservative Mexican leader Lozada.

23 NOVEMBER 1863. The republican guerrilla chief Martínez surprises 600 Algerian and conservative troops at Higueras (Sinaloa), chasing them back to Mazatlán with considerable losses.

24 NOVEMBER 1863. After clashing with some Mexican guerrillas near Maravatío (Michoacán), Castagny's 1st Infantry Division occupies Acámbaro, then Morelia six days later.

1 DECEMBER 1863. After being reinforced by Colonel Santibáñez's 450-man brigade at Huajuapam, Díaz's footsore republican army establishes its headquarters in Oaxaca City.

9 DECEMBER 1863. San Miguel Allende, Celaya, and Guanajuato are occupied by the French.

17–18 DECEMBER 1863. Uraga's forces attack the conservative Mexican General Márquez at Morelia (Michoacán), being repelled and driven south to Jalisco with heavy losses.

20 DECEMBER 1863. Threatened by Castagny's and Mejía's parallel drives north, Juárez abandons his provisional capital of San Luis Potosí in favor of Saltillo. By Christmas San Luis Potosí is occupied by the invaders.

23 DECEMBER 1863. At San Pedro (near Culiacán, Sinaloa), 500 French and conservative troops under Colonel Gazielle are routed by 400 Mexican guerrillas under Rosales and Sánchez Román.

27 DECEMBER 1863. Mejía repels a republican counterattack against San Luis Potosí under Gen. Miguel Negrete.

DECEMBER 1863. In a growing rift between Bazaine and some of his Mexican conservative allies, the French general orders Miramón and Taboada to demobilize 3,400 troops at Guanajuato.

6 JANUARY 1864. Guadalajara falls to Franco-conservative forces.

13 JANUARY 1864. Méndez arrives to besiege Arévalo's conservative garrison within Villahermosa de

Tabasco, obliging him to evacuate the stronghold by 27 February.

26 JANUARY 1864. The port of Campeche is seized by the French.

2 FEBRUARY 1864. Aguascalientes City is occupied by Franco-conservative forces.

7 FEBRUARY 1864. Zacatecas City falls to the French and Mexican conservatives.

27 FEBRUARY 1864. The former dictator Santa Anna returns from exile in Turbaco (Colombia), arriving at Veracruz aboard the British vessel *Conway.* Bazaine allows him ashore after extracting a loyalty oath to the new conservative government, Santa Anna further promising not to take part in any political activity. However, after almost immediately issuing a call to his adherents through the *Indicador* newspaper, Santa Anna is deported aboard the corvette *Colbert,* being deposited at Havana by 12 March, from where he continues back to Colombia.

7 MARCH 1864. The 38-year-old Mexican Gen. Mariano Escobedo—after separating from Díaz (*see* 27 October 1863) then being driven out of southern Mexico into the United States—recrosses the Texas border with a handful of followers and occupies Nuevo Laredo.

29 MARCH 1864. Juárez deposes Santiago Vidaurri, governor of Coahuila and Nuevo León, for hinting at switching to the conservative cause.

MARCH 1864. Bazaine directs Generals Miramón and Taboada to serve under the French commander at Guadalajara, prompting the Mexican conservatives to resign.

3 APRIL 1864. Juárez temporarily reestablishes his government in Monterrey (Nuevo León).

10 APRIL 1864. In Europe, Maximilian—having the previous day renounced all claims to the Austrian throne after receiving the favorable results of a Mexican plebiscite (*see* 3 October 1863)—accepts Mexico's crown. Napoleon promises to support him for three years, gradually reducing the size of the French expeditionary force from 38,000 to 20,000.

17 MAY 1864. Mejía and French Colonel Aymard destroy a republican force at Matehuala under General Doblado.

28 MAY 1864. Maximilian and Belgian-born Empress Charlotte (called Carlota in Mexico) reach Veracruz aboard the frigate *Novara.*

3 JUNE 1864. Acapulco is captured by five French warships; a week later 400 of its occupiers push inland, seizing La Sabana Pass.

12 JUNE 1864. Maximilian enters Mexico City to a generally warm reception. Many Mexican conservatives, however, are soon offended by some of the idealistic young monarch's more liberal opinions; republicans continue to loathe him as a foreign puppet.

1 AUGUST 1864. ***Brincourt's Offensive.*** Two French battalions reach Huajuapam to inaugurate a four-pronged offensive against Oaxaca. In addition to General Brincourt's contingent, Giraud is to march from Orizaba through Teotitlán; Mexican imperial columns are to depart Cuernavaca and Atlixco toward Chilapa and Tlapa, respectively.

Shortly after penetrating into republican-held territory, Díaz slips between both French units with 2,000 men to fall upon a company of the 7th Line Regiment and some imperial cavalry, which are garrisoning San Antonio Teotitlán in the rear. This defeat prompts Giraud and Brincourt to about-face and return to San Antonio Teotitlán by 17 August.

Once more resuming his advance southeast, Brincourt approaches Nochistlán (60 miles northwest of Oaxaca City), only to discover that it has been heavily fortified by Díaz. From Mexico City, Bazaine prohibits any direct storming of the stronghold, having insufficient reserves for a relief column should an assault miscarry. Brincourt therefore retires to his original bases.

19 AUGUST 1864. Díaz leads a Mexican counterattack against San Antonio Nanhuatipan, being repelled.

12 DECEMBER 1864. General Curtois d'Hurbal reaches Yanhuitlán with a French siege train, being part of a new, three-pronged offensive against Díaz in Oaxaca. Five days later d'Hurbal is joined at San Francisco Huitzo by another French contingent, then presses southeast against Etla, which he occupies with little difficulty on 18 December.

1 JANUARY 1865. The 27-year-old republican Gen. Ramón Corona, with 600 ill-armed guerrillas, attempts to dispute the westward passage through the Sierra Madre Mountains—from Durango to Mazatlán—of Colonel Garnier's 18th Chasseur and 31st Line Regiments with their respective artillery trains plus Lozada's

irregulars. Despite the highly defensible position chosen at Espinazo del Diablo (Devil's Spine), the Mexicans are eventually enveloped and scattered.

6 JANUARY 1865. In Mexico City, conservative General Taboada is arrested on suspicion of plotting against the emperor.

11 JANUARY 1865. Corona surprises part of General Gastagny's supply train at Veranos station (Sinaloa), defeating its escort of 150 soldiers from the 7th Chasseurs de Vincennes Regiment plus 50 armed teamsters. The 60 French and 40 teamster prisoners are then hanged, prompting Castagny to issue a decree from Mazatlán on 25 January ordering the execution of all republican guerrillas.

17 JANUARY 1865. ***Siege of Oaxaca.*** Bazaine reaches Etla to personally assume command of the 4,000 infantry advancing into Oaxaca against Díaz: two battalions of the 3rd Zouave Regiment, 12 companies of Foreign Legionnaires, plus a battalion of Infanterie Légere d'Afrique. They are supported by 1,000 troopers—a company of mounted Zouaves, three squadrons of French cavalry, four of Mexican imperial riders—plus a dozen 12-pound siege guns, eight four-pound field pieces, and six mortars manned by 80 gunners with 200 sappers and 500 auxiliaries rounding out the force.

Within a couple of days advance French elements begin harrying the republican defenders just north of Oaxaca City, prompting Díaz to order his cavalry—700 dragoons under Col. Félix Díaz—to exit, preparing the remainder of his 3,000 regulars and 4,000 militia to withstand a siege. On 21 January Col. José Guillermo Carbó's Morelos Battalion sallies and falls upon some French units at Aguilera Hacienda, this action eventually involving two other companies of the Sinaloa Battalion plus one of the Sierra Juárez.

However, the defenders otherwise mount no more counterattacks once Colonel Dutretaine commences his siege works on 1 February by installing batteries opposite the city and atop Mogote and Pelado Hills. By 8 February republican morale collapses and Díaz surrenders, being carried off into captivity along with Cols. Juan Espinosa, Manuel González, and Francisco Carrión.

28 JANUARY 1865. At Potrerillo (Jalisco), republican guerrilla Col. Antonio Rojas is surprised and killed by a Zouave contingent under Berthelin.

1 APRIL 1865. Lozada defeats Corona in a skirmish at Concordia (Sinaloa).

9 APRIL 1865. After having once been briefly occupied by republican forces under General Aguirre, Saltillo (Coahuila) is reconquered from an imperial garrison by Negrete's 3,000 troops.

12 APRIL 1865. Negrete takes Monterrey (Nuevo León) without opposition, the city having been abandoned by imperial Generals Olvera and López.

18 APRIL 1865. Lozada bests Corona at an encounter near Cacalotán (Sinaloa).

23 APRIL 1865. The republican Col. Pedro Méndez occupies Ciudad Victoria (Tamaulipas); Col. Francisco Naranjo seizes Piedras Negras (opposite Eagle Pass, Texas).

30 APRIL 1865. Two and a half weeks after occupying Monterrey, Negrete marches his 4,000 republican troops against Mejía's imperial garrison at Matamoros (opposite Brownsville, Texas)—only to retire next day upon learning of the latter's strength, plus the possible intervention of Confederates in Texas.

25 MAY 1865. French General Jeannigros reaches San Buenaventura (Coahuila) from San Luis Potosí with 1,500 troops to join Brincourt's column approaching out of the west-northwest from Parras (Durango) and attack the Mexican concentration around Saltillo under Negrete, Escobedo, and León Guzmán.

30 MAY 1865. ***La Angostura.*** Jeannigros probes north through Piñón, Carnero, Agua Nueva, and San Juan de la Vaquería, finally encountering the main republican defenses at La Angostura (site of the American victory of Buena Vista; *see* 22 February 1847 in Mexican-American War). Despite being outnumbered, the French general sends two columns of infantry into the attack on 1 June supported by four artillery pieces. The defenders scatter them with concentrated volleys, after which Jeannigros waits for his colleague, Brincourt, to close from the north, hoping to trap Negrete between. Instead, Negrete slips away the night of 6–7 June, retreating northwest to Chihuahua.

18 JUNE 1865. Republican General Arteaga overruns Uruapan (Michoacán), executing its imperial garrison commander and other officials as traitors.

16 AUGUST 1865. Gen. Albino Espinosa with 480 republican riders overtakes a rich mule train at Las Cabras Ford on the San Juan River (Tamaulipas),

which is being escorted from Monterrey to Matamoros by 100 imperial troopers, 700 infantry, and two howitzers under General Tinajero. The surprised escorts disperse, suffering 60 killed and 80 captured.

21 SEPTEMBER 1865. Republican Gen. Porfirio Díaz escapes from confinement within the Jesuit monastery at Puebla, 1,000 pesos being offered as a reward for his recapture.

3 OCTOBER 1865. The imperial government orders that all republican soldiers and guerrillas be considered bandits and summarily executed if found under arms.

21 OCTOBER 1865. Captive republican General Arteaga and four of his officers are executed in Uruapan in compliance with the 3 October decree.

23 OCTOBER 1865. ***Defense of Matamoros.*** Having concentrated several thousand followers at Cerralvo (Tamaulipas), Escobedo arrives to besiege the imperial garrison at Matamoros. After installing an eight-gun battery and siege lines southwest of the walls on 24 October, the attackers mount a three-pronged assault next dawn, with General Hinojosa storming Fort San Fernando on the right; Naranjo driving against the city center; and Cortina proceeding against Fort Freeport on the left. All are checked by heavy counterfires, after which the republicans settle down to a formal siege. Soon their ammunition supply—and patience—begins to run low; the siege is abandoned by 14 November.

23 NOVEMBER 1865. ***Monterrey.*** Nonplussed by his failure at Matamoros, Escobedo gathers another small army outside Monterrey—whose French troops have departed, leaving only an imperial garrison under Tinajero and Quiroga. They launch a sudden sally on 23 November against the republican besiegers on Guadalupe Hill, being checked by Col. Jerónimo Treviño's cavalry. Two days later Escobedo sends twin assault columns under Colonel Naranjo and Lieutenant Colonel de la Garza to storm the city's Carlota and Pueblo redoubts.

After two hours' heavy fighting they gain Monterrey's main square, only to be interrupted by the unexpected arrival of a French relief column from Saltillo under the Foreign Legion's Major La Hayrie. Learning that Jeannigros is not far behind with another 800 soldiers, Escobedo's followers break off and withdraw in two directions, bloodying a pursuit column at Los Lermas before escaping into the mountains.

EARLY JANUARY 1866. Two columns of 1,000 French and 1,200 imperial troops sortie from the Pacific port of Mazatlán in a vain attempt to chase away the republican guerrillas under Corona and Captain Miramontes, who have been hampering communications inland.

22 JANUARY 1866. In Paris, Napoleon—under increasing domestic and international pressure to withdraw from Mexico—declares the intervention a success and dispatches a delegation to Maximilian to discuss accelerating his troop withdrawal.

12 FEBRUARY 1866. At dawn republican Governor Viezca of Coahuila seizes the town of Parras.

20 FEBRUARY 1866. Major de Brian de Foussières Fousseneville marches from Saltillo with four companies of the 2nd French Foreign Legion Battalion and recuperates Parras from Viezca without opposition. However, when Brian learns on 25 February that the republican governor has withdrawn only seven miles north into the mountains with 300 men, establishing his headquarters at Santa Isabel Hacienda atop La Cruz Hill, the major sallies at midnight on 27–28 February to attack—little realizing that Viezca has been heavily reinforced by Colonels Treviño and Naranjo.

Before first light Brian's two companies (188 Legionnaires) and 250 imperial partisans approach the hacienda, only to be greeted by heavy volleys out of the darkness. The French commander falls severely wounded, his auxiliaries flee, and Captain Moulinier leads the surviving Legionnaires in a hopeless series of assaults, which cease at dawn when republican cavalry circles behind the attackers, cutting off escape. Eventually, a single French soldier crawls back to Parras, more than 80 others being killed and 100 captured.

4 MARCH 1866. At Río Frío (state of Mexico), a Belgian delegation is attacked by republican guerrillas, who kill General Forey and Captain d'Huart, traveling with the foreign visitors.

24 MARCH 1866. Lozada's imperial forces surprise Col. Perfecto Guzmán's company at Guapicori (Sonora), dispersing it before skirmishing with Corona at Concordia (Sinaloa) then retiring to Mazatlán by 11 April.

1 APRIL 1866. Escobedo attacks Matehuala (San Luis Potosí) then detaches subordinate Ruperto Martínez west to loot the rich mining camp of Real de Catorce.

11 APRIL 1866. Republican Gen. Nicolás Régules surprises Tacámbaro (Michoacán), overwhelming its garrison of four Belgian and one imperial company.

1 JUNE 1866. French units are recalled from Mexico's interior to reassemble in the capital.

12 JUNE 1866. ***Santa Gertrudis.*** Escobedo attacks a large mule train at Cerralvo (Nuevo León), which is being escorted east from Monterrey to Matamoros by two battalions of French Foreign Legionnaires under Lieutenant Colonel Tucé, numerous Belgian and imperial auxiliaries, some cavalry squadrons, and six artillery pieces.

After pinning them down with 600 dragoons under Col. Ruperto Martínez, Escobedo wheels his remaining 1,500 troops and three guns east and waits in ambush for another mule train at Derramaderos (near Santa Gertrudis). This second group is proceeding west from Matamoros to meet the first convoy and is escorted by 2,000 Austrian and imperial troops under Olvera with 13 field pieces.

On the morning of 15 June Olvera advances in skirmish line to drive back Escobedo's scouts, little realizing the hidden forces awaiting him. The republicans open fire once the enemy comes within close range then launch a devastating attack with 34-year-old Gen. Sóstenes Rocha's cavalry. Some 400 surprised enemies are killed and another 1,000 captured, Olvera fleeing the battlefield with only a handful of riders. Republican casualties total 155 killed and 78 wounded.

Upon learning of Olvera's fate, Tucé retires to Monterrey by 28 June; Mejía then evacuates half-starved Matamoros with the consent of republican General Carvajal outside.

8 JULY 1866. Empress Carlota departs Mexico City for Paris to beseech Napoleon to maintain his French army in Mexico.

11 JULY 1866. In Nayarit, Lozada abandons the imperial cause, declaring himself neutral.

26 JULY 1866. Jeannigros abandons Monterrey (Nuevo León).

7 AUGUST 1866. Tampico (Tamaulipas) is recaptured by republican forces.

14 SEPTEMBER 1866. The French evacuate the Pacific port of Guaymas (Sonora).

23 SEPTEMBER 1866. Porfirio Díaz's cavalry defeats a Hungarian contingent at Nochistlán (Oaxaca), slaying its leader, Count de Gans.

3 OCTOBER 1866. ***Miahuatlán.*** While waiting to be joined by General Ramos's republican cavalry brigade, Porfirio Díaz digs in facing northwest from Miahuatlán (Oaxaca) with Col. Manuel González's 130-man brigade; Lt. Col. Juan J. Cano's 100-man Morelos Battalion; Cmdr. Felipe Cruz's 230 Tiradores de Montaña (rangers); Col. José Segura's 96-man Patria Battalion; an 80-man Chiautla company; the 130-man Fieles de la Patria Battalion; plus 40 local militia.

They are discovered and attacked by 1,100 French and imperial troops under General Oronoz, consisting of an infantry brigade (chasseur battalion and the 9th French Line Regiment), several cavalry squadrons under General Trujeque, plus two 12-inch field pieces. The French-imperial forces close on the republican positions from Matadero Rise in three columns, preceded by a skirmishing line and long-range bombardment.

Díaz checks them along Nogales Ravine then sends his cavalry—spearheaded by the Tepejí Squadron—across Miahuatlán River to circle behind and fall upon the enemy's right rear. Oronoz flees the battlefield, leaving behind some 70 dead (including his French second-in-command, Colonel Testard) plus 400 prisoners and two artillery pieces. Republican losses total 59 killed and 140 wounded.

5 OCTOBER 1866. Having crushed the imperial forces at Miahuatlán, Col. Félix Díaz's cavalry occupies most of Oaxaca City, being joined next day by Porfirio Díaz's main body, which besieges Oronoz's remaining followers within the Santo Domingo, El Carmen, and La Soledad strongholds.

16 OCTOBER 1866. Learning that 1,500 Austrian and imperial troops are marching to the relief of Oaxaca, Díaz breaks off his siege tonight and sorties to give battle. On 17 October he is reinforced at San Juan del Estado by General Figueroa's brigade then presses northwest toward Etla.

(Also on 16 October a discouraged Maximilian quits Mexico City, determined to travel to Veracruz and depart because of his government's flagging fortunes, American opposition, and reduced French support.)

18 OCTOBER 1866. ***La Carbonera.*** Around noon Díaz's scouts discover the Austro-imperial army approaching, so his 3,000-man main body halts facing northeast, looking up the main highway bisecting the

valley beneath the hamlet of La Carbonera. On the republican right lies Figueroa's Brigade; in the center, the Chiautla and Cazadores Battalions (350 men under Col. Juan Espinosa); on the left, González's brigade (consisting of the Patria and Morelos battalions); to the rear, cavalry from the Fieles, Montaña, Guerrero, and Costa Chica Regiments plus Tlaxiaco militia and some artillery.

Shortly thereafter the enemy appears, and despite being outnumbered two-to-one, immediately deploys for battle. After marshaling on a nearby height two companies of 300 men each advance on the republican lines, only to be repelled. Both armies close and fight a general action. Eventually, the Austro-imperial right is outflanked, and their cohesion disintegrates. Díaz's victorious troops pursue the vanquished foe for 12 miles, capturing 500 prisoners and four field pieces.

20 OCTOBER 1866. Díaz returns into Oaxaca City to resume his siege of its isolated citadels. They capitulate by 31 October, the republicans capturing 350 Franco-imperial defenders and 16 guns.

21 OCTOBER 1866. Maximilian reaches Orizaba and meets French plenipotentiary Castelnau, who attempts to persuade the Emperor to abdicate and return to Europe.

Also today Washington recognizes Juárez's republican government as the sole legitimate representative of the Mexican people.

12 NOVEMBER 1866. The French having abandoned it and sailed south five days earlier, the port of Mazatlán is reoccupied by Corona.

26 NOVEMBER 1866. ***Sedgwick's Intervention.*** The republican government, having disapproved of the terms under which Matamoros surrendered to Carvajal, sends Gen. Santiago Tapia to assume command over its garrison. But Tapia is instead deposed by Colonel Canales, who is declared a rebel; Escobedo therefore arrives with 2,700 men to subdue this mutinous contingent.

In the interim, U.S. General Sedgwick has occupied Matamoros from Brownsville, citing fears over the safety of American citizens. Escobedo prepares to storm its walls at dawn on 27 November to comply with his original instructions for arresting Canales. After a half-hour bombardment republican columns fight their way into the city, and a cease-fire is requested by the Americans and the mutineers. Escobedo agrees, withdrawing to institute a siege. Canales surrenders on 30 November, the Americans evacuate, and Escobedo enters Matamoros.

1 DECEMBER 1866. After the importuning of such conservative leaders as Márquez and Miramón, Maximilian agrees to remain as emperor, even after the French withdraw.

6 DECEMBER 1866. Under mounting pressure to eliminate all foreign support for his government, Maximilian offers Austro-Belgian volunteers the option of departing Veracruz or joining the imperial Mexican army with higher ranks.

19 DECEMBER 1866. Porfirio Díaz sorties from Oaxaca City to Tehuacán to clear the Isthmus of Tehuantepec of Franco-imperial garrisons.

EARLY JANUARY 1867. With outnumbered imperial forces retreating toward the capital, San Luis Potosí is reoccupied without opposition by a northern cavalry contingent under republican General Treviño.

10 JANUARY 1867. French General Castelnau receives orders from Paris to begin reembarking the Foreign Legion, plus the Austrian and Belgian contingents, for return to Europe. Within a month most are going aboard ship at Veracruz.

16 JANUARY 1867. Escobedo's 10,000-man republican army reaches San Luis Potosí from northern Mexico, pausing to refresh.

22 JANUARY 1867. Juárez's government-in-exile reaches Zacatecas City, only to be driven out within a week by news of the approach of Miramón's 2,000-man imperial army from Querétaro.

26 JANUARY 1867. After defeating General Liceaga's 1,500 imperial troops and 22 artillery pieces outside Guanajuato, republican General Antillón reoccupies the city while his defeated foe falls back on Querétaro.

31 JANUARY 1867. ***San Jacinto.*** Learning that Escobedo is fast approaching with a much larger republican army, Miramón hastens southeast out of Zacatecas, hoping to unite near San Luis Potosí with another 2,000-man imperial army under Gen. Severo del Castillo.

Instead, Miramón unexpectedly meets Escobedo the next day at San Diego Hacienda, on the road between San Jacinto and San Francisco de Adames. The outnumbered imperial infantry occupies the hacienda, cavalry on both flanks. But Escobedo's superior force easily overwhelms the defenses, driving the enemy back into Cuisillo Ranch. Miramón is fortunate to escape to Querétaro with a handful of followers, leaving behind 100 dead, 800 captives, his artillery and supply trains, plus countless deserters.

(After this battle Escobedo executes 103 French prisoners for violating the decree recalling them to Europe.)

13 FEBRUARY 1867. Determined to maintain his throne by battlefield victories, Maximilian quits Mexico City at the head of 4,000 troops raised by Márquez, marching northwest toward Querétaro. Skirmishes occur at Lechería and Calpulalpan with republican guerrillas under Catarino Fragoso before the emperor finally reaches San Juan del Río (16 February).

19 FEBRUARY 1867. Maximilian enters Querétaro City with 1,600 troops and a dozen field pieces.

20 FEBRUARY 1867. Corona enters Morelia (Michoacán), mustering 6,000–7,000 republican troops and departing five days later to strike into the interior of imperial Mexico via Acámbaro and Celaya.

22 FEBRUARY 1867. Imperial Gen. José Ramón Méndez reenters Querétaro City from Morelia with 3,500 troops and an artillery train, augmenting the garrison to 12,000 men.

27 FEBRUARY 1867. Corona's republican army is joined at Celaya by an additional 3,000 men and ten artillery pieces under Colonels Franco and Bermúdez.

5 MARCH 1867. After conferring at Chamacuero, Escobedo and Corona agree to begin their final advance against Maximilian's stronghold at Querétaro next day in parallel columns of approximately 10,000 men each.

6 MARCH 1867. ***Siege of Querétaro.*** Advance republican cavalry units occupy Estancia de las Vacas and Castillo Hacienda outside Querétaro City, being joined two days later by Corona's column, which seizes San Juanico and Celaya Gate—just as Escobedo's contingent appears out of the north.

Together the generals command Treviño's I (Northern) Corps, consisting of two infantry divisions under Sóstenes Rocha and Francisco Arce plus a cavalry division under Francisco Aguirre; Corona's II (Western) Corps, comprising the Jalisco Infantry Division under Manuel Márquez, the Sinaloa Infantry Division under Félix Vega, the Michoacán Infantry Division under Régules, plus the 3rd Division from I Corps under Saturnino Aranda; and an artillery train under Francisco Paz. Eventually, the host swells to 32,000 troops and 100 guns, prompting the formation of a separate cavalry division under Gen. Amado Guadarrama.

Guard of the "Supreme Powers" regiment

To oppose them, Maximilian has a 12,000-man garrison under his chief-of-staff, Márquez: del Castillo's 1st Division, consisting of the 1st Brigade (Tiradores Battalion, Celaya Light Infantry, and 2nd Line Regiment) plus the 2nd Brigade (14th Line Regiment and Guardia Municipal); Casanova's 2nd Division, subdivided into 1st Brigade (Querétaro Battalion plus the 7th and 12th Line Regiments) and 2nd Brigade (Cazadores Battalion plus the 15th Line Regiment); a cavalry division under Mejía, again consisting of 1st Brigade (4th and 5th Cavalry Regiments) and 2nd Brigade (2nd and La Frontera Cavalry Regiments); Méndez's reserve, being a mixed brigade of the Emperador Battalion, 3rd Line Regiment, and Emperatriz Regiment; plus the 3rd Engineering Company under Colonel Reyes and artillery batteries under Col. Manuel Ramírez de Arellano.

Escobedo occupies the hills and roads north of Querétaro, and on 9 March he detaches 5,000 men and 14 guns to strengthen Corona's lines. After positioning his cumbersome army for several days the republican commander in chief orders a general probe of the defenses. At 10:00 A.M. on 14 March a diversionary attack commences against Las Campanas Hill, followed quickly by a three-pronged drive against La Cruz Convent (Maximilian's headquarters) under General Neri. The latter overruns its garden and cemetery but is eventually driven back when Márquez orders an imperial infantry battalion and battery to counterattack. Mejía simultaneously sallies from Pueblito Gate with his imperial cavalry, falling upon some republican dragoons opposite and scattering them, capturing 70 and killing 100 in the process. Escobedo's lone success is the seizure of San Gregorio Hill to the north, the operations costing him 1,000 casualties and 4,000 prisoners compared to 250 killed and wounded among the defenders.

Following this bloody setback the republicans settle down to a protracted siege. On 17 March Corona launches another assault against La Cruz Convent, but only to discourage a sortie being contemplated by Miramón (hoping to reestablish his prestige with the emperor). At dawn on 22 March Miramón exits with the imperial Guardia Municipal and Cazadores Battalions in his van, supported by a half-dozen field pieces and a cloud of cavalry. They surprise a republican supply train that has just reached San Juanico Hacienda, capturing and carrying it back to Querétaro with scarcely any losses.

This same night, Márquez and Vidaurri slip out of the besieged city with two cavalry brigades—1,100 troopers—having been ordered by Maximilian to cut their way through to Mexico City and hasten the dispatch of reinforcements. By sunrise on 23 March Márquez's contingent is well on its way, but instead of immediately returning with a relief column, he heads east from the capital one week later to rescue the beleaguered imperial garrison at Puebla (*see* 9 March 1867).

At noon on 24 March Escobedo—freshly reinforced by 9,000–10,000 men under Gens. Vicente Riva Palacio, Vicente Jiménez, and Francisco A. Vélez—attempts a second assault on Querétaro's walls. The main thrust is directed against Casa Blanca and the Alameda by twin columns under Generals Vélez and Joaquín Martínez, supported by numerous diversionary actions. Again the drive is repelled by timely imperial counterattacks after republicans penetrate the city. Republican losses total 2,000 killed, wounded, and captured for no gain.

Next it is the defenders' turn: Miramón sorties on 1 April with eight infantry battalions and 1,000 dragoons to attack the republican siege lines extending from San Sebastián Convent (northwest of Querétaro). Once more, an initial success is followed by quick containment, the imperial forces eventually retreating into their defenses. Morale within the city begins to sag, especially when two cavalry sallies on 12 and 16 April—attempts to reestablish contact with Mexico City—are checked.

At 5:00 A.M. on 27 March Miramón leads another sudden exit south, this time surprising Jiménez's republican troops, who are holding the México Gate and Calleja Hacienda. Brushing these aside, Miramón continues past with 3,000 troops in two columns, defeating Rivera's republican cavalry, who are belatedly hastening to Jiménez's support. The imperial forces then seize Jacal Hacienda from the Sinaloa Regiment, precipitating a wholesale republican flight from their rearmost trenches at Cimatario. In this fashion, Miramón not only seizes 21 guns and valuable provisions from supply parks in the republican rear but also breaks Querétaro's encirclement. Maximilian personally visits the battlefield to congratulate his general.

However, both emperor and staff fail to properly exploit the advantage either by leading their army out of the city or securing the breach. Instead, it is Escobedo who reacts first, throwing the Galeana Battalion—armed with repeating rifles—and San Luis Potosí Chasseurs into the gap while the Norte Cavalry Regiment recuperates much of the booty being transferred into the city. Naranjo, Guadarrama, and Tolentino then lead a massive cavalry movement behind republican lines from the southwest, recovering Jacal with a 3,000-dragoon charge. Maximilian commits the Emperatriz Cavalry Regiment in a last-ditch effort to regain his vanishing booty, but it too is repelled. The disappointed imperial troops stream back to Querétaro while Rocha reoccupies the besiegers' original positions at the México Gate and Calleja Hacienda.

At dawn on 1 May Miramón tries again, inaugurating a heavy bombardment of Calleja Hacienda, followed at 10:00 A.M. by an assault spearheaded by the Cazadores Franco-Mexicanos Battalion, 3rd Line Regiment, and Guardia Municipal under Colonel Rodríguez. They succeed in overrunning the hacienda but get no farther before being chased back into the city when Rodríguez is killed. On 3 May Miramón thrusts north toward San Gregorio, breaking through the first two republican siege lines with the 3rd and 13th Line Regiments plus the Emperador, Iturbide, and Celaya Battalions. Once more he is contained and retires. A final imperial breakout is attempted northeast toward San Sebastián on 5 May but is easily defeated.

By this time the garrison is left with only 5,000–6,000 effectives; civilians starve. Before sunrise on 15 May Col. Miguel López, commander of the La Cruz stronghold, agrees to surrender his crucial imperial redoubt to the republican besiegers in a piece of prearranged treachery. As Vélez's Supremo Poderes and 1st Nuevo León Battalions advance to seize the building the emperor flees west from his sleeping quarters, calling on his supporters to rally atop Las Campanas Hill. Dawn reveals their pathetically reduced numbers, at which point the last imperial defenders capitulate to Escobedo.

9 MARCH 1867. ***Reconquest of Puebla.*** Porfirio Díaz arrives at San Juan Hill (west of Puebla) with 3,000 republican troops to lay siege to its 3,000-man garrison under Gen. Manuel Noriega. After being reinforced by local contingents and cutting off all communication inland, the republicans inaugurate formal siege proceedings.

Within the next couple of weeks General Carrión seizes the San Javier and Penitenciaría redoubts through costly assaults, as the republicans gradually fight their way into the city limits. Díaz is unable to completely subdue the defenders, however, and on 31 March he receives word that Márquez has quit Mexico City the day before with a relief column of 3,000 imperial troops and 17 field pieces.

Acting swiftly, the republican general gathers three assault columns of 300 men apiece to storm Puebla's main stronghold—El Carmen Convent—plus 13 companies of approximately 100 men each to stealthily approach other points in the city's defenses. At 2:00 A.M. on 2 April the three-pronged attack is launched against El Carmen. After ninety minutes of noisy fighting—long enough for Noriega to commit his reserves—Díaz signals from San Juan Hill, directing his 1,300 hidden soldiers to rise and mount simultaneous attacks. They break through everywhere, only the Siempreviva trenches and Carmen Convent offering much resistance before surrendering.

Noriega's remaining defenders seek refuge in the Loreto and Guadalupe Convents, being compelled to capitulate two days later. The assault has cost Díaz 253 dead and 233 wounded compared to much higher casualties among the defenders (and 2,000 captives). The republican commander quickly detaches Colonel Lalane with 900 troopers on 4 April to monitor the approach of Márquez's imperial relief column.

8 APRIL 1867. ***San Lorenzo.*** While still camped at Guadalupe Hacienda (Tlaxcala), Márquez learns of the fall of the imperial garrison within Puebla as well as the approach of a 4,000-man republican cavalry division out of the north under Guadarrama (having been detached from Querétaro on 29 March by Escobedo).

Next day Márquez's 3,000 men make contact with Díaz's larger army at San Lorenzo near Apizaco, deploying his republicans in an extended line and commencing a long-range bombardment to pin down the imperial troops while awaiting Guadarrama. Knowing his forces to be doomed, Márquez orders a retreat in several columns next dawn—10 April—only to encounter Guadarrama barring his path at San Cristóbal Hacienda. Losing all hope, the imperial general orders most of his artillery cast into a ravine and supply carts burned before escaping into the mountains.

Meanwhile his Austro-Mexican infantry and Hungarian cavalry make a brave fighting retreat from San Lorenzo through San Cristóbal to Texcoco against overwhelming odds. Eventually, they are crushed on 10 April by republican cavalry under General Leyva, suffering 300 killed and 1,000 captured.

LATE APRIL 1867. Díaz arrives outside Mexico City and occupies the outlying towns of Chapultepec, Tacubaya, and Guadalupe, although his army is not strong enough to carry the capital itself.

24 MAY 1867. Emperor Maximilian, a captive, is put on trial at the Iturbide Theater in Querétaro along with Miramón and Mejía.

19 JUNE 1867. At 7:05 A.M. Maximilian, Miramón, and Mejía are shot atop Las Campanas Hill (Querétaro).

20 JUNE 1867. This afternoon imperial Gen. Ramón Tabera surrenders Mexico City to Porfirio Díaz, who enters next day. His troops capture and execute Vidaurri for treason.

27 JUNE 1867. The Veracruz garrison surrenders to republican forces, being the last imperial holdout of the war.

15 JULY 1867. Juárez returns triumphantly to Mexico City, being reelected president this year and again in 1871. Napoleon's failed attempt to revive an American colonial empire marks France's last major military venture in the New World.

North American Indian Wars (1861–1890)

In the United States, the second half of the nineteenth century witnesses an explosive migration inland from the original European colonies of the Atlantic seaboard. New settlers soon come into conflict with nomadic tribesmen roaming the sparsely inhabited plains, and a protracted struggle ensues for ownership over the lands. Most campaigns consist of raids and counterraids, with few large-scale battles.

January 1861. Lt. George Bascom of the 7th Infantry leads 54 mounted soldiers to Apache Pass (New Mexico) to rescue two kidnapped boys. Cochise—leader of the central Chiricahua Apache—meets the contingent and informs the commander that the captives have been taken by neighboring Coyotero Apaches, offering to intercede. Instead, Bascom accuses Cochise of collusion, prompting the Chiricahua leader to cut his way out of the tent, leaving behind his retinue as hostages.

A few days later Cochise returns with prisoners taken from the Butterfield Mail, offering to exchange them for his followers. However, a brief skirmish erupts, during which both sides kill their hostages and withdraw.

17 August 1862. ***Sioux Uprising.*** In Acton Township (Meeker County, southwestern Minnesota), an Indian hunting party treacherously kills three white men and two women gathered on their farm for Sunday dinner. This precipitates a general rebellion next morning under chief Little Crow of the Lower Sioux, who have grown resentful of the settlers' continual encroachments and broken promises.

On 18 August both the Lower and Upper Agency are ransacked; several hundred civilians are killed throughout this district while terrified survivors stream toward Fort Ridgely. Capt. John Marsh leads 47 soldiers toward the Lower Agency ferry to investigate, only to be ambushed and killed along with 26 of his men. His successor, Lt. Timothy Sheehan, musters 180 soldiers at Fort Ridgely, which is attacked on 19 August by 200 of Little Crow's warriors. Repelled by three cannons, the Indian chief makes a second attempt at noon on 21 August with 800 men, which also proves futile. The attackers draw off after suffering perhaps 100 casualties compared to three killed and 13 wounded among the defenders.

On 23 August the town of New Ulm (20 miles southeast of Fort Ridgely) is assaulted by a large number of Sioux but successfully held by Justice of the Peace Charles Flandrau. The defenders suffer 26 dead and more than 60 wounded; 190 of New Ulm's 215 buildings go up in flames, prompting the 1,000 survivors to withdraw 30 miles farther east to Mankato.

As thousands of refugees continue to flee east out of the region the cavalry vanguard of Col. Henry Sibley's 1,400-man relief column reaches Fort Ridgely from Fort Snelling by dawn on 27 August. A detachment under Maj. Joseph R. Brown is subsequently ambushed at the head of Birch Coulee, suffering 16 killed and 44 wounded before being rescued, but Sibley nonetheless presses deeper into Indian territory. At Wood Lake, his army—now increased to 1,600 men—fends off an ambush by 700–800 Sioux then scatters Little Crow's followers farther west. At a site renamed Camp Release, 269 captives are freed from Indian bondage and 2,000 Sioux are arrested. Of the latter, 38 are eventually executed in Mankato on 26 December; the rest are resettled on a reservation on the banks of the Niobrara River (Nebraska) a few years later.

Mid-August 1868. ***Beecher Island.*** Because of Washington's failure to supply aid promised at the Medicine Lodge Creek conference of almost a year earlier, Cheyenne, Sioux, and Arapaho war bands under chief Roman Nose begin raiding along the Saline and Solomon Rivers (Kansas), killing more than 100 settlers. In response, 30-year-old Maj. George A. Forsyth sets out from Fort Hays with 50 volunteer scouts on 29 August, eventually tracking some of the warriors along the Republican River into eastern Colorado and encamping the afternoon of 16 September near Arikaree Fork.

Here the scouts are assaulted at dawn on 17 September by several hundred braves. Forsyth immediately moves his outnumbered men onto an island in the partially dried riverbed and digs in. After many probes and repeated sniping, Roman Nose personally leads a massive charge around noon, which is broken when the Cheyenne chief falls mortally wounded. Nevertheless, the Indians keep the volunteers pinned down for the next nine days with galling fire until four men manage to slip out through the besiegers' ring and summon help in the form of two troops of the all-black 10th Cavalry Regiment under Lt. Col. Louis H. Carpenter. They rescue the survivors from the place that is renamed Beecher Island in honor of Forsyth's fallen second-in-command, Lt. Frederick H. Beecher (nephew to the famous abolitionist preacher Henry Ward Beecher). During the encounter five scouts have been killed and 18 wounded compared to at least 32 dead among the attackers, who disperse.

SEPTEMBER 1872. The 32-year-old Col. Ranald Slidell Mackenzie of the 4th Cavalry makes a surprise attack on a large Comanche village at McClellan's Creek (tributary of the Red River's north fork, in the Texas Panhandle), killing 20 Indians and capturing 130, along with 3,000 horses. Roving warrior bands soon recapture most of the mounts, along with some of the troopers' ponies. Cavalry losses total one dead and three wounded.

DECEMBER 1872. Major Brown—a subordinate of Brig. Gen. George Crook—runs a band of Tonto Apache to ground at Salt River Cave (a huge, shallow cavern 400–500 feet from a cliff top in New Mexico). Thinking themselves safe, the Indians make a stand, only to be decimated by bullets ricocheting down off the roof. Their desperate last-minute attempt to cut their way out ends in a massacre. A similar victory shortly thereafter at Turret Mountain secures the surrender of the majority of the remaining Tontos.

17 MAY 1873. This evening Colonel Mackenzie leads a cavalry column out of Fort Clark (Bracketville, Texas, 140 miles west of San Antonio); next dawn he splashes across the Rio Grande into Mexico to surprise a band of Kickapoo, Lipan, and Apache raiders camped on the banks of the San Rodrigo River near Remedios (Coahuila). This illegal incursion results in the killing of 19 startled Indians and the capture of another 40, along with 65 horses. Cavalry losses are one killed and two wounded. Subsequent protests from the Mexican government are ignored.

26 SEPTEMBER 1874. Mackenzie's 4th Cavalry endures a sharp skirmish with southern Cheyenne warriors in the Staked Plains region, then after feinting a march south, turn back north under cover of darkness to surprise the natives' encampment in Palo Duro Canyon next dawn. Most Indians escape to its high ground, but 1,400 ponies are taken and shot, greatly hampering later native movements.

EARLY MARCH 1876. ***Powder River.*** Brigadier General Crook marches north with 800 men from Fort Fetterman (Nebraska), his column being one of three eventually intended to invade the Black Hills Reservation (South Dakota) and put down Sioux and northern Cheyenne raiding parties being led by the Hunkpapa medicine man Sitting Bull.

Crook's vanguard consists of six troops of the 3rd Cavalry Regiment under Col. J. J. Reynolds, who chances upon and disperses an Indian encampment on the banks of the Powder River. However, Sioux and Cheyenne warriors launch a counterattack that so mauls Reynolds's command that he is obliged to rejoin Crook. The entire U.S. column retires to Fort Fetterman to refit and prepare for a second offensive.

17 JUNE 1876. ***Rosebud.*** Crook's second expeditionary force collides near the source of the Rosebud River with 1,000 braves under chief Crazy Horse, who has been sent south from the main Indian encampment to contest the soldiers' advance. After a severe action lasting most of this day Crook once again withdraws to seek reinforcements. The natives return triumphantly into camp, deciding shortly thereafter to move west to a more secure position. On the western banks of the Little Big Horn they set up a new camp three miles long.

21 JUNE 1876. This evening Brig. Gen. Alfred H. Terry, aboard the hired steamer *Far West* (anchored at the mouth of the Powder River), instructs Colonels Gibbon and Custer how they might approach and annihilate Sitting Bull's encampment on the Little Big Horn. Gibbon's force—mostly infantry—is to advance up the Big Horn River and attack the Indians from the north on 26 June while Custer's 7th Cavalry circles around and falls upon them from the south. The U.S. commanders seriously underestimate the natives' strength, believing only some 1,000 warriors are present—about one-quarter their actual number.

Next day at noon Custer leads the 7th past Terry then advances up the Rosebud and camps for the night. Upon the return of his scouts at 9:00 P.M., however, he resumes his march and, instead of proceeding farther south, strikes out directly for the ridge between the Rosebud and Little Big Horn (a distance of ten miles), hoping to gain it before daylight. Although it is impossible to understand his reasoning, obviously Custer has dispensed with the notion of cooperating with Gibbon.

23 JUNE 1876. ***Custer's Last Stand.*** At 2:00 A.M. Custer reaches Crow's Nest, a high point on the ridge overlooking the plain called Greasy Grass. At sunrise Sitting Bull's camp is faintly seen, 15 miles away; Sioux outriders in turn spot the 7th Cavalry. Custer therefore decides to attack immediately, dividing his command in three: Captain Benteen is to circle south with 125 men; Major Reno is to lead a squadron west along the

southern bank of the tributary running into the Little Big Horn (later renamed Reno Creek); Custer himself will take the remainder of the regiment in a parallel movement to eventually outflank the Indians out of the northeast.

By 2:00 P.M. Custer and Reno have advanced some nine miles opposite each other when a lone tepee is found and heavy dust clouds are spotted a few miles ahead. Erroneously believing the Indians to be scattering, Custer orders Reno to charge west while he veers north to intercept. After covering three miles at a sharp trot and crossing the Little Big Horn, Reno's squadron is engulfed and repelled by a massive Indian counterattack. This contingent is joined by Benteen's, and both survive thanks only to the natives' subsequent distraction in besetting Custer, who has meanwhile appeared four miles farther to the north. A movement to relieve Custer, led by Captain Weir of "D" Troop, is eventually repulsed.

Custer's attempt to surprise the Indian encampment via Medicine Tail Coulee is checked by a huge force of warriors under the Hunkpapa chief Gall and Oglala Sioux chief Low Dog. Driven back, his cavalrymen make a desperate last stand on the high ground, their escape route being closed by Crazy Horse's flanking charge. By 5:00 P.M. everyone in Custer's command is dead. Next morning Terry appears on the battlefield with the 2nd U.S. Cavalry and rescues Reno's survivors. The Sioux and Cheyenne have meanwhile scattered north, seeking refuge in Canada. By next spring many—including Sitting Bull and Crazy Horse—will surrender to the U.S. authorities and take up life on reservations.

OCTOBER 1876. In a surprise dawn attack Mackenzie's 4th Cavalry overruns the northern Cheyenne village of chief Dull Knife on the banks of the Powder River, killing 40 Indians and capturing 600 ponies; many survivors subsequently perish from the bitterly cold weather.

SEPTEMBER 1877. Some 300 Apaches flee the San Carlos Reservation under their leaders, Victorio and Loco. Eleven days later 187 of them (including Victorio) surrender at Fort Wingate to be taken to their preferred destination: Warm Springs Reservation.

MID-OCTOBER 1878. Learning they are to be repatriated to the San Carlos Reservation, Victorio and 80 of his followers flee Warm Springs.

Romanticized contemporary lithograph of General Custer at the Battle of Little Big Horn

FEBRUARY 1879. Victorio surrenders at Mescalero.

JULY 1879. The Apache leader Victorio flees to Mexico.

SEPTEMBER 1879. In Colorado, the White River Utes ambush a U.S. contingent under Maj. Thomas T. Thornburgh, killing him and several of his troopers. In all, 30 whites are killed and another 44 are wounded before the uprising is finally put down by the arrival of Colonel Mackenzie's 4th Cavalry.

15 OCTOBER 1880. Victorio and most of his Apache warriors are killed after a long battle with Mexican troops.

30 AUGUST 1881. Colonel Carr orders the arrest of the Apache shaman Nocadelklinny, fearful of his anti-white preaching among the tribesmen on the San Carlos Reservation. Two days later Fort Apache is besieged by angry warriors, but the clamor soon dies down.

APRIL 1882. The Apache leaders Geronimo (real name Goyakla, or the Yawner) and Juh (Whoa) secretly slip into the San Carlos Reservation, persuading several hundred of Loco's Chiricahua followers to depart with them (and killing the chief of Indian police, Albert Sterling). Pursued by U.S. regulars, including cavalry under Col. George Forsyth, the Indians succeed in reaching Mexico, only to be ambushed by Mexican troops and suffer severe losses.

SEPTEMBER 1882. Crook resumes command of the Department of Arizona, stations U.S. cavalry at the San Carlos Reservation, then crosses the border into Mexico with 50 soldiers and 200 Apache scouts to chase Geronimo in accordance with the new "hot pursuit" agreement signed between Washington and Mexico City.

MARCH 1883. Geronimo's Apaches launch lightning raids throughout northern Mexico, southeastern Arizona, and New Mexico.

1 MAY 1883. ***Sierra Madre Expedition.*** Crook sets out into the central Mexico highlands in pursuit of Geronimo, guided by a scout nicknamed Peaches, who once lived with the renegades. After tracking them through rugged ranges the column of 51 U.S. troopers and 193 loyal Apache scouts finally surround the main Apache base camp while the warriors are away raiding; they kill nine defenders. The garrison surrenders and, after three long parleys starting on 20 May, Geronimo promises to bring in the remainder of his renegades. Crook escorts 325 Apaches back to the San Carlos Reservation by June; in March 1884 Geronimo appears with another 80 plus 350 stolen Mexican cattle (which are promptly confiscated).

17 MAY 1885. Geronimo again bolts the San Carlos Reservation, this time accompanied by such hardened lieutenants as Chihuahua, Naiché (son of Cochise), the ancient Nana, and Mangas (son of Mangas Coloradas). Crook stations cavalry patrols along the Mexican border, yet Geronimo succeeds in escaping into the Sierra Madre with 43 warriors and some 60 noncombatants.

JANUARY 1886. Capt. Emmett Crawford's scouts capture Geronimo's horses and provisions in Mexico, and Crawford then opens negotiations with the renegade chieftain, only to be killed by Mexican scalp-hunters shortly thereafter.

25 MARCH 1886. After parleying with Crook, Geronimo agrees to surrender and serve two years' imprisonment in the east. The War Department reneges on this promise, however, shipping 77 Chiricahuas to Fort Marion (Oklahoma); the chieftain once more flees to Mexico with 39 followers. Crook resigns in disgust at this bad faith on 1 April, being replaced by Brig. Gen. Nelson A. "Bear Coat" Miles.

4 SEPTEMBER 1886. After a massive hunt by 5,000 U.S. regulars and hundreds of Apache scouts, Geronimo's 20 renegade warriors and 13 women surrender to Miles. Geronimo is dispatched to Fort Pickens (Florida) along with 381 of his followers; other families are sent to Fort Marion (Oklahoma).

LATE DECEMBER 1890. ***Wounded Knee.*** White authorities, increasingly alarmed by the spreading Indian practice known as ghost dances—ceremonies conceived by the Paiute shaman Wovoka in a fever the previous year, whereby dead native ancestors and buffalo herds are to be revived, thus signifying an Indian resurgence—intercept the Miniconjou Sioux band of chief Big Foot as it travels to collect reservation rations.

After being taken to and surrounded by troops at Wounded Knee Creek, the natives begin a ghost dance. At this point a concealed Indian gun is fired, setting off a heartless massacre of most of the band. More than 150 natives are slaughtered, including many women and children.

War of the Triple Alliance (1864–1870)

In April 1863 the exiled president of Uruguay, Venancio Flores—whose liberal Colorado (Red) Party has been deposed nine years previously by the rival Blancos (Whites)—invades his homeland from Argentina with support from the Brazilians of Rio Grande do Sul Province. Montevideo complains to Buenos Aires and to Rio de Janeiro about this intervention while calling on the Paraguayan government for support.

Underlying this incident are deeper, unresolved border disputes between all four nations: Paraguay asserts its boundary with Brazil runs along the Branco River while Brazil insists it is marked by the Apa; Argentina feels its dominion extends northeast to the Paraná and Paraguay Rivers, which Asunción contests; Uruguay—the least populous of the four, having 350,000 inhabitants compared to Brazil's 8 million, Argentina's 1.2 million, and Paraguay's 1 million—is squeezed in the middle.

Therefore, when Brazil masses troops on Uruguay's border and sends a squadron into the River Plate, complaining of ill treatment meted out to its citizens in this district, the 38-year-old Paraguayan dictator, Francisco Solano López, officially reproves Rio de Janeiro on 30 August 1864. The Brazilians invade Uruguay by 21 September, at which point Asunción severs diplomatic relations with its Brazilian neighbor.

13 November 1864. The Brazilian steamship *Marquês de Olinda* is seized before Asunción by Paraguayan authorities, effectively closing the river to Brazil's inland traffic.

24 December 1864. ***Offensive into Mato Grosso.*** A 6,000-man Paraguayan army departs Asunción eastward to successfully attack the Brazilians in Mato Grosso Province.

14 January 1865. Paraguay requests permission from Argentina to send troops through the Misiones District (east of the Paraná River) to attack the Brazilian province of Rio Grande do Sul, Buenos Aires—which has previously turned down a similar request from Rio de Janeiro—refuses, fueling Asunción's resentment.

10 February 1865. In Uruguay, General Flores comes into power, backed by Brazilian arms.

18 March 1865. Paraguay secretly authorizes hostilities against Argentina without advising Buenos Aires.

13 April 1865. ***Fall of Corrientes.*** Paraguayan forces seize the Argentine warships *25 de Mayo* and *Gualeguay* off Corrientes and next day occupy the city. A 1,600-man garrison is installed; the bulk of this army pushes south under Gen. Wenceslas Robles down the Paraná River for Empedrado.

1 May 1865. Argentina, Brazil, and Uruguay sign a "Triple Alliance" against Paraguay.

3 May 1865. Buenos Aires officially receives Paraguay's declaration of war and responds in kind by 9 May. The ensuing conflict will become known variously as the War of the Triple Alliance, the Paraguayan War, or the Great War.

25 May 1865. ***Argentine Counterstroke.*** General Paunero disembarks with 1,200 Argentine troops and 4,000 Brazilians near occupied Corrientes, defeating a small Paraguayan contingent on the banks of the Paraná River and a larger force that hastens to its rescue. The invaders abandon Corrientes, which the Argentines briefly reoccupy before withdrawing during the night of 26–27 May on the rumored approach of Paraguayan reinforcements from Humaitá.

10 June 1865. Tonight eight Paraguayan steamers and six gunboats under Commander Deza slip down the Paraná River, hoping to surprise nine Brazilian vessels under Vice Admiral Barroso, anchored opposite Riachuelo Creek (south of Corrientes). Mechanical difficulties aboard two of the Paraguayan steamers delay arrival until 8:00 A.M. on 11 June, at which time the Brazilians are able to repel this assault after a day-long struggle that sees three of Deza's steamers sunk and his half-dozen gunboats captured. This defeat will eventually slow Paraguayan operations downriver.

28 July 1865. Advancing down the Paraná River, Gen. Isidoro Resquín's Paraguayan invasion army reaches Bella Vista (Argentina), continuing to press south toward Goya and east toward San Roque to take up a defensive position along the banks of the Santa Lucía River.

2 August 1865. A 3,000-man Paraguayan contingent under Major Duarte, advancing down the western banks of the Uruguay River, reaches Paso de los Libres (Argentina). Three days later another 8,000 invaders under Lt. Col. Antonio de la Cruz Estigarribia

arrive at Uruguayana (Brazil), on the eastern bank opposite.

17 AUGUST 1865. ***Yatay.*** Between the confluence of Yatay and Despedida Creeks (Argentina), a 10,700-man allied army under Uruguayan Gen. Venancio Flores falls upon Duarte's heavily outnumbered Paraguayans and annihilates them with a frontal assault that ties them down and a right flanking movement that finishes them off from the rear. Paraguayan losses are 1,200 dead, 300 wounded, and 1,200 captured compared to 390 killed and 246 injured among Flores's ranks.

The victorious allies cross the Uruguay River between 21–29 August, combining with a Brazilian army arriving from the east under Generals Canabarro and Baron de Yacuhy to bottle up Estigarribia's army within Uruguayana. Eventually, the allied buildup grows to 18,600 men and three dozen cannons, overseen by Emperor Pedro II.

18 SEPTEMBER 1865. The allied army closes in on the beleaguered Paraguayan garrison within Uruguayana (Brazil), calling upon Estigarribia to surrender. Faced with overwhelming odds, his 5,400-man garrison capitulates. The triumphant allies march northwest, massing forces at Mercedes (Argentina) by 24 October.

7 OCTOBER 1865. General Resquín's 27,000-man Paraguayan army begins withdrawing north from the Santa Lucía River, pillaging the Argentine countryside and herding off 100,000 head of cattle.

30 OCTOBER 1865. Resquín's army recrosses the Paraná River into Paraguay from Argentina.

29 JANUARY 1866. Having ventured across the Paraná River from Fort Itapirú, a 1,200-man Paraguayan contingent seizes Corrales (Argentina) and probes south, only to be defeated at Pehuajó. Two days later it is driven out of Corrales and returns to home soil.

16 APRIL 1866. ***Paraná Crossing.*** An allied river squadron opens fire on Fort Itapirú (Paraguay), covering the departure one hour later of 10,000 Brazilian troops under General Osório who advance up the Paraguay River to disembark near Paso de la Patria. They are joined this evening—after a delay caused by a storm—by 5,000 allied soldiers under Uruguayan General Flores. After the so-called Combates de la Confluencia (Confluence Battles), the advance force drives the Paraguayans out of Fort Itapirú by 18 April, thus allowing the remaining 45,000 allied troops to land east of this position.

Brazilian Emperor Pedro II

2 MAY 1866. ***Estero Bellaco.*** While advancing into enemy territory and concentrating on López's main body digging in to the north behind the marshes known as Estero Bellaco Norte, the allied army is surprised when the Paraguayan leader orders Colonel Díaz's 5,500 troops to attack the invasion spearhead out of marshlands from the south—Estero Bellaco Sur. The attack develops around midday, Díaz's columns smashing into the rear of three Brazilian battalions and forcing them to abandon their artillery. Four Uruguayan (Orientales) battalions with six guns are pressed farther north before allied relief columns hasten to the rescue. Díaz is eventually driven off after suffering 1,000 casualties and 300 captured, compared to more than 2,000 casualties among the allies.

24 MAY 1866. ***Tuyutí (First Battle).*** Behind his defensive lines at Estero Bellaco Norte, López decides to deploy 22,000 of 25,000 Paraguayan troops in a preemptive assault against the 33,000 allied invaders massed opposite at Tuyutí before they can be reinforced by 15,000 Brazilians marching inland. Four columns will wend through marshy pathways: Marcó's division, which is to use Gómez Pass and fall upon the enemy's frontlines; Colonel Díaz's division,

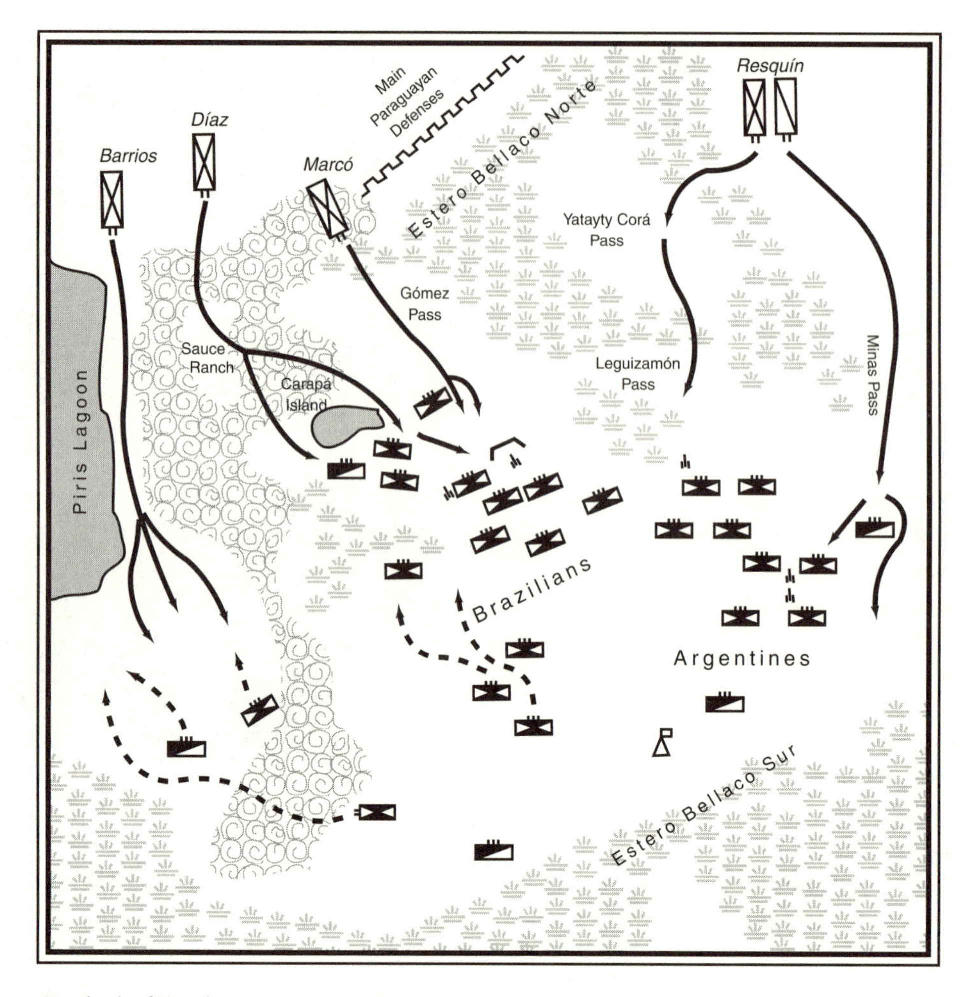

First battle of Tuyutí

which is to support Marcó on his western flank; General Resquín, who is to drive in the allied right; Gen. Vicente Barrios's division will skirt Piris Lagoon to surprise the enemy left and rear.

Díaz's division fares the best, splitting around Carapá Island in the swamp to fall upon two Uruguayan battalions at 11:30 A.M. on 24 May, only to encounter three Brazilian battalions with 26 field pieces that scatter the Paraguayans back into the jungle. Marcó comes up late and is three times repelled by the alerted allies. Resquín also makes a slow approach, his two battalions of infantry picking their way through Yatayty Corá and Leguizamón Passes while his eight cavalry regiments circle farther east via Minas Pass. The latter reach the allied right first, scattering some Argentine cavalry squadrons before being bloodily repulsed by the bulk of the infantry. Meanwhile Resquín's foot soldiers are sighted while approaching and driven off with long-range fire. Barrios's column is the last to engage, several hours after action has begun; it is also driven back.

By 4:30 P.M. all four divisions are retiring, having suffered 6,000 killed and 7,000 wounded. Allied casualties are 4,100; their invasion is halted nonetheless, so the Paraguayans claim victory.

10 JUNE 1866. Two Paraguayan battalions advance through Yatayty Corá Pass and engage the allied army, still encamped around Tuyutí. They are repelled; next day 2,500 Paraguayans return to resume action, eventually being driven off with 400 casualties—twice as many as the invaders suffer.

16 JULY 1866. The allied army at Tuyutí launches a surprise attack against the advance Paraguayan defenses around Carapá Island, only to be repulsed after suffering 1,600 casualties. The same fate befalls an attempt two days later to overrun the Paraguayan defenses at Sauce Ranch; although initially successful, the columns of storm troops are dispossessed by a counterattack and driven back with 2,500 casualties.

3 SEPTEMBER 1866. ***Curuzú.*** In order to outflank López's entrenchments at Estero Bellaco Norte, the II Brazilian Corps sails up the Paraguay River from

Itapirú, disembarking at Curuzú (a mile and a half southwest of Curupaytí) to engage 2,500 Paraguayans dug in with 13 cannons. The attackers suffer 800 dead but kill 700 Paraguayans, wound 1,700 others, and overrun the position.

22 SEPTEMBER 1866. ***Curupaytí.*** Following up their success at Curuzú, the allies advance northeast to storm the Paraguayan defenses around Curupaytí, held by 5,000 defenders and 49 guns under Gen. José Eduvigis Díaz. Brazilian Admiral Tamandaré's river squadron begins a bombardment of the defenses shortly after 8:00 A.M. and by noon signals the awaiting 10,000 Brazilian and 5,000 Argentine troops that Curupaytí's batteries have been silenced.

However, when the allied assault columns break cover, they are almost immediately engulfed in artillery fire and suffer heavy casualties while working through the mangroves. The attack is called off after 4,000 men fall—compared to 92 Paraguayans; by 5:00 P.M. the allies have returned to Curuzú.

LATE SEPTEMBER 1866. General Flores returns to Uruguay because of its unstable political situation.

OCTOBER 1866. The 63-year-old Gen. Luís Alves de Lima e Silva, marquês (later duke) de Caxias, replaces General Osório as commander in chief of the Brazilian forces in Paraguay.

9 NOVEMBER 1866. An antigovernment revolt breaks out in Mendoza (Argentina), started by recruits destined for service in Paraguay. The veteran leaders Juan and Felipe Sáa (*see* 16 November 1860, Buenos Aires versus the Argentine Confederation) plus Cols. Juan de Dios Videla and Felipe Varela take control of the uprising, calling for peace with Paraguay. General Paunero is instructed by Buenos Aires to gather troops at Río Cuarto for a pacification campaign; Col. Julio Campos advances from La Rioja with 1,200 for the same purpose.

4 DECEMBER 1866. Shortly after Paunero's Army of the Interior marches out of Río Cuarto (Argentina), the 7th Cavalry Regiment—scheduled to join his ranks—also mutinies against the government.

2 JANUARY 1867. Argentine rebel Colonel Varela defeats a government force at Guandacol under Commander Linares, thus gaining control of La Rioja Province.

5 JANUARY 1867. At Rinconada del Pocito (Argentina), Colonel Videla's rebel contingent defeats Campos's government troops, compelling the latter to flee to San Luis with only 200 followers. News of the disaster prompts Paunero to halt his drive against Mendoza at Desaguadero, where he is hounded by guerrillas under Felipe Sáa until deciding to retrace his steps to Río Cuarto by 5 February.

LATE JANUARY 1867. Colonel Arredondo returns to Argentina from the Paraguayan campaign with 3,500 troops because of its political unrest and is ordered to reinforce Paunero's Army of the Interior with four battalions—1,600 men—and two field pieces.

FEBRUARY 1867. President Mitre—commander in chief of the allied forces and accompanying his invasion army in Paraguay—returns home to Argentina because of the growing seriousness of antigovernment revolts spreading through San Luis, Mendoza, San Juan, Catamarca, and La Rioja Provinces.

4 MARCH 1867. The governor of Catamarca, Col. Melitón Córdoba, is defeated by a rebel contingent out of La Rioja Province.

19 MARCH 1867. Argentine government troops reoccupy the rebel city of La Rioja.

26 MARCH 1867. A cholera epidemic strikes the allied army in Paraguay, 2,400 troops dying at Curuzú alone. By early May 13,000 Brazilian troops are sick at Tuyutí.

LATE MARCH 1867. Having been reinforced by Arredondo, Paunero's 3,000-man army again marches into San Luis Province with ten field pieces to resume putting down its rebellion. During the advance Arredondo is sent ahead to Mercedes with a 1,600-man vanguard.

1 APRIL 1867. ***San Ignacio.*** At San Ignacio Ford over the Quinto River (Argentina), Arredondo's 1,600 government troops encounter 3,500 rebels with eight field pieces under Juan Sáa. The rebels are defeated and dispersed by nightfall; Paunero's main body reenters San Luis three days later and reclaims Mendoza by 14 April.

10 APRIL 1867. ***Pozo de Vargas.*** A mile and a half north of the city of La Rioja (Argentina), Gen. Antonino Taboada's 2,100 government troops are attacked by 4,000 rebels (including a battalion of Chilean volunteers) under Colonel Varela. In a sharp two-hour fight the rebels are routed and flee for Jáchal.

EARLY MAY 1867. A 5,000-man Brazilian contingent, advancing from Mato Grosso Province into Paraguay under Colonel Camisao, is trapped south of the Apa River by Paraguayan troops and exterminated (partly through cholera and starvation).

25 MAY 1867. The Paraguay River overflows its banks, flooding the miserable allied encampment at Curuzú and forcing survivors to seek shelter at Tuyutí.

5 JUNE 1867. A flying column of 400 Argentine government troops under Commander Charras drives Varela's rebels out of Jáchal, and by 4 August forces him into exile in Bolivia with 1,000 followers.

29 JUNE 1867. In order to break out of their Tuyutí deadlock, an allied contingent circles east of the Paraguayans' main defenses at Estero Bellaco Norte, gaining Tuyú Cué and sending 1,500 riders to San Solano (three miles north).

16 AUGUST 1867. A brief insurrection occurs in Córdoba, Argentina's war minister being detained until a column of government troops approaches under General Conesa, causing the uprising to collapse.

29 AUGUST 1867. The Argentine rebel Varela—having recrossed the border from Bolivia—defeats the government's Col. Pedro J. Frías at Rincón de Amaicha; next day he administers a second reverse in Molino Valley.

24 SEPTEMBER 1867. A Brazilian supply train carrying provisions from Tuyutí to the allied flanking army at Tuyú Cué is ambushed by Paraguayan guerrillas, suffering 200 killed as opposed to 80 dead among the attackers.

3 OCTOBER 1867. At Tayí, a clash between advancing Brazilian forces and Paraguayan raiders kills 500 Brazilians and 300 Paraguayans.

10 OCTOBER 1867. The Argentine rebel Varela fights his way into Salta, losing 125 men as opposed to 15 defenders. Soon after he is forced to abandon the city by the approach of government troops under General Navarro and withdraw to Jujuy. Eventually, Varela is chased back into Bolivia, where his guerrillas are disarmed by local authorities.

28 OCTOBER 1867. At Obella Ranch, the Brazilian army working its way around the Paraguayan eastern flank is ambushed, suffering 370 killed (compared to 140 Paraguayan dead).

2 NOVEMBER 1867. The Brazilian flanking army overruns 400 Paraguayans defending Guardia Tayí, killing them almost to the last man.

3 NOVEMBER 1867. ***Tuyutí (Second Battle).*** In order to pressure the allies into recalling their eastern flanking army, López decides to launch a dawn attack with 8,000 Paraguayan troops against the 13,000 invaders still encamped at Tuyutí. Initially it proves a great success, the attackers surprising the allied frontlines and causing four Brazilian battalions to break and flee in disorder to Itapirú. Much damage is inflicted upon the supply dumps, which are looted and fired, the flames eventually spreading throughout half the allied encampment. But heavy Brazilian and Argentine counterattacks finally drive back the raiders, inflicting 2,500 casualties—double the defenders' numbers. Despite their more numerous losses, the Paraguayans come away claiming victory, feeling they have dealt the invading host a crippling blow, thus slowing their progress.

22 DECEMBER 1867. The garrison at Santa Fe (Argentina) mutinies under Col. José Rodríguez to protest the rule of Governor Oroño. The same occurs at Rosario two days later under Col. Patricio Rodríguez. Both incidents are resolved without bloodshed.

14 JANUARY 1868. Mitre must return to Buenos Aires on account of the death of his vice president.

19 FEBRUARY 1868. The Brazilian river squadron of Adm. José Joaquim Inácio fights its way past the well-fortified Paraguayan complex at Humaitá, thus gaining control of the Paraguay River and even detaching two ironclads and a monitor under Capt. Delfin Carlos de Carvalho to bombard the outskirts of its capital, Asunción (population 15,000) five days later. This thrust, coupled with the Brazilian encirclement slowly closing in overland from the east, threatens a fatal interruption in López's flow of supplies and compels the Paraguayan leader to at last begin evacuating his Estero Bellaco Norte defenses—the so-called Cuadrilátero (Quadrilateral) stronghold—by early March.

Paraguayan contingents begin retiring north to establish a temporary defensive line on the Tebicuary River and a more permanent one at Pikiciry Creek (20 miles below Asunción) while fighting delaying actions at old positions. Eventually, López rebuilds his army to 18,000 men and 71 cannons, 5,000 troops being stationed on Pikiciry Creek; 8,000 fortified at Itaibaté (Valentinas Hills); and 5,000 and a dozen field pieces as a mobile reserve under 39-year-old Gen. Bernardino Caballero. Despite its paper strength, the Paraguayan forces include half-starved soldiers as young as 11 and as old as 60 with scant equipment or supplies.

21 MARCH 1868. A Brazilian assault on the Sauce Ranch defenses, at the western end of López's Estero Bellaco Norte entrenchments, finds only 100 defenders, who are easily overwhelmed. This is the first concrete sign of a general Paraguayan retreat and is followed by a gradual allied advance against the 3,000-man garrison still holding nearby Humaitá.

15 JULY 1868. ***Fall of Humaitá.*** After a brief siege, Brazilian troops storm the strategic Paraguayan River town of Humaitá, only to be repelled with 1,200 casualties. Nevertheless, its defense is doomed by a lack of supplies, and on the night of 22–23 July the women, children, and noncombatants are stealthily evacuated by canoe to the opposite banks. Noisy celebrations are held within Humaitá on 24 July—López's birthday—masking the garrison's intent to escape that night. When the allies finally enter they find it abandoned save for 180 cannons and 600 rifles.

5 AUGUST 1868. The allies overtake a Paraguayan contingent fleeing from Humaitá, surrounding them and thereby receiving the surrender of 1,000 troops, 300 convalescents, five cannons, and 800 firearms.

AUTUMN 1868. After delegating 6,500 Argentine, 2,200 Brazilian, and 800 Uruguayan troops to maintain pressure on López's new defensive line from Angostura up Pikiciry Creek, General Caxias slips across the Paraguay River at Palmas with 18,500 Brazilian soldiers to commence an advance up the western banks and take the enemy from the rear.

6 DECEMBER 1868. ***Itororó.*** After recrossing the Paraguay River at San Antonio, Caxias's 18,500 Brazilians are checked at Itororó Creek by General Caballero's mobile reserve of 5,000 Paraguayans, rushed north to meet the threat. The attackers make a frontal assault directly across the stream, suffering 2,400 casualties—double the defenders' numbers—but still push back the overmatched Paraguayans.

11 DECEMBER 1868. ***Avahy.*** Caballero's small Paraguayan army is annihilated after being overtaken on the southern banks of Avahy Creek by Caxias's Brazilians. The latter suffer 770 killed compared to 3,500 killed and 1,000 captured (including 600 wounded) among the Paraguayan ranks. This victory allows Caxias to rest and reorganize his weary army at Villeta before pressing southeast toward the enemy concentration in Valentinas Hills.

21 DECEMBER 1868. ***Itaibaté.*** After recuperating at Villeta, Caxias's Brazilian army attacks López's 8,000 troops at Itaibaté, seemingly carrying the defenses by sheer weight of numbers until the Acaamorotí Regiment—the Paraguayan leader's last reserve—turns the tide by driving the storm columns back out of the trenches with 1,000 dead and 3,250 wounded. A simultaneous allied offensive against the 2,000 Paraguayans holding Pikiciry Creek fails to materialize, the main frontal assault under Gen. Juan Andrés Gelly y Obes being recalled after eight hours' wait in swampy terrain because Gen. João Manuel Menna Barreto's eastern flanking movement does not appear. At 5:00 P.M., however, this overdue contingent finally bursts out of nearby woods and devastates the Paraguayan defense, killing 680, wounding 100, and capturing 100 while sending the survivors scurrying to the town of Angostura.

Six days later, after Caxias's main army has been reintegrated with 7,000 allied soldiers from Gelly y Obes's and Menna Barreto's contingents, a second attempt is made against López's 4,000 remaining troops at Itaibaté. This time the Paraguayans are routed, 1,500 being killed and a like number captured, compared to 467 dead among the 23,000 attackers. López escapes to his new capital of Luque with a small following, leaving Angostura to surrender its 1,200-man garrison under English-born Col. George H. Thompson by 30 December.

5 JANUARY 1869. Caxias's allied army takes and loots Asunción while López sets up a new government to the west, first at Luque then at Piribebuy. Paraguayan resistance is reduced to guerrilla warfare; Caxias decides to return to Brazil shortly thereafter.

12 JANUARY 1869. Having invaded Argentina from Bolivia one last time—with only 100 followers—the rebel Varela is defeated at Pastos Grandes (Salta Province) by a government contingent under Col. Pedro Corvalán. He flees to Chile and dies in 1870.

16 APRIL 1869. Marshal Guilherme Xavier de Sousa is succeeded at Luque as commander in chief of the Brazilian occupying forces by 27-year-old French-born Prince Louis Philippe Marie Ferdinand Gaston d'Orleans, Comte d'Eu, who is married to Pedro II's eldest daughter.

LATE MAY 1869. ***Piribebuy.*** After a lull in active campaigning 20,000 troops under Brazilian General Conde d'Eu drive east against the last Paraguayan stronghold at Azcurra Pass, in the hill country 30 miles from Asunción. Artillery fire pins down its overmatched defenders, allowing Mitre to slide north and turn the Paraguayan right, while the Brazilians circle southeast through Valenzuela to threaten López's makeshift capital of Piribebuy from the rear. On 12 August they overrun it, Piribebuy's 1,800 defenders suffering 700 killed and 1,000 captured, compared to 53 fatalitites among the assault forces (including General Menna Barreto).

In a desperate bid to stem this envelopment long enough for his tattered army to escape northeast, López four days later orders a stand made at Acosta Ñu near the village of Barrero Grande by his rearguard of 4,500 boys, women, and old men under Caballero. These are overwhelmed by allied cavalry charges after a desperate resistance known to Brazilian historians as the Battle of Campo Grande, enduring 2,000 killed and 2,300 captured. On 18 August, López's remaining 2,500 troops are chased across the Hondo River toward Caraguatay.

15 AUGUST 1869. The allies establish a provisional government at Asunción.

1 MARCH 1870. At Corá Hill near the confluence of Aquidabán and Nigui Creeks in northeastern Paraguay, López's last band of 500 followers is discovered by a Brazilian cavalry detachment sent by Gen. José Antônio Correia dal Câmara and wiped out. The president, vice president, cabinet ministers, and numerous military officers are all killed, only a handful of troopers surviving to be taken prisoner.

20 JUNE 1870. Brazil, Argentina, and Paraguay sign a preliminary accord ending the war. By its terms, Brazil gains the district between the Branco and Apa Rivers; Argentina acquires undisputed title to Misiones and pushes the Chaco borderline as far north as the Pilcomayo River. Paraguay thus loses 38 percent of its territory, where all its heavy and most light industry is located. Although free elections are promised within three months the last Brazilian troops do not evacuate Paraguay until six years later; Argentina continues to administer Villa Occidental until 1878, when—through the arbitration of U.S. Pres. Rutherford B. Hayes—it is restored to local control.

FENIAN RAIDS (1866–1870)

IN 1858 THE "FENIAN BROTHERHOOD"—an American branch of the Irish Republican Army—is formed in New York City to help win Ireland's independence. For a few years after the conclusion to the American Civil War, Fenian leaders contemplate crossborder raids into Canada as a means of injuring British interests.

7 MARCH 1866. Anticipating trouble on Saint Patrick's Day, Lt. Gen. Sir John Michel—commander in chief of all British forces in Canada—orders 10,000 volunteer militia mobilized; the day passes without incident.

27 MAY 1866. "Col." John O'Neill moves north by train out of Nashville with his 13th Fenian Regiment, arriving in Buffalo two days later, having gathered further reinforcements en route. By 31 May approximately 1,500 Fenians are marshaled in anticipation of advancing across the Niagara River into Canada. British authorities respond by calling up 14,000 militia volunteers, plus another 6,000 two days later.

31 MAY 1866. Tonight Colonel O'Neill takes 800 Fenians aboard two steamers and four canal barges at Lower Black Road (New York), disembarking next dawn at Fort Erie (Ontario) to commence his invasion of Canada.

Realizing the Welland Canal will likely be the enemy's objective, British General Napier concentrates 850 men of Lt. Col. Alfred Booker's 2nd Battalion (Queen's Own Rifles), the 13th Battalion (Hamilton Infantry), and the York and Caledonia Rifle Companies at Port Colborne at the canal's southern end; Col. George Peacocke's 16th Regiment, three companies of the 47th Regiment, and a detachment of artillery muster at Saint Catherine's to its north—later joined by the 10th Royal Regiment, Lincoln Militia, two more companies of regulars, and the Governor-General's Body Guard.

2 JUNE 1866. ***Ridgeway.*** After detraining at dawn, Booker's troops advance up Ridge Road toward Stevensville (Ontario), only to be unexpectedly fired upon a mile and a half away by O'Neill's Fenians, who occupy positions on Limestone Ridge. After three hours of long-range exchanges the 500 invaders are about to retreat when the Canadians mistakenly form into squares, believing they are about to be outflanked by enemy cavalry (of which the Fenians have none). The invaders fire on the easy target; Booker's redcoats break and flee in the general direction of Fort Erie, having suffered nine killed, 32 wounded, and six captured.

Later this day O'Neill overruns Fort Erie, enduring nine killed and 14 wounded in capturing its 42-man

British garrison (of whom six are injured). But realizing their prospects are now dim, the Fenians reembark for Buffalo, only to have their barge intercepted by the USS *Michigan,* whose captain arrests all participants in O'Neill's adventure.

7 JUNE 1866. Another force of 500–1,000 Fenians crosses the frontier near Saint Armand (Missisquoi Bay, Quebec) under "Brig. Gen." Samuel Spier, occupying the town as well as Pigeon Hill, Cooks Corners, Frelighsburg, and Stanbridge. The British dispatch the Prince Consort's Own Rifle Brigade, 25th Regiment, 7th Regiment, Royal Guides, Border Volunteers, and No. 2 (Hochelaga) Field Battery to confront the incursion.

9 JUNE 1866. This afternoon British defense forces enter deserted Saint Armand; the Royal Guides overtake 200 Fenians retiring south into the United States, killing several and capturing 16.

22 JUNE 1866. A small body of Fenians returns to Pigeon Hill (near Saint Armand, Quebec), firing ineffectively upon the 21st Battalion (Richelieu Light Infantry) before withdrawing.

22 MAY 1870. After a four-year hiatus of Fenian raids, British Lt. Col. W. Osborne Smith receives notice to expect another round—despite the fact Canada is no longer officially a British colony (since 1 July 1867 it has been an independent nation allied to London).

25 MAY 1870. ***Stanbridge.*** Fenian General O'Neill advances from his base camp at Franklin (Vermont), threatening the Quebec border near Saint Armand. Smith departs Montréal by rail for Saint Jean with companies of the 1st Prince of Wales Rifles, 3rd Victoria Rifles, 5th Royal Light Infantry, 6th Hochelaga Light Infantry, and Montréal Troop of Cavalry.

Disembarking at Saint Jean, Smith presses eight miles farther into Stanbridge with the Victoria Rifles and Montréal Cavalry alone, reinforcing the handful of defenders ensconced atop Eccles Hill (three miles east of Pigeon Hill). A couple of hours later 350–400 Fenians charge across the border at double-time, immediately drawing fire from Lt. Col. Brown Chamberlain's advance British detachment. Breaking for cover, the Fenians and British snipe at long range throughout most of the day until the invaders attempt to wield a field piece into position at 5:00 P.M. Smith immediately directs a rapid advance in skirmishing order, causing the Fenians to flee in disarray, the engagement ending by 6:00 P.M. Fenian losses are estimated at five dead and 15–18 wounded; the Canadians suffer no casualties.

27 MAY 1870. Another small force of Fenians advances up the Trout River and crosses into Canada near Holbrooks Corners (Quebec). It is confronted by seven militia companies of the 50th Battalion (Huntingdon Borderers) and one of the 69th Regiment regulars advancing from nearby Huntingdon to engage. Advancing at double-time and firing as they move, the Canadians and British drive the Fenians back across the border, killing three, capturing one, and wounding several while suffering no casualties of their own.

OCTOBER 1871. Aside from an attempted invasion of Pembina (Manitoba), the Fenians never again attack Canada.

RED RIVER EXPEDITION (1870)

BY 1869 BRITAIN'S PRIVATE HUDSON'S BAY COMPANY completes negotiations with the two-year-old Canadian government of Prime Minister Sir John A. Macdonald to sell its vast territory—known as Rupert's Land—and become incorporated into the new dominion. However, the local French and Indian residents (known as Métis) have not been properly consulted about the change and so form their own provisional government under one Louis David Riel to deal directly with Ottawa. Setting up his headquarters at Fort Garry (modern-day Winnipeg), Riel draws up a list of conditions, most of which are accepted when Canada passes the Manitoba Act on 12 May 1870.

Nevertheless, during the standoff an Ontario settler named Thomas Scott has been executed by a Métis firing squad; Macdonald thus orders Col. J. Garnet Wolseley (quartermaster general of the British forces in Canada and the inspiration for Gilbert and Sullivan's "very model of a modern major general" in *Pirates of Penzance*) to lead an expedition to the mouth of the Red River to depose Riel and quell further outbursts.

EARLY MAY 1870. Wolseley departs Toronto by train, his expedition consisting of 250 regulars of the 60th Regiment under Lt. Col. Randle Joseph Feilden; 370 militiamen apiece from the 1st Ontario Rifles of Lt. Col. Samuel Peters Jarvis and 2nd Quebec Rifles of Lt. Col. Louis Adolphe Casault; a Royal Artillery detachment under Lt. James Alleyne; and a detachment of Royal Engineers under Lt. Heneage. They travel to

Collingwood on Georgian Bay, where they transfer aboard the steamers *Algoma* and *Chicora,* reaching Fort William on Lake Superior by the morning of 25 May.

4 JUNE 1870. After gathering 150 boats, 280 local guides and voyageurs, and abundant provisions the advance elements of Wolseley's 1,400-man expedition begin departing Fort William westward on a epic, 500-mile march over wilderness trails.

4 AUGUST 1870. After an exhausting series of portages Wolseley reaches Fort Francis and refreshes before pressing on toward Fort Garry.

20 AUGUST 1870. Wolseley reaches Fort Alexander to find his vanguard—the regulars of the 60th Regiment with gunners and engineers—awaiting him. Rather than wait for his trailing militia to catch up, the colonel decides next day to proceed to Fort Garry.

22 AUGUST 1870. Wolseley's vanguard reaches the mouth of the Red River and next evening sights Fort Garry, bivouacking outside until 24 August, when he enters and finds it empty. Riel and his followers have withdrawn south into the United States.

29 AUGUST 1870. Wolseley begins withdrawing the first of his regulars, who return to their barracks by October while leaving Fort Garry to the Canadian militiamen and the governor-designate, Adams Archibald. Riel eventually returns to his farm at Saint Vital (south of Saint Boniface) and quietly resumes agrarian life for the next few years before again being declared an outlaw in 1875.

ARGENTINE UNREST (1870–1890)

THIS SOUTH AMERICAN NATION CONTINUES TO BE RACKED by factionalism, military coups, and civil war.

11 APRIL 1870. After nightfall a band of men under the Cordoban renegade Simón Luengo push their way into San José Palace and assassinate General Urquiza, governor of Entre Ríos Province. Three days later Gen. Ricardo López Jordán is proclaimed president at the capital of Concepción de Uruguay by a narrow vote. Pres. Domingo F. Sarmiento refuses to recognize the usurper; both sides begin marshaling armies.

20 MAY 1870. ***Arroyo Sauce.*** López Jordán, having advanced toward the Paraná River, is confronted at Sauce Creek (a branch of the Nogoyá River) by 1,700 government cavalry, 1,200 infantry, and 160 gunners manning a half-dozen field pieces under General Conesa. Although López Jordán commands 9,000 riders, they prove so ill-disciplined as to be easily scattered by the better armed regular soldiers.

7 JULY 1870. Government troops from General Gelly y Obes's Corrientes army occupy Concordia.

12 JULY 1870. López Jordán reoccupies his capital of Concepción de Uruguay.

14 JULY 1870. Government troops seize Gualeguaychú, five days later checking an assault by some of López Jordán's followers.

12 OCTOBER 1870. ***Santa Rosa.*** After avoiding action for several months López Jordán's 9,000 men attack General Rivas's 4,000 government troops at Santa Rosa Creek (affluent of the Gualeguay River, 20 miles east-southeast of Villaguay). The opening assault is a charge by 3,000 riders against Rivas's left, followed by another 1,000 troopers against his right. Nevertheless, the superior weaponry of the government forces—Remington rifles and Krupp cannons—allow them to drive off the attacks, as well as an attempt by 3,000 insurgents to fall upon Rivas's rear. After a hard-fought three-hour battle López Jordán withdraws, having killed 36 and wounded 103 government soldiers while suffering about three times as many casualties among his own ranks.

18 NOVEMBER 1870. Some 1,200 López Jordán followers wrest Gualeguaychú from its 200-man government garrison under Colonel Villar. The defenders suffer 32 dead while slaying 150 assaulters.

5 DECEMBER 1870. Col. Francisco Borges's government garrison successfully defends the city of Paraná against 3,000 of López Jordán's partisans under Col. Carmelo Campos.

26 JANUARY 1871. ***Ñaembé.*** Desperate to break out of his encirclement in Entre Ríos Province, López Jordán marches north into neighboring Corrientes

with 6,000 riders, 1,000 infantry, and nine field pieces. On the southern banks of Ñaembé Lagoon (seven miles east of Goya), he falls upon the provincial governor—Col. Santiago Baibiene—who is busily mustering 2,000 government foot soldiers, 1,000 cavalry, and a half-dozen cannons.

Despite the surprise Baibiene immediately advances with his infantry, hoping to bottle up López Jordán's larger army before it can fully deploy. López Jordán's mounted vanguard streaming back in defeat disrupts other rebel formations. At this moment Baibiene strikes frontally with his foot soldiers and along both flanks with his cavalry. López Jordán's ill-disciplined army is broken and chased to the Corrientes River, leaving behind 600 dead, 550 prisoners, all their artillery, and 52 supply wagons. Government losses total 190 casualties.

14 FEBRUARY 1871. Arredondo defeats 1,500 of López Jordán's followers under Col. Carmelo Campos at Gená Creek (affluent of the Gualeguaychú River), killing 20 and capturing 100.

6 MARCH 1871. Government Col. Donato Alvarez, commanding 620 troopers, defeats 900 insurgents under Colonel Leiva at Punta del Monte (Gualeguay Department). This action effectively marks an end to López Jordán's first rebellion, the leader fleeing into Brazil, where his 1,000 followers are disarmed.

8 MARCH 1872. ***Indian Wars.*** To avenge Calfucurá's sacking of the towns of Alvear, 25 de Mayo, and 9 de Julio with 3,500 warriors, General Rivas overtakes and defeats the raiders near San Carlos Fortress (170 miles southeast of Buenos Aires) with 1,800 troops.

1 MAY 1873. López Jordán invades Entre Ríos Province from his Brazilian exile, toppling its liberal governor. President Sarmiento dispatches Col. Luis María Campos to deal with this second rebellion; he skirmishes with López Jordán's elusive partisans at Gualeguaychú (9 May), Arroyo Ayuí (13 May), Arroyo Lucas (north of Villaguay, 29 June), Gualeguaychú again (17 October), and Arroyo Atencio (a branch of the Feliciano River, 25 October) but fails to crush the insurrection.

31 OCTOBER 1873. A 500-man government garrison under Lieutenant Colonel Méndez frantically evacuates La Paz upon the approach of 3,000 rebels. Méndez loses half his troops to enemy action or drowning and is subsequently court-martialled and demoted.

8 DECEMBER 1873. ***Don Gonzalo.*** Government Col. Juan Ayala, who has also been actively campaigning against López Jordán's followers, comes upon a 2,000-man rebel concentration under Col. Carmelo Campos at Talita Creek (branch of the Alcaraz River), killing 200, capturing 170, and scattering the rest. Nearby at Don Gonzalo Creek (affluent of the Feliciano River) lies López Jordán's main body of 5,000 riders, 1,000 infantry, and 500 gunners and auxiliaries to man eight to ten ancient field pieces.

Col. Martín de Gainza—Argentina's minister of war who is serving in the field—strikes across the Alcaraz this night and, next day, closes in on López Jordán's army. Battle begins at 3:00 P.M. on 9 December with an hour-long artillery exchange, after which the rebels attempt an enveloping movement against Gainza's right flank with three cavalry regiments, an infantry battalion, and two cannons. Thanks to their superior weaponry and discipline the government troops are able to break the assault and drive López Jordán's column to the far side of Molle Creek in disarray. The rebels fare no better in the center or farther west, being pushed across Don Gonzalo Creek by 7:30 P.M., leaving behind 250 dead, 250 prisoners, and all their artillery. (An additional 300 insurgents drown while fording the creek.) Gainza's ranks suffer some 100 killed.

22 DECEMBER 1873. Government Colonel Villar's 300 troopers defeat 600 insurgents under General Carballo at Nogoyá. A few more minor skirmishes occur, but López Jordán's second rebellion is concluded, the leader retiring to Uruguay.

24 SEPTEMBER 1874. ***Mitre's Revolution.*** After a bitterly contested, fraud-ridden election Mitre's Nationalist Party encourages an uprising to prevent Sarmiento's succession by the Autonomist candidate Dr. Nicolás Avellaneda. When the Buenos Aires newspaper *La Prensa* is closed for preaching such sedition, the crew of the gunboat *Paraná* mutinies under marine Col. Erasmo Obligado, followed by General Rivas's division outside the capital and General Arredondo's garrison at Villa Mercedes (San Luis Province)—the garrison members killing their commander, General Ivanowski.

27 SEPTEMBER 1874. Arredondo reaches Río Cuarto after a three-day forced march, hoping to surprise the Autonomist garrison under Col. Julio A. Roca; instead he finds it empty.

3 OCTOBER 1874. Arredondo's Nationalist forces enter Córdoba but soon depart to Villa Mercedes upon finding no support (and Roca closing in from Bell Ville with a gradually strengthening army).

29 October 1874. ***Santa Rosa (First Battle).*** Marching on Mendoza, Arredondo's 2,500 Nationalist troops are intercepted 45 miles to the southeast by 2,000 Autonomist troops under Lt. Col. Amaro Catalán. Arredondo smashes through the defenders' southern flank and disperses them after two hours' hard fighting in which Catalán succumbs. A total of 350 casualties are inflicted on both sides, the victors also capturing 80 prisoners. Arredondo enters Mendoza three days later.

2 November 1874. Mitre joins Rivas's rebel division at Médanos (25 miles west of Tuyú) plus 1,500 Indians under chief Catriel. Next day they proceed west, hoping to join forces with Arredondo around Mendoza.

3 November 1874. San Juan Province rises in favor of the Autonomists.

10 November 1874. Mitre's Nationalist vanguard under Commander Leyría scatters an Autonomist concentration under Col. Julio Campos at Gualicho Creek (south of Las Flores), killing 180 defenders.

13 November 1874. Learning that Roca is approaching with a large Autonomist army, Arredondo exits Mendoza and takes up a defensive position at Santa Rosa.

14 November 1874. Mitre's Nationalist army reaches Tapalqué but, being closely pursued by Autonomist forces under Cols. Julio and Luis María Campos, continues to Olavarría and San Carlos. Morale is starting to fade among Mitre's followers; four days later 600 of his Indian supporters join the enemy.

24 November 1874. ***La Verde.*** At dawn Autonomist Lieutenant Colonel Arias enters the hamlet of La Verde and learns that he is directly in the path of Mitre's approaching Nationalist army. Realizing that the latter is closely followed by other Autonomist forces, Arias decides to dig in with his 550 infantry—all well armed with Remingtons—and 350 carbine-toting troopers to check the enemy's progress.

Two days later Mitre's 5,500 followers appear and launch a four-pronged assault upon the hilltop ranch and orchard held by the Autonomists. Lacking artillery and modern weapons, the assault columns are unable to discomfit the defenders and quickly suffer 260 casualties before giving up in despair. Mitre orders his army to continue the march west, but that night at least 1,500 men desert.

2 December 1874. Arias overtakes Mitre's remaining 2,500 followers at Junín and receives the former president's surrender.

6 December 1874. ***Santa Rosa (Second Battle).*** Roca's 4,500 Autonomist troops arrive at Santa Rosa to find Arredondo's similar-sized Nationalist army dug in along the Tunuyán River bank with three cannons and two machine guns—having overestimated enemy strength and thus flooded the fields to the north of the entrenchment. Despite such obstacles Roca leaves a small detachment to threaten Arredondo's front while making a nocturnal encirclement to the rear.

By 7:00 A.M. on 7 December his main Autonomist army, stationed two and a half miles behind Arredondo, launches its attack. Caught off-guard, the Nationalists deploy their reserve to counter while fearing an attack from the front. Because of soggy terrain cavalry prove ineffective, and within three hours the Nationalists are routed, suffering 300 casualties and 2,000 prisoners (including Arredondo) as well as the loss of all their artillery and equipment. Roca's ranks suffer 200 casualties.

1 January 1876. A pursuit column under Lt. Col. Lorenzo Wintter defeats the combined Indian bands of chiefs Catriel and Namuncurá at Tigra Lagoon (southeast of Olavarría), capturing tens of thousands of cattle and other animals. Next day Col. Conrado Villegas inflicts a similar setback upon 200 natives at San Carlos (near Tapalqué).

10 March 1876. Troopers under Col. Salvador Maldonado defeat 2,000 warriors at Horqueta del

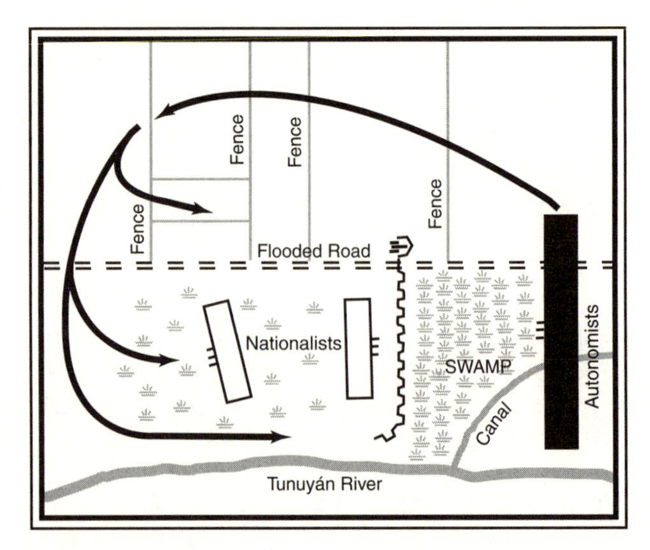

Second battle of Santa Rosa

Sauce (southern extreme of Buenos Aires Province), who are returning from a raid into Argentine territory.

18 MARCH 1876. Col. Nicolás Levalle defeats 3,000 warriors at Paragüil Lagoon (50 miles west of Juárez) before they can invade Argentine territory.

20 MARCH 1876. A month-long operation begins involving 3,700 cavalry in five distinct columns to push Argentine control farther south into Indian territory, as well as dig a 360-mile trench between Bahía Blanca and the southern portions of Córdoba Province to impede native movements.

27 NOVEMBER 1876. López Jordán reenters Entre Ríos Province from exile in Uruguay with a handful of followers. After clashing with a government cavalry patrol they penetrate the interior and attempt to raise a new revolt.

7 DECEMBER 1876. At Alcaracito (south of La Paz), López Jordán's followers—now numbering 800—are surprised by government Col. Juan Ayala's vanguard and dispersed after a brisk hour-long fight. Discouraged, López Jordán proceeds into Corrientes Province, where he is arrested. (Eventually, he escapes confinement at Rosario and returns to exile in Uruguay.)

10 APRIL 1879. ***Roca's Great Indian Sweep.*** As a climax to the lengthy struggle against Argentina's southern tribes, War Minister Roca departs Azul with one of five military columns in a coordinated strike intended to stamp out native resistance throughout the region. Almost 6,000 troopers are employed, other units being commanded by: Col. Napoleón Uriburu, departing San Rafael (Mendoza Province); Col. Eduardo Racedo, marching out of Villa Mercedes; Col. Hilario Lagos, riding out of Trenque Lauquen; and Col. Nicolás Levalle, leaving from Carhué. In a three-month campaign 1,600 Indians are killed or captured, another 11,500 submitting as vassals. Argentine cattle ranches spring up throughout the newly conquered lands.

APRIL 1880. General Roca wins the presidential election to succeed Avellaneda, but his opponent—Dr. Carlos Tejedor, governor of Buenos Aires—refuses to acknowledge the win and threatens civil war. On 10 May both men meet aboard the gunboat *Pilcomayo* to attempt to resolve this impasse but fail.

2 JUNE 1880. A shipment of 3,500 Mauser rifles reaches Buenos Aires, outgoing president Avellaneda ordering them impounded. Instead, they are brought ashore and used to arm Tejedor's followers; two days later Roca declares Belgrano to be his new capital and Tejedor to be in a state of rebellion.

17 JUNE 1880. Col. José Inocencio Arias—marching to join the Buenos Aires troop concentration at Mercedes—is overtaken by two opposing cavalry regiments under Colonel Racedo at Olivera (between Mercedes and Luján). Arias disperses them, suffering some losses in a brief pursuit before resuming his march toward the rendezvous. His numbers soon swell to 7,000, marching east to the capital next day.

20 JUNE 1880. ***Buenos Aires Assault.*** Forces loyal to President-elect Roca close in on the capital, an 800-man cavalry column under Colonel Levalle being one of the first to test the perimeter (being repelled in a probe against Barracas Bridge).

Next day Racedo's troops storm Alsina Bridge from the south, forcing Arias to redeploy at Los Corrales (modern-day Patricios Park) after a bloody engagement that causes 1,200 casualties on both sides. The defenders are again forced to retreat this afternoon into Buenos Aires proper, which is also blockaded by the Argentine navy on its seaward side. Tejedor requests terms two days later; after a week of negotiations he resigns as governor.

12 OCTOBER 1880. General Roca is officially sworn in as Argentina's new president.

15 NOVEMBER 1882. The first of three Argentine cavalry columns sets out under Col. Nicolás Palacios from Choele Choel to pacify Indian resistance in the Andes foothills around Neuquén, Río Hondo, and Chubut. Eventually, more than 1,400 troopers are deployed under the overall command of General Villegas, killing 360 natives and capturing 1,730 in a campaign that results in the creation of Neuquén Province.

1 JANUARY 1884. While probing deep into the Indian territory of Patagonia Lt. Col. Lino O. de Roa's 100 troopers are ambushed in Alto Senguer Valley by 300 natives; they repel the attack.

24 MARCH 1884. Chief Namuncurá accepts the amnesty terms offered by the Argentine government, surrendering along with 300 followers to Lt. Col. Pablo Belisle. This marks the end to most native resistance in the south.

29 SEPTEMBER 1884. The first of five military columns strikes north into the untamed Chaco district

to push Argentina's northern border as far as the Bermejo River.

26 JULY 1890. ***Campos's Coup.*** With Argentina in the grip of economic crisis, Gen. Manuel J. Campos gathers 1,300 troops—three battalions of infantry, the 1st Artillery Regiment, an engineering battalion, and senior cadets from the military academies—in Buenos Aires's Artillería Park (site of modern-day Tribunales Palace) to proclaim a revolution against the president, Dr. Miguel Juárez Celman. The naval squadron joins in, prompting Juárez Celman to depart the capital by train for Rosario, leaving his vice president—Dr. Carlos Pellegrini—to deal with the situation.

Loyal troops quickly attack the rebels, trapping them in Artillería Park and setting off a bloody night of fighting during which more than 1,000 people are killed. At dawn of 27 July Campos requests a truce to tend to the wounded; he surrenders two days later.

6 AUGUST 1890. President Juárez Celman tenders his resignation, being succeeded by Pellegrini.

PORFIRIAN DICTATORSHIP (1876–1897)

POLITICAL TURMOIL CONTINUES TO WRACK MEXICO, especially when the increasingly unpopular Juárez announces in 1871 that he will seek yet another term as president. A group of officers—Negrete, Toledo, Cosío Pontones, Chavarría, and others—stage a coup on 1 October, seizing the arsenals, the Belén jail, and La Ciudadela at Mexico City while calling for a general insurrection. They are quickly put down by troops loyal to the government under Gens. Alejandro García, Sóstenes Rocha, and 39-year-old Donato Guerra—but the retired Gen. Porfirio Díaz (hero of the struggle against the French) also proclaims his opposition to the president's reelection plans from his ranch at La Noria (Oaxaca).

Although crushed both in Oaxaca and in Zacatecas, Díaz and other Juárez enemies persist with guerrilla campaigns until the president dies of natural causes on 18 July 1872, leaving 49-year-old Sebastián Lerdo de Tejada as his successor. The latter maintains power, a 2,250-man army under Ramón Corona defeating 6,000 rebels under Manuel Lozada at La Mojonera (Jalisco) in late October 1873.

However, when Lerdo de Tejada announces he too will run for another term three years later—thus perpetuating his faction's stranglehold over power—Díaz again raises the banner of revolt, proclaiming the so-called Tuxtepec Plan on 10 January 1876, which calls for no further reelections of Mexican presidents.

16 NOVEMBER 1876. A small rebel army under Díaz defeats troops loyal to Lerdo de Tejada's government at Tecoac, prompting the president to resign office four days later.

26 NOVEMBER 1876. Lerdo de Tejada flees Mexico City to Veracruz, taking ship to New York (where he dies in exile 13 years later).

MAY 1877. Díaz is elected president of Mexico, gradually beginning the task of overhauling its bankrupt administration while installing placemen throughout the departments.

25 JUNE 1879. Nine opposition leaders are arrested and executed in Veracruz on Díaz's orders.

1 DECEMBER 1880. One-armed veteran Gen. Manuel González—a protégé of Díaz—is elected president of Mexico.

1 DECEMBER 1884. Despite his earlier opposition to presidential reelections, Díaz is once more installed into office, which he holds for 26 years (being elected eight times in all, serving six full terms).

28 JANUARY 1885. ***Yaqui Wars.*** A native war party under Loreto Molina attacks the home of 47-year-old Yaqui leader Cajeme (Hispanicized name: José María Leyva) at Guamúchiles in the remote northwestern state of Sinaloa. Failing to find the chieftain, they arrest several followers, beat his family, then loot and torch his household before withdrawing. In revenge, Cajeme declares war on his rivals, and a tribal civil war erupts.

Mexico's authorities—who because of past difficulties have ignored the Yaqui, allowing them to live autonomously—now decide to reimpose their rule over the troubled region. An expedition of 2,200 men is assembled and divided into two columns, one under Gen. José Guillermo Carbó, the other under Gen. Bonifacio Topete. While the former remains around Guaymas the latter penetrates into the Sierra Madre Range until checked by the Yaqui mountain fast at El Añil (near Vicam, Sonora). Despite bombarding the moat, stakes, and palisades with a small field piece,

Topete is unable to carry the stronghold. By July he retires with the onset of torrid summer weather.

OCTOBER 1885. Carbó dies, being temporarily succeeded by Gen. Marcos Carrillo. Angel Martínez arrives in January 1886 to assume command of all Mexican forces in Sonora and Sinaloa.

MARCH 1886. General Carrillo marches east out of Guaymas (Sonora) with 1,200 soldiers to reduce El Añil while Martínez proceeds southeast with 1,500 to subdue the neighboring Mayo tribes.

5 MAY 1886. After a fierce struggle Carrillo compels Cajeme's Yaqui to quit their mountain stronghold of El Añil (near Vicam, Sonora); most natives escape farther northeast into the mountains.

11 MAY 1886. ***Buatachive.*** Cajeme concentrates 4,000 Yaqui tribesmen at another mountain stronghold: Buatachive, located ten miles north of Tórim in the Bacatete Range (Sonora). Martínez approaches with 1,400 troops, finding a three-and-a-half mile perimeter protected by a system of trenches and stone walls.

Overnight, however, Col. Lorenzo Torres leads 300 Mexican soldiers to the heights above Buatachive, and when Martínez sees his company engaged next dawn he attacks with his main army, divided into four assault columns with artillery support. The Yaqui are defeated, suffering 200 dead and more than 2,000 noncombatants captured; Cajeme again escapes deeper into the mountains with a band of survivors. Mexican casualties total 21 dead and 48 wounded.

27 MAY 1886. A number of Yaqui and Mayo chieftains submit to Mexican authorities at Tórim (Sonora).

22 JUNE 1886. ***Guichamoco.*** At Guichamoco Beach Colonel Torres encounters Cajeme, who is leading 1,500 Yaqui warriors across open country for a surprise attack on Gen. Juan Hernández's Mexican garrison at nearby Médano (Sonora) in hopes of gaining desperately needed weapons. Torres charges and easily scatters the poorly armed host, killing 62 and effectively ending organized Yaqui resistance under Cajeme.

12 APRIL 1887. After living in Guaymas for two months under an assumed name, Cajeme is betrayed to Torres and Martínez by an Indian woman and arrested at dawn. The chief is taken aboard the frigate *Demócrata* on the night of 21 April, sailed up the Yaqui River, and executed at Cócorit four days later as a disincentive to his adherents.

20 MAY 1887. The Yaqui chieftain Anastasio Cuca—Cajeme's second-in-command—is extradited from Tucson (Arizona) and returned into Sonora, where he is executed.

JUNE 1887. Believing the Yaquis to be pacified, Martínez withdraws his troops from their lands, only to see Cócorit overrun two days later by a new leader, Tetabiate (Hispanicized name: Juan Maldonado).

JULY 1887. Torres is appointed governor of Sonora and delegates the wealthy 33-year-old local landowner Ramón Corral to carry out his duties.

FEBRUARY 1889. After a year and a half of sporadic Yaqui raids, the newly appointed military district commander, Gen. Julio M. Cervantes, offers a general amnesty, which is ignored.

MARCH 1890. Marcos Carrillo replaces Cervantes and resumes the Mexican army's patrols against rebel Yaqui bands in the mountains of Sonora and Sinaloa.

FEBRUARY 1892. Carrillo dies at Tórim (Sonora), being replaced next month by Gen. Abraham Bandala.

29 OCTOBER 1892. Porfirian *federales* wipe out the rebel town of Tomochic (Chihuahua), killing or arresting all inhabitants.

DECEMBER 1896. Col. Francisco Peinado, commander of the 5th Cavalry Regiment, begins a correspondence with the renegade Yaqui chieftain Teobiate in the Sierra Madre Range, proposing an armistice. Four months later the chief and 400 warriors accept the colonel's amnesty, meeting at La Cieneguita—between Bacatete and Tetacombiate—to finalize terms.

15 MAY 1897. At a ceremony held at Ortiz Station outside Guaymas, Teobiate's rebel band arrives from La Misa with a cavalry escort from Peinado's 5th Dragoon Regiment and submits to Gov. Luis E. Torres.

1897–1911. Ironically, Díaz's original opposition to presidential reelections will instead see him remain in power until early 1911, his military and political might helping convert him into the "strongman of the Americas." The early part of his reign is buoyed by many Mexicans' desire for peace and stable government after so many decades of fractious rule. However, his repression eventually results in the cataclysmic explosion of the Mexican Revolution.

Mexican infantry parading through a northern garrison town, 1893; by Frederic Remington

War of the Pacific (1879–1883)

In 1874, after years of bitter wrangling, Bolivia and Chile have apparently resolved their dispute over the Atacama Desert, Santiago relinquishing its claim to the southern portion and tacitly recognizing Bolivian access to the Pacific, in exchange for La Paz's promise not to increase taxation on any Chilean corporation operating in this territory. However, faced with bankruptcy four years later, the 38-year-old Bolivian dictator Gen. Hilarión Daza violates this arrangement by levying a heavy new tax on the Chilean Nitrate Co. at Antofagasta.

8 November 1878. Chile's Pres. Aníbal Pinto Garmendia—faced with considerable economic woes of his own due to collapsing international metal prices, droughts, and a lack of hard currency—sends a diplomatic note to protest Daza's tax increase, who responds by calling for even stiffer measures. When the Chilean manager at Antofagasta refuses to pay, he is imprisoned and the Nitrate Co.'s properties are seized.

16 November 1878. While entering the senate chamber in Lima, Peru's 44-year-old ex-Pres. Manuel Pardo is assassinated by Sgt. Melchor Montoya, who is disgruntled at his failure to secure an officer's commission.

10 February 1879. After three months of unavailing diplomatic protests, Santiago severs relations with La Paz.

14 February 1879. A Chilean squadron sails north from Caldera and deposits Col. Emilio Sotomayor with 200 marines in Antofagasta to prevent the Bolivian authorities from auctioning off the impounded properties of Chile's Nitrate Co. The tiny Bolivian garrison retires north toward Cobija and Tocopilla without offering resistance.

20 February 1879. Daza learns of the Chilean occupation of Antofagasta and five days later replies by requesting aid from his secret ally Peru, then declares war against Santiago on 1 March. The latter—contemptuous

of Bolivia's poverty and lack of military resources—ignores this declaration, while Peru (reluctant to become drawn into a war) merely offers to mediate.

23 MARCH 1879. Colonel Sotomayor, his unit now augmented to 500 men, defeats a hastily assembled force of Bolivian militia at Calama on the Loa River. Shortly thereafter Chilean warships also occupy Cobija and Tocopilla, being joined at this latter port by Sotomayor's land column.

2 APRIL 1879. Having learned of the secret protocol existing between Bolivia and Peru, Chile prepares to declare war against both countries within the next three days. None of the three nations is really fit to contemplate hostilities, Bolivia's population of 2 million maintaining a standing army of only 3,000 ill-equipped regulars; Peru (population 2.7 million) one of 8,000 soldiers; while Chile's 2.5 million support a like number. However, the Chileans' great advantage lies in their pair of modern, 3,500-ton, English-built ironclads *Almirante Cochrane* and *Blanco Encalada,* which their opponents' navies cannot equal.

5 APRIL 1879. Despite having been ordered to attack Peru's main naval base of Callao in a preemptive strike, the 52-year-old Chilean Adm. Juan Williams Rebolledo instead anchors off Iquique with his battle squadron, instituting a close blockade in hopes of compelling his naval opponents to seek him out for battle. (Infirm and obsessed with winning the Conservative Party's nomination for Chile's presidential elections two years hence, Williams will act with excessive caution throughout the forthcoming campaign.)

Meanwhile Chilean columns pushing out of Antofagasta clear the Atacama Desert of its last Bolivian troops, easily driving them up into the Andes.

16 MAY 1879. Stung by public criticism of his inactivity, Chilean Admiral Williams leaves the wooden corvette *Esmeralda* and wooden gunboat *Covadonga* to maintain his blockade of Iquique, while sailing his battle squadron in a feint against Arica, then continuing past to invest his main target of Callao. During his passage northward he unknowingly misses a Peruvian squadron steaming in the opposite direction under 45-year-old Adm. Miguel Grau, who intends to lift the blockade of Iquique.

21 MAY 1879. ***Iquique.*** Grau appears off this port with his 1,130-ton turreted flagship *Huáscar* and the 2,000-ton ironclad *Independencia* of Capt. Juan G. Moore. Both Peruvian vessels are quite old, but nonetheless more than a match for the wooden Chilean blockaders *Esmeralda* and *Covadonga,* which they pursue. However, during this chase *Independencia* runs aground close inshore then is totally lost when Capt. Carlos Condell's *Covadonga* turns and shells it into a wreck. (The chagrined Moore later quits Peru's navy in disgrace.) *Huáscar* meanwhile rams *Esmeralda,* whose Capt. Arturo Pratts leaps aboard the Peruvian flagship with a single follower, only to be shot down while his vessel sinks.

A few days after this encounter, Admiral Williams arrives off Callao and learns of his detachment's defeat. This news prompts him to return southeastward, searching for Grau. The latter slips past the Chileans again and reenters Callao in early June for a refit, in anticipation of launching a series of seaborne raids.

6 JULY 1879. Grau departs Callao with *Huáscar* and a few auxiliaries, surprising the blockaders of Iquique four days later and capturing one of their ships. When Chilean naval reinforcements are rushed into this area, the Peruvian admiral escapes south to seize a frigate off Antofagasta, then wreaks havoc off the ports of Chañaral and Caldera. He also intercepts the valuable Chilean troop transport *Rimac,* as well as detaching a vessel still farther south to Punta Arenas to intercept war matériel reaching Chile around the Strait of Magellan. *Huáscar* meanwhile reverses course north to shell Antofagasta, then attacks the ports of Huásco, Coquimbo, and Tongoy.

These distractions allow other Peruvian vessels to carry supplies for Gen. Juan Buendía's military buildup at Tarapacá, who is to be joined at nearby Arica by 7,000 poorly armed Bolivians marching down out of the Andes under Daza. Given the failure of Chile's navy to secure control of the seas, Admiral Williams—completely outclassed by his Peruvian counterpart Grau—is compelled to resign in favor of Adm. Galvarino Rivera.

7 OCTOBER 1879. ***Angamos.*** After three months of successful hit-and-run raids against Chilean targets, Grau reappears off Antofagasta with *Huáscar* and the swift, 1,150-ton wooden corvette *Unión,* finding its harbor empty. The Peruvian warships therefore steer north, little realizing that five of their more powerful Chilean pursuers have been alerted at nearby Mejillones and are preparing to intercept.

Next dawn *Huáscar* and *Unión* sight a trio of enemy vessels 40 miles north of Antofagasta, two of which charge *Unión* while the large ironclad *Blanco Encalada* bears directly down upon Grau's much smaller flagship. *Huáscar* turns to flee but off Angamos Point is trapped by another Chilean pair led by *Blanco Encalada*'s sister warship *Cochrane,* and the battle is joined.

The Peruvian flagship opens fire first, striking *Cochrane,* but not a crippling blow. *Cochrane*'s counterfire quickly incapacitates Grau's flagship, killing the Peruvian admiral along with his second in command, Elías Aguirre, after which *Blanco Encalada* also comes up. Both Chilean men-of-war then attempt to ram *Huáscar,* narrowly missing it and each other. However, their combined fire so rakes the Peruvian vessel that several fires break out, three-quarters of its crew are killed or wounded, and its flag is hauled down within less than two hours. Exultant Chilean boarding parties come aboard to find *Huáscar*'s sea valves open, but they are able to close them and eventually incorporate this prize into their navy.

26 OCTOBER 1879. Having gained complete mastery of the seas with the death of Grau, Gen. Erasmo Escala departs Antofagasta with an 8,000-man Chilean expedition and disembarks at Pisagua by 2 November, scaling its well-defended bluffs to seize this port and nearby Junín, thus establishing a beachhead for an overland encirclement of Iquique.

The Peruvian and Bolivian defenders fall back along its railroad line over the next couple of weeks as the invaders press inland. Finally Peruvian General Buendía has gathered 10,000 troops and marches north from Iquique to catch Escala from both front and rear, in conjunction with Daza's 7,000 Bolivians advancing south across the desert from Arica.

19 NOVEMBER 1879. ***San Francisco.*** After occupying the oasis at Dolores railway station, an advance Chilean party from Escala's main army detects the approaching host of Peruvian and Bolivian troops under Buendía. The Chileans hastily throw up defensive positions at nearby San Francisco atop a small mountain overlooking this waterhole and brace to receive an assault.

Late this afternoon the fighting commences, raging into the night. The ill-coordinated Peruvian and Bolivian thrusts are decimated by the defenders' Krupp artillery, directed by mercenary German officers who are veterans of the Franco-Prussian War. Buendía's efforts are further hampered by the failure of Daza's army to appear out of the north from Arica, most of it having turned back toward Tacna because of heat and lack of supplies. The attackers' will eventually collapses and they straggle southeastward in defeat toward Tarapacá, hoping to eventually slip north through the Andean foothills and join the main allied concentration at Tacna.

27 NOVEMBER 1879. ***Tarapacá.*** After belatedly resuming their pursuit of Buendía's defeated army, a Chilean contingent overtakes this retreating force and—through faulty intelligence and a mistaken assumption that its morale is shattered—launches a bold frontal assault on the city of Tarapacá. The Peruvians and Bolivians react well, rushing reinforcements into this encounter and crushing their pursuers. Peruvian Cols. Andrés Avelino Cáceres and Francisco Bolognesi distinguish themselves during this clash, chasing the Chileans back five miles; but despite this victory, a lack of supplies obliges Buendía's army to resume their retirement northwest toward Tacna; behind them isolated Iquique falls to Escala within a matter of days.

18 DECEMBER 1879. Having left Rear Adm. Lizardo Montero in overall command of the armies in southern Peru while himself returning from Tacna into Lima, Pres. Mariano Ignacio Prado then unexpectedly sets sail from his capital toward Europe to raise funds, ships, and other matériel for continuing his nation's war effort. Three days later his vice president—Gen. Luis La Puerta—is deposed by a popular uprising, and on 23 December Prado's longtime political rival Dr. Nicolás de Piérola is installed into office as the new president, promptly branding his predecessor a traitor for desertion.

LATE DECEMBER 1879. Disgraced by his abysmal performance in the field, Daza is overthrown in a coup directed by Col. Eliodoro Camacho and replaced as Bolivia's president by the popular Gen. Narciso Campero. Under the latter's rule Bolivia will attempt to revive its military fortunes, although its efforts still continue to be feeble.

LATE FEBRUARY 1880. A 12,000-man Chilean expedition under Gen. Manuel Baquedano quits Iquique and Pisagua, sailing north-northwest to disembark at Pacocha near Ilo, from where it is to then advance inland and threaten the main Peruvian concentration at Tacna while the fleet blockades the nearby port of Arica. Through such a strategy the outnumbered invaders hope to draw the defenders out into the open for a battle, where their superior weaponry and discipline can tell.

12 MARCH 1880. Baquedano strikes inland across the desert toward Moquegua, which he occupies on 20 March in hopes of provoking a Peruvian counterattack.

22 MARCH 1880. ***Cuesta de los Angeles.*** A short distance beyond Moquegua, Baquedano's advancing Chilean army encounters 2,000 Peruvians dug in across a defile called Cuesta de los Angeles, which proves to be an unusually strong position. Superior numbers allow the invaders to turn both the defenders' flanks as well as

overrunning their center, but Baquedano's troops suffer heavy losses in achieving this victory.

8 APRIL 1880. Still unable to lure Montero's main army out of its defenses around Tacna, Baquedano gradually pushes southeast out of Moquegua across the desert, arriving within 20 miles of his objective one month later.

26 MAY 1880. ***Tacna.*** Having encountered an army under the new Bolivian President Campero dug in atop a promontory commanding the road into Tacna, Baquedano masses his 8,500 Chilean troops opposite then orders a frontal assault. The first units attack piecemeal and suffer heavily before the entire formation can make a coordinated advance and roll up the overmatched defenders. Chilean casualties total 2,000 compared to 3,000 among the Peruvians and Bolivians, whose army disintegrates in the wake of this defeat.

The victorious Baquedano then presses on to take the nearby port of Arica from its landward side, abetted by the long-range bombardment of Chilean warships offshore. At dawn of 7 June a surprise assault is made, overwhelming the 2,000 Peruvian defenders under Bolognesi by nightfall, who "fight to the last cartridge."

SUMMER 1880. While foreign governments attempt to mediate an end to hostilities, Irish-born Gen. Patricio Lynch leads a series of seaborne descents by the Chilean navy against Chimbote and other Peruvian towns near Lima.

18 NOVEMBER 1880. After Chilean Gen. José A. Villagrán has landed at Curayaco to seize the nearby Peruvian port of Chilca as an advance bridgehead, Baquedano begins bringing another 20,000 men ashore two days later farther southeast at Pisco to unite and jointly invest Lima (population 130,000). Following two weeks of preparation, the invaders begin their overland push, reaching the southern banks of the Lurín River by mid-December. On the opposite side looms a hastily constructed line of fortifications through the San Juan foothills, held by 22,000 Peruvians—mostly raw militia and civilian conscripts.

13 JANUARY 1881. ***Chorrillos-Miraflores.*** At dawn Baquedano's 24,000 Chileans strike across the Lurín River, their main effort being directed against the Santa Teresa and Solar strongholds in the resort town of Chorrillos, defended by Gen. Miguel Iglesias. Despite heavy losses, the invaders overwhelm the Peruvians by midday, sending thousands streaming back toward Lima in disarray. The Chileans meanwhile pause to loot the wealthy summer homes throughout this district then next day visit a like treatment on Barranco, allowing the defenders time to recuperate from their setback.

Some 5,000 Peruvians reassemble in their last line of defense along the Surco River, two and a half miles outside Lima. A delegation of international diplomats led by Salvadoran Amb. Jorge Tezanos Pinto also intercedes, arranging a temporary ceasefire and peace conference at the resort town of Miraflores in the no-man's-land between both armies for 15 January. Peruvian President de Piérola and the Chilean commander in chief, Baquedano, attend, only to be interrupted by gunfire shortly after 2:00 P.M. Although the invading army has agreed to a truce, its units have also continued to redeploy for their final assault against the defenders' line, prompting a jittery Peruvian company to open fire when a Chilean artillery battery begins unlimbering within point-blank range. Spontaneous exchanges erupt all up and down both battlelines as well as from the Chilean warships offshore; the diplomats flee for their lives. By nightfall the Peruvian army is swept away; Col. Juan Martín Echenique is later blamed for his failure to commit the 6,000-man reserve, although it is unlikely to have stemmed the Chilean onslaught.

As defeated troops retreat through the capital's streets, rioting and pillage ensue. De Piérola having galloped toward Tarma to continue the resistance in Peru's mountainous interior, Mayor Rufino Torrico is left to offer to surrender Lima to the victors on the morning of 16 January. A select regiment of 3,000 Chilean troops under Gen. Cornelio Saavedra enters next day at 2:00 P.M., and order is restored. The nearby port of Callao capitulates by 18 January.

The conquest of the Peruvian capital brings a virtual end to large-scale fighting, most of Baquedano's expedition reembarking for Chile shortly thereafter. The discredited de Piérola retreats into Ayacucho and appoints the 47-year-old Cáceres as military commander for the central highlands, with Admiral Montero acting in a similar capacity farther northwest at Cajamarca. Although Cáceres in particular eventually organizes a successful guerrilla campaign in La Breña District, these efforts alone cannot hope to loosen Chile's grip on coastal Peru.

Further complicating matters is the creation on 12 March of a rival provisional Peruvian government under the lawyer Dr. Francisco García Calderón in the La Magdalena suburb of occupied Lima, which enters into negotiations with the invaders.

28 SEPTEMBER 1881. As peace talks mediated by the United States begin to collapse, the military governor of Lima—General Lynch—orders the deposal of pro-

visional Pres. García Calderón, who is later arrested and transported prisoner to Chile on 6 November.

1 OCTOBER 1881. At Arequipa in southern Peru several thousand troops mutiny against de Piérola's authority, being joined a little more than a month later by Admiral Montero, who proclaims himself the new acting president in succession to García Calderón. When Cáceres and his *montoneros* (guerrillas) in the central highlands also declare themselves against de Piérola, the latter has no choice but to resign the presidency at Tarma on 28 November and go into exile.

For the next two years, disperse Peruvian units do their best to contain Chilean incursions into the Andes, but without seriously discomfiting the invaders' occupation of the rich, populous coastland. Cáceres wins numerous small-scale encounters such as at Caxacamara in September 1882, only to finally be defeated at Huamachaca the following year while Montero is chased out of Arequipa.

Convinced peace must be restored in order for Peru to even survive, the war hero Iglesias convokes a congress at Cajamarca, which proclaims him president in spite of rival claims by Cáceres in the center and Montero in the south. Iglesias then proceeds to Ancón, a small seaside community a short distance northwest of Lima and, after considerable negotiation, signs a treaty on 20 October 1883 ending hostilities with Chile. Cáceres and Montero refuse to ratify this agreement until June 1884, and Bolivia concurs only after being threatened with a Chilean invasion.

The victors finally withdraw the last of their occupying forces in August 1884, Chile having expanded its national territory by annexing the provinces of Atacama and Tarapacá (thus gaining a monopoly over the world's nitrate deposits) while depriving Bolivia of its access to the Pacific. In one final outburst of fighting, Cáceres assaults Lima on 27 August 1884, launching a year-long Peruvian civil war to drive Iglesias from office.

RIEL REBELLION (1885)

FIFTEEN YEARS AFTER THE RED RIVER EXPEDITION, the Métis and Indians of Manitoba rise in revolt against the Canadian government, this time disappointed by the erosion of traditional ways. Riel is recalled from exile in the United States and travels to the main Métis community at Batoche to organize yet another protest movement.

11 MARCH 1885. Leif Crozier, superintendent of the Northwest Mounted Police outpost at Fort Carlton (30 miles west of Batoche), informs Ottawa that a native rebellion is imminent.

19 MARCH 1885. Riel proclaims himself president of a provisional government and two days later sends a party to demand the surrender of Fort Carlton.

26 MARCH 1885. ***Duck Lake.*** Crozier, with 98 mounted policemen and volunteers, attacks a Métis concentration under Gabriel Dumont at Duck Lake, only to be soundly beaten (12 Canadians being killed as opposed to five Métis). Crozier then retreats to Fort Carlton to be reinforced by another 90 Northwest Mounted Police from Red River under Commissioner Acheson Irvine, who assumes overall command. Feeling he cannot hold his position, Irvine orders a retirement down the North Saskatchewan River into Prince Albert.

27 MARCH 1885. The 60-year-old British Maj. Gen. Frederick Dobson Middleton—commander in chief of Canada's militia forces—reaches Winnipeg by train to begin organizing defenses.

30 MARCH 1885. Warriors under the Cree chief Poundmaker depart Cut Knife Creek Reservation and attack the Canadian settlement at Battleford. The residents seek refuge in the Northwest Mounted Police barracks while their homes are looted and burned.

2 APRIL 1885. Cree braves under chief Wandering Spirit attack Canadian settlers at Frog Lake, killing nine and capturing several others.

7 APRIL 1885. Some 600 Canadian militia reach Winnipeg, having departed Toronto a week earlier.

12 APRIL 1885. Lt. Col. William Otter reaches Swift Current by train to continue 130 miles farther north and lift the siege of Battleford with 273 men of the Queen's Own Rifles under Lt. Col. Augustus Miller; 50 men of Company "C" of the Toronto Infantry School; 100 gunners of Battery "B" of the Kingston Artillery under Maj. Charles Short; 200 teamsters; two nine-pounders under Capt. Robert Rutherford; and one Gatling gun under U.S. Lt. Arthur Howard. But the South Saskatchewan River is low, and Otter's advance is delayed by two days before proceeding overland.

14 APRIL 1885. Otter's expedition is joined at Saskatchewan crossing by 50 Northwest Mounted Police under Supt. William Herchmer aboard the steamer *Northcote.*

21 APRIL 1885. Canadian scouts from Battleford encounter refugees traveling downriver from Fort Pitt under Northwest Mounted Police Insp. Francis Dickens (son of the famous Victorian novelist Charles Dickens).

22 APRIL 1885. One of Herchmer's scouts carries word into the 500 beleaguered residents of Battleford that Otter's relief column is nearby.

24 APRIL 1885. Otter relieves Battleford, the native besiegers having withdrawn. Simultaneously, news is received that Middleton has fought an indecisive engagement against Dumont at Fish Creek (south of Batoche), 11 men having been killed and 48 wounded.

2 MAY 1885. ***Cut Knife Creek.*** Having left a garrison to hold Battleford, Otter ventures forth with 300 men in search of Poundmaker's main Cree camp. At dawn, shortly after fording Cut Knife Creek and climbing a hill beyond, he stumbles on it. Neither side is prepared for battle, fighting gradually spreading on all sides. Rather than charge the surprised Indians Otter chooses to make a stand atop the hill, where his men are surrounded and shot at from every direction. The young Cree chief Fine Day directs his warriors from a hill south of the battlefield, signaling them with a mirror.

By 11:00 A.M. Otter is so hard-pressed as to order a portion of his troops to retreat then take up covering positions farther to the rear. When his frontlines follow at noon action abruptly ceases. Eight Canadian troops have been killed and 14 wounded compared to six Cree dead and three injured. Otter abandons his ammunition train and returns to Battleford by 10:00 P.M., claiming victory.

9 MAY 1885. Middleton's column—including the 90th Winnipeg Rifles—arrives outside Batoche, and three days later charges its rifle pits, compelling the Métis defenders to flee.

The captive Louis Riel

15 MAY 1885. His followers scattered, Riel surrenders to Middleton, who then presses on to Battleford.

23 MAY 1885. Chief Poundmaker and 150 Cree warriors surrender to Middleton.

3 JUNE 1885. Insp. Samuel Steele of the Northwest Mounted Police—leading the vanguard of Major General Strange's column marching east, having relieved Edmonton in May—defeats chief Big Bear's Cree concentration at Frenchman's Butte on the North Saskatchewan River, near Fort Pitt.

2 JULY 1885. After a lengthy pursuit, Big Bear surrenders at Fort Carlton.

16 NOVEMBER 1885. Determined to put an end to Métis resistance, Canadian authorities hang Riel at Regina, followed by Wandering Spirit and seven other native leaders outside Fort Battleford on 27 November. Poundmaker and Big Bear are condemned to three-year terms in Stony Mountain Penitentiary, being released early because of their ill health; both die shortly thereafter.

BRAZILIAN STRIFE (1889–1897)

AFTER A HALF-CENTURY LIVING IN RELATIVE ISOLATION under Emperor Pedro II, this South American giant at last begins to stir, throwing off the monarchy and gradually struggling into the modern-day world.

15 NOVEMBER 1889. ***Collapse of Empire.*** At daybreak 2,500 men of the 1st and 9th Cavalry Regiments and the 2nd Artillery Battalion revolt at São Cristóvão outside Rio de Janeiro, marching into the

Deodoro da Fonseca

capital to confront the government. Liberal Prime Minister Affonso Celso, Visconde de Ouro Prêto, quickly dispatches units to put down the mutineers, but the loyal forces instead join the rebels.

Disgruntled 62-year-old Marshal Manuel Deodoro da Fonseca is behind the movement, which intends to replace the monarchy with a republic. The emperor arrives from his palace at Petrópolis that afternoon but is powerless to intervene. Next day he is informed of his banishment and sails to exile in France aboard a Brazilian warship at 8:00 A.M. on 17 November. Meanwhile Deodoro da Fonseca declares martial law and installs a provisional government with himself at its head.

3 NOVEMBER 1891. Plagued by economic deficiencies and growing political resentment, Deodoro da Fonseca sends troops to dissolve Brazil's congress.

23 NOVEMBER 1891. Rear Adm. Custódio José de Melo's squadron revolts against the Deodoro da Fonseca regime, firing a single shell into Rio de Janeiro from his 5,700-ton anchored battleship *Riachuelo* (named for a famous Brazilian naval victory; *see* 10 June 1865 under War of the Triple Alliance). Knowing himself to be surrounded by numerous other enemies, the dictator resigns rather than mount a futile resistance; next day he retires from active service. He is succeeded by his 52-year-old vice president, Adjutant Gen. Floriano Peixoto.

19 JANUARY 1892. Sgt. Silvino de Macedo leads a populist revolt at Fort Santa Cruz, being joined shortly by the garrison of Fortress Laje (both in Guanabara Bay, opposite Rio de Janeiro). Peixoto quickly deploys loyal forces and crushes the upstarts.

31 MARCH 1892. A group of 13 high-ranking Brazilian officers send Peixoto a threatening manifesto, urging quick presidential elections. He dismisses all 13 from the service, and when they organize a riot in Rio de Janeiro ten days later he arrests them, deporting many ringleaders by 11 April.

17 JUNE 1892. Youthful Júlio Prates de Castilhos leads a bloodless coup in Rio Grande do Sul Province in support of a central Brazilian state.

JULY 1892. Anticentralist Lt. Santos Lara revolts at Pôrto Alegre, shelling the city before capitulating a few days later.

9 FEBRUARY 1893. ***Rio Grandese Revolt.*** Anticentralist Brazilian exiles under their civilian leader Gumercindo Saraiva cross into Rio Grande do Sul Province from Uruguay to overthrow de Castilhos's rival regime. They are soon joined by other bands, and 3,000 united guerrillas soon come under the command of Col. João Nunes da Silva Tavares.

After overrunning the town of Dom Pedrito they march on Santana do Livramento but break off their approach upon learning it is about to be reinforced by federal troops. They are repulsed outside Pôrto Alegre but gain fresh armaments at Quaraí and come under the command of Col. Oliveira Salgado after he defects from the federal cause and supersedes Silva Tavares.

Shortly thereafter the rebels are overtaken on the banks of Inhanduí Creek and defeated by Gen. Pinheiro Machado. Salgado and Silva Tavares retreat to Uruguay, pursued by the triumphant republicans; Saraiva persists with guerrilla hit-and-run raids within Brazil.

6 JULY 1893. Adm. Eduardo Wandenkolk—one of the 13 high-ranking officers dismissed by Peixoto (*see* 31 March 1892)—commandeers the ammunition ship *Jupiter* outside Rio de Janeiro then diverts it southwest to the port of Rio Grande, where he gathers some followers and calls for a widespread antigovernment revolt. Receiving scant support, he surrenders off Santa Catarina Island to the cruiser *República.*

AUGUST 1893. Rebel Colonel Salgado returns to Rio Grande do Sul from Uruguay, joins forces with Saraiva, then inaugurates a heated guerrilla campaign throughout the province.

5 SEPTEMBER 1893. ***Naval Rebellion.*** Disaffected by the army's rule, Admiral de Melo this evening goes aboard the English-built 4,950-ton cruiser *Aquidabã* with his staff and some federal deputies, raising the

The Brazilian cruiser Aquidabã *as it appeared during peacetime*

white flag of revolt next dawn. He is joined by the 1,400 officers and men aboard the remaining 15 warships and 18 auxiliaries at anchor before Rio de Janeiro and at the naval base of Niterói opposite.

Expecting an easy capitulation—as on 23 November 1891—the mutineers are instead disappointed to find the harbor castles remaining loyal to Marshal Peixoto and no sympathetic insurrections occurring elsewhere in Brazil. Moreover, the powerful battleship *Riachuelo* is undergoing repairs in Europe, and the rest of the squadron is in such poor condition that only five vessels can actually move under their own power. As a crowning complication, the foreign warships in harbor band together under a French rear admiral aboard the 3,665-ton cruiser *Aréthuse* to protect their nationals' interests, restricting de Melo's actions (although not before he manages to commandeer about 30 merchantmen as supply ships).

Fighting between rebels and federal forces flares up on 10 September, ending next afternoon. Another round starts at 9:00 A.M. on 13 September; before dawn on 17 September the mutinous admiral detaches the cruiser *República* under Capt. Federico de Lorena and the torpedo boat *Primeiro de Março,* covering their escape past the batteries with *Aquidabã* so that they might proceed south to Destêrro (modern-day Florianópolis, capital of Santa Catarina Province) to foment a more widespread rebellion. Meanwhile Peixoto has patiently mustered 5,000 troops at Santana and reinforced Rio's defenses; a lengthy stalemate with de Melo ensues, punctuated by occasional exchanges of gunfire.

During this interval numerous foreign powers rush warships to Rio—most notably the United States, whose president, Grover Cleveland, is determined to exert influence in this American theater against European interference. Despite an embarassingly slow start because of certain deficiencies, the cruiser USS *Charleston* of Capt. Henry F. Picking eventually arrives on 27 September, followed by the cruisers *Newark* of Capt. Silas Terry, *New York* of Capt. John W. Philip, and *Detroit* of Cmdr. Willard H. Brownson plus the 500-ton wooden steam corvette *Yantic* of Lt. Cmdr. Henry W. Lyon (soon superseded by Lt. Cmdr. Seth M. Ackley).

This gives the U.S. contingent a marked superiority over the two British (flag: HMS *Sirius* of Capt. William L. Lang), two French (flag: *Aréthuse*), two Italian (*Bausan* and *Dogali*), two Portuguese, one German, one Spanish (*Cristóbal Colón*), and one Argentine (*Nueve de Mayo*) warships present in Rio's harbor. However, the first American commander—Commo. Oscar F. Stanton—compromises himself at the very outset by saluting the rebel flag upon entering port aboard *Newark,* thus precipitating a formal protest from Peixoto's government; the salute leads to his recall in early October and replacement by Rear Admiral Benham.

Also in late October, the Brazilian garrison of Fort Villegaignon joins the mutineer cause, but in November the loyalists score a victory when the ironclad *Javari* is sunk by shore batteries. Hoping to revive his flagging fortunes by personally heading southwest to raise another insurrection, de Melo breaks out of Rio on 1 December with his flagship *Aquidabã* under Capt. Alexandrino de Alencar, leaving fellow conspirator Adm. Luís Filipe de Saldanha da Gama (former commandant of Brazil's naval college) to maintain pressure on the capital. De Melo eventually disembarks in Santa Catarina Province to organize rebel activities; Saldanha grows increasingly frustrated at his idled squadron's impotence against loyalist encroachments around Rio.

On 9 February 1894 Saldanha leads 500 men ashore under covering fire from his ships to attempt to capture the eastern town of Niterói. Although initially successful, Saldahna is soon thrown back from the center by loyal troops under Cols. Fonseca Ramos and Argolo then is trapped on Armação Point. After a vicious firefight during which Saldanha is wounded the rebels are defeated and driven back aboard their ships, marking a virtual end to their resistance in the harbor. A few days later *Aquidabã*—which has returned some time earlier after depositing de Melo in Santa Catarina—again breaks out of the bay, returning to Destêrro.

The remaining mutineer ships learn on 11 March that a small loyal squadron (many of its vessels recently purchased, armed, and manned in the United States) is approaching from Pernambuco under retired Adm. Jerônimo Gonçalves. Their morale shattered, Saldanha and almost 500 of his men seek asylum aboard the tiny Portuguese corvettes *Mindelo* and *Afonso Albuquerque* of Cmdr. Augusto de Castilhos; when Gonçalves enters Rio's harbor two days later he finds the naval rebellion has ended. Peixoto demands the return of the mutineers, but de Castilhos refuses, instead exiting the harbor and setting sail for the neutral River Plate. (As Saldanha and many of his followers subsequently cross the border to join the provincial rebellion in Rio Grande do Sul, Peixoto accuses de Castilhos of sympathizing with the insurrectionists and severs diplomatic relations with Portugal.)

EARLY NOVEMBER 1893. After a 750-mile jungle campaign against the loyal Northern Division of Pinheiro Machado, rebel leaders Salgado and Saraiva fight their way across the Pelotas River into Santa Catarina

Province, seizing the coastal Laguna rail center. From here Salgado entrains to join de Melo's naval mutineers at Destêrro while Saraiva strikes north toward Lajes, shifting the main theater of operations northeast out of Rio Grande do Sul Province.

24 NOVEMBER 1893. After recapturing the town of Quaraí and defeating a republican force at Rio Negro—decapitating his captives after the latter battle—rebel Col. Silva Tavares lays siege to loyal Gen. Carlos Teles within Bagé; he disperses his followers into several columns after 45 days of fruitless watch.

28 MARCH 1894. ***De Melo's Last Gasp.*** His revolutionary movement having lost impetus because of recent military setbacks near São Paulo and dissension among its leadership, Admiral de Melo departs the captured port of Paranaguá with some contingents, heading south and being reinforced by the cruiser *República* and four armed merchant vessels out of Destêrro. Together they give him a landing force of 2,000 men, with which he intends to capture the port of Rio Grande.

However, after crossing its bar the attempt fails; discouraged, the renegades then seek to disembark in neighboring Uruguay. When interrupted by the local authorities, de Melo chooses to sail for Buenos Aires, surrendering the remnants of his fleet to Argentina in exchange for asylum.

16 APRIL 1894. Loyal Admiral Gonçalves arrives outside the Bay of Santa Catarina, torpedoing and sinking the rebel cruiser *Aquidabã.*

10 AUGUST 1894. The rebel chieftain Saraiva is killed in a skirmish; guerrilla activity declines precipitously as 2,000 tattered fighters seek asylum in Uruguay and Argentina. Peixoto emerges triumphant, earning the nickname "Iron Marshal"; numerous executions follow.

15 NOVEMBER 1894. The lawyer Prudente José de Morais e Barros succeeds Peixoto as Brazil's first civilian president; Peixoto retires modestly into private life, dying seven months later at his country estate.

MARCH 1895. Cadets at Rio de Janeiro's military academy rise against their commandant, suspecting him of being against Peixoto. The government quickly represses the outburst, discharging the insubordinate students.

8 JUNE 1895. Gen. Inocêncio Galvão de Queirós arrives from Rio de Janeiro and sets up his headquarters at Pelotas to pacify the remaining insurrectionists in Rio Grande do Sul Province. Exiled Adm. Saldanha da Gama crosses the frontier from Uruguay to attempt to keep the revolt alive.

24 JUNE 1895. Saldanha's 150 rebel navy riflemen and 550 guerrillas are attacked near Pedro Osório (north of the Quaraí River) by much larger federal forces under Gen. Hipólito Ribeiro; they are easily defeated and their leader slain.

1 JULY 1895. Rebel Col. Silva Tavares negotiates an armistice and visits General Galvão at Piratinim nine days later.

JULY 1895. Britain occupies the island of Trinidade (700 miles east of Vitória), prompting diplomatic protests from Rio de Janeiro. After a year of negotiations the island is restored to Brazil.

11 OCTOBER 1895. The Brazilian congress votes a general amnesty for all rebels of the recent disturbances despite opposition from more rancorous factions.

21 FEBRUARY 1897. After two expeditions by a small police force and a 543-man military contingent under Maj. Febrônio de Brito are repulsed by the conservative religious sect of Antônio Conselheiro headquartered at Canudos (200 miles north of Salvador, Bahia), the government decides to send in a larger unit: 1,000 soldiers under Col. Moreira César, including a cavalry squadron and artillery train. However, on 21 February they are ambushed and routed and their commander killed, provoking an outburst of antimonarchist rioting in Rio de Janeiro.

26 MAY 1897. Cadets at Rio de Janeiro's military academy mutiny against President de Morais, considering his government weak. They are quickly surrounded by loyal units, subjugated, and discharged.

5 OCTOBER 1897. ***Canudos.*** After the commitment of 6,000 troops in several columns under Gen. Artur Oscar has failed to subdue the fanatical Canudos rebels, the war minister, Marshal Machado Bittencourt, personally assumes command over the operation, his armies gradually fighting their way into the outskirts of town. Resistance ends on 5 October, no survivors being found among Conselheiro's followers; Canudos has been torched. It is estimated that the one-year campaign cost the lives of nearly 5,000 Brazilian soldiers through disease and combat.

5 NOVEMBER 1897. While reviewing some of the battalions returning from the Canudos campaign at Rio de Janeiro's arsenal, President de Morais is attacked by a young soldier named Marcelino Bispo and saved by the personal intervention of Marshal Bittencourt (who is fatally stabbed). A purge of antigovernment politicians and military officers ensues.

GERMAN OVERTURES (1890–1897)

ON 18 MARCH 1890 THE VETERAN CHANCELLOR OTTO, prinz von Bismarck, is obliged to resign from office in Berlin just before his 75th birthday. Affairs of state pass into the hands of 31-year-old Kaiser Wilhelm II, who becomes an enthusiastic proponent of sea power. Although careful never to directly challenge the United States, Britain, or France in the New World, Germany will nonetheless soon signal its rise as an imperial player.

As long ago as the winter of 1869–1870 a German squadron consisting of the warships *Arcona, Meteor,* and *Niobe* successfully blockaded Venezuela under Lt. Eduard von Knorr in retaliation for the detention of the merchantmen *Franz* and *Marie Sophie* at Maracaibo. Despite this precedent—plus the presence of several hundred thousand German emigrants resettled throughout South America and military officers advising its governments—Bismarck prevents any further adventurism until Wilhelm ascends the throne.

APRIL 1891. The kaiser orders his Far East squadron—*Leipzig, Alexandrine,* and *Sophie*—to sail from Asia and visit Valparaíso to uphold German prestige following the destruction of two of its merchantmen in Chilean waters.

22–23 AUGUST 1893. During an outbreak of unrest at Puerto Cabello (Venezuela), 100 German nationals must seek succor from French and Spanish warships in its harbor, the German vessel *Arcona* not arriving until six days later.

DECEMBER 1893. Berlin dispatches the warships *Stein* and *Stosch* on a prestige visit to La Guaira timed to coincide with the inauguration of the German-owned and -operated Great Venezuela Railroad in February 1894.

OCTOBER 1897. With disturbances in Guatemala the kaiser wishes to dispatch a warship to protect German nationals' interests, only to discover that the sole vessel available is a schoolship for cadets. Rather than send such an unprepossessing representative he cancels the order and requests an increase in naval construction from the Reichstag.

6 DECEMBER 1897. The German warships *Stein* and *Charlotte* appear off Port au Prince to intimidate Haiti's President Simon Sam into rescinding a fine levied against an alleged German national, Emil Lüders.

APRIL 1898. In Europe, Germany's state secretary of the navy, Adm. Alfred von Tirpitz, will use these and numerous other requests for patrols in South American waters as a pretext to help pass an immense naval bill authorizing the construction of 19 new battleships, eight armored cruisers, plus 12 large and 30 light cruisers. This order is nearly doubled by the appropriations bill of June 1900, the subsequent German naval buildup becoming a primary cause of World War I.

CHILEAN CIVIL WAR AND ANTI-AMERICAN ANTAGONISM (1891)

TOWARD THE END OF HIS FIVE-YEAR TERM IN OFFICE, the flamboyant 50-year-old liberal president of Chile, Dr. José Manuel Balmaceda, announces on 1 January 1891 that henceforth he will rule without congress, which has refused to approve his governmental budget. The congress declares Balmaceda deposed the very same day, placing the Chilean navy under the command of Commo. Jorge Montt on 6 January.

7 JANUARY 1891. Units of the Chilean navy mutiny at Valparaíso under the direction of Montt, senate vice president Waldo Silva, and the head of the chamber of deputies, Ramón Barros Luco. Balmaceda responds by declaring a state of martial law; next day civil war erupts. The congressionalist followers soon secure con-

trol of most of the navy; Balmaceda retains the support of its army (granting the soldiers immediate 50-percent pay raises to help ensure their loyalty).

16 FEBRUARY 1891. Unable to invest the presidential forces around Santiago, a congressionalist squadron sails north and occupies Iquique, port for the wealthy nitrate trade.

7 MARCH 1891. ***Pozo Almonte.*** Congressionalist forces defeat a small presidential contingent, thus winning possession of all of mineral-rich Tarapacá Province. Neighboring Antofagasta Province is cleared of Balmacedistas by the end of the month and Tacna is taken in April, Atacama by the end of May. Thus, all of northern Chile falls into the hands of the congressional rebels; Balmaceda and his army remain strong in the south. In order for him to prevail, the president needs to acquire warships; in order for the Balmacedistas to triumph, the congressional leaders need to buy arms and ammunition abroad to directly confront the soldiers in the field.

3 MAY 1891. ***Itata Incident.*** The congressional steamer *Itata* reaches San Diego (California) from Arica to clandestinely receive delivery of 50,000 Remington and Lee rifles with 2 million rounds. Two evenings later the vessel is impounded at the request of Balmaceda's ambassador in Washington; an apprehension order is also issued for the schooner *Robert & Minnie,* which is bringing the arms and ammunition south from Oakland.

When the U.S. marshal's tug leaves *Itata* at 4:00 P.M. on 6 May to chase the schooner into Mexican waters, the Chilean steamer avails itself of the opportunity to escape out to sea. American authorities are outraged and even more so when *Robert & Minnie* is seized near San Pedro (California) by the tug *Falcon* on the evening of 9 May only to be found empty of its cargo. It has already been transshipped to *Itata* off San Clemente; the Chilean steamer has set sail for home. The cruiser USS *Charleston* of Captain Remy is therefore sent in pursuit, and a formal protest lodged with the rebel leadership at Iquique.

3 JUNE 1891. *Itata* reaches Tocopilla (120 miles south of Iquique) but, next day, is ordered by congressionalist leaders—before it can offload its military cargo—to surrender to U.S. Rear Adm. M. B. MacCann. Thus, it departs north with *Charleston* by 13 June. Chileans are angered by this interference in their affairs, especially when an American court subsequently rules in *Itata*'s favor.

The congressionalists are left with thousands of unarmed recruits, whom they cannot train or deploy. They are also apprehensive that European-built warships *Presidente Errázuriz* and *Presidente Pinto* will soon join Balmaceda, thus shifting naval balance in his favor.

20 AUGUST 1891. Going over to the offensive, a congressionalist army disembarks at Quintero Bay (observed from a distance by Adm. George Brown's USS *San Francisco*).

LATE AUGUST 1891. Balmaceda is driven from power; he commits suicide on 18 September (the day his term officially ends).

6 OCTOBER 1891. Released under bond, *Itata* departs San Diego (California) for Valparaíso.

16 OCTOBER 1891. ***Baltimore Incident.*** This evening a fight breaks out in the red-light district of Valparaíso between a mob of Chileans—angry at perceived American interventionism—and 100 sailors on liberty from Capt. Winfield Scott Schley's USS *Baltimore.* Two American sailors are killed and 17 wounded (five seriously), leading to a downturn in diplomatic relations. Eventually, Santiago pays $75,000 in compensatory damages, and thus the crisis is defused.

Part 8: Pax Americana (1898–Present)

Victory has a hundred fathers,
but defeat is an orphan.
—President John F. Kennedy,
after the Bay of Pigs fiasco (1961)

Spanish-American War (1898)

Since the beginning of the latest Cuban insurrection, in 1895, public opinion in the United States has been building in favor of intervention against Spain, especially after the arrival of a Spanish army (which eventually swells to 20,000) under Gen. Valeriano Weyler—dubbed "the Butcher" by William Randolph Hearst's jingoistic *New York Journal*—who resorts to mass arrests, concentration camps, and executions to stifle rebel sentiment.

These tactics fail, however, Weyler being replaced by Gen. Ramón Blanco y Arenas; Spanish forces are largely defeated and driven out of rural areas by the winter of 1897–1898, being reduced to garrison duties within major towns. By this time many of Cuba's landowning elite support American intervention simply to restore public order and trade. The Hearst-Pulitzer newspaper feud in the United States also fans American passions with sensationalistic, anti-Spanish rhetoric.

1 January 1898. The American North Atlantic Squadron of Adm. Montgomery Sicard begins gathering in the Gulf of Mexico, near Florida's Dry Tortugas.

12 January 1898. A pro-Spanish riot occurs in Havana, involving numerous uniformed officers who ransack independent Cuban newspaper offices and prompt the United States consul general to request protection from Washington.

15 January 1898. Spain's governor-general establishes a guard around the U.S. consulate in Havana to protect it from attacks by pro-Spanish zealots.

24 January 1898. The 354-man, 6,700-ton battleship USS *Maine* of Capt. Charles D. Sigsbee is ordered to Havana to protect American interests, arriving next day.

9 February 1898. Enrique Dupuy de Lôme, the Spanish ambassador in Washington, writes disparagingly of Republican Pres. William McKinley in a private letter. It is published by the American press, forcing the ambassador to resign.

15 February 1898. ***Loss of the Maine.*** At 9:40 P.M., the battleship *Maine* suddenly explodes at anchor in Havana's harbor, killing 266 men and wounding 52. A naval court of inquiry is appointed by McKinley five days later; it travels to Cuba under 58-year-old Capt. William Thomas Sampson to investigate.

23 February 1898. Several American warships begin gathering at Key West, Florida.

6 March 1898. The 494-man, 10,200-ton battleship USS *Oregon* of Capt. Charles E. Clark departs Puget Sound for San Francisco, thence to Callao and around Cape Horn into the Caribbean theater, accompanied by the 144-man, 1,000-ton gunboat *Marietta*.

11 March 1898. The U.S. War Department begins mobilizing despite wavering by McKinley.

14 March 1898. Spanish Rear Adm. Pascual Cervera y Topete departs Cádiz for the Cape Verde Islands to begin marshaling an expedition to reinforce Puerto Rico and Cuba.

19 March 1898. The report of the American court of inquiry into the *Maine* explosion is completed and presented to Congress nine days later. Although unable to determine the exact cause of the explosion, court members do not believe the detonation originated within the ship—that is, from unstable ammunition—but rather from outside, suggesting a Spanish mine. Next day (29 March) resolutions declaring war against Spain and recognizing Cuban independence are introduced in Congress; they are not passed until 20 April.

5 April 1898. American consuls in Cuba are recalled.

9 April 1898. Desperately attempting to fend off war, the Spanish foreign minister informs Stewart L. Woodford, the U.S. ambassador in Madrid, that his government will grant an immediate armistice to Cuban rebels; submit the *Maine* controversy to arbitration; and accept virtually all of America's demands. War fever in the United States prevents reconciliation.

11 April 1898. McKinley asks Congress for a declaration of war, which is passed one week later and signed by the president on 20 April; hostilities are authorized to commence next day.

22 April 1898. The U.S. Navy's North Atlantic squadron begins a blockade of Cuba, the first shots being fired when the 1,400-ton American gunboat *Nashville* captures the Spanish steamer *Buenaventura* approaching Havana out of the Gulf of Mexico. Other interceptions follow.

25 April 1898. Back in Washington the Teller Amendment is added to the American declaration of war, whereby the U.S. government declares it will make no attempt to establish control over Cuba.

(This same day, 60-year-old Commo. George Dewey sails from Hong Kong to attack the Spaniards in the Philippines. He will surprise Manila six days later, completely destroying its Spanish fleet.)

27 April 1898. Shortly before 1:00 P.M., acting Rear Admiral Sampson shells the Spanish batteries at Point Rubalcava (outside Matanzas, northwestern Cuba) for half-an-hour with his 562-man, 8,150-ton armored cruiser *New York* (flag); the 339-man, 3,200-ton cruiser *Cincinnati;* and the 230-man, 6,060-ton monitor *Puritan.* Little damage is inflicted.

28–29 April 1898. At midnight Cervera slips out of San Vicente in the Cape Verde Islands with his 7,000-ton cruisers *Infanta María Teresa* (flag), *Vizcaya,* and *Almirante Oquendo;* the 6,840-ton *Cristóbal Colón* (formerly Italian *Giussepe Garibaldi II*); the 380-ton destroyers *Furor, Plutón,* and *Terror;* plus the hospital ship *Alicante.* Despite Washington's exaggerated fears as to the squadron's strength and objectives, the Spanish men-of-war are poorly armed and manned—the cruiser *Colón* mounting only two dummy ten-inch guns (the destroyers must be towed across the Atlantic to the West Indies).

29 April 1898. The 262-man, 2,000-ton cruiser *Marblehead* and the 64-man, 500-ton armed yacht *Eagle* exchange fire with the Spanish torpedo gunboat *Galicia* and the gunboat *Vasco Núñez de Balboa* at Cienfuegos (south-central Cuba), causing minor damage.

30 April 1898. The battleship *Oregon* and gunboat *Marietta* reach Rio de Janeiro, recoaling from the 6,000-ton purchased ship *Niterói* (renamed *Buffalo*) while maintaining a careful watch for the Spanish destroyer *Temerario,* which is reputedly in nearby waters.

8 May 1898. The 25-man torpedo boat *Winslow* of Lt. J. B. Bernadou enters Cárdenas Bay (northwestern Cuba) but is driven out by accurate counterfire from the 40-ton Spanish gunboats *Ligera* and *Alerta* plus the armed tug *Antonio López.*

11 May 1898. *Winslow* reenters Cárdenas Bay accompanied by the armed revenue cutter *Hudson* of Lieutenant Newcomb, backed farther out at sea by the 198-man, 1,400-ton gunboat *Wilmington* and the 154-man, 1,170-ton cruiser *Machias.* When these lighter vessels probe into shoal waters they are ambushed by a masked Spanish battery using smokeless powder. *Winslow* suffers five killed and a like number wounded during an hour-long exchange before being towed out of danger by *Hudson.* The Spaniards suffer two killed and a dozen wounded aboard the armed tug *López,* which is disabled along with *Ligera* by long-range American salvos.

This same day on Cuba's southern coast, the cruiser *Marblehead* and gunboat *Nashville* shell the beach outside Cienfuegos, providing covering fire for an attempt by 55 men aboard four boats to cut its three underwater telegraphic cables. Two are severed despite Spanish rifle fire that kills four Americans and injures five others. The armed revenue cutter *Windom* then stands close inshore, bringing down Cienfuegos's lighthouse with its four-inch gun.

12 May 1898. ***Shelling of San Juan.*** Before dawn Sampson approaches the Puerto Rican capital of San Juan out of the northeast with the 265-man, 2,000-ton cruiser *Detroit* in his van; the 590-man, 11,300-ton battleships *Iowa* (flag) and the 570-man, 10,200-ton *Indiana;* the cruiser *New York;* the 180-man, 4,000-ton monitors *Amphitrite* and *Terror;* the 32-man torpedo boat *Porter;* the 270-man, 2,000-ton cruiser *Montgomery;* plus the 32-man armed tug *Wompatuck,* hoping to catch Cervera inside.

At 5:17 A.M. *Iowa* opens fire on the outer Spanish defenses, being joined by the other American capital ships as the squadron slowly circles offshore during the next three hours. The Spaniards respond with two dozen artillery pieces; marksmanship is poor on both sides, with only minor damage being inflicted.

Realizing that the principal Spanish battle squadron is not at anchor, Sampson reverses course west—unaware that Cervera has been sighted off Martinique this same day, detaching the destroyer *Terror* and the hospital ship *Alicante* to Fort de France for repairs before continuing to Curaçao.

13 May 1898. The 11,600-ton armed auxiliary *Saint Louis* of Capt. C. F. Goodrich drags the seabed a few

miles east of San Juan de Puerto Rico, cutting its underwater telegraphic cable to Saint Thomas.

14 MAY 1898. The 12-year-old, 1,130-ton Spanish cruiser *Conde de Venadito* sorties from Havana with the equally ancient, 570-ton torpedo gunboat *Nueva España* to engage American blockaders east of the port. One hour later they encounter the 135-man, 1,000-ton gunboats *Vicksburg* and *Annapolis*—soon supported by the auxiliaries *Mayflower, Wasp, Tecumseh,* and *Osceola*—which drive the Spaniards back under the protection of the Santa Clara battery by nightfall.

At 8:00 A.M. this same day Cervera's flagship and *Vizcaya* enter Willemstad (Curaçao) for coal and provisions while *Oquendo, Colón,* and two destroyers remain outside. After hastily resupplying, the Spanish squadron departs at 5:15 P.M. on 15 May, pretending to steer north-northeast toward Puerto Rico before altering course northwest for Santiago de Cuba.

16 MAY 1898. After nightfall *Saint Louis* and *Wompatuck* stand in close to Santiago, attempting to raise and sever its two underwater telegraphic cables to Jamaica. The batteries open fire and a pair of Spanish vessels sortie, obliging the Americans to retire out of range.

Next morning at 10:00 *Saint Louis* and *Wompatuck* resume efforts, cutting one cable before withdrawing east. They try to break the Guantánamo-Haiti line as well but are chased off by the Spanish gunboat *Sandoval.*

17 MAY 1898. Racing to Key West for more precise intelligence on Cervera's movements, Sampson's flagship *New York* intercepts the 750-ton Spanish vessel *Carlos F. Rosas* off Havana. Sampson's straggling squadron overtakes the American admiral two days later.

18 MAY 1898. The battleship *Oregon* reaches Bridgetown (Barbados) alone, having taken two months to sail 14,000 miles around Cape Horn from San Francisco. (The immensely long detour will revive Washington's interest in securing a shorter passage across southern Nicaragua or the isthmus of Panama.)

19 MAY 1898. At 5:30 A.M. Cervera's squadron slips into Santiago de Cuba (population 50,000), anchoring two hours later. The city's beleaguered 9,000-man garrison under Gen. Arsenio Linares—its pay already ten months in arrears—is ill-prepared to meet the demands of an additional 2,200 seamen and their warships.

20 MAY 1898. In international waters three miles off Cap du Môle (northwestern Haiti), *Wompatuck* cuts the underwater telegraphic cable leading to Guantánamo.

23 MAY 1898. The Red Cross ship *State of Texas,* with Clara Barton aboard, reaches Tampa in anticipation of a U.S. invasion of Cuba.

24 MAY 1898. *Oregon* appears off Jupiter Inlet (Florida), reporting its arrival to Washington.

26 MAY 1898. Commo. Winfield Scott Schley arrives 20 miles off Santiago with the battleships *Iowa,* the 495-man, 10,200-ton *Massachusetts,* and the 433-man, 6,300-ton *Texas;* the 550-man, 9,100-ton armored cruiser *Brooklyn* (flag) and *Marblehead;* the armed auxiliaries *Vixen* of 165 tons, *Hawk,* plus *Eagle;* and the collier *Merrimac* to learn whether Cervera is inside. The 477-man, 8,050-ton cruiser *Minneapolis* plus the 11,600-ton armed auxiliaries *Saint Paul* and 10,800-ton *Yale* (formerly *Paris*) join him that evening.

28 MAY 1898. The U.S. tugs *Uncas* and *Leyden* demolish a Spanish blockhouse five miles east of Cárdenas (Cuba).

29 MAY 1898. After cruising indecisively off Santiago for three days, Schley sights Cervera's men-of-war lying inside at 7:40 A.M., receiving some rounds at extreme long range from *Colón.*

31 MAY 1898. Shortly after 1:00 P.M. Schley leads the battleships *Massachusetts* and *Iowa*—plus the recently joined, 365-man, 3,600-ton cruiser *New Orleans*—in toward Santiago's harbor mouth, opening fire on the outer defenses and the cruiser *Colón* one hour later. A brief exchange results in no damage.

Next dawn Sampson arrives to assume command over the U.S. fleet; the Spaniards stretch a boom across the entrance.

3 JUNE 1898. At 3:30 A.M. Lt. Richmond P. Hobson steams the collier *Merrimac* into Santiago's entrance and scuttles it under fire in an unsuccessful attempt to block its channel and trap Cervera inside. His blockship comes to rest a little out of position, thus leaving a narrow passage out to sea.

6 JUNE 1898. At 7:40 A.M. Sampson leads his fleet in two columns against Santiago's outer defenses, opening fire 20 minutes later. Although thousands of shells are expended, only three Spaniards are killed and 51 wounded ashore; another five are killed and 14 injured aboard the decrepit *Rey Alfonso XII*-class cruiser *Reina Mercedes,* after which the Americans withdraw.

7 JUNE 1898. ***Guantánamo.*** At dawn five of Sampson's vessels appear off the town of Caimanera, its Spanish batteries at Playa del Este—called Windward Point by the Americans—and Cayo Toro being destroyed by bombardments from *Marblehead* under Capt. Bowman H. McCalla; the 282-man, 6,900-ton converted cruiser *Yankee* (formerly the mail steamer *El Norte*); and *Saint Louis.* They also force the Spanish gunboat *Sandoval* to seek shelter behind minefields in the shallow upper bay.

Saint Louis then cuts the boom, allowing the Americans to penetrate as far as Fishermans Point, where they anchor and are contacted from ashore by two Cuban guerrilla officers, who report that Gen. Calixto García—of "Message to García" fame—holds the western side. The nearest Spanish concentration is the 7,000-man isolated garrison of Gen. Félix Pareja, 14 miles inland at the town of Guantánamo. The Americans therefore decide to remain off Caimanera until a U.S. landing force can arrive in support.

Two days later—9 June—*Marblehead* and the 117-man *Dolphin* again fire on the Spanish defenses, allowing 60 Marines from the battleship *Oregon* and *Marblehead* to establish a beachhead next dawn at Playa del Este. That afternoon the U.S. troop transport *Panther* (formerly the merchantman *Venezuela*) arrives with a 645-man Marine battalion and four guns under Lt. Col. Robert W. Huntington, landing near Caimanera to set up camp. Spanish resistance consists of occasional sniper rounds fired from Cuzco Hill and the surrounding jungle, four Americans being killed and another wounded.

A feeble counterattack is launched against the American encampment on 12 June; two more marines are killed and seven are wounded. At dawn on 14 June, Huntington advances to circle south around Cuzco Hill, guided by 50 Cuban scouts. The maneuver outflanks the surprised Spaniards at Cuzco well, allowing the marines and Cubans to drive them inland (killing 60 and capturing 18). Two Cubans are killed and three marines and two Cubans are wounded during the exchange.

On 16 June *Texas* and *Marblehead* again shell the Spanish fort on Cayo Toro, reducing it to rubble one hour later. This secures Guantánamo Bay as a base for U.S. naval operations along the entire coast.

10 JUNE 1898. *Saint Louis* intercepts the British collier *Twickenham,* carrying 3,000 tons of coal for Cervera, off Jamaica.

13 JUNE 1898. The Spanish torpedo gunboat *Galicia* approaches *Yankee* off Cienfuegos, apparently mistaking it for an unarmed merchantman. When the latter opens fire, the Spaniards retire into port, their retreat covered by shore batteries and their consort *Balboa.*

14 JUNE 1898. The 69-man, 930-ton "dynamite cruiser" *Vesuvius* joins Sampson off Santiago, adding its highly explosive gun-cotton shells to the intermittent bombardment of its shore emplacements.

20 JUNE 1898. After lengthy delay in assembling at Tampa, the 17,000-man 5th Corps of the 300-pound, 63-year-old gouty Maj. Gen. William Rufus Shafter arrives off Santiago aboard 32 crowded transports, beginning disembarkation two days later at Daiquirí (17 miles farther east) while Sampson's fleet shells various coastal points as a diversion. Daiquirí's 300 Spanish troops—having no artillery and menaced by Cuban guerrillas to the rear—retire quietly out of Daiquirí. Late on 22 June the first American units also reach the nearby port of Siboney (8 miles closer to Santiago), thus gaining a second landing zone for Shafter's army (plus 4,000 Cuban insurgent allies).

22 JUNE 1898. While blockading San Juan de Puerto Rico, Captain Sigsbee's 11,600-ton armed auxiliary *Saint Paul* spots the ancient, 1,130-ton cruiser *Isabel II* exiting at 1:00 P.M., followed by the as-yet unrepaired *Terror.* After pausing briefly beneath the batteries, the Spanish destroyer dashes at *Saint Paul,* only to be hit by heavy counterfire.

In a sinking condition, *Terror's* commander circles back and beaches on Puntilla Shoal (where his destroyer is eventually refloated); *Isabel* retreats into port. Sigsbee is then relieved three days later by the 285-man, 6,200-ton armed auxiliary *Yosemite* (formerly *El Sol*), sailing *Saint Paul* to New York for refitting.

24 JUNE 1898. ***Las Guásimas.*** U.S. naval authorities expect Shafter to march due west along Santiago's coast and capture its harbor castle to permit Sampson's fleet to enter and then annihilate the anchored Spanish squadron. Instead, once ashore the general decides to push northwest and invest the city

first, eliminating the military threat posed by the garrison before proceeding against the coastal defenses.

When the American vanguard advances inland from its beachhead, approximately 1,100 dismounted U.S. troopers and Rough Riders overtake a large number of Spaniards three and a half miles away at Las Guásimas, hastily retiring into Linares's defensive positions around Santiago. The column is mauled and suffers 250 losses as opposed to 16 Americans killed and 52 wounded.

28 JUNE 1898. Cuban scouts inform Shafter that 8,000 Spanish troops have broken out of a rebel encirclement at Manzanillo and are marching east to bolster Linares. This prompts the American general to hasten preparations for an assault against the Santiago defenses before the reinforcements can arrive.

30 JUNE 1898. This morning the 55-man armed yachts *Hornet* and *Hist* push into Niquero Bay (southeastern Cuba), destroying a 40-ton Spanish gunboat at long range. Joined by the tug *Wompatuck,* the American vessels then press northeast to Manzanillo, opening fire on its defenses at 3:20 P.M., only to be driven off 90 minutes later by the batteries and the 135-ton gunboat *Guantánamo,* the 85-ton *Delgado Parejo,* the 65-ton *Guardián,* and the 40-ton *Estrella.*

Also this day *Yosemite* intercepts the 3,460-ton Spanish steamer *Antonio López* as it attempts to enter San Juan de Puerto Rico out of the Atlantic. Despite a belated sally by the cruiser *Isabel II* and gunboat *General Concha,* the approaching vessel is driven aground on Salinas Point.

1 JULY 1898. ***San Juan Hill.*** At dawn Shafter launches a three-pronged attack against Santiago, sending a newly arrived half-brigade of volunteer infantry in a diversionary move along the beach toward the harbor castle and an infantry division supported by dismounted cavalry up Siboney road toward "San Juan Hill" (actually a low ridge just east of Santiago) while Brig. Gen. Henry W. Lawton's 6,200-man 2nd Infantry Division leads the main thrust by circling north and storming the isolated village of El Caney on Guantánamo road.

That place is held by 520 determined Spaniards, barricaded behind trenches and a blockhouse. For the better part of a day they check Lawton's flanking maneuver, killing 81 Americans and wounding 360 before finally being overrun at 4:00 P.M. El Caney's defenders sustain 235 casualties, almost all survivors being captured. Meanwhile 39-year-old Col. Theodore Roosevelt's 1st Volunteer Cavalry Regiment, along with 1st, 6th, 10th, and 16th Cavalry Regiments plus a battery of Gatling guns carry San Juan Hill this afternoon after a bitter struggle.

Both sides are greatly shaken by their losses. Shafter—having endured 1,100 total casualties—briefly contemplates retreat; the Spaniards—whose losses are even greater—retire into their second line of trenches on the low ground. Linares, severely wounded in the arm trying to hold San Juan Hill, is succeeded by Gen. José Toral.

2 JULY 1898. Fearful that Cervera's squadron will be lost if Santiago falls, the Spanish authorities order their admiral by telegraph to escape at all costs. He therefore recalls the 1,200 sailors who have been manning defenses ashore and, after nightfall, sends the gunboat *Alvarado* to remove six mines from the harbor entrance, thus clearing a passage out to sea.

3 JULY 1898. ***Action off Santiago.*** Cervera makes a desperate dash at 9:30 this Sunday morning with the 556-man cruiser *Infanta María Teresa* of Flag Captain Concas, 491-man *Vizcaya* of Captain Eulate, the 487-man *Almirante Oquendo* of Captain Lazaga, and the 567-man *Cristóbal Colón* under Commodore de Paredes plus the 80-man destroyers *Furor* and *Plutón* under Capt. Fernando Villaamil. Immediately they are sighted and pursued by Schley's vice-flag *Brooklyn* under Capt. Francis A. Cook plus the battleships *Iowa, Indiana, Oregon,* and *Texas* (Sampson being too far east with *New York* to engage, having gone earlier to confer with Shafter ashore; *Massachusetts* is at Guantánamo recoaling).

Wrecked remains of the Spanish cruiser Vizcaya *ablaze after the Battle of Santiago, with the American torpedo boat* Ericsson *standing by to rescue survivors*

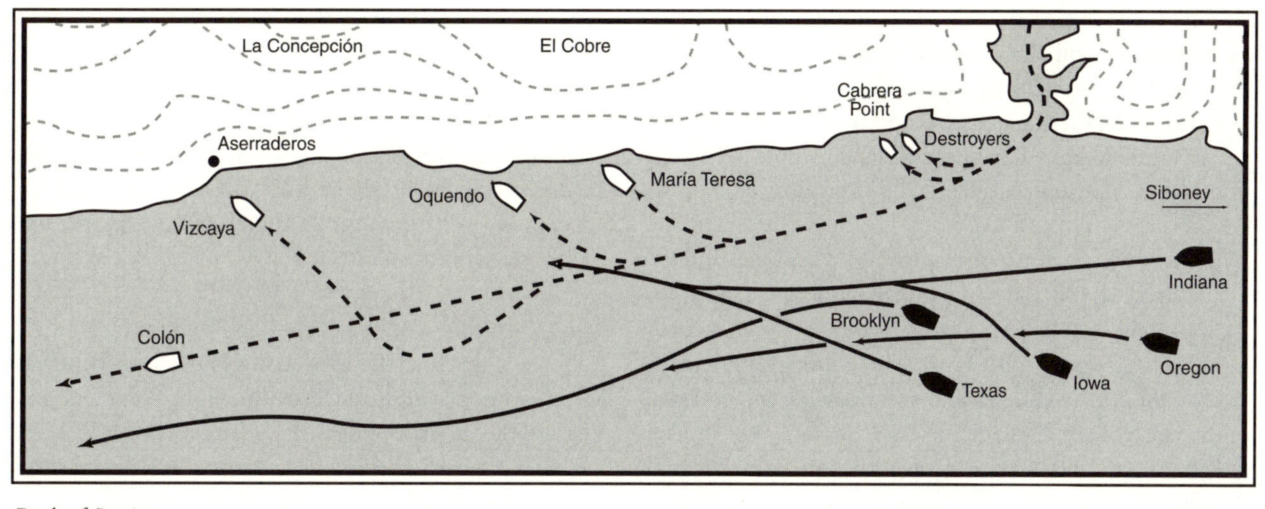

Battle of Santiago

Brooklyn, Texas of Capt. John "Jack" W. Philip, and *Iowa* of Capt. Robley D. "Fighting Bob" Evans open fire by 9:40 A.M., before Cervera can even begin turning west. Both the Spanish flagship and *Oquendo* are struck repeatedly, salvos driving them aground 20 minutes later, six and eight miles, respectively, from Santiago's entrance. *Vizcaya* is then set ablaze and runs ashore by 11:15 A.M. at Aserraderos (15 miles west of Santiago). Both *Furor* and *Plutón* are also destroyed by *Indiana* and the 93-man, 800-ton armed yacht *Gloucester* of Lt. Cmdr. R. Wainwright, succumbing near Cabrera Point. Lastly, the unarmed *Colón* leads *Brooklyn* and *Oregon* on a 50-mile chase before finally being overhauled and forced aground in ruins at 1:20 P.M. (70 miles west of Santiago, opposite Turquino Peak). All the Spanish ships are lost; 323 crewmembers are killed, 151 are wounded, and 1,700 are captured—including Cervera and *Vizcaya*'s Captain Eulate; only two American vessels sustain any damage, with one seaman being killed and another injured.

After witnessing the slaughter Santiago's garrison is further demoralized when that evening the Manzanillo relief column at last slips through a gap in the besiegers' lines, proving to be only 3,500 weary troops under Col. Federico Escario rather than the anticipated 8,000.

4 JULY 1898. In order to reblock Santiago's entrance following Cervera's sortie, the 11-year-old cruiser *Reina Mercedes*—barely able to get up steam—is scuttled in the channel at 11:30 P.M. (Later refloated, it is eventually taken to the U.S. Naval Academy at Annapolis as a prize exhibit.)

4–5 JULY 1898. At midnight the 50-man, 545-ton armed yacht *Hawk* intercepts the 4,380-ton mail steamer *Alfonso XIII* seven miles outside Havana, chasing it west. By 1:30 A.M. the Spanish vessel runs hard aground outside Mariel and is abandoned; it is shelled next morning by its pursuer along with the 153-man, 1,200-ton gunboat *Castine.*

9 JULY 1898. Having gradually extended his siege lines, Shafter closes off Santiago's last escape route when his right flank reaches the western shores of the bay.

10 JULY 1898. This afternoon a firefight erupts between Santiago's defenders and besiegers—joined by *Brooklyn, Indiana,* and *Texas* offshore—that lasts to next morning. Holding the high ground, the American soldiers suffer only two dead and two wounded, compared to seven Spaniards killed and more than 50 injured.

11 JULY 1898. While *Brooklyn, New York,* and *Indiana* continue shelling Aguadores, 59-year-old Maj. Gen. Nelson Appleton Miles arrives off Siboney with reinforcements for Shafter, visiting the subordinate's headquarters ashore next day.

12 JULY 1898. This morning *Eagle* pursues the Spanish blockade runner *Santo Domingo* west of Isla de Pinos (modern-day Juventud Island, southwestern Cuba), driving it onto Piedras Point and setting it ablaze.

16 JULY 1898. Supported by *Nashville,* Cuban insurgents occupy the small northeastern port of Gibara without resistance.

17 JULY 1898. After several days of negotiations, Toral capitulates at noon, surrendering not only Santiago's

12,000-man garrison and 97 guns but also 12,000 troops and militia at Guantánamo plus a half-dozen other Spanish outposts scattered throughout eastern Cuba. Brig. Gen. Leonard Wood is installed as Santiago's new military governor, the land campaign having cost 243 American killed and 1,445 wounded.

18 JULY 1898. Early this morning *Wilmington* and its 176-man, 1,400-ton sister gunboat *Helena* stand into Manzanillo's northern channel; the 627-ton armed auxiliary *Scorpion* and *Osceola* enter through its central channel; and *Hist, Hornet,* and *Wompatuck* go in via its southern channel to shell Spanish shipping inside. Uniting at 7:50 A.M. and opening fire from beyond range of Manzanillo's batteries, the Americans pound the harbor for two and a half hours, destroying or incapacitating the gunboats *Cuba Española* of 225 tons, *Guantánamo, Delgado Parejo, Guardián, Estrella,* and the 35-ton *Centinela,* also setting the steamers *Gloria, José García,* and *Purísima Concepción* ablaze.

21 JULY 1898. *Annapolis* and the 167-man, 1,800-ton gunboat *Topeka,* preceded by the smaller auxiliaries *Wasp* and *Leyden,* stand into Nipe Bay (northeastern Cuba), discovering the Ramón Point battery to be unarmed. Four and a half miles inside they also sight the 22-year-old, 146-man, 935-ton dispatch vessel *Jorge Juan,* opening fire at 12:45 P.M. and sinking it one hour later.

This same day, Miles departs Guantánamo with a dozen transports bearing 3,400 fresh troops—the 6th Massachusetts and 6th Illinois Volunteer Infantry Regiments plus five regular field batteries and other auxiliaries—to gain a foothold on Puerto Rico and await the arrival of contingents from Tampa and Newport News. This first expedition is escorted by the battleship *Massachusetts* of Capt. F. J. Higginson, the 181-man, 6,100-ton armed auxiliary *Dixie* (formerly *El Sud*), and *Gloucester.*

24 JULY 1898. ***Puerto Rican Invasion.*** Although originally intending to disembark at Cape Fajardo (25–30 miles east of San Juan), Miles instead changes strategy after that destination is revealed by the U.S. press. Therefore, after coasting eastward along northern Puerto Rico to deceive Spanish lookouts, his expedition reverses course after nightfall on 24 July and runs without lights around the southwestern tip of the island, appearing next dawn off the tiny port of Guánica (15 miles west of Ponce). *Gloucester* stands in and quickly secures the waterfront, thus allowing Miles's troops to occupy the town without loss. The Americans push inland on 26 July and gain the main road leading to Ponce after a bloodless skirmish.

26 JULY 1898. Spain, through France's Ambassador Cambon in Washington, asks President McKinley to name peace terms; he responds four days later. They are accepted by Madrid on 8 August and relayed to the U.S. government next day.

27 JULY 1898. Miles is joined off Guánica by another 3,300 troops from the United States: the 16th Pennsylvania plus the 2nd and 3rd Wisconsin Volunteer Infantry Regiments under Maj. Gen. James H. Wilson. Rather than disembark the troops, Miles orders the transports to proceed directly east to Ponce, which he is about to attack.

Next morning the convoy—supported inshore by *Annapolis, Dixie,* and *Wasp* plus *Massachusetts* farther out to sea—penetrates Ponce's harbor in coordination with a land assault, prompting the heavily outnumbered Spanish garrison to flee north to San Juan after token resistance. Miles issues a proclamation promising the Puerto Ricans liberty from Spain, thereby producing a friendly reception.

31 JULY 1898. Brig. Gen. Theodore Schwan joins Miles at Ponce with an additional 2,900 regulars from the 11th and 19th U.S. Infantry Regiments plus artillery and cavalrymen.

1 AUGUST 1898. Supported by *Gloucester* offshore, Miles's advancing army captures the town of Arroyo; next day Guayama capitulates after being briefly shelled by *Cincinnati* and *Saint Louis.*

3 AUGUST 1898. Brig. Gen. Peter C. Hains appears off Puerto Rico with 3,700 men of the 3rd Illinois, 4th Ohio, and 4th Pennsylvania Volunteer Infantry Regiments, disembarking at Arroyo. They are joined a couple days later by Maj. Gen. John R. Brooke, with some 2,000 cavalrymen and gunners.

Miles's command eventually swells to 17,000 men who face 8,000 demoralized Spaniards—1,300 of them concentrated inland at Aibonito to block any immediate American advance across its range to San Juan. Miles opts for a four-pronged offensive, with Schwan marching north along the coast from Guánica; a second column ascending a mountain trail to meet him at Arecibo; Wilson pressuring Aibonito frontally with a third formation; and Brooke circling behind with a fourth detachment out of Arroyo.

6 AUGUST 1898. A unit from *Amphitrite* seizes the lighthouse outside San Juan, repulsing—along with *Cincinnati*—a Spanish counterattack on the night of 8–9 August, withdrawing next morning.

8 AUGUST 1898. A minor skirmish occurs four miles north of Guayama, followed by another at Hormigueros two days later as Miles launches his northern drive. The Americans easily rout the Spaniards on all fronts, sending defeated or outflanked companies streaming back to the blockaded San Juan. (American losses total only four dead and 40 wounded in the campaign.) Schwan's troops, in particular, distinguish themselves by capturing 192 prisoners before overrunning Mayagüez on 11 August.

12 AUGUST 1898. Goodrich appears outside the Cuban port of Manzanillo with his 393-man, 4,100-ton cruiser *Newark* (flag), *Suwanee, Hist, Osceola,* and the former Spanish gunboat *Alvarado,* escorting a Marine battalion aboard the transport *Resolute.* After Goodrich calls on the governor to surrender, the warships open fire on Manzanillo's batteries at 3:40 P.M. while Cuban insurgents threaten the garrison from inland. Next morning fighting ceases when peace is announced. On 12 August 1898 Madrid signs the peace protocols, officially ending hostilities.

Although America's victory has been greatly facilitated by the 48,000 rebels fighting beside invading U.S. forces, Cuba is excluded from the subsequent treaty negotiations in Paris and must accept compromises demanded by Washington. By this accord—signed on 10 December 1898—Spain withdraws from Cuba, Puerto Rico, the Philippines, and other small islands in the West Indies and Pacific, thereby losing the last vestiges of its overseas empire. The United States assumes a protectorship over these newly liberated territories, remaining in Cuba for the next three years to supervise the installation of a national government (and inserting Sen. Orville Platt's amendment directly into the Cuban constitution allowing for future U.S. interventions). Guantánamo Bay is also leased to the American government for 99 years, starting on 2 July 1903, in exchange for annual payments of $2,000.

WAR OF THE THOUSAND DAYS (1899–1902)

AFTER THREE YEARS' PRECIPITATE DECLINE IN THE WORLD price of coffee, Colombia plunges into bankruptcy, which sparks civil unrest and rioting. The aged Conservative Party Pres. Manuel Antonio Sanclemente responds by declaring martial law on 28 July 1899, but Liberal Party opponents prepare to challenge his rule by a recourse to arms. On 18 October 1899 the northeastern department of Santander rises in revolt, and a desultory civil war ensues.

24 OCTOBER 1899. The government gunboats *Hércules* and *Colombia* overtake a hastily assembled Liberal flotilla moving up the Magdalena River that has already blocked the channel at Barranquilla and captured the river ports of Magangué and El Banco. In a violent nocturnal action the gunboats sink most of the more lightly armed Liberal vessels.

Equally ill-equipped Liberal land forces are also dispersed at Nocaima (Cundinamarca Department) and Bucaramanga (Santander Department).

15 DECEMBER 1899. ***Peralonso.*** A large but fragmented government army under Gen. Manuel Casabianca closes in on the main Liberal concentration under Gens. Rafael Uribe Uribe, Benjamín Herrera, and Justo L. Durán in the Peralonso River Valley west of Cúcuta (Santander Department, near the Venezuelan border). An indecisive action ensues around the bridge separating the armies until Uribe personally leads a charge during the afternoon of 16 December that routs the Conservatives.

By nightfall the government army is in full retreat, abandoning arms, supplies, horses, and hundreds of deserters. Despite the victory the Liberals do not follow up their advantage by marching directly on Bogotá but rather—at the suggestion of Gen. Gabriel Vargas Santos—choose to consolidate smaller local gains.

11 MAY 1900. ***Palonegro.*** After rebuilding their strength, some 14,000 government troops under Gen. Próspero Pinzón bear down on slightly less than 8,000 Liberal forces under Uribe, Herrera, and Vargas Santos in the warm, mountainous terrain around Palonegro (near Bucaramanga). During the first three days of battle—the largest in modern South American history—the defenders launch savage attacks on Conservative positions, fighting their more numerous and better-equipped opponent to a standstill. By 14

May, however, Pinzón begins to turn the tide, and next day he disperses Uribe's increasingly desperate counterthrusts.

Both armies dig in, stubbornly refusing to abandon the field while continuing limited probes throughout daylight hours and vicious patrol actions at night. Over time, disease begins claiming more lives than does combat. The stalemate is broken when the government receives several thousand reinforcements and a plentiful resupply of ammunition on 23 May, compelling the overmatched Liberals to retreat two nights later. The Liberals never recuperate from the setback, Uribe, Herrera, and Vargas Santos being individually defeated by the end of the year and obliged to flee Colombia.

31 JULY 1900. Gen. Jorge Moya Vásquez, garrison commander at Soacha (west-southwest of Bogotá), marches on the capital and topples the Sanclemente government, replacing it with another faction called the "Historical Conservatives" of Vice Pres. José Manuel Marroquín.

1900–1903. With their main army having been defeated on the battlefield at Palonegro, the Liberal cause resorts to guerrilla warfare, especially in the Cundinamarca and Tolima Departments. For the next two and a half years an increasingly vicious irregular campaign ensues, with massacres and countermassacres perpetrated by each side.

Finally, by late 1902 both camps are exhausted, some 100,000 of Colombia's 4 million people having succumbed during the conflict (mostly due to disease). In October and November the largest remaining Liberal armies, in Panama and on the Atlantic Coast, capitulate in exchange for amnesties and limited political reforms. The Conservative government then crushes guerrilla resistance in the interior.

A vestige of this war is the seizure of the American-run Panama Canal, which Washington accomplishes by backing a separatist movement in Panama—until now considered a province of Colombia. On 3 November 1903 the gunboat USS *Nashville* lends its weight to the proclamation of Panamanian independence at Colón, joined two days later by the transport *Dixie,* bearing a 400-man Marine battalion under Maj. John A. Lejeune. Despite a few tense moments the coup passes without bloodshed, the new government agreeing to a long-term lease of the canal.

PORTENTS IN MEXICO (1899–1910)

DESPITE THE IRON-FISTED RULE OF DICTATOR Porfirio Díaz, Mexico continues to simmer with discontent. Although all stirrings are repressed, they eventually lead to the Mexican Revolution of 1910.

21 JULY 1899. ***Yaqui Ultimatum.*** Chiefs from the eight major Yaqui tribes send a demand to Gen. Lorenzo Torres, calling on all whites to withdraw from Sinaloa or face hostilities.

6 AUGUST 1899. Torres defeats a Yaqui concentration at Palo Parado (Sinaloa) and is wounded in the thigh.

10 AUGUST 1899. A 784-man Mexican column—comprising units from the 11th, 12th, and 17th Infantry Battalions plus the 5th Cavalry Regiment—drive 500 Yaqui warriors from a stronghold in Sinaloa.

14 AUGUST 1899. Mexican *federales* clash with Yaqui warriors at Laguna Prieta (Sinaloa).

SEPTEMBER 1899. A Yaqui war band is decimated at Bahueca (Sinaloa), suffering 87 dead—including chief Gutmasolero.

9 NOVEMBER 1899. Yaquis and *federales* fight at Coyotes Lake; a second fight erupts nearby two days later.

18 JANUARY 1900. ***Mazocoba.*** Learning that Tetabiate's followers are concentrated in a stronghold atop Mazocoba Heights (Sinaloa), Torres approaches in three columns: 402 troops under Col. Agustín García Hernández, who reaches Semana Santa Mesa and finds a ravine separating him from the Indians; 423 men under Torres, to the right of García Hernández's formation and directly opposite the enemy; plus 240 soldiers under Col. Jesús Gándara, occupying two hills near Mazocoba.

At 10:00 A.M. the Mexicans begin shelling Tetabiate's defenses; they attack five hours later, driving the Yaquis from their trenches in hand-to-hand combat. The defenders eventually turn and flee near nightfall, many plunging to their deaths in the ravines or being

Federal *mountain battery on parade drill; uniforms are dark blue, with red trouser stripes*

finished off by skirmishers from the 4th and 11th Infantry Battalions. More than 400 natives are killed and 1,800 noncombatants are captured—fully half of the latter succumbing during a forced march into captivity at Tetacombiate. Torres's *federales* suffer 56 killed and 104 wounded.

9 JULY 1900. A company of *federales* chases eight Yaquis carrying a wounded companion a half-mile from Mazocoba, killing the latter and discovering him to be chief Tetabiate.

FEBRUARY 1902. Yaqui resistance in the Sinaloa ranges increases under a new chieftain, Luis Bule.

APRIL 1904. Mexican authorities parley with Yaqui leaders at San Miguel Horcasitas (Sinaloa) but are unable to arrange a truce.

30 APRIL 1904. *Federales* and Yaquis clash at Agua Escondida near Ures (Sinaloa).

1 JUNE 1906. ***Cananea.*** In Sonora, 5,360 Mexican workers go on strike against the Consolidated Copper Company mines at Cananea, protesting the higher wages and shorter work hours enjoyed by its 2,200 American workers. A march by 2,000 strikers toward the company lumberyard—where most Americans work—is met by rifle fire, and a riot ensues in which 23 (mostly Mexicans) die; another 22 are wounded. The strikers are chased out of Cananea and into the mountains by armed American riders but not before they have torched many buildings.

The company owner, Col. William C. Greene, requests intervention by the Mexican authorities, who not only dispatch state troops and *rurales* (federal police) under Col. Emilio Kosterlitzky but also allow 400 gun-toting American "volunteers" to enter the country from nearby Naco (Arizona), greatly offending Mexican pride. Some 50 of the strikers are subsequently identified and transported into penal servitude at the island fortress of San Juan de Ulúa (Veracruz).

7 JANUARY 1907. ***Río Blanco.*** Thousands of textile workers go on strike at Río Blanco, ransacking company stores and burning buildings. Federal troops under Gen. Rosalino Martínez are rushed in from Veracruz, Jalapa, and Mexico City, brutally restoring order by firing point-blank on the mobs. (Lt. Gabriel Arroyo, who refuses to shoot into a crowd containing women and children, is summarily executed along with his company.) By the time order is restored some 200

strikers have been killed; the cowed survivors return to work.

6 JUNE 1910. The guerrilla chief (and former butcher) Santana Rodríguez Palafox—nicknamed Santanón—briefly captures the town of San Andrés Tuxtla (Veracruz), only to be hunted down and killed shortly thereafter by *federales* under Francisco Cárdenas.

This same day (6 June 1910), the 36-year-old opposition candidate Francisco Ignacio Madero is detained on President Díaz's orders to ensure his reelection as president. Within four months Madero will escape confinement and call for a general insurrection, thereby touching off the Mexican Revolution.

EARLY POLICE ACTIONS (1901–1920)

WASHINGTON'S EASY VICTORIES IN CUBA and Panama draw it into additional Caribbean adventures, gradually supplanting the European powers that traditionally dominated the theater.

SEPTEMBER 1901. Venezuela's Pres. Cipriano Castro's refuses to fully honor his country's international debts, so the United States dispatches the warships *Hartford, Scorpion,* and *Buffalo* to La Guaira, followed by the German vessels *Vineta, Gazelle,* and *Falke.* (Although temporarily acting in accord with Washington, German Foreign Minister Oswald, Baron von Richthofen, realizes that any unilateral action will be resented as a breach of the Monroe Doctrine, adding: "The seizure of territory is precluded, as this would immediately involve us in a conflict with the United States.")

During a November 1901 visit to Virginia, the German heavy cruiser Vineta *is refurbished in dry dock.*

9 DECEMBER 1902. ***Venezuelan Blockade.*** After repeatedly requesting that Castro honor his country's debts to Britain, Germany, and Italy, the British and German ambassadors withdraw from La Guaira at 3:00 P.M. One hour later ten German and four British cutters bearing 240 men are towed into harbor, covered by the brand-new, 962-ton German gunboat *Panther* of Lieutenant Commander Eckermann. They board the 137-ton English-built gunboats *General Crespo* and *Totumo* plus the hired French steamer *Ossun,* setting 390 Venezuelan sailors ashore before towing all three vessels out to sea. (In a further hostile act the torpedo boat *Margarita* is disabled in La Guaira's dockyard; *General Crespo* and *Totumo* are scuttled after nightfall.)

The boarding parties have been sent from the 5,900-ton German cruiser *Vineta* of Commo. Georg Scheder and the cruiser HMS *Ariadne* of 60-year-old, Canadian-born Vice Adm. Sir Archibald Lucius Douglas to exact restitution from Castro's government. A contingent of 130 German sailors ventures into the suburb of Cardonal at 10:00 P.M. to protect the evacuation of foreign noncombatants; the British do the same next morning.

Also on 9 December the cruiser HMS *Charybdis* of Capt. R. A. J. Montgomerie seizes the Venezuelan gunboat *Bolívar* farther east; next day the British sloop *Alert* captures the troopship *Zamora* and the 600-ton torpedo-gunboat *23 de Mayo* in the Gulf of Paria, conveying both to Port of Spain (Trinidad). The 600-ton steamer *Restaurador* (formerly the American yacht *Atlanta*) is taken as well, so that within a couple of days virtually all of Venezuela's navy has fallen to the Anglo-German combination. With the addition of the British cruisers *Retribution, Indefatigable, Tribune,* and *Pallas;* the sloop *Fantome;* destroyers *Quail* and *Rocket;* plus German cruisers *Gazelle* of 2,650 tons and *Falke* of 1,730, the two commanders blockade the coast—the British being responsible for the Demerara–La Guaira section, the Germans for the adjacent stretch to Colombia's border.

After heated street demonstrations the Venezuelans react by arresting more than 200 foreigners at Caracas on 10 December and detaining the British freighter *Topaze* at Puerto Cabello.

13 DECEMBER 1902. The cruisers SMS *Vineta* and HMS *Charybdis* reach Puerto Cabello; after sending 50 men into the roadstead to rescue the pillaged British freighter *Topaze* (and after the Venezuelans refuse to issue a formal apology) they level the Vigía and Libertador harbor forts with a concentrated bombardment.

17 JANUARY 1903. Eckermann's *Panther* duels with Fort San Carlos outside Maracaibo, being compelled to retire when its light shells cannot penetrate the castle's ancient stone battlements. Feeling he must reassert German prestige, Scheder appears four days later with the more heavily armed *Vineta* and severely damages the fortification.

Washington responds negatively to this seemingly unprovoked escalation, lodging protests with Berlin; ominously, Adm. George Dewey conducts maneuvers in the Caribbean with more than 50 vessels. Britain and Italy are embarrassed by their German ally, drawing away from the resulting diplomatic furor so as not to worsen their relations with America.

13 FEBRUARY 1903. Castro's government comes to terms with Britain, Germany, and Italy, raising customs duties at La Guaira and Puerto Cabello in order to satisfy claims. The president is glorified by Venezuelans for resisting foreign pressure; the Germans are cast as domestic and international villains.

APRIL 1903. Former Dominican Pres. Alexandro Woss y Gil, supported by the *Jimenista* faction of former Pres. Juan Isidro Jiménez, rebels against the provisional government of Gen. Horacio Vásquez, driving him from the capital of Santo Domingo.

Shortly thereafter a second revolt occurs at Puerto Plata on the northern coast, where Gen. Carlos Morales rises against Woss. Loyalist gunboats blockade the port, but the 386-man cruiser USS *Baltimore* provides cover for foreign residents.

24 NOVEMBER 1903. After a brief siege Santo Domingo falls to General Morales's revolutionary coalition and is installed as president. Soon after, Woss's former vice president—General Deschamps—rebels at Puerto Plata.

23 DECEMBER 1903. Puerto Plata is bombarded from sea by a naval force loyal to President Morales; troops are disembarked nearby under General Cespedes to besiege General Deschamps's followers inside.

3 JANUARY 1904. The 2,575-ton cruiser HMS *Pallas* of Capt. Charles Hope Robertson arrives off beleaguered Puerto Plata to protect British interests; it is followed next day by the cruiser USS *Detroit* of Cmdr. Albert C. Dillingham to protect American residents.

On 5 January they compel the Dominican gunboat *Independencia* to withdraw without bombarding the rebel defenders, as instructed by Morales.

14 JANUARY 1904. General Cespedes informs the Anglo-American naval captains anchored off Puerto Plata that *Independencia* will return next day to bombard the place in conjunction with a land assault by his troops. In order to minimize civilian casualties and material damage, Robertson and Dillingham persuade the factions to fight a half-mile outside the city limits.

They agree, and the small armies meet on 16 January. Cespedes's advance is supported by *Independencia* until the defenders' lone field piece obliges the gunboat to retreat out of range. Nevertheless, Cespedes's 400-man main column overwhelms Morales's rebels in a 20-minute firefight after nightfall, driving him into exile and incorporating most of his men into the government ranks.

Their peacekeeping duties done, the American and British cruisers depart on 19 January.

10 NOVEMBER 1904. Rioting erupts this afternoon in Rio de Janeiro, worsening next day when cadets at the Praia Vermelha military academy join in. Order is restored during the night of 14–15 November when General Piragibe leads a loyal contingent through the streets and clears the rebels, thereby saving the administration of civilian Pres. Francisco de Paula Rodrigues Alves.

APRIL 1906. Four years after American forces have been withdrawn from Cuba, moderate Pres. Tomás Estrada Palma is pronounced reelected by the constitutional assembly despite a vigorously contested campaign. This prompts a walkout by Pino Guerra and other members of the Liberal opposition, heightening tensions on the island.

16 AUGUST 1906. Pino Guerra revolts against the government of President Estrada Palma and inaugurates a guerrilla campaign.

12 SEPTEMBER 1906. ***Guerra's Revolt.*** Four days after the ambush of a Cuban armored train west of Havana by Guerra's rebels, the cruiser USS *Denver* of Cmdr. John Colwell enters harbor, reluctantly dispatched by U.S. Pres. Theodore Roosevelt to help restore public order and protect American lives and interests.

Next day, after an interview with President Estrada Palma as to the gravity of the insurrection, 130 U.S. marines and a field piece come ashore—only to be angrily recalled on 14 September by Roosevelt.

14 SEPTEMBER 1906. The 140-man gunboat USS *Marietta* of Cmdr. William Fullam reaches Cienfuegos (Cuba), setting half the crew ashore to protect American sugar mills, which have been threatened with destruction by local rebels if they do not contribute "a small obligatory war loan." Four days later two companies of Marines arrive aboard the transport *Dixie* to augment Fullam's force.

28 SEPTEMBER 1906. Rather than call for new Cuban elections—as suggested by American Secretary of State William Howard Taft, who recently arrived from Florida aboard the cruiser USS *Des Moines*—President Estrada Palma's entire cabinet resigns at 9:00 P.M., prompting the U.S. government to intervene directly.

Next day more than 2,000 marines begin coming ashore from the battleship USS *Louisiana* and other vessels; an expeditionary force musters in the United States.

The American battleships New Jersey, Virginia, *and* Louisiana *anchored in Havana's inner harbor on 22 September 1906, with support ships*

6 OCTOBER 1906. Brig. Gen. Frederick Funston reaches Havana with the first units of a 6,000-man U.S. occupation force. He is superseded one week later by Gen. J. Franklin Bell, no resistance being encountered from Cuban rebels.

12 OCTOBER 1906. Taft appoints Charles Magoon as Cuba's provisional governor, and the island remains at peace under U.S. rule for two years until former Liberal Gen. José Miguel Gómez is elected president—in U.S.-supervised elections—and installed in office on 28 January 1909, prompting an American withdrawal.

18 MARCH 1907. ***Zelaya's War.*** Nicaragua's liberal dictator José Santos Zelaya—after encouraging an insurrection in neighboring Honduras, only to see its rebels driven into his own territory—decides to invade this country in the insurgents' support. At Namasigüe his advancing forces encounter a combined Honduran-Salvadoran army, which Zelaya's commanders massacre with machine guns (the first time these weapons have been used in Central America). The Nicaraguan victors soon enter Tegucigalpa, where Zelaya dictates terms despite diplomatic protests from Washington.

16 DECEMBER 1907. In order to reinforce the claim that the Americas are within the U.S. sphere of influence, Roosevelt dispatches Rear Adm. Robley Evans from Hampton Roads (Virginia) with 16 battleships—dubbed the Great White Fleet because of its peacetime color scheme—to cruise around South America. After stopovers in Port of Spain (Trinidad), Rio de Janeiro, Punta Arenas (Strait of Magellan), Valparaíso, Callao, and Magdalena Bay (Mexico), the warships reach California, where Evans is replaced because of his rheumatism by Rear Adm. Charles S. Sperry. He cruises as far north as Seattle before leading his 15,000-man force into the Pacific early in July 1907 to circumnavigate the globe. (The fleet reenters Hampton Roads by 22 February 1909.)

1 MAY 1908. In Peru, 36-year-old radical politician Augusto Durand leads an unsuccessful uprising against Pres. José Pardo y Barreda; it is suppressed, and hundreds are arrested.

29 MAY 1909. A band of 25 backers of opposition leader Nicolás de Piérola storms the Peruvian national

palace and seizes newly installed Pres. Augusto B. Leguía. Parading him through Lima's main streets to attempt to foment a popular insurrection, the group is quickly scattered by a small detachment of loyal troops, and Leguía is rescued.

SPRING 1910. After some bloodshed, crewmembers of the Brazilian battleships *Minas Gerais* and *São Paulo* overwhelm their officers, mutiny against the newly installed government of Marshal Hermes da Fonseca, then shell Rio de Janeiro. The rebels are eventually granted amnesty, but when a second rebellion breaks out a few days later aboard another warship and at the Cobras Island barracks, it is more severely repressed.

20 MAY 1912. An antigovernment revolt erupts in Cuba's Oriente Province, with some 10,000 impoverished, disenfranchised black residents rising under leader Evaristo Estanoz.

23 MAY 1912. ***Sugar Revolt.*** The American gunboats *Paducah, Nashville,* and *Petrel* are ordered to steam to Guantánamo and Nipe Bays to protect American sugar mills in light of Cuba's latest insurrection. A 750-man Marine detachment also boards the transport *Prairie* at League Island (Philadelphia) to sail to the trouble area.

2 JUNE 1912. Cuban rebels torch the town of La Maya, prompting President Gómez to suspend all civil liberties in Oriente Province.

5 JUNE 1912. *Prairie*'s 750-man Marine contingent goes ashore at Guantánamo Bay, accompanied by other detachments along the same coastline in response to demands from local American planters and miners. The deployment frees up the regular Cuban army to sweep through Oriente Province; it slaughters some 6,000 blacks during the next three weeks.

26 JUNE 1912. Black rebel leader Estanoz is killed near Nipe Bay (north coast of Oriente Province); his body is publicly displayed in Santiago de Cuba.

MID-JULY 1912. The Afro-Cuban revolt in Oriente Province largely ended, U.S. Marine units retire to Guantánamo Bay for rotation back to regular stations.

4 FEBRUARY 1914. This morning Col. José Urdanivia Ginés leads an assault on the Peruvian national palace; it is initially hurled back by forces loyal to Pres. Guillermo Billinghurst (grandson of an English naval officer who served in South America's wars of independence). Thanks to tacit help from the army chief of staff, Oscar R. Benavides, the rebels fight their way inside on a subsequent attempt, and Billinghurst is exiled.

OCTOBER 1914. Haitian Pres. Charles Oreste Zamor is deposed by Davilmar Théodore, who assumes office.

17 DECEMBER 1914. Concerned by the economic collapse of Haiti, Secretary of State William Jennings Bryan dispatches the U.S. gunboat *Machias,* which arrives off Port au Prince and sets 50 Marines ashore to transfer the gold reserves out of the Franco-American–controlled national bank. The government of President Théodore protests, but the gold is nonetheless conveyed to New York.

15 JANUARY 1915. Gen. Jean Vibrun Guillaume Sam, commander of Haiti's Northern Department, revolts against President Théodore at Cap Haïtien (population 25,000); he is joined a few days later by 1,000 *caco* rebels under "General" Metellus.

23 JANUARY 1915. The cruiser USS *Washington* of Capt. Edward L. "Ned" Beach—father of the future author of *Run Silent, Run Deep*—reaches Cap-Haïtien with Rear Adm. William Caperton aboard to confer with General Sam. Two days later a meeting is held at which Caperton insists on accompanying Sam's revolutionary army south to prevent excesses. Sam agrees, and the cruiser *Des Moines* and the gunboat *Wheeling* join *Washington,* shadowing the revolutionaries south.

5 FEBRUARY 1915. Sam's revolutionary army occupies Gonaïves (north-central Haiti).

22 FEBRUARY 1915. President Théodore abandons the capital of Port au Prince at noon, and three days later General Sam is acclaimed Haiti's new ruler. He will govern only five months, displaced by yet another revolutionary leader out of the north, Dr. Rosalvo Bobo.

19 MAY 1915. The French cruiser *Descartes* sets a landing party ashore at Cap-Haïtien to prevent a massacre of foreign residents by Bobo's besieging Haitian revolutionaries.

1 JULY 1915. The cruiser USS *Washington* returns to Cap-Haïtien with the armed yacht *Eagle* to protect American interests.

27 JULY 1915. At dawn the former Haitian police chief, Charles de Delva, escapes from asylum in the Portuguese embassy and, with 36 armed followers, torches and assaults President Sam's national palace in Port au Prince. Sam, wounded in the leg, flees to sanctuary at the French embassy while his police chief, Charles Oscar Etienne, massacres 200 political prisoners under his charge before seeking refuge in the Dominican embassy. An enraged mob drags Etienne into the street and hacks him to pieces; Sam shares the same fate next morning.

28 JULY 1915. ***Haitian Occupation.*** At 11:40 A.M. USS *Washington* reaches riot-torn Port au Prince (population 100,000) and that evening sets 170 marines and 170 sailors ashore at Bizoton navy yard under marine Capt. George van Orden to march two miles east to restore order in the capital. By next morning, with two Haitians dead and ten wounded, the Americans are in control; they are reinforced the evening of 29 July by the transport *Jason,* bearing a marine company from Guantánamo Bay (Cuba). At 8:00 P.M. a feeble Haitian counterattack strikes the U.S. detachment holding Fort Lerebours south of Port au Prince; it is repelled with six attackers killed and two wounded. Two Americans sailors are killed, one being William Gompers, nephew of the famous labor leader Samuel Gompers.

On 4 August the battleship *Connecticut* of Capt. E. H. Durell arrives with five companies of the 2nd Marine Regiment from League Island (Philadelphia) under Col. Eli Cole, who seizes the Haitian arsenal in Port au Prince and disbands the local factions. *Eagle* and the gunboat *Nashville* of Cmdr. Percy Olmstead bring a halt to fighting outside Cap-Haïtien in the north, and *Jason* is dispatched to convey Bobo to Port au Prince. Expecting to be greeted as president, this general is instead defeated by the American-backed candidate, Philippe Sudre Dartiguenave, in a hastily arranged election on 12 August; he goes into exile in Kingston (Jamaica).

Dartiguenave's installation is resented by many Haitians, and a revolt erupts at Port de Paix (40 miles west of Cap-Haïtien), but outright opposition is stifled by the arrival on 13 August of the armored cruiser *Tennessee,* conveying an additional 850 men and 35 machine guns of the 1st Marine Regiment under 59-year-old Col. Littleton W. T. "Tony" Waller. Three days later a sizable Marine contingent is detached to garrison Cap-Haïtien as well, and Americans assume administrative duties in lesser ports. The Haitian *cacos* retire to the interior of the island to wage a protracted guerrilla campaign against the occupiers.

27 SEPTEMBER 1915. At dawn Colonel Cole pushes inland from Cap Haïtien with 130 marines, fighting his way into Haut du Cap—four miles distant—by noon with the loss of two killed and eight wounded, compared to 60 *caco* guerrilla casualties. Next day

U.S. troops resting by a tropical roadside

Quartier Morin (five miles east along the coast) is occupied without resistance.

4 OCTOBER 1915. Waller sails east from Cap-Haïtien aboard *Nashville* and disembarks a Marine company, occupying Fort Liberté and the inland border town of Ouanaminthe without opposition.

20 OCTOBER 1915. Four Marine squads advance out of Cap-Haïtien, pushing 20 miles into *caco* territory and occupying Bahon.

2 NOVEMBER 1915. Under cover of darkness a *caco* raiding party attacks Waller's field headquarters at Le Trou (roughly between Fort Liberté and Grande Rivière du Nord). The assault is repelled, costing 38 attackers their lives.

5 NOVEMBER 1915. A marine column attempts to assault the major *caco* mountain stronghold of Fort Capois (situated on the eastern bank of Grande Rivière 40 miles west of Vallière, about halfway between Grande Rivière du Nord and Bahon), but its garrison bolts into the jungle without loss. The same occurs three days later at Forts Selon and Berthol.

16 NOVEMBER 1915. A storming force of 100 marines carries the *caco* mountain stronghold of Fort Rivière (four miles west of the Grande Rivière narrows), killing 50 among the 75-man garrison and capturing the rest without suffering a single casualty.

5 JANUARY 1916. Antoine Pierre Paul attempts to overthrow the Dartiguenave administration by having followers fire on Haiti's national palace in Port au Prince at dawn. The coup is easily repressed by the U.S. Marines, five *cacos* being killed and many others arrested.

14 APRIL 1916. After a prolonged period of political unrest, the unpopular Pres. Juan Isidro Jiménez of the Dominican Republic orders the arrest of several key supporters of his insubordinate war minister, Gen. Desiderio Arias. The latter mutinies and commandeers the main arsenal in the capital of Santo Domingo. Following a two-week standoff the general brings matters to a head by surrounding the national chamber of deputies with 250 troops on 1 May, calling for an immediate impeachment of the president. Jiménez advances from his country home with 800 loyal troops under General Pérez and orders Arias stripped of all authority.

3 MAY 1916. ***Dominican Intervention.*** This afternoon the U.S. transport *Prairie* of Commander Crosley and the gunboat *Castine* of Cmdr. Kenneth Bennett

U.S. Marines disembarking from the transport ship Prairie

arrive off Santo Domingo from Haiti; at dawn on 5 May they disembark two marine companies—150 men—under Capt. Frederic "Dopey" Wise at the foot of Fort San Gerónimo, two miles below the capital (population 30,000) to protect American interests during the ongoing Jiménez-Arias confrontation. Unwilling to cooperate with Wise in the siege against his mutinous general, Jiménez resigns as president.

Arias remains in possession of Fort Ozama until Friday, 12 May, when the U.S. dispatch vessel *Dolphin* and the storeship *Culgoa* arrive from Port au Prince with Admiral Caperton and two Marine companies under Maj. Newt H. Hall. (A third company appears next day out of Guantánamo Bay aboard the collier *Hector.*) With 400 men total, the Americans order the general to evacuate his stronghold by Monday morning, 15 May, and find Arias departed northwest by the deadline. Reinforcements continue to reach the American beachhead, as Washington intends to end the Dominican strife by full-scale intervention.

On the morning of 1 June Wise occupies the northern coastal town of Monte Cristi with 120 marines from Cmdr. Harris Lanning's transport *Panther;* 65 miles farther east 133 marines under Maj. Charles Hatch go ashore from the gunboat *Sacramento* of Cmdr. Roscoe Bulmer, wresting Puerto Plata from 500 Dominican defenders under General Rey after a heated exchange of gunfire. Three and a half weeks later—on 26 June—Col. Joseph "Uncle Joe" Pendleton leads 800 marines east out of Monte Cristi to march 75 miles inland and attack Arias's new concentration near Santiago.

Briefly checked at Las Trincheras and Guayacanas, and enduring repeated sniping, Pendleton rendezvouses on 4 July at Navarrete with 135 marines under Maj. Hiram "Hiking" Bearss, who pushed south from Puerto Plata. Next day Arias surrenders, and during the afternoon Santiago is occupied without opposition, followed by lesser towns during the next several days. The Americans take over administrative duties for the entire island and impose martial law on 29 November, inaugurating a lengthy occupation. Only Gov. Juan Pérez of San Francisco de Macorís (30 miles southeast of Santiago) mounts a brief resistance, his 300-man garrison being surprised and scattered by a marine company under Lt. Ernest Williams.

1 NOVEMBER 1916. Despite an earlier pledge not to seek reelection, conservative Cuban Pres. Mario García Menocal runs again and is seemingly defeated by his Liberal opponent amid widespread balloting irregularities. Nevertheless, when the results are announced late in December he proclaims himself victor.

An appeal to the Cuban supreme court in January 1917 is decided in favor of the Liberals, with new elections being called for in Oriente and Santa Clara Provinces; García Menocal proves slow to respond.

11 FEBRUARY 1917. ***Gómez's Revolt.*** At dawn a few Cuban soldiers at Camp Columbia outside Havana rise against García Menocal in a coordinated coup, being quickly suppressed. However, other mutinies claim the garrisons at Camagüey, Santiago, and Guantánamo, and the former president, Gómez, raises the banner of revolt in Santa Clara Province. Pino Guerra and Baldomero Acosta (a former member of the baseball Washington Senators) take the field in the west.

12 FEBRUARY 1917. To protect American interests in rebel-held Santa Clara Province, the gunboat USS *Paducah* disembarks its bluejackets.

15 FEBRUARY 1917. Before dawn the decrepit U.S. gunboat *Petrel* of Cmdr. Dudley Knox arrives outside Santiago from Guantánamo Bay; he agrees to prevent Cuban government vessels from entering in exchange for a rebel pledge not to block the channel with scuttled ships.

19 FEBRUARY 1917. Washington brands the Liberal revolt in Cuba "lawless and unconstitutional," vowing to oppose it.

25 FEBRUARY 1917. A detachment of 220 marines advance from Guantánamo Bay to occupy the city. Another 200 marines disembark from the 5th U.S. Battleship Division to protect American sugar plantations on the western hook of Oriente Province.

7 MARCH 1917. The rebel former president, Gómez, is defeated and arrested in Santa Clara Province by Cuban government forces.

8 MARCH 1917. Threatened by the steady advance of Cuban government forces, the rebel garrison at Santiago agrees to surrender control over the city at nightfall to landing parties from the cruiser USS *San Francisco* (flag), *Olympia,* and the gunboat *Machias.*

18 MARCH 1917. Cuba's short-lived "sugar revolt" officially ends when triumphant Pres. García Menocal—at U.S. urging—promulgates a general amnesty for all rebels.

17 OCTOBER 1918. The escaped former Haitian Gen. Charlemagne Masséna Péralte attacks the American-run *gendarmerie* barracks at Hinche (population 5,000) with 100 *caco* guerrillas, being repelled by the garrison with the loss of 35 followers.

10 NOVEMBER 1918. The Haitian guerrilla Charlemagne overruns the town of Maissade (upriver from Hinche), ransacking its police barracks for weapons.

MARCH 1919. ***Hunt for Charlemagne.*** Because of increased guerrilla activity in northeastern Haiti near the Dominican border, Marine Brig. Gen. Albertus Catlin requests reinforcements from Washington. Four companies of the 7th Marine Regiment arrive from Guantánamo Bay, followed on 31 March by 13 aircraft—seven HS-2 flying boats and six Curtis Jennys—which land at Bizoton.

Joining 500 marines and many Haitian *gendarmes* already deployed, all combine for a summer-long offensive against Charlemagne's elusive *cacos.* The latter responds by storming the northern gates of Port au Prince before dawn on 6 October with 300 followers. Forewarned, the defenders halt the assault with machine gun fire, killing 30 *cacos* and scattering Charlemagne and the rest.

Eventually, former *caco* Gen. Jean Baptiste Conze is bribed to lead a small party of marines into Charlemagne's camp near Grande Rivière on the night of 30–31 October; the charismatic leader is assassinated.

15 JANUARY 1920. Before sunrise Charlemagne's chief lieutenant, Benoît Brataville, launches an assault on Port au Prince with 300 *caco* irregulars. They are easily repelled, suffering more than 100 fatalities.

18 MAY 1920. Brataville's camp near Las Cahobas (Haiti) is surprised by a marine patrol; the leader is killed.

1920–1934. The Americans remain in Haiti until 15 August 1934, when the 2nd Marine Regiment is recalled by Pres. Franklin Delano Roosevelt and full autonomy restored to this island's rulers.

MEXICAN REVOLUTION (1910–1924)

IN THE SUMMER OF 1910 PORFÍRIO DÍAZ—approaching 80—stands for his eighth term as president despite growing resentment of his long reign. When the wealthy, high-minded political neophyte Madero decides to run as head of an "antireelectionist" party, the president has him arrested. When the primary of 21 June is held 5,000 of Madero's adherents are in prison; when the final elections are held on 8 July an estimated 60,000 are behind bars.

Díaz is proclaimed president on his birthday (27 September), but his government is doomed. This year also marks the centennial of Mexico's revolt against Spain, and stirrings are already being felt. Madero escapes from loose confinement in San Luis Potosí on 4 October and gains asylum in San Antonio (Texas), calling for an uprising by 20 November. The situation explodes.

19 NOVEMBER 1910. Overnight Madero recrosses the border with a few followers, attempting next day to foment insurrection at "Ciudad Porfirio Díaz" (Piedras Negras, opposite Eagle Pass, Texas); he is chased back into the United States by *federales.*

20 NOVEMBER 1910. Several small uprisings occur throughout Mexico, the most successful being led by a 28-year-old teamster named Pascual Orozco at the town of San Isidro (modern Orozco, Chihuahua). Within a month he raises sufficient men for a descent on the federal outpost at Ciudad Guerrero—100 miles west of Chihuahua City—which Orozco captures and holds after a brief siege. Pedernales, Cerro Prieto, Mal Paso, and La Mojina are also attacked.

30 JANUARY 1911. Having abandoned Ciudad Guerrero (Chihuahua) with 400 followers, Orozco destroys some rail tracks south of Ciudad Juárez (opposite El Paso, Texas), then seizes a freight and two passenger trains, using them to approach the federal garrison within Ciudad Juárez by 2 February. He is unable to reduce the outnumbered defenders; the city is relieved three days later by a federal column under Col. Antonio M. Rábago, who fights in via Bauche.

4 FEBRUARY 1911. At dawn a small revolutionary band under 49-year-old José Luis Moya takes the Zacatecan town of Nieves (population 5,000), departing that evening; he is repelled six days later at San Juan de Guadalupe.

Madero officers

13 FEBRUARY 1911. A disguised Madero recrosses the Rio Grande at Isleta (15 miles southeast of El Paso, Texas), joining José de la Luz Soto's 130 revolutionaries at the village of Zaragoza before penetrating deeper into Chihuahua.

This same day, Moya defeats a federal force under Maj. Ismael Ramos at El Ahuage then occupies the town of San Juan de Guadalupe (Durango).

26 FEBRUARY 1911. Moya's 200 revolutionaries capture the town of Chalchihuites (Zacatecas).

6 MARCH 1911. Madero attacks the depleted federal garrison at Casas Grandes (Chihuahua) with 800 revolutionaries divided into three columns. The defenders resist until relieved by Col. Samuel García Cuéllar, who drives the attackers off toward Bustillos Hacienda, capturing most of their supplies. Madero is wounded in the right arm, and his men suffer 100 casualties.

Nevertheless, he is soon joined by Orozco and many other local leaders—such as the 32-year-old bandit Doroteo Arango, better known as Francisco "Pancho" Villa—who proclaim Madero to be Mexico's true president.

10 MARCH 1911. At Anenecuilco (Morelos), Pablo Torres Burgos leads 72 peasants in revolt, striking south through sugar plantations to gather greater strength. After overrunning nearby Tlaquiltenango on 24 March and then Jojutla, Torres Burgos is dismayed by the brutalities perpetuated by some of his followers and resigns. Riding toward Moyotepec with his two sons, they are killed by a party of *federales* under Gen. Javier Rojas. Command of his 800 revolutionaries devolves to 37-year-old Emiliano Zapata.

12 MARCH 1911. Moya seizes the rich mining town of Mapimí (Durango).

26 MARCH 1911. Moya occupies Ciudad Lerdo.

9 APRIL 1911. After briefly seizing Fresnillo and being chased off by federal forces, Moya surprises Zacatecas City with his 300 revolutionaries, camping in the Mercedes suburbs before proceeding north to Veta Grande.

19 APRIL 1911. Together with 48-year-old Calixto Contreras and Martín Triana, Moya retakes the town of San Juan de Guadalupe (Zacatecas).

23 APRIL 1911. ***Ciudad Juárez.*** Four days after arriving to besiege the border town of Ciudad Juárez with 3,500 ill-disciplined revolutionaries—Orozco being their "general," Villa a "colonel"—Madero arranges a ten-day truce with the 700-man federal garrison under Gen. Juan N. Navarro to meet some Díaz plenipotentiaries from Mexico City.

Talks are broken off on 6 May; two days later the impatient Orozco and Villa arrange for rebel troops to precipitate a firefight against the *federales,* furnishing the excuse to storm Ciudad Juárez. Madero is constrained to watch as the assault pushes the outnumbered defenders back into their cavalry barracks, where they surrender by 10 May.

Three days later Orozco and Villa challenge Madero, demanding that Navarro and his federal officers—long known for their harshness—be executed, but Madero refuses and releases the captives into the United States. Both rebel commanders, although temporarily acquiescing with Madero's decision, soon leave his service.

7 MAY 1911. Beset by outbreaks throughout Mexico, Díaz offers to resign.

This same day, Moya arrives at the rich mining town of Sombrerete (Zacatecas), driving out the 200-man federal garrison under Col. Fernando Trucy Aubert after two days' heavy fighting; the revolutionary chieftain is killed by a stray bullet.

14–15 MAY 1911. Torreón (Coahuila) is overrun by the revolutionary chiefs Orestes Pereyra, Sixto Ugalde, and Agustín Castro, who defeat three federal battalions under Gen. Emiliano Lojero. The rebel victory is marred by the subsequent massacre of 303 unarmed Chinese civilians.

18 MAY 1911. Zapata's peasant army besieges the federal garrison at Cuautla (Morelos), fighting into the burning city six days later.

21 MAY 1911. Cuernavaca (Morelos) is evacuated by the federal garrison and soon taken by Zapata.

25 MAY 1911. Rioting has occurred in Mexico City's main square the previous evening, so Díaz resigns, fleeing to Veracruz on 26 May to sail aboard the German liner *Ypiranga.* Foreign Minister Francisco León de la Barra serves as interim president until elections can be held.

26 MAY 1911. This evening the revolutionary Cándido Navarro enters San Luis Potosí with more than 500 men, deposing Gov. José M. Espinosa y Cuevas next day.

7 JUNE 1911. A few hours after a heavy earthquake has killed 207 people in Mexico City, Madero makes his triumphant entry.

12 JUNE 1911. Madero visits the state of Morelos, but Zapata refuses to disarm his revolutionary followers and restore captured lands.

22 JUNE 1911. Orozco's army triumphantly enters Chihuahua City, which becomes his headquarters.

12–13 JULY 1911. Zapatista troops stationed in Puebla begin arresting civilians implicated in a plot to assassinate Madero during a forthcoming visit. Federal troops under 62-year-old Col. Aureliano Blanquet—on orders from interim President de la Barra—attack the Zapatista encampment within Puebla's bullring, killing 80 and wounding 200.

8 AUGUST 1911. Hard-bitten, 66-year-old, former Porfirian Gen. Victoriano Huerta is dispatched to Cuernavaca (Morelos) with 1,000 federal troops to keep an eye on Zapata. Under protest, Zapata grudgingly demobilizes part of his peasant army.

22 AUGUST 1911. The newly appointed federal governor of Morelos, Ambrosio Figueroa, executes 70 Zapatistas in Jojutla.

31 AUGUST 1911. Ignoring Madero's calls for restraint, Huerta occupies Cuautla (Morelos) and orders Zapata's arrest; the leader flees into the hills.

10 OCTOBER 1911. Zapata reoccupies Cuautla with 1,500 followers.

6 NOVEMBER 1911. Having won the presidential election, Madero is installed in office in Mexico City.

9 NOVEMBER 1911. From San Antonio (Texas), the former revolutionary leader Emilio Vázquez Gómez calls for a new revolt against Madero.

11 NOVEMBER 1911. Zapata narrowly escapes capture by federal troops, fleeing Cuautla (Morelos).

27 NOVEMBER 1911. Zapata publicly disavows Madero's presidency because of his apparent inability to give land to the peasants.

13 DECEMBER 1911. The 61-year-old, one-eyed, former Porfirian Gen. Bernardo Reyes crosses the border from Texas and calls for a Conservative uprising against Madero. Receiving no support, he surrenders to authorities at Linares (Nuevo León) by Christmas Day.

6 FEBRUARY 1912. The 35-year-old Zapatista leader Genovevo de la O launches a series of attacks against Cuernavaca (Morelos), prompting the federal garrison to raze the town of Santa María Ahuacatitlán in retaliation.

10 FEBRUARY 1912. Federal troops seize Zapata's mother-in-law, one of his sisters, and several brothers-in-law as hostages.

15 FEBRUARY 1912. Gen. Juvencio Robles—new federal commander for the state of Morelos—launches a terror campaign against the Zapatistas by ordering the town of Nexpa burned; over the next few days San Rafael, Los Hornos, Los Elotes, Ayala, Coajomulco, and Ocotepec suffer the same fate.

3 MARCH 1912. ***Rellano.*** In Chihuahua City, the disaffected Orozco rises against Madero, accusing him of failing to carry out the revolution (actually he resents being passed over for preferment). With 6,000 well-equipped irregulars, Orozco strikes south, prompting Gen. José González Salas—a relative of Madero's by marriage—to resign his post as war minister and march north to confront him.

A couple of weeks later near Rellano Station in southern Chihuahua González's vanguard is devastated by a runaway Orozquista locomotive filled with dynamite then attacked from the rear by rebel cavalry. During the fighting a federal battalion mutinies, drawing fire from other federal contingents. Wounded and despondent, González orders a retreat to Torreón (Coahuila) then commits suicide.

1 APRIL 1912. Zapatista forces occupy Tepoztlán (Morelos), then Jonacatepec five days later.

12 APRIL 1912. Huerta reaches Torreón (Coahuila) to take over González Salas's defeated army. After reorganizing the formation—and nearly executing "Brigadier

Villa walking away from the execution wall at Torreón after receiving a last-minute reprieve from President Madero

General" Villa for insubordination—he advances north into Chihuahua to confront Orozco.

In a summer-long campaign, Huerta inflicts a series of defeats on the rebel at Rellano, Los Conejos, La Cruz, Bachimba, Bermejillo, Chihuahua City, and Ciudad Juárez. In early September Orozco and his surviving followers are badly beaten at the border town of Ojinaga, seeking refuge in the United States.

26 APRIL 1912. Col. Pedro León's "Sierra Juárez" Battalion mutinies against Madero in Oaxaca City; he attempts to take over the capital a few days later, only to be driven into the countryside. The commander is executed by June.

1 JUNE 1912. With 60 riders Huerta defeats a 400-man Oroquista garrison at Parral (Chihuahua).

16 OCTOBER 1912. Having previously resigned his commission in the federal army, 44-year-old Brig. Gen. Félix Díaz—nephew of the departed dictator Porfirio Díaz—leads the Veracruz garrison in a Conservative rebellion against Madero. Within a week loyal forces arrive outside the port, and Félix Díaz is arrested by 23 October.

9 FEBRUARY 1913. ***Decena Trágica.*** At 2:00 this Sunday morning Gens. Manuel Mondragón and Gregorio Ruiz mutiny against Madero, marching into Mexico City from nearby Tacubaya at the head of the 1st, 2nd, and 5th Cavalry Regiments—being joined en route by the 1st Artillery Regiment, for a total of 2,400 men, six cannons, and 14 machine guns. (Some 600 cadets of the Tlalpan military college also commandeer streetcars into the capital to support the insurrection.) One column releases Gen. Bernardo Reyes from prison in Santiago Tlaltelolco, another frees Brig. Gen. Félix Díaz from Lecumberri Penitentiary.

By the time the mutineers converge on the presidential palace it has already been briefly occupied by the cadets, who have been overwhelmed by 500 loyal troops of the 24th Battalion under elderly Gen. Lauro Villar. The latter also arrests Ruiz upon entering the main square. Shooting erupts, during which Reyes and another 300 people—including many curious civilians—are killed; another 200 are wounded.

The mutineers withdraw and at 1:00 P.M. force their way into the *Ciudadela* arsenal to dig in. Meanwhile Madero arrives from Chapultepec Castle and appoints Huerta (who has been dismissed by the army and so is in the crowd) as interim commander in place of Villar, who is badly wounded. Huerta orders Ruiz and all rebel cadets shot by firing squad; Madero travels to Cuernavaca this afternoon to summon 1,000 more loyal troops under 43-year-old Brig. Gen. Felipe Ángeles.

The next day passes in silence, but at 10:00 Tuesday morning, 11 February, an artillery duel erupts with the mutineers inside the *Ciudadela;* another 500 civilians are killed. (Eventually, 5,000 die during the *Decena Trágica,* or Tragic Fortnight.) Huerta and Ángeles now command 6,000 loyal troops against 1,800 rebels under Mondragón and Díaz; still, Huerta seems incapable of reducing the ancient fortress, provoking doubts as to his loyalty. After five days of long-range shelling Madero's brother, Gustavo, arrests Huerta at 2:00 A.M. on 18 February, accusing him before the president of treachery. Unconvinced, Madero orders his general released.

At 1:30 that afternoon Huerta detains Gustavo Madero then sends General Blanquet's 29th Battalion to capture the president. He is seized after a brief struggle along with Vice Pres. José María Pino Suárez and most of the cabinet. By 9:30 P.M. Huerta meets with Díaz at the residence of U.S. Ambassador Henry Lane Wilson—a vocal critic of Madero—to sign a pact whereby the former temporarily assumes the presidency on the understanding he will support the former dictator's son during forthcoming elections. (Wilson is soon recalled to Washington and forced to retire for his role in this treachery.)

22 FEBRUARY 1913. After resigning office and being promised safe passage into Cuban exile, Madero is driven to the Lecumberri Penitentiary at night and murdered.

24 FEBRUARY 1913. Venustiano Carranza, the 53-year-old governor of Coahuila, revolts in northern Mexico against the usurper Huerta. Others join, including such guerrilla chieftains as 33-year-old Pablo González, Lucio Blanco, Eulalio and Luis Gutiérrez, the 39-year-old former photographer Francisco Murguía, Emilio Salinas, Cesáreo Castro, Jacinto B. Treviño, and many others.

9 MARCH 1913. Having escaped from prison to El Paso, Villa recrosses the Texas border to raise troops and fight Huerta.

13–14 MARCH 1913. A 33-year-old revolutionary "colonel" named Alvaro Obregón, having advanced north from Hermosillo (Sonora) six days earlier, captures the 400-man Huertista garrison in the border town of Nogales.

17 MARCH 1913. In Chihuahua, Orozco accepts the rank of brigadier in Huerta's federal army.

22 MARCH 1913. Carranza attacks Saltillo (Coahuila) with three small revolutionary columns, only to be forced to withdraw two days later for lack of ammunition.

26 MARCH 1913. The tiny government garrison at Cananea surrenders to revolutionary forces under Manuel M. Diéguez (a veteran of its 1906 strike; *see* 1 June 1906 under Portents in Mexico).

15 APRIL 1913. After heavy fighting at Naco and Agua Prieta, Sonora (south of Douglas, Arizona), Obregón and Diéguez defeat all remaining Huertista forces under Gen. Pedro Ojeda along the U.S. border.

17 APRIL 1913. After several months of peace in Morelos, Robles deposes its state government and is appointed military chief by Huerta.

18 APRIL 1913. The rebel chief Pánfilo Nátera—a former corporal in the Porfirian *rurales*—occupies Jerez (Zacatecas) by following a circuitous approach with 400 riders to surprise the 100-man federal garrison, which then joins his ranks.

19 APRIL 1913. Zapata fights his way into Jonacatepec (Morelos), defeating its Huertista garrison.

23 APRIL 1913. Zapata besieges the Huertista garrison in Cuautla (Morelos) but is unable to subdue it for lack of artillery. A fortnight later some of his revolutionaries blow up a military train, killing 100 federal troops and provoking a brutal roundup of civilians.

8 MAY 1913. Nátera circles Fresnillo (Zacatecas), being joined by almost all its federal garrison. Left with only a half-dozen loyal troops, Huertista Maj. Natividad del Toro locks himself in its stronghold. Nearly smoked out by burning sacks of chile, he commits suicide.

13 MAY 1913. ***Santa Rosa.*** Having four days earlier witnessed the arrival of a trio of warships and a pair of steamers at the Pacific port of Guaymas (Sonora) bearing 3,000 Huertista reinforcements, Obregón's small revolutionary army retreats north to the state capital of Hermosillo until ordered to make a stand by acting Gov. Ignacio L. Pesqueira. On 12 May Obregón chooses to fight at Santa Rosa and next day checks the advance of Generals Gil and Luis Medina Barrón, thereby winning the rank of brigadier.

Typical Mexican revolutionary soldier

30 MAY 1913. Zapata declares Huerta unworthy of the presidency and declares war on his regime.

1 JUNE 1913. Nátera occupies Bufa Heights, then uses the high ground to win Zacatecas City below (although it is recaptured two weeks later by Huertista Gen. José Delgado).

4 JUNE 1913. Pablo González's small revolutionary army seizes the border town of Matamoros (opposite Brownsville, Texas).

18 JUNE 1913. The 36-year-old revolutionary "Colonel" Tomás Urbina R. captures Durango (Coahuila), gaining considerable booty.

20 JUNE 1913. Obregón defeats a Huertista force under Ojeda at Santa María (Sonora) and yet another

one week later at San Alejandro, driving his beaten foes back to Guaymas and besieging them by early July.

19 AUGUST 1913. Huertista troops overrun Zapata's base at Huautla (Morelos), but the rebel chieftain escapes into the hills.

26 AUGUST 1913. ***San Andrés.*** With 700 riders and two 75-mm cannons directed by former federal artillery Col. Juan Medina, Villa defeats Gen. Félix Terrazas's 1,300-man Huertista garrison at San Andrés (near Riva Palacio, Chihuahua). Some 100 defenders are killed outright and another 236 are executed afterwards—in four-deep rows to save ammunition—compared to only 32 rebel dead.

29 SEPTEMBER 1913. ***Torreón (First Battle).*** His army—dubbed the División del Norte, or Northern Division—having swollen to 10,000 ill-disciplined followers, Villa advances on Torreón (Coahuila) in three separate columns. His own brigade drives along the right bank of the Nazas River toward Aviles; Maclovio Herrera and the Juárez Brigade follow the left bank toward the twin towns of Lerdo and Gómez Palacio; Urbina's Morelos Brigade covers Villa's right.

Aviles falls after four hours of heavy fighting, but the federal troops in Lerdo and Gómez Palacio under Huertista Gen. Eutiquio Munguía hold out for two days before finally being crushed by the Juárez Brigade. On 1 October Villa personally leads the final, costly charge that carries the revolutionaries into Torreón. Some 800 Huertista soldiers have been killed during the three days and another 120 are captured (all officers being executed).

LATE OCTOBER 1913. Having veered north, Villa launches repeated assaults against Chihuahua City but is unable to subdue the Huertista garrison under Gen. Salvador R. Mercado.

14 NOVEMBER 1913. Obregón's revolutionary Army of the Northwest captures Culiacán (Sinaloa).

15 NOVEMBER 1913. Having left some troops to watch the Huertista garrison within Chihuahua City, Villa heads north and intercepts a coal train traveling in the opposite direction from Ciudad Juárez, compelling its terrified conductor to telegraph headquarters that it is impossible to get through. Ordered to return, Villa unloads the train and hides his troops aboard, gliding into Ciudad Juárez (opposite El Paso, Texas) after nightfall on 15 November to capture it with ease. Several hundred executions follow despite Villa's personal leniency in numerous cases.

18 NOVEMBER 1913. Pablo González captures Ciudad Victoria (Tamaulipas); Nuevo Laredo and Guerrero follow.

23 NOVEMBER 1913. ***Tierra Blanca.*** Villa's 6,200-man División del Norte makes a stand along the high ground south of Ciudad Juárez, occupying a 12-mile line between Bauche and Tierra Blanca to await 5,500 *federales* traveling north out of Chihuahua City under Huertista Gen. José Inés Salazar.

The latter launches a series of ferocious assaults that bleed his army white. Leaving almost 1,000 dead upon the field, Salazar retreats southeast by the evening of 24 November to the border town of Ojinaga (opposite Presidio, Texas). Upon learning of this defeat, the 200-man Huertista garrison within Chihuahua City abandons its post.

8 DECEMBER 1913. Villa occupies Chihuahua City unopposed, the Chinese-Mexican Gen. Manuel Chao—Carranza's appointee—eventually being installed as governor despite Villa's reluctance.

LATE DECEMBER 1913. Villa detaches 31-year-old Brig. Gen. Pánfilo Nátera with 3,000 troops to besiege Salazar within Ojinaga; he fails to subdue the federal survivors.

10 JANUARY 1914. ***Ojinaga.*** Villa's main army joins Nátera before Ojinaga and in a 65-minute assault pulverizes Salazar's remaining *federales,* who stream into Presidio, Texas—where the American garrison is commanded by 53-year-old Gen. John Joseph "Black Jack" Pershing. The victory ends all Huertista resistance in Chihuahua.

11 MARCH 1914. Pablo González briefly occupies Tampico (Tamaulipas).

12 MARCH 1914. ***Siege of Cuautla.*** Having been preceded a few days earlier by contingents under subordinates Julián Blanco, Jesús Salgado, and Heliodoro Castillo, Zapata arrives to besiege Cuautla (Morelos) with 5,000 revolutionaries. The Huertista garrison is overrun by 23 March, and although Gen. Luis G. Cartón briefly escapes south toward Acapulco he is soon run down—along with 43 staff officers—and executed at Chilpancingo.

22 MARCH 1914. ***Torreón (Second Battle).*** This city having been reoccupied by Huertistas three months earlier, Villa returns to reconquer it with 12,000 troops subdivided into nine infantry and cavalry brigades plus two artillery regiments under former federal General Ángeles. After overwhelming the outlying towns Villa assaults Torreón on 28 March. Its 10,000-man Huertista garrison puts up a stout resistance under Gen. José Refugio Velasco but is driven out on 2 April with heavy losses. Villa estimates his own casualties to be 500 killed and 1,500 wounded.

23 MARCH 1914. Zapata captures Chilpancingo (Guerrero).

5 APRIL 1914. ***San Pedro de las Colonias.*** In a four-day struggle, Villa defeats Velasco's 12,000 Huertista troops at San Pedro de las Colonias Hacienda (Madero's former estate in Coahuila); the federal commander is wounded.

8 APRIL 1914. Zapata's Ejército Libertador, or Liberating Army, following its victory at Cuautla, advances west and captures Iguala (Guerrero), followed shortly thereafter by Taxco. His peasants now control all of Morelos except the Santa Clara and Tenango Haciendas, which are protected by Japanese mercenaries under a French officer.

9 APRIL 1914. At Tampico—reoccupied by federal troops under Gen. Ignacio Morelos Zaragoza and besieged by anti-Huertista rebels—eight unarmed U.S. seamen from the gunboat *Dolphin* come ashore under a 23-year-old assistant paymaster named Charles W. Copp to pick up gasoline during a lull in the fighting. Instead they are detained by ten Tamaulipas militiamen and brought before Col. Ramón H. Hinojosa, who orders their release and apologizes along with Morelos Zaragoza for the inconvenience.

The 57-year-old Rear Adm. Henry Thomas Mayo—commander of the 4th Division of the U.S. Atlantic Fleet stationed off Mexico's Gulf Coast to protect American interests—refuses to be mollified by the gesture. Without clearance from Washington he insists that the Mexican general punish the miscreants, issue a formal apology in writing, and hoist the American flag ashore, saluting it with a 21-gun salvo. The Mexicans' refusal to comply provokes a diplomatic showdown with Huerta (whom Pres. Woodrow Wilson has disliked since Huerta's brutal usurpation of power).

14 APRIL 1914. Wilson orders the U.S. Atlantic Fleet to concentrate off Mexico; Rear Adm. Charles J. Badger's battleship squadron sails from Hampton Roads (Virginia) this evening.

21 APRIL 1914. ***Veracruz Landing.*** Wishing to punish Huerta by intercepting a shipment of 200 machine guns and 15 million rounds of ammunition scheduled to arrive aboard the Hamburg-America liner *Ypiranga,* Wilson authorizes 58-year-old Rear Adm. Frank Friday Fletcher to disembark his forces and seize Veracruz (population 40,000). The American commander first advises his British counterpart, 52-year-old Rear Adm. Sir Christopher G.F.M. "Kit" Craddock aboard HMS *Essex,* plus the captain of the antique, 9,200-ton Spanish armored cruiser *Emperador Carlos V*—whose warships lie in the roadstead—of the impending hostilities. Mexican Commo. Alejandro Cerisola, commander of the 160-man garrison on the offshore island of San Juan de Ulúa, is also forewarned.

At 11:00 A.M. 800 American seamen and marines head inshore under Capt. William R. Rush of USS *Florida* and Marine Lt. Col. Wendell C. "Buck" Neville; Gen. Gustavo Maass—military commander for the city of Veracruz proper—is advised not to offer resistance with his 18th and 19th Battalions (600 regulars under Brigs. Luis B. Becerril and Francisco Figueroa). The latter withdraw ten miles inland by train to Tejería, but civilian snipers—and 90 cadets from the Mexican naval academy—open fire around noon as the invaders begin moving through the streets. Some 400 reinforcements are rushed ashore from USS *Utah* and subdue resistance by 3:00 P.M.; four Americans are killed and 20 are wounded.

Ypiranga is detained upon arrival at 2:00 P.M., its armaments proving to have originated not in Germany but from the Remington Company in the United States. Admiral Badger's battleships *Arkansas, New Hampshire, South Carolina, Vermont,* and *New Jersey* arrive after midnight on 21–22 April, setting an additional 1,500 bluejackets and marines ashore next dawn. (Eventually, as more U.S. warships join, 3,300 sailors and 2,500 marines enter Veracruz.) Sporadic sniper fire resumes, but the city is firmly under U.S. control by 11:00 A.M. on 23 April, when Col. John J. Lejeune disembarks from USS *Hancock* to assume temporary command over the occupying marines. Some 126 Mexicans have died and another 195 have been injured, compared to 17 American dead and 63 wounded.

Although directed against Huerta, the invasion is resented by all Mexicans. At Tampico, crews from the neutral HMS *Essex* and the German cruiser *Dresden* must evacuate American civilians under flag of truce. Meanwhile San Juan de Ulúa capitulates to the Americans by 26 April and is occupied by a marine company from the battleship *North Dakota* two days later. Shortly before midnight on 27 April Brig. Gen. Frederick Funston arrives from Texas City with the 5th Reinforced Brigade (4th, 7th, 19th, and 28th Infantry Regiments) aboard the transports *Kilpatrick, Meade, Sumner,* and *McClellan* to garrison Veracruz.

U.S. forces remain throughout most of the year, as Washington is bewildered by the rapid-fire changes in Mexican administration: Huerta being succeeded by Carranza, who in turn is challenged by Villa and Zapata. Finally Secretary of State Bryan announces on 13 November that Veracruz will be evacuated.

4 MAY 1914. Obregón and 36-year-old subordinate Benjamín G. Hill besiege Mazatlán (Sinaloa).

5 MAY 1914. Diéguez and Lucio Blanco capture Acaponeta (Nayarit); Tepic follows nine days later.

19 MAY 1914. Having left 3,000 revolutionaries under subordinate Ramón F. Iturbe to maintain the siege of Mazatlán, Obregón visits Tepic (Nayarit).

20 MAY 1914. ***Paredón.*** Having been diverted east from Torreón on Carranza's orders, Villa routs the remnants of Velasco's Huertista army at Paredón (Coahuila) then fights his way into Saltillo this same day.

10 JUNE 1914. ***Zacatecas.*** On Carranza's orders, Brigadier General Nátera pushes south and attempts to assail Zacatecas with only 6,000 revolutionaries—the so-called División del Centro, or Central Division, almost exclusively cavalry. It is badly beaten by the city's 12,000 Huertista defenders under Medina Barrón, who has 11 field pieces and 90 machine guns.

Once Nátera becomes engaged, Carranza telegraphs Villa to send reinforcements from his much larger, better-equipped División del Norte at Torreón. Villa refuses, instead requesting permission to lead his troops in person. When the jealous Carranza refuses, Villa mutinies and strikes south on 16 June, en route joining Nátera at Fresnillo. By the afternoon of 22 June Villa has 25,000 troops and 50 guns massed before Zacatecas. The revolutionary infantry and cavalry are deployed east at Guadalupe as well as south-southwest of the city, driving the defenders back atop their fortified hills: El Grillo west of Zacatecas and La Bufa to the east. Ángeles meanwhile installs his batteries to the north, at Veta Grande.

At 10:00 A.M. on 23 June Villa launches a massive assault, his troops scaling El Grillo by 1:30 P.M. and overwhelming La Bufa two and a half hours later. These captures prompt a stampede back into Zacatecas by the defeated *federales,* which worsens when demolition charges begin leveling public buildings at 4:30 P.M. In the resulting slaughter 5,000 Huertistas are killed, 2,500 are wounded, and 3,000 are taken prisoner (most of the survivors are executed along with numerous civilians). Wounded in his left leg, Medina Barrón is lucky to escape south to Soledad with 14 men. Villa's casualties total 4,000; several hundred Zacatecans are also killed in this ferocious exchange.

25 JUNE 1914. ***Orendáin.*** Obregón's revolutionary Ejército del Noroeste, or Army of the Northwest, arrives at Ahualulco (45 miles west of Guadalajara) and begins marshaling a large host of local auxiliaries to invest the Huertista army of Gen. José María Mier at La Vega railway station. Hoping to trap the *federales* by infiltrating his army along both sides of the rail line, Obregón's strategy is prematurely revealed when subordinate Julián Medina blows a track in Mier's rear, prompting the Huertistas to fall back on Orendáin.

But on 1 July Obregón persists with this tactic—albeit on a grander scale—by sending Brig. Gen. Lucio Blanco on a lengthy, stealthy cavalry approach due east to assault the federal outposts at El Castillo and La Capilla, thereby cutting off Guadalajara's rail communications to the south. Simultaneously, Brigadier General Diéguez is to take battalions under Eulogio Martínez, Esteban B. Calderón, Pablo Quiroga, Juan José Ríos, Severiano Talamantes, and Fermín Carpio on a forced march north through Tequila Range, circling to emerge at La Venta—directly in Mier's rear.

Obregón waits until Diéguez's column engages the Huertistas on 6 July before bombarding their paralyzed train convoy from the west with artillery and machine guns, starting at midnight. The federal army disintegrates into panic by dawn on 7 July, individual units breaking off in hopes of regaining Guadalajara. Rather than indulge in diverse chases Obregón continues swiftly to Zapopan, arriving that evening and barring all access into the capital, thereby preventing Huertistas from reinforcing the garrison.

When Mier attempts to quit Guadalajara on 8 July with his remaining 3,000 men he finds Blanco already blocking his escape at El Castillo; he is killed attempting to fight through. During these three days Huertista losses total 2,000 killed, 1,000 wounded, and 5,000 captured

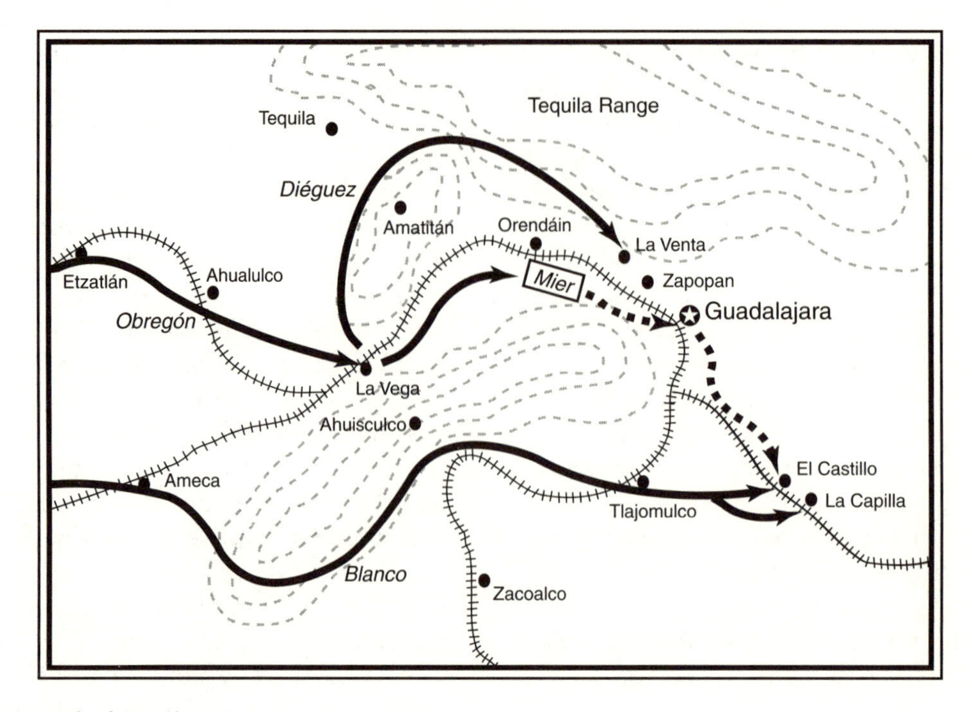

Battle of Orendáin

along with 16 field pieces, 18 trains, and 40 locomotives. The revolutionaries enter Guadalajara the same day.

10 JULY 1914. Fidencio Hernández and Guillermo Meixueiro—Conservative backers of the exiled Félix Díaz—raise three brigades in Oaxaca, capture Etla and Tlacolula, then compel its Huertista governor to resign.

14 JULY 1914. Following the twin disasters at Zacatecas and Orendáin, Huerta resigns the presidency, appointing Francisco S. Carvajal as interim successor. Shortly thereafter he flees Mexico City to Puerto Mexico and boards the German cruiser *Dresden,* eventually gaining asylum in Spain.

18 JULY 1914. Obregón assaults the federal garrison within the capital of Colima.

20 JULY 1914. Pablo González's Ejército del Noreste, or Army of the Northeast, takes the city of San Luis Potosí without opposition.

21 JULY 1914. Obregón besieges Manzanillo (Colima).

1 AUGUST 1914. Obregón's Army of the Northwest unites with Pablo González's Army of the Northeast at Querétaro, driving to Mexico City together.

13 AUGUST 1914. At Teoloyucan, outside Mexico City, Obregón signs a treaty with a representative from the federal government dissolving the Huertista administration and much of the regular army. (Only those troops deployed south of the capital to contain Zapata's peasant revolutionaries are kept in position.)

18 AUGUST 1914. Obregón's 18,000-man Army of the Northwest enters Mexico City in triumph.

20 AUGUST 1914. Carranza enters Mexico City and assumes office as president next day.

24 AUGUST 1914. The 47-year-old governor of Sonora, José María Maytorena—angered by Carranza's reproofs—attacks the border town of Nogales with 2,000 men, driving its garrison under General Hill and 36-year-old Col. Plutarco Elías Calles (future president of Mexico) back into Agua Prieta and Naco. Villa and Obregón travel by train through El Paso (Texas) in an unsuccessful bid to mediate.

5 SEPTEMBER 1914. Carranza, who has refused to allow Zapata access to Mexico City, rejects the leader's land claims in the name of peasant followers.

8 SEPTEMBER 1914. From his Cuernavaca headquarters, Zapata defies Carranza's self-proclaimed rule and begins distributing land to Morelos's peasants.

11 SEPTEMBER 1914. Mazatlán (Sinaloa) is stormed by anti-Carranza troops and is carried three days later.

Obregón—the mustachioed figure in a gray uniform seated on the left—and Villa (far right) negotiate with renegade Governor Maytorena, whose back is to the tent pole.

22 SEPTEMBER 1914. Villa also refuses to acknowledge Carranza as president; neither his followers nor the Zapatistas attend the constitutional convention held in Mexico City on 1 October.

6 NOVEMBER 1914. The constitutional convention—now transferred out of Mexico City into neutral Aguascalientes—recognizes the 34-year-old "general" (and former mine foreman) Eulalio Gutiérrez as interim president of Mexico. Carranza refuses to accept, so at 6:15 P.M. on 10 November he is labeled a rebel, and Gutiérrez appoints Villa "head of military operations" to drive Carranza out of Mexico.

12 NOVEMBER 1914. Zapata declares war against Carranza.

13 NOVEMBER 1914. American Secretary of State Bryan announces that Veracruz will be evacuated within ten days.

14 NOVEMBER 1914. Carrancista Gen. Luis Jiménez Figueroa seizes Oaxaca City, but four days later he is besieged inside El Fortín Citadel by three brigades of local revolutionaries under Meixueiro. They compel Jimémez Figueroa to flee after nightfall, overtaking and killing him at Tehuacán by 2 December.

18 NOVEMBER 1914. Threatened by the simultaneous advance of Villa's División del Norte and Zapata's guerrillas out of the southwest, Carranza quits his temporary Orizaba encampment for Veracruz.

23 NOVEMBER 1914. This morning the last of Funston's American troops depart Veracruz; Gen. Cándido Aguilar's division arrives at noon to reestablish Mexican control.

24 NOVEMBER 1914. Obregón's depleted 4,000-man garrison abandons Mexico City for Veracruz; Zapata occupies the capital's southern suburbs without opposition two days later. Carranza establishes his provisional government in Veracruz the same day (26 November).

1 DECEMBER 1914. Villa appears at Mexico City's northern suburb of Tacuba and, three days later, meets Zapata at Xochimilco. On 6 December their combined armies—totaling perhaps 50,000—parade through the capital.

12 DECEMBER 1914. Carrancista General Diéguez evacuates Guadalajara for Ciudad Guzmán, thereby allowing a Villista contingent to occupy the city uncontested five days later.

31 DECEMBER 1914. General Jesús Carranza—younger brother of Venustiano, sent to pacify the isthmus of Tehuantepec—is betrayed by local subordinate Gen. Alfonso Santibáñez and held for ransom. When Venustiano Carranza refuses to pay and sends a column of troops in pursuit, his brother is murdered at Xambao Inn (Oaxaca); Santibáñez and most of his followers then disperse into the hills.

5 JANUARY 1915. After defeating a depleted Zapatista garrison at Tecamachalco, Obregón—now "general in chief" of Carranza's army—takes Puebla City with 12,000 troops.

17 JANUARY 1915. ***Guadalajara.*** Having united with Murguía, Diéguez leads 9,000 Carrancistas north through central Jalisco to assault its capital. In a two-day battle raging over Cuatro, Gachupín, and Santa María Hills, Diéguez defeats Guadalajara's 10,000 Villista defenders under Julián Medina, Melitón F. Ortega, and Contreras, reoccupying the city.

28 JANUARY 1915. Obregón reenters Mexico City, which had been abandoned earlier by both Villista and Zapatista occupiers; their rival government transfers to Cuernavaca (Morelos) four days later.

30 JANUARY 1915. Guadalajara is hit by 3,500 Villista raiders, only to be ejected by its Carrancista garrison; 400 dead are left behind.

11 FEBRUARY 1915. Because of mounting pressure from Villa, Diéguez evacuates Guadalajara for Ciudad Guzmán but retains Jalisco's capital through a series of minor victories at El Volcán, Tuxpan, Nextipac, and Santa Ana. His Carrancistas return to Guadalajara six days later.

10 MARCH 1915. Obregón abandons starving Mexico City and reaches Tula (Hidalgo) next day, his forces massing at nearby Cazadero a fortnight later.

1 APRIL 1915. Obregón occupies Querétaro City then Celaya (Guanajuato) three days later, where he learns that Villa's approaching army is 30 miles farther west, having just entered Irapuato.

6 APRIL 1915. ***Celaya.*** This morning Villa departs Salamanca with 20,000 men and 22 artillery pieces in

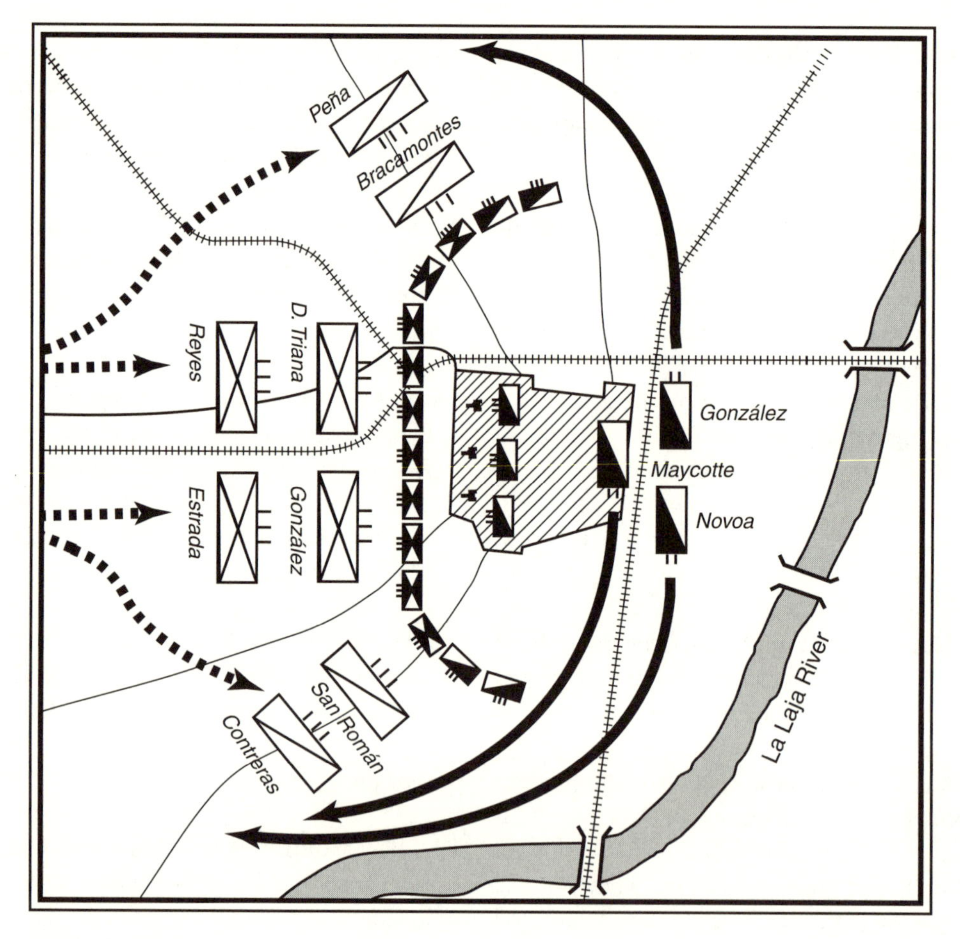

First battle of Celaya

three columns, driving directly toward Obregón, who is waiting 20 miles farther east at Celaya. Although the latter commands only 6,000 cavalry, 5,000 infantry, 86 machine guns, and 13 cannons, his army is much more disciplined and better organized than is Villa's unwieldy horde. By 2:00 P.M. this afternoon advance elements of the Villista army are arriving on the plains west of Celaya and decimating Fortunato Maycotte's brigade, quartered at El Guaje railway station. Obregón sallies by train to rescue his subordinate, the battle becoming fully joined two hours later as more and more units arrive on each side.

Throughout the night both armies blaze at one another in the darkness, then on the morning of 7 April Villa sends repeated waves against Obregón's lines, which pushes them back but fails to break through. Realizing that Villa has committed his entire strength, Obregón sends Maycotte and Novoa's cavalry brigades on a flanking movement to the south, with González's to the north, thus threatening Villa's rear. The cavalry pincers oblige the attackers to reboard trains for Irapuato, leaving behind 1,800 killed, 3,000 wounded, and 500 captured. Obregón's losses total 557 killed and 365 injured (313 and 157, respectively, from Maycotte's trapped contingent at El Guaje).

Obregón retires to his Celaya trenches while Villa—by recalling contingents from Jalisco—rebuilds his army over the next few days to 30,000 men and even attempts to telephone Obregón—only to be answered with an obscenity. The latter, through reinforcements from Veracruz, raises his numbers to 15,000, with his cavalry hidden farther east in a forest. On 13 April Villa resumes the offensive, surrounding Celaya and furiously attacking Obregón's lines throughout 14–15 April from 400 yards. The defenders once more launch a massive cavalry encirclement to the north with Gen. Cesáreo Castro's division, prompting Villa's exhausted followers to flee west into the night, leaving behind 4,000 dead, 6,000 prisoners, 1,000 horses, and their artillery.

19 APRIL 1915. Obregón occupies Salamanca (Guanajuato) and Irapuato two days later; Villa's shattered División del Norte retreats northwest toward Aguascalientes.

25 APRIL 1915. An Obregonista column occupies Guanajuato City.

28 APRIL 1915. Obregón enters Silao (Guanajuato) with his main army and next day contacts Villista forces farther northwest. Now leery of their opponent, the latter skirmish with Obregón's advance outposts over the next month, allowing Villa to regroup near León.

22 MAY 1915. Villa attacks Obregón in the Trinidad Plains northwest of Silao (Guanajuato), breaking off before any decision can be reached.

1 JUNE 1915. ***Trinidad.*** Having massed 19,500 riders and 6,000 infantry around León (Guanajuato), Villa leaves a sizable garrison behind while another portion fights a diversionary action against Obregón out in the Trinidad Plains. Such encounters have become relatively commonplace this past month, but Villa adds a bold new variant by personally leading a huge cavalry body through the hills to surprise Obregón's base at Silao, destroying trains, bridges, and telegraphs in his rear.

Obregón—with 9,400 cavalry and 14,300 infantry stretched out over an immense territory—finds this disruption worrisome, especially as it is followed by a general attack against all his forces. Fighting is raging two days later, when Obregón has his right arm shredded by a Villista shell while conferring with his officers at Santa Ana del Conde Hacienda. Hill succeeds him, and after Villa's forces exhaust their strength and ammunition in repeated assaults, he launches a massive counterattack on 5 June that routs the Villistas and breaks through to León. Having sustained 8,000 casualties—triple those of Obregón and Hill—Villa draws off north.

(Obregón's right hand, amputated by Surgeon Gen. Enrique Osornio Camarena, is today preserved in Mexico City.)

2 JUNE 1915. U.S. Pres. Woodrow Wilson gives a speech that seemingly threatens renewed intervention if Mexico's warring factions cannot achieve peace.

3 JUNE 1915. Oaxaca declares itself a sovereign state, refusing to acknowledge the authority of Carranza or any other federal leader.

8 JUNE 1915. Villista Gen. Máximo García evacuates Ciudad Victoria (Tamaulipas), his Zapatista subordinate Alberto Carrera Torres being overtaken shortly thereafter and executed.

24 JUNE 1915. Huerta and Orozco are arrested by U.S. authorities in El Paso (Texas) for violating American neutrality laws by plotting to rejoin the fighting in Mexico.

29–30 JUNE 1915. During some clashes with Villista irregulars around Lagunas de Moreno (Jalisco) Diéguez is severely wounded.

JUNE 1915. As Villa's defeated División del Norte limps north, his 35-year-old henchman Rodolfo Fierro sends a false telegram—over Obregón's signature—to the León garrison commander, ordering him to evacuate. This allows Fierro to reenter town unopposed shortly thereafter with 4,000 riders and then rampage southeast through Silao, Irapuato, Salamanca, Celaya, Querétaro, and San Juan del Río, ripping up tracks and burning bridges. At Tula (Hidalgo), he pulverizes a 1,500-man garrison then joins forces with Roque González Garza.

Obregón subordinate Pablo González feels so threatened by the incursion that he abandons Mexico City, although Fierro's small numbers do not permit any designs against the capital.

6 JULY 1915. After a brief convalescence Obregón resumes command of his army, driving north in pursuit of Villa.

8 JULY 1915. Obregón defeats Villa's rearguard at Calvillo Ravine then occupies Aguascalientes City two days later, gaining considerable stores.

28 JULY 1915. While retiring north after his successful raid into central Mexico, Fierro's 4,000 riders blunder into Obregón in the Mariscala Hills near Querétaro; he is badly beaten two days later at Jerécuaro, rejoining Villa with only 1,000 men.

30 JULY 1915. A Zapatista contingent under Gen. Amador Salazar is defeated near Mexico City.

10 AUGUST 1915. Obregón subordinate Pablo González reoccupies Mexico City.

11 AUGUST 1915. The new U.S. secretary of state, Robert Lansing, joined by diplomatic representatives from Argentina, Bolivia, Brazil, Chile, Guatemala, and Uruguay, calls on Mexico's factions to make peace. Carranza rejects the proposal one month later, branding it interference in Mexico's internal affairs.

30 AUGUST 1915. Outside El Paso (Texas), the exiled Orozco is murdered with four companions.

4 SEPTEMBER 1915. Obregón wins a clash at La Angostura (site of the Battle of Buena Vista; *see* 22 February 1847 under Mexican-American War in Part 7). Shortly thereafter he reoccupies Saltillo.

19 OCTOBER 1915. The United States, Argentina, Bolivia, Brazil, Chile, Guatemala, and Uruguay recognize Carranza as de facto president of Mexico.

1–2 NOVEMBER 1915. ***Agua Prieta.*** After a lengthy retreat north, Villa's 6,000 remaining troops make four nocturnal assaults against Calles's 6,500 fresh Carrancista defenders at Agua Prieta (Sonora). The latter win easily, killing or wounding 600 half-starved attackers; another 400 desert Villa as he retires southwest to Hermosillo on 3 November.

8 NOVEMBER 1915. Seeking to reassert federal rule over the breakaway state of Oaxaca (*see* 3 June 1915), Carrancista Gen. Jesús Agustín Castro departs Chiapas with the 21st Division and seizes Salina Cruz; he is soon followed by other contingents.

18 NOVEMBER 1915. ***Hermosillo.*** Villa's 5,000 survivors fight an inconclusive but damaging battle at Alamito—outside Sonora's capital of Hermosillo—against a superior Carrancista force under Diéguez. Four days later Villa launches an all-out, 30-hour assault against Hermosillo's garrison, during which his remaining troops are annihilated. He retires east into the mountains with only 1,400 followers, eventually reaching Chihuahua City and disbanding his column.

24 DECEMBER 1915. Villa disappears from Chihuahua City eight days before Carrancista General Treviño arrives to reoccupy it.

16 JANUARY 1916. Villa subordinates Pablo López and Rafael Castro attack a train at Santa Isabel—bound from Chihuahua City to the Cusihuiriáchic mining camp—in the process massacring 16 American passengers, which provokes outrage in neighboring Texas.

2 MARCH 1916. After pushing inland from Puerto Angel (Oaxaca), a small Carrancista army under Gens. Macario M. Hernández and Juan José Baños defeats a separatist force at Ocotlán then, three days later, occupies deserted Oaxaca City. Castro arrives by 15 March to assume office as governor.

9 MARCH 1916. ***Columbus Raid.*** In predawn hours Villa crosses the border several miles west of Columbus (New Mexico), sending 500 riders to at-

tack the town from three directions at 4:00 A.M. His followers assault the encampment of six troops—200 soldiers—of Col. H. J. Slocum's 13th U.S. Cavalry Regiment, loot numerous buildings and corrals, then set fire to Columbus's business district before withdrawing. Despite being surprised, the defenders kill about 100 Villistas. Eighteen Americans—ten of them civilians—are dead, another eight wounded.

Villa's strike not only vaults his name back into prominence but also belies the Carrancista claim to have pacified Mexico. And any U.S. pursuit onto Mexican soil will be resented by many patriots because of the recent Veracruz intervention (*see* 21 April 1914), thus drawing new recruits into Villa's ranks—while alienating Carranza from popular opinion if he should help hunt down the raiders.

13 MARCH 1916. A Carrancista column penetrating inland from Acapulco compels Zapatista General Pacheco to evacuate Huitzilac (Morelos), for which he is subsequently executed by de la O.

15 MARCH 1916. ***Pershing's "Wild Goose Chase."*** Two columns of 3,000 U.S. troops—the 13th Cavalry, 6th and 16th Infantry Regiments, plus 1st Artillery Battery—cross the border at Palomas (Chihuahua) to pursue Villa and punish his Columbus raid. Carranza offers Wilson very grudging cooperation while urging his own commanders to capture the renegade and end the excuse for American intervention.

Villa proves elusive, his troops disappearing into the hills and adopting guerrilla tactics. The local Mexican populace also views the U.S. incursion with hostility. On 12 April an American scouting party—two troops of 13th Cavalry under Maj. Frank Tompkins—approach Parral (Chihuahua), only to be set upon by a mob shouting "¡Viva Villa!" and "¡Viva México!" Three American soldiers are killed and seven wounded compared to perhaps 40 Mexican casualties.

Still more units join Pershing, so that by late April he reaches Casas Grandes with 9,000 soldiers: eight cavalry and five infantry regiments plus five artillery batteries and numerous auxiliaries (including eight Jenny biplanes of the 1st Provisional Aero Squadron out of San Antonio, Texas). In May the Americans skirmish with a small Villista force at Ojos Azules Ranch, but it quickly disappears. Early in June Villa emerges from hiding to overrun the Carrancista garrison of Gen. José Cavazos at Guerrero (Chihuahua), being wounded in the right leg. Villa orders his men to scatter and reassemble at San Juan Bautista—on the Durango border—by 6 July while he retires into a cave to convalesce.

Shortly thereafter Carranza's government informs Pershing that further penetrations west, south, or east

Double column of Pershing's troops marching through the stark landscape of northern Mexico

will be contested. On 20 June two troops of 10th Cavalry—84 black troopers under Capt. Charles T. Boyd—probe east toward Villa Ahumada, believing Villa may be there. At Carrizal they collide with a Carrancista garrison under Gen. Félix U. Gómez, who deploys his troops and forbids the Americans to advance. Boyd insists and loses his life in the ensuing exchange, during which nine of his men are also killed, ten wounded, and 23 captured. Mexican losses total 74 dead, including Gómez.

This incident halts Pershing's operations, as Washington must placate an incensed Mexican government. For the next seven months the American expeditionary force—now numbering 12,000 men and sarcastically dubbed the "Perishing Expedition"—remains largely immobile, 150 miles deep in Mexico. The U.S. government announces its withdrawal on 28 January 1917; eight days later the last American troops depart Chihuahua.

16 APRIL 1916. Zapatista General Salazar is killed by a stray round near Yautepec (Morelos).

2 MAY 1916. ***Morelos Sweep.*** Carrancista Gen. Pablo González launches an offensive—complete with air support—against the Zapatistas in Morelos, sending his Ejército del Este (Eastern Army) into this territory. His 30,000 troops occupy almost every major town within the next four days—Jojutla not falling until 25 May; he then establishes concentration camps to stifle guerrilla resistance. By the end of May 1,500 captives are on their way to incarceration at Mexico City, and much of Morelos lies looted or destroyed.

8 MAY 1916. González's subordinate, Rafael Cepeda, executes 225 Zapatista prisoners in Jiutepec (Morelos).

15 MAY 1916. Félix Díaz—nephew of Oaxaca's native son, former Pres. Porfirio Díaz—returns from exile and joins the state's separatist movement. His Ejército Reorganizador Nacional (National Reorganizer Army) is promptly defeated by Carrancista forces at Yucucundo in June and at Tlalcolula in July, obliging Díaz to retreat northeast toward the Chiapas-Veracruz border.

MID-JUNE 1916. González's forces overrun Tlaltizapán—Zapata's main hideout, south of Cuernavaca (Morelos)—slaughtering 286 unarmed men, women, and children.

6 JULY 1916. Villa rejoins his followers—now 1,000 men—at San Juan Bautista (Chihuahua-Durango border), then leads them north to forage for supplies.

16 JULY 1916. Despite being seriously weakened by González's offensive, a Zapatista column attacks the Carrancista garrison at Tlayacapan (Morelos), retiring after six hours' heavy fighting to assault Tlaltizapán next day.

1 AUGUST 1916. Carranza calls out troops to put down a general strike in Mexico City.

16 SEPTEMBER 1916. The previous night, Villa infiltrated 1,000 riders into Chihuahua City. At 3:00 A.M. on 16 September—Mexico's Independence Day—he surprises its Carrancista garrison under Treviño. After seizing much booty, giving a speech from the municipal balcony, and recruiting an additional 1,500 men, Villa disappears as suddenly as he arrived.

LATE SEPTEMBER 1916. In order to relieve his despairing followers in Morelos, Zapata advances across the mountains to threaten Mexico City, in turn prompting Carrancista Col. Jesús María Guajardo to execute 180 captives in Tlaltizapán and raze much of its district.

4 OCTOBER 1916. Zapata seizes the Xochimilco pumping station, cutting off much of Mexico City's water supply; he retires after destroying the rail lines at Peña Pobre.

7 NOVEMBER 1916. Zapatista guerrillas blow up a train, killing more than 400 passengers.

23 NOVEMBER 1916. Villa again captures Chihuahua City, occupying it for a week before emerging to confront Murguía's approaching Carrancista army on Horcasitas Plain. In a seven-hour engagement on 1 December Villa is badly beaten and compelled to abandon a trainload of provisions while retreating to Satevó.

1 DECEMBER 1916. ***Zapata's Resurrection.*** With González's occupation forces now grown weak due to neglect, desertion, and disease—7,000 Carrancistas reportedly lying sick of malaria—Zapata's battered forces are able to recuperate Tlaltizapán and launch a major offensive to regain control over the state of Morelos.

MID-DECEMBER 1916. Villa surprises the Carrancista garrison at Torreón (Coahuila), overrunning its defenses from three directions and killing two generals while driving a third to suicide. After extorting a loan from the inhabitants, the raiders depart abruptly.

7 JANUARY 1917. Villa raids Santa Rosalía (Coahuila), massacring 300 Carrancista prisoners and Chinese civilians.

This same day, Zapata reoccupies Jonacatepec (Morelos), followed by Yautepec next day, Cuautla on 10 January, and numerous other towns—including Cuernavaca.

1 MAY 1917. After holding an election on 11 March in which he receives 198,000 of 250,000 votes cast—from a pool of 3 million potential voters—Carranza officially assumes the presidency. Obregón retires to private life at Navojoa (Sonora).

7 MAY 1917. Longtime Zapata subordinate Leonardo Vázquez is executed at Buenavista de Cuéllar (Morelos) for turning against his former chief, this same fate befalling Zapata's secretary, Otilio Montaño, 11 days later.

Zapata's secretary Otilio Montaño in better days, posing in revolutionary garb

18 JUNE 1917. With supporters falling away, Zapata's brother, Eufemio, is murdered by a turncoat at Cuautla (Morelos).

19 NOVEMBER 1917. Pablo González recaptures Cuautla (Morelos) then soon overwhelms the Zapatista garrisons at Jonacatepec and Zacualpan de Amilpas.

8 FEBRUARY 1918. After being captured at San Bernardino (Oaxaca), separatist Gen. Alberto Córdova is executed in the state capital by a Carrancista firing squad.

OCTOBER 1918. González advances out of Cuautla (Morelos) with 11,000 Carrancistas, sweeping through Zapatista strongholds now weakened by starvation and disease—mostly due to an outbreak of Spanish influenza. Yautepec, Jojutla, Cuernavaca, Tetecala, and Tlaltizapán fall in quick succession, obliging Zapata to flee into the mountains with a handful of adherents.

11 DECEMBER 1918. Former Porfirian General Ángeles returns from exile in the United States and attempts to organize yet another revolution with Villa.

6 APRIL 1919. ***End of Zapata.*** In a prearranged plan, Pablo González departs Cuautla (Morelos) for Mexico City; this same night his supposedly disgruntled subordinate—Colonel Guajardo—mutinies with the 600-man 5th Cavalry Regiment, deserting to the southeast. The night of 8–9 April Guajardo seemingly confirms his switched allegiance by attacking Jonacatepec, killing a dozen Carrancista defenders while losing seven of his own men. He executes 59 followers of the former Zapatista Victoriano Bárcenas at Mancornadero before being approached—15 miles south of Jonacatepec, at Pastor railway station—by the fugitive Zapata (who has been corresponding with Guajardo for several weeks about joining the revolutionary cause).

The contingents continue together, Guajardo and his cavalry camping at San Juan Chinameca Hacienda while Zapata remains in Tepalcingo with his troops. Next morning a false alarm prompts the rebel chief to send 140 men on patrol, so when he is invited to dine with Guajardo inside Chinameca's walls at 1:30 P.M. he arrives with only a ten-man escort. The 5th Regiment's color guard, rather than fire a salute, blasts two volleys into Zapata, killing him instantly. Guajardo carries his body back to Cuautla on a mule, displaying it in the main square; he is rewarded by González with promotion to brigadier and 50,000 pesos—which he shares with his troopers.

31 MAY 1919. Separatist Gov. José Inés Dávila is defeated and killed at Ixtayutla (Oaxaca), his head being displayed in the state capital.

1 JUNE 1919. In Nogales (Sonora), Obregón announces he will contest the presidency in Mexico's forthcoming elections, running against Carranza's handpicked successor, Ignacio Bonillas. The president—already jealous of Obregón's popularity—actively obstructs the campaign.

17 JUNE 1919. Zapatista resistance having ceased with the death of the chief, Pablo González departs Morelos for Puebla, leaving occupation duties to subordinates.

JUNE 1919. Villa and Ángeles capture the border city of Juárez, only to be driven out by U.S. troops from adjacent El Paso (Texas)—this intervention again provoking a downturn in relations between Mexico City and Washington.

15 NOVEMBER 1919. Ángeles is captured in hiding near Balleza (Chihuahua), being executed 11 days later in the state capital on Carranza's orders despite widespread pleas for clemency.

27 DECEMBER 1919. Meixueiro, one of the last remaining separatist leaders in Oaxaca, surrenders to Pablo González.

JANUARY 1920. Pablo González announces that he too will run for president, on the Liga Democrática (Democratic League) ticket.

27 MARCH 1920. Protesting the arrest of 70 prominent Obregonistas in Mexico City, de la O blows up a train heading for Cuernavaca (Morelos). Among the survivors is the U.S. embassy's military attaché, who is held hostage. Next day de la O's troops sack Milpa Alta before disappearing into the hills.

EARLY APRIL 1920. Obregón is made to appear before a military tribunal in Mexico City, falsely accused of conspiring to overthrow the government with Col. Roberto Cejudo—one of Félix Díaz's minions and recently released from incarceration by Carranza's police.

13 APRIL 1920. ***Obregón's Revolt.*** After being repeatedly menaced by Carranza's police, Obregón flees Mexico City in disguise and finds sanctuary at Iguala (Guerrero) with generals Rómulo Figueroa and Maycotte. One week later he issues a proclamation from Chilpancingo calling for an uprising to depose the Carranza regime. Supporters rally to Obregón's side—including Villa, who helps capture Chihuahua City from its Carrancista garrison on 28–29 April.

4 MAY 1920. In the state of Puebla, Pablo González rises against Carranza.

7 MAY 1920. ***Carranza's Demise.*** With Murguía attempting to stave off encroaching Obregonista armies at Otumba (30 miles outside Mexico City), Carranza abandons his capital for Veracruz aboard a 15-mile-long train convoy bearing 10,000 adherents and the national treasury. At nearby Guadalupe, a dynamite-laden locomotive smashes into the lead train that afternoon, killing 200 soldiers, after which Guajardo (Zapata's killer) attacks Carranza's convoy with his cavalry troop.

The presidential column fights through to Apizaco (Tlaxcala) by next day, only 3,000 infantry, 1,100 cavalry, and two field pieces remaining. Proceeding east into the state of Puebla, another Obregonista attack occurs at San Marcos, where Carranza leaves some military cadets to fight a rearguard action. A lengthier engagement erupts at Rinconada at dawn on 11 May, Carranza having a horse shot out from under him.

Finally, his convoy is halted the morning of 14 May at Aljibes (Puebla), the tracks ahead having been destroyed by Guadalupe Sánchez; Treviño presses in from the rear—both generals commanding 20,000 troops between them. Unable to travel farther by rail, Carranza flees north into the hills with 100 followers, being joined at the village of La Unión by guerrilla chief Rodolfo Herrero. Professing loyalty, the latter leads Carranza to Tlaxcalantongo, only to murder the fallen president at 4:00 A.M. on Friday, 21 May, by firing through the back of the hut where he is sleeping.

15 MAY 1920. Pablo González withdraws his candidacy for president and retires to private life at Monterrey (Nuevo León).

24 MAY 1920. The 39-year-old governor of Sonora, Adolfo de la Huerta, is appointed interim president until elections can be held on 5 September.

2 JULY 1920. In Gómez Palacio (Durango), Guajardo—assigned to pursue Villa's guerrillas in northern Mexico—mutinies against the federal government. Advancing northeast to Monterrey (Nuevo León), his rapidly dwindling force prompts Guajardo to allege that he will soon be joined by retired Gen. Pablo González, leading to the subsequent arrest of both officers. Guajardo is executed almost immediately; González is released by President de la Huerta.

22 JULY 1920. Villa occupies Sabinas (Coahuila) with 700 troops—after destroying its rail lines to prevent any surprise by *federales*—then telegraphs President de la Huerta, requesting amnesty. The latter deeds him the 25,000-acre estate of Canutillo (Durango-Chihuahua border) and pays off his followers, thereby allowing Villa to retire to private life.

30 NOVEMBER 1920. After a highly successful campaign Obregón is inaugurated president.

20 JULY 1923. Driving his Dodge touring car back to Canutillo from Parral (Chihuahua), Villa and six bodyguards are ambushed at 7:20 A.M. at the corner of Zaragoza and Gabino Barreda Streets by eight assassins led by Melitón Lozoya—hired by local landowner Jesús Salas Barrazas (allegedly with the connivance of Obregón's interior minister, Calles). They kill the former guerrilla chief and most of his men.

23 NOVEMBER 1923. Obregón's disaffected former finance secretary, de la Huerta, announces his bid for the presidency, bringing him into conflict with former fellow minister Calles—now Obregón's designated heir apparent.

30 NOVEMBER 1923. ***De la Huerta Uprising.*** In Guerrero, Figueroa rebels against the federal government. He is soon joined by more generals in other states, and four days later de la Huerta secretly slips out of Mexico City to Veracruz by train.

On 7 December de la Huerta accuses Obregón and Calles of corruption, adding to the call for their overthrow. About 60 percent of Mexico's 110,000-man federal army eventually sides with the rebels, but Obregón's control over the treasury ensures his loyalists remain abundantly supplied with modern weapons.

28 JANUARY 1924. De la Huertista Gen. Guadalupe Sánchez is defeated at the Battle of Esperanza (Veracruz).

4 FEBRUARY 1924. Córdoba (Veracruz) falls to Obregón's forces.

5 FEBRUARY 1924. De la Huerta and his skeleton government quit Veracruz to set up their administration in Frontera (Tabasco).

12 MARCH 1924. De la Huerta flees Mexico, entering Key West (Florida) in disguise; he eventually establishes a singing academy in Los Angeles (California).

24 MARCH 1924. The last de la Huertista army under Sánchez is annihilated, the general being killed. During the next three months surviving rebels are hunted down and exterminated, including many once-famous officers: Diéguez, Chao, Maycotte, Salvador Alvarado, Ramón Treviño, José Rentería Luviano, and Rafael Buelna. In all, 7,000 people lose their lives during the abortive insurrection.

30 NOVEMBER 1924. After winning the presidential election Calles is sworn in to office.

1924. Minor revolts and mutinies continue to plague Mexico for a number of years, but large-scale fighting has run its course by 1918—mostly due to exhaustion. Some measure of Mexico's suffering can be judged by the fact that its population shrinks from 15.1 million in 1910 to 14.2 million by 1920.

WORLD WAR I (1914–1918)

THANKS TO ITS PHYSICAL DISTANCE FROM EUROPE, the Americas are spared much of this conflict until three years into the war, when the United States finally throws its weight behind Britain, France, and the other allies, effectively hastening Germany's collapse. Prior to U.S. intervention most of the fighting in the New World consists of isolated naval encounters.

6 AUGUST 1914. German Capt. Erich Köhler's light cruiser *Karlsruhe* rendezvouses 120 miles north of Watling Island (Bahamas) with the 25,000-ton liner *Kronprinz Wilhelm,* transferring two 3.4-inch guns aboard to convert the latter ship into an armed commerce raider.

The operation is interrupted at 11:00 A.M. by the British heavy cruiser *Suffolk,* which chases the German vessels north. Capt. B. H. Fanshawe's light cruiser *Bristol* then intercepts *Karlsruhe* at 8:15 P.M., opening fire at a range of six miles on a moonlit night; Fanshawe is unable to cripple Köhler's warship before it makes good its escape. On 9 August *Karlsruhe* safely reaches Puerto Rico.

13 AUGUST 1914. *Karlsruhe* is sighted off Curaçao; the German light cruiser *Dresden* of Captain Lüdecke is sighted off the mouth of the Amazon.

18 AUGUST 1914. After prowling for a week off San Francisco (California), Captain Haun's German light cruiser *Leipzig* reaches the Galapagos Islands. One week later it sinks a merchant vessel bearing sugar, and by 28 August it is hovering off Peru, hoping to intercept more British shipping.

23 AUGUST 1914. British Rear Admiral Craddock reaches the West Indian island of Saint Lucia with the heavy cruiser *Good Hope* to unite with the heavy cruiser *Berwick* and light cruiser *Bristol,* plus the 10,000-ton French cruisers *Descartes* and *Condé,* to hunt down the elusive German commerce raiders.

4 SEPTEMBER 1914. After sinking a pair of freighters off the River Plate, *Dresden* rendezvouses with the supply ship *Santa Isabel* at Orange Bay (in the Strait of Magellan) before striking out into the Pacific on 18 September.

14 SEPTEMBER 1914. The British armed merchant cruiser *Carmania* catches the German armed merchant cruiser *Cap Trafalgar* coaling off Trinidade Island (Brazil), sinking it.

18 SEPTEMBER 1914. Craddock quits Montevideo with the heavy cruisers *Good Hope* (flag) and *Monmouth,* the light cruiser *Glasgow,* and the armed merchant cruiser *Otranto* to pursue *Dresden* around the Strait of Magellan.

2–3 OCTOBER 1914. *Dresden* enters the Pacific from the Atlantic and contacts *Leipzig* by wireless from Más Afuera Island (modern Selkirk Island, westernmost of the Juan Fernández grouping), proposing a rendezvous at Easter Island.

12 OCTOBER 1914. A small but powerful German squadron under 53-year-old Vice Adm. Maximilien Graf von Spee, arrives at Easter Island, consisting of the heavy cruisers *Scharnhorst* and *Gneisenau,* the light cruiser *Nürnberg,* plus some supply ships. The force was originally stationed in China as the Kaiser's East Asiatic Squadron but was driven across the Pacific by Britain, France, and Japan's declarations of war. The warships now join with *Dreden* and *Leipzig* and, after

The German light cruiser Leipzig *coaling at Guaymas, Mexico, 8 September 1914*

coaling, set sail for the South American mainland on 18 October.

26 OCTOBER 1914. Von Spee arrives off Más Afuera (Selkirk Island, Chile), being unexpectedly rejoined by the armed merchant cruiser *Prinz Eitel Friedrich,* which is detached to Valparaíso when the rest of the squadron steers east two days later.

29 OCTOBER 1914. ***Coronel.*** HMS *Glasgow* detects German wireless traffic off Chile, prompting Craddock to sail north from Vallenar early next morning with *Good Hope* and *Monmouth*—but without awaiting the elderly battleship *Canopus,* which is rounding Cape Horn, as the British expect to encounter nothing more than the lone light cruiser *Dresden.* Instead, at 4:20 P.M. on 1 November Craddock meets almost all of Von Spee's squadron (*Nürnberg* being detached):

Ship	*Tons*	*Armament*	*Men*	*Commander*
Scharnhorst (flag)	11,600	eight 8-inch, six 6-inch	765	F. Schulz
Gneisenau	11,600	eight 8-inch, six 6-inch	765	Maerker
Dresden	3,650	ten 4-inch	360	Lüdecke
Nürnberg	3,550	ten 4-inch	320	K. von Schönberg
Leipzig	3,250	ten 4-inch	290	Haun

These clearly outclass the older British quartet:

Ship	*Tons*	*Armament*	*Men*	*Commander*
Good Hope (flag)	14,100	two 9-inch, 16 6-inch	900	P. Francklin
Monmouth	9,800	14 6-inch	675	Frank Brandt
Glasgow	4,800	two 6-inch, ten 4-inch	450	J. Luce
Otranto (liner)	12,000	eight 5-inch	?	H. M. Edwards

Nevertheless, at 5:00 P.M. Craddock bravely decides to engage until sundown, rather than lose contact. Forming a single line at 5:45 P.M., the Royal Navy vessels circle west, only to become silhouetted against the setting sun and fired upon at long range one hour and 15 minutes later. Charging in a desperate bid to close, the British suffer heavily, *Monmouth* yawing ablaze out of the line by 7:45 P.M.; *Good Hope* explodes five minutes later.

At this point *Glasgow* speeds away to warn *Canopus,* and at 9:20 P.M. *Nürnberg* overtakes the crippled *Monmouth,* sending it to the bottom with all hands eight minutes later. The Germans suffer only three wounded, although they consume half their irreplaceable heavy rounds. *Canopus, Glasgow,* and *Otranto* slowly retreat to Port Stanley in the Falklands, hoping to meet reinforcements.

3 NOVEMBER 1914. Von Spee enters Valparaíso with *Scharnhorst, Gneisenau,* and *Nürnberg; Dresden* and *Leipzig* return to Más Afuera (Selkirk) Island.

4 NOVEMBER 1914. *Karlsruhe* unexpectedly explodes and sinks east of Barbados after a detonation in its forward magazines.

15 NOVEMBER 1914. Von Spee quits Más Afuera (Selkirk) Island with his squadron, reaching San Quintín Bay (Chile) six days later to coal.

24 NOVEMBER 1914. The 55-year-old Vice Adm. Sir Doveton Sturdee reaches the Abrolhos Islands (Brazil) from England with the battlecruisers *Invincible* and *Inflexible* and, two days later, joins Rear Adm. A. C. Stoddart's *Defence, Cornwall, Carnarvon, Kent, Orama,* and *Edinburgh Castle* to prepare to scour the southern Pacific Coast in search of von Spee's squadron.

26 NOVEMBER 1914. Von Spee quits San Quintín Bay (Chile), encountering heavy weather that delays his rounding of Cape Horn into the South Atlantic until nightfall of 1 December. The Germans anchor off Picton Island (Argentina) until 6 December, taking on coal.

7 DECEMBER 1914. ***Falklands.*** At 10:30 A.M. Sturdee's fleet reaches Port William from Brazil in anticipation of coaling before rounding Cape Horn to hunt for Von Spee. Instead, the German squadron is sighted approaching at 7:56 next morning in an ill-timed attempt to destroy the Falklands' signaling stations. Expecting to encounter only light resistance, Von Spee is astonished to sight within this harbor:

Ship	*Tons*	*Armament*	*Men*	*Commander*
Invincible (flag)	17,250	eight 16-inch, 16 4-inch	780	T. P. H. Beamish
Inflexible	17,250	eight 16-inch, 16 4-inch	780	R. F. Phillimore
Canopus (beached)	12,950	four 12-inch, 12 6-inch	750	H.W. Grant
Carnarvon	10,850	four 7.5-inch, six 6-inch	650	H. L. d'E. Skipwith
Cornwall	9,800	14 6-inch	675	W. M. Ellerton
Kent	9,800	14 6-inch	675	J. D. Allen
Bristol	4,800	two 6-inch, ten 4-inch	450	B. H. Fanshawe
Glasgow	4,800	two 6-inch, 4-inch	450	J. Luceten
Macedonia (armed merchant cruiser)	?	?		?

The situation at Coronel is now reversed, the Germans having blundered into a superior British force. After receiving a long-range opening salvo from *Canopus,* von Spee breaks off the attack and turns east at 9:30 A.M. while detaching his supply ships to Picton Island. In the meantime, the British fleet frantically gets up steam, emerging half an hour later to pursue. *Bristol* and *Macedonia* are diverted at 11:00 A.M. to overhaul the fleeing German colliers, sinking *Baden* and *Santa Isabel* after taking off their crews; the faster *Seydlitz* escapes to internment at San Antonio (Argentina).

At 12:45 P.M. Sturdee surges forward with *Invincible* and *Inflexible,* opening fire on von Spee's main body at a range of 16,500 yards. Little more than half an hour later the German commander courageously turns to give battle with *Scharnhorst* and *Gneisenau* alone, hoping to cover the escape of his light cruisers. *Cornwall, Glasgow,* and *Kent* immediately obey earlier instructions by chasing *Dresden, Leipzig,* and *Nürnberg,* leaving the German heavy cruisers to *Invincible, Inflexible,* and *Carnarvon.*

Despite skillful handling, *Scharnhorst* finally sinks with all hands at 4:20 P.M., followed at 6:00 P.M. by *Gneisenau,* from which the British rescue 190 survivors. At 6:40 P.M. *Nürnberg* strikes to *Kent* and sinks 50 minutes later, only seven of its men being saved from the frigid waters. *Leipzig* too slips beneath the waves at 8:30 P.M., only 18 men being rescued by *Cornwall* and *Glasgow; Dresden* makes good its escape.

After searching in vain for their vanished opponent until 11 December, the British fleet returns to the Falklands; losses total a half-dozen killed and 16 wounded.

12 DECEMBER 1914. *Dresden* puts into Punta Arenas (Chile) to quickly take on coal, shifting into secluded Hewett Bay two days later.

8 MARCH 1915. HMS *Kent* sights *Dresden* 300 miles west of Coronel (Chile), losing contact at nightfall.

14 MARCH 1915. At sunrise HMSS *Kent* and *Cornwall* plus the armed merchant cruiser *Orama* enter Cumberland Bay on Más Afuera (Selkirk) Island, opening fire on the anchored *Dresden* by 8:50 A.M. His fuel bunkers empty, Captain Lüdecke sends Lt. Wilhelm Canaris—head of German intelligence during World War II and executed on Hitler's orders in 1944—to negotiate surrender terms. During the parley Lüdecke scuttles his light cruiser and escapes ashore with the crew.

7 MAY 1915. The British liner *Lusitania* is sunk near Ireland by a German submarine, claiming numerous American lives.

19 AUGUST 1915. The liner *Arabic* is sunk by a German submarine, taking down more American passengers.

18 SEPTEMBER 1915. In response to Washington's protests, Germany halts its unrestricted U-boat warfare around the British Isles.

23 FEBRUARY 1916. Germany resumes submarine attacks against merchantmen approaching England.

24 MARCH 1916. The liner *Sussex* is sunk by a U-boat, claiming more American lives and prompting another protest from Washington to Berlin one month later. Again, unrestricted submarine warfare is temporarily suspended.

1 MAY 1916. Germany resumes its U-boat attacks, this time even authorizing operations against British shipping off North America's coast despite Washington's complaints.

16 JANUARY 1917. German Foreign Minister Alfred Zimmerman sends a telegram to Ambassador von Eckhardt in Mexico City, advising him that Berlin is about to resume unrestricted submarine warfare on 1 February. If the United States should become a belligerent as a result, Germany proposes a military alliance with Mexico, whereby the latter should attack and reconquer Texas, New Mexico, and Arizona. The communiqué is intercepted and deciphered by British naval intelligence officers, who reveal its contents to Washington.

1 FEBRUARY 1917. Germany resumes unrestricted submarine warfare; two days later the United States breaks off diplomatic relations with Berlin.

26 FEBRUARY 1917. Congress is asked to approve the arming of U.S. merchant vessels, but 11 noninterventionist senators filibuster the bill into extinction.

1 MARCH 1917. The contents of the Zimmerman telegram are revealed to the world, embarrassing the German and Mexican governments.

9 MARCH 1917. Using his executive powers, President Wilson authorizes the arming of American merchant vessels.

18 MARCH 1917. Three U.S. merchantmen are sunk by German U-boats, sustaining heavy casualties. Three days later Wilson calls Congress into special session for 2 April to consider joining the ongoing hostilities.

6 APRIL 1917. The United States declares war against Germany.

7 JUNE 1917. U-boats operating out of Germany, Flanders, and the Adriatic commence an offensive against the U.S. East Coast.

SEPTEMBER 1917. The introduction of an Anglo-American convoy system in the North Atlantic effectively halts U-boat operations by 21 October 1918.

11 NOVEMBER 1918. At 11:00 A.M. Germany officially surrenders. Appalled at the monstrous loss of life incurred by modern weaponry in the trenches of Europe, the United States goes through a period of postwar isolationism, hoping to use the Atlantic and Pacific Oceans as barriers against the world's problems.

ISOLATED UPHEAVALS (1922–1939)

ALTHOUGH OVERALL TURMOIL IN THE AMERICAS continues to lessen, occasional outbursts still erupt, especially as the effects of the Great Depression of 1929 ripple through economies.

5 JULY 1922. Fort Igrejinha's garrison at Copacabana (Brazil) revolts against Pres. Epitácio Pessoa, being joined shortly thereafter by the military academy. The rebels lob a few shells against strategic targets within Rio de Janeiro before being put down by loyal troops and warships. A small group of Fort Igrejinha's youngest officers fight to the very end on its beach, becoming known as the "18 of Copacabana."

25 JANUARY 1923. Uprisings erupt throughout Brazil's Rio Grande do Sul state over alleged electoral fraud. They are resolved by December with the Pedras Altas Pact, which allows five-term Gov. Antônio Augusto Borges de Medeiros to remain in office.

5 JULY 1924. On the second anniversary of the *tenentes* (lieutenants) revolt, retired Brazilian Gen. Isidoro Dias Lopes leads São Paulo's garrison in a mutiny against the government of Pres. Artur da Silva Bernardes, being supported by much of the city's populace and isolated pockets throughout other states. Loyal troops soon approach, however, and compel the São Paulo rebels to retreat southwest on 27 July.

Lopes attempts to make a stand at the towns of Guaíra, Foz do Iguaçu, and Catanduvas (confluence of the Iguaçu and Paraná Rivers); he is eventually compelled to surrender his jungle stronghold by 27 March 1925 and melt deeper into the interior.

5 SEPTEMBER 1924. In Chile, a prolonged period of economic decline provokes military displeasure, resulting in the appointment of Gen. Luis Altamirano as interior minister. He in turn names Col. Juan P. Bennett and Adm. Francisco Neff to the cabinet, along with three civilians. The beleaguered 56-year-old Pres. Arturo Alessandri at this point proferrs his resignation, but congress refuses to accept it, instead granting him a six-month leave of absence. Determined to restore power to conservative hands, the military ministers then pass a popular labor legislation bill and in the resultant euphoria compel their civilian colleagues to resign on 10 September. Altamiro, Bennett, and Neff subsequently annul Alessandri's leave of absence, accept his original resignation, and then dissolve congress in a bloodless coup.

OCTOBER 1924. Young Capt. Luís Carlos Prestes rebels in the former Misiones Territory of Brazil's Rio Grande do Sul Province, heading northeast out of Alegrete (near the Uruguayan border) in the vain hope of joining Lopes's rebellion with more than 1,000 exiled former officers, adventurers, and soldiers. They arrive too late to support the cause, and during the next two and a half years Prestes's followers march more than 6,000 miles through the Brazilian jungles, avoiding loyal formations until 800 survivors seek asylum in Bolivia.

6 NOVEMBER 1924. The Brazilian warship *São Paulo* mutinies at anchor in Guanabara bay, threatening to shell Bernardes's presidential palace in nearby Rio de Janeiro. The mutineers change their minds, sailing out under fire before finally surrendering to the Uruguayan authorities in Montevideo.

23 JANUARY 1925. A group of young Chilean army officers, led by Majs. Carlos Ibáñez del Campo and Marmaduke Grove, mount a Liberal countercoup against the Conservative military junta. Although the

navy and some civilian elements at first consider resisting, thus threatening to plunge the nation into civil war, cooler heads prevail; President Alessandri is restored to office by 20 March.

AUGUST 1930. ***Peruvian Coup.*** At Arequipa, Lt. Col. Luis M. Sánchez Cerro leads a military uprising against the administration of dictator Augusto Leguía, which soon spreads to the garrisons of Puno and Cuzco. With opposition against his rule mounting even within the capital itself, Leguía soon flees Lima for the port of Callao and puts to sea aboard the cruiser *Almirante Grau.*

Sánchez Cerro meanwhile reaches the capital by airplane and receives a tumultuous reception, then quickly establishes a military junta. *Almirante Grau* eventually returns to port, and the former president is put on trial, dying from medical neglect on 6 February 1932 while incarcerated.

6 SEPTEMBER 1930. ***Argentine Coup.*** This Saturday morning—after several weeks of growing unrest in Buenos Aires's streets sparked by the worldwide effects of the Great Depression—Lt. Gen. José Félix Uriburu launches a well-planned military uprising against the second term of 78-year-old Pres. Hipólito Yrigoyen, receiving support from the Campo de Mayo military camp, the Palomar air base, and the senior military college outside the city.

At noon the mutinous general marches into the capital and occupies all government buildings by 5:30 P.M., having encountered only sporadic opposition around the congress (four cadets are slain). After peacefully inaugurating his provisional rule on Sunday, 7 September, another round of fighting erupts the next night when nervous sentries at the presidential palace (Casa Rosada, or Pink House) mistakenly fire on another rebel contingent in the gloom, resulting in one soldier and seven civilians killed; 12 soldiers and 36 civilians are wounded.

Yrigoyen goes into exile from nearby La Plata; Uriburu imposes martial law and sets about purging the Argentine government. (Upon holding new provincial elections on 5 April 1931, however, Yrigoyen's Radical Union Party emerges victorious, much to the general's dismay; he promptly annuls the results. When presidential elections are held on 8 November 1931, the Radical Unionists boycott; Uriburu engineers the victory of fellow conspirator Gen. Agustín P. Justo.)

3 OCTOBER 1930. ***Vargas Revolution.*** After months of political unrest and uncertainty in Brazil, the 47-year-old Liberal reformer Getúlio Dornelles Vargas—defeated as an opposition candidate in the 1 March presidential election—leads a revolt in Rio Grande do Sul, Minas Gerais, and Paraíba Provinces against the government of Washington Luís Pereira de Sousa and his handpicked successor, Júlio Prestes. Although poorly equipped, the rebels advance northeast out of Vargas's headquarters at Pôrto Alegre with considerable ease under Lt. Col. Góis Monteiro, soon reaching the border between Paraná and São Paulo; many federal army units either defect to their side or refuse to fight.

A major confrontation is expected in the vicinity of Itararé, but support for President Washington Luís is by now so eroded that on 24 October he is arrested in Rio de Janeiro by a junta of Generals Tasso Fragoso and Mena Barreto plus Rear Adm. Isaías de Noronha and then imprisoned in one of the Copacabana forts. The trio quickly calls for a cease-fire, subsequently sending the president and Prestes into exile while allowing Vargas to enter the capital on 3 November to a tumultuous reception. The latter immediately assumes office as head of a provisional government, suspends Brazil's constitution, and begins overhauling the government as virtual dictator.

2 JANUARY 1931. Tonight brothers Harmonio and Arnulfo Arias depose Panama's president, Florencio H. Arosemena, in a bloodless coup.

20 JULY 1931. This morning Lt. Col. Gregorio Pomar—second-in-command of Argentina's 9th Infantry Regiment stationed outside the northern provincial capital of Corrientes—revolts against the Uriburu regime, slaying immediate superior Lt. Col. Lino H. Montiel in his office. As loyal units from Brig. Gen. Luis Bruce's 3rd Division begin to close in, Pomar's followers lose heart and return to barracks. At 8:55 P.M. on 22 July the mutinous colonel goes aboard a barge with a few loyal supporters then sails up the Paraná River into exile at Humaitá (Paraguay), arriving next day.

8 DECEMBER 1931. On the day of Sánchez Cerro's installation as newly elected Peruvian president, radical opponent Victor Raúl Haya de la Torre of the Alianza Popular Revolucionaria Americana (Popular American Revolutionary Alliance, or APRA, its members being called Apristas) calls for a leftist reaction. Political violence escalates as a result, with the few Aprista representatives at the national constitutional assembly being arrested in January 1932; Sánchez Cerro is wounded in an assassination attempt on 6 March.

DECEMBER 1931. In El Salvador, the recently elected president, Arturo Araujo, is deposed by a military coup led by Gen. Maximiliano Hernández Martínez. The latter unleashes a bloody purge that allegedly kills 32,000 Indians and political opponents during the next year.

10 MAY 1932. ***Bonus March.*** In Portland (Oregon), an unemployed cannery superintendent and former sergeant in the 146th Field Artillery named Walter W. Waters calls for a pilgrimage of jobless veterans to Washington, D.C., to encourage passage of a bill introduced by Rep. Wright Patman of Texas for immediate payment of World War I veterans' adjusted compensation certificates—the so-called "soldiers' bonuses." Referred to derisively as the "Bonus Expeditionary Force," or BEF, 300 men depart Portand and reach the nation's capital 19 days later by hopping freights. They are followed by 20,000–30,000 more within the next few weeks from every state in the union.

They are greeted by a sympathetic police chief (and retired brigadier), Pelham D. Glassford, who provides temporary housing and food. However, the bill itself is voted down 62–18 in the Senate on 17 June, after which Congress recesses for the summer. Weary of the BEF shanties within the city, the District of Columbia commissioners request that Pres. Herbert Hoover send in federal troops to disperse the protesters.

A cavalry squadron, an infantry battalion, and a tank platoon appear on the afternoon of 28 July under Gen. Douglas A. MacArthur, Maj. Gen. George Van Horn Moseley, and Brig. Gen. Perry Miles (Maj. Dwight David Eisenhower serving as liaison to the police). They drive the BEF out of Washington in short order, inflicting two fatalities and many injuries.

7 JULY 1932. ***Peruvian Uprising.*** At 4:00 A.M. Aprista radicals, in their ideological capital of Trujillo, assault its powerful government garrison, subduing the defenders after five hours' fighting then arming the city populace to resist a counterattack. President Sánchez Cerro responds by ordering the cruiser *Almirante Grau* to Salaverry and dispatching loyal troops from Cajamarca and other nearby cities to converge on Trujillo.

By the afternoon of 8 July the rebels' defeat seems certain, and government airplanes begin dropping leaflets demanding the surrender of the city. The Aprista leaders flee at nightfall after ordering the execution of 60 military captives. When loyal columns fight their way in and discover the massacre a few days later they execute at least 1,000 people in retaliation.

9 JULY 1932. ***Brazil's Constitutionalist Revolution.*** Amid growing disenchantment with Vargas's dictatorial policies, Gen. Bertoldo Klinger—dismissed as commandant of the Mato Grosso military region—leads an insurrection at São Paulo against the federal government. Despite his initial surprise, the president is able to contain the rebellion and throttle it by 29 September with loyal contingents under General Monteiro with heavy loss of life.

The Paulista politicians are in turn surprised by the abrupt collapse of their army; they go into exile in Portugal. Notwithstanding the defeat, the São Paulo rebels later claim a moral victory: their action pushes Vargas into convening an assembly that writes a new constitution and authorizes elections by 1934.

31 AUGUST 1932. Aprista-inspired Peruvian adventurers occupy the Amazonian port of Leticia (population 400), ceded to Colombia four years earlier by treaty. The border incident embroils President Sánchez Cerro in an unwanted military confrontation with his Colombian neighbors.

30 APRIL 1933. After attending a military review of 25,000 troops in Lima's San Beatriz racetrack, President Sánchez Cerro is murdered by an Aprista assassin named Abelardo Mendoza Leiva.

MAY 1934. After seven months of negotiations at Rio de Janeiro, Peru agrees to withdraw its forces from the disputed port of Leticia, thus ending its conflict with Colombia.

23 NOVEMBER 1935. As part of a Comintern-inspired strategy drafted in Moscow, a group of Brazilian noncommissioned soldiers revolts this evening against officers in Natal (Rio Grande do Norte Province); this is followed by a similar uprising in Recife (Pernambuco). As loyal forces rush in to crush the mutinies, Communist Party leader Luís Carlos Prestes leads an attack against a federal barracks in Rio de Janeiro on 27 November in which many loyalists are murdered. After putting down the outbursts, President Vargas uses the threat as an excuse to suspend civil liberties and to purge all leftist political parties.

10 NOVEMBER 1937. Amid a heated campaign to elect his successor, Brazil's President Vargas denounces another alleged communist conspiracy then imposes martial law with backing from War Minister Eurico Gaspar Dutra and General Monteiro, thus continuing his own rule for another eight years.

11 MAY 1938. Political opponents of Brazilian strongman Vargas attempt a nocturnal assault on Rio de Janeiro's Guanabara palace, only to be repelled by loyal troops under General Dutra.

MARCH 1939. Peruvian troops crush a well-planned Aprista-military coup against Pres. Oscar R. Benavides.

Nicaraguan Civil War (1925–1927)

The 1924 presidential elections in this turbulent country result in the installation of Conservative Carlos Solórzano as president and Liberal Dr. Juan Bautista Sacasa as vice president. Gen. Emiliano Chamorro—himself a former president but loser in this American-sponsored campaign—refuses to honor the results.

24 October 1925. Chamorro leads a military coup that, at the cost of 20 lives, seizes the fortified La Loma Hill overlooking the capital of Managua, from where he demands the ouster of all Liberal elements from the government, plus amnesty for his action, appointment as commander-in-chief of the armed forces, and $10,000 in out-of-pocket expenses. Solórzano meekly acquiesces, and Sacasa flees to Washington.

Within the next few weeks Chamorro is appointed Nicaragua's war minister, elected to a vacant senate seat, and designated Solórzano's heir apparent.

16 January 1926. Solórzano officially resigns as president of Nicaragua and is succeeded by Chamorro. The United States refuses to recognize the legitimacy of this change, as do most other Central American and European countries.

However, Washington also refuses to uphold Sacasa's claim to the title, prompting the exiled vice president to travel to Mexico, where President Calles furnishes his followers with arms and ammunition.

2 May 1926. ***Bluefields.*** A force of Liberal exiles, supplied with Mexican arms, disembarks and occupies the eastern Nicaraguan port of Bluefields after a pitched battle. The cruiser USS *Cleveland* subsequently arrives from Panama four days later, setting ashore a landing force to "protect American lives and property."

Meanwhile in the capital, Chamorro declares a state of war, jails his Liberal political opponents, and musters 5,000 men to march east and attack the invaders.

Late August 1926. Nicaragua's former Liberal war minister, Gen. José María Moncada, captures the American company town of Puerto Cabezas, driving Chamorro's government forces inland.

October 1926. The American ambassador in Nicaragua arranges a 15-day truce between warring Liberal and Conservative factions as well as face-to-face meetings between delegations aboard the USS *Denver* at the Pacific port of Corinto.

November 1926. Chamorro resigns the presidency; former Pres. Adolfo Díaz is temporarily installed in place. Numerous protests ensue, however—both within Nicaragua and abroad—against the unpopular, American-approved choice.

1 December 1926. The exiled Liberal vice president, Sacasa, reaches Moncada's base of Puerto Cabezas and proclaims that Nicaragua's civil war will continue against Díaz. Landing parties from the American warships *Cleveland* and *Denver* disarm his supporters but otherwise do not interfere, although tensions escalate between Washington and Sacasa's backers in Mexico.

Late December 1926. ***Laguna de Perlas.*** In a four-day battle at Laguna de Perlas (midway between Puerto Cabezas and Bluefields), Moncada devastates a Díaz army, killing hundreds of troops and driving the survivors back into sanctuary at the neutral port of Bluefields.

21 December 1926. In a publicity stunt intended to highlight the U.S. government's growing interest in all of Latin America, five air corps Loening OA-1 amphibious aircraft depart Kelly Field (Texas) under Maj. Herbert Dargue on a goodwill flight throughout Central and South America. After reaching as far south as Valdivia, Chile, they return to Washington by 2 May 1927, to be greeted by Pres. Calvin Coolidge.

6 January 1927. At the request of Díaz's government, a marine contingent from the cruiser USS *Galveston* disembarks at Corinto and occupies the port, preempting an imminent fall to rebel forces. Alarmed at the prospective triumph of a Mexican-backed leftist regime, President Coolidge begins to throw his support behind Díaz by lifting the arms embargo and providing other material aid.

6 February 1927. ***Chinandega.*** Just north of the Pacific port of Corinto, Díaz suffers a crushing reversal when the 500-man garrison of Chinandega is overrun in three days of intense fighting by 1,000–2,000 rebels,

backed by a pair of aircraft. Government forces move to secure the town with U.S. Marine assistance.

19 FEBRUARY 1927. A reinforced U.S. Marine rifle company reaches devastated Chinandega, being joined next day by contingents from the U.S. cruisers *Milwaukee, Raleigh,* and *Galveston.* They declare Chinandega and the railway line running southeast into León to be neutral territory, effectively preventing their capture by rebel forces.

21 FEBRUARY 1927. Corinto is garrisoned by 200 U.S. Marines from the light cruiser USS *Trenton;* La Loma Fort outside Managua is also occupied "to afford better protection to foreign lives and property."

22 FEBRUARY 1927. Because of the inexorable rebel advance on Managua, the British government proposes sending the cruiser HMS *Colombo* to Corinto to protect their nationals' interests—galvanizing Washington into even greater efforts to stabilize Nicaragua, thus precluding the need for European intervention. Within the next few weeks the number of marines deployed throughout this country rises to more than 2,000.

MARCH 1927. ***Muymuy.*** Moncada's 3,000 troops defeat a government army at Muymuy (midway between Matagalpa and the capital), bringing Díaz's government to the verge of collapse. Direct intervention is requested from Washington; although officially refused, it is in effect implemented by the increasing U.S. presence throughout Nicaragua.

15 APRIL 1927. A U.S. envoy—Col. Henry L. Stimson—reaches Nicaragua aboard the light cruiser *Trenton* to negotiate an end to civil war.

4 MAY 1927. After securing Díaz's agreement to generous peace terms, Stimson persuades Liberal General Moncada to accept them as well at a conference held at Tipitapa (southeastern shores of Lake Managua). Only one of Moncada's rebel subcommanders refuses to ratify the arrangement eight days later—36-year-old Augusto César Sandino, who instead retires north to the Honduran border with 200 followers.

16 MAY 1927. After nightfall Marine Capt. Richard B. Buchanan leads 40 men into the railway town of La Paz Centro (between Corinto and Managua), expelling 200 demobilized Liberal soldiers who are looting the place. During a two-hour firefight, 14 Nicaraguans are killed along with Buchanan and another marine.

Smoldering devastation left behind after the rebel withdrawal from Chinandega

Female Nicaraguan rebel

19 MAY 1927. The 11th Marine Regiment reaches Corinto, being quickly deployed on garrison duty along its rail lines.

23 MAY 1927. Elements of the 5th Marine Regiment advance north from Matagalpa and occupy Jinotega, attempting to convince Sandino (at nearby Yali) to forsake his struggle. The latter withdraws farther north into Nueva Segovia Province and launches a stubborn guerrilla campaign.

16 JULY 1927. Before dawn, Sandino and military chief Rufo Marín advance out of San Fernando and infiltrate Ocotal (capital of Nueva Segovia Province) with 300 men, attacking the 40-man marine garrison under Capt. Gilbert D. Hatfield—plus a Nicaraguan national guard company—at first light. The defenders successfully resist, aided by strafing runs by five DeHavilland 4B biplanes out of Managua under Marine Maj. Ross "Rusty" Rowell. Sandino retires back into the jungle by afternoon, having lost approximately 50 men (including Marín) compared to one killed, five wounded, and four captured among the garrison.

25 JULY 1927. This afternoon a column of 50 mounted marines under Maj. Oliver Floyd surprises Sandino's headquarters at San Fernando, killing 11 Sandinistas and driving the rest into the jungle.

19 SEPTEMBER 1927. Before sunrise Sandino, with 200 men, assaults the government garrison at Telpaneca (10 miles southeast of Ocotal), which consists of 21 Marines and 25 Nicaraguan national guardsmen under Marine Lt. Herbert Keimling. The garrison repels the attackers, suffering two killed and one wounded; enemy casualties are unknown.

1927–1936. For the next five years Sandino wages a persistent guerrilla war against the U.S.-backed government of Nicaragua until signing a peace pact with newly elected president Sacasa on 3 February 1933. Little more than one year later, on the night of 21 February 1934, the guerrilla chief is murdered following a banquet held in his honor at the national palace—allegedly with the connivance of the ruthless new war minister and national guard commander, Anastasio "Tacho" Somoza García. Two years later (June 1936) Somoza drives Sacasa himself out of office and becomes dictator.

CRISTERO WAR (1926–1929)

RADICAL NEW POLICIES DRAFTED BUT NEVER ENACTED during the Mexican Revolution of 1910 are finally introduced by President Calles in January 1926, threatening Catholic Church domination in society. Archbishop José Mora y del Río of Mexico City responds with a pastoral letter restricting religious services. Calles increases the pressure on 24 June by ordering that all priests be native Mexicans, decertifying religious schools, and ordering monasteries and other church properties nationalized.

31 JULY 1926. Mexican church officials (with the backing of the Vatican) suspend all religious services and call for an economic boycott against the government.

15 AUGUST 1926. A pro-Catholic mob overruns the municipal offices at Valparaíso (Zacatecas).

26 NOVEMBER 1926. The Liga Nacional para la Defensa de la Libertad Religiosa (National League for the Defense of Religious Liberty) organizes a "war committee" from exile in the United States, headed by René Capistrán Garza.

1 JANUARY 1927. On League instructions, general hostilities against the federal government commence throughout Mexico. The mountainous backcountry of Jalisco becomes a particular hotbed for guerrilla activity, spearheaded by Anacleto González Flores. The Catholic forces—mostly impoverished peasant soldiers—call themselves *defensores de la fe* (defenders of the faith); they often shout *¡Viva Cristo rey!* (Long live Christ the king!) as a rallying cry and soon become more widely known as *cristeros*.

JANUARY 1927. Mexico's reelection law is amended to allow a former president—such as Obregón—to stand for a second term, although not in direct succession.

20 MARCH 1927. *Cristeros* waylay the Laredo–Mexico City train at San Miguel Allende (Guanajuato), killing its conductor and guards and stealing 100,000 pesos in government funds.

MID-APRIL 1927. The Mexico City–Guadalajara train is intercepted by 400 *cristeros* near La Barca (Jalisco), who not only shoot its guards and crew but set it ablaze, killing 113 passengers—many of these wounded. The government retaliates by expelling all archbishops and bishops from Mexico and sending the army on brutal sweeps through the countryside.

LATE JUNE 1927. Shortly after Obregón announces he will seek a second term as president, an "antireelectionist" party nominates Arnulfo F. Gómez as their candidate and deplores the former president's participation. Gen. Francisco R. Serrano—an old crony of Obregón—also decides to run, at the head of the National Revolutionary Party.

2 OCTOBER 1927. ***Antireelectionist Mutiny.*** Military maneuvers scheduled for Balbuena Park (east of Mexico City) are canceled by Calles, who suspects that he and former President Obregón—both scheduled to be in the reviewing stands—are to be kidnapped in a coup. Elements of the 48th and 50th Infantry Battalions plus the 25th and 26th Cavalry Regiments (1,000 men total) subsequently mutiny under Gen. Hector Ignacio Almada, marching east to Veracruz.

Fearing a more widespread conspiracy, Calles orders Serrano arrested in Cuernavaca (Morelos), where he is celebrating his birthday. Detained along with 13 companions by federal troops under Gen. Claudio Fox, Serrano is driven toward Mexico City until reaching Huitzilac, where all 14—their hands bound with barbed wire—are taken out next dawn and shot. A wave of executions follows throughout Mexico: at Torreón, Gen. Agapito Lastra, Lt. Col. Augusto Manzanilla, and all officers of the 16th Infantry Battalion; in Mexico City, Gens. Luis Hermosillo and José C. Morán; in Zacatecas, Gens. Alfredo Rodríguez and Norberto Olvera; in Sonora, Gens. Pedro Medina and Alfonso de la Huerta (brother of the exiled former president, Adolfo de la Huerta); in Pachuca, Arturo Lasso de la Vega; in Chiapas, Gen. Luis Vidal; and so on.

Most of Almada's mutinous troops surrender to loyal forces at San Juan Teotihuacán (northeast of Mexico City), leaving him to press on to Veracruz with only a small contingent, hoping to join Gómez. Pursued by federal columns under Gens. Jesús M. Aguirre and José Gonzalo Escobar, the conspirators disperse into the hills. Gómez's hiding place is eventually betrayed by a companion and he is shot on 4 November despite being so ill that he must be tied to the execution wall.

13 NOVEMBER 1927. This Sunday four pro-Catholic fanatics toss two bombs at Obregón's Cadillac as it sits in Chapultepec Park in Mexico City, awaiting a bullfight. He emerges unscathed, his attackers being captured and killed along with Jesuit priest Miguel Pro and other conspirators.

17 JULY 1928. Obregón—having been reelected president but not yet installed in office—is assassinated at a political banquet at La Bombilla restaurant in the Mexico City suburb of San Angel by the 27-year-old itinerant artist and Catholic fanatic José de León Toral.

28 OCTOBER 1928. After González Flores is captured and executed by federal troops, command of the Catholic Ejército Nacional Libertador (National Liberating Army) devolves upon military veteran Enrique Gorostieta—a West Point graduate.

30 NOVEMBER 1928. Calles leaves office, being temporarily replaced by subordinate Emilio Portes Gil.

2 MARCH 1929. ***Escobar's Revolt.*** This afternoon Aguirre mutinies at Veracruz, being seconded in Sonora by Gen. Francisco R. Manzo and Gov. Fausto Topete. They are joined next day by Escobar in Coahuila and Nuevo León and on 4 March by Gen. Francisco Urbalejo and Gov. Juan Gualberto Amaya of Durango. Other insurrections soon follow in Oaxaca and Sinaloa.

The rebels seek to depose Portes Gil in favor of Gilberto Valenzuela and rescind Calles's anti-Catholic legislation. They are quickly joined by *cristero* remnants under Gorostieta, but loyal federal troops drive north out of Mexico City under Gen. Juan Andrew Almazán, defeating the principal insurgent concentration under Escobar at Monterrey (Nuevo León).

2 JUNE 1929. Gorostieta is betrayed to federal troops by a colleague and killed. His successor, General Degollado y Guizar, proves less intractable.

1929. With the mediation of U.S. Ambassador Dwight W. Morrow, the Mexican church and government finally resolve differences, and an amnesty is declared. Minor hostilities persist for years in the hinterland.

CHACO WAR (1932–1935)

AFTER SEVERAL DECADES OF SENDING EXPLORERS and developers into the Chaco Boreal—an arid, inhospitable but potentially valuable territory between Bolivia and Paraguay—these two countries prepare to establish ownership by dint of arms. The Bolivians are motivated by their belief that a port on the Paraguay River will help give them access to the sea; the Paraguayans earn much of their foreign exchange with exports from the Chaco and wish to increase their economic returns.

15 JUNE 1932. At 5:30 A.M. 18 Bolivian soldiers under Maj. Oscar Moscoso occupy the tiny so-called Carlos Antonio López outpost on the eastern banks of Lake Pitiantuta (also called Lake Chuquisaca). Its six-man Paraguayan garrison escapes into the surrounding desert, reporting their dispossession three days later.

22 JUNE 1932. Paraguayan Lt. Col. José Félix Estigarribia sends 98 men forward to probe the Bolivian incursion at Lake Pitiantuta.

29 JUNE 1932. The Paraguayan contingent launches a probing attack against Moscoso's Bolivian garrison within the Carlos Antonio López outpost, finding it has been reinforced. The Paraguayans pull back a dozen miles and inform Estigarribia, who orders the "Palacios" Battalion of the 2nd Itororo Infantry to retake Pitiantuta at any cost.

3 JULY 1932. Directed by La Paz to retire to the west bank of Lake Pitiantuta, Moscoso instead burns the original Paraguayan outpost and installs his Bolivian troops on the northeastern corner of the lake, calling this site Fortress Mariscal Santa Cruz.

6 JULY 1932. Incensed Paraguayan officials walk out of the American-sponsored nonaggression pact conference intended to mediate boundary disputes in the Chaco.

15 JULY 1932. ***Pitiantuta.*** Paraguayan Capt. Abdón Palacios's 388-man battalion attacks Moscoso's 170 Bolivians on the northeastern shores of Lake Pitiantuta, driving them off next day thanks to the intimidating, long-range shelling of their lone Stokes-Brandt mortar.

18 JULY 1932. The Bolivian and Paraguayan armies begin secret mobilizations.

27 JULY 1932. A Bolivian contingent under Col. Enrique Peñaranda Castillo overruns the disputed Guaraní outpost of Corrales; Toledo and Boquerón soon follow.

2 AUGUST 1932. Bolivia's Pres. Daniel Salamanca proposes a suspension of hostilities, with his country retaining its latest territorial acquisitions.

8 AUGUST 1932. Bolivian forces occupy the Paraguayan outpost of Huijay (northeast of Boquerón).

15 AUGUST 1932. Dr. Eusebio Ayala is inaugurated into office as Paraguay's new president.

7 SEPTEMBER 1932. ***Boquerón.*** Estigarribia's 7,500-man I Corps advances from Isla Poí to drive the Bolivian invaders from their recently won Boquerón outpost. Next day his vanguard—Maj. Carlos

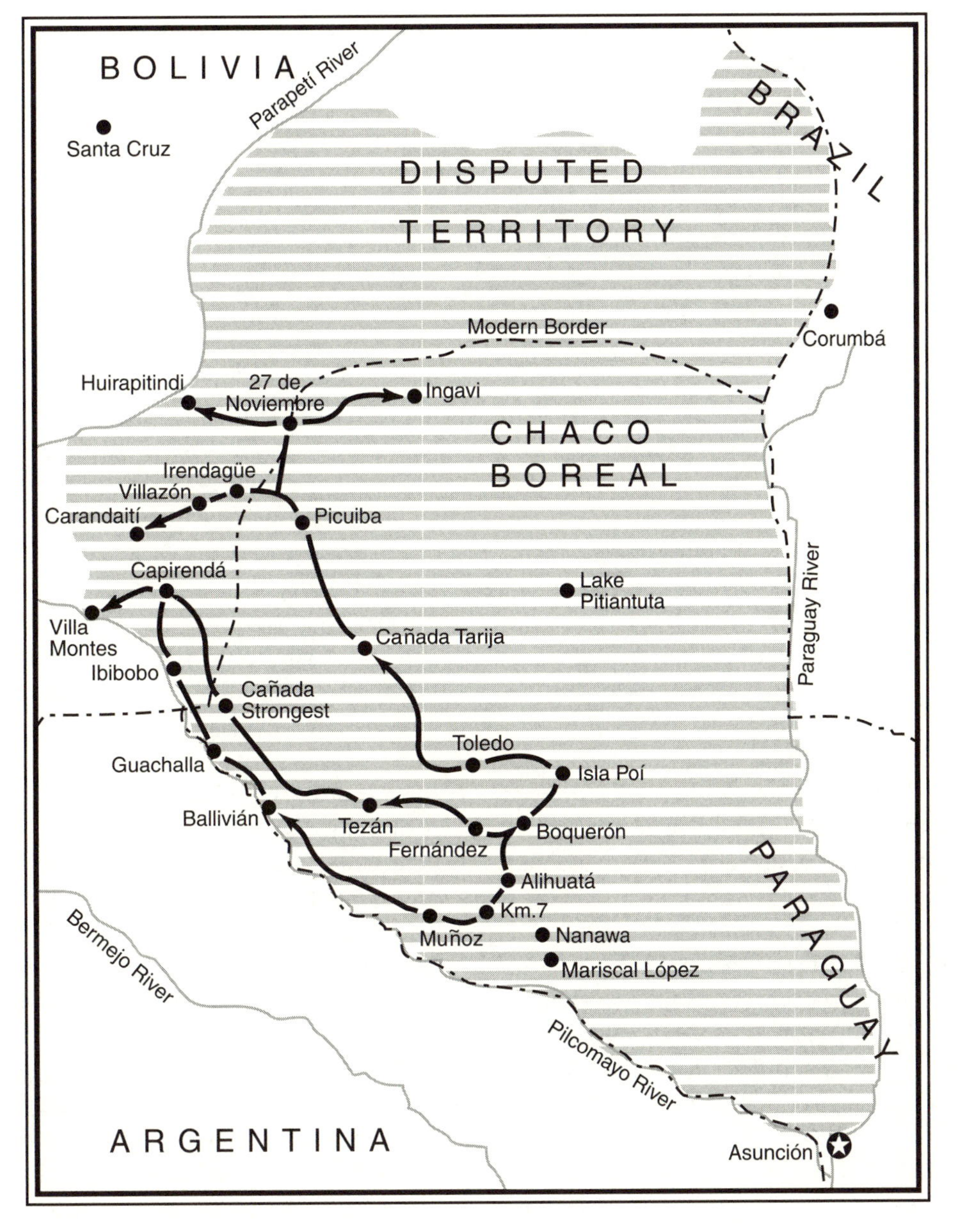

General theater map of the Chaco War

Fernández's 1st Paraguayan Division reinforced with the 3rd Infantry—pushes forward from Pozo Valencia and drives back the enemy outposts, coming within two miles of the objective.

On the morning of 9 September 5,000 Paraguayans launch a disjointed, groping attack against the Bolivian garrison, which consists of Lt. Col. Manuel Marzana's 710 men, five artillery pieces, 13 machine guns, and 27 automatic rifles. The dug-in Bolivians easily repel the assault; next day Fernández essays a flanking maneuver by having his 2nd Toledo Cavalry circle and seize Yucra (also spelled Yujra or Jujra). Although that is unsuccessful, the Bolivians underestimate Paraguayan strength, sending in small units—such as the "Lairana" Battalion of the 14th Infantry—piecemeal to clear the road; they are annihilated.

After scattered skirmishes the Paraguayans launch a renewed drive against Boquerón at dawn on 17 September with British-born Maj. Arturo Bray's 1,800-man 6th Infantry advancing out of the west. They fight all day, only to be hit in the rear at sunset by a Bolivian relief column advancing up the Lara road, crumpling two Paraguayan battalions and carrying desperately needed refreshments to Marzana's garrison. Both armies settle in for trench warfare, the besiegers pounding Boquerón from a distance; the Bolivians, under Peñaranda, Col. Francisco Peña, and Brig. Gen. Carlos Quintanilla Quiroga, prove unable to extricate their beleaguered colleagues or resupply them adequately with Fokker trimotor planes.

On 25 September Peña's 4th Bolivian Division mounts a relief effort out of the west, only to blunder into the fresh 3rd Paraguayan Cavalry Regiment, which halts the advance. Four days later Marzana finally capitulates, his garrison having suffered 320 killed, 150 wounded, and 240 captured—in addition to another 1,300 casualties sustained by other Bolivian units. Paraguayan casualties during the siege total 1,500 men.

27 SEPTEMBER 1932. Paraguayan forces recapture the outpost of Toledo.

8 OCTOBER 1932. After a lengthy reorganization following his capture of Boquerón, Estigarribia resumes his ponderous advance south to Arce with 9,200 Paraguayan troops—having been reinforced by the newly created 4th Division under Lt. Col. Nicolás Delgado.

10 OCTOBER 1932. In the Bolivian government's backlash following the Boquerón debacle, Quintanilla is recalled to La Paz and temporarily replaced as commander in chief by Colonel Peña.

11 OCTOBER 1932. Estigarribia attempts an enveloping movement against Peñaranda's 4,000-man 4th Bolivian Division, which is contesting his advance down the Yucra-Arce road. The latter withdraws his troops at nightfall, thereby escaping encirclement.

21 OCTOBER 1932. Peñaranda attempts a stand at Mula Muerta Camp with 3,000 men and some artillery, but his troops are so demoralized that most run away late this afternoon after the opening Paraguayan probes. Only the "Loa," "Campero," and 16th Infantry Battalions plus the 5th "Lanza" Cavalry Regiment remain firm, but they are too few for effective resistance. Peñaranda therefore fires Arce, then continues retreating south to Alihuatá.

23 OCTOBER 1932. Estigarribia occupies the smoldering remains of Arce.

25 OCTOBER 1932. Discovering that only 1,000 of his 4,000 Bolivians are still willing to fight, Peñaranda abandons Alihuatá.

27 OCTOBER 1932. The Paraguayan 2nd Guaraní Division occupies Alihuatá.

30 OCTOBER 1932. The Paraguayan 1st Division seizes the Fernández outpost then, one week later, captures Platanillos, as Estigarribia wishes to secure his right flank.

7 NOVEMBER 1932. ***Kilometer 7.*** Having the previous afternoon driven in the Bolivian picket line seven miles north of Saavedra, the 3rd Corrales Infantry mounts an attack against the 1,500 remaining members of the 4th Division, dug in three miles farther south under their inspirational new leader, air force Lt. Col. Bernardino Bilbao Rioja. The Bolivians repel the assault from their well-chosen defensive positions; on 8 November they use artillery to check an attempted turning of their right flank.

On 9 November the Paraguayans are reinforced by the 1st Infantry Battalion; the Bolivians receive an additional 3,500 troops and six aircraft on 10 November. When Bilbao launches a counterattack against the Paraguayan right that afternoon he encounters the newly arrived 2nd Guaraní Infantry and draws back after suffering 317 casualties compared to 139 Paraguayans. Estigarribia joins his own attacking forces with the Paraguayan 1st and 4th Divisions, launching unsuccessful assaults against Bilbao's lines on 16 and 19 November. A flanking march the night of 30 November—around the Bolivian left by 3,700 Paraguayans under Fernández—is detected after it becomes lost in the jungle, being halted by artillery batteries stationed at Montaño.

The Paraguayans try one more assault on 7 December; a week later they bring up Maj. Basiliano Caballero Irala's 1st Engineers to dig heavy fortifications and wait out the rainy season. Bilbao's stand at Kilometer 7 has effectively ended the long Bolivian retreat.

8 NOVEMBER 1932. The 1st Paraguayan Cavalry seizes Loa, Corrales, Bolívar, and Jayucubás unopposed.

6 DECEMBER 1932. German-born Gen. Hans Kundt—a mercenary who has three times served as Bolivia's chief of staff—returns to La Paz from exile abroad and is given the title "general in chief" of its field armies. (Kundt originally entered Bolivian service when Gen. José Manuel Pando requested that two dozen officers be hired in Germany in 1910 to modernize its military establishment and establish a cadet school at La Paz.)

13 DECEMBER 1932. Gen. Julio Sanjinés's newly created, 2,000-man, 8th Bolivian Division assaults Platanillos, driving its 700 defenders (of the 1st Para-

guayan Cavalry) east-southeast toward Fernández outpost.

14 DECEMBER 1932. Lt. Col. Angel Rodríguez's 3rd Bolivian Division expels the small Paraguayan garrison from Loa. A week later the Bolivian 8th Division reoccupies Jayucubás and Bolívar, forcing the Paraguayans east into Corrales.

25 DECEMBER 1932. Taking advantage of the Christmas truce, Paraguay's 1st Division retreats north from Kilometer 7 into prepared positions at Kilometer 12.

27 DECEMBER 1932. The Bolivian 4th Division launches an attack with 3,135 men—backed by artillery and low-level air support—against the Paraguayans' new positions at Kilometer 12, only to suffer 700 killed before withdrawing.

30 DECEMBER 1932. Gen. Arturo Guillén's 7th Bolivian Division captures Duarte; nine days later it overruns the Mariscal López outpost in anticipation of a major drive farther north against Nanawa.

1 JANUARY 1933. The 3rd Bolivian Division captures lightly held Corrales, pursuing its fleeing Paraguayan garrison toward Puesto Betty.

13 JANUARY 1933. The Paraguayan 7th San Martín Cavalry Regiment advances west out of Toledo and probes the new Bolivian defenses at Corrales, only to be repulsed.

20 JANUARY 1933. ***Nanawa (First Battle).*** At dawn Kundt launches a three-pronged attack against the stronghold at Nanawa with 6,000 men of the Bolivian 7th Division (ten infantry and five cavalry regiments supported by 2nd Artillery plus ten aircraft). Nanawa is held by 2,500 men of Lt. Col. Luis Irrazábal's 5th Paraguayan Division, dug-in well behind barbed-wire entangements with numerous machine guns.

(In a diversionary move, the 8th Bolivian Division also marches out of Platanillos farther to the northwest this same morning and storms Fernández outpost, only to be repelled by the 2nd Guaraní Division. A second attempt on 23 January is repulsed as well, the Bolivians withdrawing after sustaining heavy casualties. The Paraguayans for their part probe the Bolivian lines at Kilometer 7, only to find Peñaranda's 1,500-man 4th Division still holding firm.)

After his initial assault is checked, Kundt makes a second try on 24 January, sending the 41st Bolivian Infantry in an encircling movement against Ayala outpost, in Irrazábal's rear. Paraguayan cavalry advancing from Puesto Florida halts this drive, and the beleaguered defenders are resupplied by air and reinforced on the ground, Bray's 4th Division bringing Irrazábal's strength to 5,000 men. Kundt persists with small-scale attacks before calling a halt to offensive operations on 28 January, having lost 2,000 men, compared to 248 Paraguayans.

29 JANUARY 1933. Lt. Col. Juan B. Ayala's 5,000-man 6th Paraguayan Division—decimated by dysentery and typhoid—makes a feeble, uncoordinated assault against the Bolivian defenses at Corrales, being easily repelled.

2 FEBRUARY 1933. The 3,600-man 3rd Bolivian Division advances east out of Corrales, marching slowly along muddy roads to drive the Paraguayan skirmishers back from Puesto Betty one week later.

16 FEBRUARY 1933. ***Toledo.*** The 3rd Bolivian Division arrives before the outer Paraguayan defenses of Toledo and slowly deploys through the mud for an assault. This does not commence until 25 February, after a dawn raid by Bilbao Rioja's air group. During the next two days the Bolivians drive against the defenders' trench system—designed and installed by former czarist White Russian officers Belaieff and Ern—and suffer appalling losses.

Nocturnal attacks prove equally unsuccessful, and by 5 March the Bolivians have lost nearly 2,000 men. On 11 March the defenders launch an enveloping counterattack, prompting the 3rd Bolivian Division to retreat to Puesto Betty. Numerous mutinies follow, the 30th Infantry fleeing on the night of 16 March after shooting at officers. The veteran 9th Warnes Infantry also rebel along the Platanillos road, streaming to Camacho to commandeer trucks for return home.

11 MARCH 1933. ***Alihuatá.*** At dawn Col. Victorino Gutiérrez's 1,500-man 9th Andean Division—after circling overland from Sosa—takes Charata, driving the Paraguayan garrison out of nearby Alihuatá and cutting the road leading north to the Paraguayan rear. A simultaneous attack is made by Peñaranda's 4th Division against the Paraguayan front lines farther south at Kilometer 12; Capt. Germán Busch's cavalry squadron takes Campo 31.

The Paraguayans respond by extemporizing a large force under Maj. Roque Samaniego to reopen the Alihuatá road from the north. The relief column is checked, and after five days of fighting on two fronts Fernández's 1st Paraguayan Division extricates itself from Kilometer 12, retreating under cover of darkness on 16 March and reaching safety on the Gondra road two days later. Despite the victory, the Bolivians lose an opportunity to annihilate an entire enemy division.

25 MARCH 1933. The weak Bolivian 8th Division launches an unsuccessful attack against the Paraguayan garrison at Fernández outpost.

5 APRIL 1933. Col. Gaudioso Núñez's 2nd Paraguayan Division, supported by three bombers, begins flanking maneuvers against the 8th Bolivian Division, compelling it to retreat to within nine miles of Platanillos.

7 APRIL 1933. Busch's 5th Bolivian Cavalry pushes back some Paraguayan outposts below Falcón (modern-day Rojas Silva), closing the road northwest to Arce for four days. He is temporarily dislodged by a strong detachment from the 7th Guaraní Division but returns to the attack on 13 April. Eventually, a new front develops at Campo Aceval (three miles west of Rancho Ocho).

10 MAY 1933. After the collapse of U.S.-mediated attempts at achieving a truce, Paraguay officially declares war against Bolivia.

16 MAY 1933. At Gondra, Lt. Col. Rafael Franco's 1st Paraguayan Division opens a small breach in Peñaranda's left, only to be quickly contained by the redeployment of Bolivian machine guns and mortars. Both sides settle in for trench warfare, as winter is commencing in the Southern Hemisphere.

18 MAY 1933. ***Fernández.*** The 2,000-man 8th Bolivian Division storms Fernández outpost out of the west, being quickly pinned down by withering counterfire from its reinforced Paraguayan garrison. A second assault fails on 27 May, after which Lt. Col. Felipe Arrieta arrives three days later out of the east with 500 men of the Bolivian 16th and 41st Infantry plus Busch's 5th Cavalry.

They are unable to carry the outpost or completely encircle it. After another failed assault on 1 June all attackers retreat northwest to Platanillos—harassed by Paraguayan bombers—having suffered 556 killed and 314 wounded.

4 JULY 1933. ***Nanawa (Second Battle).*** In an operation designed to coincide with a League of Nations assembly to discuss the problem of the Chaco War, Kundt launches a massive new Bolivian assault against Nanawa. At 9:05 A.M. a subterranean mine is exploded beneath a fortified strongpoint in the center of the Paraguayan line, after which nearly 7,000 troops of the 7th Bolivian Division charge across the intervening no-man's land. They are supported by aircraft, 32 heavy artillery pieces, tanks, and flamethrowers.

Notwithstanding the 100-foot crater blasted in the defenders' line, the Bolivians are greeted by heavy counterfire, and their columns begin to lose cohesion. By noon their artillery shuts down for a lack of shells, and the offensive gradually grinds to a halt. Although Kundt persists with localized actions over the next two days, his main effort has failed at a cost of 2,000 Bolivian lives.

12 JULY 1933. At Gondra, Franco's 1st Paraguayan Division turns Peñaranda's right, compelling the Bolivians to retreat northwest three days later to Campo Via.

5 AUGUST 1933. A Bolivian flying column briefly occupies Falcón (Rojas Silva).

25 AUGUST 1933. Pirijayo (or Pirizal) is seized by a Bolivian task force under Col. Carlos Banzer and held for a short time.

30 AUGUST 1933. The 27th Bolivian Infantry—astride the Arce-Alihuatá road—is briefly surrounded by growing Paraguayan strength.

7 SEPTEMBER 1933. Franco shortens his Paraguayan lines, obliging Peñaranda to recall his outposts from Rancho Ocho and Pirizal.

12 SEPTEMBER 1933. ***Pozo Favorita.*** Estigarribia's latest Paraguayan offensive cuts the Pampa Grande-Alihuatá road behind the 2nd and 4th Bolivian Infantry Regiments, the incursion being strengthened next day and repelling a counterattack by the 27th Bolivian Infantry.

By 14 September part of the 18th Bolivian Infantry is trapped at Pozo Grande, Kundt trying to break through with a relief column of merely 200 soldiers—powerless against the 3,500-man 7th Guaraní Division of Lt. Col. José A. Ortiz. That afternoon more than 930 Bolivians capitulate, and both armies resume trench warfare.

(At Villa Militar, Estigarribia is promoted to brigadier for his victory; Kundt is left at Muñoz to contemplate flight into Argentina or suicide. On 2 October he is recalled to La Paz, and a major shuffle ensues among Bolivia's high command.)

23 OCTOBER 1933. Estigarribia launches a general offensive along all fronts, having mustered 26,500 Paraguayans in nine infantry divisions and two cavalry brigades—17,000 being destined for frontline duty—in a major effort aimed at ending the war.

30 OCTOBER 1933. Maintaining pressure on all fronts, Estigarribia hurls his reserves against the Bolivian trenches at Pozo Favorita, only to suffer grave losses.

4 NOVEMBER 1933. Kundt returns to Alihuatá and reassumes command over Bolivia's field armies in the face of Estigarribia's unremitting pressure.

12 NOVEMBER 1933. Gradually being forced back everywhere, 318 members of the 16th Bolivian Infantry is cut off in the trenches at Nanawa and captured.

16 NOVEMBER 1933. Estigarribia's relentless offensive recaptures the Mariscal López outpost from its Bolivian occupiers; Kundt commits his final reserves in a desperate attempt to shore up his crumbling lines.

3 DECEMBER 1933. ***Campo Via.*** Estigarribia replaces hesitant Col. Juan B. Ayala on his right flank with the more aggressive Ortiz of the 7th Guaraní Division and, next day, instructs the latter—despite torrential rains—to commence a huge envelopment of the Bolivian left by leading 14 regiments from Pampa Grande to the road west of Alihuatá. Bolivian reconnaissance flights sight the movement, but Kundt dismisses the reporting pilots as "alarmists."

On 6 December Paraguayan units cut the Alihuatá-Saavedra and Alihuatá-Pozo Negro roads, prompting Kundt to belatedly authorize Banzer's 9th Bolivian Division to retreat to Campo 31. Alihuatá is fired and abandoned by 7 December, but Kundt's retirement is further hampered by Franco's sudden attack out of Gondra, which mauls Col. Emilio González Quint's 4th Bolivian Division and seals the Campo Via-Ustares road. Estigarribia follows up the gain by directing the Paraguayans' 3rd Corrales Division to continue circling southeast from Charata to link up with Franco's 1st Division.

Kundt hopes to reestablish a new defensive line from Campo Victoria to two miles west of the Saavedra road in Campo 31, but the plan fails because of his army's utter confusion and Franco's timely occupation of the woods north of Campo Via (thereby sealing the road from Campo Victoria). A feeble Bolivian relief effort marching north from Saavedra under Peñaranda is also checked, dooming their colleagues surrounded at Campo Via. On the afternoon of 11 December 8,000 men of the 4th and 9th Bolivian Divisions surrender to Estigarribia. Paraguayan booty includes 20 guns, 25 mortars, 840 Vickers machine guns and automatic rifles, and 13,000 rifles.

12 DECEMBER 1933. Following Kundt's disastrous defeat, Peñaranda scrapes together 2,500 men this evening around the old Bolivian trench system at Kilometer 7, then is promoted brigadier general and put in command of Bolivia's field armies; Kundt flies back to La Paz to face a court-martial.

13 DECEMBER 1933. At 8:15 P.M. Estigarribia's Paraguayan forces occupy Saavedra but are too exhausted to pursue Peñaranda's few survivors, now limping west toward Muñoz.

19 DECEMBER 1933. A truce is arranged between Bolivia and Paraguay to allow foreign diplomats to negotiate a peace in Montevideo. Estigarribia attacks Peñaranda's headquarters at Muñoz just before the midnight deadline, overrunning the outpost in an action that provokes angry Bolivian recriminations at the conference table.

5 JANUARY 1934. Unable to agree on a boundary, Paraguay and Bolivia resume hostilities. Because of weariness on both sides, however, the former merely reoccupies a few small, isolated outposts—Platanillos, Loa, Jayucubás, Bolívar, and Camacho—during the next few days; the latter concentrates on reconstructing its shattered army.

1 FEBRUARY 1934. Estigarribia launches a flanking maneuver against Arrieta's 8th Bolivia Division at La China, compelling the contingent to retreat to Pozo Tortuga three days later.

9 FEBRUARY 1934. Under continuous Paraguayan pressure, the II Bolivian Corps retreats to Tezán and then farther west.

20 MARCH 1934. ***Cañada Tarija.*** After advancing 70 miles northwest from Camacho through dense jungle, Lt. Col. Federico W. Smith's 6th Paraguayan Division contacts the 1,500-man 18th Montes Infantry at Garrapatal near Cañada Tarija under Bolivian Lt. Col. Angel Bavia. Fighting erupts four days later, the Paraguayans outflanking and encircling the opposition by 26 March. Next day Bavia commits suicide, and his surviving troops surrender or die in the jungle. The defeat prompts Peñaranda to sack his subordinate, Peña, and order a general retreat to within seven miles of Ballivián, on the border with neutral Argentina.

5 APRIL 1934. In La Paz disgruntled cadets from the *colegio militar* (military academy) attempt to overthrow President Salamanca but are put down by loyal troops under General Lanza.

10 MAY 1934. ***Cañada Strongest.*** The 2nd and 7th Paraguayan Divisions come into contact with Bilbao Rioja's II Bolivian Corps, dug in along a line stretching northeast from Pilcomayo River. The defenders fall back before Estigarribia's attempts at encirclement, and Peñaranda launches a ponderous counteroffensive of his own with the 14,000-man 9th Division, stationed 20 miles north of Guachalla.

On 19 May a 7,000-man 9th Division column cuts the road behind Ortiz's 7th Paraguayan Division, heavily engaged in front. Col. Gaudioso Núñez manages to briefly check the incursion, and the Paraguayans retreat during the night of 21–22 May along a jungle trail cut by the 1st Engineers. Lt. Col. José Rosa Vera's 2nd Paraguayan Division, however, becomes trapped and disintegrates over the next few days. By 25 May 1,500 survivors surrender to the Bolivians, many others having escaped through the jungle.

MID-JUNE 1934. Franco's Paraguayan corps presses back the 3rd Bolivian Division in light fighting.

18 JUNE 1934. Despite being outnumbered almost two-to-one, Delgado's 9,000-man III Paraguayan Corps thrusts a salient into the lines of Col. David Toro Ruilova's I Bolivian Corps at Ballivián, only to be ejected shortly thereafter with extremely heavy casualties.

15 JULY 1934. Under relentless Paraguayan pressure, Peñaranda orders Toro's 16,000 Bolivian troops to retreat from Ballivián to join Bilbao Rioja's 9,000 at Guachalla, but the former refuses to withdraw, citing national honor.

14 AUGUST 1934. ***Picuiba Breakout.*** At dawn Franco's 6th Division launches a major new Paraguayan offensive by surprising and overrunning Lt. Hugo Pol's 600 Bolivians on the road leading to Picuiba (Pol escapes this evening with barely 50 survivors). Without much resistance east of Carandaití, Franco advances unimpeded in truck columns, reaching Irendagüe by 17 August, Villazón next day, "27 de Noviembre" by 19 August, and Huirapitindi on 20 August; he then compels a Bolivian battalion to surrender at Algodonal by 22 August.

On 27 August Franco reaches the Chiriguano Mountains—natural limit of the Chaco—three miles east of Carandaití, but he is soon obliged to shorten his overextended supply lines to fend off Bolivian reinforcements being dispatched north from Ballivián. Estigarribia directs Franco to make a slow fighting retirement, draining strength from Toro's concentration farther south.

5 SEPTEMBER 1934. After cobbling six Bolivian cavalry regiments into a strike force at Carandaití, Toro attempts to envelop Franco's slowly retreating column at Pozo del Burro, only to see his opponent slip east under cover of darkness to Algodonal on the night of 8 September. Fourteen trucks, some spiked guns, and 78 automatic weapons are the only booty left behind.

11 SEPTEMBER 1934. In the Bahía Negra sector, small Paraguayan contingents take Vanguardia and Vargas.

22 SEPTEMBER 1934. Toro envelops Algodonal, seizing the road three miles to the east and cutting off Franco's 6th Division from its reserves. Nevertheless, the Paraguayan commander fights east on the night of 23 September, killing 200 troopers of the 3rd Bolivian Cavalry while suffering considerable casualties among his own ranks before escaping.

5 OCTOBER 1934. Paraguayan troops capture Ingavi, threatening Bolivia's Santa Cruz Department.

6 NOVEMBER 1934. ***Villazón.*** Toro attempts a pincer movement against the 5,000-man Paraguayan stronghold at Villazón, advancing with 12,000 Bolivians in two columns: the 3rd Infantry and 2nd Cavalry Divisions to the north and the 1st Cavalry Division to the south. Heavy rains hamper progress, so it is not until 9 November that Toro's forces can close in.

Late on 10 November, however, Franco's defenders make a thrust southeast, escaping through the Bolivian siege lines toward Picuiba with help from a diversionary attack out of Irendagüe by Lt. Col. Caballero Irala's 2nd Paraguayan Engineers. Toro is able to capture only 400 prisoners and 50 trucks.

11 NOVEMBER 1934. ***El Carmen.*** Col. Carlos Fernández's I Paraguayan Corps—comprising the 1st, 2nd, 7th, and Col. Manuel Garay's 8th Divisions—begin to envelop Col. Zacharías Murillo's 1st Reserve Division, lying at El Carmen. By 13 November the 2nd Division reaches the Bolivian rear and captures Murillo's headquarters, closing the road to Oruro two days later and meeting up with the 8th Division, circling down out of the north.

On the morning of 16 November Murillo and Col. Walter Méndez's 2nd Bolivian Reserve Division mount a feeble attempt to escape; eventually they must capitulate, having suffered 2,500 killed and 4,000 captured.

13 NOVEMBER 1934. Toro's forward units link up at El Cruce with motorized elements from Bilbao's 7th Bolivian Division, advancing south out of Santa Fe (via "27 de Noviembre").

17 NOVEMBER 1934. With the Bolivians retreating northwest, Paraguayan forces occupy Ballivián.

20 NOVEMBER 1934. The Paraguayans temporarily abandon Picuiba yet make a strategic retirement only five and a half miles south in good order.

21 NOVEMBER 1934. The Paraguayan III Corps reaches Guachalla and, next day, Fernández's I Corps punches through the new Bolivian lines at Cañada Oruro, pressing on to Ibibobo.

27 NOVEMBER 1934. Bolivia's President Salamanca visits his defeated commanders at Villa Montes, intending to replace the inept Peñaranda with Lanza. Instead, the president is arrested and deposed by 300 soldiers of the 4th Artillery Group under Peñaranda, Sanjinés, Busch, and Col. Felipe Rivera Lino, commenting: "This is the only maneuver in which they have been successful." Vice President Tejada Sorzano is elevated to office.

4 DECEMBER 1934. Tejada Sorzano—an avid Liberal pacifist prior to the war—orders a general mobilization in Bolivia.

6 DECEMBER 1934. ***Irendagüe.*** Colonel Garay's 1,800-man 8th Paraguayan Division departs La Faye to drive on Irendagüe and seize its water wells. This is part of a much larger offensive by Franco's II Paraguayan Corps—which includes 5,500 men of the 6th and Reserve Divisions plus the 1st Division—aimed at destroying Toro's 12,000-man Bolivian cavalry corps, now exposed following Peñaranda's retreat west. The Paraguayan Reserve Division begins to turn the Bolivian left while the 14th Paraguayan Infantry advances down out of Ingavi in the north to threaten "27 de Noviembre" and the 1st Division moves out of the southwest toward Villazón.

Toro—his headquarters at Carandaití, 85 miles away—is slow to react, not issuing orders until almost midnight on 7 December. Shortly thereafter 200 Paraguayan troops surprise the 130-man Bolivian garrison at Irendagüe, seizing this vital water supply, and severing Toro's communications. The Bolivian commander attempts to communicate with his far-flung troops by flying overhead and dropping orders, but by noon on 9 December all cohesion is lost; his contingents stream north out of the Chaco, desperately seeking water. Some 3,000 die of thirst or surrender to the pursuing Paraguayans.

11 DECEMBER 1934. Paraguayan cavalry occupy "27 de Noviembre"; Peñaranda resigns as Bolivian commander in chief.

27 DECEMBER 1934. ***Ibibobo.*** After encountering a hastily extemporized Bolivian defense line stretching north from the Pilcomayo River at Ibibobo toward Carandaití, Delgado's 2,400-man III Paraguayan Corps pushes the 5th Cavalry through a five-mile gap, their movement hidden by gloom of night and heavy rain. Next afternoon this contingent cuts Palo Mercado road, trapping 2,000 Bolivian troops. Some 200 of these drown attempting to cross the swollen Pilcomayo River, while another 1,200 surrender after a feeble effort at breaking out. Paraguayan casualties total 46 wounded.

11 JANUARY 1935. Paraguayan forces surround two Bolivian regiments at Capirendá, killing 330 and capturing 200, thereby compelling the main enemy concentration to resume its retirement west into the Andean foothills.

16 JANUARY 1935. Paraguayan troops reach the Parapetí River, traditionally the western boundary of the Chaco.

23 JANUARY 1935. Franco's II Paraguayan Corps enters Carandaití.

28 JANUARY 1935. Boyuibé is occupied by Paraguayan forces; the Villa Montes-Santa Cruz road is severed.

7 FEBRUARY 1935. Franco's II Paraguayan Corps turns the flank of the Bolivian defenders holding Ñaincorainza Pass, only to be checked by the timely arrival of the 1st Bolivian Cavalry Division, which obliges the outnumbered attackers to withdraw in defeat four days later.

13 FEBRUARY 1935. ***Villa Montes.*** Despite being outnumbered two-to-one, Estigarribia sends 5,000 Paraguayans down Capirendá road to storm Bilbao Rioja's defenses at Villa Montes. They prove formidable, and the attackers have no shells for their siege guns. Consequently, the assault progresses slowly until 16 February, when the Paraguayans succeed in creating a two-mile salient near the mountains on the Bolivian left.

Nevertheless, the defenders contain the incursion thanks to close air support and artillery barrages. Estigarribia sends in more assault waves on 20 February, suffering heavy casualties; by March the bulge is closed, with the Paraguayans stalled in trench warfare.

8 MARCH 1935. Franco's II Paraguayan Corps strikes the 7th Bolivian Division in the narrow valley between the Aguarague and Charagua Ranges, only to have the defenders surround a battalion of 15th Infantry next day, obliging it to surrender. This raises Bolivian morale, and by 12 March the Paraguayans draw off with heavy losses.

5 APRIL 1935. Paraguayan Col. Eugenio Garay—detached from Franco's II Corps—crosses the Parapetí River with 2,600 men and captures Coperé. Pushing back the 3rd Bolivian Cavalry Division, he advances to intersect the Charagua–Santa Cruz Highway.

12 APRIL 1935. Col. Eugenio Garay turns the Bolivian flank at the village of Carandaití Moza then drives through the pass to Charagua.

14 APRIL 1935. The Bolivian defenders of Villa Montes make a number of sallies to break the Paraguayan siege trenches, which stretch in a crescent northwest from the Pilcomayo River, around the town, and toward the mountains. After three days of attempting to break through along Camatindi road, the Bolivians give up. On 19 April—despite heavy losses—they seize Tarairi, compelling Colonel Fernández's Paraguayan contingent to withdraw from this sector.

15 APRIL 1935. Col. Eugenio Garay's column, in cooperation with the 8th Paraguayan Division pushing up from the south, occupies Charagua.

16 APRIL 1935. General Guillén launches a counteroffensive from Santa Cruz with 15,000 ill-equipped Bolivian troops to reverse Eugenio Garay's incursion. Driving ponderously to cut the Casa Alta–Machareti road, Guillén fails to trap the Paraguayans—who retire in good order to Carandaití by 17 April. He retakes Mandeyapecuá on 20 April.

21 APRIL 1935. Col. Eugenio Garay's 2nd Paraguayan Division evacuates Charagua and Carandaití Moza and retires south.

23 APRIL 1935. Withdrawing south, the 8th Paraguayan Division is surrounded near Cambeiti. Five days later it breaks through the lines of the 7th Bolivian Division and escapes to Santa Fe on the Parapetí River.

24 APRIL 1935. Gen. Raimundo González Flor's 6th Bolivian Division envelops a Paraguayan force at Pozo del Tigre (nine miles north of Ingavi), only to allow it to escape shortly thereafter.

13 MAY 1935. Having retreated from the Parapetí River, 3,500 Paraguayans establish a new defensive line in front of Huirapitindi.

16 MAY 1935. Estigarribia launches a surprise counteroffensive out of Carandaití with the 6th Paraguayan Division, crossing the mountains to fall on Mandeyapecuá.

1 JUNE 1935. ***Ingavi.*** With peace talks deadlocked at Buenos Aires, an 800-man Paraguayan regiment sallies from Ingavi and mauls the 6th Bolivian Division. The latter calls for reinforcements and attempts to encircle the foe, only to become enveloped four days later.

No Bolivian reserves are available from Roboré, so when the 14th Bolivian Infantry attempts to fight its way out of encirclement it becomes cornered in the jungle and is forced to surrender by 8 June. This defeat prompts Bolivia's peace delegates to reduce demands at the conference table in the Argentine capital next day.

12 JUNE 1935. A cease-fire is signed—taking effect at noon on 14 June—which recognizes that ownership over most of the Chaco passes to Paraguay. During three years of conflict 57,000 Bolivian and 36,000 Paraguayan soldiers have died, and both countries have been driven to the brink of bankruptcy and exhaustion.

WORLD WAR II (1939–1945)

AS WITH WORLD WAR I, THE AMERICAS ARE almost entirely spared fighting on home soil during the century's second global conflict, being separated from the major theaters by the Atlantic and Pacific Oceans. More than two years elapse between Germany's invasion of Poland on 1 September 1939—sparking British and French declarations of war two days later—and the U.S. entry into hostilities following Japan's attack on Pearl Harbor on 7 December 1941. Pres. Franklin Delano Roosevelt becomes involved from the start.

5 SEPTEMBER 1939. Roosevelt orders the U.S. Navy to establish a "neutrality patrol"—also referred to as the "American defense zone"—in the mid-Atlantic to discourage belligerents from conducting operations in the Americas. The line runs south from Canadian waters along 60 degrees west longitude then roughly parallel down the coast of South America. Germany, Britain, and France by and large respect the boundary.

30 SEPTEMBER 1939. Having slipped out of Germany on 21 August (before war is declared), Capt. Hans Langsdorff's 16,200-ton "pocket battleship" *Admiral Graf Spee*—armed with six 11-inch, eight six-inch, and six four-inch guns—claims its first victim, sinking the British merchantman *Clement* off Pernambuco (Brazil). With a top speed of 26 knots, *Graf Spee* has been designed as a commerce raider capable of outgunning any Royal Navy warship it cannot outrun. It disappears east to prey on British shipping rounding South Africa's Cape of Good Hope.

NOVEMBER 1939. Washington repeals the Neutrality Act. Henceforth, war materiel can be supplied to Britain on a "cash-and-carry" basis.

13 DECEMBER 1939. ***River Plate.*** At 6:00 A.M. British Commo. Henry Harwood's hunting group "G" is stationed 150 miles east of the River Plate with *Exeter* (flag) of 8,300 tons and six eight-inch and four four-inch guns under F. S. Bell; *Ajax* (7,100/eight six-inch, eight four-inch) under C. H. L. Woodhouse; and *Achilles* of New Zealand (7,000/eight six-inch, four four-inch) under W. E. Parry. Eight minutes later they sight *Graf Spee* approaching out of the South Atlantic, making toward Uruguay to refuel.

Action commences at 6:14, when *Ajax* and *Achilles* open fire at 19,000 yards while *Exeter* turns west to divide *Graf Spee*'s targeting. Langsdorff concentrates his fire on *Exeter,* believing he has encountered only a British cruiser and two destroyers. *Exeter* is struck repeatedly by accurate German salvos, and by 6:50 A.M. has a heavy list to starboard, only one of three main turrets remaining in action. Meanwhile the two British light cruisers steadily shell *Graf Spee* while closing range. At 7:16 A.M. Langsdorff begins circling south toward the crippled *Exeter,* prompting Woodhouse and Parry to turn in the same direction and intercede, thus driving the German raider northwest. At 7:25 A.M. *Ajax* is struck by an 11-inch shell and loses use of both its aft turrets. Thirteen minutes later its topmast is also brought down by a hit; the British then make smoke and break off action two minutes later.

Graf Spee continues toward the River Plate while closely shadowed by the limping British cruisers, which it occasionally turns to bombard. Langsdorff enters Montevideo this evening, and although technically allowed to remain in a neutral port for only 24 hours he receives a 72-hour extension to repair his damaged ship. Meanwhile Harwood maintains a steady stream of false wireless traffic, suggesting that strong reinforcements—the 22,000-ton aircraft carrier *Ark Royal* and the 32,000-ton battle cruiser *Renown*—have already joined him (they are actually several hundred miles away).

Convinced he cannot break out against such odds, Langsdorff—after consulting via wireless with Hitler and Grand Adm. Erich Raeder in Berlin—weighs at 6:15 P.M. on 17 December and stands out of Montevideo, trailed by the German merchantman *Tacoma.* A short distance out he and his crew transfer aboard their consort; *Graf Spee* is scuttled at 7:56 P.M., exploding shortly thereafter. Three days later, amid criticism of his performance, Langsdorff commits suicide.

24 JULY 1940. Roosevelt declares in a speech "all aid [to Britain] short of war"; this is exemplified by his

The German pocket battleship Graf Spee *sinking after being scuttled outside Montevideo*

offer to exchange 50 old "four-piper" U.S. navy destroyers for 99-year leases on British air and sea bases from Canada to the Caribbean. The deal is ratified by 2 September 1940.

28 JULY 1940. Capt. Otto Kähler's disguised German merchant raider *Thor*—code-named *Schiff 10* by Berlin, raider "E" by London—engages the British armed merchant cruiser *Alcantara* near Trinidade Island (Brazil), severely damaging its overmatched opponent before disappearing back out into the Atlantic.

5 DECEMBER 1940. *Thor* engages the British armed merchant cruiser *Carnarvon Castle* southeast of Brazil (30 degrees 52 minutes south, 42 degrees 53 minutes west), mauling it without receiving any damage.

11 MARCH 1941. The U.S. Congress passes the Lend-Lease Act, whereby the U.S. government might lend arms, munitions, and supplies to nations whose interests "the president deems vital to the defense of the United States"—namely, Britain and its satellites.

This same month, the Atlantic Fleet Support Group is formed (part of Adm. Ernest J. King's Atlantic Fleet), consisting of three destroyer flotillas and five flying-boat squadrons.

4 APRIL 1941. British warships are allowed to refit in American yards—the battleships HMSS *Malaya* and *Resolution* being among the first to do so.

7 APRIL 1941. U.S. air bases are opened on Greenland and Bermuda.

11 APRIL 1941. Washington decides to extend the American security zone from 60 degrees to 26 degrees west out into the Atlantic, announcing the measure one week later.

19 APRIL 1941. In Mexico, Rear Adm. Luis Hurtado de Mendoza—on orders from Pres. Avila Camacho—

sends marines from the 31st Battalion to impound nine Italian vessels idled at Tampico and three German merchantmen at Veracruz.

15 MAY 1941. The U.S. Navy takes over the leased British base of Argentia (southeastern Newfoundland).

27 MAY 1941. Roosevelt announces an "unlimited national emergency."

7 JULY 1941. A U.S. Marine brigade, backed by naval forces, relieves the British garrison at Reykjavik (Iceland).

19 JULY 1941. The U.S. Navy is ordered to escort shipping of any nationality to and from Iceland.

10 AUGUST 1941. Churchill and Roosevelt meet at Argentia, signing the Atlantic Charter.

4 SEPTEMBER 1941. Washington orders implementation of Western Hemisphere Defense Plan Number 4, authorizing U.S. Navy escorts to include non-American vessels in their convoys and Canadian warships to escort American vessels.

This same day, south of Iceland, the German *U-652*—after being tracked for three hours by the U.S. destroyer *Greer*—fires two torpedoes at its tormentor; the weapons miss their target.

16 SEPTEMBER 1941. The Halifax-to-England convoy HX-150 sails with a U.S. Navy escort.

17 OCTOBER 1941. The U.S. destroyer *Kearny* is struck amidships by a torpedo, killing 11 of its crewmembers, during a nocturnal attack on convoy SC-48 by a German wolfpack.

31 OCTOBER 1941. Just after dawn the old U.S. "four-pipe" destroyer *Reuben James*—escorting con-

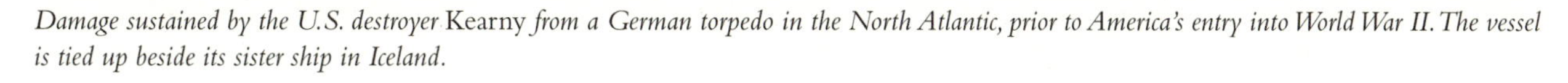

Damage sustained by the U.S. destroyer Kearny *from a German torpedo in the North Atlantic, prior to America's entry into World War II. The vessel is tied up beside its sister ship in Iceland.*

voy HX-156—is struck by a German torpedo, breaks in two, and goes down within five minutes with 115 of its 160-man crew.

7 NOVEMBER 1941. U.S. merchantmen are authorized to arm.

9 DECEMBER 1941. Two days after Pearl Harbor, Germany and Italy—Japan's Axis partners—declare war on the United States.

12 JANUARY 1942. ***U-Boat Offensive.*** Contrary to instructions from Adm. Karl Dönitz, Lt. Reinhard Hardegen's 740-ton, type IXB submarine *U-123*—after stealthily departing Lorient (occupied France) on 23 December—sinks the 9,000-ton British liner *Cyclops* of Capt. Lesley Webber Kersley 300 miles off Cape Cod (Massachusetts), thus forewarning American and Canadian authorities of the shift of U-boat operations out of the mid-Atlantic toward North America.

The German high command originally hoped to unleash a surprise offensive called Operation Paukenschlag (Drumbeat) on 13 January by launching coordinated strikes from the mouth of the Saint Lawrence River to Cape Hatteras, using Hardegen's craft plus four other type IXC boats: *U-66* of Cmdr. Richard Zapp, *U-109* of Lt. Heinrich Bleichrodt, *U-125* of Lt. Ulrich Folkers, and *U-130* of Cmdr. Ernst Kals.

At 1:00 A.M. on 13 January Kals sinks the Norwegian steamer *Frisco* in the Gulf of Saint Lawrence and, eight hours later, the Panamanian vessel *Friar Rock*. Hardegen surfaces 60 miles off Montauk Point (Long Island) the morning of 14 January, claiming the tanker *Norness,* the tanker *Coimbra* next day, and the steamer *San Jose* on 17 January. Next day *U-66* sinks the tanker *Allan Jackson;* the following day Hardegen adds another three vessels to his kills. On 21 January Kals destroys the tanker *Alexander Hoegh* south of Cape Breton; many other attacks ensue.

All told, these five U-boats claim 26 allied vessels during their two-week patrol (163,000 tons of shipping). After the fierce combat conditions experienced against Royal Navy warships closer to Europe, German submariners are delighted by their North American foes' unpreparedness: cities are fully illuminated, buoys and beacons are still in place, merchantmen run undarkened and alone, and there are but few inexperienced escorts. Recalling the easy hunts of 1940, the U-boat crews dub this their second "happy time."

As these five retire, another quintet of type IXC boats arrive—Winter's *U-103,* Rasch's *U-106,* Gelhaus's *U-107,* Scholtz's *U-108,* and Heyse's *U-128.* They claim another 19 merchantmen by 12 February (127,000 tons).

21 JANUARY 1942. Eight smaller type VIIC submarines—Rollman's *U-82,* Greger's *U-85,* Gysae's *U-98,* Suhren's *U-564,* Borchert's *U-566,* Heinicke's *U-576,* Biglak's *U-751,* and Oestermann's *U-754*—arrive to patrol from the banks of Newfoundland to Nova Scotia. Due to the harsh winter conditions they sink only 13 allied merchantmen totaling 74,000 tons before withdrawing on 19 February.

10 FEBRUARY 1942. A fourth wave of German submarines arrives off North America, consisting of three type IXC boats—Adolf Piening's *U-155,* Rostin's *U-158,* and Poske's *U-504*—plus ten VIICs: Zahn's *U-69,* Ites's *U-94,* Lehmann-Willenbrock's *U-96,* von Bulow's *U-404,* H. O. Schultze's *U-432,* Krech's *U-558,* Rehwinkel's *U-578,* Ulrich Borcherdt's *U-587,* Feiler's *U-653,* and Kröning's *U-656.* By 20 March they claim 34 allied merchantmen totaling 184,000 tons (principally south of Long Island, New York). With few escort ships or aircraft, U.S. Rear Adm. Adolphus Andrews—commander of the so-called Eastern Sea Frontier—is powerless to halt the onslaught.

16 FEBRUARY 1942. Marking a shift to Caribbean waters, Lt. Cmdr. Werner Hartenstein's *U-156* attacks three allied tankers at Aruba, sinking one and damaging the others before shelling oil tanks ashore.

19 FEBRUARY 1942. Lt. Albrecht Achilles's *U-161* enters Port of Spain (Trinidad), torpedoing an anchored American freighter and a British tanker. Other German submarine attacks follow in the Gulf of Venezuela as well as in the major shipping lane between Florida and the Bahamas as Dönitz deploys his boats into unprotected areas.

1 MARCH 1942. *U-656* goes down with all hands 25 miles south-southeast of Cape Race (Massachusetts), destroyed by American aircraft of the 88th Squadron.

MID-MARCH 1942. After repeated complaints about merchantmen being silhouetted at night against illuminated cities, U.S. Lt. Gen. Hugh Drum—chief of the army's Eastern Defense Command—introduces blackouts.

1 APRIL 1942. The first of ten British corvettes and two-dozen 900-ton antisubmarine trawlers reach New

York to bolster U.S. naval efforts against the U-boats. A convoy system is also inaugurated shortly thereafter between Hampton Roads (Virginia) and Key West (Florida). Although German submarines continue to claim a heavy toll, losses eventually decline.

20 APRIL 1942. The German supply submarine (nicknamed a "milch cow") *U-459* arrives off Bermuda, refueling 14 boats. Such measures allow U-boats to remain on patrol somewhat longer rather than risk the lengthy return home.

9 MAY 1942. Rathke's *U-352* attempts to torpedo the American coast-guard cutter *Icarus* off Cape Lookout (North Carolina), missing and being sunk in turn.

13 MAY 1942. Sailing past Miami, the neutral Mexican oil tanker *Potrero del Llano* is sunk by a U-boat with the loss of 15 of 35 crewmembers. The Mexican government files a protest with Berlin, which is ignored.

20 MAY 1942. The Mexican merchantman *Faja de Oro* is sunk near Key West by a German submarine, killing eight of 36 crewmembers.

22 MAY 1942. Mexico declares war against the Axis.

28 MAY 1942. This afternoon Rear Adm. Kakuji Kakuta sets sail from Omimato (northern Honshu, Japan) with the light carriers *Ryujo* (37 planes) and *Junyo* (53 planes); the 15,000-ton heavy cruisers *Maya* and *Takao;* the seaplane tender *Kimikawa Maru;* and the destroyers *Akebono, Ushio, Sazanami,* and *Shiokaze.* Designated the 5th Fleet, Northern Force, 2nd Strike Force, it intends to launch an air assault against Dutch Harbor in the Aleutian Islands (Alaska) six days later.

30 MAY 1942. This morning Rear Adm. Raizo Tanaka sets sail from northern Japan with the 5,600-ton light cruiser *Jintsu* and the destroyers *Kuroshio, Oyashio, Hatsukaze, Amatsukaze, Tokitsukaze, Kasumi, Kagaro, Arare,* and *Shiranuhi.* Designated the 2nd Fleet Escort Force, it intends to escort 15 transports and an oil tanker with 5,000 troops to occupy the Aleutian Islands of Attu and Kiska in an operation codenamed "AL" (intended as a diversion for Adm. Isoroku Yamamoto's much larger effort against Midway).

3 JUNE 1942. At 3:00 A.M. Kakuta—steaming 180 miles southwest of Dutch Harbor—launches 14 attack planes and three fighters from his carrier *Ruyjo* and 15 bombers and 13 fighters from *Junyo.* Because of bad weather, only nine of *Ruyjo's* attack planes and three fighters manage to find Dutch Harbor five hours later, making their attack.

Radar aboard the anchored seaplane tender USS *Gillis* has given the Americans a brief advance warning, but the destroyer *Talbot,* the submarine *S-27,* a coast-guard cutter, two army transports, and other lesser vessels are unable to exit in time. (Rear Adm. Robert A. Theobald's Task Force 8—the heavy cruisers *Indianapolis* and *Louisville;* the light cruisers *Nashville* (flag), *St. Louis,* and *Honolulu;* and the destroyers *Gridley, Gilmer, McCall,* and *Humphreys*—are on patrol several hundred miles farther south.) The Japanese planes are met with heavy antiaircraft fire, plus a few P-40 fighters, claiming one bomber. Nevertheless, the attackers set the American oil-tank farm ablaze, destroy several parked PBYs, and damage the army barracks at Fort Mears before retiring by 8:30 A.M.

The strike commander informs Kakuta that five U.S. destroyers and two submarines are also lying in Makushin Bay, prompting the Japanese admiral to launch a second wave at 9:45 A.M.: 14 attack planes, 15 bombers, 12 fighters, and four observation planes. They are unable to locate their target in the fog, returning to the carriers by 10:50 A.M. and landing during the next hour—having skirmished with some P-40s en route (one Zero is lost). Kakuta then turns southwest to make a preinvasion bombardment of Adak Island, only to turn back again because of foul weather. (The Japanese invasion of Adak is later canceled.)

This evening Rear Adm. Takeo Kurita sets sail east from Paramushiro Island with the 2nd Fleet, Occupation Support Force—the 14,000-ton heavy cruisers *Kumano, Mogami, Mikuma,* and *Suzuya;* the destroyers *Arashio, Asashio,* and *Hayashio;* and the seaplane tenders *Chitose* and *Kamikawa Maru*—to help cover the forthcoming landings on Attu and Kiska.

5 JUNE 1942. ***Aleutian Invasion.*** This morning Tanaka's expedition arrives off Attu, quickly disembarking troops and occupying the island without resistance. The Japanese garrison will eventually rise to almost 3,000 men.

At 4:00 that afternoon, several hundred miles farther east, Kakuta's carrier force launches another strike against the American base at Dutch Harbor, consisting of nine attack planes, 11 bombers, and 11 fighters. They complete the destruction of Dutch Harbor's oil-tank farm and severely damage the beached barracks ship *Northwestern.*

Simultaneously, the Japanese carriers are attacked by U.S. B-17 and B-26 bombers, which score a few near misses while losing two planes. The Japanese carrier planes return, having lost two fighters.

7 JUNE 1942. Tanaka's expedition appears off Kiska, occupying the island without opposition. The Japanese garrison eventually swells to more than 5,000 men.

4 JULY 1942. The American submarine *Triton* torpedoes the Japanese destroyer *Nenohi,* which is off the Aleutian island of Agattu as escort for the seaplane tender *Kamikawa Maru.* Only 36 of *Nenohi*'s 228 crewmembers are saved.

5 JULY 1942. Off Kiska, the U.S. submarine *Growler* sinks the Japanese destroyer *Arare* and severely damages its consorts *Shiranuhi* and *Kasumi.*

22 AUGUST 1942. Seven months after severing diplomatic relations with the Axis, Brazil declares war against Germany, Italy, and Japan. (In addition to helping defend the South Atlantic against enemy submarines, Brazil eventually sends a 25,500-man expedition under Gen. João Batista Mascarenhas de Morais in July 1944 to serve in Italy. The Força Expedicionária Brasileira—Brazilian Expeditionary Force, or FEB—will distinguish itself as part of U.S. Gen. Mark Clark's 5th Army, especially during the Battle of Monte Cassino. By the time the Germans' so-called Gothic Line is breached next spring the Brazilians have suffered 500 killed and 1,000 wounded.)

30 AUGUST 1942. American forces reoccupy Adak Island, constructing runways within the next couple of weeks suitable for air strikes against occupied Kiska and Attu farther west.

SEPTEMBER 1942. Discouraged by declining results due to regular convoys and defensive measures, Dönitz withdraws the bulk of his U-boats from U.S. coastal waters to attack Atlantic shipping beyond range of land-based aircraft. Technological innovations such as radar and sonar plus mass production of improved vessels and weaponry will eventually allow the Allies to hunt German submarines into virtual extinction.

16 OCTOBER 1942. A U.S. air raid on Kiska sinks the destroyer *Oboro* with all hands; the destroyer *Hatsuharu* is severely damaged.

12 JANUARY 1943. American forces reoccupy Amchitka—60 miles from Kiska—and begin building airstrips.

26 MARCH 1943. ***Komandorski Islands.*** At 5:00 A.M. Vice Adm. Boshiro Hosogaya is steaming north toward the Komandorski Islands with the 15,000-ton heavy cruisers *Nachi* and *Maya;* the 5,500-ton light cruisers *Tama* and *Abukuma;* the destroyers *Wakaba, Hatsushimo, Ikazuchi,* and *Inazuma;* and the transports *Asaka Maru* and *Sakito Maru.* (The destroyer *Usugumo* is supposed to join later with a third transport.)

Twenty miles southeast, on a parallel course, runs Rear Adm. C. H. McMorris's Task Force 16.6 in two columns: the destroyer *Coughlan,* the light cruiser *Richmond,* and the destroyers *Bailey* and *Dale;* with the heavy cruiser *Salt Lake City* and the destroyer *Monaghan* five miles farther east. They are part of a larger American fleet intent on disrupting Japanese supply routes between the Kamchatka Peninsula and the Aleutians.

The U.S. vessels spot their opponent on radar and begin forming into a single column; a few minutes later Japanese lookouts sight this movement, and Hosogaya turns southeast in double column at 5:30 A.M. to offer battle (detaching *Inazuma* to escort the transports northwest, away from danger). McMorris's two cruisers are by now screened on either side by a pair of U.S. destroyers and turn west in hopes of overtaking the vanishing Japanese transports.

Both sides open fire at 5:42 A.M. at about 20,000 yards. The Japanese cruisers split into two pairs, *Abukuma* and *Tama* steer southwest while *Nachi* and *Maya* continue southeast, exchanging salvos with *Salt Lake City.* There ensues a cautious long-range bombardment until 7:15 A.M., when the American heavy cruiser—after being hit a third time—requests a smoke screen from its destroyer escort (it breaks off action by 9:00 A.M.). Hosogaya leads his convoy back to Paramushiro; one month later he is retired from service for not having accomplished more during this engagement.

11 MAY 1943. ***Reconquest of Attu.*** Leap-frogging 170 miles past the main Japanese concentration on Kiska, 11,000 troops of the U.S. 7th Division disembark at three points on fog-shrouded Attu, covered by an intense naval bombardment. The 2,630 Japanese occupiers under Col. Yasuhiro Yamazaki retire to the most defensible valley on the island to make a last stand. After two and a half weeks of steady pressure, the Americans fight their way into both ends of the valley,

A 105-mm U.S. Army howitzer firing against Japanese positions atop the fog-shrouded heights of Attu Island

little realizing that the Japanese—starved and desperate, having lost radio contact with Tokyo on 27 May—are intent on resisting to the end.

On the night of 29 May Yamazaki leads his last 1,000 men out of the old Russian sealing station of Chichagof in a banzai charge, which breaks through

U.S. picket lines and overruns a field hospital and quartermaster depot despite having half their number shot down. The 500 cornered Japanese survivors commit suicide by pulling pins on their grenades; only 28 maimed prisoners are taken by the time resistance ends. American casualties for the entire campaign total 600 dead and 1,200 wounded.

26 MAY 1943. Because of Attu's fall, imperial Japanese headquarters orders Kiska resupplied by 13 I-class submarines. However, seven of the long-range vessels are quickly lost to U.S. forces, and so Japan decides to withdraw the island garrison.

21 JULY 1943. ***Evacuation of Kiska.*** Having been advised that foggy weather will cover their approach, two Japanese cruisers and six destroyers slip out of Paramushiro Island to sail east and stealthily remove Kiska's isolated 5,183-man garrison. In a brilliant feat of seamanship, the vessels enter Kiska's dangerous roadstead at 5:40 P.M. on 28 July, reemerging 55 minutes later with the island's entire contingent aboard, safely conveying it to Japan without the Americans learning of the removal.

15 AUGUST 1943. Some 29,000 U.S. troops (and 5,300 Canadians under Brig. Gen. Harry Foster) disembark on Kiska, only to find—after a two-days "sweep and search"—that the Japanese have abandoned the island altogether.

1943–1945. For the remaining two years of World War II the Allies mount enormous drives against the Axis in Europe and the Pacific, culminating in the unconditional surrender of Germany on 8 May 1945 and that of Japan on 15 August.

LATIN AMERICAN TROUBLES (1941–1989)

THE MASSIVE MOBILIZATION OF WORLD WAR II transforms the United States into a global superpower; its mastery over the Americas can no longer be challenged from overseas. Nevertheless, minor localized frictions persist throughout its sphere of influence, exacerbated by entrenched dictatorships, rural guerrilla campaigns, urban terrorism, and antigovernment coups—militarily insignificant events when compared to larger operations yet still capable of affecting geopolitical change.

JULY 1941. ***Ecuadorean-Peruvian Conflict.*** Boundary disputes more than a century old prompt Ecuador to assert ownership along the Marañón River (headwaters of the Amazon) and the town of Zarumilla, precipitating an undeclared war against Peru. The latter sends an army under Gen. Eloy G. Ureta into the trackless region; he scores a stunning victory at Zarumilla. Subsequent peace negotiations at Rio de Janeiro end on 29 January 1942 by confirming Peruvian sovereignty over 120,000 square miles of disputed territory.

9 OCTOBER 1941. Panama's profascist president, Arnulfo "El Hombre" Arias, is deposed in a bloodless military coup—with Washington's tacit approval—while visiting Cuba.

3–4 JUNE 1943. An Argentine military coup spearheaded by Gens. Arturo Rawson and Pedro Pablo Ramírez deposes Pres. Ramón S. Castillo and, by 18 June, establishes a permanent new administration, with Ramírez in charge. It soon becomes apparent, however, that the real inspiration behind the new regime is a clique of nationalistic army colonels with totalitarian leanings, popularly known as the Grupo de Oficiales Unidos (Group of United Officers, or GOU; these initials are sometimes explained as standing for *gobierno, orden, unidad*—government, order, unity) dominated by 47-year-old Col. Juan Domingo Perón.

SEPTEMBER 1943. More than 70 Argentine newspapers are forced to suspend publication for criticizing the country's military dictatorship.

26 JANUARY 1944. Under pressure from Washington because of extensive fascist activities in Argentina, Ramírez severs diplomatic relations with Nazi Germany and Japan.

24 FEBRUARY 1944. In a swiftly executed coup, an inner clique of GOU officers ousts General Ramírez as Argentina's president, fearing he is about to declare war against the Axis. He is replaced by his vice president, Gen. Edelmiro J. Farrell, but real power continues to be wielded by Perón, who is appointed war minister on 4 May and vice president by 8 July.

2 APRIL 1944. After the subservient Salvadoran National Assembly votes in February to once more ex-

tend the 13-year rule of Pres. Hernández Martínez, heated protests erupt, culminating on 2 April with an abortive rebellion led by Arturo Romero and Gen. Tito Calvo. This is suppressed, and numerous executions are ordered, precipitating renewed unrest. A student demonstration on 5 May escalates into a general strike by 8 May, prompting the dictator to resign and go into exile—after commenting it is impossible to "shoot everybody." He is succeeded by Gen. Andrés I. Menéndez.

JUNE 1944. A student strike begins in Guatemala, soon mushrooming into a general strike, which results in soldiers firing on a crowd and killing a demonstrator. Pres. Jorge Ubico subsequently ends his 13-year reign by resigning on 1 July. He is succeeded by a military triumvirate that installs Gen. Federico Ponce Vaides provisionally into office.

20 OCTOBER 1944. Dissident young Guatemalan military officers, joined by disgruntled workers and students, overthrow the administration of President Ponce. A trio—army Capt. Francisco Javier Arana and Maj. Jacobo Arbenz Guzmán plus civilian Jorge Toriello Garrido—hold elections that result in Juan José Arévalo's election on 15 March 1945.

OCTOBER 1944. Salvador's interim president, General Menéndez, is overthrown in a military uprising led by Col. Osmín Aguirre y Salinas. However, political opposition coalesces around the former chief justice of the supreme court, Miguel Tomás Molina, who establishes a government-in-exile in neighboring Honduras. The impasse is resolved on 1 March 1945, when Gen. Salvador Castañeda Castro is elected president after a campaign in which he runs unopposed.

27 MARCH 1945. In order to ingratiate his government with Washington, Argentina's President Farrell belatedly declares war on the Axis (by now virtually annihilated in Europe and the Pacific).

JULY 1945. Suspicious of the potential political threat posed by his country's Força Expedicionária Brasileira, or FEB (*see* 22 August 1942 under World War II), which is returning victorious from Europe, President Vargas quickly disbands the battle-hardened army and disperses its officers—who subsequently gain considerable influence and become known as *febianos.*

9 OCTOBER 1945. A movement led by Gen. Eduardo J. Avalos and Adm. Héctor Vernengo Lima arrests Perón, stripping him of his titles of Argentine vice president and war minister yet leaving President Farrell in power. Eight days later Perón engineers a successful countercoup with support from organized labor and marries his staunchest backer, the charismatic and politically astute actress María Eva "Evita" Duarte.

18 OCTOBER 1945. In Venezuela, beleaguered Pres. Isaías Medina Angarita orders the arrest of the 31-year-old leader of the revolutionary Unión Patriótica Militar (Patriotic Military Union, or UPM), Marcos Pérez Jiménez. The president is deposed by a rapid UPM coup and succeeded next day with a junta headed by Rómulo Betancourt of the Democratic Action Party, who sends Pérez Jiménez abroad on an extended diplomatic mission.

29 OCTOBER 1945. In Rio de Janeiro, Brazilian motorized troops mutiny and occupy the streets without opposition, bringing an end to the unpopular 15-year reign of Getúlio Vargas, who retires to his ranch in Rio Grande do Sul Province.

24 FEBRUARY 1946. Perón is elected president of Argentina, backed by the army and organized labor. He launches an ultranationalistic program of reforms.

11 DECEMBER 1947. Anti-American riots erupt in Panama to protest Washington's plans to extend the lease arrangement for numerous bases used during World War II. Eleven days later Pres. Enrique A. Jiménez is obliged to reject the deal amid great public clamor.

8 FEBRUARY 1948. After a heated electoral campaign marred by street fighting, charges of corruption, and a 15-day general strike, Costa Rica's governing Partido Nacional Republicano (PNR) candidate, Rafael Angel Calderón Guardia, is defeated by opposition leader Otilio Ulate Blanco. Outgoing Pres. Teodoro Picado Michalski refuses to honor the results, seeing to it they are annulled by the national congress and calling out the 340-man Costa Rican army in support. Ulate flees to Guatemala, but his supporters threaten rebellion.

12 MARCH 1948. ***Costa Rican Civil War.*** Col. José Figueres Ferrer, leader of Costa Rica's Social Democratic Party, rises in revolt against Picado and Calderón's PNR government. In a month's time his so-called Caribbean Legion defeats the small Costa Rican army in a campaign that claims 1,600 lives. By 20 April

a truce is arranged; Santos León Herrera is proclaimed interim president until Ulate can return from exile in Guatemala. Picado and Calderón flee to Nicaragua; on 28 April Figueres's troops enter the capital of San José in triumph to greet Ulate upon his return.

(When a new constitution is drafted in 1949 Costa Rica's army is abolished because of its recent antidemocratic stance, being replaced by an all-volunteer civil guard.)

3 OCTOBER 1948. In Callao (Peru), young civilian and military adherents of the leftist Aprista Party revolt against Pres. José Luis Bustamante y Rivero. They are quickly crushed by loyal units under Gen. Zenón Noriega, and the radical movement is banned.

27 OCTOBER 1948. ***Peru's "Restorative" Revolution.*** Amid widespread social discontent and economic difficulties, the garrison at Arequipa rises against President Bustamante, proposing 51-year-old Brig. Manuel A. Odría to replace him in office. When General Noriega, commander of the troops at the capital of Lima, refuses to obey the president and march upon Arequipa, Bustamante realizes all is lost. Two days later he withdraws from the national palace and Odría provisionally assumes power, stamping out leftist sentiment.

24 NOVEMBER 1948. After three years in office Venezuela's civilian president, Rómulo Gallegos, is overthrown by a military coup organized by Col. Pérez Jiménez.

14 DECEMBER 1948. When the Salvadoran president, Castañeda Castro, attempts to extend his term in office, he is deposed by a military uprising. Government passes to a junta of three army officers and two civilians, Lt. Col. Oscar Osorio eventually emerging as the elected president in 1950.

JULY 1949. In the highly charged atmosphere immediately prior to Guatemala's presidential elections, Defense Minister Jacobo Arbenz attempts to arrest Francisco Arana—commander in chief of the army and an openly avowed rival candidate—on charges of allegedly plotting a military coup. When the latter resists he is killed, prompting a series of uprisings by Arana supporters that are suppressed by the government. With the collapse of the last of the revolts, led by Col. Carlos Castillo Armas, Arbenz emerges as Guatemala's new president.

20 NOVEMBER 1949. When Panama's Pres. Daniel Chanís attempts to remove corrupt Gen. José "Chichi" Remón as head of the national guard, he is deposed and replaced in office by Roberto Chiari (Remón's cousin). Within a week, however, the latter is also pushed aside, succeeded by the nationalistic former president, Arnulfo Arias.

28 JULY 1950. Peruvian troops suppress a student uprising and general strike in Arequipa.

SEPTEMBER 1951. Perón stifles a military coup two months prior to Argentina's presidential election; he is easily reelected. (Because of army disapproval, however, he removes Evita from the vice presidential slate; she dies of cancer in 1952.)

26 JULY 1953. The former law student Fidel Castro Rus attacks the Moncada barracks in Santiago de Cuba with 111 followers, only to be defeated by its government garrison. After a brief incarceration he flees into exile in Mexico.

MARCH 1954. Convinced Arbenz's Guatemalan administration is a socialist front, Washington persuades the Organization of American States, meeting in Caracas, to authorize mutual defense against "communist aggression" in the Americas—in effect receiving free rein to topple the government.

15 MAY 1954. Learning that a 2,000-ton shipment of Czechoslovakian arms has reached the Arbenz government at Puerto Barrios (Guatemala) aboard the Swedish ship *Alfhem,* Washington increases its own supplies to a CIA-backed counterrevolutionary group under the exiled Castillo Armas and Gen. Miguel Ydígoras Fuentes, operating out of neighboring Honduras. Arbenz responds by declaring a state of siege within Guatemala in early June, arresting many Conservative sympathizers.

18 JUNE 1954. ***Guatemalan Coup.*** The exiled counterrevolutionary leader Castillo Armas invades Guatemala from Honduras with 160–200 men, backed by CIA-provided aircraft. Only the border town of Esquipulas is occupied, but aerial bombardments of pro-Arbenz concentrations in the capital and other Guatemalan cities sap the regime's resolve. Isolated diplomatically, and with many army officers defecting to the opposition, Arbenz resigns by 27 June. Castillo Armas enters Guatemala City aboard a U.S. embassy plane and is installed as president on 8 July. Some 9,000 Guatemalans flee into exile or are imprisoned; 8,000 peasants are killed in retribution for their reformist demands.

5 AUGUST 1954. On Toneleros Street in Copacabana, Brazilian newspaperman Carlos Lacerda is wounded and air force Maj. Rubem Florentino Vaz is murdered

by shots fired from a passing car. An investigation reveals the crime to have been instigated by Gregório Fortunato, chief of Getúlio Vargas's presidential guard; the public demands the leader's resignation.

23 AUGUST 1954. Under universal opprobrium, Brazil's President Vargas offers to temporarily step aside; when his proposal is deemed insufficient he commits suicide.

2 JANUARY 1955. Panama's Pres. José Remón is assassinated while attending horse races outside his capital. The killers are never convicted.

JANUARY 1955. Supporters of exiled leader Calderón Guardia (*see* 12 March 1948) invade the northern provinces of Costa Rica from neighboring Nicaragua with the backing of dictators Anastasio Somoza and Rafael Leónidas Trujillo Molina of the Dominican Republic.

At first the invasion makes good progress, occupying Ciudad Quesada. However, President Figueres quickly mobilizes 16,000 Costa Ricans and secures the support of Washington and the Organization of American States. Ciudad Quesada is soon retaken, and the invaders are driven back into Nicaragua.

16 JUNE 1955. In Argentina, relations between Perón's faltering government and the Catholic Church reach such a low that he is excommunicated, prompting an abortive coup by the navy and part of the air force, which is suppressed by the army.

1 SEPTEMBER 1955. ***Perón's Fall.*** With the Argentine economy in ruins due to his overambitious policies, Perón declares martial law. Two weeks later—16 September—a military revolt erupts in the interior, prompting the president to resign unconditionally three days later and flee into exile aboard a Paraguayan gunboat anchored off Buenos Aires. By 23 September 59-year-old Maj. Gen. Eduardo Lonardi is installed in office as provisional president.

11 NOVEMBER 1955. In the uncertain atmosphere following Brazilian Pres. João Café Filho's mild heart attack, War Minister Henrique Teixeira Lott leads a dawn coup that drives acting Pres. Carlos Luz, intransigent opposition leader Col. Jurandir Mamede, and Congressman Carlos Lacerda aboard the cruiser *Tamandaré*. The vessel sails out of Rio de Janeiro's harbor under fire, its occupants hoping to gain Santos and organize a resistance. Lack of support obliges Luz to return to Rio de Janeiro two days later and surrender.

13 NOVEMBER 1955. Because of his tolerant attitude toward former Peronista supporters and his appointment of ultranationalistic Catholic ministers to the cabinet, Lonardi is ousted as Argentina's interim president, being replaced by Gen. Pedro E. Aramburu.

21 SEPTEMBER 1956. Somoza is killed by Rigoberto López Pérez and succeeded as president of Nicaragua by eldest son Luis Somoza.

2 DECEMBER 1956. ***Castro's Guerrilla Campaign.*** The exile Castro returns to eastern Cuba from Tuxpan (Mexico) with 81 adherents, disembarking from the yacht *Granma* at Las Coloradas beach then disappearing into the mountain jungles of the Sierra Maestra to launch a guerrilla campaign aimed at toppling the corrupt Batista regime.

5 DECEMBER 1956. In a first encounter with Cuban troops, Castro's guerrillas are defeated. However, retreating into the mountains he is soon able to recruit an additional 500 followers and obtain fresh supplies.

EARLY 1958. Castro opens a second guerrilla front in the Escombray Mountains (in Cuba's Las Villas Province).

23 JANUARY 1958. In Venezuela, the corrupt and repressive dictator Pérez Jiménez is deposed by a coup organized by fellow military officers and exiled to the United States.

(Five years later he is extradited to Caracas to stand trial, convicted in 1968, and exiled once more—this time to Spain.)

MARCH 1958. Washington suspends its aid shipments to Batista due to his administration's human rights violations.

APRIL 1958. A general strike throughout Cuba fails to topple Batista.

MAY 1958. Batista launches a military offensive against Castro's guerrillas, which fails to defeat them then peters out two months later.

AUGUST 1958. Batista's army having become thoroughly demoralized, Castro launches a two-pronged offensive into central Cuba: one guerrilla column out of the west under subordinate Camilo Cienfuegos, another out of the east come under former Argentine Dr. Ernesto "Ché" Güevara de la Cerna.

28 DECEMBER 1958. Güevara's guerrilla column captures Santa Clara, capital of Cuba's Las Villas Province.

31 DECEMBER 1958. Tonight Batista flees Cuba into exile; next morning a temporary junta offers the government to Castro.

8 JANUARY 1959. Castro's victorious guerrillas enter Havana; shortly thereafter Manuel Urrutia Lleó is proclaimed interim president.

APRIL 1959. Panama's national guard defeats an inept disembarkation of 80 Cuban guerrillas led by wealthy playboy Roberto Arias (husband of British ballerina Margot Fonteyn), apparently intent on spreading their revolutionary cause. After Arias takes sanctuary in the Brazilian embassy, Castro angrily denounces this unauthorized operation as an attempt to bring Cuba into conflict with the United States.

JULY 1959. Dominican exiles, backed by Cuban supporters, attempt to topple the dictator Trujillo, only to be easily defeated.

JULY 1959. Urrutia is deposed by Osvaldo Dorticós Torrado, and a series of increasingly radical measures is imposed: Batista loyalists are incarcerated or executed; domestic and foreign-owned properties are confiscated; collectives are formed; and so on. Real power still rests with Castro—now head of Cuba's armed forces; thousands of fearful residents flee into exile.

At the same time in Santa Domingo, Dominican exiles—backed by Cuban supporters—attempt to topple the dictator Trujillo, only to be easily defeated.

3 NOVEMBER 1959. During Panama's independence day celebrations 120 people are injured in anti-American riots, which are quelled by national guard and U.S. troops.

13 NOVEMBER 1960. Left-wing nationalistic elements within the Guatemalan army lead a revolt; although repressed, young leaders such as Luis Turcios Lima and Marco Antonio Yon Sosa go on to establish a guerrilla force called Movimiento Revolucionario 13 de Noviembre (MR-13), which launches a protracted struggle.

3 JANUARY 1961. The United States severs diplomatic relations with Castro.

17 APRIL 1961. ***Bay of Pigs.*** This morning the CIA-backed 2506 Brigade—1,443 Cuban exiles subdivided into six 200-man battalions: the 1st Paratroopers; 2nd, 5th, and 6th Infantry; 3rd Armored; and 4th Artillery—disembark on Girón Beach in Bahía de Cochinos (Bay of Pigs, west of Cienfuegos in south-central Cuba) to mount an anti-Castro counterinsurgency. Instead, they are quickly checked by local Cuban troops and militia then overwhelmed in a fierce counterassault. By 19 April 1,200 survivors surrender.

1 MAY 1961. Castro openly announces his adherence to communist ideology and allies himself with the Soviet Union. Washington reacts bitterly.

30 MAY 1961. After more than 31 years of ruthless dictatorship, the corrupt Dominican ruler Trujillo is assassinated.

JANUARY 1962. Cuba is expelled from the U.S.-created Organization of American States.

18 JULY 1962. At dawn, ten days before his term in office is scheduled to expire, Manuel Prado y Ugarteche is toppled as Peruvian president by a military coup led by 57-year-old Gen. Ricardo Pérez Godoy.

22 OCTOBER 1962. ***Cuban Missile Crisis.*** Pres. John F. Kennedy demands the withdrawal of long-range Soviet nuclear missiles, secretly installed in close proximity to the United States. Kennedy imposes a naval blockade to prevent further shipments reaching Cuba then confronts Soviet leader Nikita Khruschev in a tense diplomatic showdown; the weapons are withdrawn and the confrontation is defused by 20 November.

EARLY MARCH 1963. Pérez Godoy is deposed as leader of Peru's military junta by Gen. Nicolás Lindley.

MARCH 1963. Guatemalan President Ydígoras is toppled in a coup led by Col. Enrique Peralta Azurdia.

25 SEPTEMBER 1963. A military coup deposes the leftist president of the Dominican Republic, professor Juan Bosch.

9 JANUARY 1964. Anti-American fighting erupts in Panama over the refusal of authorities to honor an agreement to fly the Panamanian flag in conjunction with the Stars-and-Stripes over the Canal Zone. As a result, President Chiari severs diplomatic relations with Washington next day; four U.S. soldiers and 24 Panamanians are killed and 85 Americans and 200 Panamanians are wounded before order can be restored by 13 January.

Troops are unloaded on a Cuban beach during the Bay of Pigs operation

13 MARCH 1964. Amid a debilitating economic crisis, Brazilian Pres. João Goulart stages a 150,000-person rally in Rio de Janeiro, announcing the nationalization of foreign-owned oil refineries and other socialist measures and calling for a new constitution. Fearful this might presage the establishment of a left-wing dictatorship, 500,000 counterdemonstrators take part in the March of the Family with God for Liberty six days later in São Paulo; another 150,000 march in Santos on 24 March.

Tension comes to a head a few days later when pro-Goulart sailors and marines refuse to obey superior officers at Rio de Janeiro and the president sides with the mutineers. The navy minister resigns in protest, and the military prepares to intervene.

31 MARCH 1964. ***Brazilian Overthrow.*** An anti-Goulart insurrection breaks out this morning in Minas Gerais, rebel columns from Gen. Olímpio Mourão Filho's 1st Army being dispatched under Gen. Carlos de Meira Matos to the capital, Brasilia, as well as to confront loyal forces around Rio de Janeiro. Most garrisons in the interior quickly join the uprising, and on 1 April—after attempting in vain to persuade the president to break with his communist backers—intelligence chief Gen. Amaury Kruel leads the crucial 2nd Army into revolt at São Paulo.

Goulart flies to Brasilia in a last-ditch effort to rally support, but his garrison in Rio de Janeiro mutinies during his absence and so the president instead flees into exile in Uruguay on 2 April. He is succeeded by 63-year-old Gen. Humberto de Alencar Castello Branco, chief of the army general staff, who has used his *febiano* contacts (*see* July 1945) to secretly organize the coup.

28 APRIL 1965. ***Dominican Intervention.*** After Col. Francisco Caamaño Deñó leads a pro-Bosch "constitutionalist" revolt on the Dominican Republic, U.S. Pres. Lyndon B. Johnson—fearful that the ensuing civil war might result in yet another socialist regime taking power in the region—sends 23,000 U.S. troops to intervene and prevent greater fighting against the bulk of the Dominican army under loyal Gens. Elías Wessín y Wessín and Antonio Imbert Barrera.

The conflict continues, however, so on 6 May the U.S. forces are joined by an additional 2,000 Brazilian, Paraguayan, Honduran, Nicaraguan, and Costa Rican troops, known collectively as the Fuerza Interamericana de Pacificación (Interamerican Pacification Force, or FIP). Fighting between rival Dominican factions and against the FIP lasts until August 1965, claiming some 3,000 lives. The interventionist forces finally withdraw in September 1966 after Joaquín Balaguer is reelected president and both Caamaño and Wessín go into exile.

MARCH 1967. Feeling he can most contribute to the communist cause by fomenting further insurrections throughout Latin America, 39-year-old guerrilla leader Ché Güevara leaves Cuba and enters Bolivia in disguise to set up a secret base in the mountains between Santa Cruz and Camiri. He begins with only 60 followers, led by Bolivian brothers Guido and Roberto "Coco" Peredo, who initiate attacks by ambushing an army patrol, killing seven soldiers.

EARLY JULY 1967. After sweeps by 2,500 Bolivian soldiers (Operation Cynthia) fail to locate Güevara, and some 33 troops having been killed as opposed to a handful of guerrillas—Pres. René Barrientos requests military assistance from neighboring Argentina; it is refused.

LATE JULY 1967. The 26-year-old Marxist ideologue and French journalist Jules Régis Debray is captured by Bolivian troops while walking out of one of Güevara's guerrilla camps. He is eventually sentenced to 30 years in jail for his part in the insurgency.

AUGUST 1967. In Pancasán Province (southwestern Nicaragua), the national guard of dictator Anastasio "Tachito" Somoza Debayle crushes the main forces of the Frente Sandinista de Liberación Nacional (Sandinista Front for National Liberation, or FSLN, named in honor of Augusto Sandino; *see* 4 May 1927 under Nicaraguan Civil War), prompting the latter to go underground for the next several years.

MID-OCTOBER 1967. In Yuro Ravine (75 miles north of Camiri), Güevara's jungle camp is discovered by 180 Bolivian rangers, who divide into two columns and attack around noon. After a firefight during which four soldiers and three guerrillas are slain, Güevara—wounded in the left thigh—is captured with three companions and executed next day after being carried five miles to the town of Higueras on a stretcher. His remains are displayed in nearby Valle Grande (population 7,000) for a couple of days and then cremated.

11 OCTOBER 1968. When newly elected Panamanian Pres. Arnulfo Arias attempts to strip the national guard of power and purge its officer corps, 39-year-old Col. Omar Torrijos Herrera deposes him in a military coup, exiling Arias to Miami.

12 JULY 1969. ***Soccer War.*** After two impassioned soccer playoff matches the previous month—being the final qualifying games for a single remaining berth to the 1970 World Cup championship in Mexico—relations between Salvador and Honduras reach the boiling point. Although the former wins the playoff and advances to the tournament, animosity remains high on account of retaliatory measures meted out against the 300,000 impoverished Salvadorans living and working illegally in Honduras.

Therefore, on 12 July the Salvadoran army crosses the border, occupying the towns of Nueva Ocotepeque, El Amatillo, and Nacaoné. The Honduran army retaliates, and fighting rages until the Organization of American States calls for a cease-fire six days later. Eventually economic sanctions compel the Salvadorans to withdraw by 5 August, the conflict resulting in 3,000 casualties.

DECEMBER 1969. Attending horse races in Mexico City, Panamanian strongman Torrijos is deposed by a military coup led by Col. Amado Sanjur. Returning home aboard a private plane lended to him by Nicaraguan dictator Anastasio Somoza, Torrijos rallies the national guard garrison at David and other towns, overthrows Sanjur, and reclaims power. All political parties are outlawed, and as many as 1,600 opponents are detained.

4 SEPTEMBER 1970. In Chile, Marxist candidate Dr. Salvador Allende Gossens is elected president with 36 percent of the vote, after a heated three-way race. Opposition to his ruinous leftist policies will spring up domestically and internationally—especially in Washington, where the CIA actively works toward his downfall.

21 APRIL 1971. Haiti's dictator François "Papa Doc" Duvalier dies in office.

FEBRUARY 1973. Colonel Caamaño returns to the Dominican Republic (*see* 28 April 1965), disembarking with a few followers in hopes of establishing an insurrectionist guerrilla movement. He is killed in battle within a few days.

11 SEPTEMBER 1973. ***Allende's Fall.*** At 11:52 A.M.—after months of heightened tensions and economic collapse—two Chilean Hawker Hunter fighter jets fire rocket salvos into La Moneda presidential palace, setting parts of it ablaze. From his command post in Peñalolen (a Santiago suburb in the Andean foothills), the coup leader—recently promoted Gen. Augusto Pinochet Ugarte—orders tank and infantry columns under Gen. Javier Palacios to descend on Allende's residence. They fight their way inside after 90 minutes of resistance from civilian bodyguards and nearby snipers.

Allende is found dead within an inner room, either from his own hand, from earlier exchanges of gunfire, or from triumphant soldiers. Expecting widespread leftist opposition throughout the rest of the country, other units are surprised to easily overrun ideological strongholds, arresting thousands of activists. Pinochet quickly establishes a junta with air force Gen. Gustavo Leigh, Adm. José Toribio Merino, and Gen. César Mendoza of the *carabineros* (paramilitary police), declaring martial law next day. By December at least 1,500 Chileans are dead and 45,000 have been detained; 7,000 more have fled into exile as repression sets in.

27 DECEMBER 1974. Sandinista guerrillas kidnap several top Nicaraguan officials and U.S. Ambassador Turner B. Shelton, eventually releasing them for a sizable ransom.

JANUARY 1978. Pedro Joaquín Chamorro, editor of Nicaragua's main opposition newspaper *La Prensa,* is assassinated by Somoza's national guard. The brutal act galvanizes public indignation, resulting in demonstrations and a general strike.

AUGUST 1978. Popular risings occur at Matagalpa, Jinotepa, Esteli, and Masaya against the rule of Nicaraguan dictator Somoza.

In neighboring Honduras, Policarpo Paz García assumes power in a bloodless coup.

22 AUGUST 1978. ***Sandinista Revolt.*** After several months of increasing turmoil, the two-year-old Tercerista (Third Force) guerrilla faction of brothers Daniel and Umberto Ortega Saavedra score a major propaganda triumph when 25 members under Edén Pastora Gómez—his nom de guerre being Comandante Cero, or Commander Zero—infiltrate Nicaragua's national palace and hold 2,000 people hostage before escaping to Panama. This daring coup, coupled with growing diplomatic displeasure out of Washington, emboldens opposition against Somoza's rule.

4 MAY 1979. Armed uprisings erupt in León, Matagalpa, Masaya, and even some sections of the capital Managua against Nicaraguan dictator Somoza. After initially recoiling into bases, the national guard is able to reclaim the capital one month later.

17 JULY 1979. After being pinned within Managua by 5,000 Sandinista guerrillas and 15,000 militia supporters, Somoza and many of his officers flee Nicaragua, thereby allowing Ortega's victorious columns to enter the capital two days later. The guerrilla coalition quickly splinters, having only been held together by hatred of the now absent dictator. Ortega's embracing of Marxist ideology, as well as Cuban and Soviet aid, produces a split internally and internationally, especially with Washington.

22 JANUARY 1980. An antigovernment demonstration is put down in Salvador with 200 casualties.

24 MARCH 1980. Salvadoran archbishop Oscar Romero—an outspoken critic of the right-wing government and oligarchy—is assassinated by a sniper.

APRIL 1980. Violeta Barrios de Chamorro—widow of the slain *La Prensa* editor (*see* January 1978)—forms the anti-Sandinista Alianza Revolucionaria Democrática (ARDE) coalition with Alonso Robelo and former guerrilla chieftain Edén Pastora.

OCTOBER 1980. ***Salvadoran Insurrection.*** Salvador's numerous guerrilla groups, representing 6,500–7,500 fighters, coalesce into the Frente "Farabundo Martí" de Liberación Nacional ("Farabundo Martí" Front for National Liberation, or FMLN).

DECEMBER 1980. U.S. Pres. Jimmy Carter suspends military aid to the Salvadoran government to protest human rights abuses.

JANUARY 1981. Salvador's guerrillas launch a countrywide offensive, knowing that government forces are hamstrung by lack of U.S. material support.

JULY 1981. The Republican administration of Pres. Ronald Reagan resumes military aid to the Salvadoran government, fearing a socialist takeover by leftist guerrillas.

31 JULY 1981. Panama's strongman, General Torrijos, is killed in a mysterious plane crash.

SEPTEMBER 1981. The Central American colony of Belize gains independence from Britain as well as a pledge of military support from London against any projected invasion by neighboring Guatemala.

27 JANUARY 1982. Guerrillas attack the Ilopango air force base in central Salvador, destroying or damaging a dozen aircraft and seven helicopters—approximately half the Salvadoran air strength. The losses are immediately made up by the U.S. government.

7 MARCH 1982. In Guatemala, Pres. Fernando Romeo Lucas García's handpicked successor—Gen. Angel Aníbal Güevara—is defeated at the polls yet claims victory. The attempted fraud provokes a military coup on 23 March, with Gens. Efraín Ríos Montt and Horacio Egberto Maldonado Schaad briefly sharing power along with Col. Francisco Luis Gordillo Martínez. (The latter two are jettisoned by 9 June, Ríos Montt remaining as president.)

JUNE 1982. FMLN guerrillas seize control of Chalatenango and Morazán Provinces (central and eastern Salvador, respectively).

28 JANUARY 1983. FMLN guerrillas assault I Brigade's headquarters near the capital of San Salvador.

AUGUST 1983. Guatemala's President Ríos Montt is overthrown by a military coup led by Gen. Oscar Mejía Víctores.

30 MAY 1984. At a press conference, anti-Sandinista guerrilla chief Edén Pastora narrowly escapes assassination by a bomb hidden in a journalist's camera.

7 FEBRUARY 1986. After several months of street disturbances and mounting international pressure, 34-year-old Haitian dictator Jean Claude "Baby Doc" Duvalier flees overnight into exile in France with his wife and 20 relations aboard a U.S. Air Force transport. He is temporarily replaced by a five-man junta headed by his army chief of staff, Lt. Gen. Henri Namphy.

18 JUNE 1986. Several hundred captive Sendero Luminoso (Shining Path) guerrillas, held in three separate Peruvian prisons, rise in a concerted operation—seconded by a string of bombings by outside supporters. The 37-year-old leftist Pres. Alan García responds by sending in troops to restore order. They brutally quell the prison uprisings within the next few days, slaughtering at least 300 inmates.

7–11 DECEMBER 1986. The Honduran army repels a Sandinista incursion into El Paraíso (south-central Honduras) aimed at punishing Contra activities.

15 APRIL 1987. Facing indictment in criminal court for his role in Argentina's "Dirty War" against leftist dissenters during the 1970s, Maj. Ernesto Barreiro—former interrogator at the notorious La Perla Prison—takes sanctuary at an army base outside Córdoba (400 miles northwest of Buenos Aires). He is supported by 130 local officers and soldiers but flees a few days later once 61-year-old Pres. Raúl Alfonsín flies back from his Easter vacation at Chascomas to implement vigorous countermeasures.

A second, more serious insurrection quickly erupts at Campo de Mayo 20 miles outside the capital, where Lt. Col. Aldo Rico spearheads a revolt demanding amnesty for all remaining officers accused of human rights violations plus the dismissal of 23 generals deemed weak in upholding the army's honor (including the 56-year-old chief of staff, Hector Ríos Ereñu). Alfonsín orders the base surrounded by more than 1,000 troops then helicopters in on 19 April to negotiate with Rico, returning to inform the huge throngs before his presidential palace that the rebellion is ended.

Subsequent developments, however, suggest that Alfonsín has conceded much to the mutineers: although Rico is stripped of his rank and arrested, Ríos Ereñu resigns in favor of intelligence chief José Segundo Dante Caridi, along with another 15 generals. After additional unrest at infantry garrisons in the northern provinces of Salta and Tucumán on 21 April, it becomes increasingly obvious that criminal trials of military atrocities will be indefinitely suspended.

FEBRUARY 1988. The U.S. Congress finally prevents all aid from reaching the CIA-backed Contras, who have failed in their eight-year campaign to topple Ortega's Sandinista regime in Nicaragua.

MARCH 1988. A large-scale Sandinista incursion into neighboring Honduras prompts the dispatch of U.S. reinforcements, but war along the border is averted at the last minute.

11 MAY 1988. After growing internal unrest two Guatemalan army garrisons revolt and march on the capital to depose the civilian president, Vinicio Cerezo. He manages to remain in office but with diminished authority.

19 JUNE 1988. Haitian Lt. Gen. Henri Namphy overthrows civilian Pres. Leslie Manigat, who has attempted to dismiss him from his position as army chief of staff.

18 SEPTEMBER 1988. Namphy is deposed as Haiti's president by Brig. Gen. Prosper Avril, the uprising being backed by army NCOs and the "Dessalines" Battalion.

23 JANUARY 1989. At 6:15 A.M. a band of leftist urban guerrillas from the Movimiento Todos por la

Patria (MTP; translation: All for the Nation) drive eight civilian vehicles into La Tablada army base 12 miles southwest of Buenos Aires, surprising its 3rd Argentine Infantry Regiment. Reinforced by 500 police, tanks, and artillery, the troops crush the incursion 30 hours later, killing 28 rebels and capturing another 20 while suffering nine killed and 53 wounded among their own ranks.

3 FEBRUARY 1989. ***End of Stroessner's Regime.*** Before sunrise in the Paraguayan capital of Asunción two-dozen tanks and troops of the 1st Army Corps attack the residence of the mistress of 76-year-old Alfredo Stroessner; the dictator is known to be inside, ailing from prostate cancer. After an eight-hour exchange with loyal troops that claims more than 300 lives, the despot is captured, ending a 34-year rule.

The coup has been engineered by Stroessner's second-in-command, 64-year-old Gen. Andrés Rodríguez—whose daughter is married to Stroessner's son, Freddy—who now succeeds as the dominant Colorado Party candidate for president. The deposed leader is allowed to fly into Brazilian exile two days later.

27 FEBRUARY 1989. Due to economic collapse and harsh government austerity measures, Caracas and 16 other Venezuelan cities erupt with three days of looting, resulting in 300 deaths, 2,000 injuries, and 2,000 arrests.

FALKLANDS CAMPAIGN (1982)

IN ORDER TO DISTRACT THE ARGENTINE PUBLIC from soaring inflation and political unease, a junta headed by Gen. Leopoldo Galtieri plans an early summer invasion to retake the offshore Falkland or Malvina Islands from Great Britain (they have been a bone of contention between the nations since 1833; *see* Part 7). In mid-March the date of operation is advanced when a group of Argentine scrap-metal merchants lands at Keith in South Georgia, planting their flag and thus precipitating an intense diplomatic flurry.

24 MARCH 1982. In response to escalating tensions, a detachment of 22 Royal Marines is landed at Grytviken from the lightly armed 3,600-ton ice patrol vessel HMS *Endurance.* Next day a small party of Argentine Buzo Táctico commandos (tactical divers; similar to U.S. Navy SEALS) disembark at Leith from their 3,100-ton Canadian-built transport *Bahía Buen Suceso.*

28 MARCH 1982. Argentine Task Force 20 departs Puerto Belgrano on the mainland, allegedly to participate in exercises with the Uruguayan navy. It consists of the 16,000-ton aircraft carrier *25 de Mayo* (formerly British HMS *Venerable*); the 1950s-vintage type 42 destroyer *Hércules;* the 2,400-ton *Comodoro Py,* and the 2,200-ton *Seguí* (two older former U.S. Navy destroyers); the 4,300-ton landing ship *Cabo San Antonio;* and three transports bearing the 900-man marine and army assault force (Task Force 40) intended to invade the Falklands on 1 April.

Another group of 80 marines (Task Force 60.1) is designated to capture South Georgia aboard the 9,000-ton transport *Bahía Paraíso,* escorted by the 1,000-ton French-built missile type A69 light frigates (or corvettes) *Drummond* and *Granville.* Originally codenamed Operation Rosario the entire effort is now renamed Operation Azul ("Blue").

2 APRIL 1982. ***Argentine Occupation.*** Having been delayed by a gale, Argentine Task Force 40 appears at dawn off Port Stanley, its assault force streaming ashore seven miles away at Cape Pembroke and occupying Government House and the Royal Marine "Moody Brook" barracks by 9:00 A.M. after limited resistance from 67 British defenders of Royal Marine detachment NP8901. Maj. Gen. Osvaldo J. García temporarily assumes office as military governor over the Falklands' 1,800 inhabitants, with Rear Adm. Carlos Büsser as his second.

Next day South Georgia is occupied by a detachment from the Argentine transport *Bahía Paraíso* and the frigate *Granville* after a sharp battle against its 22-man British garrison.

3 APRIL 1982. The United Nations Security Council passes Resolution 502, calling on Argentina to withdraw its troops from the Falklands.

4 APRIL 1982. The first Argentine jet fighters begin arriving at Port Stanley, having been flown out from the mainland to bolster defenses.

5 APRIL 1982. The first Royal Navy warships depart Britain to escort advance elements of a task force intended to reconquer the Falklands (code name: Oper-

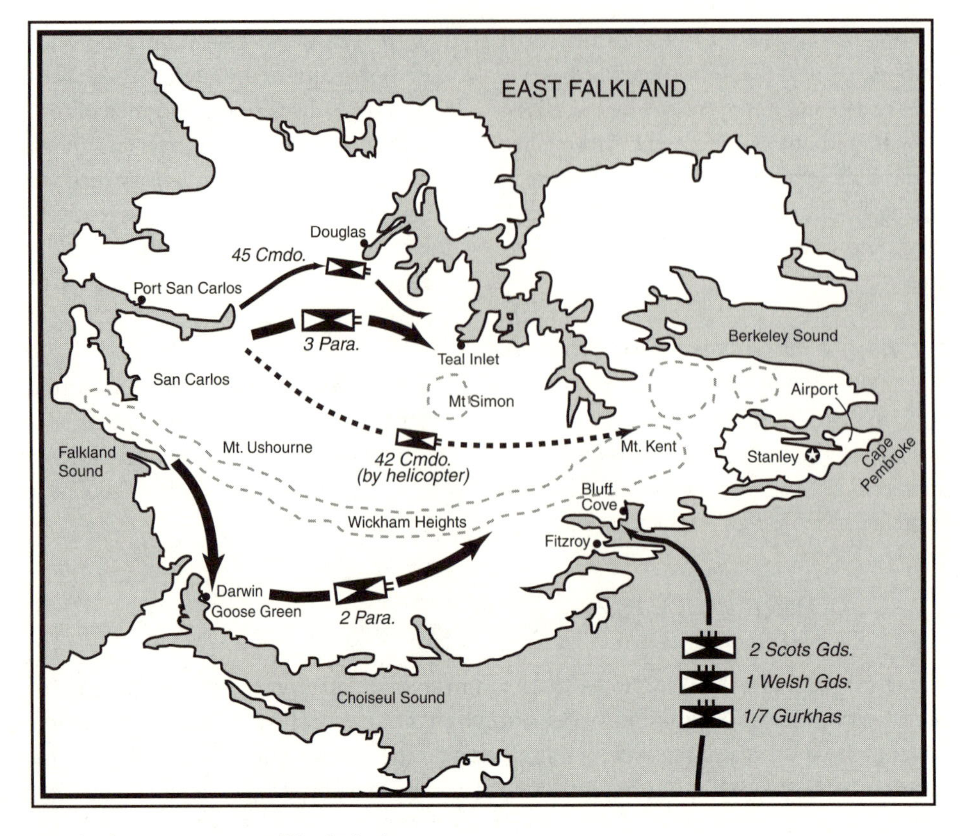

British advance across East Falkland Island

ation Corporate). Rear Adm. John "Sandy" Woodward is the battle group's commander; it includes the aircraft carriers *Hermes* and *Invincible.*

7 APRIL 1982. Brig. Gen. Mario Benjamín Menéndez arrives to assume office as governor of the Malvinas. Simultaneously, the Argentine government announces a 200-mile exclusion zone around the islands.

In Europe, meanwhile, France strongly backs ally Britain by clamping an embargo on the shipment of nine more Exocet missiles to Argentina, which leaves the invaders with only five.

9 APRIL 1982. SS *Canberra* and other British transports depart England with the first elements of the main expeditionary force, soon followed by more support vessels—including the requisitioned liner *Queen Elizabeth II.*

12 APRIL 1982. Prime Minister Margaret Thatcher announces that any Argentine warship found within 200 miles of the Falklands shall be sunk without warning. Fearing this might portend sudden attacks by the modern nuclear submarines HMSS *Superb* and *Spartan,* many of the Argentine surface ships quickly retire into territorial waters.

25 APRIL 1982. The 1,900-ton Argentine submarine *Santa Fe* (originally of the 1945 U.S. Navy "Guppy" class) is spotted leaving South Georgia after delivering supplies to occupiers and is damaged by Royal Navy helicopters; it is forced to turn back and beach at Grytviken.

26–27 APRIL 1982. South Georgia is recaptured in a predawn attack by the 22nd "Special Air Service" Regiment and the 42nd Royal Marine Commandos.

30 APRIL 1982. U.S. Secretary of State Alexander Haig abandons his attempts at mediation, and the U.S. government throws its support behind Great Britain.

1 MAY 1982. RAF Vulcan bombers and task force Harrier jets begin their first attacks on Port Stanley Airport.

2 MAY 1982. The 44-year-old, 11,000-ton Argentine cruiser *General Belgrano*—escorted by the 2,200-ton destroyers *Hipólito Bouchard* and *Piedrabuena* (formerly U.S. Navy "Sumner" class vessels)—is struck by two torpedoes fired from the British nuclear submarine *Conqueror.* Its bow blown off, it settles under the waves two hours later with the loss of 321 of 1,042 crewmembers.

4 MAY 1982. Shortly after 2:00 P.M. the 3,500-ton type 42 destroyer HMS *Sheffield* of Capt. James Salt is struck by an Exocet missile launched from Super Etendard aircraft of the Argentine navy's 2nd Fighter-Attack Squadron, flying out of Tierra del Fuego. The Royal Navy warship suffers 20 killed and 24 wounded and burns out during the next four hours, the hulk being scuttled six days later when the weather turns foul.

14 MAY 1982. The 22nd SAS Regiment raids the Argentine airfield on Pebble Island, destroying numerous parked aircraft.

21 MAY 1982. ***British Counterinvasion.*** At 8:30 A.M. the main British task force comes ashore and establishes a 5,000-man beachhead at San Carlos Bay (on the west coast of East Falkland Island) while commando feints and naval bombardments disorient the Argentine defenders. This same day, the 2,750-ton, type 21 frigate HMS *Ardent* is sunk during an air attack by the Argentine navy's 1st Attack Squadron—operating out of Port Stanley—which in turn loses at least 14 of its own aircraft.

23 MAY 1982. The 2,750-ton frigate HMS *Antelope,* supporting the San Carlos Bay disembarkation, is crippled by two 500-pound bombs dropped by an Argentine Skyhawk jet, sinking next day. At least six attacking aircraft are shot down during today's action.

24 MAY 1982. Argentine air attacks continue, resulting in the loss of eight more planes.

25 MAY 1982. The 3,500-ton destroyer HMS *Coventry* is sunk by an Argentine air attack; the 15,000-ton hired container ship *Atlantic Conveyor*—carrying important British supplies and helicopters—is struck by an Exocet AM 39 missile launched by a Super Etendard of the Argentine navy's 2nd Fighter-Attack Squadron (now flying out of Río Gallegos) and burns out.

26 MAY 1982. British troops move inland from their San Carlos beachhead via two routes.

28 MAY 1982. ***Goose Green.*** The 2nd Battalion of the British Parachute Regiment takes Darwin by midmorning and Goose Green this afternoon after fighting against stiff resistance. The 1,000 survivors from the 1,400-man Argentine garrison under Air Commo. Wilson Pedrozo officially surrender to the 600 British paratroopers next morning. British casualties total 13 killed and 34 wounded.

31 MAY 1982. Troops of the 42nd Royal Marine Commandos are helicoptered in to seize Mount Kent, a key position overlooking Port Stanley.

2 JUNE 1982. The first British troops come within sight of Port Stanley.

8 JUNE 1982. This evening two Argentine Daggers and two Skyhawks make a surprise strafing pass against the logistical landing ships (LSLs) *Sir Tristram* and *Sir Galahad* in Port Fitzroy off Bluff Cove, inflicting heavy casualties among the troops aboard; 41 are killed and 46 are wounded among the 1st Battalion of the Welsh Guards alone, with another 60 casualties.

12 JUNE 1982. ***Final Drive on Port Stanley.*** After a series of nocturnal clashes along the high ground west of Port Stanley, the British overrun Mount Longdon, Two Sisters, and Mount Harriet. During the previous night's action a jury-rigged Argentine Exocet missile was launched from land—a feat thought impossible—striking the 5,400-ton destroyer HMS *Glamorgan* offshore, killing 13 crewmembers and wounding 17 more; damage is soon brought under control.

14 JUNE 1982. Tumbledown, Mount William, and Wireless Ridge are taken in British night attacks. The Argentine troops flee their final positions before Port Stanley, and white flags begin to be seen. The Argentine commander in chief, Brigadier General Menéndez, agrees to parley with British Maj. Gen. Jeremy Moore and capitulates with his 11,000 men at 9:00 P.M. During this brief war 255 British lives have been lost as opposed to more than 1,000 Argentines.

Grenada Invasion (1983)

After a couple of centuries of British colonial rule, the Caribbean island of Grenada gains independence in 1974, its first prime minister being the eccentric Sir Eric Gairy, a former trade union organizer. In March 1979 he is overthrown in a bloodless coup by longtime political rival Maurice Bishop, who heads the New JEWEL Movement Party (Joint Endeavor for Welfare, Education, and Liberation). The organization actively seeks closer ties with Cuba and other communist states, culminating in an ambitious project to build a 9,000-foot runway at Point Salines (southwestern tip of Grenada). Although ostensibly intended to bolster the island's sagging tourist trade by receiving large jets, it will also serve as a staging base for Cuban airlifts to Africa and Soviet flights into Nicaragua.

By the summer of 1983 Bishop and one faction of the JEWEL movement has grown distinctly uneasy over this heavy-handed communist connection and wish to reestablish better relations with the West. Deputy Prime Minister Bernard Coard and another group, however, are determined to lead Grenada's conversion into a full-blown Marxist state. On 13 October 1983 Coard—after first obtaining the backing of Gen. Hudson Austin—places Bishop under house arrest to stand trial for "failing to carry out orders from the central committee." Several days of pro-Bishop demonstrations ensue upon the island, with diplomatic protests coming in from abroad.

On Wednesday, 19 October, Foreign Minister Unison Whiteman harangues a crowd in the capital, Saint George's, which then marches on the official residence at Mount Royal and frees Bishop over token opposition. Fired by this success, the mob liberates detained cabinet members from old Fort Ruppert. At this moment three armored personnel carriers and a truckload of People's Revolutionary Army (PRA) soldiers arrive under officer cadet Conrad Meyers, who gives the order to open fire. More than 100 Grenadians are killed; Bishop and several prominent supporters are then rearrested and brutally put to death inside the fort.

News of the atrocity prompts neighboring Dominica, Saint Lucia, Saint Vincent, Montserrat, Saint Kitts-Nevis, and Antigua to request military intervention from Barbados, Jamaica, and the United States. The conservative administration of U.S. Pres. Ronald Reagan—which has viewed developments in Grenada with growing distaste—reacts swiftly, being especially concerned for the fate of 1,000 U.S. citizens on the island (mostly students and faculty at Saint George's University Medical School).

20 October 1983. The Cuban government denounces the killings of Bishop and his supporters as "atrocious acts" and calls for "exemplary punishment" of his murderers.

21 October 1983. U.S. Navy Task Force 124 is diverted from a training exercise in the Caribbean to steam directly to Grenada and conduct an evacuation of American noncombatants. It comprises the helicopter carrier *Guam* and four landing ships under the command of Capt. Carl E. Erie. Aboard are 1,700 Marines of the 22nd MAU (Marine Amphibious Unit) under Col. James P. Faulkner. The carrier battle group *Independence* of Rear Adm. Richard C. Berry is also diverted from the Atlantic to reinforce the operation—designated Urgent Fury—along with its escort of cruisers and destroyers.

22 October 1983. Cuba's ambassador in Grenada informs Coard and Austin that no military aid will be sent from Havana, although the 700-man construction battalion working on the Point Salines runway will be ordered to fight alongside the PRA (under separate command). This same day, Gov.-Gen. Sir Paul Scoon—the Queen's representative in Grenada and virtual prisoner at Government House—smuggles out a request for international intervention, which the American administration chooses to honor.

23 October 1983. Vice Adm. Joseph Metcalf III arrives aboard *Guam* to assume overall command of the newly activated joint Task Force 120, with Maj. Gen. Norman H. Schwarzkopf serving as deputy. (This same Sunday, a suicide truck bomber destroys the Marine barracks in Beirut, Lebanon, killing more than 270 U.S. servicemen.)

24 October 1983. Cuban Col. Pedro Tortolo Comas flies into Pearls Airport to assume command of the Cuban construction battalion.

25 October 1983. Before dawn in a steady rain U.S. Navy SEAL teams reconnoiter Pearls Airport and its surrounding beaches, discovering them to be heavily defended. An Air Force reconnaissance AC-130 Spectre gunship also surveys the Point Salines runway,

An American soldier guarding prisoners on Grenada

which is found to be blocked with vehicles and other obstructions. At 5:00 A.M., therefore, Admiral Metcalf sends in his first marine contingent aboard CH-46 helicopters rather than risk a disembarkation. Although some antiaircraft fire is drawn while they cross the coast 20 minutes later, it is suppressed by the accompanying AH-1T Sea Cobra helicopter gunships; the marine companies occupy Pearls and nearby Grenville by 6:30 A.M. with minimal casualties on both sides.

Around 5:30 A.M. three AC-130 gunships and ten MC-130 transports approach Point Salines, only to encounter heavy antiaircraft fire. Air Force Col. Hugh Hunter therefore decides to suppress it with strafing runs before allowing the 280 Army Ranger paratroopers to jump. The latter are dropped 45 minutes later and clear the runway within 15 minutes, as most Cuban defenders are down on the beach anticipating a seaborne assault. The rangers quickly overrun their camp, Colonel Tortolo being one of the few to escape into the Russian embassy in Saint George's. Heavier fighting is encountered when the Cuban companies are broken on the beaches shortly thereafter, one counterattack being spearheaded by three BTR-60 armored personnel carriers, all of which are destroyed.

SEAL raids on the Radio Free Grenada transmitter, Richmond Hill Prison (where many prominent captives are held), and Government House experience various degrees of difficulty, during which at least four American aircraft are downed. By 2:05 P.M., however, another wave of transports begins landing at Point Salines from Pope Air Force base (North Carolina) to disgorge the 82nd Airborne. The Cuban prisoners are corralled; the medical school is secured by evening.

26 OCTOBER 1983. Two hours before sunrise marines from the LST *Manitowoc* under Lt. Col. Ray Smith disembark at Grand Mal Bay with five M-60A1 tanks to rescue the SEAL team pinned down within Government House by 7:00 A.M. A helicopter landing zone is established at Queen's Park race course, and Fort Frederick is secured by 5:00 P.M. with little opposition.

About the same time, a heliborne ranger-marine force from *Guam* assaults Grand Anse to rescue some 200 American students. A CH-46 helicopter is shot down before the rest of the force rushes the defenses and lifts out the students (a dozen rangers left behind head out to sea aboard a stolen fishing boat and are picked up by the destroyer *Caron*.)

Farther south, the 82nd Airborne advances out of its base, overwhelming Cuban and Grenadian resistance.

27 OCTOBER 1983. American units move inland to an enthusiastic greeting from Grenada's civilian population. At Frequente, a Navy A-7 air strike is mistakenly directed against a group of 82nd paratroopers, killing one and wounding 15. At 4:45 P.M. the Calivigny barracks are bombarded and stormed, its 30 defenders being subdued after a brave resistance. Three Americans are killed and a dozen injured during a multiple helicopter accident. By 10:00 P.M. the capital of Saint George's is entered without opposition, and an empty Richmond Hill Prison is seized (the guards having fled, with inmates releasing themselves).

28 OCTOBER 1983. The evacuation of American medical students to Barbados continues and mop-up operations proceed.

OCTOBER–DECEMBER 1983. Next day the first Caribbean peacekeeping forces arrive, and General Austin and his bodyguards are arrested. Nearby Carriacou Island is overrun by 31 October, but no resistance is encountered (although a large arms cache is captured).

The Cuban worker battalion and other Eastern bloc representatives are quickly deported from Grenada, and prominent JEWEL leaders are held for trial before the U.S. invaders depart by mid-December. Nineteen American servicemen have given their lives and 116 have been wounded during the operation as opposed to 70 defenders killed (including 25 Cubans) and 409 wounded (59 Cubans). Castro's prestige suffers a serious setback throughout the region, several Caribbean countries severing ties with Havana.

Panama Campaign (1989)

On 15 February 1988 51-year-old Brig. Gen. Manuel Antonio Noriega—commander in chief of the Panamanian Defense Forces (PDF) and de facto ruler—is indicted on drug-trafficking charges by grand juries in Florida. Although subsequently fired by Pres. Eric Arturo Delvalle during a live television broadcast, the general simply dismisses that official and his vice president, replacing them with the more compliant Manuel Palma. Cuba and Nicaragua are the only foreign countries to recognize this irregular change of government.

Relations between Washington and Panama—already strained because of Noriega's corruption and flirtation with anti-American factions—now takes a decidedly downward slide. When the dictator brutally annuls the presidential elections of 7 May 1989 (with opposition leader Guillermo Endara poised to win), then further begins harassing American dependents in the Canal Zone, the George Bush administration finally decides to act. A mixed brigade from the army's 7th Light Infantry Division, 5th Mechanized Infantry Division, and 2nd Marine Light Armored Infantry Division are sent to protect U.S. interests; Gen. Maxwell Thurman is appointed to command.

3 October 1989. Panamanian Maj. Moisés Giroldi Vega launches an abortive coup against Noriega, his followers being crushed by the PDF's 7th Company and "2000" battalion (so named because the canal is to be restored to Panamanian control in 2000).

15 December 1989. After weeks of escalating tension with Washington, Noriega is proclaimed "maximum leader" by Panama's rubber-stamp legislature; a "state of war" is also declared.

16 December 1989. Four unarmed marine officers are attacked at a PDF checkpoint near Noriega's headquarters, Lt. Robert Paz being killed.

17 December 1989. This Sunday President Bush authorizes the dispatch of 11,000 troops from the XVIII Airborne Corps out of the continental United States to join the 13,000 already guarding the canal and depose Noriega's regime in an operation codenamed Just Cause.

20 December 1989. After building up their numbers in the Canal Zone, the Americans launch attacks at 1:00 A.M. in four task forces: Bayonet, Red, Semper Fidelis, and Atlantic.

The first—comprising two infantry battalions, four light Sheridan tanks, and a SEAL team—advance on the PDF base at Fort Amador plus their headquarters in downtown Panama City. A SEAL team meanwhile disables Noriega's private Lear jet at Paitilla Airport, suffering four dead and 11 wounded in fierce hand-to-hand combat before retiring. Task Force Atlantic—a battalion of 75th Rangers plus two battalions of the 82nd's 1st Airborne Brigade—drop into the Torrijos-Tocumén Airport, covered by AC-130 Specter gunships. (Noriega flees from the officers' club, having been asleep.)

The Panamanian "2000" Battalion attempts to mount a counterattack by fighting west out of the Fort Cimarrón headquarters and across the Pacora River, only to be driven back by the awesome firepower of the American gunships. At 5:00 A.M. (nearly four hours late), four C-141 StarLifter and three C-130 Hercules jet transports arrive over Panama City from Pope Air Force Base (North Carolina), dropping more paratroopers. Task Force Bayonet has meanwhile overrun PDF headquarters downtown, the firefight engulfing much of the Chorillo slums in flames. Resistance does not cease until Thursday morning, 21 December.

In the meantime, air force F-117A Stealth fighter bombers out of Tonopah (Nevada) destroy the armored capabilities of the 600-man PDF concentration—the 6th and 7th Companies—at Río Hato, 55–60 miles west of Panama City, followed up by a paratroop drop of a battalion of 75th Rangers under Col. Buck Kernan from 15 transports. This effectively precludes any potential Panamanian counterattack from the base, 34 PDF troops being killed and another 260 captured at a cost of four rangers dead and 27 wounded (as well as 35 jump injuries).

Burning buildings and devastation in Panama during Operation Just Cause

23 December 1989. Having easily routed the PDF, 2,000 additional American troops of the 7th Infantry Division are flown in to restore order in Panama City—now the scene of widespread looting and rioting—and to end sporadic sniper fire.

24 December 1989. After spending four days in hiding Noriega is granted political asylum at the papal embassy in Panama City along with ten of his bodyguards. The place is immediately cordoned off by U.S. forces.

29 December 1989. Waiting for Noriega to surrender, American troops smash into the Nicaraguan embassy in Panama City, uncovering a large cache of weapons and provoking a diplomatic incident.

3 January 1990. At 8:50 P.M. Noriega exits the papal embassy and is seized by American troops. Flown to Howard Air Force Base aboard a Night Hawk helicopter, he is arrested by DEA agents and extradited to Miami aboard an MC-130 transport to stand trial for drug trafficking. Casualties from Operation Just Cause are estimated at 23 Americans killed and 330 wounded; 297 PDF members killed and 123 wounded (several hundred more being captured); plus 500 Panamanian civilians killed and hundreds others injured.

Haitian Operation (1994)

After three years of unavailing diplomatic efforts to restore the democratically elected Jean Bertrand Aristide as president of Haiti—including the use of a naval blockade and freezing of Haitian assets in the United States—U.S. Pres. Bill Clinton authorizes a military intervention, dubbed Operation Uphold Democracy.

May 1994. Frail, 80-year-old Emile Jonassaint is installed as Haiti's president and prime minister by Lt. Gen. Raoul Cédras, army chief of staff and de facto ruler over the island. The United States and most other countries refuse to recognize this as a legitimate change of government.

31 JULY 1994. The United Nations passes an American-sponsored resolution authorizing the use of force to restore the exiled Aristide to power.

23 SEPTEMBER 1994. After dispatching a 23-vessel U.S. fleet with a large landing force to Haiti the previous evening President Clinton allows a trio of emissaries—former Pres. Jimmy Carter; the former chief of the U.S. Joint Chiefs of Staff, Gen. Colin Powell; and Sen. Sam Nunn of Georgia, chairman of the Armed Services Committee—to fly to the capital, Port au Prince, on Friday to carry out last-minute negotiations. They offer inducements to Cédras, second-in-command Brig. Gen. Philippe Biamby, and police chief Lt. Col. Joseph Michel François to go into exile.

26 SEPTEMBER 1994. An American task force appears off Haiti under Adm. Paul D. Miller, consisting of the nuclear aircraft carriers *America* and *Eisenhower*, bearing more than 100 helicopters and 4,000 troops between them; the helicopter carrier *Wasp*, conveying an additional 2,000 marines; the amphibious assault vessels *Nashville* and *Mount Whitney;* the guided-missile destroyer *Comte de Grasse;* the guided-missile frigates *Aubrey Fitch, Oliver Hazard Perry,* and *Clifton Sprague;* and 14 other transports and support vessels. Together they quickly throw 19,000 men ashore, encountering no opposition from Haiti's 7,000-man army, which is ordered not to fight because of Cédras's last-minute acceptance of Washington's terms.

SEPTEMBER–OCTOBER 1994. After a three-week occupation, during which American peacekeeping forces and UN allies fully secure the island, Aristide returns to Port au Prince on 15 October; Cédras flies off to exile in Panama.

RECENT EVENTS (1990–1998)

3 DECEMBER 1990. Argentine army troops, followers of arrested Col. Mohamed Ali Seineldin—Argentine-born, but of Arab extraction—mutiny, only to be put down by loyal forces.

MID-DECEMBER 1990. In Panama, former Noriega loyalist Eduardo Hassan leads a revolt by 100 members of the newly created Fuerza Pública de Panamá (Panama Public Force, or FPP), being put down by the 193rd U.S. Infantry Brigade.

JANUARY 1995. Peruvian and Ecuadorean troops clash over four border outposts along 48 miles of still ill-charted frontier in the Condor Range between both nations. (Such outbursts usually coincide with anniversaries of the 29 January 1942 Treaty of Rio de Janeiro, whereby Ecuador lost most of this territory; *see* July 1941 under Latin American Troubles.) An estimated 31 fatalities are inflicted among both sides by the end of the month before renewed mediation attempts are made at Rio de Janeiro.

22 APRIL 1997. Following a four-month occupation of the Japanese embassy in Lima by 14 Tupac Amaru guerrillas, 140 Peruvian commandos launch a surprise attack at 3:19 P.M. while leader Nestor Cerpa Cartolini and nine followers are exercising by playing soccer inside. All the terrorists and two soldiers are killed in a half-hour shootout, which is further punctuated by numerous detonations; one of the 72 hostages dies of a heart attack.

13 JULY 1997. The exhumed remains of Ché Güevara (*see* mid-October 1967 under Latin American Troubles) are returned to Cuba, being received at the San Antonio de los Baños air base outside Havana by a full military guard headed by President Castro.

2 MARCH 1998. On Monday of the week leading up to Colombia's congressional elections, Marxist guerrillas of the Fuerzas Armadas Revolucionarias de Colombia (Revolutionary Armed Forces of Colombia, or FARC) ambush a column of government troops within El Billar Ravine along the jungle banks of the Caguan River deep in coca-producing Caquetá Province, near the Amazonian headwaters in the southernmost corner of the country. Several score fatalities are inflicted during three days of intense combat; the whole offensive is intended to frighten voters away from the polls on Sunday.

10 MARCH 1998. At 82 years of age, General Pinochet retires as the head of Chile's army, being succeeded by Gen. Ricardo Izurieta. Next day Pinochet is sworn in as senator for life, amid civilian protests against this unelected appointment.

Further Reading

The following list constitutes only a partial selection of works consulted in the compilation of this book and is reproduced here merely to help flesh out particular entries or sections. Due to space considerations a complete bibliography cannot be included.

General Works

Ballesteros y Beretta, Antonio, ed. *Historia de América y de los pueblos americanos.* Barcelona: Salvat, 1946–1963, 26 volumes.

Bethell, Leslie, ed. *The Cambridge History of Latin America.* Cambridge: Cambridge University Press, 1984–1995, eleven volumes.

Boucher, Philip P. *Cannibal Encounters: Europeans and Island Caribs, 1492–1763.* Baltimore: Johns Hopkins University Press, 1992.

Buchet, Christian. *La lutte pour l'espace caraïbe et la façade atlantique de l'Amérique centrale et du Sud (1672–1763).* Paris: Librairie de l'Inde, 1991.

Calderón Quijano, José Ignacio. *Historia de las fortificaciones en Nueva España.* Seville: Escuela de Estudios Hispano-americanos, 1953.

Catalog of the National Maritime Museum Library. *Volume Five: Naval History.* London: H.M.S.O., 1976.

Chartrand, René. *Canadian Military Heritage.* Montreal: Art Global, 1993, two volumes.

Chipman, Donald E. *Spanish Texas, 1519–1821.* Austin: University of Texas Press, 1992.

Clowes, Sir William Laird, et al. *The Royal Navy: A History from the Earliest Times to the Present.* London: Sampson Low, Marston, 1897–1903, seven volumes.

Davis, Robert H. *Historical Dictionary of Colombia.* Metuchen: Scarecrow, 1993.

Favier, Jean, and Menier, Marie-Antoinette, comps. *Guide des sources de l'histoire de l'Amérique latine et des Antilles dans les archives françaises.* Paris: Archives nationales, 1984.

Fernández Duro, Cesáreo. *Armada Española desde la unión de Castilla y de Aragón.* Madrid: Rivadeneyra, 1895–1903, nine volumes.

Fryer, Mary Beacock. *Battlefields of Canada.* Toronto: Dundern, 1986.

———. *More Battlefields of Canada.* Toronto: Dundern, 1993.

Gerhard, Peter. *A Guide to the Historical Geography of New Spain.* Norman: University of Oklahoma Press, 1993.

———. *The North Frontier of New Spain.* Norman: University of Oklahoma Press, 1993.

———. *The Southeast Frontier of New Spain.* Norman: University of Oklahoma Press, 1993.

Hefter, Joseph. *Crónica del traje militar en México, del siglo XVI al XX.* Mexico City: Artes de México (Issue No. 102), 1968.

Les troupes de marine, 1622–1984. Paris: Charles Lavauzelle, 1986.

Nickson, R. Andrew. *Historical Dictionary of Paraguay.* Metuchen: Scarecrow, 1993.

Olson, James S., et al., eds. *Historical Dictionary of the Spanish Empire, 1402–1975.* New York: Greenwood, 1992.

Pereira, Francisco, et al., eds. *Mapa: Imagens da Formação Territorial Brasileira.* Rio de Janeiro: Fundação Emílio Odebrecht, 1993.

Roncière, Charles Bourel de la. *Histoire de la Marine Française.* Paris: Plon, 1910–1932, volumes 4–6.

Suárez, Martín. *Atlas histórico-militar argentino.* Buenos Aires: Circulo Militar, 1974.

Suárez, Santiago Gerardo. *Las fuerzas armadas venezolanas en la colonia.* Caracas: Fuentes para la Historia Colonial de Venezuela, 1979.

Taillemite, Étienne. *Dictionnaire des Marins Français.* Paris: Editions Maritimes et d'Outre-Mer, 1982.

Tenenbaum, Barbara A., ed. *Encyclopedia of Latin American History and Culture.* New York: Scribner's, 1996, five volumes.

Weber, David J. *The Spanish Frontier in North America.* New Haven, Conn.: Yale University Press, 1992.

Part 1: Discovery and Conquest

Avellaneda Nayas, José Ignacio. *La expedición de Sebastián de Belalcázar al mar del norte y su llegada al Nuevo Reino de Granada.* Bogotá: Banco de la República, 1992.

Ballesteros Gaibrois, Manuel. *Descubrimiento y conquista del Perú.* Barcelona and Madrid: Salvat, 1963.

Bolton, H. E. *Coronado: Knight of the Pueblos and Plains.* Albuquerque: University of New Mexico Press, 1949.

Cerezo Martínez, Ricardo. *La proyección marítima de España en la época de los Reyes Católicos.* Madrid: Instituto de Historia y Cultura Naval, 1991.

Clayton, Lawrence A. et al., eds. *The De Soto Chronicles.* Tuscaloosa: University of Alabama Press, 1993.

Domínguez, Luis L. *The Conquest of the River Plate (1535–1556).* New York: Franklin, 1964.

Esteve Barba, Francisco. *Descubrimiento y conquista de Chile.* Barcelona and Madrid: Salvat, 1946.

Friede, Juan. *Los Welser en la conquista de Venezuela.* Caracas and Madrid: Edime, 1961.

Gabaldón Márquez, Joaquín, ed. *Descubrimiento y conquista de Venezuela: Textos históricos contemporáneos y documentos fundamentales.* Caracas: Fuentes para la Historia Colonial de Venezuela, 1962, two volumes.

Grunberg, Bernard. "The Origins of the Conquistadores of Mexico City." *Hispanic American Historical Review* 74, number 2 (May 1994), pp. 259–283.

Hemming, John. *The Conquest of the Incas.* London: Macmillan, 1970.

Lawson, Edward W. *The Discovery of Florida and Its Discoverer, Juan Ponce de León.* Saint Augustine, Fla.: self-published, 1946.

Lockhart, James, ed. and trans. *We People Here: Nahuatl Accounts of the Conquest of Mexico.* Berkeley: University of California Press, 1993.

Melón y Ruiz de Gordejuela, Amando. *Los primeros tiempos de la colonización: Cuba y las Antillas: Magallanes y la primera vuelta al mundo.* Barcelona: Salvat, 1952.

Pohl, Dr. John M. D. *Aztec, Mixtec and Zapotec Armies.* London: Osprey, 1991.

Powell, Philip Wayne. *Soldiers, Indians, and Silver: The Northward Advance of New Spain, 1550–1600.* Albuquerque: University of New Mexico Press, 1952.

Ramos, Demetrio. *Descubrimiento y conquista de Venezuela y Nueva Granada.* Barcelona and Madrid: Salvat, 1959.

Rouse, Irving. *The Tainos: Rise and Decline of the People Who Greeted Columbus.* New Haven, Conn.: Yale University Press, 1992.

Rubio y Esteban, Julián María. *Exploración y conquista del Río de la Plata, siglos XVI y XVII.* Barcelona and Madrid: Salvat, 1953.

Severin, Timothy. "The Passion of Hernando de Soto." *American Heritage* 18, number 3 (April 1967), pp. 26–31 and 91–97.

Stone, Edward T. "Columbus and Genocide." *American Heritage* 26, number 6 (October 1975), pp. 4–7, 76–79.

Thomas, Hugh. *Conquest: Montezuma, Cortés, and the Fall of Old Mexico.* New York: Simon and Schuster, 1993.

Wise, Terence. *The Conquistadores.* London: Osprey, 1980.

Part 2: Seaborne Challengers

Andrews, Kenneth Raymond. *Elizabethan Privateering: English Privateering During the Spanish War, 1585–1603.* London: Oxford University Press, 1964.

———. *English Privateering Voyages to the West Indies, 1588–1595.* Cambridge: Cambridge University Press and Hakluyt Society (2d Series, volume 111), 1959.

———. "English Voyages to the Caribbean, 1596 to 1604: An Annotated List." *William and Mary Quarterly,* 3d series, volume 31, number 2 (April 1974), pp. 243–254.

———. *The Last Voyage of Drake and Hawkins.* Cambridge: Cambridge University Press and Hakluyt Society (2d Series, volume 158), 1972.

Angulo Iñiguez, Diego. *Bautista Antonelli: las fortificaciones americanas del siglo XVI.* Madrid, 1942.

Bennett, Charles E. *Three Voyages: René Laudonnière.* Gainesville: University of Florida Press, 1975.

Boulind, Richard H. "Shipwreck and Mutiny in Spain's Galleys on the Santo Domingo Station, 1583." *Mariner's Mirror* 58 (1972), pp. 297–330.

Corbett, Sir Julian Stafford. *Papers Relating to the Navy during the Spanish War, 1585–1587.* London: Navy Records Society (volume 11), 1898.

Hampden, Janet, and John Hampton, eds. *Sir Francis Drake's Raid on the Treasure Trains: Being the Memorable Relation of His Voyage to the West Indies in 1572.* London: Folio Society, 1954.

Hampden, John, ed. *Francis Drake—Privateer: Contemporary Narratives and Documents.* London: Eyre Methuen, 1972.

Harris, Sherwood. "The Tragic Dream of Jean Ribaut." *American Heritage* 14, number 6 (October 1963), pp. 8–15 and 88–90.

Hewitt, G. R. "Drake at San Juan de Puerto Rico." *The Mariner's Mirror* 50 (August 1964), pp. 199–204.

Hitchcock, R. F. "Cavendish's Last Voyage: The Charges Against Davis." *The Mariner's Mirror* 80, number 3 (August 1994), pp. 259–269.

Hoffman, Paul E. *The Spanish Crown and the Defense of the Caribbean, 1535–1585,* 1980.

Keeler, Mary Frear, ed. *Sir Francis Drake's West Indian Voyage, 1585–1586.* London: Hakluyt, 1981.

Lorimer, Joyce, ed. *English and Irish Settlement on the River Amazon, 1550–1646.* London: Hakluyt Society, 1989.

Manucy, Albert. *Menéndez: Pedro Menéndez de Avilés, Captain General of the Ocean Sea.* Sarasota: Pineapple Press, 1992.

Marcel, G. *Les Corsaires Français au XVIe Siècle dans le Antilles.* Paris, 1902.

Markham, Clements R. *The Hawkins' Voyages during the Reigns of Henry VIII, Queen Elizabeth, and James I.* London: Hakluyt Society (1st Series, volume 57), 1878.

———. *Narratives of Voyages of Pedro Sarmiento de Gamboa to the Straits of Magellan.* London: Hakluyt Society, 1895.

Monson, Admiral Sir William. *The Naval Tracts of Sir William Monson.* London: Navy Records Society (volumes 22–23, 43, 45, 47), 1902–1914.

Ojer, Pablo. "La fundación de Santo Tomé de Guayana." *Boletín de la Academia Nacional de la Historia (Caracas)* 58, number 311 (July-September 1995), pp. 195–199.

Pérez Turrado, Gaspar. *Las armadas españolas de Indias.* Madrid: MAPFRE, 1992.

Quinn, David Beers. "Christopher Newport in 1590." *North Carolina Historical Review* 29, number 3 (July 1952), pp. 305–316.

———. "Some Spanish Reactions to Elizabethan Colonial Enterprises." *Transactions of the Royal Historical Society,* 5th series, volume 1 (1951), pp. 1–23.

Rowse, A. L. "The Elizabethans and America." *American Heritage* 10, number 3 (April 1959), pp. 4–15, 94–98; number 4 (June 1959), pp. 4–19, 105–111.

Rubio Serrano, José Luis. *Arquitectura de las naos y galeones de las flotas de Indias.* Málaga: Ediciones Seyer, 1991.

Taylor, E. G. R. *The Troublesome Voyage of Captain Edward Fenton, 1582–1583.* Cambridge: Hakluyt, 1959.

Unwin, Rayner. *The Defeat of John Hawkins: A Biography of His Third Slaving Voyage.* London: Allen and Unwin, 1960.

Warner, George F. *The Voyage of Robert Dudley, Afterwards Styled Earl of Warwick and Leicester and Duke of Northumberland, to the West Indies, 1594–1595.* London: Hakluyt Society, 1899 (reprint 1967).

Williams, Neville. *The Sea Dogs: Privateers, Plunder, and Piracy in the Elizabethan Age.* New York: Macmillan, 1975.

Williamson, George Charles. *George, Third Earl of Cumberland (1558–1605); His Life and Voyages.* Cambridge: Cambridge University Press, 1920.

Williamson, James Alexander, ed. *The Observations of Sir Richard Hawkins.* London: Hakluyt Society, 1933.

Wright, Irene Aloha, ed. *Documents Concerning English Voyages to the Spanish Main, 1569–1580.* London: Hakluyt Society (2d Series, volume 71), 1932.

———. *Further English Voyages to Spanish America, 1583–1594.* London: Hakluyt Society (2d Series, volume 99), 1949.

———. *Spanish Documents Concerning English Voyages to the Caribbean, 1527–1568: Selected from the Archive of the Indies at Seville.* London: Hakluyt Society (2d Series, volume 162), 1929.

———. "The Spanish Version of Sir Anthony Sherley's Raid on Jamaica, 1597." *Hispanic American Historical Review* 5 (1922), pp. 227–248.

Part 3: Rival Outposts

General Works

Crouse, Nellis Maynard. *French Pioneers in the West Indies, 1624–1664.* New York: Columbia University Press, 1940.

Goslinga, Cornelis Ch. *The Dutch in the Caribbean and on the Wild Coast, 1580–1680.* Gainesville: University of Florida Press, 1971.

Hurault, Jean Marcel. *Français et Indiens en Guyane, 1604–1972.* Cayenne, French Guiana: Presse Diffusion, 1989.

Pérez Bustamante, Ciriaco. *Los virreinatos en los siglos XVI y XVII.* Barcelona and Madrid: Salvat, 1959.

Early Footholds (1604–1619)

Billings, Warren M., ed. *The Old Dominion in the Seventeenth Century: A Documentary History of Virginia, 1606–1689.* Chapel Hill: University of North Carolina Press, 1975.

Davidson, David M. "Negro Slave Control and Resistance in Colonial Mexico." *Hispanic American Historical Review* 46, number 3 (August 1966), pp. 235–243.

Evreux, Yves d'. *Voyage au nord du Brésil, fait en 1613 et 1614.* Paris: Payot, 1985.

Moreau, Jean-Pierre, ed. *Un flibustier français dans la mer des Antilles en 1618–1620: Manuscrit inédit du début du XVIIe siècle.* Paris: Jean-Pierre Moreau, 1987.

Rahn Phillips, Carla. *Six Galleons for the King of Spain: Imperial Defense in the Early Seventeenth Century.* Baltimore: Johns Hopkins University Press, 1986.

Tyler, Victor Morris. "A Spanish Expedition to Chesapeake Bay in 1609." *American Neptune,* volume 17 (1957), pp. 181–194.

Holland's "Great Design" (1613–1649)

Boxer, Charles Ralph. "The Action between Pater and Oquendo, 12 September 1631." *The Mariner's Mirror* 45 (August 1959), pp. 179–199.

Cannenburg, W. Voorbeijtel, intro. *De Reis om de Wereld van de Nassausche Vloot, 1623–1626.* 's-Gravenhage: Martinus Nijhoff for the Linschoten Society, 1964.

Castillo Lara, Lucas Guillermo. *Las acciones militares del gobernador Ruy Fernández de Fuenmayor (1637–1644).* Caracas: Fuentes para la Historia Colonial de Venezuela, 1978.

Gehring, Charles T., and Schiltkamp, Jacob A., trans. and eds. *Curaçao Papers, 1640–1665.* "New Netherland Documents," volume XVII. Interlaken, N.Y.: Heart of the Lakes Publishing, 1987.

Valencia y Guzmán, Juan de. "Compendio historial de la jornada del Brasil y sucesos de ella, donde se da cuenta de como ganó el rebelde holandés la ciudad del Salvador y Bahía de Todos Santos, y de su restauración por las armas de España, cuyo general fué don Fadrique de Toledo Osorio, marqués de Villanueva de Valdueza, capitán general de la real armada del mar Océano y de la gente de guerra del reino de Portugal en el año de 1625." *Colección de documentos inéditos para la historia de España.* Madrid: Imprenta de la viuda de Calero, 1870, volume 55, pp. 43–200.

Villiers, J. A. J. de, ed. *The East and West Indian Mirror, Being an Account of Joris van Speilbergen's Voyage Round the World (1614–1617) and the Australian Navigations of Jacob le Maire.* London: Hakluyt Society, 1906 (Nendeln, Liechtenstein: Kraus reprint, 1967).

Warnsinck, J. C. M. "Een mislukte aanslag op Nederlandsch Brazilie, 1639–1640." *De Gids* (February 1940), pp. 1–33.

Wright, Irene A., comp., and Van Dam, Cornelis F. A., trans. *Nederlandsche zeevaarders op de eilanden in de Caraibische Zee en aan de Kust van Columbia en Venezuela gedurende de jaren 1621–1648.* Volumes 64–65 of the 3d Series, *Historisch Genootschap te Utrecht, Werken.* Utrecht: Kemink en Zoon, 1934–1935.

Other Colonial Struggles (1622–1640)

Boucher, Philip P. *The Shaping of the French Colonial Empire: A Bio-Bibliography of the Careers of Richelieu, Fouquet, and Colbert.* New York: Garland, 1985.

Boxer, Charles Ralph. "Blake and the Brazil Fleets in 1650." *The Mariner's Mirror* 36 (July 1950), pp. 212–228.

Ordahl Kupperman, Karen. *Providence Island, 1630–1641: The Other Puritan Colony.* Cambridge: Cambridge University Press, 1993.

England's Resurgence (1640–1659)

"Ataque y saqueo del puerto de Alvarado por piratas holandeses y franceses (1651)." *Boletín del Archivo General de la Nación* (Mexico), primera serie, volume 24, number 3 (July-September 1953), pp. 501–508.

Battick, John F. "Richard Rooth's Sea Journal of the Western Design, 1654–1655." *Jamaica Journal* 4 (1971), pp. 3–22.

Calendar of State Papers, Domestic—Commonwealth. London: Her Majesty's Stationery Office, 1875–1886 (reprinted 1965), volumes 8–10.

Incháustegui Cabral, Joaquín Marino. *La gran expedición inglesa contra las Antillas Mayores.* Mexico City: Gráfica Panamericana, 1953.

Lepart, Jean. "François Le Vasseur, de Cogners au Maine, capitaine flibustier et roi de l'Ile de la Tortue en 1652." *La Province du Maine* (October-December 1973), pp. 342–354.

Peña Batlle, Manuel Arturo. *La isla de la Tortuga: Plaza de armas, refugio y seminario de los enemigos de España en Indias.* Madrid: Ediciones Cultura Hispánica, 1951.

Powell, John Rowland. "Sir George Ayscue's Capture of Barbados in 1651." *The Mariner's Mirror* 59 (August 1973), pp. 281–290.

Richard, Robert. "A la Tortue et à Saint Domingue en 1649." Seville: *Anuario de Estudios Americanos* 29 (1972), pp. 445–467.

Richard, Robert, and Débien, Gabriel. "A la Tortue, après la mort de Le Vasseur (1652–1653)." *La Province du Maine* 81, number 32 (October-December 1979), pp. 396–405.

Rodríguez Demorizi, Emilio. *Invasión inglesa de 1655; notas adicionales de Fray Cipriano de Utrera.* Ciudad Trujillo: Montalvo, 1957.

———. "Invasión inglesa en 1655." *Boletín del Archivo General de la Nación (República Dominicana)* 20, number 92 (January-March 1957), pp. 6–70.

Taylor, S. A. G. *The Western Design: An Account of Cromwell's Expedition to the Caribbean.* London: Solstice Productions, 1969.

Venables, Robert. "Narrative; with Appendix of Papers Relative to the Expedition to the West Indies and the Conquest of Jamaica, 1654–1655." *Camden Society Miscellany* 60 (1900).

Wright, Irene Aloha, ed. and trans. "An Account of What Happened in the Island of Jamaica from May 20 of the Year 1655, When the English Laid Siege to It, Up to July 3 of the Year 1656, by Captain Julián de Castilla." *Camden Miscellany* 12 (1923).

———. "The English Conquest of Jamaica, 1655–1656." *Camden Miscellany* 12 (1924).

———. "Spanish Narratives of the English Attack on Santo Domingo, 1655." *Camden Miscellany* 14 (1926).

Part 4: Intercolonial Friction

General Works

Bradley, Peter T. *The Lure of Peru: Maritime Intrusion into the South Sea, 1598–1701.* New York: St Martin's Press, 1990.

Calendar of State Papers, Colonial Series, America and West Indies. London: Her Majesty's Stationery Office, 1893–1899, volumes 9–12.

Catalog of the National Maritime Museum Library. *Volume Four: Piracy and Privateering.* London: Her Majesty's Stationery Office, 1972.

Eugenio Martínez, María Angeles. *La defensa de Tabasco, 1600–1717.* Seville: Escuela de Estudios Hispano-americanos, 1971.

García Fuentes, Lutgardo. *El comercio español con América (1650–1700).* Seville: Escuela de Estudios Hispano-americanos, 1980.

López Cantos, Angel. *Historia de Puerto Rico (1650–1700).* Seville: Escuela de Estudios Hispano-americanos, 1975.

Lugo, Américo. *Recopilación diplomática relativa a las colonias española y francesa de la isla de Santo Domingo, 1640–1701.* Ciudad Trujillo, Dominican Republic: Editorial 'La Nación,' 1944.

Moya Pons, Frank. *Historia colonial de Santo Domingo.* Santiago, Dominican Republic: Universidad Católica Madre y Maestra, 1977.

Rubio Mañé, José Ignacio. "Las jurisdicciones de Yucatán: la creación de la plaza de teniente de Rey en Campeche, año de 1744." *Boletín del Archivo General de la Nación (México),* segunda serie, volume 7, number 3 (July-September 1966), pp. 549–631.

———. "Ocupación de la isla de Términos por los ingleses, 1658–1717." *Boletín del Archivo General de la Nación (México),* primera serie, volume 24, number 2 (April-June 1953), pp. 295–330.

Serrano Mangas, Fernando. *Los galeones de la carrera de Indias, 1650–1700.* Seville: Escuela de Estudios Hispano-americanos, 1985.

Torres Ramírez, Bibiano. *La Armada de Barlovento.* Seville: Escuela de Estudios Hispano-americanos, 1981.

Weddle, Robert S. *The French Thorn: Rival Explorers in the Spanish Sea, 1682–1762.* College Station: Texas A&M University Press, 1991.

———. *Spanish Sea: The Gulf of Mexico in North American Discovery, 1500–1685.* College Station: Texas A&M University Press, 1985.

No Peace beyond the Line (1660–1665)

Dyer, Florence. "Captain Christopher Myngs in the West Indies, 1657–1662." *The Mariner's Mirror* 18 (April 1932), pp. 168–187.

Myngs, Vice Admiral Sir Christopher. "Account of the Taking of St. Iago upon Cuba, October 1662." *Historical Manuscripts Commission Reports (Heathcote Mss).* London: HMC, 1899.

Thornton, A. P. "The Modyfords and Morgan." *Jamaican Historical Review* 2 (1952), pp. 36–60.

———. *West-India Policy Under the Restoration.* Oxford, 1956.

Second Anglo-Dutch War (1665–1667) and War of Devolution (1667)

Blok, P. J. (trans. by G. J. Renier). *The Life of Admiral de Ruyter.* London: Ernest Benn, 1933.

Calendar of State Papers—Colonial (volumes 5–12, *America and the West Indies,* 1660–1688). London: Her Majesty's Stationery Office, 1880–1899, eight volumes.

Schoolcraft, H. L. "The Capture of New Amsterdam." *English Historical Review* 23 (1908), pp. 674–693.

Verhoog, P., and Koelmans, L., eds. *De reis van Michiel Adriaanszoon de Ruyter in 1664–1665.* (Linschoten Vereeniging series, volume 62.) 's-Gravenhage: Martinus Nijhoff, 1961.

Warnsinck, J. C. M. *Abraham Crijnssen; De Verovering van Suriname en zijn Aanstag op Virginie en 1667.* Amsterdam, 1936.

Wilson, Charles H. "Who Captured New Amsterdam?" *English Historical Review* 72 (July 1957), pp. 469–474.

Buccaneer Heyday (1668–1672)

Cruikshank, E. A. *The Life of Sir Henry Morgan.* Toronto: Macmillan, 1935.

Earle, Peter. *The Sack of Panamá: Sir Henry Morgan's Adventures on the Spanish Main.* New York: Viking, 1981.

Exquemelin, Alexandre Olivier (trans. by Alexis Brown, introduction by Jack Beeching). *The Buccaneers of America.* London: Penguin, 1969.

Pawson, Michael, and Buisseret, David J. *Port Royal, Jamaica.* Oxford: Clarendon Press, 1975.

Vrijman, L. C. *Dr. David van der Sterre: Zeer aenmerkelijke reysen door Jan Erasmus Reyning.* Amsterdam: P. N. van Kampen and Zoon, 1937.

Third Anglo-Dutch War (1672–1674) and Franco-Spanish War (1673–1679)

Arana, Luis. *Infantry in Spanish Florida, 1671–1679.* University of Florida seminar paper (History 778), 1958.

Delort, Théodore. "La première escadre la la France dans les Indes; rivalité de la France et de la Hollande, 1670–1675." *Revue Maritime et Coloniale* 47 (1875), pp. 29–63, 443–471, and 841–866.

Shomette, Donald G., and Haslach, Robert D. *Raid on America: The Dutch Naval Campaign of 1672–1674.* Columbia: University of South Carolina Press, 1988.

Waard, C. de. *De Zeeuwsche Expeditie naar de West onder Cornelis Evertsen den Jonge, 1672–1674.* The Hague: Martinus Nijhoff, 1928.

Irregular Warfare (1679–1688)

Bernal Ruiz, María del Pilar. *La toma del puerto de Guayaquil en 1687.* Seville: Escuela de Estudios Hispano-americanos, 1979.

Howse, Derek, and Thrower, Norman J. W., eds. *A Buccaneer's Atlas: Basil Ringrose's South Sea Waggoner. A Sea Atlas and Sailing Directions of the Pacific Coast of the Americas 1682.* Berkeley: University of California Press, 1992.

Josephy, Alvin M., Jr. "Revolt in the Pueblos." *American Heritage* 12, number 4 (June 1961), pp. 65–77.

Juárez Moreno, Juan. *Piratas y corsarios en Veracruz y Campeche.* Seville: Escuela de Estudios Hispano-americanos, 1972.

Lussan, Ravenau de. *Journal of a Voyage into the South Seas.* Cleveland, Ohio: Arthur H. Clark, 1930.

Marley, David F. *Sack of Veracruz: The Great Pirate Raid of 1683.* Windsor, Ontario: Netherlandic Press, 1993.

Pawson, Michael, and Buisseret, David J. "A Pirate at Port Royal in 1679. *The Mariner's Mirror* 57 (1971), pp. 303–305.

Pérez Mallaína Bueno, Pablo Emilio, and Torres Ramírez, Bibiano. *La Armada del Mar del Sur.* Seville: Escuela de Estudios Hispano-americanos, 1987.

Wafer, Lionel. *A New Voyage and Description of the Isthmus of America.* London: Hakluyt Society, 1933.

King William's War (1688–1697)

Baudrit, André. *Charles de Courbon, Comte de Blénac, 1622–1696; Gouverneur Général des Antilles Françaises, 1677–1696.* Fort de France: Annales des Antilles, Société d'Histoire de la Martinique, 1967.

Dyer, Florence E. "Captain John Strong, Privateer and Treasure Hunter." *The Mariner's Mirror* 13 (1927), pp. 145–158.

Matta Rodríguez, Enrique de la. *El asalto de Pointis a Cartagena de Indias.* Seville: Escuela de Estudios Hispano-americanos, 1979.

Sigüenza y Góngora, Carlos de. *Relación de lo sucedido a la Armada de Barlovento.* Reprinted in *Obras históricas* Mexico City: Porrúa, 1960.

Tribout de Morembert, Henri. "A Saint-Domingue, Le Major Bernanos, capitaine de flibustiers." *Connaissance du Monde* 78 (1965), pp. 10–19.

The Darien Disaster (1698–1699)

Prebble, John. *The Darien Disaster.* London: Secker and Warburg, 1968.

Part 5: High Tide of Empire

General Works

Alcázar Molina, Cayetano. *Los virreinatos en el siglo XVIII.* Barcelona and Madrid: Salvat, 1959.

Calvert, Michael, and Young, Peter. *A Dictionary of Battles (1715–1815).* New York: Mayflower, 1979.

Crane, Verner W. *The Southern Frontier, 1670–1732.* Ann Arbor: University of Michigan Press, 1954.

Marichal, Carlos, and Souto Mantecón, Matilde. "Silver and Situados: New Spain and the Financing of the Spanish Empire in the Caribbean in the Eighteenth Century." *Hispanic American Historical Review* 74, number 4 (November 1994), pp. 587–614.

Maxwell, Kenneth. *Conflicts and Conspiracies: Brazil and Portugal, 1750–1808.* Cambridge: Cambridge University Press, 1973.

Rediker, Marcus. *Between the Devil and the Deep Blue Sea: Merchant Seamen, Pirates, and the Anglo-American Maritime World, 1700–1750.* Cambridge: Cambridge University Press, 1987.

TePaske, John Jay. *The Governorship of Spanish Florida, 1700–1763.* Durham, N.C.: Duke University Press, 1964.

Velázquez, María del Carmen. *Establecimiento y pérdida del septentrión de Nueva España.* Mexico City: Colegio de México, 1974.

Voelz, Peter M. *Slave and Soldier: The Military Impact of Blacks in the Colonial Americas.* New York: Garland, 1990.

Queen Anne's War (1702–1713)

Arnade, Charles W. *The Siege of St. Augustine in 1702.* Gainesville: University of Florida Press, Social Sciences Monographs (number 3), Summer 1959.

Bourne, Ruth M. *Queen Anne's Navy in the West Indies.* New Haven, Conn.: Yale University Press, 1939.

Boyd, Mark F., Smith, Hale G., and Griffin, John W. *Here They Once Stood: The Tragic End of the Apalachee Missions.* Gainesville: University of Florida Press, 1951.

Graham, Gerald Sanford, ed. *The Walker Expedition to Quebec, 1711.* Toronto: Champlain Society, 1953.

Owen, John Hely. *War at Sea Under Queen Anne, 1702–1708.* Cambridge: Cambridge University Press, 1938.

War of the Quadruple Alliance (1718–1720)

Calendar of State Papers: Colonial, volumes 30–32. London: H.M.S.O., 1930–1933.

Interwar Years (1730–1738)

Rego Monteiro, Jonathas da Costa. *A Colônia do Sacramento, 1680–1777.* Pôrto Alegre, Brazil: Livraria do Globo, 1937, two volumes.

War of Jenkins's Ear, Later King George's War (1739–1748)

Gwyn, Julian, ed. *The Royal Navy and North America: The Warren Papers, 1736–1752.* London: Navy Records Society, 1973.

Harding, Richard. *Amphibious Warfare in the Eighteenth Century: The British Expedition to the West Indies, 1740–1742.* Suffolk: Boydell Press, 1991.

Heaps, Leo. *Log of the Centurion: Based on the Original Papers of Captain Philip Saumarez on Board HMS Centurion, Lord Anson's Flagship during his Circumnavigation, 1740–1744.* New York: Macmillan, 1973.

Hinds, James R. "Captain Jenkins' Ear and American Seacoast Fortification." *Journal of the Council on America's Military Past,* volume 15, number 2 (1987), pp. 43–56.

Ivers, Larry E. *British Drums on the Southern Frontier: The Military Colonization of Georgia, 1733–1749.* Chapel Hill: University of North Carolina Press, 1974.

Kay, William Kennon. "An Expedition for King and Country." *Virginia Cavalcade* (Spring 1966), pp. 30–37.

Lanning, John Tate, introduction to *The St. Augustine Expedition of 1740: A Report to the South Carolina General Assembly, Reprinted from the Colonial Records of South Carolina.* Columbia: South Carolina Archives Department, 1954.

Nowell, Charles E. "The Defense of Cartagena." *Hispanic American Historical Review* 42, number 4 (November 1962), pp. 477–501.

Ogelsby, J. C. M. "The British Attacks on the Caracas Coast, 1743." *The Mariner's Mirror* 58 (February 1972), pp. 27–40.

Pares, Richard. *War and Trade in the West Indies, 1739–1763.* Oxford: Clarendon, 1936.

Ranft, B. McL. *The Vernon Papers.* London: Navy Records Society, 1958.

Rawlyk, G. A. *Yankees at Louisbourg.* Orono: University of Maine Press, 1967.

Richmond, Sir Herbert William. *The Navy in the War of 1739–1748.* Cambridge: Cambridge University Press, 1920, three volumes.

Rodgers, Thomas G. "Colonials Collide at Bloody Marsh." *Military History* 13, number 4 (October 1996), pp. 38–44.

Swanson, Carl E. *Predators and Prizes: American Privateering and Imperial Warfare, 1739–1748.* Columbia: University of South Carolina Press, 1991.

French and Indian War (1754–1763)

Corbett, Sir Julian. *England and the Seven Years War,* 1907.

Frégault, Guy (trans. by Margaret M. Cameron). *Canada: The War of the Conquest.* Toronto: Toronto University Press, 1955.

Hamilton, Charles, ed. *Braddock's Defeat,* 1959.

Hibbert, Christopher. *Wolfe at Quebec,* 1959.

Llaverías, Joaquín. *Papeles sobre la toma de La Habana por los ingleses en 1762.* Havana, 1948.

Lloyd, Christopher C. *The Capture of Quebec.* London: Batsford, 1959.

May, Robin. *Wolfe's Army.* London: Osprey, 1974.

Smelser, Marshall. *The Campaign for the Sugar Islands, 1759: A Study of Amphibious Warfare.* Chapel Hill: University of North Carolina Press, 1955.

Snow, Richard F. "The Debacle at Fort Carillon." *American Heritage* 23, number 4 (June 1972), pp. 80–89.

Stacey, Charles Perry. *Quebec 1759: The Siege and the Battle.* Toronto: Macmillan, 1959.

Syrett, David. *The Siege and Capture of Havana, 1762.* London: Navy Records Society, 1970.

Warner, Oliver. *With Wolfe to Quebec,* 1972.
Windrow, Martin. *Montcalm's Army.* London: Osprey, 1973.
Wood, William Charles Henry. *The Logs of the Conquest of Canada: Louisbourg, 1758; Quebec, 1759; Montreal, 1760.* Toronto: Champlain Society, 1909.

Boundary Disputes (1763–1774)

Gallagher, Robert E., ed. *Byron's Journal of his Circumnavigation, 1764–1766.* Cambridge: Hakluyt Society, 1946.
Jacobs, W. R. *Wilderness Politics and Indian Gifts: The Northern Colonial Frontier, 1748–1763.* Lincoln: University of Nebraska Press, 1950.
Moore, John Preston. *Revolt in Louisiana: The Spanish Occupation, 1766–1770,* 1976.
Quaife, Dr. Milo M., ed. "A Journal of an Indian Captivity During Pontiac's Rebellion in the Year 1763, by Mr. John Rutherford, Afterward Captain, 42nd Highland Regiment." *American Heritage* 9, number 3 (April 1958), pp. 65–81.
Tanner, H. H. *Atlas of Great Lakes Indian History.* Norman: University of Oklahoma Press, 1987.

Undeclared Hispano-Portuguese Conflict (1776–1777)

Alden, Dauril. "The Undeclared War of 1773–1777: Climax of Luso-Spanish Platine Rivalry." *Hispanic American Historical Review* 41, number 1 (February 1961), pp. 55–74.
Cal Martínez, María Consuelo. *La defensa de la integridad territorial de Guayana en tiempos de Carlos III.* Caracas: Fuentes para la Historia Colonial de Venezuela, 1979.
Caraman, Philip. *The Lost Paradise: The Jesuit Republic in South America,* 1990.

Part 6: Independence

American Revolutionary War (1775–1783)

Anderson, Troyer S. *The Command of the Howe Brothers During the American Revolution.* London: Oxford University Press, 1936.
Barton, John A. "The Battle of Valcour Island." *History Today* 9 (1959), pp. 791–799.
Bill, A. H. *The Campaign of Princeton, 1776–1777.* Princeton, N.J.: Princeton University Press, 1975.
Bonner-Smith, David, ed. *The Barrington Papers.* London: Navy Records Society, 1937–1941, two volumes.
———. "Byron in the Leeward Islands, 1779." *The Mariner's Mirror* 30 (January 1944), pp. 38–48 and 81–92.
Bourne, Russell. "The Penobscot Fiasco." *American Heritage* 25, number 6 (October 1974), pp. 28–33, 100–101.
Cappon, L., ed. *Atlas of Early American History: The Revolutionary Era, 1760–1790.* Princeton, N.J.: Princeton University Press, 1975.
Caughey, John Walton. *Bernardo de Gálvez in Louisiana, 1776–1783.* Gretna: Pelican, 1972.
Chadwick, French Ensor. *The Graves Papers and Other Documents Relating to the Naval Operations of the Yorktown Campaign, July to October 1781.* New York: Naval History Society, 1916.
Chevalier, E. *Histoire de la marine française pendant la guerre de l'indépendance américaine.* Paris: Hachette, 1877.
Clark, William Bell, and Morgan, William James, eds. *Naval Documents of the American Revolution.* Washington, D.C.: U.S. Navy Department, 1964–, six volumes.
Coker, William S., and Hazel P. *The Siege of Pensacola in Maps.* Pensacola, Fla., 1981.
Contenson, Ludovic de. "La prise de Saint-Christophe en 1782." *Revue historique des Antilles* II (1929), pp. 17–41.
Davis, Kenneth S. "'In the Name of the Great Jehovah and the Continental Congress!'" *American Heritage* 14, number 6 (October 1963), pp. 65–77.
Falkner, Leonard. "Captor of the Barefoot General." *American Heritage* 11, number 5 (August 1960), pp. 28–31, 98–100.
Forester, Cecil Scott. "The Battle of the Saintes." *American Heritage* 9, number 4 (June 1958), pp. 4–9, 108.
Froncek, Thomas. "Kosciusko." *American Heritage* 26, number 4 (June 1975), pp. 4–11, 78–81.
Guiot, Pierre. "Notes de campagne du comte Rigaud de Vaudreuil, 1781–1782." *Neptunia* 45 (January 1957), pp. 33–40; 46 (February), pp. 34–42; 47 (March), pp. 33–40; 48 (April), pp. 32–41; 49 (May), pp. 34–41; 50 (June), pp. 29–35; 51 (July), pp. 34–41; and 52 (August), pp. 31–40.
Hannay, David, ed. *Letters Written by Sir Samuel Hood (Viscount Hood) in 1781–2–3.* London: Navy Records Society, 1895.
Hubbard, Timothy William. "Battle at Valcour Island: Benedict Arnold as Hero." *American Heritage* 17, number 6 (October 1966), pp. 8–11, 87–91.
James, Sir William Milburne. *The British Navy in Adversity: A Study of the War of American Independence.* London: Longmans, 1926.
Landers, H. L. *The Virginia Campaign and the Blockade and Siege of Yorktown, 1781.* Washington, D.C.: 1931.
Langle, Fleuriot de. "Contribution de la marine française à la victoire de Yorktown." *Revue Maritime* 273 (February 1970), pp. 177–183.
Larrabee, Harold A. *Decision at the Chesapeake.* New York: Potter, 1964.
Lawrence, Alexander A. *Storm over Savannah: The Story of Count d'Estaing and the Siege of the Town in 1779.* Athens: University of Georgia Press, 1951.
Lewis, Charles Lee. *Admiral de Grasse and American Independence.* Annapolis, Md.: U.S. Naval Institute, 1945.
Lewis, James A. *The Final Campaign of the American Revolution: Rise and Fall of the Spanish Bahamas.* Columbia: University of South Carolina Press, 1991.
Marie, René. "D'Estaing aux Antilles." *Revue Maritime* 23 (December 1921), pp. 735–758.
May, Robin. *The British Army in North America, 1775–1783.* London: Osprey, 1974.
Pearson, Michael. "The Siege of Quebec, 1775–1776." *American Heritage* 23, number 2 (February 1972), pp. 8–15, 104–108.
Perkins, James Breck. *France in the American Revolution,* 1971.

Plumb, John Harold. "The French Connection." *American Heritage* 26, number 1 (December 1974), pp. 26–57, 86–87.
Pocock, Tom. *The Young Nelson in the Americas.* London: Collins, 1980.
Rathbun, Frank H. "Rathbun's Raid on Nassau." *U.S. Naval Institute Proceedings* 96 (1970), pp. 40–47.
Rice, H. C., and Brown, A. S. *The American Campaigns of Rochambeau's Army, 1780–1783.* Princeton University Press, 1973, two volumes.
Rutherford, G. "Admiral de Ternay and an English Convoy." *Mariner's Mirror* 26 (April 1940), pp. 158–162.
Scheer, George F. "The Elusive Swamp Fox." *American Heritage* 9, number 3 (April 1958), pp. 40–47, 111.
Scheer, George F., and Rankin, Hugh F. "Rebels and Redcoats." *American Heritage* 8, number 2 (February 1957), pp. 65–89.
Snow, Richard F., and Troiani, Don. "Encounter at the Brandywine." *American Heritage* 24, number 2 (February 1973), pp. 12–16.
———. "Eutaw Springs." *American Heritage* 26, number 5 (August 1975), pp. 53–56.
———. "Fort Griswold." *American Heritage* 24, number 6 (October 1973), pp. 69–72.
———. "Fort Washington." *American Heritage* 25, number 4 (June 1974), pp. 57–60.
———. "Guilford Court House." *American Heritage* 24, number 4 (June 1973), pp. 17–20.
———. "Lexington and Concord." *American Heritage* 25, number 3 (April 1974), pp. 8–11.
———. "Saratoga." *American Heritage* 27, number 1 (December 1975), pp. 29–32.
———. "Stand-Off at White Plains." *American Heritage* 24, number 3 (April 1973), pp. 41–44.
———. "Trenton." *American Heritage* 24, number 5 (August 1973), pp. 69–72.
Zlatich, Marko. *General Washington's Army.* London: Osprey, 1994.

Lesser Hostilities (1780–1790)

Dunmore, John, trans. and ed. *The Journal of Jean-François de Galaup de la Pérouse, 1785–1788.* London: Hakluyt, 1994, two volumes.
Fisher, Lillian Estelle. *The Last Inca Revolt, 1780–1783.* Norman: University of Oklahoma Press, 1966.
Phelan, John Leddy. *The People and the King: The Comunero Revolution in Colombia, 1781.* Madison: University of Wisconsin Press, 1978.

Discord in the Early American Republic and the Old Northwest Indian Wars (1786–1795)

Baldwin, Leland D. *Whiskey Rebels: The Story of a Frontier Uprising.* Pittsburgh: University of Pittsburgh Press, 1968.
Cooke, Jacob E. "The Whiskey Insurrection: A Re-Evaluation." *Pennsylvania History* 30, number 3 (1963), pp. 316–346.
McClure, James P. "'Let Us Be Independent'; David Bradford and the Whiskey Insurrection." *Pittsburgh History* 74, number 2 (1991), pp. 72–86.
Van Every, Dale. "President Washington's Calculated Risk." *American Heritage* IX, number 4 (June 1958), pp. 56–61, 109–111.
Vaughan, Alden T. "The 'Horrid and Unnatural Rebellion' of Daniel Shays." *American Heritage* 17, number 4 (June 1966), pp. 50–53, 77–81.

Haitian Revolution (1790–1803)

Chartrand, René. *Napoleon's Overseas Army.* London: Osprey, 1989.
Cole, Hubert. *Christophe: King of Haiti,* 1967.
Fick, Carolyn E. *The Making of Haiti: The Saint Domingue Revolution from Below.* Knoxville: University of Tennessee Press, 1990.
Geggus, David P. *Unexploited Sources for the History of the Haitian Revolution,* 1983.
James, Cyril L. R. *The Black Jacobins: Toussaint L'Ouverture and the San Domingo Revolution,* 1963.
Korngold, Ralph. *Citizen Toussaint,* 1965.
Ott, Thomas O. *The Haitian Revolution, 1789–1804,* 1973.
Parkinson, Wenda. *This Gilded African: Toussaint L'Ouverture,* 1978.
Stein, Robert Louis. *Léger Félicité Sonthonax: The Lost Sentinel of the Republic,* 1985.

Napoleonic Wars (1803–1810)

Costa, Ernestina, baroness Peers de Nieuwburgh. *English Invasion of the River Plate.* Buenos Aires: Guillermo Kraft, 1937.
Dudley, C. E. S. "The *Leopard* Incident, 1807." *History Today* 19 (1969), pp. 468–474.
Emmerson, John C. *The* Chesapeake *Affair of 1807: An Objective Account of the Attack by HMS* Leopard *upon the US frigate* Chesapeake *off Cape Henry, Virginia, on June 22, 1807—Compiled from Contemporary Newspaper Accounts, Official Documents, and Other Authoritative Sources.* Portsmouth, Virginia: 1954.
Graham, Gerald Sanford, ed. *The Navy and South America, 1807–1823: Correspondence of the Commanders-in-Chief on the South American Station.* London: Navy Records Society (volume 34), 1962.
Grainger, John D. "The Navy in the River Plate, 1806–1808." *The Mariner's Mirror* 81, number 3 (August 1995), pp. 287–299.
Naval Chronicle (re. conquest of Danish Virgin Islands), volume 19 (1808), pp. 156–169.
Pendle, George. "Defeat at Buenos Aires, 1806–1807." *History Today* 2, number 6 (June 1952), pp. 400–405.
Roberts, Carlos. *Las invasiones inglesas del Río de la Plata (1806–1807) y la influencia inglesa en la independencia y organización de las provincias del Río de la Plata.* Buenos Aires: Jacobo Peuser, 1938.
Rowbotham, Commander W. B. "The British Occupation of the Diamond Rock, 1804–1805." *Naval Review* 37 (1949), pp. 385–395; and 39 (1950), pp. 53–64.

Latin American Insurgencies (1808–1826)

Almaráz, Félix D., Jr. *Tragic Cavalier: Governor Manuel Salcedo of Texas, 1808–1813.* Austin: University of Texas Press, 1971.

Anna, Timothy E. *The Fall of Royal Government in Peru,* 1979.

Arnade, Charles W. *The Emergence of the Republic of Bolivia,* 1957.

Cavaliero, Roderick. *The Independence of Brazil.* London: British Academic Press, 1993.

Clissold, Stephen. *Bernardo O'Higgins and the Independence of Chile,* 1968.

Díaz Thomé, Hugo. "La Guerra de Independencia: Expedición de Mina." *Boletín del Archivo General de la Nación* (Mexico), primera serie, volume 20, number 3 (July-September 1949), pp. 365–377.

Ezquerra Abadía, Ramón. *La emancipación de Hispanoamérica.* Barcelona and Madrid: Salvat, 1959.

Friede, Juan, ed. *La batalla de Boyacá, 7 de agosto de 1819, a través de los archivos españoles.* Bogota: Banco de la República, 1969.

———. "La expedición de MacGregor a Ríohacha: año 1819." (Bogota) *Boletín Cultural y Bibliográfico* 10, number 9, 1967.

García Godoy, Cristián, ed. (trans. by Barbara Huntley and Pilar Liria). *The San Martín Papers,* 1988.

Guzmán, Martín Luis. *Javier Mina, héroe de España y México,* 1962.

Guzmán R., José R. "Actividades corsarias en el golfo de México." *Boletín del Archivo General de la Nación* (Mexico), segunda serie, volume 11, numbers 3–4 (July-December 1970), pp. 357–452.

———. "Aventureros, corsarios e insurgentes en el golfo de México." *Boletín del Archivo General de la Nación* (Mexico), segunda serie, volume 12, numbers 1–2 (January-June 1971), pp. 175–236.

———. "La correspondencia de don Luis de Onís sobre la expedición de Javier Mina." *Boletín del Archivo General de la Nación* (Mexico), segunda serie, volume 9, numbers 3–4 (July-December 1968), pp. 509–544.

———. "Francisco Javier Mina en la isla de Gálveston y Soto la Marina." *Boletín del Archivo General de la Nación* (Mexico), segunda serie, volume 7, number 4 (October-December 1966), pp. 898–1081.

Hooker, Terry, and Poulter, Ron. *The Armies of Bolívar and San Martín.* London: Osprey, 1991.

Lecuna, Vicente. *Crónica razonada de las guerras de Bolívar.* New York: Colonial Press, 1950, three volumes.

Lynch, John. *Caudillos in Spanish America, 1800–1850,* 1992.

———. *The Spanish American Revolutions, 1808–1826.* London: Weidenfeld and Nicolson, 1973 (2d edition, 1986).

Macaulay, Neill. *Dom Pedro: The Struggle for Liberty in Brazil and Portugal, 1798–1834,* 1986.

Mijares, Augusto (trans. by John Fisher). *The Liberator,* 1983.

O'Leary, General Daniel Florencio (trans. and ed. by Robert F. McNerney). *Bolívar and the War of Independence.* Austin: University of Texas Press, 1970.

Parra Pérez, Caracciolo. *Mariño y la independencia de Venezuela.* Madrid, 1954–1957, five volumes.

Rumazo González, Alfonso. *Sucre, gran mariscal de Ayacucho,* 1963.

Stoan, Stephen K. *Pablo Morillo and Venezuela, 1815–1820.* Columbus: Ohio State University Press, 1974.

Street, John. *Artigas and the Emancipation of Uruguay,* 1959.

Vale, Brian. "British Sailors and the Brazilian Navy, 1822–1850." *The Mariner's Mirror* 80, number 3 (August 1994), pp. 312–325.

———. *Independence or Death: British Sailors and Brazilian Independence, 1822–1825.* London: Tauris, 1996.

Worcester, Donald E. *Sea Power and Chilean Independence,* 1962.

Part 7: Nationhood

General Works

Barman, Roderick J. *Brazil: The Forging of a Nation, 1798–1852,* 1988.

Basadre, Jorge. *Chile, Perú y Bolivia independientes.* Barcelona and Madrid: Salvat, 1948.

Bethell, Leslie, ed. *Spanish America After Independence, c. 1820–c. 1870,* 1987.

Bushnell, David, and Macaulay, Neill. *The Emergence of Latin America in the Nineteenth Century,* 1994.

Cardozo, Efraím, and Pivel Devoto, J. E. *Paraguay y Uruguay independientes.* Barcelona and Madrid: Salvat, 1949.

Estep, Raymond. *The Military in Brazilian Politics, 1821–1970,* 1971.

Hernández, José M. *Cuba and the United States: Intervention and Militarism, 1868–1933.* Austin: University of Texas Press, 1993.

Pike, Frederick B. *The Modern History of Peru.* New York: Praeger, 1967.

Radaelli, Sigfrido. *Argentina independiente.* Barcelona and Madrid: Salvat, 1959.

St. John, Robert Bruce. *The Foreign Policy of Peru.* Boulder: Lynne Rienner, 1992.

Vayssière, Pierre. *Les révolutions de l'Amérique latine.* Paris: Seuil, 1991.

War of 1812 (1812–1815)

Berton, Pierre. *Flames across the Border, 1813–1814.* Toronto: McClelland and Stewart, 1981.

———. *Invasion of Canada, 1812–1813.* Toronto: McClelland and Stewart, 1980.

Bird, Harrison. *Navies in the Mountains: The Battles on the Waters of Lake Champlain and Lake George, 1809–1814.* New York: Oxford University Press, 1962.

Brannan, John, ed. *Official Letters of the Military and Naval Officers of the United States, during the War with Great Britain in the Years 1812, 13, 14 and 15; with Additional Letters and Documents Elucidating the History of that Period.* New York: Arno, 1971.

Brown, Wilbur S. *The Amphibious Campaign for West Florida and Louisiana, 1814–1815: A Critical Review of Strategy and Tactics at New Orleans.* Birmingham: Alabama University Press, 1969.

Carter, Samuel III. *Blaze of Glory: The Fight for New Orleans, 1814–1815.* New York: St. Martin's, 1971.

Chapelle, Howard I. "The Ships of the American Navy in the War of 1812." *The Mariner's Mirror* 18 (July 1932), pp. 287–302.

Coles, Harry L. *The War of 1812.* Chicago: University of Chicago Press, 1965.

Dudley, William S., ed. *The Naval War of 1812: A Documentary History.* Washington, D.C.: Naval Historical Center, 1985 and 1992, two volumes.

Elting, John R. *Amateurs, to Arms: A Military History of the War of 1812.*

Forester, Cecil Scott. *The Naval War of 1812.* London: Michael Joseph, 1957.

———. "Victory at New Orleans." *American Heritage* 8, number 5 (August 1957), pp. 4–9, 106–108.

———. "Victory on Lake Champlain." *American Heritage* 15, number 1 (December 1963), pp. 4–11, 88–90.

Freehoff, William Francis. "Tecumseh's Last Stand." *Military History* 13, number 4 (October 1996), pp. 30–36.

Hitsman, J. Mackay. *The Incredible War of 1812: A Military History.* Toronto: University of Toronto Press, 1965.

Horsman, Reginald. *The War of 1812.* New York: Knopf, 1969.

Katcher, Philip R. N. *The American War, 1812–1814.* London: Osprey, 1974.

Lord, Walter. "Humiliation and Triumph." *American Heritage* 23, number 5 (August 1972), pp. 50–73, 91–93.

McKee, Linda. "'By Heaven, That Ship Is Ours!'" *American Heritage* 16, number 1 (December 1964), pp. 4–11, 94–98.

Padfield, Peter. *Broke and the* Shannon. London: Hodder and Stoughton, 1968.

Pereira Salas, Eugenio. "First Contacts: The Glorious Cruise of the Frigate *Essex.*" *U.S. Naval Institute Proceedings* 66 (1940), pp. 218–223.

Pullen, Rear Admiral H. F. *The* Shannon *and the* Chesapeake. Toronto: McClelland and Stewart, 1970.

Snow, Richard F. "The Battle of Lake Erie." *American Heritage* 27, number 2 (February 1976), pp. 14–21, 88–90.

Stacey, Charles Perry. "Another Look at the Battle of Lake Erie." *Cambridge Historical Review* (March 1958), pp. 1–11.

———. "The Ships of the British Squadron on Lake Ontario, 1812–1814." *Canadian Historical Review* (December 1953), pp. 311–323.

Stagg, J. C. A. *Mr. Madison's War: Politics, Diplomacy, and Warfare in the Early American Republic, 1783–1830.* Princeton, N.J.: Princeton University Press, 1983.

Stanley, George Francis Gillman. *The War of 1812: Land Operations.* Toronto: Macmillan, 1983.

Wood, William, ed. *Select British Documents of the Canadian War of 1812.* Toronto: Champlain Society, 1920–1928, four volumes.

U.S. Expansion through Eastern Tribelands (1816–1842)

Froncek, Thomas. "'I Was Once a Great Warrior'." *American Heritage* XXIV, number 1 (December 1972), pp. 16–21, 97–99.

Mahon, John K. *History of the Second Seminole War, 1835–1842.* Gainesville: University of Florida Press, 1967.

Cisplatine War (1825–1828)

Halperín Donghi, Tulio. *Argentina: de la revolución de independencia a la confederación rosista,* 1972.

Minor Disputes (1830–1838)

Fryer, Mary Beacock. *Volunteers, Redcoats, Raiders, & Rebels: A Military History of the Rebellions in Upper Canada.* Toronto: Dundurn, 1987.

Greer, Allan. *The Patriots and the People: The Rebellion of 1837 in Rural Lower Canada.* Toronto: University of Toronto Press, 1993.

Kraay, Hendrik. "'As Terrifying as Unexpected': The Bahian Sabinada, 1837–1838." *Hispanic American Historical Review* 72, number 4 (1992), pp. 501–527.

Oates, Stephen B. "Children of Darkness." *American Heritage* 24, number 6 (October 1973), pp. 42–47, 89–91.

Texan Independence (1835–1836)

Gaddy, J. J. *Texas in Revolt.* Fort Collins: Colorado State University Press, 1973.

Haythornthwaite, Philip. *The Alamo and the War of Texan Independence, 1835–1836.* London: Osprey, 1986.

Nofi, Albert A. *The Alamo and the Texas War of Independence, September 30, 1835, to April 21, 1836: Heroes, Myths, and History.* Conshohocken, Pa.: Combined Books, 1992.

Peña, José Enrique, de la. "¡Recuerda el Alamo!" *American Heritage* 26, number 6 (October 1975), pp. 57–61, 92–97.

———, (trans. by Carmen Perry). *With Santa Anna in Texas: A Personal Narrative of the Revolution.* College Station: Texas A&M University Press, 1975.

Ramsdell, Charles. "The Storming of the Alamo." *American Heritage* 12, number 2 (February 1961), pp. 30–33, 90–93.

Tolbert, F. X. *Day of San Jacinto.* Austin: University of Texas Press, 1959.

War of the Peru-Bolivia Confederation (1836–1839)

Collier, Simon. *Ideas and Politics of Chilean Independence, 1808–1833,* 1967.

Galdames, Luis. *A History of Chile,* 1941.

Parkerson, Philip. *Andrés de Santa Cruz y la confederación Perú-boliviana, 1835–1839,* 1984.

Villalobos R., Sergio. *Portales, una falsificación histórica,* 1989.

War of the Cakes, or Pastry War (1838–1839)

Blanchard, P., and Dauzatz, A. *San Juan de Ulúa ou Rélation de l'Expédition française au Méxique sous ordres de M. le Contre-Amiral Baudin.* Paris, 1839.

Hello, J. M. *Rélation de l'Expédition de la Corvette "La Créole" au Méxique en 1838 et 1839.* Paris, 1839.

Rosas's Campaigns (1838–1852)

Lynch, John. *Argentine Dictator: Juan Manuel de Rosas, 1829–1852,* 1981.
———. *Caudillos in Spanish America, 1800–1850,* 1992.
Polnay, Peter de. *Garibaldi: The Man and the Legend,* 1961.

Mexican-American War (1846–1848)

Bauer, Karl Jack. *The Mexican War, 1846–1848.* New York: Macmillan, 1974 (reprint: University of Nebraska Press, 1992).
———. *Surfboats and Horse Marines: U.S. Naval Operations in the Mexican War, 1846–1848.* Annapolis, Md.: U.S. Naval Institute Press, 1969.
Eisenhower, John S. D. *So Far from God: The U.S. War with Mexico, 1846–1848.* New York: Random House, 1989.
Goetzmann, William F. "Our First Foreign War." *American Heritage* 17, number 4 (June 1966), pp. 18–27, 85–99.
Harlow, Neal. *California Conquered: War and Peace on the Pacific, 1846–1850.* Berkeley: University of California Press, 1982.
Katcher, Philip R. N. *The Mexican-American War, 1846–1848.* London: Osprey, 1976.
Roa Bárcena, José María. *Recuerdos de la invasión norteamericana (1846–1848),* 1971, three volumes.
Watkins, T. H. "The Taking of California." *American Heritage* 24, number 2 (February 1973), pp. 4–7, 81–86.

Filibusterism (1852–1860)

Madelence, Henri de la. *Le compte Gaston de Raousset-Boulbon: Sa vie et ses aventures (d'apres ses papiers, et sa correspondence).* Paris: 1859 and 1876.

Buenos Aires versus the Argentine Confederation (1852–1863)

Bethell, Leslie, ed. *Argentina since Independence,* 1993.
Bosch, Beatríz. *Urquiza y su tiempo,* 1980.
Campobassi, José S. *Mitre y su época,* 1980.
Criscenti, Joseph T., ed. *Sarmiento and his Argentina,* 1993.
Scobie, James R. *The Struggle for Nationhood: Argentina, 1852–1862,* 1964.

American Civil War (1861–1865)

Catton, Bruce. "Crisis at the Antietam." *American Heritage* 9, number 5 (August 1958), pp. 54–57, 93–96.
———. *This Hallowed Ground: The Story of the Union Side of the Civil War.* New York: Doubleday, 1956.
Foote, Shelby. "Du Pont Storms Charleston." *American Heritage* 14, number 4 (June 1963), pp. 28–34, 89–92.
Redding, Saunders. "Tonight for Freedom." *American Heritage* 9, number 4 (June 1958), pp. 52–55, 90.
Sims, Lydel. "The Submarine that Wouldn't Come Up." *American Heritage* 9, number 3 (April 1958), pp. 48–51, 107–111.
White, Edward. "Eyewitness at Harpers Ferry." *American Heritage* 26, number 2 (February 1975), pp. 56–59, 94–97.

French Intervention in Mexico (1861–1867)

Dabbs, Jack Autrey. *The French Army in Mexico, 1861–1867,* 1963.
Hanna, Alfred J., and Hanna, Kathryn A. *Napoleon III and Mexico: American Triumph over Monarchy,* 1971.
León Toral, general Jesús de. *Historia militar: la intervención francesa en México.* Mexico City: Sociedad Mexicana de Geografía y Estadística, 1962.
Thomas, Lately. "The Operator and the Emperors." *American Heritage* 15, number 3 (April 1964), pp. 4–23, 83–88.

North American Indian Wars (1861–1890)

Andrist, Ralph K. *The Long Death.* New York: Macmillan, 1964.
———. "Massacre!" *American Heritage* 13, number 3 (April 1962), pp. 8–17, 108–111.
Halliday, E. M. "Geronimo!" *American Heritage* 17, number 4 (June 1966), pp. 56–63, 106–111.
Hamilton, Charles. *Cry of the Thunderbird: The American Indian's Own Story.* Norman: University of Oklahoma Press, 1972.
Heinzman, George M. "'Don't Let Them Ride over Us.'" *American Heritage* 18, number 2 (February 1967), pp. 44–47, 86–89.
Hook, Jason. *The American Plains Indians.* London: Osprey, 1985.
———. *The Apaches.* London: Osprey, 1987.
Johnson, Michael G. *American Woodland Indians.* London: Osprey, 1990.
Josephy, Alvin M., Jr. "A Most Satisfactory Council." *American Heritage* 16, number 6 (October 1965), pp. 26–31, 70–76.
Katcher, Philip R. N. *The American Indian Wars, 1860–1890.* London: Osprey, 1977.
Rickey, Don, Jr. *Forty Miles a Day on Beans and Hay.* Norman: University of Oklahoma Press, 1963.
Selby, John. *U.S. Cavalry.* London: Osprey, 1972.
Stands In Timber, John. "Last Ghastly Moments at the Little Bighorn." *American Heritage* 17, number 3 (April 1966), pp. 14–21, 72–73.
Tebbel, John. *Compact History of the Indian Wars.* Hawthorn, 1966.
Vestal, Stanley. "The Man Who Killed Custer." *American Heritage* 8, number 2 (February 1957), pp. 4–9, 90–91.
Wallace, Edward S. "Border Warrior." *American Heritage* 9, number 4 (June 1958), pp. 22–25, 101–105.

War of the Triple Alliance (1864–1870)

Cárcano, Ramón J. *Guerra del Paraguay,* 1939–1941, two volumes.

Kolinski, Charles J. *Independence or Death! The Story of the Paraguayan War,* 1965.
Warren, Harris Gaylord. *Paraguay and the Triple Alliance: The Postwar Decade, 1869–1878,* 1978.
Williams, John Hoyt. *The Rise and Fall of the Paraguayan Republic, 1800–1870,* 1979.

Fenian Raids (1866–1870) and Red River Expedition (1870)

Ross, David, and Tyler, Grant. *Canadian Campaigns, 1860–1870.* London: Osprey, 1992.

Riel Rebellion (1885)

Greensword, Leonard C. "Nasty Little Fight." *Military History* 9, number 5 (December 1992), pp. 42–49.

Brazilian Strife (1889–1897)

Love, Joseph L. *Rio Grande do Sul and Brazilian Regionalism, 1882–1930,* 1971.

Chilean Civil War and Anti-American Antagonism (1891)

Pike, Frederick B. *Chile and the United States, 1880–1962: The Emergence of Chile's Social Crisis and the Challenge to United States Diplomacy.* Notre Dame, Ind.: University of Notre Dame Press, 1963.

Part 8: Pax Americana

General Works

Hale, Charles R. *Resistance and Contradiction: Miskitu Indians and the Nicaraguan State, 1894–1987.* Stanford, Calif.: Stanford University Press, 1994.
LaFrance, David G., and Jones, Errol D., comps. *Latin American Military History: An Annotated Bibliography.* New York: Garland, 1992.

Spanish-American War (1898)

Cosmas, Graham A. *An Army for Empire: The United States Army in the Spanish-American War.* Columbia: University of Missouri Press, 1971.
Feuer, A. B. *The Santiago Campaign of 1898: A Soldier's View of the Spanish American War.* Westport, Conn.: Praeger, 1993.
Freidel, Frank. *The Splendid Little War,* 1958.
Heinl, Robert D., Jr. "How We Got Guantanamo." *American Heritage* 13, number 2 (February 1962), pp. 18–21, 94–97.
Leuchtenburg, William E. "The Needless War with Spain." *American Heritage* 8, number 2 (February 1957), pp. 32–45, 95.
Pérez, Louis A., Jr. *Cuba: Between Reform and Revolution,* 1988.
Thomas, Hugh. *Cuba: or, the Pursuit of Freedom,* 1971.

Early Police Actions (1901–1920)

Healy, David. *Gunboat Diplomacy in the Wilson Era: The U.S. Navy in Haiti, 1915–1916.* Madison: University of Wisconsin Press, 1976.
Herwig, Holger H. *Germany's Vision of Empire in Venezuela, 1871–1914.* Princeton, N.J.: Princeton University Press, 1986.
Hood, Miriam. *Gunboat Diplomacy, 1895–1905: Great Power Pressure in Venezuela.* London: Allen and Unwin, 1975.
Laguerre, Michel S. *The Military and Society in Haiti.* Knoxville: University of Tennessee Press, 1993.
Major, John. *Prize Possession: The United States and the Panama Canal, 1903–1979.* Cambridge: Cambridge University Press, 1993.
Munro, D. G. *The United States and the Caribbean Republics, 1921–1933.* Princeton, N.J.: Princeton University Press, 1974.
Musicant, Ivan. *The Banana Wars: A History of United States Military Intervention in Latin America, from the Spanish-American War to the Invasion of Panama.* New York: Macmillan, 1990.
Philpott, William. "'One Had to Stiffen One's Upper Lip': The Royal Navy and the Battle of Puerto Plata, 1904." *The Mariner's Mirror* 79, number 1 (February 1993), pp. 64–70.
Uhlig, Frank, Jr. "The Great White Fleet." *American Heritage* 15, number 2 (February 1964), pp. 30–43, 103–106.
Vega, Bernardo. *Trujillo y las fuerzas armadas norteamericanas.* Santo Domingo: Fundación Cultural Dominicana, 1992.

Mexican Revolution (1910–1924)

Brenner, Anita. *The Wind That Swept Mexico: The History of the Mexican Revolution of 1910–1942.* Austin: University of Texas Press, 1971.
Clendenen, Clarence C. *Blood on the Border: The United States Army and the Mexican Irregulars.* New York: Macmillan, 1969.
Johnson, William Weber. *Heroic Mexico: The Violent Emergence of a Modern Nation.* New York: Doubleday, 1968.
Knight, Alan. *The Mexican Revolution.* Cambridge: Cambridge University Press, 1986, two volumes.
Sweetman, Jack. *Landing at Veracruz, 1914: The First Complete Chronicle of a Strange Encounter in April 1914, When the United States Navy Captured and Occupied the City of Veracruz, Mexico.* Annapolis, Md.: U.S. Naval Institute Press, 1968.
Wolff, Leon. "Black Jack's Mexican Goose Chase." *American Heritage* 13, number 4 (June 1962), pp. 22–27, 100–106.

World War I (1914–1918)

Bennett, Geoffrey. *Coronel and the Falklands.* London: Batsford, 1962.
Simpson, Michael. *Anglo-American Naval Relations, 1917–1919.* London: Navy Records Society, 1991.

Isolated Upheavals (1922–1939)

Dulles, John W. F. *Vargas of Brazil: A Political Biography,* 1967.
Hilton, Stanley E. *Brazil and the Soviet Challenge, 1917–1947,* 1991.
Levine, Robert M. *The Vargas Regime: The Critical Years, 1934–1938,* 1970.

Orona, Juan V. *La revolución del 6 de septiembre.* Buenos Aires: Imprenta López, 1966.

Skidmore, Thomas E. "Failure in Brazil: From Popular Front to Armed Revolt." *Journal of Contemporary History* 5 (1970), pp. 137–157.

Weaver, John D. "Bonus March." *American Heritage* 14, number 4 (June 1963), pp. 18–23, 92–97.

Young, Jordan M. *The Brazilian Revolution of 1930 and the Aftermath,* 1967.

Chaco War (1932–1935)

Bejarano, Ramón César. *Síntesis de la guerra del Chaco,* 1982.

Ynsfrán, Pablo Max, ed. *The Epic of the Chaco: Marshal Estigarribia's Memoirs of the Chaco War, 1932–1935.* Austin: University of Texas Press, 1950.

Zook, David H., Jr. *The Conduct of the Chaco War.* New Haven: Bookman, 1960.

World War II (1939–1945)

Dull, Paul S. *A Battle History of the Imperial Japanese Navy (1941–1945).* Annapolis, Md.: Naval Institute Press, 1978.

Hadley, Michael L. *U-Boats Against Canada: German Submarines in Canadian Waters.* Kingston and Montreal: McGill–Queen's University Press, 1985.

Hoyt, Edwin P. *The U-Boat Wars.* New York: Arbor House, 1984.

Roskill, Stephen Wentworth. *The War at Sea, 1939–1945.* London: H.M.S.O., 1954–1961, four volumes.

Latin American Troubles (1941–1989)

Benjamin, J. R. *The United States and the Origins of the Cuban Revolution: An Empire of Liberty in an Age of National Liberation.* Princeton, N.J.: Princeton University Press, 1990.

Caballero Jurado, Carlos, and Thomas, Nigel. *Central American Wars, 1959–1989.* London: Osprey, 1990.

Constable, Pamela, and Valenzuela, Arturo. *A Nation of Enemies: Chile Under Pinochet.* New York: Norton, 1991.

Gleijeses, P. *Shattered Hope: The Guatemalan Revolution and the United States, 1944–1954.* Princeton, N.J.: Princeton University Press, 1991.

Jonas, Susanne. *The Battle for Guatemala: Rebels, Death Squads, and U.S. Power.* Boulder: Westview Press, 1991.

Landau, Saul. *The Guerrilla Wars of Central America: Nicaragua, El Salvador, and Guatemala.* New York: St. Martin's Press, 1993.

Levine, D. H. *Conflict and Political Change in Venezuela.* Princeton, N.J.: Princeton University Press, 1973.

Masterson, Daniel M. *Militarism and Politics in Latin America: Peru from Sánchez Cerro to Sendero Luminoso.* Westport, Conn.: Greenwood, 1991.

Miranda, Roger, and Ratliff, William E. *The Civil War in Nicaragua: Inside the Sandinistas.* New Brunswick: Transaction, 1993.

Moss, Robert. *Chile's Marxist Experiment.* Newton Abbot, Engl.: David & Charles, 1973.

Nunn, Frederick. *The Time of the Generals: Latin American Professional Militarism in World Perspective.* Lincoln: University of Nebraska Press, 1992.

Orona, Juan V. *La revolución del 16 de septiembre.* Buenos Aires, 1971.

Pastor, R. A. *Whirlpool: U.S. Foreign Policy Toward Latin America and the Caribbean.* Princeton, N.J.: Princeton University Press, 1992.

Sandos, James A. *Rebellion in the Borderlands.* Norman: University of Oklahoma Press, 1992.

Schoultz, L. *Human Rights and United States Policy toward Latin America.* Princeton, N.J.: Princeton University Press, 1981.

———. *National Security and United States Policy toward Latin America.* Princeton, N.J.: Princeton University Press, 1987.

Simon, Jean Marie. *Guatemala: Eternal Spring, Eternal Tyranny.* New York: Norton, 1987.

Spooner, Mary Helen. *Soldiers in a Narrow Land: The Pinochet Regime in Chile.* Berkeley: University of California Press, 1994.

Walter, Knut. *The Regime of Anastasio Somoza, 1936–1956.* Chapel Hill: University of North Carolina Press, 1993.

Wickham-Crowley, Timothy P. *Guerrillas and Revolution in Latin America: A Comparative Study of Insurgents and Regimes since 1956.* Princeton, N.J.: Princeton University Press, 1991.

Wright, Thomas C. *Latin America in the Era of the Cuban Revolution.* New York: Praeger, 1991.

Falklands Campaign (1982)

Braybrook, Roy. *Battle for the Falklands (3): Air Forces.* London: Osprey, 1982.

English, Adrian, and Watts, Anthony. *Battle for the Falklands (2): Naval Forces.* London: Osprey, 1982.

Fowler, William. *Battle for the Falklands (1): Land Forces.* London: Osprey, 1982.

Freedman, L., and Gamba-Stonehouse, V. *Signals of War: The Falklands Conflict of 1982.* Princeton, N.J.: Princeton University Press, 1991.

Van der Bijl, Nicholas. *Argentine Forces in the Falklands.* London: Osprey, 1992.

Grenada Invasion (1983)

Russell, Lee E. *Grenada 1983.* London: Osprey, 1985.

Panama Campaign (1989)

Rottman, Gordon L. *Panama, 1989–1990.* London: Osprey, 1991.

Illustration Credits

All maps are copyright © 1998 by Thomas Conley, Thomas Conley Advertising, Design, and Print Management.

Images on the cover and on part opening pages are details from *Battle of the Guarapes,* a painting on the ceiling panels below the choir loft of the Church of the Immaculate Conception, Pernambuco, showing the victory obtained by the Portuguese in the first battle of the Guarapes Hills on 19 April 1648. The painting is attributed to João de Dues and Sepúlveda. Photograph copyright © Lew Parrella, Brazil.

Other images are listed below in the order in which they appear.

3 From the collection of David Marley
7 Reprinted from Artes de México, *Crónica del Traje Militar en México,* Vol. 102 (Mexico, 1960)
19 From the collection of David Marley
21 Reprinted from Artes de México, *Crónica del Traje Militar en México,* Vol. 102 (Mexico, 1960)
23 From the collection of David Marley
27 Reprinted from Artes de México, *Crónica del Traje Militar en México,* Vol. 102 (Mexico, 1960)
28 Reprinted from Artes de México, *Crónica del Traje Militar en México,* Vol. 102 (Mexico, 1960)
30 From the collection of David Marley
31 From the collection of David Marley
36 From the collection of David Marley
43 Reprinted from Artes de México, *Crónica del Traje Militar en México,* Vol. 102 (Mexico, 1960)
46 Reprinted from *Gobernantes de la Nueva España (1535–1696),* Vol. 1 (Mexico, 1985)
48 From the collection of David Marley
52 *French crossbowman in Canada, ca. 1541, dressed in the white-and-black livery of the Cartier-Roberval expedition; watercolor by Michel Pétard.* Canadian Department of National Defense.
56 Museo Naval, Madrid
58 From the collection of David Marley
60 Library of Congress
64 Reprinted from *Gobernantes de la Nueva España* (1535–1696), Vol. 1 (Mexico, 1985)
65 Archivo General de Indias
73 Library of Congress
77 Longleat House
84 Etnografisk Samling, National Museum of Denmark
86 Theodore de Bry Collection
90 Museo Naval, Madrid
95 National Maritime Museum, Greenwich
96 National Maritime Museum, Greenwich
100 *French harquebusier in Canada, 1610–1620, dressed in green tunic and pantaloons; watercolor by Pétard.* Canadian Department of National Defense.
102 From the collection of David Marley
111 Prado Museum, Madrid
117 Ashmolean Museum, Oxford
119 Museo Naval, Madrid
124 Museo Naval, Madrid
126 Archivo General de Indias
132 Etnografisk Samling, National Museum of Denmark
137 Museo Naval, Madrid
138 Reprinted from *Gobernantes de la Nueva España* (1535–1696), Vol. 1 (Mexico, 1985)
147 Archivo General de Indias
154 National Maritime Museum, Greenwich
157 National Archives of Canada, C 40695
160 *A brown-clad soldier of the French Carignan-Salières Regiment; modern drawing by Francis Back.* Parks Canada.
169 Tredegar House, Wales
174 From the collection of David Marley
179 National Maritime Museum, Greenwich
193 Archivo General de la Nación, Mexico
204 *A French-Canadian soldier dressed for a winter campaign; by Francis Back.* Parks Canada.
205 Canadian Department of National Defense
214 Archivo General de Indias
215 *Red-coated soldier of Gibsone's regiment; watercolor by Gerry A. Embleton.* Canadian Department of National Defense.
221 National Maritime Museum, Greenwich
224 *Soldier from one of the British independent companies in Newfoundland and Nova Scotia, 1698–1717; Embleton watercolor.* Canadian Department of National Defense.
227 *British "Board of Ordnance" artilleryman, clad in red and gold; this unit was stationed in Newfoundland and Nova Scotia from 1700 to 1716. Watercolor by Embleton.* Canadian Department of National Defense.

231 National Maritime Museum, Greenwich
236 Library of Parliament, Ottawa
241 Library of Parliament, Ottawa
243 Archivo General de la Nación, Mexico
252 National Maritime Museum, Greenwich
264 Archivo General de Indias
265 *A redcoat of the British 40th Regiment with his turnbacks unhooked so as to cover his thighs and lapels buttoned against the cold; also note brown field gaiters rather than white ceremonials.* Parks Canada.
271 National Maritime Museum, Greenwich
273 National Maritime Museum, Greenwich
280 *A soldier of the British 58th Regiment; modern depiction by Embleton.* Parks Canada.
281 Metro Toronto Reference Library, MTL 2653
286 National Archives of Canada, C 42249
292 National Maritime Museum, Greenwich
299 *An Iroquois chief wearing a red blanket, white tunic, and blue leggings; modern rendering by Embleton.* Parks Canada.
306 *An American ranger of Colonel Morgan's regiment, clad in white buckskins; modern depiction by Embleton.* Parks Canada.
311 *A white-coated British soldier with blue leggings, blowing into his hand; modern rendering by Embleton.* Parks Canada.
312 *A ranger of Major John Butler's Niagara-based loyalist regiment, with a red kerchief and pale green coat; modern depiction by Embleton.* Parks Canada.
317 National Maritime Museum, Greenwich
323 Reprinted from *Gobernantes de la España (1696–1821)*, Vol. 2 (Mexico, 1985)
326 National Maritime Museum, Greenwich
328 Museo Naval, Madrid
334 [both] Archivo General de la Nación, Mexico
341 National Maritime Museum, Greenwich
344 National Maritime Museum, Greenwich
349 Library of Congress
354 Library of Congress
358 National Maritime Museum, Greenwich
361 National Maritime Museum, Greenwich
368 National Maritime Museum, Greenwich
376 *Royalist medal of the Order of Isabel la Católica, 1815.* Archivo General de la Nación, Mexico.
380 Archivo General de la Nación, Mexico
381 Archivo General de la Nación, Mexico
382 Reprinted from *Gobernantes de la España (1696–1821)*, Vol. 2 (Mexico, 1985)
390 *Mexican insurgent of the Mixcoac Regiment, 1813.* Archivo General de la Nación, Mexico.
391 Museo Histórico Nacional, Buenos Aires
396 *Royalist infantryman, 1815.* Archivo General de la Nación, Mexico.
403 Museo Histórico Nacional, Buenos Aires
406 Archivo General de la Nación, Mexico
412 Museo Histórico Nacional, Buenos Aires
415 Archivo General de la Nación, Mexico
419 Archivo General de la Nación, Mexico
433 Library of Congress
439 Archivo General de la Nación, Mexico
444 Library of Congress
445 Metro Toronto Reference Library
447 *Green-clad Canadian Glengarry Light Infantryman; watercolor by Embleton.* Parks Canada.
453 *French-Canadian* voltigeur, *or light infantryman; watercolor by Embleton.* Parks Canada.
454 Library of Congress
456 *A regular U.S. line infantryman; watercolor by Hugh Charles McBarron, Jr.* Parks Canada.
460 *An officer in the New York State militia; modern painting by McBarron.* Parks Canada.
469 Reprinted from Artes de México, *Crónica del Traje Militar en México*, Vol. 102 (Mexico, 1960)
479 National Archives of Canada, C 3653
482 Library of Congress/Corbis
490 Library of Congress
506 Reprinted from Artes de México, *Crónica del Traje Militar en México*, Vol. 102 (Mexico, 1960)
514 U.S. Naval Historical Center, Washington, D.C., Ref #NH 63785 KN
517 U.S. Naval Historical Center, Washington, D.C., Ref #NH 49600
528 *Typical uniform, 1853.* Archivo General de la Nación, Mexico
529 *Chasseur under conservative General Osollo's command, 1858.* Archivo General de la Nación, Mexico.
534 Library of Congress
537 Corbis-Bettmann
541 The National Archives/Corbis
549 Corbis-Bettmann
552 *Coat of arms of Maximilian's imperial government, 1863.* Archivo General de la Nación, Mexico.
555 Reprinted from Artes de México, *Crónica del Traje Militar en México*, Vol. 102 (Mexico, 1960)
563 Reprinted from Artes de México, *Crónica del Traje Militar en México*, Vol. 102 (Mexico, 1960)
568 Library of Congress
571 Library of Congress
584 Amon Carter Museum, Dallas
589 National Archives of Canada, C 3450
590 Library of Congress
591 Mariners' Museum, Newport News
602 U.S. Naval Historical Center, Washington, D.C.
607 Casasola Archive
608 Mariners' Museum, Newport News
610 U.S. Naval Historical Center, Washington, D.C.
612 Usher Photographs, Hoover Institution
613 Clendenen Papers, Hoover Institution
616 Reprinted from Artes de México, *Crónica del Traje Militar en México*, Vol. 102 (Mexico, 1960)
618 Clendenen Papers, Hoover Institution
620 Clendenen Papers, Hoover Institution
625 Clendenen Papers, Hoover Institution

629 Clendenen Papers, Hoover Institution
631 Reprinted from Artes de México, *Crónica del Traje Militar en México,* Vol. 102 (Mexico, 1960)
634 Mariners' Museum, Newport News
641 U.S. Naval Historical Center, Washington, D.C.
642 U.S. Naval Historical Center, Washington, D.C.
654 U.S. Naval Institute
655 U.S. Naval Institute
659 U.S. Naval Institute
665 Library of Congress
673 Department of Defense Visual Center
675 Department of Defense Visual Center

Index